# Short Story Criticism

# Guide to Gale Literary Criticism Series

| For criticism on | Consult these Gale series |
|---|---|
| Authors now living or who died after December 31, 1959 | *CONTEMPORARY LITERARY CRITICISM (CLC)* |
| Authors who died between 1900 and 1959 | *TWENTIETH-CENTURY LITERARY CRITICISM (TCLC)* |
| Authors who died between 1800 and 1899 | *NINETEENTH-CENTURY LITERATURE CRITICISM (NCLC)* |
| Authors who died between 1400 and 1799 | *LITERATURE CRITICISM FROM 1400 TO 1800 (LC)*<br><br>*SHAKESPEAREAN CRITICISM (SC)* |
| Authors who died before 1400 | *CLASSICAL AND MEDIEVAL LITERATURE CRITICISM (CMLC)* |
| Authors of books for children and young adults | *CHILDREN'S LITERATURE REVIEW (CLR)* |
| Dramatists | *DRAMA CRITICISM (DC)* |
| Poets | *POETRY CRITICISM (PC)* |
| Short story writers | *SHORT STORY CRITICISM (SSC)* |
| Black writers of the past two hundred years | *BLACK LITERATURE CRITICISM (BLC)* |
| Hispanic writers of the late nineteenth and twentieth centuries | *HISPANIC LITERATURE CRITICISM (HLC)* |
| Native North American writers and orators of the eighteenth, nineteenth, and twentieth centuries | *NATIVE NORTH AMERICAN LITERATURE (NNAL)* |
| Major authors from the Renaissance to the present | *WORLD LITERATURE CRITICISM, 1500 TO THE PRESENT (WLC)* |

# Contents

Preface   vii

Acknowledgments   xi

ISSN 0895-9439

Volume 31

# Short Story Criticism

Excerpts from Criticism of the
Works of Short Fiction Writers

**Anna Sheets Nesbitt**
Editor

GALE

DETROIT · LONDON

## STAFF

Anna Sheets Nesbitt, *Editor*

Amy Francis, Lynn Koch, Susan Salas, Lawrence J. Trudeau, *Associate Editors*

Debra A. Wells, *Assistant Editors*

Susan M. Trosky, *Permissions Manager*
Kimberly F. Smilay, *Permissions Specialist*
Stephen Cusack, Kelly Quin, *Permissions Associates*
Sandy Gore, *Permissions Assistant*

Victoria B. Cariappa, *Research Manager*
Tracie A. Richardson, Norma Sawaya, Cheryl L. Warnock, *Research Associates*

Mary Beth Trimper, *Production Director*
Deborah Milliken, *Production Assistant*

C. J. Jonik, *Desktop Publisher*
Randy Bassett, *Image Database Supervisor*
Michael Ansari, Robert Duncan, *Scanner Operators*
Pamela Reed, *Photography Coordinator*

Library of Congress Catalog Card Number 88-641014
ISBN 0-7876-2054-8
ISSN 0895-9439

Printed in the United States of America

10  9  8  7  6  5  4  3  2  1

# Preface

## A Comprehensive Information Source
## on World Short Fiction

*Short Story Criticism (SSC)* presents significant passages from criticism of the world's greatest short story writers and provides supplementary biographical and bibliographical materials to guide the interested reader to a greater understanding of the authors of short fiction. This series was developed in response to suggestions from librarians serving high school, college, and public library patrons, who had noted a considerable number of requests for critical material on short story writers. Although major short story writers are covered in such Gale series as *Contemporary Literary Criticism (CLC)*, *Twentieth-Century Literary Criticism (TCLC)*, *Nineteenth-Century Literature Criticism (NCLC)*, and *Literature Criticism from 1400 to 1800 (LC)*, librarians perceived the need for a series devoted solely to writers of the short story genre.

## Coverage

*SSC* is designed to serve as an introduction to major short story writers of all eras and nationalities. Since these authors have inspired a great deal of relevant critical material, *SSC* is necessarily selective, and the editors have chosen the most important published criticism to aid readers and students in their research.

Approximately eight to ten authors are included in each volume, and each entry presents a historical survey of the critical response to that author's work. The length of an entry is intended to reflect the amount of critical attention the author has received from critics writing in English and from foreign critics in translation. Every attempt has been made to identify and include excerpts from the most significant essays on each author's work. In order to provide these important critical pieces, the editors sometimes reprint essays that have appeared elsewhere in Gale's Literary Criticism Series. Such duplication, however, never exceeds twenty percent of an *SSC* volume.

## Organization

An *SSC* author entry consists of the following elements:

- The **Author Heading** cites the name under which the author most commonly wrote, followed by birth and death dates. If the author wrote consistently under a pseudonym, the pseudonym will be listed in the author heading and the author's actual name given in parentheses on the first line of the biographical and critical introduction.

- The **Biographical and Critical Introduction** contains background information designed to introduce a reader to the author and the critical debates surrounding his or her work.

- A **Portrait of the Author** is included when available. Many entries also contain illustrations of materials pertinent to an author's career, including holographs of manuscript pages, title pages, dust jackets, letters, or representations of important people, places, and events in the author's life.

- The list of **Principal Works** is chronological by date of first publication and lists the most importantworks by the author. The first section comprises short story collections, novellas, and novella collections. The second section gives information on other major works by the author. For foreign authors, the editors have provided original foreign-language publication information and have selected what are considered the best and most complete English-language editions of their works.

- **Criticism** is arranged chronologically in each author entry to provide a useful perspective on changes in critical evaluation over the years. All short story, novella, and collection titles by the author featured in the entry are printed in boldface type to enable a reader to ascertain without difficulty the works discussed. Also for purposes of easier identification, the critic's name and the publication date of the essay are given at the beginning of each piece of criticism. Unsigned criticism is preceded by the title of the journal in which it appeared.

- Critical essays are prefaced with **Explanatory Notes** as an additional aid to students and readers using SSC. An explanatory note may provide useful information of several types, including: the reputation of the critic, the intent or scope of the critical essay, and the orientation of the criticism (biographical, psychoanalytic, structuralist, etc.).

- A complete **Bibliographical Citation,** designed to help the interested reader locate the original essay or book, precedes each piece of criticism.

- The **Further Reading List** appearing at the end of each author entry suggests additional materials on the author. In some cases it includes essays for which the editors could not obtain reprint rights. Boxed material following the further reading list provides references to other biographical and critical sources on the author in series published by Gale.

Beginning with volume six, SSC contains two additional features designed to enhance the reader's understanding of short fiction writers and their works:

- Each SSC entry now includes, when available, **Comments by the Author** that illuminate his or her own works or the short story genre in general. These statements are set within boxes or bold rules to distinguish them from the criticism.

- A **Select Bibliography of General Sources on Short Fiction** is included as an appendix. This listing of materials for further research provides readers with a selection of the best available general studies of the short story genre.

# Other Features

A **Cumulative Author Index** lists all the authors who have appeared in SSC, CLC, TCLC, NCLC, LC, and Classical and Medieval Literature Criticism (CMLC), as well as cross-references to other Gale series. Users will welcome this cumulated index as a useful tool for locating an author within the Literary Criticism Series.

A **Cumulative Nationality Index** lists all authors featured in SSC by nationality, followed by the number of the SSC volume in which their entry appears.

A **Cumulative Title Index** lists in alphabetical order all short story, novella, and collection titles contained in the SSC series. Titles of short story collections, separately published novellas, and novella collections are printed in italics, while titles of individual short stories are printed in roman type with quotation marks. Each title is followed by the author's name and corresponding volume and page numbers where commentary on the work is located. English-language translations of original foreign-language titles are cross-referenced to the foreign titles so that all references to discussion of a work are combined in one listing.

# Citing Short Story Criticism

When writing papers, students who quote directly from any volume in the Literary Criticism Series may use the following general forms to footnote reprinted criticism. The first example pertains to material drawn from periodicals, the second to material reprinted from books:

[1]Henry James, Jr., "Honoré de Balzac," The Galaxy 20 (December 1875), 814-36; excerpted and reprinted in Short Story Criticism, Vol. 5, ed. Thomas Votteler (Detroit: The Gale Group, 1990), pp. 8-11.

[2]F. R. Leavis, D. H. Lawrence: Novelist (Alfred A. Knopf, 1956); excerpted and reprinted in Short Story Criticism, Vol. 4, ed. Thomas Votteler (Detroit: The Gale Group, 1990), pp. 202-06.

# Comments

Readers who wish to suggest authors to appear in future volumes, or who have other suggestions, are invited to contact the editors by writing to The Gale Group, Literary Genres Division, 27500 Drake Rd., Farmington Hills, MI 48331-3535.

# Acknowledgments

The editors wish to thank the copyright holders of the excerpted criticism included in this volume and the permissions managers of many book and magazine publishing companies for assisting us in securing reproduction rights. We are also grateful to the staffs of the Detroit Public Library, the Library of Congress, the University of Detroit Mercy Library, Wayne State University Purdy/Kresge Library Complex, and the University of Michigan Libraries for making their resources available to us. Following is a list of the copyright holders who have granted us permission to reproduce material in this volume of SSC. Every effort has been made to trace copyright, but if omissions have been made, please let us know.

## COPYRIGHTED EXCERPTS IN *SSC*, VOLUME 31, WERE REPRODUCED FROM THE FOLLOWING PERIODICALS:

*American Literature*, v. 35, May, 1963. Copyright © 1963 by Duke University Press, Durham, NC. Reproduced by permission.—*Book World—The Washington Post*, v. 12, October 24, 1982. Copyright © 1982, Washington Post Book World Service/Washington Post Writers Group. Reproduced with permission.—*Canadian Literature*, no. 101, Summer, 1984 for "Malcolm Lowry's Comic Vision: 'Elephant and Colosseum" by Elizabeth D. Rankin. Reproduced by permission of the author.—*College English*, v. 25, November, 1963 for "Fitzgerald's 'Babylon Revisited'" by Seymour L. Gross. Copyright © 1963 by the National Council of Teachers of English. Reproduced by permission of the publisher and the author.—*College Literature*, v. 7, Winter, 1980; v. XII, Spring, 1985. Copyright © 1980, 1985 by West Chester University. Both reproduced by permission of the publisher.—*Journal of Modern Literature*, v. 13, March, 1986. © Temple University, 1986. Reproduced by permission.—*Literature and Psychology*, v. 18, 1968. © Editor 1968. Reproduced by permission of the publisher.—*MLN*, v. 102, 1987. © copyright 1987 by The Johns Hopkins University Press. All rights reserved. Reproduced by permission.—*Modern Fiction Studies*, v. 10, Winter, 1964/65. Copyright © 1964/65 by Purdue Research Foundation, West Lafayette, IN 47907. All rights reserved. Reproduced by permission of The Johns Hopkins University.—*Modern Language Studies*, v. XIII, Winter, 1983 for "The Doctor's Black Bag: William Carlos Williams' Passaic River Stories" by George Monteiro. Copyright, (c) Northeast Modern Language Association 1983. Reproduced by permission of the publisher and author.—*PMLA*, v. 84, January, 1969. Copyright 1969 by PMLA. Reproduced by permission.—*Renascence: Essays on Values in Literature*, v. XXXVIII, Autumn, 1985. © copyright 1985, Marquette University Press. Reproduced by permission.—*Renditions*, v.13, Spring, 1980. Reproduced by permission.—*Russian Literature Triquarterly*, v. 3, May, 1972. Reproduced by permission.—*Studies in Short Fiction*, v. 1, Fall, 1963; v. 2, Fall, 1964; v. 2, Spring, 1965; v. 3, Winter, 1966; v. VI, Winter, 1969; v. VII, Spring, 1970; Summer, 1981; Summer, 1982;v. 22, Summer, 1985; v. 28, Winter, 1991. Copyright © 1963, 1964, 1965, 1966, 1969, 1970, 1981, 1982, 1985, 1991 by Newberry College. All reproduced by permission.—*Style*, v. 2, Spring, 1968 for "The Poetic Narrative: A Reading of 'Flowering Judas'" by Beverly Gross. Copyright © Style, 1968. All rights reserved. Reproduced by permission of the publisher and the author.—*Tamkang Review*, v. XVII, Winter, 1986. Reproduced by permission.—*The CEA Critic*, v. 34, May, 1972. Copyright © 19-- by the College English Association, Inc. Reproduced by permission.—*The Explicator*, v. 48, Summer, 1980; v. 53, Spring, 1995. Copyright © 1980, 1995 Helen Dwight Reid Educational Foundation. Both reproduced with permission of the Helen Dwight Reid Educational Foundation, published by Heldref Publications, 1319 18th Street, NW, Washington, DC 20036-1802.—*The Georgia Review*, v. 34, Winter, 1980 for "The Man Who Loved Women: The Medical Fictions of William Carlos Williams" by Marjorie Perloff. Copyright, 1980, by the University of Georgia. Reproduced by permission of the author.—*The Massachusetts Review*, v. III, Winter, 1962. Copyright © 1962. Reproduced from The Massachusetts Review, The Massachusetts Review, Inc. by permission.—*The Psychoanalytic Review*, v. 59, Winter, 1962-73. Copyright © 1972 by The National Psychological Association for Psychoanalysis, Inc. Reproduced by permission.—*The Southern Review*, Australia , v. 1, 1963 for "The Childhood of Luvers: An Early Story of Pasternak's" by Angela Livingstone. Copyright, 1963, by the author. Reproduced by permission of the author.—*The Southern Review*, Louisiana State University, v. IV, July, 1968 for "William Carlos Williams and the Modern Short Story" by J. E. Slate. Copyright, 1968, by the author. Reproduced by permission of the author.—*Tulane Studies in English*, v. XV, 1967. Copyright © 1967 by Tulane University. All rights reserved. Reproduced by permission.—*William Carlos Williams Review*, v. XI, Fall, 1985. Reproduced by permission.

## COPYRIGHTED EXCERPTS IN *SSC*, VOLUME 31, WERE REPRODUCED FROM THE FOLLOWING BOOKS:

Baker, Carlos. From "When the Story Ends: 'Babylon Revisited'" in *The Short Stories of F. Scott Fitzgerald*. Edited by Jackson R. Bryer. The University of Wisconsin Press, 1982. Copyright © 1982 The Board of Regents of the University of Wisconsin System. All rights reserved. Reproduced by permission of the University of Wisconsin Press.—Bareham, T. From "Strange Poems of God's Mercy: The Lowry Short Stories" in *The Art of Malcolm Lowry*.

# "Babylon Revisited"
## F. Scott Fitzgerald

The following entry presents criticism of Fitzgerald's short story "Babylon Revisited." For an overview of Fitzgerald's short fiction, see *SSC*, Volume 6.

### INTRODUCTION

"Babylon Revisited" is Fitzgerald's most anthologized short story and is considered by many to be his best. First published in 1931 in the *Saturday Evening Post*, it reappeared with revisions in the 1935 collection *Taps at Reveille*. Fitzgerald wrote "Babylon Revisited" during a time of emotional and economic crisis. Like most of his work, the story reflects his own personal experience and his relationship with his wife Zelda; its tone is thoughtful and retrospective, and it is sadder than earlier stories he had written for the *Post*.

### Plot and Major Characters

"Babylon Revisited" is set against the backdrop of expatriate Europe during the 1930s and recounts the story of Charlie Wales, a onetime wealthy playboy of 1920s Paris whose excesses contributed to the death of his wife, Helen, and led to his stay in a sanitarium for alcoholism. During Charlie's recovery, his daughter Honoria was placed under the custodianship of his sister-in-law and her husband—Marion and Lincoln Peters. Since then, Charlie has reestablished himself as a successful businessman in Prague. As the story opens, he has returned to Paris to reclaim his daughter but must first prove to Marion that he has reformed. The Peterses have never been as wealthy as Charlie and Helen were, and Marion is envious and resentful of Charlie's past extravagances. This, coupled with her bitterness at Charlie's part in her sister's death, makes Marion suspicious of Charlie's reformation, and she agrees only reluctantly to return Honoria to him. Her suspicions are apparently confirmed when Lorraine and Duncan, two unrepentant friends from Charlie's past, drunkenly descend upon Charlie while he is at the Peterses' house. Marion is shocked, and changes her mind about relinquishing Honoria. The story ends as Charlie resolves to try later to regain his daughter, believing that "they couldn't make him pay forever," and that "Helen wouldn't have wanted him to be so alone."

### Major Themes

Critics have identified several major themes in "Babylon Revisited," some of which are centered upon time and its shaping of individual destiny. Joan Turner, for example, has asserted that one of the story's themes is that "the past

cannot be escaped." Similarly, Carlos Baker has remarked that no matter how sincere Charlie is in his attempt at reformation, he is "defeated by a past that he can never shed." Ronald J. Gervais viewed the story as a lament for the past and its pleasures, as well as regret for mistakes made. Numerous critics have focused on guilt in the story: James M. Harrison and Seymour L. Gross, for example, have debated whether Charlie genuinely wants to change his ways or is still attracted to his former life. Finally, while Rose Adrienne Gallo considered guilt and retribution as significant concerns in the story, she also described the pernicious influence of money as an important theme—both in its ability to waste lives, as it has with Charlie, and to foster envy and resentment, as it has in Marion Peters.

### Critical Reception

"Babylon Revisited" has been generally well-received since its publication and is now considered a masterpiece. Nevertheless, critics have pointed out inconsistencies in the plot—for example, the apparently illogical route that Charlie takes from the Ritz Bar to the Peterses, and several inaccurate references to the passage of time. For all its inconsistencies, however, most critics agree that this wistful story displays Fitzgerald's writing at its best, with its close attention to imagery and sensitive choice of words.

---

## CRITICISM

### James M. Harrison (essay date 1958)

SOURCE: "Fitzgerald's 'Babylon Revisited'," in *The Explicator*, Vol. 16, No. 4, January, 1958, pp. 1, 3.

[*In the following essay, Harrison asserts that although Charlie Wales has begun to mature, he is still drawn to his former life.*]

The usual interpretation of F. Scott Fitzgerald's **"Babylon Revisited"** has been summarized by Ray B. West (*The Short Story in America,* 1952). Charlie Wales, returning to Paris, "accidentally becomes involved with some of his old friends; and despite his present dislike of the old life—his knowledge that . . . it was something he had to escape if possible, not recover—he appears to have succumbed and thus loses, once and for all, the hope of regaining his child. The pathos in **'Babylon Revisited'** is deepend and enriched by Charlie Wales's recognition that he is, in part at least, merely reaping the harvest of his earlier years. . . . [He is] doomed because he still carries the burden of his early irresponsibility, even in the years of maturity and knowledge."

According to this interpretation the effect is, as West suggests, pathetic rather than tragic. Charlie has matured; he is reliable, sober, patient, tolerant, kind, devoted to his daughter. He is defeated by accident, and by past mistakes over which he no longer has any control. If this interpretation is sound, complaints that the story is sentimental have a certain validity.

But the situation is not really this simple. Charlie has triumphed over his past at the point where Marion Peters agrees to his taking Honoria, and the reversal—the untimely appearance of his drunken friends—cannot be attributed to accident or to past weakness; it is clearly the result of present weakness.

The point of view is Charlie's, and it is easy to read the story only on the level of his understanding; after all he is intelligent and perceptive, and his dilemma arouses our sympathy. But although we see the action through the eyes of the protagonist, and colored by his feelings and opinions, we can at the same time observe the protagonist critically. We are in a position to know everything he knows, and more. The "more" in this case is essential to our full understanding.

The central conflict is not between Charlie past and Charlie present, but between contradictory impulses operating within the latter. Charlie sees that the old, wild, gay way of life was foolish, cruel, and empty; yet it still appeals to him. He feels its temptation despite his firm desire to demonstrate his solid virtues and make a home for his daughter. Thus at the opening we see him inquiring after his old friends— motivated not by morbid curiosity but by nostalgia.

There are two Charlies in the story: Charlie the substantial man of business, the devoted father who wishes to reclaim his child; and Charlie the hedonist, who sees the waste, cruelty and senselessness of his former spree but who still feels somehow that it was gloriously wasteful, gloriously cruel and gloriously senseless—and in spite of the suffering it caused, glorious fun. It is Charlie number two who feels Lorraine Quarrles' "passionate, provocative attraction," when he suddenly encounters her. Next day Charlie number one is in control again, and he remembers her as "trite, blurred, worn away." Were he not pulled in two directions, Charlie could easily make it clear to his old friends, when he first meets them, that he is a changed man. But this he cannot do. He can brag about his moderate drinking to Lincoln Peters; he can speak of it with satisfaction even to the bartender; but he cannot bring himself to admit it to his former playmates.

At the story's climax Duncan Schaeffer and Lorraine Quarrles appear, drunk, at the Peterses' home. "For a moment Charlie was astounded; unable to understand how they ferreted out the Peterses' address." He protests to Lincoln Peters: "They wormed your name out of somebody.'" The surprise of the respectable Charlie is genuine, but the reader will remember the other Charlie inquiring at the Ritz bar about his old companions in dissipation: "Charlie scribbled an address in his notebook and tore out the page. 'If you see Mr. Schaeffer, give him this,' he said. 'It's my brother-in-law's address.'" And thus, in a passage placed for emphasis at the very opening of the story, Charlie plants the seed of his own destruction.

Charlie has come to dinner at the Peterses' at six, ignoring an invitation to meet Lorraine an hour earlier at the Ritz bar. Apparently Duncan has encountered Lorraine there, and Alix has handed him the note bearing the Peterses' address. Charlie, who has since instructed Alix not to reveal his hotel, has obviously forgotten the note. So the "reformed" Charlie is defeated, not by accident, but by an impulsive act of the other side of his nature.

Charlie's "maturity and knowledge" are still incomplete. He has turned over a new leaf, but it refuses to lie flat. The central symbol of the story is Charlie's one drink a day: he wants to give up the old way of life—almost. But for all this he is likable and admirable, a strong and tragic character wrestling with a weakness he does not completely understand.

### John V. Hagopian (essay date 1962)

SOURCE: "A Prince in Babylon," in *Fitzgerald Newsletter,* No. 19, Fall, 1962, pp. 1-3.

*[In the following essay, Hagopian examines what he describes as religious, Dantesque elements in the story.]*

Despite the obvious symbolism of the title, critics have not generally observed that F's [Fitzgerald's] **"Babylon Revisited"** is a religious story—more exactly a Catholic, Dantesque story. Not only does it evoke the mood of paralysis and defeat of the Waste Land generation following the stock market crash of 1929, but it renders with understanding and compassion the purgatorial suffering of a man for whom repentance and social readjustment alone are not enough to redeem his past. Nevertheless, as the symbolism and dramatic action both suggest, eventual redemption is probable.

F [Fitzgerald] was born into a Catholic family and had a Catholic upbringing; and his most important short story, like his most important novel *GG,* [*The Great Gatsby*] is an evocation of purgatorial suffering in the Dante-Eliot sense. Charlie Wales repents his former sins in Babylon, but it takes more than simple repentance for him to win his Honoria. He is still afflicted with the sins of pride ("he wondered if he couldn't do something to get Lincoln out of his rut at the bank") and anger ("He thought rather angrily that this was just money"). But he knows that one needn't "pay forever," though one must first endure suffering in the purgatorial fires.

There are three "vector forces" in the story, one positive and two negative: Charlie and his daughter yearning to establish the ties of paternal and filial love; Lincoln and Marion Peters, sitting in judgment over him, sanctioned by law and traditional morality; and Duncan Schaeffer and Lorraine Quarrles, emerging inexorably from his dissipated past to blast his hopes of immediate redemption. These three forces gradually converge toward the climactic scene before the denouement and give the story an admirably solid dramatic structure.

While Charlie Wales is in Paris in an effort to regain custody of his daughter, he spends three days revisiting the scenes of his former revels, places where he had been a "good-time Charlie" living with the careless abandon of the playboy Prince of "Wales." Though still occupied by dope-addicts ("Snow Bird") and homosexuals ("strident queens"), "Babylon is fallen, is fallen" (Isaiah 21:9) and is "become a desolation among nations" (Jeremiah 50:23), and Charlie finds that "the place oppressed him." He had first brought Helen to Paris; now he comes to take Honoria out.

That he is in some sort of purgatorial fire is suggested when he emerges from the Ritz Bar and observes that "the fire-red, gas-blue, ghost-green signs shone smokily through the tranquil rain." In Montmartre he notices that "the Poet's Cave had disappeared, but the two great mouths of the Cafe of Heaven and the Cafe of Hell still yawned." The artists in exile had gone, but the choice of Heaven or Hell is always with us.

That Charlie has experienced a moral rebirth and achieved a new identity is suggested not only by his control over

alcohol and money, his rejection of a prostitute and dissipated old friends, but even more subtly by his playful announcement to Honoria, "First let me introduce myself. My name is Charles J. Wales, of Prague." He is no longer from the moral wilderness of Paris (represented by the dissipated Duncan and Lorraine), nor from Burlington, Vermont (represented by Lincoln and Marion Peters); he is a respectable business man from a rich cultural center in the heart of Europe. Marion Peters, especially, is "sick" in a way diametrically opposed to the sickness of Duncan and Lorraine. Charlie resents her legal, not moral, power, but "if he modulated his resentment to the chastened attitude of the reformed sinner, he might win his point in the end."

The story opens "with a stillness in the Ritz Bar that was strange and portentous," and when it closes, again in the Ritz Bar, the portents have been confirmed. He has not regained his Honoria. But although he is suffering, he is not defeated; Purgatory is not the Inferno. "He would come back some day; they couldn't make him pay forever." The mood is one of sadness, longing, and repentance—but neither one of unutterable anguish and guilt, nor one of absolute defeat and loss. On his second night in Paris, Charlie Wales dreamed of his wife whom he had mistreated by locking her out in a snowstorm after a drunken quarrel; in the dream, dressed in white, "she said she was glad he was being good and doing better." At this point Helen has obviously become his Beatrice figure, just beyond his reach since he is in Purgatory. But she is still attainable, and at the end he does *not* collapse into drink and despair. To be sure, his sins require more than a year or two to be purged, but he has the strength to endure more and "he was absolutely sure Helen wouldn't have wanted him to be so alone."

**Richard R. Griffith  (essay date 1963)**

SOURCE: "A Note on Fitzgerald's 'Babylon Revisited'," in *American Literature,* Vol. 35, No. 2, May, 1963, pp. 236-39.

*[In the following essay, Griffith accounts for the inconsistencies in the route Charlie takes from the Ritz Bar to the home of Lincoln and Marion Peters.]*

Although **"Babylon Revisited"** is probably the most anthologized and analyzed of Fitzgerald's short stories, neither editor nor critic has noted the strange route taken by Charlie Wales from the Ritz Bar to Lincoln Peters's home in the Rue Palatine. In the opening scene Charlie discusses former days with Alix, the barman at the Ritz, and departs to visit his daughter at the Peters's home on the Left Bank. Leaving the bar, located in the Place Vendôme (on the Right Bank), he obviously walks north on the Rue de la Paix to the Place de l'Opera, where five streets intersect, including the Boulevard des Capucines and the Avenue de l'Opera. "At the corner of the Boulevard des Capucines he took a taxi."

Clearly this cab went southwest (to Charlie's left, since he was walking north) to the Place de la Madeleine, where it turned south onto the Rue Royale and into the Place de la Concorde, for we are told in the next sentence: "The Place de la Concorde moved by in pink majesty; they crossed the logical Seine, and Charlie felt the sudden provincial quality of the Left Bank." They must have crossed the river at the Pont de la Concorde, and Charlie's intent is presumably to take the Boulevard St. Germain southeast to the Rue Palatine (located just behind St. Surplice)—a reasonable enough route.

However, the opening sentence of the next paragraph asserts that "Charlie directed his taxi to the Avenue de l'Opera, which was out of his way." Fitzgerald uses litotes to good effect on occasion, but this is singularly inappropriate. There are three ways of reaching the Avenue de l'Opera from the taxi's current position at the Left Bank end of the Pont de la Concorde. They may stay on the Left Bank, going east along the river to one of the bridges opposite the Louvre, recross the Seine, and come onto the Avenue de l'Opera as it dead-ends into the Rue de Rivoli. Or they may turn around immediately, go back across the Pont de la Concorde, and take the Rue de Rivoli to the same intersection. Both these routes, unfortunately, take them to the extreme southeast end of the Avenue de l'Opera, and the only direction they can go is northwest, directly *away* from the Left Bank and their goal. The third alternative is to retrace their path exactly—back across the same bridge, through Concorde, up the Rue Royale, past the Madeleine, and via the Boulevard de la Madeleine and the Boulevard des Capucines to Charlie's original corner at the Rue de La Paix. From this point they can turn southeast on the Avenue de l'Opera; and however improbable this route may appear, especially in late afternoon traffic, it is the only one which will at least permit them to take the Avenue in the right direction.

After passing Brentano's book store, just a block south, and a middle class restaurant called Duval's, both quite accurately on Charlie's new route to the Rue Palatine via the Avenue de l'Opera, "they rolled on to the Left Bank and he felt its sudden provincialism. . . ." The wording of this passage provides the key to the problem, for Fitzgerald has used almost the identical words ("Charlie felt the sudden provincial quality of the Left Bank") to conclude the account of the first crossing. An author might conceivably become sufficiently confused to have his character cross a river twice going in the same direction, but no competent craftsman would so duplicate his phraseology, especially when it contains a striking idea like the attribution of "sudden provincialism" to the Left Bank. The obvious explanation is that the second sentence is a rewritten version of the first. If one extends this idea to the whole preceding paragraph, assuming that the entire paragraph was an expanded and revised version of the earlier sentence, intended to be substituted for it, the inconsistencies in itinerary are readily accounted for.

A brief examination of Fitzgerald's artistic purposes in the account of Charlie's taxi ride will indicate how this duplication could have occurred. He is establishing a con-

trast between the life led by Charlie and his friends before the crash (when they were "a sort of royalty") and the bourgeoise respectability represented by the "provincial" Left Bank life of Lincoln Peters (whose very name suggests democracy and rock-like stability). He achieved this very simply in first draft by mentioning the "pink majesty" of La Concorde and following it immediately with the "sudden provincial quality" of the Left Bank. However, in rewriting he found this inadequate, a mere contrast of the spirits of the two Banks. Two things were missing: the sense of glory past (for La Concorde was still there, still majestic), and the suggestion of Charlie's own regret— now that it is no longer possible to live like a king—that he had not been a member of that simpler, stabler class for which he still feels a tinge of contempt. Both these things must be established before the conversations with the Peters take place if the reader is to understand Charlie's relationship with them, and Fitzgerald achieves this very neatly by rerouting the taxi past the Palais Royale and contrasting the cab horns of the present with the trumpets of the Second Empire, by indicating the close of an age of creative literary culture by the drawing of the iron grill across Brentano's, and by Charlie's regrets, seeing the "trim little bourgeois hedge of Duval's," that "he had never eaten at a really cheap restaurant in Paris." He then revised his original sentence referring to the "sudden provincialism," with no mention of passing La Concorde, and used it to conclude the new taxi route through the Right Bank. He neglected, however, to delete the original sentence for which it substituted.

This sort of reconstruction of creative process is necessarily open to question, but in this instance the evidence seems sufficient. Traces of exactly the same sort of revision, designed to enrich through addition of suggestive symbolic detail, appear in the account of Charlie's visit to Montmartre later the same evening. Indeed, the association between the closed grill at Brentano's and the disappearance of the cafe called The Poet's Cave suggests the two passages were reworked at the same time.

A work printed during the author's lifetime and allowed to stand uncorrected by him should, no doubt, be considered as representing his final intention. However, when the choice is between perfect consistency and complete absurdity, and when the error may be accounted for readily and corrected easily—by the omission of a single sentence—it would appear an editorial obligation to do so. Presumably, Fitzgerald would have preferred having his text tampered with to being thought unversed in the geography of Paris.

**Seymour L. Gross (essay date 1963)**

SOURCE: "Fitzgerald's 'Babylon Revisited'," in *College English,* Vol. 25, No. 2, November, 1963, pp. 128-35.

[*In the following essay, Gross refutes James M. Harrison's argument that Charlie is still drawn to his former life.*]

Thus, though we cannot make our sun
Stand still, yet we will make him run.

*—Marvell*

In the little hours of the night every move from place
to place was an enormous human jump, an increase of
paying for the privilege of slower and slower motion.

**—"Babylon Revisited"**

I

The two epigraphs which introduce this essay define, in
one sense, the polar limits of Fitzgerald's life. His frenetic
attempts, almost heroic in their intensity and pathetic in
their ultimate ineffectiveness, to stay ahead of "Time's
winged chariot" (though he was afraid the race was lost at
thirty) are too well known, have been too fully documented, to need much elaboration here. "I wanted to enjoy, to
be prodigal and openhearted, to miss nothing." What
Fitzgerald wanted, finally, was to fill each moment of
life so full of living that time would stand still for him.
This was the way to "beat" time—to run a dead heat
with the galloping stallions of mortality. It is one of Fitzgerald's accomplishments that he can still make us respond
to the purity of this desire even as we recognize, as we
are so often meant to, the spurious materials and self-
defeating methods by which his characters strive to
make life go glimmering. Those of us for whom the
Twenties as Fitzgerald's metaphor of what life may
offer by way of glamour has not yet become a whip-
ping boy of middle-age can still acknowledge, as he
wrote in his notebook, how "any given moment has its
value; it can be questioned in the light of after-events,
but the moment remains. The young prince in velvet gathered in lovely domesticity around the queen amid the hush
of rich draperies may presently grow up to be Pedro the
Cruel or Charles the Mad, but the moment of beauty was
there."

But at the polar opposite of Fitzgerald's presentations of
"the romantic enlargement of the possibilities of life" (to
use Professor Bewley's phrase) emerge the results of the
toughened vision of the "spoiled priest"—as Fitzgerald
once called himself—who watches with horror as the "filled
moment" collapses of its own weight. In this region of
Fitzgerald's moral geography—whose supreme history and
topography have been written into **"Babylon Revisited"**
(1931)—there is nothing of the confusion of attitude to
be found in such essays as "Echoes of the Jazz Age" (1931)
or "My Lost City" (1932), in which the seemingly firm-
eyed recapitulation of catastrophe and self-delusion finally counts for less than the nostalgic yearnings with
which they end. Nor is there anything here of that troubled ambivalence which characterizes our response to
that fantastic ambiguity, Jay Gatsby, whose exquisite
dream moves us even as we acknowledge the cloud of
foul dust which trails in its wake. In the world of **"Babylon Revisited"** winter dreams do not drift sweetly into
sad memories, but erupt into nightmares of irrevocable
loss, leaving only the waste and horror of the twisted
shapes that lie on the decimated plains of the Babylonian Captivity.

II

The action of **"Babylon Revisited"** begins and ends in
the Ritz bar. This structural maneuver is absolutely right,
for the bar is one of the story's chief symbols of the relentless impingement of the past on the present, though it
is not until the end of the story after Charlie's defeat, that
it clearly takes on this signification. Indeed, ironically
enough, Charlie's initial appearance at the Ritz seems to
imply precisely the opposite: the apparent separation of
the past from the concerns, needs, and desires of the
present. The very fact that Charlie can return to the hub
of a life which had cost him his wife and his child does
not at all indicate, as the story's most recent commentator
has it, that the old way of life "still appeals to him," but
rather demonstrates the extent and depth of his self-mastery and the confidence he feels in his belief that his wildly squandered yesterdays are over and done with, that there
is no tab left for him to have to pick up [James M. Harrison, "Fitzgerald's 'Babylon Revisited'," *Explicator,* Vol.
16, January 1958].

The opening scene's primary function is to show how
divorced Charlie feels from the blurred life of several years
ago. His questions to the bartender about cronies from the
past are mechanically curious but fundamentally uninter-
ested. The news that "Mr. Campbell [is] a pretty sick man"
and that Claude Fessenden cheated the bar of thirty thousand francs and is now "all bloated up" evokes no comment. The pricks to memory of "familiar names from the
long list of a year and a half ago" strike no responsive
chord. Charlie feels out of place and "polite" in the bar
that, in the time of wine and roses, he had felt he had
"owned." "It had gone back into France," he thinks. When
he goes through the remembered ritual of placing his foot
firmly on the bar rail and turning to survey the room, only
a single pair of indifferent eyes "fluttered up from a newspaper in the corner." Charlie's dissociation from his past
is capped by the brief bit of dialogue with which the scene
ends:

"Here for long, Mr. Wales?"

"I'm here for four or five days to see my little girl."

"Oh-h! You have a little girl?"

In the Babylon who "saith in her heart [I] shall see no
sorrow," there can be neither children nor the risk of their
loss. The figures there float rootlessly free of human ties
and responsibilities, having sprung full-born from their
skyrocketing blue chips and capacity for dissipation. The
adults are the only children. "We *did* have such good
times that crazy spring [Lorraine wistfully recalls in the
letter to Charlie], like the night you and I stole the butcher's tricycle, and the time we tried to call on the president
and you had the old derby rim and the wire cane." But
Charlie Wales's return to Paris is an attempted return to
fatherhood, an attempt to lay the ghost of his past child-
ishness through the recovery of his lost child, Honoria.
"Oh-h! You have a little girl?" is a bitterly reasonable
question for one whose life had been nothing more than a

"catering to vice and waste . . . on an utterly childish scale." After all, children have no children.

---

**Though "Babylon Revisited" is centrally an exploration of the waste inherent in the quest for the gorgeous life, it is not thereby a paean to Main Street.**

*—Seymour L. Gross*

---

The tragedy is that Charlie no longer deserves such a question. There is in us a desire to find the present Charlie somehow deserving of his wretched fate—which is what perhaps accounts for Professor Harrison's reading—for it is easier to live with a belief in reasonable justice. But Fitzgerald does not allow us this luxury. Throughout the story he ironically stresses the splendid achievement of Charlie's reform. His sensitivity, poised intelligence, and quiet power over himself *should* be enough to get his daughter back. That moral renovation may not be enough is the injustice that lies at the center of the story.

Charlie's recovery of "character"—"the eternally valuable element"—which was implied in the opening scene in his being unafraid to confront the old life, is made explicit as he leaves the bar. Walking the street, he feels, all at once, "the sudden provincial quality of the left bank." But Charlie is not a prig: his self-mastery is too final to need the subtly corrupt support of the moral outrage of a libertine turned puritan. He can still be moved by the "pink majesty" of the Place de la Concord and "the blue hour spread over the magnificent facade" of the Avenue de l'Opera; he can even afford to indulge in the fantasy of imagining that "the cab horns, playing endlessly the first few bars of *Le Plus que Lent,* were the trumpets of the Second Empire." Paris is not, after all, Babylon. Only the Left Bank, which in the "crazy years" had seemed the epitome of romantic possibility, strikes him with "its sudden provincialism." Brentano's, cheap restaurants (in which he had never eaten), such as Duval's, with its "trim little bourgeois hedge," had never been "spoiled," because they had never been touched, by the crowd of three years ago who had made "months into days." Babylon, Charlie thinks sadly, had been an American creation.

The following scene with Marion and Lincoln Peters, Charlie's sister-in-law and her husband, who had been given custody of Honoria when Charlie's wife, Helen, was dying and he himself was broke and in a sanitarium for alcoholism, is the symbolic obverse of the opening scene at the Ritz bar, which had depicted the repudiated past. Here the "warm and comfortably American room," the intimate movements of children, "the cheer of six o'clock" as dinner is being prepared, and Honoria (in Charlie's mind) at the center of the bustle, represent the future which Charlie anticipates with excruciating need. The contrasts

between the two scenes are extensive. The mechanical exchange in the bar has become the sincerely interested conversation between Charlie and Lincoln Peters; the "single bored voice in the once-clamorous women's room" has changed into "the eager smacks of the fire and sounds of French activity in the kitchen"; the shrill group of homosexuals ("strident queens") has been replaced by a family. Honoria's ecstatic shriek of welcome—"oh, daddy, daddy, daddy, daddy, dads, dads, dads!"—is the answer to the barman's surprised question.

Yet for all the obvious contrasts between the two scenes, there is also present an ominous similarity—a similarity which functions as the first of many symbolic foreshowings of Charlie's failure to redeem his daughter (and thus himself) from the carnival years. In both scenes Charlie is fundamentally isolated from the radical quality of the life going on around him: in the bar because of his maturity, in the home because of his position as a suppliant. Despite Honoria's presence (with its infinite promise), it is Marion Peters' hostility which dominates the scene, making Charlie's heart sit "up rigidly in his body." Although it is not until Part III that we come fully to understand why Marion has set herself against Charlie's future, her animosity, interposing itself as it does between father and daughter, so serves to consign Charlie's presence to the periphery of the room that the final effect of the scene is the disturbing implication that Charlie's proximity to the symbols of the life he hopes for is as deceptive as was his proximity in the opening scene to the symbols of the life he left behind him. It is significant that Honoria never speaks again in the scene after her cry of joy and that the last bit of dialogue is Marion's frigid reply to Charlie's statement that he takes but one drink a day—"I hope you keep to it."

The parallelism between the two scenes is reinforced by the similarity of Charlie's response to both the bar and the Peters' home: relief at being able to get away and a desire to roam the streets alone to see Paris "with clearer and more judicious eyes than those of other days." His second view is more severely contemptuous, the result, no doubt, of his recent contact with Honoria. Montmartre, "where he had parted with so many hours and so much money," stripped of its alcoholic haze, reveals itself as cheap, meretriciously exuberant, and corrupt. As he watches the prowling prostitutes, devouring cafes, and "bleak and sinister cheap hotels," he "suddenly realized the meaning of the word 'dissipate'—to dissipate into thin air; to make nothing out of something." Then follows what is perhaps Fitzgerald's most profound insight into the nature of Babylon, Jazz Age style: "In the little hours of the night every move from place to place was an enormous human jump, an increase of paying for the privilege of slower and slower motion."

On the literal level, the sentence describes early morning bar-hopping: greater and greater expenditures of cash for the "privilege" of more and more uncertain physical movement. But the passage reaches out to larger significances. The impulse towards the enlargement of experience which lies behind the spree manifests itself in the *little* hours of the night (which Fitzgerald elsewhere described as "the dark night of the soul")—"little" not only in the sense of early, but also in the ironic sense of compressed and constricted. The "enormous human jump" required of the drunk in moving from place to place, for whom physical space is constantly hostile, enlarges to an understanding of the expense of spirit which the movement entails. Not only is money being spent ("an increase of paying"), but the human quality is being spent, used up, too. The desire to make the sun run by filling each moment so full of gaiety and abandon that time will seem to stand still succeeds only in so weighting down the figures that they can manage only the contrived movements of an artificially slowed-down motion picture. Life, not time, has stopped.

Part II opens deceptively. The "fine fall day," Charlie's euphoria, and lunch with Honoria at the only restaurant Charlie can think of "not reminiscent of . . . long luncheons that began at two and ended in a blurred and vague twilight," seem to promise, structurally, that the happier of the alternatives symbolically offered in Part I will occur. This scene—the only extended contact between father and daughter—is particularly poignant because in dramatizing a glimpse of the future Charlie yearns for, Fitzgerald makes us *feel* (and not merely abstractly acknowledge) the absolute rightness of Charlie's desire to be reunited with his daughter. Though Charlie knows that he needs his daughter back in order to give shape and direction to his renascence, to redeem his lost honor, and, in a sense, to recover something of his wife "escaped to a grave in Vermont," he is aware of the danger in the very intensity of his need. He knows how perilously easy it would be to make Honoria into a smothered surrogate for all that he has irremediably lost. For example, when Honoria "tranquilly" agrees that she won't always love her daddy best, but will someday "grow up and meet somebody her own age and go marry him and forget [she] ever had a daddy," Charlie is not upset. The conversation between father and daughter is tender and loving and wholly free of sinister psychiatric pressures, dramatic proof of Charlie's ability to act in terms of his understanding as it is articulated in Part IV:

> The present was the thing—work to do and someone to love. But not to love too much, for he knew the injury that a father can do to a daughter . . . by attaching [her] too closely: afterward, out in the world, the child would seek in the marriage partner the same blind tenderness and, failing probably to find it, turn against love and life.

Hawthorne once observed that every crime we commit destroys more Edens than our own. In focusing on Charlie's need it is easy to miss Honoria's. Though Fitzgerald does not cheapen the scene by sentimentalizing the unsatisfactoriness of Honoria's present life, it is clear that Honoria likes neither Marion nor Marion's daughter, though she is too well-bred and sensitive to engage in spiteful recriminations that could only serve to deepen her father's unhappiness. Her sudden "Daddy, I want to come and live with you," though unaccompanied by Dickensian emotional fanfare, is an eloquent plea that broadens the

base of the tragedy, much as does the silent presence of the children at the end of the *Oedipus*. This encounter will painfully remind us, when Charlie's undeserved defeat is at the center of our response, of Honoria's loss as well.

The past and future, which were structurally separated in Part I (though the past was made to impinge symbolically upon the future) are narratively intersected in Part II. Duncan Schaeffer and Lorraine Quarles—"Sudden ghosts out of the past"—intrude themselves upon the promise of tomorrow. They are *ghosts* not only because they will eventually haunt Charlie to defeat, but also because they are disembodied, dislocated spirits inhabiting a world which exists only in their self-conscious strivings. Lorraine's "This your little girl?" (which echoes the bartender's question) announces her exclusion from reality; similarly, when Charlie tries to stop the banal bantering about his being sober by indicating Honoria with his head, both Lorraine and Duncan can only laugh. The innocent pleasure of father and daughter attending the vaudeville at the Empire becomes, in Lorraine's "There! That's what I want to do. . . . I want to see some clowns and acrobats and jugglers," an obscene activity, a Babylonian revel of ruinous irresponsibility and desperate hilarity. But they are ghosts in yet another sense, for Lorraine and Duncan are the anonymous figures in slow motion in the passage already quoted. Doomed as they are to being out of time, where gestures pass through all the essential realities, they can only drift, "trite, blurred, worn away," in search of some vampiristic contact with those who inhabit the real world. "They liked him," Charlie thinks, "because he was serious . . . because he was stronger than they were, because they wanted to draw a certain sustenance from his strength." He has located their essential weakness; but he has miscalculated their power to destroy. Human blood cannot make vampires normally human; but vampires destroy what is human in achieving temporary sustenance.

The intrusion of the ghosts from Charlie's past accounts, symbolically, for the tableau with which Part II ends. Charlie does not accompany his daughter into the Peters's house. He waits, instead, "in the dark street until she appeared all warm and glowing, in the window above, and kissed her fingers out into the night." The distance between the shadowed father and radiant daughter, which the kiss can only symbolically but not actually traverse, is the measure of their inevitable separation. Honoria, framed in the window, has become, the passage seems to imply, a portrait—something that was once livingly available but is now only accessible as a memory in a gallery of remembrances of things past. The tableau, moreover, looks back to the terminal passage of Part I, in which Charlie eludes the "encouraging stare" of a streetwalker, though he buys her supper and gives her a twenty-franc note (as he is later to buy Honoria lunch and give her a doll), and forward to the terminal passage of Part III, when Charlie in a half-dream tries to talk to his dead wife, who "was in a swing in a white dress, and swinging faster and faster all the time, so that at the end he could not hear clearly all that she said." These structural juxtapositions indicate that although Charlie has wilfully removed himself from the sterility of his past, as represented by the prostitute, he is nevertheless actually closer to her than he is to the distanced Honoria or receding Helen. He is offered the physical presence of a non-wife, non-mother, but only the "portrait" of his child and the "ghost" of his wife.

In Part III Marion becomes a significant actor in the drama. Having dressed herself in a black dress "that just faintly suggested mourning," as if already prepared to preside over the death of Charlie's hopes, Marion sets herself squarely against her brother-in-law's dream of the future. Although she has obviously convinced herself that she is motivated solely by a concern for Honoria's welfare and duty to her dead sister, it soon becomes apparent that her hard stance is not morally unequivocal. In Marion we see a subtly corrupt desire for self-justification masking itself in the virtues of duty and responsibility. Marion, because she had never really loved her sister, jealously resented her sister's materially superior marriage. Lincoln, though a wholly decent person, has never been capable of making much money; even in the boom time he "never got ahead enough to carry anything but [his] insurance." Indeed, although Charlie has had recently to start over again from scratch, he is already making twice as much money as Lincoln. Marion's response to this "injustice" has been to take psychological refuge in the cliché that the rich are never happy; she has submerged her envy in "a curious disbelief in her sister's happiness." Marion's hostility did not originate, as Lincoln believes, in the Babylonian days—"Marion felt there was some kind of injustice in . . . you not even working toward the end, and getting richer and richer"—but long before that. The party years merely aggravated—and seemed to give justification for—an already existing mean condition of mind. Marion's vindication came in "the shock of one terrible night" when Helen was locked out in a snowstorm and barely escaped pneumonia. Convinced, because she wanted to be, that this was "one of many scenes from her sister's martyrdom," Marion's repressed envy was able to flower forth as self-righteous "hatred" for Charlie. The death of Helen (which Marion falsely insists on blaming Charlie for) and Charlie's own crack-up affirmed once and for all the superiority of her own married life. Her "investment" has paid off in the legal guardianship of Honoria; and the power to beat Charlie with this moral triumph is what she has instead of a materially lavish life.

Marion, however, is not merely an interesting piece of psychological portraiture, for she complicates what might otherwise have been an unqualified commitment to the life of the "solid citizen." Though **"Babylon Revisited"** is centrally an exploration of the waste inherent in the quest for the gorgeous life, it is not thereby a paean to Main Street. It is clear that Charlie's "plans, vistas, futures for Honoria and himself" are organized around what we have come to call middle-class values and virtues—home, responsible job, hard work, the respect of the community. But it is also clear—as Marion's presence in the story indicates—that the achievement of worth is not to be found in the middle class automatically. Every mode of life is shadowed by its own kind of treachery and means of self-aggrandizement. Marion, no less than Lorraine and Duncan, "needs" Charlie, in her case as a "tangible vil-

lain." It is therefore both ironic and apt that although Marion is revolted by people like Lorraine and Duncan—they "make her really physically sick"—she will, in Part IV, unwittingly ally herself with them to destroy Charlie. She too has set herself against Charlie's attempt to extricate himself from his past: "from the night you did that terrible thing [Charlie's accidental locking out of his wife in the snow] you haven't really existed for me." Indeed, without Marion, Lorraine and Duncan are without effect. How fully she has committed herself to keeping Charlie from escaping into the future is revealed when, after being forced to acknowledge that Charlie "had somehow arrived at control over the situation" and that Lincoln will not help her keep Honoria from her father, she responds with hysterical viciousness, "I think if she were my child I'd rather see her—" and retreats to her bed with a neurasthenic headache.

In Part IV, which ironically opens with Charlie's ecstatic feeling that the "door of the world was open again," Charlie is to feel the full weight of his history. As if duplicating the ultimate movement of the entire section, Charlie's happiness fades suddenly into the sad memory of all the plans he and Helen had made that would never materialize. Though he turns away from the past—"The present was the thing"—the arrival of a letter from Lorraine, nostalgically recalling the "good times that crazy spring," reinforces the mounting sense of an unreasonably vengeful past. It will turn out to be of no avail that Charlie can dismiss the thought of a "trite, blurred, worn away" Lorraine to "think of Sundays spent with [Honoria] . . . and knowing she was there in his house at night, drawing her breath in the darkness."

For at the very threshold of Charlie's new life, the "ghosts from the past" drift up the corridors of time. Fitzgerald's paragraph describing their emergence is appropriately eerie. First, like an annunciation of doom, the long peal of the bell; then the voices in the corridor coming closer, "which developed under the light into Duncan Schaeffer and Lorraine Quarles." Drunk, incoherent, irresponsible, the world of Babylon has shattered the world of "people together by a fire." In a brilliant symbolic gesture, Charlie, horrified, moves closer to them, "as if to force them backward down the corridor." That it is Charlie's own past that he is trying to force backward into time is amply demonstrated by the fact that Lorraine and Duncan are specifically identified with the figures in the "little hours of the night" passage: "Still in slow motion, with blurred, angry faces, with uncertain feet, they retired along the corridor."

But Charlie's power is finally useless: the door of the world opens to both the past and the future. Charlie is now more isolated than he had ever been before. Marion stands rigidly with an arm encircling each of her children and Lincoln is "swinging Honoria back and forth like a pendulum from side to side." The implications of this tableau are totally devastating. The past has set the pendulum of the future in motion; time will serve only to take Honoria further away from him; "the tangible, visible child" will swing away into dimmer and dimmer memory, like

Helen in the dream in Part III, who was "swinging faster and faster all the time, so that in the end he could not hear clearly all that she said." All that is left for Charlie to do is to return alone down the corridor, turning to say a final goodbye—"Good night, sweetheart. . . . Good night, dear children."

The story ends in the Ritz bar, where Charlie furiously goes to find Lorraine and Duncan. But he soon realizes that "there was nothing he could do." The return to the bar, as well as the first appearance of Paul, the head bar-man, "who in the latter days of the bull market had come to work in his custom-built car," symbolizes Charlie's bondage to a world which he mistakenly supposed could be cast off completely. Charlie does not change in the course of **"Babylon Revisited"**; his underserved defeat does not become an occasion for either self-pity or self-indulgence; in the bar he neither talks of his loss nor takes more than the one drink a day he has allowed himself.

But his substantial endowments have not been enough. Though he thinks that he will "come back someday; they couldn't make him pay forever," the whole movement of the story makes it bitterly clear that they can. When he asks the waiter "What do I owe you?" the answer the story supplies is "your hopes and dreams."

A part of Charlie's life had stopped in the little hours of some night when if you didn't want something to be real, "you just paid some money." Looking back, Charlie now realizes how utterly he "lost everything [he] wanted in the boom"; and Fitzgerald, in the final sentence of the story, crushes any lingering hopes by indicating that there is nothing left for Charlie to do but turn for comfort to the dead, for whom time has also stopped. "He was absolutely sure Helen wouldn't have wanted him to be so alone."

## William R. Osborne  (essay date 1964)

SOURCE: "The Wounds of Charlie Wales in Fitzgerald's 'Babylon Revisited'," in *Studies in Short Fiction,* Vol. 2, No. 1, Fall, 1964, pp. 86-7.

[*In the following essay, Osborne examines the symbolic meaning of the name "Charlie Wales."*]

Not only does the title of F. Scott Fitzgerald's short story **"Babylon Revisited"** invite symbolic interpretation, but scattered throughout the story are street names or place names like *Rue Saint-Honoré,* the *Poet's Cave,* the *Café of Heaven,* and the *Café of Hell* that seem also to have obvious symbolic overtones. In the names of the characters, too, critics have found symbolic significance. James Frakes and Isadore Traschen point out [in *Short Fiction: A Critical Collection,* 1959] that the name of Charlie Wales's daughter Honoria "suggests an allegorical play on redeeming [Charlie's] honor." Richard Griffith sees the name Lincoln Peters as being one which "suggests democracy and rock-like stability" [*American Literature,* Vol. XXXIV, May 1963]. To my knowledge, no one has

investigated the name of the protagonist, Charlie Wales, to determine whether it too might yield associations consistent with the symbolical overtones with which Fitzgerald has charged his story.

The *NED* offers several relevant meanings for *wale* as a noun: (*1*) "the mark or ridge raised on the flesh by the blow of a rod, lash, or the like. (*2*) the action or an act of choosing; choice." As a verb *wale* can mean (*1*) "to choose, select, pick out; (*2*) to mark (the flesh) with wales or weals." The idea of choice or choosing is relevant to the story since one principal theme of **"Babylon Revisited"** is that the choices Charlie Wales has made in the past have generated his present difficulties and will affect all future choices as well. But *wale* in the sense of injuring or being injured by a blow on the flesh (we still speak of "waling the daylights" out of someone) is a meaning that Fitzgerald would more likely have known. Throughout the story Charlie *wales* and is *waled* as he attempts to regain custody of his daughter. Near the end of the story, for example, he says to Marion Peters about their arguments: "Family quarrels are bitter things. They don't go according to any rules. They're not like aches or wounds; they're more like splits in the skin that won't heal because there's not enough material." Again and again, Fitzgerald writes of Charlie's pain: "An electric current of agony surged through him." "He knew now that he would have to take a beating." "The image of Helen haunted him. Helen whom he had loved so until they had senselessly begun to abuse each other's love and tear it into shreds."

With these comments in mind, we might wish to think of the story as resembling generally (but obviously not with complete consistency) a morality play, with Charlie as a short of suffering and wounded Everyman of the post-Jazz Age, trying to choose middle-class Respectability and gain Honor (Honoria) but being waled by the evil angels of his "Babylonian" past, chief of which would be Lorraine Quarrles (whose name also has appropriate connotations) and Duncan Schaeffer. On the other hand, there is the good angel of Charlie's present, the sympathetic and balanced representative of the type of middle-class respectability to which Charlie aspires—Lincoln Peters. Unable to ignore his bohemian past, assailed constantly by Marion Peters (neurotic and narrow-minded representative of the middle-class at its worst), Charlie Wales suffers the tortures of the damned.

At the end of the story both Charlie's Honor and Honoria are still hanging in the balance. To dramatize the stalemate and emphasize its importance, Fitzgerald makes a deceptively simple statement at the very climax of the story, after Lorraine and Duncan have destroyed Charlie's chances of getting custody of Honoria. When Charlie returns to the room where Marion sits in stunned but belligerent silence, he senses that his battle is now lost. At this point Fitzgerald focuses our attention on Lincoln Peters, the sane, balanced character of the story, and Honoria, the prize, the goal, the central symbol of Charlie's conflict. Writes Fitzgerald, "Lincoln was still swinging Honoria back and forth like a pendulum from side to side." On the narrative level, Lincoln Peters is merely entertaining Honoria, diverting her attention from the emotional crisis taking place in the room. Symbolically, Fitzgerald is showing that Honoria's fate still hangs in the balance, that she might go the way of Marion Peters or Charlie Wales (who himself might go the way of Lincoln Peters or Lorraine Quarrles). With this dramatic incident, this focus on Honoria, we are reminded that she too is named *Wales* and is vulnerable, liable to further injury, and dependent largely upon the choices Charlie Wales makes.

Thus, Charlie's quest for Respectability and Honor will be a continuing one, and though waled and wounded, he apparently wills to pursue his present course of action, realizing as he does so that his Honor-Honoria will be affected, perhaps affronted and injured, by choices he made long ago and by choices he must make in the present. It would seem, then, that *Wales* is a dramatically appropriate name for a father and daughter who become the center of a story involving suffering and choice, in other words, an essentially tragic story.

### Thomas F. Staley (essay date 1964-65)

SOURCE: "Time and Structure in Fitzgerald's 'Babylon Revisited'," in *Modern Fiction Studies,* Vol. 10, No. 4, Winter 1964-65, pp. 386-88.

[*In the following essay, Staley demonstrates how Charlie's past and present interact to influence his future.*]

Kant wrote that time is the most characteristic mode of our experience, and, as Hans Myerhoff has pointed out, "It is more general than space, because it applies to the inner world of impressions, emotions and ideas for which no spatial order can be given." Modern fiction is preoccupied with the concept of time; Bergson's concept of *la duree realle* and Proust's *la memoire involontaire* have of course, exerted a large influence on fiction; in fact their indirect influence has been enormous. Modern writers since Bergson and Proust have become increasingly aware of the implications of time in the structure of their fiction. F. Scott Fitzgerald was particularly preoccupied with the forces of time. His personal life, together with his reading, gave him a profound sense of the importance of time with regard to self.

Fitzgerald felt the ravages of time especially in his own life, and a great deal of his fiction touches on this theme. He was less inward in his treatment of time than either Joyce or Thomas Wolfe, but there is in his fiction a sense of the unity of past and present; the past is irrevocable because it brings about the reality of the present. An understanding of how Fitzgerald's concept of time informs his fiction can be illustrated by an analysis of his famous short story **"Babylon Revisited."** The plot of this story moves directly through time and space, and its movement conveys its theme.

The theme of **"Babylon Revisited"** suggests that the past and the future meet in the present; moreover, Fitzgerald also dramatically expresses Bergson's idea that duration is the continuous progress of the past which forces into the future. In the story, Charlie Wales relives the disastrous events of his past in a few days, and he realizes in the brilliant final scene in the Ritz Bar that time is irreversible, that the empty glass in front of him is the emptiness of his whole life, past, present, and future. At the beginning of the story, Charlie intends to shuck away the memory of his past through the recovery of his lost child, but the actuality of the past has nullified this prospect from the first.

The very title of the story suggests the movement of time and space. The scene is set in the modern city along the Seine, but we are intended to recall the ancient city on the banks of the Euphrates. Charlie Wales returns to Paris in order to claim his daughter and thus give meaning and purpose to his life. But just as Charlie has changed in the three years since he left Paris, so, too, has the world he left. In the opening scene in the Ritz Bar he inquires about his former friends, but finds they have scattered, to Switzerland, to America. He notices a group of "strident queens" in the corner and is depressed because he realizes that ". . . they go on forever" and are not affected by time.

Throughout Part I of the story Charlie is continually trying to turn back the clock. During dinner at the Peters' he looks across at Honoria and feels that ". . . he wanted to jump back a whole generation." As he walks through the Montmartre district after dinner, he recalls his dissipated life in Paris, and he realizes that his bar hopping was "an increase of paying for the privilege of slower and slower motion." As he wanders the streets of Paris, Charlie Wales' attitude toward time is that of something lost. Throughout Part I all the references to time are to the past; the hope for the future remains in the background.

There is a shift of emphasis in time as Part II opens. Charlie wants to forget the horrors of the past as he has lunch with Honoria. He deliberately chooses a restaurant that is "not reminiscent of champagne dinners and long luncheons that began at two and ended in a blurred vague twilight." Today is to be a special day; today is to be isolated into the present; but this is impossible, for out of that twilight world of the past "sudden ghosts" emerge. Two of the people who helped him to "make months into days" confront him in the restaurant, and the past impinges on the present, and also foreshadows its impingement on the future.

In this scene present, past and future fuse. Both past and future collide as Honoria, a symbol of the future, meets Lorraine and Duncan, symbols of the lurking past. This scene in which the past and future meet in the present also foreshadows the climax of the story in Part IV, when Lorraine and Duncan invade the Peters' home and in so doing both symbolically and literally destroy the future.

Part II opens at noon when the sun is high in the air and the day is full of expectation for Charlie, but it ends as Charlie stands outside in the dark street and looks up at Honoria as she blows him a kiss ". . . out into the night."

This scene also recalls the impossibility of Gatsby's dream illustrated as he stands outside in the darkness waiting for Daisy following the automobile accident in *The Great Gatsby.*

---

**Time and its ravages have left Charlie suspended in time with a nightmare for a past, an empty whiskey glass for a present, and a future full of loneliness.**

*—Thomas F. Staley*

---

In Part III Charlie is aware that he will have to submit to Marion's verbal beating in order to get Honoria back. "It would last an hour or two hours. . . ." But what is two hours in relation to a lifetime? The scene with Marion and Lincoln begins with Charlie's confidence quite high, but the desperateness of his situation shows through the conversation. He says to Marion: "'But if we wait much longer I'll lose Honoria's childhood and my chance for a home'." Charlie leaves the Peters' home and crosses through the Paris streets. With the question of Honoria's coming with him still unresolved he recalls again his past and is haunted by the image of his dead wife as he crosses the Seine, the same Seine that he crossed many times three years before with his wife Helen. His spirits rise and the Seine seems fresh and new to him. The opposition of present and past is visually reinforced by the black dress that Marion wears in the present and by the white dress that Helen has on as she swings ". . . faster and faster all the time." But this is the Helen that emerges in a dream, out of relation with time. But even in the dream, time is present in the symbol of the pendulum swinging and swinging; Helen becomes the pendulum of time herself. Dreams momentarily take the burdens of time from Charlie; they offer him an escape from the present, distort the past, and belie the future.

Charlie wakes up to another "bright, crisp day" as Part IV of the story opens. Separating past and present for a moment, Charlie looks to the future, believing for an instant that the past doesn't determine the future: "He made plans, vistas, futures for Honoria and himself." But this glimpse into the future is quickly thwarted by a glance backward at past visions: "Suddenly he grew sad, remembering all the plans he and Helen had made." Seeing the future as not quite real and the past as a crushed dream, Charlie thinks of the present: "The present was the thing—work to do and someone to love."

Each time Charlie's future with Honoria seems temporarily possible the past quickly snuffs out the hope. After having lunch with Lincoln, he returns to his hotel room to find a note from Lorraine. In the note Lorraine recalls that "crazy spring" when she and Charlie stole a butcher's tricycle. This incident again brings Charlie back to that past which in retrospect was a nightmare. Out of his feel-

ing of repugnance for the past, symbolized in Lorraine, he quickly turns to thoughts of the future, symbolized by Honoria.

At five o'clock Charlie arrives at the Peters and his dreams of the future seem realized; he seems to have finally defeated the past. But the final tension of past and present in the story comes to a climax. Duncan and Lorraine suddenly interrupt the discussion of plans concerning Honoria. These "blurred, angry faces" from the past emerge to destroy the future forever. "Charlie came closer to them, as if to force them backward down the corridor." It was impossible for Charlie to blot out the past. After Lorraine and Duncan leave, Charlie returns to the salon to see Lincoln "swinging Honoria back and forth like a pendulum from side to side." Whether Charlie realizes it or not, this action is visual testimony that time has placed Honoria in the hands of the Peters. Charlie leaves the house knowing full well that he is not to get Honoria; the past has spoiled the present and determined the future.

The final irony of Charlie's life is brought out in the final section of the story, Part V, which is set again in the Ritz Bar where the story opened. Paul, the bartender, points out the irony unknowingly when he says, "'It's a great change. . . .'" Charlie's mind goes back to the past again, but now he sees himself in the eternal present, alone. He thinks back to a fixed period of time, the Wall Street crash, and then to the time just before that when the snow wasn't real snow. "If you didn't want it to be snow, you just paid some money." To escape from the past Charlie tried to make a life for himself and Honoria, but now he must be concerned with only the hollow thought of buying her something. As the story ends, he must escape time and reality and dream again of Helen, who he is sure "wouldn't have wanted him to be so alone." Time and its ravages have left Charlie suspended in time with a nightmare for a past, an empty whiskey glass for a present, and a future full of loneliness.

### Roy R. Male (essay date 1965)

SOURCE: "'Babylon Revisited': A Story of the Exile's Return," in *Studies in Short Fiction,* Vol. 2, No. 3, Spring, 1965, pp. 270-77.

*[In the following essay, Male contends that Charlie Wales has not reformed because he is still torn between his former life and his present one.]*

F. Scott Fitzgerald's **"Babylon Revisited,"** although widely reprinted, has not produced many commentaries. James Frake and Isadore Traschen give a brief explication in their text on short fiction [*Short Fiction,* 1959], Arthur Mizener refers to the story a number of times in his biography [*The Far Side of Paradise,* 1949], and Seymour Gross has recently offered a full-length analysis [in "Fitzgerald's 'Babylon Revisited'," *College English,* Vol. XXV, November 1963]. But compared to, say, "Rappaccini's Daughter," or "The Turn of the Screw," or "The

Bear," Fitzgerald's story seems to have provoked almost no concern—mainly, I suppose, because its meaning is clear. It has some symbols, but they are not mysterious; some ambiguity, but it is not hidden; considerable irony, but it is readily discernible. It strikes us, in short, as an example of the really excellent story that is widely read and reread, usually with considerable appreciation and understanding. This paper asks, in effect, whether it is possible to write profitably about a story that everybody already understands, or nearly understands.

My basic assumption is not particularly startling, but it does run counter to that of the extreme formalists (now perhaps nearly extinct), who used to maintain that criticism and teaching of a short story should be rigorously limited to an examination of the text. "Stay inside the story," they said, as if one story is of no help in understanding another, as if the time spirit supplies nothing to shape an author's fiction, as if his life tells us nothing about his art. No, I would maintain that we should place a story in as many contexts as possible. I limit myself here to the three just mentioned: generic, historical, and biographical, paying particular attention to the first because it is the least familiar.

What kind of story is **"Babylon Revisited"**? To this deliberately broad and blunt question the answers, whether from students, English teachers, or writers, would be something short of unanimous. Here are some typical student replies: "It's a good story." "It's realistic." "No, it's impressionistic." "It's a story about life in the twenties." "It's a short story." These students were not stupid; their chaotic response simply reflects the relatively primitive state of the generic criticism of fiction. Having jettisoned the whole idea of genres somewhere in the nineteenth century, we lack descriptive terms to define fictions in any fundamental and illuminating way. The major exceptions to this generalization are terms like picaresque novel, *Bildungsroman, Künstlerroman,* and Lionel Trilling's description of the story of the Young Man from the Provinces. These terms define stories either according to the situation of the hero or according to the action imitated; they have the great advantage of being easily recognizable; and I think that their defining principle can be extended. It is not that every story can or should be classified in this way; but if we do find a group of stories imitating the same basic action, we are being critically and pedagogically provincial if we ignore their interrelationship.

From this point of view, **"Babylon Revisited"** belongs with a number of stories in which the protagonist returns after a prolonged absence, either to his home or to some substitute for it. This category we may call the story of the Exile's Return, and in American fiction it would include (among others) Washington Irving's "Rip Van Winkle," Nathaniel Hawthorne's "Ethan Brand," Hamlin Garland's "The Return of a Private," Henry James's "The Jolly Corner," Ernest Hemingway's "Soldier's Home," Theodore Dreiser's "The Old Neighborhood," Lionel Trilling's *The Middle of the Journey,* and Frederick Buechner's "The Tiger." Behind these American stories, of course, are such prototypes as Ulysses returning to Penelope, Plato's myth

of the cave, the Biblical account of the return of the prodigal son, and Dante's return from his vision of hell, purgatory, and paradise.

The advantages of placing stories together in this way are obvious: first, certain conventions and common themes emerge clearly, aiding explication of each individual story; and second, once the similarities are established, differences in execution or technique are more clearly discernible. As Henry James said, in a somewhat different connection, "our aim is to get the correspondences and equivalents that make differences mean something."

Certain themes are inherent in the basic situation of a man returning after a long absence. In fiction as in life, the most obvious and the most poignant is the mutability theme or, more specifically, the sense of permanence and change. Although some aspects of the setting seem unchanged, their apparent permanence simply emphasizes the fundamental law of life, that all things pass. Thus we have in these stories something like the *ubi sunt* formula in poetry. Rip Van Winkle asks, "Where's Nicholas Vedder? Where's Brom Dutcher? Where's Van Bummel, the schoolmaster?" Gone, all of them gone. Even Vedder's wooden tombstone, Rip learns, is "rotten and gone." This, of course, is where Fitzgerald's story begins. "Where's Mr. Campbell?" "And George Hardt?" "And where is the Snow Bird?" "What's become of Claude Fessenden?" All gone, some of them "rotten and gone." In the Babylonian Ritz Bar only the "strident queens" remain; "they go on forever."

The hero may ask about the men, his former friends, but the essential motivation for his return is always a reunion with some form of the feminine principle. She may be a person: the faithful wife as in "The Return of a Private," the daughter as in "Rip Van Winkle" and **"Babylon Revisited,"** the stable and intimate friend Alice Staverton in "The Jolly Corner." Or it may be more abstract and symbolic: the "mother earth" invoked and then rejected by Ethan Brand, the "girls" that bother Krebs in "Soldier's Home," or the alma mater as in "The Tiger." Thomas Wolfe, whose fiction flowed forth from the archetypal pattern of departure and return, described the impulse this way: "By the 'earth again' I mean simply the everlasting earth, a home, a place for the heart to come to, and earthly mortal love, the love of a woman, who, it seems to me, belongs to the earth and is a force opposed to that other great force that makes men wander, that makes them search, that makes them lonely, and that makes them both hate and love their loneliness."

As anyone who has returned home after a long absence will testify, the experience often has a dreamlike quality, a curious mixture of pain and pleasure as one feels his identity dissolving into two selves, past and present, private and public. The threatened loss of identity is explicit in "Rip Van Winkle" when he is confronted by a double, unaware, of course, that he is his son:

> Rip looked and beheld a precise counterpart of himself
> as he went up the mountain: apparently as lazy and

certainly as ragged. The poor fellow was now completely dumfounded. He doubted his own identity, and whether he was himself or another man. In the midst of his bewilderment, the man in the cocked hat demanded who he was and what was his name?

"God knows," [says Rip] "I'm not myself—I'm somebody else—that's me yonder—no—that's somebody else got into my shoes—I was myself last night, but I fell asleep on the mountain and they've changed my gun and everything's changed and I can't tell what's my name or who I am."

As Philip Young remarks in his acute, if somewhat over-elaborate interpretation of "Rip," the character has a universal quality. "If we mock him for whatever he has missed, we do it tenderly—partly because it is something hidden in ourselves we mock. It is all our own lost lives and roles, the lives and roles that once seemed possible and are possible no more" ["Fallen from Time: The Mythic Rip Van Winkle," *Kenyon Review,* Vol. XXII, Autumn 1960]. This aspect of the exile's return is central, of course, in "The Jolly Corner," where Spencer Brydon hunts down his alter ego, the self he missed becoming when he left America, "'the American fate' with which he never has come to terms." And this theme of split identity recurs, as we shall see, in **"Babylon Revisited,"** where the basic question about Charlie is whether he is indeed "the old Wales," as his former friends call him, or the new.

A final theme given in the situation of the returning exile is that of freedom and responsibility. The mere fact that he has been gone suggests the possibility of egotism and escapism. Rip, we recall, was dodging not merely his wife "but all the obligations of maturity: occupation, domestic and financial responsibility, a political position, duty to his country in time of war." This is the major issue in Trilling's short novel, *The Middle of the Journey.* The protagonist, John Laskell, has returned midway in the journey of life from an inferno of pain, a nearly fatal illness. His image on the cover of the Anchor paperback might stand for all the modern exiles, returning not "home"—Laskell's hot bachelor apartment in New York—but to friends in the country. He is "the stranger, the outlander, the foreigner from New York," and in his weakened condition he is overwhelmed by irrational terror when no one meets the train. One is reminded of Randall Jarrell's poem "On the Railway Platform" and its lines: "What we leave we leave forever: / Time has no travellers. And journeys end in / No destinations we meant." That no one met the train, it turns out, was the fault of his friends' handy man, Duck Caldwell. Later, while conversing with his friends, Laskell quickly decides to "drop the whole matter of fault and blame," but this, of course, is precisely what Trilling does not do. The book's complex though somewhat abstract plot, culminating in the death of Caldwell's daughter (who has heart trouble), turns on the question of involvement, responsibility, and guilt. So, too, in **"Babylon Revisited,"** we find Charlie Wales maintaining that he is now a responsible person but denying responsibility for his wife's death. "Helen died of heart trouble,'" he

says. "'Yes, heart trouble,'" Marion retorts, "as if the phrase had another meaning for her."

So much for the important themes these stories have in common. They are equally notable, of course, for their differences of technique. In a full-length study one might profitably observe in some detail what we will here summarize in a paragraph: the movement toward dramatization, immediacy, and restricted point of view in the modern stories as contrasted with the pictorialism, detachment, and omniscient point of view in "Rip Van Winkle," "Ethan Brand," and "The Return of a Private"; Fitzgerald's skillful transitions in this story, particularly the way he whisks Charlie out of the Ritz Bar in the first scene, as compared with Dreiser's lumbering shifts of scene in "The Old Neighborhood"; and the way in which Fitzgerald's dialogue is both realistic in tone and radiant with meaning, compared with the gritty, often trivial speech of Garland's story or the rather melodramatic rhetoric of "Ethan Brand."

To grasp some of the reasons why Fitzgerald's story came off so well, we need to see it as a product of his life and times. William Rose Benét, reviewing Fitzgerald's best novel in *The Saturday Review of Literature* (May 9, 1925), wrote, "*The Great Gatsby* reveals thoroughly matured craftsmanship. It has high occasions of felicitous, almost magic phrase. And most of all, it is out of the mirage. For the first time Fitzgerald surveys the Babylonian captivity of this era unblinded by the bright lights." In this review, which Fitzgerald quite probably read, we have important clues to the success of **"Babylon Revisited,"** written five years later. It suggests, in the first place, why he gave the story its title, avoiding the more obvious "Paris Revisited," with its narrowing of connotation. Fitzgerald was writing about the end of an era, not just some changes in a corner of tourist France.

We do not need the description of Charlie Wales—"He was good to look at. The Irish mobility of his face was sobered by a deep wrinkle between his eyes"—to know that he is close to Scott Fitzgerald. In 1930 his wife was not in a grave in Vermont, but she was in a sanitarium; his daughter, though not living with his sister-in-law, was attending school in Paris. But even though the story clearly flows from emotional autobiography, it also has the perspective that Malcolm Cowley summed up in his memorable remark about Fitzgerald's work: "It was as if all of his novels described a big dance to which he had taken . . . the prettiest girl . . . and as if at the same time he stood outside the ballroom, a little Midwestern boy with his nose to the glass, wondering how much the tickets cost and who paid for the music." This double vision of actor and spectator, with the mature spectator no longer a gawky outsider but a judge, informs all of Fitzgerald's best work, and in this story it allows him to view Charlie Wales with both sympathy and ironic detachment.

Benét's remark about Fitzgerald's "almost magic" phrasing also provides a clue to the all-important relation between art, spending, and morality in this story. When Charlie says of the old times, "We were a sort of royalty, almost infallible, with a sort of magic around us," we see the precise appeal of the rich, or at least of the spenders, for Fitzgerald. He not only wrote about how he lived; he also saw life in the high style as allied to, though not identical with, writing. It was a spending of one's resources to gain release from the rigid grip of time, space, and circumstance. "The snow of twenty-nine wasn't real snow. If you didn't want it to be snow, you just paid some money." The spenders juggled time and space as the novelist does, making "months into days," shrinking and magnifying dimensions at will. "In the little hours of the night, every move from place to place was an enormous human jump, an increase of paying for the privilege of slower and slower motion." The squandering of unearned money called forth "effort and ingenuity" and imagination; it permitted or demanded the playing of roles, wearing the old derby rim and carrying the wire cane.

The basic conflict of the story, then, is not just between Charlie and Marion; it is between Charlie Wales (who presumably takes his last name from the prince who was the epitome of the good-time Charlies in the twenties) and "Mr. Charles J. Wales of Prague," sound businessman and moralist, between the regally imaginative but destructive past and the dull, bourgeois but solid present. As Charlie now sees it, the old time spent did bring about transformations, but they were all morally destructive. To "dissipate" was to perform a magic disappearing act, "to make nothing out of something." It was all, he now realizes, on an "utterly childish scale," like the pedalling of Lorraine on a tricycle all over Paris between the small hours and dawn.

With our natural sympathy for the Charlie who at the end sees that he lost everything he wanted in the boom, we are likely to think that he wants only the honorable part of the past, that he would like to disengage himself from the rest of it, that, as he tells Marion, he *has* radically changed. But Fitzgerald is not at all sentimental on this point; he insists upon the reader's seeing more clearly than Charlie does. For the trouble with Charlie is that he *still* wants both worlds. The harsh fact is that if he had not stopped in the Ritz Bar in the first place, had not tried to get in touch with Duncan Schaefer, he would have won back his daughter. Fitzgerald has him commit this fatal act in the very beginning of the story; it comes back to haunt him inexorably in the "ghosts" of Dunc and Lorraine.

The two sides of Charlie are clearly revealed, of course, in the luncheon scene with Honoria. "'Now, how about vegetables?'" he asks. "'Oughtn't you to have some vegetables?'" This is Charlie trying to prove to himself and Honoria that he is the ordinary or garden variety of father. But he gently mocks this role by formally introducing himself as Charles J. Wales of Prague and is delighted when she quickly responds, imaginatively accepting the role of an adult woman. The game is short, however, because it rapidly evokes too many parallels with the destructive aspects of playing at life:

"Married or single?"

"No, not married. Single."

He indicated the doll. "But I see you have a child, madame."

Unwilling to disinherit it, she took it to her heart and thought quickly.

"Yes, I've been married, but I'm not married now. My husband is dead."

He went on quickly, "And the child's name?"

"Simone. That's after my best friend at school."

It is probably significant that it is Honoria who brings the conversation back to reality with this reference to school, because in this whole scene she is educating her father. She approves his suggestion that they go to the vaudeville but frowns on his approval of unlimited spending at the toy store. She is polite but cool to Lorraine, who makes clear the link between the tarnished magic of the old times and the world of childhood. "'There,'" she says, "'That's what I want to do . . . I want to see some clowns and acrobats and jugglers.'"

The acrobats, the imagery of the vaudeville, remind us, finally, that this is a story of suspension between two worlds. Charlie's dream of his wife concludes with this vision: "she was in a swing in a white dress, and swinging faster all the time, so that at the end he could not hear clearly all that she said." Fitzgerald continues this image in the climactic scene when the drunken Lorraine and Dunc invade the Peters' apartment. After they leave, Lincoln is "still swinging Honoria back and forth like a pendulum from side to side." Up to this point Charlie has virtually convinced even Marion that his feet are "planted on the earth now," but actually, as we have seen, he is caught between two worlds. Fitzgerald has arranged their representatives with a symmetry reminiscent of James. On the one hand is the pale blonde, Lorraine, with her escort Duncan Schaeffer; on the other, Marion, clothed in a "black dress that just faintly suggested mourning," with her husband, Lincoln, who appropriately works in a bank. Charlie is indebted to both of the women: to Marion for taking care of Honoria; to Lorraine, as she unpleasantly reminds him, for playing the game. "'I remember once,'" she says, "'when you hammered on my door at four A.M. I was enough of a good sport to give you a drink.'" Fitzgerald does not need to force the association, for the reader, along with Marion, silently balances the equation: Lorraine let him in at four A.M.; he locked his wife out in the snowstorm.

And so here is Charlie at the end, back at the Ritz Bar, the place where his old friend Claude Fessenden had run up a bill of thirty thousand francs, until Paul finally told him he "had to pay." Half-heartedly thinking he will send Honoria some things, lots of things, tomorrow, asking the waiter how much he owes him, Charlie is left with his remembrances of time spent and his determination to "come back some day; they couldn't make him pay forever." But he knows and we know that they can and he will. The prodigal has returned, but his effort to "conciliate something," to redress the balance, has failed, and he remains an exile.

### Robert I. Edenbaum   (essay date 1968)

SOURCE: "'Babylon Revisited': A Psychological Note on F. Scott Fitzgerald," in *Literature and Psychology,* Vol. 18, No. 1, 1968, pp. 27-9.

[*In the following essay, Edenbaum contends that, through an inconsistency in the plot, Fitzgerald reveals that he identifies with Charlie Wales.*]

F. Scott Fitzgerald's story **"Babylon Revisited"** concerns the return of Charlie Wales one-and-a-half years later to the Babylon that was—the Paris of 1929—in an attempt to retrieve what he can from the two lost years of drunken revelry that had culminated in the death of his wife, his own incarceration in a sanitarium, and the legal signing over of his daughter, Honoria, to his sister-in-law, Marion Peters. All he can hope to retrieve—other than ambivalent memories: "We were a sort of royalty"; "it was a nightmare"—is Honoria. And that possibility is destroyed, at least temporarily, when his old friends, Duncan Schaeffer and Lorraine Quarrles, appear like "sudden ghosts out of the past" at the Peters' apartment, drunk. Marion's refusal of Charlie's request for possession of Honoria follows inevitably.

Arthur Mizener, in "A Handbook of Analyses . . ." accompanying his college-text collection *Modern Short Stories,* makes the following comments upon the unexpected appearance of Charlie Wales' friends:

> We notice how unobtrusively [Fitzgerald] omits any explanation of how Lorraine and Dunc got hold of the Peters' address. We know Charlie left the address of his hotel at the Ritz bar; we can work out the rest if it becomes a problem for us, but Fitzgerald clearly prefers the question not to arise since it is irrelevant to the central interest of the story, merely a matter of the machinery of the plot. He therefore does his best— short of omitting to make the plot feasible—to keep the question from arising at all.

And, a little later:

> It is one of the story's nicest touches that Dunc and Lorraine—careless, irresponsible, uncalculating— should nonetheless have ferreted out with drunken cunning the Peters' address and tracked Charlie there.

I should say before I comment on Fitzgerald's story that I am not quoting Mizener to pick at a picayune error in, of all places, a teacher's guide. The point is not a critic's trivial misreading of a small detail, nor that other readers have made the same mistake. The interesting thing is that Fitzgerald himself was partly responsible for the misreading through what seems to be a crucial mistake that has fascinating psychological implications.

When Duncan and Lorraine walk in, Charlie, "anxious and at a loss," "was astounded; unable to understand how they ferreted out the Peters' address." A page or so earlier, in the passage Mizener refers to, we are told that, on his returning to his hotel, Charlie had found a *pneumatique* "that had been redirected from the Ritz bar where Charlie had left his address for the purpose of finding a certain man." But Fitzgerald (and his critics) seems to have forgotten the moment at the very start of the story (in *both* its original publication in the *Saturday Evening Post* and the revised version that appeared in the collection **Taps at Reveille**) when Charlie says to Alix, the barman at the Ritz, "'If you see Mr. Schaeffer, give him this . . . It's my brother-in-law's address. I haven't settled on a hotel yet.'"

Given Fitzgerald's technical virtuosity in *The Great Gatsby,* much of *Tender Is the Night,* and the best of his stories, it is tempting to credit him with an extraordinary psychological touch; to read the detail of Charlie's forgetting that he gave the Peters' address to the barman as a subtle indication of Charlie's ambivalence towards his past, towards his dead wife and their life together, and, most important of all, towards his daughter. His wife had died of "heart trouble," but Marion Peters acts as though Charlie were directly responsible for her sister's death—and Charlie himself accepts at least some of the responsibility—because some time before her death Charlie had locked her out in a snowstorm.

> On that terrible February night that Marion remembered so vividly, a slow quarrel had gone on for hours. There was a scene at the Florida, and then he attempted to take her home. . . . When he arrived home alone he turned the key in the lock in wild anger. How could he know she would arrive an hour later alone, that there would be a snowstorm in which she wandered about in slippers, too confused to find a taxi? Then the aftermath, her escaping pneumonia by a miracle, and all the attendant horror. They were "reconciled," but that was the beginning of the end. . . .

The self-justifying question—"How could he have known . . . ?" clearly indicates his defensiveness and his sense of his own guilt. His continual assertion that his wife, Helen, would have wanted him to have Honoria, indeed, in his fantasy *wants* him to have her ("He was absolutely sure Helen wouldn't have wanted him to be so alone") is further evidence of the reassurance he needs to prove to himself his right to the child.

What nicer touch, then, to suggest his fears of his own failings in the past and the future—the guilt over the past that undermines his own sense of his right to a future with Honoria—than for him to give the Peters' address to the Ritz barman, specifically for the unregenerate Dunc Schaeffer, and forget he had done so? What nicer indication of the self-destructive act?

But I think it impossible to credit Fitzgerald with that insight, for it seems clear that he intended to suggest (as he has Charlie Wales think) that Dunc and Lorraine had "ferreted out" the Peters' address, presumably through

Charlie's having left his own address at the Ritz. Since the story is framed on two visits to the Ritz, and there is no suggestion of a visit in between, it is likely that Fitzgerald was misremembering that it was the Peters' address Charlie had left with the barman. Be that as it may, it is the slip itself that provides the fascination. Fitzgerald's identification with Charlie Wales hardly needs documentation: in *The Far Side of Paradise* Arthur Mizener takes it for granted that "Wales' feelings are Fitzgerald's" and connects the snowstorm passage quoted above to Fitzgerald's disintegrating relations with Zelda. Honoria's age is given as nine years: Frances Fitzgerald was barely past her ninth birthday in December, 1930, when Fitzgerald wrote the story. Zelda was not dead, of course, but was in the middle of one of the most serious of the attacks that were to lead before long to her complete mental collapse. In the context of these details it is difficult not to see the "mistake" at the beginning of this story as significant for Fitzgerald rather than for his character. A story that the author often later mentioned as having been intended as a tribute to his daughter, the "lovely little girl of nine," masks his guilt for what he insisted was *his* role in his wife's illness. The detail in the story that might have indicated Charlie Wales' unconscious self-destructive impulse indicates instead F. Scott Fitzgerald's through the medium of Charlie Wales.

### David Toor  (essay date 1974)

SOURCE: "Guilt and Retribution in 'Babylon Revisited'," in *Fitzgerald/Hemingway Annual 1973,* edited by Matthew J. Bruccoli and C. E. Frazer Clark, Jr., Microcard Editions Books, 1974, pp. 155-64.

[*In the following essay, Toor argues that Charlie Wales is trapped between self-justification and self-recrimination.*]

Roy R. Male's perceptive article on **"Babylon Revisited"** goes far in clearing up many of the unresolved problems that have recently been discussed in relation to the story ["'Babylon Revisited': The Story of the Exile's Return," *Studies in Short Fiction,* Vol. 2, 1965]. Male has pointed out, as James Harrison had shown in an earlier note, that Charlie Wales is in a sense responsible for the appearance of Duncan and Lorraine at the Peters' house at precisely the wrong moment [Harrison, "Fitzgerald's "'Babylon Revisited'," *Explicator,* Vol. 16, January 1958]. Male has further called into serious question the general interpretation of the story, most specifically Seymour Gross' contention that Charlie has been renovated and that the punishment he suffers is brought upon him from external sources. Gross says [in "Fitzgerald's 'Babylon Revisited'," *College English,* Vol. XXV, November 1963]: "That moral renovation may not be enough is the injustice that lies at the center of the story." Both Male and Harrison point out that had Charlie not given the bartender the Peters' address at the opening of the story, Duncan and Lorraine would not have shown up there and given Marion Peters a real reason to refuse to return Honoria to Charlie.

Gross' further statement, "Nor is there anything here of that troubled ambivalence which characterizes our response to that fantastic ambiguity, Jay Gatsby," seems quite wrong, because it is precisely in the troubled ambivalence of Charlie Wales that the meaning of the story is found. But Charlie's ambivalence is not the result of the fact that, as Male argues, "his is a story of suspension between two worlds," although to a great extent the story is structured on the contrasts between the past, as represented by Lorraine and Duncan, and the present, in the persons of Marion and Lincoln, but in a deeper awareness of Charlie's own guilt and his inability to work it out. It is in a kind of personal psychological morality that the meaning of the story is found.

It is convenient for Charlie to blame the errors of his past for the pains of his present—and future. But Fitzgerald's world is not a world of external retribution—you are not made to pay for what you've done—not at least by a God, or in Hemingway's words, "what we have instead of God," a code, or even by a deterministic fate. The payment is self-punishment, and the ironically disastrous result of such punishment is the intensification of the feelings of guilt. There is no expiation, only the further degeneration of the mind—neurotic reinforcement of behavior that leads eventually to total insanity or a form of suicide.

Charlie Wales is not torn between the poles of two opposing worlds so much as he is torn by his own inner sense of guilt and his inability to expiate it. He is not morally renovated, only sicker and less able to cope with the guilt. In one part of him he wants his Honoria (honor) back, but in the deeper man, the guilt-ridden one, he knows he doesn't deserve her. He has exiled himself to a dream world free of past responsibilities—Prague—where he creates the fresh image of himself as a successful businessman. Of course the image cannot hold, and his distorted view of the real world leads him into delusion and jealousy: "He wondered if he couldn't do something to get Lincoln out of his rut at the bank." What kind of rut is Lincoln really in? A warm homelife that Charlie envies, children who love him, a neurotic wife, yes, but a reasonable contentment.

There are many hints through the story which point to these conclusions, and one of the most significant may be viewed as flaws in the technique of the tale. Fitzgerald chose a third-person limited point of view to tell the story, and the lapses, few as they are, are telling. All of the lapses—the shifts from limited to omniscient—are concerned with the Peters. The three most important ones directly involve Marion:

> She had built up all her fear of life into one wall and faced it toward him.

> Marion shuddered suddenly; part of her saw that Charlie's feet were planted on the earth now, and her own maternal feeling recognized the naturalness of his desire; but she had lived for a long time with a prejudice—a prejudice founded on a curious disbelief in her sister's happiness, and which, in the shock of one terrible night, had turned

to hatred for him. It had all happened at a point in her life where the discouragement of ill health and adverse circumstances made it necessary for her to believe in tangible villainy and a tangible villain.

Then, in the flatness that followed her outburst, she saw him plainly and she knew he had somehow arrived at control over the situation. Glancing at her husband, she found no help from him, and as abruptly as if it were a matter of no importance, she threw up the sponge.

In a way these passages are indeed flaws. Certainly a craftsman like Henry James, whose meanings so much depend on careful control of point of view, would not have allowed them to pass. But Fitzgerald, as much a conscious artist as he was, as in the excellent handling of such matters in *The Great Gatsby,* for instance, did let them pass because, I think, perhaps he might have been too involved in the problems of this tale, as he was not in *Gatsby.* There is the possibility that these few passages can be read as consistent with a limited third-person point of view and that these were indeed Charlie's reactions to the situation.

But what these flaws may represent is Charlie's attempt to somehow put himself in a position to account for the (sub-conscious) terrors that were plaguing him on this return to Babylon. All three of these cited passages are explanations of the sources of Marion's hostility and her resignation in the face of Charlie's apparent renovation. Charlie is convinced that Marion has seen that he is a changed man. But it becomes more and more clear as we examine the story that he himself was by no means convinced.

Aside from the early action of leaving the Peters' address for Duncan Schaeffer at the bar—and Charlie's subsequent denial of any knowledge of how Duncan could have found it out—we need examine in some detail what Charlie does and says through the story to understand just how completely he is caught between the psychologically necessary self-delusion that he is somehow blameless and changed, and the deeper recognition of his own guilt.

Charlie's pose, once again, is that of the reformed alcoholic, allowing himself one drink a day to prove to himself he doesn't need it. "'I'm going slow these days,'" he tells Alix at the beginning. "'I've stuck to it for over a year and a half now.'" The reassurance seems to ring true—it has been a long time. But in the way that he tells himself he can face and beat alcohol, he hasn't allowed himself to try to face and beat the deeper problems. He lives in Prague, adding to Alix, "'They don't know about me down there.'" The dream world of escape, a foreign land where maybe Charlie too, doesn't know about himself. He is cooling it—going slow these days—even the taxi horns play the opening bars of *Le Plus que Lent.*

The Peters' home reminds Charlie of what he has lost. It "was warm and comfortably American." He responds inwardly to the intimacy and comfort of the children in the house, but his outward reaction, while holding his daugh-

ter close to him, is to boast to the Peters about how well he himself is doing. He has more money than he'd ever had before. But he cuts it off when he sees "a faint restiveness in Lincoln's eye." His defensive opening had been wrong, he sees, but still he persists. He boasts also about the past: "'We were a sort of royalty, almost infallible, with a sort of magic around us.'" And twice in three lines he repeats, "'I take one drink every afternoon. . . .'"

---

**Charlie Wales is not torn between the poles of two opposing worlds so much as he is torn by his own inner sense of guilt and his inability to expiate it.**

*—David Toor*

---

In one way Charlie is ready to admit to himself—and others—that he has a large burden of blame to carry, but too often this admission is qualified with either a denial, a shifting, or a sharing of the blame. As he looks at his daughter he silently hopes that she doesn't "combine the traits of both [Charlie and Helen] that had brought them to disaster." In his lyrical reminiscences of the past in Paris, especially about the money squandered, he tries to convince and justify himself: "But it hadn't been given for nothing." Hadn't it? The next passage is really quite confused, and although it sounds meaningful, in reality it is a pastiche of attempted self-justification and escape from responsibility:

> It had been given, even the most wildly squandered sum, as an offering to destiny that he might not remember the things most worth remembering, the things that now he would always remember—his child taken from his control, his wife escaped to a grave in Vermont.

He thinks about Honoria being "taken from his control," not that "he had lost the right to her control." His wife has not "died," but has "escaped." The last part of the sentence essentially contradicts and yet reinforces the first part.

His encounters with Duncan and Lorraine demonstrate much the same kind of ineffectual self-justification: "As always, he felt Lorraine's passionate, provocative attraction, but his own rhythm was different now." After they leave the restaurant where he had been dining with Honoria, Charlie tries to separate himself from Duncan and Lorraine:

> They liked him because he was functioning, because he was serious; they wanted to see him, because he was stronger than they were now, because they wanted to draw a certain sustenance from his strength.

How do we understand this in terms of his later desire to get "Lincoln out of his rut at the bank?" We can't because of Charlie's inability to admit consciously the distorted state of his mind. Once again, it is not a conflict between the past and present, between Charlie Wales and Charles J. Wales of Prague, but between Charlie and his guilt. Charles J. Wales does not really exist, except in Charlie's limited perception.

---

**"Babylon Revisited" is not a story about the inability of the world to forgive and forget, or even about a man drawn back to the past and therefore unable to come to terms with the present. It is a story about self destruction, about the human mind's ability to delude itself into thinking that what it does is based on logic and reason.**

**—*David Toor***

---

Back at the Peters' on the evening of that first encounter with these spectres from the past, he proposes that he take Honoria back with him to Prague. He again boasts about his position and how well he is prepared to care for the girl, but he knows what he is in for—and in a way he is demanding to be punished, but he will put on an act for the Peters: "if he modulated his inevitable resentment to the chastened attitude of the reformed sinner, he might win his point in the end." But Charlie doesn't really know what his point is.

Marion, hurt and ill herself, pushes him to further self-justification: "'You know I never did drink heavily until I gave up business and came over here with nothing to do. Then Helen and I began to run around with—.'" He is cut short, but he can't help but bring Helen into it. When Marion blames him for being in a sanitarium while Helen was dying, "He had no answer." Marion pushed him further. "Charlie gripped the sides of the chair. This was more difficult than he expected; he wanted to launch out into a long expostulation and explanation, but he only said: 'The night I locked her out—.'"

When Marion asks him why he hadn't thought about what he had done before, and the damage he had caused to Honoria and himself, he again refuses to admit to the full blame:

> "I suppose I did, from time to time, but Helen and I were getting along badly. When I consented to the guardianship, I was flat on my back in a sanitarium and the market had cleaned me out. I knew I'd acted badly, and I thought if it would bring any peace to Helen, I'd agree to anything. But now it's different. I'm functioning, I'm behaving damn well, so far as—."

His guilt at the damage he'd done to Helen is further reflected in the fear of what his daughter might learn about him: "sooner or later it would come out, in a word here, a shake of the head there, and some of that distrust would be irrevocably implanted in Honoria."

Marion hits Charlie hardest when she verbalizes the real and deepest source of Charlie's guilt: "'How much you were responsible for Helen's death, I don't know. It's something you'll have to square with your own conscience.'" And this is just what Charlie can't do. "An electric current of agony surged through him. . . ." But his only outward response, after Lincoln's attempt to defend him, is, "'Helen died of heart trouble.'" There is no other answer Charlie can give, for to admit consciously, even for an instant that he might really have been to blame for Helen's death might permit him to face his guilt and thus enable him to start the cleansing process that might lead back towards balance.

In the reverie of Helen that follows the bitter scene ending with Marion's agreeing to return Honoria, we find evidence of his inability to admit to his blame. "The image of Helen haunted him. Helen whom he had loved so until they had senselessly begun to abuse each other's love, tear it into shreds." He excuses himself again for the events of the night he had locked her out. "When he arrived home alone he turned the key in the lock in wild anger. How could he know she would arrive an hour later alone, that there would be a snowstorm in which she wandered about in slippers, too confused to find a taxi?" The final scene of the vision of Helen that night is again part of his ambivalent attempt and refusal to find expiation. Helen seems to comfort him with tenderness and forgiveness, except that as she swings faster and faster the forgiveness is not complete: "at the end he could not hear clearly all that she said," leaving him to delude himself into half-believing the closing words of the story about Helen forgiving him.

The remaining two sections of the story, IV and V, reinforce what has gone before. Further self-delusions of himself as cured, even a garbled version of how best to raise a daughter:

> The present was the thing—work to do, and someone to love. But not to love too much, for he knew the injury that a father can do to a daughter or a mother to a son by attaching them too closely: afterward, out in the world, the child would seek in the marriage partner the same blind tenderness and, failing probably to find it, turn against love and life.

This is just the kind of distortion that Charlie's mind would drive him to. Certainly there is a base in Freudian psychology for what he says, but only in his conscious rationalization of "not to love too much," can Charlie make sense out of his own inability to love fully and completely. He is too warped to see that the only love worth having or giving is one without reservations and limits.

Reference has been made in footnotes to some of the changes in the above passages between the 1931 [*The Saturday Evening Post*] and 1935 [***Taps at Reveille***] versions of the story. Two of the most significant changes between the two printed versions of the story occur in part IV. Both versions open with Charlie leaving the address of the Peters with the bartender to give to Duncan Schaeffer. Lorraine's later message reaches Charlie by different means in the two stories. In the 1931 version:

> Back at his hotel, Charlie took from his pocket a *pneumatique* that Lincoln had given him at luncheon. It had been redirected by Paul from the hotel bar.

In the final version:

> Back at his hotel, Charlie found a *pneumatique* that had been redirected from the Ritz bar where Charlie had left his address for the purpose of finding a certain man.

It's likely that part of the confusion results from an oversight of Fitzgerald's in revising the manuscript. But the confusion here may also be the result of Fitzgerald's intention to emphasize that Charlie was responsible for the appearance of Duncan and Lorraine at the Peters. The "certain man" in 1935 is still Duncan at the beginning of the story. And further, that if Lincoln had given him the message, as in the earlier version, Lincoln also would have known that Charlie had given out the address, and Charlie's denial would have been seen immediately as a lie. It was important that Charlie be able to continue his self-delusion without any real fear that Lincoln would know that Charlie was responsible.

Another important change is in Lorraine's invitation to Charlie after she and Duncan have barged in at the Peters: "'Come on out to dinner. Be yourself, Charlie. Come on,'" reads the 1931 version. The final draft: "'Come and dine. Sure your cousins won' mine. See you so sel'om. Or solemn.'" In the *TAR* [*Taps at Reveille*] version Lorraine is quite drunk, obviously intended to make Marion even angrier than in the magazine version. But Fitzgerald has cut the line, "'Be yourself, Charlie.'" It is too obvious to Lorraine in that early version that Charlie is still Charlie, but more important, it is too obvious to Charlie that he is still what he was.

The ghastly scene at the Peters ends with Charlie getting what he was begging for subconsciously all along—Marion's rejection of his plea for Honoria. Before Charlie leaves he lies—consciously or not—to Lincoln: "'I wish you'd explain to her [Marion] I never dreamed these people would come here. I'm just as sore as you are.'"

Charlie cannot make amends, cannot "conciliate something," as he puts it, and the story ends on a note of almost total despair. It is not by accident that his thoughts turn back to money and his imagination of the power of money. He reflects that "the snow of twenty-nine wasn't real snow. If you didn't want it to be snow, you just paid some money." Charlie hasn't been able to deal in love, but he has been able to handle money and the things money can produce. He still isn't convinced that the two are not equal, nor can he admit to himself the possibility that the main source of his troubles was his inability to love and that his present guilt feelings stem directly from that source.

So he will turn back to the new old ways and instead of dealing with people, deal with things. "There wasn't much he could do now except send Honoria some things; he would send her a lot of things tomorrow. He thought rather angrily that this was just money—he had given so many people money. . . ." And that's all he had given.

In the tormented inner world of Charlie Wales, the world where God could not exist and therefore not punish, and where the individual retains, if not a sense of sin, at least a sense of guilt, we find the real conflict. **"Babylon Revisited"** is not a story about the inability of the world to forgive and forget, or even about a man drawn back to the past and therefore unable to come to terms with the present. It is a story about self destruction, about the human mind's ability to delude itself into thinking that what it does is based on logic and reason. The story ends with only the promise of emptiness to come in Charlie's life; it ends with the lie that may lead Charlie to destruction: "He was absolutely sure Helen wouldn't have wanted him to be so alone."

### Rose Adrienne Gallo (essay date 1978)

SOURCE: "Fable to Fantasy: The Short Fiction," in *F. Scott Fitzgerald,* Frederick Ungar Publishing Co., 1978, pp. 82-105.

[*In the following excerpt, Gallo describes the destructive power of money as an important theme in the story.*]

In **"Babylon Revisited"** (December 1930; *Post* February 21, 1931; *Taps at Reveille* 1935), Fitzgerald draws on a biblical source for his title. The inhabitants of the Old Testament city of Babylon were notorious for their licentiousness. Many of the Jews—held captive in Babylon for seventy years—were seduced by the sinful allure of Babylon, and turned from the observance of the Mosaic law to the worship of Babylonian idols.

The setting of **"Babylon Revisited"** is Paris (considered by Fitzgerald a modern Babylon in those days of unrestrained revelry just before the American stock market crash in 1929).

Using a frame device, Fitzgerald begins and ends the story in the Ritz bar—a popular haunt of wealthy Americans before the crash. Charlie Wales, one of its former habitués, has returned to Paris to visit his daughter, Honoria, who is living with her aunt and uncle, Marion and Lincoln Peters.

As the story unfolds it is revealed that Charlie Wales had left Paris, nearly two years before, after the death of his wife Helen. Reduced to poverty by the stock-market crash, and sick from excessive drinking, Charlie had relinquished custody of Honoria to his wife's sister Marion. He had then gone to Prague, where he controlled his drinking and worked hard at recouping his financial losses.

When the story proper begins, Charlie, wealthy once again, returns to Paris to regain custody of Honoria and begin a stable family life for both of them in Prague. Charlie is determined to have Honoria while she is still young enough to be formed by her father. "If we wait much longer," he pleads with the hostile Marion, "I'll lose Honoria's childhood and my chance for a home."

---

**With good reason "Babylon Revisited" ranks high among the finest short stories of the twentieth century.**

*—Rose Adrienne Gallo*

---

Charlie adopts the "chastened attitude of a reformed sinner," repeatedly assuring Marion that he now takes only one drink a day. "It's a sort of stunt I set myself," he explains. "It keeps the matter in proportion." Despite her dislike of her brother-in-law (she blames him for her sister's death), Marion is about to relent and permit Honoria to go to Prague with Charlie. At this crucial moment two of Charlie's former cronies, Duncan Schaeffer and Lorraine Quarrles, both obviously drunk, arrive unannounced at the Peter's apartment. Marion is repelled by the appearance of Charlie's inebriated friends. Fearful that Charlie may lapse into his former dissipation, Marion refuses to give up custody of Honoria. Her husband tells Charlie to wait another six months before he makes another attempt to persuade Marion.

The story ends at the Ritz bar. Despite his sorrow, Charlie, determined to prove his self-control, has his one daily whiskey and refuses the barman's attempt to refill his glass.

"They couldn't make him pay forever," Charlie declares, certain that Helen "wanted Honoria to be with him." But Marion, resentful and suspicious, may just make him pay forever. Or at least until it is too late to make Honoria truly his own daughter, "before she crystallized utterly" into a counterpart of Marion.

Charlie's purgation is far from over. There are so many subtle hints in the story that Charlie is not completely exorcised of his old life. He has experienced the fearful consequences of his former corruption. Yet he comments: "But it was nice while it lasted." His first stop in Paris is at the Ritz bar where he inquires after his old friends. Learning that Duncan Schaeffer is in town, he foolishly tells the barman to give Duncan the Peters' address. Although he does not wish to become involved again with Lorraine Quarrles, he feels her "passionate, provocative attraction."

The demons of Charlie's past are reluctant to release their hold upon him. As he rides through the streets of Paris, he notices that the lurid "fire-red, gas-blue, ghost-green signs" (perhaps of former haunts) are somewhat obscured by the "tranquil rain." But, nonetheless, they are still there—vivid reminders of the old days—just as Duncan and Lorraine are there, ghosts from the past to haunt his present.

Money, conceived as a corrosive power, is one of the principal themes of **"Babylon Revisited."** Its evil influence is obvious in the wasted lives of Charlie Wales and his friends. More subtle, however, is the deleterious effect that the desire for money has had upon the Peters' family. Marion Peters' self-righteous, moralistic stance in reality cloaks her invidious resentment of Charlie's wealth. And Lincoln Peters, humiliated by his own failure to make money, caters to his wife's whims even though he admits the justice of Charlie's claim to Honoria.

Fitzgerald expands the money theme in one of the finest features of **"Babylon Revisited"**—its brilliant evocation of place. The Paris of the present, which belongs once again to the Parisians, is juxtaposed with the Paris of the past, ruled in spirit by wealthy American expatriates. In the past Americans were "a sort of royalty, almost infallible, with a sort of magic around us," reminisces Charlie. Paris was their Babylon for American worshipers of mammon. The Parisians, seduced by American money, paid tribute to American "royalty" by catering to their basest sensual demands: illicit sex, drugs, and alcohol.

American money endowed one with a false sense of omnipotence in those days. Even the "snow of twenty-nine wasn't real snow" for the power-drunk Americans. "If you didn't want it to be snow you just paid some money." But the guilt-ridden Charlie, who had locked his wife out of their house in a snowstorm, knows now that the laws of nature are impervious to man's pitiful bribes. The snow of 1929 had weakened Helen's resistance and ultimately caused her death from heart failure. And Marion's bitterness toward Charlie has solidified into a frigid hatred that Charlie's money cannot dissolve. The snow of 1929 had cost Charlie a bitter price: his wife and his child.

The motifs of sin, guilt, and retribution are also associated, in the story, with the exaggerated emphasis placed upon money by its characters. Charlie remembers how he had spent money recklessly:

> It had been given, even the most wildly squandered sum, as an offering to destiny that he might not remember the things most worth remembering, the things that now he would aways remember—his child taken from his control, his wife escaped to a grave in Vermont.

Charlie's sinfulness is handled with admirable restraint by Fitzgerald. Although he admits to his delinquency toward his wife and child, Charlie does not wallow in maudlin expressions of remorse. He has sinned, he has repented. As a token of forgiveness—both from Helen and from Marion—Charlie wants Honoria. But Charlie's reform must go beyond the external order he has imposed upon his life. He is seeking salvation through the innocent Honoria. Salvation, however, is a personal matter. It remains for him to reclaim his vanquished manhood.

**"Babylon Revisited"** is Fitzgerald's masterpiece of short fiction. The story is perfect in plot, tone, atmosphere, dialogue, and characterization. Its thematic complexity is superbly interwoven with plot and structure. With good reason **"Babylon Revisited"** ranks high among the finest short stories of the twentieth century.

**James B. Twitchell  (essay date 1979)**

SOURCE: "'Babylon Revisited': Chronology and Characters," in *Fitzgerald/Hemingway Annual 1978,* edited by Matthew J. Bruccoli and Richard Layman, Gale Research Company, 1979, pp. 155-60.

*[In the following essay, Twitchell refutes the argument that Charlie Wales is unreformed.]*

In recent years there has been a small critical hubbub over the completeness of Charlie Wales's reformation in Fitzgerald's **"Babylon Revisited."** On the surface it does seem that Charlie has converted from wine, women, and song to one midday drink, devotion to his daughter, and serious introspection. But recently critics have questioned Charlie's conversion by pointing to a crucial scene overlooked by earlier commentators. Lorraine Quarrles and Duncan Schaeffer arrive at the Peterses' apartment because Charlie has consciously or unconsciously pointed the way by leaving his address with the bartender at the Ritz. Their appearance and subsequent rowdy behavior so upset Charlie's sister-in-law that she refuses Charlie the one thing he so desperately wants—the custody of his daughter Honoria. But that may be what Charlie has wanted all along—or so these commentators contend.

First James Harrison (1958), then Roy R. Male (1965), then Robert I. Edenbaum (1968), and most recently David Toor (1973) have made Charlie's leaving of the Peterses' address a crux in interpretation, for without it Duncan and Lorraine would never have found him out. But a careful reexamination of both chronology and character may return us to the more sensible, although less psychologically sophisticated, reading of critics like Seymour Gross, who contends that Charlie has indeed reformed, but that in this scurvy world "moral reformation may not be enough" ["Fitzgerald's 'Babylon Revisited'," *College English,* Vol. 25, November 1963]. The vagaries of fate and the perversions of character will forever make the Charlies of this postlapsarian world not tragic, but pathetic figures.

A look at the chronology of the story may exonerate Charlie from the charge of being a conscious or unconscious co-conspirator in his ultimate disappointment. In both the original publication in *The Saturday Evening Post* and in the revised version collected in **Taps at Reveille,** when Charlie arrives in Paris he gives Alix, the assistant barman at the Ritz, the Peterses' address, saying, "'If you see Mr. Schaeffer, give him this. . . . It's my brother-in-law's address. I haven't settled on a hotel yet.'" This is his first day in Paris and he has not met Duncan Schaeffer nor has he met Lorraine—an old flame and reveller from his earlier years. The next day, however, he does indeed meet his old friends, together now—Duncan, an old college chum, and Lorraine, on furlough from her stateside husband. They

are amazed to find Charlie in Paris, let alone sober, and want to get together later.

"What's your address?" said Duncan skeptically.

He hesitated, unwilling to give the name of his hotel.

"I'm not settled yet. I'd better call you."

This is not quite true, for we know Charlie has spent the night at some hotel in Paris, although we are never told specifically where. However, we do know that he does not move during the next two days, so he could have given Duncan and Lorraine an address had he wanted to. But somehow, seeing them, he understands that he must treat them like poison, and so refuses to give any address, even the Peterses'. This refusal is an act of conscious volition, and is passed over by Harrison, Male, Edenbaum, and Toor, who want to believe that Charlie secretly wants Duncan and Lorraine to disturb his in-laws, thereby allowing himself the masochistic pleasure of being denied his daughter Honoria, his honor. For these critics Charlie's guilt is so great that he must endure still more self-inflicted punishment, still more self-destruction.

The next day, his third in Paris, Charlie receives a message from Lorraine that has been redirected to him by Paul, the head bartender at the Ritz. In the note Lorraine reminds him of the jovial times they had had two years earlier, and invites him to the Ritz bar that afternoon to reminisce. Charlie's reaction is not at all ambivalent, as is implied in the psychological interpretations of Charlie as schizophrenic. He is not at all like an unreformed drunk who wants to take "just one more for the road." He knows he must avoid Lorraine. Charlie is a man of considerable control, in fact, a man who takes only one drink a day, in part to reinforce his independence, to reassert control. He knows that Lorraine is more lethal than alcohol, and thus his reaction to her invitation: "He emphatically did not want to see her, and he was glad Alix had not given away his hotel address." Fitzgerald has made it clear: if Charlie had wanted to see Duncan and Lorraine, even subconsciously, he had plenty of opportunity to show lack of restraint. But Charlie is firm. And so, when they do burst into the Peterses' apartment, Charlie is indeed genuinely astonished, consciously and subconsciously unprepared for their arrival. He instantly realizes that they got the address he left at the Ritz bar, but it was never his intention that they arrive like Mephistophelean agents from the past to collect their due, to deny him the one person he now loves the most.

Then why do they come? They come because they are vampires. They come because they need his energy, his metaphorical blood. For they are not really blood-drinking ghouls; rather they are energy leeches who parasitically thrive on the strength of their host. Charlie is more important to them now that he has reformed than he ever was before: "They liked him because he was functioning, because he was serious; they wanted to see him, because he was stronger than they were now, because they wanted to draw a certain sustenance from his strength." Duncan and Lorraine are psychic vampires, energy sponges who cannot endure alone. For instance, when they first meet Charlie at Le Grand Vatel they appear, "sudden ghosts out of the past"—not *like* ghosts, but the ghosts themselves. Hence their desperate attempt to make connections, as it were, with Charlie.

Charlie knows about the kind of aberrant love that can psychologically bleed the donor into pathetic destitution. He knows, even in terms of his affection for his daughter, that too much of the wrong kind of love can build a symbiotic relationship that will enervate both parties. At the beginning of Part IV of the *Post* text he warns himself of the danger:

> The present was the thing—work to do and someone to love. But not to love too much, for Charlie had read in D. H. Lawrence about the injury that a father can do to a daughter or a mother to a son by attaching them too closely.

This is an interesting and critically overlooked aside that reinforces Charlie's perception of human relationships and especially of the danger of "attachment." The novel by D. H. Lawrence that he doubtless has in mind is *Sons and Lovers.* Lawrence has used the metaphor of the vampire to explain a kind of love that drains without replenishing. Charlie knows this is a kind of attachment that he must be wary of with Honoria, and he knows instinctively that this is the kind of attachment that Lorraine offers. It is love as consumption. However, critics have not always agreed. In fact, David Toor claims that "this is just the kind of distortion that Charlie's mind would drive him to," and that "he is too warped to see that the only love worth having or getting is one without reservations and limits" ["Guilt and Retribution in 'Babylon Revisited'," *Fitzgerald/Hemingway Annual 1973,* 1974]. A goodly dose of D. H. Lawrence or of Lawrence's favorite interpreter of vampiritic love, Edgar Allen Poe, might remedy this sentimental and potentially maudlin view of love.

When Duncan and Lorraine arrive at the Peterses', Charlie is genuinely shocked. But Marion, Charlie's overly delicate sister-in-law, reacts with more finely tuned sensitivity. As Charlie introduces his old friends to the Peters, Marion nods, "scarcely speaking. She had drawn back a step toward the fire; her little girl stood beside her, and Marion put an arm about her shoulder." As Marion retreats with her charge to the safety of the fire (vampires are often destroyed by burning and so abhor both the light and heat of flame), Charlie advances, "as if to force them backward down the corridor." Almost on the threshold they parry—"Come and dine," Lorraine demands. But Charlie is adamant. Finally, backed across the threshold of the apartment, "Still in slow motion, with blurred, angry faces, with uncertain feet," Duncan and Lorraine "retired along the corridor."

The whole affair has made Marion, this human tuning fork, literally sick, and she has retired. And along with her have gone Charlie's hopes for Honoria. When Charlie later says to Lincoln, "'I wish you'd explain to her I never dreamed these people would come here. I'm just as sore

as you are,'" he is telling the literal, emotional, and psychological truth. It is not, as James Harrison has said, that Charlie the devoted father is trying to cover up for his alter ego, Charlie the philanderer, who wants to be punished. For here is a man who simply loves and wants his daughter and is furious that these leeches, Duncan and Lorraine, have ruined his chances.

He accepts Marion's decision to postpone her decision with the stoic resignation of one who realizes that in this fallen world he cannot expect justice to be done. He is a man who has come to believe in "character" as a lifestyle, in one drink a day and no more. He goes to the Ritz bar, furious that Lorraine and Duncan could have so sabotaged his desires, and it is here at the bar that we finally understand what Charlie means by "character." For realizing the peculiarity of fate and the perversity of being human, he concludes that "there wasn't much he could do." He calls Lincoln to inquire about his chances, is told that Marion wants to "let it slide for six months," and his response is only, "I see." For indeed, now he does see. He has had his diurnal drink, and if ever there was an appropriate time to go on a bender, it is now. But instead he says to the inquiring waiter, "No, no more. . . . What do I owe you?" His debt is paid; "they couldn't make him pay forever." He will return in six months, or twelve months, or eighteenth months, until finally Fortune allows him what is rightfully his.

## Ronald J. Gervais (essay date 1980)

SOURCE: "The Snow of Twenty-Nine: 'Babylon Revisited' as *Ubi Sunt* Lament," in *College Literature,* Vol. 7, No. 1, Winter, 1980, pp. 47-52.

[*In the following essay, Gervais contends that "Babylon Revisited" falls within the tradition of dirges for the past and compares it to François Villon's "Ballade of Dead Ladies."*]

One of the enduring themes of literature is the transitory nature of man's life, of love and beauty, of happiness. In works of this sort, an important part is sometimes played by the *ubi sunt* device, which takes its name from the first two words of the Latin sentence, *Ubi sunt qui ante nos fuerunt?* ("Where are they who were before us?"), that began numerous medieval poems. In asking the question, the writer evokes for a moment the splendor of life, symbolized by famous persons of the past, and then, by his inevitably grim answer, condemns it to death. The tone of such works will vary from the austerely admonitory to the hauntingly sad, depending on how the writer asks his question and phrases his answer: whether he sides with death or with life or tries to balance delicately between them. In the following Anglo-Saxon poem, the anonymous poet sees only that the life which was so vividly there is suddenly gone, "in a twinkling of an ye."

> Where beeth they biforen us weren,
> Houndes ledden and hawkes beren,

And hadden feel and wode?
The riche ladies in hir bowr,
That wereden gold in hir tressour,
  With hir brighte rode,
Eten and drunken maden hem glad;
Hir lif was al with gamen ylad;
  Men kneeleden hem biforen:
They beren hem wel swithe hye.
And in a twinkling of an ye
  Hir soules weren forloren.

Brief *ubi sunt* laments are also found within longer works on the theme of transitoriness. The loss of a great protector and provider is the greatest of tragedies, as in "The Wanderer."

Where now is the warrior? Where is the war horse?
Bestowal of treasure, and sharing of feast?
Alas! the bright ale-cup, the byrney-clad warrior,
The prince in his splendor—those days are long sped
In the night of the past, as if they never had been!

Without directly connecting the work with the *ubi sunt* device, several commentators have pointed out how similar motifs of impermanence, of exile and separation, and of loss and regret are interwoven in **"Babylon Revisited,"** F. Scott Fitzgerald's story of a reformed drunkard, Charlie Wales, returning to Paris to claim his daughter, Honoria. But most of these critics see mainly repugnance for a sterile past that cannot be shucked away. "It was impossible to blot out the past," writes Thomas F. Staley [in "Time and Structure in Fitzgerald's 'Babylon Revisited'," *Modern Fiction Studies,* Vol. 10, 1965]. "Time and its ravages have left Charlie suspended in time with a nightmare for a past, an empty whiskey glass for a present, and a future full of loneliness." John A. Higgins [in *F. Scott Fitzgerald: A Study of the Stories,* 1971] sees guilt and atonement for the past, but Seymour Gross shows that "moral renovation may not be enough" ["Fitzgerald's 'Babylon Revisited'," *College English,* Vol. 25, 1963]. For David A. Toor, "Charlie Wales is . . . torn by his own inner sense of guilt and his inability to expiate it" ["Guilt and Retribution in 'Babylon Revisited'," *Fitzgerald/Hemingway Annual 1973,* 1974].

But the story also expresses, especially in its images of royalty and empire, a nostalgia for the past. "It was nice while it lasted," Charlie says in valedictory to the twenties. "We were a sort of royalty, almost infallible, with a sort of magic around us." Charlie tries to catch an imaginative glimpse of this past when he directs his taxi to the Opera. "He wanted to see the blue hour spread over the magnificent facade, and imagine that the cab horns, playing endlessly the first few bars of *Le Plus que Lent,* were the trumpets of the Second Empire." An entry in Fitzgeralds's own note-book indicates an attitude of wonder for the past, as well as horror.

It is the custom now to look back on ourselves of the boom days with a disapproval that approaches horror. But it had its virtues, that old boom: Life was a great deal larger and gayer for most people, and the stampede

to the spartan virtues in time of war and famine shouldn't make us too dizzy to remember its hilarious glory.

The recognition of such "glory" suggests that **"Babylon Revisited,"** like most *ubi sunt* laments, balances between the monitory and the lyrical, between appreciation of what once was, and acknowledgement of its loss.

**"Babylon Revisited,"** then, widely anthologized and called [by Higgins] Fitzgerald's "one virtually flawless contribution to the canon of the American short story," belongs to that generic convention known as the *ubi sunt lament.* More specifically, it is organized around alusions to one of the most famous of such works, Francois Villon's "Ballade of Dead Ladies."

In the story, Charlie Wales has "spoiled" the city for himself through dissipation during the boom, but now after the crash he returns and sees it with "clearer and more judicious eyes." In the Ritz bar, he makes a series of melancholy inquiries that are Fitzgerald's version of the *ubi sunt* formula. The story opens like a medieval poem.

"And where's Mr. Campbell? Charlie asked.

"Gone to Switzerland. Mr. Campbell's a pretty sick man, Mr. Wales."

"I'm sorry to hear that. And George Hardt?" Charlie inquired.

"Back in America, gone to work."

"And where is the Snowbird?"

This slang reference to a cocaine dealer or user, the "Snowbird," is picked up later when we learn that Charlie locked his wife Helen in a snowstorm, and that she died not long afterward of "heart trouble." This event now appears as an incluctable nightmare, like certain other memories of "women and girls carried screaming with drink or drugs out of public places—" and of "The men who locked their wives out in the snow, because the snow of twenty-nine wasn't real snow. If you didn't want it to be snow, you just paid some money."

*Ubi sunt qui ante nos fuerent?* ("Where are they who were before us?"), asks Charlie. His question of "Where is the Snow Bird?" alludes to Villon's sad and lovely refrain "But where are the snows of yesteryear?" The translation below is by Dante Gabriel Rossetti.

The Ballade of Dead Ladies

Tell me now in what hidden way is
  Lady Flora the lovely Roman?
Where's Hipparchia, and where is Thais,
  Neither of them the fairer woman?
  Where is Echo, beheld of no man,
Only heard on river and mere—
  She whose beauty was more than human?
But where are the snows of yester-year?

Where's Heloise, the learned nun,
  For whose sake Abeillard, I ween,
Lost manhood and put priesthood on?
  (From Love he won such dule and teen)
  And where, I pray you, is the Queen
Who willed that Buridan should steer
  Sewed in a sack's mouth down the Seine?
But where are the snows of yester-year?

White Queen Blanche, like a queen of Lilies,
  With a voice like any mermaiden—
Bertha Broadfoot, Beatrice, Alice,
  And Ermengarde the Lady of Maine—
  And that good Joan whom Englishmen
At Rouen doomed and burned her there—
  Mother of God, where are they, then?
But where are the snows of yester-year?

Envoy

Nay, never ask this week, fair lord,
  Where they are gone, nor yet this year,
Except with this for an overword—
But where are the snows of yester-year?

Both short story and ballade are farewells to lost ladies, who represent the lost values of love, youth, and beauty that exist now only in the imagination. Each begins with a farewell to prostitutes. At the end of Part I, Charlie buys eggs and coffee for a woman who speaks to him in "the glare of a *brasserie*," but then, "eluding her encouraging stare, gave her a twenty-franc note and took a taxi to his hotel." In the first stanza of "The Ballade of Dead Ladies," Villon asks the fate of various great courtesans of antiquity: Flora, the celebrated Roman courtesan of Juvenal; the Greek courtesan, Hipparchia; and Thais, the Athenian courtesan who followed Alexander into Egypt. Villon goes on in the following stanzas to evoke Heloise and Joan of Arc, only to have them, too, disappear like "the snows of yester-year." Similarly, at the end of Part II, Charlie says goodbye to his daughter, "all warm and glowing" in a window above him as he stands in a dark street. At the end of Part III, he says good-bye to his dead wife, Helen. In his dream, she appears to him, "In a swing in a white dress, and swinging faster all the time, so that at the end he could not hear clearly all that she said." At the end of Part IV, he says good-bye again not only to his daughter, but also to her cousins, and perhaps to childhood itself. "Goodnight, sweetheart," he says, "Goodnight, dear children."

Just as the first lady in each work is a prostitute, the final one is a maiden, Fitzgerald's Honoria and Villon's Joan of Arc. One of the ghosts from Charlie's past, "a lovely pale blonde of thirty" named Lorraine Quarrels, is apparently named after Villon's ". . . Jehanne la bonne Lorraine," or "Jehanne the good maid of Lorraine," in Robert Lowell's translation. The association is, of course, ironic, since Lorraine now seems "trite, blurred, and worn away" to Charlie. Helen's name certainly evokes classical beauty, like the names of Villon's ladies, and Charlie's last name of "Wales" may suggest that he is also the "Prince"

to whom the *envoi* of a medieval French ballade was traditionally addressed. If so, he does not follow the advice Villon gives to his prince.

Part V, the conclusion of the story, like the concluding *envoi* or "send-off" of the ballade, sends Charlie off to a vague future in which the past seems lost. Told that he will have to wait at least six months for his daughter, he turns for comfort to his dead lady: "He was absolutely sure Helen wouldn't have wanted him to be so alone." In contrast, Villon advises his prince not to ask about the ladies "this week . . . nor yet this year," not unless he can also remember to ask, "But where are the snows of yester-year?"

The monitory tone of Fitzgerald's story, with Charlie's wish "to jump back a whole generation and trust in character again as the eternally valuable element," may suggest that Fitzgerald is comparing Charlie and perhaps himself with Villon, who led so disreputable a life, yet was so haunting a lyric poet that he became a legend. The chief details we have of Villon's life are of his scrapes and crimes. He was arrested several times, banished, and forced to flee Paris.

> Pardoned by a general amnesty (1461), he returned to Paris, but in 1462 he was again imprisoned and sentenced to be hanged. The punishment was later commuted to ten years' banishment. Villon was then only about thirty years old. Thereafter he disappeared completely from view.

Needless to say, Villon's career in Paris and Charlie's offer certain similarities most poignantly in their final fadeouts.

The *ubi sunt* device in both works suggests, of course, the themes usually associated with it: the impermanence of youth, beauty, and life itself. Fitzgerald's concern for such themes can be recognized as part of a tradition that goes back at least to Anglo-Saxon poetry. Since the device emphasizes the transitory nature of all things, the mood it represents is persistent and wide-spread. Even a contemporary figure like Robert Lowell "imitates" Villon's "Dames du Temps Jadis" and also asks, "Where, mother of God, is last year's snow?"

The truth that nothing which is human is enduring, permanent, or eternal reaches throughout most of ancient, medieval, and modern literature, and in using the *ubi sunt* device, Fitzgerald aligns himself with a long tradition that expresses his own themes of loss and regret, and the worth of old values. The snow of twenty-nine and the snows of yester-year evoke and then obliterate the lost ladies of the past.

**Garry N. Murphy and William C. Slattery  (essay date 1981)**

SOURCE: "The Flawed Text of 'Babylon Revisited': A Challenge to Editors, a Warning to Readers," in *Studies in Short Fiction,* Summer, 1981, pp. 315-18.

[*In the following essay, Murphy and Slattery argue that a paragraph should be deleted from the "authorized" version of "Babylon Revisited" to reflect Fitzgerald's final intentions for the story.*]

No one—not even F. Scott Fitzgerald himself—has ever seen **"Babylon Revisited"** printed in the final form intended by its author. The reason is astonishingly simple: when the "authorized" version (an extensive revision of the original 1931 *Saturday Evening Post* story) was printed by Scribners in **Taps at Reveille,** it contained a monumental editorial error, and, as far as we can determine, that error has been preserved, unremarked, in all subsequent collections and anthologies.

The error occurs early in the story, at the point where Charlie Wales leaves the Ritz Bar. We have lettered the paragraphs for easy reference.

> A. Outside, the fire-red, gas-blue, ghost-green signs shone smokily through the tranquil rain. It was late afternoon and the streets were in movement; the *bistros* gleamed. At the corner of the Boulevard des Capucines he took a taxi. The Place de la Concorde moved by in pink majesty; they crossed the logical Seine, and Charlie felt the sudden provincial quality of the left bank.

> B. Charlie directed his taxi to the Avenue de l'Opera, which was out of his way. But he wanted to see the blue hour spread over the magnificent facade, and imagine that the cab horns, playing endlessly the first few bars of *Le Plus que Lent* [sic], were the trumpets of the Second Empire. They were closing the iron grill in front of Brentano's Book-store, and people were already at dinner behind the trim little bourgeois hedge of Duval's. He had never eaten at a really cheap restaurant in Paris. Five-course dinner, four francs fifty, eighteen cents, wine included. For some odd reason he wished that he had.

> C. As they rolled on to the Left Bank and he felt its sudden provincialism, he thought, "I spoiled this city for myself. I didn't realize it, but the days came along one after another, and then two years were gone, and everything was gone, and I was gone."

Many readers, with or without first-hand knowledge of Paris, must surely have been puzzled by this strange taxi ride which takes Charlie over the Seine not once but twice. At least we were, and one of us knew Paris, one did not. As fledgling instructors at different universities, we had struggled with the problem, but to no avail. Later, in 1963, as colleagues at the same school, we shared our perplexities. We reconfirmed the absurdity of the route; we wrestled with the pointed but unconscionable repetition of the "sudden provincial quality" and "sudden provincialism" of the Left Bank; we speculated about Fitzgerald's carelessness.

Then, suddenly, the answer came to us: Paragraph B was intended as a substitute for Paragraph A, but both had been printed by mistake. Remove Paragraph A, and all would be well. In fact, all might even be better than well,

since Paragraph A reads like a poor imitation of Stephen Crane, while Paragraph B emphasizes the new, sadly ironic perspective with which Charlie now views Paris and himself.

A perusal of Fitzgerald criticism revealed that Richard R. Griffith had anticipated our wild surmise by several months and that Bernth Lindfors had anticipated Griffith by several more. However, Griffith proposed deleting only the last sentence of Paragraph A, not the whole paragraph, but that would leave us with a worse than amateurish progression of sentences: "At the corner of the Boulevard des Capucines he took a taxi. Charlie directed his taxi to the Avenue de l'Opera, which was out of his way." Nevertheless, we assumed that henceforth editors would take the cue. We were wrong; they did not. Nor did they respond when, ten years later, in 1973, Andre Le Vot discussed the matter again, supplying the motive for the revision and quoting a Fitzgerald letter which bemoans the failure of the "proofreaders" at Scribners to get things straight in **Taps at Reveille.**

Why has there been no response? Perhaps it has something to do with the unprepossessing titles of the three essays—"Paris Revisited," "A Note on Fitzgerald's **'Babylon Revisited,'**" and "Fitzgerald in Paris." None of these signals any concern with a textual problem, and unless an editor is already aware that there is one, he is likely, in scanning bibliographies, to go right past these items without an inkling that they are important to him. It is our hope that editors will not be able to do the same thing with *this* essay.

Fitzgerald had two important but different aims in reworking the stories he assembled for republication in **Taps at Reveille.** The first was to improve their quality, and this accounts for most of the more than eighty changes he made in the *Saturday Evening Post* text of **"Babylon Revisited."** A reader who compares the two texts soon discovers that the alterations—some slight, some substantial—all work in concert to give the story more depth and solidity: the time lapse before Charlie's return to Paris is lengthened from two to three years; Marion is made less spiteful; Charlie is made more sympathetic; the nemesis of the scribbled address is made more subtle, and for Charlie, more baffling.

But the second aim, which inadvertently caused the textual snarl we are concerned with, had nothing to do with improving the quality of the story. It had to do, instead, with an attempt at concealing the fact that in the throes of writing *Tender is the Night* Fitzgerald had lifted lines from his stories and used them, nearly word for word, in the novel. The only way out of the problem was to revise the passages in the stories, and he went about it in a state of agitation. Maxwell Perkins, his editor, advised him not to worry excessively over the matter, pointing out that Hemingway was guilty of much the same sort of thing, but nonetheless Fitzgerald remained anxious:

> The fact that Ernest has let himself repeat here and there a phrase would be no possible justification for

my doing the same. Each of us has his virtues and one of mine happens to be a great sense of exactitude about my work. He might be able to afford a lapse in that line where I wouldn't be and after all I have got to be the final judge of what is appropriate in these cases. Max, to repeat for the third time, this is in no way a question of laziness [the delay caused by the as yet unmade revisions]. It is a question absolutely of self-preservation.

Certain people I know read my books over and over again and I can't think of anything that would more annoy or disillusion a reader than to find an author using a phrase over and over as if his imagination were starving.

There were two passages in **"Babylon Revisited"** that Fitzgerald "borrowed" for *Tender is the Night*. One is the penultimate sentence of the story: "He wasn't young any more, with a lot of nice thoughts and dreams to have by himself." In *Tender is the Night* it appears in the opening sentences of the penultimate chapter: "The day before Doctor Diver left the Riviera he spent all his time with his children. He was not young any more with a lot of nice thoughts and dreams to have about himself, so he wanted to remember them well." Fortunately—for us and for the story—Fitzgerald overlooked this duplication. It is difficult to imagine any kind of satisfactory substitution.

He did not, however, overlook the passage about the surrealistically garish signs. In *Tender is the Night* he used it, rather better than in the story, as a contrasting and unperceived backdrop for the taxi ride during which Diver first admits to Rosemary that he loves her: "'Have you got a handkerchief?' she faltered. But there was little time to cry, and lovers now they fell ravenously on the quick seconds while outside the taxi windows the green and cream twilight faded, and the fire-red, gas-blue, ghost-green signs began to shine smokily through the tranquil rain. It was nearly six, the streets were in movement, the bistros gleamed, the Place de la Concorde moved by in pink majesty as the cab turned north." Returning to **"Babylon Revisited,"** Fitzgerald decided to cut the entire paragraph (Paragraph A above) and write a new one (Paragraph B), but because he wanted to salvage the remark about the provincialism of the Left Bank, he refashioned it as an introduction to Charlie's thoughts in the next paragraph. Originally, in the *Saturday Evening Post* that paragraph had simply begun with "'I spoiled this city for myself,' he thought. 'I didn't realize it, but. . . .'" Now, the new version read: "As they rolled on to the Left Bank and he felt its sudden provincialism, he thought, 'I spoiled this city for myself. I didn't realize it, but. . . .'"

So Fitzgerald shipped the galley back to Scribners, thinking he had removed all traces of the duplicatiton—only to discover as he was riffling through his newly-arrived copy of **Taps at Reveille** that there had been a mix-up at the print shop. He promptly wrote to Perkins: "Just found another whole paragraph in **Taps**, top of page 384, which appears in *Tender is the Night*. I'd carefully elided it and written the paragraph beneath it to replace it, but the proof-readers slipped and put them both in."

Nearly half a century has gone by since that cry of surprise and anguish. It is certainly time to do something about it. Although there are other, minor flaws in the **Taps at Reveille** text—e.g., the Debussy song should be spelled *La Plus que Lente,* not *Le Plus que Lent*—our principal challenge to editors is to remove the confusing, unwanted, unauthorized paragraph that still adulterates a very fine short story. Until such time as they do, *CAVEAT LITERATOR.*

### Elsa Nettels (essay date 1982)

SOURCE: "Howells's 'A Circle in the Water' and Fitzgerald's 'Babylon Revisited'," in *Studies in Short Fiction,* Summer, 1982, pp. 261-67.

[*In the following essay, Nettels discusses the many similarities shared by "Babylon Revisited" and a story by Howells, concluding that although the plots are alike, the perspectives on life expressed in each story are strikingly different.*]

William Dean Howells was not one of F. Scott Fitzgerald's literary heroes. Fitzgerald once included Howells along with such figures as Taft, McKinley, Bryan, Carnegie, and Rockefeller in a list of prominent men of the recent past in whom "a little boy could find little that was inspiring . . . Not one of them sounded any high note of heroism, no clear and distinct call to something beyond life" ["Wait till You Have Children of Your Own!" *F. Scott Fitzgerald in His Own Time,* ed. by Matthew J. Bruccoli and Jackson Bryer, 1971]. When his editor at Scribner's, Maxwell Perkins, asked him to soften an impious reference to God in *The Beautiful and Damned,* Fitzgerald accused Perkins of trying to bind him to the genteel and conventional, identified himself with Mark Twain, whose work, he said, exhibited a similar irreverence, and reminded Perkins that Van Wyck Brooks, in *The Ordeal of Mark Twain,* criticized Clemens for "allowing many of his statements to be toned down at the request of Wm. Dean Howells or Mrs. Clemens" [*Dear Scott/Dear Max: The Fitzgerald-Perkins Correspondence,* ed. by John Kuehl and Jackson R. Bryer, 1971].

Fitzgerald set himself in opposition to Howells, but a number of critics have noted connections between them. Sergio Perosa observes that Fitzgerald shared Howells's preoccupation with the interrelated themes of love and money and thus "linked himself with a traditional experience both human and cultural" [*The Art of F. Scott Fitzgerald,* 1965]. Kenneth Lynn identifies Kitty Ellison, the first of Howells's American heroines, as the forerunner of such later figures as the "headstrong flappers" of Fitzgerald's early stories [*William Dean Howells: An American Life,* 1970]. George N. Bennett compares Tom and Daisy Buchanan in *The Great Gatsby* with Alan and Bessie Lynde, cruel and selfish members of fashionable Boston society in *The Landlord at Lion's Head* [*The Realism of William Dean Howells, 1889-1920,* 1973]. Henry Dan Piper cites *The Rise of Silas Lapham* as the one novel about a businessman with which *The Last Tycoon,* dominated by the "doomed and heroic" figure of Monroe Stahr, can be compared [*F. Scott Fitzgerald: A Critical Portrait,* 1965]. Kermit Vanderbilt sees Howells as a linking figure who unites the psychological insights of Poe, Hawthorne, and Melville with "a vision of 'reality' as tentative as that of James, Twain, Crane, or Fitzgerald" [*The Achievement of William Dean Howells,* 1968].

Fitzgerald is also linked with Howells by the striking resemblances of his story **"Babylon Revisited"** (1931) to Howells's story "A Circle in the Water," first published in *Scribner's Magazine* in 1895 and collected in the volume of Howells's short stories *A Pair of Patient Lovers,* published by Harper's in 1901 and by Tauchnitz in 1905. There is no evidence that Fitzgerald ever read "A Circle in the Water," but if he did not, it is all the more suggestive of affinities between the two writers that without knowing it Fitzgerald should write a story so similar in plot, situation, and character to Howells's story. The stories also highlight the different outlooks of the two writers and help to explain why Fitzgerald rejected Howells as a literary mentor.

"A Circle in the Water" and **"Babylon Revisited"** both center on a middle-aged man whose wife is dead and who through folly or crime has lost custody of his only child, a daughter. Tedham, the father in Howells's story, is a convicted embezzler just released from prison, where he was sentenced to a ten year term as a warning to other peculators. Charlie Wales, Fitzgerald's protagonist, is also a perpetrator and a victim of corruption, having made a fortune through speculation in the 1920's, spent wildly, lost all in the stock market crash, entered a sanitarium to be cured of alcoholism, and finally reestablished himself in business, in Prague. When they were confined—Tedham in prison, Charlie Wales in the sanitarium—each was forced to let his wife's sister and her husband become the legal guardians of his child. Each story begins with the man's return after an absence of months or years to the city where his daughter lives with her guardians—Boston in Howells's story, Paris in Fitzgerald's. Tedham desires from his sister-in-law and her husband, the Haskeths, permission to see his daughter Fay, now aged eighteen, in hope of being reunited with her. Charlie Wales supplicates his sister-in-law, Marion Peters, and her husband Lincoln, in hopes of regaining custody of his nine-year-old daughter, Honoria. Both fathers see reunion with their daughters as the sign that they have paid the price demanded by others and fully atoned for their wrongs.

Howells presents Tedham from the point of view of a narrator, Basil March, once a friend of Tedham and still employed by the insurance company which Tedham defrauded. Like Lincoln Peters, who works in a bank, March is married and the father of two children. He is portrayed here as elsewhere in Howells's fiction as a steady, thoughtful, and humane man, an observer reluctant to involve himself in the affairs of others but often compelled by conscience or sympathy to act for them. Fitzgerald presents Charlie Wales directly, entering his mind and presenting Paris and the other characters as he sees them.

Charlie and Tedham, though seen from different perspectives, are nonetheless similar in a number of ways.

Despite their ordeals, both characters have remained physically attractive. March notes that Tedham "seemed . . . to be looking very well . . . he even looked very handsome." Charlie Wales "was thirty-five and good to look at." Both men acknowledge their wrongdoing yet maintain that their offense is not so great as others think. Tedham insists that he was drawn deeper into fraud than he ever intended and that he acted "'partly, for the sake of others.'" Charlie Wales denies that he was responsible for his wife's death although once after a drunken quarrel he locked her out of doors in a snowstorm. Nevertheless, he broods on his dead wife, "escaped to a grave in Vermont," as Tedham dwells on the memory of his wife, whose grave he visits as soon as he is released from prison.

Both characters insist that they have expiated their wrongs, that no further payment should be exacted. Neither character, however, is radically transformed; both stories show that in some ways the man is unchanged. March notes that imprisonment has not cured Tedham of his old-time shiftiness, "the abiding want of straightforwardness in [his] nature," and he concludes: "he was still the old Tedham." The reformed business man, Charles J. Wales of Prague, is also the "old Wales" of Paris hailed by his one-time companions in dissipation, Duncan Schaeffer and Lorraine Quarrles. Their drunken intrusion into the Peters's house destroys his hope of securing Honoria, but had he not sought contact with Duncan by giving the barman a note for him with the Peters's address, they could not have found him. Charlie looks back with revulsion upon the escapades of the past—"in retrospect it was a nightmare"— but he also says nostalgically to Marion and Lincoln Peters, "'it was nice while it lasted . . . We were a sort of royalty, almost infallible, with a sort of magic around us.'" Lorraine seems to him "trite, blurred, worn away"—as Tedham seems to March like "an etching of himself from a worn-out plate"—but Charlie also feels Lorraine's "passionate, provocative attraction." What March concludes after observing Tedham applies also to Fitzgerald's protagonist: "Tragedy befalls the light and foolish as well as the wise and weighty natures, but it does not render them wise and weighty."

In revealing the limited and flawed natures of their characters, Howells and Fitzgerald also create sympathy for them, primarily by portraying the father's love of his daughter, his concern for her welfare, and his desire to regain his place in her life as the strongest motives of his existence. Both fathers feel that their daughters' presence is essential to their well-being. As Tedham implores the Marches to intercede with the Haskeths on his behalf, reminding them that his daughter is "'all that I have got left in the world,'" so Charlie Wales finds his only happiness in imagining the life he will make for Honoria, and when his hopes are shattered he faces himself alone in an empty world: "he wanted his child, and nothing was much good now, beside that fact. He wasn't young any more, with a lot of nice thoughts and dreams to have by himself."

In each story, the father's love is returned by the daughter, who shares his intense desire that they be together. The daughters also possess the attractive qualities of their fathers, and as children the daughters closely resemble each other. March remembers seeing Tedham and his daughter out driving together when Tedham was thirty-five and she "looked about nine"—the ages of Charlie Wales and his daughter. The child, in March's memory, is affectionate, charming, and poised, like Honoria; "she had something of poor Tedham's own style and grace." The scene, which causes March to reflect "how happy they had both seemed," is paralleled by the scenes in which Charlie Wales entertains his daughter at lunch and at the vaudeville and she begs him, "'I want to come and live with you.'"

In both stories, the irregular past life of the father is contrasted with the sober, conventional, well-regulated household of the child's guardians. Of the Haskeths' house on a quiet street of a Boston suburb, Basil March observes: "there was an old-fashioned keeping in the place . . . it imparted to me a notion of people set in their ways, of something severe, something hopelessly forbidding." In the house on the Left Bank where the Peterses live, Charlie Wales sees what he craves—a home where the "cheer of six o'clock" speaks in the crackling fire and the play of children. But the decision made by its adult members ultimately makes this home as "hopelessly forbidding" to Charlie Wales as the Haskeths' house seems to Tedham.

In each story, the sister-in-law of the returned exile is the chief source of the distrust and hatred he suffers. March recalls that after Tedham's conviction, Mrs. Hasketh had spoken of her brother-in-law with "implacable hate" and had vowed that if she could help it, his daughter should never see him again. When March meets her ten years later, her look of severity has become habitual, and although her hatred has exhausted itself, she speaks of Tedham with aversion, wishes that they might never have anything more to do with him and tells the Marches, who have come at Tedham's request, "'I never liked him; I never wanted my sister to marry him.'"

Likewise, Marion Peters regards her brother-in-law with "unalterable distrust," speaks to him coldly and looks at him with "hard eyes." She, too, disapproved of her sister's husband from the start and refused to believe that good could come of her sister's marriage. "She had lived for a long time with a prejudice—a prejudice founded on the curious disbelief in her sister's happiness, and which, in the shock of one terrible night, had turned to hatred for him." Mrs. Hasketh's dislike of Tedham seems born of her distrust of his character; Marion Peters's hatred of Charlie Wales springs in part from her envy of his wealth, but both women reveal their need to explain and justify themselves, insisting that the father's collapse forced them to intervene and that they act solely in the child's interest. Both women appear overwrought, given to nervous illness which they can use as a weapon against the child's father. Hasketh says of his wife, "'She is never very strong,'" and she confesses to the Marches that "'the sight of Mr. Tedham would make me sick.'" After Duncan and Lorraine have gone, Lincoln Peters explains to Charlie, "'Marion's not

well and she can't stand shocks. That kind of people make her really physically sick.'"

In both stories, the sister-in-law's husband shows a certain sympathy for the child's father and indicates his willingness that father and child be reunited. Hasketh says to March, "'I was never in favour of trying to have the child forget him, or be separated from him in any way.'" Lincoln Peters greets his brother-in-law in a friendly way and carefully helps move his wife to the point where she feels forced to say that Charlie may take Honoria. In both households, however, the woman is the dominant figure. When Mrs. Hasketh enters the room, March notes that her husband, "without really stirring at all, had the effect of withdrawing into the background," leaving his wife and Mrs. March "in charge of the drama." Lincoln Peters is a more substantial and forceful presence, but his wife's will, not his, determines the fate of Charlie Wales and Honoria.

The central question in each story is raised by the sister-in-law. Mrs. Hasketh describes to the Marches her tormented effort to define her duty, to determine whether she has a right to keep from Tedham's daughter the knowledge of her father's return and the suffering that knowledge might bring. When Tedham asks Basil and Isabel March to intercede with the Haskeths for him, the Marches face the same question. At first, March questions Tedham's right to disturb the lives of his daughter and her guardians; eventually he and his wife and the Haskeths all agree that Tedham's daughter must be told of her father's desire to see her and that they cannot keep from her the suffering that is "hers by right." The moral soundness of their decision is affirmed in the loving resolution of Tedham's daughter to stand by her father and protect him from further suffering.

The daughter in **"Babylon Revisited"** is too young to determine her future; she is essentially a passive figure, last seen being swung like a pendulum by her uncle. The central question concerns not her but her father. Will he be a responsible guardian of his daughter or will he lapse again into dissipation? "'How long are you going to stay sober, Charlie?'" Marion Peters asks her brother-in-law, making her duty to Honoria dependent upon her judgment of Charlie, which only time can vindicate. Charlie's refusal to take a second drink at the end of the story when he sits alone in the bar with his shattered hopes suggests that he may, as he says, stay sober "permanently," but Marion's question, "'How can anybody count on that?'" cannot be conclusively answered. Her view of Charlie is clearly prejudiced and yet her mistrust may be justifiable. The divergence of opinion among readers—some arguing that Charlie Wales is truly reformed, others arguing that he is essentially unchanged or is divided by conflicting desires—shows that, unlike "A Circle in the Water," Fitzgerald's story does not render final judgment of the characters or reveal the ultimate effects of their actions. In both stories, a woman's feeling determines the outcome, but in Howells's story the decisive force is love, which brings Tedham's punishment to an end; in Fitzgerald's story the decisive force is hate, which leaves the reader to wonder whether Charlie will be forced to "pay forever."

In this and in other ways Howells's story is more optimistic than Fitzgerald's. In "A Circle in the Water," all the characters, including Mrs. Hasketh, come to a just perception of their duties and the rights of others and they act accordingly. Fay Tedham's love for her father remains for ten years undiminished, untainted by fear, shame, or aversion. To March, her devotion proves that a force exists which can stop the spread of evil. "Love, which can alone arrest the consequences of wrong, had ended it."

Halfway through "A Circle in the Water," when no one can foresee a happy resolution, Mrs. March exclaims: "'What a terrible thing an evil deed is! It *can't* end. It has to go on and on forever.'" The words might be spoken at the end of **"Babylon Revisited."** Unlike Mrs. Hasketh, Marion Peters remains fixed in her hatred. By reacting hysterically to the intrusion of Duncan and Lorraine, she forces Charlie to wait months before he can try again to gain Honoria. The appearance of Charlie's old friends—the intrusion of the past in the present—suggests that Charlie is not wholly weaned from his old life and that even if he were, the past at any time can erupt in the present, in evil that cannot be foreseen or controlled.

This is not to imply that there is more suffering in Fitzgerald's story than in Howells's. But in Howells's fiction, pain and failure are balanced by the promise of happiness for some of the characters. The sins of the fathers do not corrupt the children or destroy their chances of a new life unblighted by the past. Tedham is first seen by the mouldering ruins of an ampitheatre in a wood on a late November afternoon, but amidst the decay "there were young oaks and pines growing up to the border of the ampitheatre on all sides." In Howells's novels in which the father suffers a defeat or a disgrace—in *The Undiscovered Country, A Woman's Reason, The Rise of Silas Lapham, The Quality of Mercy,* and *The Son of Royal Langbrith*—the children suffer keenly through their fathers but at the end, as in "A Circle in the Water," they look to the fulfillment of love in marriage into which past evil will not intrude. For March, human love becomes the emblem of divine love, which at the end of the story he glimpses in a mystical vision of "an infinite compassion encompassing our whole being like a sea, where every trouble of our sins and sorrows must cease at last like a circle in the water."

For Fitzgerald, belief in the power of love such as March affirms belongs to an outmoded faith which has lost its reality for those of Charlie Wales's generation. Like Dick Diver, who inherits his father's genteel code but not his father's religious faith, they inhabit a world in which nothing compensates them for the loss of youth and fortune, in which creative power, once spent, is gone forever with their happiness, leaving them alone with the ghosts of a past irrecoverable and inescapable.

## Carlos Baker  (essay date 1982)

SOURCE: "When the Story Ends: 'Babylon Revisited'," in *The Short Stories of F. Scott Fitzgerald*, edited by Jackson R. Bryer, The University of Wisconsin Press, 1982, pp. 269-77.

[*In the following essay, Baker analyzes images of freedom and imprisonment in "Babylon Revisited."*]

> A kind of change came in my fate,
> My keepers grew compassionate,
> I know not what had made them so.
> They were inured to sights of woe.
> And so it was:—my broken chain
> With links unfastened did remain
> And it was liberty to stride
> Along my cell from side to side.
> 　　　　　—Byron, "The Prisoner of Chillon"

Fitzgerald once called **"Babylon Revisited"** a magnificent short story (*Letters*). The adjective still holds. It is probably his best. Written in December, 1930, it was first published February 21, 1931, in the *Saturday Evening Post,* whose editors must have recognized its superior qualities, well above the norm of the stories from his pen that this magazine had been publishing for the past ten years. Collected in **Taps at Reveille** in 1935, it stood proudly at the end of the volume, a memorable example of well-made short fiction.

The epigraph from Byron bears upon the story for many reasons, not least because "The Prisoner of Chillon" was the first poem that Fitzgerald ever heard, his father having read it aloud to him in his childhood, a circumstance that he recalled in a letter to his mother in June, 1930, when he paid a tourist visit to "Chillon's dungeons deep and old" while staying at Ouchy-Lausanne in order to be near Zelda, who was desperately ill in a nearby sanatorium (*Letters*). The story he wrote six months afterwards might have been called "Chillon Revisited," involving as it does the double theme of freedom and imprisonment, of locking out and locking in. For although Charlie Wales seems to himself to have redeemed his right to parenthood and to have regained his proper freedom, the links of his fetters are still visible when the story ends. And we, the keepers, inured as we are to sights of woe both inside and outside Fitzgerald's life and works, cannot help feeling compassion for this fictive prisoner, who tries so hard to measure up, only to be defeated by a past that he can never shed.

From the triple nadir of the Wall Street crash, months of recuperation from alcoholism in a sanatorium, and the death of his wife, Charlie Wales has now rehabilitated himself as a successful man of business in Prague, Czechoslovakia, and has returned to Paris in the hope of taking custody of his nine-year-old daughter Honoria, who has been living in the care of her aunt and uncle since her mother's death. He feels ready for the responsibility, since he has made another kind of comeback, having staved off drunkenness for a year and a half by the simple expedient of rationing himself to one whisky a day. All those sins of commission which led to the débâcle are now, he is sure, behind him. He recognizes that while he was flinging away thousand-franc notes like handfuls of confetti, even the most wildly squandered sum was being given "as an offering to destiny that he might not remember the things most worth remembering, the things that now he would always remember": Honoria taken from him and Helen buried in Vermont.

Two motifs stand opposed in the story. One is that of Babylon, ancient center of luxury and wickedness in the writings of the Fathers of the Church. The other is that of the quiet and decent homelife that Wales wishes to establish for his child. He defines the Babylon motif as a "catering to vice and waste." It is what used to happen every afternoon in the Ritz bar when expatriated Americans like himself systematically hoisted glasses on the way to the ruin, moral or physical or both, that besets so many of them now. More spectacularly, it is places of decadent entertainment like the Casino where the naked Negro dancer Josephine Baker performs "her chocolate arabesques." It is squalidly visible along the streets of Montmartre, the Rue Pigalle and the Place Blanche, where nightclubs like "the two great mouths of the Café of Heaven and the Café of Hell" used to wait, as they still do, to devour busloads of tourists, innocent foreigners eager for a glimpse of Parisian fleshpots.

Fittingly enough, it is in the Ritz bar that the story opens—and closes. The place is nothing like it used to be. A stillness, "strange and portentous," inhabits the handsome room. No longer can it be thought of as an American bar: it has "gone back into France." All the former habitués are absent—Campbell ailing in Switzerland; Hardt back at work in the United States; and Fessenden, who tried to pass a bad check to the management, wrecked at last by shame and obesity. Only Duncan Schaeffer is still around Paris. Swallowing his loneliness, Charlie Wales hands the assistant bartender a note for Schaeffer including the address of his brother-in-law in the Rue Palatine. It is his first mistake. A key clicks in the prison door. Although he does not know it yet, Schaeffer will twice seek Charlie out, only to lock him into loneliness again.

At the outset Fitzgerald alternates interior and exterior scenes, with the obvious intent of providing the Babylonian background against which the principal dramatic scenes are to occur. While Charlie is on his way to the Peters's apartment in the Rue Palatine, he is most impressed by the nocturnal beauty rather than the wickedness of Paris. Bistros gleam like jewels along the boulevards, and the "fire-red, gas-blue, ghost-green signs" blur their way "smokily through the tranquil rain." By contrast, the livingroom at his brother-in-law's place is "warm and comfortably American," with a fire on the hearth and a pleasant domestic bustle in the kitchen. Although Honoria is well, and happy enough with her small cousins, she is plainly overjoyed to see her father again. At dinner he watches her closely, wondering whom she most resembles, himself or her mother. It will be fortunate, he thinks, "if she didn't combine the traits of both that had brought them to disaster."

Marion Peters has no doubt as to whose traits must be guarded against. Between Charlie and his sister-in-law an "instinctive antipathy" prevails. In her eyes he can do nothing right. When he says how strange it seems that so few Americans are in Paris, she answers that she's delighted: "'Now at least you can go into a store without their assuming you're a millionaire.'" But Charlie replies that it was nice while it lasted. "'We were a sort of royalty, almost infallible, with a sort of magic around us. In the bar this afternoon,'"—and here he stumbles, seeing his mistake—"'there wasn't a man I knew.'" Marion looks at him keenly: "'I should think you'd have had enough of bars.'"

In Marion's mind the reference to bars has no double significance; she means only those places where drinking is done. But to the eyes of the reader, aware of Charlie's prisonlike predicament, the word might well carry an ulterior suggestiveness. For he has had enough of bars in both senses, longing instead for the freedom to live a responsible domestic life and "more and more absorbed," as he thinks next day, "by the desire of putting a little of himself into [Honoria] before she [has] crystallized utterly" into maturity.

The bars of his incipient prison move closer on the following afternoon when he takes Honoria to lunch and afterwards to a vaudeville matinée at the Empire. That morning he has awakened to a bright fall day that reminds him, as it so often reminded Fitzgerald, of football games. Charlie is naturally optimistic, sanguine by temperament, at least in the mornings. The gloom closes in when two ghosts from his past—Duncan Schaeffer and Lorraine Quarrles—intrude on the father-daughter colloquy, first at the restaurant and then at the theater. He puts them off as well as he can: they are the counterforce to all he now longs for. Going home in the taxi, Honoria says firmly that she wants to live with him. His heart leaps up. When he has delivered her to the apartment, he waits outside for her to show herself at the window. She appears, warm and glowing like an image of domesticity, and throws him a kiss in the dark street where he stands.

On his return that evening, Marion meets him with "hard eyes." She is wearing a black dinner dress that faintly suggests mourning, possibly for her dead sister. Although he understands that he will "have to take a beating," Charlie supposes that if he assumes "the chastened attitude of the reformed sinner," he may be able to carry the day and win the right to his daughter, despite Marion's legal guardianship. But she remains obdurate. Never in her life, she tells him, can she forget that early morning when Helen knocked at her door, "'soaked to the skin and shivering,'" with the news that Charlie, in drunken and jealous anger, had locked her out in the snow, where she had been wandering in slippers, "too confused to find a taxi."

Once again the imagery of keys and locks and doors rises into view. Seeing that Marion has "built up all her fear of life into one wall and faced it toward him," Charlie can only swallow his protestations. When he points out in a dull voice that Helen, after all, "'died of heart trouble,'" she picks up and echoes the phrase as if—unlike her earlier reference to "bars"—this one of "'heart trouble'" has "another meaning for her." But she has reached the end of her tether. "'Do what you like!'" she cries, springing from her chair. "'. . . You two decide it. I can't stand this. I'm sick. I'm going to bed.'"

Next day when Charlie lunches with Lincoln Peters, he finds it difficult "to keep down his exultation." The two men agree to a final conference that evening to settle all details. But Charlie's past cannot be shed so easily. Back at his hotel he finds a *pneu* from Lorraine Quarrles, reminding him of their drunken exploit in stealing a butcher's tricycle and pedalling round the Étoile until dawn. "'For old time's sake,'" she urges him to meet her at the Ritz that afternoon at five.

Lorraine as temptress has lost her charm for Charlie. At five he leaves instead for the Rue Palatine for what will amount to the obligatory scene of the story. Honoria, who has been told that she is to go with her father, can scarcely contain her delight. Even Marion seems at last to have "accepted the inevitable." Charlie nods to Peters's offer of a drink: "'I'll take my daily whisky.'" The wall that Marion erected against him has fallen now. The apartment is warm—"a home, people together by a fire," the ideal of domesticity that Charlie would like to establish on his own for his child.

At this point comes the long peal at the doorbell and the sudden intrusion of Duncan Schaeffer and Lorraine, drunken, word-slurring, "hilarious . . . roaring with laughter." When Charlie introduces his old friends, Marion freezes, drawing back toward the hearth, her arm thrown defensively around her daughter's shoulders. After he has gotten rid of the intruders, Charlie notices that she has not moved from the fire. Both of her children are now standing in the maternal shelter of her arms. Peters is still playfully "swinging Honoria back and forth like a pendulum from side to side"—a gesture to which Fitzgerald plainly attaches symbolic significance and one that even echoes, though doubtless by chance, the very words of the prisoner of Chillon. Once more, in a telling repetition of first effect, Marion rushes from the room. She is in bad shape, as Peters returns to say. Dinner is out of the question and Charlie must go.

> Charlie got up. He took his coat and hat and started down the corridor. Then he opened the door of the dining-room and said in a strange voice, "Good night, children."

> Honoria rose and ran around the table to hug him.

> "Good night, sweetheart," he said vaguely, and then trying to make his voice more tender, trying to conciliate something, "Good night, dear children."

The story returns to its opening locale. In the grip of his anger, Charlie hopes to find Lorraine and Duncan at the Ritz bar. But they have done their sorry work and vanished from his life. He orders a whisky and chats idly with the bartender about times past. Once more the memory of those days sweeps over him like a nightmare—the incoherent babbling, the sexual advances, "the women and girls

carried screaming with drink or drugs out of public places," or the men like himself "who locked their wives out in the snow" on the theory that "the snow of twenty-nine wasn't real snow. If you didn't want it to be snow, you just paid some money."

Another lock-out is imminent, which will also amount to a locking-in. When Charlie telephones, Lincoln Peters is compassionate but firm: "'Marion's sick. . . . I know this thing isn't altogether your fault, but I can't have her go to pieces about it. I'm afraid we'll have to let it slide for six months.'" Charlie returns to his table. Although he tells himself that "they couldn't make him pay forever," he knows he must serve a further sentence in the prison of his days. But he is "absolutely sure that Helen wouldn't have wanted him to be so alone."

In the spring of 1940 Fitzgerald returned finally to Babylon, at least in memory and imagination, when he began negotiations for a screenplay based upon his nine-year-old story. A producer named Lester Cowan bought the property for "something over $800.00" (*Letters*), which Fitzgerald rightly thought to be very little as Hollywood prices were going at the time. But he accepted the pittance out of sheer desperation, having to support an ailing wife and an undergraduate daughter. His hopes rose a month later when Cowan proposed that he undertake the screenplay himself. This meant that Columbia Pictures would pay him for eight weeks' work at a salary equivalent to $287.50 per week. Disgusted though he was by the penuriousness of this advance, he could still anticipate a considerably larger sum if the producer and the company should decide to carry the film to completion (*Letters*).

He began the task on April 12. The work went well and his spirits were generally high. "I've written a really brilliant continuity" (*Letters*), he told Zelda on May 11, and on June 7 he declared the job finished (*Letters*). About mid-June he seems to have been assured that while the picture would definitely be made, it would have to be postponed until the completion of another in which Laurence Olivier was to appear (*Letters*). Meantime there was the possibility that Shirley Temple, the child star, might be induced through her mother to play the role of Charlie Wales's daughter. On July 11, in pursuit of one more hope, Fitzgerald spent the day with Shirley and her mother. "She really is a sweet little girl," he told his daughter Scottie, "and reminds me of you at 11 1/2" (*Letters*). Thereafter, although he continued to tinker with the final draft of the script and to dream that Miss Temple might take part in it, the film was never made (*Letters*). *Cosmopolitan,* which was the third of his working titles, seems to have been the last of his screenplays. Before the end of that parlous year, Fitzgerald was dead.

Apart from the pleasure it gave him, the metamorphosis of **"Babylon Revisited"** from story to filmscript opened vistas into his past that enabled him to comprehend, with characteristic honesty but also with a sinking heart, the shape his career had taken over the past twenty-five years. The little girl whom Gerald Murphy had nicknamed Scottina on the Riviera in 1925 was now a young woman in her nineteenth year, already showing signs of a developing literary talent and devoting some of her energies at Vassar to the writing of a musical comedy. Her father was fearful: "You are doing exactly what I did at Princeton," he told her.

> I wore myself out on a musical comedy there for which I wrote book and lyrics, organized and mostly directed while the president played football. Result: I slipped back in my work, got T.B., lost a year in college—and, irony of ironies, because of the scholastic slip I wasn't allowed to take the presidency of the Triangle. From your letter I guess that you are doing exactly the same thing and it just makes my stomach fall out to think of it. . . . *Please, please, please* . . . keep your scholastic head above water. To see a mistake repeated twice in two generations would be just too much to bear. This is the most completely experienced advice I've ever given you.
>
> (*Letters*)

Two months later he returned to the topic. "I don't doubt your sincerity about work. I think now you will always be a worker and I'm glad. Your mother's utterly endless mulling and brooding over insolubles paved the way to her ruin. . . . She was a great original in her way, with perhaps a more intense flame at its highest than I ever had, but she tried and is still trying to solve all ethical and moral problems on her own, without benefit of the thousands dead" (*Letters*). It seemed to him that Scottie's resemblance to himself was greater than hers to Zelda. "Doubt and worry—you are as crippled by them as I am by my inability to handle money or my self-indulgence of the past. . . . What little I've accomplished has been by the most laborious and uphill work, and I wish now I'd *never* relaxed or looked back" (*Letters*).

But he was looking back still, not only to the ruination of his Princeton career but also to the time in the summer of 1924 when he had first met Gerald and Sara Murphy. "There was many a day," he told them in February, 1940, "when the fact that you and Sara did help me in a desperate moment . . . seemed the only pleasant human thing that had happened in a world where I felt prematurely passed by and forgotten. . . . So you were never out of my mind" (*Letters*). He went on to say that the child heroine of the film on which he was about to start work was named Honoria and added, almost defiantly, "I'm keeping the name" (*Letters*).

He clung to it as if it had been a kind of talisman, a means of reentering a past epoch of pleasant human things. In the same way he was somehow reassured by the image of Scottie as a child—the model, as he told her twice, for the nine-year-old daughter of Charlie Wales in the story (*Letters*). It may even be a legitimate surmise that her affectionate greeting after long separation, "Oh, daddy, daddy, daddy, daddy, dads, dads, dads," was a direct transcript of one by Scottie at some reunion in the late 1920s.

Both the Murphys and their Honoria were much in his mind in those Hollywood days. "I wish very much you would call on the Murphys during your spring vacation," he wrote his daughter. "If there is any way in which you

could help Honoria—to a date, for instance—I think it would be mutually very advantageous. . . . I know it is difficult to pick up an old thread after an interval but it would please me immensely if you could at least pay a call there" (*Letters*). In June he repeated the suggestion: "Please go in to see Gerald Murphy at Mark Cross in passing thru N.Y. this summer" (*Letters*).

Yet this picking up of old threads was precisely what his filmscript was compelling him to do. The warp and woof of two whole decades appeared in the ironic chronology he sent to Zelda that June: "Twenty years ago *This Side of Paradise* was a best seller and we were settled in Westport. Ten years ago Paris was having almost its last great American season but we had to quit the gay parade and you were gone to Switzerland. Five years ago I had my first bad stroke of illness and went to Asheville. Cards began falling badly for us much too early" (*Letters*).

These four straightforward sentences, and particularly the second, about the necessity of leaving Paris for the gray prison of Switzerland, show clearly enough that 1930 stood in Fitzgerald's mind as the watershed or turning point of his career and of that of his wife. For it was then that the onset of Zelda's illness started them both on the downgrade from which, despite the most valiant of efforts, neither of them ever wholly recovered. Another of his letters, written the summer before, summarized the crucial change. "I not only announced the birth of my young illusions in *This Side of Paradise* but pretty much the death of them in some of my last *Post* stories like **'Babylon Revisited'**" (*Letters*).

Although his memory deceived him somewhat, since more than twenty of his stories had appeared in the *Post* after the publication of **"Babylon Revisited,"** this one plainly stood out in his mind as a fictional embodiment of the great shift from false romanticism to a firmer realism in his life as a writer. Arthur Mizener states the situation exactly and eloquently [in *Afternoon of an Author*, 1958]:

> Very gradually, under the pressure of great personal suffering, out of the toughness of his Irish determination not to be beaten, with the help of the New England conscience he had developed in Minnesota, Fitzgerald achieved a kind of acceptance of this state of "lost illusion." It is impossible to say that he ever accepted it as necessary: he seems always to have felt that unnecessary personal failures were really responsible for it. But at least he learned how to live with it. Out of this attitude came the theme of his last stories with their marvelous and subtle balance between an unquestioned acceptance of what he and his world are and an acute awareness of what they might be and, indeed, in some respects at least, once were.

**Gene D. Phillips (essay date 1986)**

SOURCE: "Paradise Lost: 'The Last of the Belles' and *The Last Time I Saw Paris*," in *Fiction, Film, and F. Scott Fitzgerald*, Loyola University Press, 1986, pp. 47-61.

[*In the following excerpt, Phillips compares "Babylon Revisited" with a screenplay that Fitzgerald adapted from the story and with a film that was loosely based on the story. Phillips remarks that the quality of the story suffers with each successive adaptation.*]

### "Babylon Revisited": The Short Story

The last time that a Fitzgerald short story was made into a full-length movie for theatrical release, rather than dramatized for television, was in 1954 when MGM produced the movie version of **"Babylon Revisited,"** which was entitled *The Last Time I Saw Paris*. Even though this film was produced long before the teleplay of **"The Last of the Belles"** . . . , the short story on which *The Last Time I Saw Paris* is based takes place during the depression rather than during the earlier Jazz Age, the setting of most of the Fitzgerald stories that have been adapted to either the big screen or the little screen.

In contrast to the telefilm of **"The Last of the Belles,"** the plot of **"Babylon Revisited"** was expanded to make a feature-length film by the more conventional method of creating additional episodes for the movie version which were not in the original short story. But *The Last Time I Saw Paris* was not the first attempt to fashion a screenplay from **"Babylon."** Fitzgerald himself had tried his hand at composing a screen adaptation of **"Babylon"** toward the end of his life; and we shall of course first consider his scenario for the film, before going on to analyze the movie that was actually made of the story from a different script.

As for the short story itself, its origin is even more intimately associated with Fitzgerald's private life than was **"The Last of the Belles."** In fact it grew out of a serious crisis in Fitzgerald's life. By 1930 Zelda Fitzgerald was hospitalized in the wake of the first of a series of mental breakdowns, and Fitzgerald's continuing drinking problem was becoming more acute. Under the circumstances, he feared that his sister-in-law, Rosalind Sayre Smith, might take steps to have him declared unfit to be in charge of his daughter Scottie. After a quarrel with Rosalind Smith, in which she strongly suggested that perhaps Scottie would be better off living with her and her husband than remaining under the care of her father, Fitzgerald was moved to write **"Babylon Revisited,"** which appeared in the *Post* in early 1931.

In the story Charlie Wales forfeits the custody of his nine-year-old daughter Honoria to his mean-spirited sister-in-law Marion Peters, whereas in real life Fitzgerald never at any time lost legal guardianship of his daughter. In the short story, then, he depicted the intolerable anguish that this turn of events would have caused him, had it ever come about.

Judging by Fitzgerald's on-going correspondence with his sister-in-law, one can see that Rosalind Smith's opinion of him was no better than Marion Peters's estimation of Charlie Wales. Three years after the publication of the short story, Fitzgerald was still accusing Rosalind Smith,

with some justification, of being "irreparably prejudiced" against him. At one point she intimated in a letter to Fitzgerald that the unstable lives which he and Zelda had lived in the first decade of their marriage had been one of the principal causes of her sister's emotional collapse. Rosalind even went so far as to state in one angry letter that she wished that Zelda might die in a mental institution, rather than return to the mad world that she and Scott had created for themselves.

Although I shall subsequently have more to say about the root causes of Zelda Fitzgerald's mental illness, suffice it to say at this juncture that it is true that during the course of the Roaring Twenties the Fitzgeralds did live an unsettled existence. They were constantly on the move, restlessly traipsing around Europe as well as the United States. As a matter of fact, there were times when Zelda had felt lonely and depressed, as they found themselves temporarily sojourning in yet one more foreign capital—and her husband thoughtlessly left her alone while he went on the town without her. Yet, when Fitzgerald honestly expressed his regrets about his behavior toward his wife to Dr. Paul Bleuler, one of the psychiatrists who was treating her, the latter was reassuring. Had Fitzgerald been more sensitive and solicitous towards his wife in the past, the doctor said, he might have slowed down the progress of his wife's emotional decline; but in any case he could not have prevented her breakdown. Nonetheless, one senses in his correspondence during this period that, in the light of Zelda's present plight, he believed that he should have been more caring and dependable in his relationship with his wife; and that sense of remorse permeates **"Babylon Revisited."**

Fitzgerald was nothing if not aware of his shortcomings; so he did not really need Rosalind Smith or anyone else to tell him that he and Zelda, along with a lot of other people, had lived too high, wide, and handsome during the boom days of the twenties. Moreover, the dissipation in the decade of the twenties looked even more reprehensible from the vantage point of the Great Depression in the bleak, austere decade of the thirties. "Somebody had blundered and the most expensive orgy in history was over," he wrote in an essay [titled "Echoes"] published shortly after **"Babylon Revisited."** "Now once more the belt is tight, and we summon the proper expression of horror as we look back at our wasted youth."

If he had heralded the birth of his young illusions in his fiction of the early twenties when the nation was embarking on the Jazz Age, he once told a *Post* editor, then **"Babylon Revisited"** announced the death of those same illusions. In Charlie Wales, then, Fitzgerald compellingly expressed that disillusionment with himself and the frivolous era he had just lived through.

When Charlie returns in 1930 to Paris, where he (like Fitzgerald) had spent some time in the twenties, he finds the city still recovering from the dissolute Babylonian bacchanal that boatloads of American tourists had helped to create in the City of Lights throughout the previous decade. Charlie's own irresponsible conduct is epitomized by the mad moment the year before, when he climaxed a liquor-fueled quarrel with his wife Helen by locking her out in the snow, thereby accelerating her death from heart disease.

It never occurred to him that she would suffer serious harm as a result of his impulsive action, Charlie wails poignantly. In those days a man thought he could cavalierly toss someone out in the snow with impunity, "because the snow of twenty-nine wasn't real snow. If you didn't want it to be real snow, you just paid some money." In other words, Charlie made the mistake of thinking that one could always buy off misfortune, even when one had brought it on one's self and others. Charlie's insight into his earlier reprehensible behavior has come too late to avert his personal tragedy, but his willingness to own up to what he has done makes his story a heartbreaking tale, one of Fitzgerald's best.

### "Babylon Revisited": Fitzgerald's Scenario

During the last year of Fitzgerald's life, while he was freelancing in Hollywood, independent producer Lester Cowan (*My Little Chickadee*) purchased the screen rights to **"Babylon Revisited"** for $1,000. In addition, he offered Fitzgerald a weekly salary of $500 to cover his living expenses while he composed a movie scenario based on his story, all with a view to the film being eventually made for Columbia Pictures.

Fitzgerald wrote to Scottie that he was delighted to be able personally to adapt what he rightly termed this "magnificent story" to the screen and later wrote to his Hollywood agent that he was really sweating over the scenario. But because he was adapting one of his own fictional works for filming, it was "pleasant sweat, so to speak, and rather more fun than I've ever had in pictures."

Fitzgerald worked on his screenplay, which he called *Cosmopolitan,* throughout the spring and summer of 1940, even after Cowan stopped his salary in June. In mid-August Fitzgerald wrote to Maxwell Perkins, "I finished the job, . . . working the last weeks without pay on a gamble." He had continued laboring over the *Cosmopolitan* script without remuneration because he was betting that some producer, if not Cowan, would be willing to finance the picture, once they had read his completed script; in which case, as he explained later to his wife, he might finally gain some real status in Hollywood, "as a movie man, and not a novelist." No such luck.

Why had Cowan lost interest in a project which he himself had initiated? First of all, Cowan had originally counted on securing Shirley Temple for the key role of Charlie Wales's daughter (called Victoria, not Honoria, in the screenplay); but he failed to obtain the services of the young superstar for the part. Because Fitzgerald realized the importance of having a box office favorite like Ms. Temple appear in the picture, he spent an entire afternoon with the young actress and her mother vainly trying to charm them into accepting Cowan's offer to do the picture.

"I remember Fitzgerald as a kindly, thin and pale man," the actress said many years afterward. Like David Niven, who also met Fitzgerald during this period, Shirley Temple was impressed that Fitzgerald could consume an entire six-pack of Coca Cola in just a couple of hours. "As a young girl, I thought this to be a stunning accomplishment. In fact, I still do!" Beyond that, nothing came of the visit.

The second reason why *Cosmopolitan* never reached the screen was that, despite some reports to the contrary, the script was not nearly as good as Fitzgerald thought—or hoped—it would be. One story goes that several years after Fitzgerald's death Cowan called in another scriptwriter to revise the screenplay; but the latter returned it untouched, with the accompanying comment that *Cosmopolitan* was the most perfect movie script he had ever read. "You're absolutely right," Cowan is supposed to have replied. "I'll pay you $2,000 a week to stay out of here and keep me from changing a word of it."

This patently apocryphal anecdote has been naively recounted as Gospel by Fitzgerald's biographer Arthur Mizener, despite the fact that the same frugal producer who only paid Fitzgerald $500 a week to write the screenplay in the first place would hardly have capriciously offered someone else four times that much to leave it alone. Whatever truth there is to be found in this little tale probably derives from an actual encounter between Cowan and Budd Schulberg, whom the producer wished to rewrite Fitzgerald's script for *Cosmopolitan.* After examining the screenplay, Schulberg told Cowan that his late friend's script was "astonishingly good just as it was."

In contrast, the frank assessment of *Cosmopolitan* by another Fitzgerald scholar, Henry Piper, is that Fitzgerald's adaptation of **"Babylon Revisited"** is just not very good; and I am inclined to agree with him, for the reasons he puts forth. According to Piper, the fundamental problem with the screenplay is that, in trying to stretch the plot of one of his best short stories into a feature-length film, Fitzgerald cheapened his original story by padding out the plot of his fragile tale of love and loss with the sort of glossy melodramatic material that he all too often assumed was necessary to hold what he considered to be the limited attention span of the mass audience.

"To the story of Charles Wales's touching effort to regain custody of his small daughter," Piper writes, "he added a sentimental love story between Wales and a hospital nurse, as well as a gangster subplot," in which Charlie's crooked business partner Dwight Schuyler seeks to have him murdered in order to cash in the insurance policy their firm holds on Charlie. In the process, Piper concludes, the portrayal of the tender relationship between father and daughter is well-nigh obliterated. As film scholar Robert Gessner suggests, in essence Fitzgerald tried so hard to make his screen adaptation of **"Babylon Revisited"** a saleable commodity in the Hollywood marketplace, that he wound up altering his short masterpiece almost beyond recognition.

Just about all that is left of **"Babylon Revisited"** in the screenplay for *Cosmopolitan* is the confrontation between Charlie and his sister-in-law over the guardianship of his little daughter. In fact, this scene contains one of the few bits of dialogue brought over from the original story, as Marion tells Charlie, "My duty is entirely to Helen. . . . I try to think what she would have wanted me to do." Otherwise, as film scholar Lawrence Stewart states in his exhaustive study of *Cosmopolitan* in the *Fitzgerald/Hemingway Annual* for 1971, Fitzgerald's script has little in common with what he himself had called his magnificent short story. Indeed, Fitzgerald even cancels the tragic finale of the short story by allowing Charlie to be reunited with his daughter in *Cosmopolitan.* In consequence, Latham's claim that this particular screenplay represents the culmination of Fitzgerald's years of screenwork is simply wishful thinking and is not borne out by a close analysis of the work at hand.

But the question remains, would the shooting script of the 1954 motion picture version of **"Babylon Revisited"** be any better than Fitzgerald's earlier screenplay? There was reason to believe that it would be.

*The Last Time I Saw Paris*: The Film

After Schulberg refused to rewrite Fitzgerald's script, Cowan shelved the project for some time, until he finally decided to engage two other screenwriters to start afresh on a new adaptation of **"Babylon Revisited."** This new screenplay, which Cowan eventually sold to Fitzgerald's former employer, MGM, for $40,000, was the work of Julius and Philip Epstein, a crack writing team of identical twins, who had both already earned Oscars for the script of *Casablanca* (1943), before turning their talents to adapting **"Babylon Revisited"** to the screen.

In addition to a script that was the handiwork of two distinguished screenwriters, MGM also had the services of the prominent filmmaker Richard Brooks to direct the picture. Brooks, who would become noted for his screen versions of such literary classics as Conrad's *Lord Jim,* was the first director of consequence to film a screen adaptation of one of Fitzgerald's stories, short or long. So it might have been hoped that a creditable film version of **"Babylon Revisited"** would at last be forthcoming from Hollywood, despite the fact that the studio brass made a couple of decisions regarding the production of the picture that were less than felicitous.

Replacing the title of the short story with the name of a sentimental love song by Jerome Kern, "The Last Time I Saw Paris," was relatively harmless. But then the front office went on to make the ill-advised decision to update the setting of the story from post-World War I Paris to post-World War II Paris, on the assumption that contemporary audiences could relate more readily to a film set in the recent past than to one set in the more distant past. Brooks, who discussed with me his adaptations of literature to the screen, did not agree with this decision, which was made before he was assigned to direct the picture; he firmly believed that since Fitzgerald's story was to some

extent a requiem for the Roaring Twenties, the period setting was indigenous to the story as Fitzgerald had conceived it. But he was overruled.

As for the ways in which the Epsteins overhauled the plot of Fitzgerald's short story in order to make it fit the dimensions of a theatrical feature, the new material which the brothers invented for this purpose by and large fit into the fabric of their literary source. Fellow screenwriter Fay Kanin has since singled out Julius Epstein in particular as being adept at creating solid plot lines for films. "His stories always have good bones."

The key element in the expansion of the story line to feature-length proportions was changing Charlie's occupation from that of a businessman to that of his creator, a professional writer. Most of the additional plot material which was invented for the film was spun out of this one fundamental modification in the characterization of Charlie Wills, as he is called in the movie. It was, for example, made the basis of the growing estrangement between Charlie (Van Johnson) and Helen (Elizabeth Taylor) in the film.

Since the reasons for the gradual breakdown of their marriage could only be lightly sketched within the narrow confines of a short story, the Epsteins opted to explain it in the film by showing how the deterioration of Charlie's career as a writer causes him increasingly to take refuge in the bottle, which in turn puts a strain on his marriage. Because Fitzgerald's own drinking became more of a serious problem when his literary career went into eclipse in the thirties, film scholar Foster Hirsch is correct in stating that in the movie "Van Johnson is clearly playing a variant on the fabled author himself." I, for one, have no quarrel with this fact.

Granted, there are definite analogies between Scott Fitzgerald and Charlie Wills in the movie; but the essential parallel between them, namely, the effort which each must make to hold on to the love of a beloved daughter, was firmly embedded in **"Babylon Revisited"** long before it was turned into *The Last Time I Saw Paris.* It seems, therefore, dramatically and artistically right that the scriptwriters should follow Fitzgerald's lead in utilizing further details from the author's life, over and above those which he had himself already put into his story, in order to flesh out their screenplay. Unfortunately, although they did not introduce into the plot the kind of lurid melodramatics that Fitzgerald had laid on with a trowel in his script, the screenwriters did take other liberties with Fitzgerald's story, which cannot be so easily justified.

The crucial crisis of both short story and film is, once again, the bitter confrontation between Charlie and the small-minded Marion (Donna Reed), who turns a deaf ear to Charlie's heartfelt petition that he be allowed to have his daughter Vickie back, so that he can make up for his previous wanton behavior by being both father and mother to the girl. At this point it looks as if the film will follow the short story by dramatizing its compelling conclusion, wherein Charlie and his daughter are once more separated, this time possibly for good.

Not a bit of it. Encouraged by her husband, who has all along been sympathetic to Charlie's cause, Marion experiences a last-minute change of heart. She catches up with Charlie, whom only moments before she had driven from her home, and turns Victoria over to him. So, instead of the film closing as the story does, with Charlie musing disconsolately that he is "absolutely sure Helen wouldn't have wanted him to be so alone," Charlie's sentiments are transferred in the film to Marion, who says to him, "I don't think Helen would have wanted you to be alone."

This far-too-facile attempt in the movie's final moments to retool Marion into a much more forgiving and generous character was dictated by the myth in the film industry, still subscribed to in those days by many producers, that films with upbeat endings usually attracted a larger audience than films with downbeat endings. Such producers saw popular "tearjerkers" like *Camille* and *Three Comrades* merely as the occasional exceptions that prove the rule. In the last reel of *Paris* the attempt to realign Marion's character in a way that would justify a happy conclusion rings false, precisely because the screenplay has been fairly faithful to the short story up to this point by presenting Marion as a calculating and selfish woman. Her abrupt about-face in the closing moments of the movie is inconsistent with her character as already established in the film and is, therefore, hardly credible.

The compromised ending of *Paris* was symptomatic of the fact that, as Richard Brooks states, many studio executives at the time had a predilection for sentimental endings of this sort. When he tried to tone down the sentimentality that tinged movies like *Paris* while he was making them, he was resisted by the front office. Studio boss Louis B. Mayer told him, "You seem like a nice fellow, but if you could only make our kind of movies it would be much better." "I can't blame them" for their attitude, says Brooks; but he concedes, "I should just not have gone along with it," when it came to sending the audience away with a smile rather than a tear at the end of a picture like *Paris*.

Still *The Last Time I Saw Paris*, when all is said and done, turned out to be a better picture than *Cosmopolitan* could ever have been. The MGM movie of **"Babylon"** may have departed from its source in some ways, as with Marion's eleventh hour change of heart; but Fitzgerald's screenplay, which he hoked up with the introduction of a new love interest for Charlie, not to mention a contract killer threatening Charlie's life, nearly lost sight of his original short story altogether.

On the other hand, since *The Last Time I Saw Paris* was deprived of the rich ambience of Paris after World War I, which permeated the short story, and since the movie was likewise deprived of the hard-edged conclusion of Fitzgerald's original story, it was written off by many reviewers as a classy contemporary soap opera. "The soft soap is smeared so smoothly, and that old Jerome Kern tune is played so insistently," smirked Bosley Crowther in *The New York Times*, that the movie "may turn the public's heart to toothpaste." *Paris* was better than Crowther opined, but not as good as it could have been.

In sum, Fitzgerald's short fiction has not fared well on film, although *Bernice Bobs Her Hair* and *The Last of the Belles* do stand out as superior to the general run of adaptations of his short fiction. Nonetheless, all of the films discussed . . . that are still extant are well worth watching. For all of them can boast some sequences that retain the flavor of Fitzgerald's narrative genius and that serve to rescue each film from foundering on the shores of mediocrity.

For example, *The Last Time I Saw Paris* comes to life when, following the short story, it dramatizes in a most touching manner a frantic father's efforts to win his cherished daughter away from a calloused in-law by sincerely pleading that he has by now surely expiated his past sins. Moreover, despite the fact that the film version of **"Babylon Revisited"** departs from the original ending of Fitzgerald's story, the film still reflects Fitzgerald's abiding theme that one can only transcend one's moral transgressions by accepting responsibility for the suffering that they have caused.

**Joan Turner (essay date 1990)**

SOURCE: "Fitzgerald's 'Babylon Revisited'," in *The Explicator*, Vol. 48, No. 4, Summer, 1990, pp. 282-83.

[*In the following essay, Turner demonstrates that frequent references to time in "Babylon Revisited" support a theme important to the story.*]

F. Scott Fitzgerald uses many references to time in his short story **"Babylon Revisited."** His almost constant use of words relating to time helps reinforce one of the main themes of the story: the past cannot be escaped.

Hours and minutes are noted during the narrative present of the story. In the opening, Charlie Wales tells the bartender that he is in Paris for "four or five days" to see his daughter. It is also mentioned that it is "late afternoon" when Charlie leaves the bar. Throughout the story the current time is cited, even down to the exact hour in some cases. For example, when Charlie first sees Honoria at the Peterses', it is said that the "cheer of six o'clock" is in the room. The next day the reader learns that it is at "noon" that he eats with Honoria. The marking of the passage of time in the narrative present helps to show that while Charlie is trying to make up for his lost time with Honoria time is rapidly slipping away. Just as Charlie is aware of time passing, so is the reader.

Although Charlie is aware of lost time, he has great hopes for the future. He has dreams of being with Honoria, and the dreams are often spoken of in terms of time. He talks of bringing his sister over from America "next month" to look after Honoria. He tells his sister-in-law Marion that he plans to stay sober "permanently." In order to help his depression, he reminds himself to think of his future with Honoria, to "think of Sundays spent with her and of saying good morning to her" when she comes to live with him. The future is all that Charlie has. He has lost his past, and his present is slipping away.

Fitzgerald uses time particularly effectively in references to the sad past of Charlie Wales. Throughout the story, Charlie is reminded of his past. From the beginning, he sees all of the places from his drinking days. He asks about old friends and finds, "Two familiar names from the long list of a year and a half ago." It is this part of his past that Charlie would like to erase. But at the restaurant with Honoria, Charlie sees "Sudden ghosts out of the past," two friends of his who had helped him "make months into days in the lavish times of three years ago," or "that crazy spring."

These constant reminders help Fitzgerald demonstrate his theme. Certainly Charlie is unable to escape the fact that he had "those crazy years" and lost his wife and Honoria. He asks himself, "How many weeks or months of dissipation to arrive at that condition of utter irresponsibility?" He sees the mistakes of his past as well as their consequences. He sees that "the days came along one after another, then two years were gone, and everything was gone, and I was gone." In those two years, his wife died and he lost custody of Honoria. These facts of his past he cannot escape.

His sister-in-law, Marion, also seems unwilling to let Charlie escape from his past. She brings up the "times" that Charlie lost control. It is "those crazy years" that she remembers. Again, Charlie's mistakes are referred to in terms of time. Charlie believes that Marion has forgotten how hard he worked, "for seven years" before his drunken binge. He says that she "just remembers one night." He tells her that his drinking lasted for only "a year and a half." Marion replies that "It was time enough." When Marion finally gets upset enough to tell Charlie that she blames him for the death of her sister, Charlie has to keep his cool "for a moment." The phrase, "for a moment" is repeated three times in the one paragraph. It emphasizes how hard it is for Charlie to keep calm and also how much he wants Honoria.

For a while it looks as though Charlie will be able to escape his past and gain a future with Honoria. He realizes that if he does not gain custody, it would be "hopeless to try and know her in so short a time," during his visit to Paris. Once again, his needs and desires are expressed in terms of time. He feels that his time with Honoria is slipping away. Soon she will be grown, and he will not be a part of her life. He wants to be in her life; he believes that "the present is the thing."

Finally, Marion comes around. But just as Charlie is making arrangements for Honoria to live with him, his "ghosts from the past" arrive and spoil things for him. His failure to escape the past is told in terms of time: "We'll have to let it slide for six months." He thinks of his defeat in terms of time: he resolves to "come back someday; they couldn't make him pay forever."

Throughout **"Babylon Revisited,"** Fitzgerald uses words of time to convey his theme that people are unable to escape the past, in the story of a man trying to overcome his past mistakes, only to be constantly confronted with them.

### Cecil D. Eby (essay date 1995)

SOURCE: "Fitzgerald's 'Babylon Revisited'," in *The Explicator,* Vol. 53, No. 3, Spring, 1995, pp. 176-77.

[*In the following essay, Eby focuses on Fitzgerald's use of* double entendre *to convey the themes of the story.*]

**"Babylon Revisited"** is by any reckoning the most frequently anthologized and widely read of F. Scott Fitzgerald's short stories. It opens and closes (appropriately) in the Ritz bar in Paris, where Paul, the manager, and Charles Wales reflect on the changes wrought by the stock market crash of 1929 and the economic depression that followed. But the two men are locked in two wholly discrete dimensions. Paul conceives the crash and the depression purely in economic terms, while Charles is haunted by the dissipated lifestyle of the boom years that ended with his wife's death, his daughter Honoria's adoption by his sister-in-law, and his own stint in a sanitarium for alcoholics. Their brief verbal exchange exists on two parallel planes:

> "I heard that you lost a lot in the crash." [Paul]
>
> "I did," and he [Charles] added grimly, "but I lost everything I wanted in the boom."
>
> "Selling short."
>
> "Something like that."

The lines are deceptively simple but they convey a wealth of implication. Paul's idea of losing a lot in the crash means loss of money. Charles assents to this, but thinking of his spiritual deterioration during the flush years before the economic debacle, he adds that his losses were greater in the boom years. Paul, still locked within his money orientation, misinterprets Charles's confession. During a boom in stock prices, how can a speculator lose money? The answer for Paul—Charles must have "sold short." "Short selling" is the market term for the most speculative (and dangerous) form of stock or commodity trading, for it entails selling shares you only pretend to own on the assumption that the price will drop and you will then be able to buy them at a lower price. Unlike buying stocks, where the most you can lose is your original investment, in short selling your losses theoretically can reach astronomical proportions if the stock goes up, instead of down, and you are forced to cover your sale by buying the stock at inflated prices. Short selling is not for investors but for gamblers.

Charles Wales doubtless knows what Paul is alluding to, but his reply, "Something like that," moves on another, more commonplace, level of communication. To sell yourself short is, of course, to underestimate or undervalue your worth, to fail to come up to your potential. In this sense Charles has truly "sold himself short" by having fallen into dissolute habits through earning and spending vast sums of money during the boom years. His errors have brought him a new awareness. "He believed in character, he wanted to jump back a whole generation and trust in character again as the eternally valuable element. Everything else wore out." Although he now has a good job in Prague and his material well-being has returned, he is unable to recover what he had once lost. His wife is gone forever and he fails to recover his Honor(ia).

This *double entendre* is one of Fitzgerald's verbal masterstrokes, for it compresses and combines the two essential themes of his story—economic as well as spiritual loss—into a single poignant exchange.

## FURTHER READING

Lindfors, Bernth. "Paris Revisited." *Fitzgerald Newsletter,* No. 16 (Winter 1962): 77-8.
    Illustrates the inconsistencies in Charlie's first taxi ride.

Lueders, Edward. "Revisiting Babylon: Fitzgerald and the 1920's." *Western Humanities Review* 29, No. 3 (Summer 1975): 285-91.
    Uses the symbolism of Fitzgerald's title "Babylon Revisited" to reexamine the 1920s.

Petry, Alice Hall. *Fitzgerald's Craft of Short Fiction: The Collected Stories 1920-1935.* Ann Arbor: UMI Research Press, 1989, 235 p.
    Contains scattered references to characters and themes in "Babylon Revisited."

# Malcolm Lowry
## 1909-1957

(Full name Clarence Malcolm Lowry) English short story writer, novelist, poet, and screenwriter.

## INTRODUCTION

Lowry is known as an experimental writer who produced a small but important body of writings. Influenced by the introspective, stream-of-consciousness literature of James Joyce, he is acclaimed for his intense and highly personal fiction. His work is also noted for its dense prose, as well as its themes of heaven and hell, failure, and redemption.

### Biographical Information

Lowry was born in Liscard, Cheshire, in northwest England, the youngest of four sons. His father was a wealthy cotton broker, and Lowry had a conventional English upper-class upbringing. At the age of 17 he went to sea as a deckhand, an adventure which provided material for his first novel, *Ultramarine.* After his graduation from Cambridge, Lowry began a pattern of rootless exile. In 1935 he was confined to Bellevue Hospital's psychiatric ward in New York City for a short time for treatment of his alcoholism, an experience that inspired his novella *Lunar Caustic.* The next year Lowry traveled with his wife to Mexico. During this time he wrote a short story, "Under the Volcano," concerning three people—a alcoholic Consul, his daughter Yvonne, and her lover Hugh—and their discovery of a murdered peasant. The story, published in the winter of 1963-64, eventually became the basis for chapter eight of the novel of the same title. Lowry drank heavily throughout 1937 while working on the first draft of *Under the Volcano,* and his unruly drunkenness effectively ended his marriage. In 1939 Lowry met his second wife, Margerie Bonner, in Los Angeles. Together they moved to Vancouver, where they married in 1940. They lived in Dollarton, near Vancouver, for the next 14 years; the setting was inspirational to Lowry, and in his work he contrasted British Columbia's wild seasons with its serene beauty. It is said that these years in Canada were the happiest of Lowry's life. His masterpiece, *Under the Volcano,* was published in 1947. He never again published any major work during his lifetime. Lowry died in England from an overdose of sleeping pills and alcohol in 1957.

### Major Works of Short Fiction

Lowry completed one collection of short fiction, *Hear Us O Lord,* which was published posthumously. While five of the stories in the collection garnered little attention, the remaining two—"Through the Panama" and "The Forest Path to the Spring"—are considered among his finest compositions. "Through the Panama" portrays a troubled writ-er's rise from the depths of self-consciousness. "The Forest Path to the Spring," the most poetic and spiritual of the volume's stories, traces the psychic development Lowry experienced during his years with his wife at Dollarton. In his autobiographical novella, *Lunar Caustic,* a disoriented alcoholic is confined to Bellevue Hospital's psychiatric wing. The protagonist, Bill Plantagenet, becomes acquainted with three other patients in the ward; through his relationship with these men, he comes to realize the severity of his alcoholism.

### Critical Reception

Critics have generally provided positive reviews of Lowry's short fiction. *Lunar Caustic* has been praised as a spare, compelling, Dantesque tale. Reviewers contend that the novella is a frightening depiction of psychic limbo, a painful reminder of the horrors of earthly life, and a stunning view of human destruction and disillusionment. The stories of *Hear Us O Lord* have also been favorably received by critics, who maintain that the short fiction of the collection offers a rare vision of change and even growth in Lowry's otherwise bleak canon. In particular, "Through the Panama" and "The Forest Path to the Spring" are widely considered as brilliant and finely rendered as *Under the Volcano.*

---

## PRINCIPAL WORKS

### Short Fiction

*Hear Us O Lord from Heaven Thy Dwelling Place* 1961
*Lunar Caustic* (novella) 1968

### Other Major Works

*Ultramarine* (novel) 1933
*Under the Volcano* (novel) 1947
*Selected Poems* (poetry) 1962
*Dark As the Grave Wherein My Friend Is Laid* (unfinished novel) 1968
*October Ferry to Gabriola* (unfinished novel) 1970

---

## CRITICISM

### Malcolm Bradbury (review date 1962)

SOURCE: A review of *Hear Us O Lord from Heaven Thy Dwelling Place,* in *Critical Quarterly,* Vol. 4, No. 4, Winter, 1962, pp. 377-79.

*[In the following excerpted review, Bradbury contrasts the main themes of* Hear Us O Lord *and Lowry's novel* Under the Volcano.*]*

Malcolm Lowry has been variously claimed as an English and an American novelist, and his curious internationalism is one of the interesting things about him. Like the hero of 'Elephants and Colosseums'—one of the stories in this posthumous volume *Hear Us O Lord from Heaven Thy Dwelling Place*—Lowry's success and reputation have been in America, where he lived extensively. Like Beckett and Durrell, to both of whom he bears great similarities technically, he was a literary expatriate whose travels provided him with a range for and a seriousness about his art which he was unlikely to have acquired at home; and what makes him interesting for the contemporary reader is his sense of literature as an international art, an art which demands great dedication and technical proficiency. His ostentation of manner, his wide literary allusiveness, his evident debts to writers as various as Thomas Wolfe and James Joyce, his deliberate formal experiments, all make him interesting in a period in which the English novel seems to have retired into a provincial quietness.

Lowry was born in 1909, attended an English public school, and at the age of eighteen he went to sea. His experiences gave him material for his first novel, *Ultramarine,* which he wrote as an undergraduate; it was published in 1933 and seems now not to be available. Soon after this he went to the United States and later to Mexico and then to British Columbia. In 1947 *Under the Volcano,* the novel on which his reputation has been based, was published—it is now reprinted as a Penguin Modern Classic. He had, however, many more works in progress, and when he died suddenly in 1957, he left a novel nearing completion, notes for several more, a large number of poems and the manuscript of this collection *Hear Us O Lord . . .* to which he was putting the finishing touches. The novel, *October Ferry to Gabriola,* is soon to be published. He had planned a sequence of six or possibly seven books, to be called *The Voyage that Never Ends. Under the Volcano* was to be its centre and the character Sigbjørn Wilderness, who appears for the first time in *Hear Us O Lord . . .* the central figure. These books must have been intended to exist in an exceedingly complex relation to one another. For instance, the story 'Through the Panama', in the new volume, is presented as being "From the Journal of Sigbjørn Wilderness", but it refers to a novel which Wilderness has written, called *Through the Valley of the Shadow of Death,* in which the characters are those that appear in *Under the Volcano.* Wilderness is also described as writing another novel which merges curiously into his own life as the journal goes on. The journal also contains the marginal summaries from "The Rime of the Ancient Mariner", given at the side of the text, as well as passages from guide-books and the like. Wilderness thus appears to be a figure for Lowry himself—but then so too did Firmin in *Under the Volcano,* and so too, in a later story, does another character, likewise a writer, who knows Wilderness. In this way an extremely complex mode of presentation is set up, one of its purposes seeming to be the distancing of Lowry's various versions of himself. Many

of his characters are writers, with distinctively similar histories—with English, Manx or Scandinavian backgrounds. Themes which are present in one story are taken up and presented in another, and a repeated pattern in the stories is the violation of fiction by reality—thus the plot of 'Elephants and Colosseums' has to do with a writer's discovery of the dishonesty inherent in writing. Lowry likewise frequently builds up his characters in a highly romantic mode and then dissipates their romanticism in an extended and brilliant critique of it. One such passage occurs in 'Through the Panama'. . . . in which the romantic necessity for talent to be uncritical about itself is played off against the necessity for criticism, and then the concept of equilibrium emerges—"And yet there has never been a time in history when there was a greater necessity for the preservation of that seemingly most cold-blooded of all states, equilibrium, a greater necessity indeed for sobriety (how I hate it!)".

The use of such devices and the contrived violation of the literary probabilities he has set up for himself serves Lowry in that it enables him to pursue the honesties he is always careful to pursue; he is eternally worried about false renderings. In this respect, the wryness of his later work contrasts interestingly with *Under the Volcano,* which is a consistent and complete unity, a novel about a breaking personality handled throughout in a romantic mode. Perhaps the idea of placing this as part of the larger work is that the romanticism should be softened; at any rate, the new volume does throw light on Lowry's purposes for *Under the Volcano* itself. Lowry's heroes, as I have said, are recurrently figures for himself, for his purpose in art is to convey the experience of men of consciousness and conscience. By multiplying the figures, he is able to multiply his own experience of life, or rather to show the variety of his own interpretations. Lowry *is* a romantic; his themes are the despoliation of the world by man, and of the tragic condition of the serious spirit in the modern world. His heroes walk through landscapes of destruction and waste; they are the landscapes of hell. Lowry sees modern social institutions as in decline, man as cut off from his paradise and yet searching for peace: "The conquering of wilderness, whether in fact or in his mind, was part of his own process of self-determination." But this search leads to ruination and vulgarisation. Lowry interprets the situation differently through different characters—through Hugh the communist and Geoffrey the voice of wildness in *Under the Volcano,* through Wilderness the seafarer and other figures, including the author himself who emerges, so to speak, in the last story, in *Hear Us O Lord . . . .* The interpretations and possibilities vary, but the message is broadly apocalyptic. Geoffrey Firmin is 'doomed'—the book demands one uses the word—from the start because he is a wild spirit. But his excessive richness of manner is carefully played off against the minute, precise accuracy of description; he moves slowly through a world that is given us with the purest clarity. . . .

Lowry's recurrent theme is of man the artist in battle against the universe; his heroes are anguished men, symbolically or actually at sea and in voyage. Many are alcoholics, and most have, like Geoffrey Firmin, a beautiful woman, aristocratic in spirit, by whom they seek to be saved. These central figures recall those of Scott Fitzgerald, but the action is played out a much less realistic landscape. There are extended sea journals, done with great accuracy but carefully reinforced by an elaborate structure of literary allusion. Lowry's manner is as I have suggested enormously stylized; his landscapes are often given in order to provoke literary recollection, and he makes constant reference to an enormous barrage of reading that ranges from Prescott to Baudelaire, Marx to Thomas Wolfe. He copies down and gives at length notices, passages from travel books, poems; he creates extended set pieces from careful observation, the observation of the writer whose life has been long keeping of a journal. He puns like Joyce, and then talks about being "Joyced with his own petard". The literariness of manner often leads to literary lapses; and yet at other times it relates the experiences he is concerned with to the experience of all other writers, and so makes his work in a curious way—in Joyce's way—universal. It is not hard to find falsity and inadequacy in his work; the purpose of these comments is to suggest the largeness and the interest of his imagination, particularly to those who have deplored the limited use that most modern English novelists seem to be making of the possibilities of the novel form.

**Dale Edmonds  (essay date 1967)**

SOURCE: "The Short Fiction of Malcolm Lowry," in *Tulane Studies in English,* Vol. XV, 1967, pp. 59-80.

[*In the following essay, Edmonds provides a thematic and stylistic analysis of Lowry's short fiction.*]

To a friend and fellow writer James Stern, Malcolm Lowry once wrote, "It is possible to compose a satisfactory work of art by the simple process of writing a series of good short stories, complete in themselves, with the same characters, interrelated, correlated, good if held up to the light, watertight if held upside down, but full of effects and dissonances that are impossible in a short story, but nevertheless having its purity of form, a purity that can only be achieved by the born short story writer." Lowry was *not* a "born short story writer"; many of his works of short fiction do not succeed by themselves, nor do the later stories constitute the interrelated whole Lowry visualized. However, two of his short works, **"The Forest Path to the Spring"** and **"Through the Panama,"** may be considered minor triumphs, and several of the other stories are worthy of attention for the occasional flashes of the brilliance of *Under the Volcano.*

Lowry's short fiction may be grouped into three categories for convenience of discussion: uncollected short works, most of them early; *Lunar Caustic,* a *novella* published posthumously in 1963 after Lowry had worked on it for a number of years; and *Hear Us O Lord from Heaven Thy Dwelling Place,* a collection of pieces written after publication of *Under the Volcano* in 1947 and published posthumously in 1961. The order in which I discuss the

works indicates the ascending order of their worth and importance: The early and uncollected works are, on the whole, of little save historical and curiosity value; *Lunar Caustic* is of debatable overall merit, though it has certain undeniable strengths; *Hear Us O Lord* contains Lowry's most fully realized works of short fiction, two of which bear consideration as substantial contributions in English short fiction in the post-World War II period.

While at Cambridge University Lowry published two short stories in a campus literary magazine, *Experiment*: **"Port Swettenham"** in 1930 and **"Punctum Indifferens Skibet Gaar Videre"** in 1931. Both of these stories were based upon his experiences during a globe-circling voyage he made as a deck-hand and cabin boy on a British freighter in 1927. Lowry revised both stories slightly and incorporated them in his first novel, *Ultramarine,* which was accepted as his senior thesis at Cambridge. Thus these stories would be more properly considered in a study of *Ultramarine* than here.

Lowry took his degree in 1932, and *Ultramarine* was published in 1933. The next work of his to see print after this was a short story, **"In Le Havre,"** in the July, 1934, issue of *Life and Letters.* In the months since the publication of *Ultramarine* he had journeyed to Spain, where he met an American girl named Jan Gabrial. They went to Paris to be married, and afterwards lived together in France only a short time before Jan returned to the United States. Lowry tells **"In Le Havre,"** a fictionalized account of their parting scene, almost entirely in the form of a dialogue between an Englishman and an American who are sitting in a tavern in Le Havre. The Englishman, who has just seen his American wife, Lee, depart on a ship for New York, says that he told her at the boat that he does not love her. This information starts the American talking about the awful sights in New York, such as drunks who lie in the gutters. The Englishman says, "If only I had said then [at his wife's departure], I love you so. Why did I say, I hate you, I never loved you?" The American answers, "Listen, the hell with you and your Lee. You only love your own misery." Then he walks out; the story ends. Aside from the biographical interest, this story has little to recommend it. The dialogue in which it is framed is flat and lifeless throughout.

**"Hotel Room in Chartres,"** published in the September, 1934, issue of *Story,* focuses upon a young couple whose marriage seems much like that of Lowry and his first wife, if reports of friends are to be believed. This story is one of the most affecting of Lowry's short fictional works, although it is flawed in execution: its unevenness and occasional turgidity detract considerably. The theme is the desperation of young love and the lack of communication between marriage partners. The concrete situation concerns disagreement between the husband and wife about a proposed excursion to Chartres, which reveals a deep chasm between them. When the man wishes to be himself, his wife hates him. He longs to return to the sea: "It's a rotten life reeling from filthy port to filthy port, perhaps, but it's better than this ceaseless quarreling, this dissension. There, at any rate, our lives were sometimes in danger." "Isn't our life in danger now?" the woman asks. For a time in Chartres they find calm in the hotel room where "their own life had come into being"—they had, apparently, spent the early days of their marriage in the very room to which they now return. The story ends on what seems a happy note: ". . . the world was turning to an evening land of apple blossoms and stars. The moon drew softly the outgoing tide of the woman towards the calming sea of the man. And up in the only room in the world they were folded together in each other's arms crying with joy that they had found each other once more." But it is apparent from the rest of the story that what they find in their hotel room is nothing more than an ephemeral moment reminiscent of past bliss. The concerns of this story—the disintegration of love, the cannibalism of marriage partners—no doubt were prominent in the mind of a man who had just parted from his wife. Unfortunately, if understandably, a note of mawkishness creeps into the story. Still, it is written with some skill, and the characters' situation seems touchingly real.

John Davenport, an old friend from Cambridge days, published a short story of Lowry's called **"Economic Conference, 1934,"** in the Autumn, 1949, issue of *Arena,* a journal he edited at the time. A Contributor Note describes the story as "a passage from an unpublished pre-war novel." According to Mrs. Lowry, her husband wrote the story when he was in Cambridge, or shortly thereafter, and gave it to Davenport. Lowry did not pursue the novel and forgot about the story, which Davenport published without his permission, Mrs. Lowry states.

One can see why Lowry was displeased by the publication. This story, like **"In Le Havre,"** is told almost entirely in the form of a dialogue, this time between an American named Bill, who "writes about economics," and a Chelsea taxi-driver, also named Bill. The journalist is in England to investigate economic conditions for a paper in New York, but finds himself stranded in Chelsea at two o'clock in the morning, without a cent. The taxi-driver offers to put him up until morning at his flat. Once inside the flat, about which are found strange objects—a stuffed squirrel, a stuffed lovebird, five stopped clocks—the taxi-driver begins to talk wildly, inconsequentially, in a manner somewhat like that of the Consul of *Under the Volcano* in his more confused moments. The two men get drunk and continue to swap stories. When the journalist mentions the subject of his investigations, the taxi-driver delivers a confused, unpunctuated tirade upon economic conditions in the world. After a time, under the effect of the numerous drinks they have had, they begin to frolic about the room. To climax the evening, "The glass cases containing the stuffed squirrel and the stuffed lovebird at last fell with a dithering crack." In this story one can see at times Lowry's fine comic sense—the tirades of the taxi-driver have a kind of dazed, hallucinatory brilliance. But, the story as a whole is weak and ineffective. Lowry seems to be satirizing economic theories and those who promulgate such theories, but he never makes his point clearly. The shortcomings of the story may be explained by the fact that it was intended as part of a larger work, but by itself it is clearly not one of Lowry's better efforts.

**"Under the Volcano,"** the original short story version which was to grow into the novel of the same name, was published in the Winter, 1963/64, issue of *Prairie Schooner.* The incidents of this story, written sometime during Lowry's stay in Mexico from Autumn, 1936—Summer, 1938, were to become the central incidents of Chapter VIII of the novel. The story is interesting in that it reveals Lowry's prose style in the process of maturing—but it had not yet arrived. Also, one can see by looking at this story certain major alterations Lowry was to make to achieve the effects of the novel (for example, in the story version the Consul is Yvonne's father, not her estranged husband, and Hugh is Yvonne's boy friend, unrelated to the Consul). But, aside from such matters of historical interest, the story does not help significantly in understanding the novel, nor does it exist in its own right as a work of short fiction. What later was to become one of the novel's most compelling segments simply is unconvincing when viewed in isolation.

Of the short fiction of Lowry's later years, the only published piece not collected in *Hear Us O Lord* is a segment from the unpublished novel *October Ferry to Gabriola,* which appeared in *Show,* March, 1964, under the title **"The Element Follows You Around, Sir!"** Lowry's writing in the story as a whole is over-wrought, digressive, replete with qualifying statements. The following paragraph is typical:

> The cumulative effect [of Ethan's discovery of a series of occult correspondences] was terrifying: Yet, for all that, Ethan thought to himself again, oddly reassuring. It was all something like going into a house reputed to be—that one had always thought was—haunted, in the company of some amiable Don Quixote, and perhaps a barrel of Amontillado. Or a hogshead of gin. But haunted by spirits? Not a bit of it. Such notions were really the work of romantics. The only haunted house was the human mind. And the human mind was that of a magician . . . who had forgotten the use of his powers, but from time to time could not help using them. All of which by no means discounted the possibility of other "intelligences" inhabiting those regions so much nearer than were supposed, those near those—now he thought of it—far too near regions. Only nothing was *super*natural. Everything would be explained when the time came. Even those "imperfect" conflagrations could be explained, were not really supernatural—and it was perhaps almost a disappointment after all, could be— Jesus.

The usual Lowry preoccupations and concerns appear. Captain Ethan Llewelyn, the protagonist, has a drinking problem, which is becoming worse. Jacqueline, his wife, is a typical Lowry woman in that she is pretty and clever, but she is not as understanding as some, and she has quite a drinking problem herself. The story turns upon another of Lowry's favorite devices: mysterious coincidence. Ethan, Jacqueline, and their son Tommy have been plagued by fires. First their home in Niagara-on-the-Lake, near Toronto, burned to the ground. Then a series of inexplicable fires broke out in the vicinity of the Prince of Wales Hotel, where they moved temporarily. One of the natives of Niagara-on-the-Lake tells Ethan, "The element follows you around, sir!" Ethan thinks, "not satisfied with having taken their home, it was exactly as if something, some 'intelligence,' was searching for them *personally, or him* personally, all over the town, and preparing to strike again". The situation becomes more involved when a movie called "The Wandering Jew" comes to town. Ethan discovers that the author of the play from which this movie was made, J. Temple Thurston, died in mysterious circumstances involving fire. Ethan learns this fact by accidentally coming across Thurston's name in a book of psychic investigation to which the local police chief referred him as a result of a conversation about the local disturbances. Finally, having enough of fires, or of occult correspondence, or of both, the Llewelyns move to British Columbia. Their first sight of Vancouver from the train window is, across the inlet, a fisherman's shack built on piles, burning furiously.

As a work of short fiction this story is perhaps best described as an interesting *tour de force*. However, Lowry does succeed in giving Captain Llewelyn a life of his own (apart from that of his creator), which he did not always succeed in doing with his other characters. Perhaps the most encouraging thing about **"The Element Follows You Around, Sir!"** is that it shows that in the last months of his life Lowry had regained much of his creative power. The eventual publication of *October Ferry to Gabriola* should confirm this view.

*Lunar Caustic* is a disappointing work, particularly in view of the time and effort Lowry put into it over a period of more than twenty years. He began the *novella* sometime during his stay in New York City in 1935-36, and continued to work on it, off and, on until almost his last days. The first version published in English was in *The Paris Review* in 1963. This is not Lowry's final version, but a product of editing by Lowry's widow and Earle Birney, Canadian poet and friend of Lowry's during the Dollarton years. In a letter to the editor of *The Paris Review,* Mrs. Lowry says the editors' work was chiefly a job of splicing, in an approximation of her husband's method—"We have not added a line," she states. At the time of Lowry's death several versions of this story, of varying lengths, existed. As was his habit, he worked with these versions simultaneously, comparing, considering, rejecting, beginning over again. Despite the years of work, *Lunar Caustic* seems fragmentary and diffuse, making one regret the effort spent on this project.

The plot of *Lunar Caustic* may be described briefly. An alcoholic, who may be named Bill Plantagenet, commits himself to a New York City community hospital (much like Bellevue, where Lowry spent some time during his stay in New York). He remains there for a time, during which he becomes friends with several other patients. Then, when the hospital staff discovers that he is not American, hence ineligible for charity treatment, he is released to return to his old life of the taverns.

This is not an unpromising plot, but it does not have sufficient interest and dynamic quality in itself to "carry" the story through its weak moments (as in **"Through the**

**Panama"**), nor does Lowry create an effective story by means of his style (as he was able to do with **"The Bravest Boat,"** which actually has little plot).

---

> Lowry was *not* a "born short story writer"; many of his works of short fiction do not succeed by themselves, nor do the later stories constitute the interrelated whole Lowry visualized.
>
> **—Dale Edmonds**

---

*Lunar Caustic* is less a study of the horror of the alcoholic's withdrawal from, and subsequent return to, drink, than an occasionally effective protest against stultifying bureaucracy and disgraceful inefficiency on the part of the staff of a public hospital. In this respect the story contains the most explicit social criticism of Lowry's published writings.

Bill Plantagenet, if that is his name, is another of Lowry's sensitive drinkers, a musician this time, in the mold of the protagonists of the **Hear Us O Lord** stories. Some years before the events of the story he shipped to the Orient on a freighter which, on its return voyage, picked up a cargo of wild animals (compare Cosnahan in **"Elephant and Colosseum"** and Hugh Firmin in *Under the Volcano*). An Englishman, Plantagenet has recently been cast aside by his American wife Ruth (the correspondences with Lowry's own life are strong here). When we first see Plantagenet he is emerging from a dockside tavern. He staggers from saloon to saloon until he reaches the goal of his "pilgrimage": the hospital. He goes inside, and "With the dithering crack of a ship going on the rocks the door shuts behind him." The most noteworthy feature of the opening section is the detachment of the narrator. We are not close to the "man" (he is not identified further), do not see or feel anything through him; nor do we learn any reason for his "pilgrimage." The last point would not be disturbing if the subsequent narrative established motivation, but it does not.

The long central section of the story takes place inside the hospital. The customary Lowry themes appear: drunkenness, madness, exile, the failure of love, the sorrowful state of the world, the difficulty of communication between human beings. There are some fine descriptions in this section of the world inside the hospital and of the world outside as apprehended from within. Plantagenet's friends, Garry, Mr. Kalowsky, and Mr. Battle, are good studies in the results of neglect and misunderstanding. They are troubled and lost, but deserve more suitable treatment than they are receiving. We share Plantagenet's indignation at the hospital's "Putting the sick and the halt, the blind and the dumb, the insane and the diseased, the quick and the dead, all into one dirty room . . .".

At times Lowry incisively portrays the alcoholic mind, although not as effectively as in *Under the Volcano.* Plantagenet, watching a puppet show put on for the dubious benefit of the patients, has the feeling that he has descended into the maelstrom:

> My God, he thought suddenly, why *am* I here, in this doleful place? And without quite knowing how this had come about, he felt that he had voyaged downward to the foul core of his world; here was the true meaning underneath all the loud inflamed words, the squealing headlines, the arrogant years. But here too, equally, he thought, looking at the doctor, was perhaps the cure, the wisdom and the vision, more patient still. . . . And goodness was here too—he glanced at his two friends— yes, by what miracle did it come about that compassion and love were here too?

Plantagenet's hope regarding the doctor proves false. Hampered by the demands of his job and the inadequate facilities, the doctor can give only cursory attention to individual patients. Lowry calls this doctor "Claggart." While this name ties in with Plantagenet's interest in Melville, it seems a questionable way of suggesting the shadowy correspondence between the fates of Plantagenet and Billy Budd.

The last section of the story begins, "Once more a man paused outside the City Hospital. Once more, with a dithering crack, the hospital door had shut behind him". Plantagenet has stayed sober while in the hospital, but to what end? This is the question Lowry leaves with Plantagenet— and with the reader. Assailed as we are in fiction by outcries at the futility and horror of existence, we require something more. In this last section Lowry returns to the detached style of the first section to describe what happens to the man after he leaves the hospital. The final section is no more successful than the first and does not bring the story to a satisfactory close.

Lowry's description of Plantagenet's passage through increasingly shabby streets toward the waterfront brings to mind a similar passage in Stephen Crane's *Maggie, a Girl of the Streets.* Lowry, like Crane, attempts to present, in telescoped fashion, downward progression over a period of years. When Plantagenet smashes his bottle against the obscene sketch of a girl in the tavern washroom, one thinks of the scene in *The Catcher in the Rye* when Holden Caulfield rubs out an obscene phrase in the hallway of his sister's school. Although Lowry probably did not intend to emulate these well-known passages, the result is that the reader is likely to think that he has read all this before.

Lowry's presentation of the inner workings of a public hospital is vivid and thought-provoking; his descriptions of the mentally ill characters are effective and moving; his treatment of the drunkard is believable. But *Lunar Caustic* fails as a work of fiction because of Lowry's uncertainty of intention and inconsistency of style.

First published in 1961, *Hear Us O Lord from Heaven Thy Dwelling Place* contains seven stories, arranged in the following order: **"The Bravest Boat," "Through the Panama," "Strange Comfort Afforded by the Profession," "Elephant and Colosseum," "Present Estate of Pompeii," "Gin and Goldenrod," "The Forest Path to the Spring." "Strange Comfort"** appeared in *New World Writing* in 1953, and **"The Bravest Boat"** in *The Partisan Review* in 1954—the only stories from this collection to be published during Lowry's lifetime. At the time of his death in 1957 the other stories were in varying stages of completion. Largely through the efforts of his widow, Margerie Bonner Lowry, **"Pompeii"** was published in *The Partisan Review* in 1959, **"Through the Panama"** in *The Paris Review* in 1960, and **"The Forest Path"** in *New World Writing* in 1961. **"Elephant and Colosseum"** appeared in an Italian translation in 1960, but had not appeared in English before this collection. **"Gin and Goldenrod"** first saw print in **Hear Us O Lord.**

Although the collection won the Canadian Governor General's Award for the best work of fiction produced by a Canadian in 1961, critical reception was mixed. *The Times Literary Supplement* [May 11, 1962] called the stories "splinters" from the ambitious scheme Lowry had for all his works; "as independent units . . . they will not help his reputation. . . . the roots of this whole collection are too transparently autobiographical." Richard Mayne [writing in *New Statesman,* May 4, 1962] described the stories as "dying arias" which "weaken" the impact of *Under, the Volcano* because of their "operatic self-pity." Phoebe Adams [in *The Atlantic,* August, 1961] concluded, "As a record of private experience, the stories are interesting, if incomplete. As a comment on the experience of humanity in general, they are of debatable relevance." [In the *Saturday Review,* May 27, 1961] William Van O'Connor typified the adverse critical opinion with these observations: "*Hear Us O Lord* . . . suffers from two commonly linked limitations: self-consciousness about writing, and the absence of a true subject. Lowry clearly had talent. But in this volume the talent was powerless to overcome the limitations."

On the positive side, J. M. Edelstein asserted [in the *New Republic,* June 5, 1961] that this collection held "more of some of the finest writing of our time." [In *The Spectator,* May 4, 1962] Brian Moore said that "in these stories as in his novel . . . [Lowry] produced some of the most enduring work of any English writer of our time." Elizabeth Janeway, in a long and perceptive review [in *The New York Times Book Review,* May 21, 1961], admitted that some readers would find Lowry eccentric in these stories, but "there are surely others for whom this fresh, askant, individual view of life will come as refreshment and revelation, large, living, vibrant with humor, sympathy, and perception, where nothing is skimped." The collection, she believed, was "anything but a hash of unrelated post-humous pieces strung together simply to make a book. It is a wonderful unexpected legacy for us all from a good man and a writer of great, great talent."

Most critics commented upon the autobiographical nature of the stories. At times Lowry does include extraneous or cloying autobiographical material (as in **"Strange Comfort"**), and it is true that the most successful story in the collection, "**The Forest Path,**" is the one in which Lowry keeps the greatest distance from his protagonist's personality. However, in the second most successful story, "**Through the Panama,**" the protagonist, Sigbjørn Wilderness, bears strong resemblance to his creator, both in the external details of his life and in his emotional complex. Thus it is not the presence or absence of autobiographical elements that determines the success of the stories.

---

**The strong points, if they do not entirely compensate for the weaknesses, at least give *Hear Us O Lord* a substantial claim on the reader's attention.**

**—*Dale Edmonds***

---

Perhaps the chief weakness in the stories is a lack of movement and development ("**Through the Panama**" and, perhaps, "**Gin and Goldenrod**" may be excepted here). Often there is no satisfactory progression toward a resolution of some kind. Obviously Lowry did not attempt to provide a plot, in the usual sense of the term, but several of the stories simply do not have sufficient vitality. The protagonists of these stories, particularly of "**Strange Comfort,**" "**Elephant and Colosseum,**" and "**Pompeii,**" are virtual slaves to their introspective tendencies, with the result that the stories seem static.

The recurring motifs, themes, and symbols occasionally have the effect of boring the reader with repetitiveness, rather than tying the stories together, as Lowry hoped. At times certain themes which are relevant in one story will seem artificially engrafted onto another. For instance, the sound of the freighters' engines—"Frère Jacques, Frère Jacques"—while believable when apprehended by Wilderness on his voyage through the Panama Canal, seems incongruous amid the reflections of Kennish Drumgold Cosnahan at the Rome zoo in "**Elephant and Colosseum.**"

Several critics attacked the collection because of Lowry's preoccupation with writing and the writer's lot. Concentration upon the artistic consciousness, these critics believed, either is not of sufficient interest to the general reader, or leads to excessive introspection and self-consciousness. In a reply to his editor, Albert Erskine, who had made a similar criticism, Lowry said he felt such a theme *was* acceptable to the general public because "there is an artist, a poet in every man, hence he is a creature easy for anyone to identify themselves with: and his struggles are likely to be universal, even on the lowest plane." Lowry's thinking here is questionable. One wonders how interested a non-writer is in the agony of creation, the problems of style. The mass of excerpts from the writer's notebooks in "**Strange Comfort**" proves wearying, and makes one conclude that Lowry is giving us raw passages from *his* notebook. Lowry focused upon the writer be-

cause this was what he knew best, but he was not always successful in these stories in making the writer's problems universal ones.

There are other weaknesses in these stories. At times Lowry becomes excessively sentimental and self-pitying, as in some of Wilderness's revelations in "**Through the Panama**": ". . . this ship . . . takes him away inexorably from the only place on earth he has loved, and perhaps forever." In "**The Forest Path,**" the naivete and sense of wonder of the protagonist occasionally sound false: "I reflected how little I had known of the depths and tides of a woman until now, her tenderness, her compassion, her capacity for delight, her wistfulness, her joy and strength, and her beauty, that happened through my wild luck to be the beauty of my wife." The women in these stories are poorly drawn, although one need not go so far as one critic who described Lowry's ideal woman as "a mattress which can cook and make pretty remarks about the scenery." The Lowry woman must be pretty, gay, helpful, and understanding. The quality of understanding is most important: she must understand the almost inconceivable problems that beset a sensitive drinking writer (perhaps one should say "sensitive writing drinker"). She must remain faithfully at his side, always patient, ready to give succor, and eager to interpret natural phenomena in images of textiles and jewelry. These women may be called Primrose, Lovey, Tansy, or simply "my wife," but they are the same charming, articulate, unconvincing woman.

The character Sigbjørn Wilderness, central figure in three of the stories, is perplexing. It is difficult to reconcile the Wilderness of "**Through the Panama**" with the Wilderness of "**Gin and Goldenrod,**" and either or both of these with the Wilderness of "**Strange Comfort.**" In "**Gin and Goldenrod**" Wilderness resembles the figure Lowry once described as "a sort of underground man . . . disinterested in literature, uncultured, incredibly unobservant, in many respects ignorant, without faith in himself, and lacking nearly all the qualities you normally associate with a novelist or writer. . . . he sees practically nothing at all, save through his wife's eyes. . . ." In this story, while Wilderness feels remorse about his debauchery and loss of money to a bootlegger, he seems most interested in whether there will be a drink waiting for him at home. The Wilderness of "**Through the Panama**" has his troubles with drink, but far from being "disinterested in literature," he is obsessed by it: literary references fill his journal. Neither of these figures seems compatible with the comparatively sane and self-possessed Wilderness of "**Strange Comfort,**" an American writer in Rome on a Guggenheim Fellowship, who scrupulously takes notes and quietly reads them over a few *grappas* (albeit a letter he discovers in an early notebook suggests the problems of the other Wildernesses). Thus there is not one Sigbjørn Wilderness, but three—Lowry failed to make him consistent among all three stories, an indefensible lapse, since he used a single name.

Lowry's attempt in these stories to create the community of Eridanus does not wholly succeed. Eridanus is the name given to the little cluster of shacks on the shores of an inlet where the Wildernesses, the Fairhavens, Quaggan, and the unnamed protagonist and his wife of **"The Forest Path"** live. The settlement takes its name from a steamer lying wrecked around the point beyond the lighthouse, with the symbolic cargo of cherries-in-brine, wine, and old marble from Portugal. The steamer, in turn, took its name from the constellation Eridanus, "known both as the River of Death and the River of Life, and placed there by Jupiter in remembrance of Phaethon, who once had the splendid illusion that he could guide the fiery steeds of his sun as well as his father Phoebus." References to this community occur in all the stories of *Hear Us O Lord* except **"Elephant and Colosseum."** The community does achieve a certain life, largely through the sustained treatment in **"The Forest Path,"** but does not provide the kind of powerful link among the stories that Lowry apparently envisioned. It is merely as if the common characters happened, at one time or another, to live in the same place, to share some of the same memories, and to value some of the same things.

Lowry's style in these stories at times becomes excessively mannered. He seems to have grown more digressive, reflective, introspective than when he wrote *Under the Volcano*. There is nothing here to restrain him as effectively as did the necessities of plot in the novel (**"Gin and Goldenrod"** should be excepted here. This story is written in a virtually "straight" style—no lengthy plunges into the consciousness of the characters, no stylistic quirks, no refractions of time, space, or reality). The following passage, from **"Elephant and Colosseum,"** represents Lowry's style in general in *Hear Us O Lord*:

> [Cosnahan is reluctant to finish and pay for a glass of milk] Since it wasn't merely the milk he would be paying for (any more than anyone who bought that book would pay for the spiritual nourishment it contained) but the commanding site of the Restaurant Rupe Tarpea upon the Via Veneto, to say nothing of the three other sidewalk restaurants on the other three corners created by the crossroads with the Via Sicilia and *their* rent, or their exquisitely dressed female occupants eating ices, to whose charming activities he felt he would be expected also, obscurely, to contribute; as naturally he would be paying also for the view, should he turn around, of the gateway of the Porta Pincia, and finally for the Via Vittorio Veneto itself, with its sidewalks ten feet broad, and its plane trees casting dappled shadows on either side as it swept in great curves down toward the invisible Piazza Barberini; the Via Veneto, which, with its ceaseless traffic of horsecabs and bicycles, combined with expensive American, Italian and English motor-cars, gave one not merely the physical sense of its own spaciousness, but produced in him—when now and then he forgot his besetting unease—that expansive feeling of great riches and peace, that purring roaring feeling, yet somehow quiet as a Rolls Royce engine, of life being at a sort of permanent flood, as if there had never been a first world war, let alone a second one, which was like an evocation of 1913, of those truly pre-war days from which he retained only this curious yet powerful sensation, when with his parents he must have visited London or Dublin, or at least Weston-super-Mare, at the age of five.

In the foregoing discussion I have dealt mainly with the weak points of the stories in *Hear Us O Lord*. The strong points, if they do not entirely compensate for the weaknesses, at least give the collection a substantial claim on the reader's attention. The constantly reiterated themes do provide a certain continuity. For example, by the time he reaches the end of the book, the reader is not likely to forget the "Frère Jacques" sound of the freighters' engines. The constant repetition of this phrase, which suggests the sound of eternity, impresses upon the reader the endless cycle of existence. Elizabeth Janeway describes the successful aspect of the recurring themes as follows: "These visions of Lowry's where the world inside one's head and the world one kicks one's feet against penetrate each other, are not idle. They are visions of the reality behind the conventional habitual view we accept as life; they speak to us urgently of new meanings. . . . such bits of experience do not merely repeat each other; they reflect and heighten each other and connect the stories, making them a whole."

Of the recurring themes in *Hear Us O Lord,* one of the most prevalent is that of the opposition of nature and civilization. Throughout his life Lowry felt his greatest happiness away from cities and in close touch with nature. This Rousseauistic attitude appears in nearly all his mature writings. As Lowry sees it, the world is in a state of chaos because man has "civilized" nature. This theme is expressed powerfully in **"The Bravest Boat."** The clean, clear beauty of the park (which suggests Stanley Park in Vancouver) with its wild swans and ducks, its lagoon where a little boy sails his boat, and its strolling lovers, contrasts with the surrounding city (which suggests Vancouver): ". . . [Enochvilleport was] composed of dilapidated half-skyscrapers, at different levels, some with all kinds of scrap iron, even broken airplanes, on their roofs, others being moldy stock exchange buildings, new beer parlors crawling with verminous light even in mid-afternoon and resembling gigantic emerald-lit public lavatories for both sexes . . . cerise conflagrations of cinemas, modern apartment buildings, and other soulless behemoths . . . anyone who had ever really been in hell must have given Enochvilleport a nod of recognition."

Civilization's encroachment upon nature is the main theme of **"Gin and Goldenrod."** Sigbjørn and Primrose Wilderness emerge from their pleasant, unspoiled forest path onto the dusty main highway. They pass the office of the Rosslyn Park Real Estate and Development Company and see "the hideous slash of felled trees, bare, broken ugly land crossed by dusty roads and dotted with new ugly houses where only a few years ago rested the beautiful forest they had loved." As Wilderness ruminates, the significance of his name becomes clear: "The conquering of wilderness, whether in fact or in his mind, was part of his own process of self-determination. The plight was an old-fashioned one, that had become true again: progress was the enemy, it was not making man more happy or secure. Ruination and vulgarization had become a habit." He attributes his personal failings to the advance of civilization, remembering the time when "there hadn't been any bootlegger in Dark Rosslyn to sell you firewater on Sunday, or, come to that, any reason for drinking it." He rages against the "bene-fits" of civilization: "How easy it is for people to talk about the benefits of civilization, who've never known the far greater benefits of not having anything to do with it at all!".

---

**In these stories one finds the same rich irony and humor, the same delight in puns and word play, that suffuse *Under the Volcano*.**

*—Dale Edmonds*

---

Civilization is the creation of man; thus, Lowry believes, man himself destroys his Garden of Eden, his paradise. When man destroys his garden, he must suffer the fate of expulsion. The central stories in *Hear Us O Lord* are studies, at least partially, of expulsion and exile. The freighter which carries Wilderness through the Panama Canal takes him away inexorably from Eridanus, the only place on earth he loves. The Wilderness of **"Strange Comfort"** suffers in his exile in Rome. Cosnahan in **"El-ephant and Colosseum"** is separated from his wife, from his beloved Nantucket, and from his native Isle of Man. Roderick McGregor Fairhaven in **"Pompeii,"** although in the self-imposed exile of vacation, thinks longingly of Eridanus. Reflecting upon the ruins of Pompeii, Fairhaven wonders if man "was not beginning to stand, in some profound inexplicable sense, fundamentally in some such imperfect or dislocated relation to his environment."

After man is expelled from paradise for his sin of destruc-tion, he suffers the torments of guilt and remorse. In Lowry's fictional world alcohol is one means by which man seeks to appease this sense of guilt. Wilderness, Fairhaven, and Cosnahan are heavy drinkers, and the pro-tagonist of **"The Forest Path"** once was. In **"Through the Panama"** Lowry articulates his feelings about the use of alcohol to combat the pain of the destructiveness of civilization: "[The real cause of alcoholism is] the ugli-ness and complete baffling sterility of existence as *sold* to you."

But alcohol is a sinister anodyne—it destroys as well as appeases. For the modern malaise Lowry does offer a more salutary remedy: a life of simplicity and love in unspoiled natural surroundings. This theme is the substance of **"The Forest Path to the Spring,"** a hymn of praise to the beauty and goodness of the natural life virtually unparal-leled in all of literature.

While Lowry's style in these stories at times lapses into obscurity, overrichness, or excessive mannerism, it rises at times to the level of excellence reached in *Under the Volcano*. These stories "live" in the sense that Lowry's perception enables him to convey, in a manner both exact-ly and poetically, the texture of life. This passage from **"The Forest Path"** is typical of Lowry's style at its best in *Hear Us O Lord*:

> But then we went out to a morning of wild ducks doing sixty downwind and golden-crowned kinglets feeding in swift jingling multitudinous flight through the leafless bushes, and another day of winter companionship would draw down to an evening of wind, clouds, and seagulls blowing four ways at once, and a black sky above the trembling desolate alders, the heart clothed already in their delicate green jewelry I had never really seen, and the gulls whitely soaring against that darkness, where suddenly now appeared the moon behind the clouds, as the wind dropped, transillumining its own soaring moonshot depths in the water, the moon reflected in the half-moonlit clouds in the water down there, and behind, in the same translunar depths, the reflection of the struts and cross-braces of our simple-minded pier, safe for another day, disposed subaqueously in some ancient complex harmony of architectural beauty, an inverse moon-light geometry, beyond our conscious knowledge.

In these stories one finds the same rich irony and humor, the same delight in puns and word play, that suffuse *Under the Volcano*. Chinese coolies, imported to Panama to build a railroad, were denied their opium on moral grounds; hence, they "strangled or hanged themselves with their long queues"—"This has now become a universal habit of the English," Lowry interposes. There is the same whim-sical, illuminating use of simile. The *Salinas,* an Ameri-can ship which had caused a serious fire while unloading crude oil the day before, returns to the scene of its arson, "wearing an expression like a drunk with a hangover ap-proaching at early morning the pub from which she has been thrown out the previous night." One critic [Janeway] has said, "[In these stories] Lowry's humor, like Mark Twain's, is not only hilarious in itself, it is a deliberate technique for exploring the human psyche and the human situation." Humor practically controls **"Elephant and Colosseum."** Cosnahan's realization of the ludicrousness of his total inertia since the publication of his book, and the humorous coincidence of his discovery of Rosemary, elephantine heroine of the book, at the Rome zoo, make him see that he can and will work again.

The title of Lowry's collection comes from an old Manx Fishermen's Hymn, the words of which echo throughout the stories:

> Hear us, O Lord, from heaven Thy dwelling place,
> Like them of old in vain we toil all night,
> Unless with us Thou go who are the Light,
> Come then, O Lord, that we may see Thy face.
>
> Thou, Lord, dost rule the raging of the sea
> When loud the storm and furious is the gale,
> Strong is Thine arm, our little barks are frail,
> Send us Thy help, remember Galilee. . . .

In **"The Forest Path"** the protagonist and his wife sit with Quaggan, the old Manx boatbuilder, and sing the hymn while the tempest howls outside: "There is no hymn like this great hymn sung to the tune of Peel Castle with its booming minor chords in which sounds all the savagery of the sea yet whose words of supplication make less an appeal to, than a poem of God's mercy." The storm may be without, as that which lashes the *S.S. Diderot* on its way to Rotterdam, or it may be within, as that which rages within Sigbjørn Wilderness (or Kennish Drumgold Cosnahan, or Roderick McGregor Fairhaven). The face of God is there to light the way, Lowry says in these stories, for those who have the courage and humility to see.

Lowry arranged the stories in a basically simple pattern. The opening story, **"The Bravest Boat,"** offers a glimpse of Eridanus: ". . . a few lowly little self-built shacks and float-houses, that might have been driven out of the city altogether . . . quite evidently built or placed with some human need for beauty in mind, even if under the permanent threat of eviction . . .". The love of Sigurd and Astrid Storlesen, which began when Astrid found the tiny boat Sigurd had launched twelve years before, signifies the permanence and simplicity possible in the world, even in the harsh glare of the city.

The second story, **"Through the Panama,"** moves us away from paradise. The voyage of the *Diderot* takes place on both spiritual and literal levels: it is the voyage of the Wildernesses to Europe, and it is also Sigbjørn's passage into and through the hell of himself (the only other passenger on the freighter is named Mr. Charon).

Although the *Diderot* arrives safely, the central stories (**"Strange Comfort," "Elephant and Colosseum," "Pompeii"**) suggest that safety is an illusion when one is in an alien environment. The exiles and expatriates of these stories long for what they have left behind—most significantly, perhaps, parts of themselves.

**"Gin and Goldenrod"** brings the Wildernesses—and the reader—back to the New World, but Wilderness is unable to cope with the forces of civilization about him. It remains for the protagonist of **"The Forest Path"** to learn to live in, and with, the world he has been given, to shut off from himself the destructive aspects of civilization, and to take sustenance from nature and simple, natural love.

Thus the stories describe a "Great Circle" movement, not only in geographical terms, but also in symbolic terms: a fall from grace and subsequent laborious return to that state. The final lines of **"The Bravest Boat"** could be taken as a paradigm of the collection's structure:

> . . . And it was to this shore, through that chaos, by those currents, that their little boat with its innocent message had been brought out of the past finally to safety and a home.

> But ah, the storms they had come through!

Although the other stories in the collection contain effective passages, only in **"Through the Panama"** and **"The Forest Path"** does Lowry display in a sustained manner

the talent which produced *Under the Volcano.* On the surface, the composition of **"Through the Panama"** seems transparent: it is the log of a voyage ("From the Journal of Sigbjørn Wilderness" is its subtitle). But the story is more than simply passages lifted from Lowry's own journal of a similar voyage. This story is a spiritual autobiography of Wilderness, giving his views of literature and love, the sum of which, to him, is life. Wilderness identifies himself almost to the point of calamity with Martin Trumbaugh, protagonist of a series of novels he is writing. At times it seems to Wilderness that he is being written, rather than writing—a frequent obsession of Lowry's. The themes of alcoholism, despair, and death, and Wilderness's violent fear of losing his home at Eridanus and being separated from Primrose, are rendered effectively by Lowry. [In *Canadian Literature,* Spring, 1961], George Woodcock describes the voyage as that of "a modern Ancient Mariner, with the albatross of literary creation and its attendant curse hung around his neck." To create this effect, Lowry in parts of the story includes a marginal gloss similar to Coleridge's in "The Rime of the Ancient Mariner." In Lowry's hands the marginal material becomes both an ironic commentary on the material in Wilderness's journal and a savagely vindictive history of the development of the Panama Canal—only one history of cruelty and exploitation, Lowry contends, in a world constituted of such histories.

If **"Through the Panama"** is Lowry's best short fiction piece dealing with the dark side of the human condition, then **"The Forest Path"** is his best short work dealing with the positive aspects of man's existence. After living for a time in Eridanus, absorbing its atmosphere, learning to love it, the protagonist of **"The Forest Path"** writes a symphony of his life there. This is destroyed in a fire that consumes the shack he and his wife share. Upon the charred fragments of his symphony he builds an opera, much as he and his wife build a new house upon the charred fragments of the old. The following description of his opera is an epitome of the story itself:

> . . . The theme was suggested probably by my thoughts of cleansing and purgation and renewal and the symbols of the canister, the ladder and so on, and certainly by the inlet itself, and the spring. It was partly in the whole-tone scale . . . partly jazz, partly folksongs or songs my wife sang, even old hymns, such as Hear Us O Lord from Heaven Thy Dwelling Place. I even used canons like Frère Jacques to express the ships' engines or the rhythms of eternity; Kristbjorg, Quaggan, my wife and myself, the other inhabitants of Eridanus, my jazz friends, were all characters, or exuberant instruments on the stage or in the pit. The fire was a dramatic incident and our own life, with its withdrawals and returns, what I had learned of nature, and the tides and the sunrises I tried to express. And I tried to write of human happiness in terms of enthusiasm and high seriousness usually reserved for catastrophe and tragedy. The opera was called *The Forest Path to the Spring.*

Throughout the story Lowry successfully sustains the tone of high seriousness, and by so doing makes the protagonist a consistent character and the story an aesthetic whole.

Lowry planned to use **"The Forest Path to the Spring"** as the coda to his projected cycle of works, *The Voyage That Never Ends.* He wanted the beauty and happiness of this story to stand at the end of his work as an antithesis to the darkness and despair of some of the earlier works. He did not live to complete his *Voyage,* but **"The Forest Path"** exists to show the reader the ultimate goal he envisioned.

After viewing the body of Lowry's short fiction, one is forced to conclude that none of these pieces is of the depth, intensity, or significance of *Under the Volcano,* although **"Through the Panama"** and **"The Forest Path"** are minor triumphs. Perhaps only in the novel form was Lowry's talent given the range it needed; it is sad and ironic to reflect upon the fact that he only completed and published two novels in his lifetime, and that only one of these was successful. But, *Under the Volcano* is enough to assure his reputation. His widow, Margerie Bonner Lowry, commenting upon a similar judgment I had made elsewhere, well expressed my feelings regarding Lowry's work as a whole: ". . . [I] agree that while all the other work is interesting, unusual, often profound and witty, Malcolm will finally have to stand on the VOLCANO. If he had lived even a few years longer this would not have been true. It is too bad that he will be known as a one book author, but he is not the only great writer who is principally known for one outstanding book."

## Perle Epstein (essay date 1968)

SOURCE: "Malcolm Lowry: In Search of Equilibrium," in *A Malcolm Lowry Catalogue,* J. Howard Woolmer, 1968, pp. 15-25.

[*In the following excerpt, Epstein explores autobiographical aspects of Lowry's short fiction.*]

Malcolm Lowry was almost entirely an autobiographical writer. His stories, novels, and poems can be read as a chronicle of the man's inner life, his obsession with the sea, alcohol, nature, mystical experience, the difficulties inherent in writing and loving, war, the reconciliation of opposites, jazz, and death. At the risk of repeating himself, even to the point of reiterating word for word certain pet phrases and similes, Lowry incorporated his recurring themes into everything he wrote. Critics have condemned this concentratedly personal vision, castigating him for his self-pity and obscurantism. In recent years, however, there has been a kind of slow but sure revival of interest in and, even in some once downright hostile quarters, a capitalizing on Malcolm Lowry's genius. At this very moment *Under the Volcano* is being cast as a film; his *Selected Letters* and a second novel, edited and spliced together by Mrs. Lowry and Douglas Day, have been released and favorably reviewed; a collected poems is contemplated, and a new novel being readied for publication. No longer can Lowry be praised and pitied as the "brilliant author of one book." Obviously there must be something of the universal in that personal vision—at least enough to war-

rant all of this belated public attention. Perhaps after all, the writer himself was not joking when he said that he would become suddenly popular ten years after his death; his timing was perfect.

My own book on Lowry and the Cabbala having grown out of a shared interest in matters occult and mystical, I found on re-reading his work that, despite his erudite, often cranky thematic preoccupations, Lowry's outer framework was really glaringly simple. Stream of consciousness, hallucination, and arcane symbolism notwithstanding, the author and his protagonists are all religious, if unorthodox, men, so taken up with the problem of searching for peace and goodness that they cannot see what is immediately before them, and thus conclude by stumbling, through too much further exploration, directly into evil. If the Consul in *Under the Volcano,* for example, would only stop *thinking* so much about life, stop obsessing and intellectualizing, and just *live* it, everything would be so much easier than either he or modern civilization thinks. But then of course there would be no such novel and no such civilization. Hence, Lowry's current popularity in a world where circumventing non-heroes search for the dividing line between a form of good and evil that is no longer available since Yeats' center came unscrewed.

Lowry's literary pattern (mirroring the pattern of his life) consists of placing his personae within a revolving syndrome of:

a) recognition of a nameless personal sin and its relationship to the guilt of mankind as a whole

b) the attempt to dispel the millstone of sin by drinking

c) further guilt and suicidal notions engendered by the inability to face life, to love, to stop drinking, etc.

d) mystical illumination, usually through the medium of an aspect of unspoiled nature; animals, Lawrentian primitives

e) the spur to create, the cleansing harmoniousness of *work*

f) catharsis through selflessness in creative activity and love.

His protagonists—to a man—are haunted by the accumulated guilt of civilization and by the inability to work. To find the release he needs in order to write again, Sigbjørn Wilderness, the fictional author of *Under the Volcano,* goes back to Mexico in search of his friend Fernando. (*Dark as the Grave Wherein My Friend is Laid*) Cuernavaca, with its familiar haunts, evokes the alcoholic demons again, and the search for equilibrium, symbolized by the memory of Fernando, becomes another trek through hell.

> Suddenly it occurred to him that this was what he was doing in Mexico: was it not for him too a sort of withdrawal into the tomb? Was he the director of this film of his life? Was God? Was the devil?

When Sigbjørn learns of Fernando's death, he is somehow freed from his inertia, his self-pity, and he leaves Mexico and its burdens of the past behind him. Now too he can confront the meaning behind his debauchery as embodied in the cantino Farolito:

> . . . perhaps he had not entirely wasted his time at the Farolito. Perhaps he had grown in some inexplicable manner there. Or perhaps what he had experienced was tantamount to some kind of illumination, perhaps some sort of mystical experience that suffering caused him to undergo.

Often it seems that Lowry's characters purposely lower themselves into the abyss of the world's suffering in order to make the flame of "mystical illumination" burn all the brighter, almost as an artificial stimulus for creation. In *Lunar Caustic,* Plantagenet, or so he calls himself, having committed himself to Bellevue during a bout with delirium tremens, reminds the psychiatrist that Blake recommends 'the road of excess' and bursts out in a tirade against the so-called sane world, "the horror of man's uncomplaining acceptance of his own degeneration" from which the inmates of the asylum have withdrawn in "the necessity for change in themselves, for *rebirth,* that's the word." In order to participate in the "rebirth", he has "voyaged downward to the foul core of his world"—a favorite Lowry image used to denote the isolation and suffering that prefaces enlightenment; the enlightenment that comes too late to his greatest creation, Geoffrey Firmin, a man who humorously contemplates visiting the bottom of the barranca by lowering himself slowly into it, with an occasional swig of tequila en route.

But "Volcano" was, after all, intended to be the hell portion of a seven novel *Divine Comedy,* with **"Forest Path to the Spring"** (a novella included in the collection entitled *Hear Us O Lord From Heaven Thy Dwelling Place*) the final hopeful note of the series. This novella depicting the regeneration of the spirit through nature, represents Lowry's writing at its lyrical best. As usual in his short stories, very little physically "happens." A prodigal jazz musician and his new wife come to British Columbia on their honeymoon and decide to stay on in spite of primitive conditions. Their shack is located on a little inlet called Eridanus, named after a decaying shipwrecked steamer belonging to the "defunct Astra [star] line . . ." In addition to being a constellation, Eridanus also stands for one of the rivers of Paradise, and is referred to in the novella simultaneously as the River of Life and the River of Death. Nature here becomes an outward manifestation of "the peace that passeth understanding":

> Such a time of stillness . . . it was like what I have learned the Chinese call the Tao, that, they say, came into existence before Heaven and Earth, something so still, so changeless, and yet reaching everywhere, and in no danger of being exhausted . . .

Here the first-person narrator hopes to recoup his lost innocence, to shed the corruption of civilization. Yet, even in Paradise man's own nature will not let him be at peace.

Fetching water from a mountain spring becomes a metaphor for the churlishness that eventually caused Adam's eviction from Eden. Again confrontation—this time with a mountain lion—brings the hero an image of the truth and enables him to conquer his own fear.

> . . . it was as though I had actually been on the lookout for something on the path that had seemed ready, on every side, to spring out of our paradise at us . . . the embodiment in some frightful animal form of those nameless somnambulisms, guilts, ghouls of past delirium, wounds to other souls and lives ready to leap out and destroy me . . . so that when, as if in answer to all this I saw a mere lion, how could I be afraid? And yet mysteriously the lion was all that too.

The chore then becomes his ticket to mystical enlightenment, to joy. Thoughts of suicide give way to thoughts of creation and the eventual composition of a successful opera "suggested probably by my thoughts of cleansing and purgation and renewal."

For Lowry life only begins to assume real meaning in difficult, sometimes unbearable surroundings, places inhabited by the poor, the pariah, away from bourgeois city life, away from the sophisticated literary scene, expatriated, among animals, even in hell. Whether he lives in a Rousseauean forest hut, rises at dawn among the beggars and outcasts of the Farolito, or locks himself willingly in an insane asylum, the seeker must be cut off from ordinary life in order to find his way back into himself.

Always observing himself, the Lowry hero finds it difficult to understand other people. The very act of purgation entails a kind of egomania that precludes a capacity for unselfish love. In **"Through the Panama"** (another story in the *Hear Us O Lord . . .* collection) Sigbjørn Wilderness, again on a voyage, keeps a journal of his daily experiences. This sea journey, another of Lowry's pilgrimages, becomes a Coleridgean metaphor replete with gales, calms, with some helpful assists from brandy and wine along the way. Sigbjørn, beset by albatrosses and other "Ancient Mariner" paraphernalia, is cast into a trance by super-natural agents during a disastrous storm only to be awakened out of the whirling dream to begin his "penance" anew. In this story it is suggested that the nameless hidden guilt borne by the owner of the diary might be something sexual. In *Lunar Caustic* the babbling hint of the hallucinating Plantagenet suggests that it is pre-sexual, an infantile loss and craving for "nutrition". Nevertheless, the neurotic guilt is there—accompanied always by the desire for goodness and stability.

> Conflict is all important [writes Sigbjørn. The real cause of alcoholism, he concludes, is] ugliness and complete baffling sterility of existence as *sold* to you . . . And yet there has never been a time in history when there was a greater necessity for the preservation of that seemingly most cold-blooded of all states, equilibrium, a greater necessity indeed for sobriety (how I hate it!). Equilibrium, sobriety, moderation, wisdom: these unpopular and unpleasant virtues, without which meditation and even goodness are impossible . . .

Attempts to find this equilibrium by means of alcoholic forays into good and evil often destroys the seeker entirely (cf. the Consul). Blake's declaration was probably directed at the superman to begin with. Thus, the hypersensitive writer in **"Strange Comfort Afforded by the Profession,"** another short story, learns that even geniuses like Poe and Keats, who, it would seem, did their best to find wisdom in excess, found only sickness, strangulation of the soul, social excommunication, and death.

**"Elephant and Colosseum"** is another animal confrontation story—a humorous one this time. Another author, alone in Rome, lost, and looking for earthly fame, finds himself slipping steadily into despair. He has an almost Homeric compulsion to copy down all kinds of odd lists: news clippings about his one successful novel, signs on the street, tourist brochures, and so forth; an aesthetic means of ordering the chaotic universe in which he finds himself. An ex-sailor whose novel is based on his sea-going experience with an elephant destined for the Rome zoo, he finds himself in that very zoo on the day he learns of his actual obscurity as a writer. Miraculously, the elephant in the zoo is the one and the same Rosemary of his novel. As his own mother was a witch, and he a water diviner, he recognizes the meeting as a mystical experience, identifies the elephant with some "strange primal peace," and permits himself to accept comedy, death, separation, and above all the vain foolishness of success.

> Who are we to say that the elephant does not have some higher comprehension of the will, as do those great mystics who inhabit some of the regions whence they come? To Cosnahan the kind of animism that could read such qualities into an elephant was not based on superstition, but on personal experience.

Rosemary, at peace in the zoo, indicates that, like Noah at the end of his perilous voyage, the writer can once again identify himself as a man who must begin to work anew. This realization makes him "as happy as some old magician who had just recovered his powers . . . Good God, he really *was* a magician." Innocence rediscovered discloses his original genius to man. Unfortunately, as Goethe well knew, this condition is all too temporary and must be revived on occasion by the devil's illusions—in Lowry's case, alcohol, the artificial consciousness. (Perhaps another reason for his popularity in this period of mind expanding drugs and instant meditation.)

In **"Present Estate of Pompeii"** Roderick Fairhaven (cousin to Poe's Roderick Usher) stands in the midst of the ruins and laments the fact that "man no longer belongs to or understands the world he has created . . . Man once stood at the center of the universe . . . ", a conclusion which leads him very naturally to the old round of despair and drink.

## George Woodcock (essay date 1971)

SOURCE: "Under Seymour Mountain: A Note on Lowry's Stories," in *Malcolm Lowry: The Man and His Work,* edited by George Woodcock, University of British Columbia Press, 1971, pp. 38-41.

[*In the following essay, Woodcock discusses the influence of life in Canada on "The Bravest Boat," "Gin and Goldenrod," and "The Forest Path to the Spring."*]

Malcolm Lowry was born in England in 1909. He died there in 1957. And during the restless life that stretched between those poles of destiny he wandered over a great portion of the earth—the Far East, the United States, much of Europe, and, of course, Mexico, the setting of his now belatedly celebrated novel, *Under the Volcano.* But almost a third of his life—and the most productive third so far as his writing was concerned—he spent in Canada. He came to Vancouver just before the war, in 1939, and the next year settled in a squatter's cabin on the foreshore of Burrard Inlet at Dollarton, a settlement under the shadow of the mountains, a few miles east of Vancouver. There, with time off for trips back to Mexico and Europe and Eastern Canada, he lived until 1954, when he left for Sicily and, finally, England.

It was at Dollarton, and at Niagara-on-the-Lake, that Lowry finished the last, published version of *Under the Volcano.* It was at Dollarton also that he wrote the stories which are published in the volume entitled *Hear Us O Lord From Heaven Thy Dwelling Place.* He worked at the same time on at least two novels about Mexico, *La Mordida* and *Dark as the Grave,* of which, so far as I know, only fragments remain among the great mass of manuscript material that has recently been assembled at the University of British Columbia. Among that material is also—apart from enough poems to make a considerable volume—the almost completed manuscript of a novel, *October Ferry to Gabriola,* which is set in British Columbia, and which also will be published as soon as the editing is complete.

I do not think there is much doubt that Lowry has one foot well in the realm of Canadian literature. It is not merely that on Canadian soil he produced the final, magnificent version of what many critics regard as the best novel written in our land; nor is it merely that much of his later work was set in Canada. We do not, after all, regard D. H. Lawrence as anything but an English writer, though he wrote many of his books abroad and set them in foreign countries. Try as he might to escape from his past, Lawrence remained the travelling Englishman, refracting all he saw through a personal and alien eye; his best writing on other lands was prompted by the lyrical observations of an outsider, and when he tried to enter into the heart of Mexico and portray it from within, he produced that literary monstrosity, *The Plumed Serpent.*

Lowry's relationship to his adopted home was quite different. We read the poems he wrote on Burrard Inlet; we read the three Canadian stories in *Hear Us O Lord From Heaven Thy Dwelling Place*—"The Bravest Boat", "Gin and Golden Rod", particularly "The Forest Path to the Spring". And we realize that he is not in fact writing about Canada as a transient outsider. He is writing about it as a man who over fifteen years lived himself into the environment that centred upon his fragile home where the Pacific tides lapped and sucked under the floorboards, and who identified himself with that environment—despite trials of flesh and spirit—as passionately as those other strangers who have rendered so well the essence of their particular corners of Canada, Frederick Philip Grove and Roderick Haig-Brown. If Mexico stirred him through that combination of antagonism and attraction which so many Europeans feel there, Canada—or at least that fragment of it which stretches out from Burrard Inlet to embrace the Gulf of Georgia—stirred him through a sympathy that led towards total involvement.

It is for this reason, perhaps, that in his Canadian stories the Websterian hell of *Under the Volcano* never comes to view, though one gets a whiff of the sulphur in **"Gin and Goldenrod"**. No man goes down to destruction under Seymour Mountain, and along the beaches of Dollarton the phantoms with death's-head faces do not sing in the voices of demons as they did for Consul Firmin. On the contrary, here, in this closely and lovingly described land-and-inletscape, there is a sense of redemption; in **"The Forest Path to the Spring"** the mountain lion who sits in a tree over the path and embodies destruction runs away from the narrator's steady eye, and what the latter remembers about his trips to the spring—what he remembers most vividly—is the almost mystical experience of joy that at times seemed to carry him in a rhapsodic instant from the life-giving source back to the door of his cabin. Here, as in *Under the Volcano,* the self is immersed. But in the novel it drowns in the whirlpool of self-negation, whereas in **"The Forest Path to the Spring"** it bathes in a universal calm, the calm of a world of nature as sympathetic as ever Wordsworth wrote of, with which it identifies and from which it returns with joy enriched. It seems to me that it is in this almost rhapsodic identification with place that we find our best reason to claim much of what Lowry wrote for the literature of Canada. For it is not a sense of place that derives from mere observation, like that conveyed by a sensitive and competent travel writer; it is rather the sense of place that derives from a mental naturalization which adds to a native's sense of identity the wonder of newness a native can never experience fully after childhood.

The stories in ***Hear Us O Lord From Heaven Thy Dwelling Place*** are all worth reading for themselves; some of the non-Canadian examples, while they do not attain the intensity of feeling of **"The Forest Path to the Spring"**, are interesting for their experimental exploration of the problems of conveying multiple levels of meaning. **"Through the Panama"** is an example; the narrator, a transmuted Lowry figure, voyages to Europe by freighter, but his journey is also that of a modern Ancient Mariner, with the albatross of literary creation and its attendant curse hung around his neck as he considers his novels about novelists who are his own mirror images. For Lowry belonged in the early twentieth century cosmopolitan tradition that seemed to reach an end about the time of his death—the tradition of Proust and Gide, which came to the conclusion, inevitable after a century of

introspection, that the proper study of the writer is the writer's mind.

But all these stories are also part of a great continuum, a vast Work in Progress that filled Lowry's life and was never completed—perhaps never could be completed. In this sense Lowry was of the Proustian rather than of the Gidian tradition. The Gidians write many separate studies of experience, all related, but each self-contained; when one novel is finished a phase of investigation is ended, its record is terminated as quickly as possible, and then the writer is on to the next experience and the next novel. But the Proustians, and Lowry among them, conceive all their work as one great inter-related pattern on whose parts they work continuously and simultaneously. Proust could never leave the one great work of his life alone; he worked backwards and forwards over his manuscript, and only publication ever gave a final form to any of its parts; only death, one can be sure, put a period to the work itself, coming by coincidence at the point when Proust had reached the end of his original plan. So it was with Lowry.

### Richard Hauer Costa (essay date 1972)

SOURCE: "Lowry in Canada," in *Malcolm Lowry,* Twayne Publishers, 1972, pp. 124-45.

[*In the following excerpt, Costa examines thematic aspects of the three Canadian stories in* Hear Us O Lord, *and notes similarities between "The Forest Path into the Spring" and Henry David Thoreau's* Walden.]

Three of the stories in the posthumous collection, ***Hear Us O Lord from Heaven Thy Dwelling Place,*** have a Canadian setting. Each is self-contained, further proof that Lowry never lost the storyteller's art which first brought him to the attention of American readers in Whit Burnett's famous magazine of the best in short fiction, *Story.* Each of these three stories contains a metaphor that dramatizes poetically the tension between the promised land of *Under the Volcano*—the "Northern Paradise"—and the threat of eviction in the wake of what Lowry called in one of the stories the "suburban dementia."

Like everything he wrote, the stories are autobiographical, dealing with day-to-day slices from the Lowrys' life in their squatters' cottage on the beach near Dollarton. They stand apart in more than setting from stories like **"Through the Panama"** and **"Strange Comfort Afforded by the Profession."** Lowry is able to subsume the anguish of the artist into the more universal anguish of good people who try to hold onto their humanity despite sprawling encroachments of industrial civilization.

**"The Bravest Boat"** was suggested to Lowry by a story he read in a Vancouver newspaper about that much-repeated but never tiresome feature writer's staple, the bottle set adrift with a note in it. Lowry expands on the bare bones, develops the idea with his own mythology of the rootless voyager, and ends with a story that is considered a minor classic in France where it was first published.

**"Gin and Goldenrod"** is Lowry's most successful anecdotal story. The protagonists are the same as those in **"Through the Panama,"** but here the similarity ends. In place of Sigbjørn Wilderness's desperate search for himself through the creation of a masking fictional persona, we have an almost light-hearted yarn, the barest suggestion of the Shakespearean jester in Lowry. The title effectively juxtaposes gin—addiction as a refuge against the numbing sterility of urban litter—and goldenrod which is symbolic of the benison that nature offers, an antidote to the poison of addiction.

The best story in *Hear Us O Lord*—the purest expression of Lowry's redemptive thrust to a *Paradiso*—is **"The Forest Path to the Spring."** The story is the antiphon to the demonic voices, "the inconceivable pandemonium," that accompanied the Consul in his fall. It is not by accident that the story is the final of the seven in *Hear Us O Lord.* For, as Margerie Lowry wrote in an unsigned "publisher's note," **"The Forest Path"** foreshadowed the climactic book of the Proustian sequence Lowry had always planned: "It seems significant that Lowry should have placed this short novel, which is concerned with human happiness and ends on a note of fulfillment and resolution, at the end of what was destined to be a posthumous volume."

**"The Bravest Boat"** is a love lyric. Its tone is that of one of Lowry's earliest published stories, **"Hotel Room in Chartres"** (published in *Story* in 1934 when Lowry was 24), a story that was discussed in another connection in the first chapter. The newlyweds of the earlier story—the heroine is Lowry's romantic projection of his first wife—have been quarreling. He has given up the sea for her and he misses it. She feels his resentment. They board a train for Brest, via Chartres (where they had spent their honeymoon), barely communicating as he joins the flow of wine and song with a group of French sailors. They are happy, he assumes, because they will join their ship at Brest, and he is envious. The implicit twin threats to the marriage of drink and male camaraderie loom large. Their marriage, a series of domestic crises, drives him to wish "to join some lousy old ship . . . a rotten life reeling from filthy port to filthy port . . . but . . . better than this ceaseless quarreling. . . ." Upon learning that the sailors are homeward bound, the lovers recognize that it is a spiritual port—symbolized by a hotel room in Chartres—that they too seek

> in the only room in the world [where] they were folded together in each other's arms crying with joy that they had found each other once more.

**"The Bravest Boat"** is a companion story to **"Chartres"** although written almost two decades later. That the story is Lowry's most anthologized is a tribute to the poignancy of its theme. A side of the reader's credulity is strained by Lowry's *donnée*, a toy boat, set adrift with a child's note, has found haven years later, found by a girl (Astrid) who, though not yet born when the boy (Sigurd) released his

boat, would grow up to become his bride. Lowry wisely devotes his story to the couple's recollection of the precipitating circumstances.

The sea maintains its regal place in Lowry's iconography. **"Chartres"** ended with two contrasting metaphors, both marine: the railroad station, the potential instrument for separation, becomes for the lovers an ugly presence "like a huge ship being dismantled"; the great cathedral takes on a regenerative aspect, "the configuration of a green wave, falling along the tall rock of the spire, the blue and white sea of the cool sky rushing behind. . . ." In **"The Bravest Boat"** the metaphoric polarities are more obvious: the beauty of a public park, "seagirt . . . wisely left in places to the original wilderness . . ."; the squalor of the neon-festooned metropolis at the park's back seeming to squeeze it into the sea.

The city is Enochville, but as Anthony Kilgallin alertly observes, Lowry has used a satirical pseudonym for Vancouver. Enoch was the son of Cain. Lowry may have been thinking of Cowley's statement that "God the first garden made, and the first city Cain." The land of Cain is described in a three-page paragraph whose imagery will recur in all of Lowry's Canadian fiction: "dilapidated half-skyscrapers," "new beer parlors crawling with verminous light even in mid-afternoon," "modern apartment buildings and other soulless behemoths." The only relief is provided by a "few lowly self-built shacks and floathouses . . . driven out of the city altogether, down to the water's edge into the sea itself, where they stood on piles, like fishermen's huts. . . ." Here, Lowry might have been describing his own dwelling at Dollarton, but what is more important is that he once more casts the sea in a germinative role, as he had done in his earliest writings.

It is toward Lost Lagoon that the two lovers of **"Bravest Boat"** stroll. It is a day in June, an anniversary of the miniature boat-launching which united them. As they recall ritualistically the pure chance which brought them together, they approach a cage containing two Canadian lynxes, "demonic creatures. . . . in which seemed to be embodied in animal form all the pure ferocity of nature." Watching the desperate animal couple, the truly damned, they see again "that tiny boat, battling with the seas, at the mercy of a wilder ferocity yet, all those years before [she] was born."

For a time what passes between the lovers is rote. They remind themselves that the origins of their life together lay in the limbo of unknowable dates: unknowable for Astrid because he launched the boat five years before she was born. Another twelve years had to pass before the seven-year-old girl, playing on another beach, would find the boat and its message. More years would have to elapse before Sigurd and Astrid could marry—seven years ago.

But Lowry brushes lightly over the chronology of his love lyric. Ritual becomes incantation. A circumstantial story rises to a kind of pantheism that few other modern writers could manage. Their walk, by now a pilgrimage, takes them at last to the very edge of the water, a driftwood-littered wasteland of the entrails of marine life in wasteful burial amidst fishermen's discards. But the desolation is appearance only; the lovers feel the stir of life in a cosmic sense:

> . . . beneath the flotsam, under the very shells they crunched, within the trickling overflows of winterbournes they jumped over, down at the tide margin, existed, just as in the forest, a stirring and stretching of life, a seething of spring.

Life is a continuum, throbbing in the midst of death. The lovers, like their little boat, have braved the imponderables of time and place. The boat safe in harbor—their coming together—is a poem of God's mercy. The lovers, renewed by the example of their bravest boat, have come to see life—all human destiny—as all one with the chaos that destroys and the faith that nurtures.

> And it was to this shore, through that chaos, by those currents, that their little boat with its innocent message had been brought out of the past finally to safety and a home.

> But ah, the storms they had come through!

There is a poignant footnote to the publication of **"The Bravest Boat,"** one of the two stories in *Hear Us O Lord* (**"Strange Comfort"** is the other) which Lowry lived to see published in English. A little more than a year before his death, Lowry wrote to David Markson asking him to send the June 1954 issue of *Partisan Review*. Seeing it in print for the first time, he wrote to Markson: "I'm very fond of the old **'Bravest Boat'** though I have never managed to ascertain what anyone thought of it, if anything, in the U.S." Like a number of his shorter pieces, **"Bravest Boat"** was first published in France. Lowry lived to know that the story was listed among "Distinctive Short Stories in American Magazines . . . Foreign Authors . . . 1954," appended to *Best American Short Stories 1954*, edited by Martha Foley.

The story merits its honors. That it and the other fine stories collected in *Hear Us O Lord* were not published in those American magazines which paid commercial rates is an ironic footnote to Lowry's lifelong financial miseries. In the Lowry canon, a story like **"The Bravest Boat"** is vital because it indicates that Lowry was working in his life and art to a reconciliation that promised to put at bay the demons that threatened to overwhelm him.

Even when plunged to the depths of despair by their two-edged sword of Damocles—addiction and eviction—the Lowrys could always write "cheer keeps breaking in." The second Canadian story in *Hear Us O Lord,* **"Gin and Goldenrod,"** dramatizes one such moment. What adds an extra dimension to the story is that, in terms of what is known about Lowry's latter years in Canada, the story is a kind of whistling in the dark. The congeniality of the surface adumbrates the shadows underneath.

The hero is Sigbjørn Wilderness whom we have already met in **"Through the Panama"** and *Dark As the Grave.*

It is difficult to relate the underground man at the heart of these works to the bird watcher on a woodland trek with his wife in search of the place where he had got drunk and contracted a debt with bootleggers. Perhaps the tie between the inner-obsessed outsider and the outside-obsessed insider is that both are troubled by T. S. Eliot's need to prepare a face. Another look at **"Panama"** on top of a reading of **"Gin and Goldenrod"** reveals that the difference is only a matter of degree.

Perhaps, as Dale Edmonds suggests, [in *Tulane Studies in English,* Vol. 15, 1967], the Sigbjørn of **"Gin and Goldenrod"** is the outer side of the inner sojourner who has lost his bearings in a maze of personae; the mask-creation of the introverted Sigbjørn, the man he has named Martin Trumbaugh,

> disinterested in literature, uncultured, incredibly unobservant, in many respects ignorant, without faith in himself, and lacking nearly all the qualities you normally associate with a novelist or writer. . . . he sees practically nothing at all, save through his wife's eyes.

> (**"Panama"**)

What Lowry recaptures in this story is the diffusion of attention that was characteristic of the Consul when, for example, his concentration on the inhuman treatment accorded to the dying Indian in Chapter VIII vies with his concern about the next drink. While Sigbjørn is ashamed over having lost money to a bootlegger, he seems to be paying some implied penance to his wife and anxious to get home for a bracer.

Although Professor Edmonds is probably right in placing the story with **"The Bravest Boat"** in tracing the theme of civilization's encroachment upon nature, it fails on those terms. Sigbjørn's alcoholism—or, better, Lowry's—gets in the way. Wilderness tries to make a scapegoat of civilization. He recalls the time when "there hadn't been any bootleggers . . . to sell you firewater on Sunday, or, come to that, any reason for drinking it." Thus, the Rousseauvian romantic speaking, but a few sentences later, the alcoholic—half fighting his problem and half resenting sobriety in the wilderness:

> The bootlegger, in times of prohibition, in great cities, has one function. The bootlegger, in times of partial prohibition, has another. The bootlegger, on Sundays, where there is Sunday prohibition, is a secular savior. The bootlegger, in rural places, is as fundamental as the prostitute in the city—

> (**"Gin and Goldenrod"**)

The story almost but not quite drones off into the kind of sycophantic chatter that marred *Dark As the Grave* and will threaten *October Ferry.* They find the house where Sigbjørn got drunk. He makes out a cheque for his part of the bootleg gin. They exchange apologies. He spots a pippit and she some goldenrod. As the story ends, Primrose confesses that she has kept the last bottle of gin, the bottle he thought he had lost in the forest. They walk back to the cabin, happy in the thought that they can now mix martinis. The final sentence carries an ironic note for anyone familiar with the penalty to the alcoholic of the quick bracer back at the cabin: "In the cool silver rainy twilight of the forest a kind of hope began to bloom again." But hope for what? Salvation for their life in the woods or for the resumption of controlled drinking unassisted by bootleggers?

The story is important as one of the few Lowry left behind which deal, without the introspective longueurs, with what day-to-day life in Dollarton was like. It is only when one approaches the last and best story in *Hear Us O Lord* that he truly learns.

Early in **"Through the Panama,"** which appears like a kind of opening movement in the symphonic *Hear Us O Lord,* Sigbjørn Wilderness interrupts one of his inner monologues with the question, "Who *am* I?" He grapples to no decision with that problem throughout the rest of the novella. **"The Forest Path to the Spring,"** which concludes the collection, certainly can be regarded as the answer. But if Lowry intended this seventy-page novella as an answer to Sigbjørn's identity quest, why did he resort to the first-person narrator? Lowry learned from Aiken to believe in Henry James's injunction against using the first person, "the cursed fluidity of self-revelation." Their subjective esthetic was better served by posting another consciousness like a movie camera on the outer boundaries of Demarest's and Firmin's to record internal and external movements, in tandem, as they developed. In **"The Forest Path,"** Lowry has eschewed all ambiguity of viewpoint—all those shifting personae—for a unity of narrative stance that is absolutely without precedent in his fiction.

Although he employs the "I," Lowry appears reluctant to limit his narrator to a precise identity. He is never given a name. For once, here is no writer writing about the writer. To be sure, Lowry tells us that his narrator has been a jazz musician but one who has given up his old life of the night.

> . . . How far away that seemed now, my life in which my only stars were neon lights! I must have stumbled into a thousand alcoholic dawns, but drunk in the rumble seat I passed them by. . . . Never had I really looked at a sunrise till now.
>
> **("The Forest Path")**

But this curriculum vitae appears halfway into the story. No disquisition on drink takes over. There is a brief tribute to jazz musicians like Venuti, Satchmo, and the Duke, who have for him "the aspects of a very real glory," but no detailed digression. Lowry's thrust at all points is toward control of his materials and away from the self-indulgent ruminations that wrecked a work like *Dark As the Grave.*

What gives Lowry supreme control in **"Forest Path"** is that he has subjected the *felt* life of the protagonist to a *created* structure which elevates it to art. That structure is

much more than chronology—specifically, the cycle of the seasons around which its eight sections swing. What really unifies these sections is that Lowry has waived his usual subjective strategies for those of a kind of narrative pastoral, a poem.

To call this story a poem could lead to inter-genre problems that are outside the scope of this study. I am neither suggesting extraction of the best passages from **"Forest Path"** for stanzaic rearrangement nor calling it a "prose poem," that hybrid term I resisted earlier in discussing the love-sonnet "feel" of the Consul's unposted letter to Yvonne. What I am suggesting is the need for a technique for reading this story, which is Malcolm Lowry's finest achievement after *Under the Volcano.*

The book with which **"Forest Path"** has most in common is *Walden.* I have never seen anywhere in Lowry's notes or letters a single mention of either Thoreau or his masterpiece. The kinship between the two is accidental but pervasive, a matter that transcends any commonality of circumstances. Certainly, Thoreau and Lowry, a century apart, were searching for solitude and rejecting an economy of abundance in favor of a simple natural life. The real theme of both is the search for perfection, for a life of holiness, and for a way to endure what Thoreau called his "several more lives" away from Walden Pond and what Lowry feared would be his life after eviction from Eridanus.

Charles R. Anderson presents a persuasive case in *The Magic Circle of Walden* for thinking of the book as poetry rather than prose, if one does not insist on the mechanical distinction of verse as opposed to paragraph form. Wit and metaphor, he writes,

> serve Thoreau as the negative and positive means of his quest. These set up the direction of the book and open out its multiple contrasts. Not only are society and solitude juxtaposed but the civilized and the primitive, complexity and simplicity; also matter and spirit, animal faculties and the higher laws, earth and heaven, nature and God. Man cannot achieve his high aims by rejecting the one and leaping into the other, but must work his way up from the sty of materialism to the perfection he seeks.

This is true of *Walden* and, as will be shown, it is true of **"The Forest Path to the Spring."** The goals in both works and the journey toward them are rendered in a deceptively simple series of image clusters: animal, water, rain and shelter, the imagery of time, the quest or journey, the self reborn even as the ice thaws and the land becomes green again. Lowry's novella is as poetic as Thoreau's and the presence of *another*—wife, helpmate, guide—renders Lowry's counsels more outgoingly human, less cranky, than Thoreau's.

The novella is dedicated, in fact, "To Margerie, my wife." If Thoreau went to Walden Pond "to transact some private business with the fewest obstacles," Lowry makes it clear that retreat to the Canadian Northwest wilderness could only work as a partnership. Life became "a continual awakening. . . . until I knew her I had lived my whole life in darkness" ("**Forest Path**").

The couple arrived at Eridanus on Labor Day at the beginning of the war, intending to combine a delayed honeymoon with a last summer holiday. For a time, "the garishness and strangeness of . . . the sun . . . to me, long used to the night and sleeping fitfully. . . . [brought] the quality of a nightmare" ("**Forest Path**"). But metamorphosis soon takes place, a curious giving in to benevolent nature, a sense of their $12-a-month cabin as part of "eternal flux and change" which on the arms of the tides seemed alternately to lower and elevate "like a strange huge cave where some amphibious animal might have lived" ("**Forest Path**"). Fall gives way to the first frosts, and they are still there. In an epiphanic moment one winter's night, the poet knows why:

> . . . coming across the porch from the woodshed with a lantern in one hand and a load of wood under the other arm, I saw my shadow, gigantic, the logs of wood as big as a coffin, and this shadow seemed for a moment the glowering embodiment of all that threatened us; yes, even a projection of that dark chaotic side of myself, my ferocious destructive ignorance.

> ("**Forest Path**")

Lowry's real subject in "**The Forest Path**" is the war which Nature wins over nature, the triumph of the discovered correspondence between elemental forces and man's abiding but muted selflessness. Just as Thoreau's arguments against the railroads are among the pretended subjects of *Walden,* Lowry's diatribe against the oil refinery across the bay is a diversionary tactic against another antagonist altogether. Tonally, Thoreau's strategy is directly hortatory: go ye and do likewise. When he lashes out at the railroads, Thoreau explodes into wit and metaphor that are aimed at the rescue of time from the deception of speed. Men live life too fast, thinking

> it is essential that the *Nation* have commerce, and export ice, and talk through a telegraph, and ride thirty miles an hour . . . but whether we should live like baboons or like men, is a little uncertain. If we do not get out sleepers, and forge rails, and devote days and nights to the work, but go to tinkering upon our *lives* to improve them, who will build railroads? And if railroads are not built, how shall we get to Heaven in season? . . . We do not ride upon the railroad; it rides upon us.

> (*Walden*)

Fom this point in "What I Lived For" to the end of the section, Thoreau opens each paragraph on a cautionary note against being taken in by the lures of technology. The essence of time, he declares, is not changed by the post office or by the telegraph or by newspapers. Rather "Time is but the stream I go a-fishing in. I drink at it; but while I drink I see the sandy bottom and detect how shallow it is. Its thin current slides away, but eternity remains."

Malcolm Lowry's way is much more directly confessional. His entire thrust in "**The Forest Path**" is summed up by one of Thoreau's relatively rare acknowledgments that his life before Walden had been sham. He went to the woods so as not, "when I came to die, discover that I had not lived" (*Walden*). Near the end of "**Forest Path**" Lowry apologizes for the "mere heroics" and "vain gestures" that have characterized his life. Yet he—Everyman—must "go beyond remorse, beyond even contrition . . . pass beyond the pride I felt in my accomplishment, and to accept myself as a fool again" ("**Forest Path**"). Eridanus, finally for Lowry, is out of time altogether. The narrator gladly accepts his previous life as a necessary hell, a *felix culpa.* He and his wife have transcended the passions of the moment and their attendant fears—even the hellish fear of losing their third little house—for "now the joy and happiness of what we had known would go with us wherever we went or God sent us and would not die" ("**Forest Path**").

The real antagonist is the world which Thoreau and Lowry would banish in the interests of discovering the self. The purpose of their experiments is now clear: to withdraw from the life of civilization so that they can merge with the life of nature, to leave the artificial for the real. But the lives at Walden and Eridanus are means, not ends. *Walden* and "**Forest Path to the Spring**" are the records of quests for the buried life of the soul.

In the midst of writing "**The Forest Path**," Lowry wrote to Harold Matson that his book, as far as he knew, was "the only short novel of its type that brings the kind of majesty usually reserved for tragedy (God this sounds pompous) to bear on human integration. . . ." The last is the important word. Not only is his story a raging toward self-integration, but its poetic technique at all points a working toward an integration of man's primal urges and fears with the false buffers civilization builds against them. Like Thoreau an inveterate punster, Lowry devotes much of the first section of "**Forest Path**" to a play on the names of the beach cottages, a practice which he sees as a human's rebellion in day when "streets and houses are mere soulless numbers . . . a survival of some instinct of unique identity in regard to one's home . . . for identity itself." He concludes the section with a discussion of Eridanus, named for a wrecked steamer which still lies nearby. To show how brilliantly Lowry plays with wit and metaphor, always in the interests of discovering, in Thoreau fashion, higher laws, it is necessary to quote at some length:

> We poor folk were also Eridanus, a condemned community, perpetually under the shadow of eviction. And like Eridanus itself, in its eternal flux and flow, was the inlet. For in the heavens at night, as my wife first taught me, dark and wandering beneath blazing Orion, flowed the starry constellation Eridanus, known both as the River of Death and the River of Life, and placed there by Jupiter in remembrance of Phaethon, who once had the splendid illusion that he could guide the fiery steeds of the sun as well as his father Phoebus.

> Legend merely states that Jupiter, sensing the danger to the world, shot a thunderbolt which, striking

Phaethon, hurled him, his world on fire, into the River Po, then that, in addition to creating the constellation in Phaethon's honor, in pity he changed Phaethon's sisters into poplar trees, that they might always be near and protect their brother. But that he went to all this trouble suggests that he, even as Phoebus, was impressed by the attempt, and must have given the whole matter some thought. Recently our local paper, showing a sudden interest in classical mythology, has claimed to see something insulting in the name of our town of a political, even an international nature, or as denoting foreign influences, as a result of which there has been some agitation, on the part of some distant rate-payers, with I know not what motives, to change its name to Shellvue. And undoubtedly the view in that specified direction is very fine. with the red votive candle of the burning oil wastes flickering ceaselessly all night before the gleaming open cathedral of the oil refinery—

("The Forest Path")

One notes Lowry's ability—it was Thoreau's, eminently—to synthesize the mythological and the quotidian. Jupiter had to save the world from Phaethon's "splendid illusion," but made a protective garden of the place where he died. The Shell refinery is emblematic of waste in the guise of industrial progress, but no Jupiter destroys it (although today's ecologists might find a prophetic irony in Lowry's metaphor). Rather, "distant rate-payers" consecrate the refinery as an open cathedral.

Lowry establishes a series of polarities to warn of man's fate: squatters' shacks on one side of the bay, the refinery on the other; the finding of paradise against the threat of eviction; God's sovereignty against man-made laws; the good fishermen and boatbuilders against the real estate people and the tourists; the achievement of oneness with nature against the fatuities of progress. All are one tension, of course, and Lowry represents their reconciliation in one magnificent metaphor: the daily act of redemption in walking, at dusk, through the forest to the spring for water.

[We should] recall that his early voyages to sea—the "out-Mobying of Melville"—gave Lowry his first congenial persona and that the burning of their shack—the loss of irreplaceable manuscripts to the fire—almost destroyed him as a writer. The Consul, it will be recalled, aspired to a water-wreathed Northern Paradise but fell to his death "through the blazing of ten million burning bodies" under the volcano. **The Forest Path to the Spring** in effect resurrects the Consul, his demons purged.

Lowry's handling of the water-as-rebirth motif is pervasive but never intrusive in the story. The sheer logistics of obtaining water in the wilds—getting a boat, maneuvering it to a spring, returning a distance of miles to their house—led to frustrations and bitter resolves to return to the city. One afternoon late in the fall, everything about the water having gone wrong, he sees a ship's cannister on the beach left by the receding tide. They recover it. A light rain begins to fall. Their bitter despair forgotten, she explains with "inexpressible wonder" that "rain itself is water from

the sea, raised to heaven by the sun, transformed into clouds and falling again into the sea." He, who has been a ship's fireman, relives the story behind the discarded cannister. It does not matter that the story he tells his wife while cleaning the cannister is unlikely to have happened. What matters is that they have recharged each other's flagging spirits. One of their boatbuilder friends then shows them a spring, its running delayed by the long Indian summer, less than a hundred yards from their house.

His first walk down the path to the spring takes the form of a ten-page central section. It is an ode to recovery from life's *Sturm und Drang*; to a man's recoil from the dreadful Wendigo, the man-hating spirit of the wilderness. He sees his hatred and suffering as like a forest fire (a figure that will return with compound interest in *October Ferry to Gabriola*), "a perversion of the movement of the inlet." The fire was his hatred, turning back on himself, self-devouring.

Always standing as a counter-force to his torment is his wife, who had lived in the country as a child and who "somehow turned our limited and humble fare into works of art." She is no better characterized than other Lowry women. Failure to realize Primrose as a person was one of the many shortcomings of *Dark As the Grave,* just as a similar failure to individualize Jacqueline will be a defect in the admirable *October Ferry.* In a story like **"Forest Path,"** however, the idealizing of the wife is a kind of imperative. Hers is the role of a vital human station in the pilgrim's progress. She and the old Manx boatbuilder Quaggan and his friend Kristbjorg become archetypal of everything that is right in the felt life at Eridanus just as in *Walden* the Irish bog farmer is archetypal of everything that is wrong in life without spirit.

The onset of winter leads to contrasting strategies by Thoreau and Lowry. Thoreau's winter at the pond never threatens, is only a time for deeper reflection. "Why is it," he asks, "that a bucket of water soon becomes putrid, but frozen remains sweet forever?" Thoreau's answer is wittily metaphoric: "It is commonly said that this is the difference between the affections and the intellect." Lowry's winter at Eridanus shakes all their resolves with cosmic terror: ". . . we would lose all hope . . . the rending branches, the tumult of the sea, the sound of ruination under the house, so that we clung to one another like two little arboreal animals in some midnight jungle . . ." (**"Forest Path"**). But both winter sojourners conclude their songs on notes of apotheosis. Thoreau bathes his intellect in the Bhagavad-Gita. He lays down his book, "so remote is its sublimity from our conceptions," and goes to the well for water finding the pure Walden water mingled with the sacred water of the Ganges. Lowry's actual path to the spring is made impassable by the winter, but he still walks it in imagination "as if eternally through a series of dissolving dusks." He thinks of Renan's Isle of Delight,

> where the lamps light of themselves for the offices of religion, and never burn out for they shine with a spiritual light, and where an absolute stillness reigns, and everyone knows precisely the hour of his death,

and one feels neither cold nor heat nor sadness nor sickness of body or soul. . . . And then I thought to myself, stopping in the path: what if we should lose it? And with this thought of all-consuming anxiety I would always pause with a sigh. And then came the season of spring and I forgot this anxiety too.

("Forest Path")

Nothing in **"The Forest Path"** can compare to Thoreau's rejuvenation at the sight of the spring thaw on Walden Pond. He sees man molecularly, as but a mass of thawing clay where

one hillside illustrated the principle of all the operations of Nature. The Maker of this earth but patented a leaf. What Champollion will decipher this hieroglyphic for us, that we may turn over a new leaf at last?

(*Walden*)

But Lowry's ecstasy ascends the same pantheistic empyrean. "My God," he asks while looking at the full moon blazing clear of the pines behind the mountain, "why have you given this to us?" The remainder of the spring section is a poem to man's unworthiness. Encounters with a mountain lion and the sheer difficulty of the upward return climb take their toll until by a kind of twelve labors of Hercules he is able to face "those nameless somnambulisms, guilts, ghouls of past delirium, wounds, souls and lives, ghosts of actions approximating to murder" which threaten to destroy everything.

Thoreau's great book concludes with a chapter whose main business seems to be a series of exhortations: to explore one's "private sea"; to advance in the direction of dreams; to simplify; to step to the music one hears; to love one's life poor as it is. But the real theme of the chapter—of the whole work—is embodied in a single sentence near the beginning of the chapter: "Our voyaging is only great circle sailing." Thoreau's plea is to transcend human limitations which allow the present to be a mere replay of the past.

. . . . mere lapse of time can never make to dawn. The light which puts out our eyes is darkness to us. Only that day dawns to which we are awake. There is more day to dawn. The sun is but a morning star.

(*Walden*)

Thoreau's imprecation for transcendence of time and place is echoed at the end of **"The Forest Path"** by Lowry's rage against giving in to the tyranny of the past:

. . . It was my duty to transcend [the past] in the present. . . . Sometimes I had the feeling I was attacking the past rationally as with a clawbar and hammer, while trying to make it into something else for a supernatural end.

("Forest Path")

He must transcend the hubris that has driven him to read mystic portents in every passing moment; must return to a state of acceptance of himself as innocent of such perceptions. The story concludes in a bucolic kaleidoscope—a pastoral celebration—and, at last, a "great circle sailing" back to the regenerative fount, on the forest path to the spring.

**T. E. Bareham (essay date 1978)**

SOURCE: "Strange Poems of God's Mercy: The Lowry Short Stories," in *The Art of Malcolm Lowry*, edited by Anne Smith, Vision Press, 1978, pp. 156-68.

[*In the following essay, Bareham views the stories in* Hear Us O Lord *as interconnected.*]

***Hear Us O Lord From Heaven Thy Dwelling Place*** stands at a crossroads in Lowry's output. From this point, down one broad highway, stretches the main vista of his work— the achievement of *Under the Volcano,* the promise and near-fulfilment of the posthumous novels. But down other dark sideroads which diverge from here, we can be led a pretty dance through the quirkishness, the personal allusions and the occult world of Lowry at his most obscure and introspective. All his work is inter-connected. This makes the volume richly rewarding for the Lowry specialist, but may be daunting for the reader who comes to him for the first time through **Hear Us O Lord.** The object of this essay is to provide some preliminary guide-posts to the tracks which cross the terrain of the Lowry short stories.

Much of the material in the collection was planned towards the novel-cycle which was to be called *The Voyage That Never Ends.* Lowry was a compulsive starter rather than a diligent finisher of his material; the additions to *Under the Volcano* even in galley-proof show how the literary journey never did seem to end. He worked through an allusive inter-connecting thought-stream technique, whose patterns may not be immediately obvious to "normal" everyday logic. One must consider also whether the very nature of the triumph in *Under the Volcano* may contribute to the fact that nothing else Lowry wrote seems finished in such a way that it can stand alone in its own right. He became haunted by the spectre of a novelist who could not repeat his one success and who, increasingly, lived in a private world of self-created barriers and inhibitions. If the Consul's claim of the world in *Under the Volcano* that "this is Hell" is true, it is irresistible to continue the quotation on Lowry's behalf with "nor am I out of it". The problems are unusual enough to justify an expository account of the short stories, both for the light they shed on the mind of a man living in his self-created inferno, and for the solutions to the dilemma which they offer—solutions offered nowhere else in his work, except in the last chapters of *October Ferry to Gabriola,* with which the material in the short stories has much in common. In structure and in ideas the short stories have much to tell us about Lowry as man and as artist, and about Man as Artist in a larger and less personal sense.

The formal arrangement of the material in **Hear Us O Lord** seems to have been planned and finally decided by Lowry—a point worth making since it is not always true of his posthumous writings. The publisher's note to the Penguin edition (1969) explains:

> (he) . . . had conceived of . . . (*Hear Us O Lord*) . . . as a unit, and had arranged the tales and short novels of which it consists in a kind of curve, so that each story had a bearing upon those on either side of it.

Such an arrangement is in itself of interest, suggesting dynamic links between artistic units normally regarded as self-contained. It offered a method by which a writer, struggling for a synthesis of the disparate fragments he worked upon, could sustain a larger design.

It is commonplace that meanings and inter-dependences of the layers of work in *Under the Volcano* are only revealed with successive readings. So it is true that the bearing of each story upon the others in *Hear Us O Lord* becomes clearer and richer as one assimilates the grand design through continuing study. The stories *are* a connected curve, but the parabolic logic of the collection as an entity, as virtually a new art form, is only comprehensible in the context of the author's preoccupations in earlier phases of his writing. Most of the material in *Hear Us O Lord* stems from the period between finishing *Under the Volcano* and the final visit to Europe in 1954. The concern with the struggle for "success" is therefore obvious enough and forms a major link between all the stories. The book is also about isolation, for Lowry went into self-exile, both cultural and spiritual. He was fiercely proud of that strange integrity which he felt he was thus preserving. Most of the men in *Hear Us O Lord* explore this side of their own natures and steel themselves to test their indivduality against the world outside their chosen territory. The level at which Lowry's "curve" traces and develops this struggle may not be the deepest in the book, but it is an important one. Sigbjørn Wilderness in **"Through the Panama"** is on his way to Europe, the great testing-ground for a New World author. In **"Strange Comfort Afforded by the Profession"** the same character is visiting Italy on a Guggenheim Fellowship and experiencing a sense of dislocation which has a far greater importance than mere home-sickness. The novelist hero of **"Elephant and Colosseum"**, the schoolmaster Fairhaven in **"Present Estate of Pompeii"**, and the jazz-symphonist narrator of **"The Forest Path to the Spring"** are equally alien to the environment in which they are initially situated, though there is a steady growth through the stories towards the moment of reconciliation at the end of **"The Forest Path"**.

This is the most obvious example of linkage and development between the stories. One gradually becomes aware of numerous others. In the opening story, **"The Bravest Boat"**, the tiny balsawood craft becomes a symbol of the unquenchable spirit of love; questing, enduring, sustaining. This seems a far cry from **"Gin and Goldenrod"**, the penultimate story, yet the latter is also about endurance; and now repentance and regeneration are added as additional spiritual signs of growth, whilst in **"Present Estate of Pompeii"** the contrasts of eternity and transcience—though lightly touched upon—give the story a place in the overall picture of spiritual pilgrimage.

Lowry's world was haunted, bedevilled, illuminated by what he saw as strange coincidence, parellelisms, and omens. He lived in a fetishistic world where dates and places, brief snatches of overheard conversation, advertising slogans, and phrases from foreign languages, seemed to form repetitive patterns which he shaped into the vertebrae of his art. Wilderness's fear of sailing on the seventh day of the month was Lowry's own, but it is melted back into the texture and implication of the voyage in **"Through the Panama"** with all its Conradian and Coleridgean features, and back out again through the nearly autobiographical aspects of Wilderness's confused but hyper-sensitive mind:

> Significance of sailing on the 7th. The point is that my character Martin, in the novel I'm furiously trying to get a first draft of (knowing damned well I'd never do any work on this voyage, which is to last precisely 7 weeks), had dreaded starting a journey on the 7th of any month. To begin with we were not going to leave for Europe until January. Then the message comes that our sailing has been cancelled and we'll have to take advantage of the *Diderot's* sailing on the 6th if we want to go at all. But she doesn't—she sails on the 7th. Martin Trumbaugh's really fatal date is November 15. So as long as we don't leave Los Angeles on Nov. 15 for the long haul, all will be well. Why do I say that? The further point is that the novel is about a character who becomes enmeshed in the plot of the novel he has written, as I did in Mexico. . . .

November is, of course, the month of the Feast of the Dead in Mexico, the month in which all the action of *Under the Volcano* occurs. Naturally—or very unnaturally—they *do* leave Los Angeles on the fifteenth, having picked up another passenger: . . . "his name? Charon. Naturally." There is a puckish humour here. Lowry can take his weird preoccupation with coincidence quite seriously, and yet laugh at it and himself. *Hear Us O Lord* contains much of his best humour; his verbal acrobatics, his eye for whimsy, and his sheer love of laughter. This irreverent and sometimes flippant writing can be disconcerting, though only a misreading of *Under the Volcano* can fail to detect the same traits there. The element of consternation is calculated.

The stories which comprise the respective movements of Lowry's suite for prose orchestra in *Hear Us O Lord* are full of interlinking elements which help to explain and justify his curve. His locations seem widely disparate at first: a municipal park in seaboard British Columbia, a boat going through the Panama Canal, post-war Italy, then British Columbia again. The curve is of course present in this scheme. Yet the metaphorical setting is always the same in his work—Hell close to Eden, not far from the sea or from some natural cataclysm, where man's civilized vileness and his innate dignity are at war. He may cry "Hear Us O Lord From Heaven Thy Dwelling Place", but the burden is of man striving to be heard from his own dwelling place. For Lowry the dwelling place was a spiritual quest. Displaced between Canada, Mexico, and Europe, under threat of eviction from his shack on the Burrard Inlet, in voluntary exile from the companionship of nearly all his literary contemporaries, his insistence upon the search for an identity and for a point of stasis is not surprising. It certainly gives the work in *Hear Us O Lord* an over-all coherence within which the individual stories do form a parabola. The journey starts and ends in British Columbia, though all the tales are counterpointing tension against relaxation, Europe against America, the artist against the charlatan, past against present, and the tactile facade of sanity against the imaginary world of phantasy. For even in mid-twentieth century Canada the supernatural will rub shoulders with a Shell tanker! Roderick Fairhaven, enduring an unwanted guided tour of Pompeii (which he hates), lets his mind spiral backwards to his Canadian home:

> . . . it was this walk through the woods and back that he particularly remembered now: the stillness in the forest, the absolute peace, the stars sparkling and blazing through the trees (high on a cedar his flashlight gleamed on the four watching shining timorous curious eyes of two racoons), the stillness, the peace, but also the sense of hurt, the anxiety because of the renewed talk that evening of the possibility of the railroad's coming through, or that the forest would be slaughtered to make way for auto camps or a subsection, so that their troubles had seemed all at once, or once again, like those of country folk in a novel by George Eliot, or Finnish pioneers in the sixties (or, as Primrose Wilderness had remarked bitterly, Canadians or human beings of almost any period): and the sense too of something else topsy-turvily all the wrong way; Roderick stood quietly on his porch a moment, listening to the conversation of the tide coming in, bringing distantly, shadowily, more luminously, an oil tanker with it. To him, standing on his porch, holding his book and flashlight, it was as if Eridanus had suddenly become, like ancient Rome, a theater of prodigies, real and imaginary. As though the white whale hadn't been enough, the four o'clock news report from Vancouver heard over the Wilderness radio had related this in renewed reports from 'several accredited sources' of the famous 'flying saucers' of that period which had been witnessed that very afternoon from several different points travelling over Eridanus itself, and a sworn statement by the Chief of Police 'now released for the first time to the public, that he had, while fishing with his son beyond Eridanus Port the previous Sunday, seen, cavorting there, a sea serpent.' Good God! This was all hilariously, horribly funny, and Roderick could laugh again thinking about it now. But the truth was he wasn't really amused: these things taken together with his other deeper anxieties, agitated him with that kind of dark conviction of the monstrous and threatening in everything sometimes begotten by a hangover. And unable to fit these matters comfortably into the filing cabinet of a civilised mind it was as if willy-nilly he'd begun to think with the archaic mind of his remote ancestors instead, and the result was alarming to a degree. . . .

This sense of swirling movement, with people and places over-lapping, is present throughout the book. Sometimes Lowry asks more indulgence of his readers, or presupposes more interest in his personal shibboleths than is strictly fair or feasible. To understand fully any of his later writing one must first understand all his other writing, and this makes for a closed circle where no ready means of access

is offered. No casual reader will be aware that the re-iterative engine song of the boats in *Hear Us O Lord* echoes back through most of his other books:

> *Frère Jacques!*
> *Frère Jacques!*
> *Dormez-vous?*
> *Dormez-vous?*
> *Sonnez les matines*
> *Sonnez les matines*
> *Ding dang dong,*
> *Ding dang dong.*

No Lowry character travels anywhere without hearing this refrain. It comes from the author's own merchant-seaman days and all the imaginative processes which originate in his undergraduate voyage to the Far East as an able seaman. One fictional reflection is straight back into **"Elephant and Colosseum"** where the hero makes a similar voyage to the China Sea, befriending a young elephant who becomes a symbol of redemption from the absurdities of artistic introspection when he re-meets her in Rome zoo twenty years later. The story is witty and finely realized. Yet it is only in its proper place, between **"Strange Comfort"** and **"Present Estate"** that its full significance will be recognised.

There is a fascinating mélange of fact, fancy, and wish fulfilment behind the surface of this and most of the short stories. **"Elephant and Colosseum"** is "made up", for its hero, Cosnahan, is a Manxman, author of a supposed comic masterpiece. Yet the real interest is inwards, towards what we can learn about Lowry and about mankind at large, whilst so little does it matter *who* is telling the story in **"Through the Panama"** that we are presented with a situation where Sigbjørn Wilderness and Martin Trumbaugh (author and character) speak almost indistinguishably, and the voices of Lowry himself, of a guide book to the Panama, and of a parody of Coleridge's *Ancient Mariner,* interpose across the direction of the narrative flow. Lowry makes fresh and imaginative use of the device of marginal commentary which Coleridge had employed in his poem, in order to remind us that his hero is a Modern Mariner going his own strange and haunted voyage of discovery. Yet the casual reader, or a student coming to this book as his first Lowry, would have no means of knowing this, or of seeing the linkages between this story and so much else Lowry wrote. That "Frère Jacques" of the engines provides the link, as it alters in pitch, intensity, and implication. At one moment it becomes "*Frère Jacques, frère Jacques, frère Jacques, frère Jacques Laruelle*". Laruelle is the Consul's friend/brother/alter ego/ destroyer in *Under the Volcano.* This covert evocation of Lowry's masterpiece, which had cost him such herculean efforts, communicates a special atmosphere of tension to those who are able to pick up the reference. It must otherwise seem a very pointless piece of verbal foolery. At another moment the chant becomes . . .

> *Sonnez les matines*
> *Sans maison,*
> *Sans maison.*

and the fear of eviction, of a repetition of the fire that made the Lowrys homeless, and of all the associated traumas, rises through the other webs of plot to tug at the consciousness of the informed reader. "*Sonnez les matines*" becomes "*Sonnez lamentina*" as they pass down the coast of Mexico where the Consul had heard the bells of Oaxaca tolling "*Dolente, dolore*".

The Manx fisherman's hymn from which **Hear Us O Lord** takes its title provides another linking motif. Lowry had a special affection for this hymn, and for its tune, "Peel Castle", "with its booming minor chords" (as he puts it in **"The Forest Path to the Spring"**):

> . . . in which sounds all the savagery of the sea yet whose words of supplication make less an appeal to, than a poem of God's mercy.

That phrase itself is repeated later, when the narrator of **"The Forest Path"** speaks of his opera—here clearly an artistic equivalent of Lowry's novels:

> . . . I composed this opera, built, like our new house, on the charred foundations and fragments of the old work and our old life. The theme was suggested probably by my thoughts of cleansing the purgation and renewal and the symbols of the canister the ladder and so on, and certainly by the inlet itself, and the spring. It was partly in the whole-tone scale, like *Wozzeck,* partly jazz, partly folksongs or songs my wife sang, even old hymns, such as Hear O Lord From Heaven Thy Dwelling Place. I even used canons like Frère Jacques to express the ships' engines or the rhythms of eternity; Kristbjorg, Quaggan, my wife and myself, the other inhabitants of Eridanus, my jazz friends, were all characters, or exuberant instruments on the stage or in the pit. The fire was a dramatic incident and our own life, with its withdrawals and returns, and what I had learned of nature, and the tides and sunrises I tried to express. And I tried to write of human happiness in terms of enthusiasm and high seriousness usually reserved for catastrophe and tragedy.

There is a proud, articulate dignity about this claim which justifies the experiment in **Hear Us O Lord,** even where the attempt is not a total success. It *may* fail when the nature of linkages in ideas becomes too personal. One must also confess that there are moments when the volume fails because the quality of the writing is defective. The sentences run excitedly, but without control, several feet in front of the point Lowry's brain has got to, and his syntax can break down into a gauche, fifth-form-essay kind of enthusiasm; there is a descriptive passage on p. 261 of the Penguin text which is typical of this indiscipline. Two gargantuan sentences occupy thirty-two lines of prose during which time there are more than twenty repetitions of the conjunction "and". What happens is that as Lowry's form pushes at the boundaries of normal practice, so there is an inevitable accompanying strain upon the prose itself. He was seeking methods other than that of disjunctive thought-streaming to convey the processes and timbre of interior monologue, and neither time, nor the pressure of his own emotional excitement, allowed for a cool reflec-

tive period of reassessment. So much of the work in the book is interior monologue rather than descriptive prose, that the wonder is rather at the small amount of error than otherwise.

---

> **Lowry lived in a fetishistic world where dates and places, brief snatches of overheard conversation, advertising slogans, and phrases from foreign languages, seemed to form repetitive patterns which he shaped into the vertebrae of his art.**
>
> —*T. E. Bareham*

---

These "strange poems" are, then, work in progress, they are "*études*" rather than sonatas, but they present a rich and stimulating challenge. I hope that this survey of links in the form of the book may explain the "strange" of my chosen title. Yet, however strange, they *are* poems. Appropriately, the first and the last of them, the shortest and the longest, are the most poetic—introit and vesper to the main curve of the work. **"The Bravest Boat"**, with which the collection opens, sounds the theme of questing, of man's balance with nature, and of ghosts to be exorcised. Its tone is lyrical—almost too much so. Its themes are developed and expanded in each of the following stories, made more comic or heroic as the case may be. Yet the spirit of the balsa-wood boat with its sealed-in message of love and its indomitable but covert purpose suffuses the entire collection. It is a poem of mercy, assuredly, for the boat survives twenty years of storm-tossing before being rescued to unite Sigurd and Astrid. The scale and dimensions change in **"Through the Panama"**, yet the same themes are discernible in that boat journey—a transmutation of Lowry's voyage to Europe. In **"Strange Comfort"** the wife-figure is absent, and hence the questing and yearning can be given a fresh aspect. The artistic and the personal desires and phobias blur and mix in this story, and in the end it is a sense of humour which allows Sigbjørn to recover his balance. Quizzical though it may be, and in itself tangential and fragmentary, this story assumes its proper meaning when seen as part of a pattern and a curve.

**"Elephant and Colosseum"** takes the love and alienation themes even further. The deracinated writer is now Kennish Drumgold Cosnahan, a Manxman living in America, but visiting Italy to supervise the publication of a translation of his novel. This novel is supposed to recall his experiences as a sailor, when he nursed and grew to love a young elephant destined for Rome zoo. The encounter of man and beast is an epiphany for Cosnihan: his attempt to locate the translators of his precious book has been a farce, he has lost contact with his brothers, and just learned of the death of his mother. Yet all his tensions are released in the pure joy of the shared contact:

But it was not from the knowledge that he would now work again—though he would—that his deepest satisfaction sprang, that was now making him feel as happy as—why, as happy as some old magician who had just recovered his powers and brought off a masterstroke!

The words had almost slipped out of his mouth. And suddenly, at the realization of what he meant, a pure delight in all its renewed and ludicrous implications got the better of him, so that Cosnahan laughed aloud.

Good God, he really *was* a magician. Or this was the real wild fount of his feeling, shared suddenly, human (at the same time more than just universally ancestral), though it seemed to be; this was the real antique and secret source of his present pride, of his future salvation; this that would have caused his book to be translated, and by that, more than that, himself to be translated—his mother's son at last—into a conscious member of the human race.

"Present Estate of Pompeii" pursues the theme of opposition between Old and New World values, with all its accreted "meanings". It certainly offers an investigation of the motif of love from a new angle, since the guide, appropriately named Signor Salacci, seems to have a monomaniacal preoccupation with the sex life of the ancient and ruined city. The symbolic potential looms large, but Lowry's touch is light and deft. The story leads, with no need of a physical return journey, back to British Columbia. "Gin and Goldenrod" extends some of the ideas implicit in "Present Estate of Pompeii", but it is rich enough to add many more. In "Gin and Goldenrod" one of the best written and best directed stories in the collection, the narrative line emerges tangentially. This technique of making narrative exposition subsidiary to, but a part of, character description, is one of Lowry's contributions to the art of fiction. Sigbjørn Wilderness has been on a "bender" at a sordid little villa where the owner has been selling bootleg liquor to Sunday drinkers. Sigbjørn is now obliged to make a penitential return journey to pay the debts incurred during his binge. The day is hot, the road dusty, and the countryside ravaged by building developments which are encroaching onto the natural forestland of the Wilderness's home—their surname, of course, is no accident. This desolation of abomination is, on one level, the New World counterpart of Pompeii, the inversion being perfect, yet the analogy exact. The story is again about spiritual atrophy, about lack of love and confidence. Primrose Wilderness, half reproving, half supporting, accompanies her husband. Though the bond of sympathy has been strained by his behaviour, her love and purpose are able to transcend the horror of the moment. Even amidst the debris of the new building lots she seeks tokens of nature to refresh, revitalize, and encourage the disconsolate man by her side. The gin and the goldenrod of the story's title are to be seen as symbols of the opposing ways of life open to Sigbjørn. The entire book is about this opposition, and about the power of love (if one can find and hold it) to effect a balance between them. "Turn this into triumph: the furies into mercies . . ." notes Wil-

derness to himself with regard to his projected novel ("Through the Panama"). This suggests the creative artist as magician, and recalls Cosnahan's moment of truth, and the bravest boat which, mysteriously, through its message of love, survived the furious seas and united Sigurd and Astrid.

In **"The Forest Path to the Spring"** the transmutation of furies into mercies takes final and definitive shape. Although its narrator is a musician who has lost his *magnum opus* (a symphony) in a fire and has now turned to opera instead, he is clearly akin to Lowry himself, who after the loss of *In Ballast to the White Sea* in the conflagration which destroyed his first hut at Dollarton, turned to rather different prose kinds—as in **"The Forest Path"** itself. Through the semi-autobiography are woven all the preoccupations which inform Lowry's work: the relationship of man to nature, to other men, to himself; the value and durability of art; the causes and effects and the mysterious ways of God's mercy to his creatures. And it is an affirmation of the joy of living. Readers who know only *Under the Volcano* often misjudge Lowry. Despite his desperate moods of depression and his moments of panic and despair, he was not an habitually gloomy man. **"The Forest Path"** shows how he was able to subsume the ordinary and the visionary moments of his life into a pattern—to be a larger and more creative being, for instance, than is Geoffrey Firmin in *Under the Volcano*. Firmin's is the courage of despair, and this was not Lowry's mood for much of the time in those Canadian years, despite the hardships of life in the wild. The last words of the final story in the collection are, "Laughing we stooped down to the stream and drank." Nothing could be more fulfilled than this, both in the physical context, and through all the meanings which "spring" in both its senses takes on in the story. Here man and nature have found a perfect equipoise. The act of living has become an act of faith, and this is enough in itself.

The curve is complete. As the book began with two lovers brought together by the magical sea changes of **"The Bravest Boat"**, so it ends where spring and sea meet, and where two lovers have worked out their own salvation, where the magic comes from within. It began in a park where the lynx "in which seemed to be embodied in animal form all the pure ferocity of nature" is caged, prowling and pacing endlessly. It ends with the author facing a mountain lion in the lovely wilderness which surrounds his home. The animal is real enough, yet it is also a representation of the untamed, self-destructive side of his own nature, as he goes his peaceable path to the spring for water. Moments of a Wordsworthian despair have crippled him, even here in the forest, and the lion appears at the worst of these crises. So again man is faced by pure untamed nature, at once brutal and beautiful. It is his own courage, his instinctive grasp upon life, which now effects a purgation beyond reason or conscious will:

> So I stood traditionally and absolutely still. Then we simply waited, both of us, to see what the other would do, gazing straight into each other's eyes at short range; in fact it was only his gleaming topaz eyes and the tip

of his tail twitching almost imperceptibly that showed me he was alive at all.

> Finally I heard myself saying something like this to the mountain lion, something extraordinary and absurd, commanding yet calm . . . 'Brother, it's true. I like you in a way, but just the same, between you and me, get going!' Something like that. The lion, crouched on a branch really too small for him, caught off guard or off balance, and having perhaps already missed his spring, jumped down clumsily, and then, overwhelmed, catlike, with the indignity of this ungraceful landing, and sobered and humiliated by my calm voice—as I liked to think afterwards—slunk away guiltily into the bushes . . .

There is a metaphysical link between the beasts of first and last stories, which follows the curve of the intervening narratives, and to which the albatross of **"Through the Panama"** and the elephant of **"Elephant and Colosseum"** are united. This and other cyclic patterns, the alienation motif, the theme of redemption, the power of humour to restore the balance of life, and the value of love, makes *Hear Us O Lord* a remarkable and moving book, whilst the smaller arabesques within each story ensure that the themes do not become merely repetitive. "Strange" they may be, but assuredly they are "poems" and, triumphantly, poems of God's mercy.

## Elizabeth D. Rankin  (essay date 1984)

SOURCE: "Malcolm Lowry's Comic Vision: 'Elephant and Colosseum'," in *Canadian Literature,* No. 101, Summer, 1984, pp. 167-71.

*[In the following essay, Rankin explores the comic aspects of Lowry's short story "Elephant and Colosseum."]*

Those who know Malcolm Lowry only through *Under the Volcano* are often surprised to discover that much of his later work rejects that novel's dark and terrible vision in favour of a far more positive, even comic, outlook. *Volcano* seems such a devastating apocalyptic novel that one marvels that its author would, or could, arrive at any comic resolution whatsoever.

Actually, though, I think it is just these readers' misreading of *Volcano* that keeps them from appreciating the later work. *Volcano,* after all, is not so much a tragic novel as a novel about the possibility of tragedy. The Consul's wasted life, his terrible death, is meant to serve as a warning, just as the final words of the novel serve as a warning: "*¿LE GUSTA ESTE JARDIN QUE ES SUYO? ¡EVITE QUE SUS HIJOS LO DESTRUYAN!*" What this coda implies, I think, is that the Consul has in some sense *chosen* his tragic end, and that we have the power, if we have the courage, to choose otherwise for ourselves. Correspondingly, many of Lowry's later stories are not so much comedies themselves as stories about the possibility of a comic vision, in the Dantean sense of that term. A case in point is the much-neglected story **"Elephant and Colos-**

**seum,"** written in 1951 and published after Lowry's death as part of the volume entitled *Hear Us O Lord From Heaven Thy Dwelling Place.* In this story, which Lowry himself regarded as a "comic classic," the central character learns what *Volcano's* Consul steadfastly refused to see, what Malcolm Lowry desperately tried (who knows how successfully?) to believe: namely, that man has more options in life than absurdist drama or high tragedy; if he wants, he *can* direct his life toward meaning and fulfilment—but only if he is willing to relinquish his teleological compass and learn to steer by "dead reckoning."

To summarize briefly, **"Elephant"** is the story of Kennish Drumgold Cosnahan, a Manx-American novelist vacationing in Rome. Having recently completed a successful first novel, Cosnahan now finds himself unable to write, and the story concerns his attempts to understand and come to terms with his problem. The plot of the story is simple, if improbable. Wandering about the city after an unsuccessful attempt to locate the offices of his Italian publishers, Cosnahan stumbles upon the zoo in the Borghese Gardens. There he encounters an old acquaintance—Rosemary, the elephant he had tended on board ship when she was transported from Bangkok to Rome many years before. Thoughts of Rosemary and of his magical Manx heritage commingle to bring Cosnahan back in touch with his own 'magical' (i.e., creative) powers, and the end of the story finds him relaxed, happy, and apparently ready to begin work once more.

On the surface, the story certainly does seem as "insubstantial" as Douglas Day has alleged [in *Malcolm Lowry,* 1973] but in fact it is not—it's just that its substance depends on an unexpressed metaphor, a metaphor whose terms are revealed more openly elsewhere in Lowry. One place where that metaphor is made explicit is in **"The Forest Path to the Spring,"** the story Lowry originally planned as **"Elephant"**'s companion piece. At one point, toward the end of that longish story, the anonymous jazz musician narrator muses about the composing process: "Yet it is queer that I had to try and put all this into *words,* to see it, to try and see the thoughts even as I heard the music. But there is a sense in which everybody on this earth is a writer, the sense in which Ortega . . . means it. Ortega has it that a man's life is like a fiction that he makes up as he goes along. He becomes an engineer and converts it into reality—becomes an engineer for the sake of doing that." This allusion to the Ortega notion of man as novelist of his own existence is only one of many in Lowry's work. Although explicitly identified with Ortega in only one other fictional context (the unfinished story "Ghostkeeper"), the metaphor itself virtually permeates both *Dark As the Grave* and **"Through the Panama."** In the letters the notion is even more prominent. In one, to his friend Downie Kirk, Lowry quotes the original Ortega passage, which he has recently read. In another, written three years later, he discusses it again with his editor, Albert Erskine.

Despite the frequency of these allusions, however, few commentators on Lowry's work have seen their significance. While several have noticed a general "artist theme" running through *Hear Us O Lord,* only William New seems to see its importance *as metaphor.* In a brief but cogent comment on the story, he remarks: "The reason for Cosnahan's trip to Italy and the gift of wizardry from his Manx mother are comparably metaphoric. The translation of the novel is a way of talking about the translation of the novelist and so (circularly returning to the basic metaphor from Ortega once again) about the translation of man that takes place when he enters into a new understanding of the relationship between himself and the world" [*Malcolm Lowry,* 1971]. In seeing the Ortega metaphor that informs the story, New is able to successfully get to its very heart. For Kennish Drumgold Cosnahan, the problems of the writer are inextricably bound up with the problems of man, and in overcoming his writer's block and rediscovering his work, he is overcoming the kind of debilitating stasis that can isolate man from the process of life itself and (as in the case of *Volcano's* Consul) destroy him.

While New is right to see the translation metaphor as connected to the Ortega theme, there is another theme operating in **"Elephant and Colosseum"** which complicates and enriches the issue even more. For Cosnahan is not just a writer/man, he is a writer/magician/man, and it is to his "magical" powers that he attributes the success of his "translation" in the end.

The equation of writer with magician is one that Lowry suggests elsewhere as well—in *Volcano,* of course, but also in a passage from **"Strange Comfort Afforded by the Profession,"** the piece that immediately precedes **"Elephant"** in the *Hear Us O Lord* volume. In that story at one point the central character speaks of the poet's "magical monopoly, his possession of words," implying that the writer's ability to transmute experience into art is akin to the alchemist's ability to transform base metals into gold. In **"Elephant and Colosseum,"** the parallel is continued. Though Cosnahan's magical powers enable him to perform such tasks as halting poltergeist phenomena, solving difficult geometrical problems, and divining for water, their main application seems to be to his writing: when he hits a dry spell after his first book's publication he feels as if "albeit he wouldn't put it to himself quite like this— 'his powers had been falling off,'" and when he realizes he can write again he feels "as happy as some old magician who had just recovered his powers and brought off a master-stroke!"

It is easy to see how the magician metaphor reinforces the writer theme and hence the whole Ortega notion of man making up his life as he goes along. The power to create one's life is in many ways a magical power with potentialities for good and bad (white magic and black) which are frightening to the person who possesses the powers. He who fears his powers to such an extent that he will not use them in both cases denies an essential and vital part of himself. This, I think, is the situation Cosnahan finds himself in at the beginning of his story—a situation he overcomes, with the help of Rosemary the elephant, by the end.

Cosnahan's writer's block, as I have previously mentioned, is brought on by the completion and success of his first novel (a phenomenon not uncommon among writers, it seems). He is like the magician who, having discovered his "unlawful" powers, tests them and is frightened by the results—like the man whose life has reached some important plateau where he pauses and then is somehow afraid to go on.

The plateau in Cosnahan's life is a natural one, created by the death of his mother, his last surviving parent. Such an event in anyone's life is reason for pause: a moment when it is natural to stop and look back at the past, with all its accompanying sense of guilt and loss, and forward to the future, with its fears and uncertainties. Such pauses, as Lowry well knew, could be the occasion for asking unanswerable questions, and it is thus that Cosnahan finds himself wondering: "What on earth *was* he after?" "Yet what did he, Cosnahan, know of himself? Was he a writer? What *was* a writer?" "How did you go, how did you begin to go?"

Ostensibly, what Cosnahan is after is success: new translations, increased sales, publicity blurbs, recognition, fame. But is this what he really wants? Actually, it is not. It is his *work* that he wants, as this passage near the end of the story makes clear:

> It was success itself, oh, he'd known it, something about its effect he couldn't handle, and the futile search for which he must abandon. . . .

> And abandon for what? What but his work! Yes, his precious, ridiculous, second-rate, and yet to him, and to his wife too if they must live, all-important work: it was this he had been missing all along, seeking some stimulus, somewhere, anywhere, to begin again, and in the act of seeking, the excuse to postpone that beginning.

This passage fairly rings with significance. In his search for success, the writer resembles man in his equally teleological (and thus equally misdirected) search for "meaning." What the search comes down to, in either case, is an excuse to postpone one's real work—an excuse to postpone the living of life itself. Realizing this, Cosnahan has made the first step toward that new beginning which is, or should be, the real object of his search.

The question of how to begin, how to go, is somewhat more difficult, and yet if we look back at the context of that question we find its answer implied. "How did you go, how did you begin to go?" Cosnahan asks as he stands before the "titanic thunder and confusion of traffic" on Rome's streets. And lest we should not realize the dimensions of the question, he goes on, "Yet this momentous traffic was scarcely a symptom of the age in which he lived." The question of how to go, i.e., how to live, is answered implicitly, I think, in the way Cosnahan makes his way around the city—"steering as by dead reckoning." Cosnahan's fear of traffic, like his fear of writing, his fear of using his "magical powers" and his very fear of *being,* can be countered only by plunging into and going with the flow. (We may be reminded here, as so often in Lowry, of the Conradian injunction, "to the destructive element submit.") "Cosnahan," we are told, "was not exactly a man who walked without thinking where he was going. On the contrary, he often thought so intensely about it that every time he approached what, to another, would have seemed a logical crossing, his direction was modified by the same decision at all costs, if possible, to avoid that crossing." Once Cosnahan submits to the chaos of the traffic, however, and like the water-diviner follows the "familiar twinge of pull at his being," he is able to make some headway. Once again, the implications for the Ortega metaphor are obvious—as they are in regard to the third question, "what is a writer?"

This is a question that Lowry answers negatively, using Cosnahan's old shipmate Quattras as a perfect example of what a writer is *not.* In **"Strange Comfort,"** Lowry had gotten in some jabs at his contemporaries, poets who "dressed like, and as often as not were bank clerks" and whose work his protagonist regards as "hieroglyphics, masterly compressions, obscurities to be deciphered by experts." Now, in this story, he strikes out again at those artists, like Quattras, whose distorting aesthetic vision sacrifices life to the "higher truth" of art. For Quattras, the simple story of a rescue at sea is not romantic enough. He changes all the circumstances until the actual episode is unrecognizable: "Not from modesty, nor any aversion to the subjective, or even because he had some sage notion the truth wouldn't sell. On the contrary, he felt that what he had written *was* the truth, that it *would* sell, but only to a 'high class audience.' And if it did not, he was artist enough to admit, that would be only because it was *too* truthful, *too* realistic, too 'art for art's sake,' and in short, too much like that Sagami Sea of Japan that had all but engulfed them all, 'over their heads.'" Here, surely, is an attack not only on the "romantic" Quattras but on all those writers whose aesthetic vision results in what Lowry sees as "inauthentic" art—art which has strayed so far from lived experience that it is no longer available to the ordinary reader.

It is also an implicit critique of the "aesthetic" view of life. If the artist's role, in relation to his material, is to take it and reshape it into a preconceived form—in Quattras' case, the form of a dashing romantic novel—then man's role, by extension, is to take and reshape his experience toward a similar preconceived end (life as tragedy, for instance). The only problem, in both cases, is that in this process the material itself—lived life—is not just transmuted but destroyed. This, of course, is the real danger of the magician's art—that he will destory more than he creates—and it is the danger of the Ortega fellow as well: how to make up his life, not according to the restrictive and life-denying forms of the past, but *as he goes along,* discovering his own form.

This Cosnahan finally does, not as an act of will or through rational decision, but simply by letting go and steering by dead reckoning. Frustrated and disappointed by his failure to find his Italian publishers (and hence to "find himself translated") he wanders into the Borghese Gardens and there accidentally discovers the zoo—the very zoo in which his old friend and character Rosemary resides. Rosemary

had been part of a cargo of animals that Cosnahan had responsibility for when he worked on a steamer once in his youth. In the course of the journey he had become quite fond of her and had made her the central character, so to speak, in his comic novel, *Ark from Singapore.* His meeting with Rosemary now, several years later, is a significant one, not because of what happens (in fact, nothing actually *happens*) but simply because of the way it comes about. Earlier in the story, Cosnahan had marvelled at the number of tourists who seemed to be meeting people they knew from back home here in the faraway cities of Europe: "Yet it didn't seem that even that more romantic encounter with somebody already fallen in with in Europe was in store for him, nothing for example . . . like that felicitous meeting in Rome by the hero of a book he'd been reading with a girl named Rosemary. . . ." This comment, seen in retrospect, is of course ironic, for Cosnahan does have just such an encounter with a very different Rosemary. But he cannot have it, so it seems, until he has failed in his intended quest for his Italian publishers. If Cosnahan had been searching for Rosemary, chances are he wouldn't have found her, wouldn't have experienced the same recognition. It is the very accidental nature of the discovery "testifying to the existence of almighty God, and His wide wild humor," which releases Cosnahan from his frustration and stasis into a "passionate desire" to write and to proceed with life.

Before encountering Rosemary, Cosnahan tells us, he had congratulated himself on his "tragic sense," but now he realizes "that life, all life, must have a happy ending, that it was our tragic sense that was the more frivolous, having been given us for aesthetic reasons alone, that beyond tragedy, beyond the world, if not altogether beyond art—naturally one hoped not too soon—was reconciliation beyond our wildest dreams of optimism. . . ." Some readers have found this "happy ending" of Lowry's forced and almost cloying. Isn't Lowry's comic vision, it seems natural to ask, as "aesthetic" in its insistence on unity and preconceived form as the tragic? I think it is not. When Cosnahan discovers a unity greater than fictional unity, when he achieves a recognition more complete than any "preposterous recognition in literature," he is really seeing "beyond the world" into the realm of pure possibility. The comic vision he arrives at here is, like Dante's, not a human vision at all but the context for a human vision—a context that is religious in the broadest sense of the word. So when Lowry asserts that "all life must have a happy ending," he is asserting no more than what is *possible.* It is still up to Cosnahan, after all, to pick up his work and go on writing—something that Lowry, like his alter ego the Consul, ultimately failed to do.

### Tony Bareham (essay date 1989)

SOURCE: "The Novellas and Short Stories," in *Malcolm Lowry,* St. Martin's Press, 1989, pp. 78-101.

*[In the following essay, Bareham discusses the defining characteristics of Lowry's short fiction.]*

'Short fiction was never his forte,' says Douglas Day [in *Malcolm Lowry: A Biography,* 1973]. Time and time again Lowry begins with something that looks like a short story but uses it only as a means of expanding his ideas into some other form. There is also an intermediate stage which Lowry called 'novella'—as though this represented a finite and finished genre in itself. But often his novellas represent nothing more than short stories on their way to becoming novels. Apparently on many occasions he did not think about material and predetermine its mould; he simply worked it over and gave it whatever name suited its length at that particular juncture. He nowhere offers a precise definition of what, for him, forms the necessary boundary between short story, novella, and novel. Both *Under the Volcano* and *October Ferry* were planned as short stories, and simply grew until they had achieved novel-hood.

Equally symptomatic is the case of **'Elephant and Colosseum'**, the short story eventually placed fourth in *Hear Us O Lord.* This began as the entry for a sponsored short story competition. The sponsor imposed a limit of 1,000 words, but Lowry's final entry was something like thirty times over the prescribed limit! Material seemed to pour out, and only later to assume a name or a recognisable disciplined genre.

As early as 1950 Lowry had written to James Stern about the problems implicit in working up material for the short story. Here he first mooted the idea of interlinking the individual tales within a collection. This, of course, was a good ten years before he began work on his own major collection.

> . . . there is no . . . satisfactory design-governing posture for a true short-story writer, and I can understand how, difficult to please as to form, you kick at the amorphousness of the thing . . . It is possible to compose a satisfactory work of art by the simple process of writing a series of good short stories, complete in themselves, with the same characters, interrelated, correlated, good if held up to the light, watertight if held upside down, but full of effects and dissonances that are impossible in a short story, but nevertheless having its purity of form . . .

Lowry was to return to this notion of interlinked short narratives some fifteen years later. The publisher's 'note' to his major short story collection explains that

> Lowry had conceived of . . . [*Hear Us O Lord*] . . . as a unit, and had arranged the tales and short novels of which it consists in a kind of curve, so that each story had bearing upon those on either side of it.
>
> *(Hear Us O Lord)*

It is difficult to discern how far this is Lowry's rationalisation—or at least his own words. The letter to Stern sanctions a belief that the 'note' reflects the author's intention. Detailed scrutiny blurs this impression, however. We may identify parts of the curve and the interlinking dissonances in the version of the collection which is now published. But the extant letters reveal that the published

collection simply is not the one originally mooted by Lowry.

In October 1951 Lowry confessed quite freely to Matson that he was using his short stories as practice for the more exciting work of the full-length novels, and to provide ready-to-hand material which might induce Erskine to sign a new contract with him. This letter contains no notion of a pre-determined curve existing among all or any of this off-the-peg material. Lowry is keen to sell whatever is saleable. The stories are not all the same as those eventually collected in *Hear Us O Lord,* and the order is different from that represented by the published collection.

By May 1952 a positive sense of shape does seem to be emerging among the short stories. '*Hear Us O Lord* . . . seems to be shaping up less like an ordinary book of tales than a sort of novel of an odd aeolian kind itself, i.e. it is more interrelated than it looks . . . '. This sounds encouraging, except that the mooted interrelationships are still not between the particular story units which eventually comprise the published form of the collection. At this juncture, for instance, *October Ferry* was still intended to be the penultimate story in the volume.

A year later a bulletin of progress to Erskine is still talking about the shape of the collection—but still not the collection we now have. 'The whole thing does have a very beautiful form, and makes a very beautiful sound when taken together,' Lowry declares. *October Ferry* is regarded as a vital part of the organism, yet the same letter later asserts that *October Ferry* must be seen as a novel in its own right—so must **'The Forest Path to the Spring'**—but that 'taken in various combinations they form yet further kinds of novel'. These various 'symphonically adjacent companions' seem to be offered as cards to be shuffled and dealt in a bewildering variety of hands. Erskine may even have wondered what game he was supposed to be playing!

None of this finally precludes discussion of *Hear Us O Lord* as a fresh and interesting experiment with the form of interlinked short stories. But it must make us cautious of asserting linkages too dogmatically; it may also explain why the linkages are not all equally strong or convincing within the collection as we have it. It should also be noted that at this time—in the early 1950s—Lowry was talking of twelve 'chapters' for the complete book, not seven, as we now have. Any original concept of shape must have been pulled out of kilter or radically adapted over the years.

Still left in abeyance is the question of the intrinsic artistic merit of the material under discussion, and the value of its final formal disposition; and, even more, the decision in this chapter to discuss the two novellas, *Lunar Caustic* and **'The Forest Path to the Spring'** as a pairing, since one of them emanates from the 1930s, while the other was always intended as the conclusion to a group of tales stemming from the 1950s. The *Lunar Caustic* we now have is a splicing and reworking, made in the 1950s, of material from much earlier. It was brought out of storage for further consideration at exactly the same time as the short stories of *Hear Us O Lord* were being composed. Linkages may be stronger than hitherto argued by Lowry's critics. The gain is hopefully of a new perspective on the two works; the ostensible loss is the chance to discuss '**Forest Path**' in place as the conclusion of *Hear Us O Lord.* It is hoped that the comments made on it here will still serve to show the logic of its position as the resolution of the short stories.

The work we now call *Lunar Caustic* originated in the period Lowry spent as an inmate in New York's Bellevue Hospital in 1936, during a period of extreme alcoholic depression, following Jan's decision to live apart. Details are vague; exactly how long was the stay in hospital? How voluntary was Lowry's admission there? In any event almost as soon as he left the hospital Lowry felt the urge to write up his experiences. He called his quickly written manuscript '**The Last Address**', partly because from his hospital window he could nearly see down to the place where Melville had been living when he finished *Moby Dick*. This first draft of the Bellevue experiences is interlarded with references to Melville, and with variations on the 'great white whale' motif. This or an immediately subsequent draft was actually accepted for publication in *Story* magazine, but an ongoing process of redrafting led Lowry to withdraw the original. It became, almost inevitably, a novella. Meeting with no success from publishers the material was reworked yet again, and given another title—'**Swinging the Maelstrom**'. The various versions display substantial tonal differences. In the later version the ending is far more optimistic, and the relationship between patient and doctor is much closer.

A version of this story was given to the French translator of *Under the Volcano* in the late 1940s and eventually published by her, in French, in 1956. Lowry's commitment was stimulated by this; references to *Lunar Caustic* become frequent in the letters, as he took a fresh appraisal of this very old favourite. He attempted to bring together the whole 'bolus' of material from both earlier efforts, but he did not live to complete this task. Like *Dark as the Grave* and *October Ferry* what we have for *Lunar Caustic* is a composite text, edited by Margerie Lowry and others. Despite its vexed publishing history *Lunar Caustic* has always been among Lowry's most popular works.

By reverting to the old 'infernal' material of drunken degradation from the 1930s, and working it alongside the 'paradisal' theme of '**Forest Path**', Lowry was certainly creating dissonances, overlaps, and curves of meaning which are consistent with his declared intentions for *Hear Us O Lord.*

The first specific mention of '**Forest Path**' in Lowry's published letters comes in mid 1951. He had developed a strongly protective feeling towards the Dollarton shack upon which the novella is centred. Early work upon *October Ferry* brings the comment

> Scares of eviction come and go, and it is a situation of some universal significance I have always meant to

develop in the novel . . . the plot of the novel . . . gets into all the short stories too . . .

and a little later in the same letter he shows how material spills over from one project to another as he comments on '**Forest Path**':

> . . . I have a long short story more or less finished that is out of the Intermezzo part of the novel—this whole part will be called *Eridanus.* This part of the part is known as '**The Forest Path to the Spring**' . . . *Eridanus* is what I call Dollarton here: called such after the constellation—The River of Youth and the River of Death. Reading Dante the other day I came to the conclusion that the celestial scenery of pine trees and mountains inlet and sea here must be extremely like that in Ravenna, where he died and wrote . . . the last part of the *Paradiso.* Then I discovered that Eridanus in mythology . . . *is* the river Po and where the Po emerges to the sea *is* Ravenna . . .

The very notion of contrast between hell and paradise is consistent with contrasts to be drawn between *Lunar Caustic* and '**Forest Path**'. . . .

Within a few months the work described in the above letter had assumed major significance for Lowry. He explained that it now comprised a novella of great seriousness, which describes the happiness of his life at Dollarton. It has—and is unique in this, he claims—the kind of seriousness usually reserved for tragedy, and it deals with human integration. Again the contrast with *Lunar Caustic,* which is searingly accurate in its discussion of *disintegration,* is very germane.

The description quoted above sounds, both tonally and thematically, like '**Forest Path**' as we now have it. It appears to have been written much more *currente calamo* than many later Lowry works. '**Forest Path**' flows in a reassuring current. Any necessary layering-in has been skilfully achieved. It conveys a sense of structural integrity which helps support the work as a lyrical paean of praise, where both character development and sequential plot are virtually in abeyance.

At this date—2 October 1951—Lowry could promise '**Forest Path**' should be ready in 'about a month'; this is pretty positive even for the euphoric Lowry. Two years later the work was still on the stocks, but whether because it was under revision or because it had become bound up with other material not yet completed, it is difficult to say.

Contrast in the two novellas between purgatory and paradise is manifest enough. Whereas the mid 1930s had been a tormented period for Lowry, the very early 1950s probably represented his most stable and assured period. He was settled at Dollarton, acclaimed as author of a successful novel, domestically at peace, and apparently in control—most of the time—of his alcohol problem. Once he took *Lunar Caustic* from cold storage it is difficult to believe that Lowry would not feel the dynamic contrasts implicit in the two works. Geography, character, ethos, motive, would all point to sharp dichotomies between the two periods. One simple contrastive motif will illustrate the point.

*Lunar Caustic* describes how, outside the windows of the hospital ward, lies a ruined coal barge, which becomes a focus of attention for the inmates:

> . . . between the two wharves and fast against the poverty grass before the hospital lay the coal barge, sunken, abandoned, open, hull cracked, bollards adrift, tiller smashed, its hold still choked with coal dust, silt, and earth . . .

This passage presents a boat which symbolises destruction, waste, despair. It is in striking and direct contrast with the wrecked freighter in **'Forest Path'**:

> . . . it had been driven ashore in a wild faen wind decades ago, carrying a cargo of cherries-in-brine, wine and old marble . . .

> Gulls slept like doves on its samson posts where grasses were blowing abaft the dead galley, and in early spring pecked their old feathers off to make room for their new shiny plumage like fresh white paint. Swallows and goldfinches swept in and out of the dead fiddley . . . Grass grew too from the downfallen crosstrees, and in the dead winches wildflowers had taken root— wildflowers, spring beauties and death camass with its creamy blooms.

The wreck was called *Eridanus*—symbol of both life and death; it gave its name to the paradisal spot where the novella is set, and the passage above is typical of a work which creates a reconciliation between awareness of life and of death. The wreck itself, unlike that in *Lunar Caustic,* has become an accepted part of an essentially benign disposition. Nature, unimpeded and unvitiated by urban nightmare, has asserted her own benevolent influence upon the potential disaster wrought by man. Thus the one boat, with its coating of grime, detritus, and useless cargo, may represent Lowry's view of himself and of life during the stay in Bellevue (how ironic that name is, in context!). The boat at Dollarton symbolises a much more reposeful and accepting state of mind. Cherries-in-brine, wine and old marble evoke precisely the opposite feelings to the coal carried on that first wreck.

Taken on its own this contrast might seem forced or fanciful. It is possible to show, however, that a series of such contrasts are drawn rigorously and consistently between the two works.

The protagonist of *Lunar Caustic* is a failed musician who has involuntarily allowed his group to disperse, and has now lost all contact with them. In **'Forest Path'** the narrator-hero is an ex-jazzband leader who has made his own healthy decision to quit the urban nightlife of his vocation. But he has done so without losing touch with colleagues who still come to visit him. His musical urge has in no way been suppressed, for by the end of the book

he has set himself, very successfully, to composing his own works. Plantagenet, in *Lunar Caustic,* cannot even play adequately any more. Creative life and stultification are thus suggested as the opposing psychic centres of the two protagonists. A list of such oppositions may show just how deeply they permeate these two works when they are considered as a deliberate pairing:

### *Lunar Caustic*

Urban, enforced setting
Drink dominant and destructive
Man alienated and isolated
A world of lunatic noise
Blindness or narrowness of outlook
A world of unavailing doctors
The sordidness of public life
Struggle and suffering for tawdry possessions
Filthy urban waterway

### 'Forest Path'

Rural, voluntary setting
Drink subsumed into social harmony
Man at peace with neighbours and environment
A world of harmonious sound
Philosophical and clear-sighted prospect
A world of man self-healed
The therapy of private existence
Acceptance of Nature's gifts without desire for worldly
    things
Self-cleansing Pacific

New York is positively infernal in *Lunar Caustic.* Violent, depraved and unhealthy, the city swelters in the heat wave which becomes a significant aggravation to the hospital inmates, who cannot gain access to the natural elements of cleansing. They are even deprived of basic washing facilities. The river is a murky pathway for commerce and for traffic incomprehensible to the caged-in viewers. They react like animals to movements on its surface:

> Only nightmare ships were left in this stream. All at once, watching the strange traffic upon it, he fancied that the East River was as delirious, as haunted as the minds that brooded over it, it was a mad river . . . where everything was uncompleted while functioning in degeneration.

Supporting images drawn from Rimbaud and Baudelaire underline this sense of horror. The contrast with the entirely health-giving spring water of Eridanus is complete and radical. Moreover, where the one is a fixed and arbitrary schematisation, the other has a quiet fluidity to which man is a voluntary contributing agent. Nothing except paradigms of hell can be drawn from the East River in New York; an entire system of benevolent philosophy can be extrapolated from Eridanus and the associated spring.

It is significant that the narrator of **'Forest Path'** has to *learn* by experience to live in accord with the elements; in so doing he ensures his permanent place in the earthly paradise, for the narrator quickly realises that unless he cracks the problem of obtaining a fresh water supply he will be forced back into the city. And whereas the doctors and fellow inmates at Bellevue cannot help Plantagenet to understand or find rapport with the East River, Wilderness's wife and neighbours are active agents in helping him tap the spring.

---

**Something of both the battle and the achievement are represented in 'Forest Path'. The sense of balance, of being at one with self and nature, lend dignity to the writing. The prose of this novella is notably tranquil and unconvoluted. It achieves lyricism while avoiding mawkishness.**

**—*Tony Bareham***

---

The handling of the theme of coexistence shows a similar pattern throughout. In Bellevue Plantagenet is surrounded, on the one hand, by those much more genuinely disabled than himself, and on the other by overworked and disheartened medical staff. He struggles to find stasis or rapport with both sides. From among the patients he selects an eighty-year-old displaced Jew and a mentally retarded teenage psychopath. (It is a token of Lowry's skill that he manages to hint that both *may* be misjudged or manipulated by society, but they are 'fixed' by the roles imposed upon them by outside judgement). Kalowsky and Garry are as close as Plantagenet can come to friendship in ***Lunar Caustic***. On his other flank is the alternately sympathetic and irritated Doctor Claggart, who regards him as 'an interesting case', but whose sporadic and harassed concern is limited by pressure of time. He is forced to become the agent of authority and of eviction, who has to dismiss Plantagenet and force him back into the external hell of the city.

In **'Forest Path'** there is a cognate pattern of characters with whom the protagonist is asked to relate; the local fisherman on the one hand, his wife on the other. Instead of making essentially condescending and ultimately unavailing judgements on his fellow men, as Plantagenet did in Bellevue, Wilderness coexists with his fellow 'inmates' at Eridanus in a marvellously independent but mutually trusting rapport. He has much to learn, and once the trust of the fisherman is won, he is able to complete the learning process, to share, and to give back. His humble recognition of the paucity of his gifts is a major strand in his discovery of sanity and balance. Of all the 'Wilderness' personae present in Lowry's fiction, the one in **'Forest Path'** is by far the most complete psychologically, and by far the most congenial. And on his other side stands the therapeutic and genuinely understanding wife who offers support far more comprehensive, meaningful and wise than

that which Claggart is able to offer Plantagenet. It is from his wife that Wilderness learns many of the simple but mysterious features of nature and the universe.

Music becomes a correlative of this capacity to learn. In Bellevue the hyperactive negro, Mr Battle, sings a dislocated ballad about the sinking of the *Titanic*. In Eridanus there is communal singing of the hymn which begs protection for mariners against natural disaster at sea—Hear Us O Lord From Heaven Thy Dwelling Place. This hymn accepts that without divine intervention man alone is powerless. It demands humility and offers consolation.

Whereas Plantagenet is driven away from the asylum piano with his music despised, Wilderness has his compositions accepted by the community in which he lives. Beyond the phenomenon of music Lowry contrasts aural stimuli and moods in the two works. **'Forest Path'** is full of observation of the minute sounds of nature going about its permanently regenerative and cyclic business; the 'amours of devilfish which sound like cracking machine-gun fire', the low whistle of mating cormorants in the early spring, the swishing wash of boats as they pass, the benevolent noise of Mauger's boatbuilding activities. Conversely, Plantagenet enters Bellevue to the 'dithering crack' of the hospital door closing behind him, and is swamped by a world of cacophony:

> Voices, a prosopopeia of voices, murmured in his ears, ebbed away, murmured again, cackled, shrieked, cajoled; voices pleading with him to stop drinking, to die and be damned . . . Music mounted to a screech, subsided.

One of the major points of contrast is, of course, the shape which experience gives to the thought of the protagonists. Whereas Wilderness learns, and grows inwardly—he *changes* more than any other Lowry persona—Plantagenet's experiment in self-discovery is totally abortive. Within a few minutes of being cast out from the hospital he is reverting to the habits which first drove him into it. The initial motive forces in the two protagonists are also radically contrasted. Whereas Wilderness has a sensible plan to escape the ruinous life he is leading, but stumbles upon Eridanus by chance, Plantagenet's scheme in entering Bellevue is ill conceived, but quite probably deliberate. More than one commentator has conjectured that Lowry's own admission to the psychiatric ward was a deliberate ploy, like his very descent into the maelstrom of alcohol:

> This plunge into hell, he realised, was what was necessary. He was obsessed with Faust and he sold his soul to the demon drink in order to get a masterpiece. (BBC radio programme, 'The Lighthouse Invites the Storm', 1984)

The closed circle of Plantagenet's world, with the psychiatric ward as its nucleus, reflects this cocoon-like existence, the desire to move in a circle, not to break free. Plantagenet has been circling the hospital for hours before he finally enters. The *movement* of both work and of protagonist in **'Forest Path'** is quite different in a dynamically contrastive way.

It is true that Lowry found 'Eridanus' by accident. He and Margerie had intended renting a shack on the Dollarton beach only for a brief honeymoon. If the account in '**Forest Path**' is true, their first impressions were anything but paradisal. Yet it rapidly came to represent the only place on earth where he was genuinely happy, and where he could master drink, temper, and paranoia. The saving factor in his almost fetishistic feelings towards Dollarton is that he never lost the recognition that it was a paradise he had worked for, had achieved through spiritual and temperamental self-mastery—and through the hardest physical labour he was asked to give to anything in his entire life.

In reality there were lapses, quarrels, drinking bouts. But none of the frequency, intensity or self-destructiveness of the New York, London, Mexican, or later European phases of his life. Poverty, and distance from a ready supply of liquor undoubtedly contributed, but for most of the Dollarton period Lowry seemed a man not much less contented than the majority of his fellows, and certainly happy with much less than most desired of the world's ostensible 'goods'.

Something of both the battle and the achievement are represented in '**Forest Path**'. The sense of balance, of being at one with self and nature, lend dignity to the writing. The prose of this novella is notably tranquil and unconvoluted. It achieves lyricism while avoiding mawkishness. Lowry had no need in this work to strain for characterisation or plot development, and the feel of the piece is genuinely authoritative. It is often said that Lowry could write about nothing but himself. This must be modified; he could write about himself, and Dollarton.

For all its simplicity of outline '**Forest Path**' has palpable shape. It gradually assumes spiritual depth and natural understanding until it is able to make these carry an epiphany for its protagonist. It moves through Thoreau-esque celebration of the good and simple life, to achieve a higher dignity. Over the passage of time the narrator grows into harmony with his world. Yet, strategically placed about two-thirds of the way through the narrative, comes a sudden loss of vision and rapport. A massive and inexplicable anger shakes him as he goes about his humble task of carrying water. His equilibrium is destroyed by inability to understand or conquer this feeling:

> It was not just ordinary hatred either, it was a virulent and murderous thing that throbbed through all my veins like a passion and even seemed to make my hair stand on end . . . so all-consuming and so absolutely implacable that I was astounded at myself.

This breath from the hot furnace of hell intruding into Eden disturbs and disrupts, but it cannot destroy the integrity which has been developed through rapport with nature.

The process of understanding the irrational force springs into focus when Wilderness comes face to face with a mountain lion waiting to spring on him. The creature clearly analogises the hate feeling. It is exorcised by courage and

patience. After being stared out and banished by words of charmingly banal conjuration the cougar slinks away. The narrator can return unscathed, but enriched, to his wife and to his way of life, and the story can move onwards to its lyrical conclusion.

> **As a poem of God's mercy granted through those years of peace on the Burrard Inlet, 'Forest Path' has power, dignity, and coherence.**
>
> **—*Tony Bareham***

Within the novella itself the moment is almost understated. It gains in impact from this undramatic treatment, which serves as a reminder that even in the earthly paradise lurk untamed forces. It shakes any developing sense of complacency. This feeling is supported by the constant emphasis upon physical labour in '**Forest Path**'—which again makes it diametrically opposite to *Lunar Caustic.* It is difficult to image any other Lowry protagonist sinking foundations into a rocky foreshore, roofing a dwelling, giving practical help to a boatbuilder. All these skills the intrinsically unhandy narrator has learned for himself, and he is properly proud of his achievement.

It is not the only side of his nature we welcome. Wilderness in '**Forest Path**' is the only Lowry persona to make a success of his artistic endeavours. What a refreshing change from the agonised introversion of *Dark as the Grave,* for instance. Perhaps this aspect of the book leans towards wish-fulfilment; the reader, wise after the event, knows that this plateau of balance and stasis will fall away tragically into the rocky barranca of the post-Dollarton years, and thus to messy and tormented death. But as a poem of God's mercy granted through those years of peace on the Burrard Inlet, '**Forest Path**' has power, dignity, and coherence. It and the last few chapters of *October Ferry* are the most reposeful writing Lowry ever achieved. They offer a valid alternative to the more widely renowned passion of *Under the Volcano* and to the apparently deliberate contradistinctions made in the contemporary reworking of *Lunar Caustic.* Individually the two novellas offer extreme ends of Lowry's subject matter, style, and personality. Seen as contrastive studies in the problem of human equipoise they have genuine power, validity, and coherence.

The short stories of *Hear Us O Lord* warrant consideration alongside the novels themselves principally because they suggest an experimental interrelationship which asks us to consider them as a unit. As already noted, Lowry mooted to James Stern in 1940 a series of short stories . . . 'complete in themselves but full of effects and dissonances . . . through being interlinked'. During the 1930s Lowry had used the form of the short story comparatively little. He had published six pieces in this genre, but half of these were actually chunks of other works, or the first germs of ideas on their way to full novel-hood. His real burst of energy in the short story came after the 1947-8 trip to Europe. A good deal of the work in the early 1950s dealt with the subconscious tensions between the Old and the New Worlds—not surprising in an author who was so fraught about his own national identity and responsibility. Perhaps the amount of Henry James he had soaked up in his undergraduate days encouraged this interest. The notions of isolation, identity, and yearning homeward are strong in Lowry's writing in the period after 1950.

The interlinkages between the short stories in **Hear Us O Lord** require us to consider the collection as 'another kind of novel', though the unscheduled growth of *October Ferry* and other internal changes to the pattern may have blurred whatever shape was originally planned for the collection. The letter to [James] Matson . . . is the first time the title **Hear Us O Lord** is mentioned in the published correspondence. The hymn from which it comes was a Lowry favourite:

> There is no hymn like this great hymn sung to the tune of Peel Castle with its booming minor chords in which sounds all the savagery of the sea yet whose words of supplication make less an appeal to, than a poem of God's mercy . . .

Here, perhaps, is the first clue to the manner in which Lowry hoped to achieve his linkages, his 'curve of meaning', in this collection. The hymn itself is a motif in three of the stories. More important, the influence of the sea is felt in virtually all of them alienating, dividing, ultimately annealing. And because there is a note of confidence or hope in many of the stories, we may see how they are unified by a sense of the poetry of God's mercy.

One real problem in considering these stories as an integrated collection may be the difference in quality between them. **'The Bravest Boat'** is fearfully mawkish, while the conclusion of the incidentally interesting **'Gin and Goldenrod'** is downright silly—no matter what your spiritual tribulations, life will be OK as long as you have hidden a bottle of gin to drink when you get home! These are placed alongside the genuinely interesting and experimental **'Through the Panama'**, and the considered attempt to link comedy and epiphany in **'Elephant and Colosseum'**. Whatever linkages may be intended, the sheer difference in quality of concept and execution is too great here to allow a 'curve' of meaning to emerge with much clarity.

The extent to which the ground plan changed is revealed by the bill of sale for Matson in October 1951. The collection then comprised—and the stipulated order is Lowry's own—**'Through the Panama'**, *October Ferry*, **'In the Black Hills'**, **'Strange Comfort Afforded by the Profession'**, **'Elephant and Colosseum'** and **'The Forest Path'**. Neither number nor order looks much like the final disposition of material as published. Lowry woos Matson, rather like an importunate door-to-door salesman, 'I could throw in a couple of other short ones . . .', which

scarcely suggests that a tightly organised integrity of outline is yet an exigent part of his planning. Indeed, a version of the work had, by 11 December 1951, been scrutinised by Robert Giroux, Editor in Chief at Harcourt Brace & Co., but his letter makes it clear the collection is still in 'state One'—that is, comprising the contents and order Lowry had given to Matson above, and might have anything up to 'a dozen or more' added to it.

In January 1952 Lowry declared his desire to finish and publish **Hear Us O Lord** as soon as possible in order to clear the decks for other work, and in April he offered a confident prediction of completion by 'this fall'. A year later, however, still uncompleted, it has grown to 'twelve chapters', and we have already seen that one segment of it—*October Ferry*—is beginning to get in the way of completion of other projects, to suck in material from elsewhere, and to hover dangerously between being a separate entity and an essential part of the interlinkage in the collection.

The notion of interlinkage is still very strong, however. Lowry comments that 'The whole thing does have a very beautiful form, and makes a very beautiful sound when taken together . . .'. It is now 'less a book of short stories than a kind of novel', but—spare a thought for poor Erskine trying to stave off his superiors' disbelief—Lowry admits in the summer of 1953 that he is now unhappy with the original plan of **Hear Us O Lord** and will need to do some radical rethinking.

Probably the first hint we can take of authorial confidence in the shape we now have for the collection comes from January 1954, when Lowry writes to Matson that the collected stories have begun to take on an interrelated form and to become an independent work of art. There is more confidence in the tone of this letter than heretofore on this subject. Yet our assurance is weakened still by realisation that *October Ferry* is still planned for the penultimate place in this version of the collection.

By now the blow of losing his contact with Erskine had fallen, and Lowry was making plans for his second trip to Europe. Hereafter his work rate dropped off, and never consistently recovered. A brief look at the progress of the individual stories which eventually comprised **Hear Us O Lord** will complete the picture of its uncertain genesis and development.

> **'The Bravest Boat'**: written by November 1951. Published individually in *Partisan Review,* 1954.

> **'Through the Panama'**: voyage from which it originated, 7 November to 23 December 1947. Written up at least into a form occupying 60 ms. pages by October 1951. Probably initially called 'Homage to a Liberty Ship'. First published posthumously, *Paris Review,* 1960.

> **'Strange Comfort Afforded by the Profession'**: idea generated on first European trip, 1948. Intended for **Hear Us O Lord** by 1951. The 'Edgar Allan Poe'

material dated from a trip to Haiti as early as 1946. First worked onto the 'Keats' material, summer 1950. First published, *New World Writing,* 1953.

**'Elephant and Colosseum'**: material possibly generated from Lowry's own voyage to the Far East, late 1920s. Then from his 1948 visit to Rome. Entered for short-story competition, late 1951. Listed as item 5 for *Hear Us O Lord* in October 1951. Ms. specified as '100 pages', but still being worked over as a 'short novel', November 1953. First published in *Hear Us O Lord,* 1961.

**'The Present Estate of Pompeii'**: generated from the 1948 trip to Europe. 'Nearly finished', November 1950. First published, *Partisan Review,* 1959.

**'Gin and Goldenrod'**: 'Not so nearly finished', November 1950. Genesis may have been in an episode recorded by Day, which occurred during the Lowrys' stay in Niagara-on-the-Lake late 1944. First published in *Hear Us O Lord,* 1961, where it lies uneasily in the slot once intended for *October Ferry.*

**'The Forest Path to the Spring'**: generated out of personal experience during the earlier Dollarton years. First mentioned in *SL,* June 1951. Promised to Matson for November 1951, as containing about 100 pages. First published in *Hear Us O Lord.*

At one stage another story, entitled **Ghostkeeper'**, was intended for inclusion. Day records it as follows: '. . . another of his writer-being-written-about pieces, it was abandoned after he had written only a few pages . . .'. Mention of this abortive fragment offers a further clue at least to intended linkages across the curve of the collection. The setting for **'Ghostkeeper'** was to have been Stanley Park, Vancouver, where **'The Bravest Boat'** is also set.

These, then, are the facts from which we have to extrapolate the artistic design and intention for the finally published collection. They do not suggest a consistent dynamic shaping energy. A shape does emerge, but its outline is affected by the various vicissitudes which befell the collection over the years.

There is another major problem, concerning a lack of consistency in the central persona. The protagonist of **'The Bravest Boat'** never reappears; in **'Through the Panama'** the narrator is a deliberately whimsical *mélange* of pseudo-author, 'real' author, and fictive character, Sigbjørn Wilderness—the 'real' author above—reappears in the third story, but is replaced by Kennish Cosnahan in the fourth. **'The Present Estate of Pompeii'** uses Roderick Fairhaven as protagonist; Wilderness comes back in the sixth tale, and the narrator is anonymous, though implicitly Wilderness again, in **'The Forest Path'**. This situation is compounded when we find Lowry telling us that even Wilderness is not to be regarded as a consistent entity; he represents various aspects of the protean character of Lowry himself.

It is essential, therefore, to rid ourselves of the urge to seek consistency of outline through *character* as such. The continuum of the work is found at a more obscure level of psychic development. Fragments of personality—indeed *aspects* of a central neurosis—hold the stories into a curve of meaning. The apparent assurance in the first story breaks down in **'Through the Panama'** to such an extent that the author is in search of an author who is in search of a character. The middle stories examine further isolated aspects of a central social nervousness and inability to integrate. And the final triumphant narrative shows the author-figure at last in an aspect of repose. A number of themes are developed around this idea of the central characters' search for equipoise.

Mawkish as it is, **'The Bravest Boat'** introduces several motifs which will be sustained and built up as the collection of stories unfolds. Against the peri-urban and maritime setting of a Canadian municipal park two lovers meditate on endurance, constancy and spiritual stability. Most of the material in the later stories harks back to these points. Sigurd and Astrid have been brought together through the agency of a toy boat to which, as a boy, Sigurd had committed a message. For twelve years the tiny craft wandered the ocean, surviving storm and calm, until Astrid found it, contacted Sigurd, and became his wife. The story fails because of technical deficiencies, particularly in the exquisitely awful dialogue. Astrid's share of this comprises virtually nothing but repetition of Sigurd's not very strong lines, to the point where the reader is convinced that she must be half-witted. The *idea* of the story is admirable as a lyrical introit to material which will be explored later (fortitude, triumph over adversity, harmony with nature); its execution is very weak.

The contrast with **'Through the Panama'** is well conceived as an idea. Sigbjørn Wilderness and his wife Primrose are journeying from Canada, down the Pacific coast to the Panama Canal, then into the Caribbean and, via Curaçao, across the Atlantic to France. This is, of course, the trip which Malcolm and Margerie undertook 1947-48. Almost inevitably the protagonist is haunted by his projected next work—a novel about Martin Trumbaugh, a novelist who has written and been haunted by a novel he wrote about Mexico. The weird *mélange* of personae enables Lowry to create a good deal of comic introspection about the nature of identity, and about personal equipoise. 'How can the soul take this kind of battering and survive? It's a bit like the toy boat,' exclaims Martin, after a particularly hefty spasm of self-doubt—almost as though he had been occultly connected with **'The Bravest Boat'** itself. Later, out in the Atlantic and heading for the new trials of Europe as a spiritual testing ground, the SS *Diderot* will be battered almost as the toy boat was in the earlier tale. Through shedding care for self and being purged by the proximity of death in the storm, it is implied that the narrator may emerge as a better integrated and more understanding man.

For most of the duration of the story we are given a marginal gloss, in the manner of that provided by Coleridge for 'The Ancient Mariner', and this enables Lowry to extract further parallelisms and overlaps in the ideas-fabric of his work. Wilderness's albatross is, presumably, his social diffidence and his spiritual confusion. The vultures seen off the coast of Mexico evoke a specially potent cross-reference to the traumas previously experienced there, and the entire nexus of neurotic hang-ups is syphoned through the Panama Canal, and then purged by the near-fatal storm in the Atlantic.

The last of the marginal glosses reads:

> And the Ancient Mariner beholdeth his native country.
> And to teach by his own example, love and reverence
> to all things that God made and loveth.

For all this solemnity **'Through the Panama'** is often very funny. This aspect of the story saves it from morbidity and self-pity. Yet at bottom the bravura essay represents a touchingly serious attempt to move through the fear and pity implicit in the prayer 'Hear Us, O Lord' towards an ultimate reconciliation of a haunted man with his causes of terror. Embedded in its maritime/mariner/fraught soul themes there is a subterranean linkage back towards a central core of ideas within the volume as a whole.

**'Through the Panama'** is an inventive fantasia—one of the most original pieces of travel writing of this century. But its real travel is inwards into the haunted consciousness of its protagonist. The correlations between inner and outer states sometimes become too heavily portentous—particularly in the description of the god-like Authority figure who controls the canal locks. The work is also capable, however, of parcelling up some of Lowry's most genuine notions on character, the novel, criticism. It manages to strike a balance between clownishness and high seriousness which is rare in his writing outside *Under the Volcano.* Aspects of the inward-looking investigation, and the attribution of correlatives of despair to inanimate objects makes **'Through the Panama'** closely akin also to *Lunar Caustic.* Its calculatedly eccentric manner of presentation is initially daunting, perhaps, but once this is penetrated it justifies itself, and the story stands as one of the most satisfactory and completed things written by Lowry. The difference in intention and in execution between **'The Bravest Boat'** and **'Through the Panama'** is very large. Thus for all the arguments urging that they are progressive parts of any curve of meaning, there remains an implicit disjunction between them.

In **'Strange Comfort Afforded by the Profession'** Wilderness—here minus his wife—has arrived in Rome on a Guggenheim fellowship (Lowry had at one time hoped for such an award himself, but it never materialised). Wilderness is dislocated and thrown off balance by the intrinsic strangeness of the Old World; this Jamesian motif runs right through the 'Roman' section of the collection. In a sense it is implied that even the storm and cleansing of **'Through the Panama'** has been at best partial. The protagonists of **'Strange Comfort'**, of **'Present Estate'** and of **'Elephant and Colosseum'** all share this feeling of cultural and social apartness. After his years of self-imposed isolation it would be strange had not Lowry himself felt this when he made his return to Europe.

---

**One real problem in considering these stories [in *Hear Us O Lord*] as an integrated collection may be the difference in quality between them.**

*—Tony Bareham*

---

The story of **'Strange Comfort'** pursues the curious sense of affinity felt by Wilderness with the tragic literary and historical figures who have suffered, died, and been memorialised in Rome. He notes down phrases from the Keats and Shelley Museum as they appear to cross-refer to his own artistic *Angst,* and these become mixed in his notebook with details of the suffering of the early Christians and victims of Roman oppression. Subsidiary characterising touches reveal Wilderness as homesick, incompetent, and bewildered by the Eternal City's noise and bustle. This helps to relieve the 'arty' introspections of the story.

The 'strange comfort' of the title is, by implication, a mixture of the fellow creator's pride, together with relief about his (so far) capacity to survive crises which have annihilated fellow artists. There is a concessive touch of humour in juxtaposing the little private neuroses of Wilderness with the harrowing letters and memorials of Keats' death struggle as manifest in the museum showcases.

The narrative is enriched by Sigbjørn's discovery of the notes of a not dissimilar visit he had previously paid to the Poe memorial in Richmond, Virginia. While there he had recorded the agonised pleas Poe had made to his foster-father for support—'for God's sake pity me and save me from destruction'.

This in turn is paralleled and overlaid by the discovery of a similar letter which Sigbjørn himself had written in appeal to the Los Angeles lawyer who had charge of his affairs at the nadir of his fortunes. The themes of the struggling artist, the world's indifference, the uncaringness of Authority, and the preservation of an inner balance are thus conveyed in layers of experience set on top of each other. Those who know the Lowry biography will recognise that the author has attributed, almost verbatim, to Wilderness, a letter which had been written to his lawyer when Malcolm Lowry was first evicted from Mexico. Through the persona of Wilderness he is able to link fact and fiction, history and biography, personal and public torments. However obliquely, he is also able to stitch **'Strange Comfort'** onto **'Through the Panama'**, with its handling of storm, disruption and strange comfort. The repeated plea 'For God's sake pity me' is a variation on the leitmotif 'Hear Us O Lord'. The story is an incidental rather than a central document. It lacks the excitement which its experimental dynamics give to '**Through the Panama**'. But '**Strange Comfort**' offers a cogent and unusually well-balanced account of some of the Lowry shibboleths and nightmares.

---

'**Through the Panama**' is often very funny. This aspect of the story saves it from morbidity and self-pity. Yet at bottom the bravura essay represents a touchingly serious attempt to move through the fear and pity implicit in the prayer '**Hear Us, O Lord**' towards an ultimate reconciliation of a haunted man with his causes of terror.

—*Tony Bareham*

---

'**Elephant and Colosseum**' offers another Roman epiphany, this time in comic form. Kennish Drumgold Cosnahan, like Wilderness before him, is meditating in a Roman bar upon, *inter alia,* his incompetence in practical matters, his artistic obscurity, and his sense of loneliness in enforced isolation from his wife who has had to remain behind in the New World. The ocean divides two radically different cultures which share only the bewildering common ground of an identical language. Yet since he is in Italy—and speaks virtually no Italian—even his English is of scant use to him. The 'tower of Babel' motif is underlined by the fact that Cosnahan (who keeps breaking into Manx speech) is in Rome to check up on the non-appearance of the Italian translation of his novel, *Ark to Singapore.* This work, based on Drumgold's experience as involuntary minder of an elephant on a sea voyage from the Far East, has had a brief but flashy success in America, but none in the Old World.

Drumgold himself is caught uneasily between the two. His mother was a Manx white witch, and his brothers respectively a Catholic priest on that intensely non-conformist island, and a liberal anarchist recently unsuccessful in a *coup d'état* against the government of St Helena! Whimsical humour in abundance is woven out of these confused strands, though all clearly enough bear back upon the identity and confidence problems in Cosnahan himself.

After a comically unsuccessful attempt to trace his publishers (who are in Turin, not here in Rome at all), he wanders into the zoo and encounters the very elephant which he had nursed through a storm in the China Sea many years ago. The unexpected joy of this reunion establishes a new confidence and balance in him, and he is aware that his impetus to work has magically returned.

Here Lowry has taken a stage further the motifs present in '**Strange Comfort**'. On a literal level the 'comfort' in '**Elephant and Colosseum**' is even stranger, but more positive and tangible. The artist is preparing for a healthy

future rather than bolstering himself by drawing analogies with a morbid past. The unlikely agent of metamorphosis is the elephant, Rosemary, who—like the bravest boat—and like the protagonist of '**Through the Panama**', has survived her own *Storm und Drang* and emerged as a strange comfort to others.

The story is too long and tries to cram in too many ancillary themes, but it weaves some delightfully comic parabolas around the character of the bewildered Cosnahan, who is one of Lowry's most likeable personae. The quality of the experience at the meeting between Cosnahan and Rosemary is nicely redolent with both sentimentality and balancing humour.

Up to this point in the volume the links between the stories on an implied curve have been discernible without forcing the material, and seem to justify Lowry's claims about the novelty of the collection as an interlinking nexus of stories and ideas. The next two units seem not only among the weakest in themselves, but also the most feeble links in the chain. '**The Present Estate of Pompeii**' has New World schoolmaster Roderick Fairhaven behaving churlishly on a trip to Pompeii made for his wife's gratification. He refuses to be excited by the ruins of the ancient city. Once cajoled out of the bar and onto a guided tour he insists on counterpointing his iconoclastic interjections against the broken commentary of Signor Sallaci, the appropriately named Italian guide. The clash of Old and New Worlds is shadowly present through Fairhaven's hankering for the freshness of Eridanus as opposed to the sleazy timeless prurience of Pompeii, and a life/death schism is represented by the contrasted locations. Perhaps it can be argued that we are beginning now to slip down the curve which will carry us, two stories later, back to the Burrard Inlet. Some of Fairhaven's *sotto voce* observations on the culture schism are apposite enough: '"In Germany, England, red light"' . . . says Sr Sallaci, doing his guided tour of Pompeiian brothels . . . '"Roman better idea. Cock outside." Well, St. Malo was wiped out, Naples defaced, but a cock in the street outside a Pompeiian brothel still survived. Well, why not?' Fairhaven can throw off such whimsical *obiter dicta* which are amusing enough, but neither he nor the story itself gathers sufficient momentum to warrant much attention. The piece is ephemeral and inconsequential, a verso page from Lowry's travel notebook. Its roots are too feeble to penetrate far into the soil of the design-governing posture of *Hear Us O Lord.*

The penultimate place in the collection caused major problems once *October Ferry* outgrew its role. '**Gin and Goldenrod**' simply cannot fill the gap; it has little architectonic rationale within the overall curve of the book. Nor does it have the saving graces of sly humour and trenchant observation which save much of the 'Roman' part of the collection. This story returns to the kind of earnest but uncritical self-consciousness which caused unwitting archness of tone in '**The Bravest Boat**'.

In '**Gin and Goldenrod**' Wilderness has been forced into a penetential return visit to the sleazy house of a bootlegger where he had been on an expensive bender the previous Sunday. Here he had incurred both debt and social opprobrium. Now, accompanied by the long-suffering Primrose, he painfully retraces his steps through the desolation of abomination caused by the speculative builders who are raping the forestland around his home. We are meant to realise that through this scenery he recognises with shame and chagrin the metaphorical desolation which his alcoholism causes in his domestic life, and how this is reduplicated in the ecological theme of the ruination caused by mindless and greedy progress impinging upon the forest paradise. But the story is an intrusion upon the larger themes sounded around it. Well enough observed and written with some vigour, it evokes incidental feelings of environmental horror in which the reader may well wish to share. The problem is really in the utter feebleness of its conclusion and, such as it is, the wrongness of that conclusion at this stage on the implied curve towards purification and regeneration. Sigbjørn pays his sordid debt to the bootlegger and he and Primrose make the return journey in a more hopeful spirit, which is symbolised by the capacity of the wild flowers to survive even in the developers' wilderness. The voyage home, too, is, albeit thinly, populated with more benign figures in the landscape than the outward trip. So far so good, but the conclusion is purely bathetic:

> 'I have a confession to make Sigbjørn' . . . (Primrose)
> . . . said . . . 'You didn't lose that bottle of gin. You
> gave it to me when you came back the next morning.
> But I put it away and then you thought you'd lost it.'
>
> 'Then we can have it now.'
>
> 'Sure. And we can have a cocktail when we get back.'
>
> 'Good girl.'
>
> They stepped into their own woods and the cat came
> leaping to meet them. In the cool silver rainy twilight
> of the forest a kind of hope began to bloom again.

It is easy to see why *October Ferry* was originally intended for this moment on the curve, when 'hope began to bloom again'. In *October Ferry* this is precisely what does happen, and we are given plenty of supporting evidence as to how and why this should be so. The hope itself is a legitimate one and is validated by events in the story. But why or what the hope relates to in 'Gin and Goldenrod' must remain problematic. Nearly all Lowry's personae in *Hear Us O Lord* are drink ridden, and striving to fight it. This particular sense of progression across a curve is quite strong from 'Through the Panama' onwards. The point is that drink becomes increasingly a conquerable entity. But in 'Gin and Goldenrod' all the implications are that the earlier traumatic experience has gone for nothing. Wilderness will soon be back at his old vice—sanctioned by Primrose. If for no other reason, the story is out of place here.

Nor can it bear the burden of carrying us into the lyrical repose of 'The Forest Path'. In 'Through the Panama'

Wilderness had noted that he strove to 'turn this into triumph; the furies into mercies'. In 'Forest Path' this transmutation is achieved. *Hear Us O Lord* began with the lovers brought together by the magical sea change of 'The Bravest Boat', and it ends here where spring and sea water naturally merge on the Eridanus foreshore. Implied is the reconciliation of all the tensions which informed the voyage out and the European visit. In 'The Bravest Boat' caged cougars symbolise the manic and destructively cramped fury of nature on which urban impulses have set a cruel constraint. In 'The Forest Path' the cougar is free and passes by the vulnerable human who meets it on the path. They achieve a moment of stasis if not of rapport. The birds in 'Through the Panama' and the beast in 'Elephant and Colosseum' help pencil in this dimension to the curve arcing through the book. And in the repose and harmony which 'The Forest Path' achieves one can finally sense the purpose and the achievement of these stories as an integrated entity. It is a brave and valid experiment, vitiated in part by disruptions to the plan as work progressed, and dislocated by poor quality of both concept and execution in places. But without this collection in its attempt at a strange and new kind of unity, the Lowry canon would certainly be impoverished.

## Dominic Head (essay date 1989)

SOURCE: "Expanding Circles: Inductive Composition in *Hear Us O Lord from Heaven Thy Dwelling Place*," in *Malcolm Lowry Eighty Years On,* edited by Sue Vice, Macmillan, 1989, pp. 70-91.

[*In the following essay, Head explores the motif of expanding circles in the short stories of* Hear Us O Lord, *maintaining that it affects Lowry's use of language and functions to link the stories.*]

The stories in *Hear Us O Lord From Heaven Thy Dwelling Place* have a special significance in the Lowry canon, a significance that has not been fully acknowledged. Usually it is only *Under the Volcano* that is deemed, without serious qualification, to exhibit a highly sophisticated and innovative formal control. There is, however, a similar innovation operative in *Hear Us O Lord,* and this essay is primarily concerned with this element of textual tectonics. The design of each story conveys a sense of closure and this is an integral aspect of the short story form. Yet the real significance of these stories lies in the way their structure simultaneously cultivates and flouts this generic tendency to closure. The principle of the closed circle is played off against a concept of *expanding* circles, or widening horizons, and this formal dissonance results in certain structural fault-lines, the points which reveal (and mirror) Lowry's thematic concerns.

My argument is that the 'expanding circle' motif, which appears explicitly in key symbolic passages, also operates implicitly throughout the book governing descriptions and even syntax. The motif provides a model for the proliferation of thematic interlinking and expansion, giving free rein to Lowry's predilection for dense, associative prose. This opening out of ideas enables him to relate his personal preoccupations to public themes by stretching the boundaries of a fictional form sometimes thought to be confined to the private and the insular. The historical specificity of these 'public' issues has not yet, nor is soon likely to become anachronistic.

The expanding process depends upon a dispassionate transformation by Lowry of his autobiographical inspiration, the blending of the private with the public, the personal with the impersonal; and, since failure in this regard is a charge often levelled at Lowry, this accomplishment needs to be defended.

Lowry's fundamental principle of composition—fictional self-projection—presents an obvious stumbling block to the reader seeking a meaning beyond the individual authorial quest for self-definition. Successive critics have found the achievements of the short stories qualified, in varying degrees, by the (supposed) esotericism of their autobiographical content. This view represents a continuing echo of one early reviewer's conviction that 'as a record of private experience, the stories are interesting, if incomplete', but that 'as a comment on the experience of humanity in general, they are of debatable relevance' [Phoebe Adams, *The Atlantic,* August, 1961]. Lowry's own rootlessness and paranoiac fears contribute to the (indisputable) sense of alienation which pervades his work and these factors help explain the series of outsiders and questing artistic misfits who are the protagonists of successive stories in *Hear Us O Lord.* Yet the self-projection is designed to reveal a general significance. The debate centres on the effectiveness of this design. A measure of success is suggested by the varied characterisation, even where different protagonists share the same name. This indicates a control, through fragmentation, of the authorial persona. Lowry himself was in no doubt that the artistic struggle could provide an adequate vehicle for broader, societal themes. In a letter to Albert Erskine he wrote: 'there is an artist, a poet in every man, hence he is a creature easy for anyone to identify themselves with: and his struggles are likely to be universal, even on the lowest plane'.

While the counsel for the defence is examining the corpus delicti, the gravamen had best be admitted: short-story theorists have questioned the very generic capacity of the story form to transcend insular effects. The isolation of successive protagonists in *Hear Us O Lord* provides, on the face of it, a corroboration of Frank O'Connor's conviction, in his influential book *The Lonely Voice* [1963], that the short story inevitably conveys on 'intense awareness of human loneliness' and Bernard Bergonzi's belief [expressed in *The Situation of the Novel,* 1970] that 'the form of the short story tends to filter down experience to the prime elements of defeat and alienation'. This view of the genre's limitations effectively disqualifies the short story from the successful consideration of societal themes. For O'Connor the relationship between a society and an individual cannot be examined because the focus is always on 'outlawed figures wandering about the fringes of

society', while for Bergonzi the form is 'unhealthily limited, both in the range of literary experience it offers and its capacity to deepen our understanding of the world, or of one another'. These observations may constitute a restatement, in sociological terms, of the formalist view mentioned earlier of closure as an informing generic feature. Considered in relation to *Hear Us O Lord* this takes us back to that damaging tendency in Lowry criticism to view his work as an interconnected web of esoteric references. If the very form of the short story prohibits the consideration of themes which place the isolated individual within a social context, then all we are left with are scraps of solipsistic self-indulgence, artistic failures written during Lowry's last years in British Columbia when, according to Richard Cross, 'the artist withdrew into an isolation so profound that be became progressively less capable of defining his characters in terms of a social matrix' [*Malcolm Lowry: A Preface to His Fiction,* 1980].

It is not my intention to lay bare a hitherto undiscovered 'social matrix' in Lowry, or to argue that the short story form does not have a tendency towards isolating effects. The genre clearly does lend itself to the treatment of a single consciousness, just as Lowry's art oscillates around his own sensibility. The point is that Lowry organises his stories specifically to extend the particular into the arena of the general, and this pattern of extension—what I have termed the inductive process of composition—is coeval with an innovative expansion of the short story's formal possibilities. The lonely voice, for Lowry, is that of the visionary artist rather than that of the hermit.

**'The Forest Path to the Spring'** is a prime example of a closed, cyclic story in which broader thematic concerns are conveyed by elements which deny this closure. The story comprises a narrative cycle embracing the four seasons and involving an epiphanic experience for the questing narrator whose dwindling conviction about his artistic vocation returns. This revelation is dependent upon the concomitant resolution of the problem of social integration: positive integration and artistic creation are shown to be mutually dependent. This connection is implicit in the story's composition by virtue of Lowry's certitude that the plight of the artist is an exemplary one, and is pointed by a pattern of symbolism.

The expanding circle motif, introduced here by the narrator's wife in a description of rain falling on water, is emblematic of the thematic cross-fertilisation:

'You see, my true love, each is interlocked with other circles falling about it,' she said. 'Some are larger circles, expanding widely and engulfing others, some are weaker smaller circles that only seem to last a short while . . . The rain itself is water from the sea, raised to heaven by the sun, transformed into clouds and falling again into the sea.'

This truism is redeemed by its symbolic resonance, the social aspect of which becomes evident as the story progresses. The ripples are suggestive of a widening of horizons, and here they inspire just such a development of thought: the sight of the ripples leads into a consideration of the entire water cycle.

In contrast to this model of thematic linkage and expansion there is a formal principle of cyclic return and closure which shapes the story. The overall structure—a retrospective account framed by scenes from a notional narrative present—parallels the return to the scene of the narrator's epiphany. Within the frame an account is given of the couple's spiritual growth and development through their first year at the inlet, a growth linked to the natural annual cycle and which culminates in the spring.

Even within sections the notion of cyclic return is operative. The second section covers the reactions of the narrator and his wife on first moving into the shack at Eridanus. Their relationship is shown, at the beginning and ending of the section, to be at a stage of total introversion, despite the interposed hint that this condition may need to be transcended. To begin with they are enjoying the archetypal honeymoon state: 'That is how selfish lovers are, without an idea in their heads for anyone save themselves'. To them 'the beach emptied of its cheery crowd seemed the opposite of melancholy' and living there permanently, the narrator reflects, 'would be almost tantamount [ . . . ] to renouncing the world altogether'. There are hints of external impingement, and these are proleptic of later developments. The sight of ships carrying war cargo— even remote Eridanus witnesses evidence of World War II—pricks the narrator's social conscience and momentarily shatters the lovers' idyll: 'It's a hell of a time to live. There can't be any of this nonsense about love in a cottage', he reflects. A threat from *within* is also suggested when he conceives of his own shadow as 'the glowering embodiment of all that threatened us'. The section, a closed circle, ends as it begins, however, with the narrator's affirmation of the personal succour he draws from his wife: 'it seemed to me that until I knew her I had lived my whole life in darkness'.

The destructiveness of the reclusive impulse becomes manifest in subsequent sections, before a resolution is envisaged. This development occurs in phase with the succession of the seasons so that winter provides the background to the trough of the crisis, while the solution emerges in the spring. The ferocious winter storms cause the lovers to 'lose all hope for terror at the noise', the sounds of 'elemental despair', and reduce them, at the depth of their insularity, to 'cl[i]ng to one another like two little arboreal animals in some midnight jungle—and we were two such animals in such a jungle'. This analogy emphasises the asocial existence that has been cultivated to excess. The inability, at this stage, to sustain an outward-looking perspective is emphasised by the narrator's earlier remark concerning 'nonsense about love in a cottage' which has been emptied of its real purport and appropriated as 'a loving catchphrase'. During this 'winter' of the narrator's spiritual career he experiences a 'virulent and murderous' feeling which 'was like hatred of mankind', a state of mind which he finds 'turning inward and back upon myself, to devour my very self'. The narrator's professional and personal selves are both being consumed

here: the artist beset by misanthropy has lost his vocation since he is external to the social medium in which his work must be defined. Isolation has resulted in a state of misanthropic limbo.

The self-negation of excessive self-interest and the rejection of community is summarised in Mauger's allegorical anecdote of the eagle drowned by the salmon: to avoid sharing the fish with a flock of crows the eagle attempts to fly off and is dragged beneath the sea by its booty.

Here, as elsewhere in the story, the negative is held in tension with the positive. Having recounted the details of his disturbing hatred the narrator goes on fondly to consider his place in the Eridanus community, an ideal model of social organisation; and, having done so, he re-evaluates the feeling of hatred which he now realises is not for human beings but for 'the ugliness they made in the image of their own ignorant contempt for the earth'. Here the antinomy of nature and civilisation, a tension which informs the collection as a whole and this story in particular, is merged thematically with the narrator's artistic/spiritual quest. It is important to note that modern urban civilisation is depicted as inimical to co-operative communal living (represented by the Eridanus community) as well as to the natural world. The healthy creating self depends upon an involvement with both social community and natural environment, though these profoundly linked ideas are really different sides of the same coin. This association ensures that the self-negating immersion in his idyllic surroundings can yet provide the narrator with the basis of a positive resolution to his quest. After redefining his hatred he turns to his wife and the solace of their marital cocoon, which now reveals its positive potential: 'I forgot all my hatred and torment the moment I saw my wife'. It is this solace that enables him to understand and empathise with the natural environment. She seems to him 'the eidolon of everything we loved in Eridanus' and so 'through her I myself became susceptible to these [ . . . ] currents of nature'.

The pattern of thematic expansion is complicated by the fact that each level which reveals symbolic correlatives must also be evaluated for its actual significance. In particular, this concerns Lowry's preoccupation with the natural environment, which is no idealistic romanticism. The consternation about the destructive aspect of civilisation, 'creator of deathscapes', is more than the metaphorical analogue which, on one level, it palpably is. It is also a parallel theme in its own right. Lowry is concerned with the *literal* destruction of nature which is also the literal annihilation of human aesthetic perceptions. The ominous, encroaching city, the narrator feels, 'would almost suffocate all memory of the reality and wealth of such a life as ours'. The life source itself, which for the narrator is inextricably tied to artistic creativity, is that which the encroaching city and the oil refinery threaten. Modern ecologists, who discern a direct threat to human life sources posed by unchecked industrial and urban expansion, will find a chilling prognostication in this aspect of Lowry's work.

The chore of fetching water from the spring is the key event pertaining to the narrator's spiritual discovery. He recounts three separate occasions, when, in the process of completing this task, he experiences a moment of revelatory insight, and these three moments represent a composite epiphany. The first of these moments, . . . draws a parallel between an explosive jazz break and a sensation of happiness which heralds the spiritual rebirth. The second involves the encounter with the mountain lion the narrator's calm defusion of this mortal threat is shown to be emblematic of his resolution of the self-negating impulse. The final moment, like the encounter with the lion, occurs in the season of spring, the season of the narrator's renaissance when 'the very quality of the light was different'. The spring water provides an obvious symbol for spiritual rejuvenation and the path to the spring, according to this schema, clearly represents the pursuit of this sustenance. For the narrator, as for Lowry, this is the Proustian and Joycean quest, the search for the means of translating the past into art, and the incipient revelation involves a progression towards this capacity. The narrator, at the conclusion of his tripartite epiphany, is conscious of the path seeming progressively shorter and the job taking less and less time to complete, yet he also has 'a consciousness of a far greater duration of time having passed during which something of vast importance to me had taken place, without my knowledge and outside time altogether'. The plasticity of time and space signifies a new conception of personal time and history, a conception which will enable him 'to face th[e] past as far as possible without fear' and to 'transcend it in the present' because his 'new vocation was involved with using that past'. The accidental burning of his old work and the first shack emphasises this need to reconstruct the past 'like our new house, on the charred foundations and fragments of the old work and our old life'.

The various thematic threads coalesce when the circle image is echoed at the story's conclusion:

> Each drop falling into the sea is like a life, I thought, each producing a circle in the ocean, or the medium of life itself, and widening into infinity, though it seems to melt into the sea, and become invisible, or disappear entirely, and be lost. Each is interlocked with other circles falling about it, some are larger circles expanding widely and engulfing others, some are weaker, smaller circles that only seem to last a short while. And smiling as I remembered my lesson I thought of that first time when we had seen the rain falling into a calm sea like a dark mirror, and we had found the cannister and decided to stay.

> But last night I had seen something new; my wife had called me out of bed to the open window to see what she first thought was a school of little fishes breaking the still water just beneath, where the tide was high under the house. Then we saw that the whole dark water was covered with bright expanding phosphorescent circles. Only when my wife felt the mild warm rain on her naked shoulder did she realize it was raining. They were perfect expanding circles of light, first tiny circles bright as a coin, then becoming expanding rings growing fainter and fainter, while as the rain fell into the phosphorescent water each raindrop expanded into a ripple that was translated into light.

The multi-significance of the expanding circle 'widening into infinity' is fully embraced by the poetic progression of this passage. The theme of social integration is suggested by the notion of each droplet as a 'life' entering the ocean, or 'medium of life itself' and producing 'interlocked' circles. This interlocking, suggestive of the need for communal assimilation, also indicates the bridging of thematic interests. Here, as elsewhere, the societal theme is shown to comprise the basis of the narrator's artistic rebirth as it naturally develops into an image of artistic inspiration. This is connoted by the natural light, earlier invoked as emblematic of creative power, which here brightly illuminates the 'expanding phosphorescent circles'.

The story concludes in a visionary, symbolic phase which celebrates the positive potential of human creativity. The life source of natural light implied by the phosphorescent circles is surpassed, as the rain stops, by the appearance of three rainbows; and this is followed, significantly, by the 'beneficent signaling' of a lighthouse, the 'highest symbol' of civilisation, which is fused with the inspirational signs of natural light. Symbolic representations of social utility and artistic creativity are conjoined. Approaching once more the all-significant spring the narrator sees 'a deer swimming toward the lighthouse', a resonant image which depicts the natural and the artificial in a converging, harmonious propinquity.

The overall impact of the story's conclusion is complicated by a plethora of thematic 'tidying up'. This results in a sense of congestion which overloads the limitations of the narrative circuit, at least as far as it is conventionally perceived. Despite the neatness and circularity of the story's design there is a resonance about its dénouement which denies the formal closure: the superabundance of symbolism which accrues through the story disrupts any simple sense of finality. There is a conflict here with the couple's return to the spring, the event with which the story (and the book) ends. Despite the sensation of *closure,* the peace and fulfillment of this ending, the final effect is not a straightforward affirmation of an idyllic lifestyle and the discovery of vocation it represents: the affirmation is tempered by the potentially destructive forces, internal and external, which are always in attendance.

The interrelated themes encompassed in the story—artistic inspiration, self-definition, social integration, environmental responsibility—represent a complex layering of ideas which projects a further widening of horizons beyond the text. This metaphorical density is rarely so overt in a short story, and may cause some readers, with expectations fashioned by the converging, unified effects cultivated in many stories, to conclude that Lowry has attempted to 'put in too much' in an undisciplined loss of control. Poe's doctrine of the 'single' and 'preconceived effect', which has informed a great deal of subsequent short-story theory, is severely strained; just as a conventional view of the visionary moment as the instantaneous revelation of character and/or situation is extended by the dispersed, composite epiphany. Yet it is this very dissonance that is significant because it reinforces and clinches the topical content. The widening of horizons provides a corrective to the narrator's earlier isolation and to the insularity of the closed story form.

---

**Lowry's own rootlessness and paranoiac
fears contribute to the indisputable sense
of alienation which pervades his work
and these factors help explain the series
of outsiders and questing artistic misfits
who are the protagonists of successive
stories in *Hear Us O Lord*.**

*—Dominic Head*

---

Lowry varies the nature of the artistic quest in this story by creating a protagonist who is a jazz composer, an occupation which has an interesting bearing on the present discussion, especially as a jazz analogy is used for the first moment of insight on the forest path. On this occasion the narrator thinks of a break by Bix Beiderbecke 'that had always seemed [ . . . ] to express a moment of the most pure spontaneous happiness'. He considers, inconclusively at this stage, the possibility of translating this moment of happiness into his own life, and the implications of trying to 'make a moment permanent'. This anticipates his later reassessment of personal time and history.

There is a tacit parallel here between the jazz break and the epiphany in the short story, and this is another indication of the formal experimentation that is implicit in the story. It is interesting to note that Lowry here anticipates a recent observation by Julio Cortázar [in *The Review of Contemporary Fiction,* 1983] that 'the efficacy and *meaning* of a story rel[y] on those values that make poetry and jazz what they are: tension, rhythm, inner beat, the unforeseen within foreseen parameters'. Lowry's description of the Beiderbecke break is aptly conveyed as 'the unforeseen within fore-seen parameters', a formulation that is equally apposite in relation to Lowry's extension of the short story's parameters.

A similar tension to that discernible in '**Forest Path**' informs '**Elephant and Colosseum**', the other story I want to discuss at length. Scarcely written about and dismissed by Douglas Day [in his *Malcolm Lowry,* 1973] as 'insubstantial', '**Elephant and Colosseum**' has a density that belies its neglect. This is suggested by the fact that it was condensed, as A. C. Nyland reports [in *Malcolm Lowry: Psalms and Songs,* 1975], from an astonishing 654 pages of manuscript. As in '**Forest Path**', the plot is a circular quest in which the narrator is confronted with a significant reminder of his past which conveys to him how that past may be used as artistic inspiration in the present.

The writer Kennish Drumgold Cosnahan, a Manxman based in the USA, is on a European tour in search of the publishers of his autobiographical novel, *Ark from Singapore.*

His trip has been hastened by the need to visit his dying mother on the Isle of Man. In terms of these objectives the trip is a failure: his mother dies before he arrives and the publishing houses of Europe collectively show no interest in his work. Cosnahan is isolated and anonymous. He is redeemed, however, by a visionary encounter with the elephant Rosemary, the 'heroine' of *Ark from Singapore* and the creature he himself had nursed many years ago on the voyage fictionalised in his novel. The encounter triggers a revelation which offers the solution to his personal and professional crisis. The story is structured around this moment of epiphany—or 'anagnorisis' as Cosnahan, out-Joyceing Joyce, calls it—and it is through this revelation that Cosnahan finds meaning in his vocation as artist, receives absolution of his guilt over his dead mother, and perceives a tangible bridge between life and art as the professional and personal themes are merged. The plot itself, though structured as a closed unit, betrays a wry detachment from conventional notions of order. This is no pilgrimage to a spring at an Edenic inlet: Cosnahan's epiphanic encounter with Rosemary is pure serendipity, a happy chance on an afternoon of aimless time-killing.

The symptoms of Cosnahan's malaise are isolation and anonymity; and the diagnosis is that his (thwarted) need for recognition is a false surrogate for a genuine vocation. This point is well made when Cosnahan is pathetically reduced to leaving a copy of his novel on the café table in the hope that a stranger might recognise his photograph on the dust-jacket. In Paris, we learn, he had to be arrested before being acknowledged by some gendarmes with a common interest in rugby (he was not known as a writer), while in Rome his loneliness is only once relieved (and ironically) by the 'triumphant recognition' of truckloads of Italian soldiers who, on a whim, decide to hail him enthusiastically as they are driven past. The unnumbered doors of Cosnahan's pension, which cause him constantly to wander into the wrong room, emphasise his anonymity. The humour of these scenes is an integral part of the story's serio-comic tone (the full significance of which becomes evident at the conclusion). This pervasive alienation theme is also examined more seriously, as when he feels himself 'excluded [ . . . ] from the great circle of religion'. The serious and the comic are combined in this connection when Cosnahan observes the mutual recognition of two lovers that 'would gaze long in each other's eyes, then look away again, then laugh'. Cosnahan is struck by the simultaneous beauty and absurdity of this scene (an ambiguity which recalls the couple in '**Forest Path**'): these lovers experience a potentially positive human response, but the response is short-circuited, and consequently absurd.

In his isolation Cosnahan's literary powers have dried up, a point aptly symbolised by his loss of language power in everyday situations. He has difficulty, as a poor linguist, in communicating in a foreign city, and his phone conversation with his brother is rendered incomprehensible by a crossed line.

This symbolic isolation is Cosnahan's punishment for his pursuit of ego-enhancing recognition, which is the wrong kind of social definition. When he considers the trappings of literary fame (which he has enjoyed in the USA) he perceives that it *disrupts* rather than enhances social contact. He recalls the legal claim made by a chance acquaintance for a quarter of the profits from *Ark from Singapore,* and remembers gold-digging opportunists as well as 'those writers who would never have spoken to him before [ . . . ], but now just wanted to *look* at him, or wanted him to contribute without payment to their magazines'.

The superficial trappings of the literary life have a deleterious effect on a writer's creativity by diverting genuine artistic endeavour. This censure applies especially to notices and reviews, the commercially decisive elements in the writer's career, which wield an unwarranted and enervating power:

> Reading these later eulogies produced in Cosnahan a bizarre mental commotion as some endless mirrored reduplication, as if it were not merely that all these reviews had been written before of countless other books, but that for a moment he felt like an eternal writer eternally sitting in the eternal city, eternally reading precisely the same sort of notices from which he always derived precisely the same eternal feelings of mingled pleasure, pain, gratitude, sadness, amusement, dismay and beautiful vain-glory.

The meretricious publishing game is a closed circle of eternal puffery, a system which restrains the writer from finding a genuine purpose, and which obscures the vital connections with external experiences. This erroneous 'idea' of writing is exemplified by the literary efforts of the quartermaster Quattras whom Cosnahan recalls attempting to forge a story from the experience of an actual rescue. Quattras simulates his glamorous notion of creative exertion, 'his hair falling wildly over his face in a tangle of inspiration', ensuring to leave 'the door to his room wide open', but all for the pointless manufacture of a story in which 'there was no hint of the drama of what had occurred'. Quattras is unable to bridge art and life because his faculties are impaired by superficial notions about art, notions which seduce him into believing 'that what he had written *was* the truth'.

From the beginning of the story there are intimations of the need for positive social integration. Despite his sense of alienation Cosnahan yet has a glimmering awareness of the social ramifications of his actions, even of such minor events as the settling of his café bill:

> Since it wasn't merely the milk he would be paying for (any more than anyone who bought that book would only pay for the spiritual nourishment it contained) but the commanding site of the Restaurant Rupe Tarpea upon the Via Veneto, to say nothing of the three other sidewalk restaurants on the other three corners created by the crossroads with the Via Sicilia and *their* rent, or their exquisitely dressed female occupants eating ices, to whose charming activities he felt he would be expected also, obscurely, to contribute; as naturally he would be paying also for the view, should he turn around, of the gateway of the Porta Pincia, and finally for the Via Vittoria Veneto itself, with its sidewalks

ten feet broad, and its plane trees casting dappled shadows on either side as it swept in great curves down toward the invisible Piazza Barberini.

This passage is representative of the story as a whole: the tone is ironic, yet the expanding perspective has a serious formal significance. If the thought of inadvertently paying to watch the consumption of ice-cream is a comic touch, there is also evidence here of the recurring impulse to make connections between events and occurrences on various levels. In this case Cosnahan examines the social implications of his actions, and this expensive scene of grandeur is later recalled when he gives a beggar woman 50 lire, 'half the price of his milk'. The earlier reflections on pecuniary power are implicit in this image of social inequality which inspires a feeling of meanness in Cosnahan.

The reflections at the café, however, merely anticipate Cosnahan's eventual sense of integration, and are not sustained: seduced by a sensation of luxury, he forgets his unease in an

> expansive feeling of great riches and peace, that purring roaring feeling, yet somehow quiet as a Rolls Royce engine, of life being at a sort of permanent flood, as if there had never been a first world war, let alone a second one, which was like an evocation of 1913, of those truly pre-war days from which he retained only this curious yet powerful sensation, when with his parents he must have visited London or Dublin, or at least Weston-super-Mare, at the age of five.

The apparently 'expansive feeling' is actually one of regression, infantile and socially naïve. His mind retreats from the social implications of the episode, becomes disconnected from historical context, and finds succour in the sensation of opulent comfort that his circumstances inspire. This is a state of moral stasis, an equivalent condition to the torpor resulting from Cosnahan's preoccupation with the trappings of the literary life. As a whole this passage recalls the ripples on the water witnessed by the narrator of '**Forest Path**', but here the reflecting mind does not see the expanding horizons as the significant part of the model, and focuses on its own concentric position in relation to the 'ripples'.

The story's metaphorical pattern is complicated by the association of supernatural power and literary creativity. Cosnahan's erstwhile mystical powers have waned since the publication of his novel, just as his excessive preoccupation with success has occluded his creative energies. The supernatural theme is inextricably tied to the question of personal history: Cosnahan recalls that he has been 'conscious of something peculiar in his nature' ever since the Christmas his mother (herself a witch) 'presented him with a gray suède elephant'. This toy elephant, symbol of his inherited supernatural/literary powers, is encompassed within Rosemary's multi-significance at the moment of anagnorisis.

In literary terms Cosnahan's 'magical' powers (and those desired by Lowry himself) comprise the ability to forge art from life, and, as the necessary counterpart in this two-way process, to define himself by writing. Cosnahan's vision restores his powers (a symbolic rediscovery of his personal past) and sets him up to write again. His problems have been 'exorcised' just as he once had the capacity to exorcise possessed dwellings on the Isle of Man. Revitalised, and feeling like 'some old magician who had just recovered his powers', Cosnahan realises that 'he really *was* a magician' and that the 'source' of his 'future salvation' will be his transformation 'into a conscious member of the human race'. This consciousness of social integration, 'his sense of kinship deepening', is an integral part of his regeneration, just as his former powers of exorcism and water divining both have a community-serving function.

A further enrichment of the story's symbolic density is occasioned by the Manx motif which has an obvious generalising tendency (the Isle of *Man*). Thus the Manx faces that Cosnahan is disappointed not to encounter, in his misplaced quest for recognition ('where is Quayne, and where is Quaggan? where is Quillish? where is Qualtrough?'), become representative of a human totality at the story's conclusion:

> . . . Man was Quayne, and man was Quaggan, man was Quillish, man was Qualtrough, man was Quirk and Quayle and Looney, and Illiam Dhone, who had been hanged. And yet lived—because he was innocent?

The elephant Rosemary has a complex symbolic function in gathering together the story's thematic strands. When Cosnahan chances upon this key 'character' in his novel, art and life, past and present, merge on the narrative level. Rosemary also provides the summation of the supernatural theme as her appearance implicitly invokes Cosnahan's mother and, through his mother, his own inherited powers: she recalls their gifts to each other of a lapis lazuli elephant and the suède one. Cosnahan's epiphanic reverie makes these connections explicit: 'Rosemary was changing into a lapis lazuli elephant. And the lapis lazuli elephant changing into a portrait of a young elephant, on the cover of a novel named *Ark from Singapore*'. Rosemary is also an embodiment of the interweaving of different levels of experience: her all-encompassing significance, her inherent 'juxtaposition of the grotesque and the sublime', is emulated in the epiphany she inspires in Cosnahan, who experiences 'a hundred ideas, a hundred meanings [ . . . ] spiraling up from the same depths, from the same source in his mind'. The echo, here, of the expanding circle motif is not to be overlooked. The serio-comic tone in which the story is cast is an attempt to conjoin different levels of experience in this way.

As with **'Forest Path'**, the formal closure is denied by the symbolic overload which resonantly widens the story's horizons, an effect centred on the metaphorical multivalency of Rosemary. At one level a symbol of Cosnahan's personal regeneration, Rosemary is really no one thing, especially as she also embodies the impersonal context that must underpin that regeneration. Before his epiphany Cosnahan implicitly undercuts the personal aspect of the symbol by dismissing an anthropomorphic view of Rosemary's significance: 'If it so happened then that an ele-

phant showed you a love or intelligence you were wont to say was "almost human," as usual you were flattering to yourself'. Readerly expectations, again, will be challenged by this single symbol which conjoins so many portentous ideas but, once more, the dissonance is very much to the point since it reiterates, formally, the need to make connections and to grow beyond the insular and the superficial.

The shorter stories in the book evince the same impulse to thematic extension that I have been tracing. **'The Bravest Boat'** is a circular story in the sense that it revolves around a single image. The narrative continually returns, via the protagonists' preoccupation, to the title image and the spiritual qualities of tenacious humanism it implies. These positive human qualities are located in a broader frame of reference by virtue of the narrative context: the whole piece is posited on a tension between natural and urban worlds. The huts of the 'squatters' are seen to be 'in defiance of the town, before eternity'. A positive path is presented where man's creativity operates in concert with the natural world. The balsa boat, which (unlike the human structures of Enochvilleport) can only yield to the forces of nature, is shown to endure them.

A symbolic sea description towards the end of the story encapsulates the ambivalent view of human activity: the description of the flotsam indicates the self-destructiveness inherent in the over-reaching ambition of humankind. The 'macabre fruit of the sea', consisting of 'nightmarish bulbs of kelp' and 'sea wrack like demons', mingles with a clock, some boots, torn netting and a smashed ship's wheel and wheelhouse. This smashed human detritus—the clock, the netting, the ship's wheel—represent thwarted attempts to order or master elemental phenomena. Yet the positive potential union of human endeavour with the natural environment is also suggested here, because 'beneath the flotsam', the surface conflict, there is 'a stirring and stretching of life, a seething of spring'.

In **'Gin and Goldenrod'** the rural/urban tension is more explicitly related to modern alienated humanity. Bootleg gin provides a false relief now that the natural world, and the spiritual sustenance it represents, is on the retreat. Sigbjørn remembers 'the time when the deer used to come down through the woods and swim across the bay and there hadn't been any bootlegger in Dark Rosslyn to sell you firewater on Sunday, or, come to that, any reason for drinking it'. The story concludes with a synthesis of themes when Sigbjørn and Primrose return home, carrying their symbolic goldenrod and dogwood, to a single bottle of gin saved from the previous Sunday's drinking session. The sense of alienation cannot be overcome at a stroke and so the drinking will continue, but in a moderation that allows 'a kind of hope [ . . . ] to bloom again'. The association of modern alienation and alcoholic escape is also made in **'Forest Path'** by subverted natural images: the narrator remembers his drinking days when his 'only stars were neon lights' and when he 'must have stumbled into a thousand alcoholic dawns'.

**'Present Estate of Pompeii'** is closely allied to **'Forest Path'**. The tone and symbolic shape of the story are both emphatically prognostic of a collapse of modern civilisation to emulate the destruction of corrupt Pompeii; but, unlike the natural nemesis of Vesuvius, retribution in the modern age will be of human making. This is the point of Fairhaven's reflections on the near disaster at the Eridanus oil refinery, a brooding threat synonymous with menacing Vesuvius which, the Fairhavens learn, gave a large tremor the day before their visit. Signor Salacci, the Fairhavens' guide, takes 'enormous pride' in this 'beeg-a shake', an attitude clearly linked with his prurient interest in the provisions of ancient Pompeii for male sexual gratification. The phallic association provides a symbolic link between sexual corruption and social destruction.

In these three stories, however, though the expanding horizon principle is evident, it is not structurally disruptive. The result is a more conventional (and less arresting) fictional texture.

The element of formal conflict is more pressing in **'Strange Comfort Afforded by the Profession'**, a story explicitly about literary artifice in which the notion of closure is extended to breaking point. Sigbjørn Wilderness, on a quest for his spiritual brethren, supposes himself to be continuing a great literary tradition. The narrative is constructed around the citation of letters and biographical details pertaining to Keats, Shelley, Gogol and Poe; and these are strategically juxtaposed with Wilderness's despairing letter which is the final (and longest) artefact quoted. Wilderness exhibits a continuing uncertainty as to what to make of the literary miscellany, and this is a curiously impassive response to a body of texts testifying to artistic suffering and isolation. The 'relatively pleasurable fit of coughing' which Wilderness experiences at the story's end suggests his role as a modern suffering (tubercular) Keats; but the romantic conception of the suffering artist is dissipated by the ambiguous assessment which Wilderness makes of Poe's letter, and also of his own. The artist is continually evaluating, self-consciously, the public use to be made of private experience; and this is not a mercenary tendency, merely evidence of the continuing need of the writer to define himself in social terms.

**'Through the Panama'**, which takes this impulse to an extreme, represents the *ne plus ultra* of Lowry's experiment with the story form. The metafictional paradigm which informs the collection is recontained within another chinese-box; and this extended self-consciousness—or meta-metafiction—shatters the closed circle of convention by explicitly destroying the narrative artifice which obtains in the other stories. The discourses of author and character in the story, Sigbjørn Wilderness and Martin Trumbaugh, are almost undifferentiated, and these voices are juxtaposed with a split-column layout which begins and ends with annotations taken directly from the marginal text of Coleridge's "Ancient Mariner" but which develops, in a parody of Coleridge's commentary, into a history of the Panama Canal. The 'single effect' doctrine is overtly flouted here.

The artistic self-consciousness is most explicit in the passage about the lock-keepers of ascending power, a model

which directly links the expanding circle motif to the process of fictional composition and which admits the author's own manipulative presence in 'this celestial meccano', operated

> at the touch of that man sitting up in the control tower high above the topmost lock who, by the way, is myself, and who would feel perfectly comfortable if only he did not know that there was yet another man sitting yet higher above him in *his* invisible control tower, who also has a model of the canal locks before him, carefully built, which registers electrically the exact depth of everything *I* do, and who thus is able to see everything that is happening to me at every moment—and worse everything that is *going* to happen.

This fragmentation is really the logical extension of what Lowry does in the other stories; but whereas in **'Elephant and Colosseum'** and **'Forest Path'** meaning is generated by stretching story conventions to a point of resonating tension, here the conventions are shattered by the expanding motif. This is the unforeseen rupturing its fore-seen parameters. Those parameters are still contingent on the story's meaning, however, as a yardstick in the implicit debate on the value of literary composition.

The marriage of formal innovation and thematic content, both governed by the expanding circle principle, has a pervasive bearing on the collection, and this is true even at the level of syntax. Lowry's prose has the occasional tendency to ramble in apparently undisciplined and unwieldy sentences, yet in *Hear Us O Lord* such 'expanding syntax' is often used organically in an effort to unite the disparate threads of the topical content. The following passage from **'Forest Path'** is a good example of this:

> As the mist rolled up towards us, beginning to envelop us, the sun still trying to maintain itself like a platinum disc, it was as if the essence of a kind of music that had forever receded there, that seemed evoked from the comments of my wife as she looked through this window, out on to this porch in the first days when we'd just meant to spend a week, or in the autumn when we still stayed on, while she was making the coffee, talking to herself partly for my benefit, describing the day to me, as if I had been like a blind man recovering his sight to whom she had to teach again the beauties and oddities of the world, as if it became unlocked, began to play, to our inner ear, not music but having the effect of music, not sentimental at all, but fresh and innocent, and only moving because it was so happy, or because happiness is moving; or it was like a whispering of the ghosts of ourselves.

This free-flowing passage elides the story's various themes. Artistic regeneration for the composer (represented here by the healing 'music') is linked to the prerequisite reassessment of personal history—'a whispering of the ghosts of ourselves'—in a passage which also alludes to the first observation of the expanding circles, to the symbolism of natural light as inspiration, and to the narrator's dependence on his wife as a medium. An even longer paragraph of this nature occurs in **'Elephant and Colosseum'**. This passage, too long to quote here, summarises Cosnahan's initial state of moral stasis by conjoining images of social injustice, professional frustration and personal ineffectuality.

The nature of the formal project in **Hear Us O Lord** provides a corrective to the view of Lowry as a writer enervated by self-absorption, a view which the stories seem, superficially, to reinforce. The Lowryan quest which informs the book depends, like its modernist precursors, upon its personal roots; and there is a conviction and consistency in the collection about the need for an impersonal extension of this basis which refutes the 'bewilderment about the potential public meanings of his own type of creativity' which Malcolm Bradbury, articulating a widely held view, has discerned in Lowry. Admittedly, there is no detailed social fabric in **Hear Us O Lord** and its public themes are of a general rather than a specific nature. Yet the extension of the single consciousness (the examination of which the story form invites) into contact with broader areas is an important development in its generic context.

The densely associative narrative style in which the thematic interlinking is conducted precludes any exegetical dismantling which might dilute the richness. Despite this fact there has been a tendency amongst Lowry's critics to extenuate his achievements by installing a scale of relative importance for evaluating the work. [In *Studies in the Novel,* 1972] Richard Hauer Costa has argued that 'Lowry ought not to be taken, except in a secondary way, as a serious conservationist' and that his 'diatribe against the refinery across the bay is a diversionary tactic'. [In *Mosaic,* 1981] R. D. MacDonald has made a similar and, in my view, equally erroneous set of distinctions:

> Lowry's 'involvement' is first with his own (and perhaps mankind's) creative consciousness, second with the union of that consciousness with nature and God, third with the union of an isolated man and woman, and last (and only incidentally) with the *civitas* or the external social world.

In **Hear Us O Lord,** as I have argued, it is impossible to accord differing degrees of importance to the personal or the impersonal, the public or the private, since the ubiquitous expanding circle paradigm insists on their interdependence.

**Elsa Linguanti (essay date 1992)**

SOURCE: "*Hear Us O Lord* and Lowry's Micro/Macro Text," in *Swinging the Maelstrom: New Perspectives on Malcolm Lowry,* edited by Sherrill Grace, McGill-Queens University Press, 1992, pp. 209-19.

*[In the following essay, Linguanti views Lowry's short story collection* Hear Us O Lord *as a macrotext, or as a work of "integrated unity."]*

Like most devoted readers of Lowry I have developed my own opinions about which have to be considered the im-

portant and definitive works among all the many and often mixed-up papers he left when he died. After a few years of work on his published and unpublished works I find that I am ready to consider *Under the Volcano,* a couple of versions of **Lunar Caustic,** and the collection of short stories **Hear us O Lord from heaven thy dwelling place** as *the* bulk of literary production that Lowry has left to his readers, a bulk to which the papers so admirably collected at the Special Collections Division of the library at the University of British Columbia only add an impressive amount of material that makes the reader aware of the tremendous potential the man still had. This does not mean that I think it not worth working on those materials—I am sure that I have not yet finished with **"Ghostkeeper,"** for example, and I would still like to work on the script for *Tender Is the Night.* It only means that the works I have mentioned are not only individual works of interest, success, and beauty, but also that they constitute a macrotext. I leave aside the unprofitable question of what the macrotext would be like if Lowry had completed other works, which he did not, and of how the "case would be altered" by them.

A collection of works can be considered a macrotext when elements belonging to different organizing systems within the individual works—diegetical, structural, formal, ideological, linguistic, semantic, rhetorical, etc.—are so combined in the collection as to produce an integrated unity, and when there is a form of process and progress in the discourse so that every single text can only be where it is and not anywhere else in the succession.

If we start by thinking about **Hear us O Lord,** it is easy to see, . . . that, as Lowry wrote to Giroux, "it is a canon, or roundelay, with everyone taking up his part, dropping out, new voices joining in and dropping out, without beginning or ending." It is also true, as Lowry explained, that the seven stories are "interrelated, correlated . . . but full of effects and dissonances that are impossible in a short story." The movement is like that of a jazz suite and is based on an irregular, not linear, development of the themes, on the repetition of refrains, on occasional improvised a-solos, on self-quotation and self-parody, sonorities and brooding passages, sophisticated harmonies and strutting syncopations. The reader is given a series of clues that key him or her in to some of the codes operating through the collection.

At the beginning and at the end jazz is evoked: in the first "ouverture" story . . . after the strident discord of a loudspeaker "enthroned on a wagon" which "barked from the city," and the sound "as of a wailing and gnashing of teeth" of the sawmills, the Suspension Bridge comes into view as part of a musical score: "the road now mounting towards the Suspension Bridge in the distance much as a piece of jazz music mounts towards a break"—and then: "through whose branches . . . could be made out, from time to time, suggesting a fragment of music manuscript, a bit of the Suspension bridge itself." At the end in **"Forest Path to the Spring,"** of course, the protagonist is a jazz musician and music becomes the all-embracing energy, drive, the model of all movement, transformation, integration, and even the tides and currents in the sea become analogous to music: "not music but having the effect of music," substantiating the protagonist's symphony and the jazz opera he writes.

Between the first and the last story there are more links: the young couple of **"Bravest Boat,"** "laughing and stumbling . . . arm in arm" anticipate the anonymous couple of the final story whom we last see in a similar way: "laughing we stooped down to the stream and drank." The subjects stated at the outset in one voice are taken up again by other voices until striking themes of strongly marked character pervade the entire fabric, entering now in one voice, now in another.

After the softness of **"Bravest Boat,"** **"Through the Panama"** strikes a jarring note, but it does so while at the same time imitating or duplicating, in contrapuntal thinking, the themes presented in the first voice: we have again the voyage of a ship, a man and a wife, the new beginnings at the end ("out of the past finally to safety and a home" and, all around, "a seething of spring" become, by permutation, "dawn, and an albatross, bird of heaven, gliding astern"), and repeated mentions of hell and paradise. Within **"Through the Panama"** the repetition of the phrase "the whole is an assembly of apparently incongruous parts" refers to the ship engaged in the voyage from Vancouver to England through the canal (the ship is French, built by Americans, with a crew of Bretons), to the canal (built by Frenchmen, Englishmen, Americans, and the eight hundred Chinese who, deprived of opium for "moral" reasons, have let themselves die along its banks), to the protagonist, who is a Scot and a Norwegian, who is Wilderness, Trumbaugh, and Firmin, who progressively identifies with a voice, a lock of the canal, and the ship itself. This key phrase, of course, also refers to **"Through the Panama"** as text.

**"Through the Panama"** is a tremendous achievement: nowhere else is the dictum we all believe in today that form is content so perfectly embodied. The text is the voyage as it unfolds, organized but also subject to many unexpected events; it is a diary that is a work-in-progress; it is the novel the man is writing, which is still subject to changes; it is the canal, which is also transformed into fiction by both the historian and the novelist. Also the text parades its texture, the apparently incongruous parts of which it is made slipping past one another: fragments of the "Ancient Mariner," a history book, the two columns unfolding with reciprocal substitution from left to right, the independent lines flowing alongside each other as happens in polyphonic music. But as the ship has a ceinture put around it, so the story is there, and exactly where it is, gliding on, the tortured form still containing it. In following the different planes of movement, the reader becomes aware of the illusion of space which it is the unique capacity of counterpoint to create, and of the tensions brought into being by the simultaneous unfolding of the lines.

The three following stories all take place in Rome, but the protagonists come from and will go back to Eridanus, with

the exception of the protagonist of the central story—the central story of the three and of the collection—Cosnahan, whose topological reference points are the Isle of Man and Nantucket, the first a variant of Eridanus and the second an allusion to Melville.

The first story of the three is an a-solo from an artist away from home; the third is about a man away from home who is feeling ready to go back; in the middle is Cosnahan, completely lost in the maze of the streets of Rome and out of touch with himself. **"Elephant and Colosseum"** is the pivotal story: sheer fun, pure comedy. It is again a virtuoso piece, like **"Through the Panama,"** and it is a self-parody. While *Under the Volcano* produces and exalts contradictions, and is tragic, **"Elephant and Colosseum"** shows that any attempt to reconcile them is comic.

Here again we find the voyage on a ship and the tempest, the artist abroad, the dying-dead mother motif that **"Through the Panama"** had introduced; here the theme that had come to the fore in **"Through the Panama,"** of the artist enmeshed in his own creation, is taken up in a different register in **"Strange Comfort"**—where the artist finds a moment of liberating amusement in his own notes and in the similarity of idiosyncratic attitudes and poses between himself and other artists before him: Cosnahan is enmeshed in himself, has illusions and delusions about himself. At the beginning of the story Cosnahan is sitting with a glass of milk and an expression of "sombre panic" at the bar of the Rupe Tarpea restaurant in Via Vittorio Veneto in Rome; at the end, at sunset of the same day, he is sitting at the same place with a bottle of sparkling wine, and he laughs. All through the afternoon the "lone man" has been talking to himself, trying to rationalize his problems, to unravel perplexities, cogitating in a language slow, well-built, logical, almost Ciceronian. Cosnahan has difficulties of various types: linguistic incompetence; antagonism with the traffic in Rome; inability to write (even the letter to his mother, postponed until it is too late, or the letter to his wife); absent-mindedness (he is in Rome to get in touch with his publisher for a translation of his book into Italian, but has forgotten to bring the contract, has forgotten the publisher's name, remembers their address but has got the wrong city); difficulty in recognizing himself and in making himself be recognized: "Nobody recognized him at home; those dreamed-of moments of recognition; What on earth was he after?; What did he know of himself?; was he a writer?"

The comedy sets in because of the fundamental predicament of Cosnahan, which consists in the contrast between the illusions he has about himself and the reality of life imposed on him: the appearance is that his book is exceptionally successful, for a high-class audience, that he is a successful man and unique; reality shows to him that his book is one among others, that no one knows it or him either, that he is like everybody else. Forms of "serene confidence" and "quiet elation" make him "entranced by himself," give him a sense of "his own extraordinary rarity": "he smiled pleased by his intelligence and felt much better," but very quickly he begins to feel mean.

Cosnahan's predicament is aptly imaged in the "logical crossing" of the Roman streets he cannot face: illusion/reality, rationality/magic (something running in the family) are divarications that he illusorily tries to mediate.

The mental behaviour the text attributes to Cosnahan, counting on the reader's connivance, is quite naïve, and the syntax obviously organizes it: the syntax of Cosnahan's sentences shows a succession of logical connectives: causal (because, since, for), correlative (both . . . and, not only . . . but, not merely . . . but, no sooner . . . but) and comparative (as, so, thus, than), each of which emphatically joins together segments in an apparently faultless organization. What happens, however, is that many segments introduce diversions regardless of their semantic relevance: the irrelevant diversions engender a perception of the dissociation between the devices and contrivances in Cosnahan's reasoning and the pretence of artlessness and straightforwardness of his prose. The reader sees the process as artificial and funny, while the character produces his statements naïvely. The comic effect is not produced by puns or by the tensions that generate irony in the *Volcano* but by the attempt at rationalizing in an innocent unsophisticated way, with the naïveté and the blindness necessary for the comic element to be born. Cosnahan's discourse operates in the absence of any acknowledgment of possible objections and within a syntactic structure that takes for granted that the chosen techniques of argumentation are adequate to reach logical consequences.

Cosnahan's narcissistic axiologies, whose starting point is, in Aristotelian terms, the "locus of quality," give value to the elite over the mass, to the exceptional over the normal: while considering the possibility of being a "unique case," Cosnahan meets the "endless mirrored reduplications" of his figure among all the others in the street, of his novel among all the other novels on the publishers' bookshelves (but his own is actually missing). At the same time, Cosnahan also gives value to the "locus of quantity" because he thinks that to be appreciated by the greatest number is preferable to being known only to a few. Lowry's decision to make Cosnahan meet the elephant Rosemary and be recognized by her, and to make Cosnahan appreciate the value of the meeting and of the anagnorisis that follows on the basis of a causal link starting from magic intuitions, is so overtly and blatantly discordant and incongruous that the text becomes metalanguage of itself in a transparent way. The comic element sets in in such a gentle fashion that it is as if Lowry were showing himself using the incongruous element to his own ends.

The divarications between the "locus of essence" (according superiority to individuals who best represent the essence of genus) and the "locus of existent," between man and nature, the improper hierarchy among the elements that Cosnahan accepts uncritically, are definitely overthrown when humour replaces seriousness: "Naturam expellas pitch-fork, something or other recurret! Throw out nature with a pitch-fork but back she always comes! It was as if God, with that all-wise sense of humour that Cosnahan respected increasingly the longer he remained as a guest upon His earth, had kept Mother Drumgold . . .

up His sleeve." The Latin quotation first mentioned in relation to Cosnahan's mother and her magic powers reappears in the zoo before the elephants' cage. Between tautologies ("Because an elephant, by the way, is an elephant,") and hyperboles ("the marvellous juxtaposition of the grotesque and the sublime,") the text shows Cosnahan preparing to praise the elephant in philosophically constructed sentences:

> And an elephant, as itself, within its own paradisal and thundery being as an elephant, among other elephants . . . had its own elephantine virtues which . . . simply attested . . . to a common divinity. Since must there not have been some principle of goodness and sagaciousness first, existing in the elephants' perceptions, that the elephant was able to recognize too . . . some principle of tolerance, or above all pity, for his captor, who could not help himself, and a certain sense of interest in sportive adventure about whatever he was doing that he recognized as amusing and instructive to his elephantish faculties?

The elephant is proof of God's existence and testimony to God's sense of humour ("his wild wild humour,"); the elephant is endowed with reason, intellectual powers, and a profound sense of humour ("Freedom was of the spirit. So reasoned the elephant . . . with a practiced intellectual swirl of [its] trunk . . . Moreover watch elephants . . . smiling softly to themselves, enjoying at the same time some transcendental joke.") Above all, "an elephant may serve man, or as a spectacle for man, or as a friend of man, but what he really serves is elephant, his higher elephant." Cosnahan is ready to reconsider the quotation about "naturam" when Rosemary suddenly welcomes and hails him by trumpeting: "No preposterous recognition in literature . . . could have been more complete." The anagnorisis, "a meeting in its gently buffoonish manner nearly sublime," enables Cosnahan to disentangle himself from his dilemmas, to discover the inconsistencies of his premise, to see the way his own arguments interact: he feels himself to be "translated—his mother's son at last—into a conscious member of the human race." The syllogism—all men are unique, all men are similar, then their uniqueness consists in their similarity—becomes explicit in the final litany: "But man was Quayne and man was Quaggan, man was Quillish, man was Qualtrough, man was Quirk and Quayle and Looney, and Illiam Dhone, who had been hanged. And yet lived because he was innocent."

According to [Michel] Butor [in *Critique,* December, 1967] every literary work is a parody of the ones that have preceded it. **"Elephant and Colosseum"** is obstreperous, flagrant self-parody of the writer of *Under the Volcano*: the protagonist here mentions a brother and a friend; his wife is an actress. There are also the death of the mother, an obsession with the past and the occult, the cat as Lares (Citron-le-taciturne substituted for the Oedipus, Priapus, etc., of the *Volcano*), and the magic cabbalistic elements, although coincidences that were fiendish in *Volcano* become benevolent here. Self-parody can be identified even in small segments of the text: the "broken pillars among which the grass was green" remind the reader of the "broken pink pillars that might have been waiting to fall down on him"; the "truckloads of Italian soldiers" call up the "boys standing at the back of lorries"; the "discovery of Rosemary . . . bringing back those days of longing for home at sea" echoes the phrase "his passion for Yvonne had brought back to his heart." Because of its position at the centre of the collection, the comic character of **"Elephant and Colosseum"** has momentous consequences for the second half of the book: there will be no more "gnashing of teeth" after it, and a gentle mood will set in.

The repetition of themes distributed among various voices and in different registers safeguards the unity of the work, while the constant transformation supplies the element of variety: **Hear us O Lord** has a horizontal narrative implemented by the devices of augmentation, diminution, inversion, and canonic imitation.

After the two minor pieces of **"Present Estate"** and **"Gin and Goldenrod,"** the form of the canon really sets in with **"Forest Path,"** which is the "triumphant ending" of the collection and "a novella of great seriousness [that] starts gently, so gently." Cosnahan's final choice in favour of the value of the simple human being reappears here even more clearly: the protagonists of the story do not even receive a name. The man is reaching for some meaning that may be grasped subliminally, by means of slow approximation, in a language deliberately clumsy, interspersed with questions, with a subdued discourse scrupulously mimetic of the stages of interiorization. And Cosnahan's nature ("back she always comes") is in the foreground. The writing registers days and nights and seasons as they follow one another, the tempests and the calms, frost and thaw, snow and drizzle and all sorts of weather happenings, real close-ups of illumined surfaces with shafts of pearly colours.

The similes only touch on a series of hieratic-mystic elements: churches, cathedrals, votive lamps (recalling the "alabaster lamp illumined from within" of the dream of the northern paradise in *Volcano*). The naming process concentrates on flowers and colours, stars and constellations, crystals, diamonds, jewels. The habit of repetition, almost obsessive in *Volcano,* is toned down so that the occasional anaphoric repetition becomes all the more meaningful: "I soon learned," "Eventually I realized," "I learned," "We found," "We discovered." The search for meaning, which is the exact centre from which Lowry's writing radiates, meets the gratification of the slow, progressively diminishing resistance of the external world to the consubstantial appropriation of man. Syntax shows a high frequency of co-ordinated sentences that, at short intervals, introduce elements that are included and integrated in the process, as happens in a canon:

At dusk . . . And at dusk . . . And on other days

But apparently . . . But now . . . but we

And then . . . And I thought . . . And then I thought

And we remembered . . . And they seemed . . . And the ships . . . And the snow storms . . . And ourselves

"Less an ordinary book of tales than a sort of novel of an odd aeolian kind itself," **Hear us O Lord** is a kaleidoscope, the same elements reappearing in all the stories in different voices, registers, in contrapuntal form. But it is also an exploration in the process of writing, showing the narrator before the choices he continually has to make in order to give form to his materials: this happens in a dramatic fashion to Wilderness in **"Through the Panama"** and is shown in a metafictional parodic way in **"Elephant and Colosseum,"** while the artist musician of the **"Forest Path"** makes use of fragments stranded on the beach (the canister and the ladder are converted to use), despite his declaration that he "lacked spiritual equipment to follow such thoughts through." As if to prefigure the "odd aeolian" form of **Hear us O Lord,** Lowry had written to James Stern in 1940 that, "the best kind of novel . . . is the shortish one perfect in itself, and without being full of inventories (like Joyce), or poems (like Faulkner), or conjunctions (like Hemingway), or quotations from quotations (like me 7 years ago) . . . a satisfactory work of art by simple process of writing a series of good short stories."

It is true that intertextuality had been one of the main characteristics of the *Volcano* and of the first version of **Lunar Caustic.** Already in the second version of **Lunar Caustic** many references, allusions and quotations from other texts are dropped, and in their place Lowry uses occasional self-quotation: this will become systematic in **Hear us O Lord.**

But for all that there is one text that Lowry cannot stop alluding to: Dante's *Divine Comedy.* A miniature reproduction of *The Voyage That Never Ends,* **Hear us O Lord** follows Dante's stages, stopping on the threshold of earthly paradise. From the "selva selvaggia ad aspra e forte" to the "divina foresta spessa e viva," the journey moves through the hell of **"Through the Panama,"** the purgatory of **"Strange Comfort," "Elephant and Colosseum,"** and **"Present Estate,"** towards paradise in **"Forest Path"**: "it seemed that we were in heaven; there was everywhere an intimation of paradise." **"Bravest Boat"** shows the whole pilgrimage in a diminutive form, while Sigbjørn and Primrose of **"Through the Panama"** are similar to Adam and Eve dismissed from paradise, and Fairhaven, in **"Present Estate,"** suffers from a longing for his lost Eden, which the anonymous protagonist of **"Forest Path"** has regained.

In the same way as in Laruelle's chapter in the *Volcano,* where the reader can follow Dante's steps down to the Malebolge, so in **"Forest Path"** the twenty-seventh canto of the *Purgatorio* is always present behind Lowry's choice of material: as the path seems short and less tiring to Dante as he moves towards his Beatrix, so the path seems shorter to the man as he goes back to his wife; Beatrix is made perfect and immortal, and the man's wife does not change and the passing years do not seem to affect her at all. The woman has a Matelda function in the story, teaching the man, showing him the things he cannot see or understand by himself; the protagonist, seeing his own threatening shadow, which appears to him as a projection of the dark side of his being, recalls Dante's shadow appearing as a gloomy stain in the sunlight of purgatory, a dark and sorry recollection of the world. As Dante bathes in the Lete and Eunoè, so the man at sunrise, in the inlet, is transformed: "suddenly transilluminated by the sun's light, so that I seemed to contain the reflected sun deeply within my very soul, yet a sun which . . . was in turn transformed . . . into something perfectly simple." He becomes consubstantial with the sun and the light in the water of the bay.

The three Lowry works that I consider central (*Volcano, Lunar Caustic,* and the stories) are interrelated, correlated, full of reciprocal effects and dissonances. It is impossible to forget that the dream of a northern paradise in *Volcano* appears in exactly the same terms through *Hear us O Lord,* from the first description in "Bravest Boat" to the nostalgic memories of Wilderness in "Through the Panama" or the vivid presence in "Gin and Goldenrod" and the triumphant, almost word-by-word echoes in "Forest Path." A scene from a Canadian landscape on a calendar set to the future (because it shows the month of December) hangs on the wall in the bedroom of the prostitute in the last chapter of *Volcano,* and even in *Lunar Caustic* there are elements in the description that remind us of "Forest Path."

Also, the macrotext of these three works does show the voyage in its three main stages. If *Volcano* is obviously hell, *Lunar Caustic* is the passage through purgatory, because the man enters the hospital at the beginning—and the door opens with "a dithering crack"—and comes out at the end accompanied by the "roar of the building," which sounds like the earthquake that shakes the purgatorial mountain when a soul is ready to leave it. Plantagenet's predicament could be described as being like Dante's in the *Purgatorio*: "questi non vide mai l'ultima sera / ma per la sua follia le fu si presso / che molto poco tempo a volger era" (1:58-60). From the crowd of patients, two people move towards Plantagenet: in the same way two souls move towards Dante in canto v; Garry and Kalowsky ask Plantagenet to intercede for them ("ombre che pregar pur ch'altri prieghi," VI:26). Like Dante's *Purgatorio, Lunar Caustic* is a passage during which the protagonist cauterizes himself (with silver nitrate).

The whole journey is taken up again in *Hear us O Lord,* which ends in an earthly paradise, but the three stages must not be taken literally because experience is always flowing back on itself and starting all over again. The end of "Forest Path" reverses the order of the stages, once again with a contrapuntal technique: "if someone had charged us with the notion that we had gone to heaven and that this was the after life we would not have said him nay for long. Moreover if we had been charged with formerly having been in hell for a while we would probably have had to say yes too, though adding that on the whole we liked that fine . . . and were sometimes even homesick for it."

The reader, through the experience of the three works mentioned, is enabled to see other shapes taking form in Lowry's macrotext. The associating impulse, the analogical obsession, confines man to a form of indefinite exist-

ence in *Under the Volcano*; everything is like everything else and there is no place from where to start again. Incapable of dominating experience, the Consul clings to reality, while reality is introjected in *Lunar Caustic* and possessed by means of consubstantial appropriation in "Forest Path." The whole function of the negative drive (infernal confusion, chaos, discomposure) in *Under the Volcano* is to focus attention on the extenuation of all cultural codes and the radicalization of all contradictions: the wheel, movement without advancement, is the unstable structure from which multiple meanings hang.

Centred on a state of disequilibrium, *Lunar Caustic* is a characteristically incomplete segment, an iterated attempt at finding a way out of the vicious circle; it does not organize meanings in forms of knowledge but projects them into visions that strategically assail the rigid frontiers of conscience, of rationality. In *Hear us O Lord,* however, tensions and conflicts gather and disperse, and the exalted rejoicing of the last story is so organized as to offer a kind of direction by means of the path to the spring and at the same time make clear that no process is ever ended.

---

## FURTHER READING

### Biography

Bradbrook, M. C. *Malcolm Lowry: His Art & Early Life: A Study in Transformation.* London: Cambridge University Press, 1974, 170 p.

Introductory study interweaving biography and criticism. An appendix reprints two early stories: "A Rainy Night" and "Satan in a Barrel."

### Criticism

Bareham, Tony. *Malcolm Lowry.* New York: St. Martin's Press, 1989, 133 p.

Full-length critical study of Lowry's work.

Benham, David. "Lowry's Purgatory: Versions of *Lunar Caustic,*" in *Malcolm Lowry: The Man and His Work,* edited by George Woodcock, pp. 56-65. Vancouver: University of British Columbia Press, 1971.

Discusses various incarnation's of Lowry's novella.

Corrigan, Matthew. "Malcolm Lowry: The Phenomenology of Failure." *Boundary* 3, No. 2 (Winter 1975): 407-42.

Analyzes Lowry's fiction in terms of vision, failure, and his struggle to create order out of inner chaos.

Costa, Richard Hauer. *Malcolm Lowry.* New York: Twayne Publishers, 1972, 208 p.

Study of Lowry's major fictional themes and the significance of autobiography in his work.

———. "Lowry's Forest Path: Echoes of Walden." *Canadian Literature,* No. 62 (Autumn 1974): 61-8.

Compares and contrasts Thoreau's *Walden* and Lowry's story "The Forest Path to the Spring."

Dahlie, Hallvard. "The New Land and Malcolm Lowry," in *The New Land: Studies in a Literary Theme,* edited by Richard Chadbourne and Hallvard Dahlie, pp. 79-92. Waterloo, Ontario: Wilfred Laurier University Press, 1978.

Asserts that *Hear Us O Lord* reflects "an artistic accomplishment of a very high order, wherein the literal and symbolic properties of the British Columbia setting are exploited to heighten the human dramas being enacted."

Epstein, Perle. "'The Forest Path to the Spring': An Exercise in Contemplation." *The Art of Malcolm Lowry,* edited by Anne Smith, pp. 130-43. London: Vision Press, 1978.

Discusses the spiritual and meditative themes of "The Forest Path."

Grace, Sherrill E. "Malcolm Lowry," in *International Literature in English: Essays on the Major Writers,* edited by Robert L. Ross, pp. 363-70. New York: Garland Publishing, 1991.

Views *Hear Us O Lord* as an integral part of Lowry's artistic voyage.

Harrison, Keith. "Malcolm Lowry's *Hear Us O Lord*: Visions and Revisions of the Past." *Studies in Canadian Literature* 6, No. 1 (1981): 245-55.

Explores the significance of the past as a recurring theme in *Hear Us O Lord.*

———. "Lowry's Allusions to Melville in *Lunar Caustic.*" *Canadian Literature,* No. 94 (Autumn 1982): 1180-84.

Traces references to Herman Melville's fiction, such as *Billy Budd* and *Moby Dick,* in *Lunar Caustic.*

Kilgallin, Tony. "Lowry Posthumous." *Canadian Literature* 39 (Winter 1969): 80-3.

Offers a favorable review of *Lunar Caustic.*

MacDonald, R. D. "Canada in Lowry's Fiction." *Mosaic* 14, No. 2 (Spring 1981): 35-53.

Concludes that Canadian settings in Lowry's work exist "only to reflect the spiritual growth of his fictional personae."

McCarthy, Patrick A. "Apparently Incongruous Parts: *Hear Us O Lord from Heaven Thy Dwelling Place,*" in *Forests of Symbols: World, Text, and Self in Malcolm Lowry's Fiction,* pp. 176-208. Athens: University of Georgia Press, 1994.

Analyzes the themes, characters, and symbolism in the stories of *Hear Us O Lord.*

Miller, David. "Lunar Caustic," in *Malcolm Lowry and The Voyage That Never Ends,* pp. 31-6. London: Enitharmon Press, 1976.

Discusses the novella *Lunar Caustic* within the context of Lowry's trilogy, *The Voyage That Never Ends.*

New, W. H. "A Note on Romantic Allusions in *Hear Us O Lord.*" *Studies in Canadian Literature* 1 (Winter 1976): 130-36.

Explores the influence of the English Romantic poets on the stories of *Hear Us O Lord.*

Smith, Anne, ed. *The Art of Malcolm Lowry.* London: Vision Press, 1978, 173 p.

Collection of essays on Lowry's life and work.

**Additional coverage of Lowry's life and career is contained in the following sources published by The Gale Group:** *Contemporary Authors,* **Vols. 105, 131;** *Contemporary Authors New Revision Series,* **Vol. 62;** *Concise Dictionary of British Literary Biography, 1945-1960;* *Dictionary of Literary Biography,* **Vol. 15;** *Major 20th-Century Writers;* **and** *Twentieth Century Literary Criticism,* **Vols. 6, 40.**

# Boris Pasternak
## 1890-1960

(Full name Boris Leonidovich Pasternak) Russian poet, novelist, short story writer, essayist, memoirist, playwright, and nonfiction writer.

## INTRODUCTION

Awarded the 1958 Nobel Prize in literature, which he declined under pressure from the Soviet government, Pasternak is best known as the author of *Il dottor Zivago* (1957; *Doctor Zhivago*). An epic portrait of the Russian Revolution and its consequences, *Doctor Zhivago* ignited a political and artistic controversy that continues to overshadow Pasternak's achievements in other genres. Nevertheless, among scholars, he is critically regarded as one of the foremost poets of the twentieth century. His short fiction, though even less known than his other works, is considered stylistically and thematically unified, as well as closely linked to his work as a poet and novelist.

## Biographical Information

Pasternak was raised in a home where the arts were of prime concern. He was the son of a concert pianist and an acclaimed artist, and friends of his parents included Russian novelist Leo Tolstoy, Russian composer Aleksandr Scriabin, and German poet Rainer Maria Rilke. Influenced by Scriabin, Pasternak first studied music while in his early teens, but later studied philosophy at Marburg University in Germany. Abandoning his studies there in 1912, when childhood friend Ida Vysotskaia rejected his marriage proposal, Pasternak chose to study poetry exclusively. He joined Centrifuge, a group of innovative writers associated with the Futurist school who rejected the literary conventions of the nineteenth century and stressed the importance of poetic freedom and the realities of modern life. It was during this time that Pasternak published his first works of verse. Partially lamed by a childhood riding accident, Pasternak was declared unfit for military service, and spent the first years of World War I in the Ural Mountains as a clerical worker. He traveled to Moscow when he gained word of the Bolshevik Revolution, but soon retired to his family homestead in the surrounding countryside. There he wrote his celebrated poetry collection *Sestra moia zhizn* (1923; *My Sister, Life*). In 1923 Pasternak joined the Left Front of Art, an alliance between Futurist writers and the Communist party that used literary innovations to glorify the new social order. With time, however, Pasternak grew disillusioned with the government's increasing social and artistic restrictions, and broke away from the group in 1930. He divorced his first wife, Evgeniya Lurie, the next year, partly due to his affair with Zinaida Neigauz, whom he eventually married. Because of his literary achievements, Pasternak was invited to play a large role in the

newly formed Soviet Writer's Union, a government institution that abolished independent literary groups and promoted conformity to the precepts of social realism in the 1930s. Disturbed by Russian leader Josef Stalin's repressive policies, however, Pasternak withdrew from public life and began focusing his creative energies on his work as a translator, subsequently rendering Johann Wolfgang von Goethe's *Faust* and Shakespeare's major tragedies into Russian. During World War II, he took advantage of the government's relaxed attitude toward literature by publishing several volumes of verse, and despite his criticisms of the government, Pasternak was left untouched in the period following the war, a time during which the arts were subject to numerous restrictions and many artists were imprisoned. In 1958, following the publication of *Doctor Zhivago*, Pasternak was awarded the Nobel Prize in literature. He declined the award because of pressure from the Soviet government. Noting that the book was published in the West, one Communist party member characterized Pasternak as a "literary whore" in the employ of Western authorities, Pasternak was subsequently expelled from the Soviet Writer's Union. When he died, though the Soviet government continued to deny Pasternak the benefits accorded a literary figure of his stature, thousands of mourners accompanied his family to the grave site, which remains a place of pilgrimage today.

## Major Works of Short Fiction

Pasternak is primarily known for five pieces of short short fiction: "The Mark of Apelles," "Letters from Tula," *Povest* (1934; *A Tale*), "Detstvo Luvers" (1919) and "Aerial Ways." The first three stories all focus on artists. For example, "The Mark of Apelles," which is often considered Pasternak's earliest work in the short story genre, focuses on a rivalry that exists between two poets. Set in Italy, the tale, which is often transliterated as "The Sign of Apelles" and "The Line of Apelles," is partly an updated retelling of an ancient Greek myth about a rivalry between Greek artists Zeuxis and Apelles. In Pasternak's version about artistic identity and the relationship between art, artifice, and reality, the rivalry between his protagonists—poets—extends into their daily lives and climaxes with one poet seducing the other's mistress. The seducing poet's artifice, however, is confounded when he is engulfed with true passion for his rival's paramour. "Letters from Tula" is an epistolary tale largely concerned with a poet visiting the Urals and the group of Russian actors he watches preparing to make a historical film about Russia. They are also observed by an older actor, who upon returning to his home, re-enacts—in private—events from his past. According to some critics, the poet and the older actor are the same person. This story is considered a commentary on the nature of the true artist: one who needs only inspiration, and not an audience, to create. *A Tale,* which is also known as *The Narrative, The Story* and *The Last Summer,* similarly focuses on writers. In this piece, in which time is severely convoluted, a writer and tutor is visiting with his sister and is found, at times, reminiscing about his past. Eventually, he begins to compose a tale about a well-intentioned poet who attempts to auction off his artistic services to the highest bidder, a decision that ultimately brings only ruin and misery. Another lesser known tale, "The History of a Contraoctave," also focuses on an artist—an organist—who is responsible for his child's death. "Detstvo Luvers" is often considered Pasternak's best short story, and although its young Russian protagonist, Zhenya Luvers, is neither poet nor artist, she is often said to possess an artistic sensibility and outlook. Also known as "The Adolescence of Zhenya Luvers," "The Childhood of Luvers," and "Zhenia's Childhood," this unconventional *Bildungsroman* portrays Zhenya's growing awareness of the world around her and her changing body. For her, education is not solely gained through the active perusal of books, but often passively through sights, experiences, epiphanies, and the maturation process. The story is also said to focus on the protagonist's growing understanding of Christian morality. "Aerial Ways" is, for the most part, the only one of Pasternak's major short stories to deal with Russian politics. At the beginning of this story, a woman seeks out the help of a former lover when her child becomes lost. The story resumes, years later, when the lover has become a government official. At this time, he is petitioned by his former paramour to save the child, now a young man, who has since been charged with political crimes and is awaiting execution. Another piece of short fiction is "Without Love," which is largely a character sketch comparing an idealist and a revolutionary.

## Critical Reception

Although Pasternak remains relatively unknown to the general public for his short fiction, critics often note that there is a distinct link between Pasternak's short prose and his better known works, namely his poetry and *Doctor Zhivago.* For example, many of Pasternak's short fragments were originally intended to be parts of novels. Additionally, the character of Zhenya Luvers is often considered a forerunner of Lara, the female protagonist of *Doctor Zhivago,* and other characters, including the government official in "Aerial Ways," are also often viewed as early incarnations of characters found in Pasternak's epic masterpiece. Furthermore, commentators note that throughout all of Pasternak's short fiction there is a focus on artists, poets, the artistic sensibility, the role of the artist in contemporary society, and the relationship between suffering and art, elements that are key to all of his writing. In a highly favorable passage summarizing Pasternak's abilities as a writer of short fiction, J. W. Dyck stated: "Vague associations, visions, metamorphic powers that animate objects and nature, unexpected paradoxes and ambiguities, mixture of facts and poetry, interaction of past and future, and dangerous elements in his characters—all are characteristics of a prose which attempts to say what could not be said in poetry. It is a prose which tries to express the unspeakable: torment, joy, wildest desires of the flesh and deepest meditations of the eternal soul, most private and sacred contemplations about man's relationship to the divine and, on the other hand, efforts towards generalizations and the formulation of philosophical theories. Pasternak's prose, written out of 'almost intolerable necessity,' in a well-marked poetic epoch, unlocks new approaches and new vistas for poets and writers of generations to come." Scholar and translator Robert Payne has likewise asserted: "Writing at a time of war and revolution, during a period when the full flood of his poetry was at its height, [Pasternak] was attempting to set down his most secret thoughts, his wildest desires, his deepest philosophical theories. These stories are weighted with significance. Pasternak makes no attempt to come to terms with the accepted method of telling stories: he tells them in his own way, in a startling mixture of fact and poetry. At any moment his stories will involve unexpected paradoxes and ambiguities, sleights of hand, sudden descents into the inferno and equally sudden ascents in the upper air. We never know, when the anchor is dropped, whether the ship will sink to the bottom of the sea or take flight with its sails outspread."

---

## PRINCIPAL WORKS

### Short Fiction

*"Detstvo Luvers" ["Childhood"; also published as "The Adolescence of Zenya Luvers"] 1919

*Rasskazy*  1925
*Povest* [*A Tale*; also known as *The Story* and *The Last Summer*] (novella)  1934

**Other Major Works**

*Blitzhets tuchakh*  (poetry)  1914
*Poverkh bareov*  (poetry)  1917
*Sestra moia zhizn: Leto 1917 goda* [*My Sister, Life: Summer 1917*] (poetry)  1923
*Temi i variatsi*  (poetry)  1923
*Vysockaya bolezn*  (poetry)  1924
**Deviatsot piatyi god* [*The Year Nineteen-Five*] (poetry)  1926
*Spektorsky*  (poetry)  1926
**Leitenant Shmidt*  (poetry)  1927
*Okhrannaya gramota*  (autobiographical nonfiction)  1931
*Vtoroye rozhdenie*  (poetry)  1932
*Poemy*  (poetry)  1933
*Stikhotvoreniia v odnom tome*  (poetry)  1933
*Stikhotvoreniia*  (poetry)  1936
*Na rannikh poezdakh*  (poetry)  1943
*Zemnoy proster*  (poetry)  1945
*Il dottor Zivago* [*Doctor Zhivago*; first published in Russian as *Doktor Zivago*] (novel)  1957
*I Remember: Sketch for an Autobiography* (memoirs)  1959
*Kogda razgulyayetsya* [*Poems, 1955-1959*] (poetry)  1959
*Sochineniya*  (collected works)  1961
*Lettere agli amici georgiani* [*Letters to Georgian Friends*] (letters)  1967
*Slepaia krasavista* [*The Blind Beauty*] (drama)  1969
*The Collected Prose Works of Boris Pasternak* (prose)  1977
*Boris Pasternak: Perepiska s Ol'goi Friedenberg* [*The Correspondence of Boris Pasternak and Olga Friedenberg, 1910-1954*] (letters)  1981
*Letters, Summer 1926* (prose)  1985

*Translated and published in *The Collected Prose Works of Boris Pasternak, 1977.*

**Published together as *Deviatsot piatyi god* in 1927.

---

# CRITICISM

## Roman Jakobson (essay date 1935)

SOURCE: "Marginal Notes on the Prose of the Poet Pasternak," in *Language in Literature,* The Belknap Press of Harvard University Press, 1987, pp. 301-17.

[*In the essay below, which was originally published in German in 1935, Jakobson delineates how Pasternak's poetic disposition affected his prose works, lending insight into Pasternak's short fiction. Jakobson concludes, "Pasternak's prose is the characteristic prose of a poet in a great age of poetry."*]

Textbook categories are comfortingly simple: prose is one thing, poetry another. Nevertheless, the difference between a poet's prose and that of a prose writer, or between the poems of a prose writer and those of a poet, is very striking. A mountaineer walking in the plains can find no foothold and stumbles over the level ground. He moves either with touching awkwardness or with overemphatic artistry; in either case it is not his natural gait, but involves obvious effort and looks too much like the steps of a dancer. It is easy to distinguish a language that has been learnt, however perfect its command, from one that has been naturally acquired. Cases of complete bilingualism are, of course, undeniable, and when we read the prose of Puškin or Mácha, of Lermontov or Heine, of Pasternak or Mallarmé, we cannot help being amazed at the command these writers have of the other language; but at the same time we are bound to pick out a foreign note, as it were, in the accent and inner form of their speech. Their achievements in this second language are brilliant sallies from the mountains of poetry into the plains of prose.

It is not only a poet's prose that has a particular stamp; there is also the prose peculiar to an age of poetry, the prose of a literary current oriented towards poetry, as distinct from those literary epochs and schools that are prose-oriented. The major achievements of Russian literature in the first decades of our century belong to poetry; it is poetry that is felt to be the pure canonical voice of literature, its perfect incarnation. Both Symbolism and the later literary fermentation often summed up under the heading of "Futurism" are almost exclusively represented by poets, and if many of these occasionally try an excursion into prose, it is a conscious deviation, an experimental digression by a virtuoso of verse. With but a few exceptions the standard literary prose of this period is a typical epigone product, a more or less successful reproduction of classic models: the interest of this hackwork lies either in its successful imitation of the old or in its grotesque brutalisation of the canon, or else its novelty consists in cunningly adapting new themes to traditional forms. In contrast to the great internal tension of the poetry of the time, this prose can claim to be distinguished only in the first place because Gogol' and after him Tolstoj have lifted the qualitative norm to such a high level, and in the second place because the requirements of modern reality are themselves so exacting. In the history of artistic prose this hundredth province of Russian classic realism has little evolutionary significance, whereas the prose of Brjusov, Belyj, Xlebnikov, Majakovskij and Pasternak—that remarkable colony of modern poets—opens up hidden paths to a revival of Russian prose. In the same way the prose of Puškin and Lermontov heralded the approach of the great festival of prose that was opened by Gogol'. Pasternak's prose is the characteristic prose of a poet in a great age of poetry.

The prose of a writer in a literary movement primarily concerned with poetry is very clearly defined both in those places where it is influenced by the dominant, that is, the poetic, element, and in those where it breaks free from that influence by an intense and conscious effort. No less essential is the general context of literary activity, its role in the whole concert of the arts. The hierarchy of artistic values changes for individual artists and artistic movements: for Classicism it is the plastic arts, for Romanticism music, and for Realism literature that is the highest, the most extreme and exemplary, expression of art possible. Romantic verse is required to sing and to merge into music; in the age of Realism, on the contrary, music—in musical drama and in program music—seeks to ally itself with literature. The Romantic's slogan of art gravitating toward music was adopted to a significant degree by Symbolism. The foundations of Symbolism first begin to be undermined in painting, and in the early days of Futurist art it is painting that holds the dominant positions. And then, as plastic art is stripped of its emblematic character, poetry becomes the model of artistic innovation. A tendency to identify art with poetry is manifested by all the poets of the Futurist generation. "Art as a whole, in other words—poetry," says Pasternak. But the origin of this hierarchy of values differs from poet to poet; different paths lead them to poetry, and they start from different points. Pasternak, a convinced pupil of "the art of Scrjabin, Blok, Kommissar evskaja and Belyj," that is, of the Symbolist school, comes to poetry from music, to which he is connected by a cult relationship characteristic of the Symbolists. Majakovskij's springboard to poetry is painting. For all the variety of the artistic tasks that Xlebnikov sets himself, the written word is his sole and unchanging material. We could say that, in the development of Russian post-Symbolist poetry, Majakovskij embodies the "Storm and Stress," Xlebnikov provides its most characteristic and remarkable achievement, while Pasternak's work is, as it were, the link between Symbolism and the school that follows it. And granted that Xlebnikov reached poetic maturity earlier than Majakovskij, and Majakovskij earlier than Pasternak, nonetheless it can be said that when the reader whose starting point is Symbolism comes to tackle Pasternak, he will inevitably stumble over Majakovskij and finally, after overcoming the latter, be faced with laying a long siege to the strongholds of Xlebnikov. However, any attempt to see writers of one and the same period as individual links in a chain of uniform literary development, and to establish the sequence of these links, is always conventionally one-sided. While in certain respects the individual poet continues a tradition, in many others he breaks away from it all the more decisively; the tradition is likewise never entirely negated; the elements of negation always appear only in conjunction with persisting traditional elements. Thus Pasternak, who conceives as his literary task the continuing of Symbolist tradition, is aware that out of his efforts to recreate and perpetuate the old a new art is always arising. The imitations turn out to be "more swift and fervent" than the model, and this quantitative difference evolves naturally into a qualitative one. According to the poet's own self-observation, "the new came into being not as a substitute for the old . . . on the contrary, it arose as an enraptured reproduction of the existing model." By contrast, Majakovskij is consciously out to abolish the old poetry: nevertheless Pasternak, with his acute awareness of Symbolism, senses in Majakovskij's "romantic manner," and the sense of life underlying it, the condensed heritage of the very school of poetry that the aggressive Futurist repudiates. What then is at issue? Pasternak's and Majakovskij's innovations are just as partial as is their connection with the literary past. Suppose we imagine two related languages which differ not only in their neol-

ogisms but also in their original vocabulary: what the one has retained from the common source, the other has often rejected, and vice versa. These two languages are the poetic worlds of Majakovskij and Pasternak respectively, while the common linguistic source is the poetic system of Symbolism. The theme of the remarks that follow is that unusual element in Pasternak's work which sets him apart from his predecessors, which is in part alien and in part strikingly akin to his contemporaries, and which is most clearly to be seen in the telltale awkwardness of his prose.

I

The textbooks confidently draw a firm line between lyric and epic poetry. If we reduce the question to a simple grammatical formula, we can say that the point of departure and the main theme are, for the lyric, invariably the first person of the present tense; for the epic, the third person of the past tense. Whatever subject matter the lyric narrative may have, it is never more than an appendage and accessory, a mere background to the first person; and if the past is involved, then the lyric past always presupposes a reminiscing first-person subject. In the epic, on the contrary, the present refers expressly back to the past, and if the "I" of the narrator does find expression, it is solely as one of the characters in the action. This objectified "I" thus appears as a variant of the third person; the poet is, as it were, looking at himself from outside. So that the first person may be emphasized as the point of reception but that point never fuses with the main subject of the epic poem itself; in other words, the poet as "subject of the lyric that looks at the world through the first person" is profoundly alien to the epic.

Russian Symbolism is lyrical through and through; its excursions into the epic vein are typical attempts by lyric poets to masquerade as poets of epic. In post-Symbolist poetry the two genres diverge: while the persisting lyric strain clearly predominates, reaching its most extreme expression in the work of Majakovskij, the purely epic element finds an outlet, too, in the quite unparalleled poetry and prose of Xlebnikov. Pasternak's work is emphatically lyrical; his prose, especially, is the characteristic prose of a lyric poet, nor are his historical poems essentially different from his cycles of intimate lyric poetry.

Pasternak confesses that Xlebnikov's achievements are even now largely inaccessible to him and justifies himself with the declaration: "poetry in my view merges in history and in collaboration with real life." This reproach, with its implication that he had torn himself away from real life, would certainly have astonished Xlebnikov; for he had regarded his work as an affirmation of reality, unlike the negative literature of the preceding generations. Xlebnikov's symbolic world is so fully realized that for him every symbol, every created word, is endowed with a complete independent reality, and the question of its relations to any external object, indeed the very question of the existence of such an object, becomes entirely superfluous. For Xlebnikov, as for the little heroine in Pasternak's story, a name possesses the complete and comforting significance it has in childhood:

She could not possibly define what was happening on the other shore, far, far away: it had no name, no distinct colour or precise outlines. . . . Ženya began to cry. . . . Her father's explanation was brief: 'It's *Motovilixa.'* . . . The little girl did not understand at all and, satisfied, swallowed a falling tear. For that was all that she needed: to know the name of the incomprehensible—*Motovilixa.*

When Ženya had grown out of childhood she was struck for the first time by the suspicion that there was something which appearances concealed or else revealed only to the elect. This attitude of childhood towards appearances corresponds perfectly to Pasternak's own. An epic attitude to his environment is naturally out of the question for a poet who is convinced that, in the world of prosaic fact, the elements of everyday existence fall dully, stupidly and with crippling effect upon the soul and "sink to the bottom, real, hardened and cold, like drowsy tin spoons," and that only the passion of the elect can transform this "depressingly conscientious truth" into poetry. Only feeling proves to be obviously and absolutely authentic. "Compared with this even the sunrise took on the character of urban rumor still needing to be verified." Pasternak bases his poetics on the personal, emotional experience—indeed appropriation—of reality. "In this form the events did not belong to me," and so on. Both his adjustment of the language of poetry to the purely expressive language of music, and the fact that this conception is based on the triumphing of passion, with its animating power, over the inevitable, show Pasternak to be continuing the romantic line of Symbolism; but as his work matures and attains individuality, so his initially romantic language of the emotions evolves gradually into a language about the emotions, and it is in his prose that this descriptive character finds its most extreme expression.

## II

Whereas, despite the obvious echoes of Xlebnikov in Pasternak's work, these two poets are clearly distinguishable from each other, it is far more difficult to draw a line between Pasternak and Majakovskij. Both are lyric poets of the same generation, and Majakovskij, more than any other poet, deeply affected Pasternak in his youth and constantly won his admiration. A careful comparison of the respective tissue of metaphors of the two poets at once reveals remarkable similarities. "I was related to Majakovskij by the age and by common influences; certain things coincided in us," observes Pasternak. The metaphorical structure of Pasternak's poems reveals, too, direct traces of his enthusiasm for the author of "A Cloud in Trousers." In comparing the two poets' metaphors we must bear in mind that these have a quite different role to play in the work of each poet. In Majakovskij's poems the metaphor, sharpened by the tradition of Symbolism, is not only the most characteristic but also the most essential poetic trope, determining the structure and development of the lyric theme. In Pasternak's pertinent phrase, poetry here began "to speak in the language of sectarian parables." To define the problem: the poet's absolute commitment to metaphor is known; what remains to be determined is the

thematic structure of his poetry. The lyrical impulse is, as we have said, provided by the poet's own self. Images of the external world in the metaphorical lyric are made to harmonize with this impulse, to shift it into different levels, to establish a network of correspondences and masterful assimilations amidst the diverse aspects of the cosmos, to merge the lyric hero into the multifariousness of Being and to dissolve the manifold planes of Being in the lyric hero. Metaphor works through creative association by similarity and contrast. The hero is confronted by the antithetical image of what is mortally inimical to him, protean like all the ingredients of a primarily metaphorical lyric poetry. Such poetry inevitably culminates in the theme of the hero's duel to the death. Held together by a firm and taut chain of metaphors, the heroic lyric fuses the poet's mythology and his being into an inseparable whole, and he, as Pasternak has perfectly understood, pays for its all-embracing symbolism with his life. In this way we have deduced from the semantic structure of Majakovskij's poetry both its actual libretto and the core of the poet's biography.

However rich and refined Pasternak's metaphors may be, they are not what determines and guides his lyric theme. It is the metonymical, not the metaphorical, passages that lend his work an "expression far from common." Pasternak's lyricism, both in poetry and in prose, is imbued with metonymy; in other words, it is association by contiguity that predominates. By comparison with Majakovskij's poetry, the first person is thrust into the background. But it is only an apparent relegation—here too the eternal hero of the lyric is present. It is merely a case of his being metonymically presented; in the same way, no railway train can be seen in Chaplin's *A Woman of Paris,* but we are aware of its arrival from the reactions of the people in front of the cameras—as if the invisible, transparent train were making its way between the screen and the audience. Similarly, in Pasternak's poetry, images of the surrounding world function as contiguous reflections, or metonymical expressions, of the poet's self. Now and then the author reveals his poetics clearly, but he egocentrically applies them to art in general. He does not believe that it is possible for art to adopt a truly epic attitude to the outside world; he is convinced that genuine works of art, while relating all sorts of things, are really telling of their own birth. "Reality arises in a kind of new category. This category seems to us to be its own condition, and not ours . . . We try to name it. The result is art." Thus Constantinople seemed to the pilgrim from old Russia to be an insatiable city because he never got tired of looking at it. It is the same with Pasternak's poems and, in particular, with his prose, where the anthropomorphism of the inanimate world emerges much more clearly: instead of the hero it is, as often as not, the surrounding objects that are thrown into turmoil; the immovable outlines of roofs grow inquisitive, a door swings shut with a silent reproach, the joy of a family reconciliation is expressed by a growing warmth, zeal and devotion on the part of the lamps, and when the poet is turned away by the girl he loves he finds that "the mountain had grown taller and thinner, the town was become lean and black." We have deliberately given simple examples; there is a wealth of much more involved imagery of this sort in Pasternak's work. The substitution of an adjacent object is the simplest form of association by contiguity. The poet has other metonymical devices as well; he can proceed from the whole to the part and vice versa, from the cause to the effect and vice versa, from spatial relations to temporal ones and vice versa, etc., etc. But perhaps what is most characteristic of Pasternak is his using an action instead of an actor, a man's condition, or one of his remarks or attributes, rather than the man himself, and the consequent separating off and objectifying of these abstractions. The philosopher Brentano, who steadfastly fought against the logically illegitimate objectification of such fictions based in language, would have discovered in Pasternak's poetry and prose a most abundant collection of such alleged *entia,* treated as creatures of flesh and blood. *Sestra moja—žizn'* (My Sister Life), the really untranslatable title and leitmotif of Pasternak's most relevant collection of poems ("life" is feminine in Russian), graphically exposes the linguistic roots of this mythology. This same being repeatedly appears in his prose too.

> Life lets very few people know what it is doing with them. It loves its job too much and while at work it speaks at most with those who wish it success and who love its workbench.

In *Safe Conduct* it reappears in a more complex metonymical setting:

> Suddenly I imagined, outside beneath the window, his life, which now belonged entirely to the past. It moved sideways away from the window in the form of some quiet street, bordered with trees . . . And the first to stand upon it, right beside the wall, was our State, our unprecedented, impossible State, rushing headlong into the ages and accepted among them for ever. It stood there below, and one could call to it and take it by the hand.

Pasternak's poetry is a realm of metonymies awakened to independent life. The footsteps of the tired hero, themselves longing for sleep as he is, continue to live and move behind him. On his steep path the poet's vision gently beats: "I am the vision." In his reminiscences the author relates how

> I often heard the whistling of a nostalgia that had not originated with me. Catching up with me from the rear, it frightened me and made me feel pity . . . My silence was travelling with me, I was attached to its person for the journey, and wore its uniform, a uniform familiar to everyone from his own experience.

The sound uttered by an object assumes the latter's function:

> Somewhere nearby . . . a herd . . . was making music. . . . The music was sucked in by blue-bottles. Its skin was rippling to and fro spasmodically and surely.

Action and actor are objects in the same degree:

> Two rare diamonds were playing separately and independently in the deep nests of this half-dark bliss.

As an abstraction becomes objectified, it is overlaid with material accessories:

> Those were aerial ways, on which, like trains, the rectilinear thoughts of Liebknecht, Lenin and the few minds of their flight departed daily.

An abstraction is personified even at the cost of a catachresis:

> Midday quiet reigned. It communed with the quiet that was spread out below in the plain.

An abstraction becomes capable of independent actions, and these actions are objectified in their turn:

> Lacquered sounds of giggling from a disintegrating order of life winked at each other in the quiet.

Majakovskij, who had a predilection for continually surmounting obstacles, toyed for years with the thought of writing a novel. He even had ideas for a title—first *Two Sisters,* then *A Dozen Women.* It is no accident that the project was always postponed: Majakovskij's element is either the lyrical monologue or the dramatic dialogue; descriptive presentation is profoundly foreign to him, and he substitutes second-person for third-person themes. Everything that is not inseparably attached to the poet's self is felt by Majakovskij to be opposed and hostile to him, and he confronts his opponent face to face—challenges him to single combat, exposes, condemns, mocks and outlaws him. It is not surprising that the only undertaking he completed in the field of literary prose was the series of splendid stage plays written in the last years of his life. There is just as firm a logic about the path that Pasternak took toward narrative prose. There exist poems which are woven through and through with metonymies, while narrative prose may be studded with metaphors (a striking example is Belyj's prose), but in the main there is an undeniably closer relationship on the one hand between verse and metaphor, on the other between prose and metonymy. Verse relies upon association by similarity; the rhythmical similarity of the lines is an essential requirement for its reception, and this rhythmical parallelism is most strongly felt when it is accompanied by a similarity (or contrast) of images. An intentionally striking division into similar sections is foreign to prose. The basic impulse of narrative prose is association by contiguity, and the narrative moves from one object to an adjacent one on paths of space and time or of causality; to move from the whole to the part and vice versa is only a particular instance of this process. The more the prose is stripped of material content, the greater the independence achieved by these associations. For metaphor the line of least resistance is verse, and for metonymy it is a prose whose subject matter is either subdued or eliminated (Pasternak's short stories are an example of the first alternative, and his *Safe Conduct* of the second).

### III

The essence of poetic figures of speech does not simply lie in their recording the manifold relationships between things, but also in the way they dislocate familiar relationships. The more strained the role of the metaphor in a given poetic structure, that much the more decisively are traditional categories overthrown; things are arranged anew in the light of newly introduced generic signs. Accordingly, the creative (or, as the foes of such novelty will say, the forced) metonymy changes the accustomed order of things. Association by contiguity, which in Pasternak's work becomes the artist's flexible tool, transforms spatial distribution and temporal succession. This emerges particularly clearly from the poet's prose ventures, outlined as it is against the background of a prose that seeks to communicate in the customary way. Pasternak grounds this dislocation in emotion, or else, if one's starting point is the expressive function of literature, he uses this dislocation to help express the emotions.

A poetic world governed by metonymy blurs the outline of things, as April, in Pasternak's story **"The Childhood of Luvers,"** blurs the distinction between house and yard; similarly it turns two different aspects of one and the same object into independent objects, like the children in the same story who think that a street seen first from inside the house and then from outside it is two different streets. These two characteristic features—the mutual penetration of objects (the realization of metonymy in the strict sense of the word) and their decomposition (the realization of synecdoche)—bring Pasternak's work close to the endeavors of Cubist painters. The dimensions of things change:

> The gondola was, womanlike, gigantic, as everything is gigantic which is perfect in form and incommensurable with the place taken up by its body in space.

The distances between things change so that it becomes certain that a conversation about strangers has to be warmer than a conversation about kindred; and the vision of cosmic movement in the first part of *Safe Conduct* transforms inanimate objects into a distant, motionless horizon. A striking example of how settings are transformed:

> The lamps only accentuated the emptiness of the evening air. They did not give light, but swelled from within, like sick fruits, from the turbid and bright dropsy that puffed up their bloated shades. . . . The lamps came much less in contact with the rooms than with the spring sky which they seemed to be pushed close up to.

Pasternak himself compares, in passing, his dislocated space with the space of Gogol's eschatology: "suddenly it became possible to see far into the distance in all directions." Spatial relations are mingled with temporal ones, and the time sequence loses its strict regularity—objects "are jolted again and again from the past into the future, and from the future into the past, like sand in a frequently shaken hourglass." Any contiguity can be construed as a causal series. Pasternak is impressed by the terminology of the child who grasps the meaning of a sentence from the situation and says, "I did not understand it from the words but from the reason." The poet tends to identify the situation with the reason; he consciously prefers "the vicissitudes of guesswork to the eloquence of fact"; he proclaims that "time is permeated with the unity of a life's events," and builds bridges between them on just those prelogical "ridiculous grounds" which he openly opposes to the syllogisms of "adults." Thus it is no surprise when the chatter of Cohen's companions proves to be "uneven on account of the steplike construction of the Marburg pavements," and when the poet's numerous "therefores" not infrequently introduce clauses whose causal nature is a pure fiction.

The wider the range of the poetic figure of speech, the more thoroughly, to use Pasternak's language, "the accomplished" extinguishes "the subject of the accomplishment." A connection that has been created overshadows one that is still to be made, and governs it; "the fascination of autonomous meaning" takes on prominence, whilst material connectedness is subdued, sometimes to a mere glimmer. In this sense the metonymical connections which Pasternak establishes, no less than Majakovskij's metaphorical connections or the manifold ways of condensing speech—both internal and external—in the poetry of Xlebnikov, show a persistent tendency to dispense with the object, a tendency also characteristic of the other art forms of the period. A connection once created becomes an object in its own right. Pasternak does not tire of underlining the inessential, random nature of the thing to be connected:

> Each detail can be replaced by another . . . Any one of them, chosen at random, will serve to bear witness to the transposed condition by which the whole of reality has been seized . . . The parts of reality are mutually indifferent.

The poet defines art as the mutual interchangeability of images. Any images one cares to choose harbor more than similarity alone, and can consequently be mutual metaphors ("what cannot the sky be compared with?")—all images are in some way potentially contiguous. "Who has not something of dust, or home or a calm spring evening in him?" is Pasternak's apology for the all-embracing, metonymical elective affinity. The more unrecognizable this affinity and the more unusual the community that the poet creates, the more the juxtaposed images, and whole series of images, fall to pieces and lose their spellingbook clarity. Significantly, Pasternak consistently opposes "the meaning imported into objects" to their plasticity, for which he so delights in finding pejorative epithets—in Pasternak's world meaning is inevitably etiolating and plasticity deanimating.

### IV

To define our problem: the absolute commitment of the poet to metonymy is known; what remains to be determined is the thematic structure of his poetry. The hero is as if concealed in a picture puzzle; he is broken down into a series of constituent and subsidiary parts; he is replaced by a chain of concretized situations and surrounding objects, both animate and inanimate. "Every small detail lived and arose, without regard to me . . . in its significance," Pasternak records in his early cycle of poems *Over the Barriers,* in which, as he has admitted, he had already found his own poetic system. The theme of the poem "Marburg" is the poet's rejected proposal of marriage, but the principal characters in the action are flagstone, pavingstone, wind, "innate instinct," "new sun," chicks, cricket and dragonfly, tile, midday, Marburger, sand, impending storm, sky, etc. One and a half decades later, in his book of reminiscences *Safe Conduct,* Pasternak mentions that he is intentionally characterizing his whole life at random, that he could increase the number of significant features or replace them by others, and that, in fact, the poet's life must be looked for under other people's names.

Show us your environment and I will tell you who you are. We learn what he lives on, this lyric hero outlined by metonymies, split up by synecdoches into individual attributes, reactions, and situations; we learn to what he is related, by what he is conditioned, and to what he is condemned. But the truly heroic element, the hero's activity, eludes our perception; action is replaced by topography. If in the case of Majakovskij the collision of two worlds inevitably culminates in a duel, the polished image of Pasternak's poems—the world is a mirror to the world—says over and over again that the collision is illusory: "The enormous garden stirs in the room, raises its fist against the mirror, runs to the swing, catches, hits with the ball, shakes—and doesn't break the glass." If Majakovskij unfolds his lyric theme in the form of a cycle of transformations undergone by the hero, the favorite transitional formula of Pasternak's lyric prose is a railway journey during which his excited hero experiences a change of locality in various ways and in enforced idleness. The active voice has been erased from Pasternak's poetic grammar. In his prose ventures he employs precisely that metonymy which substitutes the action for the actor: "a fully awake and vigorous man . . . waits for the decision to get up to come of its own accord, without his contributing anything." The *agens* is excluded from his thematic material. The heroine did not call, did not arrange anything— "it was all announced to her." The height of the heroine's activity, which conjures up the inevitability of the tragedy, is the mental transformation of her surroundings; quite "fortuitously, uselessly and senselessly" she notices someone and in imagination she introduces him into her own life. Is man perhaps active in art? No, "in art," according to Pasternak's aesthetic, "man's lips are sealed"; that, indeed, is the distinctive feature of art. Is art itself active, then? No, it does not even invent metaphor, but merely reproduces it. And the poet will not present his reminiscences to the memory of the person who is their object. "On the contrary I myself received them from him as a gift." If the lyric "I" is in Pasternak's work a *patiens,* is some active third person then the real hero? No, the genuine agent has no place in Pasternak's poetic mythology; as a rule the individual has no idea of what "builds him up, tunes him and stitches him together," and the poet,

too, is "perfectly indifferent as to the name of the power that has given him his book." The third person, as it appears in Pasternak's work, denotes the instrument rather than the agent. For example in **"The Childhood of Luvers"**:

> Everything that came from the parents to the children came at the wrong moment, from one side, provoked not by them but by certain causes that had nothing to do with them.

The auxiliary, subordinate, marginal nature of the third person is often firmly underlined in Pasternak's themes:

> *Another* human being had entered her life, the third person, just anyone, without a name or with a random name which neither provoked hatred nor inspired love.

What is essential is solely his penetration into the life of the lyric self. Whatever is unrelated to this single hero is only "vague accumulations without names."

This strict body of semantic laws also determines the simple pattern of Pasternak's lyric narrative. The hero is either delighted or appalled at being governed by an external impulse; he is now branded by it, now suddenly loses contact with it, whereupon another impulse takes its place. *Safe Conduct* is an inspired account of how the author's enamoured admiration focuses in turn upon Rilke, Scrjabin, Cohen, a "dear beautiful girl," and Majakovskij, and how in this process he comes up against the "limits of his understanding" (a person's nonunderstanding is one of the most acute and compelling of Pasternak's lyric themes, just as a person's being misunderstood by others is one of Majakovskij's). Perplexed misunderstandings develop, and the inevitable passive solution follows—the hero goes off, leaving in the lurch, one after the other, music, philosophy, and romantic poetry. The hero's activity is outside Pasternak's sphere. When he does deal with action, he is banal and unoriginal, defending in theoretical digressions his right to triviality. Majakovskij, too, uses triviality as a part of his material, but with him, in contrast to Pasternak, it is used exclusively to characterize the hostile "Other." Pasternak's short stories are similarly empty of action. The most dramatic—**"Aerial Ways"**—is made up of the following "uncomplicated incidents": the former lover of the wife and friend of the husband is expected back from a sea voyage; all three are shattered by the disappearance of the child; the new arrival is shattered by the confession that the child is his son; fifteen years later he is shattered by the confirmation of this confession and then by the news of his son's death. Everything that in any way resembles action (the causes of the boy's disappearance, his rescue and the cause of his death) is left out of the picture. All that is recorded are the different stages of the emotional turmoil and their reflections.

We have tried to deduce the themes of Pasternak's and Majakovskij's work from the basic structural features of their poetics. Does that mean that the former are determined by the latter? Mechanistic Formalists would answer in the affirmative, supporting their case with Pasternak's claim that in his youth he had had formal affinities with

Majakovskij which threatened to get out of hand, thus causing him radically to alter his poetic manner and, with it, the sense of life that lay at the base of it. The position of master of metaphor was filled, so the poet became master of metonymy and drew the appropriate ideological conclusions.

---

**However rich and refined Pasternak's metaphors may be, they are not what determines and guides his lyric theme. It is the metonymical, not the metaphorical, passages that lend his work an "expression far from common."**

*—Roman Jakobson*

---

Others would try in their turn to prove the primacy of content. Mechanists of the psychoanalytical school would find the sources of Pasternak's thematic material in his confession that he had languished shamefully long "in the sphere of mistakes made by the childish imagination, boyish perversions, and the hungers of youth." From these assumptions they would infer not only the repeated theme of passive exaltation and the inevitable falls, not only the poet's agitated recourse to motifs of adolescent development, but also his metonymical deviations around every fixed object. Mechanistic materialists would note the author's witness to the apolitical nature of his environment, and would assert a socieconomic basis for his obvious blindness to social problems—particularly to the social pathos of Majakovskij's poetry—and for the mood of perplexed, inactive, elegiac distractedness which permeates both *Safe Conduct* and **"Aerial Ways."**

It is legitimate to strive to find a correspondence between the different planes of reality, as it is also to try to infer facts about one of its planes from the corresponding facts about another—the method is one of projecting a multidimensional reality onto one surface. It would be a mistake, however, to confuse this projection with reality itself and to disregard both the characteristic structure and the autonomous movement of the individual planes, that is, their transformation into mechanical stratifications. From among the actual possibilities of formal development, a person or a particular milieu can choose those that correspond most closely to the given social, ideological, psychological, and other conditions; just as a cluster of artistic forms, come by the laws of their development to the point where they are available for use, seek out the appropriate milieu, or the creative personality, that will realize them. But this harmony of dimensions should not be made idyllically absolute; it must not be forgotten that dialectical tensions are possible between the different planes of reality. Conflicts such as these are essential to the progress of cultural history. If many individual characteristics of Pasternak's poetry are in accord with the characteristic features of his

personality and his social environment, so, inevitably, there are also phenomena in his work which the contemporary poetic idiom forces upon every one of its poets, even if they contradict his own individual and social personality. (It is a question of the absolute axes of its total structure.) And if the poet rejects the demands of the idiom, he is automatically pushed off its tracks. The poet's artistic mission never penetrates his biography without a struggle, just as his biography is never entirely absorbed into his artistic mission. The hero of *Safe Conduct* is chronically unsuccessful, because Pasternak cannot do anything with the numerous successes that his original model actually achieved. (In the same way Casanova's book could not make anything of the failures that Casanova actually experienced.) The tendency which we have identified in the work of Pasternak and his contemporaries to make the sign radically independent of its object is the basic endeavor of the whole modern movement in art which has emerged as the antithesis of Naturalism. This tendency is inseparable from the progressive pathos of this movement and is to be found in all artists, independently of the details of their biography. The attempts of observers simply to attach this specific artistic phenomenon to a limited social sector or a particular ideology are typical mechanistic errors: to infer from the nonrepresentational nature of a man's art the unreality of his view of life is arbitrarily to suppress a fundamental antinomy. Rather it is the tendency of philosophy towards the concrete that corresponds most closely to the nonrepresentational tendency in art.

To belong to a compact collective group and to hold firmly to a particular direction are both repugnant to Pasternak, who is a passionate destroyer of customary affinities. He is at pains to convince Majakovskij of how splendid it would be if the latter would do away with Futurism for ever. He dislikes all "banal" affinities with his contemporaries, keeps himself separate from them, and advocates excursions off the common path. Nevertheless, despite the ideological confusion of the period, so variegated as to reach a point of mutual hatred and lack of comprehension, Pasternak's debt to his age comes out very strongly in his poetry. It is revealed both in his persistent creative annullment of the object and in his reconstruction of the grammar of art. This latter used to consist of past and present; in contrast to the simple past, the present was seen as a featureless "nonpast." It was, in fact, Futurism that wished to introduce the future into the poetic system by rubric, theory, and practice, and to introduce it as a decisive category. The poems and journalism of Xlebnikov and Majakovskij shout this tirelessly, and Pasternak's work is imbued with the same pathos, despite his profound inclination for "the deep horizon of recollection." In a new way, in the context of the new antithesis, he conceives the present as an independent category and understands that "the mere perceptibility of the present is already the future." It is not by chance that the high-flown hymn to Majakovskij which closes *Safe Conduct* ends with the words: "From his childhood he was spoiled by the future, which surrendered to him rather early and, obviously, without much difficulty." This "grammatical reform" fundamentally alters the very function of poetry in its relation to other social values.

## Angela Livingstone (essay date 1963)

SOURCE: "*The Childhood of Luvers*: An Early Story of Pasternak's," in *Southern Review*, Vol. 1, No. 1, 1963, pp. 74-84.

[*In the essay below, Livingstone analyzes "The Childhood of Luvers" from a stylistic and thematic perspective, claiming that this tale is "the most mature and perfect of [Pasternak's] early stories." Livingstone's views on Pasternak have developed considerably since the first publication of this essay; however, the position presented below is important to Pasternak scholarship.*]

'**The Childhood of Luvers**' was written in 1917 but, like nearly all of Pasternak's early work, it shows no sign of the political and social upheavals of that year in Russia. Pasternak had been working in factory towns in the Urals and there are some fine descriptions of the life and landscape there: this is the only obvious reflection in the story of his actual circumstances.

It is almost the only one of Pasternak's early prose works which is not about a poet and does not contribute to the attempt to define what art, what the artist, is or should be, although it could be seen as complementary to the main concern of the other stories. While they are concerned with different aspects of the artist's sense of inescapably acting out a role, of posing, and having to regard 'naturalness' as a special sort of task, '**The Childhood of Luvers**' depicts a life lived wholly naturally and unselfconsciously. And it is the most mature and perfect of the early stories. Unlike '**Aerial Ways**,' with its impersonal forces, it is an affirmation of personality, the personal. Unlike '**Letters from Tula**' and '**The Last Summer**,' it is structurally and linguistically clear and finished. Unlike '**The Stroke of Apelles**,' it cannot be suspected of unseriousness. In many ways, its manner and message are continued in Pasternak's autobiography of 1931, *Safe Conduct.*

Critics sometimes say that Zhenya Luvers, the story's heroine, is a sketch for the character later to appear as Lara in *Doctor Zhivago*. But although there is a similar view of woman in the two works, it is hard to find any very precise evidence for the identity of these two characters and still harder to see how, in any case, it could add anything to our appreciation either of '**The Childhood of Luvers**' or of *Doctor Zhivago*. But there are a number of more interesting similarities of thought in the story and in the novel which show that, over all Pasternak's years of comparative 'silence' as an original poet, through all the changes he made in his style (from the often esoteric complexity of his youthful writing to his later attempt at an 'unobtrusive' style), and despite the development of his thought and interest, one aspect of which might be roughly summarised as the development from an interest in man as an artist to that in the artist as a man, his view of life remained basically the same. I will mention some of these similarities at the conclusion of my account of the story.

Near the beginning of '**The Childhood of Luvers**' there comes a passage which begins:

This circumstance [i.e. of their parents' remote and capricious attitude towards them] was part of the children's upbringing. They were not conscious of this because, even among grownups, only the very rare person knows and senses that which moulds, constructs and stitches him together.

It goes on to talk of life as of some wise and provident principle which fashions us out of our chance conditions and circumstances without our knowing what is going on. All the time, we are being made, and we are not—should not be—centrally conscious of how and by what we are made; such consciousness would lead to destructive interference. It is to save us from this that 'life' provides us with all kinds of general ideas, prejudices, conventional religions, and, especially, the interest in psychology: all these are not important or necessary in themselves, they are distractions from the reality which through them protects itself and its good purposes; they are fragments of a whole which we are only just unable to survey.

The purpose of the passage seems to be to insist that there *is* a whole, for life is not just fragments, and that there is a necessary mystery: we are inscrutably directed. It also recommends a sensitive submission to the mystery and to the law of this process.

Now, in the story itself, which is an account of how a girl, Zhenya Luvers, grows up from childhood to adolescence, Pasternak has portrayed a person in process, a mind developing among the explicitly casual circumstances of its environment, and the prose of the story constantly evokes, by its images and rhythms, something of that quality of 'life itself,' that controlling principle. Elusive and unutterable, it cannot be grasped but may be sensed, both through a prolonged perception of the 'unusualness of the usual' and through the momentary comprehension of certain images.

But the story's main interest lies in the way Pasternak depicts, in Zhenya, the growth of a person who does not interfere but trusts in life, instinctively loving its way of working and letting it do as it will with her. She does not interfere, whether by deliberately conforming to a type (like the Akhmedyanov boys in the story), or by adopting too soon a rational attitude that would hold back the imagination (as her brother does), or by acquiring knowledge of things she is too young to understand without hysterics (as does her friend, Liza). As we read, we get above all a sense of the excellent naturalness of her changing and learning and gradually understanding; everything comes at the right moment for her and everything develops its destined meaning.

There are two main stages in the growth of Zhenya's understanding. In the first place, she is seen acquiring ideas, and, especially, learning the names of things. This is not told by a description of mental processes. One has the feeling of being inside the girl's mind, and yet there is very little representation of things that are usually called mental, any more than there is any description of her outward appearance. There is no interior monologue. She does not often think thoughts, endure and ponder emotions, cherish ambitions and wishes, or make decisions. But Pasternak gets us inside her mind by describing the things of the world outside her in just the way she perceives them. The prose of the story is full of extraordinary images and curious effects of unexpectedly exact and lingering description. This reflects the series of vivid perceptions and sensations which Zhenya has—one might even say, which, for much of the time, Zhenya *is*,—and these descriptions are sometimes heavy with her uncomprehending, and sometimes slowly or suddenly lightened by her little jumps of understanding. We are made to go through, again, the child's leaping moments of absolute grasping, by means of some new concept, at a powerful but hitherto mysterious fact, situation or quality, like steps taken forward in the dark upon a path becoming luminous with definitions.

The motif of names is introduced at the very opening of the story of which the first incident is Zhenya's waking in the night at three years old, frightened by the unfamiliar lights of the factory across the river; she has to be comforted by her father, who comes and tells her: 'It's Motovilikha.'

> This was all she needed: to know by what name the incomprehensible was called—Motovilikha. On that night this could still explain everything, for on that night the name still possessed its full and soothing, childhood significance.

Later—she is twelve or thirteen (the intervening years are not dwelt on)—there is her first sight of the Urals from the train window, when her family is moving to Yekaterinburg. She looks through the window and:

> What she saw can hardly be described. The noisy forest of nut-trees into which their train was pouring itself and winding like a snake, became a sea, became a world, became anything, everything. Vivid and muttering, it hurtled down, with a broad, sloping fall, then, growing small, thick and dark, it broke off sharply, now completely black. But that which towered up further off, all curls and little rings, on the other side of the rift, resembled some enormous, greenish-yellow thundercloud, stupefied, transfixed in meditation. Zhenya held her breath and straightaway felt the speed of this immense and carefree air, and straightaway understood that that thundercloud was some sort of land, some region, that had a loud and mountainous name which was rolling all around it and was flung down into the valley with the stones and sand, and that the nut-trees could do nothing but whisper and whisper the name: here, and over there, and far off in the distance; only the name.

> 'Is it the Urals?' she asked the whole compartment, leaning out.

The description of the scene is at the same time an account of how the name—the conception—of that scene grows and comes forth: a huge chaos of shapes, 'some enormous thundercloud, all curls and little rings,' becomes a 'land, a region,' and then, at last, the 'Urals,' as if the name burst forth from the phenomenon itself, sharing its shape, its 'mountainousness,' giving it a sort of relief. (In *Safe Conduct* Pasternak writes of his childhood love for botany and of the way the names of Linnaeus 'brought consolation' to the eyes of flowers).

---

**In 'The Childhood of Luvers' Pasternak has portrayed a person in process, a mind developing among the explicitly casual circumstances of its environment, and the prose of the story constantly evokes, by its images and rhythms, something of that quality of 'life itself,' that controlling principle.**

*—Angela Livingstone*

---

Something similar happens with the concept 'Asia.' The family has moved to a town in Asia and Zhenya has seen the simple signpost of the continental frontier flash by as the train passed, with the same monotonous forest after as before it, and not at all, as she had expected, comparable to the terrible iron barrier dividing the public from the cage of pumas; but, unlike her brother, Serezha, she is not satisfied and struggles to fill the concept with real meaning, with experience. She tries to crowd into it all the new sensations of the place they have come to, as well as the sense of distance they have travelled, feeling in herself, when she thinks over it:

> . . . the sensation of an astonishing mental tiredness . . . as if she too had taken part in the shifting and transporting of all that heavy beauty . . .

and she still wonders, aloud: 'Why is it Asia?', for she does not yet use words conventionally and she is not interested when her brother answers the question by pointing at the map and moving his finger down it, saying that it had been agreed to mark a natural boundary, 'that's all.'

The vague masses of experience become defined and identified by names. A thing is first of all there in immediate awareness, unrecognizable, uninterpreted, without structure, yet sharply responded to, miraculous and challengingly meaningful. Then the name is learnt; the concept comes—rightly, we are made to feel—*after* the experience. Now, throughout the story there are episodes basically of this kind, though not always including the learning of names: things that are strange to Zhenya suddenly become clear and familiar as she watches them. She is continually confronting what she cannot understand, noting it and responding to it with some kind of intense imaginative participation, then seeing it suddenly clarify itself.

Pasternak does not imply that the clarified form is the only valid one, nor *vice versa*. Both forms are obviously the true content of life. He is interested in the *process* of clarification and cares that it should take place in the right way.

Examples can be found, first of all, in all kinds of quite small incidents, such as Zhenya's looking through the huge, dusty buffet window into a station and taking it for another room into which trains silently move and from which they glide out, till she suddenly realises it is the station and out of doors, with sky between the pillars, and hills and wooden houses in the distance. Or again, there is her thinking a certain road that she glimpsed from over the fence of her yard to be mysterious and inaccessible, till Serezha tells her it is a road she often passes on her walk and she has just never noticed it is the one she saw from the fence.

The fence is the scene, also, of the best instance of the phenomenon I am discussing. The first time she looks over it Zhenya sees some people sitting on a bench:

> They were black, like the word 'nun' in the song. Three equal napes, combed up smoothly under round hats, were bending over in such a way that it seemed the one at the end, half hidden by a bush, was asleep, leaning against something, while the other two were also asleep, pressing up against her. The hats were blackish-grey and they kept sparkling and going dull in the sun, like insects. They were covered with black crape. At this moment the strangers turned their heads the other way. Something at that end of the street must have drawn their attention. For a minute they looked in that direction as one looks, in Summer, when the moment is dissolved in light and prolonged, and when you have to screw up your eyes and protect them with your hand—for just such a minute they looked, and then fell back into their former state of friendly somnolence.

The colours, the shapes, the light, the long sleepy movements—all are given as a pattern of perceptions, quite real and precise, yet somehow alien, and even more alien through the slightly uncanny interpretation which the child instinctively supplies for the strange behaviour of grown-ups. Then Zhenya sees them get up and go and the scene is explained, as if suddenly named. They had not been sleeping but reading, one looking over the other's shoulder into an atlas held by a small, crippled man, and turning their heads whenever he turned a page.

This instance is characteristic: this mixture of precision with uncanniness, of intensity with uncertainty, and this moment of something becoming clear, elements of a scene falling into a named pattern—this is characteristic of Zhenya's life and of the style of the story.

The child's vision is like the poet's vision, in at any rate one sense. Like the poet, the child has no use for words that are not full of immediate and fresh experience. And just as, for Pasternak, the 'most memorable and important thing in art is its origination, and the best productions of the world, telling of the most varied matters, in reality tell of their own birth,' so, it seems from this story, what is

most memorable and important in a person is the birth of the mind, the starting up, in the midst of concrete things and situations, of feeling and of thought. Pasternak does not explicitly indicate a comparison but one could compare, in a number of ways, the descriptions of Zhenya's ways of perceiving and recognising things with points in the theory of the origin of the work of art put forward in the autobiography, *Safe Conduct*.

I have so far discussed examples of what could be called the long process of Zhenya's learning to see and learning to use words. There are many other passages describing the sort of childhood experiences in which the child acts and feels while wholly absorbed in what is going on, without any questioning or self-awareness. The girl's mood, on such occasions, is conveyed mainly through the details of external things, especially such as evoke different kinds of weather or season, and there is often some suggestion of a miracle. Thus, in April, with its new freedom and freshness of Spring:

> the rooms became pure, transfigured, and breathed in sweetness and relief . . . the tree, as it dried, kept making its abrupt sound, where the blue air twittered piercingly and the earth gleamed, richly, like something melted.

And the first snow is described:

> The sky shook, and from it there rolled down countless white kingdoms and countries, and they were mysterious and terrible . . .

Now, through all the impressions and sensations, through all the absorptions in journeys, in illness, in excitement, in anxieties, in happiness, another kind of consciousness grows in Zhenya, which makes the second stage in the growth of her understanding. It is the awareness of a world of other people and of herself. It develops into an understanding of the words 'woman' and 'human being,' and culminates in the experience of a moral law. I will trace this development through the story.

The world of other people is first glimpsed by the child of three, for after the night when she had woken up and been comforted by her father, Zhenya was changed; for the first time she

> suspected a phenomenon of either keeping something for itself or, if it did reveal it to anyone, then revealing it only to those who were able to shout and to punish . . .

It is the beginning of complexity, of secrecy and of suspicion.

Her self-awareness starts with the sense of guilt. And the guilt increases when, at twelve, uninformed about the body's functions, and ill-treated by her governess, she sees in her first menstrual bleeding 'a disgusting and distasteful evil,' and knows she is guilty. (This incident is one of the best examples of evocation of a mood by description of surrounding things. For everything seems to reflect

Zhenya's condition; puberty is reflected in the Spring, and the Spring is 'sick and becoming mature with difficulty,' as she is, later to 'break forth broadly and tempestuously,' which suggests the dim sense she must have of a new life awaiting her. The days seem abnormally long and the lamps in the house at dusk seem to give no light but are like 'sick fruits' and 'swelling from within.')

Zhenya is in everything passive, ignorant, responsive, ready to be changed. Things keep happening to her and she does not know about them. She never knows anything with the kind of rational, articulate knowledge by means of which one may get a grip on one's experiences. Just as, while Serezha systematically learns the vocabulary of railways and stations, she is simply absorbed in the exciting sensations of the journey, and just as Asia is for her a feeling and not a region on a map, so she never *knows* about sexual or moral things systematically and abstractly as others seem to, and much of the second half of the story is about her slowly growing towards ideas about these things through the close particulars of her life.

Menstruation is an experience of sin and shame until she is saved by her mother's sudden pity. Pregnancy is likewise never a clear concept to her, but an intuition about it comes to her one day—just after the episode of her looking over the fence—when she becomes aware of a similarity between her mother and their servant, Aksinya (both, it turns out, are pregnant); the resemblance leads her to ponder resemblances altogether and to ask herself what it is that people have in common and what is meant by popular sayings such as Fate pays no respect to birth. That is, she stumbles upon truths through the spontaneous noticing of something no-one has told her about.

She does not guide her own life. 'It was declared to her' that she would start going to the high school, and at this point she notices that *everything* is in fact 'declared' to her—externally imposed and not chosen by herself. And she notices that life is no longer a 'poetic trifle' but is becoming prose, and fact. Here Pasternak introduces one of his most striking images:

> Obtusely, achingly and lustrelessly, as if in a state of eternal sobering, the elements of everyday existence fell into her opening soul. They sank down to its bottom, real, solid and cold, like drowsy pewter spoons. There, at the bottom, the pewter began to melt and fuse into clots, dripping with importunate ideas.

The image represents the hidden process of solid, external reality melting and merging to become internal, become mental, a person.

Zhenya is passive but alert, unprepared for life but ready to accept it. The reader senses a kind of blindness; as if something very valuable is being constructed in the dark. This darkness, or naturalness, surrounds her falling in love with her friend, Liza, a girl with whom she has little in common but with whom chance has brought her together. Pasternak stresses the randomness of her choice and the strength of her love. Because she is the one who loves, Zhenya is the one who suffers. Pasternak could here have written, with Thomas Mann, '*Wer am meisten liebt, ist der Unterlegene und muss leiden.*' The one who loves most is in the weaker position and has to suffer. And indeed, the relationship of Zhenya and Liza is comparable to that of Tonio Kröger and Hans Hansen: Liza seems more vigorous, extroverted and knowledgeable, and Zhenya, though sensing herself to be deeper and stranger, is envious of that tough and social life.

The second half of the story is entitled 'The Stranger' and it is largely about how other people, people 'in general,' come into Zhenya's life, and how she develops a notion of what another person is. For her to develop such a notion it is necessary that there be someone who, without being personally known to her, is nevertheless very real to her and can seem to stand for *any* body, the human being in general. Such a symbol-person is introduced in the lame man, Tzvetkov, whom Zhenya never meets but whom she sees on a number of occasions, always by chance—and here the chance factor is vital. She sees him first when she peers over the fence and finds him showing a book to some women. He is just 'someone' in her thoughts but, as we have seen, for some reason or other profound reflections follow this encounter, or glimpse. She next learns his name in a conversation in which, during an explanation about the army, she has suddenly found herself understanding that all people are individuals: the soldiers, drilling in front of her house, are all separate people:

> The veneer of lifelessness, the amazing veneer of obviousness, was removed from the picture of the white tents; the regiments dimmed and became a gathering of individual people in soldier's dress, whom one began to be sorry for at the very moment when the meaning introduced into them began to animate and elevate them, bringing them near and taking away their colour.

She feels pity: it is a moral as well as an existential development. The concept 'person' enters her mind, like other concepts, only when it has become filled with a particular feeling.

Zhenya sees Tzvetkov again at a bookshop; and after that his image is temporarily continued in that of another 'someone': walking by herself in bad weather, she comes across a man moving house, with a lurching cart heaped clumsily with furniture. Again there is the motif of an inward gait or lameness, and again Zhenya feels pity:

> 'He'll catch cold, as soon as he's unpacked his things,' she thought, of the unknown proprietor. And she pictured to herself a man—*man in general, unsteadily with unco-ordinated steps,* setting out his chattels in their places.

The italics are Pasternak's, emphasising the moment of opening consciousness, of a sudden clarity and knowledge and a sort of involvement.

Zhenya's first sight of the lame Tzvetkov coincided with her first thought about her mother's resemblance to the peasant woman, these beginnings of the two intuitions, about womanhood and about the other person, coming as if naturally together. At the end of the story both these themes, which have each developed to a crisis, are joined together by one event.

Zhenya is sent to stay with friends because her mother is ill after a miscarriage. While she is unhappy and lonely in the strange house she suddenly experiences a great pity for her mother, who seems to her

> suffering, remaining behind in the stream of yesterday's facts, as if in a crowd of people who are seeing a traveller off, and there, left behind, set whirling by the train of time that was carrying Zhenya away.

This leads to a realisation, described with great delicacy and sympathy, that she herself is 'terribly similar' to her mother.

> The feeling pierced her through and was so sharp that she groaned. *It was the sensation of a woman, who sees within, or from within, her own appearance and charm . . .*

Again we find italics, to emphasise the unique moment of change and comprehension. After this Zhenya appears to all to be profoundly different.

The second crisis is part of the same event. It comes when it turns out that her mother's miscarriage was the result of an accident in which a man was killed under the hooves of the Luvers' horse. And that man was—Tzvetkov. Under the shock of this news, Zhenya finds all her previous vague impressions of the 'other person' and unexpressed feelings of pity suddenly coalesce into a pang of sharp realisation; the knowledge which now comes to her, emerging from life itself, like a good growth, is the strange clear knowledge of a moral law:

> The impression hidden behind it all was ineffaceable. It lay outside the girl's control, because it was vitally important and meaningful, and its meaning lay in the fact that for the first time *another* human being had entered her life, a third person, anyone, with no name or with a random name which did not provoke hatred or inspire love but meant *that which the Commandments have in mind* when, addressing particular names and consciousnesses, they say: thou shalt not kill, thou shalt not steal, and so forth. 'You, who are a particular, living person,' they say, 'shall not do to *this other who is misty and universal,* that which you do not wish to have done to yourself.'

The story ends here, with the reminder that everything really important happens beyond our control, and with Zhenya once more feeling full of guilt (she caused his death because she first *noticed* him), and growing up by what is felt both as a sudden jump and as the natural completion of a long process. For the first time she makes a decision for herself, surprising her tutor by firmly putting the volume of Lermontov back on the shelf, with 'I don't want a lesson on this today.'

'The Childhood of Luvers' is a Christian story. It seems to prove that Christianity is natural. We are not shown that Zhenya goes to church or is taught Christian doctrine by anyone; there is nothing overtly Christian until the very end where, stumbling through her experiences, she falls heavily against this solid piece of morality: Do to others as you would have them do to you. Nevertheless, this is prepared for by the Christian orientation of all Zhenya's major experiences. Her first feeling is guiltiness, even as a small child, before any chance of wrongdoing. She instinctively knows original sin. At the end she is still feeling guilty but now the guilt, though still obscure, is somehow good; it is closely associated with compassion. Her sense of being painfully involved in the existence of someone she does not know, this sense which Dikikh, her tutor, sympathetically mistakes for something more sentimental and much less uncommon, is in fact the Christian experience of compassion. She finds herself loving man in general, as exemplified in one human being, no matter who he is, and selflessly suffering *for* him, feeling unaccountably responsible. All this, as well as the conception of Life as a benevolent and hidden principle that protects us and that we can get in touch with if we do not interfere wantonly with its work; and the whole mixture of difficulty and optimism that the story conveys, amounts to a teaching, in entirely unmetaphysical terms, of a religious, a Christian, view of life.

Note

In a number of respects 'The Childhood of Luvers' can be regarded as a forerunner of *Doctor Zhivago.*

The idea of "life itself," as defined at the beginning of the story and illustrated throughout it, also occurs many times both in *Doctor Zhivago* and in Pasternak's comments on his novel. That something good is happening all the time which we can never quite encompass with our minds is the most general thing he wished to show in the novel. Throughout it, moreover, we can trace a strong protest against everything which interferes in life and *is* not life, especially against cliché, 'rhetoric,' the false high-sounding phrases of a too political era, and against people who make themselves into mere 'types' by pretending these phrases are truth. This is a development of the main idea of 'The Childhood of Luvers.'

Further, a good deal of the texture of the novel, as of the story, is made of descriptions of moments in which a particular clarity or freshness is felt, or in which someone is wholly absorbed for a while in some simple, fine, life-giving activity—moments in which 'life itself,' the whole, the meaning of things, is inarticulately perceived and touched.

Both works are full of very precise details of sensation, i.e. *ordinary* perceptions analysed in such a way as to evoke the inherently *extraordinary* which is in them and in everything. Both, too, tell us that our lives consist in details, in particular things. One recalls the passage in *Doctor Zhivago* where Yury, consciously 'continuing' the thought of Tolstoy, compares history to a forest:

only its separate features are observed by us and they always seem motionless; its big changes (changes of season) are not observed, they come imperceptibly, for in fact everything is ceaselessly changing in every separate detail.

Another point of similarity is Pasternak's wholly sympathetic interest in woman, his at once realistic and reverent attempt to understand her from within and to present her as one who *suffers* in a special way, 'generates electricity'—as he says of Lara and hints of the growing Zhenya—and who is, above all, loved and to be loved. This theme is repeated in the intermediate work, *The Last Summer.*

Finally, one might mention the Christian content of both works, which also is present, explicit but very inchoate, in *The Last Summer.* Christianity is treated with incomparable delicacy—even with caution, perhaps—in 'The Childhood of Luvers' and in *Doctor Zhivago;* one might read them without feeling required to pay attention to it. Yet a Christian interpretation is, as I say, indicated in clear hints in the early story, and 'a new understanding of Christianity,' to use Vedenyapin's words, is the almost silent, but all-pervading, and finally (in Yury's poems) very powerful, message of *Doctor Zhivago.*

## Michel Aucouturier (essay date 1966)

SOURCE: "The Legend of the Poet and the Image of the Actor in the Short Stories of Pasternak," in *Studies in Short Fiction,* Vol. 3, No. 2, Winter, 1966, pp. 225-35.

[*In the essay below, Aucouturier analyzes Pasternak's focus on actors, the "legend of the poet," and ideas associated with these professions in "The Mark of Apelles," A Tale, and "Letters from Tula."*]

"You played that role so well!
I forgot that I was the prompter. . . ."
　　　　　　　　　—*My Sister, Life* (1917)

"Oh, had I known that's how it happens
when I made my stage debut. . . ."
　　　　　　　　　—*Second Birth* (1932)

"All grows still. I go onstage. . . ."
　—"Hamlet" (Poem from *Dr. Zhivago,* 1946-1953)

Written and published between 1915 and 1929, Pasternak's short stories have remained the least known and least studied part of his work. At the time of their publication they suffered from the proximity of a highly esteemed poetic output which eclipsed them in the eyes of the Russian public and critics; whereas, on the other hand, the non-Russian reader, by his ignorance of the poetry, has long been deprived of the source of light illuminating their unity. Very different in aim, form, and content, these five stories do not, in fact, appear as a homogeneous and independent whole, but as so many isolated incursions of

a poet into the domain of prose. It is mainly from this formal angle that they have been considered till now, the fiction being treated most often as merely an accessory and secondary element, as compared with an original language showing the indisputable freshness of vision of a great poet. It is therefore understandable that critical attention should have been focussed chiefly on **"The Childhood of Luvers"** which, in fact, is an unfinished novel, where the development of the subject, arbitrarily broken off, counts less than the originality of the means of investigation and description Pasternak employs to follow the paths a child's consciousness takes.

*Doctor Zhivago,* however, has modified this point of view by showing that these prose experiments are also, and above all, works of imagination whose subjects, situations, and characters already reveal Pasternak's fundamental and permanent novelistic motifs. Alongside *Doctor Zhivago,* **"The Childhood of Luvers"** thus appears as a sketch for that "novel of feminine destiny" later incarnated in the person of Lara Antipova. Similarly, in **"Aerial Ways,"** written in 1924, one already sees a first sketch for the character who, under the name of Pavel Antipov, will soon portray the drama of the revolutionist. But these two themes, however important, are subordinated to the life story of Yury Zhivago, the legendary transposition of the poet's biography, and the symbolic portrayal of his destiny. It is this "legend of the poet," constantly associated with the image of the actor, that we wish to follow through the three stories in which it takes shape, trying to show that it is not one theme among others, but the initial ferment of all the prose work of Pasternak, that which dictates and justifies his recourse to fiction and brings out its profound necessity.

With Pasternak's first story, written in 1915, we enter at once the domain of legend. He presents **"Il Tratto di Apelle,"** in fact, as a kind of apocryphal anecdote: the hero is named Heinrich Heine, but the reader quickly understands that he has to do with an imaginary character, a modern namesake, or rather, legendary double of the historical Heine. The adventure takes place in Italy, but the descriptions of Pisa or of Ferrara—Pasternak had recently visited Italy—are drawn in order to take the imagination out of its familiar element rather than to situate the action; the plot itself rests upon rather implausible psychological data; and the narrative, conducted now along the lines of a fairy tale, now along those of a play in dialogue, never seeks to create the illusion of reality. Here anecdote—and the allegory it contains—alone matters: Heine, passing through Pisa, learns that a stranger has come to his hotel and left him as a calling card a simple white card bearing the imprint of a bloody thumb. By this signature he recognizes the Italian poet Emilio Relinquimini, author of a love poem entitled "Il Sangue." The latter has previously given him notice of his visit, summoning him to reply by a message expressing in equally laconic fashion the essence of love, a message which must be at the same time his signature as a poet (whence the title of the narrative, an allusion to the famous exchange of signatures between the painters Zeuxis and Apelles). Taking up the challenge, Heine goes to Ferrara, where he hopes to find the feminine inspirer of Relinquimini. He traces her by a ruse (inserting an advertisement in the local paper, giving out that he is in possession of a bundle of the Italian poet's manuscripts); no sooner is he in her presence than he seduces her and lets himself be seduced, a brilliant improvisation on the theme furnished him by chance. Such is the signature of Heine, his "mark of Apelles."

A critique of poetry? But Heine, too, is a poet; and the favors of Camilla Ardenze are those of the Muse: their love affair thus illustrates the triumph of true poetry over an attitude in which true poetry refuses to be found. It must be recalled here that **"Il Tratto di Apelle"** belongs to the period when Pasternak, with his second collection of poems, *Above the Barriers,* was breaking with the "romantic manner" that still betrayed, in *A Twin in the Clouds,* the influence of symbolism. The name *Relinquimini,* precisely, makes one think of a cast-off skin, whereas the namesake "Heine" evokes that ironic splitting in two, with its sting of cynicism, by which the poet catches himself red-handed and confronts himself with the spectacle of his own naïveté in order to exorcise it. The romantic naïveté that Heine's reply denounces is that of wanting to *tell* love, to reach its essence by a symbol, a double illusion, about love and poetry at the same time. For the essence of love is its immediate, lived-through reality, in other words, that by which it escapes speech, rejects symbol. "Love," Pasternak was to write much later,

> . . . is as simple and absolute as consciousness and death, nitrogen and uranium. It is not a state of the soul, but the first foundation of the universe. The fundamental and primordial principle, love is thus the equivalent of creation. It is not inferior to it, and its testimony has no use for the manipulations of art. Art can conceive nothing higher than to lend its ear to the voice of love itself, that voice forever new and unprecedented.
>
> ["Translating Shakespeare," *I Remember: Sketch for an Autobiography,* 1959]

To be equal to love, poetry must be something other and more than a word about love: it must be, like love, a "second birth," an immediate experience of life in its creative principle. In love, poetry thus discovers that "alter ego" which, as in a mirror, reveals to it its own stuff: that which Pasternak was to christen, in 1917, *My Sister, Life.*

Love, in this sense, is the touchstone of symbolist metaphysics: for if it testifies to a reality superior to art, that reality is not something beyond, but on this side of speech; it does not belong to the domain of essences, but to that of existence; it is not an "idea" one can know or merely approach through language, but a force that can be lived only, in an experience identical with that of love. This is the meaning of Heine's reply, which already contains, we see, the central poetic and philosophical intuition of Pasternak's work.

But is it really a case here of love, of poetry? Heine's victory over Relinquimini ostensibly is that of the seducer over the man in love, of the Don Juan over the poet, of the rake over the simple-hearted. Nothing seems more cynical than the substitution of a casual love affair for the poetic exploit awaited by Relinquimini; nothing more immoral than the maneuver by which Heine lures Camilla Ardenze, a maneuver that the newspaper editor, after being informed, terms blackmail; nothing more false than the game he plays to seduce her, and in which she rightly denounces an actor's pose. And yet, there comes a moment when the casual affair stops being a casual affair, when the blackmail is no longer blackmail, when the pose is no longer a pose: it is the central moment of the story, marked only by the breaking off of a chapter on an unfinished sentence that is to be continued in the following chapter at the moment when the scene of seduction, apparently uninterrupted, suddenly undergoes a change of lighting and becomes a love scene. A miracle has occurred during the scarcely perceptible interval of the suspension points separating the two chapters. Heine has foreseen this miracle; before leaving for Ferrara he has sent Relinquimini the following poetic fragment: "But Rondolfina and Enrico have discarded their old names and changed them for names hitherto unprecedented, he crying wildly 'Rondolfina' and she exclaiming 'Enrico!'" But even foreseen, prepared for, staged, the miracle remains a miracle, its essence being precisely to escape the chain of cause and effect, not to let itself be reduced to the conditions that prepared for it. Enrico-Heinrich Heine is no longer the seducer, nor Rondolfina-Camilla Ardenze the fickle mistress too easily throwing over the man who loves her for a younger and more brilliant rival. They discover each other in love, this "second birth," this invisible and yet total metamorphosis that, beneath unchanged appearances, strips them, along with their "former names," of all the deadweight of their past.

Love is thus not a result justifying the artifices of the seducer, the Don Juan, the rake, but a metamorphosis that annihilates these figures. It is the expectant waiting for this metamorphosis that for Heine is a kind of justification, for it reveals the lover behind the mask of the seducer, the child behind the mask of the rake, the poet behind the mask of the adventurer. Camilla Ardenze has sensed this even before the miracle has come to pass: "For all that, you are—will you excuse my familiarity?—you are, how shall I put it, an extraordinary child. No, that's not the right word—you are a poet! Of course, how is it I didn't find the word before: it was enough to look at you." Rake and innocent at the same time, the poet is an actor who believes in a miracle and who is capable of welcoming it in himself. He knows that the actor's technique is only a way of making himself available for grace, for inspiration, which alone will make of his acting a "mark of Apelles," the infallible sign of his genius, that is to say, of that supreme spontaneity, that supreme naturalness which reveals the true artist. That naturalness is not given, and if it can no more be acquired, it is won at every moment from the inert weight of hollow words, of empty gestures, of which habit makes each of us a prisoner. Such is the paradox of the actor as Heine describes it to Camilla when she reproaches him with behaving as if he were on a stage: "We spend our whole lives on the stage," he replies, "and it is only with the greatest difficulty that some of us are capable of the naturalness which, like a role, is assigned to us at the moment of birth." True naturalness is genius, in the etymological sense of the word; but, as Goethe wrote, genius is a long patience.

One can see that this paradox of the actor is nothing else but the paradox of art, the synthesis of two apparently contradictory components: that of craft and that of inspiration, of technique and of creation, of artifice and spontaneity, of labor and gift, works and grace. In this, **"Il Tratto di Apelle"** reflects an old concern of Pasternak's, the very one that, if we are to believe *Sketch for an Autobiography,* made him give up his first calling as a musician ten years before, through having lacked the wish to acquire the indispensable technical skills:

> This discrepancy between a new musical thought, which nothing could satisfy, and its missing technical support, transformed the gift of nature which might have been a source of joy into a cause of continual suffering, which at last I could not bear. How was such a discrepancy possible? Basically, there was something that should not have existed, and should have been set right: an inadmissible adolescent arrogance, a nihilistic scorn of a half-baked scholar for all that seemed possible to him to acquire or attain. I scorned all that was not creation, all that was craft, having the cheek to think that in this matter I was a fine connoisseur. In real life, I thought, everything should be miracle and predestination, nothing premeditated or intentional, nothing arbitrary.
>
> *[Sketch for an Autobiography]*

This mystique of inspiration, which Pasternak attributes to the influence of Scriabine, is linked in a more general way to the symbolist climate in which his conceptions of art developed. The antisymbolist generation of 1910, on the contrary, emphasized the role of craftsmanship in art, to the point of defining it sometimes as a mastery (to speak with the acmeists) or as a group of technical procedures (in the language of the futurists and of the formalist criticism which grew up in their wake). It is in this sense that we are tempted to interpret the famous aphorism by which the young Pasternak, switching from music to poetry, rallied to the esthetic of the new generation: "Art, in its fashion, is nothing but a simple homework assignment, whose only requirement is to be done brilliantly" [*Sochineniya,* 1961]. If Heine's experience does not expressly contradict this formula, it nonetheless shows that the accomplishment Pasternak expects of art is not a simple technical success justifying the artifice, but a veritable metamorphosis effacing and annihilating it; that in his eyes the opposition between artisan and creator, craftsmanship and inspiration, is vain; or at least resolves itself into the paradox of the actor, which expresses the essence and the secret of genius.

This theme of the actor, like the word *genius,* which Pasternak was later to use in the same sense, retains, however, a certain ambiguity: extended from the domain of art to that of life, it makes the artist the possessor of a superior and autonomous morality which raises him above the crowd and puts him out of reach of its laws. This ambiguity is the one Pasternak later denounced in what he

called "the romantic conception of life." "This," he wrote in "Safe Conduct,"

> . . . was the conception of life as the life of the poet. It had come down to us from the Symbolists and had been adapted by them from the Romantics, principally the Germans. . . . In the poet who imagines himself the measure of life and pays for this with his life, the Romantic conception manifests itself brilliantly and irrefutably in his symbolism, that is, in everything which touches upon Orphism and Christianity imaginatively. . . . But outside the legend, the Romantic scheme is false. The poet who is its foundation is inconceivable without the non-poets who must bring him into relief, because this poet is not a living personality absorbed in the study of moral knowledge, but a visual-biographic "emblem," demanding a background to make his contours visible.

It is the sentiment of this ambiguity which inspired Pasternak's development of the actor-theme in **"Letters from Tula"** and *The Narrative.*

With **"Letters from Tula,"** written in 1918, the image of the actor finds itself challenged, precisely, by the reality of "a living personality absorbed by the study of moral knowledge." The ironic fantasy of **"Il Tratto di Apelle"** was that of a game of wits; the pathetic sincerity of **"Letters from Tula"** is that of a confession, translated into the language of fiction, but whose passionate tone suffices to betray its roots in a real experience. The form, too, is no longer that of a fairy tale, but of a realistic short story testifying to a concern for psychological verisimilitude totally absent in **"Il Tratto di Apelle."** The central event, surrounded by penumbras suggesting its connections with the whole fabric of a life, is a chance meeting that illumines, like a revelation, the conscience of a young poet, and turns him utterly against what he has been until then. The hero is at the station of Tula, where he has just parted from the woman he loves; it is to her that he relates his experience in his letters. This is the psychological context of the revelation, its realistic cause: the separation here being, as is often the case with Pasternak, the moment of discomposure, of unbalance, when love is no longer just a "state of the soul," but an impulse, a force, an unlimited power of renewal.

Like the image of love, the image of the actor is shifted here from the ground of legend to that of reality: it is materialized in the confrontation of the poet with two sorts of actors. The first are film actors, "the worst species of bohemian," who happen to be his table companions at the station buffet in Tula. "They play at being geniuses, bandying phrases with each other, theatrically flinging down their serviettes on the table, immediately after wiping their clean-shaven lips." The horror which this spectacle inspires in the poet stems from the fact that he recognizes himself in them:

> I am sick to my stomach over it. It is an exhibition of the ideals of the age. The vaporings they give off are my vaporings, all our vaporings. They are the stifling vaporings of ignorance and of the worst kind of

insolence. It is I myself. . . . Here is their vocabulary: genius, poet, *ennui,* verses, untalented, *bourgeois,* tragedy, woman, she, I. . . . How frightful to recognize one's traits in others.

And, speaking of himself in the third person: "The poet, who shall henceforth place this word in inverted commas, until it has been purified by fire, the 'poet' observes himself in actors on a spree, in a spectacle indicting his comrades and his generation." For, in his tablemates the poet recognizes an attitude that is not his alone:

> A style has come into being in life, such that there is no longer a place on earth where man can warm his soul by the fire of shame; shame has taken on water everywhere and no longer burns. Falsehood and confused debauchery. That is how all those who are out of the ordinary have lived and watered shame, the young and the old; and already it has overflowed onto the crowd, onto the unknown. For the first time since the far-off years of childhood I burn. . . .

The movement by which the poet rises against this image of himself and his time reflected back to him by the actors is a movement of shame: his revolt is a revolt of conscience. He perceives this, and formulates it, at the moment when he is aware that he is at Tula, on the very ground where Tolstoy lived: the incarnation of a literary tradition dominated by ethical preoccupations. "The adventure lies in the nature of the place. It occurs on the *territory of conscience,* in its gravitational center, in its ore-bearing regions." The revelation of Tula is that of an ethical domain where the character of the actor has no place.

The ham-actor doubtless is only a caricature of the actor. But the caricature is telling only if it hits what is effectively vulnerable. The ham-actor, who sets up the character of the actor as a universal standard, unveils his weak point, which is, precisely, that he cannot be set up as a standard. There is no morality of genius that is not fatally the caricature of one.

Denounced by the ham-actor, the character of the actor is rehabilitated, however, in the second part of the narrative, by an old trouper, long since retired from the stage, who, like the poet, was present at the arrival of the film players. This spectacle, incomprehensible to him at first, soon upsets him deeply; it makes him understand that his day is done, that he is old, that all that is left for him is to die. To escape the invasion, he shuts himself up in his room; and, to deliver himself from the inner tumult it has caused, he begins to recite mechanically an old part, finds inspiration again, and once more becomes the actor he used to be. And there he is, saved, delivered from the nightmare, in proportion as he becomes himself again by letting himself be taken over by the part he plays.

The poet has only a presentiment of the road to salvation: "He told himself everything would begin when he ceased listening to himself and when an absolute physical silence would fill his soul." The old actor is there to suggest the

way to silence this invading, autonomous ego "which makes itself the measure of life" and reduces the actor to the level of a ham. "He, too," writes Pasternak, "sought physical silence. He alone of the two heroes in the narrative had found it, by making someone else speak through his own lips." The true actor does not find his ultimate standard in himself, but in the role he incarnates. A morality of genius does really exist. It dwells in its fidelity to a destiny of which it is not author and master, but the one who is chosen.

This, henceforth, will be the fundamental theme of the poet-legend in Pasternak. Its richest and densest expression is to be found in the poem "Hamlet," a parable of the destiny of Yury Zhivago, which unites in one image the actor playing out his role to the end, the character of Shakespeare (who embodies for Pasternak the drama "of the great destiny, the heroic mission, the destiny entrusted into the hands of man") and the figure of Christ, faithful to his divine mission to the point of sacrifice ["Translating Shakespeare," in *I Remember: Sketch for an Autobiography*].

Pasternak links the idea of sacrifice to that of risk, which is already implied in the image of the actor as presented in **"Il Tratto di Apelle"**: "You would not understand half of my words," says Heine to Camilla Ardenze, "if we had not met each other in such a dangerous place. I must believe it is dangerous, although I do not know it for certain myself. . . ." The dangerous place where Heine has met Camilla is the stage of this supreme bit of acting that in his eyes represents real life. But to have knowledge of risk is to admit a limit to the acting, to recognize that it is not genuine life: one understands, consequently, that Heine resists the knowledge. Everything changes from the moment that the actor, assuming a role, admits the existence of a norm outside of his acting. For a role is not only self-subjection; it is also an engagement, thus a responsibility and the acceptance of a risk. This is the new significance **The Narrative** gives to the image of the actor.

The originality of **The Narrative,** written in 1929, is to insert the legend of the poet into a realistic context that traces it back to its birth and illuminates its essence. At first sight, **The Narrative** appears as a rather loose series of scenes evoking the life of a young poet, Serge, whom Pasternak had already made the hero of the verse-novel *Spektorski.* However, apart from some marginal episodes put in to suggest a vaster novelistic scheme, all the scenes converge in a central episode that gives them unity. This episode takes us back to the summer of 1913, when Serge, having finished his university studies, takes a post as tutor in the wealthy bourgeois Fresteln family. There he meets a young Danish girl, Anna Arild Tornskjold, a widow without means engaged as a lady-companion. She confides to him the humiliations she has had to suffer from coarse employers. He falls in love with her and asks for her hand. But at the same time he has met a prostitute, Sacha, whose distress upsets him deeply.

> All of human naturalness, howling and swearing, was there, raised up as on a strappado, at the height of a catastrophe visible from all sides. In the surroundings

descried from this elevation, one made it a duty to spiritualize oneself, on the spot and at that very moment; and, in the sound of one's own emotion, one could hear the deserted stretches of the universe, by a common impulse, and in urgent haste, become covered with rescue posts.

The humiliation of Arild, the distress of Sacha, assume for Serge the significance of an ineluctable appeal. He responds instantaneously, and without reflecting a single moment on the hopeless inadequacy of his enterprise, by making a sketch of his first narrative, the synopsis of a play which he intends submitting to a director of theatrical reviews, if only to obtain thereby a minimal fraction of the sums he knows are needed to deliver the women from their bondage. He imagines a young artist, whom he names Y3, as though to stress still more the abstract, non-realistic character of the story. Y3 decides one day to sell himself at auction. He appears in the sale room, transformed for the occasion into a theatrical hall, into which throng the elegant public of the capital. There he displays his talents as a musician and poet, and conquers the audience by the almost miraculous richness of his gifts. Then the sale begins; a rich patron of the arts carries him off, and Y3, having disposed of his acquired millions by distributing them in poor neighborhoods, gives himself up to the good pleasure of his buyer.

Serge imagines also, more vaguely, a sequel to his narrative: the bounties of Y3, far from curing the evils, provoke violence and riots that increase them; the patron, burdened by his acquisition, offers freedom to his slave, who refuses it. . . . But those, Pasternak makes one feel, are only secondary details, like all accessory developments to fill out the theme, enrich the image. The essential has been said, and can be summed up in two points. It is, first, this vision of a stage which, once again, reveals the poet beneath the features of an actor. But art, here, is no more than a sum staked: it stands for everything the actor can put into the balance; it represents at the same time his grandeur and his limitations, his power over men and his powerlessness before misery, evil, and death. The true acting by which he triumphs and fulfills himself is that complete giving of himself, that acceptance of an unlimited risk symbolized by the image of an auction at which the stage of the actor becomes identified with the sacrificial stake.

Secondly, the essential consists in the birth of legend, the pure gushing of the fiction seized at its source, at the moment when it is not yet a work of art, but merely an urgent and spontaneous response of the imagination to the position in which life has placed the poet. For, seen from this angle, the legend of the poet is not a gratuitous revery, a compensatory illusion, an arbitrary invention: it is the immediate and insistent command of an imagination directly connected to reality; it has the imperative character of inspiration. By this very fact it imposes on the poet a role that has nothing arbitrary about it, and that he is not free to choose or reject. The poet is not the author of his legend, but the servant of the destiny it traces for him: the slave of a higher and more significant work than his own person.

## Elliott Mossman (essay date 1972)

SOURCE: "Pasternak's Short Fiction," in *Russian Literature Triquarterly,* Vol. 3, May, 1972, pp. 279-302.

[*In the following excerpt, Mossman outlines Pasternak's "prose vision," discussing thematic and stylistic aspects of Pasternak's short fiction. Mossman notes in particular Pasternak's focus on history, the individual, causality, estrangement, and the relationship between art and reality.*]

The period in Soviet literature stretching from the Revolution through the 1920s represents a prolonged coming of age, both for the literature itself and for many of the writers taken in the context of their literary biographies. Following the culminal poetic tradition of Symbolism, writers sought their voice in prose. In alarm the poetic world took notice of the shift toward prose. The magnitude of historical events seemed to draw the artist away from poetry toward a regenerated tradition of prose realism.

Boris Pasternak's poetry of the 1910s, formally accomplished and innovative, seldom escapes a certain prankishness, the obscurance of contemporary theme in deference to tongue-tripping verbal artistry. The hermit poet of *My Sister Life* who troubles some children with the question, "What millennium is it outdoors?" is eccentric, but not to Pasternak's insulated poetic world. His drinking partners, Lermontov and Poe, seem as far removed from the pressing literary reality of 1917 as their drink, vermouth, from the Russian national beverage. In *My Sister Life* the hermit poet emerged, but did not set off down the road. The path to the literary reality of the day led Pasternak away from poetry toward prose. In 1917 Pasternak wrote, "I'll say goodbye to verses, my mania; / I've set a rendezvous with you in a novel" ("Autumn"). In Pasternak's long poems of the 1920s the poet made a serious effort to adapt his essentially lyrical talent to the narrative and epic modes: "The age demands the epic, and therefore I am making the transition from lyrical reflection to the epic, although this is very difficult" ["D sebe," *Stikhi 1936-1959*]. This statement of intention made light of the difficulties which Pasternak encountered along the way.

As the poetic persona faltered during the period of Soviet literature's coming of age, Pasternak came of age in his short prose. His stylized distinction between poetry and prose in **"The Childhood of Luvers"** presents the process of transition concisely:

> Having ceased to be poetic nonsense, life now fermented like a thick black fable insofar as it became prose and turned into fact. Dully, rheumatically and dimly, as if in a state of eternal sobering, elements of everyday existence dropped into her knitting soul. They sank down to the bottom, real, hardened and cold, like drowsy pewter spoons. There, on the bottom, this pewter began to run, merging into lumps, dripping with fixed ideas.
>
> [*Proza 1915-1958*]

Pasternak's short prose rehearses the poet's difficulties as he comes to struggle with the lessons of "fact" and as the "fixed ideas" of a mature literary personality take shape. His short prose recounts, as his poetry does not, the writer's coming of age.

The view that Pasternak's short prose is just the small change of his verse is not creditable. Prose was an alternative to, but not diversion from verse. As early as 1917 Pasternak thought of himself as a prose writer primarily. On March 15, 1919, he gave the following responses to a questionnaire circulated by the Union of Poets of the Moscow Professional Union of Writers:

> Q. In addition to verse, are you writing any artistic prose?

> A. Yes; and for the last two years, *mainly* prose. A novel in manuscript around fifteen signatures [i.e., approximately 250 pages], free for publication. *The central work of the undersigned is tales,* three in number, each from one-half to one signature in length.

The novel mentioned, we learn from Pasternak's second autobiography, *People and Attitudes,* was lost; Its beginning survived and was published as **"The Childhood of Luvers,"** a self-contained work with the structure of a tale. The fragment **"Uninhabitedness,"** published in 1918, in all likelihood is part of this lost novel as well. Of the three tales mentioned in Pasternak's response, one is surely **"Il tratto di Apelle,"** which is dated 1915 in Pasternak's collected prose. A second is **"Letters from Tula,"** dated 1918. The third tale mentioned is either the unpublished **"The History of a Contraoctave,"** written in 1913 and somewhat longer than one signature, or a tale which has not survived, with the exception of the recently discovered fragment, **"Three Chapters from a Tale."**

Beyond these works, Pasternak's short fiction includes the short tale **"Aerial Ways"** (1924) and the long tale ***The Tale*** (1929). The semi-philosophical, semi-autobiographical piece "Safe Conduct" (1931), like Joyce's *Portrait of an Artist,* is a special case of the imagination coming to roost in the man. Its presentation is artistic, while its content is selectively autobiographical. Worthy of mention but scarcely worthy of inclusion in the opus of Pasternak's short prose are the few wartime dispatches which Pasternak wrote in the 1940s. The several snatches of artistic prose which Pasternak published between 1937 and 1939 are properly regarded as first drafts of the novel *Doctor Zhivago* rather than part of his efforts at short prose fiction.

The unpublished tale **"The History of a Contraoctave"** was written in the summer of 1913, three years after Pasternak's return from its setting, one of those small German towns which Pasternak knew well from his experience of a summer semester's study at Marburg. **"The History"** begins in 1810, during the Napoleonic Wars, and concludes in 1820. The plot is purposely subdued: what action there is reaches us through rumor, gossip, conversation overheard, effect isolated from cause, and public consequences of private events. The town organist Knauer, improvising on the massive church organ, in a fit of ecstasy inadvertently crushes his little son in the organ's inner workings. Knauer suddenly leaves town only to return ten years later, in the capacity of tutor to a nobleman, in order to play the same organ and apply for reinstatement as organist. His application refused, he is ignominiously ushered out of town.

The most disquieting theme in nineteenth-century art (and particularly in that art touched by romantic anti-rationalism) was that of the unique destructive power which the artist wields, and of this power's utter indifference to human destinies. The power of art rendered a nearly beatific insanity in Heinrich von Kleist's "Saint Cecilia, or The Power of Music," a more mundane insanity in Gogol's "The Portrait," rivalry culminating in death in Pushkin's "Mozart and Salieri" and Tolstoy's "Kreutzer Sonata." In the phantasmagoria of Shakespeare and Beethoven Tolstoy viewed as amoral and ultimately despoiling art's indifference to human destinies. He castigated himself for having yielded to such amoralism. Art's revenge on the artist's life pervaded the thematics of the Symbolists. The living link with the nineteenth-century romantic heritage was close to Pasternak as he composed **"The History of a Contraoctave,"** an account of the terror of art over the artist, the indifference of art to human life, and the pain inflicted in the name of art on those close to the artist. This theme pursued Pasternak throughout his life, finally appearing in the novel *Doctor Zhivago,* and conditioning his portrayal of art as an illness, a dangerous delirium.

The plot of **"The History,"** while it reports the central theme of art's terrible force, does not yield a sense of the prose craftsmanship displayed in the tale. **"The History"** is a touchstone for Pasternak's prose artistry. In concert with the periphrastic presentation of the central action, Pasternak puts strict limits on the narrator's field of vision: as Knauer walks the darkened streets of Ansbach, where his son died ten years earlier, his sight and the narrator's are limited by the swath of light from a hand lantern. His excitement:

> . . . tore on ahead and expected something from the right side of the street, opposite from the side which they were walking on; it couldn't manage to stay within that swath which fell from the lantern and led the way, and when into this fully-lit swath suddenly and without warning crept the huge, bulky and solid pedestal of a Gothic church, it crossed the swath, like a little yellow river, not dislodging a single stone along its whole length, swimming across the yellow flagstone and halfway up the church, wrapped breast and stone in the night. . . .

The narrator plays off his pretended unfamiliarity with the town of Ansbach against his central character's all too particular memory of its topography. A painful psychological value is made to injure in the location of an occurrence by the narrator's suspension of foreshadowing.

The frequency of extended metonymy makes **"The History"** unmistakably Pasternak's prose. In a public room at the town inn the slightest sounds are prominent amidst the hushed silence of the late hour. The travelers' weariness inheres in the fixtures of the hotel itself: ". . . a wall clock ticks; a pendulum behind glass; swinging, it sows the room with ticking, frequent and shallow, like millet; but it brandishes about so lifelessly and tiresomely, as if it were the limp, aching arm of the sower toward evening of planting day." Metonymy extended to the point where anthropomorphized simile is discovered—such is the stamp of Pasternak in his early prose. The pendulum measuring the late hour comes, via the sower's aching arm, to measure the traveler's weariness. The fixtures of the hotel stand in for its patrons' claims upon it.

The reach of Pasternak's imagery is a specific feature of his prose. Pasternak's was a painterly eye which balanced the broad canvas against the demands of detail:

> In the ill-lit parts of the city, like words pronounced in an even voice amidst absolute silence, short, succinct lines crowded together to the point of blackness, broke loose from the gleaming sky, lines of ridge-poles, lancet cornices, soffits, trimming and further wonders of the architecture of the Middle Ages, smoke-blackened by dusk and antiquity. They were feverish from the touch of the skyey lake in which swam two hunks of cloven ice, melting and feeding the depths with a dark, chilly breeze; two large, slowly melting stars, overflowing the brim of the sky, full already of tremulous brightness. The black edges of hammerbeams and eaves came down with a slight fit of shivering all the more keen and quick for the lack of any curvatures and fluting in the structure of the roofs, to which, groping and feeling them out, the surging alluvion of this wan, unsettled night could not have made its way.

In this paragraph from **"The History"** Pasternak imposes the eye of a painter on the description of the town's skyline. In the foreground particularity of line, enhanced by the enumeration of architectural details, is balanced against the backdrop of puddled stars in a vast sky. The sharply limned foreground against the expansive background sets the picture trembling at the interstices, and the metonymy of the skyey lake results from that observation of the picture's dynamics.

In so many other ways dissimilar, here Pasternak resembles Turgenev in descriptive technique. Both writers take steps to ensure that the narrative moves through a real landscape of concrete detail ordered graphically. In the case of both writers the success of the setting is in large measure due to the accuracy of the wording. Pasternak's architectural assemblage brings to mind Turgenev's letter to Borisov in April 1870, asking for the precise Russian word for "ridge-pole." In a passage from **"The History,"** in which the child's mother founders in grief, Pasternak finds the one word which expressed her longing for release from the feeling of unfathomable loss: "If these dumb and hysterical outcries of a mother's soul had been thoughts, outcries which had wrinkled and disfigured her breasts like the creases of a soiled blouse, if her brain were able to cope with them, the thought of suicide would have come to her like the viaticum sent down from on high." The wafer of extreme unction comes to represent the sole absolution and release from her grief.

The fabric of detail in **"The History"** could not be mistaken for the plethora of details characteristic of prose in nineteenth-century Russian "naturalism" (insofar as that term can be used to apply to a literary method practiced sporadically from the 1840s through Gorky); nor is it only the accrual of details, stylistically occasioned, characteristic of ornamental prose in the 1920s. In a sketch for an article on Heinrich von Kleist, to be called "On the Ascetic in Culture," and discovered in his university notebook for 1911-1912, Pasternak maintains that the twentieth century is ready for a new concept of realism, surpassing naturalism. This new concept he termed "realism as tonality." Pasternak's technique of prose composition, "tonal realism," was an amalgam of artistic, musical and poetic techniques, as one would expect from Pasternak, his father's son, pupil of Scriabin, and poet.

In Kleist's life Pasternak saw the universalized life of the artist and the key to his creative method:

> No doubt he was a poet in the sense that he was constantly departing. In this cult of constant breaks with the natural, in this particular asceticism, bereft of a definite, singular aim and therefore representing the asceticism of creativity, in this constant self-sacrifice he discovered the essential thread of lyricism: beauty. It led him to his death.

As a result of the ascetic's "estrangement and renunciation of the natural," the artist's creation emerges. It arises at the expense of the artist himself.

Tonal realism is evident in Pasternak's prose in the context both of the visual arts and of music. The use of color in his prose is frequently tonal in quality. Pasternak was particularly consistent in his use of the color purple and its tones throughout his prose. Building upon these tones, he developed the theme of life's regenerative powers, first in the context of the natural world observed in the florists' quarter of Moscow, and later in the Christian context in *Doctor Zhivago*. The color tones vary in accord with variations on the theme of regeneration. . . .

In **"The History of a Contraoctave"** sound, rather than color, is the abstracted and then embodied vehicle of the themes. Sounds take on substance and texture. The late-night sounds of people playing bowls off the lobby of the inn become "scruples of noise tightly stoppered, monotonously weighed out on druggists' scales." At the beginning of **"The History"** the empty cathedral itself becomes the sound chamber of the organ which fills it with sound: ". . . it became cold and senselessly vacant under the vault: the interior of the soulless church came to resemble the glass bell of a huge air pump; chilled streams of white, sterile mid-day poured through the narrow vents of the long windows onto the backs of pews and onto the volutes of plaster decorations; they were sucked in here by the emptiness of the huge premises. . . ."

In the wake scene for young Gotlieb, Pasternak fashions a synesthetic, textured fabric of detail from the mourners' cries and sobs: a "catafalque, a baldaquin of muffled crying wavering over the room" fills the room in which the dead child lies with tangible sound, the wailing of a mother who, "once having fed him from her own breasts . . . now fed her own breasts, writhing from her famished convulsions, with copious sops from her generous sorrow." The synesthetic qualities of sounds are employed as variants on a scale central to the thematics of the tale, the scale of the organ music strung throughout the tale.

It is right to ask how deeply seated in his understanding of art and the artist was Pasternak's tonal compositional method. Was it merely a fanciful and inconsequential application of Scriabin's or the Impressionists' achievements to the sphere of artistic prose? Pasternak indicates that it was more than simply symbiosis in the arts. On August 6, 1913, ten years to the day after he broke his leg at age thirteen, he wrote of himself: "As if it were today he lies in his hardening plaster cast and through his delerium pass the trisyllabic syncopated rhythms of the gallop and fall. From this time forward rhythm will be an event for him, and in turn events will become rhythms; melody, tonality, and harmony will be the circumstance and reification of an event." The elements of art merged in the artist's psychology with the reified events of his existence.

This merging of art with life is at the core of **"The History of a Contraoctave."** What is lithesome and mellifluous as art there becomes clumsy and horrific in life. What is startling is that the artist cannot pay allegiance to both, without irreparable damage to one. The organist, alone in the room with his dead son, strokes the corpse absentmindedly. Distracted by the pain within him, his artistic practice overwhelms him: "But how he started when, through the dark mass of his oblivion, he noticed what his own left wrist was doing, unbeknownst to him, to the child's body. He hurriedly withdrew it. He tore it away from his son's body the way one would tear away a crawling viper or the way, burning oneself and blowing on one's fingers, one removes from the rug a firebrand from the hearth. The hand was caressing the son in octaves; it was picking out the octaves on him." This oblivious, unforgivable gesture provides the psychological motivation for the organist's flight from the town, from his family, and from art. The final proof that art and life are antithetical comes at the conclusion of the tale, when the reader learns that the much reduced Knauer is now tone deaf. No longer was he prone to "that feeling known to the artist alone . . . that property which existed at that instant between him and the cantilena, from the uneasy conjecture that it knows him equally well as he knows it. . . ."

Before the Revolution Pasternak was in the process of abandoning the romantic manner, as he later acknowledged in "Safe Conduct": "But a whole conception of life lay concealed under the romantic manner which I was to deny myself henceforth. This was the conception of life as the life of a poet. It had come down to us from the Symbolists and had been adapted by them from the romantics, principally the Germans." This essentially romantic manner proved exceptionally tenacious in Pasternak's experience, as it was in the experience of the post-symbolists throughout Europe. His understanding of romanticism was con-

cise: "Romanticism is the liberation of creativity from accepted strictures in form and content." Pasternak's short prose seeks to find these strictures in form and content which the very nature of prose itself imposes, as distinct from the strictures imposed by tradition.

In **"Il tratto di Apelle"** Pasternak again approaches the theme of art and its relationship to life and the artist, now with the ironic scepticism of a renegade from the romantic tradition. Such a renegade and cynic was Heinrich Heine, who becomes the main character of Pasternak's tale. Set in Italy, **"Il tratto di Apelle"** owes a debt to Heine's story "Florentine Nights." There the main character attempts to distract his consumptive beloved with stories from his personal experience. He tells of seeing Paganini perform, and of how Paganini related through his music the tragic events of his life. The experiences are not only auditory, but visual as well. Paganini's art is seen as "signatures." He tells of how a deaf painter composed a portrait of Paganini so accurately that the painting evoked both laughter and tears. "Why is that so astonishing? In the sure signature of his playing the deaf painter could see his tones. Are there not people for whom tones themselves are only the unsure signatures in which they hear colors and forms?" In **"Il tratto di Apelle"** the poet's signature is worked out in his fanciful courtship of a rival's mistress.

The epigraph to **"Il tratto di Apelle"** recites a parable of art from ancient Greece. In Pasternak's version the painter Apelles, finding his rival Zeuxis absent from home, leaves a line drawn upon the wall from which Zeuxis can guess the identity of his guest. Zeuxis returns the call in Apelles' absence and leaves his inimitable sign. The more common version of the parable has Zeuxis, a master of fifth-century, B.C., Greek art, entering a contest with Parrhasius, who with Zeuxis led the Ionian school of painting. Zeuxis executed a painting of grapes so realistic that birds pecked at it. Parrhasius presented Zeuxis with a representation of a curtain, which Zeuxis asked his rival to draw aside, thinking the painting to be behind it. It seems clear that it is Parrhasius' painting to which Pasternak refers as a parable of art. The signature of the artist is that textured and tangible surface which he weaves in his art seemingly from nothing at all. The identity of the artist is not the stuff of art and its relation to the artist's life, as in the romantic tradition, but the lively hide-and-seek which goes on in the art itself. Art is not the forum for the artist's views but the curtain of abstraction and estrangement which parts the artist from life. Apelles' line is drawn at the threshold between art and life.

In the antics of the fictional Heine in Pasternak's tale the implications of Apelles' parable are worked out. Heine seduces away the mistress of the Italian poet Relinquimini through a mixture of sarcastic repartee and banal highjinks. He comments: "all our lives we are on stage, and far from everyone is capable of the naturalness which, like a role, is assigned each at birth." The view of artistic activity as a stage, a screen so real as to obscure reality itself, is further developed in Pasternak's *The Tale,* in which a writer composes a story along much the same lines as Pasternak's **"Il tratto di Apelle."**

Having renounced the anthropocentrizing world view of the romantic tradition, Pasternak nevertheless experienced repeated difficulty in abandoning the manner itself in his writings. In prose the difficulty arose with special urgency. In prose, between the words set on the page and the objective world portrayed lies a third person, the even-handed voice of third-person narration. Pasternak, in coming to grips with prose, attempted to deny this third person, as did Rilke in *The Notebooks of Malte Laurids Bridge*: "And I ought to have known that this third person who never was, has no significance and must be disavowed . . . He is the noise at the threshold of the voiceless silence of a real conflict." **"Letters from Tula,"** an etude in the epistolary mode which struggles to find the necessary narrative voice between first and third persons, the success of the story depends on the achievement of "a complete silence . . . not Ibsen's, but *acoustical.*" The story concerns the observed conflict of a boisterous film crew doing a documentary on the historical Time of Troubles with an old, retired actor attempting to discover his own history through his art. The old man attains an imagined dialogue with his deceased wife, and through the medium of his art reaches the tranquil silence which eludes his rivals and transcends the significant pauses of Ibsenic dialogue. Implicit in Pasternak's story is a rejection of the artistic representation of history as objectively determined events, capable of documentary representation.

Rejection of the objective view of history does not necessarily entail migration to its opposite pole, the subjectivism which later in Soviet literature became anathema. Pasternak sought the middle ground. His Marburg training in neo-Kantian philosophy and psychology told him that what the positivist historians and ideologists condemned as the shadowy, subjective land of paradox and illogic was the fertile territory of new empirical discovery. In Pasternak's prose the objectifying descriptive function of the narrator is not abandoned but moved to the fore, as in **"Letters from Tula,"** where it is the third-person narrative which characterizes that "acoustical silence" sought on the thematic level. That silence is achieved in a landscape made desolate and lifeless:

> There was an unusual silence. The lifeless boilers and railroad cars lay on the flat earth, like heaps of low clouds on windless nights. . . . It was impossible to say where the grass was and where the cinder, and when the tired pair dragged the draught-bar in the turf, harrowing the path with the piece of iron, no dust was visible, and only the lantern at the stableyard gave a dim sense of this. The night gave a long throaty sound—and everything grew silent. This was very, very far off, beyond the horizon.

The physical silence attained is figuratively that of a lifeless world bereft of an observer, deaf and muted. In the context of the story we are led to believe that this is a silence under normal circumstances inaccessible.

We are initially puzzled to learn in **"Letters from Tula"** that the achievement of this "acoustical silence" is somehow to be associated with Tolstoy. The story encompasses "a night spent in the locale of Tolstoy's biography." The event of the story "is an occurrence on the *territory of conscience. . . .*" Pasternak's description of lifeless silence would not immediately seem to call into play Tolstoy's views on the moral function of art. Yet it is Tolstoy's view of art which Pasternak adopts and illustrates in his next prose work, **"The Childhood of Luvers."**

Pasternak had travelled to Astapovo soon after Tolstoy's death in November 1910, in the company of his father, Tolstoy's *mouleur.* Tolstoy played a central role not only in Pasternak's childhood, but throughout his life. Pasternak attributed to Tolstoy one enviable quality, "the ability to see phenomena in the abrupt finality of a separate moment." This ability, Pasternak asserts, is not the device of a writer (Pasternak evidently has in mind Viktor Shklovsky's application of the Formalist device of "estrangement" to Tolstoy's works), but rather a facility of vision peculiar to Tolstoy. Its exercise is an act of conscience. Later in Pasternak's life Tolstoy's ability is of paramount importance. In an unsent letter to the Futurist poet Sergei Durylin, Pasternak wrote:

> . . . the central and most undying aspect of Tolstoy, that which is greater than the teaching on Good and broader than his immortal artistic individuality (perhaps that which makes up his true being), is *a new kind of inspiration* in the perception of the world and of human activity; that new aspect which Tolstoy brought to the world and by which he moved ahead in the history of Christianity became and remains to this day the foundation of my existence, of my whole manner of living and perceiving. I think that I am not alone in this regard, that people from the camp which we would consider non-Tolstoyan are in the same position, that is, I want to say that despite all the appearances the historical atmosphere of the first half of the twentieth century in the whole world is a Tolstoyan atmosphere.
>
> [March 27, 1950]

Tolstoy fashioned the prose edifice in which Pasternak came to write.

By the time he began **"The Childhood of Luvers,"** Pasternak's prose vision had matured substantially. This work demonstrates the vision which he was to describe in a letter to Stephen Spender in 1959. There, Pasternak added to the usual mechanics of the prose writer's profession ("characters, their development, situations, occurrences, the plot, the subject, the content . . .") one other element: "the characterization of reality as such." He continues: "For the characterization of reality of being, as a substratum, as a common background, the nineteenth century applied the incontestable doctrine of causality, the belief that the [*sic.* Pasternak was writing in English.] objectivity was determined and ruled by an iron chain of causes and effects, that all appearances of the moral and material world were subordinate to the law of sequels and retributions." By contrast, he says: "If I had to represent a broad, a large picture of living reality, I would not hope to heighten its sense of *extant objectivity* by accentuating the fixed statics of *ananke* [necessity], of natural laws, of settled moral regularity." Pasternak in **"The Childhood of Luvers"** does not set out from the mature, nineteenth-century doctrine of causality. The events which Zhenia the child observes are wholly accidental, seldom named, let alone "caused." Time relationships, like causal relationships, are distorted, as in the title of the first part, "Long Days." Words do not characterize events satisfactorily. The French "Menteuse!" has no relationship to the bloodstains on Zhenia's shaggy white bear rug and on her pillow and sheets. The strange name "Motovilikha" does nothing to explain the awesome phenomenon of a factory which she observes floating on the nighttime horizon.

At one point in the story, Zhenia is doing her homework, a division problem. The problem is one which, contrary to the settled rules, will not come out even, and her tutor Dikikh has been teaching her the concept of infinity. She keeps dividing the repeating decimal, runs out of margin on the paper, and begins again: "'But this is the point: 3773 repeats, so may it simply be rewritten, or rounded off?' Suddenly, she recalls that Dikikh had come right out and said recently that '*you don't have to divide them; just throw them away.*'" The one and the many conflict in the girl's mind. The causal logic of an arithmetic problem is unthinkable for Zhenia, for it foresees no end but the settled universe yet incalculable ends embodied in Dikikh's rules of thumb.

Marina Tsvetaeva saw in **"The Childhood of Luvers"** the dominant theme of the artist's coming of age, and commented that Zhenia bore less resemblance to a four-teen year old girl than to Pasternak himself ["Epos i lirika sovremennoi Rossii," *Novyigrad* (Paris), Vol. 6, 1933]. One might add that she resembles the poet in Pasternak, and she comes into her own in the same way that Pasternak the poet sought to come into his own in the transition from "poetic nonsense" to the prose of everyday existence where "facts" and "fixed ideas" reign.

The key to this reading of **"The Childhood of Luvers"** is the role which Lermontov plays in the tale. We know that in 1917 Pasternak considered Lermontov a neglected writer who could play an important part in the regeneration of twentieth-century Russian literature. Pasternak spoke of him as the precursor of the modern movement of "biographical realism":

> Beginning with Pushkin we have our Russian contemporaneity, the real and the true, our modern thinking and spiritual consciousness. Pushkin erected the house of our spiritual life, the edifice of Russia's historical awareness. Lermontov was its first tenant. In Lermontov we have the independent confessional note in the subsequent intellectual tradition of our century, in poetry and prose, later enriched by the magnificent concreteness of Leo Tolstoy, then Chekhov's sharp-eyed absolute sensitiveness to reality. But whereas Pushkin is objective, tangible, and just, with generalizations of the widest meaning, Lermontov is passionate and personal, and therefore more limited; whereas Pushkin is realistic and exalted in creative activity, Lermontov is its living personal testament. . . . His operatic romanticism is apparent in part. The influence of Byron was unmistakable, because half of

Europe had been under his spell. But what we wrongly take for romanticism in Lermontov seems to me to be in fact the unbalanced nature of his modern, personal biographical realism and the foreshadowing of our modern poetry and prose.

> [Letter dated August 22, 1958, cited in *Poems,* trans. Eugene Kayden, 1959]

With Lermontov Pasternak's concerns for romanticism and realism coalesce in the hybrid concept of "biographical realism," a step away from the self-centered Byronic world view toward a realism which, nonetheless, does not deny the primacy and validity of "living personal testimony" to creative activity as a proper ingredient of art itself.

Zhenia Luvers, at the beginning of Part II, has taken her volume of Lermontov out into the yard. In the neighbor-ing yard she sees retired General Spitsyn's orderly prepar-ing to wash an ice-cream machine. As he disappears into the house after a bucket and rope, Zhenia's vivid imagi-nation floods the scene which lies before her:

> Meanwhile the Terek, prancing like a lioness with a shaggy mane on her back, continued to roar, as was her prerogative, and Zhenia was overcome with doubt only concerning whether it was precisely on her back, or rather on her neck, that all this took place. She was too lazy to do anything about the book, and the golden clouds from southern lands, from the distance, scarcely managing to see the outcast north, were already meeting at the threshold of the General's kitchen, with bucket and rope in hand.

Zhenia has merged the reality which she sees in the court-yard with the reality she imagines in Lermontov's "The Demon." Her reading of the following lines has merged with her vision:

> And the Terek, prancing like a lioness,
> With a shaggy mane on her back,
> Roared. . . .
> And the golden clouds
> From southern lands, from a distance
> Saw him north.
>
> ["The Demon," Part I, Chapter 3.]

Lermontov's Byronic poetic vision has colored the girl's perception. Her imagination evinces no interest in the separate facts of either reality. Lermontov's anomaly is widely known: it is the male, not the female, lion which is distinguished by a shaggy mane. Where an adult would insist upon the anomaly's correction, its inaccuracy passes unremarked in the child.

Next Zhenia climbs the woodpile, abandons her volume of Lermontov, and gazes across the neighboring garden into the back street beyond. There for the first time she sees the character referred to in the title of Part II, "The Out-sider." He is Tsvetkov, a friend of Zhenia's tutor. He is described as a man with a prominent limp as soon as he is first seen, and he reappears frequently in the story, seemingly to no end. Just as accidentally as Zhenia has seen him the first time, he is struck down and killed one night before the theater by the Luvers' rearing horse. Zhenia thinks she has seen his silhouetted figure two weeks after the accident, on the morning of the day she discovers that the man killed by the horse is the man she has seen time and again. She concludes from all the facts at her disposal that she has *caused* his death:

> Well *she* had introduced him into the life of the family on that day when, having noticed him on the other side of someone else's garden, and having noticed him unnecessarily, uselessly, senselessly, she thereafter began to meet him at every step of the way, constantly, directly and indirectly, and even, as it happened the last time, against all possibility.

As a result of her reasoned guilt, Zhenia renounces Lermontov, and implicitly her imaginative but careless use of Lermontov, refusing to answer to her tutor for the poet: "And without further words Lermontov was squeezed . . . back into the slightly slanting row of classics." So the work concludes.

In this scene, in the coming of age of Zhenia Luvers is portrayed the coming of age of Russian literature from romanticism to realism, from the romanticism of Byron, via Lermontov, to the realism of Tolstoy. The process encompasses the appearance and acknowledgement of a general moral relationship between the first and third persons in an integrated world. In the mature tradition of Russian prose, best exemplified by Tolstoy, indifference to life and to the consequences of individual actions has no place. The accidental interrelationships of human beings, formed by chance, are converted to moral relationships, giving rise to the conclusion, which is the Tolstoyan "lesson" of the story:

> . . . its significance lay in the fact that, for the first time, another human being had entered her life, a third person, completely indifferent, without a name or with a random name, which neither called forth hatred nor inspired love, *but such a person as the Commandments have in mind* when, addressing themselves to names and consciences, they say: thou shalt not kill, thou shalt not steal, and so on, "Thou, individual and alive, shalt not do *to this, the unknown and general,*" they say, "that which thou dost not wish upon thyself."

In the absence of all real ground for causality Zhenia Luvers has come to draw a moral relationship between herself and a third person. This is not the "settled moral regularity" with which Pasternak takes issue in nineteenth-century prose. As he comments in **"The Childhood of Luvers,"** this deep-seated feeling has no name. Rather, it is the consequence of applying Tolstoy's ability "to see phenomena in the abrupt finality of a separate moment."

Zhenia's childhood is the extended application of that ability. In Part I of **"The Childhood of Luvers"** Tolstoy's device of "estrangement" verges on the theme, so wholly is Zhenia's perception the content of the work. The narrative point of view tacitly identifies narrator and main character. As Zhenia's perception changes, the tale progresses. Characters are introduced solely at her behest. The plot follows the line of her sight, is as broad as her peripheral vision, hears the sounds which reach her ears. We sense this most keenly when the narrator moves to change the point of view, as in the following passage in which Zhenia wakes up in the railroad compartment to find that a stranger has come in while she was asleep. Zhenia, unseen, looks him over:

> She looked him over, but he could not see her: the berth sloped back steeply to the wall. He did not see her because he too occasionally looked up from behind the news, slantwise, back, and when he raised his eyes to her bunk, their looks did not meet: he either saw only the mattress, or . . . but she quickly gathered them beneath her and stretched her slack stockings.

The ellipsis is more revealing than the words themselves. The narrator drifts away from Zhenia's point of view, utilizes the precious stylization of an unmentionable, and then returns to Zhenia's point of view, which we recognize as that of a child becoming aware of her own femininity. Later, when we are told that Zhenia has recognized the fact of her resemblance to her mother, we are put in mind of Kitty Shcherbatskaya looking at herself in the mirror at the ball: "*This was the perception of a woman seeing her own exterior and charm from within herself or inwardly.*"

The sustained estrangement in **"The Childhood of Luvers"** is both the source of art in the work and the cause of the tale's culminating lesson. Pasternak succeeds in demonstrating that Tolstoy's artistic vision and his moral vision went hand in hand. One's obligation as an artist to the tangible reality of the world one describes carries with it certain moral strictures. The absence or presence and use of texture, sound, [and] color in art are determined by moral perception. Zhenia the child whiles away the time indoors by gazing out the window at the variegated world. Her imagination floods the world beyond her. She is pulled up short when made to realize that the sight which she has seen from the window is that of soldiers drilling on the field, and when she concludes that they merit her sympathy:

> An efflorescence of lifelessness, a grave efflorescence of visibility withdrew from the picture of the white tents; the squads faded and became a collection of individual people in soldier's uniform, for whom she began to feel sorry at the very moment that the meaning which had been introduced into them brought them to life, ennobled them, made them friends, and deprived them of color.

Zhehia's sympathy for and involvement with the soldiers as individuals are invoked at the expense of the color which has made them artistically attractive initially. Zhenia's moral vision absents color from the canvas in the name of life, morally differentiated.

In **"Aerial Ways"** Pasternak gives succinct expression to his understanding that the ways of man, contrary to the objectivist premise, do not lie through a reified world. The objective world in the story thrives outside of all temporal sequence, while the human world is shackled to time. No matter how the artist may attempt to anthropomorphize the objective world—"the earth, as with hayricks, was covered with forms, stunned by silence. They were resting. The spaces between them grew larger in the face of the day; just as if the better to rest, the forms had dispersed and withdrawn."—that world does not conform to the living, human temporal sequence: "The fact is that [the forms] were being shaken from the past into the future, from the future into the past, like sand in an often-turned hourglass." By contrast, the characters in the story are alien to this world, "borne only out of the past into the future, and never brought back."

In **"Aerial Ways"** Pasternak seeks to locate the place of the individual in history. Two like moments, one in 1905 and one in 1920, comprise a paradigm for the elevation of isolated events in individuals' lives to the level of historical events with their own pressing inevitability. In the first a mother loses her child on a desolate, windswept field. The ensuing search is joined by her one-time lover, the naval officer Polivanov. In the second the mother has lost her son in the maelstrom of revolution and civil war; she comes to the same Polivanov, now a Bolshevik officer, only to learn that he cannot forestall the young White recruit's impending execution. The sky above this second isolated moment is "new," the sky of the Third International. It harbors the "aerial ways" to which the title refers: "These were the aerial ways along which, like trains, the rectilinear thoughts of Liebknecht, Lenin and a few other minds of their gauge set off daily." These ways transcend the reified world: while one can hold out some hope for the discovery of a boy lost in a maelstrom on a desolate field, there is no hope for a son lost in the maelstrom of the human world of history.

Pasternak points out that writers have recognized the dichotomy between the reified world and the human world before. Alluding to the opening of *Anna Karenina,* he comments: "There exists a law by which adventures which certainly ought to happen to others can never happen to us. This rule has been invoked more than once by writers." In **"The Childhood of Luvers"** Pasternak brought Zhenia to an awareness of this rule of art and its application in life. In **"Aerial Ways"** Pasternak goes on to demonstrate that man has built for himself a second world of necessity, made up of rectilinear thoughts and existing apart from the reified world, in which causation will operate with immutability and finality. This foreshadows one of the basic premises of Pasternak's later work, *Doctor Zhivago.* Simply stated, man lives in history, not in nature.

Pasternak's artistic understanding of historical events flies in the face of modern historiography: "The more self-contained the individuality from which life derives, the more collective, without any figurative speaking, is its tale." In **The Tale** Pasternak places the self-contained individual at the center of historical events in an attempt to see history in nuance, timbre and tone. The work is one of a Proustian rummaging in the past, where scarcely articula-

ble qualities give the pre-war, pre-revolutionary years a character subsequently lost to the impelling forces of history. "Thus people moved about during that last summer, according to the calendar, when life was still apparently oriented toward individuals. . . ."

> In *The Tale* Pasternak places the self-contained individual at the center of historical events in an attempt to see history in nuance, timbre and tone.
>
> —*Elliott Mossman*

It is in many ways illegitimate to treat **The Tale** alone: to do otherwise, however, would go beyond the scope of this survey of Pasternak's short prose. **The Tale** is part of a "novel in verse," titled *Spektorsky,* which Pasternak composed between 1924 and 1929. In 1929 Pasternak wrote: "I have rendered in prose a part of the plot in the novel, a part which concerns the war years and the Revolution, because the characteristics and formulizations, most obligatory and self-evident in this of all parts, are not within the power of verse." ["Pisateli o sebe," *Na literaturnom postu,* Vol. 16, 1929]. It seems most clear that what was not within the power of verse was the Proustian shifting in memory and mind from place to place and distinct present to time past which comprises the artistic technique of *The Tale.*

As the story opens the central character, Serezha, arrives in a Siberian salt town to visit his older sister, the wife of an engineer in this industrial town of factories geared to the production of war materials. While his sister speaks on the phone in another room, he stands gazing out the window at a stranger striding at a rolling gait toward a seemingly endless fence. As Serezha's mind wanders, the man disappears behind the fence. In the meantime, Serezha thinks, his sister has hung up the phone and is now giving instructions to a seamstress at work in the bedroom. But it turns out that the sister was actually talking to the telephone operator, a part-time seamstress, at the railroad station on the other side of town. Then, with no more causation than this misunderstanding, the narration shifts in place and time to the railroad station and the arrival of the train on which Serezha travelled earlier. A fellow passenger disembarks, Fardybasov, a sailor on leave. First, Fardybasov drops in on his relative, the telephone operator; then he sets off to find his friend Otryganiev, who works in one of the new factories. Fardybasov strides off at his sailor's gait past the warehouse fences toward the factories. It is at this point that Serezha sees a man walking toward the fence, Fardybasov, whose relative at the station is sewing a blouse for the sister. Fardybasov's trip across town, particularly described, and his salty exchanges with his friends, provide a thoroughly realistic picture of the industrial landscape as seen through the eyes of a native to the place, himself in turn seen through the mind's eye of Serezha.

Pasternak achieves an anaglyphic presentation of objective reality here. The narrator disappears, while secondary characters assume the narrator's function. For the space of two pages Serezha is left out of consideration and Fardybasov roams the town making the observations of detail usually left to the narrator in realistic fiction. The tour is replete with a map-like network of spatial relations formed of fences, telephone lines, juxtapositions of time and place, and colloquial speech characteristics. Reality as such is invoked beyond the pale of the narrator, at a remove from the central character. The device attempts to convince us of the independent existence of that reality. This portrayal of reality as such through the coincidences in the daily rounds of people, analogous to Bloomsday and Dublin seen in the peregrinations of Leopold Bloom and Stephan Daedalus, is a major innovation in narrative fiction of the twentieth century. It points ahead to the formidable array of coincidence, supporting a view of reality distinct from the causational, in *Doctor Zhivago.*

The major shift in time and space in *The Tale* is one captured in the inherent ambiguity of the non-specific title, *Povest.* This work is both "a tale" of Serezha's life and "the tale" which Serezha struggles to write. From his sister's house in Siberia in 1916, Serezha traces his way back in memory to Moscow in the summer of 1913. The turbulent politics of the recent several years have had their effect on Serezha and his family. They become intertwined with his love affairs (which take up a major portion of the narration) and finally with his art. The process by which Serezha composes the tale within this tale brings us back to the starting point of this survey, back to Pasternak's first attempt at prose in the summer of 1913. Prose realism is now presented as the artist's act of conscience in a world of Raskolnikovian dilemma.

Serezha finds himself in tight straits, in need of a large sum of money to ease the burden on his beloved, a governess, that on the prostitute Sashka, and in general the burden on womankind. He determines to write a tale in order to resolve his pressing financial need, and the theme of need crosses over into the tale itself. His rough draft deals with a poet and pianist (like himself and like Pasternak) whom he names algebraically, X3. X3 is the twice-removed object of autobiographical narration. His concern as an artist for the way in which "an idea is born out of experienced situations" is the concern of Pasternak as well.

X3 decides to auction his talents in return for money, which he will distribute to the masses. At the auction he displays the virtuosity of his piano playing and poetry, filled with the striking images which are to form his audience's "future mode of feeling and recollection." His art dictates "the directions in which their future moral sensitivity and inclination toward truth will travel." The attributes ascribed to X3's art are those which Pasternak saw in Kleist: ". . . he understood living beauty as the ultimate distinction between existence and non-existence. This was his innovation, that he held this distinction, in-

telligible no longer than an instant, and transformed it into a perpetual poetic emblem." The auction of the artist results in disaster. The money distributed causes riots and disorders, rather than the longed-for regeneration of human values. Once again Pasternak has focussed on the harm inherent in the artistic act, but now it is art as a commodity which wreaks havoc. This theme of art at the service of revolution, but to the detriment of the artist, is one Pasternak followed up in his portrayal of Mayakovsky in "Safe Conduct." It is a further adumbration of Pasternak's early recognition that the act of art is one fraught with consequences which, though the art transcend them, the artist may not.

The theme of art and the artist is ever-present in Pasternak's prose. The theme is not static however. As his short prose unfolds, Pasternak's aesthetic expands to embrace within the pale of the artist a responsibility to realistic portrayal, to moral sensitivity, and finally to history. What in **"The History of a Contraoctave"** are construed as the laws binding the artist to his art, in *The Childhood of Luvers* is seen as the law morally binding the human sensibility to its fellow creatures. All the more plausible then is the outcome of *The Tale,* positing an active role for the artist in the formation of the future's moral sensibility.

The tortuous path of this aesthetic through Pasternak's short prose left many of his admirers bewildered as to his stages of growth. In 1936 Anna Akhmatova still saw in Pasternak that childlike quality which those who had known him in the 1920s never failed to single out as his most prominent characteristic. In her poem "Boris Pasternak" she wrote: "He has been accorded an eternal childhood. . . ." Pasternak's childlike vision was a long time disappearing, because it was so much the source of his art. If traces of it remained in the 1930s, they were finally effaced by the events of that decade. Kornei Chukovsky was among the few to see Pasternak finally come into his own in the late 30s, when he began to write *Doctor Zhivago:*

> . . . I well remember that every time I met him during the last, pre-war years my impression was clearer and clearer: the very same Pasternak, yet not the same. He no longer descended like a hurricane upon the person with whom he was speaking, no longer inundated him with hurried rushes of excited, explosive speech: he became quiet, slow, thoughtful and strangely soft in spirit. The long enduring childlike quality had at last left him.

> ["Iz vospominanii," *Iunost',* Vol. 8, 1965]

Pasternak came finally into his own in the thirties, after a slow and faltering coming of age stretching from before the Revolution through the twenties. His sometimes awkward maturing as a writer is evident in his prose. His heritage turned out to be that of Pushkin and Tolstoy, the two writers who shaped the broadest statement of an artist's purpose in the nineteenth century. Pasternak did not shrink from this broad statement in his later writings: "By an artist's aesthetics," he wrote in the late twenties, "I understand his conception of the nature of art, of the role of art in history, and of his own responsibility to history"

["Nashi sovremennye pisateli o klassikakh," *Na literaturn-om postu,* Vol. 5-6, 1927].

**Henry Gifford (essay date 1977)**

SOURCE: "Pasternak and the New Russian Prose," in *Pasternak: A Critical Study,* Cambridge University Press, 1977, pp. 84-97.

[*In the excerpt below, in which he discusses stylistic and thematic aspects of Pasternak's short fiction, Gifford claims there is a strong thematic relationship between Pasternak's verse and fiction, and that this fiction is often characterized by a focus on artistic and childlike sensibilities.*]

I

When in 1923 [Evgeny] Zamyatin surveyed the 'new Russian prose' [in his *Litsa*] he reserved consideration of Pasternak to the end, after making shrewd and often merciless comment on the Proletkult writers, on the Serapion Brothers (to whom, with Shklovsky, he had acted as mentor—they included Mikhail Zoshchenko and Vsevolod Ivanov), and on Pilnyak and Leonov. 'Pasternak', he observed,

> has chosen the most difficult but also the most promising path: this is a writer entirely by himself [*bez rodu i plemeni*] . . . The change [*sdvig*], the novelty he brings is not in the subject (he is without a subject) and not in vocabulary, but on a plane where almost nobody else is working: in syntax. However he has symbolism too—very effective and all his own [*ochen' ostraya i svoya*].

Zamyatin was able to judge Pasternak as a prose writer simply on the evidence of one short story—this was probably 'Letters from Tula' ['Pis'ma iz Tuly'] published in 1922—and one longer fiction that came out in the same year, 'Detstvo Lyuvers', known to English readers as 'Zhenia's Childhood' (in Alec Brown's translation) or 'The Childhood of Luvers' (in Robert Payne's). Both these stories had been written in 1918, when the creative energy released for Pasternak with *My Sister Life* was still at its height.

The others who came under Zamyatin's scrutiny differed from Pasternak in having concentrated on prose. They broke into the new Soviet literature, when books were again published after the time of shortages in the civil war, as the precursors of a generation for whom prose was to be the dominant medium. Symbolist poetry had arrived at a visible end with the death in 1921 of its greatest exponent, Blok; and after some twenty-five years that supremacy of the lyric poem which the Symbolists had brought about in Russian literature was challenged and overthrown. The poets often turned during the 1920s to narrative forms in verse, as did Pasternak; but to resurrect verse narrative, in a language and a culture that had seen

prose fiction developed to such a pitch by the great nineteenth-century masters, was bound to be very difficult. The young men who followed the pre-revolutionary generation—Zoshchenko, Babel, Yury Olesha, and countless others of lesser talent—were convinced of the need to devise a new prose drawing on common speech and looking to journalism as its arena and as the discipline that would dictate its practices. Babel, for instance, greatly admired Kipling. It was remarked by Zamyatin in his essay that 'the language of our epoch [is] rapid and pungent, like a code'. With the methods of a prose fiction that accepted this language, and worked towards the perfecting of a journalistic medium, Pasternak's own procedure had nothing in common. His prose writings, from '**Apelles-ova cherta**' ['**Il Tratto di Apelle**', or '**The Line of Apelles**', 1915] to *Safe Conduct* at the end of the next decade, supplement the poetry of those years. Sometimes, as *Povest* [*A Tale,* 1929] does in relation to the verse narrative *Spektorsky* (1924-30), the prose organises more elaborately and on a larger scale the same kind of impressions. '**The Childhood of Luvers**' actually forms part of a lost novel; but even had it been published in full, this would certainly not have put his poetry of the same years into the shade. However, Pasternak's prose is no less accomplished than his verse during this period—Weidlé actually finds it more satisfying—and in reading the stories and the autobiography one recognises that the medium comes naturally to him, and serves particular purposes more appropriately than verse. The various short or longer prose fictions in this period constitute an overflow from Pasternak's poetry: they deal with the predicament of the artist (as in '**The Line of Apelles**', '**Letters from Tula**', and *A Tale*), or they explore more persistently than a lyric can, and over a period of time, the sensibility of a child, Zhenya Luvers, which is clearly akin to the sensibility of the artist.

Zamyatin is wrong when he states that Pasternak in these stories has no subject. Even the slightest of them—the opening pair, '**The Line of Apelles**' and '**Letters from Tula**'—are not the flimsy web of impressions that he seems to imply. It is true that, in the former, descriptive writing gets out of hand, just as in Pasternak's verse of that time conceit bred conceit to the detriment of coherence. The leaning tower invades Pisa with an army of shadows that are resisted by the last rays of sunset like partisans in the streets. This image has no bearing at all on the adventure of the poet Heinrich Heine (a modern namesake); and similarly the bravura passages on the heat of a Tuscan evening, or on the sunlight that plays on the floor of the hotel room in Ferrara where he sleeps, can only be justified as attempts to make the Italian scene overwhelmingly actual. They are travel notes, impressions of Pasternak's journey to these places a few years before, that he cannot exclude. His eye is caught by the thickening patterns of sunlight as it passes through the Venetian blinds. These patterns are not symbolic; they do not subtly indicate the tone of the experience which awaits Heine. Pasternak blends all the powers of his syntax to fix that impression of the room's secret life, its changing activity all round the immobile Heine. But in this passage the only hero is syntax, the victorious power of expression. Heine becomes a device: the phrase 'Heine sleeps' merely punctuates the unfolding paragraph three times.

---

**Pasternak explores the imagination of childhood and not primarily its moral growth.**

*—Henry Gifford*

---

Yet, as Michel Aucouturier has shown, **'The Line of Apelles'** should be taken seriously for what it is—a first essay in clarifying the nature of the poet's art, and especially the relation between spontaneity and the playing of a role, like an actor's. Heine has received a challenge from the Italian poet Relinquimini. He is to prove his genius by a statement on love no less distinctive in its brevity than the single line Apelles once drew as his signature, or visiting-card, on the wall of a fellow painter. In Ferrara Heine summons by a ruse Relinquimini's mistress. He sets himself to seduce her, and then, unexpectedly for him, they fall in love. The moment of recognition on Heine's part occurs between two paragraphs. In the manner of Sterne, the narrative falters at the words 'he notices that . . .' and crossing the boundary of feeling into a new section of the story (IV) resumes '. . . that this woman is really beautiful'. The miracle takes place: Heine who was acting a part now becomes genuinely creative, the artist whose love engulfs and bears up the woman like a wave. Similarly in **'Letters from Tula'** the poet separated from his mistress recognises himself miserably in the third-rate actors who have come to Tula in order to take part in an historical film. Counterpoised to his discovery is that of the retired actor who by rehearsing a former role has found the inner peace ('physical silence') sought by the poet and found it in 'making another person [*postoronnego*] speak through his lips'. Pasternak, it is clear from *Safe Conduct,* was troubled by the affinities between actor and poet, and did not approve the way in which his contemporaries accepted 'the idea of biography as spectacle'. This illumination at Tula takes place *'on the territory of conscience':* Tolstoy had lived in those regions. The story shows an awareness of Tolstoy's demands upon art—that it should not trifle, or seek display, but communicate true feeling directly, as the poet in this story communicates his sense of self-disgust and humiliation.

Both of these stories are concerned with the themes that form the titles of lyrics in *My Sister Life:* they can be described as working towards a 'Definition of Poetry' and a 'Definition of Creative Work'. The narrative prose form enables Pasternak to dramatise the poet's self-recognition as it arises from a social relationship, and to reveal the shift from everyday life to the life of the imagination as a process sudden and unforeseen like the leap from play-acting to serious engagement in **'The Line of Apelles'**. On the evidence of these two initial stories he does not promise to develop into a novelist. They are spirited pieces, the

first in its dialogue, the second in the monologue of the letters. They move confidently, the narrator's voice holds the ear, the phases of each story are well controlled. Weidlé suggests that both **'The Line of Apelles'** and **'Letters from Tula'** are no more than trials of the pen. While the former still belongs to the experimental era of *Above the Barriers,* the latter reflects its proximity to *My Sister Life* and the poems of 1918. It seems to be a part of the poet's lightly disguised autobiography, which is also there in the fragment **'Lovelessness'** ['*Bezlyub'e*'], dating from November 1918—a chapter from some missing novel. This tells of a journey in March 1917 from the Urals on the way to Moscow, which is also described in the *Essay in Autobiography.* Some incidents from Pasternak's life appear in the poetry (the school scene from *Nineteen Five*); but a great deal of the prose writing, and not only that which announces itself as autobiography, draws freely upon his own experience. Zhenya's childhood is no nearer to his own than Ursula Brangwen's in *The Rainbow* is to Lawrence's; but both writers have recovered the quality of their self-awareness as children through imagining the early years of an isolated girl. *A Tale* as Pasternak's sister testifies in her preface to the Penguin translation, borders upon his own experience as a tutor in 1914. It is not apparent that **'Aerial Ways'** ['*Vozdushnye puti*', 1924] does this. Polivanov the revolutionary is there depicted as Pasternak's anti-self, in the way that Antipov was to Zhivago. Generally the prose fiction takes the middle ground between the poetry of Pasternak and his autobiographical writings. Both his fiction and autobiography are concerned above all with the poet's destiny and purposes.

II

The two episodes in **'The Childhood of Luvers'** are entitled 'The Long Days' ['*Dolgie dni*'] and 'The Stranger' ['*Postoronniy*']. Although forming a complete story they seem to represent no more than the prelude of the novel that was lost. Zhenya Luvers is not an artist (though conceivably she might have become one). Her perceptions and interests, however, make her an unusual child. By the choice of his title for the story, Pasternak challenges comparison with the well known works by Tolstoy and Gorky called *Childhood.* These had been told in the first person: Tolstoy's story was a fictional rendering of his own earlier years, with recognisable characters but imagined incidents; Gorky's purported to be a truthful account of his own beginnings as Alyosha Peshkov. Pasternak stands much nearer to Tolstoy than to Gorky. His nature shrank from the persistent self-regard of Gorky's chronicle, which presents a little boy as untarnishable as Oliver Twist. At the same time Pasternak in his awareness of the child's mind does not look out for unconscious hypocrisy, following Tolstoy. He explores the imagination of childhood and not primarily its moral growth. The latter does indeed become prominent in the second episode, but it fails to engross his attention as it engrossed Tolstoy's throughout the trilogy of which *Childhood* forms the first part. Pasternak resembles Tolstoy in his immediate apprehension of the way a child responds to adults and to their conventions. He resembles him too in the understanding of a child's conclusions about life.

What prompted this difficult task for a man of describing a young girl's experience at the onset of puberty? Pasternak's was a genius that invariably waited upon events. In his poetry he looks on, he overhears, he is assailed by impressions. The first appearance of menstrual blood is symbolic of this condition. Zhenya has been surprised by the workings of life, about which very early in the story Pasternak observes that few are initiated into its purposes. An artist is close to a child in his lack of shielding preconceptions—and these, with ideas of reward and punishment, and entry into a world of human obligations, come to children quickly enough. Zhenya must learn to accept the process of life with gratitude. The French governess and her mother do not encourage her to do this, though the following day her mother tells Zhenya there is no need for fear when it happens again. Pasternak has extended a tradition of Russian literature into the area of childhood. It had long used the consciousness of a young woman to examine the moral life. Instead he takes a little girl (more of a little girl in the 1900s than she would be now at a like age) to act as the recording intelligence. Zhenya replaces the writer himself in childish days and her attitudes move him to that special pity he felt towards women. When the girl forced herself to explain confusedly what had happened, and why she wanted the governess's powder, 'her mother listened, rejoicing, loving her and tormented by tenderness for this thin little body'. The tenderness Pasternak feels is not a form of narcissism, such as can be detected in the early chapters of *David Copperfield*. It attests [to] his power to imagine the role of the other sex, and to explore a child's sensibility at its most unprotected.

Zhenya's preoccupation in the first episode, which goes on to describe how the family left Perm for Ekaterinburg on the other side of the Urals, is constantly with the significance of names. When in her infancy she heard the name of the factory across the river, 'that was all that was wanted—to know what they called the thing she didn't understand—Motovilikha. On that night this still explained all to her, because on that night the name had its full and childishly reassuring significance'. Afterwards she learns that a name can hide what is most essential, when next morning she wants to know what the word 'factory' means. Most of all Zhenya finds it difficult to understand the significance of the name Asia. With her small brother Seryozha she looks out for the boundary stone between Europe and Asia; it flashes by; and the same dusty alder woods line the track in Asia as they did mile after mile previously in Europe. So what is Asia? Seryozha has an answer that evades the imaginative issue. He points to the Urals on the schoolroom map, and tells her: 'They have agreed to draw the natural boundary, that's all.' The following day Seryozha wakes up in Ekaterinburg, while Zhenya, still unresolved of her difficulty, wakes up in Asia. **'The Childhood of Luvers'** impresses by its achieved unity, the consistency of its tone—everything is brought back to the child's feeling, and through her sense of the events the narrative gains both scale and coherence. Zhenya's acuteness in weighing up what her parents mean to her (they are both inaccessible to their children) does not fall short of the little girl's in 'What Maisie Knew'; but Pasternak, unlike James, won't make her a moral umpire for the

adults. It is Zhenya who perceives the different qualities of her governesses: Miss Hawthorn is summed up in the cool justice of her lavender-scented hands; the Frenchwoman 'had been like a fly, and nobody cared for her. Her name was utterly lost, and Zhenya could not tell among what syllables and sounds you would happen upon that name.' Later, in the second episode, it is Zhenya who observes the sexton Defendov and his family, noting how they are different from hers; who sees the effect the Akhmedyanov boys have on Seryozha; who takes an interest in the Belgian Neguerat and in his friend Tsvetkov, the lame man endued by her with such a mysterious significance for her life and eventually killed in an accident involving her parents' carriage. All the impressions of the railway journey, the Ekaterinburg boulevards with their dazzling white pavements, the new flat, and the unfamiliar maid, are hers too. There was nothing remarkable in this: any story with a child at the centre will make the child's perceptions paramount. The gain for Pasternak can be measured in terms of the control that became possible. Every image, every unusual comparison in the story arises from Zhenya's mind. They are no longer irrepressible conceits, as in **'The Line of Apelles'**, but the alert perceptions and combinations of a very sensitive child's understanding. **'Letters from Tula'** begins with an ingenious image: 'in the train from Moscow they were conveying the sun that had suffocated on a multitude of striped carriage seats.' This returns in the closing paragraph: 'A train was going to Moscow and in it they were conveying a vast crimson sun on a multitude of sleepy bodies.' The conceit appears to have been imposed on the story, for the sake of pattern-making. The second sentence in **'The Childhood of Luvers'** may look rather similar: 'As at one time her little boats and dolls, so afterwards her recollections sank into the shaggy bearskins, of which there were many in the house.' Here the fusing of the material and the ideal, of toys and memories, imposes itself. The psychological fact could not be more accurately put. Her memories are confused with the toys, and both are lost in the shaggy bearskins, the first setting of childhood, beyond which a search of her past cannot go.

In the second episode Zhenya leaves her childhood behind and becomes a fully moral being, with the recognition through Tsvetkov's death that a stranger, 'without a name or with a fortuitous one, who neither provokes hatred nor inspires love', can enter into her life and must be treated as a person in his own right. The tutor who proposes to read Lermontov with her suddenly realises that she has matured into a woman—and already at the sexton's house it has dawned upon her that she is *terribly* like mamma'. Thus **'The Childhood of Luvers'**, although Zamyatin failed to see it, has a subject, and in its second episode the italicising of these two moral discoveries and their formulation as general truths show a dependence on Tolstoy's *Childhood, Boyhood* and *Youth*. Once again Pasternak has found his way to 'the territory of conscience'.

### III

This makes his prose different from that of Andrey Bely, the starting-point for much experiment in the 1920s. Bely's writing is agile, varied and fantastic. Such mannerism has its place, in the work of Proust for example, when expressing a tortuous mind in pursuit of uncommon insights. Its affectation may even be the only way for that author of achieving sincerity. Pasternak's earlier prose, *Safe Conduct* included, falls quite distinctly and regularly into mannerism, like his earlier poetry. But his principal aim was not to dazzle the reader, any more than this was Proust's. He matched syntax to the movement of thought and feeling: the order of the sentence reproduces the order of his perceptions in time. Here too he resembles Tolstoy. When demonstrating a thesis in didactic vein Tolstoy writes almost with the baldness of Chernyshevsky, but when he registers a sensation, physical or moral, his constructions can be elaborate, and sometimes indeed top-heavy. Pasternak needed a similar complication to keep up with the variety of his intuitions, which were psychological quite as often as aesthetic. It has to be admitted that **'The Childhood of Luvers'**, in view of its difficult subject, is straightforwardly written. As the drama of a child's consciousness, it can have no room for display or sophistication.

Weidlé quotes with approval of its 'limpid charm' [*bezoblachnoy prelesti*] a short paragraph that compares the tinkling of a soldier's balalaika with the sound of gnats in the yard. But 'it was even subtler and gentler. It sank lower than the gnats towards the ground and without getting dusty more lightly than any swarm could it returned to the height, twinkling and breaking off, with momentary falls [*s pripadan'yami*], unhurried.' This sudden realisation of the music and the midges in terms that become interchangeable is entirely characteristic of Pasternak. It also bears the stamp of a child's imagination. What follows in the next paragraph, as Zhenya reflects on the significance of the lame man she has just seen, is remarkable in another way:

> Zhenya went back to the house. 'Lame', she was thinking about the stranger with the album, 'lame, and a gentleman, without crutches.' She went in by the servants' entrance. In the yard there was a smell of cloying camomile infusion. 'It's some time now since Mamma got together a whole pharmacy, a lot of dark blue bottles with yellow tops.' Slowly she mounted the stairs. The iron rails were cold, the treads gnashing in answer to her scraping. All at once there came into her head an odd thought. She strode over two steps and paused on the third. It came into her head that recently there had begun to show between Mamma and the yardman's wife an unaccountable resemblance. Something most elusive. She stood still. It must be, she pondered, the kind of thing people mean when they say: we are all human beings . . . or all tarred with the same brush . . . or fate is no respecter of rank—she pushed away with the point of her shoe a medicine bottle that had rolled there, the bottle flew down, dropped on to the dusty sacks and was not broken—in a word it's something very very common, common to all people. But then why not between herself and Aksinya? or Aksinya, say, and Ulyasha? This seemed to Zhenya all the odder because it was difficult to find two women more unlike: Aksinya had about her something earthy, as of kitchen gardens, something

that brought to mind the swelling of a spud, or the primal green of a squash melon, while Mamma . . . Zhenya laughed at the very thought of comparing them.

> But meanwhile it was just Aksinya who gave the tone to this comparison that forced itself on her. She came out on top when they were brought together. It wasn't that the peasant woman gained, but the lady lost. For a moment Zhenya had a glimpse of something crazy. She fancied that the spirit of the ordinary people's life had taken possession of her mother [*vselilos' kakoe-to-nachalo prostonarodnosti*], and she thought of her mother [speaking broadly like Aksinya]—and suddenly it came to her in a flash there'd be a day when in her new silk housecoat without a sash, sailing by, she would go and blurt out: 'stand by the door!'

> The corridor smelt of medicine. Zhenya went to her father.

Here Pasternak renders the full experience of Zhenya's discovery, the physical movements and sensations that accompany her thought. The medicine bottle evokes her mother, when she is already aware of the lame man as a gentleman and preparing her mind unconsciously for the contrast between that fact and the servants' entrance she is using. And suddenly she sees her mother's position in the household as undermined by this inexplicable likeness to Aksinya. The medicine bottle that she kicks in the moment of speculation falls to the ground but is unbroken, just as her thought plunges into a void but arrives whole at a formulation. Pasternak in his prose as in his poetry recognises the way the mind working under stress of emotion grasps at and weaves into the process whatever comes before the eye. Here Zhenya seems to be helped by the bottle's safe landing to her thought, but scarcely registers any connection. On another occasion earlier at Perm when resolving to explain all to her mother, she had looked out at the night and the cold river 'and—flung herself in'. The duty of confession became for her merged entirely with the imagined sensation of the darkness outside and the icy waste. And she took the plunge.

In the passage that has been quoted one phrase—'the spirit of the ordinary people's life had taken possession of her mother'—obviously could not belong to Zhenya, though it explains in the author's own language what she had divined. And two other phrases—'something most elusive', 'the primal green [*prazelen'*] of a squash melon'—also belong to adult speech, and the second to Pasternak's idiosyncratic vocabulary. He crosses the limits of a child's lexicon whereas Mark Twain, for instance, avoids crossing them in *Huckleberry Finn*. These occasional sorties into adult expression do not, however, impair the convincingness of what Zhenya sees. It is noteworthy that Maxim Gorky, who could not make sense of Pasternak's verse, was entirely won over by **'The Childhood of Luvers'**, and astonished that its author had been able so successfully to 'reincarnate himself as a thirteen-year-old girl'. (Gorky even wrote a preface for a proposed translation to come out in New York.) Nadezhda Mandelstam finds the realisation of Zhenya more complete by far than that of Lara in *Doctor Zhivago*. **'The Childhood of Luvers'** is flawless in its rendering of an innocent and unspoilt awareness as this grows into a fuller knowledge of life. The prose is exploratory in the same way as the verse of Pasternak at this time, a mastering of new perceptions through experiment with the medium. He learns about Zhenya and about the advantages of prose simultaneously.

IV

Two other stories must be considered. . . . The first, **'Aerial Ways'**, was published six years after Pasternak had written **'The Childhood of Luvers'**. Thus it not only appears at a time when the new Soviet literature had taken root; its third and final part has a manifest connection with that literature, since it describes the contemporary scene and presents the revolutionary ethos. There Polivanov, the actual father of the child whom his friends have lost in the scene before the war, once again meets the mother of the boy, fifteen years later, in a world that has utterly estranged them. He is an overworked functionary of the new regime; matters of life and death are, if not actually in his hands, very close to them. She comes to him as a bedraggled 'former person' whose son has been involved in a plot against the Soviet state. Critics point out that Polivanov anticipates Pasha Antipov, subsequently known as Strelnikov, in *Doctor Zhivago*. The personal no longer has claims on him; and he now feels more closely linked with the sentry, whose weary indifference had been opposed to the questioning Lelya, than with Lelya herself. Polivanov talks like a newspaper article, putting in all the formal syntax and even the commas. His office momentarily recalls the lost world of St Petersburg, but this is an illusion. Outside the yard is piled with litter; normality has broken down. Their scene ends with Polivanov's total nervous prostration, and her seeming disappearance. 'Then he found her. Like a huge unbroken doll she was lying between the underpart of his desk and the chair in that very layer of shavings and rubbish which in the darkness, and while still conscious, she had taken for a carpet.' The telephone line from his room communicates with the outer darkness through which pass the aerial ways carrying the ideas of Lenin, Liebknecht and the Third International. These ideas have driven Polivanov to the verge of breakdown, like that of the country itself; they have converted his former love into a clumsy unwanted doll; they have imposed a merciless order. All this is shown, but it is also accepted. The self-engrossment of Lelya's husband, long ago, boasting of a paternity that was not his; the hysteria of Lelya herself, and the fury with which she turned on the negligent nurse; the dwarfish insignificance of their movements as they search for the child, over a widening area, in the night—all these are now doubly distanced. The whole episode had been unreal to Polivanov in its final moments when he shook off the responsibility of his parenthood by walking down to the sea. The story balances the two worlds, and it finds the later one genuinely terrible, a melodrama in which the son's return, so easily putting an end to that earlier scare, can no longer be entertained. Both Lelya and Polivanov are caught in a process that has no respect for their former relationship. The carpets have been stripped away; only shavings and litter remain. **'Aerial Ways'** is not a story of protest, or even of regret—at least on its

surface. It reveals the new situation, indelibly; and in the desire to deal honestly with [a] fact it neither grieves nor exhorts.

---

**Pasternak in his prose as in his poetry recognises the way the mind working under stress of emotion grasps at and weaves into the process whatever comes before the eye.**

*—Henry Gifford*

---

V

The other story, *A Tale,* published in 1929, has a degree of entanglement with the verse narrative *Spektorsky* (1924-30) which Pasternak says in the opening paragraphs of his prose fiction is best put out of mind. . . . *A Tale* is the recollection of a young tutor's experiences in 1914, the last summer 'when life still apparently took note of individuals', and the story begins and ends at his sister's house in the Urals, two years later. This work derives in some parts closely from Pasternak's own circumstances before the Great War, and Seryozha, not surprisingly, is a poet. Yet a further inset into the already framed narrative is made with the presentation of the scenario that Seryozha writes for a verse drama. Pasternak describes the process of creation in a passage that anticipates the famous account in *Doctor Zhivago*. His hero like the author himself is overcome by a feeling of pity for women that leads him to cast round for ways of making money to liberate them. In his verse drama a young poet and musician sells himself to the highest bidder, at a country house where he recites poetry and extemporises on the piano to the curious who have come to witness this strange transaction. His benevolent purchaser does not know what to do with him, and the huge sum the young man has spent as the proceeds of his sale to relieve the sufferings of women only brings on disorder.

*A Tale* is written with the same accomplishment as **'The Childhood of Luvers'**, and the writer's resources are more varied. He shows a considerable fluency in dramatic dialogue (anticipated in the earlier stories), and there is a scene in which Seryozha realises the full human predicament of a prostitute that takes Pasternak into a region similar to Gorky's 'lower depths'. Seryozha's sensibility is more complex than the child Zhenya's, and therefore the writing becomes in places more baroque, as in the passage where Anna is identified with the Moscow scene on a summer morning: 'he saw how, surrounded with poplars like frozen towels, she was swallowed up by the clouds and slowly tossed back her Gothic brick towers'. This returns to the manner of *Themes and Variations* at its most elliptical. But generally the notation is, though full of novelty, clear and no more complicated than the subject demands. To give one instance: Seryozha has found Anna lying on her bed in a faint.

He gasped for breath, and was himself not far from fainting. Suddenly she came round.

'You, friend?' she murmured indistinctly and closed her eyes.

The gift of speech returned not to human beings alone. Everything in the room began to talk. It was filled with noise, as though they had let children in. First of all, jumping up from the floor, Seryozha shut the door to. 'Ah, ah', aimlessly tramping round the room he repeated in something like a state of monosyllabic bliss, rushing continually now to the window, now to the chest of drawers. Although the room which faced north swam in lilac shadow, yet the medicine labels could be made out in any corner, and there was no need in deciphering phials and bottles to run with each of them separately to the window. That was done only to give vent to his joy which demanded noisy expression. Mrs Arild was fully conscious, and simply to gratify Seryozha she yielded to his insistence. To please him she agreed to sniff smelling-salts, and the pungency of ammonium chloride penetrated her in a moment as it does any healthy person. Her tear-stained face was overspread with creases of astonishment, her eyebrows were sharply pointed upwards, and she pushed away Seryozha's hand with a movement full of recovered strength. He also made her take valerian. When drinking the water she knocked her teeth against the rim of the glass, and then uttered the mooing sound with which children express the complete satisfaction of a need.

These four or five minutes of her restoration to the world, and of the world's restoration to itself, are finely imagined. The intimacy between the pair is expressed in terms that have strong sexual overtones, and it is ironic that Seryozha and Anna will have to accept this surrogate for love-making. When she comes down for their promised walk, he has already forgotten her in the fever of writing his scenario.

## VI

With *A Tale* Pasternak ends the first phase of his fictional writing. Ahead lies the autobiography *Safe Conduct,* and already in the decade that follows he will begin to make drafts for his one completed novel, *Doctor Zhivago.* The prose of a poet usually impresses by its singularity and attention to detail. Mandelstam's is a case in point. Those who are accustomed to using charged language and to the renovation of meanings will, when they leave poetry at intervals for prose, come to it with a nervous intensity that produces a prose somewhat oblique, looking towards the poetry from which it has been separated. Prose for Pasternak is truly an alternative medium to verse. He writes indeed at the opposite pole from an expert in traditional novelist's prose such as Bunin, who adds nothing to the possibilities of expression, but has schooled his mind and senses to work within the limits reached by Turgenev and Goncharov. The achievement of Pasternak in his earlier prose was to increase its range of perception and to devise an elaborate and varied syntax closely related to that developed in his poetry. He aimed to recover for verse in the 1920s its amplitude as a medium for describing man in

society. The experiment, as we shall see, was no more than partly successful; and clearly it did not persuade him that for a major statement about his time poetry could dislodge prose, the medium of the classical Russian novelists. Pasternak was able to conceive poetry and prose as equal partners in the enterprise of his imagination. For a Russian poet following Tolstoy, Dostoevsky and Chekhov—the dramatist who showed with Ibsen that prose in the modern theatre could serve poetic ends—there was every reason to make trial of prose. The stories that Pasternak wrote between 1915 and 1929 even without the poetry make Pasternak a significant artist. But they could not have been written without the poetry.

---

## FURTHER READING

### Biography

Barnes, Christopher. *Boris Pasternak: A Literary Biography, Volume One: 1890-1928.* New York: Cambridge University Press, 1990, 507 p.

> First installment in a proposed two-volume set, which provides a comprehensive portrait of Pasternak's early life and career.

de Mallac, Guy. *Boris Pasternak: His Life and Art.* Norman: University of Oklahoma Press, 1981, 450 p.

> A detailed chronicle of Pasternak's life that extensively analyzes his poetry and prose.

Fleishman, Lazar. *Boris Pasternak: The Poet and His Politics.* Cambridge, Mass.: Harvard University Press, 1990, 359 p.

> A critical study of Pasternak's career.

Pasternak, Evgeny. *Boris Pasternak: The Tragic Years 1930-1960.* London: Collins Harvell, 1990, 278 p.

> Translated from the Russian text by Pasternak's son, this volume recounts Pasternak's rise to prominence in—and subsequent rejection by—the Soviet literary community.

### Criticism

Barnes, Christopher. Introduction to *Boris Pasternak: Collected Short Prose,* pp. 3-18. New York: Praeger Publishers, 1977.

> Provides an overview of Pasternak's short fiction, including some fragments and works never published in English.

Dyck, J. W. "The Short Stories." In *Boris Pasternak,* pp. 151-77. Boston: Twayne Publishers, 1972.

> Provides a thematic and stylistic overview of Pasternak's major short stories.

Kestner, Joseph A. "The Spatiality of Pasternak's *Aerial Ways.*" *Studies in Short Fiction* 10, No. 3 (Summer 1973): 243-51.

> Examines Pasternak's focus on space, form, and the spatial arts in "Aerial Ways."

Payne, Robert. "Four Short Stories." In *The Three Worlds of Boris Pasternak,* pp. 86-122. New York: Coward-McCann, 1961.

> Provides a thematic and stylistic overview of Pasternak's major short stories.

Rudova, Larissa. *Pasternak's Short Fiction and the Cultural Vanguard.* New York: Peter Lang, 1994, 168 p.

> Provides a thorough discussion of Pasternak's short fiction. Rudova explores the era in which Pasternak was writing the majority of his short stories, as well as the influence of various contemporary literary movements, including Cubo-Futurism and Modernism, and writers, including Rainer Marie Rilke, on Pasternak's work.

---

# "Flowering Judas"
## Katherine Anne Porter

The following entry presents criticism of Porter's short story "Flowering Judas." For an overview of Porter's short fiction, see *SSC,* Volume 4.

## INTRODUCTION

The frequently anthologized "Flowering Judas" is known for its tight technical construction, its rich symbolism, and its thematic unity. Porter herself once acknowledged that this piece, which focuses on an emotionally withdrawn expatriate living in Mexico and participating in that country's revolution, was one of her best writings. She also stated that the tale was first inspired by her stay in Mexico in the early part of the twentieth century: "All the characters and episodes are based on real persons and events, but naturally, as my memory worked upon them and time passed, all assumed different shapes and colors, formed gradually around a central idea, that of self-delusion." Despite the story's autobiographical beginnings, critics acknowledge that the imagery, tensions, and language of "Flowering Judas" are the work of a master writer of fiction; in appraising Porter's work, David Madden has noted Joseph Conrad's junction that "'[a] work that aspires, however humbly, to the condition of art should carry its justification in every line.' 'Flowering Judas' realizes that aspiration to an uncommon degree."

### Plot and Major Characters

Although frequently incorporating flashbacks, "Flowering Judas" chronologically takes place in the span of one evening in 1920s Mexico shortly after the Obregon revolution. The story opens with the protagonist, an American woman named Laura, returning to the hacienda where she lives. A lapsed Catholic and a virgin known for her nun-like costume, Laura teaches English to local children, delivers messages and narcotics to political prisoners, and does various errands for leading members of the movement. Waiting for her at home is Braggioni, a leader in the revolution who attempts to seduce her through conversation and song. Laura's thoughts reveal her distaste for Braggioni, other men's ill-fated attempts to pursue a romantic relationship with her, and the lack of true emotional commitment or involvement in her life—she cares little for her teaching, finds no joy in her chastity, struggles with her religious beliefs, and participates in the revolution for strictly intellectual reasons. Eventually Braggioni leaves and returns to his long-suffering wife with whom he achieves a momentary reconciliation, but not before Laura reveals that one prisoner whom she regularly visits, Eugenio, will be dead by morning. Euge-

nio has stockpiled the drugs brought by Laura and taken them all in an attempt to kill himself. Though discovered by Laura, he has asked her not to call a doctor, a request to which she has complied. Like Laura, Braggioni honors this request, albeit out of contempt for the prisoner. "Flowering Judas" ends with Laura dreaming of Eugenio, who promises to take her to a new country—the land of death. She is lowered onto the ground by the Judas tree outside her bedroom window and finds herself in a variety of landscapes. She keeps asking Eugenio to take her hand, but he refuses, offering instead flowers from the Judas tree. Laura accepts and eats the blossoms only to discover that Eugenio's hands have been reduced to bone. Eugenio accuses her of being a murderer and a cannibal; echoing lines from the Bible, he claims the blooms are his body and blood. Laura then awakens from her nightmare, afraid to fall back asleep.

### Major Themes

Thematic analyses of "Flowering Judas" typically emphasize the story's focus on love and betrayal, the latter most obviously evoked by the name Judas, the name of the apostle who betrayed Jesus, in the title. On the most simplistic level, Laura has betrayed Eugenio by participating in his murder. Though technically a suicide, Laura is, to a degree, responsible for his death, a fact that her subconscious realizes in her dream. Braggioni is similarly a betrayer; he is guilty of adultery and, like Laura, has sent men, including Eugenio, to their deaths. Critics additionally note there are more elaborate examples of betrayal in "Flowering Judas." For instance, Laura's lack of true political conviction and enthusiasm for the revolution are often seen as acts against the movement as a whole. Laura's role in Eugenio's death and her ambivalent attitude toward her pupils—she does not feel warmth for the children but appreciates "their charming opportunist savagery"—are also seen as a betrayal, or rejection, of life in general and love in particular. Porter's thematic focus on love is further reflected in the relationship between Laura and her various suitors. She ultimately rejects each of their advances, but her misleading attitude of tolerance and her, at times, thoughtless actions are misconstrued as encouragement. Her relationship with Braggioni, specifically his visit in the story—the imagery of which contains sexual connotations—is often viewed as a brief study of sexual repression, physical erotic love, and spiritual love. Other thematic interpretations of the story emphasize the importance of revolution and religion.

## Critical Reception

"Flowering Judas" is often discussed in conjunction with Porter's "Miranda" tales and other stories of hers having a Mexican setting. Whether discussed in this light or examined for its own literary merits, "Flowering Judas" is frequently praised as a stylistically and thematically unified masterpiece of the short story genre. Critics typically focus on the final scene of "Flowering Judas," the dream sequence, as well as Laura's visit with Braggioni, and much criticism has been generated about the tale's thematic focus on death, betrayal, denial, and love. "Flowering Judas" has also garnered praise for various stylistic features, including the use of flashbacks and the present tense, as well as the lack of a formal, linear story line. Commentators have also emphasized the semi-autobiographical story's inherent religious aspects, including allusions to the apostle Judas, works by T. S. Eliot and Dante Alighieri having religious overtones, the foot-washing scene involving Jesus and Mary Magdalene, and the sacrament of eucharist as first celebrated at the Last Supper. Nevertheless, such a focus, as critics assert, does not imply that "Flowering Judas" is solely a religious tale but a rather a sophisticated exercise in mood and outlook. As M. M. Liberman has written: "'Flowering Judas' owes its greatness not at all to some opportunistic employment of a conventional religious symbol to signify theme but to a brilliant narrative practice throughout, one capable of representing a feeling that, once apprehended by the reader, permits him to see with what overriding intelligence Miss Porter knew her Laura, 'the desperate complication of her mind' and what it meant."

## CRITICISM

### Ray B. West, Jr. (essay date 1947)

SOURCE: "Katherine Anne Porter: Symbol and Theme in 'Flowering Judas'," in *Accent,* Vol. 7, Spring, 1947, pp. 182-88.

[*In the following excerpt, West analyzes religious and political symbols in "Flowering Judas."*]

Katherine Anne Porter, in writing of Katherine Mansfield's fictional method in 1937, said that she "states no belief, gives no motive, airs no theories, but simply presents to the reader a situation, a place and a character, and there it is; and the emotional content is present as implicitly as the germ in the grain of wheat." Of her own method she has written: "Now and again thousands of memories converge, harmonize, arrange themselves around a central idea in a coherent form, and I write a story."

Enlightening though these statements are concerning Miss Porter's concept of a short story, true as they appear to be of her own fiction and of the creative process, they still leave the reader with his own problem of "understanding" when he is confronted with the individual story. If we disregard the fact that the first statement was made about a fellow artist (it is still descriptive of Miss Porter's own stories), we must yet discover the "germ" which produced the emotion and which flowers into the final form of the story. Though we might say that the converging, the harmonizing, and the arranging constitute a logical, though partly subconscious, activity which serves to bring the objects of memory into some kind of order, still it is the nature of this synthesis—particularly in the predominantly social themes from *Flowering Judas* (1930) to *The Leaning Tower* (1944)—which puzzles most readers.

That Miss Porter herself was aware of the nature of her sensibility is clear from her comments concerning Miranda in a late story, who had, she says, "a powerful social sense, which was like a fine set of antennae radiating from every pore of her skin." Miss Porter's own social sense is most obvious (perhaps too obvious) in her latest long story, **"The Leaning Tower,"** but it is not with the most obvious examples that the reader wishes to concern himself; rather, with the seemingly obscure; and since I have nowhere seen published or heard expounded an examination of **"Flowering Judas,"** and since it is perhaps Miss Porter's best known story (to my mind, her most successful single work of fiction), let us examine that with the aim of understanding just what the author means by social sensibility—how it operates within the story itself.

The surface detail in **"Flowering Judas"** is relatively simple. An American girl who has been educated in a Southern convent is in Mexico teaching school and aiding a group of revolutionaries under Braggioni, a sensual hulk of a man, formerly a starving poet, but who is now in a position to indulge even his appetite for the most expensive of small luxuries. The girl (Laura) teaches her children in the daytime and at night runs errands for Braggioni, acting as go-between for him and the foreign revolutionaries, delivering messages and narcotics to members of the party who are in jail. At the point where the story opens, Braggioni has come to Laura's apartment to discover, if possible, whether it would be worth the effort to attempt an assault upon her "notorious virginity," which he, like the others, cannot understand. Laura is physically attractive, and this is not the first time that she has been courted by the Mexicans. Her first suitor was a young captain whom she evaded by spurring her horse when he attempted to take her into his arms, pretending that the horse had suddenly shied. The second was a young organizer of the typographers' union who had serenaded her and written her bad poetry which he tacked to her door. She had unwittingly encouraged him by tossing a flower from her balcony as he sang to her from the patio. A third person, Eugenio, is unknown to the reader until near the end of the story, when it turns out that he is expected to die of a self-imposed overdose of the narcotics which Laura had delivered to him at the prison. He is, however, the principal figure in a dream which ends the story, a dream in which Laura imagines him to have accused her of murdering him and in which he forces her to eat of the blossoms of the Judas tree which grows in the courtyard below her window.

All of the immediate action takes place in Laura's apartment after she has returned and found Braggioni awaiting her. He sings to her in a voice "passionately off key," talks about their curious relationship, about the revolution, and finally leaves after having Laura clean his pistol for use in a May-day disturbance between the revolutionaries and the Catholics of a near-by town. Braggioni returns to his wife, whom he has deserted for a month to pay attention to Laura, and who, despite the fact that she has been weeping over his absence, accepts his return gratefully and washes his feet. Laura goes to bed and has her dream of Eugenio.

It will be seen, even from this brief summary, that there are a great many details unexplained by the course of the action. There is the concern with revolutionary activities running throughout; there are the comments concerning Laura's religious training: the nun-like clothing, her slipping away into a small church to pray, the May-day demonstration. Obviously, a great many details have symbolic references, not least of which is the title itself.

If we turn to any standard encyclopedia, we discover that the Flowering Judas is a tree commonly known as the Judas tree or Red-bud. We learn further that a popular legend relates that it is from this tree that Judas Iscariot hanged himself. A second fact is that the exact title appears in a line from T. S. Eliot's poem "Gerontion":

> In the juvescence of the year
> Came Christ the tiger

In depraved May, dogwood and chestnut, flowering
  judas,
To be eaten, to be divided, to be drunk
Among whispers.

This is scarcely a coincidence, since Eliot's passage so clearly suggests Laura's activity at the end of the story. Our first question is: what use is made of this symbol? The dividing, the eating and drinking among whispers suggests the Christian sacrament, but it is a particular kind of sacrament. "Christ the tiger" refers to the pagan ritual in which the blood of a slain tiger is drunk in order to engender in the participants the courage of the tiger heart. In a sense this is only a more primitive form of sacrament, one which presupposes a *direct* rather than symbolic transfer of virtues from the animal to man. In the Christian ritual, the symbolic blood of Christ is drunk in remembrance of atonement; that is, symbolically to engender the virtues of Christ in the participant.

If the Judas tree, then, is a symbol for the betrayer of Christ (the legend says that its buds are red because it actually became the body of Judas, who is said to have had red hair), then the sacrament in which Laura participated—the eating of the buds of the Flowering Judas—is a sacrament, not of remembrance, but of betrayal.

This leads us to other uses of the Saviour-symbol in the story. The first is Braggioni, who, at one point, is even called a "world-saviour." It is said that "his skin has been punctured in honorable warfare"; "He has a great nobility, a love of humanity raised above mere personal affection"; finally, he is depicted, like Christ, undergoing the final purification, the foot-washing. But there are important reservations in the use of this symbol: (1) the note of irony with which Braggioni is depicted and which suggests the attitude the reader should take toward him; (2) each time the Christ-like epithet is used, it is accompanied by other, non-Christian characteristics: "His skin has been *punctured* in honorable warfare, but *he is a skilled revolutionary*"; he is a *professional* lover of humanity, a *hungry* world-saviour. It is the use of the religious symbols alongside the secular which makes Braggioni the complex and interesting character that he is.

The second use of the Christ-symbol is present in the character of Eugenio, who is seen first as one of the revolutionary workers languishing in jail, but who figures most prominently as the person in Laura's dream. His name contains the clue to his symbolic meaning—well-born. As Christ is the Son of God, he is well-born. He is, likewise, a symbol of all mankind—Man. We say he is the "Son of Man." In this respect, Eugenio is also Christ-like, for he is well-born without the reservations noted in the character of Braggioni—in the highest sense. And as Judas was the direct cause of Christ's crucifixion, so Laura becomes the murderer of Eugenio (of Man) by carrying narcotics to his prison cell, the narcotics through which he (Christ-like) surrendered himself up to death.

We can say, then, that the use of religious symbolism by Miss Porter might suggest that her story be taken as a kind of religious allegory. But there are other, complicating symbols. There is, for instance, Laura's fear of machines such as the *automobile*; there is her dislike for things made on *machines*; and finally there is the statement that *the machine is sacred* to the workers. In the last instance, we may see how the word "machine" is coupled with the religious word "sacred," thus bringing the two kinds of symbols into juxtaposition, just as the same thing is implied in the descriptions we have had of Braggioni. For instance, "His skin has been punctured in honorable warfare" suggests the act of crucifixion, but "puncture" is not a word which we would ordinarily use in describing either the nailing of Christ to the cross or the piercing of his flesh by the spear of the Roman soldier. The most common use of "puncture" now is its reference to automobile tires (of which Laura is afraid). Likewise, the word "professional" used to modify "a lover of humanity" brings the modern idea of business efficiency into conjunction with the image of Christ, as though one were to say, explicitly: "Braggioni is an impersonal, cold-blooded Christ."

A third type of symbols is composed of love-symbols (erotic, secular, and divine). The story shows Laura unable to participate in love upon any of the levels suggested: (1) as a divine lover in the Christian sense, for it is clear that she is incapable of divine passion when she occasionally sneaks into a small church to pray; (2) as a professional lover in the sense that Braggioni is one, for she cannot participate in the revolutionary fervor of the workers, which might be stated as an activity expressive of secular love for their fellow men; she cannot even feel the proper emotion for the children who scribble on their blackboards, "We lov ar ticher"; (3) as an erotic lover, for she responds to none of her three suitors, though she thoughtlessly throws one of them a rose (the symbol of erotic love), an act of profanation, since the boy wears it in his hat until it withers and dies.

Having located these symbols, it is now our problem to examine the use that is made of them. More specifically, we can say that the religious symbols represent the Christian ideology, while the secular are symbols most readily identified with the attitudes of Marxism. As philosophy, they would seem to represent the two most extreme positions possible; yet both claim as their aim the betterment of mankind. If we consider them as areas within which man may act, we might represent them as two circles. . . .

At this point, we must remember the relationship between **"Flowering Judas"** and Eliot's "Gerontion." The poem is concerned with a wasteland image; that is, with a view of life as a wasteland, sterile and barren as old-age, because of the absence of any fructifying element. Eliot's old man in the poem says:

> I have lost my passion: why should I need to keep it
> Since what is kept must be adulterated?
> I have lost my sight, smell, hearing, taste, and touch:
> How should I use them for your closer contact?

In **"Flowering Judas"** Laura has lost the use of her senses: when the children scribble their message of love, she can feel nothing for them. They are only "wise, innocent, clay-colored faces," just as the revolutionists have become "clay masks with the power of human speech." She is like the prisoners, shut off from human contact, who, when they complain to her, "'Dear little Laura, time doesn't pass in this infernal hole, and I won't know when it is time to sleep unless I have a reminder,' she brings them their favorite narcotics, and says in a tone that does not wound them with pity, 'Tonight will be really night for you.'" Seeing the colored flowers the children have painted, she remembers the young captain who has made love to her and thinks, "I must send him a box of colored crayons." She confuses the children with the prisoners, "the poor prisoners who come every day bringing flowers to their jailor." "It is monstrous," she thinks with sudden insight, "to confuse love with revolution, night with day, life with death." Laura, like the figure in Eliot's poem, has lost her passion, she has lost her sight, smell, hearing, taste, and touch. She cannot use them for closer contact. . . .

Laura may be said to be outside any of the circles. Because of her early training, she is pulled away from a belief in the revolutionary cause of Braggioni. Because of her desire to accept the principles of revolution, she is unable to accept the principles of her religious education. Without either Christianity or Marxism, it is impossible for her to respond to her suitors or to the children. She cannot even feel pity for the prisoners; she can only supply them with narcotics, which likens their condition to hers, for her life seems to be a senseless kind of existence similar to the drugged sleep of the prisoners.

Braggioni's condition is likened to Laura's ("We are more alike than you realize in some things," he tells her), but there are two important differences: (1) he has the revolutionary ideal as a guide; (2) he is capable of redemption, as the final, footwashing scene with his wife ("whose sense of reality is beyond criticism") shows. We can say, then, that Braggioni is not, as Laura is, outside the circles. He is within one of them, but it is not until he is touched with pity that he is brought wholly within the area of redemption. Laura is not redeemed, even though she desires it, as the eating of the buds of the Judas tree suggests. Her sacrament is a devouring gesture and Eugenio calls her a cannibal, because she is devouring him (Man). She is, like Judas, the betrayer; and her betrayal, like his, consisted in an inability to believe. Without faith she is incapable of passion, thence of love, finally of life itself. Reduced to the inadequacy of statement, we might say that the theme, lacking all of the story's subtle comment, might be rendered as: Man cannot live divided by materialistic and spiritual values, nor can he live in the modern world by either without faith and love.

As the Nazi landlady in **"The Leaning Tower"** is made to say when overcharging the American student who wishes to cancel his lease: "Indecision is a very expensive luxury."

Laura's world, then, is as barren and sterile as the world of Eliot's "Gerontion"; it is a living death. Said another way, the living world exists only in our sensory perception of it, and any deadening of the senses (through a denial of traditional human values) constitutes a relinquishing of moral responsibility—the betrayal of mankind into the hands of the Braggionis or, as in **"The Leaning Tower,"** into the hands of the Nazis.

This is, I suspect, what one reviewer discovered as early as 1938, when, in a review of the volume *Flowering Judas,* he wrote: "Miss Porter, I feel, is one of the most 'socially conscious' of our writers." But one might also fear that this reviewer was thinking in terms of the predominant Marxist movements of the thirties, into none of which Miss Porter could, obviously, be made to fit. "I do not mean," he continued, "simply that she is conscious of the physical suffering of her impoverished people; I mean rather that she understands the impoverishment of mind and spirit which accompanies the physical fact, and she sees too that some native goodness in these minds and spirits still lives."

But if "some native goodness" were all Miss Porter's characters had to recommend themselves to us as resolutions of our social dilemma, then every author who does not allegorize good and evil is still "socially conscious," and the reviewer's remarks represent a somewhat dubious compliment. The fact is, however, that he was right perceptually. Behind Miss Porter's elaborate structure of symbol and myth lies the psychological motivation which produces the theme. The germ which lies implicit in the grain of wheat is the central idea about which her memories cluster. An idea does not constitute her "meaning" in the usual sense of the word, but it represents a concept which makes the surface detail available to meaning. To put it another way, the very rightness of the *ideological* fact (the myth or symbol) charges the *particular* fact (the object as it exists in nature) with a meaning that is presented as an experiential whole, but which is available in all its complex relationships only when we have become aware of the entire field of reference.

### George Hendrick  (essay date 1965)

SOURCE: "My Familiar Country: Alienation" in *Katherine Anne Porter,* Twayne Publishers, Inc., 1965 pp. 39-43.

[*In the following excerpt, Hendrick provides a thematic analysis of "Flowering Judas," noting its focus on religion, self-destruction, betrayal, and the "wasteland theme."*]

**"Flowering Judas,"** (1930) can profitably be read in the light of "Where Presidents Have No Friends," Miss Porter's brilliant analysis of the Obregón revolution. Though feeling a profound respect for the aims of the movement, she sees the confusion and the cross-purposes

present at both the highest and lowest levels, as further confused by foreign opportunists who found support from many groups. "The result," she wrote, "is a hotbed of petty plotting, cross purposes between natives and foreigners, from the diplomats down to the unwashed grumbler who sits in the alameda and complains about the sorrows of the proletariat. In all this the men in present power are struggling toward practicable economic and political relations with the world." This story also marks a great change in Miss Porter's fictional presentation of the Mexican scene—for the first time, she presents an extended study of the expatriate in Mexico.

Miss Porter's own account of the composition of this justly famous story also provides a key to its meaning:

> **"Flowering Judas"** was written between seven o'clock and midnight of a very cold December, 1929, in Brooklyn. The experiences from which it was made occurred several years before, in Mexico, just after the Obregon revolution.

> All the characters and episodes are based on real persons and events, but naturally, as my memory worked upon them and time passed, all assumed different shapes and colors, formed gradually around a central idea, that of self-delusion, the order and meaning of the episodes changed, and became in a word fiction.

> The idea first came to me one evening when going to visit the girl I call Laura in the story, I passed the open window of her living room on my way to the door, through the small patio which is one of the scenes in the story. I had a brief glimpse of her sitting with an open book in her lap, but not reading, with a fixed look of pained melancholy and confusion in her face. The fat man I call Braggioni was playing the guitar and singing to her.

> In that glimpse, no more than a flash, I thought I understood, or perceived, for the first time, the desperate complications of her mind and feelings, and I knew a story; perhaps not her true story, not even the real story of the whole situation, but all the same a story that seemed symbolic truth to me. If I had not seen her face at that very moment, I should never have written just this story because I should not have known it to write.

> [*This Is My Best,* 1942]

Ray B. West wrote in "Katherine Anne Porter and 'Historic Memory'" that he was puzzled by the naming of the central character "because so many of the background facts concerning Laura were similar to those in Katherine Anne Porter's own experience, the strict Catholic upbringing, the interest in modern social causes, and the fact that Miss Porter had taught in Mexico. . . ." Mr. West asked why the character was not named Miranda, and Miss Porter replied that "Laura was modeled upon a friend" with whom she taught in Mexico, but the character was a "combination of a good many people, just as was the character Braggioni. . . ." Autobiographic qualities, therefore, may be present; for she may have combined some facets of her own character and those of the fictional Miranda into the fictional Laura.

**"Flowering Judas"** has been a favorite story for symbol hunting, and Miss Porter has recently commented pertinently [in *Recent Southern Fiction: A Panel Discussion,* 1960] "Symbolism happens of its own self and it comes out of something so deep in your own consciousness and your own experience that I don't think that most writers are at all conscious of their use of symbols. I never am until I see them. They come of themselves. . . . I have a great deal of religious symbolism in my stories because I have a very deep sense of religion and also I have a religious training. And I suppose you don't invent symbolism. You don't say, 'I am going to have the flowering Judas tree stand for betrayal,' but, of course, it does." Miss Porter's recent statement does underline, in many ways, however, the validity of much of Ray B. West's interpretation in *The Art of Modern Fiction.* According to legend, Judas hanged himself from a redbud tree, and the title occurs in Eliot's "Gerontion":

> In the juvescence of the year
> Came Christ the tiger
> In depraved May, dogwood and chestnut, flowering
> judas,
> To be eaten, to be divided, to be drunk
> Among whispers.

As West points out, the Judas tree is a symbol of betrayal, and Laura's eating of the buds is a sacrament of betrayal. Braggioni, the professional revolutionary, the professional lover of men, self-pitying and ruthless, is ironically presented as a "world-saviour." Eugenio (literally the "wellborn") is somewhat Christ-like; and, like Judas, Laura is directly responsible for the death of Eugenio since she brings the narcotics he uses in his suicide.

West's analysis of the love symbols in the story is particularly influential in recent criticism of **"Flowering Judas."** He sees Laura incapable of participating "(1) as a divine lover in the Christian sense, for it is clear that she is incapable of divine passion when she occasionally sneaks into a small church to pray; (2) as a professional lover in the sense that Braggioni is one, for she cannot participate in the revolutionary fervor of the workers, which might be stated as an activity expressive of 'love' for their fellow men; she cannot even feel the proper emotion for the children who scribble on their blackboards, 'we lov ar titcher'; (3) as an erotic lover, for she responds for none of her three suitors, though she thoughtlessly throws one of them a rose (the symbol of erotic love). . . ."

The old man in Eliot's "Gerontion" had lost his "sight, smell, hearing, taste, and touch"; and Laura is also a wasteland figure, outside of religion, revolution, and love. Braggioni, West believes, is capable of redemption, as the foot-washing scene would indicate, but Laura is not. Therefore the theme of the story may be stated: "Only in faith and love can man live."

West, however, tends to overemphasize the religious interpretation. The wasteland-Christian symbolism is, of course, clearly present in the story, and it is used to underscore Laura's disenchantment with what she knows but cannot admit is a false revolution. Without courage to disentangle herself, she drifts along in the movement, is filled with despair, feeds on the lives of others, and realizes the full extent of her betrayal only in her symbolic dream. The dream, utilizing common Christian symbols as it does, indicates the strength of the religious and ethical system she had partially put aside while she worked in the revolutionary movement. True, she sometimes sneaked into Church, but it was to no avail, and she ended by examining the tinseled, jumbled altar with the doll-saint whose drawers, trimmed in lace, had dropped about his ankles.

The scene not only enforces the wasteland theme but also shows clearly that Laura was, by the very nature of her early social training, a false revolutionist too: she could not, for example, put aside her aristocratic preference for hand-made lace. Braggioni—the name suggests his braggart nature—has equally betrayed the revolution; but he still has some ideals, can still speak of a world order built anew after the rot of centuries had been destroyed. But he spoke of his idealism as if he were addressing followers, and he quickly promised physical violence and destruction before the new order could flourish. This obscenely fat, false revolutionist, vile as he is, is at least capable of action both revolutionary and amatory; but Laura, although she had once obviously been touched with the idealism of the movement, was now paralyzed, unable to love—even betrayed love by throwing the flower to the suitor who stood by the Judas tree.

Her involvement in Eugenio's death is clear: she allows him a final act of self-destruction. Braggioni's attitude is Am I my brother's keeper? and he has nothing but contempt for Eugenio—a fool, he calls him. Braggioni is following a completely different set of values from those of Laura, and his concern is more for the movement—and his own gratification—than with individual man. But because she has no revolutionary myths deeply implanted in her subconscious, Laura sees, in the dream, the implications of her act played out in traditional Christian terms. When Eugenio offered his body and his blood, she cried "No." Had she subconsciously been able to say "Yes" without reservations, she would have been able to continue believing in the amoral (according to Christian standards) revolution; but in crying "No," while knowing that she was, as Eugenio called her, a cannibal, she realized for the first time the extent of her betrayal of herself and of her religious, ethical, and humanitarian principles. Some of her Christian precepts were as obviously flawed—her romantic concept of self as Virgin, the hiding of her body, her fear of close human contact, her aristocratic pretenses—but she was unaware of these faults.

Like a Hemingway hero, she was afraid to sleep after this dream of self-realization. Will she, frightened by her betrayal, return to her religion, a religion which in practice helped enslave the Mexicans? Will she merge Christian idealism with revolutionary idealism and find or found a more worth-while movement? Will she continue her self-isolated, wasteland existence? Miss Porter provides no answer. Laura has been a victor over self-delusion, but is not her seeming victory also ironic?

## Sister Mary Bride (essay date 1963)

SOURCE: "Laura and the Unlit Lamp," in *Studies in Short Fiction,* Vol. 1, No. 1, Fall, 1963, pp. 61-3.

[*In the brief essay below, Bride comments on the relationship between chastity, religion, and spirituality in "Flowering Judas."*]

A superficial reading of Katherine Anne Porter's **"Flowering Judas"** could very well lead one to regard it as a manifesto of what might be called the theology of the aesthete, in which chastity is the first of the capital sins and the refusal of sexual indulgence replaces the oppression of the poor as the sin crying to heaven for vengeance.

Like Browning, however, at the conclusion of "The Statue and the Bust," Porter might well have commented that sex will serve as well as anything else for her purpose; after all, it is the modern symbol of fulfillment. The real theme of **"Flowering Judas"** is still "the unlit lamp and the ungirt loin."

Laura (surely the evocation of Petrarch serves ironic purpose here) does not merely reject illicit love; she rejects all love. She rejects life. She is the essence of negation.

Laura's existence is neatly summed up in the course of the story in "the one monotonous word, 'No,'" which "holy talismanic word" preserved her from being "led into evil." Even though she was a teacher, she had no love for the little children who crowded around her each morning with fervent greetings and festooned her desk with flowers. They "remain strangers to her." A professed revolutionary, she "cannot say" precisely what holds her to the revolutionary cause. In Braggioni's service she performs deeds requiring cool courage and daring, but the people for whom she performs these acts remain indifferent to her. "Even if a known face" peers out at her from the gloom of some hideout into which she has penetrated at considerable risk with an important message, "still it is the face of a stranger." A beautiful woman, she arouses neither gossip nor jealousy because everyone knows that "nothing comes" of the ardors her beauty inspires in inexperienced admirers. She recounts the suicide of Eugenio with the complete detachment of a secretary dictating a business letter. Braggioni brings out her spiritual deadness when he asks, "Are you not in love with someone?" "No." "And no one is in love with you?" "No." "Then it is your own fault," he comments; "the legless beggar woman in the Alameda has a perfectly faithful lover."

Laura's abstention is not chastity. The "Hail Mary" uttered perfunctorily on her "golden rosary" is declared "no good." Her white collar is "not purposely nun-like." Her religion, like everything else about her, is a set of "principles derived from her early training"—a system of motions rigidly adhered to without reason or feeling. True chastity, far from being a mere matter of abstention, is a positive thing. It is not a renunciation only, but a liberation, a freeing of love from clinging preoccupation with self in order that it may give self in joyous abandonment to God. The truly chaste soul is not cold and self-contained but fired by a passionate love for all of God's creation, because in everything it sees a reflection of Him whom it loves. The chastity of a Francis of Assisi, a Francis Xavier, or a Frances Cabrini was a devouring flame.

> **"Flowering Judas" . . . is a condemnation not of chastity but of that peculiar spiritual deadness so much feared and decried in medieval spiritual treatises under the title of "accedia."**
>
> **—*Sister Mary Bride***

The revolting Braggioni emerges in the end of the story a more admirable character than Laura. He is saved by the pure love of his wife, washed clean by her tears and his own contrition. For all his bestial appearance and manners, he is a man, a leader, "his skin has been punctured in honorable warfare." No one questions his leadership or his commitment to "the cause." He is capable of loving and inspiring love. The abasement of the neglected and humiliated wife, which at first irritates the reader, is ennobled by its totality of love, by her full and free acceptance of this man to whom she has pledged herself. With the eyes of love she has been able to pierce through the mountain of obesity and infidelity which has inspired our loathing, and to see in him still the strong lover. That love and faith have power in the end to penetrate his armor of indulgence and self-complacency, to kindle the spark of nobility slumbering within him. "He is sorry for everything and bursts into tears."

**"Flowering Judas,"** then, like "The Statue and the Bust," is a condemnation not of chastity but of that peculiar spiritual deadness so much feared and decried in medieval spiritual treatises under the title of "accedia." It is a paralysis of the will, induced through a refusal on the part of the soul to make a resolute choice between good and evil. Unwilling to risk the loss of either world, the slothful soul temporizes, trying to hold on to the advantages of both without making a declaration for either. This soul finds the burden of freedom too uncomfortable; it would like, by a rigid adherence to a round of "duties" mechanically performed, to substitute an external conformity for inward commitment. To such the *Apocalypse* utters the dread sentence: "I would that thou wert hot or cold, but because thou art lukewarm I will begin to vomit thee out of my mouth."

Such chastity as Laura possessed is well characterized by William Langland, expressing in *Piers Plowman* a commonplace of medieval spirituality in the lines:

> Chastity without charity (wit you well)
> Is as senseless as a lamp that no light is in.

### Beverly Gross   (essay date 1968)

SOURCE: "The Poetic Narrative: A Reading of 'Flowering Judas'," in *Style,* Vol. 2, No. 2, Spring, 1968, pp. 129-39.

[*In the essay below, Gross discusses technical, thematic, and stylistic aspects of "Flowering Judas," delineating the story's poetic and poetical nature.*]

I would like to raise some questions about poetic narrative with the hope of making some sense out of the vague but useful recognition which the term conveys—that narrative form may at some times and in some ways take on some of the qualities of poetry. What these are and how they may affect the nature and powers of narration I propose to discuss through the example of Katherine Anne Porter's **"Flowering Judas."**

When we call a story "poetic" we may mean a variety of things. We may be saying something about its language, that it achieves the expressiveness and density of poetry. Or we may be saying something about its form, that its synthesis is spatial rather than temporal, that what it does is not to chronicle an action through a beginning, a middle, and an end, but to deploy, let us say, a succession of images, moods, epiphanies. Finally, we may be suggesting that the content of a story is "poetic," that its subject matter is particularly stirring or lyrical or sentimental. "Poetic" here has nothing at all to do with either language or form. It may be just a kind of critical *ad populum,* used in much the same way that "dramatic" often connotes exciting and "prosaic" connotes dull. I would prefer not to consider this use of "poetic" at all since it depends so much on the particular areas of soft-heartedness of the particular reader. It will be difficult enough as it is to talk about—paradoxically—the poetic form of narration and the poetic language of prose.

That paradox and the possibility of so many confusions make one wonder whether anything at all can be meant in the idea of a poetic narrative. And yet certain narratives really do contain in their language and in their form something which is more essentially what we would expect of poetry. In this discussion I will consider first what I take to be the poetic language and then the poetic form of a story which so very often and with so much vagueness gets deemed "poetic": Miss Porter's **"Flowering Judas."**

Critics have commonly recognized that the distinction between the language of prose and poetry cannot be a merely formal one. Indeed there are some—Walter Pater is one—who assert that there is no difference at all. But for what I have to say about **"Flowering Judas"** I must proceed from the assumption that there is a difference, and that the particular power of this story comes from the very fact that this difference is largely bridged. Prose is not poetry, but prose can be *poetical,* and even more than this, *poetic.* Prose language is poetical when it merely partakes of some of the devices of poetry; for prose to be poetic something more is demanded. I can explain what I mean by poetical language easily enough because it can be exemplified. Sound reinforces sense in prose as well as poetry, but instances of such reinforcement are felicitous occasions—*poetical* moments—in prose, and not really a transcendence into poetry. Rhythmic enforcement is one example of a poetical device used in this story. At various times the rhythm helps convey the hopeless monotony of Laura's life. Faced with the prospect of another of Braggioni's nightly musicales, Laura asks him if he has a new song for her. "If he says yes, she asks him to sing it. If he says no, she remembers his favorite one, and asks him to sing it again." The jingly quality of the anapests enforces the indication that they have been said again and again before, and supports the story's atmosphere of inescapable boredom and disillusion. One can also find occasional alliteration used to intensify the dramatic effect. Laura, in her anger at Braggioni's insolence, "imagines herself leaning forward suddenly, and with a sound back-handed slap wiping the suety smile from his face." The repetition of the sibilants in *suddenly, sound, slap, suety, smile, his,* and *face* produces a vocal hiss which is an audible representation of Laura's mood.

Again, these are examples of poetical, not poetic, prose. Poetic prose cannot be thus exemplified. It has much more to do with a certain use of language and with a pervasive quality in that language. We think of the language of prose as only an instrument, but the language of poetry as the poetry itself. Prose narrative is conveyed *through* language; poetry is forged *out of* language. That idea alone is often the basis for some *prima facie* distinction between prose and poetry. The remarkable thing about the language of **"Flowering Judas"** is that experience in this story is forged out of its language: the language reflects and supports the very quality of life which is established by the narrative.

It is possible to consider only a few separate aspects of language to give substance to this idea. The way the language is shaped and the vision it expresses are primarily what I want to talk about. The vision is a function of diction, description, metaphor—aspects of style which have an important bearing on the characterization of Laura and which mirror the perceptual reality of her life. But first I would like to consider the shape of the language, in particular the story's sentence patterns. As the basic structural units upon which the narrative is built they point up something fundamental about the telling of this story for they operate with the regularity and formal support of the poetic line.

There is a characteristic sentence pattern through **"Flowering Judas"** which gives a discernible weave to the story as a whole: a simple statement followed by an elaborating counter-statement. The elaboration is usually ironic, at times even back-biting. Here, for example, are three statements about the revolutionist, Braggioni:

> The gluttonous bulk of Braggioni has become a symbol of her many disillusions, for a revolutionist should be lean, animated by heroic faith, a vessel of abstract virtues.

> [Braggioni's parents] gave him the love and knowledge of music, thus: and under the rip of his thumbnail, the strings of the instrument complain like exposed nerves.

> Now he is a leader of men, crafty men who whisper in his ear, hungry men who wait for hours outside his office for a word with him, emaciated men with wild faces who waylay him at the street gate with a timid, "Comrade, let me tell you . . ." and they blow the foul breath from their empty stomachs in his face.

This weave is the dynamic tension between illusion and disillusion.

The sentences about Laura herself are especially revealing: they reflect her almost catatonic refusal to act, to think through consequences because her original, innocent notions have been so thoroughly and consistently refuted by the reality which always, though deviously, asserts itself. The counter-statements are the devious assertions: they represent not what Laura is noticing or realizing, but the more objective responses of an all-seeing narrator, less afraid, less repressed than Laura herself. Laura could know most of these things, but the amplifications give the impression of coming from someone else. Although the narrative point of view is by and large limited to Laura's consciousness, the story is written through a double vision, Laura's and the narrator's, which gives the impression that Laura will not allow herself to be conscious in her consciousness. One extended passage will show how this works. Every sentence contains a pivotal coordinating conjunction which I've italicized. Precisely at the point at which the conjunction occurs, the sentence moves into an objective amplification, sometimes even a refutation, of the opening clause:

> She was born Roman Catholic, *and* in spite of her fear of being seen by someone who might make a scandal of it, she slips now and again into some crumbling little church, kneels on the chilly stone, and says a Hail Mary on the gold rosary she bought in Tehuantepec. It is no good *and* she ends by examining the altar with its tinsel flowers and ragged brocades. . . . She has encased herself in a set of principles derived from her early training, leaving no detail of gesture or of personal taste untouched, *and* for this reason she will not wear lace made on machines. This is her private heresy, *for* in her special group the machine is sacred, and will be the salvation of the workers.

These structures of coordination, the characteristic sentence pattern in this story, allow for a very fluid relationship of ideas within the sentences themselves; they grow according to their own requirements in creating units of mood, effect, or idea. A great range of related and even apparently unrelated material is often yoked together within the same structural framework to form such a unit. The sentences are complex, abundant, even "run-on." Independent clauses frequently are "spliced" together when they bear an important enough relationship in meaning or mood to warrant incorporation within one sentence. Often the conjunctions are dispensed with and a kind of ragged coordination is produced. Indeed at times the sentences are nothing like syntactic units at all—they are units of emotion whose only principle of order is that their components mirror some mental state. "1-2-3-4-5—it is monstrous to confuse love with revolution, night with day, life with death—ah, Eugenio!" The divisions in this sentence occur right at the dashes. The first part is lexically meaningless. It is intended to convey a sense of Laura's troubled sleeplessness. We are told earlier that "numbers tick in her brain like little clocks," and the sentence just preceding records a series of confused images running through her mind. The second part of the sentence is an aphoristic statement rationalizing the confusion. The nouns are used in an abstract, non-sensory function to suggest that this succession of thought is a different kind of mental process from the production of concrete images and sounds. And finally, "ah Eugenio!" culminates the effect by revealing still a third kind of mental anguish. The first part shows a confusion which is the combined result of fatigue and a sense of failure; the second part suggests an intellectual confusion; and the third part, a succession of five syllables like the numbers of the first part, is a simple utterance of despair.

The dialogue in the story strongly contrasts with the richness and complexity of the narration. Braggioni's utterances are always composed of short, simple sentences with much verbal repetition. This is not the simplicity of eloquence, but the simplicity that suggests the speaker is incapable of any great mental formulations. Laura too seems to suffer from a language barrier. She thinks in fluid, complex English ("'It may be true I am as corrupt, in another way, as Braggioni,' she thinks in spite of herself, 'as callous, as incomplete'"); but her speeches are almost as monotonously constructed and as flat as Braggioni's: "Today, I found Eugenio going into a stupor. He refused to allow me to call the prison doctor. He had taken all the tablets I brought him yesterday. He said he took them because he was bored." The prisoners, we are told, find her Spanish amusing. Her trouble communicating with them and with everyone else is still another expression of Laura's isolation as an exile.

Notable too is the shift in language whenever a revolutionary attitude comes up. The diction changes abruptly and becomes formalized and abstract; the rhythm loses its flow and begins to stiffen. "She tells herself that throwing the flower was a mistake, for she is twenty-two years old and knows better; but she refuses to regret it, and persuades herself that her negation of all external events as they occur is a sign that she is gradually perfecting herself in the stoicism she strives to cultivate. . . ." The stilted, unnatural language of the second part of the sentence reinforces the sense of the stilted unnaturalness of Laura's self-isolation and frigidity, which is the underlying subject of the passage as a whole.

---

**One measure of the poetic vision in "Flowering Judas" is that so much of the story is realized and related metaphorically.**

*—Beverly Gross*

---

The diction thus reflects Laura's way of thinking. Descriptions in the story reflect her way of seeing: the descriptive phrases are characteristically figurative, ironic, incongruent. Their power to evoke comes from their power to surprise. Laura looks at Braggioni, for instance, and sees him "swell[ing] with ominous ripeness"; and elsewhere, "balancing his paunch between his spread knees." Concrete expressions of physical feelings are used to convey the feel of an emotional state: "She is tired of her hairpins and the feel of her long tight sleeves" suggests the physical confinement which is an extension of Laura's emotional and spiritual constraint. A kind of irony is effected through descriptive incongruities: Laura loves her students' "tender round hands and their charming opportunist savagery." In church she observes "the battered doll-shape of some male saint whose white, lace-trimmed drawers hang limply around his ankles below the hieratic dignity of his velvet robe." Epithets and descriptive phrases are especially notable for the startling, sometimes paradoxical, relation between adjective and noun: "pitiless courtesy"; "specialized insolence"; "immaculate voices"; "puzzled eyebrows"; "notorious virginity"; and "benevolent anarchy."

Descriptions using color have a special significance. Braggioni is described in purple and yellow only. This is not merely a loud combination: these are supplementary colors that are chromatically incompatible. Braggioni has yellow hair, "tawny yellow cat's eyes," wears "glossy yellow shoes," and carries a "yellow silk handkerchief." He is also sporting "mauve silk hose," a "lavender collar," and a "purple necktie." By contrast, the colors ascribed to Laura are almost monochromatic: white, gray, and dark blue. She wears a blue serge dress with a white collar, and sleeps in a white linen nightgown. Her eyes are gray, though Braggioni significantly mistakes them for green. The colors attributed to Braggioni and Laura thereby reinforce the sense of the self-indulgence of one and the self-abnegation of the other.

One measure of the poetic vision in **"Flowering Judas"** is that so much of the story is realized and related metaphorically. The story depends upon comparison for its most crucial revelations. The metaphors themselves range

from the simplest kinds of likenings to highly complex multiple associations. But the implications of even the simple metaphors are rich and revealing. "The houses lean together like conspirators" reflects Laura's sense of the hostility of her environment. "Numbers tick in her brain like little clocks" conveys her nervous sleeplessness. There is an underlying irony in "the incomprehensible fullness of her breasts, like a nursing mother's": the suggestion of maternity is antithetical to Laura's emotional frigidity. The phrase, "her notorious virginity," follows almost immediately after. This is a kind of negative metaphor: the comparison is made to contrast, rather than to compare. Another negative metaphor, more explicitly so, is "her round white collar is not purposely nun-like." This, too, is ironic simply because the collar *is* in fact nun-like. The metaphor underscores the idea that Laura's sacrifice to a political ideal is a perversion of religious devotion.

The story also abounds in more suggestive metaphors in which the comparison is only implied. They are almost always used for irony, and enable the narration to maintain the semblance of detachment and coolness even when it is conveying great contempt. Braggioni, who is usually the victim of these comparisons, is described in his singing as "taking the high notes in a prolonged painful squeal": the porcine comparison is tacit but unmistakable. Braggioni's once thin frame, we are told, is now covered with "easy billows of fat": "billows" produces an image of flesh compounded out of swelling waves. Braggioni is characterized as "a professional lover of humanity": "professional" love suggests nothing so much as prostitution. A special kind of suggestive metaphor is effected by wrenching words out of their usual contexts. Braggioni has a "*suety* smile"; he sings to Laura "in a *furry*, mournful voice" as he "sits *heaped* upon the edge of a straight-backed chair much too small for him." These words are instances of more than stylistic originality. For to describe Braggioni as "heaped" is to make the metaphoric transformation of his flesh into inert, lumpy deadweight—his corpulent presence in that chair is conveyed as something like an overstuffed sack of potatoes. And in this way Bragioni is introduced in the story's opening words.

More complex still are certain metaphors that depend upon multiple associations and certain metaphors that undergo a considerable, sometimes even a thematic, development through the course of the story. Braggioni's "cheeks are bellying with the wind of song" is a metaphor which develops through multiple associations. The image of a sail-boat is suggested here. The word "bellying," moreover, though having a verbal function meaning "to swell," also evokes its noun definition, and becomes inescapably linked with Braggioni's cheeks. There is, in addition, an appropriate pun on *bellowing*. "Wind of song" instantly suggests that the song is windy, which, according to a good desk dictionary will mean among other things: verbose, pompous, boastful, flatulent. The phrase may also have been intended as an ironic echo of "*wings* of song."

We learn that Laura's refusal to wear machine-made lace "is her private *heresy,* for in her special group the machine is *sacred,* and will be the *salvation* of the workers." The three religious terms force the connection, however ironic, between religion and revolution, a connection which is made repeatedly through **"Flowering Judas"** and which is particularly crucial for the story's ending.

One metaphoric motif undergoes a progression of effect. Through the course of the story Braggioni's guitar becomes increasingly vitalized and, as a result, increasingly tortured by its player. Braggioni begins innocently enough, merely "thumbing the strings of his guitar." But the effect starts to build almost immediately: "He scratches the guitar familiarly as though it were a pet animal"; "under the rip of his thumbnail, the strings of the instrument complain like exposed nerves"; and finally, "Braggioni curves his swollen fingers around the throat of the guitar and softly smothers the music out of it."

Metaphors in **"Flowering Judas"** are also put to a symbolic use. The betrayal of Jesus metaphorically underlies the story as a whole. The relationship is not worked out with purposeful accuracy; the elements are merely used for their suggestiveness. Eugenio and Braggioni, for instance, are both compared with Jesus. This is done for dramatic purposes in one case, for ironic purposes in the other. Braggioni fancies himself a savior and is ironically described as one: "he will live to see himself kicked out from his feeding trough by other hungry world-saviors." He is a lover of humanity, though only by profession. His description of what will happen to the world when he takes over is suggestive of the Harrowing of Hell: "Some day this world, now seemingly so composed and eternal, to the edges of every sea shall be merely a tangle of gaping trenches, of crashing walls and broken bodies." And when Braggioni comes home after a month's absence, his martyred wife washes his feet and begs his forgiveness.

The association between Eugenio and Jesus is made in Laura's dream in which, significantly, Laura figures as Judas. In her dream, a skeletal Eugenio urges Laura to eat "the warm bleeding flowers" of the Judas tree, and then suddenly and inexplicably denounces her for accepting them. His accusation is made in terms which suggest that she is partaking of an obscene Eucharist: "Murderer! said Eugenio, and Cannibal! This is my body and my blood." The Christ motif here is equivocal and confusing, but it is so to suggest something about the state of Laura's consciousness and her confused relation to herself. In the disorder of her dream she emerges as both the betrayer and the betrayed—and moreover, betrayed into her very act of betrayal. At the heart of all this is the suggestion that Laura has failed the revolutionary ideal because it has failed her. Compassion and idealism—the promptings of the revolutionist—have soured into frigidity and disillusionment. What Laura has turned into, the Laura of the story, is made more understandable through the shadowy events of her dream. Laura's dream, coming at the very end of **"Flowering Judas,"** is in a way the story's most crucial exposition. But not exposition in the usual narrative sense in which the past is brought in as a background for explaining the present. The dream in **"Flowering Judas"** is not narrative background but poetic vision: it metaphorically re-enacts the process of Laura's disillusionment.

There is, finally, one special stylistic aspect of **"Flowering Judas"** that directs us to a consideration of form. The story is told almost entirely in the present tense. Besides bringing the reader into closer intimacy with the situation by conveying the sense that the action is happening right now, before his eyes, the present tense has also the effect of suggesting habitual action with a concomitant feeling of monotony, boredom, and pointlessness. Braggioni has been visiting Laura every night for a month. She knows that this night is like all the others, and that it will probably go on this way into the future: "Braggioni is there almost every night. No matter how late she is, he will be sitting there. . . ." The use of the present tense has the further effect of investing the narrative with a kind of dreaminess. The action has not been fixed in time. This is sensed by the reader and even confirmed for him explicitly: "Laura has just come from a visit to the prison, and she is waiting for tomorrow with a bitter anxiety as if tomorrow may not come, but time may be caught immovably in this hour, with herself transfixed, Braggioni singing on forever, and Eugenio's body not yet discovered by the guard."

Paradoxically, the dream-sequence at the end of the story is related in the past tense, which gives the envisioned event a place in time and thus a sense of reality that the actual events of Laura's life do not attain. It is significant, too, that the final action of the story, Laura's awakening, is given to us in the past tense: "Laura cried No! and at the sound of her own voice, she awoke trembling, and was afraid to sleep again." For the first time in the story something *has* happened. (Throughout the story things *are* happening, but that is not at all the same.) Laura's terrified awakening is the realest event—in fact the only event—of the story. Except for the dream, which takes place only in Laura's mind, the awakening is the story's single recorded action. It is fixed in time and finalized: "Laura *cried* . . . she *awoke* . . . and *was* afraid."

The repression which is the dominant aspect of Laura's condition is supported by everything in the story including the sentence patterns. In the ending we see the painful breakdown of Laura's defense: she is forced to confront her own involvement and psychic guilt and the inadequacy of her withdrawal. But this final display is just that—it is less a denouement than a synthesizing image. The story's principle of development is not the completion of an action but the rounding off of a vision—in this case, the depiction of a moral consciousness. There is no beginning, middle, and end in this story; there is only a deepening awareness. What has happened to Laura, what will happen to Laura are ultimately less important than what *is* happening to her. In this respect, the synthesis of **"Flowering Judas"** is really more lyrical than dramatic, its deployment is more spatial than temporal, its mode is more poetic than narrational.

And yet, **"Flowering Judas"** is a story and not a poem. The final point about its poetic language and form is that they are there to support the telling of a story. The poetic language deepens our apprehension of Laura, the atmosphere of her mind, her perceptions, her very life. And the story's moral and dramatic consequence comes precisely from the subordination of its narrative energy in favor of this poetic evocation of a state of mind.


## Leon Gottfried   (essay date 1969)

SOURCE: "Death's Other Kingdom: Dantesque and Theological Symbolism in 'Flowering Judas'," in *PMLA,* Vol. 84, No. 1, January, 1969, pp. 112-24.

[*Here, Gottfried examines Porter's use of religious symbolism and ideals in "Flowering Judas," particularly those evinced in Dante Alighieri's writings, as well as her focus on negation and death.*]

### I

> I have a great deal of religious symbolism in my stories because I have a very deep sense of religion and also I have a religious training. And I suppose you don't invent symbolism. You don't say, "I'm going to have the flowering judas tree stand for betrayal," but, of course, it does.
>
> (Katherine Anne Porter, "News and Ideas," *CE,*
> Vol. XXII, April 1961)

The attempt to portray hell and its leading personages by relating them parodically to heaven, or, in other words, by using inversions of varying degrees of complexity, is traditional. Scholastic theologians like St. Thomas regularly related the various virtues and kinds of blessedness to their opposites, and both Dante and Milton, the two greatest poetic infernologists, made systematic use of parody or ironic parallelism. Katherine Anne Porter, in **"Flowering Judas,"** a story dealing with latter-day lost souls, is clearly working in this ironic mode; she uses references to the religion of the machine, two parodic saviours, symbolic perversions of the purification ceremony of foot-washing and of the sacrament of communion, and a nun-like, lapsed devotee of the religion of revolution. At the same time, certain cautions must be observed. Miss Porter is not a theologian, nor a theological poet in the same sense in which Dante is. In most of her other works, although many of them are charged with symbolism, often religious symbolism as she says, there is comparatively little explicit use of the religious and eschatological diction and imagery so prevalent in **"Flowering Judas."** In fact, even taking the word in the most extended sense, one would be unlikely to call her a "religious" writer as T. S. Eliot or François Mauriac are religious writers.

The principal difference that sets her apart from the "religious" writers, however, is not only the fact that in most of her work she has not so explicitly used the elaborate system of religious allusions so prominent in **"Flower-**ing Judas,"** but rather that her portrayal of hell (not only in **"Flowering Judas"**) is without reference to any corresponding "heaven" or given system of ultimate values, other than those of Catholicism and Marxism, both discredited. In this respect she is a typical modern secular writer, for whom meaning and value are created, not given; she enacts the characteristic doom of the modern Promethean artist struggling to carve out of the chaos of experience some order or meaning which can come into existence, if at all, only after the struggle. In her 1940 Introduction she calls the stories in *Flowering Judas and Other Stories* "fragments of a much larger plan," a plan which has never fully materialized. "They are," she goes no, "what I was then able to achieve in the way of order and form and statement in a period of grotesque dislocations in a whole society when the world was heaving in the sickness of a millenial change." For herself, she says, "most of the energies of my mind and spirit have been spent in the effort . . . to understand the logic of this majestic and terrible failure of the life of man in the Western world." Admitting that the voice of the individual artist in such times may seem inconsequential, she nevertheless concludes with a triumphant statement of faith in art itself:

> the arts do live continuously, and they live literally by faith; their names and their shapes and their uses and their basic meanings survive unchanged in all that matters through times of interruption, diminishment, neglect; they outlive governments and creeds and the societies, even the very civilizations that produced them. They cannot be destroyed altogether because they represent the substance of faith and the only reality. They are what we find again when the ruins are cleared away.

Although she is referring specifically to the period of the two world wars, Miss Porter is speaking of art in a way that might have met with ready understanding and approval any time these three hundred years or more, and assuredly for the last century and a half, and she speaks of it in much the same religious tone used by T. S. Eliot to urge the necessity of keeping alive another sort of faith during what he believed to be our spiritual Dark Ages. But faith in the vitality and reality of art itself ("the only reality") is not at all the same as faith in the existence of an order or spirit informing that other "reality" of which art has commonly been held to be a reflection. In Miss Porter's writing, such an order is implicit only by absence or negation. Yet, in her story of the failure of a young woman involved in the materialistic revolutionary movement in Mexico of the 1920's, Miss Porter's early training and background made spontaneously available to her a rich store of religious imagery and language, behind which lie centuries of systematic theological thought, to give order and form to one of her sketches of the "failure of the life of man in the Western world."

### II

> I know thy works, that thou art neither cold nor
> hot: I would thou wert cold or hot.

So then because thou art lukewarm, and neither
cold nor hot, I will spue thee out of my mouth.

(Rev. iii.15-16)

In **"Flowering Judas,"** as in a number of her other stories, Miss Porter is concerned with the problem (or sin)
of noninvolvement and the waste for which it is responsible. Among the many other writers who dealt with the
theme of the half-alive spiritual state during the period
*entre deux guerres* perhaps the most influential was
T. S. Eliot. It is therefore not surprising that we find
Miss Porter in **"Flowering Judas"** drawing, as did so
many other authors of the period, upon Eliot's poetry.
Her story owes its title and the use of the tree's blossoms as a substitute for the Host in a travesty of Christian communion directly to his "Gerontion," but the landscape of the heroine's dream at the end of the story, in
which the infernal communion takes place, is even more
reminiscent of the imagery of "The Waste Land" and "The
Hollow Men." Thematically the story has affinities to all
these poems, but "The Hollow Men" seems especially
close in theme and imagery to the problems of Laura,
Miss Porter's heroine. Like the life-in-death of the hollow men, Laura's life is characterized by "Shape without
form, shade without colour, / Paralysed force, gesture
without motion." Each of Eliot's negations is carried out
in the imagery of Laura's story.

Behind both Eliot's hollow men (and much of his other
poetry of this period) and Miss Porter's Laura, who so
much resembles them, lies the *Inferno* of Dante, and
especially the third canto, wherein is depicted the fate of
the souls who were neither good nor evil, who had never
truly lived—those "sorrowful souls" (*anime triste*) whose
eternity is spent in aimless wandering in the vestibule of
hell, as they had lived "without blame and without praise"
(*sanza infamia e sanza lodo,* ll. 35-36). Central among
these lost souls, and representative of their plight, is that
of one (perhaps Pontius Pilate) "who, through cowardice,
made the great denial" (*Che fece per viltè il gran rifiuto*). Negation or refusal of spiritual responsibility is the
keynote of the spiritual existence of these creatures, as
it was for Pilate, as it is for the hollow men, and as it has
become for Laura. Feeling that "she has been betrayed
irreparably by the disunion between her way of living and
her feeling of what life should be," Laura has sought a
point of fixity in commitment to the revolutionary cause,
but the commitment is wholly outward: "she wears the
uniform of an idea." Like the saint or mystic, "she is not
at home in the world" and tries to persuade herself that
her stoical denial of all external events "is a sign that she
is gradually perfecting herself" in a spiritual discipline
cultivated against some nameless, impending disaster. But
her stoicism is a parody of the spiritual discipline of the
saint or mystic, for her unworldliness is utterly dissociated
from joy. Totally negative, it does not stem from stirrings
of kinship with anything beyond herself and her world,
but from "the very cells of her flesh [which] reject knowledge and kinship in one monotonous word. No. No. No."

Laura, to be sure, is not entirely "without praise." We are
told, indeed, that "all praise her gray eyes, and the soft,

round under lip which promises gayety, yet is always
grave." Nevertheless, "Nobody touches her," and her
greatest fame is for the "puzzle of her notorious virginity," a virginity whose quality is purely negative. But the
thematic patterns of negation in the story are more complex than this, and far more complexly interwoven with
Dantesque imagery. The ultimate refusal is that of life
itself, and we are given an example of this in the suicide
of Eugenio, a suicide that seems the logical culmination
of his meaningless, dope-sodden, imprisoned existence.
His death was not a protest nor an act of pride, but in
keeping with the general motif of *acedia* which dominates the story—he committed suicide "because he was
bored." Laura, the uninvolved, did nothing about it. "He
refused to allow me to call the prison doctor," she says,
though in his stupor he could not have prevented her from
doing so. In Laura's dream at the end of the story, Eugenio appears to her, calls her murderer, and hands her "the
warm and bleeding flowers" that he stripped from the
Judas tree. As he holds them to her lips, she becomes
aware that he *is* the tree, "that his hand was fleshless, a
cluster of small white petrified branches," and that she is
eating his body and blood. Now the image of bleeding
and talking plants is familiar from both Virgil [*Aeneid*]
and Dante, but the association with suicide is Dante's
alone. In the *Inferno* (Canto xiii) Dante is guided through
the wood of suicides. By misusing their freedom of bodily
movement, these souls have robbed themselves of their
own form forever. They are pent up in trees and bushes,
and can find expression only in the agony of bleeding
when some chance passerby such as Dante, or when
malicious creatures such as the Harpies, break leaves or
branches from them. While they bleed they can speak.
With beautiful appropriateness, Miss Porter has blended
the image from Dante with the idea of infernal communion from Eliot's "Gerontion"—:

In depraved May, dogwood and chestnut, flowering
   judas,
To be eaten, to be divided, to be drunk
Among whispers . . .

to achieve a rich unifying statement, symbolic in form,
connecting all the negations of life and love implicit in
Laura's story with the ultimate negation of life by self-
destruction.

If we are to believe Dante, the great poet of the spiritual
life, love is the spring of all spiritual (and indeed, for
him, physical) motion. In the *Purgatory* he has Virgil
explain that neither the creator nor any creature is devoid
of love (*Nè creator, nè creatura mai . . . fu sanza amore,*
xvii. 91-92). But the whole of Dante's *Purgatory* is designed to show that our sins stem from three sorts of
perversion of love, freely chosen: love of wrong objects,
excessive love of proper but secondary objects, and finally deficiency of love (*poco di vigore,* l. 96). The last
vice is the way of the slothful, whose lack of diligence in
pursuit of the good is the sin of *acedia*. Appropriately, it
is on the cornice of the slothful in the *Purgatory* that
Virgil pauses to explain the doctrine of love and its relation to sin. In the *Inferno,* which is not organized ac-

cording to the seven deadly sins, the slothful souls are given no distinct habitation, but may have some relationship to the *cattivi* of the Antinferno (Canto iii), the souls who were kin to those angels who were neither rebellious nor faithful to God, but were for themselves (*che non furon ribelli / Nè fur fedeli a Dio, ma per sè fuoro,* iii.38-39). In **"Flowering Judas,"** it is Laura's deficiency of love that Braggioni, her revolutionary leader, finds most difficult to understand. Braggioni himself is an evil soul who becomes positive at least by virtue of action, and he cannot see why Laura "works so hard for the revolutionary idea unless she loves some man who is in it. 'Are you not in love with someone?' 'No,' says Laura. 'And no one is in love with you?' 'No.' 'Then it is your own fault'."

But to understand Laura more fully, we must direct our attention to Braggioni himself, who seems at so many points to be her opposite. Whereas she is prim in her blue serge dress and round white collar "not purposely nun-like" (it is "one of twenty precisely alike, folded in blue tissue paper in the upper drawer of her clothes chest"), he is resplendent in his expensive and gaudy dress. Whereas she is ascetic and notoriously chaste, he is a sensualist. He is frankly opportunistic, while "she has encased herself in a set of principles." She cannot love at all, but he is able to love *himself* with great "tenderness and amplitude and eternal charity." Yet in spite of these contrasts and more, Braggioni pointedly insists to Laura that "We are more alike than you realize in some things." And although she inwardly rejects the kinship, she yet admits to herself, "It may be true I am as corrupt, in another way, as Braggioni, . . . as callous, as incomplete." If there is indeed such a similarity, where can it lie?

### III

Amari habent iram permanentem propter permanentiam tristitiae, quam inter viscera tenent clausam . . .

(St. Thomas Aquinas, *Summa Theologica,*
II-II, Q. 158, Art. 5)

It is at once evident in **"Flowering Judas"** that Braggioni, though prideful and vainglorious, is preeminently a man of wrath, both by profession and inclination, and that his wrath is of the permanent sort stemming from a deep inner wound. St. Thomas in describing the wrathful follows Aristotle by distinguishing among three kinds: the quick-tempered (*acuti*), the vindictive (*difficiles*), and, in the passage quoted above, the sullen (*amari*). Dante consigns the souls of the sullen to the fifth circle of the *Inferno* (Canto vii) where they are permanently buried beneath the black slime of the sorrowful (*tristo*) Styx. Dante calls them in Italian the sorrowful (*tristi*), and he seems to echo Thomas when he fancies them describing themselves as bearing within themselves their sluggish or slothful fume (*Portando dentro accidioso fummo,* vii.123). Because they darkened the glad light of the sun and the sweet air with their sullenness, they now sadden themselves in the black muck (*Or ci attristiam ne la belletta negra,* l. 124). Completely submerged, they of

course cannot communicate directly, but Virgil is able to interpret for the sake of his disciple the bubbles they make, commenting afterwards that this is the song they gurgle inwardly, in their throats (*Quest' inno si gorgoglian ne la strozza,* l. 125). St. Thomas observes of anger (*ira*) in general that it is compounded of the contrary passions of hope (of vengeance) and sorrow (on account of some pain that has been suffered). Of the sullen specifically, we have seen that he attributes the permanence of their anger to a permanent sorrow (*tristitia*) which they nurse inside themselves.

If we examine Braggioni, beginning with his description in the first paragraph of the story, certain details are strikingly prominent. In the opening sentence we see him in an uncomfortable heap, singing in a "furry, mournful voice." Lately Laura has found him waiting for her every night with his "surly, waiting expression," "snarling a tune under his breath." Unaware in his vanity of his "miserable performance" as a singer, he refuses Laura's offer of the brown beverage chocolate, for it "thickens the voice." A few pages further on, he is described as singing another song "with tremendous emphasis, weighing his words," in sharp and perhaps ironic contrast to his normal style which is like the muddy gurgling of Dante's *tristi* who cannot speak whole words (*Chè dir nol posson con parola integra,* vii. 126) because of their situation. The song he sings is a melancholy ditty in which the singer complains of his utter loneliness with no one to console him. He finds a clear singing voice, it seems, only to indulge his meaningless and self-pitying sorrow. It is not long before his self-pity and melancholy find speech, as he tells Laura, in language suggesting both the Psalmist and Christ: "It is true everything turns to dust in the hand, to gall on the tongue." Indeed, in his abiding *tristitia,* this secular saviour recalls by travesty Isaiah's "man of sorrows, and acquainted with grief." Like the Biblical man of sorrows, Braggioni assuredly "hath no form nor comeliness." Isaiah's servant of the Lord "was wounded for our transgressions," and Braggioni sees himself as "wounded by life." In spite of his unrestrained self-indulgence, nothing satisfies him; he sighs, "I am disappointed in everything as it comes. Everything." It is at this point that he affirms his kinship with Laura; "You, poor thing, you will be disappointed too. You are born for it. We are more alike than you realize in some things. Wait and see." Braggioni's grotesque melancholy is at last appeased when he returns to his long-suffering wife. She calls him her "angel" and washes his feet in a parody of Christian ritual, and in his softened and sentimental mood, "he is sorry for everything and bursts into tears. 'Ah, yes, I am hungry, I am tired, let us eat something together,' he says between sobs." He enjoys the luxury of sobbing with his wife, who is represented as a *mater dolorosa,* endlessly weeping. In her tears she begs her idol to forgive her, "and this time he is refreshed by the solemn, endless rain of her tears."

Laura's stern self-control may seem at the opposite pole from the maudlin emotionalism of Braggioni, but at any rate she seems to share with him an abiding sorrow. She denies life, hiding her vital body with its "long, invaluably beautiful legs" and its "great round breasts . . . like a nursing mother's" in ascetic, nun-like garb, just as she has encased her soul in "the uniform of an idea." Braggioni is a minister of death, consecrated to an apocalypse of "gaping trenches, of crashing walls and broken bodies." He reserves his love for pistols and cannon and his faith for dynamite. He is an embodiment of St. Paul's warning against excessive sorrow, for "the sorrow of the world worketh death." Laura recognizes this as she hands him his gunbelt, saying: "Put that on, and go kill somebody in Morelia, and you will be happier." Braggioni the wrathful, with his infinite love and charity for himself, is a worker of death, but Laura oils and loads his pistols. She lacks even love for herself, but is allied to death through her very passiveness and through the self-delusion which monstrously confuses "love with revolution, night with day, life with death." She may abstractly love the "tender round hands" of the pupils in the school where she teaches, but they "remain strangers to her."

Braggioni is guilty of every sin, but Laura is virtuous only by negation, not by attachment to any good. "Denying everything, she may walk anywhere in safety, she looks at everything without amazement." Her "bold talismanic word," *No,* serves her in place of the Lord's prayer, for it "does not suffer her to be led into evil." Her deficiency of love renders her the victim of that spiritual sloth or *acedia* that Thomas calls *tristitia de bono spirituali,* sorrow in the face of spiritual good. If our association of *acedia* with Dante's *cattivi* be allowed, we have seen that the poet denies even a total death to the souls who die confirmed in this sin. Just as Laura lives in Mexico but is not accepted by it ("I am tempted to forgive you for being a *gringa,*" says Braggioni), so the souls of the univolved in Dante are rejected by both Heaven and Hell, where the damned might have some glory over them (*Ch' alcuna gloria i rei avrebber d' elli*). They are denied even the consummation of damnation, for they were never alive (*che mai non fur vivi*), and have no hope of death (*non hanno speranza di morte*).

Laura, we discover, who is so frightened of life, is equally frightened of death. Although she "may walk anywhere in safety," she is possessed by what may not be a wholly irrational fear "that violence, mutilation, a shocking death, wait for her." She translates this "warning in her blood" into homely terms by taking excessive precautions when crossing streets, so as not to be killed by an automobile. She has devoted herself to a cause which promised men that they might have life more abundantly only to find herself an agent of the forces of death, a cause which seemed to offer an earthly fulfillment of charity only to discover it riddled with intrigue, jealousy, and selfishness. Braggioni's "gluttonous bulk," so different from the "vessel of abstract virtues" she had imagined the ideal revolutionist to be, becomes the "symbol of her many disillusions." The life more abundant has become a "feeding trough" for him and other envious "hungry worldsaviours." But in spite of her disillusion, Laura is paralyzed. She "feels herself bogged in a nightmare," incapable of loving either man or God; she has no positive good to which she can turn and so remains motionless, the

unwilling but unrejecting agent of death. Charity is travestied in her routine, abstract attachment to the class of children she teaches and in her distribution of narcotics to the prisoners in the "infernal hole" of their prison, the narcotics which Eugenio employs to kill himself. It is not irrelevant that St. Thomas calls *acedia* a vice directly opposed to the theological virtue of charity.

> **Not only the characters but the atmosphere of the story is saturated with the feeling most characteristic of damnation—despair.**
>
> *—Leon Gottfried*

It is clear on both psychological and theological grounds that there must be some connection between those whom Dante calls the *tristi* or sullen and the spiritually indifferent (*anime triste*) of the vestibule of the Inferno. Yet the former are granted at least the dignity of damnation while the latter go mournfully sighing forever in circles, in an eternal state of alienation. The similarity is that both possess a permanent sorrow leading to a rejection of spiritual goods, but the difference seems to be between those who have made a moral choice, that is, whose wills have assented to an illicit indulgence of an appetite, and those who have vitiated their humanity by abstaining from moral choice itself. *Acedia,* that is, may be described as a state of soul or a disposition which may lead to disengagement, cowardice, negation, or indifference on the one hand, or on the other may manifest itself in that species of anger we call sullenness whose victims are punished with the other wrathful. These observations on Dante suggest the grounds, rooted in traditional Catholic psychology, of the similarity between Laura and Braggioni, as well as a pregnant contrast between them. If her activaties are a travesty of charity, so are his. Hungry men constantly wait for him outside his office or accost him on the street. "He is always sympathetic," we are told. "He gives them handfuls of small coins," and beyond this, promises. He uses them ruthlessly, and despises them. "They are stupid, they are lazy, they are treacherous, they would cut my throat for nothing," he tells Laura. When she informs him of the death of Eugenio, Braggioni's callous comment is, "He is a fool, and his death is his own business," and again, "He is a fool and we are well rid of him." By her passive acceptance of her situation and by her wilful efforts at self-delusion, Laura is a passive accomplice in his crimes. St. Thomas observes that sloth, though a special vice in relation to the Divine good, may also be a circumstance of all vices in relation to the specific goods of which they are the opposites. Laura admits to herself that she may be as incomplete as Braggioni, but their conditions of incompleteness are nevertheless different; each has his own distinct kind of damnation.

Perhaps all the major spiritual differences between them can be traced to one cause—that Laura, the idealist, feels deep attachment only to abstract principles, but none to any living thing, while Braggioni has no principles save that of expediency, but is possessed of a deep and passionate love. That this love is, however, directed toward himself accounts for the fact that, far from the Pauline "vessel of abstract virtues," he is in fact a vessel of all the deadly sins. As we have seen, the main details in his first appearance confirm him as one of the wrathful. He is devoted to destruction, telling Laura with some disappointment that "Once I dreamed of destroying this city, in case it offered resistance to General Ortiz, but it fell into his hands like an overripe pear." As a professional revolutionary, he is a "stirrer-up of strife" like the figure of Ira in *Piers Plowman,* and in this role might belong in the ninth bolgia of the eighth circle of Dante's *Inferno* with the "sowers of discord." Even his softer activities are portrayed in combative terms. His amours are vengeful—"A thousand women have paid for that," he says, referring to his early humiliation by a girl—and when he wishes to put an end to his music for the evening he "curves his swollen fingers around the throat of the guitar and softly smothers the music out of it." Indeed, Braggioni possesses the characteristics of all the kinds of the wrathful. As we have seen, there is an abiding, sullen melancholy in him which likens him to St. Thomas' *amari.* Moreover, like the *acuti,* he is quick to anger, "sensitive to slights." And finally, like the *difficiles* (also known as the *graves*), he is vindictive. He is "cruel to everyone" and it is "dangerous to offend him."

But in addition to wrath, Braggioni is also guilty of pride (*superbia*) and envy (*invidia*), the three sins which in Dante's scheme of the *Purgatory* are caused by love of the wrong objects. Of these, pride or excessive love of self, the sin of Lucifer, is primary. Braggioni is vain and sensitive, we are told, because of the "vast cureless wound of his self-esteem." Like Milton's Satan, he is an effective leader because he "loves himself with such tenderness and amplitude and eternal charity that his followers . . . warm themselves in the reflected glow" and convince themselves of his nobility. His likeness to Lucifer the arch-rebel is further borne out not only by the repeated references to his being a revolutionist, but also by inversion through the many parodic details showing him as a secular Christ. He is of vaguely foreign extraction, his father and his name having come from another country. He is a "world-saviour" whose "skin has been punctured in honorable warfare," but "he will never die of it." He is a "professional lover of humanity," "wounded by life." In the first paragraph of the story when Laura returns to her home her maid says with "a glance towards the upper room, 'He waits'." He tells his followers that "they are closer to him than his own brothers, without them he can do nothing." He urges them to be "on the watch" (for spies) and holds forth promises of a bright future—"until tomorrow, comrade!" He is obsessed by his apocalyptic vision of the destruction of the existing world, expressed by the author in the vivid language of eschatology. He joyously imagines everything "hurled skyward and distributed, cast down again clean as rain, without separate

identity . . . no one shall be left alive except the elect spirits destined to procreate a new world cleansed of cruelty and injustice, ruled by benevolent anarchy." Finally, there is the reunion with his wife, the ceremony of her washing his feet, and their communion of weeping.

---

**It is abundantly clear that the whole story is saturated in the language and imagery of theology and eschatology.**

*—Leon Gottfried*

---

Equally Satanic is the motivation of envy, and again the author has taken pains to establish the deep-rootedness of this vice in Braggioni. Although a revolutionist dedicated to the abolition of class distinctions, he boasts of his Jockey Club perfume, "imported from New York," and is proud of his "expensive garments" tricked out with diamonds and silver ornaments. These, like his conquests of women, and like the very fat that encases him, are the satisfactions of an envy traceable to his impoverished youth when "he was so scrawny all his bones showed under his thin cotton clothing . . . and he could never find enough to eat anywhere, anywhere!" All in all, Braggioni is well endowed with the attributes of the sins of malice (Dante's *malizia* comprising all the sins of violence and fraud in the *Inferno*). "He has the malice," we are told, "the cleverness, the wickedness, the sharpness of wit, the hardness of heart, stipulated for loving the world profitably."

But Miss Porter has not neglected to treat of all the possibilities of wickedness in her description of Braggioni, for he is equally devoted to the "natural" sins categorized in the *Inferno* as those of incontinence and in the *Purgatory* as those of excessive attachment to secondary goods—namely, the sins of gluttony (*gula*), avarice (*avaritia*), and lust (*luxuria*). After some of his inner qualities have been defined, we are made to see his "suety smile," his "gluttonous bulk," his oily, balloon cheeks, his "paunch between his spread knees," and his fat legs over the tops of his glossy yellow shoes swelling "with ominous ripeness," and later in the story mention is made of his "good food and abundant drink." His lustfulness is evident from his designs on Laura, his boasting of his thousand conquests, and his remark that "One woman is really as good as another for me in the dark. I prefer them all." Although he is apparently not avaricious in the common sense of stinginess, he gives his poor fellows only "small coins from his own pockets," while indulging himself with every luxury; theologically, his excessive preoccupation with material goods and his desire for more of them than is necessary are the marks of avarice. "He is not rich, not in money," he tells Laura, "but in power, and this power brings with it the blameless ownership of things, and the right to indulge his love of small luxuries," such as his expensive clothes, his hired automobile, his soft bed, and his imported perfume. Finally, there is the intermediate sin of sloth. I have already said a good deal about spiritual sloth above in discussing the relationship between sullenness, *acedia,* and *tristitia.* Of course, neither Braggioni nor Laura is guilty of that common slothfulness in the active life known as laziness (*pigritia*), she less than he, for both are energetic workers in the cause. But in keeping with what appears to be a general scheme of making Braggioni into a vessel of all the abstract vices, there is in him a trace at least of even this vice, for we are told of his enjoying "plenty of sleep in a soft bed beside a wife who dares not disturb him," and of his sitting "pampering his bones in easy billows of fat."

For Braggioni the sinner, it would seem, there is some consolation. Although everything disappoints him in the end, he at least enjoys the pleasures of his vices, revelling in his power over others and in the possession of the goods of this world. At the end of the story he is left with his wife enjoying a communion which, if it is a travesty of Christian communion, is at any rate consummated as they blend their tears, in contrast to the aborted communion in the immediately ensuing scene of Laura's dream. In the language applied by T. S. Eliot to Baudelaire, he is man enough to be damned. [*Selected Essays,* 1950]. He corresponds perhaps to the "lost violent souls" who are contrasted with Eliot's "hollow men," or to Kurtz in Conrad's *Heart of Darkness,* the story from which Eliot took the title and epigraph for his poem—the Kurtz who, through self-deification, achieved a glory of diabolism that puts him altogether beyond the wretched, papier-mâché devils of Conrad's story who had nothing inside but a little dirt. Or again, he is like the damned in Dante's *Inferno* who might glory over the souls of the indifferent if the latter were permitted to enter Hell.

For Laura, on the other hand, there is no consolation. She is un-evil, but also un-good. Her children love her; they spend their playtime writing with childish joy in tinted chalks on the blackboard "We lov ar titcher," and wreathing the words with innocent flowers, flowers in ominous contrast to the purple blooms of the judas tree which return to haunt her dreams. But she cannot love them back. She is loved and desired by men, but can feel nothing for them. Her specific failures as a woman prefigure her general failure as a human being. When she tries to pray, her lips, like those of the "hollow men," can only "Form prayers to broken stone." She continues to work for a revolutionary cause in which she no longer believes because she lacks the energy of spirit to break away. She is neat and fastidious, intelligent, intermittently perceptive, and hopelessly lost, frightened of both life and death. In spite of the likeness between her and Braggioni which he insists upon and which she partly admits, the final sense of contrast is overwhelming, and is forcefully underscored by the author's supremely disgusting but highly colored picture of Braggioni in ironic contrast with the impression of grayness left by the image of Laura.

## IV

Per me si va ne la città dolente . . .
   Lasciate ogni speranza, voi ch'entrate!
                         (*Inferno* iii. 1-9)

Not only the characters but the atmosphere of the story is saturated with the feeling most characteristic of damnation—despair. The abandonment of hope enjoined upon the damned in the legend carved upon the gate of Dante's hell may be taken more as a description of the state of damnation than as an imperative. That is, despair is less a specific punishment of the damned than a general and essential condition of, and virtually a synonym for, damnation. As St. Isidore says in a passage cited by St. Thomas, "To despair is to fall into hell." Dante himself, though under special divine protection, is forbidden to gaze upon Medusa (generally understood to represent despair), the sight of whom turns men to stone; Virgil goes so far as to cover Dante's eyes with his hands to save his charge from a sight which would forever have prevented his return to the world of light, living man though he was. This menace threatens Dante's progress through the realms of the damned at the point of his passage from upper to lower hell, the "city of Dis" (Canto ix). There is of course no special place set aside in the *Inferno* for the hopeless, since the condition of an eternity of waiting without hope is precisely what all hell is, and is shared by all the damned regardless of their special sins or special punishments. Even the virtuous pagans of Limbo (Canto iv), who suffer no special pains, are condemned to exist for eternity, as they had lived in this world, outside the pale of hope.

The fetid atmosphere of despair, of waiting without hope, hovers over the whole of the story of **"Flowering Judas,"** and the imagery of hell surrounds not only Laura and Braggioni, but is pervasive in the story. The political prisoners, for example, who are "of her own political faith," and whom Laura visits in their cells, complain that "time doesn't pass in this infernal hole." These outcast souls, who frequently "lose patience and all faith," curse their friends on the outside for not coming to their rescue, but these friends are generally little better off. They "dare not set foot in the prison for fear of disappearing into the cells kept empty for them," cells reminiscent of the special place in hell reserved for Boniface VIII in Canto xix of the *Inferno*. Laura's errands of mercy to the prison are linked with her errands to "men hiding . . . in back streets in mildewed houses, where they sit in tumbled beds and talk bitterly." Like the damned, all are waiting, fearing, cursing, in the dark, with hopes constantly being dimmed by anger and fear. In her nightmare confusion Laura even confuses the prisoners and the children she teaches, with their innocent faces and "immaculate voices," and thinks of herself as their jailer. To the extent that the outcasts have any hope or faith, it is in Braggioni, whose favor "is their disputed territory." But this false saviour cynically submits them to at least purgatorial punishment. "Let them sweat a little," he observes. "The next time they will be careful." If one is in real danger Laura will enter his hovel in the darkness, with money and the message—and it seems impossible to overlook the sardonic pun on Vera Cruz (True Cross)—"Go to Vera Cruz and wait." Laura herself both dreams and lives out a nightmare of paralysis. She too waits in dread without hope among people who "cannot understand why she is in Mexico." Like a person in a nightmare, she feels the urgent need to escape but cannot. When Braggioni, the flesh in which her revolutionary ideals have been incarnated, leaves her room, she thinks, "Now she is free . . . I must run while there is time. But she does not go." With the outcasts whom she visits (and with many of the damned souls in Dante), Laura shares an intense preoccupation with time, perhaps representing all that is arbitrary in human relationships. Her body, as she prepares for sleep, does not respond to the natural rhythm. Instead, like the prisoners, she must remind herself that it is time to sleep. "Numbers tick in her brain like little clocks, soundless doors close of themselves around her" as she enters, in sleep, her own private nightmare hell.

---

**Because of the absence of any viable faith in "Flowering Judas," it is a portrayal of a hell without a heaven.**

*—Leon Gottfried*

---

Indeed, it is abundantly clear that the whole story is saturated in the language and imagery of theology and eschatology. To the many examples already given might be added others, such as Laura's private rejection of machine-made lace, a rejection which she recognizes to be a "heresy" against the religion of "her special group" who believe that "the machine is sacred, and will be the salvation of the workers." The nameless youth who has attached himself amorously to Laura comes and sings "like a lost soul" in her patio. Words such as "faith," "charity," "love," "patience," and "forgive" are liberally distributed through the text; interestingly enough, only the word "hope" does not appear, replaced perhaps by references to Laura's "uneasy premonitions," "disillusions," and "sense of danger." More particularly, there are still other apparent allusions to Dante, in addition to those already mentioned. Laura, for example, knowing "what Braggioni would offer her" and determined to resist, "sits in her deep chair with an open book on her knees," a picture reminiscent through reversal of Francesca, whose book instead of protecting her from lust, betrayed her to it. The "violence" and "mutilation" which Laura fears suggest the punishments of the Inferno proper which she fears to visit when, in her dream, Eugenio calls her "Murderer" and commands, "follow me, I will show you a new country." Like Dante on the brink of the dolorous valley of the abyss (*la proda . . . / De la valle d'abisso dolorosa,* iv. 7-8), she is fearful of moving unless her guide takes her hand, "and she clung first to the stair rail," then to various other supports in successive downward steps suggestive of the steps of hell. Her downward motion passes "the rocky ledge of a cliff, and then to the jagged wave of a sea that was not water but a desert of crumbling stone," a forceful evocation of the general landscape of the *Inferno.* Rejecting with a cry of "No!" the recognition of evil which Eugenio attempts to force upon her,

she "awoke trembling, and was afraid to sleep again," another reversal of the situation in the *Inferno* where Dante, trusting his guide, falls "like one overcome by sleep" (*come l'uom che 'l sonno piglia,* iii.136).

Even the colors of the story (and it is, in a quite literal sense, a very colorful story) seem to form theological patterns. The main color impression of the story derives from the title itself; no one who has ever seen the judas (redbud) tree in bloom can forget the peculiar intensity of its scarlet-to-purple flowers from which, by association with the red hair of the arch-betrayer, the tree takes its name. There is such a tree in Laura's garden, and it appears twice in the story, but never in full daylight (the *Inferno* too is a place of darkness). On the first occasion it is seen by moonlight (no stars, Dante's symbol of divine light, are mentioned), with its "scarlet blossoms" dyed "dull purple" by the darkness. The imperial color of purple is, at the same time, the prevailing color associated with Braggioni with his "lavender collar," "purple necktie," and "mauve silk hose." Thus, he is linked with the judas tree in two ways—as the betrayer of his followers and of Laura's illusions, he is Judas, and again by the color conversion of scarlet, the color of blood and the theological color of charity or love, to purple, the color of empire (as the revolution intended to set men free becomes only an exchange of one set of tyrants for another). The second time the tree appears is in Laura's dream, where it serves first as one of the steps of her downward journey, then as the supplier of the "warm bleeding flowers" which Eugenio feeds her, and finally it becomes Eugenio himself. The blossoms are now their true color of blood, but it is the blood of betrayal rather than of forgiveness in this parody of the last supper: "Murderer! said Eugenio, and Cannibal! This is my body and my blood." These interpretations of the colors of red and purple are quite consistent with Dante's use of them (compare *Purgatory,* Cantos xxix, xxx), and other colors in the story bring out still further theological parallels.

All the colors of Laura's garden by moonlight are distortions of the colors of the theological virtues of faith, hope, and love, just as the virtues themselves appear in the story in perverted forms. The bright white radiance of faith becomes a dim replica of itself as "The moonlight spread a wash of gauzy silver over the clear spaces of the garden." The normally predominant color of a garden, green, the color of hope, and also of life and carnality, is obscured by the darkness and shadows into cobalt blue, in keeping with the general absence of hope in the story. Curiously enough, the color green appears only once, when Braggioni, in his song, inexplicably changes Laura's eyes from their true gray (colorlessness, chastity) to green. And finally, as we have seen, the scarlet blossoms of the tree have become dull purple. Significantly, Laura finds it impossible to feel anything for the boy singing beneath her window; instead, "the names of the colors repeated themselves automatically in her mind, while she watched not the boy, but his shadow."

One last theological symbol, and perhaps the most confusing one, is the figure (he is far too shadowy to be called a character) of Eugenio. Ray West sees in him another Christ-symbol, along with Braggioni [Ray B. West and Robert Wooster Stallman, *The Art of Modern Fiction,* 1949]. But where Mr. West perceives the irony in Miss Porter's use of Braggioni in this way, he seems to accept Eugenio at face value as a true Christ figure. He bases his presentation upon the meaning of the name "Eugenio"—well-born—and upon his allegedly Christ-like behavior in surrendering himself up to death by means of the narcotics brought by Laura, the Judas. On the face of it, this seems to be an unlikely interpretation, for there is nothing further in the story to indicate how Eugenio might in any way be a means of salvation, whether secular or theological; he is far too slender a figure in the story to carry such weight. And when we add the few details about him that are given, such an interpretation becomes even more unlikely. His death was not a martyrdom to a cause, but a suicide through boredom and despair—quite a different thing from the passion of Christ. Furthermore, in the dream, he offers himself as the way to death, not to life: "Where are you taking me? she said. . . . To death, . . . said Eugenio." When he gives her the flowers, Laura sees "that his hand was fleshless, a cluster of small white petrified branches." Instead of the Light shining in the darkness, Laura perceives that "his eye sockets were without light." Finally, his own metamorphosis into the tree, an image of damnation taken from Dante's forest of suicides in the circle of the violent (*Inferno,* Canto xiii), suggests that he is as much to be taken parodically as Braggioni himself. His betrayal of life through suicide, it is implied, is but a more violent, a more thoroughly fulfilled version of Laura's own negation of life through spiritual sloth. This would seem to be the true meaning of the infernal communion between them in Laura's dream, when Eugenio says in the language of Christ and "in a voice of pity, take and eat: . . . This is my body and my blood." But his point is to confirm her a member of the damned. In this connection, the similarity of Laura's last cry before slipping into sleep—"ah Eugenio!"—to the last agonized cry of Marlowe's Faustus—"Ah, Mephistophilis!"—may be more than fortuitous, especially since the next paragraph, immediately following Laura's cry, begins "The tolling of the midnight bell is a signal." Of course, if Eugenio is too slight and ambiguous a figure to bear the weight of being the saviour, it may be straining interpretation to make him into a devil. But certainly he is primarily associated with despair, death, and damnation, and not at all (unless ironically) with salvation.

## V

As he our darkness, cannot we his Light
Imitate when we please?

(*Paradise Lost* ii. 269-270)

The modest conclusion to which we must come, then, is not that Miss Porter has a positive religious message to transmit, but that as a chronicler of the desiccation of the soul of Western man in our time she has found in traditional religion and in Dante's poetry a valid source of language and images for dealing, intensely but obliquely, with various states of spiritual vacuity and decay. It is not necessary to assume, of course, that Miss Porter immersed herself in medieval theology, or even in Dante, in preparation for writing "Flowering Judas." Indeed, her own account of the story's long, slow gestation, and rapid, sudden composition contradicts such an idea [*Writers at Work,* 1963]. It is sufficient to note that Miss Porter's own early convent training, and her acquaintance with the works of T. S. Eliot and of Dante have put her in a position where, possibly even without full consciousness, she has been able to draw upon deep reserves of psychological and ethical thought, of imagery, and of symbolism latent in the language and teachings of the Church and of the two poets. Without direct evidence, no accumulation of detailed parallels can prove this thesis decisively, but it is striking how naturally all the details in the story reinforce the pattern here described, while the most careful search fails to yield one detail which contradicts it. That she should use this vocabulary of religious words and images most extensively in her most explicitly "political" story need occasion no surprise if we consider the degree to which politics has become, in our era, a substitute for religion, while our religions have failed to provide us with adequate solutions to our social and political problems. We are all familiar today with the equation of political creed and religion, and all the equations derived from it—political leader and saviour, political devotee and member of a religious order, political deviation and heresy, and political disillusion and apostasy. These equations or metaphors have been exploited especially by the propagandists of Nazism, Fascism, Communism, and other apocalyptic political movements, and often by their opponents as well.

What Miss Porter has done with these metaphors is basically simple. By exposing them to the light of political reality, she has converted or inverted them to reveal the full irony and danger which is latent in them. Personally, she has gone on record as being "opposed to every form of authoritarian, totalitarian government or religion." As for political expediency, she has expressed herself unequivocally: "If you are promised something new and blissful at the mere price of present violence under a new master, first examine these terms carefully. . . . If you are required to kill someone today, on the promise of a political leader that someone else shall live in peace tomorrow, believe me, you are not only a double murderer, you are a suicide, too" ["Three Statements About Writing," *The Days Before,* 1952]. "Flowering Judas" is a story about a young woman living in Mexico and working for the revolution during the 1920's. Now disillusioned, after her earlier commitment to a totalitarian political creed, she nevertheless cannot bring herself to take any decisive action, and tries to repress her internal conflict from consciousness. The story is, thus, one of self-delusion, as Miss Porter has said [in *This Is My Best,* 1942]. It is also a story about *acedia* or spiritual life-in-death, as is evidenced by its affinities to the poetry of Eliot's middle period ("The Waste Land," "Gerontion," and "The Hollow Men"). Laura "had religion" first as a childhood Roman Catholic, and later as a devoted revolutionary. She has lost her ability to believe in either faith and is consequently cut off from every possible heaven except one of private commitment and belief which she might with labor and difficulty construct, but such a labor of construction she is unable or unwilling to undertake.

Yet it is unfair to put the entire responsibility for her plight upon the heroine. Within the frame of reference of what her world has to offer her, she has, in a way, "done her best." She tries "now and again" to derive some spiritual sustenance from the faith of her childhood by slipping (at the risk of scandal) into "some crumbling little church" and kneeling "on the chilly stone," but she can no more overlook the failure of her church to meet the social injustice of the society in which she finds herself than she can overlook the vanity and cruelty of the revolutionary leaders. The "altar with its tinsel flowers and ragged brocades" and the "battered doll-shape of some male saint whose white, lace-trimmed drawers hang limply around his ankles" force themselves upon her unwilling attention. The tinsel flowers suggest a divorce from reality in contrast either to the "fresh garden flowers" left on her desk each day by the adoring children in her classroom, representing immaculate love, or to the "warm bleeding flowers" of her dream, representing a perversion of spiritual love, or even to the flower which she has heedlessly tossed to her anonymous young suitor and which he continues to wear, "withering in his hat," representing a failure of adult human love. Her religion of politics, on the other hand, seems to offer no closer tie with reality, for the "developed sense of reality" of her comrades seems to her no more than cynicism, and Mrs. Braggioni's sense of reality, which is "beyond criticism," consists merely of her recognition and acceptance of her own enslavement. Just as the eternal stasis of hell is an inversion of the unchanging bliss of heaven, so is a nightmare a horrific transformation of reality, Laura's nightmare existence is symbolized by her vision of herself sitting with Braggioni "with a bitter anxiety, as if tomorrow may not come, but time may be caught immovably in this hour, with herself transfixed, Braggioni singing on forever and Eugenio's body not yet discovered by the guard."

And yet time does move, or at any rate it conveys the illusion of movement. The seasons pass and return in endless rhythm. But for those who are fearful of death or of life the movement itself is frightful. The time of the story is April, with May rapidly approaching (the "depraved May" of Eliot's "Gerontion"), and both the Catholics and the Socialists are making their plans for the celebration of life's renewal. For the unliving and undead, however, April may be the "cruellest month," and the renewal of life is an agony to be shunned like death. Braggioni, apostle of death, is excited by the prospect of the approaching May-day, for he will come alive in his element of violence. He tells Laura "about the May-day disturbances coming on in Morelia, for the Catholics hold a festival in honor of the Blessed Virgin, and the Socialists celebrate their martyrs on that day. 'There will be two independent processions, starting from either end of town, and they will march until they meet, and the rest depends . . .'" Laura, on the other hand, reacts with fright and revulsion; as she looks down the barrel of the pistol she has been cleaning for Braggioni, "a long, slow faintness rises and subsides in her."

Two processions moving ineluctably toward mutual catastrophe—this is the metaphor for Laura's world. One procession seems to be grounded in a no longer viable past, putting its faith in unrealities, while the other, boasting a developed sense of reality, seems in fact to offer only death or another kind of tyranny. They divide the world of the story between them, and while each offers to the artist a vocabulary of words and images useful to set off the failures of the other, neither, in this context, seems to exist in relation to any other reality. Here indeed we see, behind the story of one girl's failure, a world "heaving in the sickness of millennial change." If she were an artist, Laura might devote herself to the creation of those artifacts which, as Miss Porter has said, "are what we find again when the ruins are cleared away," but not everyone can find salvation in this way. Laura might not be cut off from all life and joy if she could really love the children she teaches, or could cultivate the finer shades of interpersonal relationships, the doctrine offered in many English novels of our century. Perhaps love would offer some hope of personal redemption in the midst of chaos, as Matthew Arnold half-heartedly suggested a century ago in "Dover Beach." It does occur to Laura that love is indeed what survives, as she thinks of the youth who follows her, observing the convention of love "with all propriety, as though it were founded on a law of nature, which in the end it might very well prove to be." But even if it were possible, would such an individual salvation be enough when all around her, in the Mexico which is her Inferno, Laura sees nothing but confusion, the confusion of "love with revolution, night with day, life with death," and beyond this nothing? Such questions are at least implicit in Laura's story, and they must be considered before she can be judged or condemned.

Because of the absence of any viable faith in **"Flowering Judas,"** it is a portrayal of a hell without a heaven. It is perhaps in this sense that the story is a fragment, as the *Inferno* would be a fragment without the rest of the *Comedy*, or the first two books of *Paradise Lost* would be a fragment without the portrayal of the two paradises of heaven and earth. This in no way detracts, however, from the poetic truth or beauty of the story, for its rich symbiosis of religious and political imagery offers a profound and moving experience of the failure of two of the great faiths of our epoch. The complex, parodic symbolism of life and death, salvation and damnation, good and evil, contributes inestimably to the depth of insight offered by the story into the failure of the individual which reflects and is reflected in the "majestic and terrible failure of man in the Western world."

**Dorothy S. Redden  (essay date 1969)**

SOURCE: "'Flowering Judas': Two Voices," in *Studies in Short Fiction*, Vol. VI, No. 2, Winter, 1969, pp. 194-204.

[*In the following essay, Redden examines Porter's use of dualities and balanced tensions in "Flowering Judas."*]

Katherine Anne Porter's **"Flowering Judas,"** an unusually cryptic, complex, and challenging story, has been variously interpreted. Of the two best-known and most complete readings, that of William L. Nance maintains that Miss Porter follows "the principle of rejection" [*Katherine Anne Porter & the Art of Rejection,* 1964], while Ray B. West, Jr., argues that she "embodied an attitude that demonstrated the necessity for the application of the ancient verities of faith and love as a fructifying element in any human existence" [*Katherine Anne Porter,* 1963]. Though contradictory, both conclusions are right; each underestimates the presence of the other—an equally forcible opposite "principle," or opposite "attitude"—in the story. The paradoxes of Miss Porter's fiction, it seems to me, are insufficiently illuminated by tacit reliance on the assumption that this author holds a strictly unitary view of life. If, however, one explores the hypothesis that Miss Porter's outlook is essentially and irrevocably dual, many things fall into place, including the basic role of tension in her work.

**"Flowering Judas"** is perhaps her most remarkable story of tension sustained, threatened, and reestablished. Its protagonist is enduring an inner war between two contradictory attitudes, neither of which she can wholly accept or reject. Although "the desperate complications of her mind and feelings" [according to Porter in *This Is My Best,* 1942] must have a long history, or she would not be as troubled as she is, the story gives very little of this background, and remarks of Laura's past only that it was one of "many disillusions" and unspecified "afflictions" which she prefers to forget. To her present situation, on the other hand, Miss Porter devotes all but the final paragraph of the story in a probing analysis of the statement that Laura "cannot help feeling that she has been betrayed irreparably by the disunion between her way of living and her feeling of what life should be."

I should like to examine these two poles separately, starting with Laura's strange and painful "way of living," itself a clash of the opposing forces, seen in terms of fear. For Laura is "afraid of everything." That she fears death, even that she finds it evil, may be considered unexceptionable, at least in our civilization. An important part of her, however, feels the same way about life, and especially about its vital component of human relationships. To this part of Laura, life is not only a stifling emotional tyranny of love and sex, but a kind of death, equally vicious and sinister, equally terrifying.

Although she goes on living, she fears and hates life. At the same time, although she is drifting toward it, she fears and hates death. Obviously, these two attitudes create an insoluble dilemma. Because Laura's warring forces are evenly matched, their unresolving antagonism generates an almost overpowering tension. She feels herself mired in a perpetual waking nightmare, and for twelve pages of exposition the reader is held, with her, violently immobilized, suspended in a wild, frozen trance.

She is, in fact, barely alive. Life is motion; like wheels, human beings remain erect so long as they move ahead. They are (in our culture) propelled from behind by a fear of death, and drawn forward by a desire for life. The negative and positive forces work together to keep the organism upright and moving. Laura, however, is almost static. She is held erect not by her barely discernible motion, but by the pressures of two contradictory forces. The negative fear of death propels her from behind, it is true; but there is almost no positive force working with it to draw her forward. On the contrary, she is blocked by another negative, the fear of life.

The result is a horrible transfixion in which she feels that she must, at all costs, avoid losing her balance. As long as the two forces exert more or less equal pressure, she remains upright between them, safe. This, of course, is another delusion, for safety, if there is such a thing, lies in movement, in living, and not in a rigid stasis, which is dangerously close to extinction. But, allowed her premises, Laura is right. She cannot give up her defenses because to her they are justified; she believes that she knows the "truth" about life, what "reality" really is. If she were to relinquish her fear of life, she would have no love or hope or faith to put in its place. There would be only a vacuum, and she would topple.

Therefore, she feels that she can do nothing but try to keep the opposing pressures equal. And there is no way to do this except by complete negation. If she repudiates in one direction, she must repudiate in the other; she must deny "everything." *No* is the "one holy talismanic word which does not suffer her to be led into evil."

Laura's stance, then, is one of an almost unbearable equilibrium maintained by total denial. All of her strength is harnessed to preserving that uncertain balance, with its demand for unremitting vigilance. Fortunately, she has astonishing self-control, at least temporarily equal to the strains put upon it; it is no less impressive for being negative, and she needs every jot of it. It is her only defense against "that disaster she fears, though she cannot name it."

In a general sense the revolutionist leader Braggioni is the symbol of all that Laura hates and fears, the "reality" that seems to dominate her existence. Specifically, his characteristics are those that she finds typically human (which is to say animal), and as such they amply justify her rejection of human relationships. [The critic adds in a footnote: "As has often been observed, Laura's existence is characterized by a signal lack of love in every area, the religious (she has lost her childhood faith), the social (fellow beings are to her simply strangers in clay-colored masks), and the personal (against this, and especially erotic love, she raises her strongest defenses, indicating her deepest fears)."]

These traits, overwhelmingly repellent and menacing, center around Braggioni's vastly bloated ego. Chief among them is his sensuality, for bursting out of his binding orchid-colored clothes he resembles nothing so much as a huge tumescent phallus, the opposite of everything romantic, sentimental, and "harmless." His handling of his guitar suggests what he has in mind for Laura: he scratches it familiarly, curves his swollen fingers around its throat, rips a thumbnail across its nervous strings. Sex Laura will resist to the end; her knees cling together under her heavy "nun-like" attire. But Braggioni can wait; she will drop into his lap finally "like an overripe pear."

Why does Laura not flee while she can? Although she knows what is in store, "violence, mutilation, a shocking death," she stands immotile, waiting. There is no place for her to go; since Braggioni comprises all of "reality," there is nothing to escape to. She is an alien not only in this country, but in this world. And although her fear of death is intense, it is offset by her fear of life; in her inability to choose between them, the tension is nearly insupportable. So far as Braggioni will put an end to this terrible indecision, he is, as he insists, her "friend." If only she can do nothing long enough, the choice will be taken out of her hands.

To avoid blurring the essential issues involved, I have temporarily isolated the fears on which Laura's "way of living" is based. Actually, her attitude toward life is ambivalent, and contains an important, albeit shackled, counterforce, as the fact that she stubbornly retains a "feeling" of "what life should be" implies. This element, although in a sense allied with her fear of death, is not itself grounded in terror.

On the contrary, something in Laura yearns for an entirely different kind of life, a positive existence including faith in God and confidence in human beings both in the aggregate and individually—in short, a life rich in love, the opposite of the smothering "reality to which one side of her make-up is committed. This other part of her instinctively needs and longs for human contact; Laura's "feeling" is the involuntary cry of her half-drowned self.

But the idea of a love which is not oppressive and threatening is too alluring, with its suggestions of impossible joy and order and freedom. Since all of what Laura considers real is ugly and frightening to her, this element which does not fit into her scheme of things must be, by definition, illusive. She has had too many disappointments to dare to hope; she cannot really believe in her own insistent urge toward life. Neither can she put it aside.

In a general sense the jailed revolutionary Eugenio is the symbol of all that Laura vaguely hopes for in spite of herself. (It is not surprising that in her dream he takes on the attributes of a Christ-figure, associated with man as well as with God, with love and with life.) Specifically, Eugenio is one human being Laura might have—but has not—loved.

It is significant that Miss Porter does not mention him until late in the story, and then only briefly, to establish the fact that he is already dead. He has been much on Laura's mind, however. While solid, paunchy, callous, greasy, corrupt "reality" flourishes in her life, the pale

insubstantial "ideal" seems hardly to exist there—but its tenacity will be demonstrated, for she senses that Eugenio stands for something which can bring her relief, and she will dream that.

If Braggioni and Eugenio are antithetical symbols personifying the tension between Laura's fear of and desire for life, the third and most important symbol in the story, the blossoming redbud tree, whose name expresses its divided nature, combines both of these attitudes in one emblem. It also shifts the emphasis to love (and sexuality, although this is sternly repressed). *Flowering* is a lovely word, and flowers are indeed associated with love in Laura's mind. But these are not just any flowers—they are Judas flowers; treachery is all that she can expect from love as her fears define it. Once again, Laura is simultaneously attracted and repelled.

The Judas tree (which, like all of the symbols in this story, is multiple and complex) has another function, for it embraces a further aspect of Laura's conflicting attitudes—her self-image. Laura's feelings about herself are directly related to her feelings about other people, and consist, like them, of two incompatible elements. On the one hand she respects and defends her self; on the other she undervalues and prosecutes it. In her own eyes she resembles the Judas tree—delicate, beautiful, perfidious. She feels not only that she has made a grotesque blunder in allowing her fears to drive her to negation, but that she is to blame for doing so. In other words, Laura has somehow learned to experience her private "revolution" against life and love as worse than simply mistaken—she sees it as morally reprehensible, a betrayal of herself as well as of others. Her sense of error is intensified by a sense of guilt, and she finds herself "wrong" in both of the meanings which our language gives to that word. ("It may be true I am as corrupt, in another way, as Braggioni," she thinks, "as callous, as incomplete.") As she drifts off to sleep, this repressed feeling of culpability, reinforced by her Christian training, begins to emerge from the unconscious, and she accuses herself harshly with "it is monstrous to confuse love with revolution, night with day, life with death—ah, Eugenio!"

With this, the long, taut prelude of the story ends. Although nothing important has happened, Laura's state of paralysis and her feelings about it have been exposed with surgical precision. Now, in the final paragraph, where the entire action of the story begins, rises to its climax, and subsides, something is happening at last, if only in a dream.

It has to happen in a dream. Only in a dream can Eugenio appear as a savior, can Laura even momentarily believe in and reach out toward "life as it should be," an alternative to her death-like "way of living."

With the tolling of the midnight bell, the signal for the dead to arise, the wraith of Eugenio appears. Come, he beckons, leave this "strange house" you have built for yourself; I will guide you to death—not to physical death (that belongs to Braggioni), but to the death which is rebirth.

Laura is irresistibly drawn after him, although the goal is distant and the way tortuous. Eugenio can no longer give her physical support, and anyway, there are some things one must do for oneself. There is no time to hang back, yet she cannot brave the journey alone; perhaps the vacuum caused by the removal of her defenses will not be filled, and she will lose her precarious balance fatally in the wasteland that stretches ahead. She is still the prisoner of her wretched fears.

As if he understood this, Eugenio responds with pity. Poor creature, he seems to say, this will give you the strength you need; and he strips the pulsing flowers from the Judas tree and holds them to her lips. In promising this new life which is also the death of the old life, Eugenio seems forgiving, compassionate, Christ-like. He offers the life-bringing nourishment with Christ's words; and the flowers themselves, like the bread and wine which satisfy spiritual hunger and thirst, are warm and bleeding, suggesting Christ's corporeal being. Laura accepts them, crushes them eagerly into her mouth, for she is starving for love in all of its forms.

But these are still Judas flowers: not even in a dream can Laura wholly overcome her profound distrust. The act of acceptance makes her vulnerable to her pervasive sense of guilt, her feeling that she is unworthy of love and forgiveness. [The critic adds in a footnote: "In our tradition, as everyone knows, "morals" and sexuality have been so muddled that guilt feelings commonly acquire a sexual tinge. The religious imagery of Laura's dream tends to obscure the sexual element in her diffused sense of guilt, but it is there, and can be subsumed under her attitude toward love, which is itself an expression of her attitude toward life."] She feels responsible for Eugenio's death not because she brought him drugs, but because she has closed off in herself the springs of compassion. Laura has been taught to believe that self-betrayal is also a betrayal of others, and thus of Christ. It is a mortal sin. Eugenio turns from a figure of mercy to one of vengeful justice, the personification of her own relentless conscience.

"Murderer!" he calls her, and "Cannibal! This is my body and my blood." The ritualistic words touch a buried nerve in Laura, for they evoke the whole of her religious upbringing. It is true that she has intellectually repudiated her childhood faith, but that does not mean that it does not still have immense power over her; the "set of principles derived from her early training," in which she has rigidly "encased herself," is an iron load of moral accountability.

In this context, Laura feels that she is subverting the sacrament which is a remembrance of and a participation in Christ's atoning death and resurrection, the visible sign of an invisible grace. When one has committed a mortal sin, one must cleanse one's soul in repentance and confession before receiving the Host. Laura has not been able to do so, and she feels that she is committing another and greater sin in taking communion unworthily. This is an act of murder and cannibalism; like Judas, she has betrayed Christ to his death and yet feasts on his symbolic flesh and blood. It is to her a false communion, a desecration of the Host. Eugenio, she dreams, is pointing out to her the visible sign of her invisible damnation; she is on the brink of horrifying self-knowledge.

But Laura cannot consciously confront her mistakes, ensnarled as they are with a guilt-laden concept of "her own nature"; to do so would undermine her resistance to death and collapse the personality she is holding together by sheer will. She must negate *everything.* Recoiling in fright from the threat of disintegration, she reacts with a final "No!" and the shattering revelation goes underground again.

With this her balance is restored—but it is again a balance of tension, rather than of resolution. On one side, the secret burden of self-accusation, with its moral overtones, is heavier, for Laura stands in her own court doubly condemned—guilty first of transgression, now of refusing to confess. On the other side, the instinct of self-preservation still operates; she is "determined not to surrender her will to such expedient logic." And there is something strong and admirable about Laura's fierce resistance to annihilation. She does not go to pieces. She is not insane. She holds on.

Her future is not spelled out. So far as this story shows, Laura will remain in her private limbo indefinitely, afraid to live or to die. (As Braggioni says of the coming May-day disturbances, "There will be two independent processions, starting from either end of town, and they will march until they meet, and the rest depends. . . .") The rest depends. Possibly her two embattled forces will gradually crush her between them, but more likely Laura will survive her civil war; one feels somehow that she will never die of it, however joyless her days.

The significance of her moving and terrifying experience is, I take it, that it is impossible to break the deadlock between inner needs and inculcated precepts—at least when those precepts are founded on conventional Western ideas of moral responsibility. Miss Porter records the conflict—not dispassionately—but with her passions tightly in rein and equitably divided.

One voice in her concurs in Laura's self-condemnation, on the familiar grounds that good and evil (however hard to identify) exist, that the individual possesses—or should possess—the means (however rudimentary) to discriminate between them, and that his decisions (however well-intentioned) are subject to inexorable review. Laura has been trained in this school; she knows—or ought to know—right from wrong; she has somehow chosen the latter; and to her, the infallible sign of her guilt is her ineradicable feeling of guilt. At the same time, another voice in Miss Porter, while not directly contesting these assumptions, concurs in Laura's self-acquittal, as it were. The author clearly understands and respects her heroine's torment, and silently cries "Bravo!" to her spirited refusal to yield. Whether one chooses to consider Miss Porter half-persuaded or half-skeptical of both verdicts,

"Flowering Judas" is, in my opinion, "the testimony of a mental attitude," and that attitude is dual.

---

**While Miss Porter is not inclined to parry the thrust of the entire Judeo-Christian tradition, she effectively questions one basic aspect of it in this story, and provokes conjecture about the nature and validity of the sense of guilt, as well as of guiltiness itself.**

*—Dorothy S. Redden*

---

The contention that Miss Porter, like her protagonist, takes a double view in this story may not be subject to any concrete "proof." It is impractical to adduce here the evidence of her other work, which (again in my opinon) reflects a similar duality. Still, the reader may speculate about the effect on **"Flowering Judas"** if Miss Porter were presumed to take a single view of its dominant character and her dilemma. (It is a tribute to the authenticity of Laura that she elicits and supports such speculation.)

But which view? It would be naïve to label Miss Porter either simple moralist or simple individualist; she is too perceptive and experienced to be either, and hardly simple in any case. The only viable possibility is that she is fully aware, as Laura is not, of the nature of an estrangement such as this character feels: its origins, its symptoms, its remedy.

Suppose for a moment that Miss Porter meant to show that her protagonist is the victim of feelings she can neither understand nor control, much less trace to their source. Yet from her present situation one unmistakably infers a certain kind of past. The details cannot be guessed, but "the desperate complications of her mind and feelings" clearly indicate that Laura is following a typical neurotic pattern forced on her by early emotional deprivation, which she experienced as a betrayal of love. In such cases, the unloved child usually assumes that it is *prima facie* unlovable, somehow a "bad" rather than a "good child who understands the rules of behavior." Out of the resultant feelings of guilt and fear such a child develops a defensive personality marked by negation of the moralistic relationships that are the source of its disappointment and pain, and, by extension, of all human relationships. This movement, of course, involves a misapprehension, not of the nature of the child's experience, which it reads accurately, but of the nature of life outside of its experience—of, for example, the unconditional quality of love.

Laura has obviously constructed a large part of her existence around some such misapprehension. Irony piles upon irony. Her "reality" is not real; her "truth" is not true.

There are times when people are savage, when sex does destroy, when "love" does suffocate. But she has mistaken these qualified facts for the whole fact; human relationships are not by definition hostile to her individuality, and one cannot dismiss them without incurring the ache of loss, as she has learned.

Suppose further that Miss Porter were also showing that mistakes are not "sins," that evil, as Socrates put it long ago, is simply error. From this standpoint, Laura's mistakes were inevitable, her only protection when she was too young to question the price of survival. She could not have done other than she did. Her most self-destructive error was the assumption of guilt in the first place, but this too was a mistake she could not help making. As for her dream, Laura's refusal to confess is not at all an act of moral cowardice, but evidence that a vital spirit of independence still persists in her, still fights tenaciously for its life. She is no more treacherous than the flowering Judas tree, a pretty bush to which, because of its name, she has attached some unfortunate connotations. Her feeling that she is self-betrayed might better be replaced with self-forgiveness—or rather (for it is gratuitous to forgive oneself for trying to survive), with self-acceptance.

It this were Miss Porter's unitary view, it would cap the story with a final ironic twist—that far from being either guilty or not guilty, Laura need not be on trial at all. **"Flowering Judas"** would be a different—not a better—story, and its gist that human beings are seldom given enough light to see by.

But this is not the story Miss Porter wrote, and I am not misguidedly trying to improve on it; it is a superb achievement just as it stands: a study in irreconcilables, a portrait of stress. As such, it cannot easily be the product of a single undivided viewpoint. If Miss Porter did not stand in the same relation to both of her heroine's attitudes, one or the other would exert less force, and a disequilibrium between them would make itself felt. The whole affective power of this story results from its balance, as well as its quality, of feeling—from the high pitch of equally disposed forces. The double outlook, moreover, is integral to the success of the story, for it increases the tension which is also its subject. This reinforcement of theme extends to even the smallest details, and creates an almost electric intensity, an emotional impact of impressive voltage. [The critic adds in a footnote: "The principle of opposition permeates every element in the story, from diction (the children have wise, innocent faces and a charming opportunistic savagery; Braggioni is a professional lover of humanity, a hungry world savior) to psychology (Laura's immobility is that of rubber stretched nearly to the snapping point; her coolness masks violent emotions; her fearlessness is that of one who flees from greater terrors; her selflessness conceals complete—and necessary—preoccupation with self). The skillful use of irony alone is a study in contrast and restraint."]

Another telling indication of the dual point of view of the story is that one cannot imagine Miss Porter relaxing her allegiance either to the felt rights of the instinctual identity or to the fundamental moral strictures of our culture. Concerning individuality, she is as passionate as Hawthorne (and shows much the same cast of mind) in resenting any intrusion upon the inviolable soul. As for morality, her very language, which is scrupulously exact, protests a loyal adherence to what she has elsewhere called "some very old fashioned noble" values. For example, in saying, as she has, that this story coalesced around a central idea of "self delusion," she selects a term which, like *betrayed* and *Judas,* bows under a weight of implicit moral judgment.

This does not mean that Miss Porter accepts her heritage without qualification, however. She is also in continual, if incomplete, revolt against it. **"Flowering Judas"** is (to borrow her description of another first-rate story of her own) "a story of the most painful moral and emotional confusions" [**"Noon Wine"**]. The extent to which Laura reflects a widespread state of mind cannot be investigated here, but her tangling of the moral and the emotional is deeply relevant to at least some of the more painful confusions of modern man in the detritus of his civilization. While Miss Porter is not inclined to parry the thrust of the entire Judeo-Christian tradition, she effectively questions one basic aspect of it in this story, and provokes conjecture about the nature and validity of the sense of guilt, as well as of guiltiness itself.

**David Madden  (essay date 1970)**

SOURCE: "The Charged Image in Katherine Anne Porter's 'Flowering Judas'," in *Studies in Short Fiction,* Vol. VII, No. 2, Spring, 1970, pp. 277-89.

[*In the essay below, Madden discusses symbolism and imagery in "Flowering Judas," arguing that this story succeeds because it contains the "charged image" structure in which "a created, transcendent image [has] . . . an organic life of its own."*]

In *Writers at Work, Second Series* [1965], the interviewer asked Katherine Anne Porter whether **"Flowering Judas"** began as a visual impression that grew into a narrative. "All my senses were very keen," Miss Porter replied. "Things came to me through my eyes, through all my pores. Everything hit me at once. . . ." Without words or images, her stories began to form. Then she starts thinking "directly in words. Abstractly. Then the words transform themselves into images." On several occasions Miss Porter has testified to the potency of the real-life image that generated **"Flowering Judas."**

She chose this story for inclusion in an anthology called *This Is My Best* (1942). Commenting on the story at that time, she said: "All the characters and episodes are based on real persons and events, but naturally, as my memory worked upon them and time passed, all assumed different shapes and colors, formed gradually around a central idea, that of self-delusion. . . ." In the *Paris Review* interview some twenty years later, she elaborated:

That story had been on my mind for years, growing out of this one little thing that happened in Mexico. . . . Something I saw as I passed a window one evening. A girl I knew had asked me to come and sit with her, because a man was coming to see her, and she was a little afraid of him. And as I went through the courtyard, past the flowering judas tree, I glanced in the window and there she was sitting with an open book on her lap, and there was this great big fat man sitting beside her. Now Mary and I were friends, both American girls living in this revolutionary situation. She was teaching at an Indian school, and I was teaching dancing at a girls' technical school in Mexico City. And we were having a very strange time of it (1965).

. . . . .

I had a brief glimpse of her sitting with an open book in her lap, but not reading, with a fixed look of pained melancholy and confusion in her face.

The fat man I call Braggioni was playing the guitar and singing to her [1942].

. . . . .

And when I looked through that window that evening, I saw something in Mary's face, something in her pose, something in the whole situation, that set up a commotion in my mind [1965].

. . . . .

In that glimpse, no more than a flash, I thought I understood, or perceived, for the first time, the desperate complications of her mind and feelings, and I knew a story; perhaps not her true story, not even the real story of the whole situation, but all the same a story that seemed symbolic truth to me. If I had not seen her face at that very moment, I should never have written just this story because I should not have known it to write [1942].

. . . . .

Because until that moment I hadn't really understood that she was not able to take care of herself, because she was not able to face her own nature and was afraid of everything. I don't know why I saw it. I don't believe in intuition. When you get sudden flashes of perception, it is just the brain working faster than usual. But you've been getting ready to know it for a long time, and when it comes, you feel you've known it always [1965].

As raw material for literature, this real-life image was already, implicitly, dynamically charged with feeling and meaning. The author's physical distance from her friend that evening was an analog to the objectivity that was necessary when she transformed the real-life image into the fictive image. And out of this actual image was to grow also the structural, stylistic, and technical conceptions of **"Flowering Judas,"** a created, transcendent image with an organic life of its own. This story is one of the most lucid exemplifications I know of what Croce calls "the aesthetic image," compounded of "a tissue of images," and of what I call *the charged image.* Ezra Pound's definition of great literature as "language charged with meaning to the utmost possible degree" (to "meaning" I would add the word "feeling") suggests the source of power in **"Flowering Judas."** Before I feel out the anatomy of this charged image, I want to quote Miss Porter again.

Soon after *Flowering Judas,* her first book of stories, was published in 1930, Miss Porter wrote to a friend:

> I can't tell you what gives true intensity, but I know it when I find it, even in my own work. . . . It is not a matter of how you feel at any one moment, certainly not at the moment of writing. A calculated coldness is the best mood for that most often. Feeling is more than a mood; it is a whole way of being; it is the nature you're born with, you cannot invent it. The question is how to convey a sense of whatever is there, as feeling, within you, to the reader; and that is a problem of technical expertness.
>
> [Quoted in John V. Hagopian's review in *Studies in Short Fiction,* Vol. IV]

Mr. Hagopian's response to Miss Porter's statement reflects my own conviction: "Thus, from the beginning, Miss Porter knew what she was doing—embodying the *true intensity* of experience into literary form with *technical expertness.*" Mark Schorer, writing about technique in general, describes what Miss Porter does most brilliantly in **"Flowering Judas."** "When we speak of technique, then, we speak of nearly everything. For technique is the means by which the writer's experience, which is his subject matter, compels him to attend to it; technique is the only means he has of discovering, exploring, developing his subject, of conveying its meaning, and, finally, of evaluating it." Technique "objectifies the materials of art." The forms of the finest works of fiction, Schorer argues, are "exactly equivalent with their subjects," and "the evaluation of their subjects exists in their styles." He cites Miss Porter's work as exemplary. "The cultivated sensuosity" of Miss Porter's style has not only "charm in itself" but "esthetic value . . . its values lie in the subtle means by which sensuous details become symbols, and in the way the symbols provide a network which is the story, and which at the same time provides the writer and us with a refind moral insight by means of which to test it ["Technique as Discovery," *The World We Imagine,* 1968]. Some readers may cite Miss Porter's phrase "a calculated coldness" to explain the coldness her technique and her sensibility instill in some of her stories. But that phrase and her comments in *Writers at Work* suggest her attitude about technique as a means of discovery; although she testifies that she knew the ending of **"Flowering Judas"** before she began to write (as the *usually* knows the ending before she begins to write a story), the powerful final stroke came unconsciously (but was made possible, most probably, by her habitual consciousness of technique). "I knew that the vengeful spirit was going to come in a dream to tow her away into death, but I didn't know until I'd written it that she was going to wake up saying, 'No!' and be afraid to sleep again." Although, as friends and critics have observed, one must regard Miss Porter's comments on her own work with almost the same caution with which one regards Faulkner's self-scrutiny, it is no contradiction of our image of Miss Porter as a conscious craftsman that she claims to write her stories in single spurts of energy. "I always write a story in one sitting. I started '**Flowering Judas**' at seven p.m. and at one-thirty I was standing on a snowy windy corner putting it in the mailbox" (*Writers at Work*). Miss Porter glimpsed a girl and a man through a window in Mexico City and two years later, in a few hours in Brooklyn, recaptured and transformed that image into a work of art.

In her introduction to *The Selected Short Stories of Eudora Welty* (1954), Miss Porter describes the kind of story she prefers: one in which "external act and the internal voiceless life of the human imagination almost meet and mingle on the mysterious threshold between dream and waking, one reality refusing to admit or confirm the other, yet both conspiring toward the same end." [In their *Twelve Short Stories,* 1961] Magalaner and Volpe declare that **"Flowering Judas"** is "from the first word of the title to the last word of the text" a model of that kind of story. They go on to say that it "is a sensitive and discerning philosophical statement of human relationships, made universal by the mythic elements which intrude as early as the hint in the title." But more than that, it is a remarkable aesthetic achievement to which we may return again and again, just as we return to Keats's "Ode on a Grecian Urn"; for long after we have absorbed its universal philosophical and psychological truths, **"Flowering Judas"** remains a "thing of beauty," a "joy forever," embodying Keats's declaration that "Beauty is truth, truth beauty."

In some ways **"Flowering Judas"** resembles literary form less than it resembles dance, mother of all the arts, especially of poetry and of the most contemporary of the arts—cinema (I use these analogies simply for their suggestiveness). The dynamic imagery of dance, the compression and the expressive juxtapositions of poetry, and the montage effects of Eisenstein's cinema are transmuted by Miss Porter, unconsciously, I imagine, into fictive techniques that produce what interests and moves me most in this story—the charged image. The omniscient author's psychological analysis of and philosophical reflections about Laura's predicament and the self-delusory processes that follow from her predicament are everywhere in the story, suffusing the very style that creates the tissue of images. But overwhelming her own overt interpretations when they threaten to intimidate the life of the story, the images embody Miss Porter's meaning with expressive vitality; ultimately, of course, this vitality cannot be separated from the vitality of Miss Porter's meditations about Laura. The story exfoliates from a tight intermingling of showing and telling. And that story, were it not for the author's technique of dramatically juxtaposing tableaux, is so rich and multifaceted as to require the scope of a novel.

As the elements of Laura's exterior and interior worlds intermingle, they cohere in a developing pattern of images which expands from the charged image that inspired Miss Porter in life and that she sets forth in the beginning of her fiction:

> Braggioni sits heaped upon the edge of a straight-backed chair much too small for him, and sings to Laura in a furry, mournful voice. Laura has begun to find reasons for avoiding her own house until the latest possible moment, for Braggioni is there almost every night. No matter how late she is, he will be sitting there with a surly, waiting expression, pulling at his kinky yellow hair, thumbing the strings of his guitar, snarling a tune under his breath. Lupe the Indian maid meets Laura at the door, and says with a flicker of a glance towards the upper room, "He waits."

This central, most potent image is the hub, and all other images spoke out from it, and the author's meditating voice is the rim, and (to complete the metaphor) the reader's active participation is the energy that makes the wheel turn. Paralyzed, Laura is locked into this image, as though in a small box stage set, and we see her at a distance, as though through the original real-life window. With each image that Miss Porter shows us, we feel that Laura is withdrawing more and more deeply into herself, that her will is becoming more and more paralyzed. The controlling image (Laura and Braggioni sitting opposite each other by the table) is a simplified visual and thematic expression of the entire story; this image recurs at strategic points in the pattern, creating that sense of simultaneity that makes a work of art cohere and seem inevitable. Laura's posture varies only slightly; and though Braggioni is singing and playing his guitar, the tableau virtually does not move—it vibrates from within, sending its electrical charge in a radial fashion out into the other images connected to it.

In 1961 at Centre College in Kentucky, I discussed **"Flowering Judas"** with my two classes of freshman students. Mystification over my charged image concept only compounded their boredom with the story itself. To enable them to see Miss Porter's story, and my point, more clearly, I arranged a demonstration with the Drama Department. Using multi-level space staging and lighting as a means of isolating one acting area, one scene, from another, we mounted a series of tableaux in pantomime, while a young woman read the story over a public address system. The images enacted were these (following the sequence in the story):

Laura and Braggioni sit opposite each other by the table.

In the first image that is juxtaposed, montage-fashion, to this hub image, we see Laura sitting in church.

Cut to Braggioni at the table in Laura's house again, singing, playing the guitar.

Fade to Laura in the classroom with Indian children.

Fade to a composite image: Laura at a union meeting; Laura visiting prisoners in cells; Laura meeting men in dark doorways with messages; Laura meeting with Polish and Roumanian agitators in cafés.

Fade to another composite image: Laura riding horseback with the Captain; Laura and the Captain at a table in a restaurant; Laura in the classroom responding to a floral design and a message of affection to her drawn on the blackboard; Laura at her window responding to the youth who serenades her.

Fade to another composite: Laura and the children again; Laura at the doors of fugitives again.

Cut to Laura and Braggioni at the table again; he talks of love; her response is negative. Superimposed image of Braggioni in the streets.

Fade to a composite: Braggioni's wife weeping on the floor in her room; Eugenio's body lying on the floor of his cell.

Cut to Laura with Braggioni again; she cleans his pistols; Braggioni puts his gun belt on.

Fade to Laura in the street on errands again, meeting strange faces.

Fade to a composite: Braggioni and his wife; she washes his feet; they eat; they lie in bed together.

Cut to composite image: Laura in white in bed; Laura at dark doors;

Laura with children in classroom; Laura with prisoners.

Fade to Laura with Eugenio in a nightmare, as he leads her away, offering her the blossoms of the Judas tree to eat.

Cut to Laura awake, crying No! She is afraid to sleep again.

To this day, students tell me that this dramatic enactment of the story's charged image structure was one of the most electrifying theatrical experiences they have ever had. Re-reading the story itself, they were able to come closer to the kind of experiences the story offers readers who are more aesthetically responsive.

Miss Porter's technique of creating a dynamic interplay among images that are strategically spaced in an unfolding pattern is appropriate for the rendering of Laura's state of mind—self-delusion producing paralysis of will. Not only does she move very little in the recurrent scene set in the present, but her recent, habitual past life as well is presented in terms of static images. The reader feels the tension between these static images and Laura's impulse within the images to flee. From a positive standpoint, the static quality of the pictures is expressive of Laura's desire for stasis. The energy of the story is transmitted in the kinetic juxtaposition of one charged image to another. A few similes may make my simple point even clearer: reading the story is like watching a single photograph, simple in outline but rich in detail, yield more and more auxiliary images each time it is redeveloped and enlarged (I am thinking of the experience the photographer has in the movie *Blow-Up*); or the images are superimposed, causing a cumulative density of texture; or reading the story is like watching a cubist painting being painted, from the first stroke, the title, to the last word, No.

The contrast between the static quality of the images and the immediacy of the historical present tense generates a tension that enhances the effect of Miss Porter's basic image technique. She declares that not until someone asked her why she used it did she realize she had employed the historical present tense. In any case, it is clear that the present tense keeps the images themselves alive while they portend the incipient moribundity of Laura, the character who is at the center of each (even when, in the scene in Braggioni's hotel room, she isn't physically present). Miss Porter's technique resembles the early montage techniques of the European movies of the late Twenties and anticipates cinematic methods used by Resnais in *Hiroshima, Mon Amour* and *Last Year at Marienbad*. She shows us one scene, stops the camera, goes on to another scene, goes back to an earlier scene, holds, then goes further back to an even earlier scene, then leaps far ahead. But the image technique is also similar to one used long before the birth of the cinema—Spenser's tableau juxtapositions in *The Faerie Queen*.

Laura has just come from the prison and "is waiting for tomorrow with a bitter anxiety. . . . but time may be caught immovably in this hour, with herself transfixed, Braggioni singing on forever, and Eugenio's body not yet discovered by the guard." The result of Miss Porter's charged image technique is that the reader is left with this timeless image of Laura sitting opposite Braggioni at the table, transfixed in fear and accidie, all the other images clustered around her like spokes in a hub. Laura's one act in the present tense of the story comes toward the end: "The presence of death in the room makes her bold," so she "holds up the [gun] belt to him: 'Put that on, and go kill somebody in Morelia, and you will be happier!'" This is a futile gesture. In numerous little ways, Laura herself, we have seen, has already killed various kinds of generous human impulses toward love, including Braggioni's. So at this point, the recurrent static picture at the hub of all the other images moves, but to no purpose: Braggioni leaves, Laura goes to sleep.

Along with her use of present tense, Miss Porter's frequent use of questions—"Where could she go?"—is another technique for enlivening her overt thematicizing and the progression of static images. And the routineness of Laura's life is another element that makes Miss Porter's technique of repeating the same images in a pattern effective.

Laura has dehumanized herself by encasing herself "in a set of principles derived from early training, leaving no detail of gesture or of personal taste untouched." Miss Porter's attitude toward people like Laura is suggested in her comment on a certain kind of writer: "By accepting any system and shaping his mind and work to that mold, the artist dehumanizes himself, unfits himself for the practice of any art" (quoted in Magalaner). Braggioni tells Laura that they are more alike than she realizes; she sees the possibility of her being as "corrupt, in another way, as Braggioni . . . as callous, as incomplete," but rather than do something about these faults, she prefers "any kind of death." Figuratively, Laura and Braggioni reveal two perspectives on a single person; each exhibits aspects of the other. They also contrast with each other. But finally, Laura's personality embodies many aspects of Braggioni's, carrying them to a negative extreme. It is appropriate, then, that Miss Porter employs a modified omniscient point of view, favoring Laura, but shifting, strategically, to Braggioni near the end.

Braggioni, "a professional lover of humanity," who began as a "hungry world-savior," but who will never die of this love (one of many suggestions that he is a false Christ), tells Laura his true feelings about the common men who follow him: any of them might easily turn Judas (as, in spirit, Laura already has). In many instances, Laura is a Magdalene to one man, a false Magdalene or a Judas to others. Loyalty to one group necessitates Laura's betrayal of trust in other groups; thus "she borrows money from the Roumanian agitator to give to his bitter enemy the Polish agitator"; through her, Braggioni *uses* these people.

"Flowering Judas" delineates a maze of ambiguity of roles, beginning with Laura and Braggioni, going on down to the minor characters. Everyone seems to be both a savior and a Judas to everyone else. Braggioni is both a false and, in a purely human way of course, a real Christ to various people; but he is also a Judas. So is Laura both secular savior and betrayer of the same people. The author conceives of these complex savior-Judas relationships paradoxically and ironically and enhances them with a controlled atmosphere of ambiguity; this nexus of savior-Jesus analogies extends from the inner psychological realm of Laura and Braggioni out into the public realm and up to a symbolic level. Many kinds of service and betrayal are depicted and implied in the story; but Laura, by denying sex, love, meaningful purpose, and action, inclines too far toward betrayal, as the climactic nightmare scene stresses.

Miss Porter shifts scene and point of view deliberately for a dramatic contrast to Laura. Returning to his wife, who is still weeping, Braggioni is glad to be back in a familiar place where the smells are good and his wife does not reproach him, but offers to wash his feet (she is a genuine Magdalene to his Christ-role). We see that Braggioni is in many ways a more creative person than Laura. Out of remorse, he weeps, saying, "Ah, yes, I am hungry, I am tired, let us eat something together." His supper with his wife contrasts with Laura's devouring of the Judas flowers. His wife asks his forgiveness for failing to be sufficient to all his needs, and her tears refresh him—she weeps *for* him as well as because of him. At least with one other person, Braggioni experiences a rich sexual and affectionate relationship. He is lonely, soft, guilt-ridden, we see now, though we've sensed this all along; but because of his external public role and because of her rigid demeanor, Braggioni and Laura were unable to meet. Rilke says that "Love consists in this, that two solitudes protect, and touch and greet each other." If nothing more, Braggioni and his wife experience this touching of solitudes.

Now Miss Porter shifts point of view back to Laura as she "takes off her serge dress and puts on a white linen nightgown and goes to bed." Her virginal uniform of white mocks her sterility. She thinks of her children as prisoners who bring their jailor flowers. Numbers tick in her brain, turning her mind into a clock, a machine. Within her own solitude of mind and flesh, Laura cries out in anguish that "it is monstrous to confuse love with revolution, night with day, life with death," and invokes Eugenio's spirit "—ah, Eugenio!"

The midnight bell seems to be a signal she can't understand. Miss Porter handles the intermingling of interior and exterior worlds so adroitly that the dream passage comes with a controlled abruptness, and the change in tone does not jar, but seems inevitable. Without warning the reader, Miss Porter has Eugenio speak to Laura— without quotation marks, for his voice is pure expression, like an object. Echoing Christ's command to his followers, he tells Laura to get up and follow him. He asks her why she is in this strange house (in Mexico, in the world, in her own mind; one thinks of Lucifer's "The mind is its own place, and in itself / Can make a Heav'n of Hell, a Hell of Heav'n."). Here Miss Porter, though she is describing a dream that is happening now, shifts into the past tense to enhance our feeling that Laura's life, insofar as its capacity for responding to possibilities, is over, whether literally she dies soon after the story ends or not.

Eugenio calls Laura a murderer (she is *his* Judas, but the charge covers all her crimes of the body, the mind, and the spirit, for they affect *other* bodies, minds, and spirits, including his own.) But even to his offer to take her to a new country, death, Laura says, "No," fearing anything more than the fear to which she has grown accustomed and from which she is unable to imagine a separate identity for herself.

Miss Porter gives the reader a sense of the fluid, surrealistic changes of the nightmare landscape as Laura clings to the "stair rail, and then to the topmost branch of the Judas tree that bent down slowly and set her upon the earth, and then to the rocky ledge of a cliff, and then to the jagged wave of a sea that was not water but a desert of crumbling stone." All this suggests again Eliot's mental-physical Waste Land, and "The Love Song of J. Alfred Prufrock," and, as one critic has pointed out, "Gerontion," as well.

The ambiguous title of the story interprets all its images. The Judas tree gets its name from the belief that from such a tree Judas hanged himself. Abundant purple flowers appear in the spring before the leaves. A certain elder is called a Judas tree because it bears "Jew's ear," an edible, cup-shaped flower, resembling an ear, which is cherished as a medicine. So the tree itself and Miss Porter's title ultimately have both positive and negative connotations, and the story depicts in its charged images the gestures of both betrayers and betrayed; the reader feels his way through an ambiguity that deliberately makes it difficult to distinguish with any final clarity one from the other. Thus, Eugenio, who has qualities of Christ, as one betrayed offers *Judas* flowers to Laura, the betrayer; and thus, in eating of the body of Christ cannibalistically she is also eating of the body of Judas, for Eugenio, too, is a kind of Judas, betraying Laura. But the "flowering Judas" is Laura.

Eugenio offers her the flowers of the Judas tree, and as she devours them, he calls her "Murderer!" and "Cannibal!" "This is my body and my blood. Laura cried No! and at the sound of her own voice, she awoke trembling, and was afraid to sleep again." She wakes, but not to enlightenment (although one may argue that it is perhaps enlightenment that makes her afraid to sleep again), for the dominating idea in her life, as in the nightmare, is denial, and with this No, Miss Porter appropriately ends the story. By now the No (in contrast to the Yes with which Molly Bloom ends *Ulysses*) is both a strong auditory image and an object. Just as Eugenio's eyes, unlike Christ's, do not bring light, the dream does not result in self-revelation for Laura, and her self-delusion persists at the end, along with the paralysis of her will (reminiscent of Gabriel Conroy's predicament at the end of "The Dead," a story that concludes with a similar elegiac vision). When we discover Laura sitting at the table in the initial, persistent charged image, she has already lost in her conflict between ideal aspiration and actuality. What self-knowledge she has she fails to employ in an act of self-discovery.

While **"Flowering Judas"** is not concerned with religion in itself, suggestive religious terms and motifs recur throughout the story. The images are almost like black parodies of religious icons or such tapestries as the Bayeux, or scenes in church panel paintings, frescoes, and mosaics (scenes of worship, charity, love, and betrayal). Miss Porter's frequent use of paradox in style and characterization suggests her purpose in employing religious motifs—as analogies to patterns of human behavior and relationships on secular levels.

While politics is closer than religion to Miss Porter's concern with her characters as people alive or dying in the secular world, politics, too, functions almost expressionistically. Braggioni tells Laura about the May-day disturbances soon to occur. On the same day on which Catholics hold a festival in honor of the Virgin (a parallel to Laura, whose virginity is neither spiritual nor quite natural), the Socialists will celebrate their martyrs, and the two processions, coming from opposite ends of town, will clash. Thus, rather neatly, Miss Porter summarizes in a composite dialogue image the two conflicting public contexts (religious and political) of Laura's private despair. There is almost no sustained dialogue in the story until this scene; the fragments of dialogue are verbal parallels to the series of charged visual images. On Laura, Braggioni's voice has the same hypnotic effect it has on crowds; and as he expresses his vision of a world completely destroyed so that a better world of "benevolent anarchy" can be built upon the ruins, Laura feels he has forgotten her as a person. He will create a physical Waste Land (an objective correlative to the spiritual Waste Land of which Laura is a major exemplification). All separate identity will vanish, and "no one shall be alive except the elect spirits destined to procreate a new world" (that excludes Laura).

Institutionalized religion and political ideals, perverted in revolution, are escapes from ordinary love. Laura refuses not only Braggioni but the Captain and the youth as lovers; more crucial to her general dilemma is her failure even in non-sexual ways, for she cannot even love the children she teaches, nor Eugenio, the man to whom she offers release from the world in which she herself must continue to suffer. Failure to distinguish illusion from reality in the conflict between ideal aspiration and brutal actuality produces Laura's self-delusion and the "No" with which she arms herself against the world. Thus, she waits in fear; a sense of overwhelming futility paralyzes her.

In preparation for the public violence that is imminent, Laura, who so intensely fears violence to herself, oils and loads Braggioni's pistols; no more grotesque half-parody of Freudian symbolism can be imagined. Laura peers down Braggioni's "pistol barrel and says nothing." The barrel's sexual connotation is reinforced by the literal lethalness of its purpose. Corresponding with this double-barreled significance Laura feels "a long, slow faintness" rising and subsiding in her, while Braggioni "curves his swollen fingers around the throat of the guitar and softly smothers the music out of it." This juxtaposition is the most powerful of several in which Miss Porter makes the guitar an analogy to Laura's body.

A psychological examination of Laura will reveal the organic unity of the story more closely. One may look at Laura in light of six forces that, simultaneously, dominate her life: *1)* Laura's predominant state of mind is denial: No. Her general negativity as she waits in fear is the frame for everything else we discover about her. *2)* She rejects sex; she evades love; she substitutes a grim charity; she radiates a deadly innocence. *3)* She gives everything (though it is not enough) to revolutionary politics, while refusing social fellowship and religious transcendence. *4)* She fails to distinguish between illusion and reality. *5)* Denying everything, overwhelmed by a sense of futility, she waits in fear of violent death. *6)* These dominant elements in the story suggest a missing element: self-realization. But the reader sees what Laura fails to see. If one examine the story from beginning to end keeping in mind the pattern of images delineated earlier, one may see how each of these aspects of Laura's psychological and physical predicament is embodied in charged images that recur and cluster. I have suggested

the thematic content that Miss Porter's images embody. In his introduction to *The Nigger of the Narcissus,* Joseph Conrad said: "A work that aspires, however humbly, to the condition of art should carry its justification in every line." **"Flowering Judas"** realizes that aspiration to an uncommon degree.

## M. M. Liberman  (essay date 1971)

SOURCE: "Symbolism, the Short Story, and 'Flowering Judas'," in *Katherine Anne Porter's Fiction,* Wayne State University Press, 1971, pp. 70-9.

[*Liberman discusses the symbolism of "Flowering Judas," arguing that the symbol of the Judas tree "is employed to enhance and finally to reiterate theme, but not to be a sign of theme as if theme had not been established by other means."*]

If one opens Jean Stafford's *Collected Stories* to, say, "The Lippia Lawn," which begins, "Although its roots are clever, the trailing arbutus at Deer Lick had been wrenched out by the hogs," he is promised the work of a poet, and this promise the other stories generally keep. It is the "clever," employed for all its worth, including *its* root sense, that does it almost all, and this is as it should be if, as I suppose with a few others, the short story is, in crucial ways, most like the lyric in that its agent is neither plot nor character, but diction. When its language is felicitous, decorous, and evocative, the tone and feeling will cradle characterization, enhance idea, and imply action which the novel must nearly always dramatize or fail. But this is not to say that the short story *is* a poem and here, too, is where many fledgling writers and not a few experienced critics have gone wrong.

The short story is not quite a poem any more than it is a short novel boiled conveniently down to bite size. So it cannot, therefore, be done with sounds, sights, and symbols alone. Surely he was correct who contended that "the storyteller must have a story to tell, not merely some sweet prose to take out for a walk." And so was that editor who wrote to Katherine Anne Porter, "No plot, my dear, no story," [*The Days Before,* 1952] although how he supposed that stricture to apply to *her* work I can imagine only in a way that does him no credit.

Commentators and editors have grouped Miss Porter's stories in a variety of ways: early—late, Miranda—Laura, new order—old order, and Mexican—non-Mexican, to name a few. This habit is conventional and usually harmless enough; it does not mislead if one keeps in mind that it is usually more a descriptive than a critical practice. It is more to the point of criticism, however, to see a "story" as falling naturally into two groups which are explicitly evaluative according to degree of formal accomplishment: realized stories with sufficient verbal efficacy to compensate adequately for the absence of the explicit causal-temporal logic essential only to most longer fictional forms; and alleged stories which no amount of verbal magic can rescue from a poverty of implied plot and other indispensable narrative features.

---

**Laura is found wanting from beginning to end, and the meaning of the story does not wait on a final symbolic revelation to make accessible what would otherwise be mysterious.**

*—M. M. Liberman*

---

"During the 1940's, it was as symbolist that Miss Porter was most effusively praised by totemist critics," James William Johnson reminds us [in *Virginia Quarterly Review,* Vol. 36, Autumn, 1960]. "In fact, criticism of her work became tantamount to an intellectual parlor game: 'Let's see who can find the most abstruse symbols in **"Flowering Judas."**' Her work survived this craze, which was largely unnecessary, since the truth is that her symbols operate on the most direct level and, where she intends a multiplicity of meaning, Miss Porter almost always tells the reader so." It ought to be added to Mr. Johnson's refreshingly commonsensical observation that although her work has survived "this craze," the "craze" itself dies hard. The neo-euhemerism of the thirties and forties seems down but by no means out, and the readings of **"Flowering Judas"** which can serve as paradigms of that era's notorious and, often, hilarious symbol-mongering have, to my knowledge, never been recanted. Moreover, the epigones of the totemists are still publishing critiques of Miss Porter's stories founded on the assumption that there is nothing, given sufficient ingenuity, that cannot be read as metaphysical verse.

**"Flowering Judas"** is, to be sure, a highly figurative composition. The modern short story almost invariably is, because, perhaps paradoxically, its author is likely to write in a realistic mode. For whereas the publicly verifiable in the novel requires extended treatment, partly in order to represent time sequentially, the familiar in the short story, dealing as it does with the moment, can be represented best by a good deal of shorthand. The result has been a "symbolic realism" where the most ordinary events are imitated, but by a selective process so scrupulous as to evoke at least what the novel might show or tell. When most successful, as in **"Flowering Judas,"** the evocations are practically symbolic in that they stand for more than themselves. It follows that, mistaking the means for the end, the amateur is forever producing the unwritten. In the place of the authentic story there is fobbed off something between an impressionistic hodge-podge and a bastard lyric, known at times as the "mood piece" and at others as the "prose poem." There is also the "slice-of-life," and, more recently, the "open-ended" story, a legitimate enough form, if it is not open at both ends, top and bottom. Since on the contrary **"Flowering**

**Judas"** is so plainly a fully realized effort to tell a tale classically, that is, to move a serious theme through implied time by means of characters who act on ethical choices, and to do this, moreover, without failing to accommodate to theme, where-ever possible, the details of image and fable, it might, therefore, be wise to be a bit warier than most critics have been of reading this story as if its meaning partook of its figuration rather than, as I believe to be the case, the reverse.

There has been no slackening of published interest in **"Flowering Judas,"** but the standard reading continues to be the West-Stallman analysis which appeared in a college anthology of short fiction [entitled *The Art of Modern Fiction*] in 1949. I know of no reading that does not take off from it, at least in its basic assumption of the accessibility of theme and meaning through symbolism. The text is incorrectly titled **"The Flowering Judas."** If one believed that the causes of error are unconscious but real, the accident would be seen as a true mistake. For West and Stallman, *the* flowering Judas is virtually *the* story. The analysis itself is titled "Theme through Symbol," which, I contend, is not a viable concept for narrative fiction. The West-Stallman reading asks what the purpose of the individual symbol is, and replies that it is to "signify the theme." "In the title itself" the "most important" symbol "occurs," and the source is given as Eliot's "Gerontion." "This is scarcely a coincidence," we are told, "since Eliot's passage so clearly suggests Laura's activity at the end of the story." The five lines in which the words "flowering Judas" appear are quoted as if they are proof. The Judas tree is seen quite simply as "a symbol for the betrayer of Christ." Laura's eating the buds is a "sacrament . . . of betrayal." If we put aside the question of failure to cite evidence of Miss Porter's specific debt to Eliot in this instance, we are nonetheless free to grant her known interest in Eliot and the obviousness of the betrayal theme in both poem and story do, admittedly, constitute presumptive evidence of source. But to go further in lining up the story with the poem is to jump to conclusions about the use of the symbol, based mistakenly on the assumption that symbols are used in stories quite as they might be in poems, that is, to signify theme. In fact, in Miss Porter's story, the symbol of the flowering Judas is employed to enhance theme and finally to reiterate theme, but not to be a sign of theme as if theme had not been established by other means. Laura is found wanting from beginning to end, and the meaning of the story does not wait on a final symbolic revelation to make accessible what would otherwise be mysterious. "I have a great deal of religious symbolism in my stories," Miss Porter recently allowed, "because I have a very deep sense of religion and also I have a religious training. And I suppose you don't invent symbolism. You don't say, 'I'm going to have the flowering Judas tree stand for betrayal,' but of course it does" [*Recent Southern Fiction: A Panel Discussion, Bulletin of Wesleyan College,* Vol. 41, No. 1, January 1961]. Of course, it does, because given the association of the name Judas it can. But it does only if the author, in effect, employs it to that end. If the reader can recognize the Judas tree as a symbol of betrayal, he can do so legitimately, and not arbitrarily, only if he has been permitted to see betrayal in the story's action. It is the story, all in all, that makes of this particular tree a working symbol of anything whatever. In a work as psychologically realistic as this one, concerned as it is with the levels of a young woman's harassed consciousness (Laura's mind is in fact the work's arena), the Judas tree does not stand primarily and independently as the figure of pagan treachery, analogous to Laura's treachery. Rather it illuminates, dream image that it is, the natural depths of the bedeviled feelings of a woman who cannot, when awake, come to terms with those feelings. Seen this way, **"Flowering Judas"** is not a symbolic story in the sense that it depends on symbols to pull its thematic irons out of the fire. The entire work is in a way "symbolic" insofar as it impels the reader to attend to one striking detail and not another. But within this sense of symbol the Judas tree as a figure is not the most important. It cannot, logically, be more important than any other narrative detail which gives us insight into Laura's character. It may seem crucial because of its strategic location, that is, at the end. Thus placed, however, it can astonish only a reader who has paid little attention to the work's beginning, as might astonish the figurative phrase "my eyes burned" at the conclusion of Joyce's "Araby," a story which begins, "North Richmond Street, being blind, was a quiet street. . . ."

Miss Porter has written of **"Flowering Judas"** [in *This Is My Best,* 1942]:

> All the characters and episodes are based on real persons and events, but naturally, as my memory worked upon them and time passed, all assumed different shapes and colors, formed gradually around a central idea, that of self-delusion, the order and meaning of the episodes changed, and became in a word fiction.

> The idea first came to me one evening when going to visit the girl I call Laura in the story, I passed the open window of her living room on my way to the door, through the small patio which is one of the scenes in the story. I had a brief glimpse of her sitting with an open book in her lap, but not reading, with a fixed look of pained melancholy and confusion in her face. The fat man I call Braggioni was playing the guitar and singing to her.

> In that glimpse, no more than a flash, I thought I understood, or perceived, for the first time, *The desperate complications of her mind* and feelings, and I knew a story; perhaps not her true story, not even the real story of the whole situation, but all the same a story that seemed *symbolic truth* to me. If I had not seen her face at the very moment, I should never have written just this story because I should not have known it to write. [Italics mine]

**"Flowering Judas"** owes its greatness not at all to some opportunistic employment of a conventional religious symbol to signify theme but to a brilliant narrative practice, throughout, one capable of representing a feeling that, once apprehended by the reader, permits him to see

with what overriding intelligence Miss Porter knew her Laura, "the desperate complication of her mind" and what it meant.

---

> **Miss Porter's thrillingly intelligent narrative voice, guiding us over the landscape of Laura's mind, making sense for us of its "disunion."**
>
> —*M. M. Liberman*

---

The celebrated dream sequence on which the story ends and which is supposed to be central in its resolution and revelation through the symbol of the tree and the buds follows:

> The tolling of the midnight bell is a signal, but what does it mean? Get up, Laura, and follow me: come out of your sleep, out of your bed, out of this strange house. What are you doing in this house? Without a word, without fear she rose and reached for Eugenio's hand, but he eluded her with a sharp, sly smile and drifted away. This is not all, you shall see—Murderer, he said, follow me, I will show you a new country, but it is far away and we must hurry. No, said Laura, not unless you take my hand, no; and she clung first to the stair rail and then to the topmost branch of the Judas tree that bent down slowly and set her upon the earth, and then to the rocky ledge of a cliff, and then to the jagged wave of a sea that was not water but a desert of crumbling stone. Where are you taking me, she asked in wonder but without fear. To death, and it is a long way off, and we must hurry, said Eugenio. No, said Laura, not unless you take my hand. Then eat these flowers, poor prisoner, said Eugenio in a voice of pity, take and eat: and from the Judas tree he stripped the warm bleeding flowers, and held them to her lips. She saw that his hand was fleshless, a cluster of small white petrified branches, and his eye sockets were without light, but she ate the flowers greedily for they satisfied both hunger and thirst. Murderer! said Eugenio, and Cannibal! This is my body and my blood. Laura cried No! and at the sound of her own voice, she awoke trembling, and was afraid to sleep again.

It has been prepared for by a single reference to the Judas tree earlier in connection with a "brown, shock-haired youth" who pleaded for her love in vain. Laura, for her part, "could think of nothing to do about it."

The sense one gets of Laura's emotional stinginess is not so much that, Judas-like, she has betrayed the young man in withholding human warmth but that, like the central figure of **"Theft,"** Miss Porter's story of another young woman who is seen explicitly to have stolen life's spiritual riches from *herself,* Laura has betrayed Laura. We know next to nothing of the young man, but we know how desperately Laura needs to fulfill herself. The young man will fare badly, but it is not inevitable. Laura, on the other hand, is doomed forever to suffer her own starving soul, a fact confirmed by a negation and fear of life and truth, the note on which the very last image is played out. But nothing of what is given to the reader anywhere in the dream sequence is unprepared for, and is, moreover, explicitly *reasoned* by the narrator the moment it is possible to intrude sufficiently to explain Laura. In a work of fiction in which the narrator tells the reader what he needs to know, no symbol so arbitrary as to liken a frightened nunlike girl to the historical Judas is artistically allowable. Nor is Miss Porter guilty of such faulty aesthetic judgment.

If Miss Porter is a symbolist only in the sense we have described, that is, as a writer whose choices of vocabulary, of levels of diction, and of varieties of image work insistently to induce one to read beyond mere denotation, she is also a symbolist in **"Flowering Judas"** in the sense of her own phrase "symbolic truth," which I take to be synonymous with "meaning."

Finally, the West-Stallman reading has it that

> Laura is not redeemed, even though she desires it, as the eating of the buds of the Judas tree suggests. Her sacrament is a devouring gesture and Eugenio calls her a cannibal, because she is devouring him (Man). She is, like Judas, the betrayer—the destroyer; and her betrayal, like his, consisted in an inability to believe. Without faith she is incapable of passion, thence of love, finally of life itself.

> This is the "moral" of the story, translated as it is into the language of Christian theology: "Man cannot live by bread alone." Distilled even beyond that, into the language of statement, we might say that the theme is this: "Man cannot live if he accepts only materialistic values"; or, to put it into a positive statement: "Only in faith and love can man live." This does not, however, represent the "meaning," for the meaning is, as we have said, the total embodiment—the form. The statement is only an inadequate attempt on the part of the reader to seek out the author's intention. The question the student should ask next is, "How much does it leave unsaid?"

It is a little like shoveling sand in a windstorm to so much as begin to take issue with this crowd of New Critical pieties: the historical Christian assumptions as the ground for reading a "moral" statement; the fudging of the question of meaning by equating it simply with "form"; and the raising of the old specter of "intention." Miss Porter makes it quite clear that her intention is to elucidate the "desperate complications of her [the protagonist's] mind" and that the "meaning" of the story is in whatever general human nature can be discerned from such an elucidation. The "symbolic truth" Miss Porter speaks of is precisely in the way Laura's career corresponds to the ambiguous and paradoxical condition of recognizable modern man. Laura "is not at home in the world." In this configuration the most crucial fictional device is not the Judas tree but Laura herself. The theme, then, can hardly be stated as "man cannot live if he accepts only materialistic values." **"Flowering Judas"**

dramatizes nothing so much as the fact that modern man, especially modern political man (Braggioni), lives and thrives, but more like a pig than a human. As for Laura, who has been enlisted in Braggioni's cause, she is so far from being materialistic that, in her "notorious virginity," she has even disowned her body. She is the most spiritual of women, but her spirit has been given over to a crusade founded not on a faith in the soul of man or the love of God but on the mindless force of history. In surrendering herself thus, she has surrendered everything.

If one must state a theme, it would be that of *self*-betrayal, and, more interestingly for a fictional construct, the way in which anomic modern life can be made of it.

> But she cannot help feeling that she has been betrayed irreparably by the disunion between her way of living and her feeling of what life should be, and at times she is almost contented to rest in this sense of grievance as a private store of consolation. Sometimes she wishes to run away, but she stays.

In their haste to see the meaning of **"Flowering Judas"** as inhering in its "most important" symbol, as it "occurs," commentators after the New Critics have failed consistently to distinguish the foreground of the narration from its shadowy, memorial background, where a series of rather theoretical and underdramatized "betrayed" characters have compromised Laura's Mexican life. Even Braggioni, despite his imminence and despite his taking part in the most affecting of scenes (his homecoming), curiously resides as almost exclusively an evil presence in Laura's desolate consciousness. There is, in fact, only one character upstage, Miss Porter's thrillingly intelligent narrative voice, guiding us over the landscape of Laura's mind, making sense for us of its "disunion." This she does in the historical present, so that the truth may be held up for inspection in life's continual moment.

### John Edward Hardy (essay date 1973)

SOURCE: "By Self Possessed: 'Flowering Judas'," in *Katherine Anne Porter,* Frederick Ungar Publishing Co., 1973, pp. 68-76.

*[In the following excerpt, Hardy offers a thematic analysis of "Flowering Judas," focusing on the story's emphasis on love, religion, and revolution. Hardy characterizes this story as "perhaps the best-known of Miss Porter's stories, and a great favorite of symbolist critics."]*

**"Flowering Judas"** is perhaps the best-known of Miss Porter's stories, and a great favorite of symbolist critics. In 1947, Ray West elaborately analyzed the rather elaborately obvious religious symbolism of the story. Many later critics, taking West's study as a point of departure, have emphasized the erotic significance of the symbols. There are, I would agree with practically everybody, two most important things about Laura: she is a Catholic who has lost her faith, and she is sexually repressed.

It hardly needs saying that the two matters have a good deal to do with each other. The particular *kind* of Catholicism, from which she has lapsed, is that peculiarly North American, predominantly Irish, Jansenist cult—historically competitive with the earlier established tradition of Protestant puritanism in the United States—which makes religion all but exclusively a matter of morality, and morality all but exclusively sex morality. The ideal of sexual "purity" is the basis of all other idealisms.

For the person cast in this mold (whether officially lapsed or unlapsed), dirty, sensual Mexico (whether Catholic or socialist) exercises the ultimate charm of attraction-repulsion, offers the ultimate test of puritan idealism. Desperate sometimes because of her inability to sustain the inner conviction of her revolutionary commitment, Laura pays clandestine visits to churches. Thus she briefly and unsuccessfully tries to revive at least the emotion of her dead faith. The Roman Catholic Church in Mexico depended upon its alliance with the hereditary landowners for its wealth and political power and secured its hold on the minds of the common people through perpetuation of what the socialists regarded as superstitious beliefs and practices, such as those involved in the cult of the Blessed Virgin, the veneration of the Saints, and the Eucharistic sacrifice. It was regarded as one of the greatest enemies of the revolutionary movement. And Laura is acutely aware that simply by entering a church she is suspect as a traitor to the revolutionary cause. But it is not primarily on account of any pang of socialist conscience, not because she is no longer able to *believe,* rationally, in the doctrines of Roman Catholicism, that Laura fails in her efforts to revive the emotions of her earlier faith. Her recitation of the rosary is "no good," simply because she cannot suppress her furtive and deliciously guilty, erotic reaction to her physical surroundings:

> . . . she ends by examining the altar with its tinsel flowers and ragged brocades, and feels tender about the battered doll-shape of some male saint whose white, lace-trimmed drawers hang limply around his ankles below the hieratic dignity of his velvet robe.

The delicate fetishism of her love of fine lace, which distracts her here from her religious devotions, makes her also, in her own eyes, a "heretic" to the revolutionary faith. She cherishes a drawerful of dainty collars, all edged with handmade lace. ". . . she will not wear lace made on machines. This is her private heresy, for in her special group the machine is sacred, and will be the salvation of the workers."

The flaw that effects Laura's alienation from the church is the same flaw that prevents her from being a wholehearted revolutionist. The fault is not difficult to define. The lace of her collars, wrapped in blue tissue paper and laid away in a drawer, or worn high around her neck as a delicate armor against improper advances, symbolizes the desperate privacy of her eroticism. To the extent that she is even aware of her erotic impulses for what they are, she has been unable to reconcile them to her ideal of community faith, whether religious or sociopolitical.

The grossly sensual, vainly self-indulgent Braggioni, whose name defines his character, represents a corruption and betrayal of the humanitarian ideals of the revolution. A "professional lover of humanity," he has nothing but contempt for most men, even his fawning followers, and takes his greatest delight in killing people. His wretched wife's washing his feet, a grotesque parody of Mary's act of obeisance to Jesus (John 12:3), emphasizes with heavy irony Braggioni's falsity both in the role of repentant and forgiving husband and in that of his people's savior.

But Laura, too, has served him humbly. In the description of her dutiful submission to his request that she clean and oil his pistols, the phallic symbolism of the guns is overt. She will not sleep with Braggioni, but her fondling of the deadly weapons is, if anything, more obscene.

Laura, in truth, is no less the "professional lover of humanity" than Braggioni, her high-minded frigidity no less inhumane than his cruel sensuality. The Indian children she teaches are evidently very fond of her—covering her desk with fresh flowers every day, and on one occasion inscribing in colored chalks on the blackboard the words "We lov ar ticher"—but there is no indication that she responds with any warmth even to this innocent affection or has willingly done anything to inspire it. The teaching is a tiresome duty, like all the other tasks she performs in the abstract interest of the revolution.

The dream she has after Braggioni leaves makes it clear that Eugenio had been trying to seduce her. She had evidently felt strongly attracted to him. But to help him to sleep she had given him narcotics, not herself; and she obviously suspects that he took the overdose because he had lost hope of winning her love, not because of despair at his continuing imprisonment. That her dream of him awakens her and makes her afraid to go back to sleep is ironically appropriate to what she has done in giving him the narcotics, affording him a sleep from which he will never awaken.

From Braggioni's point of view, Eugenio's suicide is a betrayal, although not a very important one, of the revolutionary cause. Laura subconsciously attempts to convince herself of this view in her dream-identification of Eugenio with the Judas tree; his flesh and blood are the blossoms of the tree, its twigs the fingerbones of his skeletal hands. (In legend, it was from the redbud, or Judas tree, that Christ's betrayer hanged himself.) But in eating the flowers, she acknowledges herself as the traitor, and Eugenio after all as the Son of Man.

The dream's mock communion, with the body and blood of Judas substituted for that of Christ, might be seen as embodying Laura's suppressed conviction that her association with the revolutionary movement is a betrayal of her first Lord. Or the imagery will as easily support an opposite interpretation. Perhaps Laura feels guilty about her continuing, furtive flirtations with Catholicism, seeing them as a betrayal of the revolutionary cause. It is for this that Eugenio condemns her in the dream with the words "murderer" and "cannibal"—which are such words as a good socialist might use for Catholic communicants. But the important thing, either way, is that she has betrayed herself, her own humanity, in her refusal to love.

Her refusing in the dream to accompany Eugenio on the journey to death unless he will take her hand is a gesture of ambiguous significance. It is at once an acknowledgment of her need for love, and a sign of her continuing reluctance to admit it. When Eugenio finally extends his hand, it is the bony hand of death, one proferring a substance that is the food of death, not life.

Laura is afraid to go back to sleep, perhaps to reenter the dream, because she has recognized there the falsity of *all* her communions. She had gone to sleep silently repeating to herself that "it is monstrous to confuse love with revolution." But, as she senses in the dream, it is precisely in failing to achieve that confusion, or fusion, that she betrays every cause that requires her loyalty.

The point is that there is no true religion, and no true revolution, without love. The puritan mind that regards the inevitable "confusions" of the human condition—"love with revolution, night with day, life with death," spirit with body—as "monstrous" must end with making a monster of man himself. It is just this that Laura makes of Eugenio and of herself—he becoming the walking tree-skeleton, she the cannibal murderer who eats of his not-flesh. The cry of "No!" with which she awakens herself would deny her self-conviction of inhumanity. But we recognize it also as a despairing repetition of the cry with which, in the reality of waking experience, she has met all demands for human involvement. She is still bound to the lifelong habit of denial, or rejection, that has led her to the monstrous confrontation in the dream.

## Thomas F. Walsh (essay date 1985)

SOURCE: "The Making of 'Flowering Judas'," in *Journal of Modern Literature,* Vol. 12, No. 1, March, 1985, pp. 109-30.

[*In the following essay, Walsh discusses Porter's use of historical detail and personal experience in "Flowering Judas," noting in particular how historical figures became the basis for several of the story's characters.*]

Over the years Katherine Porter furnished many autobiographical details about her most celebrated story, **"Flowering Judas"** (1930), stating [in *This Is My Best,* 1942] that "all the characters and episodes are based on real persons and events, but naturally, as my memory worked upon them and time passed, all assumed different shapes and colors, formed gradually around a central idea, that of self-delusion, the order and meaning of the episodes changed, and became in a word fiction." This essay, drawing from Porter's published comments on the story, her unpublished letters, notes, and fiction, and my conversa-

tions with her and with her friend, Mary Louis Doherty, attempts to distinguish between the "real persons and events" and the "different shapes and colors" they assumed. Despite the thin record of Porter's Mexican period, the questionable accuracy of her recollections of it many years later, and her reputation for fictionalizing her life, we can discover many experiences she transformed into **"Flowering Judas,"** and the reasons those transformations took the shapes they did. Thereby we gain a clearer picture of Porter's first year in Mexico and a better understanding of her creative process.

I

Porter's earliest comment on **"Flowering Judas"** appeared in 1942:

> The idea came to me one evening when going to visit the girl I call Laura in the story. I passed the open window of her living room on my way to the door, through the small patio which is one of the scenes in the story. I had a brief glimpse of her sitting with an open book in her lap, but not reading, with a fixed look of pained melancholy and confusion in her face. The fat man I call Braggioni was playing the guitar and singing to her.
>
> [*This Is My Best*]

Porter "thought" she understood "the desperate complications" of the girl's mind and feelings, but if she did not know "her true story," she did know a story "that seemed symbolic truth" [Barbara Thompson, "An Interview," *Katherine Anne Porter: A Critical Symposium,* 1969]. In subsequent interviews Porter gave the expanded versions of the "small seed" from which her story grew. In 1963 she added the Judas tree and identified the girl as her friend "Mary" who was teaching in an Indian school and "was not able to take care of herself, because she was not able to face her own nature and was afraid of everything" [Hank Lopez, "A Country and Some People I Love," *Harper's,* Vol. 231, 1965]. In 1965 Porter added the fountain and insisted that the small apartment where "Mary Doherty" lived alone was exactly as it appears in the story. Doherty, whom a young *Zapatista* captain attempted to help from her horse, was a "virtuous, intact, straitlaced Irish Catholic . . . born with the fear of sex," who had asked Porter to sit with her because she was not sure of the man coming to sing to her. This Porter did, outwaiting him until he left in frustration. She refused to identify the man, stating that she rolled "four or five objectionable characters into one" to create Braggioni. She also claimed she was like the girl in the story, taking "messages to people living in dark alleys." A few years later she added that she visited political prisoners in their cells, two of whom she named [Enrique Hank Lopez, *Conversations with Katherine Anne Porter,* 1981]. In a lecture taped at the University of Maryland in 1972, Porter gave the fullest and least reliable account of her story's genesis, stating that both she and Doherty brought food and sleeping pills to political prisoners, one of whom persuaded Doherty to give him fifty pills with which he killed himself. When Doherty reported the man's death to "Braggioni," he told her they were well rid of him. Later she dreamed that when she refused the attempt of "Eugenio" to lead her to death, "he gave her the flowering Judas buds." "This is her dream" Porter claimed, adding, "You see, my fiction is reportage, only I do something to it; I arrange it and it is fiction, but it happened." In a film made at the University of Maryland in 1976, she stated that Doherty should have known better than to give pills to the prisoner and, for the first time, gave Yúdico as Braggioni's model. As Porter added details about **"Flowering Judas"** over the years, reality more and more resembled what grew out of it, the story becoming "reportage," mainly of the actions and motives of Mary Doherty, about whom Porter could only speculate in 1942. Porter did indeed "arrange" reality to make it fiction, both in the creation of her story and in her versions of that creation. Her story is "based on real persons and events," but not as in her versions.

II

Porter met most of the "real persons" soon after her arrival in Mexico on September 4, 1920. She found an apartment on 20 Calle de Eliseo, next door to the home of Roberto and Thorberg Haberman. Although Porter never mentioned him publicly, Roberto Haberman, a member of the labor party instrumental in bringing President Alvaro Obregón to power, introduced her to the exciting world of Mexican politics. Porter wrote to her family that she was flattered to be accepted into an exclusive group close to or actually "the holders of the government reins." This group was to change Mexico and she expected "to be connected by a small thread to the affair." She also informed her family that she planned to write for *El Heraldo,* where Thorberg Haberman worked, and to collaborate with the Habermans on a revolutionary textbook. She participated in Obregón's inaugural celebration of November 30, drinking tea and champagne with him in his official residence in Chapultepec Castle, and also attended the lottery ticket sellers' ball in company with "the greatest labor leader in Mexico," Luis N. Morones, where she danced with "marvélous carbon colored Indians in scarlet blankets" until two o'clock in the morning. On Christmas day at the Habermans' she met other labor leaders, among them her "beloved" R. H. Retinger.

Retinger, like Haberman, was advisor to Luis Morones. Working for *CROM,* he made valuable connections with international trade unionists in Europe and organized and directed Mexico's Press Agency. A participant in the League of Nations, an acquaintance of Gide, Mauriac, and Arnold Bennett, and a close friend of fellow countryman Joseph Conrad, he represented to Porter "Europe" in all its Jamesian connotations. In her notes she credits him with thoroughly educating her in international politics, but she never mentioned him publicly. They quickly fell in love, but the bickering that fills their letters is evidence enough that their relation would not survive their strong wills.

Mary Doherty, like Porter, was introduced to the labor group by Roberto Haberman. At the Rand School of Eco-

nomics she met Agnes Smedley, Thorberg Haberman's sister-in-law and later apologist for Red China, who encouraged her to visit Mexico. Doherty arrived in early 1921 and lived with the Habermans through July, briefly losing her bed to the legendary labor agitator, Mother Jones. It was to the Haberman home that Samuel O. Yúdico came to entertain her with his guitar. Doherty was soon assisting Retinger in his publicity work for *CROM* and teaching twice a week in Xochimilco, a few miles south of Mexico City. She traveled there with Yúdico or, occasionally, Porter and Retinger. Less self-centered and ambitious than Porter, more committed to Mexico's social progress, and above all, more willing to serve in whatever capacity, Doherty became Porter's confidante and, in a correspondence that spanned fifty years, a continual source of information about Mexico. From the first, Doherty deferred to her more glamorous and talented friend, even rescuing pieces of writing Porter had crumpled up and tossed into the wastepaper basket. More tolerant than Porter of Mexico's shortcomings, Doherty still remembers incidents of her early days in Mexico with pleasure, especially the Sundays she and Porter spent in Chapultepec Park with their friends. She described the happy routine in a letter to her sister in 1921:

> We passear in Chapultepec Park in a coche—those nice old family coaches with either one nice, sleek fat horse or two smaller ones with their clank clank on the pavement. Today being Sunday everyone passears from 12 to 2, the cars barely moving along—up one line and down another—much bowing, etc. You see everyone from Obregon down and since most of the people we know are gov't officials, they all come out in their cars—it is great fun.

(Porter also remembered those Sundays, for in **"Flowering Judas"** Braggioni "hires an automobile and drives in the Paseo on Sunday morning.")

On her first Sunday in Mexico, Doherty met Felipe Carrillo Puerto, then delegate from Yucatán and its next governor. She remembers him earnestly haranguing from a park bench curious passers-by on the glories of socialism. Porter first met him a few weeks before at the Habermans. They became close friends, often dining and dancing in Mexico City's nightclubs. Among Porter's papers are a description of the sinking of their rowboat in the shallow Chapultepec lagoon, his photograph inscribed to his dear friend from Felipe, and a story he told her about a woman driven mad by the Revolution. Porter planned to visit him after he became governor in 1922, but Retinger discouraged her from making the arduous trip to Yucatán.

In January 1921, Porter and Doherty attended the convention of the Pan-American Federation of Labor. They both appear in a photograph of a large group of labor leaders, including Samuel Gompers, head of the A. F. of L., Luis Morones, Carrillo Puerto, and the Habermans. Porter describes in her notes a gathering of these labor people at the Habermans' house, where she fell asleep at the feet of William Green, Gompers' successor in 1925.

According to Doherty, she and Porter were among those who saw Gompers off on his return to the United States, Porter contributing a farewell kiss. This was during the brief happy period of Porter's stay in Mexico.

### III

The bright prospects Porter anticipated in December 1920 had evaporated by May 1921. She reveals her disillusion in "The Mexican Trinity" (August 1921) and "Where Presidents Have No Friends" (July 1922), the first essay beginning,

> Uneasiness grows here daily. We are having sudden deportations of foreign agitators, street riots and parades of workers carrying red flags. Plots thicken, thin, disintegrate in the space of thirty-six hours. A general was executed today for counterrevolutionary activities. . . . Battles occur almost daily between Catholics and Socialists in many parts of the Republic: Morelia, Yucatán, Campeche, Jalisco.

What follows in both essays is highly informative political analysis, written from the point of view of one who firmly supports the goals of the Revolution, but hiding the fact that Porter herself deeply felt the growing "uneasiness." Her situation evolved into Laura's in **"Flowering Judas."**

"Uneasiness" may understate the politically unstable conditions of 1921. A clash between Catholics and Socialists on May 12 resulted in the death of J. Isaac Arriaga, head of the *Comisión Local Agraria,* which Porter lamented in her journal, connecting it to the centuries-old history of unjust seizures of Indian lands. His death provoked agrarian reformers to storm the Chamber of Deputies which became so unruly that Obregón ordered the fire department to turn on its hoses. Porter witnessed the hosing and reported it in "Where Presidents Have No Friends" About the same time, Obregón, complying with one of the conditions the United States stipulated for its recognition of Mexico, deported about thirty foreign radicals, among them several of Porter's acquaintances. Roberto Haberman was also on the list and went into hiding. This incident frightened Porter, who recorded it many time in her journal and letters, writing to friend Paul Hannah that newspapers were clamoring for Haberman's head. She visited him in hiding and described him sitting on a tumbled bed, pale and drawn, and going over a long piece he had composed about how Americans "crack the whip" over Mexico. Later she began to turn this incident into fiction: "a certain Roumanian Jew agitator" recites "romantic yarns of personal treason" and composes a thesis against giving one man absolute power. He resembles the "prisoners of [Laura's] own political faith in their cells . . . composing their memoirs, writing out manifestoes."

Even more frightening, Porter herself was on the deportation list. She wrote of rehearsing a speech she would make to the police in order to gain time to pack. George T. Summerlin, U. S. chargé d'affaires in Mexico, assured her that her name had been removed, but another informant told her later that it was not. In the meantime, her checks had been held up, and for the first time in her life she experienced hunger. She walked past secret service men sitting on the curb in front of the Haberman house, not caring whether they seized her because at least in jail she would be fed. Not finding Thorberg inside, she stole a dozen tortillas and a bowl of turkey mole. In another note she writes of crying a great deal and feeling sorry for herself: "Starvation is very hard on the flesh, and the idea of death is very hard on the nerves; I should like to deny that I am terrified but I am."

In a letter to her sister in June 1921, Doherty responds quite differently to the deportation crisis, giving in the process a rare, if brief, contemporary glimpse of Porter in Mexico:

> Of course all our crowd is on the list. . . . Bob is hiding with the papers yammering for his head. . . . Secret service people guard the house—all mail held up. All the Mexicans are with us all the while because they don't want us deported—Obregon would change his mind and cancel the order, but Americans keep up the rumpus and won't stop until they get Bob. It has been over two weeks now. . . . Strangely enough—no doubt due to the nervous tension and suspense—we who are still around loose are having a very good time—we go forth gayly with the leaders of the very government that has us on the list for deportation. Katherine, Thorberg and I have hilarious times. Of course we are really quite safe, for they won't take us until they get the more important ones and as yet we have done nothing because we can't speak Spanish—only in disrepute because of our beliefs and our associations and Katherine especially because she has refused to associate with the American colony. She is very pretty and very clever and they would like to have her and she is not very radical. . . . It will be very funny to laugh at a year from now—just now a little nervewracking.

This letter is not from somebody "afraid of everything," as Porter claimed Doherty was. Rather, the evidence shows that Porter herself was "terrified." In a note entitled "A month of uncertainties," she begins with the death of five followers of rebel General Lucio Blanco, adding "How on earth does this concern me? Yet it does." She then mentions the trouble stirring Catholics and Socialists in Morelia with "Yudico and Bob polishing their pistols," the deportation of foreign radicals, Haberman in hiding, Summerlin's information, the hosing in the Chamber of Deputies, and finally her expectations of a summons any minute. At this time her friend Retinger was in the Laredo jail where she wrote him of all her troubles. In her recital Porter intertwines her own fear of deportation with deaths and threatened violence to others. The "uneasiness" in "The Mexican Trinity" is her uneasiness, tempting one to substitute her name for Carranza's in "Where Presidents Have No Friends."

Just as Porter mingles violence and death with her personal fears, so in **"Flowering Judas"** "the sight and sound of Braggioni singing threaten to identify themselves with all Laura's remembered afflictions and add their weight to her uneasy premonition of the future." Like Porter, Laura feels engulfed by the presence of death: "Laura feels a slow chill, a purely physical sense of danger, a warning in her blood that violence, mutilation, a shocking death, wait for her with lessening patience." And just as Yúdico and Haberman polish their pistols for "a row between the Catholics and Socialists . . . scheduled in Morelia for May 1st," so Braggioni asks Laura to "oil and load his pistols" because of "the May-day disturbances in Morelia." Out of her own remembered fears of 1921 Porter created the deathly atmosphere of **"Flowering Judas."**

With Laura's "warning in her blood" of "a shocking death" awaiting her, Porter gave full expression to her all-consuming theme. In this story, earlier fictional fragments, and later stories, culminating in **"Pale Horse, Pale Rider,"** death is felt as a terrifying physical presence. In one fragment a character named Natalie complains, "There is something altogether horrible here . . . I am frightened of all sorts of things. I have terrible dreams," to which her friend Paul replies that he is "influenced by some indefinite thing in the air, a hovering and sinister presence." In **"Hacienda"** the narrator speaks of "the almost ecstatic death-expectancy which is in the air of Mexico. . . . strangers feel the acid of death in their bones whether or not any real danger is near them." Here Mexico is explicitly a place of death, symbolized by the "sour" odor of pulque, "like rotting milk and blood." In **"Pale Horse, Pale Rider,"** the air is contaminated with influenza, infecting Miranda, who smells "the stench of corruption" in her own wasted body. This story was based on Porter's near-death struggle with influenza in 1918, but, she noted in her journal, she felt "the terror of death" stronger in 1921 than in 1918. When she wrote **"Pale Horse, Pale Rider"** in 1938, the terror she expressed had been magnified by her Mexican experience. Death is the firm link between Porter's Mexican and Miranda stories. She began the outline of the novel she was writing in Mexico with "Book I: Introduction to Death," which was to include Miranda's childhood. **"The Grave"** (1935) gives that introduction and tellingly ends with odors in Mexico triggering Miranda's childhood memories: "It was a very hot day and the smell in the market, with its piles of raw flesh and wilting flowers, was like the mingled sweetness and corruption she had smelled that other day in the cemetery at home."

## IV

Porter's journal and letters give evidence that she viewed Mexico as a continual source for her creative writing. Seemingly nothing occurred that she did not weigh for its literary potential. She wrote local color sketches like "In a Mexican Patio" and "Teotihuacan" and recorded stories told to her by others. But, as we have already seen from the deportation crisis of 1921, her main interests were the political and the personal.

Among Porter's papers is an outline of all the political parties in Mexico along with a thumbnail sketch of the leaders of each party. Her thorough knowledge served her well in such objective reporting as "The Mexican Trinity," but her ultimate goal was fiction. In May 1921, she wrote Paul Hannah of her "strangely assorted contacts" with diplomats, revolutionists, government officials, and unrestrained internationalists, adding, "I am making a story of these opposed forces." Elsewhere she recorded her intention of doing sketches of her revolutionary acquaintances, but what might have begun as reportage soon became "making a story." Thus Yúdico and Morones became Braggioni; Haberman, Silberman; Carrillo Puerto, Vicente; and President Elias Calles, Velarde, the name Porter gives him in **"Hacienda."** The link between fact and fiction was her interest in the revolutionary personality, her estimate of which grew more cynical as time wore on.

Porter's personal experiences appear in her journal, often in the form of probing, guilt-ridden self-analysis, and in fictional fragments in which her alter ego Miranda makes her debut in scenes with her lover Jerome, who is based on R. H. Retinger. Porter intended to write "our story" about herself and Retinger, who was both political mentor and lover. Although she never completed the story, its fragments contributed, as we shall see, to the formation of Laura's personality.

Retinger himself influenced the composition of **"Flowering Judas"** in two different ways. While in a Laredo jail because of passport problems in May 1921, he wrote Porter to make sure that Luis Morones approved chapters of *Morones of Mexico* which she was editing. It is ironic that she, having read Retinger's adulation of Morones and Yúdico in this book, would eventually use both men as models for her negative portrait of Braggioni. Retinger wrote [in *The Rise of the Mexican Labor Movement,* 1976] that "Yudico, a tall, fair man, is a regular jack of all trades. . . . he knows every corner of the Republic, and understands the sufferings of the workers. Frank and outspoken, his equanimity is appreciated by his companions and his good heartedness makes him a friend of everybody." Apparently Porter reserved Retinger's hollow rhetoric for Braggioni's followers who "say to each other: 'He has real nobility, a love of humanity raised above mere personal affections.'"

Although Porter raised the thousand dollar bail money for Retinger with an offer of five hundred dollars more and traveled to Laredo at the request of Morones to attempt his release, their love affair was fast disintegrating. In her journal she wrote that he would be pained to know how little she cared about his predicament. In later journal entries she described him as "an Austrian Pole much given to international intrigue" and "a complex and fascinating liar." In 1943, she still held a grudge against him, calling him, in a letter to Doherty, her "old enemy and parasite." No wonder her unflattering portrait of him in **"Flowering Judas"**: "The Polish agitator talks love to [Laura] over café tables, hoping to exploit what he believes is her sentimental preference for him, and he gives her misinformation which he begs her to repeat as the solemn truth to certain persons." Behind this scene we can see Retinger professing his love for Porter in

1921 in the Café Colón on the Paseo, according to Doherty, one of their favorite meeting places. In the story, Laura is not deceived by the Pole's tactics as Porter felt she had been deceived by Retinger's. Reading the story, he would know that his former beloved had taken her revenge.

Porter also turned against Roberto Haberman, describing him in her notes as an unprincipled conniver who would practice any deception to advance his radical cause. In **"Flowering Judas"** he appears as the "Roumanian agitator": "He is generous with his money in all good causes, and lies to Laura with an air of ingenuous candor, as if he were her good friend and confidant."

As early as 1921 Porter planned to combine the political and personal in a novel called *Thieves' Market.* Through the twenties she added to it such events as Carrillo Puerto's death and Morones' fall from power. Later she conceived a three-book structure entitled *Many Redeemers* or *Midway of This Mortal Life,* which was to center on Miranda's whole life, beginning with "the history of the rise and break-up of an American family" and ending in the present with "the record of a rich and crumbling society." Mexico formed only a part of this grand scheme and was to appear as "the Mexican interval which is a tangent for Miranda, the complete negation of all she had known, a derailment up to 1928 or 30." The project would have challenged a Balzac. Begun in disconnected fragments, it ended as "fragments of a much larger plan" in the form of several short stories, **"Old Mortality"** coming closest to Porter's idea about the break-up of an American family. In the early thirties Porter visited Germany, which she apparently decided was more important than Mexico for the political statements she wished to make. The result was **"The Leaning Tower"** and *Ship of Fools,* according to most critics her least successful works, possibly because she was less acquainted with Germans than with Mexicans. But before turning away from Mexico, she did manage in **"Flowering Judas"** to unite the political and personal. She quickly knew what she had accomplished, writing to a friend in April 1930, "It's by far the best thing I ever did and is in the mood and style of the novel." Although she continued to mention a Mexican novel in the forties, there was no need to write it, for her short story was the perfect distillation of everything the novel could have been.

V

The political dimension of **"Flowering Judas,"** ignored by some of Porter's critics, is concentrated in the character of Braggioni. Since Porter did indeed roll "four or five objectionable characters" into one to create him, it is important to see how the revolutionaries she knew contributed to what was, in her jaundiced view, a portrait of *the* revolutionary.

A journal note dated 1921 begins, "Yudico came in tonight bringing his guitar, and spent the evening singing for Mary." This early record of Porter's inspiration for **"Flowering Judas"** is devoted, as we shall see, to Mary

Doherty with no other reference to Yúdico, but clearly he was the physical and moral prototype of Braggioni. The Yúdico who entertained Doherty was a tall, rather stout man with fair complexion, light brown hair, and deep green eyes, sedately dressed with no pistols in evidence. His father, like Braggioni's, was Italian. Braggioni's "tight little mouth that turns down at the corners," giving him a "surly" expression, is an accurate, if unkind, description of Yúdico. Porter lightened Yúdico's hair, but turned his green eyes into "yellow cat's eyes" and his stoutness into "gluttonous bulk" which has become "a symbol of [Laura's] many disillusions' about how revolutionists should look and act. Porter's Yúdico was not the man Mary Doherty described as a friend to her family or the one Retinger idealized in his biography of Morones. If Doherty overlooked Yúdico's defects, Porter, as other journal notes suggest, saw nothing else.

Porter was apparently fascinated with Yúdico from the start. On September 8, 1921, she wrote of doing four portraits of revolutionaries, with his portrait almost complete. Also in 1921 she wrote that she heard Retinger talking with Yúdico, "a completely savage and uneducated Indian revolutionist, a man with the eyes of a cat and the paunch of a pig and they both agreed that a woman was good for one thing." In a later note she advised herself, "Get into the scene . . . something of Braggioni's really sinister personality, the soft-spoken, hard-eyed monster." The shift here from Yúdico to Braggioni is imperceptible because Porter always saw Braggioni in Yúdico. Yúdico as sexual menace must have provoked her instinctive hatred. Another note begins, "Yudico and his wife—went home to wash feet, wife came home sobbing . . ." and then continues, "Third Wife, fiftieth concubine—not faithful to anything. Study of Mexican revolutionary. . . . Given charge of blowing up and destroying Mexico City" if it falls into the hands of the enemy. Here and in **"Flowering Judas"** the sexual and political intermesh. Braggioni revenges himself on a thousand women for the humiliation one woman caused him in his youth just as he would brutally revenge himself against his political enemies if the need arose. His behavior is pointedly typical of the revolutionary who violates at every step the principles he pretends to uphold. In another note Porter wrote that the "spirit of revolutionaries is to escape from bondage to themselves. Their desire to rule, their will to power, is sort of revenge" to compensate for "their own insignificance, their sufferings." Porter, who attended a feminist meeting with Thorberg Haberman where she became the "79th member of the woman's party in Mexico," certainly viewed the attitudes of Yúdico/Braggioni toward women as a betrayal of the Revolution and a personal affront to herself and Laura.

In 1928 Porter shifted her attention from Yúdico, who died that year, to Luis Morones, explicitly identifying him with Braggioni in her notes. In 1922 she had praised Morones for paying munitions factory workers the highest wages in Mexico. With a thirty million peso budget and a command of a large reserve of men, he enjoyed the prominence and power Porter attributes to Braggioni, with Retinger and Haberman, like the Polish and Rumanian agitators, contending for his favor. But Morones' reputation as a ruthless, corrupt politician became widespread. Porter's acquaintance, Carleton Beals, ridiculed him as "a big pig-like man . . . always meticulously dressed and perfumed, his hands glittering with diamonds." In the same vein Porter described him in her journal as a "swollen labor leader . . . who removes inordinate silk scarf, and flashes his diamond like spotlights." He has "no higher idea than simple comforts and cheap elegance and direct forthright grabbing of whatever he can get." This description fits Braggioni with his diamond hoop and "elegant refinements" of silk handkerchief and Jockey Club perfume. When Morones' presidential ambitions made him suspect in the plot to assassinate Obregón in 1928, forcing him to resign his ministry, Porter wrote that he had done badly and used his fall from power to prophesy the fall of Braggioni, who "will live to see himself kicked out from his feeding trough by other hungry world saviors." In 1922 she had written in her journal, "if Morones is next president, salvation of Mexico is assured." In **"Flowering Judas"** words like "salvation" became bitterly ironic.

Angel Gomez and Felipe Carrillo Puerto, whose portraits Porter planned along with Yúdico's, also contributed to Braggioni's character. Gomez pops up in fiction fragments and plays a major role in **"The Dove of Chapacalco,"** always as "the bomb thrower" or "the dynamiter"—for instance, "Gomez spent his time on knees as devotee, looking for chance to plan a dynamiting of the holy statue which is chief fame and revenue to church." Gomez may be Porter's pure invention or may have been a real dynamiter she met through her *CROM* contacts if Catholic claims that *CROM* was responsible for the bombing of Catholic shrines are true. In any case, she invests Braggioni, who pins his "faith to good dynamite," with Gomez's destructiveness. Braggioni envisions everything "hurled skyward" so that "nothing the poor has made for the rich shall remain." He would be more dangerous if he really believed his apocalyptic rhetoric which reveals his arrogance and hypocrisy since he enjoys the luxuries of the rich he would exterminate. To Porter he is the typical revolutionary, one of a "welter of small chattering monkeys busily making over a world to their own desires."

Carrillo Puerto did not live long enough to disillusion Porter, but her notes and fictional fragments reveal her ambivalence toward him. He is the "beautiful bandit from Yucatan," "a dreamer of violent and gorgeous dreams," and "a complete dictator." His rhetoric, like Braggioni's, was radical, as were the changes he effected in Yucatán. He claimed direct descent from pre-colonial Mayan nobility, reminding us that Braggioni's Mayan mother was "a woman of race, an aristocrat." Porter's fictional name for Carrillo is Vicente, Braggioni's first name.

More importantly, Carrillo and others are the source of the ironic Christological imagery that unifies Braggioni's portrait. Critics are probably correct in assuming that the image of **"Flowering Judas"** derives from Eliot's "Gerontion," but the large pattern derives from revolutionary rhetoric. The photograph Carrillo dedicated to

Porter had appeared in *Redención* (Redemption), a publication of the Feminist League of Merida, Yucatán, the first issue of which (May 28, 1921) is among Porter's papers. Undoubtedly, socialists, opposed to a Catholic Church that, in their opinion, promised redemption to the poor in another life while collaborating with their oppressors in this one, reinterpreted Christian language imbibed in childhood and offered political and economic redemption here and now. Porter comments on the word in "Where Presidents Have No Friends": Best Maugard's "belief is that a renascence of older Aztec arts and handicrafts among these people will aid immeasurably in their redemption. Redemption—it is a hopeful, responsible word one often hears among these men." But Porter's own hope vanished, and so Braggioni emerges as a perverse savior who, like Morones, only talks of "sacrificing himself for the worker." He is typical of *Many Redeemers,* which "is all about how men go on saving the world by starving, robbing, and killing each other—lying, meanwhile, to themselves and each other about their motives." Porter's description of her never-completed novel applies to **"Flowering Judas."**

It took nine years for Porter's views of several revolutionaries to blend and unify in her imagination. The result is the richly complex Braggioni, who is completely individualized in his brutal corpulence and perfectly typical of the revolutionary personality she came to despise. The process of Laura's creation is similar to Braggioni's, but complicated by the involvement of Porter's own personality in ways she may never have completely understood then or was willing to admit later.

## VI

In her journal note of June 1921, Porter recorded her impression of Mary Doherty seated at a table, "a little preoccupied, infallibly and kindly attentive" to Yúdico as he entertained her with his guitar. She is "a modern secular nun," "a virgin but faintly interested in love," who "wears a rigid little uniform of dark blue cloth, with immaculate collars and cuffs of narrow lace made by hand." She thinks there is something "dishonest" in lace "contrived by machinery," but "pays a handsome price" for her "one extravagance." Born an Irish Catholic, "her romantic sense of adventure has guided her to the lower strata of revolution" where she "keeps her head cool in the midst of opera bouffe plots" and "submerged international intrigue." She intended to organize working women into labor unions, but does not realize that those who thwart her efforts are not as "clear and straight minded" as she. Although she has developed "a little pucker of trouble between her wide set grey eyes," she still "has the look of one who expects shortly to find a simple and honest solution of a very complicated problem. She is never to find it."

In her portrait of Doherty, Porter's selection and interpretation of details anticipates the creation of Laura. Porter saw Doherty, as she did Yúdico, pictorially, associating her "rigid little uniform" with her nun-like virginity (a uniform Doherty was still wearing in 1926 as Edward Weston's photographs show). That uniform will eventually symbolize Laura's fearful rejection of love in contrast to Doherty's dawning interest. Doherty's lace, like Laura's, is her one extravagance, but what she "thinks" about the dishonesty of machine-made lace is already a fiction in 1921, for she bought her lace at Altman's in New York, unaware whether it was handmade or not. In **"Flowering Judas,"** Laura feels guilty about wearing the handmade lace when the machine is "sacred" to the revolutionist. From the start Doherty's dress had a meaning, but that meaning changed in the writing of **"Flowering Judas."**

Porter appropriated other details from Doherty's life to create Laura. Doherty's Irish Catholic background reinforced the image of "secular nun," although, unlike Laura, she was not a churchgoer. Like Laura, Doherty taught Indian children in Xochimilco, but never tried to organize women into labor unions. Her horse once ran away from a former *Zapatista,* Genaro Amezcua, who was head of the agrarian bureau in Cuernavaca where she first met him. Porter also knew him, describing him as "the only intelligent pro-feminist in Mexico," an ironic footnote to Laura's rejection of him and all other men in the story. However, such details do not account for Laura's personality. Doherty's honesty and genuine devotion to revolutionary reform, however naïve they seemed to Porter in her note of 1921, bear little resemblance to Laura's alienation and mechanical performance of duties in **"Flowering Judas."**

Porter's claim of coming over to Doherty's apartment at her request to protect her from Yúdico is a fiction. Her 1921 journal entry gives no hint of such circumstances. At that time Doherty was not living alone, but with the Habermans. Also, she categorically denies that she was ever afraid of Yúdico, whom she described in a postcard in 1925 as "one of my good friends." Why then Porter's fabrication? Apparently she placed herself outside and inside the scene with Doherty and Yúdico. Outside, she imagined herself coming to the rescue of Doherty, who should have been afraid instead of sitting "infallibly and kindly attentive." Porter's account of outwaiting and frustrating Yúdico is a kind of posthumous revenge on him. Inside the scene, Porter identified with Doherty/Laura's "notorious virginity," expressing her own fear of violation in a world in which men were used to having their way with women. Porter treated endangered virginity in two other works of the period. The "dove" of **"The Dove of Chapacalco"** is a young servant girl who becomes the prey of a corrupt bishop. **"Virgin Violeta"** (1924) is based on Salomón de la Selva's account of seducing a friend's young daughter. Porter noted, "Salomon is uneasy because I told a friend of his I detested his attitude toward love and women—'If Salomon met the Virgin Mary, he would introduce himself as the Holy Ghost,' I said." And so she detested what she interpreted as Yúdico's advances on the virgin Mary Doherty, in whom she saw herself, and fictionalized her detestation in **"Flowering Judas."** In this light Laura's notorious virginity is a positive virtue, other evidence to the contrary. Although it attracts Braggioni to her in the first place, thereby

placing her in danger, it is a power she has over him. He can have his way with others but not with Laura.

Laura's virginity also has its negative side and partly explains why Porter chose not to name her heroine Miranda. Although the two characters resemble each other, there is a difference. Miranda is a woman victimized from childhood by circumstances beyond her control, from a family who does not understand her to influenza that almost kills her. If she has a fault, it is expecting too much from a world that always disappoints her, thereby justifying her reaction against it. Porter's criticism of Laura is much harsher. By insisting on Doherty as the original of Laura, she makes her friend the scapegoat for qualities she found difficult to admit as her own.

Negatively Laura's virginity represents total moral disengagement. She does not, understandably, love Braggioni, but she does not love anybody. Thus she is a traitor to the Revolution and to her own religious principles. Braggioni questions Laura's coldness: "You think you are so cold, *gringita!*", but his hope that she is not is vain, for she suffers from her author's own emotional problems. In her journal Porter recorded Retinger's complaint that her "detachment from people and groups is a mark of her selfishness, is a sin against human solidarity." Another time he told her, "what you need is love. Your body will wither without it." Porter seemed torn between love and its smothering demands. After examining her attraction to Retinger, she concluded, "For I might as well acknowledge . . . love is not for me. . . . Love affects me as a great sickness of the heart, a crushing nostalgia that withers me up, that makes me fruitless and without help." In a fragment from *Thieves' Market,* Miranda "set herself perversely" against Jerome when he was "passionate," refusing to "respond" and feeling "happy in having spoiled his plan for him." Other times she was "really cold, as inaccessible as a virgin." Jerome would then call her "a Russian nun," telling her that she expected "to be taken as if [she] were the Holy Wafer." This fragment best explains Porter's ambivalent attitude toward Laura's virginity which is both revenge against Braggioni and symbol of her sexual and spiritual frigidity.

Laura's spiritual malaise results in her guilt over the death of Eugenio. The facts behind this incident and Porter's visits to prisoners in jail are impossible to verify. Porter accused Doherty of supplying pills to a prisoner and of dreaming about his death, but Doherty firmly denies ever setting foot in prison until she visited photographer Tina Modotti in 1930, whereas Porter, in tears, told me that she herself had given sleeping pills to a prisoner who saved them until he had enough with which to kill himself, adding that only the death of the man who caught influenza from her had affected her as much. Porter's memory of her friend's death in 1918 probably contributed to Laura's guilt, but no corroborating evidence of visits to prison exists.

However, Porter did write of carrying messages that will result in the death of five men against whom she holds no grudge. She wonders if she is participating in "an act of opera bouffe treachery" out of boredom when she finally blames "the enemy within" her that "lives upon sensation" and "loves the sense of power implied in the possession of these letters" so "potent" that "five men will die at dawn" upon their delivery. This fragment may be Porter's fictional attempt to involve herself in the death of Lucio Blanco's five followers, mentioned in "A month of uncertainties." Employing the present tense, it describes what she is about to do, not what she has done, and its language is melodramatic and calculated, "opera bouffe" repeating the expression she used in her portrait of Mary Doherty. On the other hand, it is in the first-person, like other autobiographical entries in her journal, whereas all the clearly fictional pieces of this period are in the third-person. If it is a true account of Porter's activities, then it explains the guilt she assigns to Laura, who also engages in deadly intrigue she is not committed to.

Whatever the facts behind Laura's relation to Eugenio, her inability to love, deeply rooted in Porter's own personality, is directly linked to her fear of death, just as Braggioni's sexual aggression is linked to his deadly power. Such power Porter feared, writing in her journal, "Now I seem unable to believe in anything, and certainly my doubts of human beings and their motives are founded in a fear of their power over me." But fear of another's power makes love as dangerous as overt aggression and explains Laura's defense system. "Her knees cling together" as she closes herself to the "spread knees" of Braggioni, who fills her with "a purely physical sense of danger." This resistance is also seen in her escape from the romantic advances of the "gentle" *Zapatista* captain and the young typographer. But Laura's protective withdrawal into self only results in a death-like stasis of noncommitment. Her desire to escape perilous human involvement paradoxically leads her to the ultimate escape, suicide. We are told, "Sometimes she wished to run away, but she stays. Now she longs to fly out of the room, down the narrow stairs, and into the street where the houses lean together like conspirators under the mottled lamp, and leave Braggioni singing to himself." Here the urge to escape life ends in futile circularity, the conspiratorial houses a nightmarish substitution for Braggioni. This passage Porter developed from a journal entry in which she complains that she would "like exceedingly to die," not having "that sense of urgency" she had when she nearly died of influenza. Then she writes, "The streets are bowl shaped, and the houses lean inward. . . . I have continually the sensation of stepping into space, and the side walk seems to curve down from the outer edges." In the next paragraph she predicts, "In a week I shall be dead." The leaning houses here are more explicitly related to suicidal impulse than they are in **"Flowering Judas."** It is as if Porter were viewing the world through a fisheye lens, a world of unreal dimension she fears entering. In 1931 she wrote her father that she had struggled a long time "against the very strong temptation just to . . . quit the whole devilish nuisance of life," but now she was "in a healthy mood of resistance and energy." Only resistance applies to Laura. Throughout the story her "No" is a rejection of life, but her "No" to Eugenio's

invitation expresses her rejection of suicide. She at least reaffirms her will to live despite her continuing state of irresolution.

Like Laura's personality, many of the story's details evolved out of Porter's own experience. For instance, the patio of "In a Mexican Patio," an unpublished sketch based on her experiences at 20 Calle del Eliseo, with its fountain and "purple" bougainvillaea, is the source of Laura's patio, with its fountain and Judas tree whose scarlet blossoms turn "a dull purple" in the moonlight. As evening falls, a young man appears as a shadowy presence, like Laura's young typographer, to communicate his love to a servant girl. Like **"Flowering Judas,"** the sketch is narrated in the present tense and ends ominously at night: "In the sunlight one may laugh, and sniff the winds, but the night is crowded with thoughts darker than the sunless world." Journal entries supply other details. Porter's servant Maria was once "the prettiest girl in Guanajuato," the hometown of Laura's servant Lupe. Porter went to union meetings to hear the spellbinding Morones speak, while Laura goes to union meetings to listen to "busy important voices." In a fragment of *Thieves' Market,* Laura in church finds nothing to pray for: "Let me set my heart on something, I don't care how poor it is . . . the legless woman in the Alameda has a perfectly faithful lover—oh God, out of your charity send me something." Porter, who told me that she often saw the legless woman on a park bench sharing money with her lover, assigned Laura's lines about the woman to Braggioni and gave a mechanical "Hail Mary" to Laura, who is soon distracted by the "battered doll-shape of some male saint whose white, lace-trimmed drawers hang limply around his ankles below the hieratic dignity of his velvet robe." The saint originally appeared in "Teotihuacan" as "St. Ignatious Loyola with chaste lace trimmed trousers showing beneath his black cassock." He is effectively denigrated by the transformation of "trousers" into "drawers." Clearly, **"Flowering Judas"** is based on Porter's own experiences, great and small.

### VII

In 1943 Porter wrote Mary Doherty, "Mexico was new to us, and beautiful, the very place to be at that moment. We believed a great deal—though I remember well that my childhood faith in the Revolution was well over in about six months." By May 1921, the time of the deportation crisis, the prototypes of Braggioni among others had sufficiently convinced her that Mexico as potential paradise was and could be nothing but a dream. But out of the dreamer's failure came the artist's success. If Mexico could not assuage her troubled psyche, it compelled her to contemplate the entwined betrayals of Revolution and of self, and to transform her disillusion and spiritual isolation into Laura's. By donning, as it were, Mary Doherty's nun-like uniform, Porter was able to give voice to all her conflicting emotions and view them with dispassionate objectivity as if they were not her own. In later comments about the creation of her story, she persisted in her disguise, claiming that her friend was model for Laura. **"Flowering Judas"** was not the "reportage" she claimed it was in 1972, but it did contain "symbolic truth" of her Mexican experience. Her transformation of purple bougainvillaea of her Mexican patio into flowering Judas is sign of the process that brought art out of life.

**Thomas F. Walsh (essay date 1985)**

SOURCE: "Braggioni's Songs in 'Flowering Judas'," in *College Literature,* Vol. XII, No. 1, Spring, 1985, pp. 147-52.

[*Here, Walsh details the relevance of Braggioni's songs and his singing to "Flowering Judas"'s plot, theme, and characterization.*]

"In Mexico, most of the birds, and all of the people, sing." So Katherine Anne Porter began her essay in 1924 on the Mexican *corrido* [*The Survey,* Vol. 50, No. 3, 1924]. She might have added later Braggioni, who, in **"Flowering Judas,"** comes with guitar to sing to Laura and win her heart although he gives a "miserable performance" and only earns her contempt. Nevertheless the two songs he sings, "La Norteña" and "A la Orilla de un Palmar," contribute to our understanding of Laura's complex personality. Porter did not choose these songs at random.

In an unpublished poem, probably written in 1921, Porter describes a blind boy playing on his flute a "song about the girl from the north, with green eyes," the last line of which includes a direct quotation from "La Norteña": "Linda, no llores. Pretty thing, don't cry." [The critic adds in a footnote: "My translation of 'La Norteña' is as follows: 'My love, the girl from the North, has eyes so translucent that they sparkle like precious stones. When they smile at me, they seem like a garden of flowers, and when they weep, they seem as if they are going to dissolve. Pretty one, don't cry. Green like the palm tree, green like the emerald, her eyes looked at me and that night she killed me with her glance. I don't know what her eyes contain when they view me with shining love. And if they weep, they seem as if they are going to dissolve. Pretty one, don't cry.' Porter once told me that her friend Castro Padilla wrote 'La Norteña' for her, but its composer was Eduardo Vigil y Robles."] In **"Flowering Judas"** Laura remembers hearing "the blind boy playing his reed-flute," his voice a sharp contrast to the "painful squeal" of one of Braggioni's high notes, but Porter assigns the song which the boy sings in the poem to Braggioni, making him its creator: "'O girl with the dark eyes,' he sings, and reconsiders. 'But yours are not dark. I can change all that. O girl with the green eyes, you have stolen my heart away!'"

Porter, through Braggioni, insists on green eyes even though the narrator two pages earlier tells us that "all praise [Laura's] gray eyes." Unless we assume that Braggioni is color-blind, which would be the least of his many flaws, there is no way to explain the inconsistency within the text. Another explanation lies outside the text. Glen-

way Wescott, whom Porter once designated her biographer, reported in 1964 [in *Images of Truth: Remembrances and Criticism*], "One of the revolutionaries wrote a song about her, 'La Norteña,' which, I have heard tell, has become a folk song. . . . I understand that another lady lays claim to it." Obviously Wescott heard tell from Porter herself, but "La Norteña," which she mentions in her sketch, "Xochimilco," published in [the *Christian Science Monitor* in] May 1921, was composed before her arrival in Mexico in September 1920. Wescott's revolutionary, then, turns out to be the fictional Braggioni, suggesting that Porter began to create a legend about herself before she wrote **"Flowering Judas"** in 1929 and embellished on it thereafter.

Porter apparently modeled her legend after that of Alma Reed, the other lady Wescott mentions. Alma Reed, a California reporter invited to Mexico by President Alvaro Obregón, became engaged to Felipe Carrillo Puerto, the radical governor of Yucatan, but he was assassinated in 1924 during the De la Huerta uprising. Shortly before his death he commissioned Ricardo Palmerín to compose in Reed's honor "Peregrina," which became a popular folk song, immortalizing their romance. Porter and Reed, as beautiful American journalists, befriended by distinguished Mexican politicians and artists, romanced by Carrillo Puerto, and honored by the government for their service to Mexico, had too much in common not to be rivals. Porter reveals her jealousy of Reed in fragments of *Historical Present,* which was to be a study of revolutionary women. She planned to begin with Reed's "cashing in on Felipe's death" and go on to her "gradually building up the legend" to become "patroness of all Mexico." It is ironic that Porter, whose fiction will be read long after Reed's derivative books on Mexican culture are forgotten, would need to create a legend about herself, patterned after a woman whose opportunism she scorned.

Porter's veiled allusion to "La Norteña" in **"Flowering Judas"** reveals her vanity, but it also operates in the text to deepen and complicate our response to Laura, whatever the color of her eyes. [In *This Is My Best,* edited by Whit Burnet, 1942] Porter stated that **"Flowering Judas"** developed around "a central idea" of "self-delusion" and "self betrayal." Expanding on Porter's statement [in *Katherine Anne Porter: A Critical Symposium,* edited by Lodwick Harthey and George Core, 1969]. Ray B. West finds that Laura "is, like Judas, the betrayer: and her betrayal, like his, consisted in an inability to believe. Without faith she is incapable of passion, thence of love, finally of life itself." However, West does not account for the reader's sympathy for Laura, despite her shortcomings. Dorothy S. Redden does, noting that while one voice "concurs in Laura's self condemnation," "another voice in Miss Porter . . . concurs in Laura's self-acquittal, as it were. The author clearly understands and respects her heroine's torment, and silently cries 'Bravo!' to her spirited refusal to yield" as she maintains "astonishing self-contol" in face of her fear of both life and death ["'Flowering Judas': Two Voices," *Studies in Short Fiction,* Vol. 6, 1969].

The allusion to "La Norteña" reinforces the reader's admiration of Laura. The girl from the North has entered an alien world, but her dedication to her ideals, however sterile, makes her unique, a figure of mystery who catches the attention of all:

> Nobody touches her, but all praise her gray eyes, and the soft round underlip which promises gayety, yet is always grave, nearly firmly closed; and they cannot understand why she is in Mexico. . . . No dancer dances more beautifully than Laura walks, and she inspires amusing, unexpected ardors, because nothing becomes of them.

Braggioni "wishes to impress this simple girl" with "her great round breasts" and "invaluably beautiful legs" and puzzles over her "notorious virginity." Because of her beauty and inaccessibility, Laura challenges Braggioni, who, like a courtly lover, composes a song to celebrate her beauty, hoping that it will melt her heart, but instead the song commemorates that mysterious inaccessibility. The reader regrets that Laura's fear of love alienates her from everyone, but takes satisfaction in her resistance to this man who is accustomed to having his way with all women. His song, when it gains popularity in Mexico, as "La Norteña" did, will be an ironic record of his defeat by Laura.

On the other hand, Laura's legendary inaccessibility, which so frustrates Braggioni, is caused by a debilitating fear of her own sexuality, as her dress symbolically reveals. In the sixth paragraph of the story, we are told, "Her knees cling together under sound blue serge, and her round white collar is not purposely nun-like. She wears the uniform of an idea, and has renounced vanities." Whether purposely or not, Laura's nun-like uniform leaves the impression of one who insists on her chastity, her closed knees, like her "firmly closed" underlip, visually affirming her notorious virginity. She wishes to renounce the corrupt world of the revolutionaries which betrays "her feeling of what life should be," but her rejection of all amorous advances, those of the young typographer and *Zapatista* captain as well as Braggioni's, suggests her feeling that life should not include a sexual dimension.

The description of Laura is followed by a contrasting description of Braggioni as he sings his other song. The combination of his song and physical appearance reveals the cause of Laura's sexual repression, her fear of pregnancy. The paragraph reads in full:

> Braggioni catches her glance solidly as if he had been waiting for it, leans forward, balancing his paunch between his *spread knees,* and sings with tremendous emphasis, weighing his words. He has, the song relates, no father and no mother, nor even a friend to console him; lonely as a wave of the sea he comes and goes, lonely as a wave. His mouth *opens round* and yearns sideways, his *balloon cheeks* grow oily with the *labor* of song. He *bulges marvelously* in his expensive garments. Over his lavender collar, crushed upon a purple necktie, held by a diamond hoop; over his ammunition belt of tooled leather worked in silver, buckled cruelly around his *gasping middle:* over the tops of his glossy yellow shoes Braggioni *swells* with *ominous ripeness,* his mauve silk hose *stretches taut,* his ankles bound with the stout thongs of his shoes. (emphasis added)

Braggioni's song Porter accurately translated from a ballad, "A la Orilla de un Palmar" ("By the Shore of a Palmgrove"), composed by her friend Tata Nacho. In it the singer relates that when he asked a beautiful young woman he met if anyone was with her, she replied in tears, "I am alone by the palm-grove. I am a little orphan, alas. I have no father and no mother, nor even a friend [*amigo*] who comes, alas, to console me. I pass my life by the shore of the palm-grove and all alone come and go like the waves of the sea," the song ending with a repetition of the girl's lament. Since the presumably male singer of the song directly quotes the girl's lament, the truncated version in **"Flowering Judas"** does no violence to the original; Braggioni can assume the roles of narrator and orphan, of potential protector and protected, or of predator and victim since the song is obvious male fantasy with the promise of sexual conquest lurking just below its sentimental surface. By catching Laura's glance, Braggioni suggests that he is aware of Laura's familiarity with the song and should identify with the girl in it, but his insinuation only increases her fear of his intentions.

Braggioni's song becomes more sinister with our knowledge of its full context. As he sings, his body induces the reader's revulsion. Critics have likened it to "a kind of overripe plum as dangerous as a grenade," "a grotesque Easter egg," and "a huge tumescent phallus," but the words I have italicized in the paragraph suggest a frightening picture of a woman in labor, Braggioni's "spread knees" and open mouth contrasting with Laura's clinging knees and closed underlip. Braggioni's song and body work subliminally on Laura as a before-and-after object lesson of what could happen to her if she relaxes her vigilance. The pregnancy his body suggests [and] gives promise, not of new life, but only of shameful, misshapen violation. And so Laura tenaciously clings to her notorious virginity and "covers her great round breasts with dark cloth, and . . . hides long, invaluably beautiful legs under a heavy skirt. She is almost thin except for the incomprehensible fullness of her breasts, like a nursing mother's. . . ." Laura's own body symbolizes her struggle between spirit and flesh. Her anorectic thinness is consistent with her thought that the ideal "revolutionist should be lean, animated by heroic faith, a vessel of abstract virtues," but her breasts, like Braggioni's paunch, undermine her ideals. The great difference between Braggioni and Laura is that he gloats over his sensuality while she attempts to suppress hers. Her choice is between sterile virginity and corrupt tumescence, and death threatens her in both.

Braggioni's songs reveal two intertwined strands of Laura's personality. "A la Orilla de un Palmar" exposes sexual fears behind her nun-like devotion to her ideals while "La Norteña" commemorates her heroic if vain struggle to cling to those ideals. Braggioni paradoxically contributes to and celebrates Laura's inner torment. Although he inspires fear, his serpent's wisdom helps us to understand her in ways she does not understand herself.

## James Walter (essay date 1985)

SOURCE: "Revolution and Time: Laura in 'Flowering Judas'," in *Renascence: Essays on Values in Literature,* Vol. XXXVIII, No. 1, Autumn, 1985, pp. 26-38.

[*In the following essay, Walter provides a thematic discussion of "Flowering Judas," detailing Porter's use of language and focus on time and temporality, revolution, and reality.*]

In Katherine Anne Porter's **"Flowering Judas,"** the following words take shape as an alienated young woman's conscious summary of her day as she awaits the narcotic of sleep to deliver her from her personal confusion: ". . . it is monstrous to confuse love with revolution, night with day, life with death—ah, Eugenio!" (*Collected Stories*). As "monstrous" and adverse to human intention as the fusions of opposites enumerated by Laura is the contradiction of motives instigating her exclamatory remembrance of Eugenio, a fellow revolutionary she visited in prison earlier in the day: although feeling guilt for having acquiesced in and aided Eugenio's suicide, she also feels envy for his having attained, she thinks, a state free of the turbulence of conscious life. The progression of Laura's aversion from life's mingling of contraries and her consequent loss of the capacity for moral initiative has been told and dramatized in the earlier parts of this story. Her flight from the United States to Mexico, a country that remains "strange" to her; her joining a Marxist revolutionary group, whose cynicism and expediency leave her disillusioned; and finally, her withdrawal into private stoicism and a "notorious virginity"—have been stages in her pursuit of a pure timeless realm where all differences are clearly drawn, entities are distinctly separated, and there is no exasperating mixture of forms of experience, categories of thought, or modes of being. Laura seeks a timeless state because she has perceived change to be her enemy; instead of bringing her to a peaceful clearness, it has only brought her deeper and deeper into a muddle of the monstrous. Her fearful closure to a creative power in time, repeatedly implied by Porter's images, causes Laura to miss signals in art and nature potentially mediating a timeless verity of love that alone could give a measure of contentment to her changing life. My title derives from Eudora Welty's suggestion that Porter makes Time serve as the helpful genie of whatever spirit is unfolding, by seeing the story and passing final judgment.

The latest evidence of time's complicity against Laura is the intermingling of Eugenio's fate with hers. Her inaction when she adhered to Eugenio's request not to summon the prison doctor to treat the effects of the narcotics she had brought him, was, she now begins to sense, a contribution to his death. In a temporal irony she is finding she cannot escape, even her choices for noninvolvement weave into time's emerging fabric of personal and communal destiny to help give it a definite texture and shape.

Laura's final gesture of withdrawal in Eugenio's case followed her successive visits to deliver articles to the revolutionaries in prison:

> If the prisoners confuse night and day, and complain, 'Dear little Laura, time doesn't pass in this infernal hole, and I won't know when it is time to sleep unless I have a reminder, she brings them their favorite narcotics, and says in a tone that does not wound them with pity, 'Tonight will really be night for you,' and though her Spanish amuses them, they find her comforting, useful.

Ironically, the prisoners desire to escape the static timeless condition that Laura desires to enter. At the nadir of despair, unable to find contentment or rest within or through the periodic revolutions of natural time, they use drug-induced aberrations of consciousness to impose an artificial and private time order. Laura, however, holds to a stoic illusion that within and against nature's unending revolutions, she can, by her own strength, achieve a calm hermitage of the self.

Two moments near the story's end indicate Laura's personal failure to create a private precinct of peace and security. The first is when she sits and passively listens to the melancholy songs of Braggioni, the revolutionary leader who has spent a month testing her virginity.

> Laura has just come from a visit to the prison, and she is waiting for tomorrow with a bitter anxiety as if tomorrow may not come, but time may be caught immovably in this hour, with herself transfixed, Braggioni singing on forever, and Eugenio's body not yet discovered by the guard.

Although part of Laura seeks refuge from time in the immediate experience of Braggioni's gross presence, another part of her longs for relief that time alone can bring, not just from Braggioni, but also from the transfixing anguish of secret and guilty knowledge. Tomorrow's coming, bitter as its revelation of Eugenio's suicide must be, at least will bring the corpse to natural and public light and thus free Laura, to a degree, from having to bear such knowledge in total privacy.

The second moment Laura seeks refuge from natural time by imposing her own construction on it is near the story's end, when she counts numbers to put herself to sleep, thus stretching a clear artificial linear gloss over time's distressful confusions. But the fragility of her construction is shown when Eugenio's spirit easily trespasses into the chamber of her well-prepared sleep.

All the human action in the present of **"Flowering Judas"** takes place in Laura's apartment, but in a number of flashbacks a broader world—including Arizona, Mexico City, its Market, a little crumbling church, fields near Cuernavaca, Laura's patio where a Judas tree flowers, the school where Laura teaches and children heap flowers on her desk, public streets, dark rooms, back alleys, and the prison—is evoked before we witness the last episode leading from Laura's high room down toward some "new country." The effect of these flashbacks provided by the narrator is to call into presence for the reader a complete believable world with its many physical qualities, natural changes, human inhabitants, social relations and political differences.

---

**We cannot understand the status and meaning of this fictional world without questioning the status and meaning of the language which presents it.**

*—James Walter*

---

We cannot understand the status and meaning of this fictional world without questioning the status and meaning of the language which presents it. As commentators have pointed out, the language is rich in religious symbolism, particularly that of the flowering Judas tree and the gesture of Braggioni's wife washing her husband's feet. Also, allegorical meanings radiate from the story in different directions. At times Braggioni, with his "gluttonous bulk," seems a conventional personification of vice, while at other times he seems to personify "the world"; his fleshly corpulence, his teeming energy, his daily recurrence at Laura's apartment, his promotion of revolutionary change, and his entropic vitality all ally him with the natural fundament and its cycles. Moreover, there are many suggestions that the physical locale of the story exists not merely as an historical setting, or as a symbol, but as an allegorical *paysage moralisé* in which high and low, natural and artificial, closed and open, covered and revealed, light and dark all resonate with psychological and spiritual meanings that expand and deepen by their interplay.

In taking note of these allegorical elements, however, it is important to recognize that in this, one of her most successful stories, Porter has approached the aesthetic ideal she articulated in her *Outline of Mexican Popular Arts and Crafts,* of "a perfect realism, a complete statement of the thing [the artist] sees". She has achieved that "fine objectivity" she admired in the stories of Katherine Mansfield: which bares "a moment of experience, real experience, in the life of some human being . . . states no belief, gives no motives, airs no theories, but simply presents to the reader a situation, a place, and a character, and there it is; and the emotional content is present implicitly as the germ is in the grain of wheat". Because Porter's own meaning in her best stories is implicit in the imagery she creates of a world—according to Welty, imagery "as likely as not to belong to a time other than the story's present . . . it is *memory* imagery, coming into the story from memory's remove"—the reader has a spe-

cial obligation to own that world and to search out the spiritual truth it mediates. Failing in this, the reader commits a mistake like Laura's of imposing his subjective meanings onto the story, in essence making the story an allegory of his own ideas and prejudices instead of its particular veiled meanings.

An example of such a misreading occurs in an article by Leon Gottfried, otherwise brilliant in its analysis of the philosophical and ethical themes in **"Flowering Judas"** drawn from Scripture, St. Thomas and Dante. [In "Death's Other Kingdom: Dantesque and Theological Symbolism in 'Flowering Judas'," *PMLA,* Vol. 84, 1969] Gottfried argues that the religious symbolism found in **"Flowering Judas"** must be understood as ironic:

> The principal difference that sets Porter apart from the 'religious' writers, however, is not only the fact that in most of her work she has not so explicitly used the elaborate system of religious allusions so prominent in **'Flowering Judas,'** but rather that her portrayal of hell (not only in **'Flowering Judas'**) is without reference to any corresponding heaven or given system of ultimate values, other than those of Catholicism and Marxism, both discredited. In this respect she is a typical modern secular writer, for whom meaning and value are created, not given; she enacts the characteristic doom of the modern Promethean artist struggling to carve out of the chaos of experience some order or meaning which can come into existence, if at all, only after the struggle.

Gottfried states, "Miss Porter's early training and background made spontaneously available to her a rich store of religious imagery and language, behind which lie centuries of systematic theological thought, to give order and form to one of her sketches of the 'failure of the life of man in the Western world.'" Yet Gottfried would have us accept that Porter uses traditional religious symbolism—having to do with saviours, purification, communion, and faith—as a merely artificial veil whose tenor contradicts the vehicle; that the veil uncovers no connection between the world of natural form, time and action which it properly signifies and a spiritual reality which both artistic veil and nature figure. This is to offer a simple and arbitrary *allegoresis* of the story, a reading which finds a content determined entirely by a subjective appropriation of linguistic convention and not by proper relations between words and things and natural relations among things signified by words. Because it neglects the importance in all of Porter's fiction of nature and the laws of nature, this way of reading risks taking us far afield from the story's true meaning. A case in point is Gottfried's own conclusion, that **"Flowering Judas"** presents an ironic account of two failed faiths, Catholicism and Marxism, and consequently allows only one sure way of salvation, the artist's Promethean creation of private existential "order or meaning." We suspect the critic has found in the story an allegory of his own belief and failed to see the story's critique of that very belief.

To discover the story's meaning in itself, it is helpful to consider an analysis of Scriptural language that was seminal for medieval hermeneutics. According to St. Thomas,

The author of Holy Writ is God, in whose power it is to signify His meaning, not by words only (as man also can do), but also by things themself. So, whereas in every other science things are signified by words, this science [of Christian analogy] has the property, that the things signified by the words have themselves also a signification. Therefore that first signification whereby words signify things belongs to the first sense, the historical or literal. That signification whereby things signified by words have themselves also a signification is called the spiritual sense, which is based on the literal and presupposes it. (*Summa*)

It was a medieval commonplace that a proper reading of the spiritual sense of a text required first a respect for the literal signification of the words of the story and for the natural world that also signified. It was believed that translation of metaphorical language demanded a respect for the substantiality of created things, the basis of all truthful linguistic and imagistic signification. According to Gregory of Vinsauf, writer of the medieval rhetoric *Poetria nova,* a figure that is totally artificial and does not refer to something real is a "vile picture, a falsified thing, a faked form, a whitewashed wall, a verbal hypocrite which pretends to be something when it is nothing. Its form covers up its deformity; it vaunts itself outwardly but has no inner substance." The medieval concern to keep allegorical writing and interpretation directly related to a real and natural base sheds light on Porter's artistic ideal, not only to *see* everything, but also to obtain "knowledge at the price of finally, utterly 'seeing through' everything" (*Days*). If her ideal of meaning in her stories is that it be implicit, "as the germ is in the grain of wheat," then we must first see the true qualities of the grain of wheat before we come to conclusions about the germ.

An instance of the implicitness of Porter's meaning in **"Flowering Judas"** and her ability to develop purely linguistic associations from the material of a realistic narrative occurs in the first flashback in the story recalling Laura's practice of slipping "now and again into some crumbling little church" to attempt, always unsuccessfully, to pray. As Laura examines the altar of the church, she "feels tender about the battered doll-shape of some male saint whose white, lace-trimmed drawers hang limply around his ankles below the hieratic dignity of his velvet robe." Perhaps it is the saint's "hieratic dignity," seeming to Laura to reflect the "vessel of abstract virtues" she had once looked for in the revolutionists, that awakens her tenderness towards its "doll-shape." Porter's description once of religious visionaries often being "God-intoxicated mystics and untidy saints with only a white blaze of divine love where their minds should have been" supports such a directly ironic interpretation of Laura's misplaced worship (*Days*).

As a poetic image, however, caught up in the play of other images, the shape of the "saint" holds a more complex potential of significance. Filtering through Laura's consciousness, the image includes elements of a baroque disorder she observes but does not recognize—the almost obscene disarray of the saint's clothing, and other marks of the saint's costly passage through time. Espe-

cially since Porter has associated white lace with both the icon and Laura, their juxtaposition is very suggestive. The stoic-seeming saint, it appears, because of "batterings" suffered in the world, must endure the comic indignity of a discomposed personal form, in contrast to Laura's tragic encasement in a set of principles "leaving no detail of gesture or of personal taste untouched." If the "white, lace-trimmed drawers" suggest something of the saint that is personal and private, innocent yet erotic in nature, then the total emblem represents the ecstatic outpouring of the saint's inward and active soul despite appearance's sake, disturbing the serenity of pure aesthetic and intellectual form but achieving by that sacrifice in time a spiritual content.

By way of a somewhat fortuitous imagistic and narrative progression, the narrator subsequently relates that Laura "loves fine lace" and keeps twenty collars "precisely alike, folded in blue tissue paper in the upper drawer of her clothes chest." Parallel imagery in this paragraph—of the blue serge dress enveloping Laura, blue tissue paper enfolding her lace—suggests further that lace is a soul metaphor and that Laura, unlike the saint, prudently preserves her soul in "upper" storage while displaying just enough of it to show the world a perfectly composed demeanor. If the homographic "drawer," while reminding us of the textuality of this intricately textured story, suggests the writer's imaginative catching of happy accidents to turn them to significance, then the responsiveness of the narrator's art to providential opportunities is very different from Laura's artful and prudent constructions against the unpredictable.

In describing Laura's caution in crossing streets, the narrator summarizes Laura's attitude toward the fortuitousness of the world: "She has translated this fear [of a shocking death] into something homely, immediate, and sometimes hesitates before crossing the street. 'My personal fate is nothing, except as the testimony of a mental attitude,' she reminds herself, quoting from some forgotten philosophic primer." An earlier description of Laura holding "an open book on her knees, resting her eyes on the consoling rigidity of the printed page" to distract her from the looming threat that in the figure of Braggioni she might recognize a sign of her whole history, already implied the power of print to stretch an idealizing gloss over the order of actual temporal experience. The passage quoted from the primer is, of course, a statement of stoic idealism that would read temporal events merely as allegories of static mental states; in making the mental order the ultimate reality, this attitude would deny time a significant role in human being. Laura remembers the passage, we suspect, for its comforting assurance of mind over matter, will over fortune. Her delusion is one that superficial readings of philosophical texts often foster and that realistic narratives, with their depiction of time passing and consequences following upon acts, usually disrupt.

Certainly the primer passage contains a truth: that character and a "mental attitude" become fate is the basis of all tragedy. But the passage does not admit of happy opportunities, those providential gifts of time which, if gratefully and hopefully taken, can be made the means of avoiding, or at least meliorating, a tragic personal fate.

Opportunities for change do come to Laura in the numerous lovers who pursue her in one way or another, but she always proves sufficiently armored to withstand their advance. Her most puzzling resistance, considering her evident maternal feeling at times and "the incomprehensible fullness of her breasts," is her denial of the children.

> She spends part of her days in Xochimilco, near by, teaching Indian children to say in English, 'The cat is on the mat.' When she appears in the classroom they crowd about her with smiles on their wise, innocent, clay-colored faces, crying, 'Good morning, my titcher!' in immaculate voices, and they make of her desk a fresh garden of flowers every day.

Later we are told, "Next morning the children made a celebration and spent their playtime writing on the blackboard, 'We love ar titcher,' and with tinted chalks they drew wreaths of flowers around the words." Yet the children "remain strangers to [Laura], though she loves their tender round hands and their charming opportunist savagery."

In these passages Porter has compactly constructed a world of implication concerning Laura's and the children's relation to language and nature. As a teacher of language, Laura is privileged to serve as midwife to the children's development of an adequate linguistic apprehension of the world, essential to all human relation and understanding. Nevertheless, it appears from her lessons that Laura remains an uninspired teacher despite her children's readiness to learn and even to instruct her. "The cat is on the mat," a synecdochal summary of her lessons, captures in a sentence Laura's peculiar catatonia. Not a statement or description of a being in action, the sentence, with its assonant circularity, mirrors a mind opposed to all but the slightest, most insignificant change. The sentence symbolizes Laura's arrestment within and by cyclic processes of time and nature in her very effort to escape them into a timeless stoic refuge.

In contrast to Laura's dominantly verbal communication to the children, they offer her a communion of words and things. The text's phonetic spelling of their words emphasizes the experiential basis of their learning and speaking, as does their impulse to relate words to things in their message. Their spoken words accentuated with a "fresh garden of flowers," and then more abstractly their written words in tinted chalk wreathed with flowers, are words assisted by nature's capacity of speech. What they represent is *a world,* known by humans who love and wish to share their knowledge. The wreaths of flowers are immediately associated in the following passage with Laura's patio garden where "The moonlight spread a wash of gauzy silver over the clear spaces of the garden, and the shadows were cobalt blue. The scarlet blossoms of the Judas tree were dull purple." In these contexts the variety of colors symbolizes the variety of the creation

made by Love to awaken love. We are told, however, that "the names of the colors repeated themselves automatically in [Laura's] mind, while she watched not [the lover in her garden], but his shadow, fallen like a dark garment across the fountain rim, trailing in the water." Characteristically, Laura turns the real order into a mere linguistic film and allows the substance of her lover to evaporate into reflections of shadows. For her, the names of the colors are Saussurean signs in which the concepts evoked by the phonic substance are arbitrarily determined by their structural position among other concepts in her closed linguistic universe.

Ironically, what Laura does love in the children—"their tender round hands and their charming opportunist savagery"—parallels qualities in Braggioni—his corpulent fleshiness and his cruel opportunist politics—that are instrumental in keeping her near him in Mexico. In her abstracted coexistence with the world, she has, it appears, chosen to find security in minimal signs of human life, flesh and amoral energy—all that remain when the human image has been deprived of soul. Laura's choice implies a desperate desire to be in the presence of life, but also a desperate refusal to risk participation in it. Afraid of real life's grotesque incongruities, she seeks a substitute that will demand less from her. This helps explain her presence in Mexico, an exotic country whose remoteness had once beckoned her romantic soul to a new life free of limitation and heightened into pure revolutionary process. If self-protecting prudence later inhibits her from full participation in the revolution, still her being near its agents, off whom she feeds, makes her *accedia* seem to be rewarding involvement. In contrast to this paralysis of will in the face of a freedom once desired but now feared, a humanly responsible stance would require Laura, first, to accept in their ordinance life's change and variety and its requirements of faith and sacrifice. In Laura's reluctance to leave Braggioni is the key to the implied cannibalism of all the revolutionists in Porter's story: like the young man of Shakespeare's first sonnet they desire something from life, from the very lives of each other; but none, except Braggioni's wife, is willing to give to life. In their revolutionary fervor "to procreate a new world cleansed of cruelty and injustice, ruled by benevolent anarchy," they neglect the procreation possible between patient love and the given earthly in accord with the changes of nature. If, as has been argued, Laura's tragic passion for the prisoner Eugenio is behind her withdrawn behavior, thus explaining her worry in the night about both "love and revolution," it is apparent that she is drawn *from* Eugenio by an equally strong attraction *to* Braggioni; perhaps her attraction to men in general subconsciously serves to keep her at a safe distance from all particular men.

The archetype of the revolution, Braggioni, needs sycophants, "hungry men who wait for hours outside his office for a word with him," since for him they seem to compensate for some of the injury to his pride when, at age fifteen, his first love laughed at him. This "vast cureless wound of his self-esteem," exacerbated by a fateful premonition that he will "see himself kicked out from his feeding trough by other hungry world-saviours," festers behind his tyrannical use and devouring of his comrades. The comrades also need Braggioni and his words to fill their spiritual emptiness with a sense of metaphysical challenge and purpose. The evil that he emphasizes they should watch out for—"spies"—serves the double function of spreading the aura of the mysterious over their secular religion and of keeping the followers mutually distrustful, and therefore as helpless meat for Braggioni's appetite. In essence, the "revolution" as Porter portrays it is not a natural or actual fact at all but merely a verbal construct maintained by a variety of linguistic deceptions: the Polish agitator gives Laura "misinformation," while the Roumanian more adroitly "lies to her"; she "never repeats anything they may say. Braggioni never asks questions." The product of a linguistic atmosphere that effectively drives persons back into their private selves and their mutually unexamined passions, the revolution is loud where silence might hear and silent where speech might find a measure of truth and a harmony of being.

With its artificial religious aura the revolution is a barrier to understanding, capable of resisting every probe or assault but one: that of death. It is Laura's mention of Eugenio's "stupor" and his certain death that changes Braggioni's casual mood and returns him home to his long-suffering wife, where he seeks some kind of renewal. We are not shown enough of his reunion with his wife to know if his refreshment at her constant center will be merely like that of the sun or a river returning to its source to begin another cyclic repetition, or will begin a true spiritual change. We are simply shown the opportunity that exists for Braggioni in his wife's willingness to forgive him and share the sacred meal with him; his future remains open as he stands at a threshold of possibility between two revolutions, the "for better or for worse" of a marriage that might still redeem time, or Promethean destruction with pistol and dynamite of the very roots and foundation of a world he views with bitter contempt.

Laura, too, is deeply affected by Eugenio's death. In her upper room as she lies in her bed she says to herself, "If you would sleep, you must not remember anything, the children will say tomorrow, good morning, my teacher, the poor prisoners who come every day bringing flowers to their jailor." The syntax and diction of the sentence condense the dreamy confusion of Laura's waking world. But at this threshold of natural sleep the words and images also hint in a strange oblique way at hidden truths: Laura, we have seen, *has* been her children's jailor, more than a teacher must be; and her children *have* brought flowers to their jailor, although she took no flowers, or other signs of hope, to the imprisoned comrades. Thus, truth is slowly intruding into the artificial room of Laura's thought before sleep takes her to a realm where truth can be more domineering.

Her dream narrative begins with the "tolling of the midnight bell," releasing ghosts from their burial chambers:

> Get up, Laura, and follow me: come out of your sleep, out of your bed, out of this strange house. What are you

doing in this house? Without a word, without fear she rose and reached for Eugenio's hand, but he eluded her with a sharp, sly smile and drifted away. This is not all, you shall see—Murderer, he said, follow me, I will show you a new country, but it is far away and we must hurry. No, said Laura, not unless you take my hand, no; and she clung first to the stair rail, and then to the topmost branch of the Judas tree that bent down slowly and set her upon the earth, and then to the rocky ledge of a cliff, and then to the jagged wave of a sea that was not water but a desert of crumbling stone. Where are you taking me, she asked in wonder but without fear. To death, and it is a long way off, and we must hurry, said Eugenio. No, said Laura, not unless you take my hand.

Despite the disturbing accusation in it, the dream gives expression to Laura's deepest desires for human communion and a transformed life in a new country. Against her will, however, it also gradually strips her of all familiar supports and carries her, through Eugenio's agency, down and down into a region where the earth time (figured in an image from tradition), and her own psyche are one. Her descent is a journey from the literal to the allegorical meanings of things. The actual stair rail outside her high room is the last token of the man-made, which she must abandon, as the Judas tree, symbol of Judas' betrayal, delivers her gently to the earth; the familiar earth, insubstantial in itself, then gives way to a harsher aspect of nature, "the jagged wave of a sea" which, to spiritual vision, is not life-giving water at all but "a desert of crumbling stone." This jagged sea and crumbling stone universalize the formless energy and energyless form that have shaped Laura's infernal waking world. Nowhere in her descent through the signs and things of the material order does Laura find an answer to her desire; instead she finds the image of death in an increasingly horrifying aspect. That which she had feared as a physical possibility, which had caused her to take precautions crossing the street, now reveals itself as a datum of inner experience.

The cause of death's presence in her imagination is revealed allegorically in the drama of the next lines:

> Then eat these flowers, poor prisoner, said Eugenio in a voice of pity, take and eat: and from the Judas tree he stripped the warm bleeding flowers, and held them to her lips. She saw that his hand was fleshless, a cluster of small white petrified branches, and his eye sockets were without light, but she ate the flowers greedily for they satisfied both hunger and thirst. Murderer! said Eugenio, and Cannibal! This is my body and blood. Laura cried No!

As one of the miserable souls who suffer in Dante's Wood of the Suicides for violating their natural bodies, Eugenio comes to accuse not only Laura but all revolutionists who join one another for self-gratification and who use human contiguity for defense against nature and fortune while refusing true friendship. The infernal imagery associated with Eugenio seems to contradict Dorothy S. Redden's view that he is a "Christ-like" life-bearing figure. Laura's devouring "the warm bleeding flowers" repeats, now allegorically and significantly, her romantic compulsion for an immediate relation to life that had been evident in her attraction to the gluttonous bulk of Braggioni and her affection for the tender warm hands of the children. What her dream manifests is that her path leads to death, to "white petrified branches," instead of to life. Her cry of "No!"—a potentially redemptive emotion in one clear-minded enough to see the insubstantiality of the face of evil—is, more likely, an expression of Laura's soul-impaled horror.

It can help us get a perspective on the complete action of **"Flowering Judas"** if we consider the reference to the story's central symbol in its title. Except for the tinsel flowers in the crumbling church Laura visited, which were emblematic reflectors of her own false religious devotion, other flowers appear in the story to symbolize a creative love that communicates itself temporally through nature. The flowers of the Judas tree, in its two appearances in the narrative, are no different in their essential meaning. Even Judas' guilt, which typifies the guilt of all men in their betrayal of Christ, is turned by the Word's creative love into a potential basis for hope—thus the mysterious gentleness of the Judas tree as it sets Laura on the earth. As the arch-symbol of this story, that in some ways brings all events within its radius of implication, the Judas tree, it must be noticed, is "flowering"; thus, it is [as Samuel Taylor Coleridge once wrote] a vital "part of . . . the whole of which it is representative": the living process of nature which, in Porter's vision, is the medium of Divine care.

Here then is Laura's only future hope: having seen spiritual death, in the April of her temporal revolution she still has time to search for life. The possibility of finding it was already insinuated by the narrator into Laura's earlier reflections on the youth who serenaded her from her garden:

> Now Laura is accustomed to him, it means nothing except that he is nineteen years old and is observing a convention with all propriety, as though it were founded on a law of nature, *which in the end it might well prove to be,* (italics my own).

By mentally reducing the youth's eros entirely to the category of a comprehensible convention, Laura had domesticated and trivialized not only the youth's passion but also her own experience. The termination of this mental habit in a death's head means that her return to life must wait on her discovery of a spirit of life communicating itself in nature and history. The key to Porter's own persistence in creative venture might be looked for here: just as the youth's eros for Laura moved him to write poetry, Porter's *kairos* for the world in all its charming opportunist savagery, and her hope that a meaning might be discerned through it, moved her to write her excellent stories.

If, as Gottfried argues, Porter placed a high faith in the redemptive power of art, then we must examine her art closely to understand her faith. In her 1940 "Introduction" to *Flowering Judas and Other Stories,* she wrote:

> . . . the arts do live continuously, and they live literally by faith; their names and their shapes and their uses and their basic meanings survive unchanged in all that matters through times of interruption, diminishment, neglect; they outlive the governments and creeds and the societies, even the very civilizations that produced them. They cannot be destroyed altogether because they represent the substance of faith and the only reality. They are what we find again when the ruins are cleared away.

A crucial word in this statement is "represent," which means more than merely "to typify"; it means also to *re-present* in the form of a sign or symbol. In Porter's fiction "the only reality," of which art is a representing symbol, is in essence a spiritual action originated in time's openness contextually ordered by nature. The poet's task, as **"Flowering Judas"** implies in the difference between Laura's failure and the children's aptitude, is to make a language articulate of human freedom within nature's ordinance. That language, freedom and ordinance, then, in all their interdependencies, "might well prove to be" mediators of "the only reality" that endures.

### John Gerlach (essay date 1985)

SOURCE: "The Twentieth Century: New Forms: Imagist Form," in *Toward the End: Closure and Structure in the American Short Story,* The University of Alabama Press, 1985, pp. 94-107.

[*In the excerpt below, Gerlach examines thematic and stylistic aspects of "Flowering Judas," citing the relationship between Braggioni and Laura as the pivotal element in the story.*]

[Katherine Anne Porter's] fastidiousness and the consequent diminution of her total output are legendary. Consequently, we might expect her to be more conscious of closure, and her comments on endings and their relation to structure have a familiar ring: "If I didn't know the ending of a story, I wouldn't begin. I always write my last lines, my last paragraph, my last page first, and then I go back and work towards it. I know where I'm going. I know what my goal is" [Interview with Barbara Thompson in *Writers at Work,* 1963]. **"Flowering Judas"** (1930) was clearly a story she had in mind when referring to endings; in the same interview just quoted she mentions it as the one case when her expectations were denied: "In the vision of death at the end of **'Flowering Judas'** I knew the real ending—that she was not going to be able to face her life, what she'd done. And I knew that the vengeful spirit was going to come in a dream to tow her away into death, but I didn't know until I'd written it that she was going to wake up saying, 'No!' and be afraid to go to sleep again."

Despite the resemblance of her method of aiming for the end to Poe's method, her stories bear little structural resemblance to his. She does not commonly write a linear, direct story; her technique in **"Flowering Judas,"** like Anderson's, is characterized by a controlling central image (Braggioni sitting before Laura, playing his guitar), and although the image implies pressure and anticipates release, it does not suggest normal narrative sequence.

The departure from traditional form in **"Flowering Judas"** is what has caught the attention of most critics. Beverly Gross, for instance, has argued [in "The Poetic Narrative," *Style,* Vol. 2, Spring 1968] that "there is no beginning, middle and end in this story; there is only a deepening awareness." "Narrative energy," she argues, is subordinated to "poetic evocation of a state of mind." The final paragraph is thus "less a denouement than a synthesizing image." David Madden sees the structure of the story as a wheel, with the image of Braggioni in Laura's room at the hub and the other incidents arranged as spokes [Madden, "The Charged Image in Katherine Anne Porter's 'Flowering Judas'," *Studies in Short Fiction,* Vol. 7, Spring 1970]. These nonlinear views of the story are reasonable when one thinks of **"Flowering Judas"** in relation to its nineteenth-century predecessors. Porter does not seem to rely on an extensive action or movement from point to point or return, as, for instance, Hawthorne did by beginning "Roger Malvin's Burial" in the wilderness, then drawing Reuben back to the same spot eighteen years later. Furthermore, the climax of the story may seem blurred. When Braggioni exits, his leaving is a false ending—the story continues past it, actually ending with a dream of Eugenio and Laura's awakening.

Nevertheless, it is profitable to look at the story in the terms used so far. A problem is immediately identifiable: the initial image of Braggioni heaped in a chair, singing to Laura in her bedroom, and Laura, resenting the need to listen to him play his guitar, avoiding her house until the last possible moment (Braggioni has appeared every night for two months) is a tableau that demands resolution. Either Braggioni will satisfy his needs and cease his caterwauling, or she will rid herself of him and sleep in peace.

The difference between this and nineteenth-century narrative lies in the way the problem level controls what follows. Laura devises resolutions in response to her needs, and these are disposed in a logical array that constitutes a mental equivalent of a developing action. This array of potential resolutions carries the suggestion of linear movement, though in fact the resolutions end in indecision, and in that sense movement seems circular. The original image is simply deepening in its irony, not progressing toward resolution, thus creating the illusion of motionlessness.

One consequence of the transfer of movement from action to thought is that endings seem constantly imminent. Laura's first proposed ending is simply to lie down and ignore Braggioni, a form of wish fulfillment. She thinks only briefly of this solution and then asks Braggioni to sing, thus initiating the nightly recurrence of the tableau. Why she does so is explained at least on the simple

level—no one crosses Braggioni, no one would "lay a finger on the vast cureless wound of his self-esteem." Laura proposes a tentative explanation of the significance of the scene, thinking of Braggioni in his "gluttonous bulk" as "a symbol of her many disillusions," an explanation that accounts for him but not for her own part in the tableau.

---

> **The difference between this and nineteenth-century narrative lies in the way the problem level controls what follows.**
>
> *—John Gerlach*

---

Her next "ending" is the culmination of these unpleasant thoughts—she longs to "fly out of this room," leaving Braggioni to sing by himself, and, because no longer present, she would no longer need to account for herself. This aspiration immediately vanishes, as did her first wish: "Instead she looks at Braggioni." What follows is an explication that sums up the incongruities of the situation, deepening the irony of the second, nonnarrative level. Laura's background, her Roman Catholic upbringing, her fascination with lace, contradict her revolutionary fervor and make the tableau seem all the more incongruous. Matched with the description of her is that of Braggioni, dressed in yellow and purple, his belt "buckled cruelly around his gasping middle." He swells with an "ominous ripeness," as if he were fruit on a tree ready to drop, perhaps a reference to the tree of the story's title. The ominousness is part of a building pressure in the story, pushing toward a bursting point. This pressure is not the result of plot, but it produces an equivalent suspense.

As Braggioni talks to her he introduces an idea that Laura does not understand: "We are more alike than you realize in some things," he claims. The statement evokes in Laura "a slow chill," a "sense of danger," an anticipation of "a shocking death" that waits for her with "lessening patience." His assertion offers a new meaning for the tableau, one that accounts for her as well as him, contrary to the distancing she would choose to practice. She tentatively accepts this in spite of herself—"It may be true I am as corrupt, in another way, as Braggioni . . . as callous, as incomplete." The conception reduces her to immobility: "She sits quietly, she does not run." More of her past is introduced, initially with the theme of her revolutionary activities but blending them with a relation of two courtships, one with a captain who had been a soldier in Zapata's army and another with a shock-haired youth who sings to her on her patio by the scarlet blossoms of the Judas tree. The soldier she escapes by spurring her horse at an opportune moment; but the youth she has thrown a flower, on the advice of her maid. These incidents generalize Braggioni's significance; he seems another manifestation of Laura's more general dilemma. This summary of her past concludes with the lesson that she draws from all her activities: the power of the talismanic word "no," a word that appropriately characterizes both the temporary, stalled position of Laura in her current relation with Braggioni and her more general stagnation. The story seems nowhere closer to not ending at all—as if it were an archetypal indirect story—than at any other point.

---

**The structure creates a syncopated effect, seeming to lead to a close before the story is over, then opening up again.**

*—John Gerlach*

---

But ironically, when nothing seems likely to happen, the tension breaks. If all of Laura's proposals to herself are false endings, the most false ending comes now when Braggioni, for no particular reason, asks Laura if she is going to sleep. What follows divides into two parts: the oiling of Braggioni's pistol and then the tying up of the remaining threads, Braggioni returning to his wife and Laura preparing for sleep, one of the conventional forms of natural termination. Read for its overtones, as a Freudian message, the pistol scene is a parody of resolution. Braggioni is enabled to disrobe at least partially, unbuckling his ammunition belt. While she cleans and oils, he advises her that no woman need go begging for satisfaction—even "the legless beggar woman in the Alameda has a perfectly faithful lover." Braggioni does not get what he came for, but he leaves with his pistol oiled. Then, by accounting for a final reconciliation scene between Braggioni and his wife, Porter provides closure for him; putting Laura to bed by herself should at least get her what she has wanted from the beginning of the story.

Closure underlines not how much but rather how little has been accomplished. One question remains: Braggioni's coming and going has been a meaningful experience for Laura, but in what sense has she been altered by her understanding of him? The question is answered in the last paragraph, not by Laura's consciousness but by her unconscious self, as her thoughts of a character named Eugenio lead to a dream:

> Eat these flowers, poor prisoner, said Eugenio in a voice of pity, take and eat: and from the Judas tree he stripped the warm bleeding flowers and held them to her lips. She saw that his hand was fleshless, a cluster of small white petrified branches, and his eye sockets were without light, but she ate the flowers greedily for they satisfied both hunger and thirst. Murderer! said Eugenio, and Cannibal! This is my body and my blood. Laura cried No! and at the sound of her own voice, she awoke trembling, and was afraid to sleep again.

Instead of lapsing into sleep, into natural termination, Laura is left wide awake, trembling. She experiences more disequilibrium than she did when the story opened. Furthermore, Eugenio, who had been a minor character throughout, now appears in a puzzling role. A communion is shockingly inverted, and Laura's hunger, both literal and spiritual, is unfulfilled. Readers, however, expect closure and will search for equilibrium.

To some extent resolution is possible. One can, for example, reconstruct the role of Eugenio. Initially he appears in a passage in which Laura reflects on how she feels herself "caught immovably in this hour, with herself transfixed, Braggioni singing on forever, and Eugenio's body not yet discovered by the guard." Why his body should concern her is revealed later when we learn that he has taken an overdose of the narcotic tablets she brought him and so killed himself. Eugenio serves two contradictory functions (and for that reason he may appear as a curious amalgam in the dream, as man and tree, as savior and accuser): he is, on the one hand, similar to Laura, like her, a prisoner of Braggioni, bored, unwilling to wait for Braggioni to set him free; on the other hand, he is her victim. She has killed him by giving him the narcotics. In this sense it is she who plays the role of Braggioni, who himself is a betrayer of his country as well as its savior, a Judas as much as a Christ. Insofar as Laura is linked to Braggioni, Braggioni's assertion of their identity is fulfilled. The attribution of new significance to phrases as well as solutions to puzzles such as the meaning of the dream of Eugenio might satisfy some of the reader's desire for order and balance, but we could question whether they redress the essential instability. Has the dream, for instance, changed Laura?

Probably not. The dominant word of the ending is still "no," occurring three times in the paragraph before the quoted passage and once in the passage itself. Leon Gottfried has provided a compelling analysis, based on the story's allusions to Dante, of Laura as a character in limbo, permanently fixed in inaction, and this characterization of her is not changed by her posture at the end ["Death's Other Kingdom: Dantesque and Theological Symbolism in 'Flowering Judas'," *PMLA*, Vol. 84, January 1969].

Even so, we should note that Laura has been "awakened." She may no more change her ways than Wakefield might, but Porter has ended her story with the suggestion that Laura's unconscious is at least at work, sending her messages. No integration of her personality is predicted, but there is not, as in Hawthorne's "Wakefield," a narrative voice declaring the impossibility of alteration.

In sum, the reader can sense stability but not total balance. The structure creates a syncopated effect, seeming to lead to a close before the story is over, then opening up again. The sense of negation, the trembling and fear of the final sentence, suspend the ending, and the dual attitude the reader might have toward Laura's change complements this suspension. Laura is fixed in her attitudes, but the reader can see, even if she cannot, the process of change potentially at work. In nineteenth-century stories such as "Bartleby the Scrivener," the reader is also responsible for holding in suspension several themes—guilt and responsibility, for instance—but natural termination and encapsulation round off a straightforward structure, as if the writer could not risk raising unsettling moral issues until he had provided the reader with a structurally closed experience.

Nineteenth-century stories that end on a note of uncertainty do, to be sure, exist: witness Hawthorne's "My Kinsman, Major Molineux." After Robin's ambiguous outburst of laughter directed at his kinsman during the symbolic parricide of tar and feathers, celebrated by onlookers with "counterfeited pomp, in senseless uproar, in frenzied merriment, trampling all on an old man's heart," Hawthorne adds a touch that opens up the story. Robin wants to go home, to leave town to return to his village—"Will you show me the way to the ferry?" he repeats—but the gentleman with him defers showing him, suggesting to Robin that he rise in the world without the help of his kinsman. We never learn whether Robin chooses his own village and consequently stagnation or an urban American destiny ambiguously short on decorum and stability.

Robin's experience is left as undetermined as Laura's in **"Flowering Judas"**; the gentleman's tap on his shoulder has awakened him from a dreamlike state and left him with a major moral choice. The difference, however, is the effect of this openness on the rest of the story. By placing the climax so near the end and by bringing back the cast of characters whom Robin met earlier, Hawthorne creates a traditional, formally balanced pattern. Though different from the dominant expectation of total closure common in a direct story of this period, the open ending is an isolated effect with no structural consequences for the work as a whole. Not until the twentieth century do we see suspension thoroughly worked into the structure of a story, and not until the twentieth century does this openness become almost a norm, which the reader expects in a story that identifies itself as modern.

## Darlene Harbour Unrue (essay date 1985)

SOURCE: "The Inner Darkness," in *Truth and Vision in Katherine Anne Porter's Fiction,* The University of Georgia Press, 1985, pp. 12-59.

[*In the following excerpt, Unrue analyzes Porter's emphasis on betrayal and the female principle in "Flowering Judas."*]

[**"Flowering Judas"**] almost always is interpreted as a story about revolution and betrayal, and any critical confusion has revolved around the extent to which Laura is in fact the betrayer, the "Judas." Ray West's elaborate analysis of Laura as betrayer because she brings no love to the revolution has been the most widely accepted interpretation for many years ["Katherine Anne Porter:

Symbol and Theme in 'Flowering Judas'," *Accent,* Vol. 7, 1947]. However, even West's theory does not answer all the important questions about the story, as Liberman, among others, has pointed out. Porter has identified the model for Laura as her friend Mary Doherty, who like Laura taught Indian children in Xochimilco and participated in the revolution. Some critics, however, have correctly seen Laura as a combination of Mary Doherty and Porter herself and thus Laura as a somewhat autobiographical character, an embryonic version of Miranda, who first appears as a character in Porter's fiction five years after the publication of **"Flowering Judas."** If Laura is examined as a version of the grown-up Miranda and her "betrayal" examined in the light of Miranda's experiences in **"The Circus," "The Fig Tree,"** and **"The Grave,"** Laura herself emerges as a character better understood and the theme of betrayal in the story is more clearly defined. **"Flowering Judas"** is a link between Porter's concern with primitivism and her childhood experiences that created the Miranda cycle.

Laura's betrayal is indeed the crux of the story. However, Laura as the betrayer of the revolution because she brings no love to it, or Laura as the betrayer of herself because she does not allow herself love, or Laura as Eugenio's betrayer because she makes his suicide possible seems inconclusive. Moreover, the label that associates Laura with Judas Iscariot seems too strong, especially when her acts of "betrayal" are measured against those acts of "betrayal" by other characters in the story. The evidence that is cited as proof of Laura's self-betrayal centers on two elements in the story: Laura's "frigidity," symbolically grounded in her nunlike appearance and her "notorious virginity," and the dream at the story's conclusion, in which Eugenio's calling Laura "murderer" seems to hit its mark so directly that Laura is terrified of returning to sleep. Porter, however, does not intend to portray a frigid or even sexually repressed Laura. She shows a Laura who has simply withheld love, as "the incomprehensible fullness" of her breasts, "like a nursing mother's," indicates. In fact, the complete withholding of love has been Laura's protection against brutal violation from revolutionists like Braggioni, who swells "in ominous ripeness" but who will grudgingly honor the ideal of chastity.

Laura's withholding of love thus has a practical cause. But she has justified the withholding in two ways that defy rationality. She has displaced love on the one hand, and on the other she has idealized it. In her total commitment to the revolution, Laura has transferred libidinous passion into revolutionary fervor, as the conclusion of her scene with Braggioni clearly illustrates. Braggioni asks Laura to clean and oil his pistol, and the dialogue between them as Laura "peers down the pistol barrel" is heavy with sexual imagery and illustrates a subconscious collusion between them that Laura already has dreadfully intuited. Braggioni has told her, "We are more alike than you realize in some things," and after feeling "a slow chill, a purely physical sense of danger, a warning in her blood that violence, mutilation, a shocking death, wait for her," Laura thinks, "It may be true that I'm as corrupt, in another way, as Braggioni, . . . as callous, as incomplete." In a parody of a consummating love scene, Braggioni speaks of the revolution as a process that engenders a new life: "No one shall be left alive except the elect spirits destined to procreate a new world cleansed of cruelty and injustice." He "strokes the pistol lying in . . . [Laura's] hands, and declares, "Pistols are good, I love them, cannon are even better, but in the end I pin my faith on good dynamite." Laura's response would be appropriate were she responding to a lover's sweet appeal. But the gentleness is in contrast to the content of her words. She holds up the prepared ammunition belt and says softly, "Put that on, and go kill somebody in Morelia, and you will be happier."

Laura shows no aversion to the phallic suggestions in the scene. But if she has displaced her sexuality in the revolutionary moment, she also has idealized it, as is apparent in other important scenes. Her "tender" feelings about "the battered doll shape of some male saint whose white, lace-trimmed drawers hang limply around his ankles below the hieratic dignity of his velvet robe" point to an idealized phallic appreciation ("she loves fine lace") and show how her encasement of principles has removed her from the intimacy of human love in any form. The children she teaches "remain strangers to her." Indeed, she does not love *them,* but she does love "their tender round hands and their charming opportunistic savagery."

Both Laura and Braggioni have substituted revolution for love, or death for life, as Laura's sleep-filling consciousness deduces immediately before she slips into the dream. Laura indeed betrays herself insofar as she denies herself the highest human fulfillment, which love makes possible. The dream, however, is cited as evidence that Laura is also the betrayer of Eugenio, who calls her "Murderer" and "Cannibal." In most interpretations the dream is seen as combining the two forms of Laura's betrayal. In betraying herself by refusing to give her love, she also has betrayed Eugenio by being unable to love him. Her providing the drugs which he uses for his suicide also supports the charge that Laura has betrayed Eugenio by making his death possible. The dream is of course crucial to the resolution of the story's theme, and it does merit careful consideration. It is important to remember, however, that the dream is created in Laura's subconscious with the symbols of her childhood religion and that it externalizes Laura's own fears rather than offering objective proof of Laura's responsibility for Eugenio's death.

In the dream Laura is called out of sleep by Eugenio and instructed in a parody of the words of Christ, "Follow me." When it is clear that he is taking her to the land of death, rather than life, Laura resists, saying she will not go unless Eugenio takes her hand. Eugenio is already dead, and instead of giving Laura his fleshless hand [he] gives her flowers from the Judas tree, which she devours greedily. However, when Eugenio calls her "Cannibal!" and says, "This is my body and my blood," Laura cries "No!" and awakes trembling, "afraid to sleep again."

The most important symbol in the story, the flowering Judas tree, reaches its culmination in the dream. Flower imagery in fact has permeated the story, although the only flower named and described in the story is that of the Judas tree. The children Laura teaches "make her desk a fresh garden of flowers everyday," and when they write "We lov ar ticher" on the chalkboard, they draw "wreathes of flowers around the words." Flowers are traditionally a symbol of the female archetype, and there is sufficient reason to believe that Porter was using flowers in this sense in **"Flowering Judas."** Once when she was discussing symbolism, Porter remarked that the rose "begins as a female sexual symbol and ends as the rose of fire in Highest Heaven." And in her sketch about Xochitl, whose name means "flower," she described the goddess of pulque as also the earth mother who "sends rain . . . and makes the crops grow—the maguey [from which pulque is made] and the maize and the sweet fruits and pumpkin." Thus Xochitl in Porter's sketch is the Great Mother who both gives life and provides pulque, a drug. If flower symbolizes the female principle as it is embodied in Xochitl, then one can easily see how Laura has betrayed it, just as Miranda fears she has betrayed it in **"The Fig Tree."** If we recall Miranda's refusing the figs, another symbol of the female principle, and avoiding the baby animals at the farm because she thinks she has "given" death to the baby chicken, then Laura's detachment from the children she teaches is more easily understood. Her betrayal of her female self is represented by her throwing a flower to the youth who serenades her, not according to the custom of the culture to encourage his "love" for her, but in contradiction to make him "go away." The flower symbolically withers in his hat as he follows her through the city for several days.

Trees themselves, as the centers of vegetative symbolism, are another archetype of the female principle, and in this story flower and tree come together ironically in the Judas tree, the tree of betrayal, when the descriptive "Judas" is interpreted by Laura's discarded Christianity. The title and the dominant symbols in the story support the theory that Laura is betrayer of the female principle more than she is of anything else, and it is the recognition of this betrayal that terrifies her, much as it terrifies the young Miranda of **"The Fig Tree"** and **"The Grave."** The symbolism is completed in the dream when Laura devours greedily the "bleeding flowers" which satisfy "both hunger and thirst" in an attempt to integrate herself with the flower. Laura as the carrier of drugs has fulfilled only one role of the Great Mother and has denied the more significant role, that of giving nourishment, or life. Thus, Eugenio's telling her, "This is my body and my blood," horrifies her because what she had thought was an act of self-nourishment is actually an act of murder and cannibalism. Her awaking "trembling" is as understandable as Miranda's beginning "to tremble without knowing why" when she discovers the blood on the dead baby rabbits and understands at some place of "secret, formless" intuition that she has participated in death rather than life.

When Porter was writing **"Flowering Judas"** as well as some stories in the Miranda cycle, she would have been in her late thirties and early forties and, according to

Joan Givner, unhappy over her childlessness. Letters Porter wrote to Eugene Pressly while they were separated in 1932 hint at a troubled relationship that may have been caused largely by Porter's unfulfilled maternalism. In one such letter, after saying that happiness for the two of them "seems possible, if not altogether reasonable," she immediately adds, as if by association, "I had the damndest dream last night." She then recounts a complicated dream in which she was a bystander who saw dead men, one with a heavy cross of flowers weighing him down, and dead women "clasping newly born babies." Her sister Alice was in the dream with another baby, which was Porter's, and regarded Porter with a "censorious look on her face." She tells Pressly that the dream was "very sinister, mysterious and portentous . . . and yet without meaning." The elements of guilt, flowers, and death—particularly in the form of dead mothers who could not nourish their babies—indicate that the dream may have related in a profound way to the stories Porter already had written and some she was planning. She later recorded the details of a similar dream from the same period; it included both her and Pressly as well as a monkey that was starving to death in spite of her efforts to find milk and food for him. She says, "The dream ended I do not remember precisely how or when, except that my uneasiness was growing and the monkey was shrivelling up and lying in the palm of my hand almost perfectly still and silent. It was a very anxious and unhappy dream and very hopeless."

The important flower symbolism in the story is supported by other symbolism, that of machinery and oil. In contrast to her concept of flowers, Porter consistently thought of machinery as life-negating, observing in "The Flower of Flowers" that "the world of evil is mechanistic," furnished with "the wheel, but not the rose." And she once told a former lover that she knew their love affair was dead when it became clear that he wanted them to "be machines . . . functioning with hair's breadth precision." Laura senses this hovering negation, because she has a proper fear of machines ("I shall not be killed by an automobile if I can help it," she says) and a revulsion for them ("her private heresy" is that "she will not wear lace made on machines"). Braggioni's threat to Laura is suggested in imagery that links him to machines and particularly to the automobile. "His skin has been punctured in honorable warfare" ("puncture" is a word directly related to automobile tires), and when he asks Laura to oil and load his pistols, she "sits with the shells slipping through the cleaning cloth dipped in oil." When Braggioni sings, his cheeks grow "oily," and his smile is "suety." Thus his Sunday morning ride down the Reforma, the avenue that is dedicated to revolutionary vision and bravery, is highly ironic.

Machine and oil metaphors are particularly interesting here, as well as in **"Hacienda,"** because they have specialized meaning to Porter that they could not have had to Faulkner, for example, who also used them as symbols of antilife and antinature, notably in *The Sound and the Fury* and *Sanctuary.* Porter's arrival in Mexico City coincided with the explosion of the so-called petroleum

problem. Because Obregón stepped into the presidency during the depression that was the aftermath of World War I, he was immediately faced with many problems that grew out of the worldwide economic collapse. The Mexican federal treasury in 1921 was drained by the need to support the numberous unemployed in Mexico as well as to send help and railroad passage to the thousands of workers who had gone to the United States only to discover that depression and unemployment were there also. Thus, prices of raw materials dropped sharply, and Obregón had to suspend production taxes on silver, copper, and lead. However, the petroleum industry during these same years was remarkably healthy (1921 and 1922 were peak years in the production and exportation of Mexican crude oil). In order to replenish the treasury, depleted by loss of taxes on other raw materials, Obregón cited and upheld Article 27 of the Mexican Constitution as amended by Carranza in 1917; it was essentially a decree that the Mexican government had full title to all the lands in Mexico, both surface and subsoil, and had the power not only to break up and divide among the Indians certain unwieldy landholdings but also to tax subsoil products. The oil interests were enraged and suspended operations, throwing another four thousand persons out of work. A compromise between the oil companies and the government was reached in which the payment of taxes was linked to the redemption of Mexico's defaulted foreign bonds, and although it was a compromise that would plague the Mexican government for more than a decade, it did lead to the United States's recognition of the Obregón government in 1924.

Because Porter's reasons for going to Mexico in the first place were idealistic, she felt an immediate aversion to the capitalists and to oilmen, it seems, in particular. Shortly after her arrival there she described to her sister Gay her association with "rich men who are clever enough, but smell offensively of money, and who wish to hold your hand, and be a father to you—or rather, three fathers. And I tell one of them," she says, that "I am handsomely supplied with a perfectly spiffing father, and a brother beside, and a lover into the bargain, and I can only be a 'talking friend' to him. At which he sulks in his fat oil magnate way, and I order my favorite dessert." Within seven months, she was able to write an incisive article she called "The Mexican Trinity," in which she analyzed the intricate relationships among "the great triumvirate, Land, Oil, and the Church."

The crucial imagery in **"Flowering Judas"** is tied directly to Porter's experiences in Mexico, especially her research into primitive myths and her observation of the effects of machines and oil on Mexican society. The machine and flower imagery represent Laura's dilemma. The machine has been linked to the revolution because it was to free the peon from bondage, an illusion Porter elaborates upon in **"Hacienda,"** but Laura's aversion to it is an instinctual female response to its antilife associations. The dilemma represents Laura's whole experience in the Mexican revolution, a subject Porter had put away by the time she started the Miranda saga in earnest. But she retained the most universal theme from **"Flowering**

Judas," fidelity to the female principle, and integrated it into **"The Old Order."**

### Darlene Harbour Unrue  (essay date 1988)

SOURCE: "Mexico," in *Understanding Katherine Anne Porter,* University of South Carolina Press, 1988, pp. 22-46.

[*In the following excerpt, Unrue briefly assesses theme and symbolism in "Flowering Judas."*]

Porter did not include **"The Martyr"** or **"Virgin Violeta"** in her first collection of stories. She told a student that she had omitted them because she had not been satisfied with them once she saw them in print. A story which did satisfy her was **"Flowering Judas,"** one of her best-known and most often anthologized stories. Although she took notes for the story in 1921, she did not complete it until 1929, the year before her last sustained visit to Mexico. She described the writing of **"Flowering Judas"** in Whit Burnett's *This Is My Best.* It developed from the state of revolutionary affairs in Mexico in 1920 and a memory of an experience with her friend Mary Doherty, who became the real-life counterpart of Laura, even though Porter included something of herself in the character as well.

When Porter took notes for the story in 1921 she still had some idealistic faith in the revolution, but by the time she wrote the story she had become disillusioned, and this cynicism is evident in the story's tone. The first paragraph describes Braggioni in repugnant images. At the end of the paragraph, the maid greets the returning Laura at the door saying "with a flicker of a glance towards the upper room 'He Waits.'" The allusion to Christ and the Last Supper (Mark 14. 12-16) establishes at once the central paradox of religion vs. revolution and anticipates the theme of betrayal. It is already clear that this representative of the revolution, Braggioni, is particularly unworthy of the comparison. As the story unfolds, the conflict is amplified. The revolutionary ideal has replaced Laura's discarded faith, her childhood Catholicism, but Laura has not settled everything because "she cannot help feeling that she has been betrayed irreparably by the disunion between her way of living and her feeling of what life should be."

Betrayal is the dominant theme of this story. Laura feels betrayed by the revolution that did not fulfill the early idealistic aims of the movement. Braggioni, who was a poet in those early days, can sing now only of unrequited love, as does the shock-haired youth, who sings in Laura's patio. Laura also betrays the revolution's ideal by stepping into a church to pray, knowing that discovery will cause a scandal, and by rejecting the machine, which is sacred to the movement (her private heresy is that she refuses to wear lace made on machines). If she feels betrayed by the Church that promised something Laura has not found, she also betrays her religion, which promises spiritual life, by replacing it with the revolution that practices death.

---

### Betrayal is the dominant theme of this story.

*—Darlene Harbour Unrue*

---

It is too simplistic to say that Laura betrays Eugenio by providing the drugs that make his suicide possible, but she does betray herself, and in a way that includes her responsibility to Eugenio. Laura has rejected her femininity, her materialism, her nurturing nature. She has done so partly in unconscious self-protection because she knows that only as long as she is a virgin will she be safe among Braggioni and others, who honor the ideal of chastity in their inherited chivalric code. But unconscious or not, the defense constitutes a rejection. Laura has managed the rejection by denying everything and encasing herself in a set of principles rather than facing reality ("she is not at home in the world"). By denying everything, by negating "all external events," she must also deny herself love. Every day she teaches children she does not love; they remain strangers to her, even though "she loves their tender round hands and their charming opportunist savagery." As a courier for the revolutionists, she is required to knock on the door of strangers, kinship with whom she rejects with a "No. No. No." She is gradually perfecting herself "in the stoicism she strives to cultivate."

The theme of betrayal is focused in the primary symbol in the story, the flowering Judas trees, which was inspired by T. S. Eliot's poem "Gerontion." According to legend, Judas hanged himself from a redbud tree, and Eliot's poem names the tree "flowering judas." The symbolism of the Judas tree is completed in the dream when Laura eats the "bleeding" flowers as a ritual of Christian communion, but when she discovers they are Eugenio's body and blood, not Christ's, she awakes "trembling" and "afraid to sleep." What she thought was an act of contrition proves to be an act of destruction. Porter's use of the dream in this story is developing into a means by which her characters confront elemental truths.

Flowers are symbols in the story, and Porter identifies flowers with the female principle in her essay "Flower of Flowers" (1950) and in an unpublished sketch she wrote in the twenties about Xochitl, an ancient Mayan goddess, whose name means "flower." The children whom Laura teaches "make her desk a fresh garden of flowers everyday," and when they write "We lov ar ticher" on the chalkboard, they draw "wreaths of flowers around the words." Also she throws flowers (that symbolically wither) to the youth who serenades her. Other important symbolism in the story is that of machinery and oil, which Porter thought of as anti-life and opposite to flowers. Laura's fear and abhorrence of machines (identified with the revolution that was to free the peon from bondage) is linked to Braggioni, described as "oily" and "suety." Braggioni also is associated with animal imagery in the story. His voice is "furry," he has "yellow cat's eyes," and he "squeels" his songs.

Laura's partial awakening has been the result of a spiritual journey, symbolized by her walking through the streets of Mexico City. References in the story to the Sixteenth of September Street, the Merced Market, the Zócolo, Francisco I. Madero Avenue, the Paseo de la Reforma, Chapultepec Park (all names that have significance in the honorable history of Mexico's revolutions) provide a backdrop that has given momentary legitimacy to present revolutionary activity but also create a contrast between past honor and present corruption. Another journey, to death, which Eugenio offers her in her dream at the story's end, she chooses not to take. It remains for Miranda to make that journey in **"Pale Horse, Pale Rider"** and thus to complete the rite of passage that Laura barely begins.

## Norman Lavers   (essay date 1991)

SOURCE: "'Flowering Judas' and the Failure of Amour Courtois," in *Studies in Short Fiction,* Vol. 28, No. 1, Winter, 1991, pp. 77-82.

*[In the essay below, in part a response to an essay by Ray B. West, Lavers analyzes the pattern and influence of the tradition of courtly love on "Flowering Judas."]*

[In Lodwick Hartley and George Core's 1969 *Katherine Anne Porter: A Critical Symposium*] Ray B. West, in his essay, "Symbol and Theme in **'Flowering Judas,'**" points out that Katherine Anne Porter's most famous story is symbolical, and therefore needs to be interpreted. He then proceeds to give the story a very sensitive reading, examining symbols, and unraveling meanings. He does his work so convincingly that later critics evidently have felt no need to go further. But while everything West says in his celebrated essay is essentially correct, he is by no means exhaustive. In fact, what he has left out of his interpretation is not merely a few ancillary images but the central controlling symbolical pattern itself. He writes at the conclusion of his essay, "The meaning [of the story] . . . is available in all its complex relationships only when we have become aware of the entire field of reference." My intention here is to put into the reader's hands that "entire field of reference."

To refresh the reader's memory, let me briefly summarize the story, and then West's interpretation of it.

The story takes place in Mexico shortly after the Obregon revolution in the early 1920s. Laura, a beautiful American girl, has been helping the revolutionaries in various small ways, mostly by carrying messages to men who are in hiding or in jail. Lately, Braggioni, their leader, a fat, self-indulgent, childishly vain, but also very dangerous man, has begun courting her. Every night when she gets home he is waiting to play for her on his squealing guitar and to sing passionately off key to her. Having no choice, she endures this with an expression of "pitiless courtesy." Inwardly she feels terror, "a warning in her blood that violence, mutilation, and shocking death wait for her with lessening patience." Two other men have courted her here, but she has refused to respond to their signals.

As she sits listening to Braggioni, she is thinking about Eugenio, whom she has been visiting in his prison cell. She had been bringing him drugs to help him pass the time; he had saved them up and taken them all that day, unable to endure any further incarceration. Braggioni is increasingly restless. He tells her that May Day disturbances are coming in the city of Morelia. Catholics will have a procession marching one way, socialists the other way, until they meet. Laura cleans his revolver for him. "Put that on, and go kill somebody in Morelia, and you will be happier," she says softly. He leaves, and she feels she has finally gotten rid of him for a while. When she goes to sleep, she at once dreams of Eugenio, who calls her "murderer," makes her eat from the bleeding flowers of the Judas tree, and takes her on a journey to death.

The story, barely ten pages long, is so rich and packed it immediately suggests itself for symbolical interpretation. Here is what West says about it.

He sees the story as a religious allegory involving love in three guises: religious, secular, and erotic. One series of images has to do with the revolutionaries, who are socialists. Braggioni, their leader, is "a professional lover of humanity"—the sarcastic tone suggesting a union of the material with the Christ-like. Braggioni and the other two men who at some time in the story court Laura, represent erotic love. Religious symbols accrete around Laura's childhood Catholicism and her sneaking off to visit a church to say a Hail Mary. The Catholic parade that will march toward the socialists in Morelia, and finally, the overarching image of the Flowering Judas tree are further religious references. Yet Laura is unable to pray meaningfully in the church and is unable to receive the advances of the men; her chief action in the revolution is to bring Eugenio the narcotics with which he kills himself. In her dream at the end he calls her "cannibal" and "murderer" and makes her eat of the Judas flowers. "This is my body and my blood" he tells her, for it has been a negative sacrament of betrayal, and Laura, the only character in the story incapable of love on any of the levels, has finally betrayed life itself.

West has read the story so intelligently that his interpretation is essentially correct in spite of missing the central symbolical pattern. What is that pattern? I believe I can demonstrate that it is the pattern of the tradition of Courtly Love.

The Courtly Love tradition developed in the Middle Ages and early Renaissance. In this tradition (the rules were so rigid handbooks could be written about it), the young bachelor paid court to a woman who was married, or for other social or ethical reasons unavailable to him, winning jousts for her, serenading her, writing poems, or in Renaissance versions, sequences of sonnets to her, and otherwise giving her the sincerest protestations of love, not only before the eyes of society, but before the eyes of her husband himself. The entire process was acceptable to all so long as it did not pass its prescribed boundaries. That, of course, was up to the woman. She was allowed to accept her suitor's adoration, but could never give in to him physically. Therefore the tradition depended on the virtue of the beloved.

However, in the greatest flowering of the tradition, it was not enough for the woman to have the mere negative virtue of being able to say no. If the lover were honorable, and the beloved compassionate, though she could not yield to him in the flesh (she could not, in the usual term of the sonnets, show him *pity*), she might feel concerned for his welfare, knowing he was spending his energy and sometimes wealth out of his devotion to her. There was the possibility they could have a kind of spiritual union.

This aspect of the tradition developed out of Plato's *Symposium,* with the notion that man in his unenlightened state could not perceive true Beauty (always identified with the Good); however by a kind of instinct he could at least recognize carnal beauty in a sexually attractive beloved. This beloved person, if truly virtuous, could gradually raise the suitor from contemplating only erotic beauty, little by little to the contemplation of spiritual beauty. Plato's idea, linked to the Courtly Love Tradition, said that the beloved woman, who had attracted her lover first with her physical beauty, should bend every effort to raise him to a love of spiritual (in this case, religious) beauty, at which time they could become "platonic" lovers.

It is some generalized form of this tradition, I maintain, that Katherine Anne Porter means us to see at the center of her story. Laura has three courtly lovers in the story, each pursuing her in a prescribed manner. There is the young typographer who serenades her outside her window, and writes poems to her, and walks a set distance behind her everywhere she goes, "observing a convention with all propriety." There is the dashing and impulsive captain who tries to take her down off her horse and kiss her—when she spurns him, he apologizes later for not having done things in the proper order. Finally there is Braggioni, who comes to her house every evening with a new song to sing her. In each case she follows the minimal courtly rule of chaste denial: "There is nothing to do [she concludes] but sit patiently and say 'No,' when the moment comes."

But this does not seem to be enough. She is curiously dissatisfied with her life. "She is not at home in the world"; she feels "betrayed irreparably by the disunion between her way of living and her feeling of what life should be." "She persuades herself that her negation of all external events as they occur is a sign that she is gradually perfecting herself in the stoicism she strives to cultivate against that disaster she fears." The disaster is more than a fear of disunion, it is a fear of "violence, mutilation, a shocking death." The disunion, the mutilation, is the separation of self from self.

Braggioni also is dissatisfied. In quite biblical terms he says "It is true everything turns to dust in the hand, to gall on the tongue." "I am disappointed in everything as it comes. Everything. . . . You, poor thing, you will be disappointed too." And finally he tells her, "We are more alike than you realize in some things." She herself thinks, "It may be true I am as corrupt, in another way, as Braggioni . . . as callous, as incomplete."

Incompleteness is the point, and here we see another traditional pattern. The descriptions of Braggioni are all grossly animal: his "Gluttonous bulk," his belt that "creaks like a saddle girth," his eyes that are "the true tawny yellow cat's eyes." He sings in a "furry" voice, "snarling" a tune, and so on. In contradistinction, the descriptions of Laura are so devoid of the animal as to be ethereal: "No dancer dances more beautifully than Laura walks." "She longs to fly out of this room." Laura and Braggioni represent spirit and flesh, the two aspects of being, which need each other for completeness. But to her nun-like spiritual being, the very thought of the flesh (Braggioni) is revolting. Although Braggioni is the symbol of it, symbol of her own animality she has rejected, this rejection makes her reject the flesh in all of its forms: her suitors, and even the innocent children whom she teaches but cannot quite love. Continually we are told of her lack of connection with others. "Nobody touches her." Everyone remains a stranger to her: "The very cells of her flesh reject knowledge and kinship in one monotonous word. No."

West is percipient when he speaks of the three kinds of love: erotic, secular, and divine or Christian. Because he does not recognize the source of these increasingly refined forms of love in the *Symposium* and the Courtly Love tradition, he does not realize they form a sort of progression. But he is exactly right when he says the two poles of the story are the socialist-secular and the Christian-spiritual. I have just suggested that at a deeper level in the symbolical structure, they are body and soul. He is further correct when he says that either one by itself is barren, and only when the two are united by a fructifying love are they vital.

This was Laura's obligation, her role to play in the Courtly Love tradition, to connect the fleshly, through her love, to the spiritual. Braggioni tells Laura of the upcoming May Day disturbances in Morelia: "There will be two independent processions, starting from either end of town [the socialists and the Catholics], and they will march until they meet, and the rest depends. . . ." It depends on Laura to unite these two factions by accepting her own flesh, and by raising the spirituality of her lover by bringing together body and soul. Instead, "Laura holds up the [pistol] belt to him: 'Put that on, and go kill somebody in Morelia, and you will be happier.'" At that very moment Eugenio is dying from the drugs she gave him.

Braggioni now returns to his wife. West says—and in the first part he is correct—that Laura has failed as a complete human being because she has failed at love, whereas Braggioni has succeeded, because he feels pity for his wife, and when she washes his feet there is the suggestion that he is to be interpreted as a Christ-like character, a lover of man. But this scene needs to be looked at more closely, with reference to the Courtly Love Tradition. The scene indeed closely parallels the scene in Luke: "And, behold, a woman in the city, which was a sinner . . . began to wash his feet with tears." But a point has just been made in **"Flowering Judas"** that his wife is not a sinner: she is perfect and good. When she washes his feet, bathing him with her tears and asking his forgiveness, she is doing what Laura did not do: she is purposely making of him a Christ, a lover of man, raising him up in that way, uniting his flesh with her spirit. Her actions are an example for what Laura's ought to have been.

Laura's name, I believe, was carefully chosen. It reminds us of Petrarch's Laura, which in turn reminds us of one of the most famous life-long examples of a courtly lover writing the poems of the *Canzoniere* to his virtuous mistress, just as Braggioni writes his songs for the modern Laura. Petrarch was himself a social idealist who hobnobbed with bloodthirsty despots, but his Laura's goodness, if it could not do much to clarify his ambiguous politics, at least raised his original erotic desire for her to an increasingly spiritual union. In case the reader has still missed the connection with Petrarch, Braggioni goes out of his way to tell Laura that he is a poet with a Tuscan background. "Traditionally," he tells Laura, "he must sing in spite of his life which drives him to bloodshed."

"Sing, then," Laura tells him. Conventionally, the courtly lover hopes for pity from his mistress. But Laura can only listen with "pitiless courtesy." The cost to her is that violent dissociation she had feared. When she goes to sleep, her spirit finally forsakes all union with her flesh (the dead Eugenio says, "Come out of your sleep, out of your bed, out of this strange house"). But shorn of the nourishment of the body, her spirit can only be led to death, over a sea so barren "it was not water but a desert of crumbling stone."

Do we then take the last line of the story to mark a hopeful turn? "Laura cried No! and at the sound of her own voice, she awoke trembling, and was afraid to sleep again." This time the "No!" seems to be a denial of her former denials. She is saying, No, she will not allow her fleshless spirit to be carried off to barren death, and the sound of her voice awakens her back into her bed, back into her house, back into her body, and we are told that her fear at the vision that has been vouchsafed her will prevent her from sleeping again.

## FURTHER READING

Heilman, Robert B. "Katherine Anne Porter: 'Flowering Judas'." In *Modern Short Stories: A Critical Anthology,* pp. 180-94. New York: Harcourt, Brace and Company, 1950.

    Reprints "Flowering Judas" and then provides a brief critical discussion of the tale.

Ibieta, Gabriella. "The North-American Exile's Vision of Mexico According to Katherine Anne Porter." In *Proceedings of the Xth Congress of the International Comparative Literature Association,* edited by Anna Balakian and James J. Wilhelm, pp. 233-38. New York: Garland Publishing Inc., 1985.

    Examines Porter's depiction of Mexico in "Flowering Judas" and "Hacienda," concluding: "These texts are particularly valuable as outstanding examples of intercultural relations between two countries that still hold a conflictive fascination for each other. In both instances a process of mediation is effectively achieved by North Americans who, from a seemingly safe, although existentially precarious existence, refract an implicitly double image of the Mexican reality."

Nance, William L. "The Emerging Pattern." In *Katherine Anne Porter & the Art of Rejection,* pp. 12-54. Chapel Hill: The University of North Carolina Press, 1964.

    Discusses "Flowering Judas" in relation to Porter's artistic development, highlighting thematic and stylistic features of the story.

Patridge, Colin. "'My Familiar Country': An Image of Mexico in the Work of Katherine Anne Porter." *Studies in Short Fiction* VII, No. 4 (Fall 1970): 597-614.

    Examines various tales by Porter with Mexican settings. Patridge asserts that "'Flowering Judas' is an advance upon the previous tales. The movement from levels of psychological conflict to levels of social and political implication is handled with conciseness and skill."

Vukmirovich, John. "Porter's 'Flowering Judas' and Pynchon's *V.*" *Pynchon Notes,* Nos. 22-23 (Spring-Fall 1988): 71-3.

    Notes similarities between "Flowering Judas," particularly those scenes encompassing the Judas tree and Braggioni, and the seventh chapter of Thomas Pynchon's *V.* The critic asserts: "In fact, [Porter's] story, and its central image of the Judas tree, can be seen as a seed for this crucial chapter in Pynchon's novel."

Walsh, Thomas F. "Braggioni's Jockey Club in Porter's 'Flowering Judas'." *Studies in Short Fiction* 20, Nos. 2-3 (Spring-Summer 1983): 136-38.

    Discusses Porter's inspiration for "Flowering Judas."

# P'u Sung-ling
## 1640-1715

Chinese short story writer, novelist, poet, songwriter, and essayist.

## INTRODUCTION

A prolific storyteller, P'u is regarded as a monumental figure in Chinese literature for his entertaining collection of supernatural and satiric folk tales, *Liao-chai chih-i* (*Strange Stories from a Chinese Studio*). Written in a highly allusive, traditional style, *Strange Stories* both attacked and appeased the oppressive Manchu government of P'u's time. Known as a serious writer to few people beyond a small circle of scholars and writers in his day, P'u attained enormous status in the centuries after his death because of the enduring intellectual and aesthetic appeal of the tales, many of which were imitated by later Chinese writers or adapted to the stage.

## Biographical Information

P'u was born into a well-educated merchant's family in Tzu-ch'uan, Shantung, near the end of the Ming dynasty, a period during which the warring Manchus of northern China systematically overthrew the Ming empire. He aspired to a scholar's life at an early age. After completing his prefectural examination with high honors in 1658, P'u resolved to pass the more difficult provincial exam, which would enable him to enter government service. Although P'u never attained this goal despite concerted attempts throughout his life, biographers believe that it was his questioning, humanitarian sensibility, and not a deficiency in scholarship, which barred him from obtaining an official position, as the Manchu testing system was designed to promote only those who displayed allegiance to the elitist views upheld by the state. Thus excluded from enjoying the material comforts and elevated status that accompanied official appointment, P'u earned his living largely as a teacher, factotum, and scribe. In 1670 he became secretary to the magistrate in the southern province of Chiang-su; two years later he left southern China after obtaining a position as administrator for a wealthy friend, with whom he and his family resided for over thirty years. During this period, P'u also worked as a licentiate for the district school.

## Major Works of Short Fiction

Although historians believe that P'u began compiling and writing tales early in life, exact composition dates are not ascertainable. It is known that during his return from Chiang-su, following completion of his duties there, he visited many notable landmarks and amassed numerous regional stories along the way. In 1679 P'u composed a preface for his collection, signifying the near-final form of the work. For approximately the next eighty years *Strange Stories* circulated in manuscript until an admiring scholar undertook its publication.

P'u's stories are modeled upon the genre *ch'uan-ch'i,* a short narrative form that originated during the T'ang dynasty (618-907 A.D.). Considered a singularly successful revival of this early literary tradition, *Strange Stories* closely adheres to the *ch'uan-ch'i* mode of compact, semi-poetic prose embroidered with esoteric allusion. Critics note, however, that P'u surpassed his T'ang predecessors through a greatly refined style and innovative fusion of social criticism with entertainment. Largely drawn from imaginative folk tales and legends, his stories contain ghosts, fairies, and various birds and animals symbolizing both the ruling and ruled classes. Thus carefully masking his social criticism, P'u protested the harsh Manchu domination of his people, which he had witnessed since a child. His stories depict a dualistic world in which forces of evil, though initially triumphant, are ultimately overcome by forces of good. P'u's verbal attacks on corrupt landlords and government officials firmly demonstrate his desire for social reform within the feudal system.

## Critical Reception

Scholars have observed that in *Strange Stories* P'u wrote unevenly, at times liberating his narrative from reference to antecedent works, writers, and events, while at other times overloading it with these elements. Although P'u has been criticized by Maoist critics for failing to acknowledge that the Manchu system itself was the fundamental cause of injustice and cruel abuse, other scholars believe the frequently sharp satirical commentary found in *Strange Stories* outrivals more recognized examples of political satire, including Wu Ching-tzu's eighteenth-century novel, *Ju-lin wai-shih* (1768-1779; *The Scholars*). In addition, despite the otherworldly features and romantic sensibility of the tales, critics unanimously assert the realistic effect of *Strange Stories* and credit P'u for his ability to develop fantastic situations into readily visualized and even believable scenes.

While P'u wrote in several genres, he is best remembered for his *Strange Stories,* a work that has appealed to readers for over three hundred years. In tribute to this long-standing classic, Tsung Shu has claimed that it "surpasses any previous collection of ghost and fairy tales in scope, literary merit, and profundity of ideas, serving as a landmark in the history of Chinese fiction." As one of the first Chinese writers to imbue the short narrative with a serious authorial voice, P'u commands an important and unique place in the history of Oriental literature.

## PRINCIPAL WORKS

### Short Fiction

*Liao-chai chih-i* [*Strange Stories from a Chinese Studio*] 1765
*Liao-chai chih-i wei-k' an kao* 1936
*Liao-chai ch'uan-chi.* 2 vols. (essays, poetry, short stories, and songs) 1936

### Other Major Works

†*Hsing-shih yin-yuan chuan* [*Marriage as Retribution*] (novel) 1870

*Exact years of composition remain unestablished for any of P'u's works. *Liao-chai chih-i* is believed to have been in near-final form in 1679, though scholars agree that later additions and emendations to the collection were made. *Strange Stories from a Chinese Studio* (1880) is only a partial translation.

†*Hsing-shih yin-yuan chuan*, according to some sources, may have appeared in book form as early as 1728, though this too has not been conclusively verified. *Marriage as Retribution* (1984) is only a partial translation.

## CRITICISM

### Herbert A. Giles (essay date 1908)

Introduction to *Strange Stories from a Chinese Studio*, Boni and Liveright, 1925, pp. xi-xxiii.

[*A highly regarded English sinologist, Giles, through his numerous lectures and publications in the late eighteenth and early nineteenth centuries, was instrumental in conveying the rich variety of Chinese culture to ill-informed Western audiences. In 1880 Giles published* Strange Stories from a Chinese Studio, *the first and most extensive translation of P'u's* Liao-chai chih-i. *In the following introduction, which was originally written in 1908, Giles comments on P'u's stature in Chinese literature. In his discussion, Giles also includes a 1679 essay by P'u, as well as an 1842 essay by T'ang Mêng-lai.*]

The barest skeleton of a biography is all that can be formed from the very scanty materials which remain to mark the career of a writer whose work has been for the best part of two centuries as familiar throughout the length and breadth of China as are the tales of the "Arabian Nights" in all English-speaking communities. The author of ***Strange Stories*** was a native of Tzŭ-ch'uan, in the province of Shan-tung. His family name was P'u; his particular name was Sung-ling; and the designation or literary epithet by which, in accordance with Chinese usage, he was com-

monly known among his friends, was Liu-hsien, or "Last of the Immortals." A further fancy name, given to him probably by some enthusiastic admirer, was Liu-ch'üan, or "Willow Spring;" but he is now familiarly spoken of simply as P'u Sung-ling. We are unacquainted with the years of his birth or death; however, by the aid of a meagre entry in the *History of Tzŭ-ch'uan* it is possible to make a pretty good guess at the date of the former event. For we are there told that P'u Sung-ling successfully competed for the lowest or bachelor's degree before he had reached the age of twenty; and that in 1651 he was in the position of a graduate of ten years' standing, having failed in the interim to take the second, or master's, degree. To this failure, due, as we are informed in the history above quoted, to his neglect of the beaten track of academic study, we owe the existence of his great work; not, indeed, his only production, though the one by which, as Confucius said of his own "Spring and Autumn,"[1] men will know him. All else that we have on record of P'u Sung-ling, besides the fact that he lived in close companionship with several eminent scholars of the day, is gathered from his own words, written when, in 1679, he laid down his pen upon the completion of a task which was to raise him within a short period to a foremost rank in the Chinese world of letters. Of that record I here append a close translation, accompanied by such notes as are absolutely necessary to make it intelligible to non-students of Chinese.

### AUTHOR'S OWN RECORD

"Clad in wistaria, girdled with ivy:"[2] thus sang Ch'ü-P'ing[3] in his *Falling into Trouble*.[4] Of ox-headed devils and serpent Gods,[5] he of the long-nails[6] never wearied to tell. Each interprets in his own way the music of heaven;[7] and whether it be discord or not, depends upon antecedent causes.[8] As for me, I cannot, with my poor autumn firefly's light, match myself against the hobgoblins of the age.[9] I am but the dust in the sunbeam, a fit laughing-stock for devils.[10] For my talents are not those of Kan Pao,[11] elegant explorer of the records of the Gods; I am rather animated by the spirit of Su Tung-p'o,[12] who loved to hear men speak of the supernatural. I get people to commit what they tell me to writing and subsequently I dress it up in the form of a story; and thus in the lapse of time my friends from all quarters have supplied me with quantities of material, which, from my habit of collecting, has grown into a vast pile.[13]

Human beings, I would point out, are not beyond the pale of fixed laws, and yet there are more remarkable phenomena in their midst than in the country of those who crop their hair;[14] antiquity is unrolled before us, and many tales are to be found therein stranger than that of the nation of Flying Heads.[15] "Irrepressible bursts, and luxurious ease,"[16]—such was always his enthusiastic strain. "For ever indulging in liberal thought,"[17]—thus he spoke openly without restraint. Were men like these to open my book, I should be a laughing-stock to them indeed. At the crossroad[18] men will not listen to me, and yet I have some knowledge of the three states of existence[19] spoken of beneath the cliff;[20] neither should the words I utter be set aside because of him that utters them.[21] When the bow[22] was hung at my father's door, he dreamed that a sickly-looking Buddhist priest, but half covered by his stole, entered the chamber. On one of his breasts was a round piece of plaster like a *cash*;[23] and my father, waking from sleep, found that I, just born, had a similar black patch on my body. As a child, I was thin and constantly ailing, and unable to hold my own in the battle of life. Our own home was chill and desolate as a monastery; and working there for my livelihood with my pen,[24] I was as poor as a priest with his alms-bowl.[25] Often and often I put my hand to my head[26] and exclaimed, "Surely he who sat with his face to the wall[27] was myself in a previous state of existence;" and thus I referred my non-success in this life to the influence of a destiny surviving from the last. I have been tossed hither and thither in the direction of the ruling wind, like a flower falling in filthy places; but the six paths[28] of transmigration are inscrutable indeed, and I have no right to complain. As it is, midnight finds me with an expiring lamp, while the wind whistles mournfully without; and over my cheerless table I piece together my tales,[29] vainly hoping to produce a sequel to the *Infernal Regions*.[30] With a bumper I stimulate my pen, yet I only succeed thereby in "venting my excited feelings,"[31] and as I thus commit my thoughts to writing, truly I am an object worthy of commiseration. Alas! I am but the bird, that dreading the winter frost, finds no shelter in the tree; the autumn insect that chirps to the moon, and hugs the door for warmth. For where are they who know me?[32] They are "in the bosky grove, and at the frontier pass"[33]—wrapped in an impenetrable gloom!

From the above curious document the reader will gain some insight into the abstruse, but at the same time marvellously beautiful, style of this gifted writer. The whole essay—for such it is, and among the most perfect of its kind—is intended chiefly as a satire upon the scholarship of the age; scholarship which had turned the author back to the disappointment of a private life, himself conscious all the time of the inward fire that had been lent him by heaven. It is the keynote of his own subsequent career, spent in the retirement of home, in the society of books and friends; as also to the numerous uncomplimentary allusions which occur in all his stories relating to official life. Whether or not the world at large has been a gainer by this instance of the fallibility of competitive examinations has been already decided in the affirmative by the millions of P'u Sung-ling's own countrymen, who for the past two hundred years have more than made up to him by a posthumous and enduring reverence for the loss of those earthly and ephemeral honours which he seems to have coveted so much.

***Strange Stories from a Chinese Studio,*** known to the Chinese as the ***Liao Chai Chih I,*** or more familiarly, the ***Liao Chai,*** has hardly been mentioned by a single foreigner without some inaccuracy on the part of the writer concerned. For instance, the late Mr. Mayers states in his *Chinese Reader's Manual,* p. 176, that this work was composed "circa A.D. 1710," the fact being that the collection was actually completed in 1679, as we know by the date attached to the "Author's Own Record" given above. I should mention, however, that the ***Liao Chai*** was

originally, and for many years, circulated in manuscript only. P'u Sung-ling, as we are told in a colophon by his grandson to the first edition, was too poor to meet the heavy expense of block-cutting; and it was not until so late as 1740, when the author must have been already for some time a denizen of the dark land he so much loved to describe, that his aforesaid grandson printed and published the collection now universally famous. Since then many editions have been laid before the Chinese public, the best of which is that by Tan Ming-lun, a Salt Commissioner, who flourished during the reign of Tao Kuang, and who in 1842 produced, at his own expense, an excellent edition in sixteen small octavo volumes of about 160 pages each. And as various editions will occasionally be found to contain various readings, I would here warn students of Chinese who wish to compare my rendering with the text, that it is from the edition of Tan Ming-lun, collated with that of Yü Chi, published in 1766, that this translation has been made. Many have been the commentaries and disquisitions upon the meaning of obscure passages and the general scope of this work; to say nothing of the prefaces with which the several editions have been ushered into the world. Of the latter, I have selected one specimen, from which the reader will be able to form a tolerably accurate opinion as to the true nature of these always singular and usually difficult compositions. Here it is:—

### T'ANG MÊNG-LAI'S PREFACE

The common saying, "He regards a camel as a horse with a swelled back," trivial of itself, may be used in illustration of greater matters. Men are wont to attribute an existence only to such things as they daily see with their own eyes, and they marvel at whatsoever, appearing before them at one instant, vanishes at the next. And yet it is not at the sprouting and falling of foliage, nor at the metamorphosis of insects that they marvel, but only at the manifestations of the supernatural world; though of a truth, the whistling of the wind and the movement of streams, with nothing to set the one in motion or give sound to the other, might well be ranked among extraordinary phenomena. We are accustomed to these, and therefore do not note them. We marvel at devils and foxes: we do not marvel at man. But who is it that causes a man to move and to speak?—to which question comes the ready answer of each individual so questioned, "*I* do." This "I do," however, is merely a personal consciousness of the facts under discussion. For a man can see with his eyes, but he cannot see what it is that makes him see; he can hear with his ears, but he cannot hear what it is that makes him hear; how, then, is it possible for him to understand the rationale of things he can neither see nor hear? Whatever has come within the bounds of their own ocular or auricular experience men regard as proved to be actually existing; and only such things.[34] But this term "experience" may be understood in various senses. For instance, people speak of something which has certain attributes as *form,* and of something else which has certain other attributes as *substance*; ignorant as they are that form and substance are to be found existing without those particular attributes. Things which are thus constituted are inappreciable, indeed, by our ears and eyes; but we cannot argue that therefore they do not exist. Some persons can see a mosquito's eye, while to others even a mountain is invisible; some can hear the sound of ants battling together, while others, again, fail to catch the roar of a thunder-peal. Powers of seeing and hearing vary; there should be no reckless imputations of blindness. According to the schoolmen, man at his death is dispersed like wind or fire, the origin and end of his vitality being alike unknown; and as those who have seen strange phenomena are few, the number of those who marvel at them is proportionately great, and the "horse with a swelled back" parallel is very widely applicable. And ever quoting the fact that Confucius would have nothing to say on these topics, these schoolmen half discredit such works as the *Ch'i chieh chih kuai* and the *Yü ch'u-chii*,[35] ignorant that the Sage's unwillingness to speak had reference only to persons of an inferior mental calibre; for his own *Spring and Autumn* can hardly be said to be devoid of all allusions of the kind. Now P'u Liu-hsien devoted himself in his youth to the marvellous, and as he grew older was specially remarkable for his comprehension thereof; and being moreover a most elegant writer, he occupied his leisure in recording whatever came to his knowledge of a particularly marvellous nature. A volume of these compositions of his formerly fell into my hands, and was constantly borrowed by friends; now, I have another volume, and of what I read only about three-tenths was known to me before. What there is, should be sufficient to open the eyes of those schoolmen, though I much fear it will be like talking of ice to a butterfly. Personally, I disbelieve in the irregularity of natural phenomena, and regard as evil spirits only those who injure their neighbours. For eclipses, falling stars, the flight of herons, the nest of a mainah, talking stones, and the combats of dragons, can hardly be classed as irregular; while the phenomena of nature occurring out of season, wars, rebellions, and so forth, may certainly be relegated to the category of evil. In my opinion the morality of P'u Liuhsien's work is of a very high standard, its object being distinctly to glorify virtue and to censure vice; and as a book calculated to elevate mankind, it may be safely placed side by side with the philosophical treatises of Yang Hsiung[36] which Huan Tan[37] declared to be so worthy of a wide circulation.

With regard to the meaning of the Chinese words *Liao Chai Chih I,* this title has received indifferent treatment at the hands of different writers. Dr. Williams chose to render it by "Pastimes of the Study," and Mr. Mayers by "The Record of Marvels, or Tales of the Genii;" neither of which is sufficiently near to be regarded in the light of a translation. Taken literally and in order, these words stand for "Liao—library—record—strange," "Liao" being simply a fanciful name given by our author to his private library or studio. An apocryphal anecdote traces the origin of this selection to a remark once made by himself with reference to his failure for the second degree. "Alas!" he is reported to have said, "I shall now have no resource (*Liao*) for my old age"; and accordingly he so named his study, meaning that in his pen he would seek that resource which fate had denied to him as an official. For this untranslatable "Liao" I have ventured to substitute "Chinese," as indicating more clearly the nature of what is to follow. No such title as "Tales of the Genii" fully expresses the scope of this work, which embraces alike weird stories of Taoist devilry and magic, marvellous accounts of impos-

sible countries beyond the sea, simple scenes of Chinese everyday life, and notices of extraordinary natural phenomena. Indeed, the author once had it in contemplation to publish only the more imaginative of the tales in the present collection under the title of "Devil and Fox Stories"; but from this scheme he was ultimately dissuaded by his friends, the result being the heterogeneous mass which is more aptly described by the title I have given to this volume. In a similar manner, I too had originally determined to publish a full and complete translation of the whole of these sixteen volumes; but on a closer acquaintance many of the stories turned out to be quite unsuitable for the age in which we live, forcibly recalling the coarseness of our own writers of fiction in the eighteenth century. Others, again, were utterly pointless, or mere repetitions in a slightly altered form. From the whole, I therefore selected one hundred and sixty-four of the best and most characteristic stories, of which eight had previously been published by Mr. Allen in the *China Review,* one by Mr. Mayers in *Notes and Queries on China and Japan,* two by myself in the columns of the *Celestial Empire,* and four by Dr. Williams in a now forgotten handbook of Chinese. The remaining one hundred and forty-nine have never before, to my knowledge, been translated into English. To those, however, who can enjoy the **Liao Chai** in the original text, the distinctions between the various stories in felicity of plot, originality, and so on, are far less sharply defined, so impressed as each competent reader must be by the incomparable *style* in which even the meanest is arrayed. For in this respect, as important now in Chinese eyes as it was with ourselves in days not long gone by, the author of the **Liao Chai** and the rejected candidate succeeded in founding a school of his own, in which he has since been followed by hosts of servile imitators with more or less success. Terseness is pushed to extreme limits; each particle that can be safely dispensed with is scrupulously eliminated; and every here and there some new and original combination invests perhaps a single word with a force it could never have possessed except under the hands of a perfect master of his art. Add to the above, copious allusions and adaptations from a course of reading which would seem to have been co-extensive with the whole range of Chinese literature, a wealth of metaphor and an artistic use of figures generally to which only the writings of Carlyle form an adequate parallel; and the result is a work which for purity and beauty of style is now universally accepted in China as the best and most perfect model. Sometimes the story runs along plainly and smoothly enough; but the next moment we may be plunged into pages of abstruse text, the meaning of which is so involved in quotations from and allusions to the poetry or history of the past three thousand years as to be recoverable only after diligent perusal of the commentary and much searching in other works of reference. In illustration of the popularity of this book, Mr. Mayers once stated that "the porter at his gate, the boatman at his midday rest, the chair-coolie at his stand, no less than the man of letters among his books, may be seen poring with delight over the elegantly-narrated marvels of the **Liao Chai**;" but he would doubtless have withdrawn this statement in later years, with the work lying open before him. During many years in China, I made a point of never, when feasible, passing by a reading Chinaman without asking permission to glance at the volume in his hand; and at my various stations in China I always kept up a borrowing acquaintance with the libraries of my private or official servants; but I can safely affirm that I never once detected the ***Liao Chai*** in the hands of an ill-educated man. In the same connection, Mr. Mayers observed that "fairytales told in the style of the *Anatomy of Melancholy* would scarcely be a popular book in Great Britain;" but except in some particular points of contact, the styles of these two works could scarcely claim even the most distant of relationships.

---

**Terseness is pushed to extreme limits; each particle that can be safely dispensed with is scrupulously eliminated; and every here and there some new and original combination invests perhaps a single word with a force it could never have possessed except under the hands of a perfect master of his art.**

*—Herbert A. Giles*

---

Such, then, is the setting of this collection of ***Strange Stories from a Chinese Studio,*** many of which contain, in addition to the advantages of style and plot, a very excellent moral. The intention of most of them is, in the actual words of T'ang Mêng-lai, "to glorify virtue and to censure vice,"—always, it must be borne in mind, according to the Chinese and not to a European interpretation of these terms. As an addition to our knowledge of the folk-lore of China, and as a guide to the manners, customs, and social life of that vast Empire, my translation of the ***Liao Chai*** may not be wholly devoid of interest. It has now been carefully revised, all inaccuracies of the first edition having been, so far as possible, corrected.

*Notes*

[1] Annals of the Lu State.

[2] Said of the bogies of the hills, in allusion to their *clothes.* Here quoted with reference to the official classes, in ridicule of the title under which they hold posts which, from a literary point of view, they are totally unfit to occupy.

[3] A celebrated statesman (B.C. 332-295) who, having lost his master's favour by the intrigues of a rival, finally drowned himself in despair. The annual Dragon Festival is said by some to be a "search" for his body. The term *San Lü* used here was the name of an office held by Ch'ü-P'ing.

[4] A poem addressed by Ch'ü-P'ing to his Prince, after his disgrace. Its non-success was the immediate cause of his death.

[5] That is, of the supernatural generally.

[6] A poet of the T'ang dynasty whose eyebrows met, whose nails were very long, and who could write very fast.

[7] "You know the music of earth," said Chuang Tz ; "but you have not heard the music of heaven."

[8] That is, to the operation of some influence surviving from a previous existence.

[9] This is another hit at the ruling classes. Hsi K'ang, a celebrated musician and alchemist (A.D. 223-262), was sitting one night alone, playing upon his lute, when suddenly a man with a tiny face walked in, and began to stare hard at him, the stranger's face enlarging all the time. "I'm not going to match myself against a devil!" cried the musician, after a few moments, and instantly blew out the light.

[10] When Liu Chüan, Governor of Wu-ling, determined to relieve his poverty by trade, he saw a devil standing by his side, laughing and rubbing its hands for glee. "Poverty and wealth are matters of destiny," said Liu Chüan; "but to be laughed at by a devil—," and accordingly he desisted from his intention.

[11] A writer who flourished in the early part of the fourth century, and composed a work in thirty books entitled *Supernatural Researches.*

[12] The famous poet, statesman, and essayist, who flourished A.D. 1036-1101.

[13] "And his friends had the habit of jotting down for his unfailing delight anything quaint or comic that they came across."—*The World* on Charles Dickens, July 24, 1878.

[14] It is related in the *Historical Record* that when T'ai Po and Yü Chung fled to the southern savages they saw men with tattooed bodies and short hair.

[15] A fabulous community, so called because the heads of the men are in the habit of leaving their bodies, and flying down to marshy places to feed on worms and crabs. A red ring is seen the night before the flight encircling the neck of the man whose head is about to fly; at daylight the head returns. Some say that the ears are used as wings; others that the hands also leave the body and fly away.

[16] A quotation from the admired works of Wang Po, a brilliant scholar and poet, who was drowned at the early age of twenty-eight, A.D. 676.

[17] I have hitherto failed in all attempts to identify the particular writer here intended. The phrase is used by the poet Li T'ai-po and others.

[18] The cross-road of the "Five Fathers" is here mentioned, which the commentator tells us is merely the name of the place.

[19] The past, present, and future life of the Buddhist system of metempsychosis.

[20] A certain man, who was staying at a temple, dreamt that an old priest appeared to him beneath a jade-storfe cliff, and, pointing to a stick of burning incense, said to him, "That incense represents a vow to be fulfilled; but I say unto you, that ere its smoke shall have curled away, your three states of existence will have been already accomplished." The meaning is that time on earth is as nothing to the Gods.

[21] This remark occurs in the fifteenth chapter of the Analects or Confucian Gospels.

[22] The birth of a boy was formerly signalled by hanging a bow at the door; that of a girl, by displaying a small towel—indicative of the parts that each would hereafter play in the drama of life.

[23] See Note 2 to No. II.

[24] Literally, "ploughing with my pen."

[25] The *patra* or bowl, used by Buddhist mendicants, in imitation of the celebrated alms-dish of Shâkyamuni Buddha.

[26] Literally, "scratched my head," as is often done by the Chinese in perplexity or doubt.

[27] Alluding to Bôdhidharma, who came from India to China, and tried

to convert the Emperor Wu Ti of the Liang dynasty; but, failing in his attempt, because he insisted that real merit lay not in works but in purity and wisdom combined, he retired full of mortification to a temple at Sung-shan, where he sat for nine years before a rock, until his own image was imprinted thereon.

[28] The six *gâti* or conditions of existence, namely:—angels, men, demons, hungry devils, brute beasts, and tortured sinners.

[29] Literally, "putting together the pieces under the forelegs (of foxes) to make robes." This part of the fox-skin is the most valuable for making fur clothes.

[30] The work of a well-known writer, named Lin I-ch'ing, who flourished during the Sung Dynasty.

[31] Alluding to an essay by Han Fei, a philosopher of the third century B.C., in which he laments the iniquity of the age in general, and the corruption of officials in particular. He finally committed suicide in prison, where he had been cast by the intrigues of a rival minister.

[32] Confucius (*Anal.* xiv.) said, "Alas! there is no one who knows me (to be what I am)."

[33] The great poet Tu Fu (A.D. 712-770) dreamt that his greater predecessor, Li T'ai-po (A.D. 705-762) appeared to him, "coming when the maple-grove was in darkness, and returning while the frontier-pass was still obscured;"—that is, at night, when no one could see him; the meaning being that he never came at all, and that those "who know me (P'u Sung-ling)" are equally non-existent.

[34] "Thus, since countless things exist that the senses *can* take account of, it is evident that nothing exists that the senses can *not* take account of."—The "Professor" in W. H. Mallock's *New Paul and Virginia.*

This passage recalls another curious classification by the great Chinese philosopher Han Wên-kung. "There are some things which possess form but are devoid of sound, as, for instance, jade and stones; others have sound, but are without form, such as wind and thunder; others, again, have both form and sound, such as men and animals; and lastly, there is a class devoid of both, namely, *devils and spirits.*"

[35] I have never seen any of these works, but I believe they treat, as implied by their titles, chiefly of the supernatural world.

[36] B.C. 53-A.D. 18.

[37] B.C. 13-A.D. 56.

## Martin Buber  (essay date 1911)

Introduction to *Chinese Ghost & Love Stories,* by P'u Sung-ling, Pantheon, 1946, pp. 9-13.

[*An Austrian-born Israeli religious and social thinker, Buber is highly regarded for his research of popular myths and legends and, especially, for his translations of traditional Hasidic tales. In the following excerpt from an essay originally published in 1911 as an introduction to his German translation of P'u's tales, Buber notes the engaging subject matter and fascinating supernatural figures in* Strange Stories.]

During my studies in the myths of demons and spirits, I became familiar, first through translations, and later under the friendly instruction of Mr. Chingdao Wang, with the Chinese collections of ghost stories, and particularly with the classic *Liao Chai Chih Yi.* I was especially drawn by one characteristic of the tales, not possessed to this extent in the ghostlore of any other people—the atmosphere of intimacy and concord. In these stories spirits are loved and possessed by human beings, and human beings by spirits. But the spirits who come to woo or to take possession of mortals are not Incubi and Succubi surrounded by the vaguely terrifying aura of the other world, but beings of our own experience, only born into a deeper, darker plane of existence.

In their accuracy of imagery and expression the Chinese tales remind us of the accounts of Celtic peasants of their contacts with ghosts; but here it is not the mystic vision perceived in lucid terror that becomes articulate, but natural magic operating in a familiar world. The order of Nature is not broken, its perceptible limits merely extend; the abundant flow of the life force is nowhere arrested, and all that lives bears the seed of the spirit. Not only in animals, plants, and stones does the spirit blossom forth, yearning toward a human form as a flower toward the fruit. What your hand has created longs for the breath of life and for union with living, breathing creatures; what your mind has devised becomes animated and projects itself forth into reality before your eyes. Any act of yours can beget a spirit who will henceforth enter your house as your friend, your wife or your son, and reward you according to your merits. But there is nothing uncanny in all this—it is your home, it is your life.

This people, in whom are fused Lao-tse's doctrine of the All-embracing Way and Buddha's doctrine of the All-effecting Deed, has devised in its ghost stories a song of all the congenial and loving elements, a song for gods and men.

It was the Chinese people that conceived the ghost stories in the *Liao Chai* collection. They were given poetic form by Pu Sung-ling, called by his friends "Liu-hsien, the Last of the Immortals." . . .

Wherever possible he retained the actual record of the people who reported the occurrence, though, as the uniform style of his book proves (which is still admired in China today more than that of any other modern prose work), he always retold it in his own words. . . .

The title of the book might be roughly translated thus: ***Strange Stories from the Refuge of my Study.*** And that the approximately four hundred tales truly are: very strange stories. They relate all kinds of weird and wondrous things—tales of wanderers on their travels, of the dreams of the lonely in their solitude, of singing frogs and acting mice, of sea-monsters and giant birds, of snowfall in summer, of floods and earthquakes, of rare diseases and unusual ways of dying, of travels in the land of cannibals and in the land where ugliness is taken for beauty and beauty for ugliness, of experiences in the underworld, of seeming deaths and of resurrections, of every type of magic art, of buried treasures, of alchemists and prophecies and prophetic dreams; and mingled with all this there is a wealth of satire: on prejudiced officials, unfair examination judges, ignorant doctors, deceitful priests—often described in such a way that the social conditions of the underworld are portrayed, which prove very similar to those in the world of man.

Most numerous and most significant, however, are the stories dealing with spirits—animal spirits, plant spirits, water spirits, cloud spirits, spirits living in a picture, spirits living in the eyes, departed spirits of human beings, spirits of all sorts and descriptions in their manifold relations to human beings, and primarily of the joys and dangers entailed in their love for man. For they all seek man—to play with him as with a toy or to play with him as with a friend, to punish him or to instruct him, to carouse with him or to work with him, to help him or to receive help from him, to give him a kind of love that no being of his own kind can bestow and through his love to receive the gift of life, accessible for them only through association with human beings. For the man or woman involved, this love is sometimes a menace, though often unmingled bliss; for the spirit, it always means fulfillment.

Fox spirits play a particularly important rôle in these stories. They appear in many guises, but mostly in that of a beautiful girl who approaches a man, wins his love, bears his children, runs his house for him, and by this union wins a more tangible and brighter form of existence. This strange preference for the fox has been accounted for, among other things, by the fact that in winter, when this animal crosses a frozen lake or river, he continually lowers his head to the ice and listens to the water flowing beneath it. In this way he combines the realm under the ice, the domain of Yin, the dark primeval feminine force, with the bright world of Yang, the masculine and constructive element.

### Jaroslav Prušek (essay date 1962)

"P'u Sung-ling and His Work," in *Chinese History and Literature: Collection of Studies,* D. Reidel Publishing Company, 1970, pp. 109-38.

*[A well-known Czechoslovakian scholar specializing in Oriental studies, Prušek is highly esteemed for his interpretive and investigative treatment of P'u's works and life. In 1962 he translated into his native language several selections from* Strange Stories. *In the following excerpt from his preface to this collection, Prušek places P'u's stories in their historical context, highlighting several pieces for their fusion of reality, fantasy, and satire.]*

The eighteenth century . . . appears more and more clearly to us as the dawn of a new era in Chinese literature, as a kind of ouverture to modern literature. During this time narrative prose came to occupy the dominant place in Chinese literature, while the character of this genre was undergoing a profound change.

In the seventeenth century China lived through one of the greatest popular uprisings of her whole history, led by Li Tzŭ-ch'eng: it swept away the Ming dynasty (1368-1644). The causes of this rebellion were the same as in all the uprisings that stirred the surface of Chinese history from time to time: the expansion of the great estates both in private and official hands, corruption among the officials and the ruling gentry, the breakdown of central government, etc. The rebels gained possession of Peking and the last of the Ming emperors hanged himself. The panic-stricken Chinese gentry called on the Tunguz Manchus to help, from the powerful kingdom they had established in the north-east provinces. It was the Ming general Wu San-kuei, who appears in one of P'u Sung-ling's stories **"Pao Chu"**, who sent for them, hoping that the barbarians would help him to seize the throne for himself. But the Manchus were not content to be the instrument in the hands of an ambitious general, and seized China for themselves. . . .

> **P'u's conscious attempt to serve his people through his writing brings him near to modern Chinese writers, across the abyss of the ages.**
>
> —*Jaroslav Prušek*

The greater part of the Chinese ruling class seem to have accepted this situation—and the Manchus were cruel in their repression of any expression of hostility towards themselves, particularly in literature; on the other hand it can of course be debated to what degree the critical note heard in Chinese literature from the eighteenth century onwards was due to the feeling that the whole of the traditional order had collapsed in the period immediately preceding. It is not impossible that at least those among the educated Chinese who pondered things more deeply asked themselves what had caused that vast catastrophe, and felt the urgent need to seek for the very pillars on which Chinese society stood. It is possible that some such feeling brought the great novelist Wu Ching-tzŭ to look with open eyes at his own class, to see through their hypocrisy, falsehood, grudging selfishness, dishonesty, moral sterility and narrow-minded self-satisfaction. On the other hand it is not impossible that these critical notes are the harbingers of the ultimate final crisis of the old Chinese social order which began at the end of the eighteenth century and ends with the contemporary revolution. It is of course also possible that both these series of causes are combined: on the one hand the Manchus saved and protected the old feudal order which was already profoundly shaken, but on the other hand they intensified the crisis, for they added to the existing burdens weighing down the people of China a numerous and exacting class of their own parasitic elements.

The work of P'u Sung-ling appears to open this new epoch in Chinese literature. He openly declares that his volume of tales [*Liao-chai chih-i*] is the expression of his own views and feelings, and there is a strong note of indignant social criticism running through his writing, so much so that his ideas sometimes seem to be reflecting the ideas of the broad mass of the people. In his characters P'u Sung-ling embodied many ideals which could not be realized until our own time. Finally, his conscious attempt to serve his people through his writing brings him near to modern Chinese writers, across the abyss of the ages. . . .

P'u Sung-ling, although he was probably endowed with the richest fantasy of all Chinese writers, seems to have made use of his imagination in his mind rather than in his real life, and on first acquaintance struck people most by his hesitation and awkwardness. This is the impression we get from his oldest portrait, sketched by the author of his epitaph: 'Alas! When I did not yet know the Master and had only read his works and heard how famous he was, I pictured him as an eloquent orator and brilliant debater, as a person with charming and captivating manners and behaviour, in short I imagined him an aristocrat such as had not his equal anywhere in the world. When, however, I went and was received by him, I found an old man, somewhat slow and very precise, and when he spoke it seemed as if he found difficulty in speaking, as if he could not get the words off his tongue. But when one looked into his innermost being, it was at once apparent how wide and well-founded was his knowledge and how deep and daring his spirit, and that in his heart he could find the answer to all the questions in the world.' This is clearly the portrait of a deeply reflective man, thoughtful, with a satisfying inner life, a man who did not care to reveal his soul to the world at large. How much more profoundly, then, must he have been affected by every impression which gave him no peace until he had absorbed and assimilated it. This, as we shall see, was the main principle of his art. Nor shall we neglect his pedantic precision; it explains the accuracy of his character drawing and his descriptions of the background.

Yet beneath this apparent passivity and lack of vitality there lay exceptional perseverance, energy and ardent fantasy such as the world has rarely seen. He struggled persistently against fate, attempting the state examinations up [to] the age of fifty: he was still working at seventy, as a teacher in other people's houses, travelling back and fore between his home and the place where he was employed; and at the same time he wrote his vast collection of educational and literary works. By his remarkable perseverance he managed to rise above poverty and acquire a degree of prosperity. It is not improbable that this ability to look life in the face and not give in to defeat are at the root of P'u Sung-ling's stern realism, which is at times almost naturalism—his ability to see the world as it is, without frills and without illusions, but with all its cruelties; this is the second great source of his art. His imagination conjured up pictures of unheard-of beauty, but his sharp sense of reality never allowed them to become shallow pretty-pretty lies hiding the real truth about life. No less remarkable is the firmness of his principles, in spite of all the ups and downs fate prepared for him and all the changes his life underwent; we can trace throughout his work certain principles to which he remained loyal all his life, and which were most unusual principles for his time. His serious mind is enlivened by a sense of humour and appre-

ciation of the ironic, which we feel in all his stories and with which in his poems he treated, for instance, his own old age. . . .

[At] the worst period of his life, he wrote his wonderful collection of fairy tales. It is perhaps the greatest contrast of all those that accompanied his life, for all its monotony, that these stories of such magic and beauty were written at the darkest moments of his life. He wrote the foreword to the collection, a touching cry of pain and helpless sorrow when he had been ill for a long time and perhaps even feared for his life. He seems to have looked upon his writings as the only way to achieve fame and immortalize his memory, thus outweighing to some degree the failures of his lifetime; that is why when he found himself in the deepest distress, he began to give the book its final form. . . .

As we have already suggested, P'u Sung-ling's main purpose in writing his collection of stories was probably (besides his liking for stories of the supernatural, mentioned in his foreword) his longing for fame and a great name. In a poem of 1679 he said: 'Hopeless is my lot—and the book still unwritten'. The fact that he decided to write a collection of literary stories to fulfill his ambition, however, is another and perhaps the most striking proof of his original mind. At that time scholars seeking literary fame either wrote literary essays for the state examinations, or poems, or devoted themselves to learned interpretation of the Classical Books. P'u Sung-ling's decision to write a book of stories is already a sign of the new spirit of the age, the growing interest in story-writing referred to above.

On the other hand, the scholarly environment from which he came and the training he had undergone would not allow P'u Sung-ling to forsake the traditions entirely and write in the vernacular, the language of narrative prose for a long time past and the language of such outstanding works as the "Stories of the Water Margin", *Shui-hu-chuan,* "Journey to the West", (*Hsi-yu-chi*), and many stories. In the eyes of scholars these were not literary works because they were written in 'the language of servants and coachmen'.

If P'u Sung-ling wished to write something his own circles would acknowledge, then he had to write in the old literary language. He may also have been moved by the desire to prove that he, a student who had failed to pass the examinations, could handle the instrument of the learned—the literary language—at least as well as his more successful colleagues. This is also suggested by the absolutely fantastic number of hidden allusions to classical literature to be found in the stories, for these allusions were considered the chief adornment of literary style, and a sign of literary accomplishment. . . .

For all these reasons P'u Sung-ling took up the tradition of the old Chinese story written in the classical language, and in particular the tradition of tales of the supernatural, miracles, the doings of saints and magicians, and so on. . . .

It is clear at first sight that in his stories P'u Sung-ling did not follow directly in the tradition of the T'ang stories, but that in between there lay several centuries during which the story in the vernacular developed; thanks to the professional story-tellers and some highly talented writers who wrote for the people (and probably the upper class too) this genre opened up the realm of fantasy and miraculous adventure, discovering new themes and new ways of stimulating the audience's imagination. With a few rare exceptions the T'ang story showed itself incapable of developing beyond the stage of mere chronicling of events, in which it originated, and the authors as a rule sketched merely the outline of a plot. What P'u Sung-ling learned from the creators of folk tales was primarily how to develop his theme in a subtle and involved composition; for instance, the idea of a man finding himself among insects (e.g. ants) in a dream, and experiencing various adventures there, had already been used in T'ang novels, but not one of these stories can be compared with the lovely **"Princess Lotus Bloom"**, **"Lien-hua kung-chu"**, of P'u Sung-ling, for the perfect mingling of reality and fantasy, for the wealth of detail and the subtlety of the descriptions. From this point of view P'u Sung-ling has no equal in Chinese literature, and if we take into account the poetic nature of his tales, we shall find few to equal him in the literature of the world.

Certainly the popular fiction also influenced P'u Sung-ling in his choice of certain themes. There are a number of crime stories in his collection—the equivalent of our detective stories today—a type of story which was extremely popular among the people. Such are his **"A Just Verdict"**, **"Che yü"** and **"A Poem as the Corpus Delicti"**, **"Shih-yen"**, etc. In the Sung period (960-1279) the folk story-tellers developed a type of very intricate crime story, which had all the elements of the modern detective story; since then no collection of stories in either the vernacular or the literary language would be without one. The interest in these blood-curdling tales was so great that P'u Sung-ling worked such themes even into stories which are decidedly mythological; such is the murder of the faithless wife in the story **"Ch'eng the Immortal"**, **"Ch'eng hsien"**, the head without its body in **"Judge Lu"**, **"Lu p'an"**, and elsewhere. It appears that the best way to rouse the readers' interest was by working a murder into the narrative.

As I pointed out at the beginning of this study, it was a completely new feature of the novels and romances of this period—at least as far as the work of outstanding writers was concerned—that there is a strong personal note heard in them, giving them quite a new significance. These works primarily serve a clearly personal aim, the author is trying to say something about himself, express his feelings and give his views on the world. . . . It is not at all unlikely that the form of fantastic stories appeared very suitable for saying much that he would not have dared to say in a straightforward piece of writing. On the other hand, this basically allegorical form has the disadvantage that the hints and images are fully understood only by the inner circle of the writer's friends, while later attempts to decipher such tales are always doubtful and open to the danger of arbitrary interpretation. It has helped the understanding of his book a great deal to know that for the most part it was written during the unfortunate period of his life when he was a struggling secretary and teacher, and not—as students of his work had assumed up to now—when he was living in the relative luxury of the Pi household. An immense amount of work will still be necessary, however, before we can understand many of his images, and the feelings from which various spellbinding pictures sprang we shall probably never appreciate to the full. We must be content with the beauty and colourful charm of them, although their sense is often hidden from us.

Sometimes his stories speak quite clearly. If, for example, we read carefully the description of the crimes of Doctor Tseng . . . and the punishments the author heaps on him in this world and in hell, we feel at once that this is not just a drastic literary image, but a real cry of hatred such as can only be felt by one who has suffered the consequences of such evil himself, or watched those dear to him falling victim to it. The title of the story stresses its significance even more: in the original it is called **"Continuation of the Yellow Millet"**, **"Hsü huang-liang"**, by which P'u Sung-ling made it clear that he was relating his story to the T'ang story of the "Yellow Millet". In the latter an unsuccessful scholar meets a Taoist priest who is cooking himself some millet in an inn. He complains of his lack of success, and the priest lends him a pillow; the moment he puts his head on this pillow the scholar falls asleep and in his dreams lives through all the ups and downs of an official career. He is completely cured of his ambitions, and when he wakes up he sees that the millet is still not cooked. In the original story it is a general theme, the vanity of human ambition and longing for an imposing career. P'u Sung-ling's story has a definite target: it is a passionate expression of hatred, and harking back to the older story only makes his purpose stand out more. Was P'u Sung-ling thinking of any one person, so that his contemporaries would see his intention quite clearly, or was he attacking all evil officials who made life a purgatory and often a hell for those they had to deal with? This we unfortunately cannot know.

Noteworthy in this story, too, is the terrible picture of the life of the women. Yet not even this is invented; frequent references in literature show that the burning of women on the most sensitive parts of their bodies was a common punishment.

The author's views are equally clear when he describes the pompous, arrogant and heartless rich who figure in many of his stories. We can see from them what his own experiences must have been, dependent as he was for years on people of this type. . . . P'u Sung-ling's stories are full of such cruel rich and powerful criminals among the upper class; this makes his work a far sharper social satire than the famous "Chronicle of Scholars" by Wu Ching-tzŭ. What is particularly amazing is the breadth of his observation: he penetrates the furthest corners of life, bringing to the light of day all the many parasites and tyrants, presenting them in one guise after another. It may be the rich man robbing the poor man of his only treasure just for the fun of it, in the **"Stone from Heaven"**, **"Shih Ch'ing-hsü"**: or the greed of those who open a coal-mine near a burial ground but leave the victims of their thirst for wealth unburied, in **"Minister Dragon's Flight"**, **"Lung-fei hsiang kung"**: (in this story, incidentally, we are given the first glimpse of coal miners in Chinese literature). Or there is the mad prince who throws away a fortune for a fighting quail in **"Wang Ch'eng"** P'u Sung-ling probably reached the highest point of his literary achievement in the story **"The Cricket"**, **"Tsu-chih"**: the miraculous element serves to create a magic atmosphere, but it is nevertheless one of the most realistic pictures of the misery of the Chinese people to be found in the whole of the country's older literature.

With the help of this story we can also consider the question of P'u Sung-ling's political attitude. There is no doubt that the social criticism running through this story confirms . . . P'u Sung-ling's deep feeling of bonds with the common people: he saw life through the eyes of the broad mass of the peasantry and turned his hatred and his irony on those who exploited and oppressed them. The two stories we have just been considering, **"The Cricket"** and **"Wang Ch'eng"** may also suggest what the author's attitude was to the immense change that occurred in the country during his own childhood, when the Ming dynasty was replaced by the Manchus. Many of the older interpreters of his work were convinced that P'u Sung-ling revealed in it a strong anti-Manchu attitude. I do not feel that the material so far known to me lends any support to this interpretation, nor is it even probable. The Manchus would have seen to it that both the author and his work disappeared if it had revealed even the slightest hint of opposition to their rule. In such cases the literary inquisition liquidated not a few authors, and usually their whole families as well. In fact we can find in P'u Sung-ling's work proof that he regarded those who took part in fighting against the Manchus with scorn—in the story **"Rebel Families"**, **"Tao-hu"**, for instance. All through his life P'u Sung-ling wanted to pass the state examinations, which means that he had no objections to serving the new dynasty, and at his death his papers included a large number of practice pieces for the examinations, addressed to the ruling dynasty.

The two stories we are considering (for it seems that **"Wang Ch'eng"** is also set in the Ming period) show that P'u Sung-ling regarded the Ming dynasty as corrupt and inefficient rulers whose conduct of affairs brought about the great rebellion, so that the gentry could see in the Manchu dynasty rulers who would restore order to the country.

The most important fact to bear in mind, however, is that for the broad masses of the peasants it did not matter so much who was on the throne, but primarily what sort of people they had immediately above them, what sort of people enjoyed wealth and power—even though naturally the character of these men was often influenced by the character of the central government. The interests of the general run of the people, however, were primarily social, and their content or discontent depended on their relations with the whole of the ruling class, on the situation all along the line where their lives came into contact with the wealthy and the officials. And as far as this aspect goes, P'u Sung-ling clearly expressed the views of the broad masses of the people; it is here that the progressive character of his work is apparent, and not in his attitude to the dynasty alone. When P'u Sung-ling stood out against those who were oppressing the people, he was standing out against the whole class of exploiters, and there was no need for him to specify individual elements in that class. It was the same whether the dynasty was a Chinese one or a foreign one, and in addition the mythological atmosphere of his stories permitted the widest possible interpretation and their lesson could be applied to all similar cases. There is a certain parallel to the fact that secret Chinese sects and societies organized revolts both under the Chinese and under the barbarian dynasties. On the other hand, we must stress that P'u Sung-ling did not and could not have developed a revolutionary standpoint. The time was not favourable to such a development, nor the society in which he lived—let us not forget that he belonged to the educated class, as we have said above. He cannot propose more than the age-old solution: replace the bad officials by honest ones and everything will be put right. That is why his criticism is directed at individuals, and he describes good officials and good rich men as well as evil ones. . . .

It is not only in his attacks on evil officials and wicked rich men and all their works that P'u Sung-ling shows himself a man of the people; the whole current of his work is such, the very thing that makes his stories stand out in Chinese literature as a whole—their fairy-tale quality. . . . [It] is in the way he looked at the world, the way every incident became a fairy-tale in his mind, the way everything he imagined came to life, the way the frontiers between the world of man and the world of other creatures of nature disappeared, the way he hinted at something mysterious behind every apparently natural and simple phenomenon, the way he flooded the whole of life with an air of inexplicable but unlimited possibilities, that he came closest to the world of the peasants of his day; in this he gave us a clear insight into the psychology and attitudes of the masses of common people in his day. This is pointed out by Ho Man-tzŭ, the author of an excellent study in Chinese on the work of P'u Sung-ling; he explains in this way the fact that although written in the literary language, the works of P'u Sung-ling found their way to the common reader and became extremely popular. . . .

For the people of the feudal age supernatural beings were often the only way of explaining the forces and processes that constantly threatened them; their belief in the supernatural made the real cruel world more human and brought incidentally a ray of hope into it. Their faith was often a comfort, the belief that somewhere, even if not until after death, justice would be done and evil punished, or that somewhere there were people endowed with super-human strength and powers who could avenge the victims of injustice. It is in this type of story that P'u Sung-ling comes closest to the imagination of folklore, as when he invented the figure of a king-avenger endowed with mysterious supernatural powers, living somewhere in the wild hills, in the story **"The Royal Man"**, **"Wang-che"**, or when he gave new form to the legends of wandering knights avenging the innocent victims. It tells us much of P'u Sung-ling's view of women that he turned the traditional knight-avenger into a woman, giving us a most convincing portrait of her in the story **"The Heroine"**, **"Hsieh-nü"**. . . .

It would of course be misunderstanding P'u Sung-ling's intentions and an absolute caricature of his work, to take literally the themes he adopted from religious mythology whether Taoist or Buddhist, and to seek naive religious faith in them. For him the mythological view of the world, the fairy-tale atmosphere, the supernatural and the miraculous are purely artistic means, ways of dealing with reality and presenting it to the reader, and not an expression of faith or even its propagation. . . .

The fantastic element also enabled P'u Sung-ling to give more effective expression to his ideas; the only concept which could be invoked against that of despotic rule, for example, was that of the bandits in the hills. They were significant, though, only in times of social breakdown; under such rulers as the first of the Manchus, the bandits were no more than brigands and robbers on occasion. What P'u Sung-ling set up in contrast to his omnipotent officials was a vision—a mysterious king in the mountains, ruling not only with many subjects, but with magical means. A certain social fact thus grew in the author's imagination to gigantic proportions, and acquired the ability to serve a general purpose.

Endowing a certain phenomenon with universal proportions is one of the most effective satirical weapons of P'u Sung-ling, enabling him to express to perfection the general validity and the terrible implications of a given social fact. One of the commonest themes used by bourgeois critical realists in Chinese literature at the beginning of this century, for instance, is the corruption, greed and arrogance of officials; their works are full of dozens and hundreds of anecdotes showing the incredible corruption of government officials. Yet all these instances taken together cannot equal in their power one single story by P'u Sung-ling, **"Kung-sun Hsia"**, because each is concerned with a detail which can always be shrugged off with the excuse that it is nothing of general validity but a biassed and distorted report. P'u Sung-ling maliciously shows that corruption is a widespread evil, which is even current in the underworld. At the same time he makes the god of war himself, Kuan-ti, punish the corrupt seeker after office. In this way he puts a specific fact before his readers as a general typical phenomenon, which is the purpose of every great artist. . . .

Fantasy was probably often called upon to supply what life itself could not give. There was little place in Chinese life of that time, for instance, for love; marriage was arranged by the parents and nobody cared what the young people felt about it—indeed, they often met for the first time on their wedding night. Besides these forced marriages, which were simply taken as a duty, there existed prostitution, or the husband could take a concubine—but

this was always a question of money and never of love. A writer like P'u Sung-ling who wanted to describe the beauties of love and write a story about real lovers was forced to include in his world beings not bound by the bonds of convention. This was certainly one of the reasons why love stories almost always contained some mythological elements, as in the earlier T'ang stories. Since however the emotion P'u Sung-ling is describing is that of natural love, his love stories are truer than the sentimental tales within the bounds of feudal convention, although the actors in the former are foxes, vampires and other supernatural beings. His enchanting love stories like [**"Miss Chiao-no"**, **"Ying-ning"**, and **"Nieh Hsiao-ch'ien"**] present a convincing picture seen through an artist's eyes, the vision of a new and different world in which women would no longer be the oppressed suffering creatures of his day and where free and happy love between two equal partners would be possible, unfettered by the inequalities of feudalism and its cruel conventions. . . .

P'u Sung-ling seeks in his visionary scenes the antidote to all the evil and misery he saw in the life around him. In contrast to the cruelty and greed of his world he described self-sacrificing friendship, as in **"Ch'eng the Immortal"** and passionate enthusiasm for beauty and beautiful things as in **"Miss Huan-niang"** and there can be no doubt that the author achieved a profound didactic effect through these visions. In [**"The Heroine"**] P'u Sung-ling even gave a foretaste of the image of those Chinese women who dedicated their whole lives to revenge (avenging their nation, not themselves), and who became the most passionate fighters for the revolution. . . .

P'u Sung-ling's extremely fertile imagination enabled him to think up such surprising fantasies that we are amazed every time that he could still think of a new original plot. Naturally in his immense collection of 445 stories, (with those recently discovered the total will be about 500), there are subjects which are related to each other. Nor have the majority of the stories the perfect story form of those normally translated for publication in European selections. A large part of his tales are merely notes of strange events which do not differ much from thousands of such notes in the *pi-chi,* the notebooks, of Chinese scholars, a very popular literary form. Two instances of this unfinished form are e.g. the stories of animal performers, **"The Frog Song"**, **"Wa-ch'ü"**, and the **"Mouse Performance"**, **"Shu-hsi"**. These notes also suggest that P'u Sung-ling probably drew much of his material for his stories from the tales told by his contemporaries to which he refers in his Foreword and in the notes to various stories.

Some of the stories, however, are in a very finished form and probably show the highest point reached by the Chinese novella in the old literature. For the most part P'u Sung-ling preserves the old classical form of short story in which the hero is introduced at the beginning and the plot unfolds in chronological order. The form probably developed from the historical biographies. This is nothing new, but P'u Sung-ling limits his narration to one main episode or several important incidents, and suppresses all irrelevant detail. He carries to the utmost the principle of brevity and economy which was always the aim of the classical, as contrasted with the popular, literature. A few lines are enough to present the background and create the atmosphere in a masterly way. These enchanting sketches undoubtedly show the influence of Chinese lyric poetry in which writers for thousands of years endeavoured to evoke their images as effectively and as briefly as possible.

Up to recent times there have rarely been novellas in China, in the European sense of the word, that is to say narratives concerned with a single psychological situation, in which all the elements are parts of a single whole. Many of P'u Sung-ling's stories, for example, could easily be expanded and even made into complete novels, by the insertion of extra episodes. Nevertheless the economy of his writing brings his stories close to the finest European short stories on another plane. The style also corresponds to the same principle of economy in the structure of the story; the style is indeed the culmination of a thousand years' development of the written language in China. . . .

Chinese critics have emphasized the conflict between the realist tendency of P'u Sung-ling's stories and the highly artificial style in which they are written, which forced the author to pay more attention to his choice of words and the order in which he used them than to the accurate depiction of his subject. P'u Sung-ling was also the last writer with the genius to create a great literary work in this classical style, and he succeeded because he began to write stories instead of literary essays. All that was written afterwards in the classical language, absorbing the energy and infinite patience of generations of scholars, has little greater value than schoolroom essays for us. Nor have any of the imitators of P'u Sung-ling, of whom there were many up to the time of the literary revolution, ever been more than average in achievement. P'u Sung-ling's work brings to a close the thousand years' development of Chinese literature in the classical language.

It is also possible that P'u Sung-ling himself felt the instrument he was using to be dead and blunt, although he tried to sharpen it to perfection; this may be why in the second half of his life, in particular, he began to write in the vernacular as well. He composed eighteen long narrative songs and theatrical plays, partly by working over subjects and stories from his own collection. This extensive body of works intended for the common reader, or rather listener, is a major work of art and testifies to the genuine affection for the common people which we have already referred to in P'u Sung-ling's character. It is characteristic of the firmness of his convictions that in these works, which must for the most part have been written in the Pi household, the note of social criticism is even sharper than in the stories. . . .

Another proof of P'u Sung-ling's close bonds with the people is to be found in his extensive popular didactic works, which probably date from the same period. He wrote on each of the basic aspects of life important for the peasants: on morality, which in the Confucian system of thought was the backbone of society: on the calendar, according to which the peasant's work must be organised;

on weddings, which assured the continuity of the race; on the vulgar characters necessary for the peasant to deal with the simplest of written matters; on agriculture and on silk-worm rearing, the basis of life for most of the Chinese; and finally on means to overcome or palliate pain and sickness. Taken all round it is a remarkably compact and well-balanced outline of knowledge needed by everyone, and the most important point is that these writings (as the author repeatedly stressed in his Forewords) were intended for the common people. . . .

I feel that this thought for the needs of the simple people is the most eloquent testimony of all to the character of this great Chinese writer of fairytales living in the eighteenth century. Studying his work constantly brings to mind the figure of Božena Němcová, the Czech writer of the revival period in the nineteenth century, who was so like him not only in the fairytales she wrote, but in her affection for the simple people too.

## Chun-shu Chang and Hsueh-lun Chang (essay date 1980)

"P'u Sung-ling and His 'Liao-chai Chih-I'—Literary Imagination and Intellectual Consciousness in Early Ch'ing China," in *Renditions,* Vol. 13, Spring, 1980, pp. 60-81.

[*In the following essay, the critics provide a thematic overview of P'u's* Liaozhai zhiyi.]

I

One of the major tasks of an historian is the search for and depiction of the spirit of an age. But the spirit of an age is forever elusive and tantalizing. This is particularly so if the historian follows only the traditional politico-socio-economic approach in his research and analysis. The gist of the spirit of an age is what Raymond Williams has called "the structure of feeling" and it is nowhere more manifest than in the imaginative literature of an age. Therefore, unless an historian uses literary works as one of the major sources in his studies, he never feels the presence of a "living" age in his mind, and hence misses a critical part of his understanding of the age under study. Through the ideas, emotions, and imaginations of creative literature one feels the spirit of an age unfolding in front of his eyes. Furthermore, the conditions, values, aspirations, and consciousness of a society can become alive again through the fiction and drama of an era.

The age of the Ming-Ch'ing dynastic transition, during the mid and late seventeenth century, is a good example of the need for this type of study. Our comprehension and appreciation of this critical age in Chinese history would be far from complete and, in fact, greatly hindered, without a thorough understanding of the rich fiction and dramatic writings of that era. Our venture on the short stories by P'u Sung-ling (1640-1715), in a collection entitled *Liao-chai chih-i* (Tales of the Unusual from the Leisure Studio), is intended to illustrate this point.

Among the popular literary works of the early Ch'ing period, P'u Sung-ling's **Liao-chai chih-i** is one of the most widely read. Its main manuscript was completed in 1679, but for many decades this collection of short stories was circulated in manuscript form only. Not until 1766 was it first printed and published. Within a short period it gained a wide circulation in imperial China. Since then, as its English translator Herbert Giles rightly pointed out, it has been as familiar throughout the length and breadth of China as have the tales of *The Arabian Nights* in all English-speaking communities [Introduction to *Strange Stories from a Chinese Studio*, 1929]. "Almost in every household there is a volume of this collection," recorded one Chinese writer in the middle of the nineteenth century. Even Chi Yün (1724-1805), the chief editor of the great *Complete Library of the Four Treasuries* (*Ssu-k'u ch'üanshu*), recognized the literary power of the **Liao-chai chih-i,** although he did not approve of its writing style [*Yüeh-wei ts'ao-t'ang pi-chi,* 1934].

The **Liao-chai chih-i** is the best-written collection of short stories from the early Ch'ing period. In its traditional popular edition, the collection includes 431 short stories, many of which are ghost stories, fox-fairies, and other fantasies that make the outlook of the book very much similar to the tales of *The Arabian Nights*. However, it is of a much more serious nature. The author makes it rather plain in his preface that he wrote the book for the purpose of venting his excited feelings of distress and frustration. What we gather from reading these stories are the author's strong feelings toward the injustices of his day. Many tales in the book, beneath the cover of ghosts and fairies, actually aim at attacking, exposing, and satirizing the society of his time. Yet, at the same time, other stories conform with the established values of the society. Their contradiction in ideas appears throughout the book. To obtain a better understanding of such a book, the author's social and family background should first be taken into consideration.

P'u Sung-ling, a native of Tzu-ch'uan District of Shantung, was born into a once-prosperous landlord-merchant family. Scholars have long suggested that P'u's ancestors were not Chinese, and that he may have been descended from P'u Shoukeng—the famous Arab who served both the Sung and the Yüan dynasties and accumulated incredible wealth in the thirteenth century—or from Turkish or Mongol peoples. Recent studies have demonstrably proved that P'u's ancestry was Islamic. However, no records of P'u Sung-ling's days indicate that members of the P'u clan were then still Moslems. P'u Sung-ling's own account of his family background reads, in part, as follows:

> My father P'u Min-wu showed talent in his youth and was fond of study; he followed T'ao and Teng in his literary style but failed to pass the first-degree examination. As the family was poor, he gave up study and went in for trade; and in about twenty years became well off. But when he was over forty and had no son, he stopped trying to make money and stayed at home to study, never leaving his books, so that even well-learned scholars could no longer equal the erudition and depth of his scholarship. He helped the poor,

contributed to the building of temples, and neglected his own estates. Then his first wife gave birth to three sons, his second wife to one; and when they reached their teens he taught them himself. Since there were many mouths to feed and little money coming in, however, our family gradually grew poor.

["Shu Liu-shih hsing-shih," *P'u Sung-ling chi,*
ed. by Lu Ta-huang, 1962]

P'u's family lived near the eastern coast, where commerce had been highly developed since ancient times, and his father had engaged in trade; P'u was naturally influenced by this urban background. Many heroes and heroines in his stories are merchants and prostitutes, and he did not show any of the traditional Confucian disrespect for them. On the other hand, when P'u Sung-ling was born, his father had already retired from urban life and was living as a country squire. His father was fond of study; the fact that he failed to obtain any degree must have been a life-long regret for him. And he taught his sons to study. All his life P'u Sung-ling, a holder of an elementary degree, was haunted by the desire to be successful through the imperial examination system.

The combination of merchant-landlord family background and varied ideological orientations is one of the key factors that cause a sharp conflict of ideas in P'u Sung-ling's writing. For example, there is the conflict between free marriages and the traditional marriages arranged by parents through the medium of go-betweens; the conflict between ideas of fatalism and ideas of retribution; the conflict between his hatred for the examination system and his helpless longing for position and wealth through this system; the conflict between individualism and conformism; and the conflict between Confucianism and Taoism.

The life of P'u Sung-ling can be summed up with a simple description: he lived a poor and frustrated man. Many of his poems describe or reflect his extremely poor living conditions. As an unsuccessful scholar who obtained only the elementary degree, he made his living as a private tutor all his life, except for one period in 1670-1671 when he was an invited guest and private secratary. When he was an old man, his son wrote about him: "My father is now seventy-four; only in the recent four years has he not taught as a private tutor" [*P'u Sung-ling chi*]. The life of a private tutor was lonely and boring; the income was small; and he had to be separated from his family most of the time. P'u Sung-ling once wrote a long satirical drumsong (*ku-tz'u*) to describe the life of a private tutor and concluded it with "If I could have any choice, I would not want to be the master of children" [*P'u Sung-ling chi*]. But fortune never fell upon him, and year after year he failed in all higher (provincial) examinations, after being granted the first degree at the age of nineteen. The lonely life of a private tutor and his frustration at failing examinations led him to commit his thoughts to writing. His voluminous writings include not only his famous short stories—represented by the celebrated collection **Liao-chai chih-i**—but also a considerable variety of other works:

volumes of classical poems and lyrics, and essays of more than sixteen forms; three musical plays; six drum-songs and fourteen narrative folksongs (*li-ch'ü*); extensive popular instructions on almost all basic aspects of daily country life—such as rites, rituals, morality, calendar, wedding customs, popular worship, medicine, plants and animals, agriculture, and silkworm rearing; learned commentaries on religious matters (Taoism, Buddhism, popular beliefs); discussions on the colloquial usage of the Chinese language; and so forth. However, of all these works, only the ***Liao-chai chih-i*** has brought P'u Sung-ling fame and popularity. The rest received little attention until recent time. Some of them still remained in hand-copied manuscript form at the time of their discovery; some were represented only by their short prefaces; and some, except for their titles, were completely lost. But the fact that P'u Sung-ling was such a productive, versatile writer and scholar provides us with new insights into his mind. He was a man of broad interests and knowledge, a scholar of admirable erudition. An examination of his writings reveals a remarkable range of intellectual pursuits: literature, classics, biographies, politics, history, social customs, folklore, law, language, philosophy, technology, science, medicine, and religion.

Although P'u Sung-ling was ahead of his time in many of his ideas, particularly his conscious use of various types of colloquial literature for expressing his moral, social, and political ideas, he was also conditioned by the prevailing ideals and values of his time. He spent much of his time writing the so-called "Pretended Memorials" (*i-piao*)—memorials to the throne that were written in the name of high-ranking officials but never made known to the emperor or the officials. These memorials, altogether seventy-nine, constitute a noticeable portion of P'u's writings. But, written in stock style, as a whole they demonstrate nothing but his feverish longing for official position and success. Some of P'u's narrative folksongs and short stories also show his constant indulgence in pornographic subjects and details. It seems clear that P'u Sung-ling was typical of the frustrated intellectuals who were searching with all their intellectual resources for the relevance and meaning of their life in a trying age of dynastic transition.

P'u Sung-ling's times made a significant impact upon him and his works. P'u belonged to the first generation under the new Manchu regime. He was born in 1640, four years before the Manchu conquest, and grew up in the turbulent period when the Ming resistance force were still active in South China. However, in 1659, the last Southern Ming remnant regime in South China under Emperor Yung-li (1646-1659) was driven out to Burma by the Ch'ing forces, and the last strong Southern Ming loyalist forces under Cheng Ch'eng-kung (Koxinga, 1624-1662) and Chang Huang-yen (1620-1664) suffered disastrous defeat by the Manchu armies. With these defeats, the hope of restoring the Ming regime was gone forever. It was just the year before that P'u, at nineteen, participated in the district examination and won distinction. Also about this time, P'u started to write the short stories that were to be put into a collection later named ***Liao-chai chih-i.*** The main manuscript of the ***Liao-chai*** was completed in 1679. Thus

the creative period of the book lies in the twenty years from about 1660 to 1679. The period itself is an important factor in the creation of the ***Liao-chai.*** It was a period characterized by a tense political atmosphere within the Chinese empire, before the Manchu's high-handed policy changed to one of appeasement of defiant Chinese scholars, as expressed by the special *Po-hsüeh hung-tz'u* examination in 1679. The newly established regime still faced various resistance forces and rebellions. Under the circumstances, being much more sensitive to and conscious of its alien rule, the court launched a literary inquisition and persecution of Chinese scholars, as in the cases of Chuang T'ing-lung and Chuang T'ing-yüeh in 1661-1663, Chin Sheng-t'an in 1661, Shen T'ien-fu and Lü Chung and Hsia Lin-ch'i in 1667; as a result, hundreds of scholars were killed. This "reign of terror" overshadowed the academic world for a long, long time. Under such circumstances, it was natural for men of letters to retreat to a world of fantasy to express their realistic feelings through an imaginative world of ghosts and fairies.

Although we are not writing a literary history and do not propose to give an intrinsic treatment in an artistic sense, we should point out that the literary style of the short stories of the ***Liao-chai*** follows a combination of the styles of *chih-kuai* stories of the Six Dynasties (220-589) and *ch'uan-ch'i* tales of the T'ang period (618-907). Only in the ***Liao-chai*** did the artistic and thematic achievements reach their maturity, compared with similar attempts of earlier periods—such as the Ming dynasty Ch'ü Yu (1341-1427)'s *Chien-teng hsin-hua* (New Tales of Wick-trimming Hours), which influenced the writing of the ***Liao-chai.*** It also should be noted here that the romantic spirit of P'u Sung-ling, as well as those of his contemporary dramatists, such as Hung Sheng (1645-1704) and K'ung Shang-jen (1648-1718), were influenced by the romantic movement of the late Ming, called the movement of "ardent Zen" (*k'uang-Ch'an yun-tung*). The impact of this movement upon the popular literature as a whole is seen in two characteristics, individualism and sentimentalism. The individualism, as represented by Li Chih (1527-1602) and others, provoked general reaction among scholars who were strongly opposed to the threat of moral and social anarchy in Li Chih's thought; however, in the world of letters its romantic spirit satisfied the individual writer's yearning for freedom in pursuing a happier life. The sentimentalism, with its emphasis on love as the most essential element in life, is represented by the dramatist T'ang Hsien-tsu (1550-1617), under whose influence the style of Ming drama passed on to Hung Sheng and K'ung Shang-jen in the Ch'ing period.

The outlook of the ***Liao-chai*** is, as Lu Hsün once pointed out, a collection of strange stories. The strange stories at the end of the Ming dynasty are usually so brief and absurd that they seem incredible. But the stories of the ***Liao-chai*** contain such detailed descriptions and normal incidents that even flower-spirits and fox-fairies appear humane and approachable. Yet, just as we forget that they are not human beings, the author introduces some peculiar happenings to remind us that they are supernatural after all.

Among the short stories in the **Liao-chai,** the largest portion consists of love stories. If we try to group the rest of the collection according to their themes, they can be divided into three major categories: stories that exposed the corruptions of the bureaucracy; stories intended chiefly as a satire upon the civil service examination system and upon the scholarship of the age as a whole; and stories that reflected the anti-Manchu feelings of the Chinese people. Of course, some of the stories are for other purposes or merely for amusement, such as some ghost stories that emphasize only the thrill of horror. Since it is not our intention to give an intrinsic treatment of the writing in an artistic sense, we shall examine in this study the stories according to the four major themes that represent the author's thought: love, bureaucratic corruption, scholarship and the examination system, and anti-Manchu sentiments.

## II

The love stories in the **Liao-chai** are very colorful; they reveal a world of fantasies in which love becomes the symbol of passion, and outruns time and space. Some of the love stories deal strictly with mortals—men and women. Others deal with men and ghosts, men and goddesses, men and fox-fairies, or men and the spirits of insects, birds, flowers, and trees. The reason for the existence of this fantastic world is obvious. The author realized that in the real life of the traditional society, true love between men and women was so rare and so hard to find that he had to create another world to satisfy his yearning for happiness. However, the author never forgot the reality; he used these incredible romances to depict real human society.

As pointed out before, under the influence of the romantic movement of the late Ming, the author created his heroes and heroines as rebels, somewhat defiant of convention and alienated from their society. They represented the author's protest against the social ethics of his day. One of P'u's characteristic protest is his concept of feminity. Protesting against the prevailing idea of "A woman without talent is a woman of virtue," the author embodies his heroines with so much wisdom, courage, talent and wit that they sometimes surpass the men in the stories. In the story of **"Yen Shih"** (The Daughter of the Yen Family), the young woman whose husband was frustrated by constant failures in the civil service examinations disguised herself as a man and took the examinations. She succeeded in all examinations and finally won the highest degree, *chin-shih* (doctor). There are many talented girls in the world of the **Liao-chai**: the expert surgeon Miss Chiao-nu in the story of **"Chiao-nu"**; the learned sisters in the story of **"Hsien-jen tao"** (The Island of Fairies); the maiden poet Hsiang-yü in the story of **"Hsiang-yü"** (The Flower Maiden Hsiang-yü); and the expert lady fencer in the story of **"Hsia-nü"** (The Lady Knight-errant), to name only a few.

Another important aspect of these love stories is the author's emphasis on devotion. There are many love stories in which the heroes are faithful to their beloved: the honest and devoted scholar, Feng, in the story of **"Hsin Shih-ssu niang"** (Hsin Shih-ssu Niang, the Fox-lady); the foolish lover, Sun Tzu-ch'u, in the story of **"A-pao"** (Miss A-pao); the faithful scholar, Huang, in the story of **"Hsiang-yü"**; the book worm, Lang Yü-chu, in the story of **"Shu-chih"** (The Bookworm); the brilliant and affectionate young scholar, Wang Tzu-fu, in the story of **"Ying-ning"** (Ying-ning, the Laughing Girl), and so on.

> **Many tales in the book, beneath the cover of ghosts and fairies, actually aim at attacking, exposing, and satirizing the society of his time. Yet, at the same time, other stories conform with the established values of the society.**
>
> —*Chun-shu Chang and Hsueh-lun Chang*

On the other hand, the heroines in these love stories show not only deep devotion but also courage and endurance. The story of **"Ya-t'ou"** (Ya-t'ou, the Faithful Girl) is a good example. In the story, a young girl, Ya-t'ou, falls in love at first sight with a poor scholar, Wang Wen. But Ya-t'ou's mother is a greedy woman who wants Ya-t'ou to become a prostitute to make money. The two young lovers elope to another town and make an honest living by keeping a small shop, but the mother later finds out where Ya-t'ou lives and forces her to come home. To separate the two young lovers, the mother moves the family north and demands that Ya-t'ou to change her mind. Ya-t'ou refuses, and is beaten almost to death. She is asked again and again, and she refuses repeatedly; each time she refuses, she suffers a more severe punishment. But nothing can change her deep devotion for Wang Wen. Finally, her mother gives up and imprisons her. Only after eighteen years of separation do the two lovers finally have a happy reunion.

Another typical love story is **"Hsiang-yü."** In this story, the heroine is a beautiful maiden transformed from the spirit of a flower, a white peony, that grows in the courtyard of a temple. Her lover, the scholar Huang, happens to live in a nearby cottage. They meet and fall in love. One day the white peony is picked by a traveller who passes by the temple, and as a result, the flower maiden Hsiang-yü also dies. Huang mourns over her death so sincerely that he at last moves the Flower Goddess, who then allows the spirit of the white peony to revive. It takes Huang one year to water and take good care of the peony plant before its spirit finally is embodied again as Hsiang-yü.

The theme of this story is very simple; yet the author recounts it in such an exuberant, concise, and classic style that it delights its readers as a true story. Moreover, it also carries a message to the readers: If one concentrates one's emotion, one can reach the spiritual essence of things; the spirit of flowers can thus be related to the soul of man.

In the story of **"A-pao,"** the hero is A-pao's foolish lover, Sun. Sun is so crazy about A-pao that he cuts off one of his fingers when he is told that she wants him to do so. A man of extremely simple nature, Sun always readily believes in people and does what he is told. After he has done a number of crazy things, he finally wins the girl's heart. The author is so sympathetic with this simple but honest man that at the end of the story he makes the following comment:

> Only those who are crazy have both the will and the perseverance that are necessary to succeed in life. Whoever is crazy about writing may become a successful writer; whoever is crazy about art may become a successful artist. Only the unsuccessful are not crazy at all!

This belief in "craziness' actually represents the force behind the author's drive towards imaginative writing. It is manifested not only in the "crazy" devotion of the love stories, but also in extreme devotion to objects in other stories in the *Liao-chai.* For example, in the story of the crazy bookworm, **"Shu-chih,"** the poor scholar loves his books to the point of being crazy about them, and then becomes crazy to the point of being bewitched by them. Nevertheless, the author's sympathy with this crazy bookworm is obvious; he arranges a happy development for him by having a beauty from a book conduct an incredible romance with him. Another example of this lies in the story of the stone-lover of **"Shih Ch'ing-hsü"** (A Stone from Heaven). The story is about a man who is so crazy about a piece of strange stone that he chooses to die for it rather than part with it. The strange stone returns its master's affection by crushing itself into a hundred pieces rather than ailowing itself to be taken away from its master. Here again, the message is identical to the one in the story of the Flower Maiden.

Not only flowers and stones have "love and affection." Animals, such as birds, also have it. In the story of **"Ko-yi"** (The Strange Dove), the man who is fond of doves one day receives a pair of unusually beautiful white doves from the fairy of the doves. After two years, this pair of white doves gives birth to six doves. One day a high-ranking official visits this man and admires his doves. To please this high-ranking official, the man gives him two white doves as a precious present. But the official, who has no fondness for doves, turns them over to the cook and then eats them. As a punishment for this man's betrayal of their trust, the rest of the white doves leave him and fly away. The message is that love should be perfect; anything less than perfect love is unacceptable. The doves stayed with the man only because the man loved them; once they found that the man treated them as less than a devoted friend, they left him forever.

Similiar search for perfection is seen in the creation of the many idealized heroines in the *Liao-chai.* There is a remarkable contrast here between the real and the ideal. In reality, the women in the traditional society were pitiable.

Submitted to the ideology of male supremacy, they were weak and incapable of taking care of themselves, both mentally and physically. In addition the women, who lived in a large, compound family, tended to be tricky, jealous, and quarrelsome; they fought with each other to win the favor of their men. In the idealistic world the heroines were strong and talented; they were simple, charming, passionate, and courageous; they dared to defy their parents and their society with the great courage to face their fate. The aboved-mentioned Ya-t'ou in the story of **"Ya-t'ou"** is an example. In the story of **"Ying-ning,"** the sunny character of the irresistible Ying-ning gives another unforgettable example: she is pure and innocent, witty and full of life, and her lovely face that beams with laughter all the time makes people forget about all their worries. In a word, Ying-ning represents everything opposite to the traditional image of a girl.

One may say that in the world of *Liao-chai,* most of the heroines were girls transformed from goddesses, fox-fairies, and ghosts, and thus it was much easier for them to be brave and independent. But is it not exactly because the author was dissatisfied with the real human situation that he himself escaped to the loving world of fantasy?

### III

The second category of stories includes those that expose the corruption and injustice of the bureaucracy. The most explicit example is the story of **"Meng-lang"** (A Dream of Wolves). The story is about an old man who has a bad dream about his older son, a magistrate of a distant district. In his dream, the old father visits his son's *yamen* and finds that it is thronged within and without by wolves, some sitting and some lying, while a great heap of white bones is piled in the courtyard. Then the old man sees his son changed into a tiger hounded by two warriors in gilded mail. Awake and worried, the old man sends his second son to visit his older brother. The younger brother goes to see the magistrate brother and stays with him for a few days; in the magistrate's *yamen,* he sees nothing but corruptive runners and bribe-givers who stream in from morning till night. The younger brother begs the magistrate with tears to mend his way, but is only scoffed at by the latter, who says, "What do you know of official life? Promotion depends upon a man's superiors and not upon the people. If your superiors approve of you, you are a good official; but if you love the people, how can you please those above you?" Unable to persuade the magistrate, the younger brother returns to tell his father about all that has occurred. Soon, news comes that the magistrate has been promoted to a post in the Ministry of Civil Officials. Before long, it is reported that the older brother, the former magistrate, has been killed by robbers on his way to his new post. It is also reported that before his head was cut off, the former magistrate begged the robbers for his life but the robbers said: "We are here to avenge the wrongs of the people of the whole district, not just to take your money."

The theme of this story is very clear, as the author commented on it at the end of the story: Many officials in this world are tigers, and their subordinates wolves. Even if an official is not a tiger, his subordinates may be wolves; and some officials are worse than tigers.

If the story of **"A Dream of Wolves"** symbolizes hatred for corrupt officials, a similar theme is fully elaborated in a remarkable short satire, **"Ts'u-chih"** (The Cricket)—officials only try to please their superiors and never care about the people. In this story, the crickets become favorite pets in the palace, for the royal family likes to watch them fighting with each other. To please the royalty, all the officials in the empire send their running-dogs to the countryside to look for strong crickets that can fight bravely. Thus the tribute of crickets becomes a ladder to success in the officialdom. In the story, Ch'en Ming's rise from obscurity shows how a cricket can affect a man's destiny. As a poor and unsuccessful scholar, before he finds the right cricket, he is scolded, beaten and extorted by local petty officials. But after he finds the right cricket, fortune smiles on him and everything comes his way. The right cricket makes him a rich and powerful official. Here P'u Sung-ling clearly says that in the eyes of officials, the lives of people are worth less than the life of a cricket.

In the story of **"Han Fang"** the author satirizes officials who use every pretext to rob the people, just as he narrates how ghosts extort money from the people while on their way to hell. In the story, Han Fang's parents are very sick; as a poor farmer, Han can do nothing but go to a nearby temple to pray for them. Heaven hears his prayer and sends a local deity to help him. The local deity tells Han Fang that the Jade Emperor (Supreme God) in Heaven has summoned all evil ghosts to report themselves to Hell; while on their way, some of the evil ghosts cannot help extorting money from the people they meet. Han's parents are among those preyed upon by these evil ghosts. The only way to cure this is to put a yellow paper on the bed and say aloud: "I will report you to the Jade Emperor if you do not stop bothering us." So Han Fang does as he is told, and his parents are immediately cured. At the end of the story, we read the following comment by the author:

> In either the thirty-third or thirty-fourth year of K'ang-hsi [1694 or 1695], as I recall it, the authorities decreed a new grain tax, which they called the "Voluntary Contribution." The different prefectures and districts also levied additional sums for themselves. Moreover, at that time, as a result of flood, the seven districts of North Shantung had a very poor harvest; so it was exceptionally difficult for the peasants to pay up. Han-lin Compiler T'ang of our district, who happened to visit Li-chin [district], saw about a dozen arrested men on the road and stopped to ask what their offense was. "The authorities are taking us to the district city to make us pay the 'Voluntary Contribution'," they told him. The peasants did not know what the "Voluntary Contribution" meant, and thought it the name for some new form of labor conscription or extortion! This is laughable, but sad too.

There are many other stories in the *Liao-chai* that expose the corruption and tyranny of the officials. In the story of **"Hung-yü,"** a discharged censor, Sung, fancies a poor

scholar's wife. First, Sung attempts to buy her from her husband; he is refused. Then he sends several scoundrels to the poor scholar's house. Both the scholar and his father are beaten on the floor while the scoundrels take away the young wife and leave the baby crying in bed. Badly wounded, the old man dies. The scholar then appeals to the authorities for justice, but is turned down several times, for although discharged from office, Sung still had powerful influence over the local authorities.

In the story of **"Mei-nü"** (The Daughter of the Mei Family), an innocent girl is forced to hang herself because a petty official accepts a small amount of cash and lets the girl's reputation be spoiled by a scoundrel. The story begins one night when the girl's father catches a thief and sends him to the authorities. The thief bribes the jail warden with three hundred coins; the warden releases the thief and announces that the accused merely had an affair with the daughter of the accuser. Thus, for the small amount of three hundred coins, the greedy jail warden causes the death of an innocent girl. In those days, a girl's chastity was more important than her life.

Perhaps the most forceful satire of all is the story of **"K'ao-pi ssu"** (The Bureau of Frauds). The head of the Bureau of Frauds in the world of the dead is portrayed as a greedy, cruel hypocrite called Hsü-tu Kuei-wang (The Empty-stomach Ghost King) who institutes the most evil practice of requiring all dead degree-holders to cut a piece of their rump as a tribute to him. Only those who can make a costly bribe can be excused from this painful exploitation. P'u Sung-ling then describes the details of the cruel torture of cutting rump and the horrible cries of the victims. Thus the world of exploitation of helpless scholars by cruel, corrupt superiors was a world of horror. In the story, a scholar finally appeals to Hades; the latter, who usually represented the opposite of justice in traditional thinking, actually grants justice to the poor scholars by punishing the head of the Bureau. One may raise the question: Why not appeal to the Supreme God, who was the symbol of justice in traditional times? The answer given by the author was a simple one: "The Supreme God of Heaven was far in the blue sky; where can He be found and told about our grievance? Only Hades, in the world of ghosts, is near and can be the possible access to justice." In a word, evil officials can be checked only by evil means; true justice is beyond reach.

IV

Related to the corruption of the bureaucracy was the whole system of imperial civil service examinations. Many stories in the *Liao-chai* reveal the dark side of this system and form the third category of the *Liao-chai* collection. Being a victim of this system, P'u Sung-ling attacked it most vigorously. Yet he never questioned the existence of this system, he only exposed and ridiculed its many abuses. There are two central themes in this category of stories: the corrupt and incompetent examiners on the one hand and the ill fate of the mass of *hsiu-ts'ai* (holders of the elementary degree) on the other. We shall choose a few stories to elaborate on these themes.

In the story of **"Ssu-wen lang,"** the author made up a story of Hades to satirize the injustice of the examination system. In the world of ghosts, a minor office known as a clerk in charge of writings in the office of God of Literature is temporarily filled by a deaf boy. As a result, the writings which show real talent cannot be found. In the mortal world, the examiners were even worse. The author uses a blind monk to exaggerate his criticism: "Although I am blind, I still can use my nose to tell good writing from bad; but those [the examiners] are not only blind but they also have lost their [sense of] smell."

In the story of **"Chia Feng-chih,"** Chia is a learned scholar, but he fails the examination every time. He is told that his thought is too profound and his writing too smooth and lucid, and that he has to learn the current stale style in order to pass the examination. But he is too honest a scholar to make himself accept this advice. He fails again and again, until one year he is forced by a spirit to write the examination paper in a stale, ridiculous style. Not only does he make it this time, but he passes the examination with the highest honor. He is so ashamed of what he has written that whenever he thinks of it, his face becomes flushed. Burdened by this sense of shame, he eventually leaves home for the seclusion of the mountains.

In the story of **"Yü Ch'ü-wo,"** the author uses a ghost named Yü Ch'ü-wo to express his criticism of the examination system. The ghost Yü once says to a mortal friend T'ao Sheng-yü: Those who are successful through all examinations know nothing about historical classics. When they are young, study is only a steppingstone to an official career. Once they pass the examinations and become officials they never study again. After their appointment as officials, having spent more than ten years in taking care of official writing, even the "men of letters" cannot know anything of real learning. But it is from among these half-educated bureaucrats that examiners are chosen; how could they be expected to advance the talent?

While many stories in the *Liao-chai* ridicule the examiners of the examination system, even more describe the general disposition of the poor scholars as a whole. In this regard, the author obviously had mixed feelings. On the one hand, he praised the honest, self-respected and learned scholars who held on to their beliefs, such as Chia Feng-chih in the story of **"Chia Feng-chih"**; Wang P'ing-tzu in the story of **"Ssu-wen lang"**; and T'ao Sheng-yü in the story of **"Yü Ch'ü-wo."** On the other hand, the author satirized the vanity, love of money, and self-importance of scholars who were products of the examination system. For example, in the stories of **"Ishui hsiu-ts'ai"** (A Scholar from I-shui), and **"Yü-ch'ien"** (The Money-rain), the scholars' love for money is sharply deplored. In the story of **"Hsien-jen Tao,"** the ignorant but self-esteemed, egoistic scholar becomes the laughingstock among the fairies. In the story of **"Chai-p'ing kung-tzu"** (A Young Gentleman from Chia-p'ing), the young gentleman, although handsome and good mannered in his physical appearance, is empty and ignorant inside. In the story of **"Hsü Huang-liang"** (A Continuation of the Huang-liang Story), the scholar's hunt for fame and wealth is satirized most force-

fully. The story describes a scholar, Tseng, who has just passed the examination for the highest degree, *chin-shih.* He is overjoyed at this great success and takes a trip to the suburbs with friends. Someone happens to suggest that there is a fortune-teller in a nearby temple. So the group goes to see the fortune-teller. The fortune-teller observes Tseng's joy and wants to please him. He therefore announces that Tseng is going to be a prime minister for twenty years. Overwhelmed by this prediction, Tseng later has a fantastic dream. The whole story is mainly a description of this dream. In the dream, Tseng becomes the prime minister and has all power and wealth at his disposal. First, he grants favors to a friend who once helped him with money; then he revenges an acquaintance who was not nice to him. From then on P'u Sung-ling describes how Tseng abuses his power to the extreme of killing innocents, robbing other people of their properties, taking in young and beautiful girls by force, and so forth. In a word, he uses Tseng's dream to expose the darkness and corruption in the inner soul of a scholar. He reminds the readers of the basic question: What is the examination system for? Is it only for the purpose of seeking power and wealth? If it is so, then the end is very clear: The end of the corruption of power is total self-destruction.

Besides analyzing the scholar's inner soul, P'u Sung-ling also wrote about the state of mind of scholars from their entering the examination hall until leaving; from their handing in their papers until preparing to sit again. In the story of **"Wang Tzu-an"** (A Scholar Named Wang Tzu-an), P'u gives us a vivid picture of the psychology of scholars in the process of examination. Due to tension, exhaustion, humiliation, and anxiety, the *hsiu-ts'ai* candidate Wang Tzu-an falls, after the examination, into a delirium in which he sees himself a successful *chin-shih* degree holder and a *han-lin* academician. Although he eventually wakes up to the suffering world, he thinks he has been tricked by the spirit of a fox. But such a traumatic ordeal is quite understandable to P'u Sung-ling, a long-time victim of the examination system. Commenting on the story, P'u asserts the insanity of the examination process, and describes the process and a candidate's state of mind as affected by it in terms of seven analogies. At the time of entering the examination enclosure, the candidate is like a beggar; he is like a felon when his name is called and checked by an examiner; he feels like a bee at the end of autumn when he is in his examination cell, and like a moulting bird leaving its cage when he comes out of the examination enclosure; he is like a chained monkey when he is restlessly waiting for the result of the examination; he feels just like a poisoned fly—dropping dead—when he is informed of his failure at the examination; and finally he comes to be like a pigeon whose eggs have been broken and which can only rebuild its nest anew, after a period of anguish, dispiritedness, and complete hostility towards the examination.

It is interesting to note that Wang Tzu-an's delirium readily finds an echo in the nineteenth century rebel leader Hung Hsiu-ch'üan (1814-1864). After failing four times at a *hsiu-ts'ai* examination, Hung Hsiu-ch'üan fell into a delirium in which he finally found liberation from the cruel experiences of the examinations by proclaming himself the son of (the Christian) God and launching into a total denunciation of the evils of Confucius, the man whose teachings were the subject matter of the examinations in traditional China. It is clear that the traumatic, pathetic experiences of Wang Tzu-an under P'u Sung-ling's pen were a common and real ordeal for all candidates of the imperial examinations. P'u's picture of the scholars' humiliation and degradation is the sharpest and most penetrating criticism of the evils of the examination system and of its effects on the character and personality of the candidate-scholars who were the elite, and future leaders, of traditional Chinese society.

V

The last category of stories in the *Liao-chai* are those that reflect the racial hatred of the Chinese people for their Manchu rulers. Here we should first point out that P'u Sung-ling was not a Ming loyalist of the caliber of the great thinkers of his time, like Ku Yen-wu (1613-1682) and Huang Tsung-hsi (1610-1695). He was not even close to it. In his collection of works, we find many distasteful "Pretended Memorials" that a Ming loyalist would never write. Nevertheless, as a writer he shared the general anti-Manchu emotion of his day. The fact that a considerable number of the stories in the *Liao-chai* were adopted by P'u from folk-tales makes him more or less a spokesman of his day. It is naturally for this reason that the anti-Manchu emotions exist in the *Liao-chai.* Thus one may reasonably assume that P'u Sung-ling's anti-Manchu feeling is more a reflection of the flavor of his age than a deliberate, sophisticated, well-engineered effort.

Generally speaking, these anti-Manchu feelings are expressed by P'u in a subtle and indirect style. For example, in the famous story of **"Lo-ch'a hai-shih"** (The Rākshasas and the Sea Market), he imagined an appallingly ugly race and named its country the Rākshasa—a Buddhist term meaning both *barbarians* and man-devouring demons. The hero of this story is a young Chinese travelling merchant whom all the people of the Rākshasa view as the most extraordinary-looking man they have ever seen. The author implies that the Rākshasas represent the Manchus, for he describes the dresses of Rākshasa women in terms of the Manchu style, which was different from that of the Han Chinese. Moreover, in the story, the author has the young Chinese put on a false ugly face everytime he goes to the Rākshasa court, where his disguise wins him tremendous praise. This reflects the fact that the Manchus wore their hair differently from the Han Chinese, and when they came to China they demanded that all Chinese shave and braid their hair the way the Manchus did. This was a big, bitter issue of the day and the Chinese, although revolted at seeing men with braided hair and Manchu clothes, were forced to accept this custom after bloody struggles. So it is also possible that the author expressed his disgusted feeling by describing how ugly those Rākshasas were without mentioning their hair-style, because that would be too obvious and too dangerous. At the end of the story, the author comments rather explicity:

> Men must put on false, ugly faces to please their superiors—such is the hypocritical way of the world. The foul and hideous are prized the world over. Something of which you feel a little ashamed may win praise, while something you feel exceedingly ashamed of may win much higher praise. But any man who dares to reveal his true self in public is almost certain to shock the multitude and make them shun him.

A part of these comments and criticisms is evidently directed to the Ming officials who served the new alien Manchu court by putting on new masks to spiritually and physically please the new master.

Along the same line of approach, in the story of **"Yeh-ch'a kuo"** (The Land of Yakshas), the author seems to use the ugly Yakshas (man-devouring demons) to express his disgust of the Manchus. For not only does his description of the female Yaksha styles correspond to that of the Manchus, but he also repeatedly mentions the custom of wearing a bead necklace when the Yakshas greeted their king. This is exactly the custom of the Manchu court: the high-ranking officials (grade five and above) in the Manchu court had to wear a bead necklace.

If the above two tales are too subtle to represent the author's anti-Manchu feelings, other stories are more explicit. Using ghost stories as a form of narration, the author reveals the terror of the Manchu massacres. In the story of **"Kung-sun Chiu-niang"** (The Lady Ghost Kung-sun Chiu-niang), the author plainly states the fact at the very beginning.

> In the case of Yü Ch'i (Revolt) [1661], most of the people who were involved with this case and got killed were from the two districts of Ch'i-hsia and Lai-yang. There were so many people killed—several hundreds a day—in the field of military training that the field was all soaked up by blood and the white bones of corpses were piled up to the sky.

Again, at the very beginning of another story, **"Yeh-kou"** (The Wild Dog), the author repeats: "In the case of Yü Ch'i (Revolt), there was a frightful mass slaughter." In the story of **"Kuei-li"** (The Ghost Clerks), P'u Sung-ling mentions the massacre of Chi-nan (Capital of Shantung) in plain language: "Shortly after the northern army [the Manchus] came, there was a massacre in Chi-nan and corpses were counted up to a million."

Another story in the *Liao-chai* directly exposes how the Manchu soldiers debauched women and girls. It is the story of **"Chang-shih fu"** (The Wife of a Man from the Chang Family), which begins with the following statement:

> In the year of *Chia-yin* [1674], the rebellion of the Three Feudatories took place. The southern expeditionary armies reached Yen-Chou [in southern Shantung]. The soldiers looted the area and debauched the women folks.

Besides exposing the terror of war and disorder, the author reveals the universal feelings of disgust toward those who ranked high but betrayed their loyalties. Using the notorious Ch'in Kuei (1090-1155) as a symbol (the Southern Sung prime minister who was traditionally regarded as a symbol of a Chinese traitor, and who was responsible for executing the national hero Yüeh Fei in 1141), P'u Sung-ling applied the Buddhist theory of karma to the story of **"Ch'in Kuei"** to illustrate the punishment of those who betrayed their loyalties. In the story, Ch'in Kuei is reincarnated as a pig and is butchered. But even as a pig, the meat of Ch'in Kuei is so rotten that nobody wants to eat it.

In the story of **"San-ch'ao Yüan-lao"** (The Elder Statesman of Three Reigns), P'u Sung-ling satirized Hung Ch'eng-ch'ou (1593-1665) who served as an elder statesman in both the Ming and the Ch'ing dynasties. He did not directly blame Hung, who surrendered to the Manchus when defeated, but made up a story based on the ironic event that the last Ming emperor Ch'ung-chen (1628-1644) received a false report of Hung's death in the battle and decreed a temple to be built in Peking in honor of Hung. In the story, a former student goes to see Hung, who has just reached Nanking after his victorious southern expedition for the Manchus. The former student tells Hung that he has a paper in hand and wishes Hung to see it. Hung refuses, with the excuse that he cannot see well. Then the student insists on reading it aloud, and does. The paper is the eulogy that Emperor Ch'ung-chen of the Ming wrote in honor of Hung upon hearing the false report of Hung's death.

In another story, **"She Chiang-chün"** (General She), the same theme of loyalty is repeated. General She is a military officer under the command of Tsu Shu-shun, who is very kind to She and promotes him several times until he becomes a Brigade General. Later on, when She feels that Tsu is fighting a losing war, he rebels against Tsu and captures him in order to surrender to the new regime. Bothered by his conscience, one night General She dreams that he has gone to Hell. Hades is so furious over She's treachery that he orders the ghosts to pour boiling oil over She's feet. When General She awakes, he feels a fiery burning pain over his feet. His health grows worse and worse, and he finally dies. In his dying bed, his last words are: "It is indeed very treacherous of me to betray my loyalty!"

In contrast to his deploring disloyalty in these stories, P'u has high praise for the loyal hero General Huang Te-kung (d. 1645), of the Hung-kuang reign (1645) of the Southern Ming, in the story **"Huang Chiang-chün."** Huang is painted as a brave man, who fights the robbers with his bare hands and wins, while his travelling companions—two *chü-jen* degree holders—kneel down in front of the robbers and present their money to them.

When one considers all of these stories—fables, tales depicting the terror of massacres, stories satirizing the disloyal high-ranking official or praising loyalty, it is clear that anti-Manchu feelings do exist in the *Liao-chai.* The fact that some stories are very subtle and some are very explicit reflects their different time background, for P'u

Sung-ling wrote these short stories over a span of twenty years. During this long period, the new regime's policy alternated between high pressure and appeasement. It is understandable that P'u Sung-ling was sometimes especially cautious and at other times more relaxed. Moreover, this collection was circulated in manuscript form for many decades. The first printed edition, which was also the most current edition until the 1950's, was published in 1766. In this edition, most of the anti-Manchu wordings were modified and some explicit stories were missing. These omissions and changes for the sake of political considerations can be seen only by a thorough comparison of the 1766 popular printed edition and the various existing hand-copied manuscripts of the *Liao-chai,* one of which is the recently discovered incomplete original manuscript of P'u Sung-ling. Our conclusions are based on such research.

## VI

To conclude our study of P'u Sung-ling's short stories, it is important to point out what they mean to our study of ideas. As pointed out earlier, in his preface to the collection of *Liao-chai chih-i,* P'u Sung-ling made it very plain that he wrote the book to vent his feelings of distress and frustration. To the modern reader, this statement is nothing new; it merely conforms to the established modern concept that literature describes human experience. But to a student of Chinese intellectual history, the statement is highly significant. P'u's preface was written in 1679, at a time when literature was still viewed as "vehicle of the Way." To announce to the world that his writing is "venting his excited feelings" is rather unusual. It represents not only a deep sense of pessimistic protest, but also a spirit that was searching for a new meaning in life. Only when we keep this basic sentiment in mind can we obtain a better understanding of P'u Sung-ling and his work.

To understand P'u Sung-ling's thought, it is necessary to discern the intellectual influences and ethical values which lie behind his writing. In this regard, we are very fortunate, because in P'u Sung-ling's own preface to the collection of *Liao-chai chih-i,* he candidly admits the influences on his writing:

> "Clad in wisteria, girdled with ivy," thus sang San-lü [Ch'ü Yüan, ca. 343-277 B.C.] in his *On Encountering Sorrow;* of ox-headed devils and serpent Gods, he of the long nails [Li Ho, a T'ang poet, 791-817, noted for his long nails] never wearied to tell. Each interprets in his own way the music of heaven; and whether it be discord or not, depends upon antecedent causes. As for me, [following Hsi K'ang, 223-262] I cannot, with my poor autumn fire-fly's light, match myself against the hobgoblins of the age. I am but the dust in the sunbeam, a fit laughingstock for devils. For my talents are not those of Kan Pao [fl. 323 A.D., author of the famous *Sou-shen chi* (Records of the Supernatural)] who was fond of exploring the supernatural; I am rather akin to the temperament of Huang-chou [Su Tung-p'o, the famous Sung statesman, poet, and essayist, 1036-1101] who loved to hear people talk about ghosts. Having heard what people say, I would put it in writing and subsequently dress it up in the form of a story. Thus in the lapse of time my friends from all quarters

have supplied me with quantities of material, which, from my habit of collecting, has grown into a vast pile.

Human beings, I would point out, are not beyond the pale of fixed laws, and yet there are more unbelievable phenomena in their midst than in the country of those who crop their hair [southern savages of early ages]; and even before our very own eyes, many tales are to be found therein stranger than that of the nation of Flying Heads [a fabulous race mentioned in *Yu-yang tsa-tsu* (Yu-yang Miscellany) by Tuan Ch'eng-shih (d. 863 A.D.)]. [As the poet Wang Po (648-675) rightly says,] "Irrepressible bursts and refreshing ease," I was indeed but wild! "Forever indulging in farreaching thought" [as did Li Po (701-762)], I did not try to hide my foolishness. Were men like these to open my book, I should be a laughingstock to them indeed. However, although the stories heard at the crossroads might, like the story about [Confucius burying his mother at] the Wu-fu Crossroads [in modern Shantung], be nonsense, yet they might make sense if one views them through the Buddhist theory of the three states of human existence [—the present, the past, and the future]. Furthermore, [as Confucius once cautioned us,] never set aside words because of the man who utters them.

When the bow [a small towel announcing the birth of a boy] was hung at my father's door, he dreamed that a sickly-looking [Buddha], Ch'ü-t'an [Gautama], but half-covered by his stole, entered the chamber. On one of his breasts was a piece of plaster like a coin; and my father, waking from sleep, found that I, just born, had a similar black patch on my body. As a child I was thin and constantly ailing, and unable to hold my own in the battle of life. Our home was chilly and desolate as a monastery; and working there for my livelihood with my pen, I was as poor as a priest with his almsbowl. Often I put my hand to my head and exclaimed, "Surely he who sat with his face to the wall [referring to the Buddhist patriarch Bodhidharma who came as a missionary to China in the late fifth century] was myself in a previous incarnation," and thus I referred my non-success in this life to the influence of a destiny surviving from the last.

I have been tossed hither and thither in the direction of the ruling wind, like a flower falling in filthy places; but the [Buddhist] six paths of transmigrations [i.e., the paths of heaven, men, demons, hell (tortured sinners), hungry devils, and brute beasts] are inscrutable indeed, and I have no right to complain. As it is, midnight finds me with an expiring lamp, while the wind whistles mournfully without; and over my cheerless table I piece together my tales, vainly hoping to produce a sequel to the *Yu-ming lu* (The Infernal Regions) [written by Liu I-ch'ing (A.D. 403-444)]. With a bumper I stimulate my pen, yet I only succeed thereby in "venting my excited feelings," [as expressed by the philosopher Han Fei (ca. 281-233 B.C.) in his "Ku-fen" (Solitary Indignation)]. If I am obliged to vent my feelings in this way alone, it is sad enough. Alas! I am but the bird that, dreading the winter frost, finds no shelter in the tree; the autumn insect that chirps to the moon, and hugs the door for warmth. For where are they who know me? They are [as Tu Fu (712-770) once said in a poem to Li Po] "in the bosky

grove and at the dark frontier pass"—wrapped in an impenetrable gloom!

The melancholy and emotional tone of the Preface reveals the inner soul of a lonely man who sees himself as one of the great writers in history who were unsuccessful in life, but achieved immortality after death. Four significant points are worthy of notice.

> **No matter that his ideas were in many ways ahead of his time, he was still the child of his age, conditioned by the social, political, and cultural environment of that age.**
>
> —*Chun-shu Chang and Hsueh-lun Chang*

First, it seems that P'u Sung-ling identified himself as a spiritual brother among the great poets and essayists in Chinese history; Ch'ü Yüan, Li Ho, Su Tung-p'o, Wang Po, Tu Fu, and Li Po are the great poets he cherished. It is especially notable that the Preface begins with a quotation from the ancient Ch'u poet and statesman Ch'ü Yüan, who drowned himself in the Mi-lo River after having been unjustly dismissed from favor of the Ch'u Court, and ends by identifying the *Liao-chai chih-i* with the chapter "Ku-fen" (Solitary Indignation) of the *Han Fei Tzu* by Han Fei who, after rising to distinction, was unjustly thrown into prison in 233 B.C. All of these tell of P'u Sung-ling's strong feeling of being deserted and unappreciated and, above all, his sorrows and frustrations.

Second, it is interesting to note that while P'u Sung-ling admits that his tales are "wild" and "foolish," he reminds his reader: "Never set aside words because of the man who utters them," for no matter how absurd they seem, we might still learn something from them. It is obvious that P'u Sung-ling wants his reader to learn something from his tales.

The third notable aspect of the Preface is P'u Sung-ling's sense of predestination. He refers his "non-success" in his life to "the influence of a destiny surviving from the last." It seems that he really believes this when he tells about the possibility of his previous incarnation as a Buddhist monk. P'u Sung-ling's belief in a previous state of existence reveals the tremendous religious—mainly Buddhist and Taoist—influence on his life. This explains the many superstitious fears, customs, and beliefs that fill up the pages of his *Liao-chai chih-i.* P'u Sung-ling was living in a superstitious rural society in seventeenth-century China. No matter that his ideas were in many ways ahead of his time, he was still the child of his age, conditioned by the social, political, and cultural environment of that age. He wrote on a variety of subjects, not because he consciously attempted to serve his people and society, as portrayed by an eminent Western scholar, but because he felt the urge to express his ideas and feelings in writing. It is especially significant that, as already pointed out, he wrote in classical as well as vernacular language and also in every style and form: poems, essays, short stories, popular dramas, drum-songs, narrative folksongs, popular didactic works, and so on. He wrote in classical language because that was the established written language of his day; scholars seeking literary success wrote either classical essays (mostly for imperial examinations) and traditional poems, or devoted themselves to learning the interpretations of the Confucian Classics. Yet the fact that he wrote not only classical essays and poems, but also classical stories shows that he had already found the orthodox literature—essays and poetry—no longer the only effective, useful vehicle of literary expression. Furthermore, he also wrote various pieces in the vernacular because it was the spoken language of the day, and he desired his works to be widely read. That he attempted to use all possible literary media to express himself shows not only his original mind but also the new spirit of his age. The rising demand for popular literature among the people demonstrated its strength in the styles of P'u Sung-ling's writings. Without realizing its true historical significance, P'u wrote popular literature of every sort, going wherever his fancies led him.

The last but not the least notable impression one gathers from reading P'u Sung-ling's preface to the *Liao-chai chih-i* is its strong personal note of irony and disillusionment. This glum view of life is in sharp contrast to the generally lively and colorful outlook of the world of the *Liao-chai chih-i.* The *Liao-chai* stories, with all their popularity, had been generally viewed by their traditional readers as a form of entertainment and aesthetic enjoyment. The famous early Ch'ing scholar, writer, and critic Wang Shih-chen (1631-1711) exhibits the contemporaneous and traditional view of the *Liao-chai chih-i.* In a poem commenting on the book, he humorously referred to P'u's stories as "those that are told light-heartedly should be received with the same light spirit." Responding to this comment, P'u Sung-ling himself admitted: "When the book *Liao-chai* was completed, people who read it have indeed felt it amusing" [Lu Ta-huang, ed., "P'u Liu-ch'üan hsien-sheng nien-p'u," in *P'u Sung-ling chi,* Vol. 2, p. 1778; both Wang Shih-chen's poem and P'u Sung-ling's reply are recorded under the year 1689 in this *nien-p'u.*]. But P'u Sung-ling did not write the book merely for the sake of amusement. In a poem dated 1671, the year he went home from the South, ending his brief connection with the government as a secretary to Sun Hui (1632-1686), the district magistrate of Pao Ying and of Kao-yu (in modern Kiangsu), he described his book as his only hope for fame and success in life after all hopes of an official career were gone [P'u Sung-ling, *P'u Sung-ling shih-chi, chüan* 1 in *P'u Sung-ling chi,* Vol. 1, p. 483].

As we pointed out earlier, the greater part of the *Liao-chai chih-i* took form in the gloomiest period of P'u Sung-ling's life. Thus P'u wrote the stories to vent his excited feelings, and to compensate, by expressing profound ideas through popular literary means, for his sad failure in the examinations and his official career. Both of these motives were clearly revealed in his Preface. But to contemporary and later traditional scholars and readers, both intentions seem to have been lost. Take the previously-mentioned views of Wang Shih-chen and Chi Yün. Both scholars were fascinated by the literary power and imagination of P'u Sung-ling's *Liao-chai chih-i* as a piece of entertainment, but they did not consider it an expression of deep-grounded ideas and personal feelings. To the general reader, the *Liao-chai chih-i* was only a collection of fantastic, amusing tales, although readers were strongly influenced subconsciously by the ideas behind the stories. P'u Sung-ling's reputation as a truly great writer in Chinese history was, in general, not recognized until modern times—particularly recent decades. It is his ideas and thought, more than anything else, that have won him the respect and sympathy of modern readers.

In short, P'u Sung-ling's ideas and thought, and his means of expressing them as fiction, generally transcended his time and eluded most readers of the traditional period. Electrified by his fantastic tales, his readers gradually and subconsciously accepted his vivid and penetrating analysis of the comedies and tragedies of the human condition during a great dynastic transition; his revealing description of the intolerable tensions between the intellectuals and the government and the devastating consequences of these tensions; his views and criticisms of his time and his society; and his ideals of life and government. P'u Sung-ling's traditional readers thus unconsciously appreciated his work without recognizing its true literary merit.

We have seen P'u Sung-ling as an analyst of his life and his inner ego, as a teller of unusual tales, as an observer of human nature and human society, as a recorder of the local and national memories of the Ming-Ch'ing dynastic transition, and as a molder of the images of his age and the Chinese culture. Through his short stories, he communicates his sense of his country's culture and history; he allows his readers to see and share his perceptions of the inner orders and structures of the individual, the society, and the times. Some scholar may raise the question of the originality of some of P'u Sung-ling's stories: what was his own creation and what was only his re-creation based on old stories? But this misses a point of critical importance in understanding the spirit and methodology of traditional Chinese intellectual and literary pursuits. Re-creation has always been a form—in fact, the most prevailing form—of creation. This has been a unique character of Chinese thinking and intellectual endeavor, a tradition that has gone all the way back to Confucius (551-479 B.C.) and is well attested to by the fact that the most original Chinese philosophical ideas have been made in the form of commentaries on the Classics. Thus, through his short stories, P'u Sung-ling revealed not only the style and vision of his literary imagination, but also the creative process of Chinese intellectual consciousness, a process that has actually remained unchanged in the contemporary Chinese world of ideas and intellectual exercise.

## Fatima Wu (essay date 1986)

"Foxes in Chinese Supernatural Tales (Part I)," in *Tamkang Review,* Vol. XVII, No. 2, Winter, 1986, pp. 121-54.

[*In the following excerpt, Wu demonstrates how P'u reinvented the traditional Chinese fox tale.*]

### Fox Spirits in P'u Sung-ling's *Liao-chai chih-yi*

It can be said that P'u wrote the most fox tales up to his time in his one collection of *Liao-chai chih-yi.* There are almost seventy-one fox tales in his book. P'u's fox spirits can be put into two categories: the good and the bad. There are also vengeful foxes that are used to emphasize a satiric viewpoint, such as in the tale named **"Yi yüan kuan"** and **"Tao-hu,"** the fox spirit in the first story dares speak the truth in contrast to others who are timid and quiet. The fox in **"Tao-hu"** is used to satirize the impotence of the government officials at that time.

The fox spirit from the tale **"Ch'ou hu"** is an ambivalent character. She is both good and bad. She is good to Mu when he agrees to love her. Whenever she comes, she gives presents of gold and silk to the entire household. Yet when Mu gets tired of her and plans to get rid of her, she takes full revenge on him. She hurts him physically with a cat; she ruins his home, and snatches all his property, causing him to be as poor as he once was.

**"Hu ch'êng yin"** has another "bad" character. In the tale, there is a typical cunning and dangerous fox spirit. It damages the new landlord's clothes and puts dirt in his food. Moreover, it secretly places aphrodisiacs in the mistress' food when the master is away. The mistress has to run to her guest, who insults and refuses her. She almost dies of shame afterwards. Yet the reader must not be distracted just by the fox's bad behavior; he must also be aware of why the fox is acting that way toward the humans. The two fox spirits mentioned above are actually doing the man a favor by teaching him a lesson: that he should value genuine love over monetary gains and mere physical pleasure. By using a fox which is lewd in character to punish a lewd human-being, P'u shows his skillful hand in writing satire. Can there be a worse man when even the lewd fox thinks him lascivious? These in-between fox characters are important characters for P'u, for they help him to illustrate his view of life and comment on the moral character of men. In a sense, these foxes are good foxes to P'u, for they know what is right and wrong, while the mortals in the tales do not. These fox spirits act as P'u's didactic agents to punish the bad and the immoral.

P'u's bad fox characters are very traditional, so much so that they are simply repetitions of their predecessors. Examples of these negative fox characters from *Liao-chai* are in: **"Chia êrh," "Tung shêng," "Hu Ssŭ-chieh," "Hsia nü," "Chi shêng,"** and finally, **"Nung-jên,"** and **"Chiao Mi."** These bad fox spirits usually bewitch and possess their victims, ruining their health and causing their families' concern. In most of these tales, the fox spirits are exorcised by a Taoist priest or a helper who drives away or kills the spirit. Many of these bad spirits die of lasciviousness. In **"Chia êrh,"** the young boy kills the fox because he bewitches his mother and forces her into an illicit relationship. The fox in **"Nung-jên"** also has his eyes on a young girl. The unluckiest fox is the one in **"Hsia nü."** He does not have a chance to do anything yet before he is killed. The female foxes in **"Tung shêng"** and **"Hu Ssŭ-chieh"** catch their victims. In **"Tung shêng,"** though the fox lady is successful in assimilating the vital spirit from the scholar and causing his death at the end, this death is avenged by another man. This second man takes the place of the exorcist in destroying the fox lady.

**"Hu Ssŭ-chieh"** is an unusual story in that in the same story, there are simultaneously good and bad fox ladies. First there is Miss Hu the Fourth, a good fox, but her older sister, Miss Wu the Third, plans to kill the scholar after they have met. Although Miss Hu the Fourth truly loves the man and saves him from her vicious sister, she is astonished to find that he is again bewitched by another fox. Both sisters at this time join forces to save him from the third spirit. P'u is having a lot of fun here, confusing the reader with both good and bad foxes interacting with one man. This is one of the ways in which P'u makes his stories interesting, filling them with excitement and suspense. A similar story to the above can be found in **"Chou San."** In this story, a man's house is pestered by a fox spirit. The master of the house asks another fox to perform the exorcism. The second fox refuses because he thinks that there is another fox who is better qualified for the job. He recommends a third fox, who after the exorcism, stays at the master's house for good. Both **"Hu Ssŭ-chieh"** and **"Chou San"** indicate that there are different ranks among the fox spirits. As I have discussed earlier, there are fox fairies and fox spirits. The former have devoted more years to their Taoist training and hence are more powerful than the latter, who are just beginning theirs. The difference in rank in the fox spirits allows P'u to create stories which sometimes act as a reflection of the human world, which has both positive and negative characteristics.

P'u's fox tales are different from the collection in *T'ai-p'ing kuang-chi* [977-981] in that almost eighty percent of P'u's fox tales have good fox characters. In *T'ai-p'ing kuang-chi,* only less than one-fourth of the tales carry good fox images. It is in the writing of good fox characters that P'u is best. His good fox characters include: 1) scholars or educated and refined individuals who help men in their studies, 2) drinking foxes who develop with men a relationship of trust and love, 3) female or male fox spirits who assist men in various matters, for example, to achieve a fortune and to drive away a shrewish wife, and, 4) single women who become involved with men, help men in their career, and start a family with them.

Since the time of *So shên chi,* fox scholars have been popular characters in tales. P'u picks up this tradition but adds his own imagination to create new fox stories. The story **"Hu-shih"** is a good example. Mr. Hu, who is a fox spirit, turns himself into an educated man and works as a tutor in a prominent man's house. Even though the family later finds out the tutor's identity, they still respect him because of his good will and literary talent. At the end, he is even accepted as a family member when the master agrees to marry his son to Mr. Hu's sister. Another story **"Lêng shêng"** has a talented fox spirit. We do not know whether this fox is female or male; we do not even get to see its face. Yet we know it is very talented scholastically because the fox has transformed the young retarded student, Lêng, into a quick and intelligent scholar. Before Lêng meets the fox, he could not familiarize himself with any one of the great books, even at over the age of twenty. Only days after they have been together, Mr. Lêng's personality is totally changed. He loves to laugh no matter where he is, and he can finish a good essay in one sitting. At the end, he is remembered by the books he has written. **"Kuo shêng"** also has an intelligent and witty fox. In this tale, we do not see the fox's face either, yet we see its pen strokes. Kuo, the man of the house, is very upset by his essays because they have been ruined by a fox who blots and covers part of them with ink. Slowly, his friends realize that the fox was trying to correct his essays by cutting the bad parts out. Since then, Kuo follows the fox's instructions and manages to pass his examinations. Again, we see a scholarly fox guiding a man's studies without any intention of hurting him or receiving any rewards from him. Educated, talented, and witty foxes also appear in **"Hu hsieh," "Hu Ssŭ-hsiang-kung," "Hu lien,"** and **"Yi yüan kuan."**

Fox spirits tend to adore drinking. Through the medium of wine, fox spirits become good friends with humans. In a story called **"Chiu yu,"** a male fox spirit carries on a relationship with his drinking friend, who is mortal. Instead of hurting him, the spirit uses his power of prediction to make his friend rich. **"Hu Ssŭ-hsiang-kung"** and **"Hu hsieh"** are tales of male and female fox spirits who drink and write poems with their human companions. The fox spirit in **"Chi shêng"** also loves to steal wine and food from the master's house. The protagonist in **"Ch'in shêng"** dies because he has drunk some poisonous wine. A fox spirit comes by and heals him, saying that she has just rescued her husband who has died of the same cause. The scholar in **"Hê-chien shêng"** loves to drink, and so does the fox spirit that lives in the dry weeds in his fields. In the form of an old man, the fox goes out every night to his friends' drinking parties. The fox spirit in **"Chin-ling Yi"** steals wine from a brewer. When he is caught, he has to take the brewer on an amorous adventure in order to save himself. Here is another example in which a fox spirit gets into trouble because of his affinity for wine.

The third category of good fox spirits in the *Liao-chai,* male or female spirits which assist humans in various situations, excludes a love relationship between the spirit and the human. The assistance rendered by the spirits in most cases is voluntary, and they are not rewarded. The spirits help humans for the following reasons: a) they are repaying what the man has done for them in the past, b) they do it totally out of sympathy and compassion, or the feeling of indignation at the situation, and lastly, c) the spirits are involved in a very trusting and close friendship

with the humans. **"Chiao-na"** is a moving story of friendship. Scholar Kung is in love with Chiao-na at first sight, yet he does not pursue her when he knows that she is not available. The feeling Kung has for her enables him to fight the monster. In return, Chiao-na for the second time cures him and saves his life. The two lead a relationship between a man and a woman rare in classical tales. It is a friendship based on trust, love, and the will to sacrifice oneself.

The story **"Hêng-niang"** involves a deep and trusting relationship between two women, a fox spirit and a housewife. The spirit, in the course of helping the mistress to gain back her husband's heart from another concubine, has become a good friend of the concubine. Their relationship is described by the spirit as *"ch'ing jo yi t'i,"* which literally means "two in one." Because of the trust that exists between the two of them, the spirit even discloses to her good friend that she is actually a fox. Another story of friendship is **"Ma Chieh-fu."** The fox spirit, a sworn brother to the protagonist, out of compassion and love for him raises his nephew, takes care of his father, and helps him, as much as he can, to counteract his shrewish wife. Moreover, the spirit respects him when he chooses not to condemn his wife. Though possessing supernatural power, the spirit does not take the liberty to get rid of this vicious woman himself. This shows that he cares for and loves Ma, who is a kind but cowardly man. This spirit, like the other spirits mentioned earlier, receives no reward for what he has done for his friend.

Another moving fox tale comes at the end of the *Liao-chai* collection. In **"Liu Liang-ts'ai,"** since the spirit has made a lasting relationship with Liu's father, he decides to be reborn as Liu's heir. His reason for doing that is because Liu has never rejected or despised him though he knows that he is a fox. The trust and respect which Liu has bestowed on the spirit move him. In return for the favor, the fox is born as the only heir for his friend.

One can see that these fox spirits are human in their actions, thoughts, and beliefs. They value friendship, trust and love. They show their gratitude with whatever they can do: healing the human of sickness, saving a man from death, helping a man out of poverty, teaching a man a lesson in life, warning him of imminent danger, or helping him to have an heir. Other fox spirits in **"Lêng shêng," "Chou San," "Kuo shêng," "Ssŭ-hsün," "Ch'in shêng,"** and **"Nien yang"** help men simply out of good will, compassion, indignation, or just plain enthusiasm.

By presenting foxes with human qualities, P'u has created in his tales an inseparable link between fox and man. This is something the authors in the past have failed to do. P'u has the ability and power to make the reader forget the identity of the animal. He does so totally by his narrative art. His descriptions, settings and dialogue are vivid and natural, given the limitations of classical Chinese. His fox spirits live, feel, laugh, and cry like men. As a result, they lose their animal identity and merge with that of the humans. Lu Hsün has said in his book, *A Brief History of Chinese Fiction,*

*The Strange Tales of Liao-chai,* however, contain such detailed and realistic descriptions that even flower spirits and fox fairies appear human and approachable. . . .

The reader is so absorbed by such characters as Chiao-na and the aunt from **"Wang Ch'êng"** that he can follow the story without remembering that both characters are not human but foxes. This is exactly the illusion that P'u tries to create in his tales.

### P'u's Female Fox Spirits

Though P'u writes about both male and female fox spirits in his **Liao-chai,** he puts much more emphasis on the female ones. Female spirit tales take up about eighty percent of his fox tales. For this reason, I would like to devote the last part of this section to a discussion of this topic.

Female fox spirits, from the early *So shên chi* to the *Jên-shih chuan* in the Tang Dynasty, slowly acquire a new image. They begin to shake off their negative and bestial qualities. From the dangerous, lewd, selfish, greedy, and cunning animals in the ancient tales, they slowly become kind, self-sacrificing, faithful, sincere, and caring individuals in the later ones. *Jên-shih chuan* is a very good example. She is the image of perfect womanhood. Very likely, *Jên-shih chuan* was one of the tales P'u had in mind when he began his own writing on female fox spirits.

As was stated earlier, many of P'u's foxes are human in that they possess human traits and respect human values. These human factors in P'u's foxes are revealed intricately through social injustice and human relations. We see scenes of touching friendship in **"Chiao-na"** and **"Chiu yu."** Kung and Chiao-na can be said to be the most truthful friends because they respect and love each other, yet they are not involved sexually. Chiao-na, the female fox here, has shaken off the traditional lewd image of female foxes. Also many of P'u's foxes have a sense of human dignity. In **"Hsin Shih-ssŭ-niang"** the female fox protagonist is portrayed as a quiet, submitting but dignified woman. She is not promiscuous, for she refuses the man's advances and even his marriage proposal. She only yields to his request when he is backed up by a powerful aunt. At this point, though she has no choice, she insists on a decent marriage. It is obvious that the character of the fox in this tale, Lady Hsin, is a proud and dignified person. Even though she is forced to marry a man of low moral character, she has kept her values. She is a good wife in that she shows concern for and obeys her husband. It is also the fox spirit who saves him from jail. She is intelligent enough to know that her husband is not the man for her, yet she is considerate enough to find him a mate before she leaves. This story shows the fox's concern, care and submission even for a man whom she does not love but is only bound to by a marriage oath. Though it is an unwanted relationship, the fox never tries to use her supernatural power to control or to desert him. She is willing to submit, as best she can, to do what is required of her.

The **"Hsin Shih-ssŭ-niang"** tale leads our discussion to a fox spirit's reaction against various kinds of treatment from human society. P'u's fox spirits possess love and trust for their mortal friends, yet they also manifest hatred and mistrust when mistreated. The fox in **"Chou hu"** has much more human dignity than her human lover. Although she is ugly and swarthy, she is generous to the men she loves. She gives them gold in return for their love. Everything she does is very straightforward and fair. When deserted by her men, she regards it as fair to retrieve her gold. Her clean-cut way in dealing with a love relationship, though it may seem commercial or unsincere, is far better than the man's attempt to hurt her while he is claiming love for her. In this story, P'u is emphasizing his point by using a fox spirit: the spirit, which is traditionally regarded as lewd, cunning, and dangerous, has changed places with man, who is usually thought of as distinguished from beasts because of his conscience and dignity.

Another story that exemplifies a similar idea is **"Wu hsiao-lien."** Shih, an educated man, at his worst stage in life, in sickness and poverty, is rescued by a woman who cures him and supports him financially. When he becomes well and has found himself an official post, he deserts his benefactor and marries another woman. Although eventually the fox lady comes and joins him at his house without causing any trouble with the concubine he has acquired, she does not have his love or respect. Instead, he wants to kill her when he finds out that she is really a fox spirit. Again, this is P'u's satire on the humanity of the animal versus the inhumanity of man. Shih, an educated and renowned court official, is heartless and ungrateful to the companion who has saved his life. But the fox lady is obedient, faithful, reliant and generous to him. She stays with him and helps him in his career until her life is threatened. Unlike the ugly fox, who demands all her belongings when she leaves, she only asks for her medicine back. She does not cause any trouble to anybody or to anything in the house. The story of **"Wu hsiao-lien"** suggests a moral degradation among the official class. The fox is a symbol of the good wife that is upheld in Chinese society.

P'u's female fox spirits are not just dignified, loving, and financially generous but are also magnanimous. Jealousy is a common theme in P'u's tales in **Liao-chai,** as it was a common practice for man to have more than one mate in old China. When a woman was sterile, the husband had a justified excuse in acquiring a concubine for the purpose of family heir. When more than one woman served the same man in the house, the situation sometimes was uncomfortable. Jealousy plays a big role in many of P'u's stories, which disclose his view on the subject. P'u thinks it is the man's fault if he is unable to insure his family's prosperity. But it is the woman's, especially the wife's, task to organize and pacify the concubines by being generous and kind to them. The fox in **"Wu hsiao-lien"** is a perfect model of a wife who loves and respects the concubine Wang. The latter, touched by her kindness, becomes very close to her. Very soon, they live just like sisters in harmony. It is only the man who causes a rift between the two by loving one and detesting the other.

In **"Ch'ing-mei"** the fox spirit arranges a wedding between her husband and her former mistress, not even for the purpose of reproduction. In **"Ch'ang-ê"** the fox spirit, after having a relationship with her man, even gives him money to marry a mortal woman. At the end of the story, the two women stay happily with the same husband. Some of P'u's mortal women, when compared with the fox spirits, are much more selfish and dangerous. A good example is **"Ma Chieh-fu,"** mentioned earlier. Ma's wife has no children. Though her husband acquires a concubine for the reason of propagation, he never dares talk to the concubine in the wife's presence. When the concubine becomes pregnant, the wife beats her on a pretext and causes her to have a miscarriage. At the end, P'u gives her a miserable end, showing his disapproval of her behavior. The jealous wife in **"Shao nü"** is again a senior wife who tortures two concubines to death until she is moved by the kindness of the third one.

Many of P'u's fox spirits possess the virtues which are found in a mortal woman. These inhuman beings turn into human beings in P'u's hands. They become traditional virtuous Chinese women with flesh and blood, with feelings and emotions. **"Ya-t'ou"** is a perfect model of a chaste and virtuous wife. Coming from a brothel, Ya-t'ou is different from her fox sister in that she is not promiscuous even by trade. Once she devotes herself to Wang, she swears fidelity to him. Despite physical torture inflicted by her fox mother, Ya-t'ou remains faithful. She suffers under her mother's hands for years until her son grows up to be a young man and rescues her from agony. Yet she does not want her mother to be hurt. She is heartbroken when she finds out that her half-human son has killed both her mother and sister. Ya-t'ou is a woman who dares to love and is willing to die for her daring. She is defeated only by her own kindness towards her family. She is very human, as she values chastity and family ties and is willing to sacrifice herself for both.

### P'u Sung-ling's Use of Fox as Symbol

When P'u writes about foxes, he is actually writing about human beings. The human world involves many limitations: social injustice, moral obligations, lack of freedom, illness and mortality. Men also need good friends, true love, an amiable family, a prosperous career and wealth. Because of various reasons, many of these needs and limitations will never be satisfied or overcome by certain individuals except in fantasy or dreams. For example, a man who is impotent by birth would in those days never be able to overcome the deformity and live like a normal man. In P'u's **"Ch'iao-niang,"** the elderly ghost cures the young man Fu of his impotence, while the fox spirit teaches him his first lesson in sex. Another similar example can be found in the story of **"Lêng shêng."** The scholar is born retarded. In his life he would never be expected to have a scholastic career until a fox spirit comes to him one day, and cures him of his retardation. **"Hsiao Ts'ui"** is almost the same story, in which the fox spirit is able to cure her companion Wang of his imbecility. Physical deformity imposes a limit in a person's life in different forms. In **"Ch'iao-niang,"** Fu's impotence deprives him of sex-

ual pleasure in life, while Scholar Lêng and Wang are kept from having a career. By putting in his fox characters, P'u instills hope into the human world. In P'u's gothic world, miracles do happen to the hopeless.

---

**When P'u writes about foxes, he is actually writing about human beings.**

—*Fatima Wu*

---

By using foxes with supernatural powers, P'u's tales help to relieve the pain of death. In **"Ch'in shêng,"** the scholar is poisoned by his own wine and dies at his prime. While the wife is mourning for him, a fox spirit comes by and raises him from death.

P'u's fox spirits also help man to satisfy his secret desire for love. A stable but monotonous family life sometimes causes one to daydream and fantasize. **"Shuang teng"** is such a story. Wei, an ordinary young man who has no purpose in life except living and working for his in-laws, meets a fox spirit one evening when he is alone upstairs in a winery. For half a year, he has nothing but fun and sex with her, until one evening, the spirit comes to say good-bye and disappears in the dark. The spirit could be interpreted today as a figment of Wei's imagination and as a relief from everyday monotony, although P'u may not have intended such a psychological interpretation. Wei, a young man in his twenties, is already settled down for life. His lack of excitement and freedom in love helps build this fantasy tale. **"Fên-chou hu"** is another tale which can be interpreted as an elderly man's secret wish to have an extramarital affair. Ch'u is a state official. Because of his social standing, his secret desire to have a relationship cannot be fulfilled easily. The fox spirit appears in his house right in his room. Moreover, she is not just the casual type but cares for and loves the man. Her sincerity in this affair shows itself when he asks her to go home with him. Although it is forbidden for a fox to cross a river, she tries her best to obtain permission from the river god, who allows her to cross the river and stay with the official for ten more days. These two tales, on the surface, are simple short stories. Yet they are symbolic of a man's aspiration in a free and true love relationship. It is free because it is outside wedlock and free of obligation. It is true because the man and the fox usually get together for no reason at all but love. Often the fox spirit asks nothing from the man, and when their love calms down eventually, usually the spirit will disappear, leaving no obligations for the man, but only beautiful memories.

The fox spirit world for P'u also represents the ethical world to which he aspires. By using these spirits, P'u is able to create his idea of a Utopia in front of our eyes. He uses foxes to redress social injustice and family disputes; to remind and warn man of his moral obligation; and to reflect corruption in the governmental and examination systems. Many scholars claim that P'u's tales are very didactic, that he emphasizes especially the Buddhist idea of cause and effect, in which the good will be rewarded while the bad will be punished for their deeds. P'u, in order to give the weak and oppressed emotional and poetic justice, takes the reader into a world of the supernatural, in which the weak are protected by a certain magical power. Not only are they able to escape oppression, but they are also given a chance to redress the injustice done to them.

The story of **"Chiu-shan wang"** tells us of the fate of the Li family when the master of the house decides to burn his tenant and his family to death. His tenant, an old fox spirit, offers a hundred pieces of gold to rent a deserted part of Li's residence. The fox family then invite Mr. Li over for dinner, during which he is offered very good food. Thinking it strange that his tenant has changed the deserted house into a fine mansion in such a short time, he decides that his new tenants must be foxes. In secret, he buys some sulphur and niter and one day sets fire on the whole house-hold. Up to this point, P'u shows us the injustice Li has done to the foxes. Li, who has received a good rent from the foxes, has never been bothered by his tenants. Rather, his deserted house becomes very well decorated and taken care of. Moreover, the old fox spirit is friendly and respectful towards Li. Li is presented here as an obnoxious, cruel and greedy person. After the conflagration, the fox says to him,

> "There has not been any rejection or complaint between us. I have paid a hundred pieces of gold for your deserted land, no small amount. How can you then bear to kill us all? There is slim chance that I would not avenge this most obnoxious feud."

The old fox's revenge against him takes advantage of Li's greediness. As a fox, he is able to transform himself into a respectable fortune-teller who appears to Li a year later. By telling Li that he is destined to be king, and by assembling followers for him, the fox turns Li into a rebel leader. Li's end comes when the emperor's army is surrounding his fortress and the fortune-teller has disappeared. Li is captured and executed together with his whole family. At the end, P'u makes his comments in the guise of the Historian of the Strange. He says that Li's end serves him right, for his cruelty is seen when he murders the foxes. If Li had been a good man, the fox would never have been able to trap him. The fox's vengeance would not have been possible if the fox had not been a supernatural character. A mortal tenant would have died after the fire. Neither would he be able to change himself into another man in order to win Li's confidence or be able to recruit soldiers and win battles for Li. The fox spirit here is presented as a respectable, polite, and educated individual in the beginning. But at the end, in order to avenge himself, he has turned into a cunning and cruel old man.

The fox lady in **"Wu hsiao-lien"** is also able to avenge herself on her husband Shih only because she is a supernatural creature. She demands her medicine back. The

result leads to Shih's death. If she were a mortal woman, she would have been deserted, insulted, cheated or even hurt by him. P'u makes use of his fox spirits as his didactic tools in teaching these human malefactors a lesson. By the end of his tales, the author is able to reinstall social justice.

Such tales as the **"Chou hu,"** **"Wu hsiao-lien,"** **"Chiu-shan wang,"** carry at least two messages from P'u Sungling. First, they are moral satires in which man, who is at the top of the scale in the animal world, is compared to the foxes, a rather low animal. The irony is that man (like the protagonists Mu, Shih and Li in the above three tales), who is educated and intelligent, does not act as he should. Yet the foxes, though they are bestial, act with human dignity and love. Shih, a man with a military degree and a government post, should be a man of understanding and discretion. He should be able to tell what is wrong and what is right. His unwillingness and inability to recognize the fox spirit's virtues and to accept her put him morally below the animal.

In **"Chou hu,"** Mu's fault lies in his greediness, ingratitude and cruelty. Compared with him, the fox lady is more generous, kind, fair and frank. P'u comments in the voice of the Historian of the Strange that even though she is a fox, for all she has done for Mu, she does not deserve such treatment. The moral character of the fox is elevated above the male protagonist in the tale. In **"Chiu-shan wang,"** Li kills the old fox and his family just because they are animal spirits. He fails to see them as polite, respectable and generous individuals.

The second message of these tales lies in P'u's intention to present to the reader his ideal world—an ethical world in which love, generosity, and kindness are highly valued. In his Utopia, human or unhuman beings with the above moral qualities will win over the immoral. P'u is disappointed by mankind and its vices and so creates a supernatural world in which improbable characters and events can correct these wrongs.

### The Function of the Female in P'u's Fox Spirits

When one looks at the fox tales in *T'ai-p'ing kuan-chi,* it is not difficult to find that most Chinese traditional fox spirits are female. Many more than half of the fox characters in the tales are female. Female fox spirits are especially common when the tale is concerned with a man-and-woman relationship. When the woman is the seducer, she is always a fox spirit. This is such a traditional pattern that it has now become a modern cliche, which the Chinese still use in their daily speech. The modern expression *hu-li-ching,* "fox spirit," refers to a "bad" woman who seduces a man sexually and tricks him into giving her whatever she desires. In modern language, the term is never used to refer to the male sex.

As in the past, some of P'u's less interesting female foxes do carry their traditional lewd image, such as the two foxes in **"Fu hu."** Both men in the two tales come across sexually demanding fox spirits. The man in the first tale becomes sick and weak as a result. One day a doctor gives him a kind of aphrodisiac which makes him so potent that he conquers the fox in bed and takes its life. The man in the second tale is born so sexually strong that when the fox spirit goes to him, his strength is enough to scare her away.

Descriptions of the sexual relationship between fox and man appear in many of P'u's fox tales. They indeed form a pattern of an initiation process, by which the male and female protagonists are attracted to each other and fall in love. In P'u's best fox tales, this apparently loose relationship later develops into a relationship of true love, devotion and sincerity. The female fox spirit's lewd image at the beginning of the tale, when she comes on her own accord to seduce the man she loves, can be explained as a female's expression of her need for free love in a morally restricted Confucian society. In such an environment, the human female does not have the right to choose her own lover, or the freedom to go out of her house to visit him. The Chinese tradition requires the young woman to follow the order of her parents, who decide her marriage and her life:

> With Confucianism, two barriers are erected to insure the cohesion of the feudal social order: the first is the door to the bedchamber, the second is writing and knowledge in general. A woman cannot cross them both at once.

In ancient Chinese society, only the males are free to visit friends, roam the streets, and join different social activities. P'u bestows supernatural power on the female foxes, so that they are able to express their love and hate without obstruction.

As I have mentioned earlier in the story of **"Wu hsiao-lien"** and **"Hsin Shih-ssŭ-niang,"** the female protagonists in these tales are able to avenge themselves on men because they are foxes possessing supernatural power. This is probably the only way that P'u can give emotional and poetic justice to the social imbalance that he sees in the world around him: that females are often oppressed by males, or sometimes by a more powerful female agent, such as the old aunt in **"Hsin Shih-ssŭ-niang."** The old aunt in the tale represents the powerful, prominent and vicious forces against which the weak, the poor and the powerless have to fight in society.

P'u's foxes, then, are mostly female for the following reasons:

1) Foxes are traditionally regarded as a lewd animal. Therefore, female foxes are ideal characters in a free love relationship.

2) These female foxes are used as symbols for mortal women who, in a sexist society, are oppressed and controlled by men and other superiors.

3) The female foxes with supernatural powers give vent to social injustice. With their superhuman power, they are able to correct the wrongs done to them.

4) By using female foxes in place of mortal females in his tales, P'u elevates the animal spirits to a higher level of existence. At the same time, since these animals are virtuous, they give an exaggerated effect. P'u is saying that even among mortals such virtuous women cannot be found. But for him, such virtuous women are essential in building an ethical world.

His tales of good female fox spirits are numerous. Among these are **"Ch'ing-mei," "Ya-t'ou," "Chiao-na," "Lien-hsiang," "Ch'iao-niang," "Hung-yü," "Hsin Shih-ssŭ-niang," "Fêng San-niang," "Hsiao-ts'ui," "Fêng hsien," "Ch'ang-ê,"** and **"Wu hsiao-lien."** Most of these tales consist of a female fox spirit who falls in love with a mortal, helps him in various ways, and finally establishes a stable and longlasting relationship with him. The ending of these tales, in which the fox spirit is allowed to stay with her husband or lover, is the almost unique contribution of P'u Sung-ling. The fox tale section in *T'ai-p'ing kuang-chi* has only one tale, "Chi Chên," in which the female fox is allowed to marry a man and stay with him until she dies of a natural cause. All female spirits in other tales are either killed, driven away or leave on their own accord at the end. P'u's fox tales are different in that he unites man and animal not only on a love basis but also on an ethical one. Moral virtues and everlasting love are enough for P'u to break through the man-animal barrier. This barrier is dissolved in a very subtle way. P'u's fox spirits are so humanized that they not only look human but also act, think, and speak like mortals. The fox spirit's double identity, fox and mortal, overlap and mix to form a model character for P'u.

To end this essay, I would like to discuss two tales: **"Ch'ing-mei"** and **"Ya-t'ou."** I choose these two because they have much in common and both pertain to the points I have explicated above on P'u's good female fox spirits. 1) Both Ch'ing-mei and Ya-t'ou are fox spirits. Ya-t'ou is from a family of foxes, and Ch'ing-mei is the child of a fox and a mortal. 2) They both fall in love with a mortal man, who is rejected by the fox's family members. 3) Both fox spirits fight for freedom in love, acting against their own families. 4) Both foxes, after much suffering and patience, are able to reunite with their loved ones and to enjoy the fruit of their struggle at the end. 5) Both foxes give birth to children. 6) Both spirits are virtuous, intelligent, sincere and loving individuals. 7) Neither of them has much if any supernatural power. Ch'ing-mei has none whatsoever. 8) In both tales, two generations of foxes show contrast between one another.

In **"Ya-t'ou,"** P'u places the female protagonist in the environment of a brothel in order to emphasize her background. Ya-t'ou is both fox and prostitute. Her mother and sister are typically greedy and lewd women. But out of this moral pollution, Ya-t'ou emerges as a perfect daughter, wife and mother. She is obedient to her mother. She loves and forgives her family, even though they have tortured her physically and separated her from her husband and son. She is a good wife because she is chaste. After she has spent her first night and has fallen in love with Wang, she will not take another man. She would rather suffer beating from her mother. After the elopement, it is also Ya-t'ou who works hard to support the family. As a mother, she is concerned about her son, who is impulsive and brutal. She uses tears to teach him love and forgiveness. Ya-t'ou is a spirit which possesses superhuman power, yet she does not use it unless she has to do so. In only two instances does she display her magical power. First, she speeds up the elopement by tying a talisman on the servant and on the donkey's rear. Secondly, she takes off the "evil tendons" from her son's hands and feet. But she does not use any magic to help herself while she is imprisoned by her mother for eighteen years. Nor does she use it to acquire money in order to help her husband when they first start life in a strange city. The two magical deeds she has performed could be left out without changing the tale substantially. This tale would then be just an ordinary tale without any supernatural elements. With the fox, the story becomes partly a fantasy and a fairy tale.

P'u emphasizes Ya-t'ou's moral character by contrasting her with her fox mother and sister. The fox mother in the tale has the image of a greedy and cruel parent. She forces her daughters to sell their bodies to the customers who come to the brothel. When her wish is ignored, she does all that she can to inflict pain and suffering on them. She does not value true love or family ties. Although Ya-t'ou's older sister, Ni-tzŭ, is a minor character in the tale, she does not leave the reader with a good impression. She comes to fetch Ya-t'ou home after the elopement without trying to understand her younger sister. When Ya-t'ou is suffering at home, she does not even try to help her. Ni-tzŭ, like her mother, does not have love and concern for her own family members. Ya-t'ou is exactly the opposite of her mother and her older sister.

**"Ch'ing-mei"** is another of P'u's good fox tales. She is half human and half fox, born of a mortal father and fox spirit mother. Again P'u is ingenious in bringing out Ch'ing-mei's moral character by putting her in a low social stratum. Ch'ing-mei first starts out as an innocent child caught in her parents' dispute. Her father Ch'ing, impatient to have a male heir, marries Madam Wang, while Ch'ing-mei's mother, angry at being jilted by her husband, leaves the infant Ch'ing-mei to her own fate and disappears. When the father dies, Ch'ing-mei lives with her uncle, who is a heartless man. He sells her as a maid into another Wang family, in which she serves the master's daughter. Ch'ing-mei turns from a happy child with a family into an orphan and a maid in a stranger's house. With such a complicated and discouraging background, Ch'ing-mei could have been just an ordinary maid with no education, no money and no social status. She could have spent her life serving in the Wang family and marrying a fellow servant. Yet, because of her merits, she turns into the wife of a prominent court official, enjoying a happy family and prosperous life. Although she is a maid who must obey orders, Ch'ing-mei is portrayed as a strong character who recognizes what she wants and decides her own actions. Once she discovers that the poor scholar Chang is a kind, hard-working and filial man, Ch'ing-mei decides to match him with her mistress. She is not selfish, because she thinks of her mistress first when she sees a

good man. Later, when her plan to unite the two fails, Ch'ing-mei volunteers herself to be the bride. She is confident that she has made the right decision. No matter what happens, she will not be swayed. When she tells her mistress of her decision to marry Chang, her mistress says:

"You foolish maid, can you act on your own?"

"If nothing avails, I'm ready to die!"

Although she successfully marries herself to Chang, she has nonetheless plunged into another difficult situation. Chang's family is extremely poor. His father is very sick and needs to be taken care of constantly. Chang himself needs time to study for the examination. Once Ch'ing-mei joins the Changs, she takes up the responsibility to serve her in-laws. At the same time, she embroiders to make a living, allowing her husband to have the time and money to go on with his studies. Here our heroine is portrayed as a diligent, self-sacrificing (for she eats rice bran herself and gives the rice to her in-laws) and filial daughter-in-law.

Ch'ing-mei remains a humble and kind person after she has become a government official's wife. Her magnanimity is manifested in her treatment of her former mistress when the latter is in great distress. Although now A-hsi is no longer her mistress, Ch'ing-mei still respects and loves her. When she knows that A-hsi is homeless, she insists on bringing her to her house. Far from being jealous, Ch'ing-mei is the one who arranges A-hsi to marry her husband. We are told in the tale that, for the rest of her life, she serves and respects A-hsi as she did before, even though she is the senior wife in the family. Ch'ing-mei is a person who values friendship, love and righteousness.

Ch'ing-mei serves as a strong contrast to her mother, the fox lady. Although in the tale, the daughter is said to resemble her mother physically, they have completely different characters. Ch'ing-mei's mother is promiscuous. She hangs on a man's belt and follows him home. But when she finds that he is fickle, she leaves the man and her own child without a second thought. This fox spirit gives us the impression of a lewd, selfish and cruel woman. Yet Ch'ing-mei, the fox's daughter, is humane and kind. When she reunites with her former mistress A-hsi, she takes up the responsibility to marry A-hsi to her husband. This is the crucial difference between the mother and daughter. The mother fox, enraged with jealousy, breaks up the family and ruins her daughter, while her child Ch'ing-mei harbors no jealous feelings at all but only love and understanding for the new couple. Rather than breaking up her relationship with her husband, Ch'ing-mei unites the couple and herself into one family, which prospers with wealth and children. For all this, Ch'ing-mei turns from a fox's daughter into a perfect model of a mortal woman. The reader should also notice that Ch'ing-mei has absolutely no superhuman power at all. At the beginning, she is not even able to save herself from being sold as a maid. In her early married life, she has to work even harder than a maid for a living. Ch'ing-mei has elevated herself from her animal status (as a fox), and her social status (as a maid) to an intelligent, sincere and virtuous woman in P'u's world.

One can say that many of P'u Sung-ling's fox tales are didactic tales. Everytime he tells a tale, he has in the back of his mind an ethical framework from which he never strays. In all of his tales, there exists a strong tendency to elucidate cause and effect. If a fox spirit is good, P'u never fails to reward it. If a man is bad, at the end, he will surely get his due. This has become a literary formula which underlies the whole collection of *Liao-chai.* As C. T. Hsia has said about the colloquial tales, the cause and effect formula limits the realism in the tales. Not only is the reader able to predict the ending while he is still reading the story, but the author has also limited his imagination and his art if he has to follow a certain pattern. The good foxes in P'u's stories all are rewarded with more or less the same thing: a successful and loving husband, with a prosperous family and children. Apparently, these are the only things that a woman would want in that social environment. Ch'ing-mei, Ya-t'ou, and Ch'iao-niang are examples. Since our author insists on staying inside his own ethical fence, he is not able to write such stories as *Jên-shih chuan* of the Tang Dynasty. Shên Chi-chi wrote the story because he thought that Miss Jên was a rare female who was understanding and righteous. He felt sorry for her and so wanted to record her life. This is different from P'u's purpose of expounding morals with his imagination.

---

**Yu on P'u Sung-ling's ghost tales:**

Because its author has a declared intention in social polemics, *Liao-chai* is an anthology in which the satiric jostles the fantastic in claiming the reader's attention. Many venerable institutions and structures of traditional Chinese society become the ready targets of P'u Sung-ling's irony. Under his prolific brush, there are marvelously entertaining—and often, riotously funny—tales of drunkard ghosts, jealous wives and concubines, corrupt officials, ghosts desperate to pass civil service examinations, and incorrigible gamblers whose legal problems endure even in hell. In virtually all of these stories, the variegated experiences of the world of light are transplanted wholesale into the world of darkness.

Anthony C. Yu, "'Rest, Rest, Perturbed Spirit!' Ghosts in Traditional Chinese Prose Fiction," Harvard Journal of Asiatic Studies, Vol. 47, No. 2, December, 1987, pp. 397-434.

---

## Judith T. Zeitlin   (essay date 1993)

"The Discourse on the Strange," in *Historian of the Strange: Pu Songling and the Chinese Classical Tale,* Stanford University Press, 1993, pp. 15-42.

[*In the following essay, Zeitlin reviews how P'u's* Strange Stories *has been received over time and comments on the many varied interpretations of the stories.*]

The Master did not speak of prodigies, feats of strength, disorder, and gods.

—*The Analects of Confucius,* 7.21

"Here is that crazy scholar who didn't believe in ghosts and spirits and who presecuted our minions when he was alive." The King of the Ghosts glared irately at the prisoner: "You possess five sound limbs and inborn intelligence—haven't you heard the line 'Abundant are the virtues of ghosts and spirits'? Confucius was a sage, but still he said: 'Revere them but keep your distance from them!' . . . What kind of man are *you* that you alone say we don't exist?"

—Qu You, *New Tales Under the Lamplight*

"A literary work is not an object that stands by itself and that offers the same view to each reader in each period." Hans Robert Jauss's now almost-commonplace pronouncement [in *Toward an Aesthetic of Reception,* 1982] is given strikingly new visual force in the standard edition of *Liaozhai's Records of the Strange,* Zhang Youhe's collated and annotated version, which amalgamates editions and the writings that circulated with them before the twentieth century. Embedded in a welter of prefaces, colophons, dedicatory verses, interlinear glosses, and interpretive commentaries, and crowned with a new foreword and appendix, this edition encompasses a virtual, though incomplete, history of *Liaozhai*'s interpretation.

This format derives directly from traditional Chinese critical discourse, which was not simply interpretive but interactive as well. There was a snowballing effect: as a book or manuscript circulated, readers recorded their reactions all over its pages, even between the lines. New readers might even treat the comments of their predecessors as part of the book and comment on them accordingly. In this way, the text became the site of an ongoing dialogue not only between the author and his readers but also between generations of readers. A later reader thus finds it increasingly difficult to ignore this organic process of interpretation, to screen out comment from text in reading.

Although the collation of editions, a mainstay of Chinese scholarly activity past and present, has resulted in redactions in which the amount of commentary far exceeds the amount of original text, the unusual volume of writings in Zhang's edition of *Liaozhai* is unprecedented for a collection of classical tales. It consists of three full-length commentaries, two extensive glossaries, and a mass of prefaces, colophons, and poems. These waves of literary activity attest both to *Liaozhai*'s great popularity and to the continuous printing of new editions. But these writings also reveal a strong underlying need to interpret the work.

This need to interpret *Liaozhai* is bound up with the problem of the strange posed by the tales. An understanding of what the strange represents and of the importance or value of the strange within *Liaozhai* is thus tightly intertwined with the history of the book's overall interpretation. This history began even before the collection had been completed. Pu Songling's literary friends wrote two prefaces, several poems, and scattered comments for the manuscript well before it reached its final form in the early 1700's. After the author's death in 1715, additional prefaces and colophons were written as the collection circulated in manuscript for fifty years. The first printed edition was published in 1766 and, not surprisingly, contributed its own influential preface and foreword. The ambitious full-length commentaries written in the first half of the nineteenth century mark another watershed.

The traditional critical discourse on *Liaozhai,* like that surrounding vernacular fiction and pornography, is on the whole apologetic and defensive; each contribution must justify anew the value of the work to a sometimes implicit, sometimes explicit, hostile interlocutor. An attentive ear thus enables us to detect elements of the negative reception of *Liaozhai* as well, even if we allow that for rhetorical purposes the defenders of the book might have altered or exaggerated their opponents' arguments.

An examination of the traditional writings surrounding *Liaozhai* uncovers three major interpretive strategies: (1) legitimating the practice of recording the strange; (2) understanding the work as an allegorical vehicle for serious self-expression; and (3) acknowledging the work as a model of stylistic brilliance and as a great work of fiction. A fourth approach, a conventional moral didacticism, drones softly through the discourse on *Liaozhai,* but with one or two exceptions, notably in funerary writings about Pu Songling, this argument seems to have been taken for granted as the most obvious line of defense and is rarely elaborated with much vigor. These approaches, all of which appeared well before the twentieth century, have profoundly shaped modern readings of the work.

In providing this selective interpretive survey, I necessarily simplify and impose order on many often contradictory and sketchy arguments. Since previous arguments are often repeated perfunctorily in later writings, I try to trace changes in emphasis rather than note mere inclusion. Finally, I have concentrated on prefaces and colophons rather than on dedicatory verses because prose writings by necessity entail exposition and argument. Dedicatory verses, in contrast, tend to be written in an altogether lighter and more bantering vein, caring more for a witty turn of phrase than for advancing an argument.

### The First Wave: Legitimating the Strange

In 1679, Gao Heng (1612-97), an eminent, retired scholar-official from a prominent gentry family in Pu Songling's hometown of Zichuan and a man of eclectic interests in literature and religion, composed the first preface for *Liaozhai.* Three years later in 1682, Tang Menglai (1627-98), another retired high official, a leading member of the local Zichuan gentry, and a writer of some renown, completed a second preface for the manuscript. The social and literary prestige of these two men ranked among the highest in the community and extended well beyond Shandong provincial circles. As personal friends of the author, who were also featured as informants or even as protagonists

in several tales in the collection, their prefaces offer valuable insight into the immediate circle of readers for whom *Liaozhai* was written and the social and intellectual climate from which the book emerged.

Gao and Tang's prefaces share a similar orientation: both redefine an interest in the strange in morally and intellectually acceptable terms with the aid of precedents from the Confucian classics. A corollary of their effort was to widen the boundaries of the mainstream literary and philosophical tradition to incorporate the more marginal tradition of recording the strange. To this end, they rehearse many arguments that had become almost standard by the seventeenth century in prefaces to collections of strange accounts.

Tang begins by scrutinizing the concept of the strange. He argues that we cannot base our understanding of the strange on our own empirical experience because the latter is far too limited and individual powers of perception vary too greatly. What is commonly deemed strange is based on convention rather than on any identifiable qualities inherent in strangeness; conversely, familiarity blinds us to the potential strangeness that lies before us.

> Now, people consider that what they see with their eyes exists, and that what they don't see, doesn't exist. They say, "This is normal," and what suddenly appears and suddenly vanishes amazes them. As for the flourishing and fading of plants, the metamorphoses of insects, which suddenly appear and suddenly vanish, this does not amaze them; only divine dragons amaze them. But the whistling of the wind, which sounds without stimulus, the currents of rivers, which move without agitation—aren't these amazing? But we are accustomed to these and are at peace with them. We are amazed only at wraiths and fox-spirits; we are not amazed at humankind.

Tang's contention that strangeness is a subjective rather than an objective category echoes a late third-century inquiry into the strange, Guo Pu's (276-324) influential neo-Daoist preface to the mysterious *Classic of Mountains and Seas* (*Shanhai jing*), an ancient book of geographic marvels. As Guo Pu argued: "We know not why what the world calls strange is strange; we know not why what the world does not call strange is not strange. How is this? Things are not strange in and of themselves—they must wait for me before they can be strange. Thus the strange lies within *me*—it is not that *things* are strange" [Chen Hsiao-chie, *Shan hai ching,* 1985].

Casting the strange as an epistemological problem to refute skeptics had its seeds in the Daoist parables about great and petty understanding in *Zhuangzi.* Guo Pu declares, in fact, that he took as his point of departure *Zhuangzi*'s dictum: "What human beings know is far less than what they don't know." It is worth recalling here part of the famous dialogue that *Zhuangzi* uses to illustrate this point. The North Sea lectures the Yellow River:

> "You can't discuss the ocean with a well frog—he's limited by the space he lives in. You can't discuss ice

with a summer insect—he's bound to a single season. You can't discuss the Way with a cramped scholar— he's shackled by his doctrines. Now you have come out beyond your banks and borders and have seen the great sea—so you realize your own pettiness. From now on it will be possible to talk to you about the Great Principle."

Although elsewhere *Zhuangzi* draws upon marvels to illustrate these epistemological points, Guo Pu was probably the first Chinese thinker to ask what the strange is and to ponder what makes something strange. His radical conclusion, reached through an elaborate series of double negatives, is that the strange exists only in the perceiver's mind, not in any objective reality, and that therefore "nothing is impossible."

Guo Pu's and Tang Menglai's arguments will seem oddly familiar to a reader who has encountered Montaigne's celebrated essay, "Of Custom, and Not Easily Changing an Accepted Law": "These examples from strange lands are not strange if we consider what we regularly experience: how much habit stupefies our senses." Like Montaigne, who developed this stance after confronting ethnographic accounts of the New World, Guo Pu was responding to the depiction of exotic lands. Not so Tang Menglai, in whose preface the conventional image of the strange is represented by the otherworldly beings in our midst rather than by the inhabitants of distant barbarian lands: "We are amazed only at wraiths and fox-spirits; we are not amazed at humankind."

But Tang's preface to *Liaozhai* represents another turn in understanding the strange. Although he borrows Guo Pu's neo-Daoist arguments, profound differences exist. Guo Pu was ultimately arguing for the veracity of the places and creatures depicted in the *Classic of Mountains and Seas* and for its practical use as an omen book and as an encyclopedia of knowledge. Tang is neither confirmin nor denying the factuality of books like *Liaozhai*; rather, he is contending that unless we allow a greater tolerance for the discussion of things that lie beyond empirical experience and ordinary discourse, "the beginnings and endings of the Way" are in danger of being "obscured to the world." If our curiosity is entirely suppressed, then ignorance will triumph and "what we see becomes less and less and what amazes us becomes greater and greater."

Tang's preface shares some of the concerns voiced in sixteenth- and seventeenth-century prefaces to both strange tales and vernacular fiction. For instance, Jiang Yingk's (1553-1605) comic preface to *Tales of Hearsay* (*Er-tan*), a collection of strange anecdotes, also admonishes the reader to reconsider what is really strange. Jiang mischievously selects the ear of the title as something that is not amazing because it is too commonplace: "Now an ear measures only one inch in width, twice that in length, and about three inches inside—that's just a couple of inches. And yet it can receive anywhere from a single syllable to millions of words, far too many to count. Now isn't that exceedingly odd? But no one considers it odd."

Similarly, Ling Mengchu's (1580-1644) preface to his first collection of vernacular stories, *Slapping the Table in Amazement* (*Pai'an jingqi*) (dated 1628), closely resembles Tang's preface. Both begin with different halves of the same proverb ("To see a camel and call it a hump-backed horse"—Tang; "To the man of little experience, everything is strange"—Ling), and both demonstrate that ordinary experience is far more extraordinary than is commonly recognized. The two men draw different inferences, however; Tang justifies recording otherworldly beings ("wraiths, fox-spirits, and prodigies"), whereas Ling advocates depicting "the wonders before our very eyes," by which he seems to mean the curiosities to be found in daily life.

Tang insists that accounts of the strange should not be dismissed as untrue or subversive. Strange tales are valuable because they can break down the limitations of petty understanding and reason, just as Daoist parables do. His arguments, penned to an obscure manuscript with no immediate hope of publication, were presumably aimed at a small hypothetical audience of Neo-Confucian skeptics. Ling Mengchu, on the other hand, is arguing that stories of daily life can compete in interest and novelty with more fantastical and exotic accounts. This is clearly an appeal to a broad, existing reading public, one that Ling was trying to wean from what he perceived to be a considerable appetite for supernatural tales. Ling is thus distinguishing the intriguing and novel sense of strange from the supernatural and exotic sense; the former he tries to capture in his fiction, the latter he vehemently rejects, at least in principle.

**"The Rakshas and the Sea Market" ("Luosha haishi")**, one of the few *Liaozhai* tales about a voyage to a foreign country, vividly plays out the argument that strangeness and normality lie in the eyes of the beholder. A young Chinese merchant is blown ashore on a strange island populated by a race of hideously deformed people, who are in turn appalled by *his* monstrosity. A slightly more human-looking inhabitant finally plucks up his courage and explains the native point of view: "I once heard my grandfather say that 26,000 miles to the west lies the land of China whose inhabitants are all of a weird physical appearance. But this was hearsay; only today do I believe it." Pu Songling is here mocking those proverbial cramped scholars who refuse to believe anything that they have not seen with their own eyes. On this isolated island, the ordinary appearance of the Chinese merchant becomes truly extraordinary. However, the merchant quickly becomes habituated to the sight of these monstrous natives, and he is no longer frightened by them; indeed, he quickly learns how to profit by frightening them. In the world of *Liaozhai*, the extraordinary is made to seem ordinary, but the ordinary is also made to seem extraordinary.

In the first half of his preface, Tang argues that the strange is a subjective and relative concept. In the second half, in a radical shift, he attacks the common understanding of strangeness as anomaly and its subsequent equation with monstrosity and evil. In his hands, the strange is redefined exclusively in human ethical terms.

> I consider that regardless of whether something is normal or abnormal, only things that are harmful to human beings are monstrous. Thus [evil omens like] eclipses and meteorites, "fishhawks in flight and mynah birds nesting," rocks that can speak and the battles of dragons, cannot be considered strange. Only military and civil conscription out of season or rebellious sons and ministers are monstrous and strange.

By relocating the strange to the human world and moving the marginal to the center, Tang has diffused any potential threat that anomaly poses to the moral order. For Tang, strangeness in the sense of evil can exist only in the realm of human events, especially in the political arena. In this regard, he sets the stage for the satiric demystification of the strange often found within *Liaozhai* itself. At the end of the tale **"Guo An,"** for example, it is announced that this court case is amazing not because a servant saw a ghost but because of the utter stupidity of the presiding magistrate and his miscarriage of justice.

In the other seventeenth-century preface, Gao Heng also argues that the strange is primarily a moral category with canonical roots. He begins by defining the term "strange" to explain its inclusion in the title of the book: "To say that something recorded is 'strange' clearly means that it differs from the norm." This definition is presented as the common understanding of strange, and indeed, judging from other examples, it seems to be so. Like Tang, however, Gao seeks to demonstrate the inadequacy and even the inappropriateness of such a simple definition: by juggling a quotation from the *Book of Changes* and an audacious pun, he glosses yi (strangeness, difference) as *yi* (righteousness), one of the cardinal Confucian virtues. This is possible, he declares, because "the principles of Heaven, Earth, and Man, the writings of the Six Classics, and the meanings of the sages, can be 'bound together with a single thread'." Thus this strangeness, this difference, is not external to the proper workings of the universe and moral concerns but is incorporated within them. The potential threat that irregularity poses to order, as deviation or heterodoxy, is neutralized. The strange is no longer unfathomable, but coherent and intelligible.

Both Gao and Tang are clearly operating within what Charlotte Furth has described [in *Late Imperial China,* Vol. 9, No. 2, December 1988] as "a long-standing Chinese view of cosmological pattern that sought to incorporate anomaly rather than reject the irregular as inconsistent with the harmony of natural pattern." In this tradition of correlative thinking, anomalies were taken as omens manifesting Heaven's will and played a powerful role in political discourse, especially during the Han dynasty. But if we accept the argument that by the late Ming people were "beginning to question the tradition of correlative thinking which assumed that natural moral and cosmological phenomena were rendered intelligible by an underlying pattern of affinities," [Furth] we can perhaps understand Gao's sophistry and Tang's brashness as efforts to reassert the old moral and political implications of anomalies in the face of the age's increasing dissatisfaction with correlative thinking.

Aware that his rhetorical conflation of strangeness and righteousness is shaky, Gao goes on to upbraid would-be critics for construing the great cultural tradition too narrowly. To this end, he refutes the staunchest attack against an interest in the strange, the statement in *The Analects of Confucius* that "the Master did not speak of prodigies, feats of strength, disorder, and gods." Like many other apologists for recording the strange, Gao argues that Confucius was also the author of the canonical *Spring and Autumn Annals,* a repository of the very subjects that the Master supposedly avoided speaking of:

> The narrow-minded scholars of later generations, whose pupils are as tiny as peas . . . explain away everything they haven't seen with their own eyes with the phrase "the Master didn't speak of it." Don't they know whose pen recorded [the omens of] "fishhawks in flight and meteors falling"? To blame Master Zuo [commentator on the *Spring and Autumn Annals*] for such errors is no different from covering one's ears and loudly declaring there is no thunder.

Gao also exploits other loopholes opened by contradictory remarks within *The Analects* itself to justify such Buddhist-influenced preserves of the strange as a belief in hell and the workings of karma and retribution. Modern critics may explain such textual contradictions as stemming from different strata of scriptural transmission, but for scholars such as Gao and Tang the Classics were a unified whole; any apparent contradiction arose from an inadequate understanding of the lines rather than from a problem inherent in the text. This attitude still prevailed in the seventeenth century, despite the new advances in philological studies (*kaozheng*), which were subjecting the Classics to increasingly rigorous modes of scholarship.

Instead Gao and Tang prefer to resolve such contradictions in the canon by appealing to the role of the listener or reader. Gao in particular emphasizes the power of the interpretive act to activate the moral potential of a written text:

> For the intelligent men of this world, even "what the Master didn't speak of" can help in the places that conventional teachings don't reach. [The strange accounts of] *The Librarian's Miscellany* [*Youyang zazu*] and *Records of the Listener* [*Yijian zhi*] can thus accomplish the same as the Six Classics. But for other types of men, even *daily* recitations of what Confucius *always* spoke of can be used to abet evil.

Thus, the good reader can glean enlightenment from any text; the bad reader can find a justification for evil in the most canonical of texts. What is striking in this formulation is not that esoteric or subversive texts require discerning and enlightened readers—appealing to the superior and understanding reader is a conventional move—but that bad readers can pervert a sacred text. Although Gao grounds this point in historical precedent, he is chipping away at the privileged authority of the Classics over other texts: moral authority is contingent not on a superior *text* but on a superior *reader*.

We thus find a merging of two seemingly unrelated and even contradictory arguments: since strangeness is a subjective perception, the morality of strange accounts ultimately depends on the reader and his interpretation of the text. This is a particularly powerful method of challenging the canon to include non-canonical texts and non-canonical traditions. But this concern with the superior reader is also symptomatic of an anxiety that *Liaozhai* will be misread. And for a book to be in danger of being misread, there must be a marked disjunction between the content and the underlying meaning that the inferior reader would miss.

Although Tang and Gao argue along similar lines, Gao's final discussion of the relationship between the strange and the fictive imagination is unique. The last in Gao's series of skeptical interlocutors reluctantly allows that strange things do occasionally occur in this world and that one can chat about them, but he bristles at taking imaginative license with them. "To allow the imagination to gallop beyond the heavens and to realize illusions in the human sphere, isn't this modeled on Qixie['s legendary book of marvels]?" Gao's first defense is rather predictable: he cites textual precedents for indulging the imagination in Sima Qian's biographies of court jesters and the fanciful parables of *Zhuangzi.* But his next defense is more startling, for he openly calls into question the veracity of the official histories: "And is *every* record in the twenty-four histories solid [*shi*]?" Once this point has been granted, he can logically argue that since we tolerate fictions in the histories, we ought also to tolerate fictions in other works.

Gao begs allowance for authorial inspiration and invention, "for the swift literary mind whose pen supplements the process of creation, not only by embellishing the surface but even by smelting the material." The allusion is to the myth of the goddess Nü Wa repairing the toppling sky with molten rock. Thus "supplement" is meant in the sense of "filling in the holes"—of placing new material where it belongs within a pre-existing structure, of mixing small doses of fiction with history. In this metaphor, literary invention bolsters and reinforces order rather than distorting and subverting it. This is not the Western image of the writer who freely imitates the Creation but rather a view of the writer as an assistant to the natural process of creation who selectively fills in gaps as needed. This image of the fictional imagination as a "rock filling in holes" culminates in the opening of the eighteenth-century novel *Story of the Stone*: the novel itself originates as a rock rejected from the celestial repair process, who becomes both the protagonist of the story and the surface upon which the story is inscribed.

But for Gao, the hard-earned license of literary invention is not to be squandered; it must be well spent in refining human beings. The polarity between exceptional and non-canonical (qi) and orthodox and canonical (zheng) that permeates the discourse on the strange is hereby introduced. Literary invention is qi, refining human beings is zheng; they are two sides of the same coin, not incompatible extremes.

## The Second Wave: Self-expression and Allegory

The earliest discourse on *Liaozhai* primarily defends the tradition of recording anomalies: *Liaozhai* itself is hailed as a superior but typical example of the zhiguai genre. To this end, an attempt is made to redefine the notion of the strange and to widen the margins of mainstream literature. But the next group of writers, particularly those seeking to publish the manuscript in the fifty years following Pu Songling's death, advanced a radically different approach. These new champions of *Liaozhai* sought to distance it or even to remove it altogether from the anomalies tradition, claiming that the book was not really about the strange at all.

This tendency was reflected in the first published edition of *Liaozhai.* The prefect Zhao Qigao (d. 1766), who sponsored the publication, mentions in his foreword that he had excised forty-eight of the shorter, more insipid, and more commonplace items. Although much attention has been paid to Zhao's censorship of a group of supposedly anti-Manchu tales, these number only a handful; the rest are standard records of anomalies in style and content: unembellished, factual reports of strange events such as **"A Freak Melon" ("Gua yi"), "A Passion for Snakes" ("She pi"),** or **"The Clam" ("Ge").** Moreover, Zhao tells us he had originally planned to publish only the tales he considered the best, but he eventually decided to append the ones left over after his initial selection to the end of the book. According to Allan Barr [in "The Textual Transmission of *Liaozhai zhiyi,*" *HJAS,* Vol. 44, No. 2, 1984], "The tales which were later incorporated . . . are by no means lacking in interest, but have much more in common with the short anecdotes recorded by other seventeenth and eighteenth century writers, and as such, are rather unexceptional." In other words, these last tales, which tend to accentuate *Liaozhai*'s similarity to conventional collections, are relegated to the most inconspicuous place in the book and grouped together as an afterthought.

Although Zhao does acknowledge *Liaozhai*'s affiliation with the anomalies tradition, the aim implied in his selection of tales is to distinguish *Liaozhai* from a stereotypical image of strange accounts. Zhao's secretary and the collator of the edition, the painter and poet YuJi (1739-1823), explicitly states this idea in his preface: "Comparing it to Qixie's book of marvels or saying that it differs little from collections of rare phenomena or strange tales is a very shallow view and one that greatly contradicts the author's intent."

Pu Lide (1683-1751), Pu Songling's grandson and a keen advocate of *Liaozhai*'s publication, makes this point even more forcefully in a colophon to an edition that he never succeeded in publishing:

> Since this book has the word "strange" in the title, someone who doesn't know the work will assume that it must be like *The Magician's Records* [*Yu Chu zhi*] or *Seeking the Spirits* [*Soushen ji*], or else that it's something like Su Shi's ghost stories, randomly selected and casually prolonged, which are told simply as

material for conversation, otherwise they'll say the title is unfair. Someone who knows the work, on the other hand, will say that it uses the supernatural to demonstrate rewards and punishments. But none of these understand this book.

In Pu Lide's scheme, the ideal reader of *Liaozhai* is not one who reads the stories for pleasure or one who understands the work as a didactic tract, but one who realizes that the book is an act of serious self-expression.

Earlier, Gao Heng had introduced the dichotomy between *Liaozhai*'s surface content and its underlying meaning, appealing to a superior reader capable of discerning this meaning, but he was still interested in the subject matter of the tales and the implications of the strange. In contrast, the second wave of writings on *Liaozhai* vehemently denies the importance of its content. The bizarre subject matter of the tales is dismissed as a smoke screen, one that veils not so much a concrete meaning as the presence and intention of the author.

Writers adopting this new approach interpreted the strange almost exclusively as a vehicle for the author's self-expression. *Liaozhai* is lifted into the highest reaches of the literary tradition, not by challenging the conventional boundaries of that tradition but by assimilating strange tales to the autobiographical reading conventions of the major literary genres, especially poetry. The ancient definition of poetry, "that it speaks of what is intently on the mind," had long been extended to other literary genres and other arts; by the late Ming and early Qing, this theory of self-expression could be applied to virtually any field of human endeavor, no matter how trivial or eccentric.

In this mode of interpretation, recording the strange was merely the means through which Pu Songling articulated "what was intently on his mind"; the very outlandishness of the material alerted the reader to the personal distress behind the work. For the reader who styled himself a knowing reader, a *zhiyin* (literally, "one who understands the tone"), the primary question was no longer "What is the strange?" or "What can we learn from the strange?" Rather, it was "Why would a man channel such extraordinary talent into a work of such a dubious genre?" Read against the background of Pu Songling's lifelong failure to realize his political and social ambitions, the strange content of *Liaozhai* was familiarized and excused. As the collator Yu Ji lamented [in *Wusheng xi*], "He entrusted to this book all the extraordinary *qi* [energy] that otherwise had no outlet in his life. And so in the end he did not care that his accounts often involve things so weird and unorthodox that the world is shocked by them." (This mechanistic view of qì, which here seems to mean something like creative energy, may remind the twentieth-century reader of the Freudian model of libido: if denied access to a proper outlet, it will involuntarily force its way out through some other channel.)

The promotion of *Liaozhai* as the author's self-expression probably began to take shape toward the end of Pu Songling's life. By this time, it had become clear that Pu

Songling would never achieve conventional success and that *Liaozhai,* which had expanded in size and scope over the years, would be his lifework. The first written evidence of this view appears in a grave inscription commissioned by Pu Songling's family: since the normal channels were insufficient for Pu to unleash his pent-up sorrow, he "sought out the strange and composed his *Records of the Strange.* Although things in it involve the fantastic, his judgments are sober and serve to warn the people." This eulogist, Zhang Yuan (1672-1756), bore a strong resemblance to the man he was eulogizing. Like Pu, he was a first-degree holder who spent most of his life failing higher examinations, the only avenue to success for intellectuals of limited means; like Pu, he was a man of literary talent forced to support himself as a tutor in a wealthy household, separated from his own family. Both Pu and Zhang, then, epitomized the frustrated, public-minded literary man unable to realize his ambitions in the political, social, or literary system. This resemblance reveals not so much an uncanny correspondence between the two men as the typicality of Pu Songling's career during the Qing. Yuan Shishuo's painstaking study of Pu Songling's friends and family demonstrates that this pattern applies by and large not only to Pu's childhood friends and his pupils, but even to his sons and his favorite grandson, Pu Lide. The literary work of such frustrated scholars, especially if it betrayed any originality or impropriety, was invariably interpreted to fit the ancient paradigm of the worthy man who meets unjustly with failure and so vents his sorrow and disaffection in literature. Zhang Yuan's eulogy introduces the self-expression theory not only because he felt sympathy and admiration for his subject, but because it was by then virtually required to confer literary value on an unusual work and to explain its emotional power.

The pervasiveness of this reading tradition ensured that a brief biography of Pu Songling would be inserted in the first published edition of *Liaozhai* and appear in the many subsequent reprints. Later readers thus began their reading of the book with a strong impression of the author's personal failure. One such reader, the late Qing scholar Fang Junyi (1815-89), professes wonder that a writer of such exceptional talent chose to squander it on fantastic tales rather than employing it more fruitfully in poetry and prose essays. But the question already contained within it the answer: the choice of form and subject matter was given meaning as a desperate act. Thus Fang concludes: "This work must certainly have been written by a great man who met with failure in his time. I ache on his behalf." Here we see a two-way process at work: an image of the author's life gleaned from his writing is reinforced by his biography, and this knowledge is then read back into his work.

What caused this shift in interpretation? We cannot explain it as a result of historical differences between the intellectual climate of the seventeenth century and that of the eighteenth. Seventeenth-century readers were just as prone as eighteenth-century ones to interpret problematic works as acts of self-expression. Seventeenth-century readings of the macabre and visionary poetry of Li He (791-817), for instance, reveal exactly the same impulse to locate stereotypical political motivations behind a difficult work (although in the case of Li He's poetry these explanations seem much more forced). Alternatively, a famous eighteenth-century recorder of the strange, the prolific and successful Yuan Mei (1716-98), specifically forestalls such an interpretation of his work by telling the reader that the contents of his collection were gathered purely for fun, "*not* because I was moved by something."

A better explanation for this shift may be found in the aging of *Liaozhai.* Often the process of interpretation follows its own pattern, one that may have less to do with a specific historical period than with the passage of time and how this alters subsequent views of a work. In this light, the reinterpretation of *Liaozhai* as a vehicle for self-expression, that is, as a plaint of personal failure and a diatribe against the failings of the age, is a highly predictable move. It is predictable not only because it was an ancient way to reclaim works that otherwise threatened the tradition, but also because the work itself had become gilded with the patina of age. To Pu Songling's senior contemporaries Gao Heng and Tang Menglai, he may have been a man of talent, but he was an insignificant figure. Moreover, when they wrote their prefaces, it was still not too late to hope for an improvement in Pu Songling's career, and the collection was much more modest in scope. For those writing later (and for critics of our times who may identify with Pu Songling's plight), the author's personal failure, which seemed merely pathetic in its own time, lent a tragic glamor and profundity to *Liaozhai.* One treats the work of a dead author differently from that of a living writer.

As the emphasis shifted from the content of *Liaozhai* to its author's intention, a general allegorical reading of the tales perhaps became inevitable. In this reading of *Liaozhai,* the evil demons and ghosts in the stories are transparent symbols of human wickedness, the bureaucratic hells of the underworld satires on corrupt human officialdom. Pu Songling was certainly cognizant of the metaphorical possibilities of the strange, a tradition that preceded the zhiguai genre and could be traced back as far as *Zhuangzi* and *Liezi,* works he particularly loved. In many tales he calls attention to an allegorical reading, usually in the evaluative comments following a story, under his sobriquet Historian of the Strange. For example, in **"The Painted Skin"** (**"Hua pi"**), a man who has been dallying with a beautiful woman peeps through the window one day and discovers a hideous demon using a paintbrush to touch up a human skin spread out on the couch. She lifts up the skin, and "as though shaking out a garment," drapes it over her body, transforming herself back into a beautiful woman. When he seeks to exorcise her through a Daoist charm, she flies into a rage and tears out his heart. The Historian of the Strange underlines the obvious moral allegory in his final comments to the story: "How stupid are the people of this world! Someone is obviously a demon, but people consider her beautiful." This exact point, that beautiful appearances can conceal souls blacker than any demon's, is in fact offered in collator Yu Ji's preface as an example of how to read the strange in *Liaozhai.*

Gao Heng, the author of the first seventeenth-century preface to *Liaozhai,* had already hinted that the more fanciful subject matter of the tales could be explained as *yuyan*— literally as "loaded words," a common, all-purpose Chinese figure variously translated as "allegory," "metaphor," and "parable." In its broadest sense, *yuyan* designates fiction as opposed to fact. A comment to the seventeenth-century novel *The Carnal Prayer Mat* (*Rou putuan*) makes this usage quite clear: "Fiction is 'loaded words.' To say that words are loaded means they're not fact." Since the term *yuyan* is employed so broadly in this period, it may be best to think of it simply as "figurative language"— something not meant to be taken as literally true that points to a larger truth.

Although Gao Heng introduced the figurative possibilities of *Liaozhai,* he was still willing to tolerate the coexistence of several levels of meaning, and he enjoyed playing with the intellectual paradoxes posed by the concept of strangeness. The lapses in logic and wide leaps in his preface reveal a refreshing lack of dogmatism. The next generation of readers, men like Yu Ji and Pu Lide, however, are rigorous allegorists: they reject the literal sense altogether and retain only the figurative moral sense. By reducing a story to only one possible meaning, they eliminate *Liaozhai*'s strangeness; they try to homogenize the collection, both in terms of itself (all the stories are alike) and in terms of other works (all great literature is alike).

One of the most original discussions of the interpretive problems posed by *Liaozhai* appears in a preface that has only recently come to light. Written by the philologist and official Kong Jihan (1739-89), a member of the illustrious Kong clan that traced its origins back to Confucius, this preface was preserved in Kong's collected works. This preface may be seen to some extent as a bridge between the first wave of interpretation and the second, or as a compromise between the two.

For Kong, the central problem raised by *Liaozhai* is still its strangeness (yi), which he explores in terms of its related meaning, difference. He begins by setting out the common understanding of the strange: "People always consider that what runs counter to the norm and counter to nature is strange." But he immediately wonders what happens when so many tales about the strange are read collectively: "When you put together all these many piled-up stories and compare them, it's like fishing in a dried-up marsh—though every fish head is strange or different, they no longer seem strange or different." When so many tales are assembled, the impression of strangeness disappears, for the tales resemble one another more than they differ.

This point repeats an earlier objection leveled at the truly voluminous twelfth-century zhiguai collection, *Records of the Listener*: "Now it is only because things that run counter to the norm and counter to nature are rare that we say they're amazing. If, however, they're too numerous to record, then we can no longer find them strange." But Kong refuses to conclude that *Liaozhai* transcends strangeness or that strangeness is only relative. He continues:

"Then why did the author put the word 'strange' in the title? Because it *can* be considered strange."

Kong's fish-head analogy exposes the paradox that in quantity unusual things seem to lose their singularity. This leads him to introduce the opposite paradox: when ordinary things we take for granted become rare, they suddenly become strange. Kong's examples are the biographies of "singular conduct" (*duxing zhuan*) in the dynastic histories. "Transmitting biographies of 'singular conduct' in the histories began with [the historian] Fan Ye. He placed them in a separate category because they differed from ordinary biographies, that is, because of their strangeness. But all the biographies of singular conduct that he transmitted display loyalty, filial piety, and virtuous principles. These are qualities present in everybody's heart; so how could they be considered strange or different?" Kong resolves this contradiction, one that has profound implications for *Liaozhai,* by suggesting that in Fan Ye's time morals were so odious and rebellions so frequent that ordinary behavior deserved to be singled out. Then why, he objects, when the ethical climate had presumably improved, did later histories continue the practice of singling out ordinary morality as extraordinary?

Kong is exploring the possibilities of how something can simultaneously be both strange and commonplace. For him, this paradox is the key to *Liaozhai*'s bipartite structure of meaning: "All of what *Records of the Strange* relates here are things that are seldom seen or heard; so of course people will say they're strange. But nine out of ten are allegories [*yuyan*], and if we generalize [*tong*] their meaning, then none of them are about things that people would say are strange."

Kong locates the structure of allegory in the term *yuyan* itself, where *yu* is the figurative meaning and *yan* the literal meaning. The things the stories describe are strange because they are unusual, but the ethical values they convey are commonplace. Unlike his contemporaries Pu Lide and Yu Ji, Kong is not entirely willing to dismiss the literal content of the tales and concede that *Liaozhai* is not strange. Nor is he quite willing to follow his predecessor Tang Menglai and dismiss strangeness as purely subjective perception. For Kong is quite frank about the pleasure that people (including himself) take in reading about the strange, a pleasure that is not necessarily diminished by grasping the underlying moral significance. "If people don't find strange the meaning of the allegory but find strange only the words as written, it is because of people's fondness for the strange. But if this fondness for the strange is pushed to the opposite extreme [i.e., completely negating it?], then I don't know what happens to the notion of strangeness!"

Kong posits two levels of reading and three kinds of readers for *Liaozhai*: the frivolous reader who sees only the obvious allure of the strange; the dogmatic reader who sees only the hidden moral or satirical meaning; and the hybrid reader who sees the surface and underlying meanings and is affected by both. The third reader in his scheme is naturally the best. Thus Kong resembles other interpret-

ers of *Liaozhai* who attempt to prescribe an ideal reader. He concludes, however, with another paradox:

> We can't know whether future readers of *Records of the Strange* will be startled at its strangeness and take delight in it. We can't know whether some will despise the allegory and grow furious or enraged at it. And likewise, we can't know whether some will comprehend the strangeness of both the allegory and the words and sigh passionately, shedding tears over it. For we see that people call strange what they find strange and don't call strange what they don't find strange. Someone might even deny that *Records of the Strange* is strange and argue instead that it is only *reading* it that is strange, thus arguing that there's nothing really strange about the work at all—but how could this be?

Kong's scheme presents strangeness as an elusive concept, in constant danger of disappearing into relativity, subjectivity, or allegory. He is ambivalent about whether as a concept strangeness exists independently in the abstract or whether it must be grounded in concrete readers and reading. In the end, he seems to propose a two-tiered reading method, in which the strange is accepted as both a subjective and an objective phenomenon, and in which the surface allure of strangeness and the internal moral balance each other out.

Wang Jinfan, a contemporary of Kong's who published a rather drastically altered edition of *Liaozhai* in 1767, also explores some paradoxical implications of the strange. Like Kong, Wang distinguishes between the content of the tales, which is admittedly strange, and their underlying morality, which is decidedly ordinary: "There are certainly strange events in this world whose underlying principle is ordinary, and extraordinary language whose intent is orthodox." Nevertheless, Wang is more interested than Kong in the didactic potential of *Liaozhai.* Thus, rather than propose an ideal reader who perceives the author's true intentions, Wang posits two inferior extremes who are manipulated by the author, the uneducated reader and the overly sophisticated reader: the former is aroused by the satiric moral of the tales, the latter finds new delight in conventional morality. From a stock appeal to the vastness of the universe to support the claim that strange things really do exist, Wang shifts to another important topic related to the discourse on the strange: fiction making. If the principle behind an event is true, he claims, then it does not matter if the event occurred or not. In the end, he attempts to collapse the disjunction between story and message by appealing to the ancient principle that opposites become each other at their extreme: "Thus, there is nothing that is not figurative and nothing that is not real."

The Third Wave: Style and the Analogy to
Vernacular Fiction

The approaches introduced above may differ over the meaning and import of the strange in *Liaozhai,* but they basically agree that the content of the book is at stake. But the third wave, the authors of detailed, full-length commentaries on published editions of *Liaozhai,* circumvents this debate almost entirely. The strange is no longer a charged issue for them. What is most valuable in *Liaozhai* is no longer insight into the workings of the universe that it contains, the intellectual paradoxes that it poses, or the allegorical self-expression that it conceals. Instead nineteenth-century interpreters defend *Liaozhai* largely on grounds of literary style and narrative technique, and these concerns shape their entire commentary project.

To summarize, because of their subjective and relativistic understanding of the strange, previous defenders of *Liaozhai* had in some way to situate the strange in the reader. For them, the strange was not an absolute value or independent quality but was realized only in the reading process, for it required interpretation and mediation. In the nineteenth-century discourse on *Liaozhai,* the concern with the strange per se evaporates; what remains is essentially an interest in the reading process itself. *Liaozhai* is now defended because its mastery of language and allusion can teach one to read other more important texts, such as the Classics and histories. Commentator Dan Minglun (1795-1853) exemplifies this new approach in his 1842 preface:

> I remember that when I was losing my baby teeth, I'd come home from school and read *Liaozhai's Records of the Strange.* I couldn't bear to put it down. My father used to scold me: "How can a boy whose knowledge is still unformed like to read about ghosts, fox-spirits, and freaks!" A friend of my father's once happened to be sitting there, and he asked me why I loved this book. "Well," I replied, "all I know is I enjoy how in some places it's allusive like *The Classic of Documents,* valuable like the *Zhou Rites,* or vigorous like the *Ritual Canon,* and how in others the narrative is profound like the *Zuo Commentary, The Conversations of the States,* or *Intrigues of the Warring States.* From *Liaozhai,* I also gain insight into literary methods." When my father heard this, his wrath turned to laughter.

The child Dan has precociously demonstrated himself to be a "better" reader than his father by divorcing *Liaozhai*'s problematic content from its brilliant literary style. Once again an obvious pleasure in the strange has been deflected onto another, subtler level of reading. To borrow Formalist terms, we may say that our child-commentator has distinguished *discourse* ("the world of the author-reader") from *story* ("the world of the characters"). This favoring of discourse over story characterizes the great Jin Shengtan's (1610-61) influential approach as commentator and reader of fiction and drama. Jin's annotated and amended editions of *The Water Margin* (*Shuihu zhuan*) and *The Western Wing* (*Xixiang ji*) were so successful that they virtually drove previous editions of these famous vernacular works off the market until the twentieth century. Scores of readers, writers, and commentators were trained in Jin's method of literary analysis, in which every word and every sentence were considered deliberate and meaningful within the structure of the work as a whole.

Dan's own commentary clearly reveals that he was well schooled in Jin Shengtan's reading methods. We even begin to suspect that Dan may have been a bit less precocious

than he pretends since the gist of his schoolboy eloquence comes directly from Jin's "Reading Instructions for the Fifth Book of Genius" (i.e., *The Water Margin*). Jin's edition of this novel was specifically addressed to his young son.

> In the past when children read *The Water Margin,* all they learned were some trivial episodes. Now when they read *this* edition, they'll learn some literary methods; and they won't learn literary methods only in *The Water Margin,* they'll also be able to detect them in books like *Intrigues of the States* and *Records of the Historian.* In the past when children read books like *Intrigues* and *Records of the Historian,* all they saw were some trivial episodes—how absolutely ridiculous! . . . Once children gain some sense of literary methods, they'll be unable to tear themselves away from such books. *The Water Margin* can do quite a lot for children.

In fact, even Dan's recollection of his boyish love for *Liaozhai* echoes Jin's own account of his childhood passion for *The Water Margin,* which "he clasped to his bosom day and night."

These commentators are by no means the only devotees of fiction to ground their strong attachment to a particular work in childhood reading experience. Wu Cheng'en, the supposed author of the fantastic novel *Journey to the West* (*Xiyou ji*), wrote in the preface to his zhiguai collection of the youthful delight that he took in such books.

> In my childhood, I loved marvelous accounts. As a pupil at the boy's academy, whenever I sneaked off to buy unofficial histories and fiction, I was always afraid that my father or teacher would bawl me out and confiscate them; so I'd read them in secret. But as I grew up, my passion became ever more intense, the accounts ever more marvelous. By the time I was an adult, I sought them in every way until I had accumulated a vast store.

All these writers may have been influenced by the ideology of childhood in the philosophy of Li Zhi (1527-1602). In his famous essay "On the Childlike Heart" ("Tongxin shuo"), Li Zhi argued that all great literature derived from an author's "childlike heart," that is, from a mind that had not lost its original authenticity and spontaneity.

The nineteenth-century commentators' debt to Jin Shengtan is essentially threefold. First, their prefaces to *Liaozhai* borrow wholesale his defense of vernacular literature—that if properly read, it can teach children, and by extension adults, the literary methods necessary to read beneath the surface of canonical texts, especially the histories. Second, their commentaries adopt the literary methods and criteria Jin and his followers had developed for vernacular literature. Finally, Jin's example showed them that commentary could be as important and taxing as authorship itself.

Feng Zhenluan, an important nineteenth-century commentator on *Liaozhai,* explicitly modeled himself on Jin, to whose literary prowess he attributed the very survival of the masterpieces of vernacular literature. As he wrote in his 1819 "Random Remarks on Reading *Liaozhai*" ("Du *Liaozhai* zashuo"): "Jin Shengtan's commentaries on *The Water Margin* and *The Western Wing* are so insightful and cleverly worded that they constantly open the eyes and minds of later readers. This is why these works [belonging to the lowly genres] of the novel and drama have not been discarded in our own day."

Jin Shengtan's favoring of discourse over story provides the cornerstone for Feng's understanding of *Liaozhai.* From the beginning of his "Random Remarks," Feng emphasizes that *Liaozhai*'s aim is "to create literature" (*zuowen*), not merely "to record events" (*jishi*). "Anyone who reads *Liaozhai* only as stories and not as a literary work is a blockhead!" he warns. The eighteenth-century distinction between literal and figurative readings of *Liaozhai* has given way to a distinction between literal and *literary* readings. This new literary reading is not synonymous with a purely formal reading; rather, an attention to formal features alerts the reader to the moral nuances of a text. Although this approach ultimately derived from the traditional method of combing the *Spring and Autumn Annals'* laconic text for its "subtle meaning" (*weizhi*), Feng concentrates on the stylistic techniques through which the moral nuances are uncovered rather than on the moral nuances themselves. This emphasis becomes obvious when he castigates the vogue for *Liaozhai* imitations: "Lacking *Liaozhai*'s ability, these are just stories of wraiths and fox-spirits, exaggerated accounts of strange phenomena. *Since their literary style is negligible, their purport is unintelligible.*"

Feng makes a halfhearted attempt to defend *Liaozhai*'s strange content by echoing an old seventeenth-century argument: numerous accounts of ghosts and prodigies are also included in the histories; *Liaozhai* cannot be blamed for doing likewise. But Feng's solution is more daring: he suggests that the reader simply "take the writing itself." It does not matter whether the strange events in a story are true or not if the writing is good. Feng has arrived at a full-fledged defense of *Liaozhai* as creative fiction.

In Feng's "Random Remarks" we encounter for the first time an explicit comparison between *Liaozhai* and the masterpieces of vernacular fiction and drama. Feng likens *Liaozhai* to *The Water Margin* and *The Western Wing* because all three works have "large structures, finely wrought ideas, extraordinary writing, and orthodox meanings." Unlike eighteenth-century literary claims for *Liaozhai* that assimilated the work into the autobiographical reading tradition, the nineteenth-century arguments for *Liaozhai*'s literary merit derive from analogies drawn between vernacular fiction and historical narrative. This is a great change, one that attests to the improved status of vernacular literature. In this new environment, *Liaozhai* is understood as an offspring of a genuine fictional tradition.

By the early nineteenth century, *Liaozhai* had become so identified with fiction that Feng was compelled to point out that the book records many historical events and per-

sonalities. Compare this with original publisher Zhao Qigao's caveat that although *Liaozhai* contains some verifiable accounts, it is difficult to take most of it as "reliable history." The emphasis has unmistakably shifted. With the passage of more than a century and with the expansion of the readership outside Pu Songling's native Shandong province, the historical nature of many events and characters in the tales would inevitably fade and be forgotten; the fictional impression of the tales would be correspondingly enhanced. Indeed, a major task of the nineteenth-century annotators was to signal which characters and events had a basis in history and to provide necessary facts about them for the common reader. The impression of *Liaozhai*'s fictionality has accelerated with the immensely greater distance separating the modern reader from Pu Songling's world.

Feng's reading of *Liaozhai* as literature in which writing takes precedence over event obliges him both to uphold the practice of writing fiction and to defend *Liaozhai* against the charge of being bad history. The disparaging of the fictional imagination has deep roots in the Chinese tradition. Even fiction's chief defender, Jin Shengtan, argued that it is easier to write fiction than history, for in fiction the author can give free reign to his imagination, whereas in history the author is constrained by the facts. Jin's insight recalls the ancient philosopher Han Fei's famous remark on representation in painting: it is easier to paint a phantom or a demon than a horse or a dog; since no one knows what a phantom looks like, the artist need not worry about painting a recognizable likeness as he would in painting familiar creatures. Although this valuing of mimetic representation in painting was eclipsed quite early in China, vernacular fiction writers frequently used Han Fei's remark to attack the supernatural orientation of popular literature and to defend the focus on daily life in their own work. Feng refutes this charge of reckless imagination by arguing that even when writing about phantoms, Pu Songling always conforms to the logic of the human world; he makes the incredible detailed and vivid enough to *seem* credible.

Pu Songling's use of fictional detail and dialogue lies at the heart of Ji Yun's (1724-1805) well-known complaints against *Liaozhai.* Ji, a leading scholar-official who wrote the late eighteenth-century's finest collection of strange accounts, objected to Pu's inclusion of both "short anecdotes" (*xiaoshuo*) and "narratives in the biographical style" (*zhuanji*) in a single work. In light of this complaint and the abbreviated style of his own stories, it is clear that Ji Yun's real objection to *Liaozhai* was primarily epistemological. He maintained that as varieties of historical narrative, both short anecdotes and narratives in the biographical style had to be based on plausible sources—autobiographical experience or eyewitness testimony—and not freely invented by the author, "like plot elements in a play." All stories need not be true, but they must at least persuade the reader that they *might* have been seen or heard by an actual source. Thus Ji Yun complains: "Now P'u Sung-ling [Pu Songling] gives a vivid picture of the smallest details down to amorous gestures and the secrets whispered before lovers. It would be unreasonable to assume that the writer experienced these things himself; but if he was describing what happened to others, how could he have known so much?"

Pu Songling's stories are too detailed and too vividly dramatized for Ji Yun to accept as based on something heard or experienced by the author himself. For Ji Yun, verisimilitude *decreases* the impression of a narrative's realness, since he understands realness as "the claim to historicity," that is, as the claim that the events in a narrative really happened. It is not the strangeness of *Liaozhai* that bothers Ji Yun; rather, Pu Songling's narrative techniques too obviously betray authorial fabrication.

Feng Zhenluan defends *Liaozhai* against these charges by applying these rigid epistemological standards to the histories. Are the histories always true accounts of events? Are their sources impeccable? Or does their narrative technique also betray traces of overt fabrication? As an example of fictionalizing in the histories, Feng singles out a famous speech in the *Zuo Commentary* delivered by the assassin-retainer Chu Ni just before he smashed his head against a tree and killed himself. "Who heard the words of Chu Ni beneath the locust tree? How could Master Zuo have known them?" Feng's solution to this and the related problem of discrepancies between different historical accounts of the same event is once again to distinguish between discourse and story: the mode of telling a story may vary without harming the essence of the story. This example in turn helps justify Feng's assertion that he reads the *Zuo Commentary* as fiction and *Liaozhai* as the *Zuo Commentary*.

This argument for fictional license in narrative did not originate with Feng. A letter nearly two centuries earlier from a seventeenth-century collection had cited the identical incident from the *Zuo Commentary* for the identical purpose: "As far as Ch'u Ni's [Chu Ni's] utterance is concerned, there was no one else to know what he had said, so how did Tso Ch'iu [Master Zuo] know about it?" The letter's bold conclusion is to hail Master Zuo as "the progenitor of a whole line of literary lies." Feng accepts the definition of fiction as literary lies, but argues that "even lies must be told fully," that is, fleshed out with sufficient skill and logic to convince the listener. Feng's defense of lies is thus essentially the same as his defense of painting phantoms. But what is a lie? A lie is an utterance that the speaker knows is untrue. In understanding the *Liaozhai* tales as literary lies, Feng reflects another nineteenth-century view, that the ghosts and fox-spirits in *Liaozhai* are nothing but a game, a trick played by the author on the naive reader. Once again, a two-tiered level of meaning is posited; an appeal is made to a superior reader aware of the discrepancy between content and intent who does not let himself be hoodwinked by the author's literary lies. In this last formulation, the strange in *Liaozhai* has finally become a purely fictional and ironic construct, one predicated on the author's and reader's mutual suspension of disbelief.

To conclude, we may also understand the development of these three interpretive approaches in terms of the circumstances behind their adoption and the context in which

they were written. Pu Songling's personal friends wrote the first prefaces and dedicatory verses when his manuscript was still unfinished. Their efforts were inherently *social* in nature. They wrote to help introduce his work into society, that is, to a limited circle of like-minded readers. These established literary figures and statesmen lent their authoritative voices to an obscure and potentially suspect manuscript, supplying it with a pedigree and moral approbation. To this end, they tried to carve a niche for records of the strange within the dominant literary and intellectual tradition.

The advocates of *Liaozhai*'s publication primarily constituted the second wave. They were arguing to a new class of readers, the general reading public, why people ought to read an unknown author's work. For this reason, they sought to distinguish *Liaozhai* from the plentiful collections of strange tales on the market, attempting to convince the public that something special about *this* book warranted purchase and persual. These writers strove to elevate a mere collection of strange tales by reclassifying it as an allegorical work of self-expression, a high literary value not ordinarily associated with works of this kind. At the same time, social networks also shaped this second generation of interpreters. Pu Lide composed one of his postfaces to enlist the help of the sons of his grandfather's friend Zhu Xiang, who had expressed interest in helping him get *Liaozhai* published. Yu Ji, the collator of the first published edition, wrote his preface at the behest of the publisher, the prefect Zhao Qigao, who was also his friend and employer. Yu Ji's dedicatory verse for the edition is essentially a eulogy to Zhao, who died before the book came out.

The nineteenth-century commentators who constituted the third wave were associating themselves with an already famous book. By elaborating the book's literary methods, by "scratching the author's itch," as Feng Zhenluan put it, they hoped to win literary fame for themselves. (And to some extent, they have succeeded. We remember these men today solely as commentators on *Liaozhai*.) Because a fictional tradition had been firmly established by this period, the third wave was able to transcend the problem of the book's strange content by "simply taking the writing itself."

---

## FURTHER READING

Barr, Allan. "The Textual Transmission of *Liaozhai zhiyi*." *Harvard Journal of Asiatic Studies* 44, No. 2 (December 1984): 515-62.

> Surveys the *Strange Stories'* textual history in an attempt to place P'u's stories in chronological order.

———. "A Comparative Study of Early and Late Tales in *Liaozhai zhiyi*." *Harvard Journal of Asiatic Studies* 45, No. 1 (June 1985): 157-202.

> Contrasts P'u's early and late stories, offering insight into the author's creative development.

————. "Disarming Intruders: Alien Women in *Liaozhai zhiyi*" *Harvard Journal of Asiatic Studies* 49, No. 2 (December 1989): 501-17.
Discusses the many types of ghost women in P'u's *Strange Stories.*

Chun-shu Chang and Hsüeh-lun Chang. "The World of P'u Sung-ling's 'Liao-chai chih-I': Literature and the Intelligentsia During the Ming-Ch'ing Dynastic Transition." *Journal of the Institute of Chinese Studies of the Chinese University of Hong Kong* 6, No. 2 (1973): 401-21.
The critics examine unresolved tensions between Confucianism and Taoism, individualism and conformism, and fatalism and justice in *Strange Stories.*

Lin Lien-hsiang. "The Examination Syndrome in *Liao-chai-chih-yi.*" *Tamkang Review,* Vol. XIII, No. 4 (Summer 1983): 367-96.
Analyzes those stories concerning government examinations.

Prušek, Jaroslav. "Two Documents Relating to the Life of P'u Sung-ling" and "*Liao-chai-chih-I* by P'u Sung-ling: An Inquiry into the Circumstances Under Which the Collection Arose." In *Chinese History and Literature,* pp. 84-91; 92-108. Dordrecht, Holland: D. Reidel Publishing Co., 1970.
Translations of P'u's biography of his wife and of the inscription that appeared on P'u's tomb; examination of new information concerning P'u's life. Prušek contends that the biographical material necessarily alters one's understanding of *Strange Stories.*

Tsung Shu. "An Outstanding Collection of Tales." *Chinese Literature,* No. 10 (October 1962): 89-94.
Discusses the importance of P'u's essentially optimistic, romantic outlook as a key to understanding the popularity of *Strange Stories.*

Yu, Anthony C. "'Rest, Rest, Perturbed Spirit!' Ghosts in Traditional Chinese Prose Fiction." *Harvard Journal of Asiatic Studies* 47, No. 2 (December 1987): 397-434.
Places P'u's tales within the genre of traditional Chinese ghost fiction.

Zeitlin, Judith T. *Historian of the Strange: Pu Songling and the Chinese Classical Tale.* Stanford: Stanford University Press, 1993, 332 p.
Comprehensive overview of P'u's stories, which includes several translations and an extensive bibliography containing Chinese, Japanese, and Western sources.

---

Additional coverage of P'u Sung-ling's life and career is contained in the following source published by The Gale Group: *Literature Criticism,* Vol. 3.

# Jesse Stuart
## 1907-1984

American short story writer, novelist, autobiographer, biographer, essayist, editor, and poet.

## INTRODUCTION

Stuart is considered a regionalist writer whose short stories explore life in the Appalachian hills of Greenup County, Kentucky. His short fiction is noted for its use of folklore and its themes of family, community, survival, and man's love of the land. Stuart is praised for the insightful nature of his work, as well as his lyrical, simple language.

## Biographical Information

Stuart was born in a log cabin in Greenup County, Kentucky. His father was an itinerant sharecropper and Stuart's family moved several times in his youth. As a result, he missed school often and eventually dropped out. When he was fifteen, Stuart quit his job as a concrete worker and returned to high school, where he was influenced by the work of Robert Burns, Walt Whitman, and Edgar Allan Poe. In 1926 he began attending Lincoln Memorial University in Harrogate, Tennessee, and during his senior year his poetry was published in several periodicals. After graduation he returned to his native Greenup County and became a teacher and administrator in the area. His first collection of short fiction, *Head o' W-Hollow,* was published in 1936. In 1939 he left teaching and bought a sheep farm. During his life Stuart traveled extensively as a lecturer and educator, but always returned to Kentucky. A prolific writer of fiction, poetry, and essays, he published nearly 500 short stories. He died in 1984 after a long illness.

## Major Works of Short Fiction

Although he is considered a regionalist writer, the themes of Stuart's short fiction are universal in nature. In "Thanksgiving Hunter," a sensitive young boy on his first dove hunt finds himself unable to kill a bird. Ashamed of what he perceives as a weakness, he resolves to kill his first dove. Using a special dove call, he lures a beautiful bird. Upon closer inspection, the boy realizes that the bird is blind; another hunter has shot away both of its eyes. When the dove's mate calls and the blind dove flies away, the boy is left to ponder the harshness of life. In "Another Hanging," the hanging of a murderer provides a social occasion for the citizens of the county. Stuart juxtaposes the suffering of the murderer's wife and family against the

excitement of the young narrator as he puts on his new clothes and meets a pretty girl at the hanging. The story "Clearing in the Sky" reflects Stuart's belief that the land and nature hold a healing power for people. In this story, a father shows his son his vegetable garden on the top of a mountain. The father claims that in maintaining the garden, he has been able to stave off a terminal illness despite the dire prognosis that his doctor had given him.

## Critical Reception

Although some commentators have categorized Stuart as a regionalist writer, many critics have acknowledged that his work transcends strictly regional concerns, embodying such universal themes as community, individuality, poverty, and survival. Many critics have discussed the role of folklore in his short fiction, especially his use of local legends and their place in the modern world. Several commentators have noted the autobiographical aspects of the stories, most of them set in Stuart's home county of Greenup, Kentucky. Several of his short stories deal with animals, and critics have discussed his engaging portrayal of animals fighting for survival among humans or in the wild. Stuart has been noted for his often compelling presentation of plot and character, in particular his use of humor, insight, and dialect. Moreover, he has been praised for his simple, evocative stories, especially his unaffected language, warm and amusing characters, deft descriptions, and the incorporation of the natural world in his work.

## PRINCIPAL WORKS

### Short Fiction

*Head o' W-Hollow*  1936
*Men of the Mountains*  1936
*Tales from the Plum Groves*  1946
*Clearing in the Sky*  1950
*Plowshare in Heaven*  1958
*My Land Has a Voice*  1966
*Best-Loved Short Stories of Jesse Stuart*  1982

### Other Major Works

*Harvest of Youth*  (poetry)  1930
*Man with a Bull-Tongue Plow*  (poetry)  1934
*Beyond Dark Hills*  (autobiography)  1938
*Trees of Heaven*  (novel)  1940
*Taps for Private Tussie*  (novel)  1943
*Album of Destiny*  (poetry)  1944
*Mongrel Mettle*  (novel)  1944
*Foretaste of Glory*  (novel)  1946
*The Thread That Runs So True*  (autobiography)  1949
*Kentucky is My Land*  (poetry)  1952
*The Year of My Rebirth*  (autobiography)  1956
*God's Oddling: The Story of Mick Stuart, My Father*  (biography)  1960
*Hold April*  (poetry)  1962
*To Teach, To Love*  (memoirs)  1970
*The Land beyond the River*  (novel)  1973
*My World*  (memoirs)  1975
*Dandelion on the Acropolis: A Journal of Greece*  (memoirs)  1978
*Lost Sandstones and Lonely Skies and Other Essays*  (essays)  1979
*If I Were Seventeen Again and Other Essays*  (essays)  1980

## CRITICISM

### W. S. Wabnitz (essay date 1937)

SOURCE: "Jesse Stuart and the Old and New in Short Stories," in *The New Mexico Quarterly,* Vol. VII, 1937, pp. 183-88.

[*In the following essay, Wabnitz explores the role of suspense in Stuart's short stories.*]

Jesse Stuart is young, spirited, stockily built, hair rumpled, hands strong, well-shaped, and large; although himself one of the mountain people of Kentucky, in manner and appearance he has nothing of the grotesqueness that he so often makes us see in his mountain characters. Make allowance for attire and he looks like Robert Burns with whose poetry his has been compared; praise which Jesse Stuart disclaims in one of the sonnets in *Man With a Bull-Tongue Plow,* a sonnet which he likes well enough to use again in his credo at the end of his volume of short stories, *Head o' W-Hollow*:

I cannot sing tunes that great men have sung,
I cannot follow roads great men have gone.
I am not here to sing the songs they've sung,
I think I'm here to make a road my own.
I shall go forth not knowing where I go.
I shall go forth and I shall not go alone.
The road I'll travel on is mud, I know,
But it's a road that I can call my own.
The sun and stars and moon will give me light.
The winds will whisper songs I love to hear;
Oak leaves will make for me a bed at night
And dawn will break to find me lying here.
The winey sunlight of another day
Will find me plodding on my muddy way.

He speaks and reads with a natural purity of accent, giving a heightened value to words and syllables slurred over in the speech of the mountain people; he has rendered his native dialect into poetry and prose that retains its savor, yet by its rhythms escapes the effect of slovenliness.

Enough of raillery and irony tinge Stuart's exuberance to give his "biography" a story flavor. His mother's family felt disgraced when she married because the Stuarts were Republicans. (He has dramatized this theme in the story, entitled **"One of the Lost Tribe."**) His grandfather Stuart from over on the Big Sandy was shot three times during the Civil War. The Stuarts work a little farm in W-Hollow, which gets its name from its shape. His mother can hoe corn faster than her husband or any of her sons.

He liked school, was glad to walk four miles to get there; every hour in school was free of farm-chores. The teacher gave him a book of Burns' poetry. He wanted to go to high school. His father said: "I'd like to see you go. I'd like to see you get through. No Stuart ever got through high school."

One summer the streets of Greenup, Kentucky, were dug up for paving. Jesse Stuart was water boy. When the sun got too hot for the man who was running the concrete mixer, Jesse Stuart got that job. It was his first "big" money, five dollars a day. Later he worked on a ferris wheel and was fired for giving free rides to the children. He was strong and husky and a fighter. In the steel mills he took a beating from a millworker and wrote—on the back of a Hershey-bar wrapper—the sonnet *Batter me down, you who are strong, I plead.*

He set out for Vanderbilt college with twenty-nine dollars, registered and was put to work in a hayfield. The other boys wanted him not to rake so fast. One of them, they said, got fainting spells if he had to rake too hard in the heat. Jesse Stuart prodded him in the stomach with a fork handle and the faintness never came back. The boy, later his roommate, helped him to become editor of the college paper, in which Jesse Stuart printed his first poem and thereby satisfied the desire to see his name in print. At Vanderbilt he announced that he would earn his way writing term papers. Dr. Mims said: "Young man, you'll be lucky if you pass yourself." He worked first as a janitor. His papers had as many red marks, he says, as there are blades of grass in a lawn. Toward the end of the year his chance came: an assignment to write an eighteen-page paper on an original subject; his philosophy of life, for instance. He wrote three hundred pages which his professor liked well enough to send to a contest sponsored by *The Atlantic Monthly.* France Winwar's *Poor Splendid Wings* won the prize, which was five thousand dollars, and Jesse Stuart's manuscript was second. Now after five years it will be published as his third book *Beyond Dark Hills,* but then the sting of defeat was bitter. His disappointment led him to complete the set of 700 sonnets which make up *Man With a Bull-Tongue Plow.* The first section of this book was written at the ends of corn-rows, while plowing; the second during the winter, when he was a County Superintendent of Schools with little money and thirty law suits; the last section in a graveyard during vacation. "There was never a word changed. I slapped them down like this from the start. But I might not write them like that now," he says.

II

With about forty stories published since his first, **"Battle Keaton Dies,"** appeared in *Story* two years ago, Jesse Stuart is outstanding among the newer writers. He is less spectacular than William Saroyan whose "Daring Young Man on the Flying Trapeze" ends in an inspired outburst not quite equalled in any of Stuart's stories. The latter's less subjective output is richer and more varied in theme than Saroyan's which is inclined to sound too thinly a single note; that of the vague dissatisfactions of a restless young man.

Certainly the one quality more than any other that makes a story is the feeling that here is an actor striving for a goal. Opposition, or the threat of it, gives the story its dramatic texture. By infinite and subtle variations the actor's success or failure is made to satisfy the reader or to impress him with a sense of the irony of life. But there is rarely ever an outstanding story unless a struggle is present. Thus for more than a century, during which the short story may be said to have existed as a recognized form (although in reality it has existed as long as mankind), it has been well-grounded in the Rousseauistic ideal of self-realization. Every short story has been in some measure an exhibition of the doctrine of individualism, rugged or not, and suspense has been one of its valued elements; suspense manifesting itself in the reader as a strong partisan interest in the actor's struggle.

Lately we hear about a new type of story in which suspense is not important. Outwardly, of course, stories have been changing. The leisurely, abstract, commentarial style of Nathaniel Hawthorne, already giving way to a terser realism in the days of Maupassant and O'Henry, becomes the clipped objective recording of behaviour in Hemingway, or the packed imagism of Katherine Mansfield. On the other hand, commentary rather than action, as pursued to its extreme in Proust, has not been without its effect, for example in William Faulkner or Conrad Aiken. Gertrude Stein toying with words in patterns of repetition has directly influenced Hemingway and through him newer writers. Jesse Stuart, with a natural tendency for repetition, indulges in it more than he would if it were not in the air. Closely allied to repetition has been a kind of rhapsody, also repetitious, that is strong in Thomas Wolfe, often noticeable in Saroyan, and accompanied in Jesse Stuart by a nervous but sometimes effective use of the present tense.

> **Jesse Stuart is an honest new writer; people like him. If his work may be taken as a token, short stories, for a while at least, will not be fundamentally different from those in the past.**
>
> *—W. S. Wabnitz*

The greatest recent development in the technique of story telling has been that labeled stream-of-consciousness. The author, instead of analyzing or commenting upon the thoughts and feelings of the actor in the struggle, endeavors to give the reader the illusion of floating in the stream of the actor's consciousness of events, and seeks to have the reader identify himself with the actor in thought and feeling; become the actor, as it were, for the time being. This technique of which Proust and James Joyce seem the fountainheads and Virginia Woolf the exemplar may be seen at its clearest in a story called "The New Dress" from Virginia Woolf's *Mrs. Dalloway.* One of the sparing and subtle users of the device was Katharine Mansfield.

With the above developments has come also the plea for sincerity in story telling voiced by the editors of *Story* magazine, Whit Burnett and his wife, Martha Foley, and by Edward J. O'Brien, editor of the *Yearbook of the Short Story.* This plea has had good results. It has also had bad results; too often interpreted by writers, who have nothing worth saying, as a command to record and publish their run-of-the-mill personal and especially sexual experiences, the demand for sincerity has helped bring about a peculiar lack of reticence in stories, which was at first novel and exciting, then boresome, proving nothing except that sincerity alone does not make an artist.

With this wealth of new devices an author like Katharine Mansfield, a super-sensitive soul, was able to produce brief masterpieces of fiction illusively formless and fragile as puffs of wind. No central actor, no striving against an obstacle, just a delicate recording of impressions, says the hasty imitator, and aspirants, trying Katharine Mansfield's wings, fall flat. True in her stories the suspense is often hard to define and the struggle deeply concealed or esoteric as in her final story "The Fly," which her husband interprets as her own struggle against death.

Memorable new stories have this in common with the old: they still present a hero in struggle, with drama rising out of the opposition, and suspense as one of the delights for the reader.

What then is to be said for the story without suspense? If it is purely rhapsody, or if it depends for its interest upon sensationalism or lack of reticence, it is beside the point. But if it is a story which represents a new spirit of the times, it must be considered. Obviously three elements determine the course that stories will take; the writers, the readers, and the spirit of the age. The spirit of the last century, though growing more and more realistic through the knowledge of science, has never lost its romantic interest in the aspirations of the individual. Now, however, with one-sixth of the world's population Soviet and presumably communistic, and Nazi and Fascist presenting another aspect of collectivism and regimentation, we may stop to ask: Does the old spectacle of an individual winning a struggle (or losing if he be a villain) cease to be of interest? It would hardly seem so yet. The portion of the public most collectivistic in its state of mind still seems to be the portion that buys its fiction from the drug store rack, where the "pulps" contain nothing but stories of the old pattern. Nevertheless the matter bears watching.

One of Jesse Stuart's acquaintances says: "Jesse can go into a room in his boarding house or anywhere and come out after a little while with a long story written, and he doesn't know how he does it." This spontaneity is one of his engaging traits, bursting as it often does into hyperbole, travesty, burlesque. Sometimes his actors are distasteful, yet they exert a fascination struggling in the maze of their own imperfectness. He usually achieves suspense. The exception which proves the rule is a story in August, 1937, *Esquire,* called **"Huey the Engineer."** Read it and you will find that in spite of the wealth of mountain lore that it has to offer, it is dull and will hardly keep you awake because the central actor is engaged in no struggle. It does not stand up beside the same author's **"Snake Teeth,"** or **"Red Jacket: The Knocking Spirit,"** or **"Governor of Kentucky."**

Jesse Stuart is an honest new writer; people like him. If his work may be taken as a token, short stories, for a while at least, will not be fundamentally different from those in the past.

**Winston Bode (essay date 1959)**

SOURCE: "Jesse Stuart's Story Harvest," in *Southwest Revew,* Vol. 44, No. 1, Winter, 1959, pp. 83-6.

[*In the following essay, Bode offers a mixed review of* Plowshare in Heaven.]

Jesse Stuart is a goodhearted writer. A writer is not to be judged by good intentions; but, nevertheless, Stuart's desire to communicate the look and feel of his country, to tell of his people's needs, griefs, joys, and pretensions—this remains after one has got through worrying about his anecdotal superficiality, mannered lyricism, or Al Capp crudity of stroke. And one must admit that by main strength and enthusiasm, if not always by artistic mobility, Stuart does get a message on humanity across, does hew out, sometimes with woodcut broadness (and with some of the woodcut's effectiveness) a picture of his Appalachian hills and the people inhabiting them.

Stuart continues to stretch his Kentucky tapestry with publication of *Plowshare in Heaven,* a pleasant collection of his stories, nearly all of which appeared first in magazines. The magazines are of striking range—from *Country Gentleman* to the *Atlantic Monthly,* from *Fantasy Magazine,* which ran the title piece, to *Progressive Farmer.* Two of the stories appeared in *Southwest Review*: **"Walk in the Moon Shadows"** and **"Before the Grand Jury."**

This makes the twentieth book, including three juveniles, for the poet-novelist-lecturer-storyteller from Greenup County, Kentucky. Unlike Wolfe, Stuart is a "tight" writer, who deals in short, economically-worded blocks. But he just keeps a-writin' and a-writin'.

The latest crop is varied and a little confusing. A story like **"Zeke Hammertight,"** which tells of the running down by a posse of a cracked old head-clansman, seems to be a display of the things that are dubious in Stuart. Like twenty of the twenty-one stories in the book, it is told in the first person singular. The style here is a free-wheeling, simile-slinging, heightened colloquialism which smacks of that muscular, formulized literary rusticity so fervently embraced through the years by various literary forces in America:

Old Zeke Hammertight—you ought to see him. . . . You ought to see his steady blue eyes that the years cannot dim any more than they can the eternal Kentucky rocks—wear a little, tear a little—just a little by the wind, the sun, the rain, the sleet and the snow. Freeze a little, thaw a little, and fade a little as the years go by.

It is this kind of sophomoric incantation, with its rocking rhythms, maddening repetitions, and doubling back, its stagy diction, choppy declarative sentences, and parade of bucolic speech figures, not to mention vagueness of effect, that constitutes something of a blight on the whole body of our indigenous literature.

At its worst, this Sing-of-America style simply obtrudes like a bumpkin in the parlor. It comprises an essentially egoistic performance, a stylized manhandling of material and lack of artistic humility (and the effectiveness that goes with it). The chanter-narrator doesn't listen to nature with all her nuances of rhythm; he is too busy talking.

Humanity is not depicted in all its interior convolutions, its intricacy of relationship; the storyteller is too busy trying to startle with giants and heroic deeds. And there is a kind of lack of civility: the narrator comes on like thunder, spouting idiom and dropping g's, without so much as a howdy.

---

**It seems to this reviewer that Stuart, in his tales-from-the-hills version of this American genre, never satisfactorily handles the broad content and the broad effect.**

*—Winston Bode*

---

It seems to this reviewer that Stuart, in his tales-from-the-hills version of this American genre, never satisfactorily handles the broad content and the broad effect. It is, to repeat, partially a matter of improper preparation of the reader; and the material seems to shift in the course of a story from a context of relative realism to a framework somewhere beyond, not shocking or amusing, but simply straining credulity.

There is certainly nothing wrong with grotesque or exaggerated material, and Washington Irving, to name an easy example, handled it beautifully. But when Stuart has members of the Old and New Faiths fighting at a gravesite, or the boys of Carver College falling out of a towering tree, he simply seems to deteriorate into Li'l Abner or Barney Google. Giant men knock each other through the air and shoot at each other and plunge great distances with a tree branch in tow, but about all that happens is that they're "knocked cuckoo."

Prepared as we are by the tradition of Bunyanesque mountain men, we can be made to accept, possibly, men who are routinely six feet six, weigh from 240 to 300 pounds, have hands like shovels, chop trees in zero weather without shirts on, eat two dozen eggs, drink a gallon of moonshine while plowing and then dance all night; or sleep in eight inches of snow, melt it four and five feet around them in all directions, and get up the next morning without even a stopped nostril.

But you can't mix these in with mortal surroundings and events without a rather choppy effect.

Stuart has considerably more success with the grotesque when its intent is not so pointedly humorous, or not humorous at all. **"Walk in the Moon Shadows"** is effective because of the strong sense of the pregnant mother's mystic, ritual communion with the dead couple in the moonlight at their old home. **"Sylvania Is Dead,"** telling of the death of a 650-pound woman moonshiner, seems to grow naturally out of the country.

(Sylvania could not be arrested by revenue men because they could neither get her out of the house nor down the mountain to the jail; to bury her, the men must tear down the chimney wall.) The grandma who comes back from death during the "settin' up," and has a good report on her wayward deceased son; and Bird-Neck, who cheats the hospital he has sold his body to by seeing that his bones bleach from the top of a tall hickory tree in his field—these also are examples of gothic material handled without strain.

As one moves forward in *Plowshare in Heaven,* it becomes harder to make generalizations about the author. The clamorous monologue of Zeke Hammertight gives way to the controlled, eloquently idiomatic narrative of the grandpa telling about the Roman-holiday Sunday afternoon hangings they used to have in Blakesburg.

The doubtful humor of the college boys in **"How Sportsmanship Came to Carver College"** is relieved by a smiling portrayal of a smitten youth in **"Love in the Spring,"** and by the lighthearted **"The Devil and Television,"** which tells of the deacon who is "churched" for installing a "worldly device"—TV. ("Brothers and Sisters, the devil has pulled a fast one.")

The broad brush is put aside as we swing from an epic paean to the river and river men, **"Land Beyond the River,"** with its stereotyped, quickly sketched characters, to the more intimate pictures of **"Alec's Cabin,"** the story of a squatter with a strong claim to the cabin he takes over; **"Old Dick,"** a telling sketch of men mourning a good mule; and a sharp, inside account of a rustic grand jury.

One becomes aware that, in the over-all, Stuart's first person narrative device is used with vividness and impact; that the pacing is good and the structure tight; the dialogue rips along. There are sharp images: "Soon, after we had staggered and stumbled along," says the boy in **"Walk in the Moon Shadows,"** "I looked ahead and saw a vast opening beyond the trees. It was like leaving the night and walking into the day to leave the woods and walk into a vast space where only waist-high bushes grew."

It gets October, and they can't find Bird-Neck's body. "I started shuckin' Bird-Neck's corn. . . . The great sweeps o' fall-time winds would whip like a buggy-whip through the trees. Then the leaves would fall in swarms, jist like birds gettin' ready for the South. The treetops got bare."

The only thing is that, as you go along, the stories don't get more complex. One enters the genial warmth of **"Love in the Spring,"** and says, "Ah, now we're going to get a little psychological subtlety, a little involvement for a change." And the whole episode is resolved into naught with a knock on the boy's head. One is swept along with the promise of the tale of burying the patriarchal timber-cutter, with its complications of two sets of relatives with opposing faiths (**"Death and Decision"**). But we leave the story by way of a boring, unconvincing free-for-all in the graveyard, told with what seems much gusto.

It becomes apparent at the end that some of the best stories have been pure anecdote or sketch; that virtually none of the stories goes past the anecdotal level. There are in the volume few, if any, short stories, which work out character revelation in a systematized fashion.

One begins to conjecture as to what effect Stuart's love affair with Kentucky has had on his vision as he reads the final, title piece, in which the boy-narrator sorrows for a departed woman who will have to leave Kentucky ("the pink crab-apple blossoms, and the wild plum blossoms . . . the white listing sails of the dogwood blossoms . . .") for heaven. "How will she feel among strangers from all lands and in a great multitude of people? How will she feel among many tongues when she has only heard one?"

"Surely," he says, "for a hill Kentuckian God would let us have our Heaven here in Kentucky! We have lived in it so long, shut away from the outer rim of the hills, that we do not know it is Heaven until we get away."

Has this infatuation with, attachment to, a single region involved not only a not looking beyond the hills, but an insular adjustment that does not permit looking too far beneath the surface? What psychic drag is reflected in the boy's inability to leave home in **"Love in the Spring"**? What crippling ancestor worship is reflected in a preoccupation with family giants and their heroic deeds? The consistent device of using a family-oriented narrator, frequently a boy or young man, and the superficiality of treatment—not necessarily theme—suggest a reluctance to go beyond the anecdotal framework, past folklore, beyond the traditional tongue of the people.

The hearthstone is not the proper framework for the artist, who must be brutal and hypercritical, as well as loving.

Stuart is productive, but is he furrowing deep enough?

## Max Bogart (essay date 1963)

SOURCE: A foreword to *A Jesse Stuart Reader,* by Jesse Stuart, McGraw-Hill Book Company, 1963, pp. iii-vii.

[*In the following essay, Bogart discusses the universal appeal of Stuart's short fiction.*]

You enter the world of Jesse Stuart. The scene is eastern Kentucky, the hills, the mountains, the forests, the rivers, a land of primitive beauty, far, far away from any large city. You meet the people of this land. They may seem strange to you. Who are these people? They are determined pioneers, bold frontiersmen, feuding clansmen, brave settlers, and all of them are fierce fighters. And they are tender too. They are Jesse Stuart's people, the key to his world.

At first you may find it difficult to understand these people and to comprehend a pattern of life so different from your own. But as you move further into the world of Jesse

Stuart, you will make a curious discovery. As you meet more and more of the people he writes about, you begin to feel less and less isolated from them. Though the scene is Kentucky, his people share the condition of men everywhere. The themes of Jesse Stuart expose the foundations of human emotion. He has brought the humble, independent people of his land into the world of literature, where there are not Kentuckians, Californians, or New Yorkers but human beings yielding to their fate or mastering it. The result is literature with a universal appeal.

The world of Jesse Stuart, then, is people. What are they like? They are proud and loyal and tough "like the muscles of a hickory sprout." They are individuals, and one of their most cherished traditions is the sacredness of that individuality. They live with a fierce and deep-rooted love of the land. Jesse Stuart describes the closeness between the people and the land in many of his poems, essays, and stories.

> Our roots are deep, for we are a part of this land—and it is a part of us.
>
> Land to us, to men whose ancestors fought and died for it and whose people have lived on it over a century, is a dear possession. Those who are forced to leave it never feel the same.

This land and its people are his raw material. How does Jesse Stuart use the treasury of material that is his in the Kentucky mountains? Several ways. For example, he selects an ordinary occurrence from the daily life of one of his Kentucky people, and then with a kind of magic he creates a story that fascinates thousands of readers. Take Hester King, the 135-pound weakling in the story called **"No Hero."** He is quite an ordinary fellow. All he wants is to be a good farmer and to make a living for his wife and children. But when crops fail and Hester is desperate for money, he agrees to go into the ring against a 386-pound wrestler. Hester becomes at that moment quite extraordinary. The Jesse Stuart storytelling magic has been applied to Hester King, and he emerges as the hero of **"No Hero."**

Jesse Stuart also uses folk material of his land to create a story. Take Pappie in **"Rain in Tanyard Hollow."** Pappie wants rain because his crops are burning up in the heat. For weeks Pappie has been trying the only cure for drought he knows: he has been killing black snakes and hanging them on the fence. He believes this will do the trick. Many of his neighbors believe it too. But somehow it is not working for Pappie. He resorts to prayer, something he had never tried for rainmaking. The results are fantastic. Jesse Stuart has woven a folk superstition into a kind of folk comedy.

All Jesse Stuart's work is filled with characters like Hester and Pappie. He has created a gallery of memorable portraits: an Indian named Cherokee Bill who modestly admitted he was "great"; Grandpa Powderjay, who had no book learning but was an "educated man"; Buck, the fighting dog in **"Fight Number Twenty-five,"** who managed to avoid the fate of the twenty-four dogs before him; Miss Anna, who taught first grade for fifty years. Stuart's genius as a storyteller is his uncanny ability to reveal a personality in one or two paragraphs as in this one from **"No Petty Thief"**:

> and I watched the buggies, hug-me-tights, and the fancy express wagons. . . . It was fun to watch the wheels roll. I'd stand and watch them for hours, and what I wanted most in the world was to own something with wheels. Whether I could find level ground enough around our house or not for wheels to roll, if I just had something with wheels I could have sat and looked at it for hours, admiring the wheels and machinery.

Even absurd and exaggerated characters like Ezra Alcorn, who became moon-maddened in April, appear credible because of the art of Jesse Stuart.

The physical world of Jesse Stuart, its sights, sounds, and smells, comes alive in his descriptions of mountains, valleys, woodlands, and rivers. These passages are inspirational, creating a radiant and ethereal mood, lifting us out of the humdrum and heightening our sensitivity to the beautiful in nature. For example, as Stuart fondles a handful of sassafras leaves, he thinks: "I held beauty within my hand."

---

**Because a writer chooses to limit his stories and poems to a region, this does not necessarily mean that his work lacks universal implications. Jesse Stuart is a regional writer in the same way that Mark Twain, William Faulkner, and Robert Frost may be cataloged as regionalists.**

*—Max Bogart*

---

As he narrates the early pioneers' efforts to build new communities in the wilderness and the feuds between individuals and families, he treats the reader to the folklore of the Kentucky mountain regions.

When the major portion of an author's literary work pertains to a particular geographic region or territory, critics and historians label the writer a regionalist, or local-colorist. Generally, regional literature is literature which presents the physical landscape, the dominant features and peculiarities of a locale and its inhabitants, including the dialect, beliefs and attitudes, and folkways and customs. This literary form usually focuses upon local history, often stressing the glories and virtues of past generations in backcountry America. Hamlin Garland wrote that regional literature has ". . . such quality of texture and background that it could not have been written in any other place or by anyone else than a native."

All too often, however, this literary label is applied in a negative and restrictive sense. To many readers it suggests that the author's outlook is limited and that he has little knowledge of the world beyond this region.

Because a writer chooses to limit his stories and poems to a region, this does not necessarily mean that his work lacks universal implications. Jesse Stuart is a regional writer in the same way that Mark Twain, William Faulkner, and Robert Frost may be cataloged as regionalists. After all, many of Mark Twain's novels are limited to life along the Mississippi River; Faulkner's stories, with rare exceptions, are set in a mythical county in northern Mississippi; and many poems by Frost deal with northern New England and its inhabitants. Each has created a cosmos, using the geographic area as the symbol.

Readers will find the study of the language of Jesse Stuart's world a source of interest and delight. As a regionalist he has a predilection for dialect, colloquialisms, and the rhythms of frontier speech which give the English language a colorful and sprightly flavor. By including picturesque mountain expressions which are gradually becoming obsolete, Jesse preserves the country-folk vocabulary and presents realistic dialogue. Often the language is reminiscent of the sweet music of a folk song. In terms of language alone, Stuart's stories are a fine achievement, for they appeal to the ear as well as the eye.

The world of Jesse Stuart is one of conflicting currents. Generally, the main current is tenderness versus violence, but the variations are abundant. The contrasts are incessant and interwoven in Jesse Stuart's stories: compassion and kindness toward man and animal life contrasted with cruelty and meanness; the goodness of mountain people confronted with the corruption of urban influences; seemingly simple Kentucky people behaving in complex ways; deep-seated, violent conflicts between families versus peaceful coexistence; the hardships of the tenant farmer when crops fail, followed by happy days when yields are successful; a narrow provincialism balanced with a worldly outlook; primitive versus highly civilized behavior; the sneers of mountain people toward the educated person, yet the fostering of education for their children; the beauty of natural phenomena and the ugliness of particular human behavior; birth and death on the same page, occurring at the same instant; and the tragic response to death, but acceptance of it as a segment of the life cycle.

Yet in the midst of the pathos in these serious and tragic tales, he sprinkles a unique brand of frontier humor, causing the reader to laugh at many passages. A rich vein of humor and satire not unlike Mark Twain's runs through Jesse Stuart's work.

Jesse Stuart elicits the enthusiasm of readers because they quickly discover that his stories and poems are connected to their own experiences—and they respond emotionally and intellectually. In particular, his writing provides escape from daily routine, vicarious adventures into the Kentucky hills, and for all enjoyment, first and last.

In all probability Stuart's novels, short stories, and poems could not have been written in any other place or at any other time—and the depicted way of life, which we cannot forget, has all but disappeared from the American scene. It is preserved in Jesse Stuart's art, and we relive it each time we read one of his books, for his people and his world are not exclusively his. His people, and the people like him, made this country, and so they belong to all of us. The world of Jesse Stuart is, in a very real sense, your world.

**Everetta Love Blair  (essay date 1967)**

SOURCE: "The Short Story," in *Jesse Stuart: His Life and Works.* University of South Carolina Press, 1967, pp. 82-129.

[*In the following excerpt, Blair provides a thematic and stylistic analysis of Stuart's short stories.*]

In 1936, the first of Jesse Stuart's collection of short stories was published. That collection was *Head o' W-Hollow.*

When *Head o' W-Hollow* made its appearance, Ralph Thompson, of *The New York Times,* wrote: "What Brete Harte was to the outcasts of Poker Flat, and Joel Chandler Harris to the plantation negro, Jesse Stuart is to the folk of the Kentucky mountains. There aren't many originals among American writers of the past few years; it is hard to think of one who can beat Stuart at his best." [*New York Times Book Review,* March 21, 1936].

[In the *New York Herald-Tribune Books,* March 21, 1936] Lewis Gannett was equally enthusiastic in his estimate of the Stuart collection. He said: "There is music of the American tongue in his stories. He is an authentic writer, worth a hundred city slicker products."

**"Battle Keaton Dies,"** a story which is included in the *Head o' W-Hollow* collection, is one of Stuart's most dramatic and moving short stories. This story was his first. He tells about its sale in *Beyond Dark Hills:*

> A letter comes to me. It is from *Story* magazine. It says: "We are accepting your **'Battle Keaton Dies.'** Enclosed is our check for $25." Strange, the first story I ever wrote! Strange It got the same money that I did for my first poem. Sold a story! It didn't have a plot. Just a man died and wanted to be buried in his shirt-tail. But it was not the same kind of money the poetry money was. It was fun-money. Poetry was blood money.

**"Battle Keaton Dies"** is a striking example of Jesse Stuart's distinctive treatment of the short story. Instead of a plot the story has a powerful, impressionistic summary of the life and incidents surrounding a single theme, the death and burial of a rugged old mountain man. No detail is left out which will portray the elementary, almost primitive folkways of the region concerning the treatment of death.

The realism with which Stuart invests his story produces the calculated effect of placing the reader in the presence of death in its simplest, most unadorned state. Stuart spares the reader nothing in presenting his picture of Battle's death, with the result that the brutally frank, the naturalistic descriptions throughout the story may easily turn away the faint hearted.

Battle Keaton's last hours are shown through the use of stream-of-consciousness technique to show the old man's dying thoughts. His unending monologue is interspersed with the "sip-sip-sip," as he quenches a burning thirst from water brought in answer to his constant demands by his grieving daughter, Fronnie. Battle is obsessed by the sight of a spider on the ceiling above him:

> Well, I lay here and I think I can reach up there and get that old she-striped-back spider sometimes. I want to cut its guts out with a knife. I want to crush that spider between my thumb and my index finger so bad I can taste it. God knows I ain't got no use for no damn fly, but I can't stand to see them lay up there in them webs and have to die by degrees. I have to lay here on this bed and I can't lift my arm sometimes to reach for that spider. . . . And I think of Old Tid Coons who used to run a sawmill and work his men eleven hours for a dollar and ten cents a day. He was a striped-back spider like that one up there on the wall . . . old Tid took the blood out'n twelve men instead of twelve flies.

The old man admonishes his daughter for weeping, "I want you to quit actin like you are actin. Don't you know this is goin to come to you like it is comin to me and it is goin to come to everybody else that's born in this world." Then, he gives her specific instructions for his burial:

> See that I'm put in my coffin just like I go to bed—that I have my shirt on and no necktie—my shirt and my long underwear. I don't want any shoes 'r' socks on my feet neither. I want to lay down in my coffin just like I lay down in my bed—to bed is where this old clay temple is goin, Fronnie. To bed. Yes. I don't want no hat on me neither, for no one ever goes to bed with a hat on. I want a blue work shirt on and my long heavy drawers—I want my clothes clean and no smell of sweat in them or smell of brush smoke. I want to be laid over there on the Runyan Hill by Daid near them old cornfields where we used to work together, from sunrise till sunset together.

When Battle dies, his last breath is:

> . . . a sharp sizzle of wind and it goes like wind pressed in a vise, if wind could be pressed in a vise. It is wind come out where the walls fall in . . . wind that if it could speak would say, "Wind has come in here and gone out for the last eighty-four years—but now the wind time is over and past."

There follows the description of the care and preparation of the corpse by the daughter, son-in-law, and neighbors who come to the rude little cabin to help. The mood of the world outside is depicted: "The sun is red behind the mountain. The wind stirs the green July corn . . . and now time would slowly disintegrate his [Battle's] burned-out clay to mix forever with the elements."

Recollections of Battle are recounted by the people at his "settin-up." There is a wail of guitar music in the night, and religious songs are sung by the group surrounding the corpse. "Holy-Joe Madden" speaks words over Battle, with a lot of "Thee's, Thou's and Thy's," but Fronnie is not comforted. She cries, "Poor Pa . . . Dead . . . Dead . . . Dead as a beef. Over there—See!" The coffin is constructed with a half-lid, so people will not see that Battle has on only his work shirt and drawers. His daughter and son-in-law see to it, in spite of the neighbors' protests, that the old man's dying wish is carried out. On the night of his burial, people from far and near come over the hills to pay their respects to an old friend. The welcoming speech of Sweetbird, the son-in-law, is indicative of the hill custom of making a funeral a social event. His words, too, show the spirit of feuding which characterized that area.

> Come on in, folks—just set any place you can find a seat. Anybody is welcome in my house but a person that has the last name of Turner. No Turner is welcome in my house. If a Turner is here now I want that Turner to get out before I put him out. I mean business, too. If a Turner goes to Heaven I don't want to go there. If one goes to Hell I don't want to go there. I hate a Turner and Dad didn't allow none here when he was livin and by hell Sweetbird Bradberry ain't goin to allow none here this night when poor old Dad Keaton lays a corpse. No, Dad is too near and too dear to me. Dad got on the Lord's side of the fence, but he could never forget the Turners.

The story ends on a note that is reminiscent of the lyricism which is found in Stuart's poetry:

> Out on the wind there are words floating among the leaves—floating on the wind. There are stars in the sky. There is wind in the corn. There is a red-oak-chip-colored moon riding in a pretty color-of-pond sky. See it all—See Battle too. He is in his coffin—if Battle could only see this night.

Man's life ends and Nature continues in endless cycle of day and night. But, in the old mountain man's wish to be buried in his usual garment for sleeping there is the feeling that, though his life on earth is to be ended, Battle will merge his life with that of Nature and that he will continue through infinity to arise to meet the day. Jesse Stuart emphasizes the two time levels with his dramatic use of the present tense, directing the reader to observe Battle dead while Nature, ungrieving, and in timeless pattern, provides a canopy for him brilliant with red moon and with starlight. Death is natural. "I want you to stop grievin," the old man had said to his daughter. The symbolism of the story is that of acceptance. In the sympathetic tone which Stuart achieves throughout the story, there is shown the author's identification with Battle, giving insight to his belief of acceptance. **"Battle Keaton Dies,"** with its implicit moral of affirmation, is in direct contrast to such

sonnets of protest over the briefness of life as Sonnet 27, "Man's Life Is Like the Season of a Flower," in *Man With a Bull-Tongue Plow*, and "Why Ever Grieve," in *Hold April.*

**Head o' W-Hollow** contains a number of stories which dwell on the theme of death as it is met by hardy hill characters like Battle Keaton. Among such stories is **"Uncle Jeff,"** a simple recounting of a visit to a city hospital of a mountain man and his two sons to see their brother and uncle, an old railroad man, as he lies dying. **"Battle Keaton Dies"** might be said to be somewhat diffuse with its prodigious amount of detail. **"Uncle Jeff"** is tautly told. Although, it, too, has a wealth of atmospheric description, in action **"Uncle Jeff"** maintains the straight narrative line, achieving notable unity in plot. **"Uncle Jeff"** is included in the aforementioned college textbook, *The Literature of the South.*

**"The Bellin' of the Bride"** is a story of a very different mood from the death stories of **Head o' W-Hollow.** This sketch shows the custom of serenading a couple who have just married. The couple in the story, T. J. Lester and Daisy Bee Redfern, hide behind the big chimney, which is built onto the lower half of their cabin where the fireplace is, and which leans away from the house enough to provide space for hiding. The "bellin party" probes behind the chimney with a clothesline pole, and the hapless couple come out. After the gunshooting and the cowbell-ringing which follow, the beating on wash-tubs and "plow pints," a sixty gallon barrel of hard cider is opened, and there are cider, food, candy, and square-dancing for everybody.

This collection has such varied stories as **"Snake Teeth,"** which describes the religious primitivism of the people who believe in "the Unknown Tongue"; **"The Governor of Kentucky,"** a hilarious account of a bus trip to Chicago by a man who is known as "the Herb King of Kentucky." The man resembles the Governor of Kentucky, Governor Randall Spoon, so he and his friends decide that he shall pose as the Governor on this pleasure trip into the city. Everywhere the bus stops, the "Herb King" is presented as Governor Spoon, and this practice is continued at a ball game which he and his party attend in Chicago. His attendants have been sampling generously the "herbs" which they have brought along for the trip, and when they say "We have Governor Randall Spoon of Kentucky with us" to the world at large, the results constitute a high point of humor in Jesse Stuart's writing. "The Governor" enjoys his role tremendously. The climax of his adventure comes when he reaches home and hurries out to his barn to keep an early-morning date with a flirtatious widow. His wife has gone to the barn early to attend to the chickens. In the dark, he mistakes her for the widow, and grabs her in his arms. The wife, who hasn't spoken to her husband in two months, is thrilled to think that he still loves her. They make up then and there. The "Governor of Kentucky" is elated. This story, in its exaggeration of character, is in the "tall story" tradition.

**Men of the Mountains,** Stuart's second collection of short stories, was published in 1941. This book has such stories as that of "old Flem," who looks ahead to dying, digs his own grave, and tries it out for size. The grave's a good place to be when a man's tired, Flem theorizes. There's no worrying there about getting bread, or having land to tend. He savors his mountaintop restingplace, with the wind blowing through the chestnut oaks and the sound of foxhorns in the distance.

**"For the Love of Brass"** is a fascinating yarn about a little "bird-necked man" who says "just call me Bud," who came to stay overnight at Thorny Kirk's farm. He stays, to become a valued handyman on the farm. Thorny and his wife wonder about "Bud," who tells them nothing of himself, just attends to his work, and seems to love being with them. One day the Sheriff comes to pick up Bud, to take him back to the penitentiary. The Sheriff tells them that Bud is making his fourth trip to the "pen" for stealing brass. Bud has committed no other offense. His weakness is for stealing brass. Years later, Thorny gets a package of clothes. "I don't like my old home nigh as well as I liked my home with you. I'm 42 years old next month. Have spent 21 of my 42 here. Take care and keep the farm going." Thorny keeps Bud's big hoe hanging in the barn. Bud was a good corn hoer. He could outhoe Thorny. Some day, Thorny and his wife hope, they will look down the road and see Bud returning.

The *New York Herald-Tribune* book reviewer, Milton Rugoff, in writing about **Men of the Mountains** and Jesse Stuart, has this to say [March 16, 1941]: "There is, in sum, nothing slick or tricky in Stuart's work, nothing even sophisticated. And yet, neither is there the rawness of the Southland etchings of Erskine Caldwell nor the horrifying decadence of Faulkner. Next to Caldwell, Stuart seems lyrical and classic and next to Faulkner, wholesome and conventional."

Once or twice, this reviewer observed, Stuart dropped into the "feuding" and "moonshinin'" themes of the caricature hillbillies of radio and vaudeville, but the percentage of stories below standard in **Men of the Mountains** was very slight.

The Stuart short story collection entitled **Tales From the Plum Grove Hills** (1946), contains **"Another April,"** a story thought by many critics to be Jesse Stuart's finest. **"Another April"** is included in *The Literature of the South.* It appears in Donald Davidson's college textook, *American Composition and Rhetoric.* Davidson uses only three stories for illustration of style in the short story— one from Thomas Hardy, one from James Joyce, and Jesse Stuart's **"Another April."**

*The World of Endless Horizons,* a textbook for secondary-level schools, has **"Another April"** in its section headed "The World of Human Kinship, Currents of Understanding in Families." Under the "Twentieth Century" division in this textbook's section listing writers "Across the Ages," W. Somerset Maugham and Jesse Stuart lead the list.

This association of the names of Maugham and Stuart seems a happy one when Maugham's introduction to his

book *Maugham's Choice of Kipling's Best* is read. Maugham says in that introduction:

> One of the most absurd charges brought against him [Kipling] was that his stories were anecdotes, which the critics who made it thought was to condemn him (as they sometimes still do); but, if they had troubled to consult the *Oxford Dictionary* they would have seen that a meaning it gives the word is: "The narration of a detached incident, or of a single event, told as being in itself interesting or striking." That is a perfect definition of a short story.

Jesse Stuart, in his writing of anecdotal or "plotless," short stories, would seem to be championed, along with Kipling, by Somerset Maugham.

**"Another April"** has the *tenderness* which is one of the outstanding qualities of Jesse Stuart's writing. There is no action in the story except the development in the mind of a little boy of the meaning of old age. The boy's grandfather, who is ninety-one, is allowed out of the house for the first time after a long winter. Grandpa's daughter, the boy's mother, fusses over the old man to see that he is clothed warmly enough. The boy laughs at his grandfather's ludicrous, bundled-up appearance. Grandpa goes out eagerly to enjoy "another April," and to greet an old friend. The friend is a terrapin who has spent fifteen years under the smokehouse. He has 1847 cut on his shell. He's ninety-five years old, Mom tells the little boy, maybe older. Grandpa calls the turtle "my old friend." He says to him, "Old fellow, it's been a hard winter. How have you fared under the smokehouse floor?" The boy is amazed, but sees that the terrapin seems to understand Grandpa. Grandpa stops to examine very carefully the blossoms from a dogwood and a redwood tree. He tells the terrapin that he is "a-gettin' a little chilly; I'll be gettin' back to the house," and he says good-bye to his old friend. The little boy watches, as Grandpa takes his cane and hobbles slowly toward the house. The reader understands that the boy has come to a realization that the terrapin will outlive humanity, but that Grandpa is spiritually unconquered.

Skillfully, Stuart has interwoven the levels of time. The past is represented in Mom's recitals of Grandpa's exploits and in the boy's memories, and the present fuses dramatically with the relentless future as Grandpa completes his last walk, still "enjoying April." The emphasis upon Grandpa as a physical creature, at one with Nature, is subtly felt in the brief, symbolic, almost nebulous action.

Jesse Stuart's stories are not consciously didactic. Stuart presents his incidents or sketches from life in photographic detail for the building of a mood or of a judgment. The morals drawn from them are created in the mind of the reader; rarely are they stated by the author. **"Another April,"** with is unity and conciseness, might be called Jesse Stuart's most distinguished short story.

**Tales from the Plum Grove Hills** contains another of Stuart's most poignant stories, **"My Father is an Educated Man."** The author's father could not read or write his name, but he knew the land, he knew railroading, mining, and buildings, his son writes here. He has "raised food for his family to eat." He has given them a roof over their heads. He has encouraged his children to go to school. "And as I think of my father's autumn-colored face, of this small hickory-tough figure of the earth, I think of the many men in America still like him. And I say they are educated men."

---

**Jesse Stuart's stories are not consciously didactic. Stuart presents his incidents or sketches from life in photographic detail for the building of a mood or of a judgment. The morals drawn from them are created in the mind of the reader; rarely are they stated by the author.**

*—Everetta Love Blair*

---

Jesse Stuart's father, dressed in his overalls, clean blue work shirt, and overall jacket, would go to town every Saturday to join the men grouped on the courthouse square. A simple figure of earth, he is one of Stuart's greatest creations from life. He recurs throughout his son's writing, but is never given more sincere tribute than in the story, **"My Father is an Educated Man."**

**"The Storm"** tells of domestic troubles that vie with the gloom of the elements. A storm is brewing outside, but Mom has decided to leave her husband and go home to "Pap." She has had enough, she says. She and her husband are different, that's all. Mick, the husband, tries to talk Mom into staying. She is determined to go this time. The storm hits the clapboards of the little cabin, with a fury of wind and rain, and plays the dramatic role of mediator. Mom weakens, decides not to go. She cannot leave her husband, and the homely, everyday things that have meant their life together. As the storm subsides, Mick puts his pipe in his pocket, pulls his wife outside happily for a walk, to look over their sweet potato bed.

A story with more substance than **"Storm"** is **"Nest Egg,"** which is also found in *Tales from the Plum Grove Hills.* **"Nest Egg,"** like **"Another April,"** is one of Jesse Stuart's more famous stories. It was written when he was a high school student in 1924, then dug up and mailed to a magazine in 1944. *The Atlantic* published it. "Later, this story 'Nest Egg' was placed by Homer A. Watt and Oscar Cargill in their college textbook for English and American literature, *College Reader,* as an illustration of one of the better short stories." This textbook also includes short story illustrations from Jack London, Ring Lardner, Ernest Hemingway, Thomas Hardy, and Thomas Wolfe.

**"Nest Egg"** is a saga of a powerful "fightin' rooster," which was hatched from an egg that was supposed to have been destroyed. The nest egg had been guarded zealously by a stubborn "old Sebright hen," who had resisted all attempts to take it from her. When her chicken came, she took it to the woods and lived there with it. The chicken grew up to be a tall rooster, with big legs and little straight spurs that "looked like long locust thorns." When winter came, the Sebright hen brought the young rooster down to the corn crib for food, as there was none left in the woods. The fledging was dubbed "Nest Egg" by the boy who was supposed to have taken the egg from the Sebright hen. The boy knew the rooster to be the product of the egg he had failed to remove. Nest Egg was attacked by the five old roosters who ruled the barnyard, but he fought them off stoutly. When Nest Egg killed the veteran rooster, War Hawk, he became king of the lot. His fame spread, and the neighbors insisted on bringing their roosters around for matches with Nest Egg. Nest Egg was always the victor. The neighbors' chickens flocked to be with him. Hen's nests were found everywhere—under the ferns, under the rock-cliffs, under the smokehouse corncrib, in hollow logs and stumps. The neighbors accused the boy's father of being a chicken thief, but he maintained that "It's a good-lookin' rooster Nest Egg that all the hens all take to; he tolls the hens here." The neighbors brought the father into court, but the judge threw the case out. The chickens continued to be charmed by Nest Egg. The whole community seemed turned against the boy's father. Then, fate stepped in and settled matters. A little screech owl flew into the chicken roost where Nest Egg was sleeping, lit on the mighty warrior's back, and killed him by pecking a hole in his head.

**"Nest Egg"** is an entertaining little animal fable, with a distinctly Chaucerian flavor. Nest Egg is given personification, as is Chantecleer of the Chaucer tale, but his human quality of overweening pride in his exploits is in contrast with that of the timidity of Chantecleer, who must always be bolstered by his wife, and who, in the end, saves himself through a craftiness born of sheer desperation. **"Nest Egg"** has an unmistakable moral, the moral being, of course, that the powerful, when taken unaware, can be destroyed by the weak. But the story is remembered chiefly for its humor of situation and for its characterization.

Among the remaining stories which appear in *Tales from the Plum Grove Hills,* **"Weep No More, My Lady"** is notable for its description of the custom of "funeralizing," the custom of having a funeral preached every year for the deceased. "Funeralizing" occasions the "norrating" of the news of a community gathering at the home of the departed one. The people who participate in the "funeralizing" enjoy festive meals and the contents of the gallon jugs that are brought out at the deceased's home. There is singing of hymns, accompanied by guitar music, and the giving of "testimonials" in the house. Afterward, the group moves to the graveside and continues the hymn singing and the drinking. The preacher delivers a long sermon, which consists mainly of eulogies for the departed neighbor. The Mountain Baptists are the people who practice "funeralizing." The Free-Will Baptists don't believe in it.

The religious primitivism of the region is set forth graphically in **"Weep No More, My Lady."**

**"Another Hanging"** describes the custom of the region in making a social occasion of a hanging. This story, with its theme of a crass, almost unbelievable, mob brutality, is painful to read. **"Another Hanging"** is one of the best examples of naturalism in Stuart's works. "Naturalism" is employed in connection with the study of Stuart in the sense of the use of unsparing detail in the description of a scene from life, or in the delineation of character, with disregard for its effect of shock or of revulsion upon the reader. "Naturalism," in this study, does not refer to scientific determinism. Stuart is the opposite of the scientific determinist. His strong belief, which has been borne out in his own life story, is that one can rise above the restrictions and frustrations of an environment.

**"Frog-Trouncin' Contest"** shows the love of the people of Stuart's area for physical activities. The story contains exaggeration and the boisterous spirit of triumph in outwitting an opponent by fair means or foul, elements of broad frontier humor such as that found in Augustus B. Longstreet's "The Gander Pulling" in his *Georgia Scenes.* This sport of frog-trouncing was popular in Shakespeare's day, Stuart points out, and is, thus, another custom handed down directly from English forebears to the folk of his region.

**"Dawn of Remembered Spring"** is one of the most original Stuart's stories. The subject matter, that of snakes making love, comes as a surprise to the reader, in view of the highly poetic title of the story. Stuart says that he sent **"Dawn of Remembered Spring"** out to publications thirty-seven times. The thirty-eight time he sent it out, it was accepted by *Harper's Bazaar,* and subsequently was included in a Martha Foley collection of *Best American Short Stories.* The history of this story, he says, provides a real lesson in perseverance for young writers who believe that their stories are doomed to receive only rejection slips.

*Tales from the Plum Grove Hills* may be considered Stuart's most outstanding collection of short stories, since it contains his most diversified and best-known works in that field.

*Clearing in the Sky,* which was published in 1950, is Jesse Stuart's fourth and most studied book of short stories. This book is dedicated to his father, Mitchell Stuart. It is illustrated with beautiful woodcuts by Stanley Rice. On the whole, *Clearing in the Sky* seems more restrained in style and has fewer of the elemental themes than have the earlier story collections. There is less violence in the language and, it seems, a somewhat more limited use of localism. This would tend to bear out Stuart's previously mentioned statement that he is striving to "tone down" his use of the vernacular of the hills, and that his earlier stories show more of the "exactness" of his region. In this statement, he reiterated that those early stories "do not exaggerate."

One of the stories in *Clearing in the Sky* which is written in Stuart's earlier style is the lead story, **"The Champion."** This story is another rustic, frontier-type tale which Stuart insists is not exaggerated but is a true picture of his region. The story is featured in the section entitled "Enjoying Humour" in the secondary school textbook, *Adventures in Reading.*

**"The Champion"** is included in *Story,* an anthology of "the fiction of the forties" which has appeared in that magazine. This anthology was published in 1949, with Whit and Hallie Burnett, the editors of Story, serving as editors of the collection. In this anthology, the editors, claim Jesse Stuart as "an early discovery of *Story,*" since that magazine published his first story, **"Battle Keaton Dies."**

**"The Champion"** recounts the adventure of a notorious glutton when, as "eatin' champion" of Raccoon Creek, he is pitted against a game rooster in a private eating contest. The instigator of the contest says that he will give his rooster a grain of corn every time he gives one to the glutton, Sam Whiteapple. Sam accepts the challenge. His "nail-keg stummick" rebels, however, after he has swallowed what "'pears like . . . a bushel of shelled corn." Doc Hornbuckle is sent for; Sam is hauled away on a wagon to recuperate. The rooster walks away with his flock of hens.

**"The Slipover Sweater"** is among the numerous stories by Jesse Stuart which have been reprinted for their simplicity of style and of theme. The theme emphasizes a common human desire, the desire to own something equal to or better than that owned by another who is in competition with one. This Stuart story has an autobiographical flavor. The protagonist is a young high-school football player who wants a slipover sweater to give to his girl. The name of the boy is "Shan," a name often used by Stuart to represent himself in stories. Shan is very resentful of the fact that his girl is wearing a sweater that belongs to Roy Tomlinson, his rival. Working his way through school, Shan finds it difficult to meet daily expenses, and there is no money for such luxuries as the sweater. He broods about the matter, and finally gets up the courage to go to the town bank and ask for a ten-dollar loan. Since Shan is a football star, the banker lends him the money, after taking out twenty-five cents of the amount for interest. Shan gets the sweater. It is the only one in school with three stripes on the sleeve. Shan is elated when his girl friend Jo-Ann accepts his sweater and gives Roy Tomlinson's back. As time passes, however, he becomes despondent about repaying the ten dollars to the bank. Jo-Ann tires of him and humiliates him by returning his sweater to him publicly. A mountain girl, Grace, who has had a longing for Shan, comes to his aid and helps him to gather roots and herbs for selling, so that he can pay off his loan. The loan is repaid. Shan comes to recognize the difference between the loyal mountain girl and the fickle Jo-Ann. He knows that one day Grace will wear his slipover sweater. He dreams of building a house for himself and Grace on Seaton Ridge on the path that leads from her family's house to his.

The most poignant story in **Clearing in the Sky** is that from which the collection takes its title. Jesse Suart discusses this story in an article entitled "Backgrounds and Results of Regional Writing," which he wrote for *The Peabody Reflector,* the alumni magazine for George Peabody College for Teachers.

> . . . I wrote an article, **"Clearing in the Sky,"** which was a truthful account of my father and a garden he had hidden on a high hill top. It wouldn't go for an article, but an editor accepted it, didn't ask for a word to be changed, and published it as a short story. Since the publication of **"Clearing in the Sky,"** it has been reprinted eight times. One of the reprints was in South Africa. The background was the center of our farm. The character in the story, one of the people on this earth I know best, is my father.

**"Clearing in the Sky"** combines two of Jesse Stuart's most beloved themes, the land and his father. His father had been told that he had a bad heart, that he would have to take it easy, that he probably would not live long. Instead of "taking it easy," Jesse's father, Mitch Stuart, had followed a secret desire, and had planted a garden on "new ground" on the highest point of their native mountain. He had been climbing up to his small secret clearing on the top of the mountain, in defiance of the doctors' orders, to find the fresh, fertile soil that he had tilled as a young man. One day, Mitch Stuart shows his "clearing in the sky" to his amazed son. He tries to explain about it:

> . . . the doctors told me to sit still and take life easy. I couldn't do it. I had to work. I had to go back. I had to smell this rich loam again. This land is not like the land I had to build to grow alfalfa. This is real land. It's the land that God left. I had to come back and dig in it. I had to smell it, sift it through my fingers again. And I wanted to taste yams, tomatoes and potatoes grown in this land.

Jesse asks his father why he has so many paths coming from the flat up the steep second bluff. The father explains that the spring before, when the doctor had not given him a week to live, he had found that he could not climb the steep path. He had made a longer, easier path, then, so he would not have to do so much climbing. Then, as he got better, he made another, steeper path. He had continued this procedure, as the days went by. That was one way, he said, that he had had of knowing that he was getting better all the time!

The story ends with Jesse's following his father down the path that "wound this way and that, three times the length of the path we had climbed."

Jesse Stuart told the writer in the previously noted interview of March 27, 1953, that he enjoyed writing in the medium of the short story more than he did the writing in any other literary form, more even than the writing of poetry, his first love.

> I just love to write a short story. I can get ideas for short stories and put them right down on paper. Then I wonder why I don't go on and work them into novels. But the novel is too much longer. I can't sustain the mood. I can sustain a single mood in a short story, but I can't in a novel. This was pointed out to me by a critic, J. Donald Adams, of *The New York Times.* When he wrote about *Taps for Private Tussie,* he said that he could tell when I had written half of the book, and when I wrote the other half. He said that he knew they were written at different periods, and he was right. There were two weeks between the the two periods, and, in that time, little things had happened, not serious things, but little things in my life that had caused me to change moods in my writing. Adams picked that out in my book.

When Jesse Stuart's fifth volume of short stories, **Plowshare in Heaven,** appeared in 1958, it seemed a happy omen to his public that the author had turned again to his favorite medium. The gusto and dramatic sweep, humor, realism, and tenderness displayed in this new collection was reminiscent of Stuart's younger days. Though some of the stories had been written in earlier days, others were new and seemed to signify an exuberant return to full, normal living for the man who had been so close to death as a result of the heart attack, in 1954, and who had fought his way back for two slow, agonizing years to a semblance of his former life.

Those years of recovery had produced *The Year of My Rebirth,* a quiet journal of Jesse Stuart's reawakening to the beauties of the world of Nature and of the life about him. **Plowshare in Heaven** swung Stuart back into the orbit of his youth when his rugged mountain sonnets and stories caught the attention of the American literary world and won for him, from a number of critics, the accolade of being a new and vital force on the native scene.

Though *The New York Times* reviewer Charles Lee Snyder stated that Stuart would add much more to his reputation by writing another novel as amusing as *Taps for Private Tussie,* he hailed the new short story collection for its wide range and its general artistry, particularly for the poetic style.

> Mr. Stuart is a poet, and one of the secrets of his charm as a story-teller is a certain poetic touch in his description. Of the twenty-one tales in this collection, some deal with humorous or pathetic incidents in the lives of more or less ordinary hill people. Others deal in humorous or satirical fashion with odd and outlandish characters, rugged or ragged individuals from away back.

> [*NYTBR,* September 21, 1958]

To Borden Deal, writing in the *Saturday Review* [September 20, 1958], Stuart's stories were "mountain magic." He wrote, "He [Stuart] has, from the beginning, worked in an artful simplicity that has the solid, enduring shape of legend."

"Walk in the Moon Shadows" is an example of this simplicity—a story, told in the first person from the viewpoint of a young boy (the young Stuart), centers about the pathetic loneliness of a mountain mother who takes her children for a walk in the moonlight to look for the ghosts of happier days as she is about to become a mother again. Atmospheric description throughout "Walk in the Moon Shadows" deepens the symbolic meaning of loneliness and the wonder and fear of the children for their mother's withdrawal into a world beyond their understanding, as she takes them over the mountain paths to the deserted cabin of her friends of former years.

> There were a few dim stars in the sky but over the meadows, down where there were long moon shadows from the tall trees, thousands of lightning bugs lighted their ways, going here, there, and nowhere. Upon Press Moore's high hill where Pa had found a wild bee tree, and cut his initial on the bark, a whippoorwill began singing a lonesome song.

The whippoorwills' lonesome songs on the ridges, and the falling apple blossoms from the trees which encircle the old house form an imagery of death in the young boy's mind. He is frightened, and wishes to return home. There is no moon as the little party trudges back, after Mom has given up her vigil by the haunted house. It is dark, and the boy trembles with relief as his father, who has skeptically refused to go on the moonlight expedition, comes up the path to meet them and accompany them home. There is no plot here, only an incident related from the childhood memory of the narrator, an incident in which the protagonist, the mother, shows a primordial yearning for happiness and for assurance as her time of trial and of danger approaches. It is of interest in the study of Stuart to note that this story has a universality which caused it to be selected for featuring over the Danish Radio Network. It was read to a nationwide audience on Sunday, November 27, 1960, by Karin Nellemose, actress of the Royal Danish Theatre.

"Alec's Cabin" in *Plowshare in Heaven* has the same theme of loneliness as that of "Walk in the Moon Shadows." It portrays an individual who clings doggedly to a symbol of happier days, then destroys it when he leaves for new scenes.

Among stories to which Borden Deal gave special mention, along with those of serious mood, was "The Devil and Television," a story in a different vein. He noted its "funny and touching" conflict between the old Kentucky and the new.

Indeed, this story may be cited as an example of Stuart's realism in pointing up the changing attitudes of his region toward encroachment of the modern world. The tale concerns a man's mental struggle when he is threatened with being "churched" for owning a television set. Stubbornly, he decides in favor of the devil and TV.

"Whatever the story," Deal concluded in his review, "Stuart's prose and his people remain."

Even in his most ribald and wildly exaggerated tales, as in "The Governor of Kentucky," in *Head o' W-Hollow,* the story of a busload of drunken hill men on a trip to Chicago, or as in "Death and Decision," in this later collection, in which there is a donnybrook between two factions in a funeral party following the burial of a relative, it seems that Jesse Stuart can convey a poetic undertone. There is a feeling of the compelling force of the hills, of the lonely landlocked lives which find an outlet in actions grotesque, pathetic, or beautiful, according to the personalities of the protagonists.

---

**Often it seems that Jesse Stuart is overly preoccupied with the grotesque, the weird and distasteful in life. This would seem to represent a dichotomy in the writer who is most often acclaimed for the air of optimism and of poetic beauty in his writing, yet it is really his way of accentuating the juxtaposition of good and evil in life.**

**—*Everetta Love Blair***

---

Often it seems, however, that Jesse Stuart is overly preoccupied with the grotesque, the weird and distasteful in life, and seems to derive a sadistic pleasure in lending an eye to unsparing realistic detail that is like "the wielding of an axe"—in centering his readers' attention on the ugly, instead of on the beautiful. This would seem to represent a dichotomy in the writer who is most often acclaimed for the air of optimism and of poetic beauty in his writing, yet it is really his way of accentuating the juxtaposition of good and evil in life.

In *Head o' W-Hollow* one of the most painful stories in the reading is "Sunday Afternoon Hanging," recalling "Another Hanging," of an earlier volume. The description of the event is bruising, told in the rugged vernacular of the frontier, yet there is dramatic poetry, an epic-like quality, in the narrative of this early Kentucky pastime of a people who sought amusement in such a way because of the restricted choice of diversions in the isolation of their lives.

A classic in the category of the grotesque is "Sylvania Is Dead," which is included in *Plowshare in Heaven.* This unbelievably weird tale is a story from life, as most of his stories are, Mr. Stuart insists.

"Yes, 'Sylvania Is Dead' is based on facts," he wrote in a letter from Cairo, Egypt, dated June 5, 1961, in answer to the writer's query. "The story came from Hancock County in East Tennessee. Many people there will know about this story—which is quite a story. I wrote it in college."

Outlandish to the point of hyperbole, both in selection of subject and in descriptive details, the account of the life, death, and attendant difficulties of the burial of a 650-pound female bootlegger has an artistic unity for which Jesse Stuart has been commended by such previously noted critics as Robert Penn Warren and Edward J. O'Brien. With careful craftsmanship, Stuart approached the architectonics of his story with the selection of a name for his protagonist.

"Sylvania" is the incongruous poetic name evoking visions of willowy, ethereal heroine, which he gives to the mountain of flesh who is his central character. Having selected the name, he chooses the most dramatic title for the story, giving it the "spoken," the oral, flavor—not "Sylvania's Death," or "Sylvania's Burial," but **"Sylvania Is Dead."**

This sets the tone, and, from the first line, when Bert Pratt says, "it's too bad about Sylvania," as he pulls himself up another step of the mountain incline by catching a sassafras sprout, on his way with his fellow mourners to dig the bootlegger's grave, the story moves forward with dramatic pace, in the dialogue of the men, as well as in the concise but vivid account of the action. Sylvania had long enjoyed immunity from the law because officers could not drag the 650 pounds of her through the doorway of her house. She had spent all of her life, from the days of her young girlhood, in the house. To move her out would have meant tearing down the house, so her parents moved out, instead, when Sylvania married, leaving the house to the newlyweds. In the vein of incongruity, Stuart naturally makes Sylvia's husband "Skinny," a hundred-pound man who speaks with a pathetic formality of "my wife" at her burial.

As in all Stuart stories, the human action is given a harmonizing backdrop by the elements. Nature is in sympathy and takes a symbolic part in the events, as in the scene when the men are climbing the mountain towards the house of the deceased:

> September was here and the leaves were falling from the oaks and beeches. The backbone of the mountain was gray and hard as the bleached bone of a carcass. The buzzards floated in high circles and craned their necks.

The men reminisce about Sylvania, whose heart was as big as her frame, who would trade moonshine for pistols, butter, turnips, corn meal, or almost any commodity the men had on hand if they did not have money. Now, they are increasingly disturbed by the buzzards which swoop low toward the death shack. Lonnie shoots into the swarm of scavengers. This brings Skinny out of the shack in hysterical protest against "the boys'" bad manners, yelling to them, "Shooting around here, and my wife a corpse!"

Crestfallen, the men explain that they are trying to scatter the buzzards. They proceed to the spot where they are to dig the graves, and again Nature plays an active part:

> The lazy wind blew over the mountaintop. Leaves swarmed in the wind. Leaves fell into the grave the men were digging for Sylvania. Buzzards flew above the shack while Flora Fitch and Vie Bostick worked in the shack and prepared Sylvania for burial.

The grave is dug, but there is the problem of getting Sylvania out of the shack. In a quandary, the men consider taking up the floor. But this might cause "disturbances," and they didn't want "no disturbances" attributed to Sylvania, because "Sylvania's been a mother to all of us." Skinny might want "to jump the broom again," and he wouldn't want his first wife buried under the floor, they reason.

The expression "jump the broom," for "get married" is a colorful colloquialism which occurs throughout Stuart's writing. Stuart does not strive to be picturesque or intentionally regional, but he uses words and phrases to which he, as a man of his region, is accustomed in his simple, unaffected American-English. Thus his diction fits theme and tone of his subject matter, that of men living close to the soil whether in devout, superstitious or in crude and boisterous mood.

In these passages, some might question Jesse Stuart's use of the word "disturbance," along with his colloquialisms. Is it not "unnatural" to use the formal with the colloquial in this man's speech? Is such a word current in the ordinary conversation of the region and time? Would not the hill man have said "ruckus" or "trouble"? Certainly there were formal words used naturally in the hills as quaint relics of Chaucerian English or of seventeenth-century English, such as the word "oddling" for one who was different. But use of "disturbance" here and of "replenish" in the following sentence invites questioning. "All they [the revenuers] could do was pour out a barrel of good licker. It wasn't no time until Sylvania had the barrel replenished and we were going back again."

For another example of what might appear to be inattention to diction, there is this passage: "There never was a better woman than Sylvania. When she sold you a gallon of moonshine you got a gallon of unadulterated moonshine and not two quarts of moonshine with a quart of water and a quart of carbide all stirred up well and shook before drinking. I don't know what we'll do without her. We won't have no market fer our corn."

Would not the man of the region who said "stirred up well and shook," and "we won't have no market," have said "pure moonshine," instead of "unadulterated moonshine"? Is this a fault of diction, as some critic unfamiliar with the hill people might infer, or an instance of carelessness toward detail of treatment which, now and then, one finds in Stuart's works? At times, Jesse Stuart is reluctant to reread and revise his work after setting it down on paper when he is in the grip of mood. He is a spontaneous writer and an impatient editor of his own works. In this, he is closely allied in temperament to Thomas Wolfe.

The problem of getting Sylvania out of the shack is solved when it is decided to tear down the chimney which almost covers one end of the house. Placed in her coffin at last with great difficulty, Sylvania has an almost lifelike domination of the scene, as Skinny announces to the men her legacy to them: "It was my wife's dyin' request that she didn't have her funeral preached, nor no songs sung. . . . See that barrel over there! It's the last my wife made. It's all fer you, boys. There's the dipper over there. What you can't finish today you can finish Monday when you come back to hep me make my new chimney."

The "boys" gather around the barrel, and begin to carry out the dying request with alacrity. They look at Sylvania and weep.

"Just a lot of drunk men crying," is Rodney's tart observation in a short while, saying that they should have had the "licker" last. But Skinny says he is "conducting" the funeral, and he is doing what Sylvania requested.

Before the men are past walking, Bert, who has charge of the actual burying, gets them under way. Fourteen men lift the black-oak coffin and inch slowly out of the open end of the house where the chimney had been.

"Just like picking up a house with the family in it," Rodney groans, as they make their way laboriously to the pine tree under which Sylvania is to be buried. Here again is an example of Stuart's very apt and homely similes.

The funeral fervor, characteristic of the hills, is evidenced in Skinny's hysterical scream, "I wish I was planted by 'er side!" Piety ingrained in these rough men, even in their inebriated state, is shown by Bert's words, "May God rest Sylvania's soul" after she has been lowered into her grave.

The conversation of the men during the process of the lowering of the coffin is staccato and graphic, like dramatic dialogue, as it forwards the action. Stuart is particularly adept at this stark, Greek-like technique of using sparse description in favor of de-development of theme by use of powerful dialogue, thus bringing a strong sense of reality through few words. In this, and in numerous other short stories, his treatment of narrative may be likened to Faulkner's taut, dramatic style in *As I Lay Dying,* as contrasted with Faulkner's usual convoluted, rhetorical and obscurantistic style.

In **"Sylvania Is Dead"** alternation between present and past is skillfully integrated—the present, constituting the action of getting the corpse of Sylvania from the house and burying it; the past, in the men's recollecting of Sylvania's role in their lives, and in their alcoholic celebration at her funeral, for which Sylvania, in character, her generosity following her to the grave, has provided.

The focus which Stuart maintains in this story is sharp and clear. Sylvania's character and personality dominate throughout, and the exaggerated dignity with which the bootlegger is treated in death, as though she were a leading citizen, is beneath its surface satire, indicative of a deep Stuart belief. Sylvania was one of Nature's freaks, but she had her place in life. She built a niche of immor-

tality for herself in the heart of her husband and in the affections of her moonshine customers. The tone maintains the exaggerated, bizarre effect, yet underlying it is a tenderness of perception which is characteristically Stuart, in his belief that each individual, no matter how grotesque or useless in the eyes of the world, may still develop an innate dignity to give life meaning, no matter how small the periphery of influence.

In the category of the grotesque, **"Zeke Hammertight"** takes its place beside **"Sylvania Is Dead,"** though its theme of violence differs drastically from the baroque note of sympathy interweaving theme and treatment of Sylvania's story.

Charles Snyder of *The New York Times* took special note of Zeke Hammertight as an "odd and outlandish character, patriarch of a pestiferous, prolific and pesky clan," who is shanghaied out of the way by his neighbors in a frighteningly brutal manner.

There is no tenderness of tone here. The subject matter, as in that of *Taps for Private Tussie,* is of a shiftless tribe of people who refuse to work, and who overrun the hills like the sassafras sprouts, leaving their destructive mark on everything they touch. The Hammertights, especially crazy old Zeke Hammertight, should be killed out, just like the sassafras, in the opinion of the other hill people. Objectively, in relentless detail, Stuart recounts the carrying out of the brutal plan for the elimination of old Zeke. He tells the story from the point of view of a young man who is a member of the posse that brings Zeke in. But there is nothing of the subjective Stuart in that youth. He is selected as narrator to point up the unwitting callousness of the hill mob which pursues its murderous objective with a sinister delight.

"The crazy, damned Hammertights and the sassafras sprouts are taking this country. They are taking Kentucky," is the flat statement of Cousin Milt, who has been the object of Zeke's hallucination that someone is "pizenin'" his cattle. Zeke, at least, "crazy as a bedbug," a useless member of the hill society, should be eliminated.

Milt enlists the unwilling aid of the sheriff, who in his election had bought the Hammertight vote from old Zeke for forty dollars. A posse is organized to clean out the hills of the Hammertights, beginning with bringing in the crazy head of the family. Around the barn in which Zeke has hidden himself, upon receiving the "noration" of the news via the mysterious hill grapevine, there is a whole ring of Hammertights, armed with gooseneck hoes, briar scythes, broadaxes, apple-butter stirs, clubs, and rocks. But they scatter into the brush when the sheriff's reinforcements storm the barn with their double-barreled shotguns, members of the posse screaming with glee as they charge up the hill after them. In the words of the narrator, "Whooppee! Whooppee! . . . We are after the Hammertights."

Old Zeke is pulled out, "a-spitting and biting and fighting," and thrown into a big hog crate, and the men bring him triumphantly into town. "You ought to see us going to Greenbriar. Like a big bunch of men been to the hills and caught a bear. Just that away: a long line of men behind the wagon and Sheriff Watkins up front, just riding as big with the bloodhounds with broken noses strapped to the saddle."

Although this story is told objectively, two moralizing passages enter in. There is the sheriff's statement: "He's not safe among civilized people. . . . He'll know where he is when he wakes up in the asylum. He's lucky to get there. All this expense on the county taking him over there. W'y he's not any more good. He ought to be left out there among the sassafras sprouts. Out there for the crows and the buzzards. Making us fight the Battle o' Bunker Hill over again to get him."

And, in a rhythmic concluding paragraph, typical of Stuart prose, which might often be free verse, there is the moralization which reflects the feeling of the author as a man of Nature, who thinks that Zeke should have been left to run free-crazy or not. "Maybe the hills know we got old Zeke Hammertight. Maybe the eternal rocks of Kentucky know it and the lizard knows about it. The sassafras sprouts know that we got him. Like the buzzard, the crow, the lizard, the snake, old Zeke would love to get out of that hog crate and run wild over the hills that have produced him and his generations thick as the hair on a dog's back, thick as the sassafras sprouts on a Kentucky poor-clay bank and under the Kentucky wind, and sun, and moon and stars."

This is one of the rare instances in which the moral is stated in a Stuart story. Zeke Hammertight has been hunted by his neighbors, with intent to murder him, has been caught and caged like a wild animal. Even though contemptuous of the shiftless Hammertights, Stuart states his disapproval of the brutality shown, a disapproval that would encompass all forcing of the wild from their habitats.

Though it would be sheer loss to the reader to eliminate this concluding paragraph, with its poetic strength, it would seem to be in the interest of artistic unity to do so, for it weakens the effectiveness of the story as an unrelieved picture of naturalism. It is not artistically acceptable for the author to intrude at the end of the story, when he has been consciously out of it throughout the narration. He should maintain objectivity to the finish.

The author has shown in the story that the world of Nature is aware of what is taking place. As usual, Jesse Stuart gives the elements and birds and beasts a part in the action: "The wind lap-laps the poplar leaves about our heads. It is a lazy wind. The sun is hot and the lizards are sleepy on the rocks. They lift their heads when a green fly passes over and swallow the flies like a toad frog catching yellow jackets. The ground sparrows twitter in the seeding crab grass. The voices of the men are lazy as the wind."

As the victim is pursued, there is this passage which foreshadows Nature's awareness of the outcome: "We take over the hill, down the path, across the rocks, the stumps, the fallen trees, Cousin Milt in front with the pistol in his

hand. . . . Maybe the lizard is watching us, maybe the rocks that have seen men kill before and men go crazy. Rocks that have seen stories they've no tongues to tell."

Here is the cosmic touch, the suggestion of Nature's endurance and indulgence for the wickedness and foibles of mankind. This passage makes sufficient moral comment, and in an expressionistic way, renders superfluous the author's intrusive didacticism at the close of the story, his preachment against the hill men's way of solving their problem concerning Zeke Hammertight—and against any such solving of the geriatrics problem.

*In Sunday Afternoon Hanging,* the moral is unstated, and the single effect is thus more artistically attained—that of a cruel, unsparing naturalism that often may be shocking in the reading, for Jesse Stuart in this vein of objective savagery is not for the timid reader. The story shows an artistic unity in construction—a unity that is weakened in **"Zeke Hammertight"** by statement of the moral.

Three of Jesse Stuart's short stories deserve special mention for their treatment of the theme of the strong hill man beaten by the machine—the natural man in conflict with civilization, defeated in the end by the rise of industrialization. These stories are **"Uncle Jeff," "Huey, the Engineer,"** and **"Tim." "Uncle Jeff"** is the best known of these stories.

In **"Uncle Jeff,"** the problem is stated in the beginning of the story: the uneducated versus the educated in life. Shan, who is young Jesse Stuart, asks his father, "What is the matter with Uncle Jeff?" Shan and his brother are walking with their father in the town of Ferton, West Virginia, on their way to the railroad hospital to see Uncle Jeff.

"He is a broke-down man," the father replies. "He is like I am. Look at me—I am a broke-down man. If you follow workin on a section long as your Uncle Jeff, then you would have one foot in the grave and the other ready to slide in, too. He's been on that Chatworth section for thirty-three years. Could have been a boss if he had the education. Can't read. Just like I am. Now you boys see that it pays to take education. I couldn't take it for there was none offered here in these Kentucky hills when I was a boy."

In the ensuing conversation, the father explains Uncle Jeff's condition, and the similes used are sharp and homespun. Jeff and eighteen other men on a motor car had been hit by a Big Sandy train in a fog. Uncle Jeff had leaped "like a frog," or he would have been dead like some of the others, when part of the motor car and several of the men "flew through the air and lit on them like a bird. Brother Jeff was knocked cold as a icicle." When he woke up, he was in this railroad hospital in West Virginia. He hadn't been able to work since. "He is like a horse too old to plow but has to pull the plow just the same. I am a horse too broke-down to pull the plow, but I have to pull it just the same."

The boys are planning to take Pa to his first picture show after they leave the hospital, so they are walking to the hospital, to save money, instead of riding on a street car. Shan describes in detail the peculiar clothing that they are wearing, old clothes that do not fit, except for the new overcoat that Shan himself has on. Pa wears a big gray overcoat that strikes him around the ankles. It is a coat that Shan found in an old house and gave to him, but Shan says, "I believe he [Pa] sorty thinks I stole it." Pa resents the way "these damn big-headed people" of West Virginia hold their heads in disdain above the Kentuckians. He would like to tell those people about the time when he was sixteen years old and worked in the mines in West Virginia, and the place where he boarded had so many bedbugs he had to leave. "I'd like to tell these people about the bedbugs they got in this state—more than any State in the Union."

When they get to the hospital, at the reception desk, a woman "who looks mean out of a pair of glasses" tells them that they can not see Jeff Powderjay. Pa is ready to make a scene, when the boys grab his arm and take him to see the hospital doctor. The doctor says that it is good they have come to see Jeff. "None of his kin have come to see him and he will not get back to Kentucky alive." Pa is fascinated by the doctor's soft hands, contrasts them with his own work-worn ones. This descriptive aside to the story illustrates Jesse Stuart's eye to detail in making his characters and incidents realistic.

Pa goes first into the hospital room, greets Jeff and asks if he knows him.

"Know you? What do you think I am? I'd know you in hell, Mick. You are boy number eleven, and I am number ten. Ain't that right. . . . And you come up to see me kick the bucket."

Uncle Jeff wants the boys to come over "and say goodbye and old-Satan-bless-you Uncle Jeff." He has been praying to die, to get out of that place. The nurse, "that big-tailed thing they got waitin' on me" is trying to kill him too soon, he says. God won't have him. He wants to go some place, so he has been "cussin and praying for the Devil to get me."

Here it is interesting to note that the Devil of the hill people is a real personality, as is the devil "Auld Nickie-ben," of Robert Burns, and is invested by the hill sinners, anyway, with human qualities of understanding and comradeship. The Devil will take in Uncle Jeff, the old man believes, since God would not have him.

While he is talking, Uncle Jeff has been holding tightly to Shan's hand. Shan does not like holding his uncle's hand.

"His hand is soft and warm and wrinkled like a thawed-out black snake. His lips have fallen down at the corners, beard is over his face—a white and red-sandy beard. His eyes are the color of faded slate."

Uncle Jeff asks for a chew of Red-Horse. "Give me a chew of Red-Horse, and I'll give you a cup of water in hell," he pleads, and Pa, with tears in his eyes, says he

will give him a chew, even if the doctor throws him out of the hospital. Jeff wants to go back to the Big Sandy and die, "back where Pap and Ma died." He insists that he is going back. The nurse comes in to run the visitors out, saying that it is time for the patient to take his medicine. Uncle Jeff refuses.

"No, by God."

"Die then."

The doctor comes in and Jeff is more tractable. The visitors say good-bye.

"You boys don't work on no goddamn railroad," Uncle Jeff says, as they leave, and Pa, in grief, tells his sons, "Brother Jeff is a goner."

There follows a description of Pa's first trip to a picture show, which the boys have maneuvered him into making with them, while they wait for the bus that will take them back to Kentucky. They arrive home, they do their chores by lantern light and by starlight on their small rented farm. Pa lectures his sons throughout on getting an education so that they can stay away from working on a railroad section, where "you get the least wages in the world and do the hardest work."

The story ends with the arrival of the telegram announcing Uncle Jeff's death, and Pa's catching "Number 8" to ride up to the Big Sandy country to oversee Jeff's burial. Shan understands that Uncle Jeff will be hauled on a wagon over an old woods road, overgrown with weeds and brush, to the spot by a little peach tree "near Ma," which is the place he has specified for his last resting place. "It will be where the green peach tree leaves and the pink peach tree blossoms were crumbled down last year. There will not be the sound of a train whistle back there."

Thus ending his narrative with pungent words and with calculated artistic effect, Jesse Stuart evokes the symbolism of the peace and quiet of the woods where the man of nature has found his reunion with earth, in contrast to the cruel life of the machine age represented by the railroad—a sharp lesson which he desired in the mind of the reader. He does this without pointing a moral. He does not add the final paragraph which weakens some of his stories by a statement of that which has already been achieved by selection of theme and of protagonist, by colorful, incisive imagery and diction and by taut, dramatic treatment. For its embodiment of all of these essentials for attaining artistic unity, **"Uncle Jeff"** is rightfully considered a classic.

Its humor, which understates a larger theme of pathos, is typical of Jesse Stuart's attitude toward life, representing as it does a fatalistic acceptance of the triumph of industrialization, after salty individualism has gone down fighting. There are overtones of bitterness in the story for the poverty of men like "Uncle Jeff" and "Pa," who lack an opportunity for acquiring an education, and who spend their lives in comparative slavery as a result. The note of social protest wherever it appears in Stuart's works is mainly concerned with this imbalance of educational opportunities, or, as in *Taps for Private Tussie,* with the government's paternalistic humoring of people who will not work but prefer to live on "relief."

Sharply opposed in tone to **"Uncle Jeff"** is a more recent story, evidencing Stuart's ability to turn easily from bawdy humor to poetic quietness.

**"Angel in the Pasture,"** published in the June 1959 issue of *Esquire,* is a perspicuous example of Jesse Stuart's sublimity of mind, as reflected in his writings, following his miraculous recovery from the heart attack which almost claimed his life.

Labeled a short story in the magazine, **"Angel in the Pasture"** is hardly more than a vignette of a mood. It is a dream sequence, an hallucination experienced under an oxygen tent, which might well have been taken from *The Year of My Rebirth,* Stuart's journal of his recovery and of his reunion with the natural world.

If **"Angel in the Pasture"** is a short story, it is a "short short," the briefest of Stuart's stories. Yet the insight which it gives into Jesse Stuart's thinking, his approach to life in his mature years, gives this story a real significance. It is important, also, as an example of the restrained style which is in marked contrast to the rugged "slice of life" style characteristic of Stuart's earlier works. Here experience is interpreted subjectively through the imagination of the writer and becomes a strong poetic expression through evocation of mood.

The theme of nostalgia, which embodies two time levels, the past and the present, and points up the ephemeral quality of life, is set in the opening paragraph: "Shan slowly closed his eyes and entered a beautiful world long past, with sun he could not hold in the sky, flowers he could not keep fresh on their stems and sumac leaves he could not keep from going into an autumn season, coloring and dying and blowing hither and thither in the autumn winds of 1916."

The imagery is of a bright, sunlit world, the world of a nine-year-old boy, sent to find a cow in a pasture, as contrasted with the present world of gloom under an oxygen tent—"death-colored" (to use one of Stuart's favorite descriptive terms)—when the leaves of spring have darkened into autumn colors and are being scattered by autumn winds to their resting place on earth.

The young boy dawdles at his task, while he is alive to the natural world about him, seeing birds, animals, flowers, and trees through the perspective of the embryo poet. He goes first to the hollow where the tall beeches grow, to watch the squirrels return from their early morning breakfast and play on the big, leafy branches of the trees where they have their holes. He watches the sudden flight of a pheasant which he has startled from a cluster of saw briers at his feet. He listens to young hawks and crows as they are fed in their nests, and visits again the nest of an old hummingbird which he had long tried to catch, "but he'd

always fly off and whistle through the air like a bullet. Like the whine of a .22 rifle."

This simile of the bird's take-off as sounding like the whine of a bullet is an excellent example of Stuart's objective: always to find the exact descriptive words—as was the objective of the Imagist poets—to bring the sharp image, or correlative, which was in the mind of the writer, to the mind of the reader.

Similar sharp similes are to be found in this story:

> There were dewdrops on the pine-tree needles. These dewdrops weighted them like little lumps of polished silver until the sun lifted them skyward in white ribbons of mist. There were dewdrops on the red-tinted sand-brier leaves, on the hard stems of the sand briers, on the milkweed and silkweed leaves that were shaped like stiff hogs' ears, only they were green. And the bright wind above him was filled with streamers of mists.

Although only those familiar with farm life might appreciate the homely simile of the milkweed leaves as being "like stiff hogs' ears," any reader with vision can see the dewdrops on the pine-tree needles as "little lumps of polished silver" and the metaphoric "streamers" with which the mist laces the bright wind.

As stated, the name which Jesse Stuart gives to himself in much of his fictional writing is "Shan." Here we are in sympathy with young Shan as his revery is interrupted by the arrival of his mother in the pasture to speed up his search for Gypsy, the cow, so that she can milk her under the big white oak.

> He wouldn't have time now, since his mother had come, to talk to the birds, squirrels, hawks and crows, and pretend he was a brother to them. he didn't have a brother and he talked to everything when he was out in the woods alone. . . . He wanted to be among the good wind, songs of the birds, beauty of flowers, leaf and brier forever.

> *If only I could command the sun to stop where it is in the sky and hold all the white mists where they are in the air, Shan thought. If I could only keep the birds singing like they are singing now, and keep the soft, warm June winds blowing. If I could keep the pasture daisies as white and the wild roses as pink as they are now. If I could keep the saw briers in clusters with red-tinted leaves and the little pines and sumacs the same size as they are now. If I could make this pasture and this world and time stand still I'd do it!*

This wish for the immutability of time is followed by Shan's description of his mother, with more apt similes, as she suddenly appears before him in the pasture, "five feet eleven inches tall," her hair "black as the crows' wings," her eyes, "grey as the bark on the poplar tree" and her teeth "white as daisy petals."

Again, the similes come from Nature, from the world close to the soil which is Jesse Stuart's individual world, as it is the universal world. Again, in the wish for time to talk as to a brother with the birds, animals, flowers and trees, and to hold them forever in that perfect moment of communion, there is the strong feeling of transcendentalism which is evidenced throughout the life and works of Jesse Stuart.

But time will not hold still. Shan has found Gypsy under the sweet-apple tree, and he stretches out dreamily on the ground, to observe sky and earth, in close harmony with his mother, his "angel" in the pasture, as she milks Gypsy. But into his fantasy of an unchanging world steals the realization that he cannot keep it, this perfect world, from its degeneration and death.

> He couldn't keep the pine seedlings from growing into saw-log timber. He couldn't stay the hunters' guns from pheasants, crows, hawks and squirrels. He couldn't hold the wild rose and the blooming daisy beyond their seasons. He couldn't keep the young spring wind blowing over him. He suddenly wanted his mother to finish milking. He listened to hear her say, "Shan, let's be goin'." For he was waking from this dream world he couldn't hold into a world of reality.

> Instead of a warm, June wind and green leaves above him there was a clear, cool tent. That wasn't his mother standing there. It was a nurse. Reality. His mother no longer milked Gypsy under the white oak. She rested at Plum Grove. This wasn't 1916. This was 1956. Dream world or real world, there was one thing he was certain of: he had been with an angel in that pasture.

Despite the banality of the closing sentence, **"Angel in the Pasture"** remains a clear example of beauty of language and thought, of atmospheric feeling and of psychological depth. It is scarcely more than an etching, yet it is deserving of a unique place among the hundreds of Stuart short stories.

## Mary Washington Clarke (essay date 1968)

SOURCE: "The Hill Man's Religion," in *Jesse Stuart's Kentucky,* McGraw-Hill, 1968, pp. 55-90.

[*In the following excerpt, Clark examines the role of religion in Stuart's short fiction.*]

> But the hill people still saw God. . . .
>                                                    *Beyond Dark Hills*

With less of social protest than of humor, Jesse Stuart has brought alive the *old-time religion* with its narrow intolerance, its dark superstition, and at the same time its undeniable sustaining power. The strange blend of self-contradictory elements that made up hill church doctrine was as basic in hill thinking as were the religious gatherings in the social life and in the personal relationships of the people. Stuart's vivid descriptions of the highly emotional scenes of *a hill revival, a spring baptizing, a footwashing,* an *Association,* a *funeralizing,* and other religious meetings have communicated the hill man's concepts of Heaven, Hell, God, the Devil, sin, and *living by the Word,* with each detail concretely envisioned. Here, as in other phases of hill life, Stuart's use of folk speech has provided the outsider with a key to help him understand the concepts, attitudes, and conduct of the of hill people.

The Good Book, the Holy Bible, was often the only book a hill family owned, and the reverence that even illiterate people felt for it was closely akin to magic. Stuart recalled of his early childhood: "We had only one book in our shack. That was the Bible." The *Word* could refer to the Bible, to God, or to a *call to preach* (*got the Word*). The Bible was the one book which the hill people considered worth reading; and they were thoroughly convinced—many of them—that its meaning would be divinely revealed to true believers: "Don't have to go to school. . . . Just have the faith and open the Word and read." The preachers in Stuart's stories, like their real life counterparts, have consequently quoted and misquoted the Bible in support of farfetched notions of right and wrong and to explain very peculiar conduct. When a hill man said, "Don't it say in the Word," he was not asking a question but making a confident assertion, no matter how bizarre his thinking may have seemed to an outsider. The Word, based on the Scriptures or distorted from the Bible passages, was the key expression to hill religion.

When the Tussies gained the prosperity of Kim's $10,000 government insurance, Grandma made a remark that illustrated a typically grotesque application of Biblical language to everyday living and the hill tendency to interweave religion and folklore: "Money's like *manna* from heaven. . . . I've always dreamed of finding a pot of gold where a shootin' star fell. . . . This is the pot of gold I've always looked for!" Grandma could foresee that the Tussies' riches would bring relatives down upon them *like locusts in their seasons to eat up the trees.* Uncle George Tussie, one of the *locusts,* was sure that he had Scriptural basis for thinking that Vittie, Kim's widow, would get her reward in Heaven for the way she was using her dead husband's insurance money: "I was given plenty to eat, a good bed to sleep in, and today *you clothed me.* Ain't there something in the Word about clothin' a man?" When the owner of the big Rayburn house gave the eviction notice, Grandpa Tussie was even more certain that he had Biblical support for his advice to the forty-six Tussies who had come to live with him: "That's what the Word tells us. *Dance and be merry for tomorrow you may die.*" He accepted the supposed death of his son and the loss of his old-age pension with fortitude: *Man born of woman is full of trouble*; and *every man must have his Judas.* Grandma distorted the Biblical proverb only a little in reference to Vittie's marriage to Uncle George: *Give 'em the wind. That is what they've sown, and the wind's what they'll reap.* Not for the primitive Tussies, but in reference to his own energetic family was Stuart's mention of the ancient fable of the ant and the grasshopper: *Go, thou sluggard, like the ant and be wise.*

The lusting of the flesh led some hill men to *know* a woman before marriage, but most of them felt that once they had married they should not *put asunder what God had jined together.* When a logger killed his rival logger for committing adultery with his wife, the murderer went free in court; but the relatives of the dead man pointed out the sign on the courthouse: *God is not mocked. Whatsoever a man soweth that shall he also reap.* They were threatening him with the stern mountain code that called for *an eye for an eye, a man for a man.* Ronnie, who had "two livin' wives right down there together" was *a-livin' in adult'ry,* for which he was much at fault *in the eyes of the Lord.* When Brother Fain Groan tried to show his faith in the Word by resurrecting his dead wife, even his *Disciples* felt doubtful about carrying husbandly affection so far: "It is against the *Word* to *prank* with the dead. Don't the Word say, 'Let the dead rest. Bury the dead and let them rest'?" Phoeby's husband Dave took a more usual attitude when he submitted stoically and said over her coffin, with characteristic mountain fatalism, *Thy will be done.*

Unexpected associations of Biblical terminology with details of hill life have sometimes shown evidence of the hill man's straight-faced humor, but even then have indicated the far-reaching influences of the Bible on hill speech and thought: a reference to Kentucky hill Republicans as the *Lost Tribe of Israel,* a revenue officer's badge as the *Mark o' the Beast,* a clever trader as a *wolf in sheep's clothing.* Less intentional on the part of the illiterate hill preacher than on the part of Jesse Stuart was the humor of a somewhat jumbled funeral tribute to soldier Kim Tussie: "Like *David* of old, who *slew the Philistines with the jawbone of an ass,* Kim *barked* our enemies with his rifle. I know that Kim has entered the *pearly gates* of Heaven!" The context was hardly that of the original when Arn Sparks consoled her son whose hound dog had been poisoned, *Don't let your heart be troubled.* Old Op, annoyed at his city visitor's disbelief in ghosts, asked him indignantly, "Don't the speret leave the body atter we wear out these old clay temples of ourn? . . . Don't ye believe in the *Good Book?*" More literally perhaps than Enoch of old, the Stuart children, on their way to school and Sunday school, *walked with God*—"What did we care about the bull in Wheeler's pasture?"

The love of nature has prompted Stuart's repeated use of the Bible verse, *the Heavens declare the glory of God.* In various contexts he has also repeatedly referred to man's *bringing forth fruit in his season,* and to Bible terms associated with death: when a person had lived his *threescore years and ten* (often Stuart refers to his *fourscore years and ten*) and *had neared the end of his travail upon God's footstool,* he *confessed his sins before men* and hoped to find his name written in the *Lamb's Book of Life.* All except the most *wicked* hill men looked forward to taking their places before the *Throne of God* where *God would wipe away all tears,* and there would be no hunger or thirst or any other troubles that had beset the person on

---

earth. The book of Revelation has had a particular fascination for the hill people, and their interpretations have been fearfully and wonderfully concrete and literal. Yet never has this apocalyptic vision affected their trust in God's personal and benevolent concern for them, as expressed in Uncle John the Baptist's ringing song, *His eye is on the sparrow, and I know he watches me.* Judge Allie Anderson's illegitimate son, Rufus Litteral, unclaimed until the supposed *day of doom,* also found great comfort in the Scriptures.

---

**Stuart's portrayal of hill preachers has often leaned toward the extremes of corruptness and fanaticism, and he has been inclined to deal with the uniquely grotesque incidents rather than the typical.**

—*Mary Washington Clarke*

---

When a hill preacher *got the Word,* his belief that God had divinely called and inspired him to lead others in the paths of righteousness, most of the members of his congregations shared the attitude of the child Jesse Stuart, "I thought all the preacher said just had to be true." Some of them *got the Word* very suddenly, as did Brother Melvin P. Hankas. He *got under conviction* at one of Brother Peter Leadingham's revivals: ". . . the next day I was on a mowin' machine and I felt like I had a sunstroke. Right there me and my Lord got right, and He put his hand on my head and said, 'Preach.' I went to preachin' in three days." The real-life incident that inspired this story was a reiterated story in Brother Tobbie's sermons at Plum Grove. Stuart's mother told him during one of his college vacations: "Yes, he [Brother Tobbie] did go over that old story again about the Lord calling him to preach when he was a-cuttin' hay on that piece of ground back of the barn." An unlooked-for answer to a skeptic's prayer launched another hill man into the ministry. Silas Woodberry, amazed into conversion by the storm that washed out his milldam, prayed that God would help him to catch the *drifting souls* and give him the *heaviest cross to bear.* Hank Redfern also *got the Word* suddenly and began to preach. When the Reverend Adam Flint was preaching the funeral of a man who resembled Stuart's maternal grandfather, he spoke of boyhood visions in the cornfield and how he could suddenly read the Word, preach, and *line out* hymns from the *Old Sweet Songster.*

The illiteracy of the preachers and a widespread tendency to argue over doctrine and take pride in considering one's own interpretations direct messages from God himself led to unreasoning intolerance among denominations and to divisiveness within denominations. In **"The Anglo-Saxons of Auxierville"** Stuart was being more truthful than facetious when he wrote: "Their spirits will leave their temples of clay for one of the eight Baptist Heavens." Revivals with their supercharge of emotionalism did much to encourage the dogmatic attitude that the hill people took toward their chosen churches, each believing that only his church had the *right kind of Faith* and a *prom-*

*ise of the Glory Land.* Although Methodist, Holy Roller, Unknown Tongue, and certain other sects have found a place in Stuart's writings, as they have in hill religious life, his stories have reflected the overwhelming predominance of the Baptist doctrine in the region. His comic muse has been much in evidence in stories picturing the difficulties that Mountain Baptists have had in agreeing, or disagreeing, among themselves.

In **"Love in the Spring"** Elster's fourth-generation Methodist parents threatened to disown him if he yielded to his love in the spring and married that *infidel,* the *Slab Baptis'* girl Effie; but it was a knockout blow from her *Slab Baptis'* boyfriend following his declaration that he "ain't no damned *infidental*" that sent Elster back home and into the Methodist fold. In **"Weep No More My Lady"** it was only because of her misunderstanding that the Mountain Baptist widow married a Free Will Baptist as her second husband. In **"Three Hundred Acres of Elbow Room"** Big Eif Porter insisted upon his son's *norrating* among his neighbors—especially the *Free Willers*—the news of his *token* that he was to *change worlds* that night at ten o'clock and urged them to be present so that they would know that the *Forty-Gallon Baptists* (the name Stuart has given one of the divisions of Mountain Baptists who approved of drinking mountain whisky) had the *right kind of faith* and the *true religion.* "Uncle John the Baptist" in the story of that title was just as thoroughly convinced that the *Free Willers* had the inside track to Heaven. Uncle Mel Shelton, who was considered by many to be an *infidel* standing in the way of many with his *set idears on the Bible,* inspired his nephew to have a vision of the afterlife:

> If you could see all of us Republicans, Democrats, Methodists, Forty-Gallon Baptists, Hard-shelled Baptists, Free-will Baptists, Primitive Baptists, Regular Baptists, United Baptists, Missionary Baptists, Union Baptists, Independent Baptists—all of us out'n the graves a-shaking hands and asking the other how he is after the long night o'sleep . . . how great it all is. . . .

When Baptist and Methodist preachers stopped preaching *holiness* and the *coming of the millennium* and discouraged shouting and other such displays, some of the oldtimers became uncomfortable and formed new sects, each stubbornly holding that its members were *the only people right.* Stuart has coined and often used as a blanket term for these sects that split off from the Baptist and Methodist churches the name the *Church of the Old-Fashioned Faith.* The rapid growth of such sects as the Church of God, Pilgrim Holiness, Church of the Nazarene, Pentecostal, and others during the depression years of the 1930s when Stuart was publishing his first books and stories unquestionably influenced his writings.

Stuart's portrayal of hill preachers has often leaned toward the extremes of corruptness and fanaticism, and he has been inclined to deal with the uniquely grotesque incidents rather than the typical; but he has also shown insight in his occasional incidents dealing with hill preachers who were sincere men of integrity and sympathetic concern for the hill people. In the former category were such men as the preacher the boy Jesse Stuart saw with a woman in the weeds by the creek bank. "He gave me twenty-five cents and . . . told me not to say anything about seeing him there." Brother Hammertight collected *sinful* jewelry from repentant sinners and sold it across the river in West Virginia, following the practice of corrupt churchmen since pre-Reformation days. Brother Tobbie, who committed suicide by putting a double-barreled shotgun to his temple, *wasn't nigh right with the Lord*; Brother Fain Groan, who said of the ten virgins parable, "You know there was ten of them, don't you? And you know one of them was Virgin Mary, don't you?" was not typical in his ignorance nor in his fanatical faith—nor was he alone! It would not be difficult, however, in the 1960s to find preachers still haranguing against television, swimming, and women's clothing; people believing that a person who does not show emotion and shout and testify during a church service has not been *born again*.

Brother Osborne represented the better type of hill preacher:

> He is the shepherd to the flock of hill people in Greenup Country. He preaches to them. He marries them. He preaches their funerals. He comes to their bed in time of sickness. He rides on horseback or walks. He goes to them in their time of need.

At the funeral of Mrs. Waters, the insane suicide, his words were gentle and compassionate—unlike the preaching of so many old-time preachers—full of God's love for his struggling people.

When the preachers' faults were born of ignorance and naïveté rather than of greed, lust, and deceit, Stuart has portrayed them as pathetic rather than evil. For example, the young girl snake-handler of the *Unknown Tongue* church was presented with almost idyllic sweetness in **"Snake Teeth."** Humor took the reins in **"Red Jacket: The Knockin' Spirit,"** when Old Brother Peter Leadingham fell prey to prankster Judd Sluss. Brother Peter boasted: "God is just a common man. . . . God is about the size of Judd Sluss. . . . God smokes a pipe just like I do and the same brand of tobacco. . . . I'm the only skunk livin' that has seen his Saviour face to face."

In the Kentucky hills, unlike some of the highland communities, very few immigrant Catholics were attracted by the development of public works, and the preachers and members of their congregations alike were militantly Protestant. Stuart reflected this antipathy toward Roman Catholics in his account of a hitchhiking incident. The Catholic truck driver with whom he had ridden the night before had been invited along with Stuart to eat breakfast in a Kentucky mountain home, and the farmer's wife had offered him ham and gravy. "'No, madam. I don't eat meat on Friday. It is against my religion. I am a Catholic.' Mrs. Tillman acted like she had been hit above the eye." In the course of the conversation Mr. Tillman felt impelled to knock the man down from the table. The next person to give Stuart a ride, upon hearing of the inci-

dent, expressed just as strong anti-Catholic feeling, saying meaningfully, "I'm a Klansman."

Most of the hill preachers and members of their congregations had a dual concept of God as a fearful physical presence and as a benevolent protector. The young Jesse Stuart thought of God as ready to "jump from behind a tree and hit me with a stick."

> . . . Everybody there had the same picture of God. He was a strong man that rode the clouds. He saw through a tree. He took the good people home and sent the bad people to the Devil. God and the Devil were at war. They had many fights there at Plum Grove.

Granny Flaugherty's dream of Heaven with its harp-playing angels and a fatherly God on his *Great Throne* is one of many Stuart picture of God's benevolence. The details of this vision were impressed upon the young Stuart by Granny's much-repeated account of her visit there. Relatives, neighbors, and friends who had *gone to Glory* met her there with as warm a welcome as if she had been paying a neighborly visit in Kentucky. It seemed a most democratic place in which God smiled upon his *sanctified* followers. When *the good old Soul* died at ninety-three her neighbors felt sure she had become *one of God's angels*. Sister Combs of the Unknown Tongue faith preached in a hill revival: "What will you do in Heaven for whisky and terbacker? There will be no saloons there. There will be no spittoons there. You will not want to dirty the *streets of gold* with old black *ambeer* spit. You will not want to get drunk in Heaven." Young Sid, listening to the funeral sermon for his uncle Kim in *Taps for Private Tussie,* wonders about Brother Baggs' picture of Heaven: "I don't think that Heaven with golden streets and good people would suit Uncle Kim," rough, profane, hard-drinking, pistol-shooting mountain man that he had been on earth.

Big Eif Porter deviated a little further from the Scriptures when he hoped that Heaven would provide him with a "farm where I can work, and I hope they have winter, summer, springtime, and fall there just like we have here." He thought of death as "somethin' like a-goin' from my farm over to Wormwood's farm," and he hoped that his neighbors would "live on adjoining farms" in Heaven. He thought it might take "a hour to get up that long ladder a body's got to go up before he gets to Heaven." Old Peter Leadingham also thought of Heaven as quite near—just a mile or two above his head. The title *Plowshare in Heaven* (1958) suggests this tendency toward concreteness in religious concepts as a basic element in hill religion. As in certain traditional folk ballads, characters were unable—or unwilling—to distinguish between the flesh and the spirit. Phoeby in the title story **"Plowshare in Heaven"** saved money to buy a new dress, "the dress I want to wear in Heaven. . . ." Shan, the small boy in this story, doubted that Phoeby would be happy in Heaven as the Bible has described it.

> It will not be home unless she can walk barefooted over the fields of growing corn and feel the soft earth

beneath her feet; unless she can feel the handle of a hoe in her hand and smell the good clean wind of a Kentucky spring. . . .

The funeral songs of the mountain people, as Stuart has recorded them, have shown the deep need of hard-working men and women to think of Heaven as a place of eternal rest: "The Land Beyond the River," "Rock of Ages," "Leaning on the Everlasting Arms," and "Where the Living Waters Flow":

> There is a land of wondrous beauty
> Where the "Living Waters" flow,
> The word of God to all has said it
> And it surely must be so.
>
> No tears are there, no blighting sorrow
> From the cruel hand of Death;
> No flowers fade, no summers perish
> By the winter's chilling breath.
>
> I've loved ones there who passed before me,
> They'll rejoice to see me come,
> But best of all, I'll see my Saviour,
> Who will bid me welcome home.

Other favorites have been "Amazing Grace," "From Greenland's Icy Mountains," "When Winter's Darkling Waves We'll Ferry O'er," "We'll Meet You in the Morning Over There," "Safe in the Arms of Jesus," and "The Sweet Bye and Bye."

The mountain man's visualizing of Hell and the Devil has been equally vivid. Anse Bushman, during his period of unconsciousness after a tree had fallen on him, saw himself in the *lake of fire and brimstone* trying to swim amid serpents and scorpions that wore the heads of his sinful earthly neighbors. Old Peter Leadingham's concept, however phony his vision in the beech grove, was of a fierce Devil carrying a pitchfork in his hand: "He has the horns of a two-year-old bull and he looks somethin' like a black cow walkin' on her hind feet." Old Op, too, had a tall-tale experience with the Devil. These stories, partaking of practical joking and folk tale, are extreme; but the picture of a physical devil in the image of man—but with horns, tail, and cloven hoof—was as widely held among the hill people of the past as was the anthropomorphic concept of God.

Literal, too, was the hill man's belief that the body would be resurrected in physical form on the *Judgment Day.* Uncle Mel Shelton in **"This Is the Place"** spoke for many:

> "We shall be as we have been—have the same color of hair, shapes of noses, the same voice—We shall run with our old company—I expect to have my farm here and do the things as I have always done. How can that which is the real Mel Shelton die? . . . It was not born to die—only the husk that encloses it was born to die."

The belief in *Christ's Second Coming* in the clouds followed by the *millennium,* or thousand years of peace, that

had been revived by European pietists from the beliefs of the early Christians has been the subject of much discussion among the highland population, particularly in time of war or the threat of war. It has lost ground in recent years, but only two decades ago events that took place one night in Blakesburg (Greenup) demonstrated conclusively that the concept of the *Judgment Day* was almost universal among the townspeople there as well as among the Red Necks, or country people.

---

**The Calvinistic, Puritan identification of hard work with the good life is a recurrent theme in Stuart's writings and an integral trait of mountain character.**

*—Mary Washington Clarke*

---

An unusually brilliant showing of the aurora borealis on September 18 was mistaken for *the end of the world, the end of time, the Judgment Day, Christ's coming on a cloud.* This naïve interpretation of a natural phenomenon uncommon so far south inspired a whole gallery of portraits of frightened men and women in Stuart's *Foretaste of Glory.* People so visual-minded, whose very lives depended often on elemental nature, found it easy to explain natural phenomena and uneasy states of mind in terms of the supernatural. Some—not all—hill preachers and *exhorters* exploited this tendency to the full. The Reverend Mr. Whetstone, retired minister, could not get an audience when he tried to quiet the people with the scientific explanation. Sister Spence, assisted by *exhorter* Bert Edgwater in the courthouse square, pleaded: "This will be your last time to repent! Oh, why not be saved before it is too late! A home in Glory and the promise of eternal life is better than a-goin' to a Devil's hell to spend your eternity in fire and brimstone! . . ." As his fellow townsmen rushed about taking advantage of what they thought was a last chance to *get right* with God and man, the gravedigger Uncle Uglybird Skinner and Judge Allie Anderson down at his hogpen remarked uncertainly: *The end of time comes in a twinkling. . . . Not even the angels in Heaven will know when it comes.* The majority of characters in *Foretaste of Glory,* however, brought to the surface their innermost, and often guilty, secrets as they looked fearfully upon the signs in the skies; until they had fully confessed their sins, they felt unprepared *to meet their Maker* on the *Day of Doom.*

Mountain religion is full of contradictions. Kentucky historian Thomas D. Clarke has written in *A History of Kentucky* of the early pioneers as applying "a practical religious belief of foreordination to their daily lives." The passage continues:

> . . . Nearly everyone believed that his fate was a sealed book and very philosophically accepted his hardships

as God-sent. This belief is typical of people who live close to nature. Religion on the frontier was as rugged and hard as the virgin oak . . .

Even within his own family Stuart has recognized this fatalistic element in hill belief. But this does not in the least rule out an equally strong belief that each individual participated in his own salvation.

The Calvinistic, Puritan identification of hard work with the good life is a recurrent theme in Stuart's writings and an integral trait of mountain character. Grandpa in the story **"Grandpa"** states a widely held moral code and religious viewpoint in the following passage of conversation:

> . . . I am the last leaf. I'm waitin' fer the Master's call. He will call me, too, when he wants me. I'll hear His call. I'll heed that call, fer I am ready. I've cheated no man. I've given away in my lifetime. I have come to the end without land or money. I've wronged no woman, killed no man, stole no chickens, I've cut as many saw logs and cleaned as much of briers and sprouts and trees as any man in Kentucky.

This feeling of a direct, personal relationship between God and man appears everywhere in Jesse Stuart's stories and autobiographies, and is attributed to many types of mountain men and women.

*The Word,* then, sometimes means the Bible and the good life based on the hill man's understanding or misunderstanding of the Bible; or it may be an illiterate hill preacher's prohibitions of wearing jewelry, using tobacco, dancing, or watching television. *Living by the Word* involves plenty of hard work, occasional *wrestlings with the Devil, owing no man anything,* and accepting whatever comes as *the will of God,* who put everyone and everything here *for a purpose.* Incredibly naïve at times, mountain religion is an intensely personal experience, inseparable from folk custom and the practical details of everyday living; and each sect is sure that its followers alone have *the right kind of faith.*

Almost everyone in the hills, no matter how *wicked* (*weaked*), intended someday to *get right with God.* In Stuart's accounts of mountain religious conversions humor, sympathetic insight, and critical comment are blended. He has focused attention especially on the spring revivals, which were often rightly called *protracted meetings,* for they sometimes lasted four and five weeks instead of the originally planned two weeks. Some church members backslid repeatedly during the long pent-up winters or during the hard summer work in *crop time,* and had to *get right in their hearts* year after year.

Conversion was due from the time one's *accountability* began at the age of twelve, but in some Stuart stories the lusty old figures of earth had passed their fourscore years and ten before they could bring themselves to give up *worldly things.* Battle Keaton, for example, was past eighty when he *got saved* and *come across on the Lord's side* at a protracted meeting in the schoolhouse on Hog Branch.

*Getting saved* followed a rather definite pattern, which might extend over hours, days, weeks, or even longer. As soon as the sinner *got under conviction* and went up to kneel at the *mourners' bench,* he began to *wrestle with the devil* in prayer. The praying continued until the *burden was rolled away* and he could bring himself to *confess his sins before men.* Usually his confession was followed by a trance-like state of exaltation proving to him and to all present that God had forgiven his sins. He was then ready to *follow his Lord in baptism* by immersion in the waters of Little Sandy at Put-Off Ford, and live *on Jesus' side (on the Lord's side).* Unless a person had committed the blackest sins or unless he himself felt impatience, the baptism was usually delayed until the big *spring baptizing*; but Stuart's parents' experience of being baptized in weather so cold that a hole had to be chopped in the ice was by no means unique. Only the fortunate few among the converts were righteous enough to achieve *Second Blessing* and *Sanctification* that made it impossible for them to sin thereafter.

The typical hill revival service was noisy and emotional, often with several preachers participating. Although it was the exception rather than the rule for preachers to wear long, flowing white robes, some of the young girl evangelists and a few of the more fanatical men preachers imitated the robes in the Sunday-school card pictures of Christ performing His earthly ministry. The *meetings* often took place in schoolhouses or church houses; but the largest and most exciting ones were held in the groves with the congregation sitting on split-log benches and lanterns hanging from the trees.

The loud harmonized hymn singing, sweet to mountain ears, sounded across the countryside, sometimes to organ or guitar accompaniment, sometimes *lined out* by a leader in churches that ruled out musical instruments and even tuning forks—but nevertheless loved to sing. The revival songs were widely diversified, including many of the old hymns familiar to Evangelical Protestants in the highlands and throughout the South, less familiar old-fashioned selections from the *Old Sweet Songster* and others of its type, and newer songs showing the influence of outland slang and jazz. The style of singing showed the influence of old-style ballad singing in the little grace notes and sharp intake of breath at the end of a phrase, and also the influence of the loud and lusty harmonies of the camp meeting. Stuart has included texts—and has mentioned many additional songs—in all three categories. . . . .

After the spirited song service, several hours of preaching, exhorting, and praying were accompanied by shouting on the part of anyone in the congregation that the spirit moved to shout (no one, least of all the preacher, considered the *Amens* and *Glory hallelujahs* to be interruptions). The typical sermons concentrated on contrasting the horrors of Hell with the beauties of Heaven, with the former receiving by far the greater emphasis. *Burning forever* in the *lake of fire and brimstone* was pictured as the awful consequence of such *mortal sins* as the following: raising or smoking the *filthy and evil weed* tobacco—less frequently of drinking whisky; playing cards, going to cockfights, and otherwise gambling; stealing, even so much as a chicken; committing adultery; dancing to fiddle music, or playing it; wearing cosmetics and jewelry; attending movies, baseball games, and carnivals; women's wearing bathing suits, shorts, low-necked and sleeveless dresses; and, more recently, watching television.

When a repentant hill tobacco farmer went home from the revival service and cut his green tobacco by moonlight, some of his fellow church members were worldly enough to wonder how he would feed and clothe his family without the money from his crop. Some sons of pipe-smoking mountain women doubted Brother Toady Leadingham's preaching that a person had to change the color of his spit before he could go to Heaven, and accused the preacher of getting *off'n the Gospel.* One fiery old hill preacher kept a *Scandal Board* where he mounted the sinful objects—pipes, plugs of tobacco, rings, guns, knives, steel knucks, and even ten-dollar bills. Since mountain preachers and their listeners usually felt that it was wrong for them to take money for their preaching, the temptation was great to take the sinful objects across a state line and sell them. Brother Doubty, who preached just as vociferously against those evils, was greatly admired for his integrity in refusing all money. Whether or not they gave up their *pleasures,* the hill men usually agreed with the preacher that the foregoing things were *sinful.*

Whatever the subject of his harangue, the preacher accompanied his shouted sermon with a good deal of near-acrobatic action, although Brother Hammertight may have carried it to a greater extreme than was usual:

> Brother Hammertight is trying to climb the stovepipe.
> . . . He tears the whole works down. . . . He shouts on.
> . . . "There's the work of the Devil. See that terbacker
> up there. The old Devil has went out of this room by
> now. . . . We've got him on the run. Shout on, Brother,
> Amen, Sister. Shout on. Glory be to God."

Women breast-fed their babies to stop them from crying. Drunken, pistol-toting young men *carvarted* about and mocked at the choir as they parodied their song, "I would not be pop-eyed."

When the sinners began to squirm and feel the presence of the Devil right at their shoulders, it was time to give the *invitation,* which was the climax of every revival service. Stuart's accounts of the religious hysteria at Plum Grove and in the outdoor tabernacles of the *Unknown Tongues* are hardly less extreme than historical accounts of the Cane Ridge revivals of 1801. Stuart captured the spirit of a hill revival in *Beyond Dark Hills:*

> There is great rejoicing in Heaven tonight. A sinner
> here at Plum Grove has repented. . . . Sing the last
> stanza of "Nearer, My God, to Thee!" O won't you
> come? The Lord and the Devil are waiting to see how
> this meeting is a-comin' out. That's right, sister. Come
> right up. Now don't be afraid. Others want to, but the
> Devil won't let them. The Lord is knocking at all their
> hearts. O won't you come? Praise the Lord they are
> coming. The Devil is going. . . .

The saved people tried by song and entreaty to get the sinners down front to the *mourners' bench,* reminding them that *tomorrow's sun may never rise,* this could be their last chance to accept God's promise of *a home in Glory* and *everlasting life.* And the choir sang *Almost persuaded—but lost!* The sinners writhed under their *jolt-wagon loads of sin* until they *prayed through.* The confession of a newly saved soul sometimes caused a less repentant sinner to leave the congregation, especially if he had been an accomplice in adultery. In one story Stuart tells of an *exhorter* of the old logging days who *packed the sinners—* even big lumberjacks, colliers, and ore diggers—down the aisle on his shoulder if they were too slow in going of their own accord. According to Old Op, their confessions were worth hearing. Sometimes the church bell rang out across the fields and hills in the early-morning hours to let the people know that the sinners had all *pulled through.*

The day after a revival or an especially successful Sunday-night service, the conversions would be the talk of the neighborhood:

> "Well, Mrs. Fort came through last night. . . . She
> finally told the Lord what was the matter with her. She
> told him she had killed a lot of young babies. . . .
> When she said these words she began shouting." "I
> want to tell you Sy Mullins got religion last night.
> He's been trying for years. But he could never get
> right with the Lord. He told all he'd ever done last
> night. Since Hilder Kameen's wife died he confessed
> being with her down in the cornfield one time. He
> would never confess when she was living. . . ."

The big *Spring Baptizing* was a social event that drew people from a radius of five and six miles around. Converts who could afford to buy new clothes bought white dresses if they were young girls, flashy pants, silk shirts, and loud neckties if they were young men. The preacher and two strong men went out to measure the depth of the water with a light fence rail until they found a place free from snags and rocks where the water was the right depth. Meanwhile, the people made their wagons and buggies secure or hitched their mules and horses where they would not be in danger of sliding into the water.

The same baptizing seems to have inspired the detailed descriptions in *Beyond Dark Hills* and in **"Braska Comes Through."** When each person being baptized went down into the water, the choir sang "Shall We Gather at the River," and after he had been immersed the people sang "Where the Healing Waters Flow."

> Sister Tister is the first to follow the preacher into the
> brown swirling water. It gathers up her clothes tight
> around her legs and body. When the water is close
> under her arms, they stand. He waves his hand for the
> choir on the bank to sing:

> Yes, we shall gather at the river.
> There the saints of our fathers trod,
> Yes, we shall gather at the river,

The beautiful, the beautiful river
That flows by the throne of God.

There is a splash of water. Words have been said. Sister Tister is up and she is shouting. The two strong men keep her from running into the deep water or from hitting a snag. Women on the river bank are sobbing and shouting. She comes out of the river shouting. She shouts all over the bank. She goes down exhausted. She begins to jerk, lying stretched out in her wet clothes on the sand.

Some of the wet men and women went into the bushes to change their clothing, but others wore their clinging garments home, as the more modest way. Until the following year, there would not be another such *baptizing.*

Not all mountain churches practiced *footwashing,* not even all Mountain Baptist churches; but among those who practiced it, the ceremonial was significant and private. Stuart has given a detailed description of a *footwashing* in the short story **"Love in the Spring,"** which he localized as taking place at Put-Off Ford in Little Sandy, scene of many *baptizings.* The Slab Baptists looked upon visitors from other denominations as the *Devil in sheep's clothing,* and did not hesitate to let the Plum Grove Methodist boy know that he was not welcome. *Bitten by the love bug right above the heart* when he saw Effie, the Slab Baptist girl, he stayed and watched:

> . . . A whole row up and a whole row down. The row standing up was a-washing the feet of them on the ground. Just setting there on the ground as unconcerned and washing feet. Then they would sing another verse of "Where the Healing Waters Flow."

> . . . . .

> . . . Some man had his back to me. He was washing her foot. He had an old chipped washpan and a big towel and a bar of home-made soap made from oak-tree ashes. He'd put it on her foot till it would look pink as a wild crab-apple blossom.

Effie's Slab Baptist sweetheart glared at Elster: "Go on about your business . . . and leave us Baptis alone. This ain't no side show. We are here worshiping the Lord."

Uncle Uglybird in one of his stories of an earlier day at Six Hickories Church on Laurel Ridge referred to the big *protracted meetings* and the *footwashings.* In response to a question as to where the people got water to wash one another's feet, he replied:

> Took lanterns and pine torches and went down to that sulphur spring under the hill in the beech grove. . . . There was a path worn over the hill to that spring in them days slick as the path to a groundhog hole.

As at so many of the hill gatherings, fights were not unusual at the footwashings. Stuart also has made other references to them, but the details seem to have been less familiar to him than those of the revival meetings and baptizings. In **"A Yard of String"** the narrator told of breaking his little finger in two places when he *hit a fellow at a footwashing.*

The Baptist *Association* held annually throughout the denomination had a particular social significance in the hill communities. Baptists from one or more counties met to report on the year's work and make plans for the coming year; they *fellowshiped* together, listened to budget reports and long sermons, ate much fried chicken, and gloried in being Baptists. In *Trees of Heaven* the mountain woman Fronnie told her neighbors at the *molasses-making* about attending the Big Baptist Association at Mountain Chapel—"about this Baptist preacher and that Baptist preacher and how long each preached and she can tell a few things that each said in his two-, three-, and four-hour sermons."

Probably the same event gave rise to the story **"Uncle John, the Baptist,"** describing a *Free Willer Baptist Association* that lasted three days at Mountain Chapel, while much trading went on nearby: "Just can't trade within two hundred yards of the preacher," Uncle John explained. The description of the scene at Mountain Chapel suggested similar meetings throughout the Southern mountains:

> . . . We walk across the tradin' grounds to the head of a little stream. . . . People are sittin' under the trees on rocks, on the ground, on half-split logs. Down below them is a big platform built . . . five logs high and covered with a puncheon floor. Across this are logs split in two and held up by huge blocks of round trees. Men with long beards are settin' on these seats sayin' "Amen" to the "Word" Brother High is preachin'.

> "Amen," says Uncle John, walkin' up to the platform. "Praise the Lord."

> Uncle John . . . greets each brother while Brother High beats his fists together and preaches the "word." Uncle John sits down on a split log, claps his big hairy hands and pats his brogan shoes on the puncheon floor and sanctions all Brother High says.

Women and men passed baskets of *good Baptist grub* among the people as they listened to the long sermons. Later the preachers ate at a special table set for them under the beech trees.

Uncle John, whose son had accused him of going to the *Association* mainly to show off his new teeth, found the *grub* and the new teeth the cause of considerable suffering: he choked on a bit of meat and could swallow nothing until the eleventh day when he coughed up the offending particle and proclaimed loudly that he had *whopped the Devil.* (His family had feared that they would have to take him home in a *wooden overcoat.*)

To a greater extent, perhaps, than any other religious gathering in the hills, the *Association* was a get-together where *saved* people *got happy* and *praised the Lord* long and loudly. It tended more to emphasize the pleasures of being Baptists than to stress the awful threat of hell-fire and damnation to sinners. The Baptist preachers tried to outdo one another in courtesies to their colleagues as well as in the length of their sermons. The women gave an all-out demonstration of their cooking and baking ability; and everyone fellowshiped in a spirit of the greatest generosity and mutual helpfulness.

A more frequent and popular church social was the *basket dinner,* or *dinner on the grounds.* When an all-day service made it practical, the women of the church prepared abundant food on Saturday for dinner on the church grounds preceding the evening preaching services. Like the *pie socials,* these were the scene of much laughing, talking, and courting among the young people—and, not infrequently, the scene of fights. The usual pattern when all ran smoothly was for the families to spread their picnic meal on the ground or for families to get together and share what their baskets contained, then for everyone to move about the churchyard and socialize, and finally go into the church house for the *meeting.*

Stuart has referred to *basket dinners* in several stories, but his only detailed account of one was much involved with a feud, and at least two families loaded their wounded into their wagons after bloody fighting and went home before the evening service. The story, nevertheless, illustrated the basic customs associated with the traditional hill *basket dinner.* Each family had brought abundant food, the best their larders afforded; each spread a tablecloth in the churchyard a slight distance from other families. The boys wearing their silk shirts and flashy ties hoped to *catch us some girls.* "Be a lot of good-lookin' girls there. Allus is at a basket dinner at the Gap Church."

The Dinguses feasted on

> . . . dumplings, pickles, cake, pie, ham, fried chicken, apple preserves, plum preserves, apricots, apples, cornbread, biscuits, light-bread, jelly, Irish 'taters, sweet 'taters, squirrel, soup beans, green beans, leatherbritches beans, blackberry cobbler, raspberries, dewberries, strawberries, wild-plum jelly, wild-grape jelly. . . .

The older women usually exchanged news and gossip, and the men indulged in theological disputes as well as exchanging crop news. The women always hoped that no violence would take place, although it was not uncommon for members of certain families to attend the same small church for many years without speaking to one another, except in anger, as had the Dinguses and Bridgewaters of this story. Ma urged the Dinguses: ". . . Fill yourselves on good grub now and this evenin' we'll fill our hearts on the word of the Scriptures. Goin' to be some good preachin' in th' house this evenin'." A *basket dinner* was always a part of the Baptist Association, but other denominations also had basket dinners.

Equally exciting, but a more serious occasion, was the meeting in which a church member was threatened with excommunication, or in mountain speech *churched.* The exercising of strong disciplinary measures over the church members from seventeenth-century New England to modern times in certain churches has sometimes seemed harsh

to those outside the church. By Stuart's time the regular monthly meeting of Baptists no longer took place (with all members present) to discipline those guilty of fighting, lying, and harmful gossip, stealing, adultery, horse racing, dishonest business dealings, and drunkenness; but in one or another of Stuart's stories every one of these sins has been dealt with. Frolicking and dancing, treating the church with contempt, and other ancient offenses have also received repeated mention in Stuart's writings. Not all offenses were serious enough to justify one's being *churched*; and, no matter how serious the offense, if the sinner repented with enough humility, the measure would serve as a purification rather than as a complete excommunication.

In Stuart's story **"The Devil and Television"** a man was *churched* for having a television set in his home. It might have occurred in this *Church of the Old-Fashioned Faith* for any of the other offenses mentioned in the following section of a sermon on **"The Devil Has Many Faces"**:

> The devil loves company and he is always with the crowd at these places of amusement. If he was there walking among these people they would run and scream. And God's Houses would be full and running over with people. But that's not the way the devil does things. He is a devil with many faces, visiting many places. And now the devil has the slickest way he has ever had of getting into the homes, homes of good people, religious people. He comes in this newfangled thing called television. I believe that's what it's called. I've never seen it. But these places of amusement, these singers and dancers and baseball players and wrestlers and women in shorts and low-necked dresses above the elbows are brought right inside the homes for the family to see. Brothers and Sisters, the devil has pulled a fast one.

Had Pa repented, as other backsliders had done, he would have fallen to his knees and prayed along with the Moderator and the congregation that his sins be forgiven, amid shouts of *Glory* and *Amen.* But Pa is a transitional figure and is not convinced of the sinfulness of his new diversion: "'Come, let's go to your church for a change,' Pa said. 'I'm not movin' my television set out of our home. And I'm still goin' on to church.'" The usual procedure was to warn the offender in advance of the trial; preach a sermon against the specific sin of which the offender had been accused; then call on the person to say "what he had to say for himself," giving him the opportunity to fall trembling to his knees; and finally to give the verdict, which in Pa's case would, of course, be excommunication. The story related that more than thirty of the sixty members of this group had been *churched,* but only Pa and one other had remained unrepentant. In **"Weep No More, My Lady,"** Stuart attributed the practice of *churching* members for worldly pleasures (or the threat of doing so) to the Mountain Baptists, the purpose, of course, being to purify rather than to get rid of the member.

Whether a hill man had ever brought himself to the point of making a public confession of sin earlier in life and whether or not he had belonged to a religious body that practiced *churching* to keep its members on the straight-

and-narrow path, he nearly always wanted to *cut the last rotten speck out of this good apple* when he felt the approach of death. The sins most often confessed on deathbeds were adultery, theft, and murder. Through dreams, the hearing of voices on the wind, or the visualizing of an embodiment of death, he seemed to know when the time had come for him to die. Only the rare exception was unconcerned in that extremity as to where he would spend eternity:

> Where will you spend eternity?
> The question comes to you and me!
> Tell me, what shall your answer be?
> Where will you spend eternity?
>
> Leaving the straight-and-narrow way,
> Going the downward road today,
> Sad will their final ending be,
> —Lost through a long eternity!
>
> Refrain
> ETERNITY! ETERNITY!
> Lost through a long eternity!
> Repent, believe this very hour,
> Trust in the Saviour's grace and power,
> Then will your joyous answer be
> SAVED THROUGH A LONG ETERNITY!

Battle Keaton, for whom the song was sung, was counted *among the blest*; but not so fortunate, the hill people thought, were Annis Bealer and Old Harmon Manley who "died cussing the Lord." Old Man Slackburn, of course, was *saved,* for he "left the world a-clapping his hands and saying, 'Glory to God. They ain't no doubt now. I'm bound for the Promised Land. All you people meet me there.'"

---

**Stuart's many stories and poems dealing with death and the folk beliefs and customs associated with it have reflected the hill man's continual awareness of its immincence and his acceptance of death with the same fatalism that he has accepted the hardships of life.**

*—Mary Washington Clarke*

---

Stuart's many stories and poems dealing with death and the folk beliefs and customs associated with it have reflected the hill man's continual awareness of its imminence and his acceptance of death with the same fatalism that he has accepted the hardships of life. Inseparable from folklore were the interpretations of birthmarks, *tokens,* heavenly visions, and the beliefs out of which the *settin'-up* and the *funeralizing* grew. The hill folk of the past would have associated all such matters with the *one*

*true religion* of their *Old-Fashioned Faith.* Some of the customs relating to death and burial, like those in other phases of hill life, became dissociated from the beliefs out of which they developed and by Stuart's time were known simply as *the way of the hills.*

The behavior of family and neighbors at the time of a death in the Kentucky hills, as pictured in **"Battle Keaton Dies," "300 Acres of Elbow Room," "Plowshare in Heaven,"** and **"She Kept Her Distance,"** was typical of the culture. The death having been *norrated around,* neighbors came to wash, dress, and *lay out* the corpse (women if a woman had died, and men if the deceased were a man). Not often perhaps did these persons comment, as they did of old Battle Keaton, that the water they had washed him in was "damn black" when they emptied the washtub over the bank from the back porch.

As mentioned earlier, every effort was made to comply with deathbed requests as to the details of the funeral and burial. In **"She Kept Her Distance,"** Effie Pratt felt honored by the dying Lommie Wilburn's request that Effie prepare her for her casket: "I want you to wash me clean and put new clothes on me. . . . I don't want an undertaker to touch me." (An ironic detail suggesting, as Stuart often does, the transition at work in his region, was the fact that Lommie's son was an undertaker.) Battle Keaton's daughter, over the protest of some of her friends, honored old Battle's request that he be buried in his long underwear and a blue work shirt. Many agreed that she was doing the right thing, even though the coffin the five men down in the barn were making of wild-cherry and oak planks had to be worked over, so that only part of the lid could be opened and his long white drawers would not show.

The coffins were often shaped to fit the body: "It was shaped like a guitar-box," Billy Auxier said of his mother's homemade coffin. The coffin might be of cedar, poplar, or any other well-seasoned lumber that was available. As they did for the beautiful orphan girl Fern, the women lined the coffin when the men brought it to the house. "The girls went down in the hollow and gathered wreaths of the blue sandflower, goldenrod, and farewell-to-summer," and laid them around the room in which the person *laid a corpse.* A typical *settin'-up* appears in **"She Kept Her Distance"**:

> People came by twos, tens, twenties. They came to sit
> up with the corpse. It was a custom here. They laughed
> and talked in the front room. They sang a hymn. They
> spoke of life. They spoke of crops to be planted. They
> did not talk about death. They kept the lamp burning
> low in the backroom with Lommie all night. . . .

In **"Sittin' up with Grandma"** and in **"A Close Shave"** the observance of this custom proved somewhat premature. Grandma *returned from the dead*; the man in **"A Close Shave"** who had been kicked by a mule could hear all that was said and see all that was done around him, but was unable to communicate the fact that he still lived until after he had been fully prepared for his coffin:

Neighbors . . . telling her what a fine man and a good neighbor I'd been all my life. They told her that I was better off than their husbands who sat around the dining-room table looking at the white two-gallon jug with the long brown neck plugged with a corn-cob stopper.

The men talked of the dead before they began swigging from the jug. Meanwhile the young people played post office, and the sons and daughters quarreled over the division of their father's estate. During the midnight supper someone became aware of the *dead* man's movements. "Before sunrise," he said, "I had chopped up my coffin and made my will."

Some *settin'-ups* became rather disgraceful affairs, such as the one for Uncle Jeff, at which his drinking companions "tried to drown their cares and grief about Uncle Jeff's passing." Some were very quiet, like Phoeby's in **"Plowshare in Heaven."** Phoeby had a store-bought coffin with shiny handles. The house was filled with people, but they sat quietly around the big log fire, at times some of them breaking the silence or soft-spoken conversation to sing a favorite old hymn.

> There are two chairs in the back of the big front room. On these two chairs is the coffin. . . . It is a bluish-gray-colored coffin and it has a glass lid. . . . Phoeby is in the coffin. I know she is in the dress she told Mom about and she has the pennies that she covered with dark cloth over her eyes.

About four o'clock the people who had sat up during the night went home to do their morning chores, but others took their places. Many of the men did not go to the fields even in crop time or to their jobs on public works when a neighbor was *laying a corpse.*

The corpse was never left alone. It would have been difficult for an old-time hill man to express to an outsider exactly what he meant by *showing respect to the dead,* but Stuart has communicated the peculiar atmosphere of the *settin'-up* with its socializing in the foreground and always in the background a superstitious awe in the presence of a great mystery.

It is credible that someone of Stuart's acquaintance, like Flem in **"Men of the Mountains,"** had stored several barrels of salt to preserve himself and his wife in their graves so that they would "keep like a jar of apples till the Judgment Day." But surely his tall-tale brand of humor prompted his account of six months of play parties at weekly *settin'-ups* for old Doug Grayhouse, salted down in the attic at age ninety-six, while relatives all over the country recovered from illnesses, bought new clothes, and otherwise made ready to attend the funeral on the money Grandpa had bequeathed to them for the purpose.

Waning of the prejudice against embalming and removing the corpse from the home before removal to the burial place has been reflected in the otherwise grotesque situation of competing undertakers rushing to the scene of a homicide in **"Competition at Slush Creek."** The old-fashioned *settin'-up,* or *wake,* with rare exceptions belongs to the past.

Another means of *showing respect for the dead* was the mountain funeral, such as Mrs. Auxier's: "Took three preachers four hours to preach Ma's funeral," said Billie. Equally long were the funeral sermons in **"Fern," "Death and Decision,"** and *Taps for Private Tussie.* In the days before embalming, when deaths took place in remote sections of the hills, it was understandable that the *buryin'* took place with little ceremony, and the real memorial service was delayed until a minister could attend—or several ministers. In bad weather it was a considerable undertaking to get the body to the place of burial. In **"I Remember Mollie"** the husband sat on the coffin of his dead wife to keep it from bouncing off the wagon, and the people following in the funeral procession were splashed with mud from the chugholes in the rough country road. In **"Death and Decision"** the male descendants carried Old Dad to the *new-fangled deadwagon,* the ambulance that waited at the main road. In *Taps* six stout Tussie men carried the coffin all the way up the steep mountainside in the heat of summer.

A more unusual custom in the northeastern Kentucky hills has been the *funeralizing* that memorialized a person long dead or paid respect to the same person repeatedly, as in Stuart's story **"Weep No More, My Lady."** In this story a man who had been funeralized each year on the anniversary of his first funeral was being honored for the seventh time by his Mountain Baptist wife. Her second husband, at first acting *like a sheep that had got into the wrong pasture,* mellowed under the influence of the mountain whisky that circulated freely during the service, and by the end of it, was mourning along with his wife for his predecessor.

The *funeralizing* began at the house with a period of *fellowshiping,* singing, and taking inventory of past conduct under the threat of being *churched.* When no one confessed to making love to another man's wife, gambling, or attending street fairs, circuses, or picture shows, the first part of the service ended with everyone's singing "Leaning on the Everlasting Arms." Then all ate a hearty dinner before climbing up the steep mountain to the graveside.

When everyone reached the burial spot, Sister Ebbie lined out the hymn "From Greenland's Icy Mountains" to the accompaniment of Brother Amos' wailing guitar. The preacher, Brother Cyrus, stood with his hands lifted high, one holding a Bible. Next Brother Tobbie Lennix prayed a long prayer.

Then Brother Cyrus started his long sermon.

> He preached about Pa from the time he was a small boy riding a mule to the water mill barefooted with a turn of corn to grind for meal. He took Pa all through his young days, what a sinner he was then and how he finally knelt at the altar where Brother Cyrus was still a young preacher. Then he preached about the change

that had come over Pa, how he married Ma, a pretty young girl of seventeen summers from Beaver Branch. He preached about how he had replenished the earth with seven fine children, all saved but . . . me. . . . Then he brought Pa's life up to the day of his death. He spoke of what a powerful man Pa was when he worked in the fields or when he worked for the Lord.

Jason, the second husband, got along very well until the preacher got to the part of his sermon about no other man's being able to "fill the dead man's shoes, to run his farm, and all that." But by the end of the four-hour sermon Jason was a strong link in the *chain of fellowship* as the people held hands to help one another get safely down from the mountaintop.

---

> **Stuart has clearly demonstrated his awareness of the bad effects of bigotry and superstition in hill religion; but humor has everywhere dominated protest.**
>
> *—Mary Washington Clarke*

---

Stuart has pictured the loud weeping and wailing of the bereaved widows, the occasional *put-on* of a surviving partner already eager to marry someone else, the socializing of the young people, and the occasional fighting among relatives over differences of religious opinion or over the estate of the deceased. The service ended in **"Weep No More"** with the singing of the hymn "Amazing Grace":

When we've been there ten thousand years,
Bright shining as the sun;
We've no less days to sing God's praise
Than when we first begun.

The gathering broke up amid much "handshaking and slapping each other on the back," while everybody tried to talk at the same time and "everybody was happy in fellowship and love." The suggestion of transition was expressed by Pa's children at the beginning of the story: ". . . I don't see any use having his funeral preached every year. It brings back old memories. And it brings back old griefs." Pa had been a *strong* Mountain Baptist who *got a token* of his approaching death, went to the barn, and made his coffin of seasoned boards he had kept there in case of a death in the family, and cleared the place in the thicket where he wanted to be buried. Ma insisted on having the *funeralizing*: ". . . if we didn't have the funeral preached every year, he'd turn over in his grave."

Stuart has given only brief attention to the old custom of *cleaning up the burial grounds.* Subrinea Tussie and Tarvin Bushman set aside a day to clean away the weeds from the final resting place of her people under the trees of heaven in the squatters' graveyard:

Tarvin cuts the briars with his hoe. He whacks them down. He rakes them from the graves with his hoe. He picks up armloads of briars and carries them from this ancient graveyard. . . . Subrinea gets down on her knees and places bits of torn sod back in place. She pulls weeds from the graves. She lays bunches of wild roses, dusty miller, wild trillium, blue ageratum, blood-root, and eggplant on the graves. She pushed the dead leaves away from the head stones.

Subrinea's feeling "like I just haf to decorate my people's graves" is typical among the hill people. In most families or communities it would have been an all-day social occasion with many helping and perhaps with dinner on the grounds.

The importance of looking after the dead was vivid in Stuart's memories of his own family: of his small brothers being hauled in bad weather the long country miles to be buried on land owned by his grandfather; later, of his father's having them moved to the Plum Grove Churchyard so that the whole family could *sleep* there together (less than a year later his father was buried there beside them).

Throughout the mountains it has been a matter of the utmost concern to a family for their dead to receive *decent burial.* Whatever confusion of flesh and spirit, whatever of superstition and sentimentality may have influenced these customs, Stuart has pictured their integral place in the culture of northeastern Kentucky.

Stuart has clearly demonstrated his awareness of the bad effects of bigotry and superstition in hill religion; but humor has everywhere dominated protest. He has mentioned the midweek prayer service and Sunday services not interrupted by the excitement of a practical joker impersonating God or free-for-all fighting in the churchyard; but the extreme incidents, in his opinion, make better *yarns.* He has sometimes, but not always, rationalized the hill man's views. He has understood the need of his people for the emotional outlet of the hill revival, but he fully recognizes the suggestibility of the fiery sermons that can mislead as often as lead. His own family respected the deathbed requests that his father made in 1954, but they were reasonable. At times he has seemed regretful at the passing of old neighborly customs, as the hill people have toned down their church activities and accepted the services of professional morticians. The over-all impression, however, has been good-humored tolerance of both old and new.

**Mary Washington Clarke (essay date 1977)**

SOURCE: "Jesse Stuart's Use of Local Legends," in *Jack London Newsletter,* Vol. 10, No. 2, May-August, 1977, pp. 63-70.

[*In the following essay, Clarke perceives Stuart's use of local legend as "providing a felicitous vehicle for his perception of a changing society within a framework of timeless nature."*]

It is a truism of Jesse Stuart scholarship that the author's literary projection of his native W-Hollow setting, with all that such a projection implies, has provided him with his most successful literary capital. Two biographical facts have given strong direction to his use of it—his early formative years of being locked into an extremely conservative and primitive way of life and his exposure during a year at Vanderbilt University to influences from some of the most sophisticated Southern literati of the 1920s and 1930s. This superficially incongruous yoking together of influences proved fortuitous, producing a unique corpus that can be examined from many points of view. In this essay I shall attempt to examine only one, the author's use of local legendry as a distinctive facet of his narrative art.

Stuart's fiction most typically exploits what Francis Lee Utley called "the juncture between oral and written literature," and nowhere is this more apparent than in his use of local legends. With his awareness of the past living on in the present, his quick grasp of the continuing effects of older modes of thought and older codes of conduct on contemporary patterns of behavior is that of a poet and humorist. When the humorist predominates, the poet is in the background. When the poet is in control, the humorist is in the wings. The result is that when Stuart draws upon local legendry he produces larger than life characters, at times caricatures, involving narrative motifs that have appealed perennially to something basic in American character. The action illustrates Stuart's compassionate and affirmative view of life as zestful individual experience within a tragi-comic continuum.

In no instance does Stuart retain to the letter the authentic detail or oral style of analogous items collected for Kentucky archives of oral history and folklore. The motifs are, however, in Kentucky tradition, and Stuart's storytelling techniques reflect familiarity with the folk narrator's style. He uses legendry as he uses other materials, with much freedom and sometimes repeatedly. In one context the entire story may develop out of a bit of legend; in another the motif may function as a detail of characterization or setting.

The definition of legend and fine distinctions that identify its subtypes are matters beyond the scope of this essay. I am using *legend* to designate materials that have or purport to have some tie with reality—a place, a person, an event, or all three—and that also have some traditional circulation as oral narrations. The same motifs may attach to different persons widely separated in time and space. The motifs may be superhuman, supernatural, or merely memorable.

The element of belief in far-fetched supernatural motifs is once or twice removed in most tellings. Typically, Stuart's presentation is deadpan, but a careful reader will note the character of the teller, the effects of alcohol, scientific phenomena, a bit of moralizing humor, a tongue-in-cheek suggestion of an ulterior motive on the part of the narrator. An element of social history is implicit in oral material which for any reason lives in a community for generations. Disarming, even offhand, informality in the presentation makes it possible for casual readers to enjoy the colorful local lore for its own sake. More thoughtful readers will often find complicated social values and serious commentary on the human condition running inconspicuously through Stuart's main current of humor.

In a Foreword to David Brandenburg's 1968 reissue of *Tim* (written in 1927, first published in 1939), Stuart remarks on the cultural matrix of his early fiction: "Many of the people living here then couldn't read and write. But I believe everybody could tell a story better than the one just told. . . . In those days our greatest entertainment was telling stories," truthful stories he thought at the time. Then in his 1957 journal *The Year of My Rebirth* he comments that "the great tall tales about this place have flown with the winds of yesteryear." Although they have not altogether flown, as evidenced by continuing additions to Kentucky archives of oral history and folklore, they no longer function as they did during Stuart's boyhood before good roads, radios, and television made their impact on rural life. Whether presented as past or present, in his own person or through a narrator, Stuart's use of legend demonstrates among other things the sanctioned attitudes toward character, class structure, nature, and religion in his native region during his lifetime. Among his acknowledged sources of legendry are older members of his family, neighbors, and especially a longtime squatter and occasional farmhand on the author's land.

Op Akers, as Stuart calls the old squatter in his 1953 novel, *The Good Spirit of Laurel Ridge,* always makes his tales incidental to his actions. He is fishing, cutting brush, or at the very least walking past some reminder of the legendary happening while he talks. The thin plot of the novel is clearly subordinate to characterization, setting, and theme. During World War II Op's daughter Lucretia and two friends from Dayton, Ohio, invade the old man's solitude in his self-sufficient little world of the ridge with its many memories and ghosts of the past. The ghosts are shades of ore-diggers, lumberjacks, Civil War guerilla fighters, his dead wife, old friends, all linking Op with a livelier personal and historical past. Memory and imagination of narrator and author mingle to evoke significant facets of the real and mythic W-Hollow.

One of Op's narratives illustrates Stuart's repeated use of the same motif for different purposes. The story of a butting contest between a man and a ram appeared as a short story, **"A Goin' to the Buttin'"** in *Esquire* magazine in 1937. The same motif turns up as just one of Op Akers' many narratives in *The Good Spirit of Laurel Ridge.* Op tells the story of a butting to Lucretia in the first person as "one of the funniest things" he ever saw. This story, especially in the abbreviated form Op gives it, is strongly suggestive of a legendary incident told of Kentucky's colorful historical figure Cassius Marcellus Clay, in adult life a hardheaded abolitionist and friend of Abraham Lincoln. Charles T. Morgan in *Fruit of This Tree.*(1946) gives a telling:

On at least one occasion Cassius lost his fight as a lad. His father had just imported a fine merino buck and had him tied to a tree. While Mr. Clay was at dinner, his son amused himself by playing with the animal. The buck became a little warlike. The boy in his childish ignorance was in the act of putting his head down to see whose head was the harder, his or the buck's. It happened that his father returned just in the nick of time and with his own hand slapped his son farther than the sheep would have done if it had butted him. It was said in later years that the father took needless precautions, for the head of Cassius would certainly have proved harder than the head of the buck.

Sally Bly refers briefly to the incident in a Louisville *Courier-Journal* (April 9, 1967) feature article.

In Stuart's story the character bears little physical resemblance to Clay, and the butting takes place as a well-publicized and well-attended event. Op, whose real-life counterpart may well have been Stuart's source for the story, tells it this way to his newfound daughter as he walks with her on the ridge near his cabin:

> . . . Minton was a short bullish man with shoulders broad as a corncrib door and had a head not much bigger than the ram's, on a short thick neck stuck in the middle of his shoulders. When he got down to run on his all fours and butt against Charlie Worthington's ram, a lot of people yelled fer Minton. But there were more people a-yellin' for the ram. Minton had fit too many men with his head. He's butted them nearly to death. But when Minton and the ram clashed head on, he had found his match. Ye could hear their heads pop when they went head on a half mile away. A lot of people felt sorry fer Minton, since the blood ran from his nose, his eyes, and his ears. But Minton did something that turned about everybody fer the ram.

In good story-telling fashion, Op pauses to arouse his listener's suspense before he finishes the story:

> Old Minton squirmed around and got in line with a tree, and when the ram charged, he jumped outten the path and let it hit the tree. The ram broke his neck and Minton winned the buttin'. The people didn't like it when Minton outwitted the ram. They didn't think he butted fair.

Whether a real butting contest between a man and a ram ever took place in Kentucky or elsewhere, whether the story began with the boyhood exploits of Clay or whether it was a much older story suitable to attach to him, whether Minton Artner had a real-life counterpart who might have undertaken such a reckless display of strength, the story is rooted in folk literature and the values of Appalachian culture. In Stith Thompson's *Motif-Index of Folk Literature* (6 vols., 1955-1958) and in Ernest Baughman's *Motif and Tale-Type Index to of the Folktales of England and North America* (1966) similar and related motifs are indexed from many sources. Nowhere does the specific motif appear in these volumes of a contest between a man and a ram, but the type—contests between man and animal—is widespread.

A man heedless enough to risk his head by butting against a ram is on the periphery of legendry proclaiming the fabulous exploits of American frontier demigods such as Mike Fink and Davy Crockett, themselves recent offshoots in the long folk and literary history of boastful strongmen heroes. The final touch in the story—that some people didn't think Minton had butted fair—is typical deadpan Stuart humor. And it is typical of his perception of violence as an accepted part of the code of his forebears, with an implication that fascination with cruelty and mortal danger is part of being human. Among other narrative motifs of brute strength in the Stuart canon is one of a man who could kill a beef with his fist, a motif repeated almost to the point of cliche.

---

In the context of the author's entire corpus of mainly autobiographical writing, motifs of strength, size, ingenuity, courage, as well as supernatural motifs, often take on symbolic force as instruments of moral and spiritual victory, as they have time immemorial in folk literature.

*—Mary Washington Clarke*

---

Remarkable strength and remarkable size figure about equally in folk legendry. Stuart reflects the tendency to elevate remarkable size to hyperbole in his repeated incorporation of the legend of a giant woman moonshiner who had a real-life counterpart in the mountains of eastern Tennessee not far from Harrogate, where Stuart attended Lincoln Memorial University. His short story **"Sylvania is Dead"** appeared in *Commonweal* in 1942, and was reprinted in **Plowshare in Heaven** in 1958. He makes other references to her and tells the story of her funeral with slight variations in *Daughter of the Legend* in 1965. This novel, written almost a generation before its publication, tells about the Melungeons, a relatively isolated group whose unknown origin accounts for *legend* in Stuart's title. In *Daughter of the Legend* the narrator is presented as an outsider who marries a beautiful Melungeon girl and lives with her on "Sanctuary Mountain" in a situation which gives Stuart the opportunity to present many aspects of an isolated, traditional way of life. The real existence and huge dimensions of "Sylvania" are documented in photographs as well as in the oral folk history of East Tennessee. She is pictured as Big Betsy Mullins in the Tennessee Writers' Project volume *God Bless the Devil* (1940). Although the real life counterpart of Stuart's character is documented in history, the humor of Stuart's story is broad, much of it undoubtedly embellishment.

In the same story, Stuart's reflections of social history include the snake-handling cult, which still exists in the Appalachian region. Sylvania wanted no Bible reading or songs and prayers at her funeral, but shortly before her death "Brother Dusty tested her with the serpent right in her own shanty." This reassured her family and neighbors that "she won't be smellin' any brimstone and black curlin' smoke from a Devil's hell."

In spite of these humorous embellishments, the principal legendary motif is Sylvania's size. Stuart's version is that the men remove the chimney wall of the mountain shack to permit them to bring her enormous home-made black oak coffin into the house, and remove it with her 650-pound corpse inside. It took fourteen men to carry her out, and ten plowlines (heavy ropes) manned by twenty men to lower her into the grave. One of the recurrent jokes about her size is that she could make moonshine with impunity because the officers of the law could not get her out of the house. Stuart adds the touch that both the "High Sheriff of Cantwell County" and his deputy were among the appreciative longtime customers who assisted with her burial. Some otherwise admiring readers of Stuart have chided him for an "Al Capp approach" to such material as this. The mourner who periodically shoots into a cloud of buzzards to keep them away from the shack and the coffin is a case in point. I must disagree with these critics on the basis that what may sometimes appear to outsiders as a Dogpatch-type caricature has grown out of the regional esthetic and reflects the lusty enjoyment of such exaggerations by insiders in the culture. Jesse Stuart as critic and interpreter shows beneath the rough surface of the funeral activities the warmth and strength of clan loyalty and the practical ingenuity of life in an earlier and more primitive era. The story also illustrates the fine line between reality and legend as source material for a writer who has been immersed in the culture with which he deals.

The next story has a Kentucky setting and belongs to Old Op's repertory. In Stuart's early autobiography *Beyond Dark Hills,* the story is told from family legends of the exploits of Stuart's maternal great-grandfather, Preston Hilton. Hilton's attempt to defeat Morgan near Lexington was a complete fiasco. Op attaches his story to a spot near Stuart's home, a locality that has no historical records to support it. According to Op, General John Hunt Morgan and his "Raiders" attempted a Confederate raid into Ohio, but were forced to fall back from a point on Laurel Ridge near the Artner Rocks. A band of old men and young boys from the neighborhood who were Union sympathizers armed themselves with rifles and hid behind the rocks until Morgan's cavalry covered the full arc of the ridge. These impromptu guerrillas short first the horses and then Morgan's men. Morgan and his remaining men made a hurried retreat, carrying away their dead and wounded on the horses that had escaped injury, but their losses forced a postponement of the invasion into Ohio. Local tradition has it that ghostly riders head in the night along the ridge (once the main road through the area) are Morgan's men returning to get their revenge. Kentucky historian Thomas D. Clark portrays Morgan and his mounted infantrymen as daring and colorful and as having gaps in their record which could give credence to Op's (Stuart's) telling of the legend. This is the version he tells to his daughter Lucretia:

Young lady, many a night I've heard the sound of hosses' hooves a-poundin' this Laurel Ridge road . . . I know who it is a-ridin' past in a hurry. It's General Morgan and his Cavalry. Back there at that arc on Laurel Ridge, down behind the big rocks, the old men and boys stopped 'im once and made 'im turn tail when he was a-goin' to raid Ohio in the days of the Rebellion. My father was one of the men behind those rocks. Bones of their horses were left to whiten on the ridge. . . . But Morgan got out of that death-trap in a hurry. Carried away his dead and wounded. . . . But they come back here now and ride this ridge and worry me because I'm the son of George Akers, who had behind a rock with his long rifle and helped stop 'em.

*(Good spirit)*

The reckless courage of John Hunt Morgan and his Raiders was admirable even to his enemies, and guerilla warfare was inevitable in a state as divided in its Civil War loyalties as Kentucky. The sound of ghostly horses' hooves is common in Kentucky tradition, much of which is Civil War inheritance.

Stuart's use of legendry includes treacherous murder motivated by greed, the effect sharpened by his comic spirit. Paul Henson devotes a small book to *Lost Silver Mines and Buried Treasures of Kentucky* (1972), stating his own belief that some exist despite reports to the contrary by Kentucky geologists. Thomas D. Clark in *The Kentucky* refers to legends growing out of Old Sailor John Swift's silver mining and his death at the hands of Indians. Jesse Stuart's story **"Red Jacket: The Knockin' Spirit"** seems to have developed out of old stories of buried treasure and the murder of an old Indian medicine man. It appears in **Head o' W-Hollow.** An old Indian medicine man who wore his black hair in a long braid and had a headdress of feathers spent a week in "Jimpson Burr" selling liver remedies and hair tonic and pulling old snaggle teeth with his bare hands. Stuart's story holds that about 1850, money-mad local men who were convinced that Red Jacket had a treasure hidden somewhere waylaid him in the dark. "Red Jacket keep gold to shoe Indian's horse and buy firewater. Red Jacket don't tell," goes Stuart's story. Old Preacher Leadingham prayed for God to help him find Red Jacket's gold, but to no avail. The grim humor of the story has a serious undercurrent. Red Jacket was hit over the head with a mattock handle and left in Widow Skaggs' hoglot, where the hogs got a little, the crows a little, and Alf Sinnett's foxhounds a little. "The hungry hounds packed away the bones. Jim Kearns found thigh bones and a man's skull near the head of Leadingham Branch." Notwithstanding this tale's grisly contents, Stuart's accounts of Red Jacket as a knocking spirit are comic. In the earlier story the knocking activities become involved with a medium who can do table-tipping and call forth voices of the dead. The spirits expose unfaithful husbands and wives, the magic rationalized to a degree by the presence of a white-clad girl assistant to the medium who appears and disappears from behind a screen. The treasure was never found. In Old Op's repertory the knocking spirit of Red Jacket becomes his alter ego who helps Op drive from the ridge the city intruders who are interfering with his simple way of life.

Younger readers can enjoy the romance and comedy of this ghostlore. More mature readers can grasp Stuart's commentary on the ugliness of greed and poverty, the violence they breed,and more subtly the cyclic vision of life, death, and resurrection that is seldom absent from either his poetry or prose.

An even more variable cluster of legendary details has been associated with an old hand-dug well near the site of Stuart's home. These have provided what is probably the best example of Stuart's use of local legend as a blend of creative imagination and social history. About midway of the nineteenth century an old peddler who was believed by the local people to be rich was horribly murdered and robbed, and his beheaded corpse along with the remains of his blood-soaked, broken buggy were thrown into the well. Here is a perfect situation to give rise to road ghosts, headless apparitions, ghostly lights, and other motifs that keep past events alive. Baughman's index reflects the variety and persistence of such motifs in England and North America.

One telling of the Peddler's Well story appears in a sequence of four sonnets in *Man With a Bull-Tongue Plow*, with no significant changes in the narrative from the 1934 to the 1959 revision. He begins, "I've heard the old men say . . . ," and the story unfolds of a headless ghost rising from an uncovered well in the moonlight, sometimes carrying a pack on his back and sometimes leading a sorrel horse or riding headless in his buggy. A number of conflicting testimonies are attributed to people of the W-Hollow community whose real names appear in Stuart's journal *The Year of My Rebirth*. Peddler Nick was reported to have been killed by three young men. In this telling, human bones and some curly hair wrapped in leaves were found in the well later as evidence. In this context Stuart attached to the tale of horror one of his most serious and compelling poetic themes, the cycle of life. He refers to the trees growing around the well:

> A carpet of dead leaves around the tomb,
> But in the Spring are thick-bark black gum
>  blooms.

(Sonnet 260)

And he closes the sequence with the lines:

> And if we could be by that well, they say,
> We would see Nick arise on Resurrection Day.

(Sonnet 262)

Among those real persons Stuart reports as having professed to seeing the ghosts or the ghostly lights or both at an old well on a farm owned by the Myers family were old Mr. Daugherty, "who wasn't a cowardly or superstitious man," but who saw so many strange sights in this area that he would not drink water from the well or pass that way at night; his son W. W. Daugherty, who drank enough whiskey "to float the biggest saw log in W-Hollow from the source to the mouth of W-Branch"; Lydia Collins, a God-fearing pillar of the community known

for her courage and truthfulness; Stuart's cousin Ben Stuart; Martin Hilton, the Uncle Mel of Stuart's fiction, who weighed 220 pounds and had no fear of man nor beast until one morning about four o'clock when he "heard a whirring sound overhead and looked up in time to see a pair of white wings pass over, felt his bank cap lifted off"; and Stuart's parents. In *The Year of My Rebirth* Stuart conjectures that natural gas, which is abundant in the region and which bubbled in the creek near the well, could be a partial explanation; but as a child he himself believed in the ghosts to such a degree that he never ventured into the area at night.

In the youth novel *Hie to the Hunters* Stuart associates the ghost of a jilted woman suicide with the old well. She appears only to false lovers and men too slow to marry, often snatching their caps or hats. A ghostly milk-woman and a ghostly dog that tears at the roof shingles are associated with the site of Stuart's home, where a mother of small children hanged herself by tying a bed-sheet around her neck and to the bedpost and then jumping out the upstairs window. In various contexts these stories seem to intermingle with those of the Peddler's Well.

In an August entry in *The Year of My Rebirth* (1956) Stuart tells of walking down the valley from his home toward Dead Man's Curve and the Old Peddler's Well, and he is reminded of the legend of the murdered peddler:

> He was fished from the water, the buggy and all the debris cleaned out, and the well's rock wall scalded and washed down so the water could be used again. But even a century later most people in W-Hollow wouldn't touch this water. . . .

The complex of ghost stories involving the old well and its environs become overlapping and vary in both content and mood, but the stories clearly had a fascination for Stuart. His literary rendition of them communicates tragic loneliness and poetic acceptance of death as well as the more obvious and usually humorous moralizing.

As in the context of the author's entire corpus of mainly autobiographical writing, motifs of strength, size, ingenuity, courage, as well as the supernatural motifs, often take on symbolic force as instruments of moral and spiritual victory, as they have time immemorial in folk literature.

Much attention has already been given to Stuart's use of natural metaphors to express his affirmative view of life. His use of his regional folklore represents an equally natural drawing upon resources at hand, local legend providing a felicitous vehicle for his perception of a changing society within a framework of timeless nature. He establishes locale, communicates insider-outsider relationships in his community, and shows transitional values. He entertains as an appreciative purveyor of the legends, and informs as a poet whose perspective forever separates him from modern writers who feel disinherited.

## Kenneth Clarke  (essay date 1977)

SOURCE: "Jesse Stuart's Use of Folklore," in *Jesse Stuart: Essays on His Work,* edited by J. R. LeMaster and Mary Washington Clarke, The University Press of Kentucky, 1977, pp. 115-29.

*[In the following essay, Clarke explores Stuart's use of folklore in his short stories, contending that, like Ralph Waldo Emerson and Walt Whitman, Stuart provides an original, authentic voice to American literature.]*

Assessment of the extent and function of folklore in Stuart's writing is a task made relatively easy because of his time and place. His writing career has coincided with development of academic folklore studies in major universities, and some aspects of Kentucky folklore have been collected and analyzed more carefully than those of some other regions, making it possible to compare field-collected data with an author's rendition. In addition, Stuart has been remarkably cooperative with investigators of his life and works, freely responding to inquiries and sometimes volunteering information to aid them in their studies. The fact that a considerable portion of his writing has been in some way autobiographical has been useful to the folklorist in that it cues the investigator to specific inquiries. Stuart's forthright responses facilitate separation of fact from fiction in a way that has not often been possible in such investigations.

For the purpose of this discussion Archer Taylor's succinct definition of folklore is most useful: "Folklore is the material that is handed on by tradition, either by word of mouth or by custom and practice" [*Pacific Spectator,* Vol. 2, 1948]. This covers a wide range of material. What is handed on by word of mouth may be a traditional folktale, a family legend, a home-town joke, a riddle, a proverb, a superstition, or a remedy. It would include country dance calls, songs, weather prediction formulas, game rhymes, taunts, and nicknames. Running through all these and other kinds of word-of-mouth traditions is the language itself, a regional dialect of American English characterized by traditional vocabulary, pronunciation, and syntax. Folklore handed on by custom and practice rather than by word of mouth includes ways of doing or of making things such as patchwork quilts, log houses, oak-split baskets, and sorghum molasses. It includes the ordinary life of people who learn by tradition most of their domestic activities—animal care, farming methods, food preservation, hunting, fishing, and recreation. Most of these nonlinguistic kinds of folklore, especially those dealing with material culture, are called folklife.

Even the most casual reader of Stuart's works will recognize immediately that all the examples listed above occur in his writing, and once reminded of the scope of folklore and folklife, the perceptive reader should be able to add to the list. An extensive catalog of specific songs, tales, beliefs, and practices abstracted from Stuart's works would not be as useful as a comment on how they serve the writer's purpose and how their use fits into some general ideas about American literature, and thus by inference

how their use defines one aspect of Stuart's role as an American writer.

A convenient category for initial examination is the smallest expressive unit, the word. Stuart's use of folk speech has been mentioned by many writers, and it received careful attention in Mary Washington (Clarke), "Folklore of the Cumberlands as Reflected in the Writings of Jesse Stuart" (Ph.D. diss., University of Pennsylvania, 1960), and most particularly in articles by the same author in *Southern Folklore Quarterly*: "Jesse Stuart's Writings Preserve Passing Folk Idiom" (September 1964), and "Proverbs, Proverbial Phrases, and Proverbial Comparisons in the Writings of Jesse Stuart" (September 1965). In these articles Mary Clarke checked a large catalog of folk idiom abstracted from Stuart's work against regional word lists, standard references works, her personal field collecting in Stuart's general culture area, and finally with Stuart himself. The end result is a reliable assessment whereby one can answer such questions as these: Is this an authentic example of regional speech, or just a "folksy" coinage? Is this a traditionally used proverbial comparison, or did Stuart invent it? Is this ancient proverb a part of folk usage in Greenup County, or has it been transplanted there by the author? Is this colorful exaggeration presented as it is commonly uttered by the folk, or has the author improved upon what he has heard?

Stuart uses authentic regional dialect, faithfully rendering his time and place, combining his knowledge of life with imagination to create a unique literary expression. This would seem inevitable in the light of his lifelong ties with the rural areas of his nativity and his choice of that setting for most of his fiction. Most of his characters are drawn from direct observation, sometimes lacking even the mask of a fictional name, and their speech is the speech Stuart has heard and used all his life. Although the reader who is unfamiliar with authentic Kentucky hill speech may feel that a rendition is exaggerated, careful examination suggests that Stuart's recollection and rendition are reliable, and that exaggeration, where it does occur, is a device employed for dramatic or comic purposes. In any case, he has usually avoided the gross errors of "eye" dialect characterized by misspelling and overworked archaisms that flawed the work of many earlier regional writers, especially those self-conscious local colorists described by Calvin Brown [in his foreword to *Yesterday in the Hills* by Floyd C. Watkins and Hubert Watkins, 1973] as almost always "sentimentalists on an intellectual slumming tour," whose characters "are mere puppets being put through antics that will illustrate the regional idiosyncrasies." Brown went on to say that such writing is "always condescendingly genteel, and usually smugly and offensively so." Stuart is most emphatically not of this stripe, for he is also one of his own principal characters, many of the others being his family and neighbors. Their folklife is his, as he recalls it and lives it. Where he does describe the expressions and antics of a "low-down trashy set" is in the light of the values and judgments of a regional culture rather than in the mode of condescending gentility. The wisdom and worth of some of his relatively uneducated hill people is not diminished by their use of folk speech;

similarly, the shoddy character of some of his better-educated townsmen is not concealed by their use of "standard" English.

Stuart's use of brief traditional formulas is a significant aid in characterization as well as a means of reinforcing a sense of a time and a place. Some of these are sayings or expressions of traditional wisdom upon which characters act or upon which they judge an event. Stuart uses the expressions as they occur in actual oral tradition instead of correcting them to make them conform to scriptures or other literary sources. Consider these examples drawn at random from his writing: "Everything has a season." "Every man must have his Judas." "You can't larn an old dog new tricks." "Killin two birds with one stone." "When you dance you got to pay the fiddler." His proverbial comparisons are similarly apt for character, situation, and setting: "like a fox when he goes to get chickens," "rough as a gritter," "tough as a hickory," "slick as a meatskin," and "clean as a hound-dog's tooth."

Omens, or tokens, as many folk call them, are similarly functional in that they faithfully portray traditional beliefs about foreknowledge. In addition, they may establish tension, tone, and foreshadowing:

> I got uneasy when a whippoorwill
> Came on the porch last night. That is a sign
> Death takes one of the house.

Birdlore, dreamlore, and similar ancient devices for folk prognostication survive as an active element in the folk community, and they sometimes surface in the context of the oral tale, another kind of folklore Stuart uses freely. His use of the folktale is a rewarding subject for the investigating folklorist. Here one finds a range from direct use of an identifiable local legend to so skillful a fabrication that it sends the investigator to his library in a futile effort to document it. Some contemporary folklorists find it useful to distinguish between transcriptive folklore and functional folklore in a writer's works. They label transcriptive the tale, song, or other expression which is entertaining or instructive on its own merits and appears, therefore, virtually unchanged as it exists in oral tradition. The writer merely creates a situation in which it can be presented. The flimsy frame of an old man answering the questions of a little boy in the works of Joel Chandler Harris is an example of this device, and the reworked folktales the old man tells illustrate the transcriptive use of folklore.

Functional use of folklore is more subtle. Here the folkloric expression or the allusion to it is subordinated to a specific literary requirement such as the development of character or setting. The tale-telling bent of two fictional characters reveals how functional the folktale is in Stuart's writing.

Old Op Akers is the herb-gathering yarnspinner in *The Good Spirit of Laurel Ridge* (1953). He is familiar with the old legends of the area, has a firm conviction that there are ghosts (or sperets) about, and participates in the whole range of folklife on the ridge. When he and his daughter Lucretia hear foxhounds in the distance, he identifies them and predicts the development of the chase: "'That's Penny Shelton's horn,' Op told her, a note of excitement in his voice. 'The fox hunters are on Laurel Ridge tonight.'" Op explains that the horn sounded at Six Hickories, the location of a fox den. He identifies the barking of Penny's Blue Boy, a cold trailer. "He's a-takin' that fox toward Wince Leffard Gap. . . . Lissen fer more hounds to open up! Every fox hunter on Laurel Ridge'll let his hounds loose."

As other hounds join the chase he identifies them. He tells where the fox is, where it will go. "He'll come up Shinglemill Hollow, up the fox path from the old pasture field, and cross the ridge right out yander. I know the way foxes run here. Lissen to the music of them barkin' hounds."

This interlude of foxhunting on an April night is but one of many kinds of folklife worked into a novel whose central character is a walking encyclopedia of folklore. Op chews on a piece of calamus root he carries in his pocket as faithfully as some city dwellers carry a tin of aspirin. He gathers medicinal plants and digs their roots. He relates the legend of a Civil War skirmish with Morgan's Raiders. Above all, he tells tales—ghost tales and tall tales about fishing and hunting. The first one in the novel is the ubiquitous tale of the vanishing hitchhiker, highly localized by old Op, and set in an earlier period. "One Sunday, back when Teddy Roosevelt was President, old Doc Burton drove his two-hoss surrey out Laurel Ridge to see Mort Doore who got blood pizen from runnin' a rusty nail in his foot." Op goes on to recount how a young couple, closely described, hitched a ride with Doc Burton on his return trip, how Doc, busy with his team on the downgrade, hardly noticed that the young couple had stopped talking to him, and how he discovered with shock that only the armload of flowers the girl had been carrying remained in the back seat. The ghostly couple were later identified as local people who had drowned while swimming at Sandy Falls.

Although Op tells several kinds of tales, the ghost tale is most useful in this novel because it ties in with a mysterious "ghost" on Laurel Ridge—which finally turns out to be a living person. Old Op reports on so many beliefs, practices, and local happenings that one is inclined to think of him as a kind of Appalachian Uncle Remus, a fictional creation used for presentation of transcriptive folklore. The book is a novel, however, and it does have a plot. Examination of its folklore and folklife content shows that it is largely functional in the sense that it serves to enhance characterization, make vivid the setting, and advance the plot.

Stuart injects a subtle ambiguity into his presentation of Op Akers as a naïve backwoodsman who is completely comfortable with his belief in ghosts. Old Op drives off city intruders who claim they are not superstitious by telling them hair-raising tales about snakes and ghosts. It is never quite clear whether he is being merely ingenuous or crafty, in the time-honored American tradition of the countryman getting the best of "sophisticated" urbanites. In any case, the situation is traditional in both oral and written literature, as much an expression of American folklore as the exploits of Mike Fink.

---

**Partly as a result of his familiarity with the folklore and folklife of his region, Stuart has added a strong, original voice to the main thrust of American literature.**

*—Kenneth Clarke*

---

Another narrator, Grandpa Tussie, exhibits a different repertoire. The fact that *Taps for Private Tussie* (1943) was winner of the 1943 Thomas Jefferson Southern Award and a selection for the Book-of-the-Month Club is more than casually related to the fact that its pages are replete with folk speech, folk beliefs, folklife, and snatches of folksong and folk narration. Grandpa Tussie, addicted to the "gravy train" of relief grub and afflicted with an incurable aversion to work, tells whoppers. He can stop patting his foot to the tune of Uncle George's magic fiddle and tell a tall tale about lumbering in Michigan on cue: "'Tell Sid about your train ride in Michigan, Press,' Grandma said, wheezin on her long pipestem. 'I got on a train in Michigan,' Grandpa said. 'Traveled two days and nights through the timber. Never saw a town. Never saw anybody but the people on the train. We only stopped for water and coal. We passed through timber tracts where the trees were big around the butts as sixty-gallon mash barrels.'"

Whether the tales Op Akers and Grandpa Tussie tell in their respective novels are identifiable as traditional oral narratives or are creations of the author does not alter their folkloric role. The fact is that Stuart, intimately familiar with long, windy yarns, first-person hunting and fishing whoppers, legends, and scary ghost stories in oral tradition, has created two believable folk types, each one presented as a raconteur. The distinctive functional aspect of their renditions is that their narrations help to maintain tone and theme as well as to extend characterization. Old Op is a gentle recluse, a healer and believer. His tales, even if gross exaggerations, are presented in a positive way, reflecting the author's approval of his creation. Grandpa Tussie's repertoire gives more emphasis to tall tales rendered in keeping with an entirely different kind of characterization and in a very different kind of novel. *The Good Spirit* is a gentle romance; *Taps* is a "Dogpatch" style caricature of the welfare syndrome, a comedy containing a considerable element of satire.

As *The Road to Xanadu* so profoundly illustrates, a prolific, spontaneous writer soaks up many impressions and recombines them in manifold and sometimes marvelous ways. Examination of Stuart's works suggests that he freely combines a rich heritage of folklore with his literary education in a variety of creative moods, and that he rarely makes a conscious effort to use folklore as a special focus. He does, however, use a good tale or custom as a springboard for a composition. Two short stories, **"Rain on Tanyard Hollow"** and **"Frog-Trouncin' Contest"** (both in *Tales from the Plum Grove Hills*), are illustrative.

**"Rain on Tanyard Hollow"** is Stuart's adaptation of a tale type widely known in oral tradition. Essentially, the tale concerns a man who buys or prays for a change of weather and gets more than he bargained for. Maritime versions of the tale involve the superstitious belief that a becalmed sailor can buy wind by tossing a coin overboard. This act usually brings on a storm rather than a beneficial breeze, whereupon the sailor observes that a smaller purchase would have been in order. A dry-land version has the farmer pray for rain, get a gullywasher, then observe that a more modest prayer would have been better. Stuart uses this theme, having Pappie get down on his knees in the dried-up strawberry patch and utter a mighty prayer for rain. Because his wife has taunted him about his faith, he overreaches, praying for a storm. "Send rain, Lord, that will wash gully-ditches in this strawberry patch big enough to bury a mule in."

Pappie gets exactly what he prays for. Lightning splits big oak trees and chickens go to roost in the midday gloom. The resulting flood washes away the corn crop and sends mud and rocks into the house. So fearful is the thunder "rollin' like tater wagons across the sky" that a flock of visiting relatives who have been eating Pappie out of house and home pray for relief and promise the Lord they will leave Tanyard Hollow and never return if they survive.

Surveying the damage, Pappie can see the bright side: "'It wasn't the brazen images of snakes,' Pappie said, 'that done all of this. Tanyard Hollow is washed clean of most of its topsoil and lost a lot of its trees. But it got rid of a lot of its rubbish and it's a more fitten place to live.'"

The "brazen image of snakes" refers to the black snakes Pappie had hung on the rail fence before his prayer. This was in response to the folk belief that hanging up a dead snake will bring rain. The black snakes failed to produce, but prayer did, hence the "brazen images," an example of the hillman's familiar use of biblical allusion.

**"Rain on Tanyard Hollow"** is clearly an expanded and highly localized rendition of a folktale. Stuart weaves in the weather superstition involving snakes, and he skillfully keeps it before his readers by using numerous snake-associated images throughout the story. He adds the locustlike flock of relatives who have squatted in Tanyard Hollow. He also introduces the conflict between husband and wife (the pesky relatives are her kin), with special focus on her objection to his hanging up dead snakes and her taunting him for his lack of faith. The point of view is effective in that the observer-narrator is Tracey, a young son, who nervously responds to Pappie's prayer by saying, "I don't want to wish you any bad luck, but I hope you don't get all you ast for."

Folklore here includes the folktale itself, regional speech, beliefs, regional life-style, and the hillman's ambiguous involvement with fundamentalist religion and superstition. The folktale itself, sometimes only a paragraph-length anecdote with a punch line such as "A quarter's worth would have been enough," is just one element of the mixture that bears Stuart's hallmark for humorous effect—exaggeration and incongruity.

These are the same elements that elevate an almost forgotten cruel pastime to a mock epic struggle in **"Frog-Trouncing Contest."** In this instance the curious survival of cruelty to frogs or toads provides the seed of the story. Mary Clarke, field collecting in Stuart's Big Sandy region, found informants who recalled frog trouncing. The activity involves fastening a frog to one end of a plank balanced over a fulcrum, then hitting the other end of the plank to bounce the frog high into the air—with fatal results for the frog, of course. Survival of this custom is a curiosity in that the practice has been verified as far back as Elizabethan England.

As he does in **"Rain on Tanyard Hollow,"** Stuart uses the folk activity as a seed from which the short story can grow. Instead of a dimly remembered activity, frog trouncin' in the story becomes a tournament-style annual contest with training, defending champions, elimination, and judges. In the well-worn folk tradition of youngest-best, the least favored nephew manages to win the contest by training for it secretly and using a special mallet (also in the folk tradition of a remarkable weapon) to deliver the winning blow. The preparation of the mallet appears to involve some borrowing from Mark Twain's "The Celebrated Jumping Frog of Calaveras County," another story that depends in part on folklore. In Stuart's story the mallet instead of a frog is secretly filled with lead shot.

Folklore in Stuart's fiction cannot be fully evaluated by merely cataloging the songs, tales, beliefs, regional lexicon, or other specific elements. Cataloging can be an instructive exercise for an undergraduate student learning to use the library tools of folklore research, but merely to label a song fragment by a Child number or to tag a narrative passage with a Thompson motif number is a classroom exercise rather than an evaluation. A knowledge of field-collected folklore materials is, of course, essential, just as biographical knowledge of Stuart will reveal his authentic "insider" view of the culture. Equally important, his mode of comic exaggeration must be taken into account, so that the critic can avoid the error of assuming that there really is or was a frog-trouncing day in Greenup County.

Beyond those elements of folklore that can be cataloged, however, there is a matrix that holds them together which is fully as traditional as a folksong or a folktale, yet too diffuse to be neatly abstracted and verified on a checklist. This omnipresent element is the collective folkways that produce stereotyped values, attitudes, and responses. Some

of the best folklore in Stuart's writing is his evocation of the matrix rather than specific bits of folklore embedded in it.

**"Testimony of Trees"** (*Clearing in the Sky*) provides a good example. The story is about a land dispute in which a man in the hills tries to cheat a neighbor out of his land by misrepresenting an old deed. An aggressive land hog can take advantage of the fact that old "meets and bounds" deeds were often inaccurate, that the calls were to such impermanent or movable markers as trees and rocks. Stuart's resolution of this simple conflict is to have the put-upon landowner call in Uncle Mel, an ancient and woods-wise timber cutter. Uncle Mel studies the deed, having the boy narrator in the story read the difficult words for him, then goes to the seventy-year-old property line and verifies the blaze on each tree left standing. He chops into each old blaze scar with his keen double-bitted ax, then counts the annual growth rings to discover the age of the scar. In each instance the scar is seventy years old; the original survey line is verified, and the land hog is foiled.

**"Testimony of Trees"** is a very short story with a simple linear development to the resolution of an unambiguous conflict. Except for regional dialect the story contains none of the "genres" of folklore. But it is as fully charged with the lore of the hill people as anything Stuart has written.

Rural Kentuckians love politics and courthouse jockeying. They are also perennially concerned about property lines, easements, and access. It may seem odd that old boundary disputes can carry on from one generation to another, sometimes leading to bloodshed or chronic enmity between neighbors, especially if the matter can be settled by the simple expedient of an official survey. But a licensed, impartial surveyor's services are expensive, a luxury beyond the means of many impoverished hill folk, who have trouble enough paying their taxes. The old disputes go on to such a degree that long, quasi-legal narrations recounting the complicated histories of land transactions become a part of the oral literature of a neighborhood.

**"Testimony of Trees"** capitalizes on this more general aspect of the folklife of rural Kentucky. Despite the improbable accuracy of Uncle Mel's dendrochronology, the hillman's wary attitude toward his property lines is faithfully revealed. **"Hell's Acre"** is similarly based on a property dispute, though much overdrawn in its "battle" scenes. As the title suggests, the dispute involves only one acre of land, but the attitude of the belligerents is no less fierce than if the disputed land were a thousand acres. "I jest decided powder and lead was cheaper than lawyers' fees and court costs. That's the reason we've been fighting another ten years fer that acre of land."

The short story **"Uncle Casper"** takes its title from the name of a half-educated, windy old ex-preacher, ex-teacher, candidate for political office. He is a folk type, a man of words, the talkative center of attention beside the pot-bellied stove in the country store, the oral historian in the courthouse square, the ambulatory archive of folk medicine, kinship, natural history, and scriptural interpretation. Finding a young man old enough to vote, Uncle Casper launches into a series of narrations. One of these is his recollection of watching a black snake in mortal combat with a rattlesnake. The black snake killed the big rattler ("Twenty-seven rattlers and nine buttons"), apparently with the restorative aid of a medicinal weed. "The black snake took out of there and run out and bit him off a little chew of a weed. Munched it in his flat jaws like a rabbit munches clover."

As he rambles on, Uncle Casper recalls encountering a huge rattlesnake "big as a cow's leg" while digging ginseng with Chuck, a companion. The two men tried to hold the snake to draw its fangs, but it "shot a stream of pizen from the gall bladder through the fang" into Chuck's eye. Uncle Casper took a big chew of "taste-bud tobacco," worked up a mouthful of tobacco juice, and squirted it into Chuck's eye. "He squalled a little, but I knowed it was a case of life or death."

This reminds Uncle Casper of the time he was cutting dry poles for firewood. In an encounter with a racer which struck at his throat, he drove the snake into a knothole in a sourwood pole. "It stuck its head out and licked its tongue out at me. I thought 'Old Boy, I'll fix you.' So I climbs up the pole with a wooden glut in my hand and drove it down in the hole with a stick." A year later, cutting wood on the same hillside, he recalled the trapped snake, chopped down the sourwood, and "out popped that snake poor as Job's turkey. I could a-counted its ribs if I'd had time." The snake remembered him, wrapped itself around his leg "like a rope around a well windlass." Uncle Casper had to get his wife's aid to save himself. "Liz just reached down with that butcher knife and she cut that snake into ten pieces. It was wropped around my ankle five times if I am right." Liz saved Uncle Casper, but when her baby was born it was marked with the prints of a black racer over its heart.

Uncle Casper's narratives continue in the story, but these portions are particularly suitable for further illustration of Stuart's use of folklore. The general matrix of folklife forms a kind of backdrop in a mildly satiric story about politics at the grassroots level. Embedded in the rambling recollections are elements of two traveling anecdotes about snakes. The fact that snake tales turn up regularly in conversations of country people seems inevitable in a state having a large population of timber rattlesnakes and copperheads. There is a traditional way of describing snakes— usually by girth, and usually by anatomical comparison. Hence "big as my wrist," "big as my arm," or "big as my leg" are customary. Uncle Casper's black snake in combat with a rattlesnake was "bigger than a baby's leg," and the rattlesnake in the ginseng patch was "big as a cow's leg." Also, it is customary to count the rattles and always add the "button" in reporting the size of a rattlesnake. Stuart allows Uncle Casper a little exaggeration: "Twenty-seven rattlers and nine buttons."

The tale about a weed-chewing snake is traditional. Ordinarily the victorious snake is nonpoisonous, and its victory over the copperhead or rattlesnake is attributed to the curative power of a nearby plant. A more elaborate version of the tale has a human observer become the victim of snakebite, whereupon he uses the same weed to effect a miraculous cure.

The mortally dangerous constricting power of a nonpoisonous snake in Kentucky exists only in folk imagination. The motif occurs in oral narratives in various contexts, one of which has the snake get under the long skirts of a woman and coil about her waist. This titillating version then presents a dilemma for a black servant. Dare he lift his mistress's skirts to save her life? Stuart used the basic folk motif of the potentially lethal constrictor in a highly original piece of creative writing, a capsule example of his multilevel adaptation of folklore for literary purposes.

This sampling of folkloric elements in Stuart's works reveals the variety of both the folklore and the ways in which it serves the author's literary purposes. It reveals also the naturalness of the use of traditional materials by an "insider" in the culture. Certainly Stuart is not condescendingly genteel, and he is not on an intellectual slumming tour. He is, rather, the kind of American author some nineteenth-century critics, especially Emerson and Whitman, were calling for when they stressed the American experience in terms of strongly local, natural language rather than effete borrowing from cultivated European expression. They extolled the American workman close to the soil or the frontier rather than the aristocrat insulated from grassroots experience and expression. Development of authentic American literature, they felt, must come from the vigor of the folk experience, necessarily local, idiomatic, and relatively independent of refined antecedent models. Such writing is enhanced by accurate use of regional folklore. Partly as a result of his familiarity with the folklore and folklife of his region, Stuart has added a strong, original voice to the main thrust of American literature.

### Katherine Paterson (essay date 1982)

SOURCE: "Jesse Stuart's Stories of Old Kentucky Homes," in *Washington Post Book World,* Vol. 12, October 24, 1982, pp. 3, 13.

[*In the following essay, Paterson provides a positive review of* The Best-Loved Short Stories of Jesse Stuart.]

"They really brought men to justice back in them days when they had to have someone to hang every Sunday after church." This is a throwaway sentence buried in the middle of a paragraph about halfway through a story with the straightforward title: **"Sunday Afternoon Hanging."** Yet there is in this sentence the deviousness of a poet. It jars the mind from bend to bend like Donne's, "A bracelet of bright hair about the bone." But Jesse Stuart's prose has so much poetry in it that he often seems to throw away great lines. It is a trait of mountain people not to suspect that their ordinary speech rolls with the rhythm of the Psalms and lights up with bursts of Shakespearean imagery. But Jesse Stuart, although he has lived nearly all his life in the Kentucky hills, is not an unlettered Appalachian. He knows what he's doing.

In **"Sunday Afternoon Hanging,"** a mountaineer is telling his grandson about the good old days before baseball games and the "hot seat," when, on a Sunday "people came for forty miles to see a hanging." There follows a marvelous, terrible Brueghelian scene gone round the bend with the uniformed band playing "My Old Kentucky Home," screaming babies being forced to nurse by mothers intent on hearing the last words of the condemned, boys hired to fling water on fighting dogs or beautiful fainting girls, men chewing tobacco while chatting about "crops and the cattle and the doings of the Lord to the wicked people for their sins." Madame Defarge, eat your heart out.

It is this powerful, often comedic, moral irony of Stuart's tales which makes me wonder why the editor chose to call this collection, "The Best-Loved Short Stories . . ." Such a title leads the first-time Stuart reader to expect an Edgar Guest telling tales from his porch rocker as he gazes, tear on cheek, over the lavender hills. How can you "best love" a story that gruesomely, albeit hilariously, details in sequence five public hangings? Or love a painful account of adultery and murder in two generations like **"A Land Beyond the River,"** even if the title does belong to a beloved old country hymn? Moreover, by choosing a mere 34 out of Stuart's nearly 500 published stories, you're bound to invoke grumblings from Stuart admirers that their particular favorites have been left out, as indeed Robert Penn Warren seems to be doing in the introduction to this book.

Well, no matter. It is a good collection and well balanced. The violence of stories like those already mentioned is intermingled with tender stories of married love and aggravation like **"The Storm,"** macabre tales like **"Word and the Flesh"** which gives Poe a run for his money, and high comedy like **"Nest Egg,"** the tale of a Don Giovanni of the hen-yard who kills every fighting rooster in the district and seduces all the female fowls in the hollow, only to be brought low by "a little screech owl no bigger than [Pa's] fist."

Jesse Stuart is often referred to as a "regional writer." And certainly he devoted his life as a writer to poetry and tales of the Kentucky mountain people he knew so well. "I write of what has actually happened," he once said to a Princeton University audience, "and in the only way I can—the way that comes naturally to me." But Stuart's natural way of writing is the way of the artist, the selection of revelatory detail. He achieves what Conrad indicated was the task of the writer of fiction—"by the power of the written word to make you hear, to make you feel . . . to make you *see.*"

Stuart makes us see his world. Most of his stories are more extended picture than formal plot. Usually this doesn't matter, the pictures are so vivid that they can live without more formal construction. Occasionally, however, this becomes a weakness, as in in the story, **"Eustacia,"** which begins strongly but winds down to a platitude. On the other hand, there is the last story in the book, **"This Is the Place,"** in which an old man wants all his relatives buried in the same plot of mountain soil, so that on judgment day they will all rise together. This piece has far less story line than **"Eustacia,"** yet somehow manages to rise above platitude and sentimentality on the back of lyrical language.

> "And what do we do while we are waiting—while our dust is sleeping the long night," I say to Uncle Mel, "in the narrow confines of our small world—in the village of this silent city of Powderjays and Sheltons with our in-laws plus that have come to sleep beside their wives." "My son," says Uncle Mel, "we shall go on living in the same way we lived here—only we'll be light as the wind. We shall be as we have been—have the same color of hair, shapes of noses, the same voice—we shall run with our old company—I expect to have my farm here and do the things as I have always done. How can that which is the real Mel Shelton die? It can't die. You can't take a hammer and beat it to death even if you beat my head off. The real Mel Shelton will be here. You can't kill it. It was not born to die—only the husk that encloses it was born to die. We are going to bring all these husks right here and crib them."

A particular favorite of mine is another story about life and death. **"Uncle Fonse Laughed"** describes the friendship of two hill farmers who built good fences between their lands and then shared food and worries and practical jokes and good-natured arguments about religion. When Fonse predicts his own death, Mick, the narrator's father, assumes that Fonse is joking again. But he is mistaken.

> "Fonse is dead as a piece of dirt," said Pa. "He died last night sometime. I was there just a few minutes ago. I took the mole along to slip in his pocket. But he was dead. The family is all crying and going on something awful. I didn't stay. I couldn't stay. Fonse, there so quiet—not laughing! W'y he laughed when he was going to have the James boys to make his coffin. I thought he was joking. He didn't care to die. He laughed quietly into the arms of Death. I've always thought God would want a man that could laugh no matter what church he belonged to . . . Fonse there so quiet, so silent. He didn't speak to me. I couldn't stand it."

I think one reason I like this particular story so much is that I have heard it read aloud. Jesse Stuart's pictures are meant to be heard as well as seen. They are full of music.

**Ruel E. Foster  (essay date 1984)**

SOURCE: A foreword to *Clearing in the Sky and Other Stories* by Jesse Stuart, The University Press of Kentucky, 1984, pp. ix-xiv.

[*In the following essay, written for the reprint of Stuart's* Clearing in the Sky, *Foster surveys the major themes of the collection.*]

When literary historians a hundred years hence write a history of the American short story, Jesse Stuart's name may well be near the top. Stuart has written well in the genres of the novel, essay, and poetry, but for many of us his greatest talent has been shown in the short story which has always been his special delight. Doubtless he has written too many short stories (some five hundred at the last count), but we should not hold this against him since he has lodged so many of that five hundred everlastingly in the imagination of America. Stuart, like many American writers, has created a magic sense of place. He has brought to lasting fictional life the world of W-Hollow, the locale of most of his short stories. W-Hollow now joins Faulkner's Yoknapatawpha County, Elizabeth M. Roberts's Pigeon River country, and Thomas Wolfe's Altamont as one of the places we visit imaginatively and lose ourselves in.

The present volume, *Clearing in the Sky,* clearly has about it that talismanic sense of place which fascinates American readers. This book gives us in generous portions a mountain way of life which is now long past but which was once prickly hard with the thorny individualism of Kentucky mountaineers. W-Hollow is a world of hills and mountains, dark hills in the wintertime but marvellous flowering hills in the spring. It is a hard land where people make their living by hardscrabble farming, cattletrading, mining, timbering, or moonshining. The people are primarily of Scotch-Irish or English stock with old-fashioned names—Sam Whiteapple, Cief Salyers, Battle Keaton, and the Powderjays, Pa and Ma and children Finn and Shan; Shan frequently functions as the first person narrator in the stories.

What has made this world of Stuart's short fiction so lively, so compelling that readers for the past fifty years have followed it with timeless fascination? Though genius can never be analyzed to its ultimate source, it can at least be annotated and described. Among the obvious virtues of Stuart's short stories are their convincing primitivism, humor, natural talk style, and epiphanic insight.

Take, for example, his hard primitivism. If the term seems needlessly abstruse, let us say his short fiction is of the earth, earthy. In Stuart's phrase he is "just a dirt-colored man." He is a "one horse farmer singing at the plow." His fictional creatures are children of the earth, a voice from the clods. His stories call us ever to the outdoors. They give a poet's voice to the far and lost land of the Appalachians. We open *Clearing in the Sky* and get the odors of new plowed ground and feel the fine mist of nature blow into our face. A father hoists a handful of rich loam from the virginal soil of the story **"A Clearing in the Sky"** and smells its fecund odors with a kind of ecstasy. Stuart stops under the oaktrees and prays an earth-prayer— "Give me life close to the earth." "Get close to the soil and know Him" (*Beyond Dark Hills*).

The story **"Clearing in the Sky"** is an excellent example of Stuart's belief that earth and nature provide a healing, annealing power to men. In that story a father conducts his son to the top of a mountain where the father has a vegetable garden in virgin soil. The father explains that the doctors had given him up, had told him he had no chance to live. He has been saved by his work in the virginal garden soil. "The best days are the first to flee" wrote Willa Cather in *My Antonia,* translating a line from Virgil's *Georgics.* This is the classic theme of the primitivist and it is stated succinctly here by Mitch Stuart who yearns back to the garden world of his youth. **"Clearing in the Sky"** is his therapy which does for him what physicians could not do. Later Stuart mulling over the earth tie that both his mother and father had, wrote: "They were the least book-educated but the best earth-educated people I have ever known."

> **Stuart has written from within a great globe of actual event and of myth and oral tales of which he is the center.**
>
> —*Ruel E. Foster*

Stuart as a short story writer learned to follow his own life and his instincts. Like Robert Frost, Stuart can say that almost all of his stories are based on events that either happened to him or were told to him. He has written from within a great globe of actual event and of myth and oral tales of which he is the center. More than that the greater part of his work falls for the most part into readily discernible categories. Stuart and his editors have already recognized these categories by bringing out a volume of short stories, *Save Every Lamb,* in which all the stories have to do with farm animals. Later Stuart published *Dawn of Remembered Spring* in which every story features a snake. One familiar with Stuart's work could easily pick stories for a volume simply on dog stories, or one on political stories, or one on politics, moonshine, etc. Please note that the present volume mingles several categories. Stuart's strong primitivistic, agrarian bent is featured in the title story, **"Clearing in the Sky,"** as well as in **"Testimony of Trees,"** where Uncle Mel foils a land thief by demonstrating that an old blaze mark never completely disappears from a tree; i.e., nature, which provides so many norms to man, can also be a silent witness in a court battle. Other categories found in the stories that follow are animals, politics, feuds, and moonshine. An important mode in the above categories is Stuart's brand of southwestern humor. Although there is a streak of surrealistic or "black bile" humor in Stuart, a mixture of the comic and horrible, this does not appear in *Clearing in the Sky.* In the present work, Stuart's humor is a good natured reveling in comic incongruities, as in Sam Whiteapple's corn eating duel with Lester Pratt's game rooster (**"The Champion"**).

Stuart is a true devotee of animals. He finds them splendid, courageous, and admirable. In the present volume, at least six stories revolve about animals and one about bees. In **"The Champion,"** champion eater Sam White-apple matches himself against a cock-of-the-walk rooster at eating raw corn with farcical results. **"To Market, to Market"** trots out Pa and his prize bull trained to walk on his hind legs at Pa's command. Pa takes him to market and has a run-in with the local pin-hookers where, in classic comic fashion, the con man gets conned. **"Fight Number Twenty-five"** enlists our sympathies for a mongrel dog who has to take on a wildcat that has slaughtered a vast number of dogs. **"Horse-trading Trembles"** is a traditional tale of the old South (A. B. Longstreet's "The Horse Swap") and of Faulkner's *The Hamlet* translated into an Appalachian milieu. Once again the cheater gets cheated. **"No Hero"** pits a six-foot five-inch bean pole who weighs 135 pounds against a 385-pound bear in a wrestling match which comes to a miraculously gentle conclusion. **"Battle with the Bees"** shows the organized mayhem which results when a hundred beehives are turned over by marauding hogs and the bees invade the family farm house in a mad orgy of stinging. **"Hot-collared Mule"** shows how Pa learns a lot more about mules from a retired mule skinner who cuts down Pa's braggadocio. Essentially a third of the stories in this book treat animals, their habits, devotion, and idiosyncrasies. These stories record Stuart's deep kinship with the animals of the earth and his almost mystical feeling for the wild life of the earth, a feeling very similar to Thoreau's thoroughly primitive "Brute Neighbors" chapter in *Walden.* This sentiment is italicized for us by Stuart's final line in *Save Every Lamb*—"And the saddest and loneliest countries in the world are those without wildlife."

Lesser categories in this volume are the stories of politics—**"Thirty-two Votes before Breakfast," "Road Number One,"** and **"Governor Warburton's Right-hand Man."** These confirm the Kentucky cliché that "politics are the damnedest in Kentucky." Then there are the moonshine stories, **"Coming Down the Mountain"** and **"Evidence Is High Proof."** The remaining stories treat feuding, social consciousness, and young love.

Please note that all the stories in this book were published between 1941 and 1950. The years from 1930 to the mid 1950s were Stuart's freshest and more spontaneous period. The stories written in this period are closer to the elements of nature that he enjoyed so much as a young man; the dialect is stronger, the language more evocative. This early fiction becomes in the aggregate a great sustained elegy to a lost world of Appalachian experience, a nostalgic greeting and farewell to an important part of America's past.

I would argue that this short fiction is essentially optimistic. Stuart believes in and practices Allen Tate's concept of "Knowledge Carried to the Heart." He has continued to live so close to his material that he can, as he says, "hear it snore." As a good primitivist he is *not out of time with nature* and his best short stories are not out of time with nature. Even city people—in some cases especially city people—will find the timeless archetypes of Stuart's fiction attractive. Animal fables are as old as civilization, their appeal timeless.

The reader who comes to the present work will find that the author is indeed a genuine, original, marvelously fecund writing man. These stories are well representative of his genuineness and his great vitality. They are the incarnation of a matchless individuality. Stuart says "yes" to life all along the way. He obviously belongs to what R.W.B. Lewis in *The American Adam* calls "the party of hope." These stories are a welcome part of his affirmation.

## Mary Rohrberger (essay date 1984)

SOURCE: "The Question of Regionalism: Limitation and Transcendence," in *The American Short Story 1900-1945: A Critical History,* edited by Philip Stevick, Twayne Publishers, 1984, pp. 147-82.

[*In the following excerpt, Rohrberger discusses Stuart as a regionalist writer.*]

[A writer] clearly in the regionalist tradition is Jesse Stuart, who does for the culture of the Appalachian region of eastern Kentucky what Ruth Suckow did for rural Iowa. One of our country's most prolific writers, Stuart wrote more than 350 short stories, many of which appeared in seven collections dating from 1936 to 1966. In addition to short stories, he has published seven autobiographical volumes, hundreds of poems, seven novels, five juvenile books, and scores of articles and lectures. Born in an isolated log cabin in Kentucky, Stuart appears to have lived a life fast passing into mythology, where boys roamed the hills shooting squirrels and, grown into men, continued male pleasures of fighting, handling guns, and shooting them whenever there was a chance; where the women were likely to be more educated, having attended a couple of years of school; where there was in the house one book, a Bible; and where, in spite of the paucity of reading material (or maybe a Bible is enough), education is sometimes valued, as Stuart came to value it along with firmly held democratic ideals.

Stuart is an optimist, an affirmer, in love with his people and his region, and though his stories sometimes tend to broad comedy and even black humor where grotesquerie is dominant, the world he presents is for the most part realistic, three-dimensional and characterized by solidity and depth. Stuart's hill and mountain people are strongly passionate, fiercely religious, loyal within families, and hardworking. And as hard as they work is as hard as they play. Buttressed by moonshine, they give themselves over to relaxations—courtships, basket dinners, fox hunting, and always fights. But the simple verities prevail, and, in this, Stuart is a cultural primitivist, blending in his stories of W-Hollow a romantic exuberance with realistic detail and an ear for idiom that cause the people and the region to come alive. The cumulative effect of the stories is of the presentation of authentic mountain folk, come alive by vigorous force. Also characteristic are the oral character of the narrative (mainly first person and present tense) and the abundance of visual and auditory images. For the most part, the stories are plotless, primarily incidents recording a response to an action. They are also simple and direct, so that a person used to and valuing the complexities of the modern short story must find Stuart's value as a writer of short stories in accumulated detail rather than in story valued as story.

*Tales from the Plum Grove Hills* is typical Stuart. Most of the stories are told in the first person by a boy (adolescent or a young man, depending on the story) named Shan who is Stuart's persona. The stories range from character sketch to incident to story with well-developed plot, and from the serious to the playful and humorous to the farcical and absurd.

**"Another April,"** the first story in the collection, characterizes Grandpa, who is ninety-one and did not retire from cutting timber and farming until he was eighty. Grandpa is Shan's mother's father, and as the story opens, the mother is carefully putting layer after layer of clothes on the old man to prepare him for his first walk in the spring after the long winter. During his walk, Grandpa stops frequently to look at things in a careful manner, apparently making contact with life around him. When he returns, instead of coming in through the front door, he toddles around toward the back. Before long it becomes apparent that Grandpa is having a conversation with an old terrapin that is, at the least, ninety-five years old.

The boy wonders about who cut the date in the terrapin's back and about whether and how long that person lived in Plum Grove and whether that person, also, like Grandpa in the spring, enjoyed the April and his walks, and looked at the blossoming trees, and talked to the terrapin. At the end of the story, in order to make the identification clear, Stuart has the boy say, "Gee, Grandpa looks like the terrapin." In the identification of Grandpa and terrapin and in boy and grandfather and in boy and grandfather with the person who carved the date in the terrapin's shell, Stuart comments on processes where birth and death are no more than part of a natural order.

**"My Father Is an Educated Man"** makes clear a relationship between father and son and explains why the son of his father went to school and got educated and became a "book-writer." The scene is a town, the center of the father's universe, four miles from his home, where he meets a group of men on the courthouse square; they talk and tell stories and chew tobacco and whittle. The situation concerns the narrator's overhearing a schoolteacher talking to another group of men, telling them that the father never amounted to anything and never would. The narrator wants to walk over to the schoolteacher and tell him a few things—how his father could read his name and, if he wanted to, piece together letter sounds to make words, how his father came from a heroic race, tillers of the earth who brought plows to rocky mountain slopes, who helped to build the railroads and provide the coal, who helped to build the cities and the highways and the churchhouses. What use to them was book learning? But they were educated, Shan would insist. The father's tragedy was that he was educated in a time when that kind of education was not valued as much as sitting behind a desk and

wearing a neat suit and tie. But the father knows enough to encourage his son's education; he knows also that an "educated" son can no longer kill his enemies, since the son will be caught in abstractions of the kind the father will never understand, for the father's life is based in the real, the solid, and the durable.

In **"Thanksgiving Hunter,"** Stuart recounts how Shan could not kill doves, though his Uncle Walt had carefully taught him how to shoot and care for his gun and hunt. The occasion is a dove hunt, but the boy has two memories that interfere with his desire to join in the kill and please his uncle. The first is of live doves, singing their mournful songs, carrying straws to build their nest, flying in pairs, carrying food, and feeding the young. The other is of a time when he was younger and killed a groundhog with a sassafras stick because the groundhog was eating a blister-ear of corn; he remembers hitting the groundhog over and over again for no good reason. The boy waits for the hunting party, sunning himself on a rock and noting the death around him as the season changes to winter. Everything, he thinks, is dead but a few birds and rabbits: the gun, for him, means death, too.

But the hunters know nothing of these thoughts as they hunt doves for Thanksgiving dinner. Still, the boy, hearing them, believes that he has let his uncle down, and he hopes that he can overcome his feelings and kill one dove before the hunting party returns. So he whistles his dove calls, and he is answered. As the dove comes closer to him he lifts his gun; then seeing that the dove appears unafraid, the boy thinks that the dove is a pet and lowers the gun. The dove comes closer, and the boy sees that the dove is blind in one eye, caused by a hunter's bullet. The dove turns its head, and the boy sees that both eyes have been blinded. Nevertheless, though blind, the dove calls to its mate, and soon its mate answers, its whistle becoming a beckoning voice.

These kinds of stories, told from the perspective of a sensitive boy, are different from ones in which the narrator participates as part of a ritual experience. Apparently now a feisty young man in **"Death Has Two Good Eyes,"** Shan and his cousin, Finn, have been summoned by other cousins who live at Blanton on the Big Sandy River. Shan and Finn are met at the station by their cousin Frank, who tells them there is trouble at home with "blood-kin" whom they respect enough to put aside pistols and knives to fight with fists, clubs, and rocks. The problem has been precipitated by their Uncle Melvin, who, it appears, has seven boys by a legal wife and seven boys and two girls by another woman. The knowledge that her husband has gone to live for good with another and younger woman is driving Aunt Mallie to her grave. Since seven brothers have been pitted against seven brothers, the fight has been in stalemate; therefore, Cousin Frank has sent for reinforcements with whom he intends to win the battle. So brothers fight brothers with a couple of cousins thrown in, and, indeed, the cousins do make the difference. The fight is stopped, mighty as it is, when the other woman, wringing her bony hands and pushing her coarse black hair back from her face comes crying, "My true love is dead."

It seems Uncle Melvin complained of a pain in his heart and then died in the outhouse. But dead or alive, Uncle Melvin is carried back to his lawful wedded wife while the unlawful wedded wife screams out her despair.

More like a tall tale in the local color tradition celebrating the rites of manhood than the kind of account celebrating kinship knowledge experienced by Shan in **"Death Has Two Good Eyes,"** the story ends on the comment that Finn, who is a mighty fighter, must take after the father's side of the family, while Shan, who is not so good in a fight, undoubtedly takes after his mother's people.

At an even greater distance from the Shan of **"Death Has Two Good Eyes"** is the narrator of **"Another Hanging."** He speaks in a dialect, is overjoyed at the prospect of a hanging, joins crowds of drunken people on the way to the site, picks up a girl to watch the hanging with, and "loves her all the way home." The man who is being hanged is a murderer who has been too free with a razor and has finally slit someone's throat from ear to ear. The drunken crowd of people on their way to the hanging includes young men with pistols and girls. One is tempted to tie together these image patterns and those in **"Death Has Two Good Eyes"** and see in them grotesqueries of the male psyche, at least the male psyche in W-Hollow. Given, however, that Stuart's life experiences as presented in his autobiographical writing seem to deny such a meaning, and given that the story has been called an example of Stuart's "exuberant lyricism," a "wild and delirious ride" through the night proceeding with "joyous abandon," it might be better just to agree with Ruel Foster in his book on Jesse Stuart that the story is one of Stuart's "most potent and economical" and leave it at that. The narrator, Eif, is not Shan, and one can say that the callous views expressed are his and

his neighbors', friends', and parents', not Stuart's. "Comic gusto," Foster goes on to tell us, "is a very American brand of humor."

---

## FURTHER READING

Blair, Everetta Love. *Jesse Stuart: His Life and Works.* Columbia: University of South Carolina Press, 1967, 288 p.

    Provides critical and biographical information on Stuart.

Clarke, Mary Washington. *Jesse Stuart's Kentucky.* New York: McGraw-Hill Book Co., 1968, 240 p.

    Explores the major themes of Stuart's work.

Foster, Ruel E. *Jesse Stuart.* New York: Twayne Publishers, 1968, 168 p.

    Full-length critical study of Stuart's work.

————. "Jesse Stuart's W-Hollow—Microcosm of the Appalachians." *Kansas Quarterly* 2, No. 2 (Spring 1970): 66-72.

    Offers a stylistic and thematic analysis of Stuart's short fiction.

————. "Jesse Stuart's Way with Short Fiction." *Kansas Quarterly* 9, No. 2 (Spring 1977): 21-9.

    Contends that the body of Stuart's work, "of which the short stories are the finest portion, represents the most significant work of any Appalachian writer."

Patrick, Nancy. "A Delineation of Folklore Elements in Jesse Stuart's *Tales from the Plum Grove Hills.*" *Jack London Newsletter* XIII, No. 2 (May-August 1980): 66-71.

    Outlines the different types of folklore found in the stories comprising *Tales from the Plum Grove Hills.*

# Ludwig Tieck
## 1773-1853

(Full name Johann Ludwig Tieck; also wrote under the pseudonym of Peter Leberecht) German novella writer, novelist, dramatist, poet, translator, essayist, critic, and editor.

## INTRODUCTION

A seminal figure in the German Romantic movement, Tieck is best known for his *märchen,* novellas derived from traditional fairy and folk tales, his novel *Franz Sternbalds Wanderungen* (1798), and his dramas *Der gestiefelte Kater* (1797, *Puss in Boots*) and *Leben und Tod der heiligen Genoveva* (1799). In his works, Tieck combined realism with the inexplicable, thus rebelling against the literalism of the Rationalists who preceded him. "The stated aim of Tieck's fiction," wrote Maria Tatar, "was to drive readers to the point of distraction, to mystify and bewilder them until they reached that blissful state that Tieck designated as 'poetic madness'."

## Biographical Information

Tieck was born into a middle-class family in Berlin, which was then the capital of Prussia. Encouraged to read by his mother, Tieck was influenced at an early age by the works of William Shakespeare and Johann Wolfgang von Goethe. He attended a progressive secondary school where he is believed to have written as many as thirty works in various genres. Tieck studied theology, philosophy, and literature at universities in Halle, Erlangen, and Göttingen. In 1794 he found employment as a writer for the Berlin publisher Christoph Friedrich Nicolai. Shortly thereafter, Tieck produced *Volksmährchen* (1797), which contained his most celebrated novella—*Der blonde Eckbert*—as well as the play *Puss in Boots*. The success of Tieck's 1798 novel *Franz Sternbalds Wanderungen* liberated him from Nicolai, a welcome parting after Nicolai published an unauthorized edition of Tieck's writings.

Around this time, Tieck became involved with the Jena Romanticists, an elite literary circle that included such notable figures as Friedrich Schlegel, August Wilhelm Schlegel, Friedrich Wilhelm Schelling, and Novalis. In 1798 Tieck married Amalie Alberti; the couple later had two daughters. After 1800 Tieck's literary output waned, partly because of his perfectionist ways but also because of frequent lapses into depression. He desperately sought regular income, and eventually moved his family into the home of his friend and benefactor Wilhelm von Burgsdorff. In 1819 Tieck was appointed *Dramaturg,* dramatic advisor, of the Dresden Theater. He then began writing the bulk of his novellas, the majority of

which were historical works. Tieck spent the remaining years of his life as writer-in-residence at the court of King Frederick Wilhelm IV of Prussia. He died in Berlin in 1853.

## Major Works of Short Fiction

Tieck is best known for his imaginative reworkings of fairy tales and traditional folktales. Among his most popular works is the novella *Der blonde Eckbert,* which combines psychological examination of its protagonist's mental states with typically fantastic and supernatural plot elements drawn from folklore. In many of the stories that comprise *Volksmährchen,* Tieck explores the relationship between reality and the imagination. Using a dense, poetic style, he creates an atmosphere that enables his readers to accept improbable occurrences as possible, even inevitable. In 1811 he published *Phantasus,* which includes plays, tales, and novellas. The framing story of the collection revolves around a group of young people conversing about literature and reading aloud the stories that comprise the volume. Their remarks provide a highly self-conscious literary commentary on the individual pieces. The novellas of this volume, in addition to Tieck's later novellas, are less Romantic than his earlier works, reflecting Tieck's age and outlook at the time they were written.

## Critical Reception

Tieck's works were so popular in his lifetime that he and Goethe were together hailed as Germany's most distinguished men of letters. His influence was not lasting, however, as Tieck's works are seldom read today. Critics commend Tieck's introduction of fantastic elements into otherwise realistic narratives, and he is consistently praised for his effective portrayal of the mental states of his characters. He is also praised for his integration of numerous themes, such as the loss of innocence, dualism in nature, guilt, fatalism, and the destructive power of love. However, some commentators criticize his confusing interweaving of different time periods, sudden interjections of unrelated action, and a perceived lack of cohesion in his plots.

---

## PRINCIPAL WORKS

### Short Fiction

*Volksmährchen* [as Peter Leberecht] (novellas and dramas) 1797
*Phantasus.* 3 vols. (novellas) 1812-16
*Die Verlobung* (novella) 1823
†*Novellen.* 7 vols. (novellas) 1823-28
*Musikalische Leiden und Freuden* (novella) 1824
*Die Reisenden* (novella) 1824
*Pietro von Abano oder Petrus Apone* [*Pietro of Abano*] (novella) 1825
*Der Aufruhr in den Cevennen* [*The Rebellion in the Cévennes Mountains*] (novella) 1826
*Der Alte vom Berge, und: Die Gesellschaft auf dem Lande* [*The Old Man of the Mountain*] (novellas) 1828
*Schriften.* 28 vols. (novels, novellas, drama, poetry, and essays) 1828-54

### Other Major Works

*Geschichte des Herrn William Lovell.* 3 vols. (novel) 1795-96
*Der gestiefelte Kater* [*Puss in Boots*] (drama) 1797
*Franz Sternbalds Wanderungen.* 2 vols. (novel) 1798
‡*Romantische Dichtungen.* 2 vols. (dramas) 1799-1800
*Kaiser Octavianus* (drama) 1804
*Gedichte.* 3 vols. (poetry) 1821-23
*Vittoria Accorombona.* 2 vols. [*The Roman Matron*] (novel) 1840
*Five Dramas of Ludwig Tieck Hitherto Unpublished* (dramas) 1959

---

*This collection includes the novella Der blonde Eckbert.

†*This work includes the novellas* Der blonde Eckbert, Der Runenberg, *and* Die Elfen.

‡This work includes the drama *Leben und Tod der heiligen Genoveva.*

## CRITICISM

### Edwin H. Zeydel  (essay date 1935)

SOURCE: "The Early 'Novellen'," in *Ludwig Tieck, The German Romanticist: A Critical Study,* Princeton University Press, 1935, pp. 284-300.

*[In the following excerpt, Zeydel discusses the themes and critical reception of Tieck's early novellas.]*

The classification of Tieck's "novellen" for purposes of individual discussion presents problems arising not only from their number and bulk but also from the multiplicity of topics. Two attempts have been made to class them according to subject matter. The first was by J. L. Hoffmann in 1856 [in *L. T., eine literarische skizze*]; he discussed three types, fantastic, social and historical—an utterly inadequate classification. The second more important attempt was made in 1884 by Jakob Minor in an enlightening article [in *T. als Novellendichter*]. He found that apart from **Der junge Tischlermeister** and *Vittoria Accorombona,* which defied systematization, there were eight categories, namely "novellen" dealing with questions of the day, those dealing with great writers, historical "novellen," stories of ghosts and magic, "novellen" of roguery, satires against the Young Germans, mere anecdotes and epic narratives.

The weakness of Minor's mode of procedure is due to several reasons. His compartments are not always mutually exclusive. Not every "novelle" fits into a single group; some belong in two or three. Besides, plot and subject matter are not as essential to Tieck as is his critique of the times. We shall, therefore, avoid every form of classification and observe a purely chronological method of treatment, devoting [this essay] to the "novellen" written before the July revolution of 1830 (an important event in the political and literary history of Germany). . . . This seems desirable not only for practical reasons, but also because [the early and later novellen show], in a rough way, a unity of purpose. The "novellen" of the first group are generally aimed against some form of ultraconservatism, while those of the latter group usually attack one of the doctrines of the Young Germans.

The first of the "novellen," **Die Gemälde** (1821), is one of the most characteristic. The plot is so simple that Wilhelm Grimm called it trivial and complained that when he reached the end he was still waiting for the beginning. A young man wastes his large patrimony but is saved by some fine pictures which are hidden in the wainscotting. They are accidentally discovered at a drunken revel (the discovery constitutes the turning point) and enable him to marry the girl of his choice and to live to a ripe, respected age.

Far more important than the plot is the underlying purpose—a discussion of the conflict of opinions aroused by the opposite tendencies in the prevailing theories of art.

These divided the artists of the time into two camps. In the one were the adherents of the old classical tradition, in the other the devotees of the more recent school, which had arisen as the result of Wackenroder's and Tieck's meditations, studies and writings on art. Like literary Romanticism, this Romantic school of esthetics, launched in defense of old German and Nazarene art, had degenerated. It had developed a reactionary form of religionism and an ultramontanism which banished all worldly beauty. Tieck, the well informed critic, realized that he himself was partly responsible for this development and wanted to present a true, unprejudiced picture of the situation. So in *Die Gemälde* he praised the sensual, happy classical beauty of Giulio Romano and overlooked the objections against him in his *Geschichte und Theorie der bildenden Künste*. On the other hand, he did not altogether reject religious painting, although he censured the exaggerated veneration of old German customs (Deutschtümelei) externally manifested even in clothing and coiffure, which had been suggested by himself and Wackenroder but brought distinctly into vogue by A. W. Schlegel's Romantic colloquies on paintings in the *Athenäum* (1799). Tieck's young painter Dietrich represents this fatuous trend. And yet the representatives of academic classicism are also slyly ridiculed.

Tieck writes with calmness and circumspection. He shows more animation, and bitterness, too, when he argues against the self-styled connoisseurs (represented by the prince—is Burgsdorff his prototype?) who claim omniscience but are really ignoramuses. This deceiving nobleman is himself deceived by a tippling forger named Eulenböck, one of the most delightful creations in German "novellen" literature, who of all of Tieck's characters comes closest to being more than merely a typical figure. His is one of the many genial ironists in the "novellen." His remark that a given brand of wine represents the poetry of its native locality has become famous. But the frequently repeated statement that Eulenböck is a counterpart of the architect and writer on art Genelli is refuted by Tieck in a letter. Count Schack's suggestion that he represents Tieck's nephew Gustav Waagen must also be taken with a grain of salt. As for the principal character, he bears many of Tieck's own characteristics. His predilection for humorous speeches in praise of good victuals and drink was also Tieck's. Three English translations appeared between 1825 and 1833.

The interest in art, particularly in old paintings, evinced by Tieck in *Die Gemälde* accompanied him through life. We have had previous occasion to refer to it in discussing his relations with Wackenroder, the Schlegels and Runge, and in commenting upon the unpublished manuscript *Geschichte und Theorie der bildenden Künste* reposing in Vienna. It appears very markedly, too, in his correspondence with the noted art collector Sulpiz Boisserée, whom he met about 1808. Boisserée had an unbounded admiration for Tieck and justly considered him an able connoisseur. Some of Tieck's judgments in his letters to Boisserée are indeed sound, as that on the painting of a Dying Virgin owned by Boisserée (now in the Munich Pinakothek), which, Tieck readily discerned, was the work of a German artist who lived after Dürer and spent some time in Italy. In the course of his Dresden period his preoccupation with painting also earned him the friendship of the noted artist Vogel von Vogelstein, whose portraits of Tieck have been mentioned.

Not long after *Die Gemälde* Tieck wrote *Der Geheimnisvolle* (1821). With it he sounded one of his favorite "novellen" themes, a typical social problem, namely insincerity in political and social life and the perniciousness of lies. The germ of the tale lies in an incident to which allusion has been made. In 1804 his brother-in-law Reichardt, using material furnished him by Count Schlabrendorf, secretly published a pamphlet against Napoleon. Though shielded by the Prussian chancellor, Count Hardenberg, he was forced to flee from the emperor's wrath. Around this nucleus of fact Tieck builds his plot, the locale of which is clearly Ziebingen. Kronenberg, a vain secretmonger and liar, who pharisaically censures others for the same fault of which he is guilty, falsely claims the authorship of a book against Napoleon. His prevarication involves him in serious trouble and almost costs him his life. Most of the other characters in the "novelle" are also untruthful, conspicuous exceptions being noble Cäcilie and young Emmerich. The latter gives expression to Tieck's own patriotic sentiments, his belief in the necessity of German unity, and his disbelief in excessive outspokenness of the public press. Tieck's semi-dramatic treatment has been referred to in the previous chapter.

As *Der Geheimnisvolle* depicts a gallery of prevaricators, so *Die Reisenden,* written in the spring of 1822, pictures an assemblage of fools. A tourist travelling incognito—a fad in Tieck's day—is mistaken for a madman and incarcerated in an asylum. Here most of the happenings, largely of a ludicrous nature, take place. We are introduced to many well drawn types, some really insane, while others are merely eccentric and hover on the borderline separating sanity from lunacy. One of Tieck's best figures is young Raimund. Though sane, he is suspected of being deranged, and every attempt to clear himself of this mistrust makes him more suspicious in the eyes of the "experts." His chief handicap arises from a false belief, which becomes an obsession, that his sweetheart has died. Minutes seem as years to him; this earns him the nickname of Methuselah. In the end the old physician in charge of the asylum loses his own mind and dismisses all the inmates. Tieck's ultimate purpose in composing this modern catalog of fools seems to be to deal in a realistic, satiric way with the typically Romantic question: Where does rational thinking end and madness begin? The "novelle" well illustrates his abiding interest in demonism. But from his nature demonism of 1797 to his new realistic demonism is a far cry. *Die Reisenden* contains many reminiscences of Burgsdorff. A certain similarity to *Los Locos de Valencia* of Lope, from whom he borrowed numerous motifs for the "novellen," is evident. A French version appeared in 1833.

*Die Verlobung* (1822) is a polemic against exaggerated and complacent piety and against Tieck's old Romantic theory that art and religion are identical. Orthodoxy, he felt, had been labored to such an extent that it had led to mere lip-service, external religionism and intellectual flaccidity, and had undermined mental and moral discipline. The lesson which he would point seems to be that a cultured man may possess truly religious instincts without being orthodox. This idea is pressed with some insistence and stamps *Die Verlobung* as the first markedly programmatic "novelle."

Apparently the protest it voices was timely. Shortly after its appearance the publisher F. A. Brockhaus noted in his diary that it contains "words spoken in the nick of time, for conditions are now bad, indeed. People care less whether a man does right and fulfils his duty than whether he observes the externalities of religion." Similarly, Goethe felt that Tieck has dispelled gloomy clouds and revealed a clear blue sky of common sense and pure morals.

As usual when Tieck's chief purpose is argumentative and not narrative, the plot is thin and insignificant, serving merely as an illustration of the subject of controversy. A young and beautiful but poor girl consents with reluctance to marry a very pious young baron. She is saved from him by an equally rich but less pious count, who marries her and settles the mortgage on the family mansion. The characters, however, are well portrayed. The principal one bears the name of Tieck's elder daughter Dorothea and mirrors the noblest aspects of her personality. An English translation by Connop Thirlwall came out in 1825.

*Musikalische Leiden und Freuden* (1822), suggesting in title Hoffmann's *Johannes Kreislers des Kapellmeisters Musikalische Leiden* and written one year after Weber's *Der Freischütz,* is composed in a bright, humorous vein. It is of twofold interest and value as an historical document, showing Tieck's own reaction to music and reflecting conditions in the musical world of his day. The autobiographical element is strong. Early in life he had come to understand and appreciate music at Reichardt's home in Berlin and later in Halle and Giebichenstein. He conceived a boyish admiration for Mozart. But his own attempt to play the violin, delightfully described by the "layman" in the story, was an utter failure. Wackenroder had opened his eyes to the close relationship of music and the rest of the arts, with the result that many of his works possess a strong musicalness and marked synaesthesia. His friend Burgsdorff was very musical. And in the home of Count Finckenstein at Madlitz (he was the model for Baron Fernow in the story) Tieck also heard much music.

The trend of his argument in this "novelle" is against spuriousness in music, particularly against ignorant "lovers" of music, stupid amateur performers and the caprices of audiences and singers, in short against all the various abuses of the art. There is no mistaking the types which he introduces, for instance the dilettante enthusiast Kellermann, who is always ecstatic, generally over some composition which he has never heard; Count Alten, the "concert hound"; the musical director tortured by the whims of the public; and the Italian singing teacher, in whom the soulless virtuosos are attacked. It is in this "novelle" that we find Tieck's charge that Beethoven is guilty of far-fetched originality. As often in Tieck, the "novelle" is a story framed within a story, so constructed that in the end framework and narrative proper are blended into a unit.

The setting of *Die Gesellschaft auf dem Lande* (1824) is eighteenth century Brandenburg. The theme, the evil of untruthfulness, is identical with that of *Der Geheimnisvolle.* Though Tieck opposed the "fanaticism for veraciousness" ascribed to the Teutons, and could condone a white lie, he demanded truth and frankness in all matters of importance, making this demand one of his leading motifs.

As usual the plot is simple. Franz has seen Adelheid at a ball and fallen in love with her. By her brother, his friend, he is invited to the family's country estate. There he poses as a painter. But Adelheid, repulsed by his disingenuous mode of courting, conceals her love for him and encourages another suitor, until the latter has a serious quarrel with her father, the baron. The father, a champion of the "good old times," wears a queue and expects all his friends to do likewise. His steward Römer, who poses as a former hussar, has a particularly fine queue, which is cut off half in jest by Zipfmantel, the miller. The resulting ignominy is too much for Römer, and he dies. Thereupon it turns out that he was a base charlatan, who had lied so long and persistently about his past that he had come to believe his own prevarications. Needless to say, Franz wins Adelheid, and a happy ending is achieved. The tale is written in a pleasantly humorous vein. Some of the characters are well portrayed, especially Römer (modelled on a figure Tieck met in Ziebingen), the old baron (a take-off on the ultra-conservatives of the time) and the baroness (who, like Tieck's Ziebingen friends, unable to distinguish between "mir" and "mich," always uses the accusative in addressing servants and the dative in social intercourse).

In its day this "novelle" was praised. A. W. Schlegel read it "with unending delight" and felt that nothing since *Don Quixote* could compare with it [Lüdeke, *L. T. u. d. Brüder Schlegel*]. Of interest are a fine tribute to Frederick the Great, also the mature fatalism and belief in supernaturalism affirmed in the words: "Do we toy with ourselves, or does a higher hand shuffle the cards? Perhaps in the very important moments of our lives these two possibilities come to the same thing."

*Pietro von Abano oder Petrus Apone, Zaubergeschichte* (1824) deals with medieval superstitions, spooks and magic and is charged with an atmosphere of fantasticalness. In being more a narrative portrait than a disquisition it is hardly a "novelle" in Tieck's sense, rather a fairy tale in the Romantic style. Like *Dichterleben,* which was to follow, it marks a transition from the "novelle" of contemporary conditions to the historical type. But instead of allowing the magic element to be manifested in nature, as he had done in *Der blonde Eckbert,* he makes the devil and his human underlings its ministers. The hellish medieval magician Apone of Padua, in love with dead Crescentia, calls her back from the grave. Hovering between life and death, she is promised full life by the sorcerer if she will marry him. But her yearning for death is stronger than her will to be resuscitated under such conditions. In the end it turns out that Apone was under the influence of Berecynth, a demon, who restores him to life, only to spirit him away. And Crescentia has a twin sister, who had been kidnaped in infancy and is now rescued and married by Antonio, Crescentia's lover. Of interest is Tieck's belief that childlike faith works greater miracles than sophisticated sorcery.

The source which Tieck used is the *Storia della letteratura italiana* of Girolamo Tiraboschi. Though lacking unity, the difficult subject, which Brentano also used in his *Romanzen vom Rosenkranz,* is handled cleverly (as Niebuhr, too, thought) and with a degree of skill. As in his earlier Romantic tales, Tieck banishes realism and all reference to contemporary everyday life. In later works, when he mixed spiritualism, magic and realism, as in the modern tale **Der Schutzgeist** (1839), he was less successful. A continuation of **Pietro von Abano,** announced in 1824, did not appear. In 1827 the tale was used as the basis for an opera by Spohr (text by Karl Pfeiffer). Two English translations were published in 1831 and 1839, respectively.

**Dichterleben** (1824), with a prolog **Das Fest zu Kenilworth** (1828) and a second part (1829), is again more narrative than argumentative and rates higher than any of the "novellen" preceding it except **Pietro von Abano.** As early as 1800 he had planned a novel on the early English drama. The three "novellen" comprising **Dichterleben,** together covering three hundred fifty pages in the *Schriften,* are in a sense the consummation of this plan. They deal with that period in the history of English dramatics, the first thirty years of Shakespeare's life, which held the greatest interest for Tieck. On the model of the "Künstlerdrama" made popular by Goethe's *Tasso,* Kind's *Van Dykes Landleben,* Castelli's *Rafael* and Oehlenschläger's *Correggio,* they introduce a new type of "novelle," which deals with the lives of great poets.

Considering the three "novellen" as an entity, we may call them a sort of repository for the unused materials of the book on Shakespeare. We become acquainted first with Shakespeare, the highly precocious child, and with the environment in which Tieck pictured him. The Middle Ages and the heyday of the Catholic Church in England still cast their shadows. The influence of a gloomy, harsh and prosaic father (who is modelled somewhat on the plan of Tieck's own father) is outweighed by the more buoyant, tender and poetic nature of the mother (Tieck's mother). We meet Ann Hathaway, who early calls the boy "meinen kleinen Mann," and with Shakespeare we are participants in the festivities at Kenilworth in 1575. In the first part of the "novelle" we accompany the obscure beginner to London and witness him wresting the poetic laurels from Greene and Marlowe, the leading playwrights of their day, and finding a friend in wealthy Southampton.

Thus far Shakespeare, the harmonious genius, free of all demonic passion, is seen only in the background, while his more experienced but utterly unbalanced rivals play the principal parts. There is irony in the fact that although their ideas seem to impress him, he never puts them into practice. There is fatalism in the prophecy of a soothsayer that he will be a great poet.

At the opening of the second part Shakespeare is seen at the inn of Davenant in Oxford. The time is about 1593, and *Love's Labour's Lost* has been half finished. Two sections constitute this latter portion, Shakespeare's narrative of his own life up to his flight to London, omitted between the prolog and part 1, and his visit to Stratford with Southampton. While he was almost a mythical figure in the first part, without blemish or reproach, he is brought closer to us in the latter part, where we witness him in a struggle with himself. Unfortunately, however, the nearer he is brought, the smaller he seems. His views on poetry are those of Tieck, the nineteenth century critic. His Protestant faith, with its contempt for Puritanism and the Anglican Church but its kindly feeling for Catholicism, is also Tieck's.

From a letter to his publisher Max of 1840 we learn that Tieck planned a continuation in the form of a full-length novel. In another letter to Max of 1842 we read that it was to deal with Shakespeare's "later relation to Ben Jonson and the other poets, but particularly with the story of Essex and his private secretary Cuffe." Tieck adds: "The building materials for this work have been ready for many years, and it is quite possible that you, my friend, will publish it in a year or two." This promise was not fulfilled.

Among his works of this type written thus far he considered **Dichterleben** his favorite. At the time of its appearance it created a furore. The critics practically agreed that it was the finest piece which had flowed from his pen in at least a generation, an oustanding literary masterpiece, superior to any of Scott's novels. [In *Allgem. Zeitung,* 1892], Wilhelm Grimn thought it showed remarkable insight into the human heart; Immermann and Hebbel [in *Tagebucher*] had words of high praise for it. As early as 1824 Tieck suggested that Brockhaus publish an English rendering. In 1828 A. W. Schlegel thought that if translated into English it would cause quite a stir [*L. T. u. d. Brüder Schlegel*]. Such a translation (of the first part) appeared at Leipzig in 1830 but passed unnoticed. In 1837 *Blackwood's* brought selections from the prolog and both parts. A Danish version of the first part came out in 1826. In 1832 two French translations, one of the prolog and the two parts, the other of parts 1 and 2, appeared. A three-act drama, *Shakespeare* (1836), by Braun von Braunthal, is based upon the first part. A novel by H. C. König (1839), a drama by Holtei (1840) and Wildenbruch's *Christoph Marlowe* (1884) also owe much to Tieck.

The chief basis of **Dichterleben** is not, as might be expected, historical source material or tradition, but his own intuition as a poet. A recent English critic, Professor John G. Robertson, has given an interesting appraisal of the work [in *Modern Language Review,* Vol. 18]. He calls Tieck's interpretation of Shakespeare thoroughly Romantic and characterizes the novel as mediocre, inanimate and devoid of all English atmosphere. However this may be, it is true that, in comparison with Scott's *Kenilworth* and such modern novels of Elizabethan England as Virginia Woolf's *Orlando* and Eduard Stucken's *Im Schatten Shakespeares,* Tieck's effort seems futile.

***Der Aufruhr in den Cevennen,*** of which four sections were planned but only two appeared, is Tieck's first real historical "novelle," or more properly novel. The historical background is the uprising of the Calvinist Camisards in the Cévennes mountains of southern France in 1703.

He explained his first acquaintance with the subject and the genesis of his work as follows. His attention, he reported, was first attracted to the theme in 1806, upon his return from Italy, through three dramas of J. von Sinclair. Some years later he chanced to read a story by Mission entitled *Le théâtre sacré des Cévennes* (London, 1707), containing the visions and vicissitudes of Camisard refugees in England. This and the fact that the fate of the Camisards had never found objective treatment appealed to him so strongly that he decided to treat the material himself. Now he set to work reading numerous pertinent sources, among them the *Lettres des Protestants des Cévennes aux Réfugiés François-Allemands* (Berlin, 1704), a French *Histoire des Camisards* (London, 1744) and the memoirs of the Catholic Duke of Villars (1734-1736). But one important work, *Histoire des troubles des Cévennes* (1760), he did not discover until after he had practically completed the work, which he began in 1820 and finished in 1826.

But in the summer of 1829 Brentano told Johann Emmanuel Veith that he was responsible for calling Tieck's attention to the subject, having confidentially communicated to him "eine längere Dichtung" on the theme. The truth of this is borne out by the fact that in October 1806 Brentano recommended Sinclair's dramas to Arnim. Moreover, Brentano started a play on the same subject. It would seem, therefore, that Tieck either met Sinclair, or became acquainted with his works, through Brentano.

Nor is Tieck's catalog of his specific sources for the "novelle" complete, as shown by Lebede's recent research into the records of his loans from the Dresden library. To be sure, Tieck quotes his chief source for purely historical facts, the pro-Protestant and rather subjective *Histoire des Camisards,* which he drew from the library for thirteen months (1822-1823). But he used at least seven other important works, the Catholic and pro-Camisard *Histoire du Fanatisme* of Brueys, the more objective *Histoire de France sous le règne de Louis XIV* by Larrey, the *Mémoires* of Guiscard, a *Histoire de l'Edit de Nantes* (1693-1695), a *Histoire générale de Languedoc* (1733-1745), the *Monumens de la Monarchie Françoise* by Montfauçon, and, for geographic orientation, Herbin's *Statistique générale et particulière de la France.*

He adheres with fidelity to the historical facts as he ascertained them from the gloomy account of would-be prophets, cruelties, carnage and pillage which his sources gave. Even the miracles which he reports are in the sources. The Camisard leaders Cavalier, Catinat, Roland, Ravenel and Mazel, like their opponents Basville, Montrevel and Julien, are a poet's recreations of extravagant historical characters. Because he found them ready-made in the sources, they are among his best figures. The masses are also effectively introduced, sometimes to the detriment of plot development.

But the main plot, the story of Edmund and his family, is his own free invention. In development it may be compared roughly with Schiller's *Wilhelm Tell,* Edmund's father being a sort of Attinghausen and Edmund himself a combination of Rudenz and Melchthal. Edmund, at first a fanatical Catholic, is converted by a sort of miracle into an equally zealous Calvinist. The scene in which he is forced to destroy his own house, marked by gloomy fatalism (of which there are many traces in the work), is one of the finest among a wealth of stirring scenes. In the end the hero is cured of all fanaticism, whatever may be its hue, and led to peace and conciliation, by Father Watelet, a wise old priest who has obviously studied Jacob Böhme and like Tieck been influenced by him. His discussions with Edmund on the subject of faith are an important part of this "novelle" and reproduce Tieck's own clarified, unbiased views. While adhering to his inherited creed, Father Watelet opposes belief in supernaturalism and superstition. Miracles, he holds, are to be found not in deviations from the laws of God and nature, but in these laws themselves. And Christianity is to him an elastic religion, which permits every man to make his own code. The character of the unbeliever, Lacoste, may owe traits to Schopenhauer.

It is significant that Tieck here reverts, as he does also in ***Der Hexensabbath,*** to one of his favorite themes, the gradual development of a psychic disturbance. Such disturbance he now prefers to study under the aspect of religious superstition, which becomes a menace in times of fanaticism. Here, as in *Vittoria Accorombona,* his chief characters are demonic men and women impelled by magic or mysticism, who trespass beyond the bounds set for human beings. In this sense they are akin to William Lovell, Eckbert and Tannenhäuser.

Of course religion plays a weighty rôle. And yet religion is important chiefly as a part of the historical milieu. The latter is paramount. Moreover, the work is significant in giving us a picture of his purpose in writing historical "novellen." He would use them as a means of revealing a relationship between bygone ages and his own times, and of thus discovering a general human significance in history.

Although most contemporary reviewers did not greet the work with great warmth, many notable critics, among them Jacobs, von Hauch, Menzel, Johanna Schopenhauer, A. W. Schlegel, Immermann, Gries, Schleiermacher and Joseph von Hormayr, were loud in their praises and implored Tieck to finish it. Raumer felt that he deserved a theological degree for it. The historical novelist Häring (Wilibald Alexis) credited him with discovering in it the secret of the poetical treatment of history in novellistic form. His failure to complete the "novelle," despite these many encouragements, led to various rumors, the most pernicious being that of Varnhagen von Ense previously referred to. The unedited correspondence with Reimer, the publisher of the work, throws new light on the question. As late as April 1838 Tieck promised him to complete it that summer, but in July 1845 he wrote to the younger Reimer that he never finished it because old Reimer was opposed to a continuation. That this is probably true and that the publisher's opposition was due to external economic reasons, is indicated by the fact that in 1846, twenty years after its appearance, the edition of the extant section was not yet exhausted.

Even today critics do not agree as to its merits. Witkowski feels that it cannot be rated highly as a work of art. But Berend calls it a masterpiece of historical fresco painting and Willoughby gives it the palm among the later works. No doubt it has elements of greatness, but it lacks vitality. This fatal defect, brought about less by such minor flaws as the verbal perversions of Frau Barbe, or the precociousness of little Eveline (a typical Tieckean child), and less by the sentimental ending than by the obtrusiveness of the argument on religion, deprives the work of truly lasting significance. But after all is said and done, it remains one of the most compelling works of the aging poet, and visualizes his ideas of tolerance, as *Nathan der Weise* does Lessing's.

Madame Burette's English translation (1845) is fairly readable. In 1880 A. Langert based an opera upon the "novelle."

In view of the energy devoted by Tieck to the last three works, it is no wonder that his next "novelle," **Glück gibt Verstand** (1826), shows a marked slackening of his powers. Bäring, an old country parson, is a philistine, but also a gruff and stern parent. He has lofty ambitions for his exceedingly modest son Simon, who has studied law. He wants him to apply for a high judicial post. With misgivings Simon departs to the city to submit to the necessary examination, taking a fond leave of Sidonie, his sweetheart, of whom his father disapproves, not because she is older than he, but because she is a poor orphan. Before Simon can present himself to the minister to seek the desired appointment, he falls into the hands of some friendly adventurers, who pose as influential noblemen. One plays the part of the ruling prince and treats Simon with such kindness that he develops enough courage to apply successfully for the position. The real prince takes a fancy to him and at the same time gives his father a promotion in rank. Better still, Simon is permitted to marry Sidonie, who unexpectedly receives a handsome sum of money.

The triviality of this plot is relieved by occasional clever incidents and digs against philistinism. There is an amusing conversation on the joys of pipe-smoking and of wearing a nightcap. As in Tieck's earliest comedies, particularly **Der letzte Betrug ist ärger als der erste,** proverbs play an important part. Not only is the title proverbial, but the actions of the hero throughout are guided by proverbs which he had heard discussed at the beginning. But the critic who wrote of this "novelle" that "few poets make it as clear as Tieck that substance is inconsequential and form or mode of treatment all-important" must have been strongly prejudiced in his favor.

Although **Der funfzehnte November** (1827) is not one of his best "novellen," either, it is significant from one point of view. A program "novelle," the trend of its plot and indeed its very title (a mockery of such titles as *Der 24, Februar*) serve as a disputation against the "fate dramas"

and their mechanical conception of fate. But it presents his case not by argument or mere talk, rather through the medium of the story itself. His reasoning is that a higher, divine conception of fate and a nobler fatalism exist than that espoused by such dramatists as Werner and Houwald. The essence of this exalted fatalism is absolute faith in the inscrutable wisdom of God. The tale which illustrates this idea and pictures his mature conception of demonic force is the most soulful and pious of all his "novellen," but the plot is too far-fetched, the motivation too deficient, and the characterization too conventional.

The son of a wealthy Dutch merchant, a gifted young man, is suddenly deprived of part of his reason and power of speech. Though very strong physically, he is now a moron in all his actions. But one aptitude has remained with him—he is very clever at building. Sensing some terrible misfortune, he sets to work constructing a huge boat. This occupies him for two years; on his birthday it is finished. Then the dike breaks. With almost superhuman exertion he saves numerous lives in his craft. Exhausted, he sinks into a long, deep sleep. When he awakens, he is completely cured. He marries the girl who has nursed him through his illness with loving care, and they live a happy, genuinely pious life ever after.

Except for an amusing minor incident, which describes how a Werther enthusiast is hoaxed by some robbers, the unity is well observed. The main idea came to Tieck from a Dutch copperplate representing a flood. Incidentally he takes occasion to defend the Dutch against the then prevalent charge of stolidity. He paints them much more favorably than he does a German swaggerer.

**Der Gelehrte** (1827) is one of the best "novellen," free of propagandistic purpose and bizarre effect, artistically sound, and rich in harmless humor and excellent characterization. A very bookish professor, who has been an inveterate celibate, suddenly decides to marry. With unerring instinct he selects that one of three eligible daughters who will make him the best wife. She is Helena, the Cinderella of her family. Marriage soon serves to cause an electrifying transformation in the morose ascetic. He becomes quite human, adopts a more mellow outlook upon the world and becomes aware of countless amenities of life to which he had been blind.

Tieck has woven many autobiographic touches into his "novelle." The professor's passion for books, abhorrence of street noises, philanthropic bent and contempt for money were traits of Tieck himself. Helena's charming womanliness, combined with a love for learning, was a characteristic of Dorothea, while her domesticity was a quality of his other daughter Agnes. Among the many apt humorous touches, the episode in which the butler Werner proposes to the housekeeper is prominent.

The little story served Freytag as the model for incidents in his novel *Die verlorene Handschrift.* Freytag's hero, Felix Werner, bears the name of Tieck's butler, while the butler Gabriel in the Freytag novel is patterned on the same model. In Freytag a lost manuscript of Tacitus plays an important part; in Tieck a misplaced slip bearing an emendation of Quintilian.

But the present-day reader, interested in the psychological study of character, seeks in vain a depiction of the various steps in the transformation, which takes place too suddenly in the soul of Tieck's professor. Tieck's successors in the "novelle" would undoubtedly have considered this metamorphosis of the bookworm the most alluring phase of the subject.

*Der Alte vom Berge* (1828) is characteristic in introducing as its protagonist one of those "queer birds" who are as numerous in the "novellen" as in Jean Paul's novels and in the narratives of such successors as Raabe and Keller. In this case he is a man who, professing theoretical misanthropy and leading the life of a recluse, is in reality a very warm-blooded philanthropist. Blessed with wealth, he gives large sums for factories and human betterment. But he dies before he can make a will to prevent his fortune from coming into the possession of relatives who he thinks are frivolous and wasteful. As frequently in the "novellen," however, God disposes more wisely than man proposes. What was looked upon as a misfortune turns out a blessing in disguise, for, as the sequel proves, the money gets into the right hands after all. While the plot is clever, the motivation, as usual, leaves much to be desired.

On April 3, 1828, Tieck wrote to the publisher Max that no work had caused him more trouble and been so much delayed as *Der Alte vom Berge.* While he had begun it "with pleasure" (mit Freude), he was soon interrupted by illness and other distractions. Max preferred it to *Der Aufruhr in den Cevennen,* Tieck not. An English translation appeared in 1831, a French version in 1833. A new French translation, by Bournac and Hella, appeared in 1931.

One of the brightest, most humorous and most entertaining of the "novellen" is *Das Zauberschloss* (1829), a parody of E. T. A. Hoffmann's spook stories and Müllner's "fate dramas," also a burlesque of contemporary bluestockings and their affected writings. A Herr von Freimund, who wishes to marry his daughter to an elderly "Landrat," resolves to celebrate the betrothal in Schloss Graupenheim, an old castle which he has just purchased and which, as popular tradition has it, is haunted. Two friends of the family precede the rest to make the necessary preparations. On the way they meet a poetess, who has composed verse in honor of the occasion. Only with difficulty is she prevented from reading it and other effusions to them *in extenso.* Arriving at the castle, they find it locked. Then a terrific shower surprises them, and they are quite marooned. To make matters worse, the deaf gardener takes them for burglars. Finally the rest of the party arrive. But the fiancé is missing, and worse, the commissary wagon fails to come. Potatoes are the only available fare. There is but one small lamp, which is accidentally overturned. Mysterious noises, as well as other terrifying circumstances practically convince the frightened assemblage that the castle is really haunted. To cap the climax, the bride's horses shy and run away with her into the black night. Her aged fiancé, a belated arrival, is

less perturbed by this than by his hunger. When the bride returns the next day as the happy wife of her real lover, a young army captain, it becomes clear that the runaway was merely part of a scheme devised by the captain's father, an old friend of Herr von Freimund.

To his brother Tieck described *Das Zauberschloss* aptly as "ein Spass, wo ich mir den Spass gemacht, viel Spass aus einem nichts zu entwickeln." Next to *Die Gesellschaft auf dem Lande* it was A. W. Schlegel's favorite.

Into this jovial "novelle" Tieck has woven another little tale, *Die wilde Engläderin,* which is a masterpiece of realistic fiction. It is read by one of the characters to prevent the poetess from presenting her poetry. The plot relates how a coy, prudish girl devotes herself to astronomy and mathematics, but spurns love and a noble, wealthy lover until after he has accidentally seen her partially nude as she dismounted from her horse. This twenty-page story on the theme of a woman's chastity (similar in motif to Hebbel's drama *Gyges und sein Ring*) is done very delicately and has a well managed turning point. The development of the girl is described with psychological finesse, yet with grace and naturalness. It would be prudish to charge Tieck with impropriety in his mode of treatment. A comparison of the egregiously few piquant incidents found in his later writings— such episodes occur in *Däumchen, Die Vogelscheuche, Der junge Tischlermeister* and *Eigensinn und Laune*—with those in almost any present-day novelist, shows how intent he was to spare his readers' blushes and how closely allied to that spirit which developed into the Victorian tradition.

The feverish search for contacts with the supernatural world, characteristic of Tieck's day, is exposed in *Die Wundersüchtigen* (1829). The career of Cagliostro and the activities of the Rosicruceans and Illuminati at the end of the eighteenth century, attacked by Goethe in *Der Grosskophta,* had furnished crass illustrations of how fanatics, deceivers and deceived, working hand in hand, resorted to cunning means of cheating a gullible public, who craved for some form of supernaturalism which the Age of Reason had tabooed. Tieck looks upon this rage for miracles as though it were a social or moral disease. Animal magnetism and somnambulism are the particular targets of his attack. Two types of "wonder workers" are presented, Feliciano, an unconscionable Cagliostro, and Sangerheim, a more principled imposter. In practice one is as pernicious as the other.

His moral purpose in writing this tale, which we distinguish from such a "novelle" as *Das Zauberschloss* by its stern tone and the absence of humor, is a variation of his favorite doctrine: That miracles *do* exist, but that they are not as crass and tawdry as those spurious ones of the professional mongers. Real miracles, he finds, are marked by divine benevolence and occur in the broad daylight of routinary life. And since they proceed from God, it behooves man neither to construct systems upon them nor to draw conclusions therefrom.

Such a "novelle" as *Die Wundersüchtigen* can have little more than antiquarian interest today. But in its time it was praised as an opportune document and considered superior to Goethe's drama in effectiveness. An English writer in the *Foreign Quarterly Review,* after discussing the "novellen" in general and this one in particular, assures his readers "that with respect to purity of style, moral tendency and philosophic truth, no more estimable works can be found in the whole range of German literature."

Though not published until late in 1830, ***Der wiederkehrende griechische Kaiser*** was begun in 1829 and finished before July, 1830, as Tieck's letters to Brockhaus show. It is a long historical "novelle," originally planned as a drama, a sort of exposé of the machinations of politicians and statesmen. The scene is laid in Ghent in 1202 during the fourth crusade; the plot, dealing with a pretender, is of the type of Schiller's *Demetrius.* Johanna rules as regent of Flanders while her father, Count Balduin, is absent in the Holy Land. There he acquires the Greek imperial crown but dies soon after. When word of his death reaches Flanders, trouble begins to brew. Most of it is caused by two intriguing grandees, each of whom plots to force Johanna to marry his son. One of the factions, to thwart the other, spreads the rumor that Balduin is still alive and trumps up an imposter who claims to be the emperor. The king of France appears as the *deus ex machina.* Through him the pretender is unmasked and the warring factions are brought to rest. He also effects the recognition of Ferdinand, a hitherto obscure kinsman of Balduin who had himself lived in ignorance of his lineage. Ferdinand loves Johanna, who requites his affection, and all ends well.

Tieck's contemporaries regarded the "novelle" highly. One reviewer praised the masterly portrayal of the historical background, the rich variety of characters, the colorful individual scenes and the genuinely poetic conception. Another deemed his characters incomparable, his scenes very lively and his humor in a class by himself. Laube claimed that the tale converted him definitively to realism. But the present-day reader is disappointed by the work. He finds a mass of irrelevant detail and great prolixity. The background seems vague, the characters untrue to life, the speeches long-winded and tiresome, and the foolery of the jester trite. There are many indications that the subject matter was quite alien to Tieck's talent.

As an historical "novelle," however, ***Der wiederkehrende griechische Kaiser*** shows certain improvements over ***Dichterleben*** and ***Der Aufruhr in den Cevennen.*** Above all, it contains more frequent realistic touches. There is also a noticeable effort on Tieck's part to individualize the characters more sharply and to achieve plastic effects. This applies particularly to the figures of the two grandees, who are well contrasted. No doubt he was gradually learning a useful lesson from Scott.

## Gordon Birrell (essay date 1979)

SOURCE: "Split Terrain: Space in the *Märchen* of Tieck," in *The Boundless Present: Space and Time in the Literary Fairy Tales of Novalis and Tieck,* The University of North Carolina Press, 1979, pp. 39-62.

*[In the following excerpt, Birrell explores how Tieck's use of spatial and temporal space is related to thematic and structural qualities of* Der blonde Eckbert.*]*

### *Der blonde Eckbert*

In contrast to Novalis's tales, which are intellectually engaging but rather short on emotional appeal, the *Märchen* of Ludwig Tieck speak directly to the feelings and senses. ***Der blonde Eckbert,*** for instance, is so lyrically evocative that some critics have been inclined to interpret it more as poetry than as prose, writing off the plot as inconsequential and meaningless. While Novalis sublimated his intense emotional energies into creations of exquisite refinement, the young Tieck tended to let himself go, turning out works which sometimes reflect all too clearly the neurotic preoccupations of their creator. The two tales under consideration here, ***Der blonde Eckbert*** and ***Der Runenberg,*** while easily the best that Tieck produced in the genre, are divergent enough in quality to give some indication of the unevenness of Tieck's work. As a freelance writer, of course, he was dependent on sheer volume of output, rather than artistic excellence, for a livelihood. Also, the partisan encouragement that he as the first official practitioner of literary Romanticism received from the Schlegels may well have blunted his sense of fastidiousness, never very strong to begin with. Whatever may be said for or against the Schlegels' influence, however, it was ***Der blonde Eckbert*** (1796) that first drew their enthusiastic attention to Tieck. By almost any standard, this brief, uncanny tale remains a masterpiece of narrative fiction, surely one of the finest pieces of writing to emerge from Early Romanticism.

At first glance, ***Der blonde Eckbert,*** which chronicles the gradual disintegration of a troubled mind, seems so fundamentally different from Novalis's tales that there is almost no common ground for a comparison. One of the advantages of an analysis of spatial and temporal organization, however, is that it offers a more abstract basis for comparison than an analysis of thematic material in the conventional sense. As it turns out, both ***Eckbert*** and the Novalis *Märchen* share a most crucial structural feature. In all of them, space is split into a polar configuration that appears as the juxtaposition of two internal spaces. In ***Eckbert,*** precisely as in "Atlantis," a house in the woods confronts a castle. The two spatial foci serve as headquarters for opposing forces. But although the house and castle in Novalis's tale both represented incomplete, one-dimensional entities in need of—and in search of—synthesis, the confrontation in ***Der blonde Eckbert*** is between a state of utopian perfection and a state of dire inadequacy, and relations between the two realms are anything but pleasant.

The opening pages of ***Der blonde Eckbert*** are full of hints of trouble at Eckbert's and Bertha's castle. The lonely, secluded location of the little fortress; the orderly, austere, childless existence of the couple; their lack of guests and friends; Eckbert's bent toward melancholy: all of these details point to a state of withdrawal, a defensively private existence, a life pared back to the barest minimum of joy and warmth. One senses immediately the presence of an uncomfortable secret behind all this privacy. One evening Eckbert invites his only close friend, Philipp Walther, to spend the night at the castle, and in the intimate glow of the fireside, Bertha relates the strange story of her childhood.

On this particular evening, the isolation of the castle from the outside world seems more pronounced than ever:

> Es war schon im Herbst, als Eckbert an einem neblichten Abend mit seinem Freunde und seinem Weibe Bertha um das Feuer eines Kamines sass. Die Flamme warf einen hellen Schein durch das Gemach und spielte oben an der Decke, die Nacht sah schwarz zu den Fenstern herein, und die Bäume schüttelten sich vor nasser Kälte. . . . Nun ward Wein und die Abendmahlzeit hereingebracht, das Feuer durch Holz vermehrt, und das Gespräch der Freunde heitrer und vertraulicher. . . . Es war jetzt gerade Mitternacht, der Mond sah abwechselnd durch die vorüberflatternden Wolken.

In almost every respect, the interior scene represents an antithesis to the external world. The castle room is warm and cozy while the night outside is wet and cold. The room is bright with the cheery blaze of the fire while the external world is only sporadically illuminated by the moon. Moreover, in contrast to the more or less stationary group around the hearth, the natural world outside is constantly in motion, an indefinite landscape of trees and clouds moving in the wind and in the eerie interplay of light and darkness. This nature is full of eyes which peer malignantly into the castle as if to keep its inhabitants under constant surveillance and to observe the revelation, at last, of Bertha's dreadful secret. To judge from the opening scene, then, Eckbert's castle represents a defensive and rather vulnerable little stronghold of internal space surrounded by the hostile external space of nature.

The second spatial focal point of the tale is the old woman's hut in the forest, where Bertha spends six years of her childhood. She first views the hut from the top of a hill: "Wir stiegen nun einen Hügel hinan, der mit Birken bepflanzt war, von oben sah man in ein grünes Tal voller Birken hinein, und unten mitten in den Bäumen lag eine kleine Hütte." Like Eckbert's castle, the hut is surrounded by, and indeed even engulfed in, the world of nature; but there the similarity ends. If the castle represented a complete disjunction of inside and outside space, the interior of the hut is coordinated with the forest outside in a most remarkable way. Bertha's description of her first night in the hut makes the nature of this correspondence clear:

> Ich blieb nicht lange munter, ich war halb betäubt, aber in der Nacht wachte ich einigemal auf, und dann hörte ich die Alte husten und mit dem Hunde sprechen, und den Vogel dazwishen, der im Traum zu sein schien, und immer nur einzelne Worte von seinem Liede sang. Das machte mit den Birken, die vor dem Fenster rauschten, und mit dem Gesang einer entfernten Nachtigall ein so

> wunderbares Gemisch, daß es mir immer nicht war, als sei ich erwacht, sondern als fiele ich nur in einen andern noch seltsamern Traum.

In this initial impression, inside and outside are conjoined by sound, as the two birds sing together and the coughing of the old woman mingles with the rustling of the birches. The correspondence also extends to a visual level. The ever-changing colors of the bird's feathers and the ceaseless mobility of the old woman's face find their counterpart outside in the shimmering leaves of the birch trees. Finally, after Bertha has adjusted herself to the routine at the hut, a significant daily pattern is established: the bird sings in his cage, Bertha spins away in the hut, and the birches rustle and shimmer in the valley outside. The image that emerges is one of concentric circles of complementary activity, activity which fills time with color and sound but does not lead to change or any sense of temporal progression. The inside of the hut is totally integrated with the outside; each sphere of activity is self-sufficient but coordinated harmoniously with the others. Here again we find a kind of boundless presence, in which near and far are nothing more than variations on a single theme, and in which space (representing diversity) merely affirms the essential spacelessness of unified existence. It is worth noting that Bertha herself is not at the center of this spatial scheme. The innermost circle is occupied by the magic bird in his cage, who may be taken to represent the creative heart of nature. Thus it is appropriate that Bertha's later crimes are directed primarily toward the bird: she not only displaces it from its central location in order to utilize its productivity for her own gain, but later strangles it in a paroxysm of guilt and fear.

In comparison with the conclusions of Novalis's tales, there is something rather modest and domesticated about Tieck's utopia. The notion of completion and self-fulfillment within the confines of one's own snug little circle is strongly reminiscent of Classicism, even *Biedermeier*. At the heart of this eminently Romantic tale are unmistakable signs of the cozy conservatism that Tieck was to adopt as his personal and literary style a decade or so later.

By the time Bertha has finished her tale of betrayal and murder, the implications of the discrepancy between inside and outside space at Eckbert's castle have become fairly evident. The castle is a spatial image of self-protective guilt, a retreat from the existential and moral necessity of meaningful interaction between man and man, and between man and nature. Castle and hut thus function as spatial manifestations of one of the most important conflicts in the tale: on the one hand, the impulse toward independence, narcissism, isolation, and repression of guilt; on the other, the need for openness and integration.

Secondary literature is sharply divided on the problem of the ultimate significance of *Der blonde Eckbert*. One well-defended view argues that the tale revolves around moral issues such as transgression, unatoned guilt, and retribution. On the other side, an equally convinced group of critics contends that ethical considerations are irrelevant in the overall context of the tale, and that Eckbert and

Bertha, guilty or not, fall victim to an irrationally vindictive, a demonic force residing in nature. The fact that critical opinion has taken such divergent directions suggests certain tensions in the tale itself, and I would argue that *Der blonde Eckbert* does in fact accommodate *both* readings. Critics who espouse the second interpretation usually focus their attention on Eckbert's horrifying epiphany in the concluding episode. The revelations voiced there by the old woman, they maintain, retroactively invalidate any interpretation of the tale in moral terms. Nevertheless, the ethical problems that are raised in the preceding twenty-four pages of the text are simply too prominent, and too insistent, to be dismissed out of hand as irrelevant. Whether or not Eckbert's final fate is sealed by a demonic or inscrutable force, there is no denying that he has played an active role in his own destruction.

Because the spatial scheme of the tale generally supports an ethical reading, this [essay] will take up the line of interpretation advanced by the first group of critics. . . .

While Valentine C. Hubbs could, as late as 1956, defend Eckbert as the innocent victim of Bertha's transgressions [in "Tieck, Eckbert und das kollektive Unbewußte"], later studies have agreed that Eckbert is no less culpable than his sister. There are indications that he shared Bertha's greed for the jewels and married her at least partly for her money. He says, for instance, to Walther: "Ich hatte kein Vermögen, aber durch ihre Liebe kam ich in diesen Wohlstand." And he murders Walther with the same impulsiveness with which Bertha murdered the bird. More important, however, are his union with Bertha and his friendship with Walther, which point to a deeper source of guilt. By marrying—not entirely unwittingly—his own half-sister and by choosing as his best friend a man in whom he found "approximately the kind of thinking to which he himself was most devoted," Eckbert reveals a narcissistic need to surround himself with people who reflect his own image. Bertha and Walther do not function as total human beings for him, but are reduced to mirrors that fortify him in his isolation. Thus as his mind begins to collapse, he wonders whether Bertha had ever even existed: "Jetzt war es um das Bewußtsein, um die Sinne Eckberts geschehn; er konnte sich nicht aus dem Rätsel herausfinden, ob er jetzt träume, oder ehemals von einem Weibe Bertha geträumt habe."

It would be wrong, however, to assume that Eckbert is fully conscious of his narcissistic impulses. Not until the cataclysmic revelations of the old woman at the conclusion is he aware of the terrible loneliness of his existence. There are signs that the marriage with Bertha has been preying on his conscience: his occasional moodiness; his hasty assurance to Walther that "unsere Verbindung hat uns bis jetzt noch keinen Augenblick gereut"; and his anguished cry at the conclusion, "Warum habe ich diesen schrecklichen Gedanken immer geahndet?" When he becomes conscious of the extent to which he has been dominated by the drive toward selfishness and isolation, he perishes in anguish. One of the truly modern, and at the same time deeply pessimistic, premises of *Der blonde Eckbert* is that the impulse toward community and integration, as well as the impulse toward self-glorification, independence, and detachment, are both imbedded in the unconscious mind. Bertha's description of her internal struggle before leaving the old woman's hut is most telling: "Es war mir eng und bedrängt zu Sinne, ich wünschte wieder dazubleiben, und doch war mir der Gedanke widerwärtig; es war ein seltsamer Kampf in meiner Seele, wie ein Streiten von *zwei widerspenstigen Geistern* in mir" (emphasis added). In contrast, the conscious mind proves to be tragically impotent in times of crisis. The most important actions in the tale are carried out without the conscious control of the characters. Bertha, for instance, departs from her parents' house propelled by blind need: "Als der Tag graute, stand ich auf und eröffnete, fast ohne daß ich es wußte, die Tür unsrer kleinen Hütte. Ich stand auf dem freien Felde, bald darauf war ich in einem Walde." In a similar fashion, Eckbert loses command of his actions when he murders Walther: "Plötzlich sah er sich etwas in der Ferne bewegen, es war Walther, der Moos von den Bäumen sammelte; ohne zu wissen, was er tat, legte er an, Walther sah sich um, und drohte mit einer stummen Gebärde, aber indem flog der Bolzen ab, und Walther stürzte nieder."

Not only is the conscious mind unable to superintend the powerful impulses emanating from the subliminal self, but to a certain extent it seems actually to be directed by the subconscious. In contrast to the wonderful interplay of order and disorder that characterized the old woman's hut, Eckbert's castle seems to be a model of rational control: "Nur selten wurde Eckbert von Gästen besucht, und wenn es auch geschah, so wurde ihretwegen fast nichts in dem gewöhnlichen Gange des Lebens geändert, die Mässigkeit wohnte dort, und die Sparsamkeit selbst schien alles anzuordnen." The stable and rather Spartan regime at Eckbert's castle serves to put the lid on emotions that, once released, could engulf the loveless couple in guilt and despair; it fortifies Eckbert and Bertha in their independence and isolation. The conscious mind with its loyalty to order and control thus operates—unwittingly, of course—in the service of a corrupt subconscious. Bertha herself points out the connection between conscious awareness and guilt midway through her story: "Ich war jetzt vierzehn Jahr alt, und es ist ein Unglück für den Menschen, daß er seinen Verstand nur darum bekömmt, um die Unschuld seiner Seele zu verlieren." Those critics who have been quick to blame the "demonic forces" of nature and/or the old woman for Eckbert's and Bertha's downfall overlook the very real presence of demonic impulses *within* Eckbert and Bertha, impulses that effectively sabotage every attempt to breach the walls of loneliness and mistrust.

What follows in the tale proper (as opposed to Bertha's narrative) is a systematic destruction of the sanctuary of repressed guilt that Eckbert and Bertha have established. The agents of destruction are Walther, Hugo, and the old woman herself, all representatives of the world of nature, which in turn embodies an absolute and pitiless moral law. If in Novalis's tales Nature was willing and eager to proceed hand in hand with Mind toward mutual perfection, Tieck presents what might be termed Old Testament pantheism: the supernatural force that manifests itself in this nature (and through the old woman) has the judgmental authority to reward the childlike and selfless and to deal out a terrible punishment to the wicked. Hyazinth's initial withdrawal from nature marks the beginning of his journey toward reconciliation on a higher and total level. In *Eckbert,* the crime of withdrawal provokes a relentless persecution from the external world.

> *Der blonde Eckbert* . . . **remains a masterpiece of narrative fiction, surely one of the finest pieces of writing to emerge from Early Romanticism.**
>
> *—Gordon Birrell*

In spatial terms, the primary focus of attack is, predictably enough, the discrepancy between inside and outside which characterizes Eckbert's castle. The strategy which the external world adopts to puncture Eckbert's and Bertha's insular existence displays the intricacy of a carefully planned field campaign in psychological warfare. There are at least four distinct maneuvers. First, the state of isolation must be made more and more uncomfortable, thereby (secondly) forcing Eckbert and Bertha into a confession. Thirdly, if either one of them is so hapless as to annual the effect of the confession by reverting to suspicion and mistrust, then their suspicions are to be mercilessly confirmed. Finally, if sanity has operated in the service of isolation, it must be destroyed.

The first step is at work on the night of Walther's visit to the castle. As we have noted, the outside world on this particular evening seems more than usually agitated and menacing. Bertha's confession, which she relates at Eckbert's behest, would appear to be a response to the threatening countenance of the external world, an attempt to fortify themselves by drawing Walther into the circle: "Es gibt Stunden, in denen es den Menschen ängstigt, wenn er vor seinem Freunde ein Geheimnis haben soll, was er bis dahin oft mit vieler Sorgfalt verborgen hat, die Seele fühlt dann einen unwiderstehlichen Trieb, sich ganz mitzuteilen, dem Freunde auch das Innerste aufzuschliessen, damit er um so mehr unser Freund werde." In spite of the rather conspiratorial atmosphere in which it is presented, Bertha's story has the earmarks of a true confession. It represents a movement outward, an attempt at communication and responsibility, an act of humility and contrition. By the time Bertha has finished her tale, however, Eckbert's negative, secretive side has begun to reassert itself, and he hurriedly throws in a defensive lie that severely compromises any redemptive effect the confession may have had: "Unsere Verbindung hat uns bis jetzt noch keinen Augenblick gereut." It is significant that Walther's mention of the dog's name—his seemingly offhand but devastating form of retribution—*follows* Eckbert's initial act of bad faith. The comment that Bertha makes after

Eckbert's remark (and before Walther's parting shot) is also of interest: "Aber über unser Schwatzen ist es schon tief in die Nacht geworden." It seems more than a little incongruous that she should use the word *Schwatzen* to describe a lengthy confession of betrayal and murder. Through her choice of words she makes light of something that is extremely serious, thereby departing from her former attitude of remorse and penitence.

After the other two have retired for the night, Eckbert paces back and forth, animated by a deepening sense of mistrust toward Walther: "Ist der Mensch nicht ein Tor? . . . Ich bin erst die Veranlassung, daß meine Frau ihre Geschichte erzählt, und jetzt gereut mich diese Vertraulichkeit!—Wird er sie nicht mißbrauchen? Wird er sie nicht andern mitteilen? Wird er nicht vielleicht, denn das ist die Natur des Menschen, eine unselige Habsucht nach unsern Edelgesteinen empfinden, und deswegen Plane anlegen und sich verstellen?" The positive impulse toward confession is followed, then, by the negative impulse toward suspicion, withdrawal, and greed. The effect of this night in the castle is to liberate both sides of Eckbert's psyche and to bring the internal ambivalence to a head. Significantly, as the emotional forces within him are unleashed, Eckbert becomes spatially mobile. From the time Bertha's confession has concluded to the end of the tale, he is constantly in motion: "Auch Walther legte sich schlafen, nur Eckbert ging noch unruhig im Saale auf und ab. . . . In einem abgelegenen Gemache ging er in unbeschreiblicher Unruhe auf und ab. . . . Wie ein unruhiger Geist eilte er jetzt von Gemach zu Gemach, kein Gedanke hielt ihm stand, er verfiel von entsetzlichen Vorstellungen auf noch entsetzlichere." Eckbert's desperate pacing back and forth is a reflection of the increasing lack of comfort which the internal space of his castle affords him. Soon, he who otherwise was "only rarely seen outside the walls of his castle," is driven out into the external world. The last pages of the tale are characterized, in spatial terms, by Eckbert's increasingly hysterical oscillation between outside and inside space, between interaction and retreat (neither of which provides any enduring solace or satisfaction), as the two conflicting aspects of his subconscious are more and more intensely mobilized. The dynamics of this process are worth examining in some detail. After Bertha reveals that Walther's inexplicable knowledge of the dog's name is responsible for her illness, Eckbert retreats to a remote room in the recesses of the castle. Finding no peace there, he bursts out of the castle full of murderous intent of which, as we have seen, he is barely conscious. He finds Walther and kills him, far out in the hostile external space of the forest: "Es war ein rauher stürmischer Wintertag. . . . Er hatte einen großen Weg zu machen, denn er war weit hinein in die Wälder verirrt." Then he flees—or, more precisely, is mindlessly propelled—back to the castle: "[Es] trieb ihn ein Schauder nach seiner Burg zurück." Soon the loneliness of his existence becomes unbearable, and he emerges again from the castle in search of companionship. In a rather grim parallel to Fabel's movements in the Klingsohr tale, each successive excursion into the external world takes Eckbert further away from the seemingly protective shelter of his castle. He begins to take part in social functions in the nearby city and meets a young knight named Hugo, who makes a special point of befriending Eckbert. This latest experiment in human communication cluminates again in a confession, as Eckbert reveals his dreadful secret to Hugo while the two are "out on a lonely ride" (external space). Once more, however, the confession backfires. Back in a hall in the city (an internal space), Eckbert's negative side reasserts itself, and he begins to mistrust Hugo. To his horror, he sees his suspicions affirmed, as Hugo assumes Walther's features. Half mad with fear, he races out into the night and returns to his castle.

The former citadel of moderation and rational control is by this time no longer capable of providing even the slightest comfort for his deranged mind. Isolation is unberable, communication impossible; the two opposing directions of Eckbert's tormented psyche have *both* been defeated, and by each other. Under the illusion that he will be able to "order his thoughts again," he sets out in blind flight. Having rejected his castle once and for all, however, he delivers himself into the clutches of the external world and is drawn, with terrible consistency, directly toward the opposite spatial pole, the old woman's valley, the site of the lost paradise. When Eckbert hears the bird and the dog, the last underpinnings of his sanity give way. He is, however, granted one last moment of lucidity. The old woman appears and delivers with brutal directness the insight that Eckbert has avoided all of his married life: that Bertha is his own half-sister. Having provided Eckbert with three test situations (Walther, Hugo, the peasant), three opportunities for interaction, all of which he has failed, the old woman herself must now provide him with the final and annihilating confession which he would not or could not bring himself to make. There is a cruel irony in the fact that his one interaction of pure communication—the only such interaction that Eckbert has ever known—must inevitably destroy him. As his last mental defences fall, the internal void which he has sheltered and never admitted becomes his only reality. Unable to perceive space at all, he hears only crisscrossing voices and sounds: "Eckbert lag wahnsinnig und verscheidend auf dem Boden; dumpf und verworren hörte er die Alte sprechen, den Hund bellen, und den Vogel sein Lied wiederholen."

The spatial indefiniteness that Eckbert experiences at his death is a far cry from the wondrous synthesis of space and spacelessness at the conclusions of Novalis's tales. There is no fusion of former polarities here, no participation of the entire community or cosmos. Eckbert's fate is agonizingly private, the culmination of a life characterized by withdrawal and the repeated failure to establish true contact with other human beings. Bertha's childhood existence in the old woman's valley, with its coordination of inside and outside space, order and disorder, is as close as Tieck ever came to a depiction of utopia. The whole movement of the tale is *away* from this state of synthesis. Initially, internal and external space are severed in the situation at Eckbert's castle. Then, gradually, external space comes to predominate exclusively. In the final scenes, Eckbert is utterly exposed to the open landscape. Although he has apparently returned to the old woman's valley, there

is, appropriately, no further mention of the cozy internal space of her hut.

In comparing Tieck's employment of space with that of Novalis, it is useful to examine Bertha's journey to the old woman's valley. Like Hyazinth, Bertha runs away from her home village as fast as her legs will take her. While Hyazinth was obsessed with the desire to find the "Mother of All Things," however, Bertha's only thought is escape, headlong flight from the intolerable situation at her parents' house. Despite their differing motivations, the two figures traverse landscapes that are all but identical. As was the case with Hyazinth, Bertha's journey takes her through forests and mountains, which become increasingly wild and desolate. One morning she wakes up to find herself in a landscape that, like Hyazinth's deserts, appears to be a monstrous void: "Als ich aber oben stand, war alles, so weit nur mein Auge reichte, ebenso, wie um mich her, alles war mit einem neblichten Dufte überzogen, der Tag war grau und trübe, und keinen Baum, keine Wiese, selbst kein Gebüsch konnte mein Auge erspähn, einzelne Sträucher ausgenommen, die einsam und betrübt in engen Felsenritzen emporgeschossen waren."

For both characters, the experience of an utterly barren landscape represents a critical turning point in their development. The spatial indefiniteness of the desert reflected a gradual settling of Hyazinth's aggressive drive, a clearing of all fragmentary scraps of knowledge from his mind, and the beginning of his facility to experience nature in its totality. Bertha's response to the barren landscape around her is rather more specific: "Es ist unbeschreiblich, welche Sehnsucht ich empfand, nur eines Menschen ansichtig zu werden, wäre es auch, daß ich mich vor ihm hätte fürchten müssen." Having tasted the anguish of absolute isolation, Bertha is prepared to establish human contact again, no matter what the consequences. As if to reward her for her inner conversion, the natural world gradually becomes much more hospitable than she has ever known it to be: "Gegen Abend schien die Gegend umher etwas freundlicher zu werden, meine Gedanken, meine Wünsche lebten wieder auf, die Lust zum Leben erwachte in allen meinen Adern. . . . Ich sah Wälder und Wiesen mit fernen angenehmen Bergen wieder vor mir liegen. Mir war, als wenn ich aus der Hölle in ein Paradies getreten wäre." The mountains, once a source of terror, are now suddenly pleasant. Stopping by a brook, she scoops up a drink—like Hyazinth's drink from the spring, the action suggests a sacrament with nature—and in that very moment hears the approach of the old woman. After a supper of bread and wine (a second sacrament), the old woman leads Bertha further away from the wilderness, and as the two emerge from the forest, a magnificent panorama opens before them in the sunset: "Ich werde den Anblick und die Empfindung dieses Abends nie vergessen. In das sanfteste Rot und Gold war alles verschmolzen, die Bäume standen mit ihren Wipfeln in der Abendröte, und über den Feldern lag der entzückende Schein, die Wälder und die Blätter der Bäume standen still, der reine Himmel sah aus wie ein aufgeschlossenes Paradies, und das Rieseln der Quellen und von Zeit zu Zeit das Flüstern der Bäume tönte durch die heitre Stille wie in wehmütiger Freude."

In the corresponding phases of Hyazinth's journey, the landscape is described in general as becoming fuller, brighter, more substantial, while a discrete number of specific details are reintroduced. Significantly enough, Tieck's landscape also appears as a marvelous mixture of definite and indefinite space. One's first impression is not of an articulated landscape at all, but of a wash of color ("In das sanfteste Rot und Gold war alles verschmolzen"), followed by a few details ("die Bäume mit ihren Wipfeln," "die Felder") in an indefinite setting of light ("die Abendröte," "der entzückende Schein"). One sees the vast open space of the sky and notes at the same time such an intimate detail as the leaves of the trees. The fusion of determined and nondetermined space is reinforced by similar muted combinations of sound and silence, motion and rest, and various moods (as in the oxymoron "wehmütige Freude"). In every respect, the panorama that Bertha views here is a herald of the life which she is about to lead at the old woman's hut; she too, at her own level and in her own sphere, is to integrate herself into this landscape. It is most significant, in light of the central ethical conflict of the tale, that her response to this natural spectacle is one of *selfless* awe and total immersion: "Ich vergass mich und meine Führerin, mein Geist und meine Augen schwärmten nur zwischen den goldnen Wolken."

There is, however, an important distinction in the way Novalis and Tieck use space in these passages. In "Hyazinth und Rosenblüte," the external landscape consistently corresponded to the internal situation in Hyazinth's mind; operating in unison, mind and nature developed together toward perfection. In the description of Bertha's journey, on the other hand, the natural world seems to be all but autonomous. Rather than accompanying Bertha's internal development, it directs it. The whole sequence of landscapes during her journey serves to prepare her for entrance into the old woman's valley. Bertha is transformed from an awkward, dreamstruck child to a person who is willing—and able—to take part in a community. The natural world has a decidedly pedagogical function, educating Bertha to the horrors of loneliness and rewarding her after she has learned her lesson. Unlike "Hyazinth und Rosenblüte," where nature and mind were peers, mutually dependent on each other, nature here is of a higher order than mind. As we noted earlier, the natural world in *Der blonde Eckbert* functions as the executor of an absolute moral law, whose prime commandment is an extension of Kant's categorical imperative to all of nature as well as humanity: treat each living creature not as a means, but as an end in himself. It is precisely this commandment which Eckbert and Bertha repeatedly break, in their greedy and selfish dealings with the old woman, the bird, and themselves. Neither the conscious nor the unconscious mind is able to mount any kind of effective defense against the primal force that resides in nature. It is through the generosity of the natural world and the responsiveness of her still innocent soul that Bertha is permitted to participate in the harmonious community at the old woman's valley. Eckbert's castle, on the other hand, is an affront to the moral law of nature, and both Eckbert and Bertha are ultimately driven from its questionable shelter.

From the perspective of the old woman, and from the traditional standpoint of Western ethics, Eckbert and Bertha are clearly culpable, and the retribution visited on them is appropriate and just. But this ethical system presupposes, as a fundamental and necessary condition, the freedom to choose between good and evil. Eckbert and Bertha do not enjoy such freedom. Throughout the tale they are manipulated by subconscious impulses that make a mockery of free will and unclouded moral choice. On this point the ethical interpretation of *Der blonde Eckbert* founders. While an absolute and unconditional moral viewpoint will not hesitate to find Eckbert and Bertha guilty as charged, a psychologically informed reading must consider them more sympathetically and with a certain measure of forbearance—though it can scarcely exonerate them altogether. We may justifiably deplore Eckbert's and Bertha's behavior, and we may even take some satisfaction from Eckbert's final collapse, since his horror and despair are only comprehensible as the reaction of a man who has the stature to regard himself to the end as accountable for his actions. But we cannot applaud the old woman's harsh tactics in bringing Eckbert and Bertha to justice, much less her insistence on exacting the death penalty for human frailty and involuntary evil.

The triumph of external forces over a weak and divided mind in *Der blonde Eckbert* is indicative of Tieck's rather eccentric position in Early Romanticism. Like his close friend Wilhelm Heinrich Wackenroder, Tieck never felt very comfortable with Fichte's and Schelling's conceptions of the mind as an endlessly creative force capable of transcending itself and transforming nature. It may well be said that Tieck experienced the crisis of Romantic subjectivity before he ever joined forces with the Schlegels, Schelling, and Novalis. His philosophical affinity with the leading spirits of the movement was at best a tenuous one. Even the so-called Romantic irony of his *Der gestiefelte Kater* is more a matter of clever mischievousness than a serious attempt to juxtapose the limited and incomplete world of empirical experience with the higher world of abstract thought. While Tieck was willing to acknowledge the attractiveness of Fichtean idealism, he was inclined to regard nature as a more valid source of authority than the mind. Ludwig Wandel, the hero of Tieck's short story, **"Die Freunde"** (1797), experiences a series of dreams which are encapsuled in each other in a manner reminiscent of Fichte's process of reflection. Unlike Hyazinth, however, who travels through the endless chambers of his dream into the "realm of the holiest," Ludwig becomes successively alienated from the external world of love and friendship and enticed into a fantasy world of self-gratification. The caveat that Tieck expresses here is not merely a compromise of his Romantic impulses for the sake of his conservative reading audience. Rather it stems from his conviction, gained from personal experience, that unbridled subjectivity leads to a state of lovelessness and self-indulgence.

In *Der blonde Eckbert,* however, Tieck entertains at least the *possibility* that the mind can rise above itself to create a new utopia. Here we come to the most crucial distinction between Bertha's development and Hyazinth's. Although it is possible to interpret Bertha's life in the valley of birches as a "second paradise," as Janis Gellinek has done [in *"Der blonde Eckbert*: A Tieckian Fall from Paradise"], this paradise must not be equated with Novalis's second Golden Age. To be sure, the synthesis of space and spacelessness as well as unity and diversity corresponds in many respects to the conclusions of Novalis's tales. What is missing in Tieck, however, is the participation of mind in this state of perfection. *Waldeinsamkeit* is, in effect, a second Golden Age scaled down to the dimensions of a child's mind. Nevertheless, it is to serve as a model for the adults Bertha and Eckbert. The naive synthesis of internal and external space that is presented to Bertha as a reward for her innocence and unselfishness must be reachieved on a higher level through an active process of moral will, as an accomplishment of the mature mind. Thus the qualities of openness, integration, and self-fulfillment on one's own level, which Bertha experiences in the old woman's valley, are to be transformed into the ethical categories of responsibility, generosity, repentance, and self-knowledge. The natural world cannot bestow these latter qualities on Eckbert and Bertha. The most it can do is to force them into a position where they must choose for themselves and to punish them if they make the wrong decision. Again, however, we must note that the old woman's tactics, although defensible from an absolute ethical standpoint, are predicated on the erroneous assumption of free moral will in Eckbert and Bertha.

To a certain extent, Eckbert and Bertha are in the same position as Hyazinth in the second phase of Novalis's tale. Alienated from nature and from each other, they lack the ability to free themselves from a perpetual state of inadequacy. Unlike Hyazinth, however, they are incapable of recognizing and acting on the advice of the old woman in the wood, and it is questionable whether their lives could be salvaged even if they *were* to undertake the task of regeneration through confession, repentance, and self-scrutiny. The second Golden Age, in which an original harmony is recreated on a higher level through the activity of the mind, is in Tieck's tale only a remote possibility. While Novalis outlines the methods by which the new perfection is to be achieved, Tieck explores the depths of human fallibility and weakness that make this perfection unattainable.

### Roger Paulin (essay date 1985)

SOURCE: *"Vittoria Accorombona*: The Literary Works of the Later Dresden Years," in *Ludwig Tieck: A Literary Biography,* Clarendon Press, 1985, pp. 304-31.

[*In the following excerpt, Paulin provides a thematic and stylistic analysis of Tieck's later short fiction.*]

There were some works written in Tieck's later years in Dresden which were mere passing reactions to the 'charivari of the times', others a proof that a seasoned practitioner could write a Novelle with his little finger if he needed the money. Sometimes, the chance to write a preface for a friend's work or for one of the many translations he

superintended, gave him the opportunity for extemporized literary criticism, most of it highly readable, much of it very percipient.

From the later 1820s until the 1840s, Tieck lent his name to Friedrich von Uechtritz, or Anton Dietrich, or Eduard von Bülow, or to the memory of his sister or of Adelheid Reinbold; his name was associated with editions, or translations, of *Die Insel Felsenburg, Marcos Obregón* or Cervantes' *Persiles y Sigismunda.* They are a record—though hardly a monument—of his loyalty to friends, his continued assistance to the inexperienced and young—but also of his remarkable ability to produce the well-turned essay, the fireside chat, where he gives away so much of his real literary persona. The essay may often, as with *Die Insel Felsenburg* (he had nothing to do with the actual edition) or the *Novellenbuch,* have little bearing, sometimes almost none at all, on the text. Yet, if we wish to understand Tieck and the theatre, we must go to Bülow's edition of Schröder; for his notions on prose fiction, to the *Novellenbuch* or *Marcos Obregón.* We gain an impression—but little else—of his knowledge of Cervantes from *Persiles* and wish that we could have had more. Brockhaus and Max would, of course, be assured that there was a wealth of material on Shakespeare or Cervantes or the Spanish theatre or the drama (it could be written up at short notice); or that he would edit Lessing's correspondence or August Wilhelm Schlegel's with Goethe, or write his memoirs. It again—we must add—naturally, came to nothing. We must be grateful for the fragments we do have.

But there were other works that Tieck had pondered and mulled over, in some cases, for decades. The Novelle about Shakespeare, *Dichterleben,* can be related to the early vision of *Die Sommernacht*; *Der junge Tischlermeister* has much of the Rossstrasse; the germ of *Vittoria Accorombona* was sown in Göttingen. It seemed appropriate, therefore, that Tieck should enter into the last decade of his creative career with a statement of his position, the reissue of his works in 1828-9: *Ludwig Tieck's Schriften.*

We have already seen some of the background to this edition, that it proceeded from the promptings of both author and publisher. The main considerations were obviously the writer's image, the publisher's profit, and the author's payment. In the case of Tieck and his publishers, it would be difficult to place these in order of priority. Ever since Weigand and Göschen had started the practice as a commercial enterprise in the 1780s, the issue of collected editions had proved satisfactory for both author and publisher alike. The 1820s, with the book trade fully recovered from its Napoleonic uncertainties, were good times commercially and strategically for a Romantic to reissue his works. For not only, as Brockhaus had reminded him, were the 'classics' appearing in large editions, but one would find a Zschokke or a Raupach or a Houwald or a Tromlitz also claiming a brief multi-volume immortality.

Tieck was no stranger to such issues of his works, from the infamous *Sämmtliche Werke* to the *Romantische Dichtungen,* to *Phantasus* and the *Gedichte.* Then there had been the Vienna set of *Sämmtliche Werke* issued by the pirate publisher Leopold Grund. Grund, charlatan though he may have been, produced an edition of some bibliophile pretentions. Above all, the astute bookseller brought all the texts by Tieck on to the market that he thought would sell: many of the larger earlier works, nearly all of the translations and editions, and all the poems.

> Tieck's Novellen are going to be somewhat hit-or-miss affairs: they may be a mere passing reaction to an event or a mood, or they may transcend the historical moment of their origin. One thing is certain: most of them do not stand close analysis as 'models' of their genre.
>
> —*Roger Paulin*

Tieck may have had Grund in mind with his own *Schriften,* but in the event it turned out otherwise. There is next to nothing of the translator or editor, no poems, and, as the edition progressed, no major work like *Vittoria Accorombona.* One may welcome the reissue of juvenilia like *Alla-Moddin* or *Das grüne Band,* but some of the schoolboy's best work remains at this stage unpublished. Works like *Abdallah* and *William Lovell* are heavily reworked and are not the strident texts of the 1790s. The Romantic poet is in the forefront, with *Kaiser Octavianus,* the progress of romance, the kaleidoscopic changes of colour, the symphony of strophes and metres, the conjunction of poetry, love, faith, and playfulness, leading the procession in volume one.

*Sternbald* is as yet missing, pending completion; it will not appear until 1843, and then rather lamely, and in a revised form. Other works, like the *Straussfedern* or *Fortunat,* are put in contexts different from the original. It is all with the aim of bestowing some kind of coherence to an *œuvre* disparate in origin and nature. The prefaces, which several volumes have, are to foster the same impression, and often they contain all that we know of how some works came about—or how it may have seemed to have been. These prefaces, like those to Lenz or Kleist, or like the *Dramaturgische Blätter,* are major statements of aesthetic standards and decorum; but they give a semblance of consistency to the inconsistent or they abstract the Romantic poet from the whole host of interesting areas which make up his life and work. Much—like the famous 'Wendepunkt'—will carry a spurious canonicity which but little suits an author most accommodating and heterdox. As with the prefaces to different friends, Tieck succeeds in creating the impression of the loyal concerned friend, an image of himself which is appealing and convenient, but, alas, not all the truth. Yet the old Romantic magician has spoken with such plausible charm that generations have taken him at his word. In short, **Ludwig Tieck's Schriften,** if the only satisfactory collected edition that we have, are to be treated with great care.

But a writer who is to retain esteem, and stand for many as the representative of his national literature, cannot in 1829 simply sit back and rest on sixteen volumes of collected works, most of them written before 1820. He cannot be content with being a local celebrity. His reputation will rest on his continuing activity, a daunting responsibility. Yet, if there is a moment in Tieck's life when his name seems most secure, then it is probably around 1829; when he can survey the ranks of his past work and find some pleasure in his own development, give an account to the world of himself, when his critical authority has been established, when the first volumes of the new Shakespeare edition are appearing; when a good ten Novellen of the new sort have made his name inseparable from the genre; when two long Novellen, which are in effect novels, **Der Aufruhr in den Cevennen** and **Dichterleben,** show his growing commitment to the large-scale prose work, in a decade when the conventional novel in German seems difficult to write. He has his publishers organized; there is no cause to despair yet of the Dresden theatre. Above all, Goethe is still alive, and one can take comfort in being the one 'whom his countrymen rank only below Goethe'. Once that mighty figure is gone, once—if Tieck really did use the phrase—we are all 'verwaist', orphaned, once one emerges from the shadow into the glare, as the figure on whom both adulators and detractors visit their attentions, the position is different. For Goethe's late work—as we can now see it—can stand and withstand any amount of criticism, any number of campaigns against its 'obscurity' or 'impiety' or 'terseness' (can even transcend hagiography). Tieck's work is not made for this kind of treatment: there is less that is obviously 'great' or 'monumental'; his work has a more subtle consistency. We have, between 1825 and 1841, to pick our way between around thirty Novellen, many of them, alas, of but indifferent quality, but very much part of the Tieck whom we are trying to see as he really was. There is a body of editions, translations, and prefaces, which has never really been allowed to coexist with the Novellen. There are two major novels, **Der junge Tischlermeister** and *Vittoria Accorombona*—the charm of one and the mastery of the other have often not been appreciated, as coming 'too late' to rescue an already sliding reputation. Goethe, on the other hand, can stand secure on one or two late works; there is no real need to draw on, say, his considerable corpus of reviews after 1820, however enhancing they may be. In the case of Tieck, we have to gather everything together, works poetical and critical. His contemporaries did not see it this way; critical studies of his work have seldom done so. It is not enough to concentrate solely on one aspect. When he, for instance, writes Novellen for money, they rarely outlast the metal in which they were paid, even if they can command temporary importance. Tieck was however to come under such attack after 1836, that, by the time the masterpiece of his late maturity, *Vittoria Accorombona,* appeared, his contemporaries, emerging into years of journalistic polemics much tougher than in the 1820s, were largely prevented from seeing what they still had in their midst.

It is not easy to characterize twenty-nine Novellen, written between 1827 and 1841, let alone another four, large enough to be classed as novels, or indeed called that by the author. The Novellen are a very mixed bag; they reflect their author's admission to Brokhaus that he has a 'Musterkarte'—a book of patterns—to hand and can produce a Novelle on any given subject for any given occasion. They are thus going to be somewhat hit-or-miss affairs: they may be a mere passing reaction to an event or a mood, or they may transcend the historical moment of their origin. One thing is certain: most of them do not stand close analysis as 'models' of their genre. The rather dismissive words of a reviewer in *Blackwood's Magazine* in 1837 are not without some truth:

> After glancing back to the long list of Tieck's performances in this department, we in vain endeavour to recollect one scene or one character which has firmly imprinted itself on our minds. We find ourselves in the situation of honest Cassio, after his potation.—'We remember a mass of things, but nothing distinctly.'

Very few get into Heyse's *Novellenschatz* of 1871; they are no use for those for whom the Novelle is a genre represented by formal restraint and stringency, tightened knots and dense story, for those for whom the study of this kind of prose is a hunt-the-slipper for symbols and turning-points and other strictly formal narrative devices. They do not suit the non-historical approach which would see in a series of model interpretations all that needs to be said about a highly complex and slightly wayward genre. In short, for many, Tieck's Novellen are a nuisance. The strict formalists among the historians of the German Novelle approve highly his coining, 'Wendepunkt' (it is actually August Wilhelm Schlegel's), to stand nicely beside 'Begebenheit' or 'Falke' or 'Schwester des Dramas' as pegs on which to hang suitably economical and laconic stories. But his practice baffles them. Either they search, often vainly, for a 'Wendepunkt' where there is none, or, even worse, they declare his Novellen to be spurious. It never pays to seize on a term or a phrase of Tieck's—he is notoriously indifferent to precise aesthetic distinctions and niceties—without, as it were, reading the small print. For the famous idea that the genuine Novelle should contain a turning-point, as formulated in volume eleven of the **Schriften** in 1829, is in itself a problem.

It is, again, a question of the canonical authority of these prefaces as pronouncements; but it is also a matter of noting what the author actually says. Tieck is not speaking of a formal, tectonic device, but of a moment in the story where 'das Wunderbare'—a higher force, a religious awe, an awareness of the transcendent—may intervene and give everyday events a new significance. It can be love, moral sense, or what Tieck calls 'Mährchen'—a feeling of wonder, of the irrational and inexplicable origin of all things, the inaccessibility of the mysteries of life to reason and measure. The Novelle **Das alte Buch und die Reise ins Blaue hinein** of 1835 formulates this credo which never lost its validity for Tieck:

> Das echte Mährchen, so sagte ich ungefähr, erschließt mit seinem Kinderton und dem Spielen mit dem Wunder eine Gegend unsers Gemüthes, in welche die übrige Kunst und Poesie nicht hineinreicht. Unsre ersten

und heiligsten Verhältnisse zur Natur und der unsichtbaren Welt, die Basis unsers Glaubens, die Elemente unsers Erkennens, Geburt und Grab, die Schöpfung um uns her, die Bedürfnisse unsers Lebens, Alles dies ist wie Mährchen und Traum und läßt sich nicht in das auflösen, was wir vernünftig und folgerecht nennen. Darum die Heiligkeit und das Wunderliche, Unbegreifliche aller alten Sagen. Die Schöpfung, die Entstehung des Guten und Bösen, der Fall der Engel, die Erlösung, man nenne, was man will, bei Griechen, Heiden, Juden oder Christen, das Ursprüngliche der Legende sowohl wie unsers nächsten alltäglichen Lebens ist, wenn wir das Wort heilig und ernst nehmen, ein Mährchen. Wer nun durch Erfindung sich auf diesen ersten Standpunkt des Lebens versetzen kann, dem klingt das innerste Gemüth der Menschen entgegen, aller Derer, die sich nicht schon ein einseitiges System von Kunst und Kritik auferbaut haben. Wir werden an unsre räthselhafte Stellung und Bestimmung durch diese erinnert, und zwar in einer lieblichen Gestaltung, in der das Gemüth nicht sogleich jene tiefsinnige Hinweisung erkennt. Alles Geschichtliche, Politische, Historische ist schon, wenn auch edel und groß, ein Abgeleitetes; hier werden schon jene ersten Urbestimmungen der Menschheit als etwas Unerschütterliches, das sich von selbst versteht, vorausgesetzt, als etwas, das keine Verwunderung, keine Untersuchung mehr erregen soll. Dieses blitzende, sehnsüchtige oder kindliche Hinweisen auf die Natur und die frühsten Bedingungen der Existenz geschieht, und so vielleicht am lieblichsten, auf kindliche, spielende Weise, indem sich eine süsse Rührung mit dem Schauer vermählt, der jeden durchzieht, der zum ersten Mal die Alpen oder das Meer erblickt. Es kann aber auch witzig, neckend, geistreich geschehn.

[The true fairy-tale (this was more or less what I said) opens up with its child-like tone and its play with the wondrous, an area of our spirit into which other kinds of art and poetry cannot find their way. Our first, and most sacred, relations with nature and the invisible world, the basis of our faith, the elements of our perception, birth, and grave, the creation around us, the necessities of our life, all this is as fairy-tale and dream and cannot be resolved into what we call rational or consequent. Hence the sacredness and strange mysteriousness of all old romances. The creation, the origin of good and evil, the fall of the angels, redemption, call it what you will, in Greeks, Gentiles, Jews, or Christians, the fresh originality of legend as well as of our closest everyday life, if we take the word in a sacred and serious way, is a fairy-tale. If we can through invention put ourselves back into this first position of life, then the inner spirit of man will waft over to us in sound, the spirit of all those who have not constructed for themselves a one-sided system of art and criticism. They remind us of our mysterious position and end, and in such appealing forms that the mind does not immediately apprehend the deeper meaning behind it. All the events of history and politics, noble and great as they may be, are but derived; but here those first primeval things that man was created for are presupposed as something unshakable, that goes without saying, as something that should no longer elicit wonderment or investigation. When—in the flash of a moment, in longing, or in childlike fashion—we are led to nature and to the earliest circumstances of existence, it happens, perhaps most appealingly, in a child-like, playful way; when we feel sweet emotion come over us mingled with the thrill that runs through us when we first catch sight of the alps or the sea. But it can also be in a witty, teasing, and ingenious fashion.]

It is Romantic vocabulary and a restatement of Romantic values. But it is also related to experience; it is not that art offers 'all ye need to know'. Art gives intimations of the deepest processes of life and death, not by systems and actualities, but by 'Spielén mit dem Wunder', by placing us in that half-way state between waking and dreaming, where we glimpse, fleetingly, an inkling of universal truth. It is only 'religious' in the very broadest sense; it is not Friedrich Schlegel's or Görres' Catholic mysticism; it lacks the, often tortured, Christian message of Brentano or Eichendorff. It is not Hoffmann's or Arnim's surrender to the irrational, demonic, or bizarre. It is naïve and playful, sceptical and worldly-wise, at the same time. It tries to utter mystery, but also to find a consensus of human experience, where those of goodwill and unshackled moral sense may follow.

The notion of 'Wendepunkt', accordingly, has very much to do with the content of a story, a moment of recognition, 'wunderbar und doch natürlich', such as Cervantes' *Novelas ejemplares* contain. And that moment, that 'desengaño', or opening out into the wondrous, is not incompatible with looseness of texture, discursiveness, reflection, or plain garrulity:

> Bizarr, eigensinnig, phantastisch, leicht witzig, geschwätzig und sich ganz in Darstellung auch von Nebensachen verlierend, tragisch wie komisch, tiefsinnig und neckisch, alle diese Farben und Charaktere lässt die ächte Novelle zu, nur wird sie immer jenen sonderbaren auffallenden Wendepunkt haben, der sie von allen andern Gattungen der Erzählung unterscheidet. Aber alle Stände, alle Verhältnisse der neuen Zeit, ihre Bedingungen und Eigenthümlichkeiten sind dem klaren dichterischen Auge gewiß nicht minder zur Poesie und edlen Darstellung geeignet, als es dem Cervantes seine Zeit und Umgebung war, und es ist wohl nur Verwöhnung einiger vorzüglichen Critiker, in der Zeit selbst einen unbedingten Gegensatz vom Poetischen und Unpoetischen anzunehmen.

[Bizarre, self-willed, fantastic, with a touch of wit, loquacious, and getting lost completely in the presentation of irrelevances, tragic as well as comic, serious-minded and teasing, all of these shades and characters can be permitted in the genuine Novelle, only it will always have that strange and striking turning-point that distinguishes it from all other kinds of narrative. But all estates and conditions of modern times, their circumstances and peculiarities are by no means less suited to the clear eye of the poet for poetry and noble presentation, than were for Cervantes his times and surroundings, and it is only the self-indulgence of some of our most prominent critics to see in those times an absolute contradiction between poetic and unpoetic.]

Indeed, this heterogeneousness, this admixture of the romantic and the real, was something on which Tieck's contemporaries were already divided. Those who expected plot, incident, clear happenings, to be sitting on the edge of their chairs as they read, were to be disappointed. Doubtless they read his stories as they appeared singly, and disregarded the preface to his collected works.

No doubt, too, they paid little attention to the highly significant—and much neglected—prefaces written between 1827 and 1828: for the edition of *Marcos Obregón,* for *Die Insel Felsenburg*; these, along with the *Bücherschau* he had contributed to the short-lived *Morgen-Zeitung* of Karl Constantin Kraukling and Friedrich Kind in 1827, tell us many revealing things about the later Tieck's attitude to prose-writing. For he cannot suppress a love of the picaresque, the *roman à tiroir,* with its mixture of plan and improvisation; he throws out, seemingly as an aside, the highly important statement that the novel can, in aesthetic dignity, stand with the epic and the drama. Witnesses are Cervantes and Goethe, but even Scott, Fielding, Le Sage, and Balzac. It is Friedrich Schlegel's emphasis from Jena days, on prose as a medium of 'Poesie'. In those days, Tieck, although translating *Don Quixote,* was not prepared to draw any significant theoretical conclusions from it; and *Sternbald* scarcely lent itself either. Now he can cast his whole authority behind a notion which had once been formulated, two generations earlier, by Friedrich von Blanckenburg, as an early attempt in Germany to establish the legitimacy of prose. Tieck, too, has an indulgent word for the lower echelons; he realizes that works, which produce a sensation in one age, may give rise to modish trivia in the next. If novels become mere 'Fabrikaten', this is because human nature has that side to it which cannot always be gratified by masterpieces. The interrelation of high and low quality is part of the 'Gang der Weltbegebenheiten'. You cannot have 'ächte Dichtung' without base imitation; you cannot appreciate Jean Paul or Scott, or even Cramer or Clauren, without knowing what they owe to the conventions of eighteenth-century fiction. In this, Tieck himself gives us the key to the understanding of so much of his own prose-writing—but also one of the basic tenets for the writing of literary history. He now, after some twenty-five years, gives us the reason why he so venerates Cervantes above all prose-writers—there is also a translation of *Persiles y Sigismunda,* done by Dorothea—and this can tell us quite an amount about Tieck himself: it is that fine balance between Cervantes' loving esteem of his famous hero, and smiling at his weakness; the interrelation of parody and heroism, 'das Alltägliche und Geringe' and 'das Wunderbare'. It is not the 'sentimental' reading of *Don Quixote* which is so typical of European Romanticism: it stands more in the 'ironic' tradition of Fielding and *Wilhelm Meister.* Much of this will be said in the preface which Tieck writes for Bülow's *Novellenbuch* in 1834. There he will offer no definition of the Novelle; indeed it will emerge that there is no strict distinction at all between Novelle and 'Roman'. It seems that the words spoken in the story of 1830, **Das Zauberschloss,** in a moment of agreeable self-parody, could also apply to Tieck's definition of the Novelle: 'ein Titel, der jetzt für alles Mögliche beliebt wird' [a title popularly used today for all sorts of things].

Perhaps more important than all these questions of definition is the tone of Tieck's Novellen. In the preface to the

*Insel Felsenburg* we find words of some dignity and nobility which characterize the best of Tieck's concern in these years, indeed which sum up what the writer had been pursuing for decades:

> Neu sein, und doch alt, fortgehen in der Zeit, und doch nicht der Sklave jeder Thorheit werden, die Weisheit des Bestehenden, Festen, mit dem spielenden Witz des Wandelbaren verknüpfen, diese Widersprüche zu lösen, war die große Aufgabe aller Zeiten

> [To be new, and still old, to progress in time and yet not to be the slave of every folly, to conjoin the wisdom of that which is lasting and permanent with the interplay of wit and the ever-changing, solving these contradictions was the great task of all times]

If, in the light of this statement, we seek the quintessence of Tieck's Novellen, we could say that they address themselves to the needs of an existing, present, identifiable society; that they are concerned with the matters faced by people in their general experience, with a consensus of accumulated wisdom, with friendship and conversation. They are not esoteric, they do not conjur up frenzies of 'Weltschmerz' or visions of a 'Höllenbreughel'. They are not, even if both may have learned from Tieck, Hoffmann, or Edgar Allen Poe; they are not Victor Hugo, whose Gothick Paris he sees as a travesty of everything historical or medieval; not Maturin or Byron. With Raumer, he detests the 'Poesie des Teufels, der Zerrissenheit, des Hochmuths, der Nacht, des Hässlichen', the predilection for what seems the gratuitous use of tragic subjects in painting, 'das Blutige, Grässliche, Atroce' which passes for the sublime. This does not mean that he cannot, as he wishes, draw on his own Romantic background, in stories of black magic (*Pietro von Abano*) or revenants (*Die Klausenburg*), whose serious nature can also be parodied in the likes of *Das Zauberschloss*; or introduces his own Romantic persona in stories changing effortlessly from humorous present to an evocation of 'Wunder' (*Das alte Buch, Die Vogelscheuche, Waldeinsamkeit*).

These stories are flexible, allowing for change of tone, story within story, 'Märchen' within Novelle. The feature they all have in common is the use of conversational technique. As in *Phantasus,* the Novellen reflect the tone of a social and literary salon; only the boorish, the egoistic, those in need of correction, raise their voices out of turn. Conversation will bring the shy or retiring out of their shells (*Waldeinsamkeit, Der Gelehrte*), will make plain the Zeitgeist and its manifestations (*Die Verlobung, Liebeswerben, Die Vogelscheuche*), will contrast bombast, platitude, or prejudice with tolerance and elegance (*Die Gemälde, Musikalische Leiden und Freuden, Die Wundersüchtigen*), will confront old and new, conservative and progressive, extreme and moderate (*Die Gesellschaft auf dem Lande, Die Ahnenprobe*). Characters are less described than allowed to present themselves, or give themselves away, by the way they converse: it is typical for these Novellen to start in mid-conversation with a question or an expostulation. This use and manipulation of conversation affects the style: the author aims for a 'middle tone', polished, elegant, articulate, the style which Fontane is to perfect. Conversation also enables reflection—a 'message', if one will—to enter unannounced into a story; it means that Tieck is avoiding both the crassness of trick and sensation of the Gothic, and the restrictions of the tightly-knit Italian novella in the Boccaccian tradition. In fact, Rumohr, like others, noting how far Tieck had strayed from Italian models, has Tieck's use of 'raisonnement' in mind when he postulates a 'didaktische Novelle' as one of the possibilities open to the writer of the genre.

If we choose two Novellen for closer analysis, then not because they stand as 'exemplary' or represent the 'main stream' of nineteenth-century shorter prose fiction (although one, *Des Lebens Überfluss,* frequently finds its way into selections and anthologies). Indeed, both show how little formal considerations are binding for Tieck. Of *Das Zauberschloss,* Tieck writes to Brockhaus: 'diese Erzählung sollte, meiner Laune nach, aus lauter kleinen, scheinbar unwichtigen Details bestehn, und das Ganze nur einen Anstrich von Wunderbarem enthalten. Etwas Wahrheit, wie bei meinen meisten *Novellen,* liegt wiederum zum Grunde'; [this story should, as my mood suits me, consist of just a set of little, seemingly unimportant details, and the whole should have the faintest touch of the wondrous. A little truth, as in most of my Novellen, is still the foundation] and to Friedrich Tieck: 'Ein Spaß, wo ich mir den Spaß gemacht, viel Spaß aus einem Nichts zu entwickeln' [A jest, where I make the jest of developing a good deal of jest out of a trifle].

Something improvised, dashed off, which the old *routinier* can do almost without trying? Certainly the highly improbable story, with its young lovers parted by parental intransigence, and stratagems to bring them together—using a 'haunted' castle as the main precinct—is told with much wit and absolute control of comic situation. That would be 'Spaß aus einem Nichts', with jaunty conversation as the chief medium of entertainment. But Tieck had something else up his sleeve; can he, too, not produce something like Boccaccio? A seemingly gratuitous situation is arranged for a character to take out of his pocket a Novelle:

> Es rührt, was ich mittheile, von jenem Verfasser her, von dem schon manche Erzählungen bekannt geworden sind. Er scheint sich bei dem Titel Novelle etwas Bestimmtes, Eigenthümliches zu denken, welches diese Dichtungen charakterisiren und von allen andern erzählenden scharf absondern soll. Doch ist es nicht mein Beruf, ihn zu kommentiren, ich theile Ihnen die Geschichte selber mit, die überdies für eine wahre Anekdote ausgegeben wird.

> [What I am about to tell you comes from the pen of that author who has produced quite a number of well-known stories. He seems to have his own special and peculiar notion about the title *Novelle,* that is supposed to characterize this kind of writing and distinguish it sharply from all other kinds of narration. But it is not my business to do a commentary on him, and so I give you the story, which incidentally claims to be a true anecdote.]

'Erzählung', 'Novelle', 'Geschichte', 'Anekdote': take your pick. A pleasant self-parody. Yet the story itself, *Die wilde Engländerin,* shows another side of Tieck's sophistication as a prose-writer. Here all is condensed, no detail superfluous, every incident carefully planned; the style has that elegant feeling of ease and mastery found at the time only in the interspersed Novellen in *Wilhelm Meisters Wanderjahre.* Here is a young woman preferring her bookish inclinations to the wooings of a lord, older than she, but of great dignity and worthiness. After being spurned, he tries one last time to open his heart to her: the moment is chosen when they are out riding. She responds—and rejects him—with even greater vehemence. The narrator proceeds:

> Sterben eher! rief sie mit dem heftigsten Ausdruck des Widerwillens. Sie selbst wollen mir es recht leicht machen, Ihre Abwesenheit zu ertragen. So leben Sie denn wohl!

> Sie trieb das Pferd an, und Beide waren im höchsten Unmuth bald vor dem Schlosse angelangt. Er stieg ab, um ihr zu helfen, sie wendete sich mit dem Ausdruck des höchsten Unwillens, sie wollte sich eilig vom Pferde schwingen, und das Reitkleid blieb fest am Sattelbogen, ein Moment, und sie stand halb nackt vor dem Erstaunten. Mit einer Schnelligkeit, die unmöglich schien, rannte sie ins Haus und der Lord gab die Pferde ab und begab sich nachdenkend träumend in den Park.

> ['I would sooner die!' she cried with the most violent expression of repugnance. 'You yourself want to make it easy for me to bear your absence. Farewell then!'

> She spurred on the horse, and both had soon arrived in high dudgeon in front of the castle. He dismounted to assist her, she turned with an expression of utmost annoyance, she was about to slip down hastily from her horse, when her riding habit got caught in the saddle-bow, an instant, and she stood half-naked before the astonished beholder. With a swiftness that seemed incredible she sped into the house and the lord handed over the horses and walked into the park, thinking as in a dream about what had happened.]

It is the 'Wendepunkt' to end them all. But it is not bawdy or salacious (not Boccaccio). With great tact and economy, the author leads his heroine to matrimony (children, grandchildren, and living happily ever after), not before having hinted, again with much delicacy and worldly wisdom, at the origin of such tenacious chastity ('Ich liebte ihn, so wie er zum ersten Mal unser Haus betrat. Das Gefühl ängstigte mich eben, und ich wollte ihn dafür bestrafen, daß er mich mir selbst entwendet, dass er mich den Gefühlen untreu gemachte hatte, die ich für meine besten hielt'). [I loved him the very moment he set foot in our house. The feeling disturbed me, and I wanted to punish him for making me unfaithful to the feelings that I considered to be my best.]

*Des Lebens Überfluss* is not called upon to cope with such stylistic or psychological subtleties. Whereas *Das*

*Zauberschloss* keeps its two sides in separate compartments, this story—an eloped couple in a garret breaking up the staircase in their house for firewood—is more discursive. It is a series of clichés and stock situations—the Spitzweg-like idyll in the garret, the resourceful servant, the situational comedy, the love transcending social bounds—which come and go like the references to Jean Paul or Cervantes or Tasso. We never for a moment doubt that there will be a happy ending, that 'Treue, Pflicht, Ordnung' will reassert themselves, that society will find ways of integrating this seeming misalliance into its structure and that nothing will change—except the material fortune of the lovers. It has much of the fairy—tale set in the present day: the outcome is entirely predictable. And yet in the midst of such situations we have—in a conversation—Tieck's conservative credo (the year is 1839). The lines from *Tasso* (somewhat adapted)

> Und wie der Mensch nur sagen kann: 'Hier bin ich';
> Daß *Freunde* seiner *schonend* sich erfreun!

provide the opportunity for Tieck to set out his notion of benign criticism, mild censure, showing up the errors of society, but not changing the texture or presuppositions of that same entity. In matters of state, in religion, in art, the 'Sucht und Kraft zu vernichten'—negative criticism, seditious stirrings—proves inadequate to deal with the ultimate mysteries of human intercourse and interdependence.

Both of these stories appear in Brockhaus's *Urania,* an almanac now greatly enhanced by Tieck's authoritative presence. But Tieck also graces Reimer's *Novellenkranz.* Max, in the mean time, receives the occasional story, but also issues an important set of collected Novellen. If Brockhaus has dark blue covers and gilt edging, Reimer has engravings. Reviewers may carp about unevenness of quality and garrulity of style in Tieck's Novellen, but his authority is still secure and seemingly unassailable. Brockhaus is doubtless pleased to read in his own *Blätter für literarische Unterhaltung* that Tieck's Novellen are 'classische Kunstwerke', but it is also his private opinion. Alexis and Immermann naturally agree, but so also do the so-called Young Germans. That is, until his stories become polemical and controversial—and point in their direction. For in many, if not most, of Tieck's stories, society is identifiable as being contemporary and typical of an age and its foibles. Only rarely, as with *Die Vogelscheuche,* does one particular group (the Liederkreis) come in for special—satirical—treatment.

The other group of Novellen from the Dresden period seek more universal application for their message. The four major poetic works—as opposed to criticism—on which Tieck's later reputation rests—*Der Aufruhr in den Cevennen, Dichterleben, Der junge Tischlermeister,* and *Vittoria Accorombona*—belong together in scope, and, to some extent, in quality. Above all, they are more reflective, more serious, and, in most cases, represent the maturing process of decades.

*Der Aufruhr in den Cevennen,* begun in 1820 and appearing in 1826, shows Tieck aware that the poet who uses history needs to study the sources as much as the historiographer: on this, he and Raumer, indeed, every historian and historical novelist before 1870 are in absolute agreement. And the preface to the novel makes it plain that Tieck pursued such studies conscientiously. Somewhere enters into all this a new factor: Tieck's short-lived enthusiasm for Scott. Of what brevity this is we learn from his rejection, already in 1821, of Scott's less than punctilious approach to history in *Kenilworth.* But, if in 1820, or 1826, a historical novel is not to follow Scott, whom then? If one is to find models different from those which provoke *Sur Walter Scott. A propos de Quentin Durward* or inspire *Les Chouans,* where is one to look? Clearly the friend of Raumer will have no time for Fouqué's flights into Nordic fancy or Arnim's unfinished, broken-backed novel, *Die Kronenwächter.*

The dilemma is set out, not by Tieck himself, but by a young writer whom in 1824 he already finds preferable to the Scott of *St Ronan's Well* or *Peveril of the Peak*: Willibald Alexis. A long review by Alexis, *The Romances of Walter Scott,* in the *Wiener Jahrbücher* of 1823, tells us much that is symptomatic of German attitudes to the historical novel, and much that explains its vicissitudes before about 1870. We sense that Alexis is constrained to make a case for Scott's novels, that he needs to defend him against charges of intellectual poverty, 'Gedanken- und Ideenarmuth' in the face of a more reflective German tradition; that he is forced to pay obeisance to the novel's mighty rival in Germany—the historical drama; that he needs to establish the historical novel's credentials as 'accurate' and 'true'. Indeed, while nineteenth-century historians as various as Thierry, the young Ranke, Carlyle, or Macaulay admitted their debt to the historical novel, Scott himself never claimed to be a historian 'polluting the well of history with modern inventions'. But historical accuracy Alexis takes very seriously, no less than Hauff's preface to his *Lichtenstein* of 1826 or still Stifter's to *Witiko* in 1865. Alexis wants a Scott who is respectable in German terms, who can stand comparison with both epic and drama, who has even, if need be, 'Gemüth'. There will be less about his Udolphean tricks and short cuts, his indebtedness, as he freely admits in his general preface of 1829, to the *Castle of Otranto* and Miss Edgeworth. Small wonder that Alexis, once he launches into the genre himself, is hedged about by so many concerns and checked by a native tradition of fiction so different from the Scotsman's, that his novels, while laudable, show evidence of this unfortunate need to satisfy everybody.

In 1826, with *Der Aufruhr in den Cevennen,* Tieck, too, was trying to satisfy a number of demands—with the result that the work never really 'comes off'. His strictures on Scott of 1821 had related to Scott's highly liberal chronology in the interests of bringing all his characters together—and giving the story life. But, with the age of Elizabeth, where for Tieck every year is significant, as contributing to the knowledge of Shakespeare, one may not be so free. We can adduce from his other remarks on Scott from the period, that, for all his recognition of the other's art, there was, bound up with it, too much of the 'Gothic', too much story, incident, devices—and not

enough reflection. It is in this quality of stating positions through reasoned argument and measured discussion that Tieck wishes to establish the legitimacy of his art, not through feints and frights. Tieck's primary interest in his subject was also different from Scott's; the German is concerned with religious fanaticism as a general phenomenon; the Scotsman, in his memorable novels at least, is trying to recapture moments and personalities in the history of his native land. Tieck is to be commended for not attempting merely to superimpose Scott's patterns on to some incident in German history. For Scott cannot be imitated; the nineteenth century is littered with the wrecks of historical novels which have failed to recognize his uniqueness. When we, however, examine *Der Aufruhr in den Cevennen* more closely, we notice that Tieck is in fact treating a subject already found in one of Scott's truly great novels, *Old Mortality.*

The revolt in the Cevennes, and the uprising of the Covenanters, clearly have much in common. But for Scott, this is part of that native history, native soil if one will, without which his Scotland would not have been what it was, a country with a notoriously long memory and a highly touchy sense of justice. This is what gives *Old Mortality* its greatness. But, if Tieck chooses to be different, to go outside his own native sphere of experience, to rely on that which is acquired rather than inborn, this also has its legitimacy. Yet, if an Episcopalian may find his way into the manners, speech, and terrifying Old Testament fanaticism, of Cameronian Presbyterians, it is because he is close to the speech, customs, attitudes of such people, and to their 'worthies'. It may be different for a latitudinarian Lutheran to enter into the spirit of a Calvinist uprising in a part of a country he had never visited. It is clear that Tieck is fascinated by the manifestation of visions, dreams, intimations, prophecies; the descriptions of these, and the bloody deeds they inspire, provide some memorable passages in the book. They are noteworthy in revealing that Tieck's life-long concern with mysticism had not ceased with his rejection of Jacob Böhme. There is much in *Der Aufruhr* to remind us of Moritz's *Magazin für Erfahrungsseelenkunde* or Jung-Stilling's *Leben* or Gotthilf Heinrich Schubert's *Ansichten über die Nachtseite der Naturwissenschaft*; much that is the common property of Romanticism, a movement given, more than is credited, to the hope of a 'Gemeinschaft der Bessern', of the truly religious, regardless of confession, a movement concerned with the universality of religious experience.

None of this, is, historically speaking, exactly relevant to the subject; English Puritanism or Scots Covenanting might well be closer. But we should not condemn Tieck for failing to do what for other traditions would seem appropriate. This 'historical' novel is much more concerned with the basic human questions raised by history: truth, tolerance, humanity. It does not, indeed cannot, create local colour; it has a uniform level of style; it fails to reproduce satisfactorily the words of the young or the humble. Above all, Tieck falls back on his tried device of conversation; characters will reveal themselves more in the positions they adopt in debate. Here, we will hear from M. de Beauvais or Father Watelet, the voice of reasoned tolerance, religious inwardness free of zealotry, a sense of awe and wonderment and respect for the divine. It is clearly Tieck's own position, amid the pillage, burning, and carnage of the extremes, the 'große Blutwunde der ganzen Welt'. Tieck never finished it. Did he despair of a harmonious ending? Or was he simply overtaken by events and commitments? He certainly did not abandon the historical Novelle. One, not especially memorable, **Der griechische Kaiser,** takes the question of political legitimacy—in the year 1830. Another, **Der Hexen-Sabbath** (1831) returns us to late-medieval Burgundy to bring a story—worthy, in its subject at least, of *The Scarlet Letter* or *The Crucible*—of fanaticism, superstition, and persecution, where nothing—neither tolerance, nor decency, nor political moderation, nor art, nor civilization—can withstand the dark forces of destruction. It is a black and desperate vision, the far extreme of Tieck's growing sense of isolation, of a threat from all sides to civilized values.

Where politics and systems of state may fail, poetry remains lasting and imperishable. This is certainly the message of the two 'Künstlernovellen', **Dichterleben** and **Tod des Dichters. Dichterleben** is about Shakespeare, the first years of his career, up to his friendship with Southampton. It may not be the 'slight *novella*' which Schoenbaum chooses to call it, but its importance is more symptomatic than intrinsic. In other words, it tells us more about Tieck's continuing wrestling with the angel of Shakespeare's genius than about the Bard himself. We learn yet another corner of his meandering path to Shakespeare, of how the byways of scholarship can somehow merge with the straight road of fiction. Already the *Briefe über W. Shakspeare,* and the preface of 1823 to *Shakspeare's Vorschule* had made it clear that Tieck's approach was becoming increasingly biographical. He could, however, certainly enter into both the letter and the spirit of the arch-biographer, Carlyle, who had exclaimed:

> How shall that unhappy Biographic brotherhood, instead of writing like Index-makers and Government-clerks, suddenly become enkindled with some sparks of intellect, or even of genial fire; and not only collecting dates and facts, but making use of them, look beyond the surface and economical form of a man's life, into its substance and spirit?

Bringing Shakespeare into *Kenilworth* might be one thing—and bad history and bad biography at that; but how does the writer of fiction achieve the 'substance and spirit' of a man's life? He can, as Tieck did, read that storehouse of anecdote, Nathan Drake's *Shakespeare and His Times,* and study the sonnets. Tieck has Dorothea translate the sonnets and issues a selection in Theodor Hell's *Penelope* of 1826, stating: 'Man hat mich oft aufgefordert, ein Leben Shakspears zu schreiben. Das Meiste, was ich von ihm weiß, habe ich in diesen Sonetten erfahren.' [I have often been asked to write a life of Shakespeare. Most of what I know of him I have learned in these sonnets.] The first part of **Dichterleben** is issued in 1826 in *Urania,* with a Lips engraving incorporating the Chandos portrait. What for Shakespeare's countrymen was never successfully accomplished—a novel on the Bard's life—might seem an

easier task for a German writer. For Tieck could look back to Goethe's *Tasso* and his own *Sternbald* as the works which had inaugurated the fashion for 'Künstlerdramen' and 'Künstlernovellen', by 1826 firmly established in the patterns of those genres; and both of those works find their places among that interesting interplay of literature and painting in the nineteenth century when eventually 'Seni Contemplates the Dead Wallenstein' or 'Chaucer Reads at the Court of Edward III'. But does Tieck's Shakespeare novel work? The answer is: no, it does not. But not for lack of trying; Tieck is so concerned to avoid a *Kenilworth* that he never really takes flight. Peele, Marlowe, Nash, Henslow, are all there in their appointed places; Shakespeare and Southampton go on a journey almost the same as Tieck's and Burgsdorff's in 1817. The young poet, alas, never becomes truly alive, and the story falls into a series of conversations. And yet, if we remove these discussions from their context—they could almost occur in **Phantasus** or *Goethe und seine Zeit*—we have as clear a statement from Tieck of his own poetic ideal: it is Goethe's 'Weltfrömmigkeit' which speaks in this statement:

> . . . so das Leibliche mit dem Geistigen, das Ewige mit dem Irdischen, Cupido und Psyche, im Sinne des alten Mährchens, auf das Innigste in Gegenwart und mit dem Beifall aller Götter zu vermählen.

> [thus to marry the physical with the spiritual, the eternal with the earthly, Cupid and Psyche, in the spirit of the old fairy-tale, inextricably bound together and with all the gods giving their approval.]

More specifically, Tieck will have his hero speak of the intimate relationship between patriotism, an abiding order of state, and poetic enthusiasm; indeed, true poetry will always have this as its well-spring. But poetry is not frenzy or undisciplined prating; it arises in that moment—beyond analysis—where technique and mystery are conjoined. Against Shakespeare, Tieck sets Marlowe. It is not fair to Marlowe as we now know him; it is not 'historical' in the true sense. In fact, Tieck wishes us to read for Marlowe—or Tasso, or Lenz, or Kleist—those who have not achieved mastery of life and poetic imagination, whose 'Zerrissenheit' has kept them from true greatness. These, says Tieck to his own generation, we will not emulate, while appreciating the merits they may undoubtedly have. We must look to purity, not to imperfection. It will mean making Marlowe into something 'atroce', in the same way as Tieck elsewhere compares Webster with Young Germany or the French Romantics; Marlowe will praise 'Entsetzen', 'Grauen', 'fratzenhafte komische Gegebenheiten' in tragedy, at the cost of patriotic concern.

We find a similar duality in the Novelle **Tod des Dichters** of 1833. It is the story of the last days of Camões, who, while missing from the Romantic canon in *Zerbino,* now emerges—largely through Friedrich Schlegel's advocacy—as the paradigm of a national patriotic endeavour and as a tragic symbol of his country's downfall. This story comes over more convincingly than **Dichterleben**: we see a poet, at the end of his days, bowed down by poverty, deprivation, and grief, denied true recognition, but drawing comfort from the realization that those who serve their country and sing its glories, rarely find fame in their own day. Camões' career has been one succession of rejections and misunderstandings—but there is still the proud moment of the *Lusiads,* the work which will, for nearly two centuries, stand for the nation's lost identity. Camões' poetry is of his native land; it is not the fantastic airy realm of Ariosto; Tieck has chosen as his tragic poet, not Tasso, not Chatterton, not Richard Savage, not the 'zerrissen' or feckless. He has moved away from the 'unpatriotic' Italian poets, once such prominent denizens of his garden of poetry. Perhaps *Tod des Dichters,* while not in every part memorable, deserves to be better known. Together with *Dichterleben,* it reasserts much of what the preface to Lenz's *Schriften* had stated. These stories are not the *Herzensergiessungen* revived in middle age: they are biography *and* poetic manifesto. They do, however, provide the link between that early Romantic world of the Klosterbruder and Sternbald, and later development. They combine, as Wilhelm Waetzold noted, both 'Bildungsgeschichte' and 'Versenkung'; they rise like plants from the real to the ideal. Their true successors are the great art biographies of Carl Justi and Herman Grimm later in the nineteenth century.

Yet when Tieck is talking of poets and their ideals, he is, as experience now shows, inevitably speaking of Goethe. Shakespeare and Camões stay true to their principles; they do not lose touch with national themes and national values; they keep free of courts (Tasso's undoing); they are not ministers of state. Their bearing is modest; for them poetry is all—they are merely the chosen vessel. There have been those who have read *Dichterleben* as a *Dichtung und Wahrheit* as it, in Tieck's eyes, should have been, without the aberrations into classicism and cosmopolitanism. Be this as it may, Tieck's ambivalent attitude to Goethe stands. On the one hand, he has stated his ideal of the poet, one which sets its face against 'Zerrissenheit' und 'Epigonentum'; not art for its own sake, but to record with 'Begeisterung' the wonder and mystery of the world and of the divine; on the other, he has raised Goethe among the highest, among Shakespeare or Dante or Camões or Cervantes. But he has also made full use of the words attributed to Goethe: 'Nur wer mich liebt, soll mich tadeln'. [Only those who love me should chide me.]

It is not, therefore, altogether by chance that Tieck's last long Novelle—or novel—of the mid-1830s, *Der junge Tischlermeister,* should reflect this same ambivalence towards Goethe. Not that this story is about Goethe or necessarily accessible only in terms of him. It is, as it were, the other side of *Der Hexen-Sabbath* or *Tod des Dichters:* a last, positive, affirmation of those cultural values which accompanied the writer throughout his career. It reminisces, but not on the purely anecdotal level of the rather ephemeral little *Eine Sommerreise* of 1833; it takes stock of, and evaluates, what, since 1795, can stand and what cannot. Tieck informs us in the preface that the earliest plans went back to the spring of that year. Was it as a result of reading the first book of *Wilhelm Meisters Lehrjahre?* Instead, the real influence, we are

told, was Cervantes' *Novelas.* For we see in this work both the quirky and the unpredictable, but basically integrated, world of those stories; but also much of Sterne or Hippel or Jean Paul, even of the *Straussfedern;* yet also that tradition, too, in which, following Fielding, and in German, Friedrich von Blanckenburg and Wieland, the 'Bürger' is led through sets of circumstances to a full unfolding of character and personality. All the same, *Der junge Tischlermeister* (to its credit, perhaps) is not a 'Bildungsroman'; the hero, an educated craftsman, does not, like Goethe's merchant son, find a new world and destination as a result of anabases and misapprehensions: he returns whence he came. The theatre—a theme common to both authors—is in Tieck not there for the hero to indulge his illusions and delusions; it is a means of finding true, temporary, escape from oneself, an enriching release from reality.

When the work was published in 1836, Tieck could not resist using the preface for some timely polemics against the young and impudent, quoting, with Goethe, the dictum that one is never too old to learn and add to experience. He puts in, for good measure: 'nur in seinem wahren Beruf kann der Mensch stark seyn, irgendwo muß er ganz zu Hause seyn und fest-stehen.' [Man can only be strong in his true profession; somewhere he has to be completely at home and stand fast.] This might seem to be the motto of the book: the craftsman hero, who enteres into a series of adventures in aristocratic circles, returning at the end to the limitations of bourgeois existence, is destined to see the truth of this statement. The beginning and end of the novel, with their mingling of nature and the hum of trade, seem to assert that what lies between is merely aberration; that home, wife, family, peace, and order are best, and all. We seem to be in the world of Biedermeier painting, of Rayski or Waldmüller or Winterhalter; a picture of 1826 by Erasmus von Engert, 'Im Hausgarten' could almost have been done to illustrate this novel: a woman sitting in an arbour beside sunflowers, knitting in her hand and book in her lap, while in the background—the ultimate source of this leisure—we see the stacked timber of a builder's workshop. It may be that the model for Leonhard, the hero, is none other than that intelligent, enterprising and well-read master craftsman, Johann Ludwig Tieck senior. But this is not a social novel—the order of classes is accepted from the beginning. When Theodor Mundt, reviewing it in 1837, noted with disapproval the almost patriarchal attitude to society, he was nevertheless right in stressing 'Annäherung der Stände' through 'Bildung'. It is essentially the success story of the Tieck family, exploiting the opportunities of education to find social mobility. A master craftsman, then, while 'bürgerlich', need not be the cultural inferior of the nobility. For indeed, this Novelle is not, as Mundt supposed, about 'gesellschaftliche Realitäten', but about the wisdom and release imparted by the experience of culture in the theatre.

In the centre of the story, amid the journeyings to old Romantic haunts (Franconia) and discussion of favourite Romantic themes (Mozart, Cervantes, Goethe, Shakespeare) is the experience of the theatre. The assembled society performs three plays: *Götz von Berlichingen, Die*

*Räuber,* and *Twelfth Night.* The first two involve crass naturalism, chaos, and disharmony, each actor choosing the
role that suits his own temperament, and everybody falling flat on their faces. In *Twelfth Night,* however, roles are
apportioned, not chosen; each character can satisfy his
inner desire to be something he is not, to wear a mask, to
escape from the restrictions of the everyday. At the performance, all is poetry and magic, lightness and harmony.
Unreality, make-believe, have benign sway—but only for
those who can enter into the true spirit, who do not with-
hold themselves, who are able to return to reality after it
is all over. That is the sense of the Novelle's ending: one
has confronted the unruly spirit in one's nature, has given
it its head in an artificial world of fancy, and makes one's
way, enriched with wisdom, back to normal, responsible
existence.

But, as a Novelle also about the theatre, it cannot resist
setting out many of Tieck's favourite ideas, so frustrated
by real directors and real audiences. It takes Goethe to
task for failing to make himself part of the living German
theatre tradition, for neglecting to accommodate himself
to its needs. This is much franker even than *Goethe und
seine Zeit.* We come, inevitably to the contrast between
Goethe and Shakespeare; here, the Bard must win the day,
as he always will when Tieck is discussing that total experience which is 'Zauber' and 'Wunder' and theatre. *Der
junge Tischlermeister* is Tieck's last real assertion on this
scale of his moderate, wise, Romantic position. It is never
querulous; it looks benignly, sometimes ruefully, on human folly, on the triumph of Bottom over the fairy world
of the imagination. It shares his still unshaken belief in
social decorum, agreed rules of restraint, moderate discussion. From then on, with perhaps only the point of light
afforded by *Des Lebens Überfluss,* his vision becomes
increasingly sombre . . .

## Maria Tatar (essay date 1987)

SOURCE: "Unholy Alliances: Narrative Ambiguity in
Tieck's 'Der Blonde Eckbert'," in *MLN: Modern Language Notes,* Vol. 102, 1987, pp. 608-26.

[*In the following essay, Tatar examines the narrative structure of Tieck's novella, maintaining that the ambiguity of
the text "engages the reader's mind in a never-ending
process of interpretation, in an endless search that becomes its own end."*]

While most authors have at one time or another professed
a preference for entertaining or for instructing their readers (unless they have prided themselves on their ability to
do both), Ludwig Tieck never really harbored the one
ambition or the other. The stated aim of his fiction was to
drive readers to the point of distraction, to mystify and
bewilder them until they reached that blissful state that
Tieck designated by the name "poetic madness." That he
very nearly achieved his aim can be verified by virtually
any reader of the *Märchennovellen* produced in the early
phases of Tieck's literary career. These texts seem de-

signed to develop enigmas rather than to resolve them.
The search for solutions to their mysteries is forever ob-
structed by the presence of conflicting codes within the
text.

The common generic designation for many of Tieck's
shorter fictional texts reveals something about the source
of confusion generated by his narrative strategies. The
term *Märchennovelle* points to the presence of two normally separate and discrete modes: the one admitting the
presence of the supernatural, the other knowing nothing
more than natural laws. This co-presence of two contradictory levels of fictional reality can produce a radical
sense of disorientation: in a world governed by natural
laws, the supernatural is forever making its presence felt.
Both the characters who inhabit the fictional world and its
readers are faced with an interpretive challenge. Have the
apparently supernatural events represented in the text actually taken place or are they merely phantoms of the
fictional characters' minds? The hesitation between these
two interpretive propositions stands as the hallmark of
what [Tzvetan] Todorov has called [in *The Fantastic: A
Structural Approach to a Literary Genre,* 1975] the fantastic tale. In the pure fantastic tale, it becomes impossible to choose between the two options, for the question
concerning the substantiality of the seemingly supernatural events is sustained right to the very end of the text.

While Todorov has focused primarily on the effects (shock,
uncanny sensations, hesitation) produced by apparently
supernatural events to formulate his definition of the fantastic tale, other, more recent, critics have shifted attention to the source of the interpretive dilemmas that surface
in fantastic tales. For them, narrative ambiguity and unresolved antinomies build the enigmas that stand at the heart
of the fantastic tale. Shlomith Rimmon reminds us [in her
*The Concept of Ambiguity—The Example of James,* 1977]
that ambiguity is predicated on the principle of choice:
*either* A *or* B. The ambiguous text invites us to make a
choice between two equally cogent literal interpretations
that are charged with a kind of nervous tension by virtue
of their incompatibility. As she puts it in her study of
narrative ambiguity: "When . . . two hypotheses are mutually exclusive, and yet each is equally coherent, equally
consistent, equally plenary and convincing, so that we
cannot choose between them, we are confronted with
narrative ambiguity." One hypothesis accepts the possibility of supernatural causality and requires the reader
to suspend disbelief; the other searches for natural
causes (e.g., delirium, intoxication, derangement) to
explain what a character or the narrator perceives to be
a supernatural event. Other critics have proposed definitions along similar lines. Amaryll Chanady [in her *Magical
Realism and the Fantastic: Resolved versus Unresolved
Antinomy,* 1985], for example, finds that "unresolved
antinomy," or "the simultaneous presence of two conflicting codes" (the supernatural and the natural), constitutes the distinguishing feature of the fantastic tale. Here
once again, double meanings do not operate in unison
to create a rich, complex design; rather they create interpretive enigmas by standing in flagrant contradiction to
each other.

Ambiguous texts, as Rimmon has further proposed, perform on a literary level the kind of visual trick enacted by drawings that simultaneously represent both a rabbit and a duck, or an urn and two profiles. Gestalt psychologists remind us that viewers of such drawings see either the rabbit or the duck, the urn or the two profiles, but not both at the same time. As one becomes the figure, the other turns into the ground. Like the ambiguous text, these drawings offer two conflicting "readings": both are equally valid, yet mutually exclusive. It requires a radical shift in perspective to move from one to the other.

In Germany, the fantastic tale made its debut with the stories of Ludwig Tieck, E. T. A. Hoffmann, and Joseph von Eichendorff. In their own way, the tales of these authors can be as maddening as the rabbit/duck figure that engages our intellectual faculties in a process of perpetual interpretation and reinterpretation. But few of the tales written by the German Romantics succeeded so well in challenging the interpretive prowess of critics and in testing their tolerance for ambiguity as Tieck's **Der blonde Eckbert.** At first sight, the narrative ambiguity of this particular text seems to turn on the question of whether the protagonist is the victim of supernatural powers or a madman suffering from hallucinations. *Either* the Old Woman who pronounces Eckbert's death sentence is a real phantom *or* she is merely a phantom of the mind. The first reading would draw the story into the realm of what Todorov calls "the marvelous"; the second reading moves it into the domain of what he labels "the strange." Yet on closer inspection, it becomes evident that the Old Woman, who was Bertha's childhood mentor and who later masquerades as Walther, Hugo, and a peasant, must be more than a figment of Eckbert's deranged sensibilities. By pronouncing the name "Strohmian," Walther at once authenticates Bertha's retrospective narrative about her childhood (which we might otherwise be tempted to dismiss as a fanciful account) and suggests that he too, like Bertha, can not only traverse the frontier dividing the fairy-tale world from reality but also transform himself from a fairy-tale creature into an ordinary human. This single textual detail, Walther's revelation of the name "Strohmian," weighs the scales in favor of an interpretation that accepts the supernatural as part and parcel of the fictional world created in the text.

In view of the seemingly unambiguous status of Eckbert's friend Walther as the emissary of a marvelous world, it is not surprising to find that critics of **Der blonde Eckbert** have almost without exception followed the lead of the tale's two protagonists and adopted their interpretation of events. If Bertha's voice guides us through the past, Eckbert's perceptions orient us once Walther makes his momentous pronouncement. As focalizer, Eckbert becomes our sole source of information—his conviction that he is haunted by a supernatural presence gradually becomes our conviction. In the absence of skeptical authorial intrusions, we suspend disbelief. For this very reason, the endless debates about Tieck's story focus less on the two kinds of readings that can be abstracted from the text than on the figurative meaning of the superhuman personage who disrupts the tranquillity of Eckbert and Bertha's domestic life. Once critics agree that a text belongs to the category of the marvelous, they still have the privilege of disagreeing about the symbolic meaning of the supernatural agents or events in the text. The Old Woman, alias Walther, has been seen alternately as an agent of justice, as nature personified, as the spirit of revenge, and as the incarnation of fate.

> **The stated aim of Tieck's fiction was to drive readers to the point of distraction, to mystify and bewilder them until they reached that blissful state that Tieck designated as "poetic madness."**
>
> *—Maria Tatar*

Characters persecuted by supernatural powers larger than life tend to lose their capacity to act as free agents and to become victims of forces beyond their control. Fantastic literature, especially when it shades into the marvelous, is primarily a literature of victimization. "What has happened to me?" the startled protagonists ask with the same sense of bewilderment that Gregor Samsa voices upon awakening from his strange dreams into an even stranger reality. But supernatural agents, especially the Romantic variety, are rarely so capricious as to invade the ordinary world without some anterior cause or provocation, and if Bertha and Eckbert become the targets of the Old Woman's wrath, there must be a reason why they are singled out for persecution. As we learn from Bertha herself, the Old Woman does in fact have a score to settle with her. Before the fourteen-year-old Bertha abandoned Strohmian and absconded with the Old Woman's bird and jewels, she was given fair warning about the consequences of straying from the path of virtue: "Nie gedeiht es, wenn man von der rechten Bahn abweicht, die Strafe folgt nach, wenn auch noch so spät." Just as Bertha first invited, then violated the trust of her guardian, so Walther, alias the Old Woman, retaliates by first winning, then betraying Bertha's confidence.

The story of Bertha's life, in enacting the lesson that crime inevitably leads to punishment ("die Strafe folgt nach, wenn auch noch so spät"), contains within it a kind of sober and sobering logic. The Old Woman's disquisition to Bertha on the wages of sin has its counterpart in the less than logical maxim she addresses to Eckbert in the coda to the narrative. After demanding the return of her bird, her pearls, and her dog from Eckbert, the Old Woman, in a statement that seems to patently contradict the reality of the situation, declares: "Siehe, das Unrecht bestraft sich selbst." The phrase suggests that Eckbert is not so much the victim of her vengeance as he is the victim of his own tormented conscience. Yet in the litany of crimes recited by the Old Woman to the dying Eckbert, it is difficult to identify a single one that might lead Eckbert to engage in the kind of endless self-reproaches that constitute a form of self-punishment. The theft of the bird and the jewels was, after all, Bertha's crime. The sin of adultery was committed by the father. And even the murder of Walther, Eckbert's one manifestly guilty act, is evidently not a real murder, for Walther lives on in the guise of the Old Woman.

Of the Old Woman's many alarming pronouncements, the one that literally floors Eckbert concerns the identity of his wife Bertha. That statement alone touches on a guilty secret that Eckbert responds with the words: "Warum hab ich diesen schrecklichen Gedanken immer geahndet?" The question reveals that Eckbert, like Bertha, has long been guarding a dark secret, and it is precisely that secret which serves as the matrix of the anxieties besetting Eckbert during the years of his marriage. If Eckbert all along has been harboring premonitions of incest but has kept such thoughts both to himself and from himself, then surely he has more to fear from his own consciousness and conscience than from any external agent of retribution. If supernatural powers conspire to punish Bertha for her transgressions, it is primarily human guilt that haunts Eckbert and brings him to his ruin. The process by which Eckbert's guilty secret nonetheless draws him into the marvelous world of Bertha's past offers one key to understanding the narrative ambiguity of Tieck's text, and for this reason it is imperative to review the stations of Eckbert's sufferings as he moves from his secure castle fortress to the domain of the Old Woman.

Eckbert and Bertha spend their married lives in a kind of nervous solitude and studied seclusion. Their mountain retreat, encircled and secured by a protective wall, stands as a fitting emblem of the need to shield themselves against intrusions from the outside world. They seldom receive guests and, over the many years of their marriage, they develop only one "friendship"—and even this one friend turns out to be more fiend than friend. Taking the cues of the narrator at face value, critics have repeatedly traced the source of the couple's isolation to a desire to protect the secrets of Bertha's past. But Eckbert, as we learn only at the end of his story, also has a secret to guard, a secret that generates far greater anxiety in him than the story of Bertha's unprincipled accession to wealth.

The presence of a guilty secret in Eckbert's psyche is first introduced in a gnomic pronouncement from the narrator: "Es gibt Stunden, in denen es den Menschen ängstigt, wenn er vor seinem Freunde ein Geheimnis haben soll, was er bis dahin oft mit vieler Sorgfalt verborgen hat." The narrator's reflections on such secrets and the compulsion to reveal them ("sich ganz mitzuteilen, dem Freunde auch das Innerste aufzuschließen") prepares us for a full confession from Eckbert, who has after all figured as the principal subject of the narrator's opening remarks. But instead, what follows is Eckbert's amiable offer to share with Walther the story of Bertha's life—the secret story of her childhood. The telling of this tale culminates in Walther's dire revelation of the name *Strohmian.* On the following morning, Bertha, presumably overtaxed by the task of narrating her story, takes to her bed. But only a few days later, she confesses to her husband that her illness stems

from Walther's evident familiarity with her past. Eckbert remains strangely laconic on the occasion of this revelation: he looks at Bertha "mit einem tiefen Gefühle," engages in a moment of silent meditation, offers his wife a few words of consolation, and leaves. Eckbert's reaction to Bertha's troubled confession comes perilously close to callousness. To offer a few comforting phrases to a spouse in a state of physical and emotional shock seems to reflect a staggering insensitivity on his part. Yet Eckbert is anything but calm and collected once he leaves his wife's chambers. As he nervously paces the floors of his castle, he banishes Bertha's illness from his thoughts and instead reflects with growing irritation on his friendship with Walther: "Walther war seit vielen Jahren sein einziger Umgang gewesen, und doch war dieser Mensch jetzt der einzige in der Welt, dessen Dasein *ihn* drückte und peinigte. Es schien ihm, als würde *ihm* froh und leicht sein, wenn nur dieses einzige Wesen *aus seinem Wege* gerückt werden könnte" (my emphasis). Oddly enough, Eckbert seems to see himself alone, and not Bertha, as the victim of Walther's oppressive influence. To be sure, he must feel threatened by Walther's evident knowledge of Bertha's past, but he appears less agitated by the implications of that knowledge than by Walther's seemingly preternatural powers to divine a name that has been forgotten. What disturbs Eckbert is that Walther has the ability to aid others in renewing lost memories. "Ein gewaltiges Entsetzen befiel mich, *als mir ein fremder Mensch so zu meinen Erinnerungen half. Was sagst du, Eckbert?*" (my emphasis). These are the words that Bertha addresses to Eckbert after disclosing the source of her fears. Eckbert has precious little to say in response, for he is nearly speechless with anxiety about the possibility that this "stranger," who is so adept at naming names, may also have the power to assist him in recovering the memory of a name that he once heard in his own childhood.

Both partners of the incestuous marriage in ***Der blonde Eckbert*** suffer from lapses in memory. But of the two occasions on which the half-siblings are reminded of names that they have forgotten, only the first—which marks the classical "Wendepunkt" of this particular tale—has received widespread critical attention. For Ernst Bloch and Walter Benjamin, who discussed ***Das Märchen vom blonden Eckbert*** on an autumn evening in Capri into the early hours of the dawn, Philipp Walther's naming of the dog Strohmian figured as the most arresting moment of the narrative [See Bloch's "Bilder des Déjà vu," *Literarische Aufsätze,* Vol. IX of *Ernst Bloch: Gesamtausgabe,* 1965]. But Eckbert, like Bertha, also "forgets" a name that played a prominent role in his childhood experiences, and he too remains unable to recall that name until a stranger ("ein fremder Mensch," to use Bertha's words) pronounces it for him. It is the Old Woman, alias Philipp Walther, who tells Eckbert that Bertha is his own father's daughter and that once, in his early youth, Eckbert had overheard his father speak of an illegitimate child. Had Eckbert not at one time known the name of this half-sister, it is highly unlikely that he would ever have suspected that his wife was a true blood relative. Without some knowledge (however deeply buried in the depths of his psyche) of his half-sister's name, there would be no reason for him to be haunted by the premonition that his wife and his half-sister are one and the same.

---

**In building ambiguity by fusing two discrete narrative modes, the text of *Der blonde Eckbert* creates a situation in which it becomes impossible to pin down even the bare essentials of the plot.**

—*Maria Tatar*

---

That Eckbert had in fact worried about the propriety of his marriage long before the Old Woman's pronouncement becomes evident when we contemplate his response to Bertha's account of her childhood. At the conclusion of Bertha's retrospective narrative, Eckbert makes no attempt to exonerate his wife's behavior—as one might expect; instead he hastens to justify his choice of Bertha as a marriage partner in a series of back-handed compliments. "'Ihr hättet sie *damals* sehen sollen,' *fiel Eckbert hastig ein—, '*ihre Jugend, ihre Schönheit, und welch einen unbegreiflichen Reiz ihr ihre einsame Erziehung gegeben hatte. *Sie kam mir vor wie ein Wunder. . . .* Wir zogen hierher und unsere Verbindung hat uns *bis jetzt* noch keinen Augenblick gereut'" (my emphasis). Eckbert's compelling need to vindicate his alliance with Bertha by emphasizing her spellbinding attractiveness seems to point to the possibility that his conscience is not altogether clear on the score of his marriage. And his observation that the union between him and Bertha has "up until now" occasioned no cause for remorse only underscores his awareness that, at some future time, he may have good reason to regret the marriage. It is more than odd that Eckbert chooses to extol the virtues of marital bliss by pointing to the absence of remorse; that he should focus on the absence of this particular emotion only strengthens the suspicion that for some reason he fears its presence. At some level, therefore, Eckbert appears to know that something is amiss in his marriage, and the final revelation of the Old Woman thus only echoes his deepest fears. Yet much as he suspects that his wife Bertha may in fact be his father's daughter, he stubbornly refuses to allow the childhood memory of his father's adultery to rise to the threshold of consciousness. Just how intensely he fears the surfacing of this memory—with the attendant surfacing of the name Bertha—becomes evident in the anxiety that besets him when Philipp Walther casually displays his uncanny ability to retrieve lost memories (names in particular) from the depths of consciousness.

As Freud has pointed out for us [in *Gesammelte Werke*, edited by Anna Freud, 1952], those who try to forget a painful memory that contains within it an intolerable idea are undertaking an impossible task: "Sowohl die Gedächtnisspur als auch der der Vorstellung anhaftende Affekt sind einmal da und nicht mehr auszutilgen." As desperate-

ly as Eckbert tries to suppress his childhood memory, which threatens to implicate him in the sin of incest, his efforts are doomed to failure. All the same, it is possible to diminish the strength of an intolerable idea by depriving it of its affect, either by translating the affect into a somatic form of expression (as in conversion hysteria) or by transferring the affect to other related ideas. In this second process, in which an unbearable anxiety seizes upon and hides behind another more tolerable anxiety, Freud saw the source of obsessive behavior, of the many compulsions and phobias that are erected as defense barriers against ideas incompatible with consciousness.

Through an effective combination of denial and projection, Eckbert succeeds both in exonerating himself from guilt yet also in talking constantly about it as a defect in others. It is Bertha who has terrible secrets to hide; the betrayal of her guardian has generated an intolerable atmosphere of distrust and paranoid fears over the years. While it is not without logic that Bertha's fears should have a contagious effect on her husband or that those fears should be absorbed by her half-brother through a process of consanguineous association, it is surprising to find that Eckbert develops those fears to a degree far more intense than does Bertha. Yet once we recall that Bertha's sense of guilt arose in connection with her infidelity to a mother figure and that the sin of Eckbert's father consisted of infidelity to the mother of Eckbert, then the intensity with which Eckbert fixes on Bertha's transgression acquires a new dimension of plausibility. Eckbert's manifest fears and obsessions are linked by a train of psychological associations to the content of his latent fears. And this train of associations makes it all the easier for Eckbert to engage in denial and projection: to substitute fears concerning Bertha's act of treachery for his own far more pronounced anxiety concerning the revelation of his father's act of infidelity and the consequent recognition that his marriage is an incestuous one.

Philipp Walther's naming of the dog Strohmian represents the point at which Eckbert's guilty secret becomes enmeshed with Bertha's guilty secret. In dropping the name Strohmian, Philipp Walther transforms himself from a benevolent confidante into a menacing judgmental figure. This single word becomes the signature of his supernatural powers: it signals the imminence of punishment for Bertha's crimes and at the same time stands as an emblem of his power to bring Eckbert's secrets to light. The possibility that Philipp Walther can help to recall a name from the past may never enter Eckbert's consciousness, yet it remains the only plausible explanation for the wave of anxiety that nearly overwhelms the protagonist of Tieck's tale. Instead of searching for the real source of that anxiety and thereby coming to terms with his own guilt, Eckbert endlessly torments himself with the kinds of fears that beset Bertha after she left the hut of the Old Woman. He nervously speculates on the possibility that human greed will lead to an act of treachery: "Wird er [Philipp Walther] nicht vielleicht, denn das ist die Natur des Menschen, eine unselige Habsucht nach unsern Edelgesteinen empfinden, und deswegen Plane anlegen und sich verstellen?"

In order to "divert himself" from his troubles, Eckbert undertakes a hunting expedition. In vain he searches for his quarry until he sees Walther collecting moss from trees: "Ohne zu wissen was er tat, legte er an." Walther menaces Eckbert with a silent gesture, but too late. The arrow reaches its intended target. The narrator's words concerning the alleged lack of intentionality behind the deed only highlight Eckbert's failure to come to terms with his own subconscious motives. In effect, Eckbert has performed the one deed that offers relief from his tortured thoughts. After the murder of Walther, he feels "leicht und beruhigt" even if a vague sense of apprehension drives him back to his castle. When Eckbert returns to find that Bertha has died, he is nearly at his wit's end, though surprisingly not because of his wife's death: "Die Ermordung seines Freundes stand ihm unaufhörlich vor Augen, er lebte unter ewigen innern Vorwürfen."

Just as Eckbert has suppressed the content of his childhood memory, so too he has withheld from consciousness the self-reproach attached to that memory. And if he manages to prevent the rekindling of the childhood memory by dressing his real fears in Bertha's anxieties, he also succeeds in delaying recognition of the self-reproach attached to his own guilty secret by translating his silent, inner accusations into the audible, external accusations of Bertha's persecutors. Even in his death throes at the end of the story, the mad Eckbert can still hear the Old Woman speaking, the dog barking, and the bird singing. Once Walther implicitly threatens to reveal Eckbert's secret, he is transformed into a ubiquitous persecutor whose accusations for various evils only mask the real reproach that hounds Eckbert.

Eckbert's manifest guilt is repeatedly projected onto the outer world until he comes to live in a world inhabited by multiple persecutors. The mechanism of substituting Bertha's sins (greed and treachery) for his own allows him to post a small gain in the battle to suppress his childhood memory, but it also compels him to sustain a serious loss. By projecting reproaches concerning Bertha's crimes onto the outer world, he succeeds in withholding and delaying recognition of his own guilty act. But at the same time, as in all cases of paranoia, he begins to lose protection against the real self-reproach as his delusions of persecution gain in strength. By the end of Tieck's narrative, Eckbert's anxiety is so intense that even a harmless peasant offering directions is transformed into Philipp Walther. The psychic reality of Eckbert's mental life develops so powerful a sway over him that he cuts himself off entirely from the physical realities of his existence and takes flight in madness.

Eckbert's flight is represented in both psychological and physical terms. In fleeing from reality, he also abandons his mountain fortress to enter the world of Bertha's childhood. His journey takes him past the stations of Bertha's youthful pilgrimage to the world of "Waldeinsamkeit." Still laboring under the delusion that he must expiate Bertha's sins and that her transgressions figure as the source of his malaise, he enters a world in which punishment will be meted out for those wrongs. And in fact the Old Woman

first voices the reproach that Eckbert has been expecting: she demands the return of her bird, her pearls, and her dog. Her next revelation concerns the fact of her identity with Walther and Hugo: all these persecutors were in fact one. It is only the third revelation, however, that truly stuns Eckbert: "Und Bertha war deine Schwester." With this pronouncement, the Old Woman proceeds to reveal exactly why Eckbert had always suspected the kinship to Bertha, and the riddle of Eckbert's existence is solved at last.

Eckbert, like Bertha, dies from the shock of recollection. Once the secret of his guilt comes to light, he finds himself unable to tolerate the knowledge of his misdeed. And in this sense, the Old Woman's words, "Siehe, das Unrecht bestraft sich selbst," take on a terrifying reality. For Eckbert's suppression of his childhood memory, his marriage to Bertha, and his subsequent repression of the knowledge of incest themselves appear to generate the guilt that conjures up the figure of the fiendish Old Woman. As Tieck pointed out in an essay on Shakespeare, self-reproaches silenced by the mind invariably return in the form of reproaches addressed to the self by phantoms of the mind. Eckbert may be as much the victim of his own subconscious thoughts as he is the victim of an external agent of retribution.

The story of Eckbert's guilt and punishment is grounded in a psychologically realistic situation. To ward off the knowledge of incest, Eckbert suppresses the childhood memory of his father's adultery and seizes on Bertha's anxieties to mask his own, but ultimately descends into a world of hallucinatory confusion in which he projects the accusations of his own guilt-ridden mind onto the external world. The story of Bertha's guilt and punishment, on the other hand, stands under the sign of the supernatural. Bertha brings to her marriage with Eckbert a sinister dowry: the fabulous jewels stolen from the Old Woman may provide relief from material cares, but at the same time the guilt attached to their theft fosters a kind of nervous anxiety about the possibility of retribution. Bertha herself is less troubled by a guilty conscience than by the fear that a superhuman power may, at any moment, invade her life.

The marriage of Eckbert and Bertha brings together two persons already joined by a biological tie. From the start, the kinship of these two half-siblings is graphically intimated in the single syllable that the Christian names of the marriage partners share. If the union of Eckbert with Bertha marks the transgression of a normative cultural law, it also violates the integrity of two separate and distinct narrative modes. The marriage of Eckbert to Bertha may fail to produce children, but more importantly it breeds a disturbing atmosphere in their secluded mountain retreat. For that marriage not only joins unsuitable partners in unholy matrimony, but also draws together two normally incompatible spheres: the world of natural laws and the world of a supernatural order. The unholy alliance of Eckbert with Bertha is emblematic of the unholy alliance of the realistic narrative with the supernatural tale. Once the marriage of the two figures is consummated, the commonplace existence of the groom is wedded to the fairy-tale origins of his bride to produce a condition conducive to narrative ambiguity. Whether the couple inhabits an ordinary world where events are psychologically motivated or a fairy-tale world in which events are determined by supernatural causality becomes unclear. It is hardly surprising to find that Eckbert himself begins to wonder whether his life is "ein wirklicher Lebenslauf" or "ein seltsames Märchen." Life at the castle may take on a certain routine quality, but the world of Bertha's past forever threatens to invade this ordinary world and to overturn its ground rules.

The point at which this potential threat becomes a menacing reality can be precisely located in the narrative. When Philipp Walther drops the name Strohmian, he also drops the mask of human friendship to reveal that he may be a powerful enemy who is more deeply implicated than he has let on in Bertha's past. That Walther is a masculine incarnation of Bertha's mentor is suggested by the letters of his name, for a simple deletion of the letters "w" and "h" from "Walther" yields the masculine form of the Old Woman's appellation (*die Alte*). Nonetheless, the botanist and geologist Philipp Walther remains firmly anchored in the domain of everyday life. And in fact, Bertha, who has every reason to believe that Walther is an emissary of her childhood world, is bent on divesting Walther of his uncanny powers. "Ist das Zufall? Hat er den Namen erraten, weiß er ihn und hat er ihn mit Vorsatz genannt?" she speculates as she tries to silence her fears. If Bertha dies with the hope that Walther is nothing more than a human who has succeeded in guessing the name Strohmian, Eckbert dies in the belief that Walther is nothing more than a superhuman incarnation of the implacable Old Woman.

The true status of the "stranger" who names Bertha's dog remains enigmatic. Both Bertha and Eckbert chat by the fireside with their friend Philipp Walther; and both Bertha and Eckbert also meet the Old Woman in her secluded retreat. Thus we can be assured that Philipp Walther and the Old Woman exist as actual characters who inhabit two discrete and separate arenas in the narrative. The transformation of Philipp Walther into the Old Woman is, however, witnessed only by Eckbert. Once Philipp Walther names the dog, he begins to lose his distinctive human identity and to take on the supernatural powers, if not yet the actual physical shape, of the Old Woman. At that point, however, his existence still hovers between two polarized extremes: a human friend named Philipp Walther and a supernatural adversary known as the Old Woman.

The visual analogue that is appropriate for displaying Philipp Walther's ambiguous status is, in this particular case, not the rabbit/duck figure, but rather a work entitled "Night and Day" by the Dutch artist M. C. Escher. In Escher's woodcut, we find that a group of black birds flying in one direction gradually transforms itself into a group of white birds flying in the opposite direction. If the black birds maintain their distinct identity to the left side of the work and the white birds maintain their distinct identity to the right side of it, black birds and white birds remain perfectly fused in the middle ground. Escher's "Night and Day" is, however, not quite the right example to illustrate the ambiguities of *Der blonde Eckbert,* for

both sides of that work give us a realistic situation: to the left we have birds flying in the daytime, to the right we have birds flying at night. But to see how a similar visual trick can illustrate the meeting ground of the natural and the supernatural, we need only look at Escher's lithograph "Encounter," where a procession of what Escher called white optimists meets and greets a procession of black pessimists. If we think of Escher's optimists as ordinary humans and of his pessimists as supernatural fiends and focus solely on the background of the lithograph, then we have a more accurate illustration of the fantastic ambiguity in *Der blonde Eckbert.*

Walther and the Old Woman, while maintaining their separate identities as emissaries from two different worlds, converge in Tieck's text to produce a wholly ambiguous figure that weds the human friend to the supernatural adversary. This situation, in which human characters or natural events blend with supernatural characters or supernatural events to create a condition of narrative ambiguity, represents a special case of the fantastic tale. In its purest form, the fantastic tale charges every textual detail with ambiguity. Its reader questions the nature of each and every event—is it the work of supernatural forces or can it be explained by natural laws? *Der blonde Eckbert,* by contrast, first polarizes the natural and the supernatural by locating them in two separate settings, then fuses elements of those two settings to produce narrative ambiguity. The technique appears in countless texts from the German Romantic period, texts that cannot be aligned with either the novella or the fairy tale, but rather occupy a unique position between these two literary vehicles. The protagonists of these tales inhabit a world in which the real and the surreal are seamlessly joined to produce a world of bewildering ambiguities.

In *Der blonde Eckbert,* the central ambiguity of the text is evidently resolved when the Old Woman announces that all along she has been masquerading as Philipp Walther and as Hugo. That declaration, in leading Eckbert to conclude that Philipp Walther and Hugo were nothing more than human incarnations of a super-human power, tips the plot of his life in the direction of the marvelous. Yet by the time the Old Woman finally appears in the wooded preserve that constitutes her domain, Eckbert is in the final stages of his descent into madness. And it is by no means certain to the reader that this Old Woman is a real phantom, for at this point she may simply be a phantom of Eckbert's deranged mind. In the plot of Bertha's life, the Old Woman stood as a full-fledged supernatural power. By contrast, when she appears to Eckbert, she may be nothing more than an impalpable figment of his imagination. If the ambiguities of Eckbert's existence are resolved *for Eckbert* by the Old Woman's declaration, these same ambiguities persist and resonate with renewed energy in the mind of the reader, who hesitates between natural and supernatural explanations for Eckbert's final, fatal meeting with the Old Woman.

In building ambiguity by fusing two discrete narrative modes, the text of *Der blonde Eckbert* creates a situation in which it becomes impossible to pin down even the bare essentials of the plot. We are faced with a riddle that yields no single, straightforward solution. The marvelous world of Bertha's past has become so enmeshed with the strange course of Eckbert's life that it becomes impossible to distinguish the supernatural realities of Bertha's life from the psychological realities of Eckbert's life. If the first part of Tieck's narrative establishes the *coexistence* of two separate domains—one admitting the supernatural, the other knowing only natural laws—the remainder of the text draws us into a middle ground where the two worlds are *copresent.* With this unexpected turn of events, we experience a radical loss of orientation that subverts our capacity to interpret the narrated events. Whatever interpretive avenue we take to analyze the tale, we reach a deadlock with its conclusion. This interpretive deadlock corresponds to the visual stalemate depicted in the middle regions of Escher's "Day and Night" and "Encounter." It becomes impossible to interpret the events in the story unequivocally, for the space in which those events are grounded is characterized by a radical lack of stability—a lack of stability that obliges us to sift through textual clues and to review the evidence that points us first in the direction of the ordinary, then in the direction of the supernatural. If this lack of stability fails to engender in the reader the kind of "poetic madness" that figured as Tieck's stated aim in composing the text, it nevertheless engages the reader's mind in a never-ending process of interpretation, in an endless search that becomes its own end.

---

## FURTHER READING

### Bibliography

Klett, Dwight A. *Ludwig Tieck: An Annotated Guide to Research.* New York: Garland Publishing, 1993, 201 p.
 Full-length bibliography of secondary material on Tieck.

Paulin, Roger. *Ludwig Tieck.* Stuttgart: J. B. Metzler, 1987, 133 p.
 Contains a complete primary bibliography of Tieck's literary and critical works.

### Criticism

Birrell, Gordon. *The Boundless Present: Space and Time in the Literary Fairy Tales of Novalis and Tieck.* Chapel Hill: The University of North Carolina Press, 1979, 160 p.
 Examines Tieck's use of space and time motifs, and compares his technique with that of Novalis.

Crisman, William. "Names, Naming and the Presentation of Language in the Fairy Tales from Tieck's *Phantasus.*" *Michigan Germanic Studies* XI, No. 2 (Fall 1985): 127-43.
 Considers Tieck's use of names in the *Phantasus* fairy tales in relation to his linguistic attitudes generally.

————. "The Status of Adult Rationality in Tieck's Fairy Tales." *Colloquia Germanica* 21, Nos. 2-3 (1988): 111-26.
 Counters a critical tendency to interpret Tieck's fairy tales as parables about the corrupting influence of adult rationality.

Ewton, Ralph W., Jr. "Childhood Without End: Tieck's *Der Blonde Eckbert.*" *The German Quarterly* XLVI, No. 3 (May 1973): 410-27.
 Asserts that the central theme of the novella *Der Blonde Eckbert* is a desire to escape reality and return to the protected, magical world of childhood.

Knight, Victor. "The Perceptive Non-Artist: A Study of Tieck's *Der Runenberg.*" *New German Studies* 10, No. 1 (Spring 1982): 21-31.
 Explores Tieck's portrayal of artists and poets and their relationship to society.

Paulin, Roger. *Ludwig Tieck: A Literary Biography.* London: Clarendon Press, 1985, 434 p.
 Critical and biographical study of Tieck and his work.

Sellner, Timothy F. "Jungian Psychology and the Romantic Fairy Tale: A New Look at Tieck's *Der blonde Eckbert.*" *The Germanic Review* LV, No. 3 (Summer 1980): 89-97.
 Applies a Jungian interpretation to *Der blonde Eckbert.*

Trainer, James. "Ludwig Tieck." In *German Men of Letters: Twelve Literary Essays,* edited by Alex Natan, pp. 39-57. London: Oswald Wolff Limited, 1961.
 Provides an overview of Tieck's life and work, particularly his short fiction.

Zeydel, Edwin H. *Ludwig Tieck, The German Romanticist: A Critical Study.* Princeton: Princeton University Press, 1935, 406 p.
 Offers a chronological account of Tieck's life and career, as well as general critical commentary on his works.

---

Additional coverage of Tieck's life and career is contained in the following sources published by The Gale Group: *Dictionary of Literary Biography,* Vol. 90; and *Nineteenth-Century Literature Criticism,* Vols. 5, 46.

# William Carlos Williams
## 1883-1963

American poet, novelist, short story writer, playwright, essayist, and autobiographer.

## INTRODUCTION

An important American poet, Williams also wrote short stories, most notably the collections *The Knife of the Times* (1932) and *Life along the Passaic River* (1938). Williams was a devoted, practicing physician during most of his literary career, and much of his work demonstrates his respect and concern for his patients and their life situations. The poverty, suffering, and means of survival among the ordinary, poor people of his native New Jersey inform most of Williams's short fiction, which often features conversations written in "the American idiom," his term for the vernacular language essential to shaping his vision of the American experience. Unconventional in form and episodic in construction, his realistic, and sometimes graphic, stories often juxtapose vivid images from life to convey their messages. Williams received a lukewarm critical reception to his short fiction during much of his career. However, many scholars have since recognized that his stories significantly influenced the development of the short story form in twentieth-century American literature.

### Biographical Information

Williams was born in Rutherford, New Jersey, where he spent his entire life. During his adolescence, a heart ailment forced him off the sports fields and led him to study literature. Nevertheless, from 1902 to 1906 Williams attended medical school at the University of Pennsylvania, where he made lasting friendships with American poets Ezra Pound and H. D. By the time Williams had established his own medical practice in 1910, he had published his first book, *Poems* (1909). During the next decade, Williams married Florence ("Flossie") Herman in 1912, started a family in 1914, and published two more books of poetry. In the 1920s Williams extended his literary efforts to prose, producing the prose "improvisations" of *Kora in Hell* (1920), the short novel *The Great American Novel* (1923), the historical essays of *In the American Grain* (1925), and his first full-length novel, *A Voyage to Pagany* (1928). Williams's short stories began appearing in the 1930s. Scholars have surmised that his growing frustration at the mild response to his poetry prompted Williams to write fiction, including the novels *White Mule* (1937)—his first popularly acclaimed work—and the first volume of *The Stecher Trilogy,* which is based on the people and the circumstances of his wife's youth. The 1940s and 1950s marked Williams's most productive period. He published two novels, three plays and a libretto,

another collection of stories entitled *Make Light of It* (1950), his autobiography, and many collections of new and previously published poetry, most notably the five-book epic poem *Paterson* (1946-1958), which is widely considered a masterpiece of American literature, and *Selected Poems* (1948), which won the 1949 National Book Award. Following a series of heart attacks and a bout of depression from 1948 to 1953, Williams retired from his medical practice, but continued to write. In 1961 he published his final collections of stories, *The Farmers' Daughters,* and plays, *Many Loves and Other Plays.* After he died on March 4, 1963, Williams was awarded the Pulitzer Prize in poetry for *Pictures from Brueghel* (1962) and the National Institute of Arts and Letters gold medal for poetry.

### Major Works of Short Fiction

Williams, the doctor-narrator in most of his short fiction, believed that the short story form was "a good medium for nailing down a single conviction. Emotionally." Most of the eleven stories in *The Knife of the Times* represent Williams's experiences with some of his patients and neigh-

bors during the early years of the Great Depression, showing their fortitude and perseverance while dealing with
social and individual suffering. The "knife" in each of
these stories refers to more than the hardships of dire
economic reversal, often focusing on "couples" and their
unions and separations. The title story, for instance, portrays a lesbian relationship between Ethel and Maura, who
cope with the "knife" of their homosexuality. "Old Doc
Rivers," perhaps the best known story of the collection,
relates the anecdotes of a legendary small-town doctor,
who "would go anywhere, anytime, for anybody," but tragically succumbs to shifting American cultural values and
ultimately to the "knife" of drugs and alcohol. *Life along
the Passaic River* contains nineteen stories about similar
themes and situations, but the tone is darker, the focus
turned more toward children characters, and the locale
assumes significance, reflecting Williams's belief that "In
a work of art place is everything." In a series of vignettes
that dissolve into one another, the title story offers detailed descriptions of the industrialized riverscape and the
people who live there, focusing on the conflict between
industry and nature. In "The Use of Force," Williams's
most frequently anthologized story, a doctor attempts to
diagnose a child's fever, but the child refuses to allow an
examination, so the doctor must resort to forceful methods. "Jean Beicke," one of Williams's favorite stories,
centers on the life and death of an eleven-month-old girl,
including a vivid description of the child's autopsy. *Make
Light of It* comprises the stories from Williams's first two
volumes and twenty-one other stories in a section entitled
"Beer and Cold Cuts," of which all but two had been
previously published. *The Farmers' Daughters* includes
all of Williams's previously collected short fiction and the
uncollected title story, which recounts the relationship
between two southern farmers' daughters and their doctor.
*The Doctor Stories* (1984) collects several doctor-themed
stories from *Life along the Passaic River.*

## Critical Reception

The technique and style of Williams's stories have often
been compared to that of Gertrude Stein, Sherwood Anderson, early Ernest Hemingway, and D. H. Lawrence. The
stories of *Life along the Passaic River* have received the
most critical attention, particularly "The Use of Force,"
which has been interpreted variously in terms of its implications about violence, practical applications in the field
of medical ethics, sexual connotations, psychological aspects, and autobiographical factors. Many critics have
emphasized the autobiographical quality of much of Williams's work: "His temperament . . . was neatly split between that of a feeling, observing doctor and that of the
practicing poet. . . . He was a poet-physician. These two-
parted identities stand behind his every word," observed
George Monteiro. Most scholars have agreed that Williams's innovations in the short story form were revolutionary. Linda Welshimer Wagner has pointed out that
"the apparently effortless telling, the informal (and often
unresolved) plot, the emphasis on character presented
through salient details, and above all, the reliance on dialogue—these trademarks of a Williams's story occur re-

peatedly in contemporary writing." James G. Watson has
likewise remarked on Williams's contributions to the
American short story: "Declining the formulas of tradition
and the acceptable contemporary conventions, Williams
chose to state frankly the intimate passions and passionate
brutalities that he said were flashes struck from the materials of life." Commenting on Williams's literary accomplishments, Wagner concluded that his "short stories may
have had as deep an effect on contemporary fiction as his
poems have had on modern poetry."

---

## PRINCIPAL WORKS

### Short Fiction

*The Knife of the Times, and Other Stories*  1932
*A Novelette and Other Prose* (novella and prose)  1932
*Life along the Passaic River*  1938
*Make Light of It: Collected Stories*  1950
*The Farmers' Daughters: The Collected Stories*  1961
*The Doctor Stories*  1984

### Other Major Works

*Poems* (poetry)  1909
*The Tempers* (poetry)  1913
*Al que quiere!* (poetry)  1917
*Kora in Hell: Improvisations* (poetry)  1920
*Sour Grapes* (poetry)  1921
*GO GO* (poetry)  1923
*The Great American Novel* (novel)  1923
*Spring and All* (poetry)  1923
*In the American Grain* (essays)  1925
*A Voyage to Pagany* (novel)  1928
*The Cod Head* (poetry)  1932
*Collected Poems, 1921-1931* (poetry)  1934
*An Early Martyr and Other Poems* (poetry)  1935
*Adam & Eve & the City* (poetry)  1936
*\*White Mule* (novel)  1937
*The Complete Collected Poems of William Carlos Will-
    iams, 1906-1938* (poetry)  1938
*\*In the Money: White Mule—Part II* (novel)  1940
*The Wedge* (poetry)  1944
*†Paterson (Book One)* (poetry)  1946
*The Clouds* (poetry)  1948
*A Dream of Love: A Play in Three Acts and Eight Scenes*
    (drama)  1948
*†Paterson (Book Two)* (poetry)  1948
*†Paterson (Book Three)* (poetry)  1949
*The Pink Church* (poetry)  1949
*Selected Poems* (poetry)  1949
*A Beginning on the Short Story [Notes]* (essay)  1950
*The Collected Later Poems* (poetry)  1950
*The Autobiography* (autobiography)  1951
*The Collected Earlier Poems* (poetry)  1951
*†Paterson (Book Four)* (poetry)  1951
*\*The Build-Up: A Novel* (novel)  1952
*The Desert Music, and Other Poems* (poetry)  1954
*Selected Essays* (essays)  1954

*Journey to Love* (poetry) 1955
*I Wanted to Write a Poem: The Autobiography of the Works of a Poet* 1958
†*Paterson (Book Five)* (poetry) 1958
*Yes, Mrs. Williams: A Personal Record of My Mother* (biography) 1959
*Many Loves and Other Plays: The Collected Plays* (dramas) 1961
*Pictures from Brueghel, and Other Poems* (poetry) 1962
*The Collected Poems of William Carlos Williams.* 2 vols. (poetry) 1986-1988

*These works are commonly referred to collectively as *The Stecher Trilogy.*

†These volumes, together with notes for a proposed sixth book, were collected and published as *Paterson* in 1963.

---

## CRITICISM

### Philip Rahv (essay date 1938)

SOURCE: "Dr. Williams in His Short Stories," in *Image and Idea: Twenty Essays on Literary Themes,* New Directions Paperbook, 1957, pp. 155-58.

[*In the following essay, which originally appeared in* Partisan Review *in March 1938, Rahv summarizes the themes of* Life on the Passaic River.]

In his prose as in his poetry William Carlos Williams is too hardy a frontiersman of the word to permit himself the idle luxuries of aestheticism. There are too many things to be seen and touched, too many cadences of living speech to be listened to and recorded. Kenneth Burke once said of Williams that he was engaged in "discovering the shortest route between subject and object." Perhaps that explains why in *Life on the Passaic River,* a collection of nineteen short stories, not one imitates in any way the conventional patterns of the genre. The directness of this writer's approach to his material excludes its subjection to the researches of plot and calculated form. What Williams tells us is much too close to him to lend itself to the alienation of design; none of his perceptions can be communicated through the agency of invented equivalents. The phenomena he observes and their meanings are so intimately involved with one another, the cohabitation of language and object is so harmonious, that formal means of expression would not only be superfluous but might actually nullify the incentive to creation.

These notations in a doctor's notebook, these fragments salvaged from grime and squalor, these insights gained during the routines of humble labor—such would only be given the lie by the professional mannerisms of authorship, its pomposities and braggadocio. Where a writer usually takes the attitude of an impresario toward his themes, calculating each entrance and exit, Williams will begin or end his story as the spirit moves him; pausing to face his reader, he will take him into his confidence and

speak his mind without recourse to stratagems of ingratiation. Elliptical in some passages and naturalistic in others, Williams is perfectly conscious of writing but hostile to "literature." Out of "a straight impulse, without borrowing, without lie or complaint," he puts down on paper that which stirs him. His subjects are few and often minute, their scope is sharply circumscribed by his personal experience and by his voluntary seclusion within the local and immediate, he repeats himself frequently—yet these stories are exceptional for their authenticity and told not to provoke but to record. It is pain which is the source of values here. The dread of annihilation is ever present. "Christ, Christ! . . . How can a man live in the face of this daily uncertainty? How can a man not go mad with grief, with apprehension?" No grand conceits, no gratuitous excitements, no melodrama. There is no doing away with the staples of existence; no gallivanting on the banks of the Passaic River.

For what could be more dismal than life in these small industrial towns of New Jersey? The mills are worked by immigrant laborers, and their youngsters are "all over the city as soon as they can walk and say, Paper!" The doctor visits these uprooted households, often angry at himself because of the tenderness in him that reaches out to these people, quite as often resigned to doing his job, to immersing himself in the finalities of human life. "To me," he writes, "it is a hard, barren life, where I am alone and unmolested (work as I do in the thick of it), though in constant danger lest some slip send me to perdition but which, being covetous not at all, I enjoy for the seclusion and primitive air of it."

The little girl, both of whose tonsils are covered with membrane, fights furiously to keep him from knowing her secret. Another one, a lank-haired girl of fifteen, is a powerful little animal upon whom you can stumble on the roof, behind the stairs "any time at all." A whole gang is on her trail. Cured of her pimples, how will this tenacious creature ever slash her way to the bliss recited on the radio? "The pure products of America go crazy," Williams once wrote in a poem. And these stories are familiar images of the same, released by that active element of sympathy which is to be prized above all else in the equipment of an artist. But this writer has no hankering for consistent explanations, for the constancy of reason; he seldom permits himself to ask why. "What are you going to do with a guy like that. Or why want to do anything with him. Except not miss him," he says of one of his characters. This last is the point. He is content with grasping the fact, with creating a phenomenology; but the relations, social and historic, that might unify these facts and significate them on a plane beyond sensation or nostalgia or pathos he has no mind for. And this absence of what one might call, in his terms, ideological presumptuousness, while admirable in its modesty, also constitutes his defeat. However much of value there is in these facts of "hard history" and in the scrupulous gathering of their detail, the larger implications are systematically neglected. Thought is proscribed as anti-aesthetic. Yet, though habitually confined to the suggestive and purely descriptive, this prose nevertheless holds within itself some of the raw elements of a comprehensive consciousness.

But Williams does think about America, if only to sketch it in psychic outline. He is under the spell of its *mystique* and strains to encompass it in a vision. This need in him provides a contrast and relief to the phenomenological principle informing his work; and much of his charm flows from the interaction of his precise facts with his American mysticism. In his novel, *White Mule,* the fusion of these two qualities allowed a visible direction to emerge. "What then is it like, America?" asks Fraulein Von J. in **"The Venus,"** which seems to me the best story in the collection. This German girl is a genuine Weimar-period object. She has a genius for formulating the most complex modern problems in the simplest terms. The daughter of a general, she comes to Italy to become a nun. But perhaps America—she questions the American, Evans, who carries a flint arrowhead in his pocket—could prove a satisfactory alternative to the Church? Evans speaks of the old pioneer houses of his ancestors, and of that "early phase" of America whose peculiar significance has been forgotten or misunderstood. The German girl holds the arrowhead in her hand, feeling its point and edge. "It must be even more lonesome and frightening in America than in Germany," she finally says. The story recalls us to the Williams of *In the American Grain,* a writer ravaged by this hemisphere's occult aboriginal past. In some ways Dr. Williams is really a medicine-man.

### Vivienne Koch (essay date 1950)

SOURCE: "The Novels and Short Stories," in *William Carlos Williams,* New Directions Books, 1950, pp. 187-246.

[*In the following excerpt from a detailed assessment of Williams's fiction to 1950, Koch reviews the stories in* The Knife of the Times *and* Life along the Passaic River, *indicating their significance in the development of Williams's career and of the modern American short story form.*]

The logic of Williams' allegiance to the quest for a knowledge of localism, for a defining of the American grain, has compelled in his fiction a restriction to American materials. The notable exception to this is his first novel, *A Voyage to Pagany.* While its subject-matter is ostensibly Europe, the Old World, it is, in reality, an assessment of that world through the eyes of an American, its hero, and thus, in effect, an assessment of America too. The Jamesian pattern of New World meets Old has in Williams' novel a similar function. While this encounter does not always change the two worlds, it nevertheless mutually illuminates their two systems of value. And with Williams (seemingly the last writer in the world to compare on *technical* grounds with James) the result, as in James, is a judgment of America, a judgment perhaps as ambivalent as James's although disguised by a more visible affection.

The years 1920-23 . . . were dedicated by Williams to a reconsideration of the various aesthetic points of view with which it seemed possible for a writer to identify himself.

His editing of *Contact* must have sharpened the focus for such revaluation and, indeed, the discussions of policy in the five issues of that periodical reveal an awareness of the choices and, at the same time, an almost fanatical resistance to the contemporary pressures toward aesthetic conformity. The nexus of belief and value from which Williams' fiction has sprung is precisely the same nexus from which his poems, plays and criticism derive.

Perhaps the best measure of Williams' particular development of the concept of "the local" would be to fix its relationship to other formulations of the "American" problem in the arts during his time. The decade 1915-25 (roughly) while witness to a large exodus of writers and artists from the United States to other countries, at the same time, and perhaps for the same reasons, marked an attempt to create an "American" culture. This impulse was crudely nationalistic in many of its manifestations. It could be seen, for example, in the blatant "new localism" of Lindsay dedicated to the wish that smaller American communities might be enabled to survive by creating their own arts and crafts. The regional poetry of Sandburg sentimentalized in heroic terms the achievement of the pioneers and industrial leaders of the West. Robert Coady, in "The Soil," "a magazine of art," sought for an American art in the immediate and familiar. Coady tried, naïvely, no doubt, to find a native and popular aesthetic for America by drawing on photography, engineering, sports, the dime novel, etc., for his materials. Perhaps the most sophisticated attempt to define the American task in letters was to be found in the pages of *The Seven Arts* which had on its editorial board writers like Waldo Frank, Van Wyck Brooks, and Randolph Bourne who, at distinct levels of intellect and outlook, were all similarly engaged in evaluating the American scene, its past and its future. Bourne's dissident, brilliant, and querulous anti-imperialist, anti-war stand differed sharply from the increasingly conservative, nationalistic orientation of the former expatriate Brooks. The quest for the Grail in each instance is pursued in the spirit not of the Grail but of the man who seeks it.

It is reasonable to assume that Williams could not have been unaffected by the powerful stream of investigation and, more dangerously, *wish,* represented by this search for the meaning of American experience. The significance of his own search is, as I have suggested, defined by his greater integrity of purpose, his sharper assessment of the problem. In 1928 Gorham Munson could say [in *Destinations: A Canvass,*] when comparing Williams' interest in American materials with that of his contemporaries, that "Williams differs . . . in that he has observed the limitations of his program and thereby kept it pure, he has confined himself to the strictly aesthetic problems of choice of subject-matter and the fashion of perceiving and handling it." *Contact* had set forth a program for American writing which stressed the necessity for contact between "words and the locality which breeds them, in this case America." The distance between this kind of localism and that of the mid-western regionalists is, of course, radical. The former stems from a recognition of the relationship between experience and the modes by which it is ordered; that is to say, it recognizes the problem of technique and craft. The latter emphasizes merely the authenticity of the "local" as subject matter; it is essentially disinterested in form. . . .

When Williams' first collection of short stories came out during the days of the Depression, it had a grimly appropriate title. *The Knife of the Times,* published in 1932, appears to represent the "real" world Dev Williams had gone back to at the end of *A Voyage to Pagany. Pagany* is no longer an operative ideal in these powerful, often humorously forthright stories of the bleak and sometimes heroic lives of the small people of America, many of whom are the cast-off spawn of that Europe which Dev could not accept.

The social types represented are diverse. Farm-boys, professional men, Negro servant-girls, middle-class housewives, local playboys, school teachers, the range of caste and personality is as wide as the landscape of a semiurban American community permits, although the locale shifts from industrial towns like Paterson, to near-by farm communities, and to unnamed suburban villages. The stories, although various in theme, seem to cluster about two poles: the present, represented by the title piece, **"The Knife of the Times,"** and the past, seen with a nostalgic authenticity of detail, and cherished for its greater fluidity of personality, its slower levelling-down of conduct and individuality. Sometimes, as in **"An Old Time Raid"** or **"The Colored Girls of Passenack—Old and New,"** the present serves as ironic counterpoint to the freer, more careless style of American life in the early decades of the century.

Williams utilizes, perhaps not at all consciously, three sources for the predominant narrative style in this collection. Gertrude Stein's cadenced, clear, syntactically functional prose is suggested over and over again in the easy colloquial flow of the writing. The brilliantly swift title story is a small masterpiece (under six pages in length) of understatement, dealing with great delicacy of the curious, overpowering love of a middle-aged mother of six for her childhood friend, Maura, also the mother of a family. The lucid, almost transparently simple prose races along with Ethel's mounting lust, without any of the locutions of Miss Stein's later mannered writing, and more in the style of her early *Three Lives.*

At the time the stories in *The Knife of the Times* were being written, Williams was carefully studying Gertrude Stein's work, as a magazine piece in which her emphasis on the "play" (or music) of sight, sense and sound contrasts were suggestively compared to that of Sterne's, especially as seen in Chapter 43 of *Tristram Shandy.* "Stein's theme," says Williams, "is writing." This had, of course, been his own theme in *The Great American Novel.* Further: "It is simply the skeleton, the 'formal' parts of writing, those that make form, that she has to do with, apart from the 'burden' which they carry." Williams does not deflesh the skeleton, as does Miss Stein in her later writing (this was not her practice in *Three Lives* and Williams in this article shows that he is aware of it), but instead makes the skeleton *compose* or bear the burden. A short passage from *The Knife of the Times* will show how

much Williams has learned from the prose of Miss Stein's "Melanctha" (which he calls "one of the best bits of characterization produced in the United States") and how freely he employs it for narrative movement:

> Ethel wrote letters now such as Maura wished she might at some time in her life have received from a man. She was told that all these years she had been dreamed of, passionately, without rival, without relief. Now, surely, Maura did not dare show the letters any longer to her husband. He would not understand.

The story moves with a compelling intensity to its surprising denouement in which the passive Maura is swept through sympathy into the vortex of her more aggressive friend's desire. The taut austerity of the style both heightens and contends with the desperately purposive passion of the distraught woman. The title of the story, suggesting as it does, another dimension of social reference for Maura's capitulation to Ethel, clarifies the ironic symbolism of lives, turned by the cruel edge of a mechanical society back upon themselves (upon their own narcissistic love-images) for enrichment and satisfaction.

In **"The Sailor's Son,"** Williams handles the complementary situation to Lesbianism, in the behavior of the docile and dependent Manuel. The plot is clever, although not in the fashionable way. The revelation at the end does not depend on a trick of withheld knowledge for its shock, but derives from the actual opening up of the meaning of Manuel's conduct before the outraged eyes of his employer, Mrs. Cuthbertson. When Margie, the woman whom Manuel plans to marry and who supports him in periods of unemployment, is told by Mrs. Cuthbertson that she has fired Manual because of her discovery of his homosexuality, she completely reverses the direction of Mrs. Cuthbertson's judgment as well as the actual events of the story:

> The boy is lonesome up here, said the woman. Why do you keep his friends away? I am engaged to marry him, I don't care what he does. Why should you worry? . . . Finally the fiancée grew abusive and Mrs. Cuthbertson losing her temper very nearly struck her. It was a wild moment. But in the end Manual was fired. And the woman took him back to the city with her where she told him she would pay for a room until she could find work for him elsewhere.

**"The Descendant of Kings"** is another story whose narrative cadences suggest a close reading of Stein. The process of Stewie's being and becoming are appropriately woven together in a supple, limpid prose. The handsome, summer playboy, Stewie, grows up in ignorance and want under the possessive guardianship of a poetic grandmother who keeps him out of school so that she can remain near her beloved sea. The story for its overtones of inarticulate, almost pathological deprivation stands alongside Sherwood Anderson's memorable portrait in "I'm A Fool" of another American possessed by his social inadequacies. When Stewie, still in his teens, gets out of the Navy up to which time "he had gone on like a straw on the stream of the old lady's will" he faces up to the fact that he knows nothing to do. Aimlessly, he falls for a sophisticated summer visitor, an artist's model, Muriel, who in her wisdom clarifies for him what is to be his role.

When he catches Muriel with another man (the inevitable Yale graduate), he gets the first of a series of singularly ironic blows which he is to get from women—always where it hurts him most. Later Stewie becomes a performer in the local hotel orchestra and his triumphs become almost epical. But the second time Stewie really falls, this time for a pretty schoolteacher, her double-crossing is fatal to his chief excellence. The understatedly symbolic denouement comes in Stewie's curious tussle with a bull in which, injured and bleeding, he finally conquers the animal by a heroic wrench of the nose-ring. It is the first time Stewie has ever tested his strength against another male. The struggle restores his psychic potentials for once again fulfilling his male nature. A revitalization or rebirth has taken place, and we know that Stewie will resume the career destined for him by his motherless, seahaunted childhood. But the wry ending lowers the key of this victory over self, and we see that the protagonist is not immune from time any more than he is from the paradoxes of his own conquests: "For he did get over it fairly well in the end tho' he was never again as able as he had been as a kid—naturally."

Belle, the plump, middle-aged country Venus of **"Pink and Blue"** is a female Stewie in the fervor and single-mindedness of her pursuit of the opposite sex. But her touching addiction to the outer proprieties of caste, such as clothes, calling cards, and legal titles are seen at the level of a semicomic social criticism, different from the more inward conflict which determines Stewie's downward path to wisdom. For Belle is placidly at peace with herself in the amorous adventures which prove so destructive to the men who love her. Her confusions are merely social in their nature and it is the man who can give her the greatest quantity of matched "outfit" who, in the end, may keep her love. The story is told from the point of view of Mrs. Bandler, the employer of one of Belle's indeterminately numbered husbands. The tone of controlled irony derived from her gracious, kindly and equally caste-conscious viewpoint lends a quiet dignity to the pathetic events of this rural comedy.

**"Mind and Body,"** as the title indicates, is similarly polarized around a conflict in values, a conflict which is finally resolved by the somewhat unsatisfactory deus-ex-machina of science, an engine the doctor employs when all other attempts to explain his psychotic patient to herself have failed. His reliance on the findings of capillaroscopy "a study of the microscopic terminal blood vessels," is used self-consciously and with a deliberate obliquity of intention. The woman, a self-described manic-depressive with a background of institutionalization, is a fine study of the conflict between a primitive cultural inheritance and a veneer of the most esoteric sort of book-learning. Brilliant, educated, and miscast in her social and sexual role as wife to a kindly, lame, and womanish little male-nurse, she alternates between superstitious misapprehensions of her own physical condition and learned speculations on literature and philosophy. The factor of suppressed

Lesbianism in her personality which the doctor boorishly brings to the surface is appropriately left unresolved.

The sources of her problems in an inheritance from one of the "old country families" with its increment of insanity and pathology are only lightly sketched in. Nevertheless, by the time the rambling story, largely told by the patient herself, is completed we have a bold character drawing of a ruined human potential for social responsibility. These meanings do not lie close to the surface in **"Mind and Body"** any more than they do elsewhere in Williams' deceptively simple prose.

By now we can see that one of Williams' recurring aims in the short story is to achieve a reversal of values. **"The Buffalos"** because of its theme of the power-conflict between male and female, its rather explicit symbolism and the way in which the action is narrowed down to a male and female actor (thus intensifying the character of the conflict) reminds one of some of D. H. Lawrence's stories. A love affair between a beautiful suffragette and a man who is at first amused and then bored by her political ardors is brought to its frustrating, almost cruel, conclusion by the careful analogy with which the now disenchanted lover confronts the lady, for he has rightly suspected her motivation. The situation has been completely reversed: the suitor is the victor, but he has suffered a loss in the winning. Similarly, the lady has won her point: she has been theoretically granted the possession of the male privileges she envies. But having been taken at her word, she loses her man.

Two stories in *The Knife of the Times* reveal a special attempt to come to grips with character as it responds to or stems from American social habit and values. When character is treated on a humorous, anecdotal level as in **"An Old Time Raid,"** the story becomes essentially a study in manners. But in **"Old Doc Rivers"** the study of a brilliant, hopped-up suburban doctor, one of the richest character drawings of comparable length in recent American fiction, the problem of motivation is more deeply investigated. The social environment is reported, as in **"An Old Time Raid,"** but it is also questioned. In **"An Old Time Raid"** the result is comedy, while in **"Old Doc Rivers,"** although comic elements are present, the effect is one of tragedy.

In the first story "Dago" Schultz, the professional roisterer and good-time Charlie of a cocky, crude-mannered semiurban culture, expresses the gross animal vitality and instinctive insubordination of a raw, vital people. Dago's death (he was an expert train-hopper), while hopping a train after a drinking bout, is meaningless as "tragedy" but has a cultural significance. As the first-person narrator, commenting on his death, says: "Makes me think of an old man I knew, when they'd ask him how far back he could remember he'd say: I can remember back to when the U.S. was a republic.—That's where 'Dago' Schultz belongs. You know."

But if Dago is seen as a type of socially misdirected energy, still he is essentially part of his community, while

Old Doc Rivers, the most able, talented and sensitive man in the New Jersey town where he practises, is shown as a man in conflict with his environment, his profession and his times. His drug-taking, which at first fortifies and then increasingly hampers the execution of his brilliant diagnostic insights, is evaluated by the young colleague who is narrator:

> It came of his sensitivity, his civility; it was this that made him do it, I'm sure; the antithesis rather of that hog-like complacency that comes to so many men following the successful scamper for cash.

The crude environment of the turn of the century times "in the provincial bottom of the New Jersey" in which Rivers lived, made it impossible for him to find a release there, although at first he had great popularity and great power.

Rivers' personality is built up through the younger doctor's investigation of old hospital records for evidence of Rivers' medical results, as well as through the various eye-witness anecdotes which he collects from older patients and physicians. The social data are looked into with the detachment of a field sociologist, but the cumulative detail mounts to a profound study of individual character while, curiously, forcing the social implications to a higher level of abstraction. The

> awful fever of overwork . . . A trembling in the arms and thighs, a tightness of the neck and in the head above the eyes—fast breath, vague pains in the muscles and in the feet. Followed by an orgasm, crashing the job through, putting it over in a feverish heat. Then the feeling of looseness afterward. Not pleasant. But there it is. Then cigarettes, a shot of gin. And that's all there is to it. Women the same, more and more . . . He had no time, had to be fast, he had to improvise and did—to a marvel.

These are the social terms by which sensitive men like Rivers must live. But as the tempo of the American malady makes deeper inroads on Rivers' interior resources and capacity for rebound, he grows more dependent on drugs. Finally, he makes errors in judgment and eventually whispers of malpractice spring up. But still the humble butchers, the peasant mill-workers and street laborers go to him, for now his name has come to have mythic properties and the visible evidence of his professional defections are discounted. What the people of Creston want is what the unheeded voice of a collective Paterson cries out for in the poem *Paterson*: "A marvel, a marvel!" Even when he was almost "finished," the town's ritualistic faith in Rivers persists.

Rivers does not die in the gutter, as a conventional oracle might predict, but, what is worse, he is *brough* before he quits. He is a man robbed of his full scope for action by the slow attrition of his personality through the very means by which it is completed. **"Old Doc Rivers"** is a self-contained, under-stated, and, perhaps, minor American tragedy. But in the compass of a forty-page story Williams has succeeded by a quiet, almost statistical investi-

gation in piecing together the social meaning of the failure of a superb talent, "a serious indictment against all the evangelism of American life which I most hated."

In his next volume of stories **Life Along the Passaic River** (1938) Williams confines himself almost entirely to the people who live along its banks. The collection, without being "regional," builds up a solid feeling of community, of place. Written during the Depression years, they reflect some of the curious dislocations in caste and character precipitated by the times. The Poles, the Italian mothers, the wild children, the unemployed, the furtive adolescents, all these aspects of the life of a small industrial town in America are explored with that warm authenticity of observation which sheds clarity and illumination into the disordered areas of the human soul. Many of the stories, like Chekhov's, have quite patently grown out of Williams' medical experience. Of these the best are **"The Girl With the Pimply Face," "The Use of Force," "A Night in June," "Four Bottles of Beer,"** and **"A Face of Stone."** The last is one of Williams' finest stories, and demonstrates his secure movement in the limpid, Flaubertian prose which he was to consolidate so powerfully in *White Mule*.

In **"A Face of Stone,"** a busy pediatrician is irritated by the seemingly deliberate obtuseness of a Jewish immigrant couple who come to him for the care of their child. The pattern follows that of Williams' most successful stories—a situation in which a reversal of values is achieved by the slow impact of character upon character. The story opens on a note of annoyance:

> He was one of these fresh Jewish types you want to kill at sight, the presuming poor whose looks change the minute cash is mentioned. But they're insistent, trying to force attention, taking advantage of good nature at the first crack. You come when I call you, that type. . . . She, on the other hand, looked Italian, a goaty slant to her eyes, a face often seen among Italian immigrants . . . A face of stone. It was an animal distrust, not shyness . . . She looked dirty. So did he . . .

The patients do not follow the doctor's directions either in the care of their child or in calling upon his services. The overtones of the doctor's distaste for these uncooperative and unattractive people is expressed in terms of "racial prejudice." Yet, in a gradual way, he begins to be involved in their problems. First it is the baby, with "a perfectly happy fresh mug on him" that amuses him in spite of himself. Then he becomes interested in the curious dull flush which comes over the greasy little husband whenever the inarticulate wife's health is discussed. Eventually, he learns that she is only twenty-four, that all her relatives were killed in Poland, and that she had almost no food as a child. The bare, medical description of the woman's physical features builds up the pathos of her deprived past, but yet supports the doctor's wish to hold on to his negative attitudes.

When he learns that the woman herself has recently arrived from Poland he slowly begins to understand her absorption in the baby. As the husband, on the last call, describes how he must dissolve aspirin for her "His face reddened again and suddenly I understood his half shameful love for the woman and at the same time the extent of her reliance on him. I was touched." The doctor's own growth in understanding seems to invade the woman with the face of stone. When he shows her some pills for her rheumatic pains, "She looked at them again. Then for the first time since I had known her a broad smile spread all over her face. Yeah, she said, I swallow him." That is the end of the story. There is no explicit referral to the nature of the exchange. But what has happened, in this restrained narrative, its detail grounded in the natural orbit of the doctor's job, is that a social miracle of a sort has been accomplished. Two opposed sets of impulse, training, and value as represented by the worn, small-town American physician (working in a milieu remarkably like Williams' own Rutherford), and the obdurate, immigrant couple are brought into conflict. The outcome is that each begins to accept something from the other's realm of meaning. The harsh undertones of prejudice on the one hand and mistrust on the other are ruled out of the story by the expansive warmth of the final sentence.

In **"The Girl With the Pimply Face"** there is a similar struggle between two sets of values. The doctor-narrator, who in reality is the hero of the piece, takes a warm and understanding interest in a Russian working-class family. While visiting their sick baby, the doctor gets interested in a pimply-faced girl of sixteen, the sister, who by her tough, straightforward self-reliance amuses him. He learns that she has left school and advises her on how to care for her face. Later, he meets the family's former physician who tells him they are drunks, on the charity rolls, that they mistreat the baby and that the girl is a "little bitch. Say, if I had my way I'd run her out of town tomorrow morning . . . Boy, they sure took you in." But when the doctor returns he finds the baby improved, the girl's face clearing up and the girl going back to school. There is no attempt to whitewash the people. The doctor, as opposed to his cynical colleague, may have been "taken in." He doesn't know, nor do we. But he has been fulfilling his function as healer. He has cured, and his fulfillment is in his willingness to accept the reward proper to his function, a reward which lies entirely in the curing. It is this type of subtle revaluation of a crass popular morality, which reveals Williams as a writer with the greatest responsiveness to the questions of social ethics.

In **"The Use of Force,"** a very short story, the doctor-narrator emerges as the villain of the piece. The way in which the physician, in spite of his recognition that he is contending with a sick child, is gradually drawn into a violent contest of wills is depicted with honesty and power. The brutality with which the doctor, now in a blind rage, forces open the child's mouth and discovers the nature of the illness is a startling exposure of those subrational wells of impulse which invade the conduct of supposedly disciplined adults.

On the other side of the psychological scale, in **"Jean Beicke,"** is the curiously unexpected love and tenderness which a very ill infant, dying of a seemingly undiagnosable ailment, arouses in the breasts of the hard-boiled doctor-narrator and the attending physicians and nurses. The miracle of human personality is the beautiful center of the relationship. Williams is one of the few writers of fiction who are aware of the dynamics of this force in infants:

> Somehow or other, I hated to see that kid go. Everybody felt rotten. She was such a scrawny, misshapen, worthless piece of humanity that I had said many times that somebody ought to chuck her in the garbage chute—but after a month watching her suck up her milk and thrive on it—and to see those alert blue eyes in that face—well, it wasn't pleasant.

The tiny thread by which the potentials of personality develop or are cut off is revealed, at the end, to have been a slip-up in diagnostic procedure for which several interested and capable physicians are jointly responsible.

**"A Night in June"** is a warmly stated tale of a physician's home delivery of a child to a simple Italian woman who can hardly talk with him. There is profound humility in the doctor's awareness of how his own responses to the woman have changed: "This woman in her present condition would have seemed repulsive to me ten years ago—now, poor soul, I saw her to be as clean as a cow that calves. The flesh of my arm lay against the flesh of her knee gratefully. It was I who was being comforted and soothed." Her child is born, the doctor and the mother jointly assisting the delivery. In the end, the doctor has been strengthened and renewed by his closeness to the woman's experience.

**"At the Front,"** like **"Four Bottles of Beer,"** relies on first-person narrative for a brief and humorously anecdotal tale of World War I. Both this and the series of small vignettes collected in the end-piece, **"World's End,"** seem to have been set down because of Williams' persistent interest in speech patterns as ends in themselves, as well as hallmarks of personality. Several sketches in **"World's End"** deal with the meaningless but nevertheless deadly violence with which the human and the animal worlds combat one another. The one of the old hospital infested with cats which the internes hunt down and destroy for twenty-five cent bonuses, or that of the laboratory where the clotted blood on slides is eaten overnight by invading cockroaches are curiously moving glimpses of man's vulnerability to physical degradation. These tales grow out of experiences Williams had over thirty years before when interning in the ramshackly, ill-administered Nursery and Child's Hospital in a New York slum district.

In **"Dance Pseudo Macabre"** in which the reader follows a doctor on his emergency rounds in the middle of the night, Williams defends the use of this kind of material. He defies those who would accuse him of a "shallow" morbidity to prove that health alone is inevitable: "I defend the normality of every distortion to which the flesh is susceptible, every disease, every amputation." Although **"Dance Pseudo Macabre"** is not one of Williams' successful pieces, others of these tales of death and illness compel us to accept his valuation. These stories do not depress us but instead instruct us in a greater comprehension of the narrow boundaries between living and dying, between health and disease, between reason and impulse. For Williams' sane, compassionate and scientific intellect orders these complex relationships from the uniquely privileged vantage point of one whose profession is equally among the quick and the dead. These stories will prove revealing sources for Williams' future biographers.

The most ambitious story of *Life Along the Passaic* is **"The Dawn of Another Day."** The time is the Depression and a young man of background and wealth has, in desperation, left his wife and children who are now living off his mother-in-law, to stay on an old unsaleable yacht. His companion is a chronic drunk, Fred, who drinks his liquor and stimulates him by his undisciplined talk of revolution, and the defections of the class to which Ed, the younger man, belongs. The servants are loyal to Ed's family, even supplying them with food, and Ed himself has his laundry cared for by a young colored woman, Pauline.

On the particular dark evening of the story, the two odd friends are drinking and arguing about Communism on Ed's boat. Finally, Fred falls into a drunken sleep and Ed, going ashore, meets Pauline who has called for his wash. He is grateful and offers to walk her down the road. He is troubled and lonely and begins to talk to her. She, however, is responding on another level and suggests as much. Ed is startled but, nevertheless, attracted by her offer, although earlier in the evening he had warned Fred to stay away from the Negro women living along the river-bank unless he wished to risk a venereal disease. Now Pauline, with a curious dignity, withdraws until she is sure she is really wanted.

The two go back to the yacht where Fred lies in a drunken stupor and the colored woman (who perhaps has had an encounter with Fred) keeps urging that Ed "throw the bum out." Pauline's sexual vitality restores Ed's sense of belief in himself. He tries to communicate to her that it has shaken up his scale of values. "'Do you know where I feel it most?' Ed went on slowly. 'In the head.' She chuckled and moved against him." The "class-consciousness" in which Fred has tried to instruct him is illuminated by his random but meaningful experience with Pauline. As they walk along on her way to her home she again tells Ed to "kick that dirty bum out . . . He isn't in your class." Ed's attitude toward Pauline is grateful but clean-cut: ". . . I'm not getting rid of that guy. That's final . . ." It is clear, too, that he is not going to turn to his family for release from the hard way he has chosen. A victory is implied for Ed, although we do not know precisely what kind. We sense that he has chosen what is, in effect, a novitiate toward a better understanding of life.

The irony of the revelation that Ed has experienced lies, of course, in the fact that its instrument, Pauline, has no consciousness of it. But Ed sees, and this is the point at which the story is relieved from a possible charge of romanticism, that it was the disorganized Fred who led him in the direction of the revolt which Pauline merely symbolically fulfilled.

The weakness of this story is not in its tone which is subtly and beautifully modulated to catch the undercurrents of insecurity and tension between the colored woman and the white man, between the professional has-not and the amateur has-been, but in an inadequate development of the connection between Ed's physical knowledge of Pauline and his implied acceptance of Fred's analysis of society.

## William Carlos Williams (essay date 1950)

SOURCE: "A Beginning on the Short Story (Notes)," in *Selected Essays of William Carlos Williams,* Random House, 1954, pp. 295-310.

[*In the following essay, which was originally published in 1950, the author comments on the art of the short story.*]

The principal feature re the short story is that it is short—and so must pack in what it has to say (unless it be snipped off a large piece of writing as a sort of prose for quality of writing which might be justifiable).

It seems to me to be a good medium for nailing down a single conviction. Emotionally.

There's "Melanctha" (and there are the Poe stories), a means of writing, practice sheet for the novel one might *discover,* in it. But a novel is many related things, a short story one.

Plato's discourses: the *Republic,* a walk up from the port of Athens, the stopping with a friend and talking until morning. Socrates as a hero.

You can't "learn" to write a short story—either from De Maupassant or Henry James. All you can learn is what De M. or H. J. did. Or take a reader of the short story like Charles Demuth—and observe what he *did* in the way of painting following the texts.

It isn't a snippet from the newspaper. It isn't realism. It is, as in all forms of art, taking the materials of every day (or otherwise) and using them to raise the consciousness of our lives to higher aesthetic and moral levels by the use of the art.

As in the poem it must be stressed, that the short story uses the same materials as newsprint, the same dregs—the same in fact as Shakespeare and Greek tragedy: the elevation of spirit that occurs when a consciousness of form, art in short, is imposed upon materials debased by dispirited and crassly cynical handling. What the newspaper uses on the lowest (sentimental) level, the short story had best elevate to the level of other interests.

This should make apparent that a mere "thrilling" account of an occurrence from daily life, a transcription of a fact, is not of itself and for that reason a short story. You get the fact, it interests you for whatever reason; of that fact you *make,* using words, a story. A thing. A piece of writing, as in the case of De Maup't, "A Piece of String."

---

**When you begin to write a short story you should really know what you're writing about—because, if you write skillfully enough, sooner or later someone is going to find it out and judge you as a man for it.**

*—William Carlos Williams*

---

In plainest words, it isn't the mere interest of the event that makes the short story, it is the way it raises the newspaper level to distinction that counts.

This is not easy. At first or perhaps at any time, it won't sell. Hemingway's "Two Fisted" or "Two-hearted River"—was that way. And to *make* a story of any sort, short or long, we use words: writing is made of words—all writing is made of words, *formal things.*

We have Kipling's famous short stories, we have Gogol, we have Dickens' "Christmas Carol."

We also have agents who, seeing some spark of novelty (but a big slab of conventionality) in some recent graduate—will teach her to write *Ladies Home Journal* or *Sat. Eve. Post*—at the rate of $200 to $2000 a throw. And do it every day, more or less. We also have the picture of an "accepted" writer, someone known by her style, that she will not offend or shock us, who long after her final deterioration (repeating the same stock) will go on selling the *Delineator* (note the use of "selling") for $50,000. A THROW. (There's a good story with that, the mag saying the price is too high, dropping the serial or whatever and getting another "good" writer to take on the stint for $25,000. The only trouble was that they, the mag, lost money on the deal, made more money by hiring the first lady at $50,000 to write for it. Except that after that experience her fee went up to $75,000. And they paid it!)

I should think, for myself, that the short story is the best form for the "slice of life" incident. It deals with people and dogs and cats, sometimes horses—those creatures who are the commonest sublimation of man's sexual approaches to woman: Big eyes, magnificently curved haunches and slender ankles, the mane, the dilating nostrils—how exquisitely Shakespeare sketched one in the *Venus and Adonis*—like Dürer at his best. They top monuments and sometimes cathedrals—as at St. Marco in Venice. Kafka and the cockroach.

It is for all that man (as man and woman) from the "Boule de Suif" to the "Murders in the Rue Morgue," a trait of some person raised from the groveling, debasing as it is debased jargon, fixed by rule and precedent, of reportage—to the exquisite distinction of that particular man, woman, horse or child that is depicted. The finest short stories are those that raise, in short, one particular man or woman, from that Gehenna, the newspapers, where at last all men are equal, to the distinction of being an individual. To be responsive not to the ordinances of the herd (Russia-like) but to the extraordinary responsibility of being a person.

Can we not anticipate and look forward with eagerness amounting to despair to the time (past most of our lives) when there will appear those journals, those poems and short stories, being written underground now in Russia as in Ireland of this century by the literary heroes of the future? For it has to be so. And the Russians of all people will be the most persistent, the bravest and the most, I think, brilliant. Any nation that has braved Siberia for eight generations and survived to catch a glimpse of freedom so often dragged, as it has been today, from before their eyes, will be writing the masterpieces of the future.

As we write for the magazines today so they write, officially, for the Politburo. But the real writing, the real short story will be written privately, in secret, despairingly—for the individual. For it will be the individual.

Thus and for that purpose, the great writer will use his materials formally, in his own style, the words, the choice and the mode of his words—like Boccaccio, Stein and Faulkner.

But what right have I who never wrote a successful, that is to say salable, moneymaking short story in my life, to speak to you in this way? I feel like an impostor. I'm just a literary guy, not *practical*—like a one-time atomic physicist. Even a poet, of all things. What a nerve to come to a going institution of learning to teach you how to write?! Even to sell? Why, you might as well have an Einstein. HE at least can play the violin, this is, fairly well.

There's something to it. And so I object also.

But Hemingway did at first sit at the feet of Gertrude Stein and Ezra Pound. They taught him a lot. And then he went out and capitalized on it—to at least *her* disgust, so they say. And she had written at least one magnificent short story. Pound not even one. But then again Hemingway's not a bad poet and might have been a better one.

So if they did that may we not, conceivably, do this? I'll go the limit, as far as I know any limit. From me perhaps you'll pick up a point or two and make use of it. At the worst we'll fool the trusting faculties who invited me here while you get a laugh.

Nobody knows who's going to be successful. Moreover nobody knows who's going to be good. Now it's Paul Bowles.

So let's look at short stories and see what CAN be done with them. How many ways they CAN be written, torturing the material in every way we can think of—from that YOU draw what you want to.

The art would be, by the style, to wed the subject to its own time and have it live there and then. Have it live.

Take one of Kipling's best tales. Can we learn anything from it for our use today? Take O. Henry's ending. They are out of date "an O. Henry ending." Obviously not. Take a Gogol story, the woman who ran wild and naked at night baying like a dog on her hands and feet through the country. I speak of this from memory. Take a Kafka story more recently dead—the sliding of consciousness, a lateral slip that stands up to nothing but fantasy and is yet firm.

What is the common quality in all these changing styles? Not a stereotyped snaring of the interest, a filling in of necessary documentary details and a smash finish. That is merely the cheap surface of the ten-cent customers. What about Hemingway's "Short Happy Life"? or Poe's "Gold Bug"?

They all have a frame—like a picture. There is a punch, if you like. But what *is* that punch? What kind of a punch do you want: philosophic as Plato's *Republic* and—what in a woman shooting her husband's head off with an elephant gun? What in "The Gold Bug?" Murder is nothing at all but death—and what's new about death? Violence is the mood today. Now it's something if a son cuts his mother's throat as in the Agamemnon. Maybe Plato was a bit fed up on the Sophocles. His endings are arguments: that he did give Socrates the hemlock (and a termagant for a wife) finally: who could even outtalk her.

What today will be the punch paragraph or maybe today we'll shift the emphasis and get a punch from having no punch. Maybe the buildup and the documentation will be merely hinted. The rough stuff (lying usually) or the capitalizing of the Negro comic (so-called) at a dime a throw— to flatter a certain snob sense of fixed values? To flatter a buyer—in good old 6th Avenue style? Oh, but don't let's be so vulgar!

In other words when you begin to write a short story you should really know what you're writing about—because, if you write skillfully enough, sooner or later someone is going to find it out and judge you as a man for it.

Oh, but am I making a mistake? Perhaps all you want is to write a story and not be judged a liar because you lie. I'm really afraid I'm in the wrong bin. I'm taking the art of the short story seriously.

What will it *do*?

For instance—what was my problem or urge or opportunity for realization of my insights in 1932?

What was going on?

How did I solve it? Why did I choose the short story and how much must it have been modified from a stereotype to be serviceable to me?

(I do not mean to imply that the choice was a conscious one altogether. I mean, looking back upon it, what were the elements involved in my coming upon the short story as a means?)—that is during the Depression?

Answer: The character of the evidence: to accommodate itself to the heterogeneous character of the people, the elements involved, the situation in hand. In other words, the materials and the temporal situation dictated the terms.

I lived among these people. I know them and saw the essential qualities (not stereotype), the courage, the humor (an accident), the deformity, the basic tragedy of their lives—and the *importance* of it. You can't write about something unimportant to yourself. I was involved.

That wasn't all. I saw how they were maligned by their institutions of church and state—and "betters." I saw how all that was acceptable to the ear about them maligned them. I saw how stereotype falsified them.

Nobody was writing about them, anywhere, as they ought to be written about. There was no chance of writing anything acceptable, certainly not salable, about them.

It was my duty to raise the level of consciousness, not to say discussion, of them to a higher level, a higher plane. Really to tell.

Why the short story? Not for a sales article but as I had conceived them. The briefness of their chronicles, its brokenness and heterogeneity—isolation, color. A novel was unthinkable.

And so to the very style of the stories themselves.

This wasn't the "acceptable," the unshocking stuff, the slippery, in the sense that it can be slipped into them while they are semiconscious of a Saturday evening. Not acceptable to a mag and didn't get into them.

To continue our study:

What sort of a short story must a Gogol have written or a Kipling in India—in their time?

And so, practically speaking, what sort of short story must be written in the U. S. or the Northwest today? I use the word *must,* I don't ask what you would care to do. Each man or woman is born facing a *must.* Who will drive it through or even see it? The one who will, will be at least justified and happy in his own eyes doing it. But he will know what he must do.

In other words, to write a short story of parts one must know what he is writing *about,* see it, smell it—be compelled by it—and be writing what ordinarily one doesn't want to hear.

Is that extraordinary?

We forget the meaning of art. Art means the skillful lie—what doesn't exist—as Aristotle pointed out.

To be an artist, one must deceive, make up a story. One must get the punch in, the shocking punch so skillfully that no one will suspect it. The art covers that. The shock is necessary. Necessary to make them stop, look, listen—in other words, read and say, 1) how awful, and 2) how fascinating. What a wonderful writer!

The artist always has his tongue in his cheek.

It must be so artful with the truth that above and beyond anything else its beauty of style or accurate statement will negate all its petty and thoroughly excusable lies. For its lies, never of statement, originate from its affection.

It must be written so well that that in itself becomes its truth while the deformity informs it.

I say a man must know what he is writing *about* but the short story, as a form, must be demanded.

Down to your own Jack London: what do Jack London's stories *mean*?

They mean, as far as I can tell,—take "To Build a Fire," they mean, the impact between civilization and the wild. For, note, that he isn't interested in the pioneer who goes native and survives fairly well. He means (when he is any good at all and not a pure sentimentalist) the terror and lonesomeness of the wilderness in its impact on civilized man. That, as far as I can see, is the best of him.

His failure?

When he tries to talk big—which reveals no more than his littleness.

12/22

So how shall we write today (unpredictable—or to predict the genius who will answer) of what shall we write today? Let us try to predict. What will the short story consist of and what will be its terms?

The hero? Who is a hero? The peasantry? There is none. Men and women faithful to a belief? What belief?

One thing I found out for myself by writing a short story once that almost broke up the faculty of Arizona University and was finally published obscurely in Berkeley, Calif. It is this:

Most of us are not individuals any more but parts of something. We are no one of us "all" of anything. It is too big for us. So why not write of three people as one? That's what my story tried to do, make itself more than one, three in one. Imagine a woman looking at herself three ways. Wouldn't that break up the faculty of any university?

I cannot tell you how to write a short story, I can only tell you how you must write it.

It is not to place adjectives, it is to learn to employ the verbs in imitation of nature—so that the pieces move naturally—and watch, often breathlessly, what they *do*.

That is the enlargement of nature which we call art. The *additions* to nature which we call art.

You do not *copy* nature, you make something which is an *imitation* of nature—read your Aristotle again.

That is the *work* of the imagination, as the late Virginia Woolf pointed out. You have to work, you have to imagine the character, which is for your mind to *be* the creator.

Arrived at that condition, the imagination inflamed, the excitement of it is that you no longer copy but *make* a natural object. (Something comparable to nature: an other nature.) You yourself become the instrument of nature—the helpless instrument.

You must tell the truth. You can't lie because the moment you attempt to fall off you destroy yourself.

It *is* nature. I don't think you know in a short story what's coming out. That is the excitement of it.

Take "Death in Venice," take "Boule de Suif," take "Melanctha." They are creations. Natural objects. Not copying. But by housing a spirit, as nature houses juice in an apple, they live.

It is perhaps a transit from adjective (the ideal "copy") to verb (showing process).

There are no beginnings and ends in nature—except birth and death—which are meaningless to us. Religion imitates nature with the imagination—a once moving fable—which we have to know is a lie before we can believe it.

There is only, we might say, flux in nature.

But there is also an apple, a flower and a man.

The artist adds, "There is also a work of art." Now how absurd it is to dwell upon cherries so real that the birds peck at them (I knew a man who had a whole canvas full of cherries in a heap which to him was art). How absurd it is to make a statue so copied that it is mistaken for a woman: The story of Pygmalion and Galatea is merely a best seller—a very second-rate fable for jokesters.

The secret lies elsewhere—in the *marble* of it. If it is merely mistaken for a woman it is senseless: a copy.

But as an *imitation* of nature (not a mere woman's body) it becomes something a woman never was, something a woman at her best may imitate—a work of art. A work of man to lay beside nature and enlarge it. Engrandize it. Make a Caesar greater than Caesar or, if not that at least a Caesar, an undying Caesar whose other works have crumbled—a *completion* of his greatness. It is what the imagination *adds* to the woman that makes the statue great.

Something of this sort is what Oscar Wilde must have meant when he said, "God created man, then woman, then the child and finally the doll. And the greatest of these was the doll."

Carnal desire for a statue is for adolescents and senility if not the pathological (at least the stupid). But to take decay, despair and elevate the details to an action, to greatness as in "Death in Venice"—to make by an action a thing that is deformed clean, salutory—*that* is an addition to nature.

To take a lump of fat and transform it by imitating nature—goes beyond copy—to transform a cockroach, the same—into a work of illuminating penetration—gives us a glimpse of the process.

Braque would take his pictures out of doors and place them *beside* nature to see if his imitations had *worked.*

So you see how it opens up sculpture, painting and writing. In the Greek tragedies the imitation of the gods.

The short story is no different.

(I didn't say not to copy, not, for instance, accurately to observe conversation. But I did say that *that* is not the short story. It *might* be, but only when there is something else as well.) A view, a room with a view, something heard through a knothole—a secret.

Now what are some of the advantages of the short story as an art form—bearing what I have said, in mind.

It should be a brush stroke—as compared with a picture.

One chief advantage as against a novel—which is its nearest cousin—is that you do not have to bear in mind the complex structural paraphernalia of a novel in writing a short story and so may dwell on the manner, the writing. On the process itself. A single stroke, uncomplicated but complete. Not like a chapter or paragraph.

Thus, bearing a possible novel in mind, if you will, you can play with the words as materials. You can try various modes of writing—more freely.

Try all sorts of effects. The short story is a wonderful medium for prose experimentation. You may, economically, try devices—varied devices—for making the word count toward a particular effect. I'd say write a story—as Joyce did. *Dubliners* to *Stephen Hero* to *Ulysses* to *Finnegans Wake.* I say that it took off from the short story. It makes a delightful Field of Mars—for exercises in the Manual of Arms. I think that's its chief value.

And be careful not to imitate yourself—like how many others. Remember: the imagination! The short story has all the elements of a larger work—but in petto. Dash off

a story in an evening—any old way, trying to follow the action of some characters you can *imagine.* Sit down blind and start to fling the words around like pigments—try to see what nature would do under the same circumstances—let 'em go and (without thinking or caring) see where they'll lead you. You may be surprised—you may even end up as a disciplined writer.

---

> **The short story is a wonderful medium for prose experimentation. You may, economically, try devices—varied devices—for making the word count toward a particular effect.**
>
> —*William Carlos Williams*

---

12/23/29

Crawl into the man's head and how get inside a woman's head, being a man? That is the *work* of the imagination (of which V. Woolf speaks). This is where the *imitation* of nature takes place. There is no copying here.

You *are* now nature: given a set of circumstances—a woman: a man—names:

What is there to do?

Now go ahead and do it. Name the actions and perform them—yourself.

This is something that you yourself (as "Jim Higgins") have very little to say about (you become a nonentity, like Shakespeare). You are in the creative process—a function in nature—relegated to the deity.

You have now entered what is referred to as the divine function of the artist.

Let's keep away from frightening words and say you are nature—in action.

It is an action, a moving process—the verb dominates; you are to *make.*

And who are you, anyway?—with your small personal limitations of age, sex and other sundry features like race and religion?

Unimportant.

You, even you are at the moment—the artist, good or bad—but a new creature.

You must let yourself go—release it and be that transcendence (but in control by your technique which you have learned—like the voice of an opera singer) but inside that frame of reference you must *release* yourself to act.

How, in *The Sheltering Sky* (a novel) is Bowles going to get the girl undressed. He is going to *act* to do it.

By setting the imagination to *work*. WORK. The artist is now a woman, a particular woman. He is therefore bound by her conditions and so he works at it. And in this case what comes out?

The woman is going to be undressed *willingly*—within a time limitation of a train schedule. She will *want* to be undressed even while she fights against it—by running out.

So he gets her soaked to the skin. But on a train? in Africa. How?

Read it. Lesson No. 1.

December 30/49

It is the transit to the imagination from the plebeian plodding of ordinary consciousness which is the important thing—the sometimes impossible thing for any of us, the always impossible thing for many of us—or so it seems. To take to the imagination is the first requisite.

How does one take to the imagination? One may recognize its approach in that its first signs are like those of falling asleep—which anyone may observe for himself. It is likewise governed by the conditions of sleep.

At first all the images, one or many which fill the mind, are fixed. I have passed through it and studied it for years. We look at the ceiling and review the fixities of the day, the month, the year, the lifetime. Then it begins; that happy time when the image becomes broken or begins to break up, becomes a little fluid—or is affected, floats brokenly in the fluid. The rigidities yield—like ice in March, the magic month. They coalesce and, finally, merciful sleep intervenes. Sleep is black. But before we awaken it begins again, in reverse—with dreams. Ending in waking and we return to consciousness, refreshed. By the imagination?

That is the way sleep goes. But we are now looking for cues to something else, we are speaking of the resemblance between falling asleep and the awakening of the imagination that sometime impossible step to be taken before the writing begins (tho' it is wavelike and even during the writing, of many qualities, it rises and falls—tho' it remain of the same texture).

Possessed by the imagination, we are really asleep tho' we may awake: it explains much bravery. We do not hear what is said to us, we do not see the danger.

Kenneth Burke once said to me that the way to write or perhaps to learn to write is to sit down and to begin to write. Write down anything that seems pertinent to the subject or to no subject. Get into the fluid state, for unless you do, all you will say will be valueless. Continue to write until you have begun to say what you find to be necessary to the subject. Tear up the first eight to twenty pages and you have made a start!

Arrived! we think on a different plane. All the lines—the complex arrangement of reins lie free in the hand.

What distresses can happen in the effort to let go! to release ourselves to the imagination, with this we are all familiar. It is because we are really afraid. We can be struck to the ground by a realization of how we have been conditioned in our lives. The realization of it may be a terrific blow. In all our conscious lives we stick to what we call standards—to precepts—to those bulwarks against quicksands—so we say. Think of Rimbaud etc.

Then to reverse the process: Where might we not land? What fences we put up in the past are precisely our stumbling blocks now. I once wrote down: How did Shakespeare become great? By begetting twins, abandoning his wife, running away to London and falling in love with men. In other words—to let go the imagination.

I don't especially recommend it. How can I?

I am now stressing the diseases. We get fixed in squirrel cages of thought. Everyone does. Drink, drugs—anything you can think of is practiced to escape. The Yeats story about his London lecture.

All I am trying to point out is that it is all the effort to take that step into the imagination. Queer dress. Nocturnal habits like Balzac who went to bed at 10 A.M. etc. Do not forget the tremendous advantages of prison and far greater Cervantes wrote *Don Quixote.* The imagination is freed. To raise the beat of the brain to bring it oxygen.

March 26/50

We speak of a man's "mettle"—it might better be metal. It is as with other metals, when it is heated it melts. It is when the metal is fluid the imagination can be said to become active; it is the melting, the rendering fluid of the imagination that describes the mind as entering upon creative work.

It must be melted to create; fluid, unfettered by anything.

The characteristic of being melted is for the object to have lost the form it was in. It can be played with, made into a new form as we desire.

With the short story as with any sort of creation, I am trying to say, the imagination (that is the mind in a fluid state or a melted state) has to be given play.

Now, we know by knowledge of the physiology of the brain that it acts only when it has been supplied oxygen in abundance. So it glows and sweats when it is active—as with anything else.

What is the origin of that heat? Something has stirred us, some perception linked with emotion. We are angry, we are committed to something in our lives, as with the poem. It doesn't matter what it has been—anything. We heat up. This incentive is usually secret, it is guided by our fears perhaps. But we are heated and (if we can get quiet enough, as in jail, or running away—finally) we melt and the imagination is set to flow into its new mold.

April 24/50

What shall the short story be written about. Obviously not, if it is serious, the mere sentimental characters. How write about a poor Wop, a Polish gal in her kitchen, a foreign peasant who is barely articulate.

What then? Something that interests the writer seriously, as a writer (not necessarily a man for in that case the interest would be moral and perhaps best NOT as a short story). It is the way his interests, as a writer, impinge upon the material—graphically, told.

The result is life, not morals. It is THE LIFE which comes alive in the telling. It is the life under specified conditions—so that it is relived in the reading—as it strikes off flashes from the material. The material is the metal against which a flint makes sparks.

Anything, thus anything can be used without fear of sentimentality. The THING we are writing, directing all our wit, our intelligence to discovering and setting down—is revealed as it hits against anything at all. That's the modern understanding—and I guess it is pretty hard to realize. Whatever that may be for each man who writes. What good are you? Prove it. Or what do you see, young as you are? Do you think a prostitute is "bad" because she's a prostitute. And yet how shall you show her "good" except by speaking of her in the conditions of her prostitution. By using that material, graphically, specifically you must learn to tell all you want to tell—whatever YOU want to say. That is the art.

## Cid Corman (essay date 1962)

SOURCE: "*The Farmers' Daughters:* A True Story about People," in *The Massachusetts Review,* Vol. III, No. 2, Winter, 1962, pp. 319-24.

[*In the following essay, Corman discusses the chief literary qualities of Williams's writing style in* The Farmers' Daughters.]

Bill was upstairs. (I was visiting 9 Ridge Road, 1954.) Floss was explaining his nervousness whenever the phone rang. He thinks it's for him, a patient. Few seem to realize that 70% of his life has been given to his practice.

She was implying, perhaps, that writing occupied only part of the remaining 30%. But life, like death, has a funny way of getting round percentages. And to read [*The*

*Farmers' Daughters: The Collected Stories of William Carlos Williams*], without exception relating, directly or indirectly, to his work as a G.P. in and out of his office (at home) in Rutherford, New Jersey, is to realize rather that writing of this order is an extension, not an escape or evasion or diminution, of a man's days and nights.

These sketches, "verbal transcriptions," histories, anecdotes, tales, are all instances of one man's remarkable capacity for love. Love of people, foremost, but no less—with enduring respect—a love of human expressiveness, of language, particular speech, its trickiness, vivacity, penetration.

If I had to choose which, of all the "pieces," I preferred most, I suppose I'd say: **"Old Doc Rivers,"** for its groping toward understanding, the openness and clarity of its relations, the way the local is a universe and is again itself; **"The Use of Force,"** for all its anthologizing, a beautiful clean thing, prose, direct in its attack, sure in its sense of when to leave off, its language crisp and true, touching; and **"The Farmers' Daughters,"** perhaps the most ambitious work, with its broken chronology, weaving incident and anecdote, perception and experience, with honest feeling, words falling for words, free and fluent and with complete control.

In some of the earliest pieces I have gritted my teeth at the too heavy sense of the "dialect." The writer seems too much "outside" and making a thing up, not wholly with it, *not* recounting it, trying too hard to impress. The commitment uncertain, off. But with **"Mind and Body"** the inside opens:

> . . . I know people think I am a nut. I was an epileptic as a child. I know I am a manic depressive. But doctors are mostly fools. . . .

(I begin to hear the voice of a "later" poet, Robert Creeley, foreshadowed.)

How often, as here, the good doctor tries to project a woman's sense of things, her involvement in body, person, place, in things and in "relations." "It is life, what we see and decide for ourselves, that counts."

For response to and a gathering-up of language, in the same story, consider this:

> . . . When I was talking to the Jesuit, who came to teach me what the church meant, I told him I could not believe that. He said, I should. I asked him, Do you? But he did not answer me. . . .

Set this against Charles Olson's "Pastoral Letter" in his recent *Maximus Poems,* if you want to see evidence of what Dr. Williams has quietly effected "in the art":

> . . . "I don't believe
> I know your name." Given.
> How do you do,
> how do you do. And then:

"Pardon me, but
what church
do you belong to,
may I ask?"


     . . . . .


I sd, you may, sir.
He sd, what, sir.
I sd, none,
sir. . . .


The short punched-out speech, sporadic, laconic, easy, but not facile, straight-on. Not exaggerated, for the true is crazy enough and hard enough to hang on to. And as he gradually works his way open, into the open, he is what he is, William Carlos Williams, half Spanish, half English, part Jewish, part this and part that, man and woman, Pater-son, make no mistake, "Doc," and his wife is Floss, and there are the two boys, and there is the neighborhood. And Rutherford-Paterson opens to contain and be contained to brimming. As a flower in fertile soil. Red roses or "white weeds." Jonquils that "want affection," lore, and raspberries, as one learns, to be picked from a roadside and brought "home" to share.

But is it "art"? The question *is* asked, in and out of school. Sadly. For to express relation with feeling this cleanly, this precisely, without any phoney theatricalism, without resorting to a pompous rhetoric, or a desire to overwhelm with literary machinery, if art is anything, is what this is. There is a glory in people, his glory (as well as ours), the stuff they are made of, we are, stubbornness, indomitability, even within the confines of ignorance, stupidity, poverty. "He was liked," would be the simplest comment one would expect his townsfolk to say, if asked about him. How could he not be? Concerned about payment, on a visit at whatever hour, but not overly concerned, willing to do it for "nothing," for a laugh or a lark sometimes, for a word or a gesture, a look, for the love of it, for the love of them. For the Polish mother who smiled when she lost her "first daughter" at birth, for the Italian peasant who paid him in snuff. For the love of Mike, sentimental! How, if the feeling is accurate. He is guilty and proud, moved and obdurate, sensible and sensitive. "I have found . . . that we must live for others, that we are not alone in the world and we cannot live alone."

". . . What was he going to do? How did he know? Where was he going to stay when it got cold? Whose the hell's business was that? What would he eat? Beans and bananas, chewing gum, caviar and roast duck. With that she left him. And later on it grew cold. . . ." A love for the weak and the strong, respect for the offbeat, for the independent soul, for dignity, for sheer doggedness and spite, for a thin body holding out for life, for candor, for generosity, for care.

Do they get "under"? Does anything that is not there? The majority of these recountings, if not all of them, strike me as probably having been written "at the moment," at the spur; they are so close to event. Yet, as often as not, there

is a "history" involved and I see that much more goes on here than meets the eye: a world, inside. The cadences of speech, the speed and the relaxation, the deftness and alertness of ear and mind, bespeak authority.

In **"Old Doc Rivers"** he can attack and defend at the same time, and he mutes verdicts:

> Well, Mary, what is it?
>
> I have a pain in my side, doctor.
>
> How long have you had it, Mary?
>
> Today, doctor. It's the first time.
>
> Just today.
>
> Yes, doctor.
>
> Climb up on the table. Pull up your dress. Throw that sheet over you. Come on, come on. Up with you. Come on now, Mary. Pull up your knees.
>
> Oooh!
>
> He could be cruel and crude. And like all who are so, he could be sentimentally tender also, and painstaking without measure. . . .

As against practitioners of the "tough guy" school, like Hemingway, say, his language is at once more convincing and accurate, and out of the body, out of the mouth, less manufactured, less "literary." And yet not at all unaware of the problems of what goes, what sticks. He had written, as early as 1932, answering academicism and snobbery:

> . . . I cannot swallow the half-alive poetry which knows nothing of totality. . . . Nothing is beyond poetry. It is the one solid element on which our lives can rely, the "word" of so many disguises, including as it does man's full consciousness, high and low, in living objectivity. . . . It is, in its rare major form, a world in fact come to arrest of self realization: that eternity of the present which most stumble over in seeking—or drug themselves into littleness to attain. . . .

The vision, no matter the structure of prose, is a poet's, making poets of us too. Each relation relates one to another. I think any reader will find a coherence; they are all "of a piece." And the "form"? The living speech of a time, a place, a people. All elements of society come to his feast: children, adults, old folk, animals, Polacks, Wops, Jews, the Irish and Scotch and English, the southerner, the negro, lady and bum, the wise-guy and the tease, the professional and the conversationalist. William Carlos Williams. It may be that I recognize a world my own and so feel "at home" and drawn to it. But there's also "more."

It has to do with a man's zest, his brio, his appetite for life, his disgust, or the confrontation of death, an eagerness for detail, a nose, an ear, an unfailing willingness, desire, to know and know more, to encounter "them." He doesn't blink at what he sees either. On the contrary, what he sees is what makes him want to see more, to speak to a "patient" always as a person, as this man or this woman or this child and no other. He makes me want to address my world, wherever I touch it, with equal frankness and affection. Unblinking. Perceiving.

"Down to earth," I'd say. American archaeology, as a friend where I now am staying might say. Not the classical bit of fancy goods and dream-boats, but the bones, the beads, the chipping stones, flints, arrowheads, artifacts of a difficult and often bare existence, a raw country building. Silver-dollars on a skeleton's eye-sockets. Money plastered everywhere. Seen. Faced. Not pandered to or for. A knowledge, I'd say, that the most beautiful vases are also made of clay. He makes the pot and paints it, with earth's colors.

And no slouch is he as a weaver, out of the so-called "common" thread—to show us, we onlookers, how uncommon our lives may be and often are, as in **"The Farmers' Daughters,"** where he moderates lovingly between two women he knew professionally and as friends, throughout a long career, the very image of his career, the poetry of their lives touching his, or his touch lifting them into a world of poetry, a world where what is true shines.

His order is that of disorder, but sensed, grasped, embraced, danced with, released. He says it himself, as of a house of an admired patient:

> . . . I have seldom seen such disorder and brokenness— such a mass of unrelated parts of things lying about. That's it! I concluded to myself. An unrecognizable order! Actually—the new! And so good-natured and calm. So definitely the thing! And so compact. Excellent. And with such patina of use. Everything definitely "painty" . . .

"I'm struck by his honesty and concern, the openness of both."

These are love-stories, all, and one of the quietest of them, **"Country Rain,"** speaks for both himself and Floss of their relation and our relation to them, to others. It opens towards the request for it ("commissioned" by the heart):

> If this were Switzerland, I thought, we'd call it lovely: wisps of low cloud rising slowly among the heavily wooded hills. But since it's America we call it simply wet. Wet and someone at another of the tables asks if it's going to stop raining or keep it up all day. . . .

To write as simply and fluently and perceptively as that may suggest to some that it's "easy." Don't you believe it. It takes years of listening, of speaking well, of caring to. It requires the mind of a poet.

Perhaps this is more obvious, or will be, in this quote from the end of the same piece. He and Floss, on a wet summer morning gone to pick up the mail for the country house where they are vacationing, find they have "time"

and drive on into the old landscape, discussing some of the people they have recently met.

> I stopped the car in a dark, heavily wooded portion of the road dripping with the rain from the overhanging spruces. Floss looked at me. There was a sharp drop to the left beyond the half-rotten section of a crude guard rail where in the intense silence a small stream could be heard talking to itself among the stones.

> What are you stopping here for?

> I want to look at a rock. As I spoke I backed the car about twenty feet, drew in toward the embankment and shut off the engine.

> The rock day at about eye level close to my side of the road, the upper surface of it sloping slightly toward me with the hillside. Not a very big rock. What had stopped me was the shaggy covering which completely inundated it. The ferns, a cropped-short, dark-green fern, was the outstanding feature, growing thickly over an underlying cover of dense moss. But there was also a broad-leafed vine running lightly among the ferns, weaving the pattern together.

> That wasn't all. The back portion of the rock, which wasn't much larger than the top of an ordinary dining-room table slightly raised at one side and a little tilted, supported both the rotten stump of a tree long since decayed but, also, a brother to that tree—coming in fact from the same root and very much alive, as big as a man's arm, a good solid arm—a ten-foot tree about whose base a small thicket of brambles clustered. Ferns of three sorts closed in from the sides completing the picture. A most ungrammatical rock.

> Isn't this magnificent! Let's bring the two school teachers out here for a ride tomorrow, said Floss. They'd love it. Have you ever talked to them? she added. They're sweet.

> No, I said, observing the woods ascending the hillside in the rain, but their situation among the dones, the aints and the seens amuses me. I've been wondering what they are thinking.

> Don't worry, said Floss. They know what it's all about.

> Look, I said, after we had rolled forward another half mile or so, do you see what I see?

> Oh, said Floss, raspberries!

> We stopped again, it was still raining, so I told her to stay where she was while I got down to pick some of the fruit, the remainder of what I could see had been an abundant crop recently growing at the side of the road sloping toward the stream.

> Oh, taste them! said Flossie when I had brought them to her in my hand. They're dripping with juice. Anyone

who would put sugar on such berries, well, would be just a barbarian. Perhaps we could stop again here tomorrow and pick enough for everybody.

A steady, heavy rain, she added. The farmers will like that. And then as an afterthought: Do you think Ruth will ever marry?

Why? I answered her.

I'd be a barbarian to add more. But I can't refrain adding a bit from the beginning of the next story **"Inquest"** and let that be it:

What we save, what we have, what we do. No matter. That which we most dearly cherish, *that* we shall lose, the one thing we most desire. What remains?

To be and remain interesting—with reservations—perhaps. . . .

Stories? Yes: "a world in fact come."

## R. F. Dietrich  (essay date 1966)

SOURCE: "Connotations of Rape in 'The Use of Force'," in *Studies in Short Fiction,* Vol. III, No. 4, Summer, 1966, pp. 446-50.

[*In the essay below, Dietrich analyzes sexually suggestive aspects in the language and tone of "The Use of Force."*]

It is difficult to pick up a collection of short stories these days without finding William Carlos Williams' odd little story **"The Use of Force."** Its ubiquity in college anthologies is not surprising, really, in that it simply, quickly, effectively illustrates many of the conventions of short story writing, and thus provides easy means for the instructor's first assault on the elements of fiction. Readily identifiable in this thesis story are theme, conflict, character, tone, point of view. The freshman or sophomore feels secure in his mastery of at least *this* simple little story, however muddy things may get later on. Sadly, however, such undergraduate confidence is unfounded, for the art of this story is more complex than at first seems the case.

My title advertises rape, but it is perhaps best to begin more innocently, as does the tone of the story, and save the sex for later. The physician who tells the story in a very casual and frank manner fashions himself in the familiar image of the family doctor, who of course achieves great villainy only when he collects an exorbitant fee. As for any pain that a physician might cause, we reason that it is but the necessary prelude to health, and we freely forgive him for it. And we have a rather settled image of our doctor: he is supposed to be cool and calm on all occasions, disciplined to evince only one emotion—sympathetic cheerfulness. When children refuse to open their mouths, he is supposed to make a funny face, and, abracadabra, the innermost depths of Johnny's being are ex-

posed to view. The reader expects as much of the physician of this story, and certainly the tone of his voice is reassuring.

As the doctor begins telling his story, there is no indication of anything out of the way. The doctor-patient relationship is established in a rather wry manner, but the situation perhaps calls for it. He is new to the Olsons, making them a bit nervous and distrustful. They proceed on the assumption that since he is the physician he should tell them what is wrong, not vice versa. The narrator counters with the time-honored tradition of the bedside physician. He attempts to coax Mathilda into opening her mouth, and Williams phrases the girl's response in comic tones—"nothing doing." The mother then helpfully promises that the doctor won't hurt her, and at this false promise the doctor grinds his teeth "in disgust." This is the first indication of an excessive response on the part of the doctor, and as if to balance it he insists that he did not allow himself "to be hurried or disturbed." He spoke "quietly and slowly" as he approached the child again.

But the physician's calm rationality encounters a rather unexpected obstacle—the girl knocks his glasses off; and when the mother admonishes her and tells her what a "nice man" the doctor is, the doctor responds in a most curious way. He sees that he is not at all a nice man to her and that her having diphtheria and possibly dying of it is not the real issue ("nothing to her."). There is something more important at stake here than merely dying.

The physician does not suddenly abandon all reason. He sees that "the battle" is on, but he explains quite coolly and professionally to the parents the alternatives. It was entirely up to them. "He would not insist upon a throat examination so long as they would take the responsibility." At the mention of responsibility, the mother threatens the girl with going to the hospital, thus putting it back upon the physician, whose attitude now takes another strange turn. He scoffs at the mother's threat ("Oh yeah?") almost in words the child her self might have used. An identification has begun to take place, not with the adult world, as represented by the parents, for they were "contemptible" to him, but with the irrational world of the "savage brat." He responds to the challenge of the girl in a quite elemental fashion, scorning the parents, who in the ensuing struggle "grew more and more abject, crushed, exhausted. . . ." They are crushed by the vital powers of unreason, in which the physician strangely finds only glory. As he says, "she surely rose to magnificent heights of insane fury of effort bread of her terror of me." The manner in which he responds to this "fury" is seldom recorded in medical journals. He begins to attack the inviolable throat, with the father as a weak and ashamed accomplice, until the doctor "almost wanted to kill him" for always releasing her at the critical moment when he had almost achieved success.

The parents are now beside themselves with shame and "agony of apprehension." Part of their adulthood lies in their being tamed and disciplined in the expression of emotion. The assumption of reason has only made them timid. Violent, unashamed expressions of emotion produce in them the discomforts of embarrassment, since only the pathetic and the sentimental are socially allowed in the adult world. Such scenes of passion remind the adults that they have been cast out of the child's garden of spontaneity, with the curse of shame as the penalty for their original sin. The physician quite spontaneously "had grown furious at a child," but the parents know only one response to fury. "'Aren't you ashamed,' the mother yelled at her. 'Aren't you ashamed to act like that in front of the doctor?'" Especially in front of the doctor, who is the human symbol of that discipline which is at once the idol-god and the frustration of the ordinary, civilized adult, and nothing is more unseemly, more shameful, than to express the fundamental unreason of humanity before this correct and condescending god. "'Aren't you ashamed,' the mother yelled at her . . . ?"

But this is no ordinary physician, or at least he is not behaving in the conventional manner. The encounter with the vital, screaming denial of his symbolic status loosens the hold of his medical code and renews the admiration for that vital force that was and always is the primitive antagonist of man's pretensions of rationality, the antagonist before which the ordinary adult is merely cowed. Thus the physician lends himself to the immortal struggle, with respect for the enemy and scorn for those who surrender meekly to it.

Or so it seems. At least this is the way the physician would have us see it. And the casual, confident tone of the story-telling is almost enough to make us see it that way, too. But then we begin to notice something. It is all right to speak of "immortal struggle" on the heroic plane, but objectively we still must face the fact of a full-sized, furious adult brutally handling a small, sick child. The doctor in understanding the elemental nature of their conflict has allowed its emotional power to sweep him along in some obsession. He is rationally aware that he is contending with a sick child and at the same time allows himself to be drawn into a violent contest of wills. His brutal methods in discovering the nature of the illness expose with rare honesty how a supposedly disciplined adult can be overwhelmed by the subrational wells of impulse within him. The casual tone of the story is achieved by the physician's ironic awareness of his own lapse of discipline. He too "had got beyond reason." And "a blind fury, a feeling of adult shame, bred of a longing for muscular release are the operatives. One goes on to the end."

"The end" is nothing so glorious. The sickness of her inner physical being now bared to the world, the girl is initiated into the world of shame. She had only been trying previously to protect herself, to keep from knowing the shame; but now that she has been violated, defense is useless, and she can compensate for her loss of innocence only by a hateful revenge upon her conqueror.

This leads us to notice certain overtones of the language of the story. The choice of words at crucial spots is highly suggestive of a sexual encounter. The physician-patient conflict seems to have been subverted by a more primitive conflict—that of male-female.

When the doctor first sees the child, he notices that she "was fairly eating me up with her cold, steady eyes," indicating immediate recognition of a basic antagonism. The doctor thinks that she is "an unusually attractive little thing, and as strong as a heifer in appearance." We need not make too much of the obvious parallel between a heifer and the virginal Mathilde, but it does suggest the basis of his attraction to her. Further, in the attack, "her face was flushed, she was breathing rapidly," symptoms of disease of course but also symptoms of sexual excitement. The doctor is quite honest in his emphasis upon her physical attraction, being well aware that she has "magnificent blond hair, in profusion." The girl cannot take her eyes off him, in this almost Strindbergian encounter.

The intensity of the love-hate conflict heightens after the girl knocks his glasses off. The glasses, which enable him to "see," (*i.e.,* to reason, to understand), as a product of civilization are symbolic of the artificial devices that stand between the "savage brat" and the physician. As Williams describes it, "with one catlike movement both her hands clawed instinctively" for his glasses. A cat clawing instinctively connotes a female-like reaction against a male aggression. Then "her breaths were coming faster and faster" as the struggle surges to a climax. The physician sees that he "had already fallen in love with the savage brat."

He then makes the parents accomplices to his "assault." The girl screams in hysterical negation. It is possible, I suppose, to speak of the attack upon the "mouth cavity" with the wooden spatula in sexual terms, although an apocryphal story has it that even Freud put his foot down when someone pointed out to him that the cigar he was enjoying was a phallic symbol. But if one wishes to go that far, then we might as well notice that the girl reduced the wooden blade to splinters, thus calling into use a "smooth-handled spoon of some sort." The result is that the girl begins to bleed. At this point the doctor decides it would be best to go away for an hour or so before trying again. But the obsession has control of him. Williams puts it very graphically: "I could have torn the child apart in my own fury and enjoyed it. It was a pleasure to attack her. My face was burning with it." The connotations of rape are unmistakable. The girl is "overpowered" as the physician forces the spoon down her throat, thus exposing the "membrane" that is her secret.

Well, what does all this mean? Is the sexual antagonism cause or effect of the doctor-patient conflict? Is the physician a villain? Or is he simply more perceptively aware of a usual relationship than most physicians are supposed to be?

At this point it is always good to reassure the undergraduate that the girl was not "really" raped, despite the suggestive language. Rather the prevalence of sexual connotation is simply testimony to the animal nature of this conflict. The sexual connotations are there because they express the savagery in human nature that, lying so close to the surface, can erupt at any moment in a flow of irrational behavior, especially in moments of crisis, moments when primitive force is required to achieve some civilized end, as in preventing diphtheria. There is no more revealing use of force, I suppose, than sexual aggression to show how close man lies to the savage within himself. Williams has seasoned his story with suggestive language to bring out the deeper flavors of life, the strong taste of life in the raw.

What of the curious tone of the story? The whole affair is treated as a momentary lapse of an eventually restored discipline, the event reflected upon with an ironic eye; but there are other, modifying tones. It is important to keep in mind that everything is presented from the doctor's point of view. Perhaps this event is not as casual as the physician has tried to make it seem. Perhaps it did permanent damage to his conventional role, and so the ironic reflection is tinged with a bit of awe, the wry tone and comic effects merely an attempt to gain control of an overpoweringly emotional experience, as with Conrad in *Heart of Darkness*. Certainly the understanding that one has within oneself the potential of savagery breeds new respect for the powers of darkness.

### J. E. Slate  (essay date 1968)

SOURCE: "William Carlos Williams and the Modern Short Story," in *The Southern Review,* Vol. IV, No. 3, July, 1968, pp. 647-64.

[*In the essay below, Slate relates Williams's theories about writing short fiction to the stories themselves, demonstrating the modern qualities of Williams's thought and practice.*]

William Carlos Williams' **"The Use of Force"** needs no defense in academic circles. Endorsed by the critics and teachers who print it in anthologies, **"The Use of Force"** now indisputably belongs. Though the other fifty-one stories in Williams' largest collection are still relatively unknown, fifteen years in the right circles have established this single piece of fiction. Success is always paradoxical for an artist, but Williams' success with **"The Use of Force"** contains an especially sharp self-contradiction: Williams was an esthetic revolutionary who never stopped thinking of himself as a dangerous outsider or—at the very least—a subversive agent. He usually wrote to attack academic assumptions about the short story and continually questioned the premises of successful fiction.

**"The Use of Force"** conceals Williams' intentions better than his other stories; and it is not surprising that Williams' destructive role escaped notice, for he often pretended sympathy for the intellectual establishments in order to undermine them from within. When they finally listened to him, though never as they had listened to T. S. Eliot, he was happy to speak to groups of young writers about the need for formal revolution. His lecture at the University of Washington published in 1950 as *A Beginning on the Short Story,* is typical in its contrast between

the classic, which aspires to the timeless, and the modern, which formally reflects its own time. Although his words openly urged undergraduates to revolt, they were either ignored or misunderstood, because **"The Use of Force"** was enshrined in a college text that same year.

The brief analysis of the story in Robert Heilman's *Modern Short Stories* ignored Williams' theories but was notable for its refusal to categorize Williams as a primitive or proletarian writer. This error had been encouraged by Williams himself, who not only published five of his best stories in a magazine called *Blast: Proletarian Short Stories* but also acted as its advisory editor. Nevertheless, even in 1934, the idea of Williams as a primitive was so ridiculous that Ezra Pound could enjoy the irony of naming him "the Communists' white-haired boy" while reporting that one story had been rejected by a doctrinaire Communist magazine as lacking in class consciousness. "One of the editors pointed out that the 'doctor' seemed unaware of the implications of giving the girl a prescription that would cost not less than fifty cents, when her father was receiving ten dollars a week."

Philip Rahv knew better than to expect party orthodoxy of Williams, but he, too, missed the point when he reviewed the collection containing these stories in 1938. He described Williams as the kind of writer who rejects all ideas ("thought is proscribed as anti-aesthetic") and merely wants to record facts ("the relations, social and historic, that might unify these facts and significate them on a higher plane beyond sensation or nostalgia or pathos he has no mind for"). By 1950 the ideas implicit in Williams' "facts" were beginning to emerge, so that Heilman stressed the "symbolic value" of **"The Use of Force."** Yet its values for him turn out to be moral rather than esthetic and not at all revolutionary. Although "it would be a mistake . . . to read the story as a treatise against the use of force," it illuminates "the kind of hostility, love of conquest, and madness that the use of force brings into play, whatever the apparent justification for vigorous action." As a matter of fact, violence has no more moral value than it has political meaning in Williams' world, though its broad metaphoric use makes it a valuable key for discovering what sort of esthetic blast Williams wanted to set off with stories like **"The Use of Force."**

I

In Williams' *Beginning on the Short Story,* the basic problem of the writer in twentieth-century America is clearly articulated. "How shall we write today? The hero? Who is a hero? The peasantry? There is none. Men and women faithful to a belief? What belief?" In the past there were heroes, whole men, and traditional systems of values; but today, and especially in America, "we are no one of us 'all' of anything." We are still too new to have inherited any of the old values, yet we are too frightened by our new world to live independent of the past. In art we still value the old forms for the stability implicit in them, paying the commercial artist to produce familiar shapes. But if our world is actually new—modern, American, or both— we must face the terror of the unfamiliar and find our values in it rather than in the past or in distant places. Valueless, offering as yet no perfect art, the new world is all we have that is truly ours.

---

> Williams' new world is as violent as Poe's because it is still a wilderness violently resisting all efforts to cultivate it, and because, in its violently accelerated change, it is even more difficult to grasp than before.
>
> —*J. E. Slate*

---

In the new and terrifying world of the imagination, cut off from the comfortable certainties of the past, the serious artist creates in the fullest sense of the term. "You do not *copy* nature, you make something which is an *imitation* of nature," Williams told the Washington students. In the imagination, the artist, like nature, evolves new forms out of his new material; or, in terms closer to the center of Williams' theory, the artist faces the poverty and isolation of his world and embraces it violently, shaping it formally in its own terms while rejecting the alien and the old.

The distinction between *copying* and *imitation* appears as early as 1925 in the contrast between Hawthorne and Poe developed in Williams' *American Grain*. Despite Hawthorne's "willing closeness to the life of his locality in its vague humors; his lifelike copying of the New England melancholy; his reposeful closeness to the town pump," his tales are formally too old to have much value for a new world. Poe, Williams argued, is actually much more valuable, though he might at first seem to have fled the scene before him by refusing to write about "trees and Indians." Poe not only used new materials—his language was American, not English—and expressed the terror of life in a new world over and over again, but he also kept in mind "a beginning literature . . . that must establish its own rules, own framework." Behind the appearance of a wealth of new material, an illusion which trapped most of his contemporaries, Poe recognized a world lacking in value but so stubborn and savage in character that only the greatest formal skill, employed with imitative savagery, could allow the artist to survive and create. Williams imagined Poe as a frontiersman who survived by refusing to trust "the great natural beauty of the New World," by relying on his murderous skill as Boone had done, and by losing his alien ways in the violence of our new world. Because Poe understood the need for violence, "in all he says there is a sense of him *surrounded* by his time, tearing at it, ever with more rancour, but always at battle, taking hold."

Williams' new world is as violent as Poe's because it is still a wilderness violently resisting all efforts to cultivate it, and because, in its violently accelerated change, it is

even more difficult to grasp than before. For Doctor Williams, daily faced with poverty-stricken patients too ignorant to help themselves, the available material was indeed raw. Instead of complete actions he found isolated moments; instead of whole persons he found unrelated parts. These materials and the temporal situation, he says, "dictated the terms" in which they must be shaped, while the short story specifically had to "accommodate itself to the heterogeneous character of the people, the elements involved, the situation in hand."

Inventing truly new forms demands involvement in our time. Writing what Pound called "histoire morale contemporaine,'" Williams was so deeply involved in his time that his active political concerns could have no place in his short stories: to him, being a "proletarian writer" meant imitating the antisocial attitude of the deprived citizen, a man who clings to the myth of the self-made man so stubbornly that he cannot conceive of a revolutionary social movement which will not threaten his freedom. The central idea of the story and the collection called *Life Along the Passaic River* is "Nobody's gonna teach it to you; you got to learn it yourself." This is a significant statement of Williams' artistic creed made more significant because it is spoken with the accents of the poor. He is so determined to save them from cultural poverty that he becomes them, sharing their language and its limitations, their stubborn ignorance and their violence.

## II

In theme, language and physical detail, **"The Use of Force"** is unquestionably modern, reflecting its time exactly as Williams' theory demands. Its broad outlines, however, are more classic than modern, and this fact explains why the story has been more popular with critics than with Williams himself, who identified another story written the same year as his favorite. **"The Use of Force"** suggests classical tragedy, as one 1965 textbook explains, because the protagonist fights against overwhelming forces so well that her courage and determination take on values which outlast her ultimate defeat. Even though Mathilda Olson is not Antigone but a little girl lacking in real tragic stature, there is enough of the heroine in her to make the doctor into a kind of scientific Creon: his sense of social responsibility and his personal passion combine in a familiar pattern. Yet the story is more than a miniature tragedy in modern dress. In **"The Use of Force"** classical form is joined—though not successfully in my opinion—to a number of modern themes which, like violence, are characteristic of Williams' fiction in general. Ironically, the presence of the classic formula does not prevent the story from functioning as a good introduction to Williams' theory of modern fiction.

In all Williams' fiction, but most fully in his novel *White Mule,* children and childish adults represent modern or American man. As in **"The Use of Force,"** the child's helpless struggle to retain her independence often generates admiration and other powerful emotions, but her character remains incomplete, material too raw to be valuable in itself. The central figure of **"Jean Beicke,"** Williams' favorite story, is an infant resembling Mathilda in her resistance and her hidden disease. "A worthless piece of humanity," Jean dies despite the affection of the nurses and the intense professional interest of two good doctors. They attempt to make sense out of the child's condition but are left "dumb," defeated by their lack of knowledge and of words to express their feelings.

Jean, Mathilda, and the Flossie Stecher of *White Mule* share a capacity for self-destruction, irrational behavior, and violence. Jean's death spurs the narrator to say, "Vote the straight Communist ticket," suggesting—among other things—a revolutionary new view of life; and the little girl called "white mule" or moonshine is irrationally stubborn and as violent as a shot of raw whisky. Commenting on *White Mule,* Williams said, "I was crazy about babies, the contempt that all babies have for adults. They don't give a damn what goes on." In other words, the emotions associated with children are in themselves not only worthless but even self-destructive; yet these violent emotions are all we as new or unformed men have to give. The artist's social function is to invent forms for these emotions, to arrest the suicidal movement and to give the subjective emotion objective value.

Just as the child replaces the whole man or hero in Williams' fiction, circular movement or anticlimax often replaces a classical resolution of the plot. The last paragraph of **"The Use of Force"** imperfectly illustrates the difference, for after the doctor finally defeats the child and seems to resolve the conflict, the child attacks him again as if to renew the struggle. To invent a new ending suitable for his time, Williams has to make the ending a beginning, returning the plot from the moment of peace— a kind of death—to violence and life. Because defeat and death are the major premises of classical tragedy, the new form must go beyond it, suggesting a larger view in which life, though lacking in real value, goes on.

In his lecture on the short story Williams declared, "Murder is nothing at all but death—and what's new about death? Violence is the mood today." He sincerely admired the classic use of death as a means of defining life and intensifying human values, from Aeschylus ("a son cuts his mother's throat") to Hemingway ("a woman shooting her husband's head off"). But he suspected this was already old to the Hellenistic Greeks. "Maybe Plato was a bit fed up on the Sophocles" and invented the new form of the dialogue as a way of replacing murder with verbal violence. Williams notes that Plato's dialogues have arguments rather than deaths for endings, though he finally gave Socrates, his hero, the hemlock as well as a wife who could outtalk him.

In one of Williams' earliest stories, first published in 1920, art opposes death exactly as verbal violence opposes murder in the dialogues. **"Danse Pseudomacabre"** criticizes the traditional literary form, the dance of death, for putting its emphasis on *death* rather than *dance,* for the work of art can outlive death. In one part of the story death is imaginary—a childish man with erysipelas calls the doctor to witness his will—and in the other a baby

twitches in agonies that are coldly final. The doctor finds death the abstraction in both scenes but is searching for something more nearly like life, a way of defeating death. "Either dance or annihilation," the theme of this story, might well be the motto of all Williams' stories involving doctors and patients. In them the doctor is always reluctantly embracing his worthless material, moving with it in constantly changing patterns in order to rescue it from lifeless insignificance.

Another early story, **"The Accident,"** published in 1921, further developed the distinction between death and violence. In it Williams says, "Death is difficult for the senses to alight on. There is no help from familiarity with the location. There is a cold body to be put away but what is that? The life has gone out of it and death has come into it. Whither? The sense has no footspace." Violence is not only sensuous and therefore easier to grasp, but it is also capable of singling out moments in the stream of time and individuals in the mass of humanity without finishing the action or killing the individual. However, violence loses power if not apprehended as immediate experience. The newspapers give us violence enough but fail to present it in its own terms; adding nothing to life, the news actually debases it. In Washington, Williams declared that "the finest short stories are those that raise, in short, one particular man or woman, from that Gehenna, the newspaper, where at last all men are equal, to the distinction of being an individual."

Not surprisingly, the metamorphosis of Mathilda in **"The Use of Force"** follows this pattern. The girl's beauty is at first seen in stereo-typed images: she's "one of those picture children often reproduced in advertising leaflets and the photogravure sections of the Sunday papers." But her snatching of the doctor's glasses not only begins the process of making him "blind" with fury but also forces him to look at her with new eyes, raising her out of the exploiter's reach. Finally, when her hidden violence has become overt and she is understood in her own terms as a "savage brat," the doctor sees as an individual.

Impersonal violence, represented chiefly by war rather than by newspaper stories, has been a major problem for writers of the last hundred years. For Williams, the formal treatment of the inhuman event contained the solution: the artist captures the initiative from impersonal violence if he is able to imitate its destruction creatively, in the imagination. There the impersonal event—even war—can be given human meaning, though it may be imperfectly disciplined. Williams was close to the dadaists in 1914-16 and to the surrealists in the early forties when the wars of Europe brought refugees and violent new forms to New York; but his greatest productions of new prose forms coincide, not with international wars, but with the violent influenza epidemics of 1917-18 and 1929, and with other localized battles. He grasped violently new forms such as dada or invented his own—the *Improvisations* are a good example—to fight his enemy, impersonal violence.

Mathilda, too, attacks all the impersonal forces of society. Like the writer, she gains a temporary victory for humanity by her instinctive and ignorant seizure of the initiative from the one who threatens to expose her secret. She can do this and succeed, temporarily, because death as yet holds no fear: "that's nothing to her." But she ultimately fails: she acknowledges death in her scream, "You're killing me," and—under still greater force—her open mouth makes her secret public. In this context Mathilda's attack in the last lines of the story becomes a pitiful attempt to seize the initiative again. She will fail, no longer acting in self-confident ignorance, because successful new violence requires clear insight and technical skill, but her eyes are blind with tears.

The relationship between doctor and child, between passion and skill, between raw and formal violence, is obviously the central theme of **"The Use of Force."** The interaction of the two, and not the superiority of one over the other, is the point. The doctor's objectivity, his sense of social purpose and his accumulated knowledge are all modified in the course of the action, so that his violence is affected by that of the "savage brat." Her all-too-human violence, in turn, is beaten by the greater forces of time and death; only in the shape of the story does her formless passion take on meaning. Only in art does modern life have coherence, Williams implies.

### III

In 1917-18, in the chaos and violence of the great epidemic, Williams met death's impersonal violence with the distorted forms of the short prose pieces later collected as *Kora in Hell: Improvisations*. Their relationship to the short stories exists on several levels, but their commitment to violence is the most easily demonstrated connection: "Richard worked years to conquer the descending cadence, idiotic sentimentalist. Ha, for happiness! This tore the dress in ribbons from her maid's back and not spared the nails either; wild anger spit from her pinched eyes! This is the better part. Or a child under a table to be dragged out coughing and biting, eyes glittering evilly. I'll have it my own way! Nothing is any pleasure but misery and brokenness. THIS is the only up-cadence." Techniques from the past, such as the metrical problem preoccupying Richard, have only a "sentimental" relevance to the violence and fragmentation of life today. But wild scenes reminiscent of **"The Use of Force"** and other short stories offer a solution for the modern artist: deformity, insanity, wounds, amputation, disease may be clues to the shape of new forms. This argument is continued in **"Danse Pseudomacabre,"** where the narrator asserts "the normality of every distortion to which flesh is susceptible, every disease, every amputation." Like violence, disease is normal in its opposition to death; unlike violence, disease is what Williams called "the illuminating element."

In **"The Use of Force"** all three Olsons are called "patients" because all their secret lives are illuminated by the child's disease. The story's action centers around force or violence, and a secret is literally forced out of each character in the story. But violence, like the idea or suspicion of disease, has been present in them from the beginning.

It is insubstantial until it breaks into the open and makes itself fully concrete in the membrane on the child's tonsils. The meaninglessness of violence without disease, of emotion without its image, lies at the basis of the dramatic poem "The Raper from Passenack," published the same year as *Life Along the Passaic River.*

This poem focuses on the victim's attempts to understand the act of violence:

> Only a man who is sick, she said
> would do a thing like that.
> It must be so.
>
> No one who is not diseased could be
> so insanely cruel. He wants to give it
> to someone else—
>
> to justify himself.

She comprehends something of his motives but "can't yet understand / it" in terms of herself, because not even the experience of personal violence is self-illuminating. So she creates a disease, an explanation, just as the artist creates an image to match his emotion. But in her ability to see how the violence might in simpler times have contained the seeds of life ("I'd rather a million times / have been got pregnant") she fails to understand the need to make disease breed life rather than death:

> if I get a
> venereal infection out of this
> I won't be treated.
>
> I refuse. You'll find me dead in bed
> first.

Without art violence failed to find its proper image, its "right" disease, and the result was "hatred of all men /— and disgust."

Rejecting the symbol in favor of the image, its modern counterpart, Williams necessarily rejects the values familiarly attached to disease. Eliot's assertion in "East Coker" that "Our only health is the disease / If we obey the dying nurse" finally depends on these old, familiar associations even though its emphases, such as the insistence on the savior's imperfection, are modern. Eliot gives the classic symbolism of disease a new twist which allows the past to offer an ironic contrast with the present, while Williams attempts to use disease objectively, giving it only an esthetic value as "the illuminating element." **"The Knife of the Times,"** one of many Williams stories dealing with sexual perversion, presents disease in precisely this objective manner. A knife cuts objectively, regardless of the patient, to reveal the truth; this knife is doubly objective, for the times—our modern times—do not treat the disease of homosexuality with traditional horror, nor do these times have any values to impose upon the truth they reveal. The knife of the times enables an ordinary woman to discover the "disease" in her best friend and then in herself; facing the possibility of a new, though "abnormal," life, she asks,

"Why not?" The diseased world of Lesbian love offers no basis for horror, and after all, she has nothing else. The disease, radiating its own objective truth, has no more moral significance than the knife which lays it open: both are images of art rather than morality.

All the world is a hospital to Williams as much as to Eliot, yet Eliot's institution, a kind of purgatory, specializes in the curing of souls, while Williams' corridors have no surgeons in them and he minimizes the importance of cures. "Any worth-his-salt physician knows that no one is 'cured,'" Williams says in his *Autobiography.* Ignorant of this simple fact and living in the old world of absolutes, his patients demand bigger and better cures, "home runs, antibiotics to cure man with a single shot in the buttocks." "It is noteworthy," he says, "that the sulfonamids, penicillin, came in about simultaneously with Ted Williams, Ralph Kiner and the rubber ball." Without scorning humanity's weakness for absolutes, he treats us as children who will get, not what we want, but what is good for us in the way of art. Just as the doctor is obliged by social expectations to strive toward a total "cure" or immortality, the artist is obliged to aspire toward completeness and a final fixed form; but Williams secretly believes that "discovery is the great goal."

"There is only, we might say, flux in nature." If this is true, as Williams asserts in *A Beginning on the Short Story,* movement and change characterize life, while death, in essence, is fixity. By analogy, a cure, as a moment of pause in the course of a disease, is a kind of death. In the realm of art, as in medicine, some temporary fixing of life is necessary, but concentration on the end rather than the means leads directly to denial of movement and change, to dead form. Gazing too long at the still beauty of perfection, an artist forgets his humanity, his ultimate commitment to change. To counteract this Williams recommends "Drink, drugs—anything you can think of" to free the artist's mind from fixity, especially from past forms embodying values irrelevant to our times. Like the doctor in **"The Use of Force,"** the artist needs release from rational restraints before he can begin to see the values inherent in his crude materials. He must be willing to come down to their own level, where abnormality, disease and violence are expected. And the familiarity of violence to us, for whom it has been called "idiomatic," makes old literary treatments of such material less truthful than non-literary ones.

Freedom being as essential to fictional technique as to the basic imagination, Williams suggested to his audience in 1950 that "release" be followed by improvisation. "Sit down *blind* and start to fling the words around like pigments . . . let 'em go and (without thinking or caring) see where they'll lead you." The words, freed of their habitual and traditional uses, become concrete objects rather than ideas and the shape of the entire work is deformed by the violence of the method. Its deformities, both surface roughness and structural imperfection, deny its own completeness, sacrificing wholeness for connections with life as an ongoing process and with our unformed and incomplete new world. It is writing rather than literature.

Viewed from a different position, deformities are the memories of violence made permanent, testimony to the violence of the creative act. The woman with the broken nose in episode 17 of *Paterson* is "marked up / Beautiful Thing / for memory's sake / to be credible." In the last word Williams puns on *credit,* the nation's self-created wealth, to suggest that the values of art, after all, constitute our least tangible and yet our only true source of wealth. Here, and in many other passages, he insists on retaining the physical marks of the process by formal invention rather than by freedom from form. Although techniques of improvisation cannot be perfected and still remain improvisatory, those techniques may be improved by closer imitation of the violence and deformity of our daily life, constantly reinventing forms nearer and nearer to the truth about us. The truth about the modern world does not exist except in its art, so that the responsibility for writing truthfully ultimately becomes the responsibility to write well. The short story, Williams says, "must be written so well that that in itself becomes its truth while the deformity informs it."

### IV

In fiction, truth is always reached by means of a life. In this sense, all fiction must be deformed. Williams' emphasis on deformity, however, forces him to emphasize the lie to an unusual degree. His *Autobiography* tells of a libel suit rising out of a short story, which he was happy to settle out of court for $5000, though every word in the story was factually true. Williams seems to offer this incident as a parable: since he was writing fiction, he was indeed guilty, both of lying and of telling the truth. He was happy to pay the price to go on writing fiction. But he was also paying for the privilege of producing an unsalable lie, telling a truth so unpleasant and so crudely disguised that it was certain to be offensive. The ignorant citizen of the new world prefers a familiar kind of lie and also has spirit enough to aspire toward perfection, if it is only a mechanically perfect technique in the fiction he buys. The new world is sensitive enough to resent seeing its own deformities made public and seeing its lack of refinement reflected in its art, for it childishly wants to deny its own newness.

Among Williams' stories, **"Frankie the Newspaperman"** probably puts the motives of vanity, ignorance, and a pitiful aspiration together in the neatest structure. In high school English, Frankie Weber, the bright son of a washerwoman, is always in trouble. Most recently, he made a fool of his teacher by a crudely inventive twist of colloquial speech: everybody should chip in a dollar and take up a collection for the teacher "because she is so flat busted!" But the cruel joke, puncturing the teacher's vanity, is on him, too: the newspaper writing he aspires to will inevitably lack the pleasure and force of his improvisation and lack the basic American crudity that permits the joke to flash the truth about him, his teacher, and their world—that all are culturally indigent, "flat busted." Newspapers function similarly in **"The Use of Force."** Mathilda's apologetic parents, acutely self-conscious and aware of their lack of refinement, cannot help being upset when the doctor's first impression of their daughter, as "one of those picture children . . . of the Sunday papers," is quickly destroyed. The crude behavior of the child forces them into the open, turns them "inside out" just as most newspaper facts, if twisted or otherwise deformed, can be forced to reveal their implicit truths.

---

> "The Use of Force" and most of Williams' other stories might be described as fictions in which Williams involves himself as the narrator; but they are more accurately stories in which the point of view is missing, formal structures in which the flaw functions as a part of the whole, giving it its meaning.
>
> —*J. E. Slate*

---

Referring to his libelous story, Williams said with his usual false naïvete that pressures of time and place kept him from refining it: "I planned to change the names later." Conditions prevented him from protecting his readers from the truth about themselves, forced him to use "real names" and made his crude failure more significant than a slick success. Once again, **"The Use of Force"** may be read as a dramatization of a critical principle. Mathilda's lies about her throat fail, forcing her to violence that reveals her true worth; the doctor's false smile—in his "best professional manner"—fails, forcing him also to violence. However, he would still prefer to achieve his goal in some less physical manner, and his familiarity with successful lies makes him furious with Mrs. Olson's unsuccessful "He won't hurt you." "If only they wouldn't use the word 'hurt' I might be able to get somewhere." Of all the characters, only Mrs. Olson fails to realize that her lies are lies, so that she remains ignorant to the end and refuses to give up her interjections of "nice" and "kind" for the crude action which is an admission of failure and a deformed kind of success.

"I lived among these people," Williams said of the patients who were the chief characters of his stories. "I was involved." Involvement, of course, meant lack of esthetic distance or a point of view, a technical deformity Williams was conscious of almost to the point of "shame." But as usual, he attempted to exploit this flaw, to make the deformity inform his work. Since the fictional narrator belonged to the past and a modern substitute had not yet appeared, he had nothing from which to invent a new form except his own shameful involvement. Thus **"The Use of Force"** and most of Williams' other stories might be described as fictions in which Williams involves himself as the narrator; but they are more accurately stories in which the point of view is missing, formal structures in which the flaw functions as a part of the whole, giving it

its meaning. His closeness to the action of the story must appear as a deformity, a failure to invent, until the meaning of the story becomes radiantly clear. Then the form is seen as new rather than old and the imperfection becomes a kind of refinement.

The technical refinements in Williams' stories like **"The Use of Force"** are so new that they can seldom be described except in terms of the old. In language, for example, Williams' stories appear careless, crude or unfinished. One, called **"Verbal Transcription: 6 A.M.,"** pretends to be nothing more than a crude set of notes, and its material, like Frankie's joke, is often cliché. But the language is not copied; instead, it imitates the rough talk of the new world, recreating that world in its own terms. The careless effect of the first paragraph of **"The Use of Force"** comes from two sentences combining inaccurate statement with loose and illogical connections of ideas. And although one sentence is spoken by one of the Olsons and the other by the doctor, the speaker's individuality seems to be denied by the stylistic flatness of both. Yet in the end, we see that the whole family *are* patients, that the two speakers are close-knit in speech because they are related in several significant ways, and that subtle distinctions between parental nervousness and professional calm are present in the two speeches. [The critic adds in a footnote: "Punctuation divides each sentence into two major units. Of the paragraph's four units, the first and the last are single phrases of minimum length grouped around a single primary stress, the repetition functioning to call attention to the similarities and differences in the two middle units, which subdivide into two parts. These differ so clearly in pauses and primary stresses that the doctor's slower and the parent's more rapid speech can be distinctly heard."]

Similarly, the diction of **"The Use of Force"** appears flat and its metaphors seem clichés. The words and phrases describing Mathilda—*eating me up, strong as a heifer, with one cat-like movement, clawed, savage, wild, damned*—do not call attention to themselves; lacking commercial beauty or obvious newness, they generate meaning through their arrangement within individual sentences and within the story. *Damned,* the climactic word, is probably the best of all the calculated failures. It does, of course, fail to convey the doctor's frustration or his need to express himself violently; a banal blasphemy, it expresses only failure. But attached to a child who contains all the new world, it takes on the solid new meanings of *doomed* and *lost.*

Looking back, Williams said of his stories, "I kept the literary thing to myself. No one knew I felt that the stories might be literary." It is this attitude which distinguishes Williams from his contemporaries, Gertrude Stein, Sherwood Anderson, and Ernest Hemingway, each of whom shared some part of his theory of modern fiction. All these others refined their materials in the classical manner: their writing quickly became independent of its sources in everyday diction, the rhythms of the spoken language, the mind of the nonliterary and anti-intellectual citizen. Hemingway, Williams complained to Pound in 1928, misused the formal qualities implicit in conversation: "I am afraid

Hem doesn't at all understand, since it is rarely as expressive as he makes it and twice as succinct." Later Williams returned to the same point to say "Hemingway's not a bad poet and might have been a better one." Both comments seem to be references to the techniques of refinement which made Hemingway a successful and even salable writer. Prose so obviously patterned that it became poetic was for Williams a betrayal of the new and its inherent deformity; it was neo-orthodox writing, the old masquerading as something new.

Like Williams' famous but misunderstood criticism of T. S. Eliot's neo-orthodoxy, his opposition to Hemingway's style was an outgrowth of his theory more than it was jealousy of one more successful than himself. Williams' theory of the new could not accommodate a successful writer, even one whom he had helped and who had arrived only after years of neglect. Williams assumed the existence of a new world always new and therefore never wholly conquered; its writers must always be on the way, in the midst of their work, and never in a position of having arrived. Furthermore, Williams' world of perpetual change claims the artist's whole attention, leaving him no time to compare himself with the great men of the past as Hemingway was so fond of doing. For all these reasons, Williams' approach will appeal strongly to the young or unsuccessful writer even where its appeal to basic American prejudices does not touch him. It was entirely appropriate that Williams' fullest statement of his theory of fiction be made to college students, and that it be called *A Beginning on the Short Story.*

### V

William Carlos Williams demanded so much of the modern artist that he could not always satisfy his own demands. A few of his stories, like **"The Dawn of Another Day,"** cannot be distinguished from the commercial formulas he said he was attacking; a great many more, like the ones mentioned through this essay, are fascinating attempts to make the deformity inform the modern short story. **"The Use of Force,"** however, stands out. Its critical and commercial success calls attention to its failure as a modern work, its failure to deal with the people and the times completely in the contemporary patterns of deformity and failure.

The deficiencies of **"The Use of Force"** as a modern short story become apparent when it is contrasted with a more anecdotal fragment like the following narrative from Williams' *Autobiography.* "One day I was examining a fifteen-year-old white girl—a cute kid who had been brought into the clinic for diagnosis by her mother who wanted to know what made her belly so big. The kid was not dumb and fought us every step of the way. Finally after threats by her mother and persuasion on my part, we got her dress off, but at that point she flew at us all and in her underwear dashed out the door and up the street like a young doe. That's the last I saw of her." Like some of *Kora in Hell: Improvisations* and all of the miniature narratives that make up the story **"World's End,"** this expresses the fragmentary nature of Williams' world more

clearly than **"The Use of Force,"** as well as avoiding the suggestion of any classic pattern. Her escape is not the comic success of the underdog, for her secret can be concealed even less successfully than Mathilda's; and her deformity is full of human meaning which has no relationship to her rather temporary escape. In escaping the doctor's clutches, she is also life escaping the artist no matter how many times he tries to bring his work to perfection. The diagnosis is incomplete and the "cure" for pregnancy is such an unlikely possibility that it is not mentioned in the narrative.

As this example suggests, Williams' theory and practice both make it necessary to redefine the term *fiction,* at least for him, to include almost all his prose: novels, short stories, improvisations, autobiographical works. R. P. Blackmur called *In the American Grain* and *The Great American Novel* fictions; they are certainly not essays and ought to be read as fiction if not as poems. And it might even be useful to extend the term to include Williams' peculiar alternating form of verse and prose—exemplified in *Spring & All, The Descent of Winter,* and *Paterson*—if this would, as I believe, increase the appreciation of his art. Along with such a redefinition, the fact must be faced that Williams' critical essays, like Poe's, are absolutely essential for reading his work, because the real subject of it all is art and his critical statements are the best keys to what he was attempting to do.

The critical problem of Williams' basic assumption of a perpetually new world, of course, remains, for understanding of the importance of the assumption to him should precede any attack on this problem. It is certainly far from the simple primitivism which a number of critics have claimed. I have tried to show how much misunderstanding exists in spite of Williams' coherence and consistency. I have been especially eager to correct the confusion between traditional morality, for which Williams has no artistic use, and the morality of art that operates in all of Williams' work. His dedication to art was as single-minded as that of his "saint" Edgar Allan Poe, and his dedication to the new world was as great as that of his other guide and patron, Walt Whitman.

### Thomas R. Whitaker (essay date 1968)

SOURCE: "On the Ground," in *William Carlos Williams,* Twayne Publishers, 1968, pp. 97-118.

[*In the excerpt below, Whitaker gives a thematic overview of Williams's short fiction.*]

Though Williams had written short stories during the previous decade or so, not until the 1930's did this form become of major importance to him. In the people among whom he worked, the Depression was now revealing qualities that demanded a brief narrative form: "brokenness and heterogeneity—isolation, color." Temporary uncertainty about his direction in poetry also led him to prose—as a "laboratory for metrics" in which he could listen to live speech, hoping to discover the new. And behind these immediate reasons there was, I think, his increasing need to explore more intensively the minute particulars of that ground to which Dev Evans had returned—that ground on which Williams walked daily. Indeed, the primary stylistic meaning of these stories results from their movement beyond what he had called in 1927 "my formerly important irritability, diffuseness," toward annihilation of the self-regarding ego and a clearer acquaintance with the ground. This movement required a difficult honesty: "In order to be plain myself I must be assured that I am speaking true. That is the style, true to the sharpest, firmest present vision of which I am capable."

The stories collected in *The Knife of the Times* (1932) sometimes recall Gertrude Stein, Sherwood Anderson, and D. H. Lawrence, for Williams employs an oral style that relies heavily upon rapid and generalized narration and upon strategic focus on a few banal but authentic details. In understated sketches (**"The Knife of the Times,"** **"The Sailor's Son"**) characters reach blindly toward some fulfillment, their need answered half-comprehendingly perhaps by another. More extended studies (**"A Descendant of Kings,"** **"Pink and Blue"**) balance pathos and comedy as they move toward a grotesque inflation made possible by their anecdotal mode.

The accurately heard speaking voice is a key to greater intensity in **"An Old Time Raid,"** where the first-person narration stylistically renders the theme—a vacuous violence, without self-comprehension, born of hidden frustration. In this instance, an anecdote widens to become a character study and a study of an entire deformed milieu. A similar intensity charges **"Mind and Body,"** in which a neurotic patient reveals her complex rhythm of being through her own lengthy utterances. Here too appears another device of great importance in later stories: Williams focuses upon a human predicament through the doctor-patient relationship, allowing the shadowily present doctor to serve as explicit or implicit locus of observation. The deepest meaning of such stories may be found less in the predicaments observed than in the difficult but unself-conscious openness of the doctor's attention. The conclusion of **"Mind and Body"** itself points ironically to that fact: pressing for a somatic diagnosis, the woman invites from her doctor a drastic reduction of that total human interpretation implicit in his arrangement of the story's details.

The major piece in this volume is the long story **"Old Doc Rivers."** In it, a doctor-narrator's inquiries combine with related anecdotes in a *progression d'effet* which leads into a complex awareness of both Old Doc Rivers and his provincial environment, with its walling-in and its limited releases. The opening paragraph plunges us into the rhythm of the narrator's repeated drama of sudden discovery and ruminative assessment: "Horses. These definitely should be taken into consideration in estimating Rivers position, along with the bad roads, the difficult means of communication of those times." As the story proceeds through neatly fitted blocks of material, the meanings of "horses" and "bad roads" widen to include Rivers' pride in occu-

pation, his dashing readiness and fevered rush, his isolation and need for release—and, with a sardonic modulation, his final doped decline amid changing times. We last see him as owner of "two cars always ready for service," riding out on calls with one of his wife's Blue Pomeranians on his lap; "for in those days he himself never sat at the wheel."

---

**Williams employs an oral style that relies heavily upon rapid and generalized narration and upon strategic focus on a few banal but authentic details.**

*—Thomas R. Whitaker*

---

Between that opening and that close, the story follows a seemingly devious but subtly direct line of understanding. First, there are glimpses of Rivers' practice and of his drive across the County Bridge toward some release in the "dark spring night." Then follows the narrator's inquiry into hospital record books, where he characteristically finds at first "something other than the thing desired" but with unexpected relevance: data about the human occupations, misery, and fatalities of the time, among which he slips new information for us about Rivers, "dead surely of the effects of his addiction." The story then moves (by way of alcoholism as a ledger entry) through exploration of Rivers' use of dope, inquiries of surgeons who had assisted him, and the narrator's own memory of the two occasions on which he had helped Rivers with an operation.

By now our distance from the narrator has decreased—as has his own distance from the past that he is exploring. We may thus join him in searching the meaning of Rivers' tenderness and cruelty, carelessness and painstaking attention. Then, with the outlines of a character and a predicament before us, we can actually follow Rivers on those drives away from town: toward the Jeannette Mansion, toward the Maine woods and the North Jersey mountains, and (after another "digression," telling of his stays in the Insane Asylum and his marriage, and locating us in the consciousness of a youthful eye-witness) toward that most important of "favorite places," the isolated farm where a woman provided—in her own abandonment—a more necessary asylum.

As the friend tells of those visits (appropriately beginning with the inclusive phrase, "You know how it used to be," and incorporating a running account of his own youth), it becomes increasingly hard to distinguish his voice from that of the narrator. And in a sudden detail—"Killy-fish rippled the road ditch, a diminutive tempest, as the carriage and the hoof beats of the horses slightly shook the ground in passing"—we are momentarily swept through the minds of narrator and informant into that of Rivers himself, as we now fully sense the meaning of that drive across the County Bridge. Williams has led us back into what James called a "visitable past," a past that is also ours.

In doing so, Williams has given the larger meaning of Rivers' predicament: a complex nature hemmed in by a "crude environment," a "refinement of the sensibilities that made him, though able, the victim of the very things he best served." Rivers was "by natural endowment the ablest individual of our environment"; and—unlike most in the cities who "have lost touch" with themselves, "have become indeed not authentic persons, but fantastic shapes in some gigantic fever dream"—he had "the courage to break with it and to go."

As the story tails off with anecdotes of decline and of legendary competence (rendering the despairing faith of a population which, as in *Paterson,* seeks a "marvel"), we find two summary statements casually included among other data. The first: "A cure for disease? He knew what that amounted to. For of what shall one be cured? Work, in this case, through sheer intuitive ability flooded him under." Ironically enough, Rivers' own amazing diagnostic ability makes him a focus for the ills of his time, which take in him a peculiarly revelatory form. And the second statement: "He was one of the few that ever in these parts knew the meaning of all, to give himself completely." We suddenly recognize—in and through the distortions of temperament and time—a spiritual descendant of Rasles and Boone—and a true colleague of the writer himself.

*Life Along the Passaic River* (1938) continues the double interest in people and place, and also focuses on that overwhelming question: "Of what shall one be cured?" Through the panoramic sketch (**"Life Along the Passaic River"**), the neatly plotted episode (**"The Dawn of Another Day"**), the series of vignettes (**"World's End"**), and the character drawing (**"Under the Greenwood Tree"**), Williams explores the blockages and perversions of the time and implies a cure: attentive acceptance. One of several earlier pieces collected here—**"Danse Pseudomacabre"** (1920)—presents a rather strident version of such acceptance. But other stories, relating encounters of doctors and patients, more firmly realize both disease and cure.

In **"The Girl with a Pimply Face"** the "hard, straight thing" that the doctor-narrator admires in the girl appears also, complicated and refracted, in his own attention to her warping milieu. We accept his compassion for the alcoholic mother partly because it is one genuine emotion among others—puzzlement, irritation, inarticulate rage, enthusiasm. Hence in its closing dialogue the story can accomplish the very difficult task of allowing both narrator and fifteen-year-old girl to emerge as implicit signs of life in a venal and oppressive environment.

In **"The Use of Force"** the same frank acknowledgment of what *is* allows the doctor to move from impatience to love, to pleasure in his own fury, and on to self-recognition: "The damned little brat must be protected against her own idiocy, one says to one's self at such times. Others must

be protected against her. It is social necessity. And all these things are true. But a blind fury, a feeling of adult shame, bred of a longing for muscular release are the operatives. One goes on to the end." This doctor's curative insight is, among other things, an awareness of how he shares in those desires which, uncomprehended, make for conflict and tyranny.

In **"A Night in June"** the burden of self-knowledge for such a doctor emerges unobtrusively in the midst of an early morning delivery of a child to an Italian immigrant woman. The first sentences of the story establish an ironic point of reference by alluding to the delivery of her first baby (eighteen years earlier) when the narrator was "a young man . . . full of information and tenderness." The story has about six pages of detail concerning the routine preparations for the present delivery in order to render the quality of experience of a man honestly aware of his own sources of gratification—a man for whom the self-conscious imparting of "information and tenderness" are signs of youth.

After this preparation we can approach a statement that would otherwise be quite misleading: "With my left hand steering the child's head, I used my ungloved right hand outside on her bare abdomen to press upon the fundus. The woman and I then got to work. Her two hands grabbed me at first a little timidly about the right wrist and forearm. Go ahead, I said. Pull hard. I welcomed the feel of her hands and the strong pull. It quieted me in the way the whole house had quieted me all night." He recognizes that it is he who is "being comforted and soothed." But the story must continue even beyond this climax for another page—through a variety of medical concerns and family reactions to the final question from the sister-in-law: "What shall I do? Put a little boric acid powder on the belly button to help dry it up?" Only amid equal attention to details of this kind can such gratification or release be of another order than Rivers' dope or the use of force.

The very different doctor-narrator of **"Jean Beicke"** projects in his rambling discourse a mask of callousness, verve, curiosity, and wry humor through which tenderness emerges only obliquely or in disguise. The story's most striking device is its limiting of the baby Jean's hospital life to a three-page block in the middle of some eight pages. The long introduction establishes the tonal complexity of the narrator's voice against a background of human deprivation and a range of simpler attitudes toward it: the "doctor who has given the parents a ride," parents who were habitual drunkards ("No fault of theirs maybe"), and nurses who "break their hearts over those kinds, many times, when I, for one, wish they'd never get well."

But why should Williams inform us of Jean's mastoiditis and death and then go *back* through the details of the autopsy that had revealed the nature of her illness? By eliminating suspense, he enables us to join the narrator in focussing with equanimity upon the medical details—against a background, once more, of simpler and more extreme human responses: the mother's sorrow and her sister's sense of relief. Sharing both impulses, the narrator yet proceeds with what needs to be done. However, the final interchange with the "ear man" points beyond the narrator for the full meaning of a normative awareness:

> A clear miss, he said. I think if we'd gone in there earlier, we'd have saved her.
>
> For what? said I. Vote the straight Communist ticket.
>
> Would it make us any dumber? said the ear man.

The human condition requires a more delicately vulnerable witnessing than the narrator's own armor of defensive abstraction and sardonic solutions may allow. But the difficulty of such witnessing is also part of the meaning of little Jean herself: "She was just skin and bones but her eyes were good and she looked straight at you. Only if you touched her anywhere, she started to whine and then cry with a shrieking, distressing sort of cry that no one wanted to hear." In Jean, as in all the adults of the story, potential awareness has been crippled as a raw sensitivity defends itself.

The use of a doctor-narrator is most striking in **"A Face of Stone."** There the narrator himself begins with responses to experience that are habitual and self-enclosing. In the opening description of the couple who seek his help, his irritation and prejudice are manifest: "He was one of these fresh Jewish types you want to kill at sight, the presuming poor whose looks change the minute cash is mentioned. But they're insistent, trying to force attention, taking advantage of good nature at the first crack. You come when I call you, that type." The tone is convincing: this narrator is a man whom the author thoroughly understands.

Turning from one half-projected mode of defensiveness to another, the doctor describes the woman, who "stood beside her smiling husband and looked at me with no expression at all on her pointed face, unless no expression is an expression. A face of stone. It was an animal distrust, not shyness. She wasn't shy but seemed as if sensing danger, as though she were on guard against it." There *is* danger, of course, which the narrator does not see because it is in himself.

Toward the end of the story, as he realizes the woman's suffering and the nature of the husband's devotion to her, his view of the couple begins to alter: "suddenly I understood his half shameful love for the woman and at the same time the extent of her reliance on him. I was touched." His own stoniness is explicitly dissolved; but the fuller meanings of that process are only implied by the woman's response as he explains the medicine she is to take: "Then for the first time since I had known her a broad smile spread all over her face. Yeah, she said, I swallow him." What the narrator does not know, or at least cannot say, is the fact that his own new condition has enabled in the woman a comparable opening, of which her words are symptom and symbol. "Of what shall one be cured?" This story dramatizes with firm and tactful detail the narrator's movement toward re-acquaintance with not merely a local but a spiritual ground.

Williams' awareness of this meaning is evident from a canceled preface, written during a moment of doubt over the clarity of the story's structure:

> What shall I say? The truth only, of a life tortured, but no more than others, and unfeeling. It is even somewhat shameful to speak of these things. . . . Of what is there to confess? Loss of love? Why pretend a love that doubtless never quite existed? . . .
>
> How shall I say it? I who have wished to embrace the world with love have succeeded only in binding to myself a wife and children . . . ? I who wished, in a general way, to die for love have suffered only the small accidents of fatigue, bewilderment and loss? . . .
>
> Who feels enough confidence to say anything? All I know is that no matter what we have dreamed or desired it slips away unless by a supreme effort we struggle to detain it. And often, in spite of all that we can do, it is to someone else we owe the little we can hold. . . . I want to explain, for once, not only the story, but to go besides outside it and stress what it means to me—returning to a life as I had planned it.
>
> It is only a story, good enough, and there is a desperation in the very triviality of situations, since we know well what they signify but being unable to quite convince ourselves of their importance we allow them to pile up . . .

And in this earlier draft, Williams included a more explicit account of the narrator's feeling toward the husband:

> There is in a defenseless thing something that infuriates us. . . . We find ourselves beaten by the meanness of our own lives, the squalor of it, the grossness, the moral weakness. And not daring, out of cowardice, to attack the real enemy, ourselves, we wreak our vengeance on the meanest thing before us.
>
> Even knowing I was cruel, cowardly, I couldn't stop myself. There was a pleasure in it. . . . That pity, even tenderness could at the same time be alive seems impossible, yet it is so. But once the attack is launched, even against reason, against desire, the object of our hatred becomes fixed and we go on to the bitter end. Only a deeper power, as I will show, can wake us finally to all that life can mean—and save us.

Though, as autobiographical statements, these are moving in their tortured honesty, Williams was right to omit them. His narrator enacts a process that he cannot (without self-contradiction) fully articulate. **"A Face of Stone"** stands firmly as it is: a rendering of that "deeper power" and that "waking."

*Make Light of It* (1950) includes many brief sketches that are important mainly as reflecting Williams' search for the illuminating detail and the cadences of live speech. But several stories are more difficult contrapuntal structures, rendering a hitherto unrecognized order. In **"The**

**Burden of Loveliness"** a central anecdote appears in a seemingly digressive context that is really "conversation as design." The result is a subtle exploration, through interlocking trivial situations and obliquely symbolic detail, of what happens to esthetic appreciation and sexuality in a market economy. No doctrinaire diatribe, it is a sympathetic presentation of the human costs borne by those who buy or sell or try to do neither.

In **"Country Rain"** the meaning expands mainly through symbolic details and characters. The relationship of Helen and her friend Ruth, who have left city and men for an unconventional new start as operators of a country inn, is counterpointed by that of two lady school teachers and that of the narrator and his wife. Early drafts treated at some length the repressed school teachers' obsession with grammar, their conservatism and prejudice, and their readiness to discover political subversion. But Williams reduced such material to brief hints and to a closing symbolic comment, which juxtaposes "their situation among the dones, the aints and the seens" and an "ungrammatical rock." The richly regenerative details of that rock summarize what we have seen beneath the neat surfaces of Helen's and Ruth's life together. The story ends with another counterpoint—Floss' question, "Do you think Ruth will every marry?" and the narrator's counterquestion: "Why?" Growth here does not result from insistence upon some grammar—linguistic, political, or sexual.

The most successful story of this kind, however, is **"Comedy Entombed."** Central in it is the doctor's response to the woman and the mode of life in the house: "There was nothing properly recognizable, nothing straight, nothing in what might have been called its predictable relationships. Complete disorder." But he comes to see it as an "unrecognizable order" and implicitly discerns the meaning of its resemblance to the woman, with her smiling ease amid fifth-month contractions. The final page, through conversation alone, subtly rounds off a double pattern: the comedy entombed alive in the woman herself (by oppressive environment and unwanted child) and the further entombing which results from it:

> It was alive when it was born though, she said. I looked and I could see it open its mouth like it wanted to breathe. What is it, Doc, . . . a boy or a girl?

> Oh, boy! said the husband, have I got a bellyache tonight. She laughed. Guss he's having a baby. He's worse than I am. . . . Say, Doc, she continued, you haven't told me. What was it? . . .

> I looked. Yes, it would have been a girl.

> There, she said, you see! Now you've got your girl. I hope you're satisfied.

> I haven't got any girl, he answered quietly.

> I'm hungry, yelled a sleepy voice from the other room.

> Shut up! said the father.

The narrator's attention has focused a family pattern of conflicting "hungers" or desires to "breathe" which lead to frustration, shutting up, entombment. . . .

A late story, **"The Farmers' Daughters"** (1957), may remind us where Williams' strengths lie; for it avoids the dangers that attend dramatic action and also those of the writer's egocentric involvement. Though the story may seem a random sequence of glimpses, it is really a firm composition of selected narrative blocks. The narrator, an anonymous member of the community, is little more than a voice. Through him we share the story's real point of view: that of the doctor who is friend and confidant of the two lonely women, Helen and Margaret. The doctor, however, is no center of conflict, nor does he search into the meaning of the events he witnesses. Often no more than implicitly present, he is at most a shadowy figure. Yet for that reason he gradually focuses the story's most important meanings.

The first seven narrative blocks suggest the frustration and violence in the women's past and their continuing loneliness and self-destructiveness. We see, however, that, while Margaret is still victim of a compulsive sexuality, Helen is pulling out of her similarly compulsive drinking. We also see that the doctor's mere attention to Helen—his good-humored, sympathetic, and honest response—has been an important curative force. After brief description of the developing friendship between the two women, the next five blocks bring the story to its first climax. We see Helen's home situation more fully—including her intense yet obliquely expressed love for the doctor. The doctor's response appears in his reaction to the photograph she gives him: "The trees blossoming with ice seemed to them both a triumphant thing; it made their hearts sing, therefore he was grateful to her for the picture, wanted to keep it where he could see it when he was depressed." We then follow corresponding material concerning Margaret—including her growing desperation and her imperfectly acknowledged affection for the doctor. Here too we find hints of his own fascination. The last block of material, spanning several years, moves with stark swiftness from the symbolic Thanksgiving celebration with the doctor ("a love feast, . . . a despairing avowal and celebration") into the first major crisis: Margaret's drunken fracas, her attempt to kill herself and her children, and her flight with boyfriend Mac.

In the next section—another twelve blocks—this established rhythm is expanded. With minor variations, we move through Helen's situation and then through Margaret's. Again the last block moves swiftly from a kind of domestic felicity into catastrophe: the shooting of Margaret by her new husband. Two other blocks provide a coda on the meaning of human relatedness. First, Helen's hysterical reconstruction of the murder, concluding with her plea to the doctor: "Take good care of yourself 'cause I can't afford to lose you. When she [Margaret] died, I died too, you're the only one I have left." Second, the dry account—after the inquest—of the trajectory of the bullet.

Many details in this half of the story have developed its central triangular relationship. There are little parallels: Helen yearns toward her china doll as the doctor implicitly does toward Helen—with her "Dresden china blue eyes blinking at him above a house-coat of mixed colors and faded blue slacks." Yet such pathetic attempts to overcome isolation have their beauty: "*You're* not the one to judge: when you talk about that doll you're beautiful." There is even something curative and pastoral in the doctor's relation to Helen, as there is not in the visit made by the Episcopal minister or in the baptism which she recalls. Their mutual need is doomed, however, to imperfect manifestations—even as the doctor says "all the great dramas with love as their theme are tragedies."

Indeed, the murder of Margaret itself arises from a more frenzied acting out of this very need to love and be loved, as the doctor's comments on her vulnerability to exploitation may suggest: "You'll do it all over again and nobody can stop you. You've done things to *us* which are inexcusable. And yet . . . I don't blame you. That's a trait that people like you exhibit—to our envy—and despair—a sort of power that you have over us. I still believe in you, that you are not guilty. . . . Not only that, but in many ways you are the best of us, the most direct, the most honest—yes, and in the end, the most virtuous." Each of these three persons is partly mirrored in the others, and in the trees blooming in ice, the roses, and the jonquils. Yet each sums up one facet of their common predicament: in Margaret, the most desperate and naked loneliness; in Helen, a more vigorous if precarious thriving despite that loneliness; and, in the doctor—imperfectly manifest through his own need—that non-possessive love which might cure the alienation from which all suffer.

Emphasizing the doctor's role in this way, I have necessarily shifted the apparent focus of the story. Its own narrative tact makes the doctor hardly more than a mode of relating. ("Nothing like careful snipping," advised Williams, "for the bringing out of the profile.") The story thus avoids the pitfall of self-indulgence that awaits any fuller attempt to dramatize such a figure. And that tact also requires that the doctor not search for meaning but merely be attentive to what unfolds—and vulnerable to it. The narrative structure causes us then not to look *at* him so much as to see with his eyes. We find ourselves not driving toward some goal of understanding but merely paying attention—now to Helen, now to Margaret. But "attention" is a pale word to describe what is happening as we share in the partial failure of love—the story's tragic burden.

## Linda Welshimer Wagner (essay date 1970)

SOURCE: "'The Shape of Men's Lives',," in *The Prose of William Carlos Williams,* Wesleyan University Press, 1970, pp. 104-20.

[*In the following essay, Wagner surveys Williams's short fiction, relating its subjects and techniques to those of other contemporaneous writings.*]

Williams' short stories may have had as deep an effect on contemporary fiction as his poems have had on modern poetry. Denis Donoghue feels that "his stories will wear better than his poems, because the stories keep him rooted in the particular incident" [*Connoisseurs of Chaos,* 1965]. Many modern writers, ranging from Flannery O'Connor to Robert Creeley, share this view. The apparently effortless telling, the informal (and often unresolved) plot, the emphasis on character presented through salient details, and above all, the reliance on dialogue—these trademarks of a Williams' story occur repeatedly in contemporary writing. Yet mere copying of one stylistic device or another has never insured success, as many imitators of the supposed "Hemingway" style or "Faulkner" style have discovered. There are two primary difficulties in discussing Williams' short stories: first, the great variety of them; and second, the poet's insistence that a story is an amoral art form, that—as the most free of art forms—it has no responsibility to be anything other than a "formal" arrangement of words. Because the tradition in the American short story is didactic (Hawthorne instructed, whereas Poe only bewildered), critics have attempted too often to find explicit messages in stories which Williams intended rather as "a good medium for nailing down a single conviction. Emotionally" ["A Beginning on the Short Story (Notes)," *The Selected Essays of William Carlos Williams,* 1954]. As he explained in 1950,

What shall the short story be written about?. . . . Something that interests the writer seriously, as a writer (not necessarily a man for in that case the interest would be moral and perhaps best NOT represented as a short story). He writes about the way his interests, as a writer, strike upon the material, of some event, graphically presented.

The result is life, not morals. It is THE LIFE which comes alive in the telling. . . .
[*A Beginning on the Short Story,* 1950]

Warren Tallman discusses the problem of reading contemporary fiction in his perceptive introduction to *New American Story,* an essay which begins with praise for Williams and Stein as two "battlers" for new American writing:

Change forces other changes, and as a direct result of these efforts to rediscover the sources of vitality the longtime ascendency over fiction of chronological continuity weakens as markedly as representational form had already weakened in painting. Obviously, you can't make it down to more primary levels of consciousness by walking in the same old ways down the same old streets. Consequently, the firm progress from a beginning to a middle to an end gives way to stream of consciousness, free association, improvisation. And this shift to a circling, side-winding, wandering progression opens out liberating possibilities for the man of words. However, the consternation among readers who couldn't stand to ride on a novel without a plot track was at least as great as had been the consternation among viewers who refused to look at a painting unless they could find a picture. Because this consternation was shared by readers and critics alike, a mistaken generation focused attention not upon the new energy and variety in the writing but upon unpuzzling in the old ways the new works that emerged. Works that should have been studied in light of their linguistic potential were studied instead in light of their semantic potential. The consequences go on to this day in the vast collection of explications and interpretations that have plowed through the masterworks of our century in attempts to turn up Truth, Wisdom, Reality and Morality. Patient and praiseworthy as the best of these attempts have been, the general effect has been to conceal the new art that has emerged by handing it over to the old Jehovahs.

But if the semantics of the works ("the science of meanings") carried the critics and the colleges, the syntax ("the ordering of word forms") carried the writers. For critics, stream of consciousness, free association and improvisation have been so many twists and turns that lead—once straightened out—straight home from at sea. But for writers these leaping, crisscross and erratic—because pathless—pacings open out new beauty, variety and power in the language. No man can ever go beyond that form of writing life which leads to words. . . .

The chief difference, then, between the older American writing and the new is that between writing considered as a means to an end, sentences used as corridors leading to further rooms, and writing considered as an end to itself. The latter will seem limited only to readers who fail to realize that books contain not persons, places and things but words. . . .

Just as Williams had, throughout the 1920's, berated authors who considered writing as philosophy or theology instead of as literature, so he continued his attempts to do "something new with the words" ["A Note on the Recent Work of James Joyce," *Selected Essays*]. His admiration for the techniques of Stein and Joyce directed his fiction, his own work in their media. Yet Williams was honest enough to maintain his own discipline: art must never copy anything, even other successful art. He had to find his own way—a way likely more simple and direct than Joyce's and yet richer and more humane than Stein's. The results of his experiments in writing short stories show that Williams was as apt in using organic form here as he was in poetry. They also show that, for Williams, "the life" that most often comes alive in the telling is of a person he understands, admires, or even loves. Although many of his stories were written during the 1930's, most of them are neither cynical nor dispirited. More of them reveal what the poet was to declare a decade later [in "To All Gentleness"]: "damned if I do not believe you find the greatest tenderness only among the most coarse."

### Early Fiction

Despite much talk of Williams' easy use of autobiographical elements in his fiction, his earliest stories are strained and self-conscious. The doctor-poet who appears frequently as narrator or participant is not the Williams we have come to expect. In later writing the doctor is comparatively unobtrusive; in contrast, the use Williams makes of that persona in his first published fiction, *Three Professional Studies* (1919), which opens with **"The Doctor"**:

I go in one house and out of another practicing my illicit trade of smelling, seeing, hearing, touching, tasting, weighing. . . . I am a young man, I am in perfect health, I am agile, good-looking. I do not smoke since it drugs the intelligence; I want all my reactions. . . .

After declaring that he needs no "courage" to write and to practice medicine, Williams next describes two cases, two "everyday" problems of which he makes both literary use and medical (the "professional" of the title can well be ambivalent). **"Mrs. M."** and **"Something"** describe women who do show courage of a sort; yet that is not the connection Williams makes. His emphasis is on the doctor's reactions to these women and their situations—and in 1919 his reaction is one of near disgust:

The children dig into the mush and chew it off the spoons. The largest boy age eight glances sidewise, sees mother is not looking, shovels out a spoonful from brother's dish. My God do they like it? Haven't they enough? Screams. Mother rushes at him, slaps his face. The children do not even know I am in the room.

Perhaps a more pervasive impression is that of Williams' self-consciousness. Attention is on the doctor, not the patient, as the ending of the last sketch indicates: "I walk out of the back door, I lift my nose. I smell the wind."

**"Danse Pseudomacabre"** (1920) followed a similar approach: two brief anecdotes of death, connected only through the doctor's use of them as material. The transitory paragraph between the two echoes a passage from *Kora in Hell,* the idea of life as a dance, here subverted to the deaths as "danse." The second vignette, much the stronger of the two, concerns a baby dying from meningitis. Instead of focusing on the doctor, this story ends with the ironic revelation of the probable cause of the child's disease, its baptism. In its use of understatement and the rhythms of actual speech, this closing paragraph foreshadows much of Williams' later fiction:

It is an infection?

Yes.

My wife is Catholic—not I. She had him for baptism. They pour water from a can on his head, so. It runs down in front of him, there where they baptize all kinds of babies, into his eye perhaps. It is a funny thing.

In 1923 Williams published **"Three Letters,"** another story with an episodic structure, and **"The Accident,"** which, although it begins with a death, assumes as subject a much less weighty incident. The latter is in many ways the beginning of Williams' concentration on unimportant but real happenings. As he was to write [in "A Beginning on the Short Story"],

a mere "thrilling" account of an occurrence from daily life, a transcription of a fact, is not of itself and for that reason a short story. You get the fact, it interests you for whatever reason; of that fact you make, using words, a story. A thing. A piece of writing.

In **"The Accident,"** the setting is spring. A child falls down. The sympathy evoked by his dirty face brings six factory workers into the story. But, again characteristic of Williams' avoidance of "moral," this sympathy in no way changes the child's world. Neither does it unite the observers. It simply exists, and the child recovers by himself.

---

**Williams was honest enough to maintain his own discipline: art must never copy anything, even other successful art. He had to find his own way—a way likely more simple and direct than Joyce's and yet richer and more humane than Stein's.**

**—*Linda Welshimer Wagner***

---

In most of his earliest stories, Williams as doctor-poet is himself the narrator. But as he writes more fiction, he begins to use other points of view. His employment of a narrator other than the doctor becomes an important device: it allows him to avoid either a conventional moral judgment or a reaction consistent with the doctor's persona. It also gives him the chance to use various idioms, a means to display what he has learned from his years of "listening." Most important, the interplay between patient and doctor serves a valuable function in itself, that of supplying a wider social context for the story proper. One of Williams' primary concerns in his fiction is presenting a full story. Although he defines the story form as that which raises "one particular man or woman . . . to the distinction of being an individual" ["A Beginning on the Short Story"], he criticizes Gertrude Stein's "Melanctha" (even while admiring it immensely) because it does not include a sense of the whole:

> "Melanctha" is a thrilling clinical record of the life of a colored woman in the present-day United States, told with directness and truth. It is without question one of the best bits of characterization produced in America. It is universally admired. This is where Stein began. But for Stein to tell a story of that sort, even with the utmost genius, was not enough *under the conditions in which we live,* since by the very nature of its composition such a story does violence to *the larger scene which should be portrayed.*

In many of his stories, Williams succeeds in this wider purpose. Whether his sense of the times and conditions comes from his inclusive detail ("two large iron double beds standing there as if they had been two boats floating in a small docking space, no carpet, no other furniture"); from his rare understanding of people ("What you gonna

do to my mother? the boy asked"); or from his constant use of seemingly real speech ("Oh, he makes me tired. He says it's all my fault"), Williams does quickly establish setting and cultural level. The narrator is not only a vehicle for getting a story told but an integral part of the circumstance which has produced the story. It is not surprising, then, that the story itself can often be told very briefly because Williams has already provided much background for the characters to come and for their behavior.

### The Knife of the Times

That this collection of short stories was published in 1932 gives some explanation for its title. Williams' patients were particularly hard hit by the Depression; he is to write his most socially aware prose and poetry during this decade. "The plight of the poor in a rich country, I wrote it down as I saw it. The times—that was the knife that was killing them" [*I Wanted to Write a Poem,* 1958]. In Williams' 1949 lectures on the short story, he describes in detail his own impetus toward writing stories on more than an accidental basis. In 1932, he recalls [in his *Selected Essays*], the story form seemed viable because of "the heterogeneous character of the people":

> I lived among these people. I know them and saw the essential qualities (not stereotype), the courage, the humor (an accident), the deformity, the basic tragedy of their lives—and the *importance* of it. You can't write about something unimportant to yourself. I was involved.

> That wasn't all. I saw how they were maligned by their institutions of church and state—and "betters." I saw how all that was acceptable to the ear about them maligned them. I saw how stereotype falsified them.

> Nobody was writing about them, anywhere, as they ought to be written about. There was no chance of writing anything acceptable, certainly not salable, about them.

> It was my duty to raise the level of consciousness, not to say discussion, of them to a higher level, a higher plane. Really to tell.

> Why the short story? Not for a sales article but as I had conceived them. The briefness of their chronicles, its brokenness and heterogeneity—isolation, color. A novel was unthinkable.

> And so to the very style of the stories themselves.

"My duty," "involved," "maligned," "falsified"—Williams leaves no question about his motives for writing these stories. Feeling so deeply as he does about many of his subjects, the amazing thing is his ability to avoid the maudlin or proletarian literature which permeated the 1930's. Williams' devices for objectifying the story (a variety of narrators, the seemingly tough doctor and tougher milieu, the sharp focus and usually brief narration) and his preference for the *telling* episode over the merely exciting help him avoid most of the common traps. But it is interesting that, of Williams' three story collections, *The Knife of the Times* is the most slanted toward evoking a reader's sympathy for the situation of its characters.

The title story, for example, describes a Lesbian relationship. As lead-off story, such an episode will receive disproportionate emphasis and falsely leads critics such as J. E. Slate to conclude that "many Williams stories deal[ing] with sexual perversion," when very few do ["William Carlos Williams and the Modern Short Story," *Southern Review*, Vol. IV, No. 3, Summer 1968]. The title implies that circumstances affected Ethel and Maura's behavior; yet such inference is false. They have sufficient money; in fact, they meet as Ethel comes to New York to join her sister, who has been abroad. Told in third person, the story is less immediate than most of those in the collection. Williams recalls the impetus for this story [in *I Wanted . . .*]: "to find a woman telling me about her experience intrigued me. She was not shocked, just amazed." Similar weaknesses plague **"The Sailor's Son,"** the story of homosexuals. Again told to the doctor by a woman, the tale of Manuel is also fragmentary. Perhaps the best of these sexually oriented stories is **"A Descendant of Kings,"** the somewhat ironic account of beachboy Stewie, who has been reared by his fierce grandmother to be a stud. "There was damn little for him to do," never having finished the eighth grade, being used by numerous women until his sexual prowess ended. Williams uses an omniscient point of view here, to make the boy more understandable. In many respects Stewie is a victim of "the knife of the times."

More typical of Williams' later stories, and more compatible blendings of technique and theme, are **"Mind and Body," "A Visit to the Fair,"** and **"Pink and Blue."** In the monologue and dialogue of the first story Williams characterizes Ingrid, the Norwegian woman whose identity comes to us through the physical symptoms of her illness as well as through her speech. Her reminiscence and philosophy show a complex woman, seemingly at great variance to her deformed husband. Much like Corydon of *Paterson IV,* the woman has few appealing qualities. Because her depiction is important to Williams (he refers to a similar character in the *Autobiography* and also in *Paterson V*), she presents an interesting artistic problem. How to draw an unsympathetic person so that she attains dignity? As he did so often in other writings, Williams relied on Ingrid's speech: "I have found," she says with surprising gentleness, "that we must live for others, that we are not alone in the world."

In the friendship of Bess and Mr. Tibbet lies an illustration of this same need. **"A Visit to the Fair"** is one of Williams' strongest arguments for people to enjoy life, to be treated as though they have value. Again, the camouflage of woman as narrator; again, the possibly objectionable situation, one man escorting another man's wife; again, the sense of the poverty of the 1930's.

**"Pink and Blue"** continues the depiction of the times, here with brides like Belle Tompkins whose simple depravity leads her from husband to husband in search of

social approval. Again using an observer-narrator, Williams manages to depict lonely people in their misdirected search for love (Cupid's Clubs, violence, sex). The poverty here is personal, spiritual, as well as financial.

The best story of this first collection, perhaps Williams' "Melanctha," is the longer **"Old Doc Rivers."** For one of the first times in this period of his fiction, Williams narrates the story himself. He knew Doc Rivers and in him saw much to admire—dope, junkie, drunk that he became. As Williams presents him, "confident, a little disdainful, but not unfriendly. He knew them all," Doc Rivers' life was his work. He would go "anywhere, anytime, for anybody." Yet something was missing, and Rivers became the victim of the culture he was ostensibly saving. In a description much like his view of Poe, Williams summarizes:

> He was far and away by natural endowment the ablest individual of our environment, a serious indictment against all the evangelism of American life which I most hated—at the same time a man trying to fill his place among those lacking the power to grasp his innate capabilities. . . .

> Intelligence he had and force—but he also had nerves, a refinement of the sensibilities that made him, though able, the victim of the very things he best served.

A fitting conclusion to the collection in that Rivers represents the best of men cut down by the times, this story is also Williams' attempt to portray that life with which he too was involved. In his various methods of characterizing the older doctor, he is able to include the operations they shared, patients they had in common, and the social milieu which surrounded them both. Understanding Rivers is easy for Williams because he too can feel the waste, the impact of city life ("we have lost touch with ourselves"), and "the awful fever of overwork."

Williams tries hard to create sympathy for Rivers. He draws from actual medical records, conversations with other doctors and patients, and his own knowledge, always creating scenes painstakingly to give us the rough yet kindly doctor. "He was one of the few that ever in these parts knew the meaning of all, to give himself completely." And yet the story is in no sense a paean. For, once well into his dope habit, Rivers is a real danger to his patients. It is then that his society deifies him, reacting to the legends and the wild charisma rather than to his formerly valuable qualities ("always the wrong reasons," as Williams said about Poe's acceptance).

A "pure product of America" like Elsie of the 1923 poem, Doc Rivers went "crazy" in his own way, and Williams closes the long narrative with an image reminiscent of the ending of "To Elsie." The story of Rivers has begun with the one-word sentence, "Horses." Williams emphasizes then the satisfaction a man received from his dependence on the horse and how quickly changed was that simplicity with the coming of the car. The story ends, ironically, with Rivers being driven out in his car, holding one of his wife's Blue poms on his lap, "for in those days he himself never sat at the wheel." Rivers was a man, yes, but a man out of control.

### Life Along the Passaic River

Williams' strongest collection of stories is the second, published in 1938 after *Blast* had used many of the stories in 1934 and 1935. Using an episodic narrative structure much like that of **"The Colored Girls of Passenack—Old and New,"** Williams relishes the anecdotes and details of that life both in the opening title story and in **"World's End,"** the closing piece. Most of the other stories—**"Jean Beicke," "The Girl with a Pimply Face," "A Face of Stone"**—treat individually the same kinds of character in the doctor-oriented narratives that are Williams' forte. It is as if only the size and shape of the story determined its structure, whether it fitted into the longer sequences as an episode or stood on its own as a full story. As Williams wrote [in *A Beginning . . .*], "The short story consists of one single flight of the imagination, complete: up and down."

The tone of these stories, and of the collection as a whole, differs radically from that of *The Knife of the Times.* **"Colored Girls"** is one of the few stories in the earlier collection that do not berate the culture of the 1930's. *Life Along the Passaic River,* for the most part, uses understanding rather than vindication as its dominant tone. The role of the title story is to establish the kind of life in question; the subsequent stories illustrate the bravery or humor or solidarity of that life; and the closing story summarizes it all, with a tweak of the nose for the traditional source of strength in a culture like this, its religion.

Like the scenario for a movie, **"Life Along the Passaic River"** zooms in on "a spot of a canoe filled by the small boy who no doubt made it . . . west of the new Third Street Bridge, midstream." Williams is at home here, in the details of the town bordering the river, the description of the young boy and others like him. He moves to the men lined up, waiting for work; and then picks out a few and gives us dialogue from the hitchhiker and the tough six-footer. Next he swings to describe the young suicide at the morgue, five months pregnant with twins. "If you can make sense out of that, go to it. It's all right to be wise, but you got to watch that too. There's no way to learn it easy."

Williams' compassion colors the portraits of this life that he knows so well. He has dropped the device of having someone other than the doctor narrate the story, perhaps because he is following the same pattern he has taken in poetry: maturity and command of techniques enable him to use "I" effectively, with no hedges, no subterfuge. This is truly the doctor's view of his people. The tone is lightly ironic, almost sardonic. "Further downstream at the Country Bridge," the story progresses, and Williams remarks none too slyly, "It's an eye opener what you have time for these days." Each character we meet is out of work, lost, involved in crime because there's nothing else; yet in the mass of these men, Williams finds those of nobility and honor.

The persona's language is an apt cover for his reactions to the characters. "Swell looking muscles. What for?" "All you gotta do is rake in the old coin. Is that so?" The question undercutting the initial assumption, the reliance on vernacular (but rarely on slang), the short statement—all contribute to the terse idiom that seems to characterize the narrator. Such an idiom is, of course, highly effective when broken.

---

**Time and time again Williams' stories praise the characters who swim against the current.**

*—Linda Welshimer Wagner*

---

**"A Night in June"** illustrates a turn from the brusque to the gentle. The tired doctor, delivering a child to a woman he hasn't even remembered as a former patient, is brought through a long night to this realization:

> With my left hand steering the child's head, I used my ungloved right hand outside her bare abdomen to press upon the fundus. The woman and I then got to work. Her two hands grabbed me at first a little timidly about the right wrist and forearm. Go ahead, I said. Pull hard. I welcomed the feel of her hands and the strong pull. It quieted me in the way the whole house had quieted me all night.

> This woman in her present condition would have seemed repulsive to me ten years ago—now, poor soul, I see her to be as clean as a cow that calves. The flesh of my arm lay against the flesh of her knee gratefully. It was I who was being comforted and soothed.

After this profession of love for the experience, Williams again avoids the sentimental by returning quickly to the business at hand, putting drops in the baby's eyes, burying the afterbirth, taking count of the other children. The closing scene similarly rests on that objective detail which draws attention away from the doctor:

> How many is that? I asked the other woman. Five boys and three girls, she said. I've forgotten how to fix a baby, she went on. What shall I do? Put a little boric acid powder on the belly button to help dry it up?

This particular story, one of the most direct recountings of Williams' experiences as a doctor, cannot help but suggest the 1919 **"Something."** We are struck with the difference in Williams' attitude toward the suffering women. The woman of the earlier story he described as if she were a block of wood, a "thing" as the title suggests: "Oh. Agh. Ah—Hold this. Hold her head. She subsides into bovine passivity. Trembles a little like a cow about to be slaughtered. . . . What is this woman?" No later story except **"A**

Face of Stone" approaches this tone; but since it is a study of the doctor's gradual initiation into understanding, there are more differences than similarities.

---

**That some of Williams' late short stories do not reach the quality of those written in the 1930's suggests, more than any technical deficiency, his change of emphasis. . . . Just as Williams' short poems were try pieces for his late longer work, so the short story led him to the more inclusive shapes to come.**

*—Linda Welshimer Wagner*

---

"Four Bottles of Beer" is another central story, important thematically and technically. Much in keeping with the doctor's attitude in "A Night in June," the narrator-doctor admires the woman whose child is ill. Like the later Clara in *Many Loves,* this mother questions the doctor about his personal life ("Does she cook for you? / Yes. / And you eat it? / Why yes. / I couldn't eat nigger cooking"). Williams likes the openness of the young Polish woman. He leaves after his call with the four bottles of home brew and the accomplishment of having used only dialogue throughout the story. Even the opening is the woman's greeting, "He's asleep." Stories such as this give credence to Williams' description of his stories as being "written in the form of a conversation which I was partaking in."

Several other stories from this second collection are entirely dialogue. Often, these are the particularly short accounts, similar in effect to the group of short poems collectively titled "Detail." Long interested in the language as spoken, Williams creates a variety of effects by changing narrators—his mother, an ex-serviceman, the many patients. True to his belief that a man's language is a way into his character, Williams shapes some stories around the conversation: the story opens with "Hello" and closes with "Goodbye." Structurally, Williams can do little more to stress the importance of the characters' effects on one another.

For Williams, fiction was a way to re-create a genuine existence, perhaps his own as well as that of the other characters in his stories. As he reminisced [in *I Wanted . . .*] about the 1938 collection, "The subject matter is the same as that of the earlier stories but I had matured as a writer. I was much freer. I could say what I had to say." And what Williams "had to say" was about his "townspeople." He no longer considered himself an oracle to his patients; he too had learned humility. As he wrote in his *Autobiography*:

> They had no knowledge and no skill at all. They flunked out, got jailed, got "Mamie" with child, and fell away, if they survived, from their perfections.

There again, a word: their perfections. They were perfect, they seem to have been born perfect, to need nothing else. They were there, living before me. . . .

Jack O'Brien in "Under the Greenwood Tree" is a good illustration of Williams' admiration. A handyman, usually down and out, O'Brien wins the doctor's respect because he "lives uncomplaining. Self respecting. . . . It's the way he rides evenly over the times. The way he takes the weather." O'Brien's story is one of the few Williams prefaces with explanation, a paragraph interesting for its statement about both Williams and O'Brien:

> The chief cultural influence in a community is not always self apparent. If, as Keyserling says: localism alone can lead to culture (and this I give my life willingly to experience and to prove) Jack O'Brien is to me one of the princes of the world that I know.

Time and time again Williams' stories praise the characters who swim against the current. The "savage brat" of "The Use of Force," Belle Tomkins in "Pink and Blue," Margaret and Helen from "The Farmers' Daughters," "Jean Beicke," "The Girl with a Pimply Face," and many others share the quality Williams once described as "Toughminded. Tough. To be able to take it," with a quick qualification that the best way to take it is to be "soft enough, yielding enough."

Technically, emphasizing character tends to strip much material from the episode. In Williams' stories there is seldom any preliminary description: a patient enters, the phone rings, the doctor enters a house. The conflict is identified early, that the labor is difficult or the patient, hostile. Description of even the central character is minimized; in one case we hear about "ugly bunches of varicose veins" rather than about a face. Most stories move quickly to the end because Williams focuses on single episodes (a "brush stroke" rather than a picture). Often, endings are incomplete. They answer the central conflict rather than including all the implied points.

Mona Van Duyn takes her cue from the title Williams first gave his collected stories, *Make Light of It.* She relates the title to his prose technique, "The actual direction of the stories is almost always 'made light of' and this offhand effect is accomplished through . . . the causal dropping of the crucial insight along the way, while the story hurries on to end in non-symbolic detail." She also points out Williams' "cutting across the main line of the story with both seemingly and genuinely extraneous detail" ["To 'Make Light of It' As Fictional Technique," *Perspective,* Vol. 6, Autumn-Winter 1953].

Later Stories

*Beer and Cold Cuts,* the third group of stories Williams included in his 1950 collection, contains several major pieces and a number of fragmentary glimpses of the people he loved. "Ancient Gentility" describes the old Italian migrant sharing his innate dignity with his snuff. "Comedy Entombed" refers to another spirited woman, this one undergoing a miscarriage. Several of the stories are as much **"Exercises in the Variable Foot"** as his late sequence of poems: **"Above the River," "In Northern Waters," "Frankie," "The Final Embarrassment," "The Good Old Days,"** and particularly **"Verbal Transcription—6 A.M."** The latter story is a one-page masterpiece of a wife's monologue after her husband has suffered a heart attack. Another impressive story is **"The Red Head."** "I'm going to have a baby!" the twelve-year-old girl repeats. "And then she'd sob and blow her nose and they'd walk on and on, round and round the block . . . the two girls in front and the two boys a few paces back of them." The terror in the scene is framed by society's view, "They're so cute," and underlined by the doctor's concern. "Where can they turn for advice if we cut them off?" In two pages Williams evokes a convincing picture of the trapped adolescents—and their unresponsive culture.

That some of Williams' late short stories do not reach the quality of those written in the 1930's suggests, more than any technical deficiency, his change of emphasis. After 1938, short fiction is less interesting to him because most of his energy is going into the Stecher novels, the plays, and *Paterson.* Just as Williams' short poems were try pieces for his late longer work, so the short story led him to the more inclusive shapes to come: as he saw Joyce's progress, "*Dubliners* to *Stephen Hero* to *Ulysses* to *Finnegans Wake.* I say that it took off from the short story. It makes a delightful Field of Mars—for exercises in the Manual of Arms. I think that's its chief value" [*Selected Essays*]. Yet the techniques of these stories were to serve Williams well in his later work, largely because his rationale for fiction was so expansive.

In 1949 he defined the objectives of the short story: "The art would be, by the style, to wed the subject to its own time and have it live there and then. Have it live" [*Selected Essays*]. Reminiscent of Henry James's concept of freedom in the novel, this suggestion is detailed by correspondingly free corollary principles. Speaking of Kipling, O. Henry, Kafka, Poe, and Hemingway, Williams asks, "What is the common quality in all these changing styles?" In answer, he refutes the usual assumption of "plot" ("not a stereotyped snaring of the interest, a filling in of necessary documentary details and a smash finish") and goes on to list two particulars of the structure he admires: (1) "They all have a frame—like a picture" and (2) "There is a punch, if you like. But . . . maybe today we'll shift the emphasis and get a punch from having no punch. Maybe the buildup and the documentation will be merely hinted." The object of the form of a story is to be "natural," Williams contends.

In these remarks, Williams emphasizes action rather than description: "It is not to place adjectives, it is to learn to employ the verbs . . . so that the pieces move naturally—and watch, often breathlessly, what they do." As illustration Williams recalls Thomas Mann's "Death in Venice," a story more passive in its apparent plot structure than most; "to take decay, despair and elevate the details to an action, to greatness"—that act had Williams' admiration.

"Try all sorts of effects," advises Williams the craftsman. "You can try various modes of writing—more freely. . . . The short story is a wonderful medium for prose experimentation." Once again coming to the heart of his approach to literature, Williams suggests that the writer "try to follow the action of some characters you can *imagine.* . . . Crawl into the man's head and how get inside a woman's head, being a man? That is the work of the imagination." Actual dialogue is important in re-creating the character, as is a thorough knowledge of the subjects. But as for any preconception about what kind of characters should be the subject for fiction, Williams only questions, "The hero? Who is a hero? The peasantry? There is none. Men and women faithful to a belief? What belief?" Williams was also concerned with the writer's tendency to oversimplify character. In several of his later stories he experimented to show the complexities of characters who could have been one-dimensional. Helen and Margaret, **"The Farmers' Daughters"**; the hitchhiker in **"Around the World Fliers"**; the unnamed woman in **"Inquest."** Of the latter story Williams noted,

> Most of us are not individuals any more but parts of something. We are no one of us "all" of anything. . . . So why not write of three people as one? That's what my story tried to do, make itself more than one, three in one. Imagine a woman looking at herself three ways.

The woman waiting for the bus prompts three characterizations, one of a factory worker, another of an instructor in philosophy (a little drunk), a third of a dancer—all women somewhat less than virtuous. The last two pages present the woman's relationship with "good old Doc" who advises her to "quit it" but does what he can to help her out of her promiscuity.

**"The Burden of Loveliness"** dwells on the same need, of a woman to give her sex freely. These stories of the 1940's point increasingly toward Williams' concern with the virgin-whore distinction of *Paterson V.* What constitutes virtue, the giving or the withdrawing? [In the introduction to *William Carlos Williams Readers,* 1966] M. L. Rosenthal describes this recurring theme as Williams'

> special interest in women—what they are really like, how they grow into their maturity, their sources of strength and weakness, their real relationship to the oversimplified visions of male sexuality. . . . It is at once a matter of the normal erotic range of interest and of curiosity and of something else, a romantic sense of mystery pursued through the unorthodox methods of the realist.

Striking evidence of this interest, I think, is the fact that **"The Knife of the Times"** and **"The Farmers' Daughters,"** those stories which open and close the collected stories, are much the same. Two women, incapable of being understood by the men who love them, find solace in each other. That the lesbian relationship in the earlier story has given way to a limitless friendship in the later suggests Williams' move away from the sensational elements in his culture. In **"The Farmers' Daughters,"**

Helen's love for Margaret is in no way selfish. Helen gains nothing but sorrow for her affection. Both the doctor and Helen admire the whore, for, as the doctor tells her, "in many ways you are the best of us, the most direct, the most honest—yes, and in the end, the most virtuous." Murdered finally by her young husband of four months, Margaret was Williams' last short-story character. He had worked fifteen years on the long story, retitling his collected stories after the final version. In it, he seemed to have unified many single impressions of the shorter sketches through the years. In the stories of Helen and Margaret—first written separately, and then in several different versions of the final—we surely find the evidences of "the knife of the times"—a times that Williams found, to his sorrow, went beyond the physical poverty of the Depression and into the spiritual poverty of the prosperity to come. In what kind of culture, the story asks, can a man shoot his wife in the back and have the death be labeled "accidental"? And, more important, in what kind of culture can a man shoot his wife in the back?

"No one came to the funeral but her family and me," Helen tells the doctor after it is all over. "They didn't open the casket. There were no flowers beside the bunch of red roses I'd sent her."

A letter from Margaret has stated earlier, phrased with Williams' sad irony, that "New Orleans was beautiful, so much better than New York to live in." This suggestion of the betrayal of place, one of Williams' principal tenets, brings to mind his early praise of Kenneth Burke's stories. They were effective, Williams thought, because Burke was writing from his own knowledge, his own location: "From the shapes of men's lives imparted by the places where they have experience, good writing springs" ["Kenneth Burke," *Selected Essays*]. Or, as Faulkner, another writer Williams admired, once phrased it [in *The Faulkner-Cowley File, 1944-1962*, 1966]: "Art is simpler than people think because there is so little to write about. All the moving things are eternal in man's history. . . ."

## Fergal Gallagher (essay date 1972)

SOURCE: "Further Freudian Implications in William Carlos Williams' 'The Use of Force'," in *The CEA Critic*, Vol. 34, No. 4, May, 1972, pp. 20-1.

[*In the essay below, Gallagher identifies the characters of the child, the doctor, and the parents in "The Use of Force" with the function of id, the ego, and the superego in the human psyche.*]

In his interesting article on William Carlos Williams' **"The Use of Force,"** R. F. Dietrich points out the sexual connotations of the story that "are there because they express the savagery in human nature that, lying so close to the surface, can erupt at any moment in a flow of irrational behavior . . ." (*Studies in Short Fiction,* Summer 1966). The interpretation of the doctor-child conflict in terms of a sexual encounter does indeed appear to be valid when

one considers the sexual overtones of the language of the story as Dietrich does. However, I would like to suggest a further interpretation based upon Freudian theory. I believe that the three sets of characters in **"The Use of Force"**—the doctor, the parents, and the child—are motivated by the three zones of the human psyche, the ego, the super-ego, and the id, respectively, and I also believe that the doctor, at first governed by the ego, permits his id to dominate him during his encounter with the child.

It is evident that the child, in her unrestrained passion and aggression, is acting entirely according to the dictates of the id, which Freud describes in his *New Introductory Lectures on Psychoanalysis* as "striving to bring about the satisfaction of the instinctual needs subject to the observance of the pleasure principle." The aim of the id is to seek pleasure and to avoid pain, functioning without regard for the conventional restraints of society or morality, and even without regard for self-preservation. The id, as Freud remarks, "knows no judgements of value: no good and evil, no morality." Mathilda's blind fury and her instinctual, hysterical attack on the doctor, when he moves closer to examine her, indicate that she is completely unconcerned about the doctor either as someone capable of helping her or in his role in society as someone to be respected. Describing her as lunging at him with "one catlike movement" while "both her hands clawed instinctively" for his eyes, the doctor emphasizes Mathilda's instinctual, animal-like aggressiveness, characteristic of an individual governed by the id. In other words, the child appears to be dominated by the id, and reason or conventional morality (the ego and the super-ego) form little part of her psyche.

According to Freud, the instinctual aggressions and passions of the normal adult psyche are regulated and repressed by the reason (the ego) and the conventions of society and morality (the super-ego). As Mathilda's behavior would seem to indicate that she is dominated by the id, the control and repression of her untamed aggression must be supplied from some external source. Freud points out that "young children are amoral and possess no internal inhibitions against their impulses striving for pleasure. The part which is later taken on by the super-ego is played to begin with by an external power, by parental authority." In their physical attempt to hold their daughter still so that the doctor can examine her throat, the parents are, in effect, attempting to repress her passion and aggression. In Freudian terms the super-ego is attempting to repress the id. In regarding the parents as the super-ego, I think it is worth noting that their reaction to Mathilda's behavior is not one of anger, but rather one of extreme embarrassment and mortification. At the child's first attack on the doctor, "both the mother and father almost turned themselves inside out in embarrassment and apology." The father releases her at the critical moment because of his "shame at her behavior and his dread of hurting her." When Mathilda reduces the wooden spatula to splinters, her mother asks her: "Aren't you ashamed to act like that in front of the doctor?" Rather than considering the doctor as one who can help their child, the parents seem to regard him as one socially superior to them because of his professional status. This is why they are embarrassed rather than angered at their child's behavior. And this display of embarrassment on the part of the parents is indicative of the feelings of guilt associated with the super-ego.

Whereas the parents are governed by the super-ego, the doctor, understanding the practical nature of the problem, is governed by the ego, which, Freud says, "stands for reason and good sense." The physician realizes that he "had to have a throat culture for her own protection." He is annoyed with the mother when she refers to him as a nice man. He realizes he has a job to do: "For heaven's sake, I broke in. Don't call me a nice man to her. I'm here to look at her throat on the chance that she might have diphtheria and possibly die of it." This is the reasonableness of the ego opposing the super-ego's concern with social convention.

No change occurs in the behavior of the parents or the child. Throughout the story the parents remain dominated by the super-ego, and Mathilda is governed by the id. But there is a remarkable change in the behavior of the physician. He loses control of himself, or, in Freudian terms, he permits his id to dominate the ego. As he first encounters the patient he behaves with reason and circumspection. He is annoyed at the stupidity of the parents and is determined to obtain the necessary throat culture. After the second fruitless assault, the doctor reasons with himself whether he should continue or try again later. But he realizes the urgency of the situation and tries again to force open the patient's mouth. Up to this point the doctor is controlled by the ego, and even in the motivation for his final forceful attempt to obtain the throat culture he is behaving rationally, for he realizes the necessity of force under the circumstances. But, in the use of force, he loses his ability to reason as he attacks the girl with the same blind fury with which she resists him: "But the worst of it was that I too had got beyond reason. I could have torn the child apart in my own fury and enjoyed it. It was a pleasure to attack her." So in a "final unreasoning assault" the doctor manages to force open Mathilda's mouth and examine her throat. But, in so doing, he loses his ability to reason and permits his passions and aggressions to govern him. The doctor's ego submits to the id as he enjoys the momentary release of instinctual aggression. It should be noticed here, however, that this is not a total domination of the ego. For if the doctor were totally governed by the id, he would have probably merely struck the girl in blind fury. Perhaps it was Williams' intention here to demonstrate the *usefulness* of force in such a crisis. Without the use of force, it would not have been possible for the doctor to obtain the necessary throat culture. Nevertheless, there is no doubt that the doctor derives pleasure from his attack, even if only for a moment.

According to Freud, in the normal individual the ego acts as a mediator between the id and the super-ego. At the beginning of **"The Use of Force"** the doctor, governed by the ego, serves as the intermediary between the parents dominated by the super-ego and the child controlled by the id. Thus, as we should expect, the physician is the one

who acts with reason and circumspection. But in the process of examining his patient he, too, becomes momentarily unbalanced. Therefore, **"The Use of Force"** deals not only with the conflict between doctor and patient, but also with the inner conflict between the psychic forces of reason and aggressive passion, between the ego and the id.

**Murray M. Schwartz (essay date 1972-73)**

SOURCE: "'The Use of Force' and the Dilemma of Violence," in *The Psychoanalytic Review*, Vol. 59, No. 4, Winter, 1972-73, pp. 617-25.

[*In the following essay, Schwartz offers a psychoanalytic reading of "The Use of Force," focusing on Williams's representation of violence in the story.*]

My subject is a very short story by William Carlos Williams called **"The Use of Force,"** about a doctor who forces a spoon into a little girl's mouth to reveal diphtherial membranes that she has been hiding for three days. But, as so much else in Williams' art, it also represents the dynamics of violence, the convergence of motive and situation which transforms the apparently ordinary into the revelation and partial recognition of sadistic desire enclosed by it. In this condensed expression of a critical incident in the life of a doctor we see the precarious closeness of therapeutic and destructive motives. I want to subject the story to a detailed psychoanalytic reading, to identify its core fantasies, to explore the relationship between manifest and unconsciously acted roles, and to suggest some explanations of its violence. In spite of its brevity, **"The Use of Force"** brings together central aspects of our current concern with the psychodynamics of aggression. It provides the literary critic with an opportunity to relate careful textual analysis to the more comprehensive concerns usurping our energies.

A doctor, who remains anonymous, is called to the house of "new patients" named Olson. He enters an atmosphere which he perceives as distrustful. In the kitchen he attempts to examine the throat of the daughter, named Mathilda. The girl refuses to open her mouth. Fearing the presence of diphtheria, the parents and doctor coax, threaten, and finally overpower the child, who resists violently, tearing at the doctor's eyes, crushing his tongue depressor and, finally, lunging at him after the exposure of her throat is complete. The doctor himself oscillates between his professional role, with its emphasis on social welfare, money exchange, and controlled authority, and his more basic impulses. He "fall[s] in love with the savage brat," finds "pleasure" in attacking her, grows furious. The girl's parents act in collusion with the doctor's wishes, and in the short space of five pages all four characters regress to levels of behavior which the doctor-patient relationship is usually designed to defend against.

The story deals with the breakdown of what is typically a highly ritualized situation. Doctors are called when the capacities of real parents (known by the child) are inadequate to meet the real demands of a situation. They are bound to be seen, on one level, as rescuers embodying both maternal (nurturing) and paternal (prescriptive, authoritarian) powers, and as surrogates for the parents (specifically, in the story, the mother). As surrogates who take up the nurturing task where the parents leave off (in the story, the mother's giving "don't do no good"), they are bound to be viewed ambivalently by both parents and child, for in seeking recourse to the doctor's mysterious powers, the parents become symbolic children. The burden of ritualization is very great, partly because the doctor represents a "pseudo-species," a class of intimate strangers who rescue us from disease or death, like "gods." Ritualization regulates the power over others and the gratification of unconscious aims which can be exercised or derived from a situation. Anyone who has been treated by a doctor who does not speak his language will realize the potential for anxiety generated by the situation over and above the dangers presented by the disease. It is no accident, then, that the father in the story asks the doctor to "come down" to them, and that the parents seem to view him both as a figure beyond reproach and as a repository of true words which they will buy for money. For them he is depersonalized; for him, they are "patients."

In the course of the examination, the boundaries which regulate the situation are violated, so that the role difference between parent and child, doctor and patient, fails to defend against underlying erotic and aggressive impulses. The reader is made to experience the conflict in the doctor between the wish to preserve psychic distance and the wish to make the girl an object of his own violent, libidinal desires. Professional defenses and techniques become instruments in the service of id aims they are meant to control. The result of the doctor's regressive response to the girl's violence is reciprocal violence, the behavioral opposite of ritualized cooperation. The characters become identified in violence and through violence. Sadism replaces the professional mask of caring, and parental collusion replaces autonomy.

Given this situation and this collective regression, how can we account for the specific form of these violent events? In a partial Freudian reading of the story, R. F. Dietrich observes that a close examination of the text reveals "connotations of rape." The girl is "flushed" and "breathing rapidly;" as the "battle" begins, "her breaths were coming faster and faster." The doctor "tried to hold [himself] down but [he] couldn't." When he inserts the tongue depressor, "she reduced it to splinters before [he] could get it out again." The girl begins to bleed, grows "hysterical," and a "heavy silver spoon" exposes the membrane, which is called her "secret." Certainly, the accumulation of language appropriate to disease *and* sexuality seems to revolve around a fantasy of rape. Not only does the story convey violence through genital symbolism, it mobilizes (at least in this reader) castration anxiety, fear of the mouth as a displacement upward of the *vagina dentata,* ambivalence toward the brutal act, and a wish both to subjugate and to glorify the object of sadistic attack. But if Dietrich points out the symbolic weight of Williams' language, he stops short of the story's psycho-

analytically accessible meaning. It is not enough to say, "The prevalence of sexual connotation is simply testimony to the animal nature of the conflict." Animals do not confuse sexuality and violence. Besides, the girl is described as a "heifer" before the doctor attacks her. The degradation is a prelude to the "rape."

If the fantasy of rape organizes Williams' representation of the violent encounter, why is this fantasy provoked by the doctor's situation? And does the latent desire to possess the girl sexually adequately explain the doctor's treatment of her? I think not. The prevalence of sexual connotation in the story is symptomatic of a more basic crisis of identity and identification than the idea of the return of repressed sexual impulses suggests. Here is the doctor's description of the girl:

> The child was fairly eating me up with her cold, steady eyes, and no expression on her face whatsoever. She did not move and seemed, inwardly, quiet; an unusually attractive little thing, and as strong as a heifer in appearance. But her face was flushed, she was breathing rapidly, and I realized that she had a high fever. She had magnificent blond hair in profusion. One of those picture children often reproduced in advertising leaflets and the photogravure sections of the Sunday papers.

The emphasis here is on the visual attraction of the girl; she is like a picture, to be taken in with the eyes. Yet she is paradoxical and threatening, at once a "little thing" and "as strong as a heifer," someone who seems to be "eating [him] up." Even as he first encounters the girl, the doctor describes her more as an image than as an independent person. We may find phallic significance in her profusion of hair, but symbolic labeling misses another, more significant aspect of her presence. He experiences her as powerful, perhaps threatening, but she is *excluding* him. She is blank, cold, a depersonalized surface. The doctor imagines this inaccessibility as a form of incorporation, as if the boundary between them were jeopardized not by the experience of fusion but by the perception of unbridgeable otherness. The violence in the story has its genesis in this motionless inaccessibility.

It is not surprising to find the story filled with language whose psychological referent is the oral phase of childhood. The story's visual and oral language emphasizes the failure of basic trust and its replacement by suspicion and shame. We are located in a "warm" kitchen meant to protect the girl, a place obviously associated with nourishment. The parents are "eyeing [him] up and down distrustfully." The doctor, they think, should "look her over." Twice he asks the girl to let him "take a look." "Just open up and let me see." As the professional smile gets nowhere, the mother prods the girl with, "He won't hurt you," and the doctor's response suggests controlled oral aggression: "At that I ground my teeth in disgust." (Disgust: an appropriately oral word.) In their habitual language the parents regard sight as a moral category: "Look how kind he is to you." "Look what you've done." Taking things in, visually or orally, has become an activity bound up with superego inhibitions, not an activity of pleasure.

As often in scoptophilic people, the eye has become an organ which admonishes or robs or eats. Ocular control comes to replace ocular pleasure. The girl's fixed stare may be an unconscious attempt to ward off or take in threatening others (or, perhaps, an attempt to ward them off by taking them in), a strategy designed to prevent their attempts to take her in with words. ("'Look here,' I said to the child, 'we're going to look at your throat.'") When her eyes fail in their magic, when she is immobilized by the men, she "shriek[s] terrifyingly," and in the end "tears of defeat [blind] her eyes." We move anxiously from eyes to mouth to eyes as the psychological and physical space between her and the doctor closes to penetration. Psychoanalytically, the dominant loci of gratification in early infancy are experienced as focal regions of pain. No defense supports trust, and distrust supports the permission of the will which releases violence.

In the course of the story, the doctor tries to approach the child with coaxing words, with his best professional smile, with a display of harmless intentions. But as he moves closer she attacks like a cat, clawing at his eyes and knocking his glasses off. She would rather have her private disease, it seems, than be penetrated in any sense by the adults in her world. Her attempt at symbolic castration evokes guilt-inducing words from the mother. When the mother threatens to send the girl to a hospital, the doctor's response expresses his perception of the psychological structure of the situation; by now he has abandoned the pretense of a formalized doctor-patient relationship:

> Oh yeah? I had to smile to myself. After all, I had already fallen in love with the savage brat; the parents were contemptible to me. In the ensuing struggle they grew more and more abject, crushed, exhausted while she surely rose to magnificent heights of insane fury of effort bred of her terror of me.

"Oh yeah?" reveals a childish defiance of separation. Now that the child has been provoked, and has provoked him, he does not want to lose her. Having projected responsibility onto the parents, they now become impotent participants in the sadistic love affair, and, in his mind, the child gains the potency they lose. When the girl's blankness gives way to violent exclusion, the doctor moves from professional gesture to an *imaginary* relationship of love in which the girl is given an identity by him. Now she is seen as actively different from him ("the savage brat"), and her excitement is perceived solely as a function of his power: "bred of her terror of me." Is there not an implication in this phrase that she is his creation, the product of his omnipotence? In the face of exclusion the doctor is affirming in fantasy his conception of himself as godlike and his conception of the girl as "savage" and, a few paragraphs later, as a "damned little brat." When the ritualized situation designed to prevent violence fails, the doctor fills the vaccum with a structure of relationships based on reciprocal violence, as if his violence could create her or rescue her from death.

In the forced penetration which follows the girl's repeated efforts to escape examination, the doctor's instrument is described first as a "wooden tongue depressor," then as a "wooden spatula," and finally as a "wooden blade," a progression (or regression) which suggests increasingly aggressive genitalization. The blade is "reduced to splinters," an exaggeration which reinforces the reader's anxiety and emphasizes the regressive loss of differentiation between professional and sexual objects. While the violence escalates, the father's participation is confined to a role of sheer force (he pins her to his lap) and the mother is reduced to rhythmic futility, "raising and lowering her hands in an agony of apprehension." The confusion of identities claims them all; the parents are not the only ones turned "inside out."

**"The Use of Force,"** then, reaches down to the level at which identities are formed and dissolved, and it depicts the doctor's attempt to act in accordance with and then to reclaim his professional identity by answering his patient's inaccessibility and violent exclusion of him with a violent attack of his own. He mirrors the "savagery" he finds in the girl. First he rejects the possibility of delay, although he sees delay as a positive moral alternative:

> Perhaps I should have desisted and come back in an hour or more. No doubt it would have been better.

Then he utterly depersonalizes his relationship with the girl:

> But I have seen at least two children lying dead in bed of neglect in such cases, and feeling that I must get a diagnosis now or never I went at it again.

To "get a diagnosis" is a far cry from concern for the girl. The doctor pretends rationality to butter his illegitimate pleasure. As Freud recognized, depersonalization leads to a split in the ego, and the professional rationalization is immediately followed by a confession of pleasure in attack:

> But the worst of it was that I too had got beyond reason. I could have torn the child apart in my own fury and enjoyed it. It was a pleasure to attack her. My face was burning with it.

The girl's attempt to negate him, expressed in imagery of incorporation and castration, elicits his reciprocal negation of her as an independent person, also expressed in imagery of castration and sexual arousal. The collapse of social differentiation (the doctor-patient relationship) and familial differentiation (parent figure and child) reduces the doctor and the girl to an identity; each is furious and each is blind. The reciprocal incorporation of one personality by another here takes the paradoxical form of mutual repudiation, each by the other. In the structure of their violence, the more the doctor finds himself appealing to differences based on social role and professional self-esteem ("I know how to expose a throat for inspection"), the closer he comes to a premoral and prepersonal assault, and the more bound they become as mirror images of one another. First she attacks, then he attacks, then she does.

In the telling of the story Williams sharply separates the "higher" forms of self-justification from the "lower" drive for release:

> But a blind fury, a feeling of adult shame, bred of a longing for muscular release are the operatives. One goes on to the end.

The doctor himself has become a kind of reflex mechanism. His shame accompanies the symptoms of sexual arousal, but sexual arousal does not account for it fully. As the psychoanalyst Heinz Lichtenstein has shown, the sense of shame is more fundamental than the feeling of sexual exposure it often accompanies or hides. Although the story's pervasive visual emphasis and the exposure of a hidden, "secret," and diseased membrane point to the fantasy of a sexual revelation, shame can be interpreted in a more extensive sense "as the breakdown of the capacity for identity maintenance, carrying with it the threat of metamorphosis" [H. Lichtenstein, "The Dilemma of Human Identity," *Journal of the Psychoanalytic Association,* Vol. II, 1963]. The doctor's assault can be seen as a desperate attempt to reconstitute his identity by abandoning it.

> Shame occurs in such situations where the burden of identity and separateness, the loneliness of autonomy has become unbearable: the temptation to abandon it, to give up one's will, to become a slave, a physical thing, triumphs over our defenses.
>
> [Lichtenstein]

As he "creates" the object of his attack, the shock of physical contact seems to validate his image of her as a "valiant" antagonist, and her violence and disease seem to validate his need for confirmation and release. The longing for motor release which breeds shame becomes in the assault on the girl the doctor's means of reconfirming his professional ego. He does get an accurate diagnosis. Like the release provided by festivals or orgies, the violence in the story becomes a way back to the identity it threatens to subvert. The articulation of motives for restraint becomes a way of neutralizing the power of those motives to restrain. The deritualization which collapses hierarchy orients each antagonist toward a rival who exposes his (or her) secret.

But a secret may be exposed without its implications recognized, and in the final lines of the story Williams focuses almost completely on the girl. It is *she* who has been hiding her "secret," the secret of disease and, on an unconscious level, the secret of her sexuality. It is *she* who is blind with fury. It is *she* who lies to her parents to avoid the disclosure of her disease. The doctor's massive projection of guilt and responsibility is made possible by the actual presence of diphtheria. Inaccessible as a person, the girl becomes humanized as the projected embodiment of what is denied in the shame of adulthood, at once "magnificent" and "insane." And the doctor's violence seems for the moment to be vindicated. "The sadistic act," Fenichel writes [in *The Psychoanalytic Theory of Neurosis,* 1945], "not only means, 'I kill to avoid being killed,' but also, 'I punish to avoid being punished,' or, rather, 'I

enforce forgiveness by violence.'" Certainly the compliant parents in the story will forgive his violence, even if he retains his contempt for them. He has saved the girl's life.

At a price. Mathilda, whose name means "might and battle," does not forgive him, and the story ends in her violent reaction to defeat. She is an embodied creature, displaying no capacity to differentiate intention from experience or action from meaning. For her the examination can only be experienced as a sadistic impingement on her private space. In defeat, she too would reclaim her identity through violence. As the story ends, we have come full circle in this pattern, this antidance of violence. The dilemma of violence is that it restores autonomous identity only at the expense of the other. Reciprocal violence excludes the possibility of mutuality.

Williams tells the story in the past tense, a technique which permits clarifying distinctions among motives that were merged in the event. Written in 1932, during the depression, "in white heat," perhaps as a means of mastering the anxiety associated with an actual episode in his life as a doctor, **"The Use of Force"** provides us now with more than the experience of the pleasure-pain of its fantasies. It crystallizes an interaction of drive and defense, intensifies the antithesis, in such a way that we are made to see the components of its violence with retrospective precision. The boundaries ruptured in the experience are again demarcated by language. Finally, if Williams the doctor sought to vindicate himself through violence, Williams the writer sought a more therapeutic action. For Freud the beginning of catharsis consisted in putting affects into words. For Williams this was the use of imagination.

## Majorie Perloff (essay date 1980)

SOURCE: "The Man Who Loved Women: The Medical Fictions of William Carlos Williams," in *The Georgia Review,* Vol. 34, No. 4, Winter, 1980, pp. 840-53.

[*In the essay below, Perloff examines psychosexual aspects of the doctor-patient relationships in several medical stories from* Life along the Passaic River.]

In one of William Carlos Williams' autobiographical sketches about the world of the big city hospital, a story called **"World's End,"** the doctor-narrator recalls a particularly difficult little girl about six years old who was brought to the hospital kicking and screaming so violently that she could not be placed in a ward. The doctor decides to see what he can do: he takes the child to his office where she promptly bites him in the thigh, knocks off his glasses, and carries on like a wild little animal. Finally, not knowing what else to do, the doctor opens his desk drawer, takes out some crackers, and starts to chew on one. Here is the sequence that follows:

> The child quit her tantrums, came over to me and held out her hand. I gave her a cracker which she ate. Then

she stood and looked at me. I reached over and lifted her unresisting into my lap. After eating two more crackers she cuddled down there and in two minutes was asleep. I hugged her to myself with the greatest feeling of contentment—happiness—imaginable. I kissed her hot little head and decided nobody was going to disturb her. I sat there and let her sleep.

The amazing thing was that after another half hour—two hours in all—when I carried her still sleeping to the door, unlocked it and let the others in—she wakened and would let no one else touch her. She clung to me, perfectly docile. To the rest she was the same hell cat as before. But when I spoke severely to her in the end she went with one of the nurses as I commanded.

This little incident provides us with a paradigm for all the medical stories collected in the volume called **Life Along the Passaic River** (1938). Consider the following points: (1) the patient, whether a child as in this case, or a teenager as in **"The Girl with a Pimply Face,"** or an adult as in **"A Night in June,"** is always female. In only one instance, **"A Face of Stone,"** is the baby a boy, and then Williams, who, by his own account [in *I Wanted to Write a Poem,* 1968], wrote these stories "at white heat" and "seldom revised at all," makes a remarkable slip:

The man turned to his wife. Gimme the baby he said. . . . Give him to me. . . .

I hold her, the woman said keeping the child firmly in her arms.

(2) The doctor-narrator, Williams' projected image of himself, is regularly presented as a no-nonsense, matter-of-fact type; if, in **"World's End,"** he takes great pains for the little girl, he is also remarkably unflappable—a man who knows what needs to be done and does it. On the other hand, (3) although the doctor keeps his distance in the proper professional way and is designated throughout the *Passaic* stories as a married man whose emotional life lies elsewhere, his references to the treatment of the female patient are regularly couched in sexual language: in this case, he lifts the little girl "unresisting" into his lap where she "cuddled down," and he recalls that "I hugged her to myself" and "I kissed her hot little head." (4) In keeping with this subliminal erotic response of doctor to patient, the success of the "treatment" induces a sense of elation or victory that seems quite in excess of the actual event: "I hugged her to myself with the greatest feeling of contentment—happiness—imaginable." At the same time, (5) the patient is wary of all other doctors, which is to say of men who would or could have similar power over her. When the little girl wakens, she "would let no one else touch her. She clung to me perfectly docile. To the rest she was the same hell cat as before." Only his "severe" words can make her finally go with one of the nurses "as I commanded."

Critical commentary on these medical fictions has tended to rationalize their sexual component more or less as follows. Williams, both in his life and in his art, so the rea-

soning goes, was unusually sensitive and responsive to the human condition—especially to the condition of the ordinary poor people, many of them immigrants, who came to him as patients in his native Rutherford, New Jersey. His stance toward these people who become the characters of his short stories is, in James Breslin's words, at once "tough *and* sympathetic" [*William Carlos Williams,* 1970]. Williams does not sentimentalize their plight, yet he can see—in even the homeliest woman in her ninth month of pregnancy or in the "girl with a pimply face"—a glimpse of what he calls "the hard straight thing in itself," the "Beautiful Thing" he was to celebrate in *Paterson.* Williams' unillusioned toughness and direct treatment of the thing gives the short stories their air of remarkable "authenticity." Or, as J. Hillis Miller has suggested [in *Poets of Reality,* 1965]:

> Williams' fiction is based on the power to put oneself within the life of another person and make him comprehensible by an objective report of his speech, movements, and facial expressions. There is none of the problem of knowing others which has long been a thematic resource in fiction—all that play of perspectives and points of view, product of the assumption that each man is locked in the prison of his consciousness. . . . Williams' characters, like those of Virginia Woolf, penetrate one another completely and are known by a narrator who has transcended point of view so that he stands everywhere in his story at once. His fiction, like that of the French "new novelists," is evidence of a Copernican revolution in the art of the novel. . . . Williams' people are not fixed personalities persisting through time, but are flowing centers of strength, polarizing themselves differently according to each situation.

But how *does* the poet enter the lives of those around him? "The reaction which gives Williams possession," Miller observes, "is strongly sexual." But since, in the Williams universe, one knows human bodies in the same way that one penetrates the life of flowers or fish, the sexual, Miller would argue, is more or less equated with the larger vitalistic, erotic pulse of the universe, the spirit celebrated from *Kora in Hell* to *Paterson* and beyond. In this context, Williams' ecstatic participation in the birth process of his patients (as, for example, in **"A Night in June"**), is read as emblematic of the poet's sense of creation, perpetual beginning. Birth is the opening of the field; the poet's mission is "to make a start out of particulars."

No doubt Williams wanted his fiction to be read in this way. In his remarkably evasive *Autobiography,* Williams plays the role of genial innocent, the good fellow who has never quite figured out what, in his own words, makes women "tick." "I was an innocent sort of child," the first chapter begins, "and have remained so to this day. Only yesterday, reading Chapman's *The Iliad of Homer,* did I realize for the first time that the derivation of the adjective venereal is from Venus! And I a physician practicing medicine for the past forty years! I was stunned!" But this "gee-whiz!" tone gives way, at moments, to its opposite: a cocky reminder that this poet-physician has been around. Consider the following passage in the Foreword:

I do not intend to tell the particulars of the women I have been to bed with, or anything about them. Don't look for it. . . . I am extremely sexual in my desires: I carry them everywhere and at all times. I think that from that arises the drive which empowers us all. Given that drive, a man does with it what his mind directs. In the manner in which he directs that power lies his secret. We always try to hide the secret of our lives from the general stare. What I believe to be the hidden core of my life will not easily be deciphered, even when I tell, as here, the outer circumstances.

This is, as Herbert Leibowitz notes in a fascinating new essay on the *Autobiography,* "at once a warning and a challenge to the reader," as if to say, "keep your distance. Don't expect an easy intimacy with me" ["You Can't Beat Innocence: The Autobiography of William Carlos Williams," *American Poetry Review*]. In a later chapter of the autobiography called "Of Medicine and Poetry," Williams dangles the same key to his "secret life"—the "secret life I wanted to tell openly—if only I could"—in front of our eyes when he remarks:

> . . . my "medicine" was the thing which gained me entrance to these secret gardens of the self. It lay there, another world, in the self. I was permitted by my medical badge to follow the poor, defeated body into those gulfs and grottos. And the astonishing thing is that at such times and such places—foul as they may be . . . just there, the thing, in all its greatest beauty may for a moment be freed to fly for a moment guiltily around the room. In illness, in the permission I as a physician have had to be present at deaths and birth . . . just there—for a split second . . . it has fluttered before me for a moment, a phrase which I quickly write down on anything at hand, any piece of paper I can grab.

This astonishing passage is not just another account of the coming of the privileged moments that yield poetic vision. For the key word here is surely *guiltily:* "the permission I as a physician have had to be present," the poet's "medical badge," are what give him access to the "secret gardens of the self," but such access is perceived as somehow *guilty.* The medical metaphor, in other words, allows the narrator to present his true feelings about women in the guise of safety and respectability. It would seem, then, that this narrator has not so much "transcended point of view," as Miller suggests, as he has carefully displaced it. In hugging the little girl who has finally stopped screaming and kicking, the doctor is, after all, behaving not abnormally or inappropriately; his gestures are, in his own words, "not easily deciphered," and so the "hidden core" of his life is not violated. Indeed, it is the poet's peculiar oscillation between "normalcy" (another routine house call with its trivial incident and predictable dialogue) and the pressure of desire, a desire neither acted upon nor fully understood, that gives the short stories of the thirties their particular poignancy.

**"The Girl with a Pimply Face,"** for example, begins on a matter-of-fact note:

> One of the local druggists sent in the call: 50 Summer St., second floor, the door to the left. It's a baby they've just brought from the hospital. Pretty bad condition I should imagine. Do you want to make it? I think they've had somebody else but don't like him, he added as an afterthought.

Challenged by his "afterthought" which presents him with an unknown rival, the physician-as-knight sets out on a quest to rescue, ultimately, three damsels in distress: baby girl, mother, and surrogate patient in the person of the baby's sister—"a lank haired girl of about fifteen standing chewing gum and eyeing me curiously from beside the kitchen table." The narrator's immediate response to this girl is "Boy, she was tough and no kidding but I fell for her immediately." And after some desultory talk about the baby's diarrhea, he notes: "This young kid in charge of the house did something to me that I liked. She was just a child but nobody was putting anything over on her if she knew it."

Although, or perhaps perversely *because* her legs are covered with scabby sores, her feet with big brown spots, and her face with terrible acne, the unnamed girl attracts the doctor and he mentally undresses her: "But after all she wasn't such a child. She had breasts you knew would be like small stones to the hand, good muscular arms and fine hard legs. . . . She was heavily tanned too, wherever her skin showed." The physician's sensible advice as to what soap the girl should use for her face, and his gentle reprimand that she should be in school must be seen in the context of these fleeting thoughts about her breasts and legs; she is not just any patient but an ignorant, helpless girl to whom he can minister in the role of masterful, efficient male. Imagine Williams' story as "The Boy with a Pimply Face," and the point will become clear.

When the baby's mother finally arrives and the doctor examines the real patient, he finds that the infant has a severe congenital heart defect. Calmly and professionally, he notes that "she was no good, never would be," but he prescribes formula, calms down the mother, and writes out a prescription for "lotio alba comp." for the teen-age girl's acne. "The two older women looked at me in astonishment—wondering, I suppose, how I knew the girl." To them, he evidently appears as a miracle worker. It is a response nicely balanced in the story by the tolerant skepticism of the doctor's wife:

> What's it all about, my wife asked me in the evening. She had heard about the case. Gee! I sure met a wonderful girl, I told her.
>
> What! another?
>
> Some tough baby. I'm crazy about her. Talk about straight stuff . . . And I recounted to her the sort of case it was and what I had done. The mother's an odd one too. I don't quite make her out.
>
> Did they pay you?
>
> No. I don't suppose they have any cash.
>
> Going back?

Sure. Have to.

Well, I don't see why you have to do all this charity work. Now that's a case you should report to the Emergency Relief. You'll get at least two dollars a call from them.

There is a fine irony in this last speech, for the wife cannot understand—as the reader does by this time—that her husband is getting much more than "two dollars" for his "charity work." He too is in need of a kind of "emergency relief." Indeed, the doctor is, in his own words, so "keenly interested," that even a colleague's account of the case—his warning that the mother is an alcoholic, the father a liar who pretends to have no money, and that the "pimply faced little bitch," as he calls her, has "a dozen wise guys on her trail every night in the week" and deserves to be run out of town—cannot alter the narrator's feelings. And in an oblique way, his "sympathy game," as the other doctor calls it, is rewarded. Here is Williams' conclusion:

The last time I went I heard the, Come in! from the front of the house. The fifteen-year-old was in there at the window in a rocking chair with the tightly wrapped baby in her arms. She got up. Her legs were bare to the hips. A powerful little animal.

What are you doing? Going swimming? I asked.

Naw, that's my gym suit. What the kids wear for Physical Training in school.

How's the baby?

She's all right.

Do you mean it?

Sure, she eats fine now.

Tell your mother to bring it to the office some day so I can weigh it. The food'll need increasing in another week or two anyway.

I'll tell her.

How's your face?

Gettin' better.

My God, it *is,* I said. And it was much better. Going back to school now?

Yeah, I had tuh.

This is not the inconsequential ending it appears to be. For the implication is that, consciously or unconsciously, the girl goes back to school in response to the doctor's wish. The baby is getting better, the mother is placated, the girl's skin is clearing up. Thus the "powerful little animal" with the bare legs has responded to the doctor's power.

To read **"The Girl with a Pimply Face"** as a story about the beauty, vitality and strength latent in even the most "venal and oppressive environment" is, I think, to sentimentalize it. Like "The Young Housewife," in which the poet compares the woman to "a fallen leaf" and then declares, with humorous asperity, "The noiseless wheels of my car / rush with a crackling sound over / dried leaves as I bow and pass smiling," this short story is a fantasy of sexual possession. But it is important to note that unlike the fictions of such postmodern writers as Coover or Sorrentino or Kozinski, Williams' story is firmly wedded to the mimetic convention. The narrator, that is to say, is not about to engage in kinky sex with the pimply-faced girl. Rather, the focus is on the disparity between the doctor's external manner—so composed and matter-of-fact—and his sexual urges.

Another interesting variation on the paradigm I have described is found in **"A Night in June."** Here the doctor's quest romance takes him across town to deliver the ninth baby of an Italian woman named Angelina. He approaches the prospect of the delivery (he has brought all but one of Angelina's children into the world and remembers with grief her first baby which he lost) as one would contemplate a love affair. Fondly, he prepares his instruments and puts them in an old satchel; lovingly, he sets out into the "beautiful June night." All is peaceful and still: "The lighted clock in the tower over the factory said 3:20." At the house, there is much to do and the doctor once again becomes his efficient self, selecting artery clamps and scissors, preparing the hot water, ordering an enema, and so on. Labor has not yet begun and he sleeps briefly, awakening to "the peace of the room" that strikes him as "delicious." Later, he gives Angelina a dose of pituitrin; "She had stronger pains but without effect." Here is the poet's reaction:

Maybe I'd better give you a still larger dose, I said. She made no demur. Well, let me see if I can help you first. I sat on the edge of the bed while the sister-in-law held the candle again glancing at the window where the daylight was growing. With my left hand steering the child's head, I used my ungloved right hand outside on her bare abdomen to press upon the fundus. The woman and I then got to work. Her two hands grabbed me at first a little timidly about the right wrist and forearm. Go ahead, I said. Pull hard. I welcomed the feel of her hands and the strong pull. It quieted me in the way the whole house had quieted me all night.

This woman in her present condition would have seemed repulsive to me ten years ago—now, poor soul, I see her to be as clean as a cow that calves. The flesh of my arm lay against the flesh of her knee gratefully. It was I who was being comforted and soothed.

Here delivery becomes deliverance. The physical ritual of the birth process becomes, in Williams' account, a variation on the act of love—the welcome feel of the woman's hands, the pressing down, the strong pull, the relief and relaxation: "The flesh of my arm lay against the flesh of her knee gratefully." By such contact, the doctor is "comforted and soothed." And yet this erotic experience is "permitted by the poet's medical badge" and hence domesticated, made safe. Within minutes, he is worrying about putting drops into the new baby's eyes and getting rid of the afterbirth. Again, he asserts his down-to-earth, "sensible" role as doctor, prescribing boric-acid powder to dry up the belly button. Even this new belly button, I might add, belongs to a baby girl.

The medical metaphor thus provides Williams with a plausible evasion of a persistent problem. For curiously, in the rare stories in which the challenge becomes real, as it does in **"The Venus"** (the story originally at the center of *A Voyage to Pagany* which Williams removed, presumably because the publisher found the manuscript too long), the self-assurance of the narrator dissolves. Here is the reaction of Dev (the protagonist of *Pagany* who is a thinly disguised version of Williams himself) to the German girl he meets on an outing to Frascati:

> This day it was hot. Fraülein von J. seemed very simple, very direct, and to his Roman mood miraculously beautiful. In her unstylish long-sleeved German clothes, her rough stockings and heavy walking-shoes, Evans found her, nevertheless, ethereally graceful. But the clear features, the high forehead, the brilliant perfect lips, the well-shaped nose, and best of all the shining mistlike palegold hair unaffectedly drawn back— frightened him. For himself he did not know where to begin.

On Roman soil, stripped of his medical props and defining role, the Williams hero is like a knight stripped of his armor and his magic talisman which will open the gates to the castle. Face to face with a beautiful woman who has no reason to be dependent on him, he is frightened. "Not knowing what else to do or to say, he too looked (as the tram went through some bare vineyards) straight back into her clear blue eyes with his evasive dark ones." Confronted by this Venus who keeps asking him what America is like, the poet-doctor retreats. For to be an American is, as Williams knew only too well, to fear eros even as one is obsessed with it. America, he tells the Fraülein, "is a world where no man dare learn anything that concerns him intimately—but sorrow—for should we learn pleasure, it is instantly and violently torn from us as by a pack of hungry wolves so starved for it are we." But when the German Venus then asks him why, given his attitude, he should want to return to America, Dev replies: "It is that I may the better hide everything that is secretly valuable in myself, or have it defiled. So safety in crowds."

Here again is the guilty secret to which Williams alludes again and again. The "pagan grove" of Frascati is too openly erotic; Dev's last words to the German girl are "come on . . . let's get out of this." And we recall that it is "medicine" that gives him entrance to the "secret gardens of the self."

Indeed, the failure of medicine is oddly equated with the failure of desire. The very short story **"The Accident,"** written as early as 1921 but included in the *Passaic* volume, begins with the sentence, "Death is difficult for the

senses to alight on." The surprising word here is "senses" where we would expect "mind" or "heart." The narrator now explains: "After twelve days struggling with a girl to keep life in her, losing, winning, it is not easy to give her up. One has studied her inch by inch, one has grown used to the life in her. It is natural." From this deathbed image, the story now cuts abruptly to the following morning, a morning of spring sunshine in which the poet is driving somewhere with his baby son. Having so recently witnessed the girl's death, his mood is one of unrelieved sexual tension:

> What are you stopping here for! To show him the four goats. Come on. No? Ah! She blushes and hides her face. Down the road come three boys in long pants. Good God, good God! How a man will waste himself. She is no more than a piece of cake to be eaten by anyone. Her hips beside me have set me into a fever. I was up half the night last night, my nerves have the insulation worn off them.

In the Laurentian sequence that follows, the doctor converts his sexual energy into some "harmless" play with the goats; he tries, for example, to back the smallest goat "around the tree till it can go no further," whereupon the goat "tries to crowd between me and the tree." The doctor wins this particular struggle and lets the baby touch the goat's "hairy cheek" and stroke its flanks. We read: "The nozzle is hairy, the nose narrow; the moist black skin at the tip, slit either side by curled nostrils, vibrates sensitively." Here it is, of course, the father rather than the child who finds relief. Accordingly, when (on their way back to the car) the baby stumbles and "falls forward on his hands," his face in the dirt, the doctor-father is struck with guilt. For why did he bring the child here in the first place? And although the baby's fall is in fact a pure "accident," the narrator's guilt is oddly confirmed by the response of the "six women" whose heads appear, suddenly and mysteriously, "in the windows of the Franco-American Chemical Co. across the way." "They watch the baby, wondering if he is hurt. They linger to look out. They open the windows." The eyes of these strange women seem to penetrate what Williams calls the "hidden core" of his life; it is as if they challenge his erotic fantasy. But then, in a sudden transformation that recalls Surrealist film, the women are transformed: "They laugh and wave their hands." And indeed life, seemingly cut off by the death of the little girl as well as by his own baby's accident, goes on:

> Over against them in an open field a man and a boy on their hands and knees are planting out slender green slips in the fresh dirt, row after row.

> We enter the car. The baby waves his hand. Good-bye!

To read a story like **"The Accident"** is rather like looking at a relief map of what appear to be flatlands, only to see little mountain-shapes well up from beneath the surface and create peculiar irregularities. But before we can take the measure of these new mountains, canyons, and watercourses, the map collapses from somewhere within and flattens out once again. So in **"The Accident,"** the baby's waving of the hand and the word "Good-bye" break the spell; the narrator's desire is once again enclosed in its secret chamber and "normalcy" is restored.

But what happens when the map undergoes no such transformations, when the tension between desire and the need for safety disappears? In such later fictions as **"The Farmers' Daughters"** (1957), the medical paradigm I have been describing undergoes some curious changes. The patient or patients are, as always in Williams, female: in this case, Margaret and Helen—both lonely and self-destructive women who turn to the doctor (here presented in the third person) for help. But this doctor is not called upon to deliver babies; rather he gives vitamin shots, advises the persistent Margaret on how to improve her breasts, and counsels Helen on her alcoholism. More important, the doctor of this story is no longer the tough but sympathetic narrator of **"The Use of Force"** or **"A Face of Stone"**; he is, on the contrary, deeply involved in the lives of the two women, even though he is himself safely married.

Throughout the story, there are allusions to his lovemaking, whether or not it is fully acted out, with both women, and especially with Helen, the stronger of the two, who turns out to be the survivor. Interestingly, in this story where the doctor's sexual interest in his patient becomes quite overt, there is never the moment of satisfaction that occurs in **"A Night in June"** or in **"World's End"**—the moment of bliss when the doctor finds the proper "treatment" for the patient. It is as if Williams needed to hide what he calls the "inner core" of his life, to keep the "Beautiful Thing" buried in the recesses of his being. When, as in **"The Farmers' Daughters,"** the sexual encounter moves from the realm of fantasy to reality, a curious apathy—a kind of *post coitum tristia*—occurs, an apathy coupled with a new irritatingly patronizing tone toward women. Consider this passage:

> The doctor had a climbing rose in his garden named Jacquot which his wife and he both very much admired. It was a peachpink rambler, the petals fading to a delicate lavender after the first flowering. More than that, the rose throve in their garden against odds thought by the man who sold them the plant to be overwhelming. . . .

> In spite of that its vigor was phenomenal, you couldn't kill it. It covered the trellis with a profusion of blossoms that in early June were a wonder to see. In addition it was delicately scented so that their whole yard smelled of it when it was in bloom. He had never encountered it in any other garden.

> Once he spoke of it to Helen and invited her to come over and see it and whiff its odor during the flowering season.

> They gave her a layered shoot; she planted it and it took hold at once.

So the doctor keeps the rosebush for his wife but gives a shoot to Helen: he has his cake and eats it too. Both

Margaret and Helen have had lovers and husbands, but they constantly assure their doctor that he is the only man they can really love and trust, their only friend and confidant. He is the recipient of Helen's favorite photograph, of Margaret's post-Thanksgiving banquet ("a poetic occasion, a love feast"). It is he who yearns for Helen's "Dresden china blue eyes," just as she yearns for her little Dresden china doll—he who tells Helen, "When you talk about that doll you're beautiful." Again, when Margaret decides to leave town in search of new adventure, he chides her gently but tells her: "in many ways you are the best of us, the most direct, the most honest—yes, and in the end, the most virtuous." Hearing these words, Margaret predictably "wrapped her arms around his neck, curled up on his knees and sobbed quietly." Finally, after Margaret's terrible death (she is murdered by her most recent fly-by-night husband), Helen tells the doctor:

> No one came to the funeral but her family and me. They didn't open the casket. There were no flowers beside the bunch of red roses I'd sent her, her favorite flower.—How are you, my sweet? Take good care of yourself 'cause I can't afford to lose you. When she died, I died too, you're the only one I have left.

In his discussion of **"The Farmers' Daughters,"** [in *William Carlos Williams*, 1968] Thomas Whitaker concludes that each of the three characters sums up one facet of their common predicament: "in Margaret, the most desperate and naked loneliness; in Helen, a more vigorous if precarious thriving despite that loneliness; and in the doctor—imperfectly manifest through his own need—that non-possessive love which might cure the alienation from which all suffer." This is, I think, to sugercoat the pill. For the doctor's "love" is *not* as nonpossessive as all that: he is, after all, charmed and titillated by the attentions of Margaret and Helen, by their openly declared love, their kisses and embraces. As opposed to the two women who are, in their different ways, losers, the doctor (however unfulfilled some of his yearnings may be) retains his position and his equilibrium; he is left, finally, with bittersweet and tender memories—memories that form the substance of the fiction itself.

Whitaker rightly points out that the doctor in this story is not the real focus of attention, that he is "hardly more than a mode of relating. . . . The narrative structure causes us . . . not to look *at* him so much as to see with his eyes." But it is precisely this narrative stance that makes **"The Farmers' Daughters"** problematic. For whereas the earlier fictions delineate the quandaries attendant upon a dimly understood sexual tension, **"Farmers' Daughters"** is, as it were, carefully censored so as to give the reader no choice but to accept the narrator's overt evaluation of himself and of his two "patients." Unlike the protagonist of the earlier story, **"The Use of Force,"** who suddenly remarks: "I could have torn the child apart in my own fury and enjoyed it. It was a pleasure to attack her," this doctor is careful not to drop his guard. Indeed, he resembles the speaker of "Asphodel, that Greeny Flower," who believes he can justify his countless infidelities to his wife by telling her:

Imagine you saw

a field made up of women
    all silver-white
        What should you do

but love them?

It sounds so simple, so earthy and natural. But as the recently published manuscript called "Rome" (the first version of *Voyage to Pagany*) reminds us—and as Williams' best work makes clear—the Man who Loved Women never had quite so easy a time of it. For the "beautiful thing" flies only for a moment "guiltily about the room." Or, as Williams put it in a cancelled preface to **"The Girl with a Pimply Face"**:

How shall I say it? I who have wished to embrace the world with love have succeeded only in binding to myself a wife and children . . . ? I who have wished, in a general way, to die for love have suffered only the small accidents of fatigue, bewilderment and loss?

Who feels enough confidence to say anything? All I know is that no matter what we have dreamed or desired it slips away unless by a supreme effort we struggle to detain it.

It is this "struggle to detain" what "we have dreamed or desired" that gives force to Williams' finest stories, such as **"The Accident"** or **"A Face of Stone."** And the younger Williams knew, as perhaps the mature poet no longer cared to admit, that such struggle was a bloody business. In the ecstasy of the "guilty" moment, the poet's "medical badge" could become a kind of "open sesame." But, as Dev tells the beautiful Fräulein in **"The Venus"**: "To me it is a hard, barren life, where I am 'alone' and unmolested (work as I do in the thick of it) though in constant danger lest some slip send me to perdition."

## George Monteiro (essay date 1980)

SOURCE: "The Doctor's Black Bag: William Carlos Williams' Passaic River Stories," in *Modern Language Studies*, Vol. XIII, No. 1, Winter, 1983, pp. 77-84.

[*In the essay below, which originally was presented as a paper at the Eastern Comparative Literature Meetings in May 1980, Monteiro shows how Williams's own identity as "poet-physician" informs several of his doctor stories.*]

All day long the doctor carries on this work, observing, weighing, comparing values of which neither he nor his patients may know the significance. . . . He is half-ashamed to have people suspect him of carrying on a clandestine, a sort of underhand piece of spying on the public at large. . . . His only fear is that the source of his interest, his daily going about among human beings of all sorts, all ages, all conditions will be terminated. That he will be found out.

    William Carlos Williams, *Autobiography* (1951)

*Black bag* (adj., as in *black bag jobs*): illegal, surreptitious, undercover operations with the purpose of securing information, such as warrantless wiretaps, break-ins, and mail-openings.

William Carlos Williams was luckier than most people. He seemed always to know what he was about. Or at least, writing at the age of sixty-eight, he knew what he had been about. "As a writer, I have been a physician, and as a physician a writer," he said simply in the "Foreword" to his *Autobiography* in 1951.

Although it is accurate to say that William Carlos Williams' stories are a doctor's stories, saying that does not indicate that they are to be judged less strictly or rigorously than are the stories of, say, Stephen Crane or Henry James. The point in calling them a doctor's stories is that at their best they draw essentially both from the doctor's quotidian experiences and upon his embodied conflicts between his learned professionalism and his affective impulses. His practice was his avenue to particular kinds of sociological experience that would otherwise have been unknown to him. His profession, however, placed him in a peculiarly vulnerable position as a participant-observer. His temperament, moreover, was neatly split between that of the feeling, observing doctor and that of the practicing poet. He was a doer and a maker. He was a contemplator and an actor. He was a poet-physician. These two-parted identities stand behind his every word.

Such complementary/conflicting identities shape the substance of his "doctor" stories, four of which I shall examine here: **"The Use of Force," "Jean Beicke," "A Night in June,"** and the superb late tale, **"Comedy Entombed: 1930."** Spanning Williams' entire career as a writer of fiction, these four stories, taken as a block, are representative of Williams' interests and techniques.

**"The Use of Force"** was first collected in *Life Along the Passaic River* (1938). Readings of the story frequently conclude that the doctor-narrator's encounter with his young female patient, understood psychoanalytically, evolves into an adventure in displaced sexuality. But the story can also be read in terms of affective neutrality, which sociologist Talcott Parsons defines as the encouraged capacity within a physician to set aside normal human emotions and to depend instead upon medical training and learned technique to guide professional behavior. That control, in turn, enhances the possibility that his procedures will be technically successful. Paradoxically, the practice of medicine, seen by many as an art in the service of humanity, calls for a practitioner to put aside, indeed to suppress even the possibility of his ever feeling emotion toward a patient. **"The Use of Force"** explores on a small scale the human consequences of the physician's having to live with this paradox.

The story starts out quietly enough. The narrator (a doctor) reports having smiled at his "new" child-patient in his "best professional manner." The smile leads to other "professional" devices. Mixing questions with suggestions, he asks the child to tell him her given name; he asks her to open her mouth; and when she does not immediately accede, he gently coaxes her. All to no avail. So far the doctor is still in control. Careful as he has been, however, he has already slipped up once. He has not taken the child's parents into account and the failure to do so begins to affect his relationship with the child. First, the well-meaning mother tells the child that the "nice man" will not "hurt" her. "At that I ground my teeth in disgust," reports the doctor. "If only they wouldn't use the word 'hurt.'" After further futile efforts at getting the child to open her mouth, during which she knocks the doctor's glasses off, the mother again takes the initiative, shaking her by one arm and chastising her for her bad behavior towards "the nice man." This time the doctor turns on the mother. "For heaven's sake," he breaks in. "Don't call me a nice man to her." There is nothing "nice" in what he is there to do, he insists. It is a matter to be handled with professionalism. "I'm here to look at her throat on the chance that she might have diphtheria and possibly die of it." Another direct appeal to the child fails. This is followed by the doctor's rather unprofessional threat to shift the burden for the child's safety to the parents. "Then the battle began. I had to do it. I had to have a throat culture for her own protection," he insists. "But first I told the parents that it was entirely up to them. I explained the danger but said that *I would not insist* on a throat examination so long as *they would take the responsibility.*" (Emphasis added).

Again the mother admonishes the child. "If you don't do what the doctor says you'll have to go to the hospital." By this time, much too emotionally involved in the conflicts, the doctor admits that while "the parents were contemptible" to him, he had already "fallen in love with the savage brat." In the ensuing, accelerating struggle, the doctor loses more and more of his professional neutrality. With a start he realizes that he has "grown furious" and, worse, that his fury is directed at the child. Fury at a child, in an adult, is ugly enough. Fury at a child who is also a patient, in a doctor, is, of course, professionally inexcusable. Worse still, although he recognizes his behavior for what it is, he can do little about it. "I tried to hold myself down but I couldn't," he admits. His continued efforts to force her mouth open with a wooden spatula have cut her tongue and caused her mouth to bleed. At that moment he realizes that perhaps he should have desisted and come back in an hour or so, that is to say, when, perhaps, both the doctor-adult and his patient-child had cooled off. But he rationalized his need to gain his clear-cut immediate victory over the child by observing that he has already "seen at least two children lying dead in bed of neglect in such cases." The rub, however, is that he "too had got beyond reason." Indeed, he "could have torn the child apart" in his "own fury and enjoyed it. It was a pleasure to attack her." His rationalizing continues. "The damned little brat must be protected against her own idiocy," he begins righteously, adding, in a moment of great self-knowledge, or so "one says to one's self at such times." To this he adds a saving professional rationalization: "Others must be protected against her. It is social necessity. And all these things are true," he insists. But it is neither professional duty nor objectivity that is now operative. "But a blind

fury, a feeling of adult shame, bred of a longing for muscular release are the operatives." All ideals and duties aside, "One goes on to the end." The child is then overpowered in a "final unreasoning assault." And sure enough, the doctor has his victory and his discovery of the child's "secret." The tonsils are "covered with membrane," the child does have a sore throat, and the diagnosis is diphtheria.

**"The Use of Force"** tests the doctor's ability to function as a professional. There is a "best professional manner," as Dr. Williams well knew, and it goes beyond the possibilities inherent in a friendly smile. But in **"The Use of Force"** he presents us with a self-contained segment in which a medical practitioner willfully permits first the erosion and then the collapse of his own affective neutrality. Faced with a situation that calls only for a rather simple diagnosis, the doctor all too quickly succumbs to his own feelings. In his emotional reactions to the parents who, it is immediately obvious, remain ineffective before the child's obstinacy and his anxious willingness to redefine his physician's role into that of antagonist to his patient, the narrator allows his own emotions precedence over professionalism. Williams' account of the doctor's impetuous and dogged struggle with his young patient renders brilliantly the fragility of that professional's affective neutrality by which the physician would do his life's work.

In **"Jean Beicke,"** a second story from his collection *Life Along the Passaic River,* the relationship between the physician and his patient is all on the side of the physician. Perhaps the best place to begin discussing **"Jean Beicke"** is the end of the story: the account of the autopsy. The child with the too long legs, with an omniverous appetite that compelled her to eat everything given her, has succumbed at last, having first won the emotional support of her nurses and doctors. So much so, in fact, that her nurse, despite the doctor's attempts, has not gone down to the postmortem. "I may be a sap, she said, but I can't do it, that's all. I can't. Not when I've taken care of them. I feel as if they're my own." It is important that we hear this, for the nurse's behavior, with her attendant explanation, serves as a necessary prelude to the doctor's account of the autopsy.

> I was amazed to see how completely the lungs had cleared up. They were almost normal except for a very small patch of residual pneumonia here and there which really amounted to nothing. Chest and abdomen were in excellent shape, otherwise, throughout—not a thing aside from the negligible pneumonia. Then he opened the head. It seemed to me the poor kid's convolutions were unusually well developed. I kept thinking it's incredible that that complicated mechanism of the brain has come into being just for this. I never can quite get used to an autopsy.

> The first evidence of the real trouble—for there had been no gross evidence of meningitis—was when the pathologist took the brain in his hand and made the long steady cut which opened up the left lateral ventricle. There was just a faint color of pus on the bulb of the choroid plexus there. Then the diagnosis

all cleared up quickly. The left lateral sinus was completely thrombosed and on going into the left temporal bone from the inside the mastoid process was all broken down.

As one would expect, the doctor, who had been so solicitous, always looking for signs of progress and dreading the possibility of deterioration, even to the point of rooting like a fan for the scrappy kid, is now coolly clinical. Look at what he notices, and remember that the child is dead. "The lungs had *cleared up.* They were *almost normal.*" The patch of pneumonia that remains "really *amounted to nothing.*" Chest and abdomen are in "*excellent* shape." Then the doctor opens the head. As for its convolutions, they were "unusually *well developed.*" Then the coolness falters, when he admits that he kept thinking that it was incredible "that that complicated mechanism of the brain has come into being just for this," an autopsy. It is in the head that the doctors succeed in their quest—their inquest—as the pathologist takes up the brain. Here Williams describes his next professional move. He "made the *long steady cut* which opened the left lateral ventricle." Only at second or third thought, perhaps, does one realize the violence of the pathologist's act and its attending violation of the child's brain. But the clinical cut "opens" that part of the brain, and reveals the mystery. "The left lateral sinus was completely thrombosed and on going into the left temporal bone from the inside the mastoid process was all broken down." The breakdown is exposed, and the "diagnosis" cleared up. It should be noted that diagnoses are usually in the service of life and potential health, and therefore patient-oriented. But here there is no longer a patient, merely a cadaver for which all diagnoses are bootless. In what sense is it still a satisfying diagnosis? And in what sense is it still health-oriented? Uncovering the breakdown of the mastoid process, discovering the logic of the disease, serves the doctors, of course. When a third physician, the "ear man," is called down to see for himself what has been found, he conjectures that they made a mistake. "A clear miss, he said. I think if we'd gone in there earlier, we'd have saved her." But the narrator-physician will have none of such talk. The autopsy has apparently served its neutralizing purpose. The doctor dismisses the "ear man's" comment with a political quip. "For what? said I. Vote the straight Communist ticket." To which the ear man counters: "Would it make us any dumber?" Satisfaction has come with postmortem knowledge. The child has disappeared into the inquest. The physician's faith in his science and craft is intact. And besides, who needs another unwanted child, let alone an unwanted voter? The doctor, after his infatuation with the child ("we all got to be crazy about Jean"), has reverted to the self who, making rounds in the morning, would tell the nurses that the "miserable specimens" who would survive would "grow up into a cheap prostitute or something." Of course, what gives this story its power is that the wisecracking and the running diagnosis cum treatment cannot eradicate the narrator's affections. They can, from time to time, encapsulate them.

Collected in *Make Light of It* (1950), **"A Night in June,"** set in that fabled month for love and marriage, calls for a doctor to attend a woman at term. Settling in for a night of waiting for the delivery of what will be the woman's ninth baby, the doctor falls asleep. He sleeps at the kitchen table in a pleasant and comfortable position. He dreams; and in his half sleep he begins to argue with himself—"or some imaginary power." The argument turns on a conflict between "science and humanity." The dream, as the doctor describes it, runs like this:

> Our exaggerated ways will have to pull in their hours, I said. We've learned from one teacher and neglected another. Now that I'm older, I'm finding the older school.

> The pituitary extract and other simple devices represent science. Science, I dreamed, has crowded the stage more than is necessary. The process of selection will simplify the application. It touches us too crudely now, all newness is over—complex. I couldn't tell whether I was asleep or awake.

> But without science, without pituitrin, I'd be here till noon or maybe—what? Some others wouldn't wait so long but rush her now. A carefully guarded shot of pituitrin—ought to save her at least much exhaustion—if not more. But I don't want to have anything happen to her.

Within the dream the doctor's options take the form of conflict. Shall he use a substance that will speed up the processes of labor or shall he wait patiently for nature's course? Shall he risk injecting pituitrin in the case of a woman whose uterus after eight deliveries is more than commonly susceptible to tearing to save them both time and fatiguing effort, and in her case possibly something "more," a something that he does not name? This conflict he sees as one between Science and Humanity. What makes its resolution into professional action difficult—after all, the doctor will choose to inject the pituitrin or he will choose not to do so—is that within the doctor another antagonism is playing itself out: the desire to act under the control of neutralized feelings in the face of emotions that threaten to break through the technique with which the doctor practices his artful science. In his dream the doctor sees such conflicts in terms of competing schools that are "older" and "newer." Significant, too, is his claim that as he gets older, he is finding "the older." It is the school of Humanity that is older, the school of Science younger. It has been hardly casual, one recalls at this point, that the doctor began his narrative with a two-paragraph summary of his failure years earlier—as a young man—to deliver successfully the woman's first baby. "It was a difficult forceps delivery"—of course that delivery would call for Science—"and I lost the child, to my disgust." Significant, as well, is the feeling that this failure engenders in the young doctor. He does not feel *disappointment,* which would be more neutral, more professional, nor *grief* or *pain,* which would be more humane. Rather, he feels *disgust.* He feels aversion, abhorrence; he is, perhaps, offended. If he feels that he is at all to blame for the failure, however, he quickly exonerates himself: "without nurse, anesthetist, or even enough hot water in the place, I shouldn't have been over-much blamed. I must have been fairly able not to have done worse." In short, we are to infer, the doctor had done the best he could given limitations and circumstances outside his professional control. There was no failure of technique, obviously, and therefore no reason for disgust, at least not self-directed disgust.

---

> **The dream of the artist, and the artist's reward, is that his skill and technique and vision will discover for him the new order, and that there will always be such new orders. Williams displayed this most often and most lyrically in his poetry. But these truths were also there, amidst the everyday dust and dirt of his realist's observations, in his stories.**
>
> —*George Monteiro*

---

But all this is preliminary to a story centering, years later, on still another delivery. And by this time the doctor is a seasoned professional. The story celebrates his preparation and judgment, and, in the end, his success. There runs through the narrative a strong sense of contentment and self-congratulation. For example, because seldom are women any longer delivered at home, the doctor must seek out that "relic" of a satchel he had tossed under a table "two or three years" before. Nevertheless, a check shows that it contains just about everything the doctor will need.

> There was just one sterile unbilical tie left, two, really, in the same envelope, as always, for possible twins, but that detail aside, everything was ample and in order. I complimented myself. Even the Argyrol was there, in tablet form, insuring the full potency of a fresh solution. Nothing so satisfying as a kit of any sort prepared and in order even when picked up in an emergency after an interval of years.

In the course of the early morning hours the doctor periodically examines the woman, assesses probabilities, and decides on procedures. All runs largely on course until the moment for delivery. "The woman and I then got to work," announces the doctor. Her "hands grabbed me at first a little timidly about the right wrist and forearm. Go ahead, I said. Pull hard. I welcomed the feel of her hands and the strong pull. It quieted me . . ." No forceps are needed. There is no need for the doctor to resort to instrumental intervention. The delivery will be natural, becoming a collaboration of the woman and her doctor. The situation provides the doctor with a moment of quiet self-perception: "This woman in her present condition would have seemed repulsive to me ten years ago—now, poor soul, I see her to be as clean as a cow that calves." The head is born, and then the rest of the baby. There has been no

injection of pituitrin, no need for forceps; it has been in every way, a natural delivery. It is as an afterthought that the doctor reminds himself: "Oh yes, the drops in the baby's eyes." But, he quickly decides, there is "no need. She's as clean as a beast." Yet, the professionalism within him reminds him that he can't know for sure. Again there is a professional conflict. "Medical discipline says every case must have drops in the eyes. No chance of gonorrhea though here—but—Do it." The resolution to the allegorical conflict between Science and Humanity—the claims of the younger school and those of the older—is that they can go hand-in-hand when united by the experienced, judicious doctor. There have been employed no "exaggerated ways"; the horns of Science have been pulled in. For once, all's right in Doctor Williams' medical world. Mother and baby are doing fine.

**"A Night in June"** had begun with a doctor's memory of a forceps-delivered child he had lost. Although he had rather quickly absolved himself of blame, he nevertheless was disturbed by his failure. And, of course, the infant was dead. In **"Jean Beicke,"** the eleven-month child loses her fight, and she, too, is dead. If the Beicke autopsy serves to bring the doctors back to the right professional note, there is no sense that all's right with the world. Curiously enough, though, that is exactly the note sounded in Williams' **"Comedy Entombed: 1930,"** also collected in *Make Light of It* (1950). The story is thoroughly comic, or would be if it were not for one thing: the culminating event of the story is the delivery of a dead fetus. On second thought, there is no exception to the story's comic thrust. Not only does everything turn out for the best but, in certain respects, rather well. It is, as the doctor says, "just a five months' miss." The fetus was a girl, information the mother uses to taunt her husband who, after several boys, wants a girl. It is the mother, as it turns out, who controls the emotional ambiance of the whole procedure, who "knew it was all right," and who laughs at her husband's bellyache. She taunts him about his couvade: "You'd be more famous than the Dionne quintuplets . . . You'd get your pictures in the papers and talk over the radio and everything." In all likelihood the mother's sustained equanimity has given the doctor's narration its particular coloration and its sense of order-within-disorder. The story is about the discovery of that order, one unexpected and certainly unsuspected. The details of the house—its "greasy" smell to its "soiled sheets"—anticipate the potential messiness of a "birth" four months short of term.

> The whole place had a curious excitement about it for me, resembling in that the woman herself, I couldn't precisely tell why. There was nothing properly recognizable, nothing straight, nothing in what ordinarily might have been called its predictable relationships. Complete disorder. Tables, chairs, worn-out shoes piled in one corner. A range that didn't seem to be lighted. Every angle of the room jammed with something or other ill-assorted and of the rarest sort.

In a story in which a dead fetus occasions a mother's not-so-black humor, however, matters are not readily predictable, and the observant doctor does not stop with these observations. He has an insight, an artist's epiphany.

> I have seldom seen such disorder and brokenness— such a mass of unrelated parts of things lying about. That's it! I concluded to myself. An unrecognizable order! Actually—the new! And so good-natured and calm. So definitely the thing! And so compact. Excellent. And with such patina of use. Everything definitely "painty." Even the table, that way, pushed off from the center of the room.

"An unrecognizable order! Actually—the new!" That new knowledge will inform the doctor's experience with the collected mother and her dead fetus of a daughter (it's 'born' "still in the sack . . . It all came together . . . the whole mass was intact"). Indeed, since death and disorder are seen to be very much in the nature of things, it is almost as if the whole thing were a joke on the comic father.

**"Comedy Entombed: 1930"** offers an unmatchable key into Williams Carlos Williams the physician-poet. Williams' aesthetic impulse was in certain ways at odds with his doctor's scientific training. His aesthetic was profoundly Dionysian ("a new order") but his profession calls for an Apollonian temperament. The artist was always looking for new order; the physician always trying to engender the known, predictive, scientific order. As in the past—the scientist would say—so again, so now. The artist: never so before, but now, anew, so.

For the physician the fear would always be that the order would breed chaos, that it would be discovered that at the heart of order will be a disorder (an unknown, unrecognized, unrecognizable disease). The dream of the artist, and the artist's reward, is that his skill and technique and vision will discover for him the new order, and that there will always be such new orders. Williams displayed this most often and most lyrically in his poetry. But these truths were also there, amidst the everyday dust and dirt of his realist's observations, in his stories.

## James G. Watson (essay date 1984)

SOURCE: "The American Short Story: 1930-1945," in *The American Short Story, 1900-1945: A Critical History,* G. K. Hall & Company, 1984, pp. 103-46.

[*In the following excerpt, Watson surveys Williams's contributions to the short story form.*]

Other native sons and daughters whose work significantly contributed to the contours of the short story between the wars include two at apparently opposite ends of the spectrum: the American expatriate writer, Kay Boyle, and the doctor-poet of Rutherford, New Jersey, William Carlos Williams. Expatriate and poet are delimiting labels for these two, but they help to account for divergences in the pattern I have been tracing. In her stories, many of them in the 1930s and 1940s written in England and Austria

and France, Kay Boyle appeals obliquely to the rich resources of the Adamic myth. Her sophisticated short fiction draws on the American Adam as a frame or context for plots and values in the way that the poetry of T. S. Eliot and Ezra Pound draws on myth and literary precedent as artificial ordering devices. It is a sign of her modernity and her Americanness.

---

**Williams's America of the 1920s and 1930s is less bound by traditions; it is more fragmentary and, in that, more modern.**

*—James G. Watson*

---

William Carlos Williams commonly abjures such literariness. He relies instead on acute attention to the telling concrete details of American life to give his stories their shape and significance. His long battle against Eliot's classroom classicism carried naturally from his poetry into his fiction, where likewise the ideas in things have metaphysical value. What Boyle works for through tradition, Williams tries to do with bare perception. Yet they are not so different as this makes them appear, and given another axis of comparison they might occupy some of the same space. In an essay titled "Style and Sacrament in Modernist Writing," Herbert Schneidau says of twentieth-century prose generally that it "seems to welcome more poetic effects and structures than does that of the preceding century. . . . This poetic quality is not a matter of atmospherics, nor even of reliance on images; at bottom we may see that it is the metaphoric pattern of language that is being used to cross-fertilize prose." Boyle's and Williams's stories mark an advance over those of Farrell and Wright and others of the second level of American short story writers in this regard. With some reservations for individual writers and individual works, the very best American short fiction is characterized by its range and intensity of poetic effect. . . .

In Boyle's fictional world, no less than in Richard Wright's, the generative American myths of innocence and opportunity are dispelled by inversions that assert, by mocking, the national identity. In the postlapsarian darkness of the 1930s, her stories of idealism wasted and abused take place always in broken gardens, lonely corners, and isolated lives. Her 1932 *New Yorker* story "Black Boy," for example, makes the beach where the child narrator and her black friend meet into childhood's last refuge: she calls it "the forsaken part, . . . the other end of the city," where waves "as indolent as ladies gathered up their skirts in their hands and, with a murmur, came tiptoeing in across the velvet sand." All too predictably, American racism intrudes on the metaphoric garden, in the person of the girl's grandfather, to drive the children into the world. "Keep Your Pity" (1936) tells the opposite story, of sheltered love impoverished by selfishness and hardened by pride, and of the unredeeming idealism of a well-meaning American innocent abroad named Mr. Jefferson. Like some under-developed Jamesian hero, Jefferson's innocence remains undisturbed and ironically unbetrayed by the equally symbolic Benedict Wycherley and his witchy wife.

The title story from the same collection puts such overtly American materials at a still further remove from America proper. "The White Horses of Vienna" also is set in a place apart, this one a white house high on a mountain above an Austrian village. The time is the mid-1930s. Austria is politically in disarray. Boyle's protagonist is a doctor, a former prisoner of war in Siberia, who intends his house on the mountain as a refuge from the world. In this reconstituted Eden, however, white is not only the color of the doctor's idealism but also of his blonde Nordic wife's belief in racial supremacy. The doctor injures a leg at a secret political rally, and the replacement called from Vienna turns out to be a Jew, Dr. Heine. Heine's story of a crippled Lippizaner stallion at the Spanish Riding School in Vienna symbolizes lost Austrian ideals and forecasts the doctor's destruction. And his own. The anti-Semitic wife accuses him of money grubbing, serves him pig for dinner, and in one terribly prophetic scene actually sets him afire. The situation of European Jews as Kay Boyle envisions it in this fine story is as severe and as frightening as that of American blacks in the stories of Richard Wright. And it is cast in the same metaphoric form as Wright's. Boyle uses the fall of the doctor's family as an allegory of the coming fall of Europe, but the Adamic substructure, like the allegory itself, makes it a particularly American expression. If the values and the dreams at issue here are not specifically American, the method and materials of the story are. In the words of a more famous American expatriate, in his memoir *A Moveable Feast,* "all generations were lost by something and always had been and always would be." Hemingway was speaking of Paris in the 1920s and of mental carelessness, but whether the something was carelessness or racism or fascism, destructive pride or simple American cupidity, the common sense of loss and the common forms of its expression underlie the short fiction of this as well as his own American generation.

William Carlos Williams came to these themes differently, as he came by different ways to the short story form. For two decades a poet, though not yet the poet of *Paterson,* he published two volumes of short fiction in the 1930s, *The Knife of the Times* (1932) and *Life Along the Passaic River* (1938). In his 1949 retrospective essay, "A Beginning on the Short Story (Notes)," he said that the heterogeneous character of the people was centrally responsible for his coming to the short story in the early years of the Depression. "I lived among these people," he said. "I know them and saw the essential qualities (not stereotyped), the courage, the humor (an accident), the deformity, the basic tragedy of their lives—and the *importance* of it. You can't write about something unimportant to yourself. I was involved." Williams was involved aesthetically as well as personally, as a poet as well as a doctor, and in both cases he was ideologically involved.

He despised the institutions of the church and state that falsified by stereotyping such lives, and he found in the short story the artistic means to raise people from "that Gehenna, the newspapers, where at last all men are equal, to the distinction of being an individual." "The pure products of America / go crazy," he had written in 1923 in the poem "To Elsie," and it is significant of his social idealism that he chose to publish five stories in the little magazine *Blast: Proletarian Short Stories.* Yet Williams was no Marxist. His objections to social formulas made him impatient, too, of formulas of objection, and the best of his stories are no more typical of proletarian realism than of any other convention of expression, including conventionally American ones.

He could not, in any case did not, name a character of his Adams, as Hemingway so pointedly did. Nor does he appeal to mythic models to portray Passaic River lives in the way that Farrell does to express immigrant hopes, or Wright the hopelessness of black Americans. Williams's America of the 1920s and 1930s is less bound by traditions; it is more fragmentary and, in that, more modern. "How shall we write today?" he asks in "A Beginning on the Short Story." "The hero? Who is a hero? The peasantry? There is none. Men and women faithful to a belief? What belief?" Whatever the quality of their disaffection, Farrell and Wright (not to mention Saroyan) *want* to believe in the American Adam, and the myth informs their fictions. Because of the allegorical implications of that myth, their stories have a finished quality and a sense of closure that Williams's often do not. Kay Boyle's carefully made stories are still more finished: she is less concerned with the substance of the Adamic story than with its outlines, less inclined to it as a system of values than as a pattern of human behavior.

Williams claimed membership in no school of storywriters, subscribed to no modernist or even national creed. His characters seem often to enter and leave his stories as his patients entered and left his office. They come briefly under his eye and hand and are gone, fragments themselves of a hardly definable whole. Yet the stories are carefully, often poetically crafted. Whatever Williams might have seen that was Adamic in the people of Rutherford, to portray them in terms of a national literary convention would have been to sentimentalize their lives and condition. He was interested in overcoming traditions, not copying them. He tried, as he said, to impose form on material in such a way as "to wed the subject to its own time," and of that conjunction the result is "life, not morals. It is THE LIFE which comes alive in the telling. It is the life under specified conditions—so that it is relieved in the reading—as it strikes off flashes from the material. The material is the metal against which a flint makes sparks."

In the best of Williams's short fiction, both the subject matter and the form are revolutionary in this way. Each of the first four stories in *The Knife of the Times,* for example, deals with a sexual relationship that violates social norms: lesbianism in the title story, adultery in **"A Visit to the Fair"** and **"Hands across the Sea,"** and bisexuality in **"The Sailor's Son."** Each subject is figuratively a *knife* of the times, a painful fact of the heterogeneous life in Depression-era America that challenges social definitions of love and family and upsets preconceptions of normalcy. In **"The Knife of the Times,"** a middle-aged married woman is courted in letters and then in person by a childhood friend, herself a married woman and a mother. At first Maura shares Ethel's newsy letters with her husband, but the personal note becomes more confidential, then passionate, until the letters are "full love missives . . . without the least restraint." Maura is simultaneously frightened and attracted by them: now she hides them from her husband with Ethel's gifts, indulges Ethel's franker and franker fantasies, and finally agrees to meet her friend in New York. There Maura's last reservations about the relationship are overcome. Ethel draws her into a pay toilet where she kisses and caresses her, and though Maura tries to appease the passion she cannot modify it. At a public luncheon, she frankly responds to Ethel's under-the-table pressures. All these elements—the letters, the fetishism, the pay toilet, and the excitement of forbidden caresses—might be no more than symbolic elements in a loveless woman's fantasy life were they not first so frankly granted as realities. Maura is not a frustrated wife in a loveless home, and however abnormal her attraction to Ethel's advances, Williams is at pains to show that it is not entirely unnatural. The opening sentence establishes that "the girls who had been such intimates as children remained true to one another," and the intimacy of shared secrets gives way naturally to that of shared love, first in Ethel's letters and then in their lives. At the conclusion of the story, Ethel begs her lover "to visit her, to go to her, to spend a week at least with her, to sleep with her," and Maura's answer is, "Why not?" Knifelike itself, the story cuts away the easy affirmations and surface assumptions of the times to pose the same question that Maura asks herself. Given the importance of life in its essential qualities—not stereotypes—*why not* be true to the imperatives of intimacy, in life and in art?

Speaking of such stories in 1949, Williams acknowledged with a wry sexual twist and a jab at the *Post* that he had remained true to this principle. He said, "This wasn't the 'acceptable,' the unshocking stuff, the slippery, in the sense that it can be slipped into them while they are semiconscious of a Saturday evening." What writers for the *Saturday Evening Post* accomplished by innuendo or altogether ignored, Williams tried to portray frankly in individualized characters. Unsparing of his patients in his "doctor" stories, he was as unsparing of himself. The life that interested and involved him in the stories of *Life along the Passaic River* was "THE LIFE which comes alive in the telling," his own included, and he resisted the slippery standards of *Post* fiction with the same fervor he reserved for the Gehenna of the newspapers. The knifecuts that reveal the deformities, the tragedies, and the courage of his patients in **"A Face of Stone"** and **"Jean Beicke"** and **"The Use of Force"** also uncover the buried life of the doctor-narrator. In these opening sentences, for example, the doctor's stony reserve is no less a mask than the expressive face of the patient as he describes it: "He was one of these fresh Jewish types you want to kill at sight, the presuming poor whose looks change the minute cash is mentioned. But they're insistent, trying to force attention, taking advantage of good nature at the first crack. You come when I call you, that type." A "type" at the outset, the patient emerges as a father and husband, and the doctor's stone face cracks to reveal his compassionate nature. They are softened into individuality by their shared concern for a third masked character, the patient's deformed but stoic wife, whose sudden smile concludes the story.

In **"Jean Beicke"** the doctor's compassion slips past the mask of cynicism he constructs to hide it; his otherwise inexpressible feeling finds expression in its opposite. "Give it an enema," he says of a starving child, "maybe it will get well and grow up into a cheap prostitute or something. The country needs you, brat." Too many of his "brats" will grow up to be cheap prostitutes, he knows, but when they fail to get well the failing is his, not society's. "We did everything we knew how to do except the right thing," he says of Jean Beicke's death. But in **"The Use of Force"** the right thing is drastically wrong and another kind of failure. Mathilda Olson has diphtheria, which she hides by clamping her jaws shut and refusing to be examined. The doctor describes her initially as "one of those picture children often reproduced in advertising leaflets and photogravure sections of the Sunday papers." But Mathilda's violent resistance to the "nice man" who wants to look at her throat belies the newspaper stereotype: she rises above it to "magnificent heights of insane fury of effort bred of her terror." Simultaneously, the doctor's professional zeal becomes "a pleasure to attack her," and he forces her mouth open with a cooking spoon. The scene is elemental, savage, sexually charged, and he knows it:

> The damned little brat must be protected against her own idiocy, one says to one's self at such times. Others must be protected against her. It is social necessity. And all these things are true. But a blind fury, a feeling of adult shame, bred of longing for muscular release are the operatives. One goes on to the end.

At the end, the doctor and Mathilda have used force against each other: he to confirm his diagnosis, she to express her fear of him. Typing each other, each fails to communicate with the other, and their mute frustrations erupt into violence that reveals while it demeans their individual dignity.

Like this one, many of Williams's stories are concerned with obstacles to communication, in life and in art. Mathilda Olso refuses to speak; the wife in **"A Face of Stone"** speaks English haltingly; Jean Beicke cannot speak at all and so she screams. The problem for the doctor-narrator of the stories is to understand, so that he can treat, people who cannot or will not express themselves—the physically ill and the deformed, the children, and all the impoverished of language who come to him in need or hide in fear. The problem for the storyteller, of course, is to express them himself: to assert his authority as author over their limitations and his own in order to make stories. In this large sense, Williams's work in the short story is one attempt of many significant attempts to make the fragmented modern world possible for art. Some American writers found a solution in the Adamic forms of Hawthorne and Melville and Twain, others, like Kay Boyle, in the mythical method of Joyce and Eliot. Declining the formulas of tradition and the acceptable contemporary conventions, Williams chose to state frankly the intimate passions and passionate brutalities that he said were flashes struck from the materials of life. His stories fall into that space between revolutionary fictions and the fiction of revolution, and if he is less sure of his form than the great innovators, his stories are more powerfully expressive than those of the committed ideologues. The short story, he said, "must be written so well that that in itself becomes the truth while the deformity informs it."

Some of Williams's stories meet that high standard, and some do not. As a poet writing short stories, he was not always at home with his own form as he was not always at ease in his time. But the best of his work weds the materials to the form the times dictated, as he said, and marks a significant contour of the genre.

**Joseph M. Gratto  (essay date 1985)**

SOURCE: "An Analysis of William Carlos Williams' 'Mind and Body'," in *Studies in Short Fiction,* Vol. 22, No. 3, Summer, 1985, pp. 347-51.

[*In the essay below, Gratto details the autobiographical, medical, and literary components of "Mind and Body."*]

William Carlos Williams' short story **"Mind and Body"** takes a vignette about a woman who obviously fascinated Williams, melds it with the substance of a chapter from a highly popular medical book of the depression era, and illustrates in a very effective literary way the main elements of an important medical issue—the relationship of psychiatric medicine to general practice.

The case of Martha Darby, first mentioned by Williams in his essay "Jataqua," provides the general biographical outlines of a character whom Williams would subsequently develop into the central figure in **"Mind and Body."**

> Intelligent, our girls are, their minds are whip-like, if they don't rot, as did Martha's, she who beat the record of all years at Cornell; was secretary to Altman; was graduated as a trained nurse and, what a volcano of energy! taught Greek in a school till she went mad at the slowness of the pupils—and married that marvelous little lame Irishman, Darby—who has the moods of a rose. What a woman! spending her life now as servitor to women in the Insane Hospital on Ward's Island—after being an inmate there herself—and recovering. What an energy wasted there! No place for it in the world save among the insane. Especially no place for it in the United States.

A decade later Martha Darby reemerges as Ingrid Yates in the short story **"Mind and Body."** Like Martha, Ingrid

had won a scholarship from a Brooklyn High School to Cornell where she majored in Latin, Greek and Logic, and again won a fellowship in Logic. The instructors retreated in disorder before her attacks till she quit the game and, needing money, went to teach Latin in a high school from which, after a month, she ran away. The slowness of her pupils drove her mad. From there she went to a New York business schools, graduated in no time and became private secretary to one of New York's leading merchants. . . .

. . . . .

Yates, she had met, incredibly, in an asylum where she had been confined after her breakdown. She had gone there of her own will to be cured and there she had decided to remain, to become a nurse to attend the insane. And there she had encountered Yates, the gentle-voiced and kindly nurse—employed in the care of male patients—as she was in the care of females. It had been a most happy marriage, she with her erratic voluble disposition, he with his placid mind.

In the short story, Ingrid is undergoing an examination because of intestinal pains for which the doctor has difficulty finding a cause. He is not alone in his diagnostic difficulty; other physicians before him have also apparently failed, as Ingrid admits, for the condition lacks a physiological basis:

> "I know people think I am a nut. I was an epileptic as a child. I know I am a manic depressive. But doctors are mostly fools. I have been very sick. They say it is my imagination. What is that?"

Williams, in an essay written about 1931, [titled "Imaginations"], commented on the relationship of the body and the wits, referring somewhat favorably to "Dr. Clendening's book" on this subject. The reference is almost certainly to Logan Clendening's *The Human Body,* originally published in 1927. Clendening's book contains a chapter entitled "The Relations of Mind and Body" which deals, as does Williams' story of similar name, with the general issue of psychosomatic illness. Clendening notes that telling a patient that his illness is "imaginary" is "resented more than anything. The patient will insist, 'I can tell you this is not imaginary,' . . . and they are perfectly right."

The difficulty for the physician in dealing with such a patient is recognized by Clendening, who views cases such as Ingrid's as conversion reactions. Clendening notes that such cases represent psychological "adaptation of the patient to his life up to the time of . . . [the symptom's] . . . origin."

Williams' physician attending Ingrid initially proceeds essentially as Clendening suggests would be appropriate: "Tell me more of your life," he says. Ingrid has obviously encountered this line of questioning before, because after telling him about an operation eighteen years earlier she remarks, "I am compensating for my childhood now." There follows an outpouring of dialogue, which Ingrid dominates, as she rambles erratically for several pages in a manner typical of a person a clinical psychologist would diagnose as a hysterical personality. Finally she remarks, "Someone to tell our troubles to is what we need. I suppose I bore you with all I am saying today but I must talk. You must think I'm crazy."

Clendening notes that patients whose illnesses are essentially psychosomatic are likely to find relief only from "regular physicians who devote themselves to rational psychotherapy," rather than from a "dreary round of specialists or mechanists," or from the average physician, whose psychiatric training is inadequate to the problem:

> "The reason for this attitude of mind lies largely in the training of the average physician. All his professional life he is urged to look upon diseases from a mechanistic view-point. Therefore when a patient with many symptoms and no signs appears, he is apt to think that, no matter if you do call it hysteria or neurasthenia, still there must be some obscure infection, or some derangement of a ductless gland, or some metabolic disorder temporarily beyond his powers of demonstration. When the patient's complaints become so absolutely unreasonable as to force him to the conviction that no physical basis for them exists, the spiritual equipment of the average practitioner is inadequate to a sympathetic interpretation."

The patient, on the other hand, does, in fact, experience symptoms like those of actual disease, Clendening notes. Furthermore, the patient is unaware of the psychological adaptiveness of the illness, "totally unconscious of the steps by which he got sick," and thus essentially incurable in a normal medical sense.

The dilemma of a patient who can't accept the psychosomatic nature of her illness, and the doctor, who suspects it, but by training and temperament still perhaps seeks an organic cause is well illustrated in **"Mind and Body."** Ingrid ultimately insists on a physical examination. The doctor agrees. He

> carefully palpatated her abdomen but could find nothing at all. . . . Her heart action was even and regular. Only flushed cheeks, the suggestively maniacal eyes, the quiver of the small muscles of her face, her trembling fingers told her stress. She awaited my verdict in silence. I could find nothing. "Yes," she said, "only two men have found the exact spot, and she pointed to a place in her right iliac quadrant. One was a young doctor at the Post Graduate Hospital who has become famous since then, and another was the surgeon who operated on me the first time. The rest just feel around the abdomen as you have done."

The doctor responds rather absurdly with a reference to an ancient medical belief, "But do not forget, I said in my own defense, that there is a place in the abdomen of major hysteria which if it is pressed upon will definitely bring on a convulsive attack."

A short discussion of this comment ensues, but the doctor quickly stops any further speculation with a diagnosis of exactly the sort Clendening abhorred: "I believe you are suffering merely—but that is quite enough—from what

Llewelyn C. Barker calls—I have forgotten the term—what we used to call mucuous colitis." He explains the condition briefly, but the explanation in actuality is vague and uninformative. Furthermore, Ingrid apparently does not choose to hear it, presumably because she cannot psychologically endure the loss of her illness, anyway. At any rate, after the doctor takes her to the bus stop she remarks, "Well, you haven't told me what is the matter with me. What is it? Don't tell me I am nervous?" The doctor responds remarkably:

> "There has never been an anatomic basis discovered for an opinion in cases like yours . . . until recently. Apparently the cause was laid down in the germ plasma when you were created. . . ."

> . . . . .

> "The anatomic basis of your condition . . . seems to have been detected in a new study called capillaroscopy, a study of the microscopic terminal blood vessels. In people of your type these terminal loops between the arteries and the veins are long and gracile. They are frail, expand and contract easily, it is the cause of all the unstable nervous phenomena, you see."

Ingrid is now satisfied. "Yes, I can feel it often, she agreed. The blood goes into my face or into my brain. I often want to run and scream out, it is so hard for me to stand it."

The doctor begins to elaborate, but the arrival of Ingrid's bus mercifully interrupts this curbstone diagnosis the doctor is improvising.

Dr. Clendening, in his chapter on "The Relations of the Mind and Body" has outlined the difficulties for both patient and doctor when a physician who is untrained in psychiatric medicine encounters a patient who presents a psychosomatic disorder. Dr. Williams, in his story **"Mind and Body,"** has effectively illustrated those difficulties.

Williams, of course, may have been dealing ironically with the issue. He did not fully agree with Clendening, who had embraced Freudian thought in a way Williams never would. Thus, while Williams' general practitioner in **"Mind and Body"** may have been inadequate by Clendening's standards to work Ingrid through her psychologically based conversion reaction, he obviously was ultimately perceptive enough to recognize a psychosomatic issue when he saw one. He did not rashly strip away Ingrid's defense mechanism. He recognized that Ingrid was rather hysterical, to be sure, but that she was also functional and in no apparent danger. The doctor could not cure Ingrid, and maybe she didn't need curing. At any rate, true to the Hippocratic oath, the doctor did the patient no harm.

**Paul Mariani (essay date 1985)**

SOURCE: *"La Giaconda's Smile,"* in *William Carlos Williams Review,* Vol. XI, No. 2, Fall, 1985, pp. 55-60.

*[In the following essay, Mariani closely analyzes Williams's use of language and its effect on meaning in "Country Rain."]*

"Why don't you write a story about the place while it's raining, now you've got your typewriter set up." So Williams has his wife, Floss, ask him in his short story, **"The Country Doctor."**

And Williams, art reflecting life: "*Country Rain,* said I, looking out of our bedroom window over the ploughed field. Or, *The Dark Helen,* huh?"

In early August, 1946, with the hardest part of the war rationing all but over, Williams and his wife drove up along the Mohawk Trail in western Massachusetts to Charlemont for a two week's vacation. Two young women, Helen Grieder and Ruth Borklund, who had formerly worked in the Passaic National Bank, had decided to settle up in Charlemont and earn a living by converting an early nineteenth century house located on upland pasture into an inn. They called the place *Viewcrest* and they had learned to run it pretty much themselves, keeping only one man on the place, Helen Grieder's eighty-three-year-old father, an old Swiss from Basle, whose job it was to prepare the vegetables for the guests and keep an old tom named District out of the house. The only other man around was a neighbor, Horace Warfield, of old Yankee stock, born in the farm perched on the hilltop above *Viewcrest.*

Though Williams met the farmer and liked him, liked his ways and his Yankee speech—he was "extremely able and intelligent"—and though Williams and Floss spent hours walking over the farmer's property following the streams and examining the various ferns in the area—Warfield, called Tilford in Williams' story—he appears in *Country Rain* only in a segment of a home movie made by Helen Grieder. This absence of the male except indirectly reminds us of Williams' use of the movies—a clip from Eisenstein's suppressed Marxist film, *Viva Mexico*—to present the Mexican peasant in *Paterson 2,* on which he was about to begin work again. But the absence of the male from the female (Mary, the Italian immigrant woman) on Garrett Mountain also registers as a sign of divorce, and it is a strategy which mutely but powerfully reinforces the independence of the two women from the male in **"Country Rain."**

As simple as Williams' story looks on its surface, however, as though it were little more than a verbal transcript of several inconsequential conversations which seem to go nowhere, this is really a complex story whose multifoliate meanings keep slipping away from the reader. During this vacation Williams himself was working primarily on an essay on Ezra Pound's *Cantos* and literary influence, an essay which took the form of a letter to an Australian editor [*Briarcliff Quarterly,* Vol. 3.2, October 1946]. The key point of that essay (Creeley for one thought it one of Williams' most important pieces) is no doubt Williams' rejection of literary androgyny, in which "the classics . . . father every thought," by which he means something like Harold Bloom's male-to-male and text-to-text literary development.

But that sort of lineage, Williams' insists, leads to sterility. For there is another source, he points out, which is every bit as important as the first, though we often take it for granted, or worse, are blind to it. And that is the pressure of the present moment, of the language as it is actually spoken, with its infinite subtleties and constant idiomatic and rhythmic mutations. That complementary source, Williams suggests, is what he calls by analogy the feminine, the fructifying female, the mother tongue. Where Pound, then, has come to rely too heavily on prior texts and not enough on the spoken word, Williams believes, Pound's work will become dry and lifeless. Williams, of course, is thinking of his own risks in *Paterson* and of the importance of getting figures not like Jefferson and Adams and Confucius into the fabric of his poem, but rather the letters of an angry and frustrated woman and some of Paterson's early history into the text as well. No wonder Williams laughed with relief listening to the idiom of western Massachusetts farmers during his vacation, a language he found as fresh and as varied as the ferns and apples grown locally on these small hill farms, something distinctively in the American grain, as it still is.

But how is Williams' preoccupation with words translated into this story about two women? It is a complex issue and perhaps one which Williams does not so much answer as present to us for us to answer. We know he could offer his opinions when the mood moved him, as he did in a story he published back in 1918 when he was thirty-four. In **"The Buffalos"** he had also talked about women and women's rights and the division of power. Let women have all the political power, he had mused somewhat simplistically and sardonically, and send men out to the plains like herds of buffalo to hunt and fish and fight:

> Then once a year, at the proper times certain women of the cities would send out chosen emissaries, eunuchs perhaps, to treat with the tribes—then in the pink of condition, trained, hardened by their rigorous life out of doors—and those most able, most vigorous, most desirable would be admitted for the breeding.

That is Williams at thirty-four. At sixty-two he had softened somewhat, though the attraction-repulsion between the sexes remains a mystery to him. He has also learned how to tell a better story.

Consider for example the narrative frame of **"Country Rain."** It's vacation time for Williams and the small group of teachers and the Diesel engineer who have come together to this country inn. But the rain threatens to spoil their fun. It has been raining and looks as if it will continue to rain, and in fact Williams complains afterwards about how cold and generally vile the weather had been while he'd been in western Massachusetts. The weather: a condition everyone talks about—as Mark Twain said—but about which nobody does anything. And so with the real issue of the story: the nature of relationships between the sexes. Everybody talks about men and women, but who has the answers? And what answers will resolve the complex tensions between the sexes? In his mid-seventies Williams would write that long after the race issue in this country had resolved itself there would still be unresolved tensions between the sexes to contend with.

Williams' strategies in many of his mature stories are so extraordinary and yet so simple that we are in danger of simply missing them, for the problem is not only within us, the problem is that we ourselves are part of the problem. Another part of the problem of course is the language we use and the sorts of implied value judgments we are forever making, as if the language itself would answer the questions when there may not even be any questions. "If this were Switzerland, I thought," Williams begins his story, "we'd call it lovely: wisps of low cloud rising slowly among the heavy wooded hills. But since it's America we call it simply wet." And Floss, two pages later, telling Williams that in fact the place is just that: lovely. "There are so many things lovely about this place," Floss says, "and the charming atmosphere of it!" Cross purposes? A comic misreading? Or just the way we talk past each other—*and ourselves*—a hundred times a day?

The answer of how we read these lines depends on whether a man is doing the reading, or a woman. "The charming atmosphere of it," Floss notes. And Williams answers: "That's the girls—and the others." And Floss: "Vegetables taste so sweet." And Williams: "That's because they're so fresh." Because, because . . . simple cause and effect. Everything neatly tied up with answers. Williams knows men in particular tend to think this way, by habit. So the other man with Williams, a Diesel engineer from New Jersey on vacation, as he and Williams watch a Diesel shunting an empty freight into a siding along the Deerfield River in the valley below the inn. "No," George the engineer explains, "they're not clean, you can't say that [George just in fact having said precisely that]—but they got a big future." And then Williams' comment: "It was something, here on vacation from the big city, which he could talk about with authority." The need to speak with authority.

Or take George's other speech, about the fire which destroyed Mr. Tilford's house in February, so that the volunteer fire department could do nothing but watch the flames consume the house and all of its possessions. Williams too laments the loss. "I'll bet they had some pretty fine old things in there too," he says. "What a shame to lose them that way." And George answers—with knowing authority—"That's the way it is." The finality of the comment answers for the meaning of fate itself.

A key word: authority. Speech for many men seems practical, assertive, authoritative. You say something and that's the way it is. Take language itself, for example, and meaning. Who is not an authority on the words if not Williams? And yet, and yet . . . he knows that the words continue to slip away, that at the heart of the experience there is a mystery, the smile of La Giaconda. "Leonardo / saw it," Williams writes in his late poem "Tribute to the Painters," the "it" slippery, but suggesting perhaps the word Logos, as meaning, the design from without: "Leonardo saw it, / the obsession / and ridiculed it / in *La Giaconda*."

Design, Williams says, is from within, is something imposed on a complex mystery—that which remains other—and which will not reveal itself. But the women among themselves also seem to have their own kind of quiet authority. They listen to men or ignore them as they wish. And it is Floss who tells her husband, in talking about two of the other guests—two elderly school teachers—not to worry about them interacting with the other more worldly guests, for she is sure they "know what it's all about."

But do they? And do we? And what about men and women? Do they really need each other, then? Look at Ruth and Helen, the dark Helen, a woman with his mysterious mother's name, a reminder of the one whose face launched, we say. . . . How explain the relationship between these two women, who have so ably managed to divide the work of a paying household between them? Watching the home movies of Ruth and Helen working the place, the other women act as a kind of chorus, lending their implicit support to what in the east was a daring experiment in living some forty years ago:

> Helen is all for the movies; Ruth takes the still shots and does all her own developing and printing. Helen and her sister do the cooking and Ruth does all the baking, said one of the women in a low voice. Her mother takes care of the rooms.

But we have questions. What about the heavy work, the work usually assigned to men as the physically stronger of the species? And what about sexuality and the propagation of the race? These questions are "answered" as well as the story develops, not of course in front of the women, but in private, between Williams and Floss as they take a quiet morning drive up into the hills and across an old covered bridge (closed to traffic) and down a quiet country road in rain.

Floss wonders if Ruth will ever get married. After all, she's young, pretty, and men are attracted to her. Then, as so often happens when the real issue is other than the one being discussed, something like an antagonistic dialectic is set up between the man and the woman: "Be done with men and all that sort of thing if she likes it; that's her business," Floss says to the man she has been married to for the past thirty-three years. But then she adds, thinking in terms of her own priorities and her own necessarily limited knowledge: "But she's too pretty and smart to have it last, I think." What does this suggest? That the social and sexual pressures on a woman are too great to be successfully avoided? An unstated complicity on the part of most heterosexual people—men *and* women—to get the qualified unmarried out of that condition and into marriage?

But instead of demurring, protesting that there is more to this attraction and fear between the sexes than drayhorse drudgery or the yearly implantation of the seed, Williams seems to agree, complicating the issue as men often do by using what women perceive as an aggressive sort of self-protecting irony. As a baby doctor he can speak on this issue as well with some authority. He knows that women "can get along all right together without a man, unless they want an alligator in the bathtub or something of the sort."

Floss ignores the crude alligator metaphor and continues her own train of thought. Granted, women do need men, she says, the way a farmer occasionally needs a horse. "But if they have ability and aren't particularly amused by sexual diversions they can get along all right; even save time and energy for more productive things." What these more productive things are she does not enumerate, but we have seen one example of productivity in the rows of jars of beans and tomatoes and other vegetables stacked neatly in the cellar. And another example—as surely Williams knows—is writing itself, surely one "more productive" way of spending one's time away from sexual diversion. (Remember that a few months earlier Williams had had the protagonist of his fragmentary improvisation, **"Man Orchid,"** typing away late into the night while his wife, getting angrier and angrier, had told him that all he was really doing with that typewriter was playing with himself.)

The discussion tapers off—its various points made. Yet Williams continues to drive on. But look at what has been left unsaid or only implied. In this philosophical disquisition, like something out of a book on Eugenics or Thomas More's *Utopia,* what may escape us is that it is a woman and a man who are addressing each other, alone, in a car, on a road closed to traffic, as if the scene were a re-enactment of Adam and Eve in the Garden. Floss has even repeated her husband's phrasing in responding to her husband: "Women can get along all right," Williams says, and Floss responds a moment later: "They can get along all right." But where Williams goes on to qualify his comment with an "unless," Floss follows her comment with a more emphatic comment: women can get along all right without men AND this would "even save time and energy for more productive things."

We are at an impasse. Both Adam and Eve have spoken, as if with authority, on the issue of women's independence. The thing can be done, just as Williams would admit such independence can in large degree be achieved by men. So there. But this is not a pro- or anti-feminist tract Williams is writing and, happily, this is not where he chooses to end his story. Instead, poet that he is, Williams provides us with an image, a silence, a rock with its attendant tree to meditate upon. The image is worse than the complicated jigsaw puzzle he'd seen the women trying to solve in the dining room of the inn the day before. Now Williams suddenly stops the car in the rain and backs up, he explains to Floss, to look at a rock.

Interestingly, no words transpire between Williams and Floss as they look hard at it. For Williams seems simply to present the rock itself as an "answer" to the issues the two have raised. What Williams suggests here is that language itself—especially dialogue—has been able to take this man and woman only so far, an antagonistic co-operation active between them, where the deeper attractions and needs and potentially murderous differences between

the interested parties are obliquely felt but left unstated. If Williams could have described the rock without words at this point and instead given us the experience of the rock itself, he probably would have. But, as Apeneck Sweeney say, "I gotta use words when I talk to you." And so, with a show of objectivity, Williams presents the rock itself: a permanence, being itself, primordial, being carrying on a dialogue with itself, like the small stream in the "intense silence" of this ruined garden, "talking to itself among the stones."

Listen, Williams says—and he sounds very much like a Zen master at this juncture—listen to the rock in the midst of it all:

> The rock lay at about eye level close to my side of the road, the upper surface of it sloping slightly toward me with the hillside. Not a very big rock. What had stopped me was the shaggy covering which completely inundated it. The ferns, a cropped-short, dark-green fern, was the outstanding feature, growing thickly over an underlying cover of dense moss. But there was also a broad-leafed vine running lightly among the ferns, weaving the pattern together.

> That wasn't all. The back portion of the rock, which wasn't much larger than the top of an ordinary dining-room table slightly raised at one side and a little tilted supported both the rotten stump of a tree long since decayed but, also, a brother to that tree—coming in fact from the same root and very much alive, as big as a man's arm, a good solid arm—a ten-foot tree about whose base a small thicket of brambles clustered. Ferns of three sorts closed in from the sides completing the picture. A most ungrammatical rock.

A most ungrammatical rock. Williams slips in at the end, watching his readers and throwing the whole image onto a new self-conscious level of language. A reality, a thing, even a pattern, which refuses to reveal any meaning beyond itself. A rock and moss and ferns, a living tree and a dead, the living stemming from the root of the dead, and "brother" to that tree. A rock outside of our ordering, as if to say that what we call meanings are like the moss on the rock, added afterwards: that at the core of thought itself there is not a prescription, a grammar, or a text, but a rock atop which there is the disorder of brambles and—simultaneously—the weaving of a pattern together. Men and women will continue to be attracted to each other in a symbiosis, attracted AND repelled, needing each other and stemming out of each other, woman from man, man out of woman, a mystery of which—like country rain—we are forever complaining that we get either too little or too much.

But the story is still not quite over. Williams spots some raspberries growing along the road and tells Floss to stay where she is while he picks some to share with her. How are we to read this gesture, then? The protective male telling the woman to stay in out of the rain? Surely Floss could handle the weather as well as her husband, which is one of the reasons Williams married Floss in the first place. Or is the gesture a caring for the other, a generosity, an ornament in our behavior towards the other, male or female, done for the same reason Ruth had grown gourds: for the gourd flowers and for the gourds themselves, useless, except that, as Floss says in a phrasing very dear to Williams: that the useless flower is a beautiful thing. How are we to read the motives for our words? Pascal's imaginary sister might have a field day with this scene.

Yes, but. . . . Floss accepts the gesture and the gift of raspberries from her husband, extending the gesture of generosity—double-edged though it might be—to include the others. Nor is her response lost on her husband: "Perhaps we could stop again here tomorrow and pick enough for everybody," she offers. She has even come to accept the inevitable rain for the sake of the farmers, turning the fact of the rainy weather into a generous gesture extended outward toward the farmers who at least profit from the wet.

And at the very end of the story, as an afterthought which is anything but, Floss adds: "Do you think Ruth will ever marry?" To which Williams replies, as much to us and himself as to Floss: Why?

Why indeed. That is precisely the question.

## Robert F. Gish  (essay date 1989)

SOURCE: "Rare Presences: *The Knife of the Times* and *Life Along the Passaic River*," in *William Carlos Williams, A Study of the Short Fiction*, G. K. Hall & Co., 1989, pp. 39-78.

[*In the following excerpt, Gish elucidates the thematic, stylistic, and technical characteristics of Williams's short fiction.*]

Williams's first two volumes of short stories, *The Knife of the Times* (1932) and *Life Along the Passaic River* (1938), represent the kinds of "rare presences" he found as a doctor in his various encounters with his patients and with people in general; in listening to what they said and how they said it—with the ear not just of a physician formulating a diagnosis or prescription but of a poet tuned in for the music and dance of their words and voicings. Williams's stories are records of those times, those meetings, those places, and of his remembering of them; they are his attempt to turn case history into story and back again through writing. His stories become their own kind of rare presences both as things in and of themselves and in relation to each other. Williams's own rare presence permeates all of the stories—a "new meaning beginning to intervene," the "poetry" under the language that represents the lives of the people who are his characters, his life and his character as author-narrator.

Outside of two or three of the eleven stories in *The Knife of the Times*—namely "Old Doc Rivers," "The Colored

Girls of Passenack—Old and New," and the titular story, "The Knife of the Times"—the eight other stories are relatively neglected by critics, as is the volume as a whole, which has been overlooked in favor of *Life Along the Passaic River* and, most certainly, *In the American Grain. Knife,* admittedly, includes only about one quarter of his stories, and early ones at that. But the stories in this first volume are some of Williams's finest, and reveal some of the techniques—style, structure, point of view, and theme—that he carried through and developed in his later stories and that mark the "presence" of a Williams story.

> **Given Williams's interest in storytelling, it is not surprising that his stories thus often take the form of stories within stories, making for multiple narrators and for a succession of linked stories rather than for predictable and formulaic frame narratives.**
>
> **—Robert F. Gish**

Much of what characterizes his stories must be demonstrated by analyzing individual stories, and by noting comparisons between them. Williams would be the first to admit that different readers find different things to see in a story: "So, let's look at short stories and see what CAN be done with them. How many ways they CAN be written, torturing the material in every way we can think of—from which YOU are to draw what you want." There are, however, a few general traits that bear mention as well as more extensive comment in the discussions below. Williams's stories, it must be reiterated, gain much of their motive and nature from the process of storytelling itself, from the oral tradition and the ancient native voice; he was preoccupied with the native voice, the American idiom, and dedicated himself to finding and experiencing it in daily life. By transferring the voice and the experiences to writing, Williams made a lasting thing out of those experiences for himself and for readers.

Given Williams's interest in storytelling, it is not surprising that his stories thus often take the form of stories within stories, making for multiple narrators and for a succession of linked stories rather than for predictable and formulaic frame narratives. The stories are often recounted in series or layers, much as an event might be related by various individuals, from various perspectives, to one central inquisitor or listener trying to make sense of it all, or trying to find the truth of the matter and then to relate that through the larger telling, which is the frame or "container" identifiable by title as the Williams story.

Significantly, this is the method and form of the case study, written by the scientist or investigator who knows that there are many sides to any story, many versions of character or action or setting that may appear as "truth." This method is also reminiscent of gossip, of hearing and telling about a person and what happened or did not happen to that person, from people who knew, each in their own way, portions of the story, who may have added to the story or even fabricated portions of it. These case stories or reports, or gossipy stories told to an inquisitor-listener who then relates incidents—often in retrospect—give an abiding anecdotal quality to a Williams story. This is not to say that his stories are completely without plot, or without sequenced events. Rather, even in stories that utilize sequenced events and motives, plot takes a decidedly anecdotal and digressive turn. Given an implied listener, Williams's stories seem like a prose variant of the dramatic monologue.

In keeping with their "oral," anecdotal, conversational, reportorial quality, his stories offer some fascinating examples of dialogue that is not really dialogue so much as it is, again, reporting, partially because the reporting is reported as it was reported. Moreover, the narrator does not pronounce judgment on the significance of these conversations. There is, however, more editorializing, more political and moral judgment, more overall value judgment in a Williams story than is commonly pointed out. There are, too, implicit judgments to be drawn, but by and large Williams's stories are not explicitly didactic in the sense that they draw a heavy-handed moral, unless the point is not to draw a moral, certainly not a "puritanical" moral. This is not to say that there is no moral center in his stories, at times even moral indignation. Williams's moral center, his "opinions" are decidedly not bourgeois, at least not overtly. His middle-classness, such as it is—physician, family man, citizen—is subservient to a more radical, left-of-center posturing and self-dramatization.

Because Williams is writing his stories quickly, with a brush stroke here and a fling of paint there (as he describes the process), the spontaneity, as technique, determines some of the form of the story; exposition blends with dialogue, the present of the story proper blends with the present (now the past) of the story related to the principal narrator (for example, the narrator closest in time, place, and psyche to Williams the man, but oftentimes a persona, variously close to or distanced from Williams himself). As a result, there is limited use of quotation and transition, unlike the more traditional short stories of Williams's day.

In terms of personae, point of view, and tone, Williams's stories are, like his other prose fiction, highly autobiographical. A doctor very much like Williams, with a wife like Flossie, with two sons like Williams's, with friends like Williams's, with a philosophy like Williams's, and so on, is quite often the principal narrator. Despite these similarities, the stories are ultimately fiction and not autobiography. At a minimum all characters' names are changed—a need Williams learned with a vengeance when he was used for not doing so in **"The Five Dollar Guy,"** a story he had tucked away in a drawer and later submitted to the *New Masses* (in 1926) without changing the names as he had intended. The evolution of case history into story, however, goes much beyond mere cosmetic name changes. The vernacular voicings, especially of the narrator, but also of the characters; the finely pared and crafted structures—patterns, rhythms, openings and closures; the usually ironic and oftentimes cynical tonalities; the minimalist "style" and "presence" that is uniquely Williams—all of these ingredients work the marvelous transformations of art.

The case study as source and foundational form notwithstanding, the narrator in these stories, particularly in the early stories, is not always a doctor. Roughly half of the stories in **Knife** are not stories told by a doctor, nor are they, strictly speaking, about a doctor—though the overall attitude of the narrator and/or persona behind the narrator is keenly aware—as a writer and chronicler of humanity and mortality must be aware—of the miseries, "la tristeza," of the human condition as a doctor stereotypically is thought to be. When Williams's stories are about neither physicians nor writers as such, they are nevertheless, invariably (albeit oftentimes obliquely) about the writing process, and most expressly about the storytelling process.

Williams's diction is for the most part decidedly casual and, in keeping with whatever character is speaking, utterly colloquial. The common language of ordinary working class, not particularly well-educated Americans—the "American idiom"—pervades each story. There are also, however, instances in which highly technical language, usually medical language, intervenes. "Profanity" occurs, but there is never "obscene" language as such, for as iconoclastic and "shocking" as he is, Williams makes an attempt to tone down, for the sake of literary presentation or public reception, the blue hues of the people's language and his own language. In his letters and notes to friends and other writers his use of the vernacular illustrates just how fully he toned down his own eloquent use of profanity for the more public, artistically crafted stories—texts especially susceptible to public standards of taste or editorial censorship in the 1920s and 1930s.

Certainly the places Williams writes about and the kind of people he writes about (including himself as dramatized by his narrators and characters) give his stories the stamp of local color. In **Knife** he echoes local colorists of Rahv's "Red Skin" variety, such as Mark Twain and company. Somewhat more refined voicings are also heard—Hardy, T. F. Powys (in his village sketches), and behind these the austere voice of George Crabb. And ever so seldom, in a story like **"Hands Across the Sea,"** even Henry James is heard—he is present in the writing to the extent that he is being rejected and replaced by what Williams considered his better ear for American place and people. In more general terms, perhaps part of Williams's voice is the voicing of the modern, an Arnoldian "plangent threnody" of recognition of the "buried life," the Sophoclean tragic "turbid ebb and flow of human misery," flowing mysteriously from the Aegean to the English Channel to the Passaic River, turning, anxious and forlorn, not so much on the intruding forces of naturalism as on the anguish met firsthand by a physician working with disease, illness, and death in the cutting and killing times of the American depression.

The stories in *Knife* are not all depression stories in any all-encompassing sense, in the sense that all the characters depicted are not suffering as a direct result of poverty or economic reversal caused by the failure of the economy. The "knife" and the "times" in the title may well be seen as metaphors for cuts in and cutbacks to the amenities otherwise available in more solvent, stable times. The "knife," however, as it appears literally and figuratively in these stories, takes on many different meanings. In one sense the knife is the stress, the neurosis, the anxiety caused by modern living—separations caused by city/country, love/hate, health/sickness, and other lesions associated with family and self, husband and wife, parent and child, individual and others, home and homelessness, youth and age, or, more uniformly in these stories, of middle age set against youth and old age. Not only are many of these stories "couples" stories or "love" stories that deal with the battle of the sexes, they also deal with the crises of middle age, and appropriately so, given that Williams himself was facing the personal and artistic crossroads of middle age when he turned to writing stories. In certain instances the "knife" is a cutting tongue of verbal insults and abuses; in other instances it is the looming threat of insanity and nervous breakdown, of losing control of one's life, one's job, one's mental as well as physical health. In some instances it is the "knife" of drug addiction and alcoholism; of homosexual rather than heterosexual yearnings; of racism and rape and violence in real and imagined forms; of apprehension about and recognition of infidelity—the "knife" that cuts the knot of marriage, of human emotional and sexual solidarity, whether of lovers, friends, or fellow human beings. In some instances the knife is one of jealousy, of real and metaphorical back stabs and gut stabs and violent assault. As a backdrop to some of the stories, World War I presents one version of the metaphorical "knife." In rare instances it is a literal scalpel, used to remove surgically a major disease or tumor or to perform something as minor as circumcision, tonsillectomy, or appendectomy. And in a somewhat more far-fetched sense the knife is not just the tongue but the pen, the stories themselves that bring to the reader short, close cuts of "realism," slices of life. There are then many ramifications of the title in these early stories, ramifications of theme and character and form, of style and technique, which though capable of being isolated in these stories also carry over to Williams's other stories, to his other prose works, and to his longer poetry.

In *The Knife of the Times,* Williams is in a real sense not just involved in a literary experiment or a literary creation for its own sake; he is working through, in writing as healing, his own doubts and despairs as a man who is compelled—like Coleridge's Mariner or the poet persona of Wordsworth—to give relief through a timely utterance and thereby avoid the despondency and madness that comes from an inability to express something akin to "emotion recollected in tranquility" in the face of the observable. There is a certain dimension of the romantic crisis lyric, as well as the conversation poem, in these stories, which

also owe something of their form, as well as their impulse, to the tradition of the biographical sketch or life telling, the autobiographical confessional.

"Hands across the Sea" is particularly revealing of Williams's autobiography; however, in **"Mind and Body,"** **"The Colored Girls of Passenack,"** and **"Old Doc Rivers,"** Williams also makes appearances as narrator/character that place him as close as possible to his actual self. This quartet of stories does not represent his best stories (except, perhaps, **"Doc Rivers"**), only some of his most characteristically autobiographical. These four stories provide Williams with the means and ways of looking at some of the knives of his own disturbing middle age as his autobiographical presence (who he was able to become as a good, productive male and human, and who he might have been, in the fashion of Conrad's Kurtz in the potential of his own and humanity's darker self) shuttles back and forth, in and out of the stories. If one recognizes Williams's presence in these four stories, his already very much felt presence in companion stories is made yet more easily identifiable if we compare **"Hands"** (to mention just one of the most directly autobiographical quartet) with **"The Knife of the Times"** and **"The Sailor's Son"** (where the psychic and physical unions and splits involve more bizarre sexuality), and with **"A Visit to the Fair," "An Old Time Raid," "Pink and Blue," "The Buffalos,"** and **"A Descendant of Kings"** (where the unions and separations run the gamut of age, friendship, marriage and parentage). . . .

In **"Mind and Body"** Williams's fictional counterpart is the unnamed doctor and friend who listens to and examines an unnamed woman patient. Only the patient's husband, Yates, and the doctor's wife, Emily, are known by name. The main characters—doctor and patient—are not named, and effectively so, since they know each other well, both as friends and as patient/doctor. The woman patient and Yates are, moreover, family friends. Because of the relative anonymity of the characters Williams achieves a kind of authenticity about the confidentiality obligatory between doctor and patient. Names seem to be changed or not given to protect Williams's actual patients and friends.

The setting for this story, the doctor's home with an office upstairs, is very similar to Williams's own residence at 9 Ridge Road in Rutherford. The place is in the northeast—for all practical purposes, New Jersey—and the ambiance is urban. Much of the story involves the doctor's attempts to diagnose what ails the woman, her attempts to explain her symptoms, and in the process her beliefs and opinions on a number of subjects. The knife that is whittling down this patient is anxiety concerning just what is wrong with her and how it relates to what has been wrong with her in the past: her operation some eighteen years ago, and her nervous breakdown, which placed her in a hospital for a time, a hospital where she met Yates, a man with his own kind of problems.

Their conversation is followed by the doctor's physical examination of the woman. Both the mind and the body of the patient are thus considered and ministered to by a physician who offers advice on sexual matters and marriage in a most matter-of-fact way—especially since the physician goes to the extent of telling the woman that perhaps she needs a woman to love rather than a man. The woman's husband, Yates, seems much more the friend than the lover; but there is no real evidence in the story that the woman actually would prefer a female lover in place of Yates. Maybe she prefers a more masculine one—like the doctor, for their "appointment," has its erotic overtones. (This same kind of acceptance of lesbianism and homosexuality as either a biological or a psychological fact pervades Williams's other stories that address the subject, including **"The Knife of the Times"** and **"The Sailor's Son."**)

**"Mind and Body"** has a convincing air of reality about it: the physician knows his stuff and demonstrates wide past experience as well as familiarity with the latest research found in professional journals. From the attitudes and methods demonstrated one can infer some of the techniques Williams no doubt approved of and demonstrated in his own methods and bedside, examining room manner as a physician. To a certain extent the physician acts more like a psychoanalyst than a general practitioner.

What is impressive about the story, and unusual by today's impersonal clinical standards, is the extent to which the physician talks to the woman as a friend and even escorts her to the bus stop, insisting that she and her husband return for a visit. The basis for this relationship only partially resides in the fact that the doctor and woman are friends. They discuss religion, education, culture, medicine—many subjects all of which ultimately have a bearing on the woman's condition—and on her relationship to her husband. One infers that in Williams's assumptions of what a doctor does, both "mind and body" are important, and society is both part of the ailment and the cure. As in the prototypical portrait of the physician of an earlier era, this doctor, like a writer, listens and counsels, proving very much a human being and not a sterile, faultless scientist detached from the humanity he serves.

As in **"Hands Across the Sea,"** couples—the woman and Yates, the doctor and Emily—again provide a pattern that Williams uses to great effect to describe the patient-doctor/husband-wife types here. Both marriages are vulnerable to being cut asunder given the numerous pressures of the time, such as the selfishness or narcissism announced in the woman's half-believed assertion, which is the first sentence of the story: "For ourselves are we not each of us the center of the universe?" Williams both gives evidence of egocentrism as a true and almost instinctive aspect of life and attempts, through the words and actions of the physician and his wife, to disprove this view. Not only mind and body but minds and bodies need contact, need to converse, need to care reciprocally about each other.

Williams fuses the woman's narrations with the doctor's narrations, her past and her present, in such a way—without the use of quotation marks or paragraphing, for example—to underscore visually on the page the story's need

for greater fusing and welding of hitherto disparate architectonic parts. The woman, as well as the doctor, is quite opinionated about literature, art, and cultural issues, and yet they are both listening to each other and in key instances conceding points of argument to each other. It is no happenstance that the woman is trained in logic and very intelligent and that the doctor is operating throughout by means of the logical processes taught him.

As intelligent and intellectual and reasonable as the doctor and the patient are, they both hold out for a certain pragmatic primitivism, a superstitious belief in what works over what is explainable in their culture's logic about mind and body. She believes in intuition and "second sight," or animal knowledge. And the doctor does not refute her—he even agrees. Although people view the woman as a "nut" and an eccentric, and conjecture that much of her problem is imagined, she knows, as does the doctor, that natural remedies and nostrums, even superstitious religious ceremonials, can be effective—if there is belief. The doctor/narrator advises that everyone should avoid priests with only one answer, one way to be saved, saying that a ceremonial dance by a medicine man "with beating of tom toms to conduct . . . [him] into the other world" would be more comforting "than the formula of some kindly priest." Williams himself preferred the "poetry" of the satyrs, as he says in *Paterson*. And his analogue Evans in **"The Venus"** carries the emblematic arrowhead in his pocket, ready to express its secrets to those who care. But the arrowhead is emblematic of much more than words—as are the satyrs. A similar "no one has all the answers" attitude is also found in **"Doc Rivers."**

Williams's own individualism as a writer, his iconoclasm in the face of traditions of one kind or another, carry over to his characterizations found here in the woman and in the characters of other stories: the story asserts the implicit value of individualism, even quirky individualism. Intellectually, the woman sets herself above many of her former doctors who, she thinks, do not even understand her charts and the terminology on them to the extent that she does. As she tells the doctor her history, offers him her biography, the doctor is simultaneously drawing conclusions based on what he hears and what he is observing—and these processes, too, are blended with the woman's narrative in such a way as to make the disparate pieces whole, and his thinking process organic to the woman's "storytelling," which is her case, her life. The doctor, in coming finally to what he believes is the right diagnosis—attributes her symptoms not so much to a pathological condition ("mucous colitis" or intestinal spasms) as to an anatomical basis (her "short more inert [capillary] loops which account for [her] more lethargic demeanor")—offers an explanation of first causes: "apparently [it] was laid down in the germ plasm when you were created." The diagnosis tends to have a calming effect on the woman, because it helps her to accept who she is, how she came to be herself. As simple and all-inclusive as the explanation is, it does give her a better sense of what is wrong with her. It seems as good an explanation as any for her anxiety, reconciling in a way that other doctors had yet to do, her "mind and body."

At the end of the story, what the woman tells Emily—whose place in life is as a housekeeper, looking after her husband—is contrary to what she says as the story opens. Now she asserts that "we must live for others, that we are not alone in the world and we cannot live alone." In part she knows this before she visits the doctor; but the doctor, in his actions and in his listening to her case history, and in his willingness to talk with her and express his own views, has had a healing effect on the woman. One also knows, and can infer from the telling, that the doctor has benefited from the rather bizarre (yet natural) visit from this woman and her nervous, rare presence as a person. . . .

The other stories in *Knife* have little to do directly with physicians or with Williams's autobiography, at least his life as a doctor. Williams is not as present—at least some of the more prominent and documented aspects of his life as a physician or husband are not as present—in these relatively lesser-known stories. They do, however, reveal a physician's (and a writer's) caring involvement with the miseries of humanity. Furthermore, most of these stories share with the other stories in the volume a concern with couples, their fidelities and infidelities, their bondings and their separations—all set against the cutting tensions of individual and social hard times: homosexual psychic and physical unions and splits; young and old; longtime friends and cronies; mail-order bride and crazed husband; would-be patriarch and liberated wife; mother and son; sons and lovers.

**"The Knife of the Times"** and **"The Sailor's Son"** have received more critical attention than **"A Visit to the Fair,"** **"An Old Time Raid," "The Buffalos," "A Descendant of Kings,"** and **"Pink and Blue."** But Williams's stylistic presence is so successful in all of these stories that one can only wish he had written fewer stories about the physician's life and more stories like these, which go about their business outside of the more focused world of doctors and medicine. This is not to say that these stories are not autobiographical, for they still deal with the crises of middle age that Williams faced, and they allow him a way to objectify some of these crises, empathetically, through self-as-other portrayals. . . .

In **"An Old Time Raid,"** and **"The Sailor's Son,"** the two sets of male friends try to survive the pressures against their mutual personal commitment. In the former story that commitment is rowdy friendship; in the latter story the commitment is rowdy homosexual love. Moreover, in the latter story the male companionship is set against the complications of two women—one a disapproving employer of young Manuel, the other an assenting fiancée who is not bothered in the least by his carousing in the haystack with the wild motorcycler and bad influence from the city: "the Kid."

**"An Old Time Raid"** is one of Williams's most colloquial stories. Another retrospective accounting of a friend's life, the narrator here relates some of the wild times of his youth with a crazy prankster of a fellow—a good but wild old buddy, Dago Schultz. As such, the story functions as a eulogy of sorts both to the memory of Schultz and to the good old days when a fellow could carouse through the town with a friend. Prank follows prank, mischief follows mischief as the narrator confesses to some meanness carried out with Schultz one day in New York City. They raid restaurants, fruit stands, theaters, businesses and disturb the civic peace and order, hastening a police raid or two.

> In *Passaic* more than in any other collection of his stories, memorable characters come to the forefront as living people, people with names and desires that at once typify and transcend their kind.
>
> —*Robert F. Gish*

Williams's expert handling of the opening and the ending of the story makes it clear that Dago's days are surely numbered. In the opening paragraph (which deals with events some three years later) he is presumably clipped by "a freight coming from nowhere in the opposite direction." But that destiny is not known for sure until the ending, and the ending of the story is nicely reflexive to the opening as the reader learns conclusively from the narrator and crony, "Well, whether he was drunk or not or just didn't see, as he swung out after getting a grip on the rail, a freight coming from nowhere . . . , just clipped him—." It is a fitting outcome for Dago's life, another aspiring roamer, a free-spirited hobo whose freedom and daring lead to death. The consolation, and another ironic, ambivalent one, is that he literally did not know what hit him and thus went out in his own kind of style and gory glory.

Schultz's kindred spirit in **"The Sailor's Son"** is "the Kid," a free spirit who leads a gang of motorcycle rebels lawlessly through the city streets, and every now and again goes out to the country for a sexual tryst with young Manuel, who is employed by Mrs. Cuthbertson. Once she is aware of what she considers outrageous goings on, Mrs. Cuthbertson orders a stop to it and fires Manuel. Manuel's lovesick and lonesome attitude, his longings for both the Kid's attentions and for letters and visits from his fiancée, Margy, and Mrs. Cuthbertson's overall outrage, are all ironically undercut by Margy's arrival on the scene and her berating of the older woman: "I am engaged to marry him, I don't care what he does. Why should you worry?" Here again, the narrator takes no puritanical stand on so-called aberrant sexual liaisons. Although Margy seems rather too nonchalant, it is her opinion that rings beyond the story—another commentary on Williams's live and let live physician's acceptance of the human condition in all its forms and manifestations. The Kid provides yet another instance of Williams's alterego, the wild and free rebel ready to live beyond the pale of society's approvals and conventions in an urban counterpart of America's former frontier. Part delinquent, part hero, he is the stuff not just of stereotype but of an American archetype that fascinated Williams—whether as aborigine, frontiersman, mountain man, cowboy, or biker.

In the much-talked-about title story, **"The Knife of the Times,"** the narrator takes a similar live-and-let-live attitude in recounting the long-pent-up lesbian love of Ethel for her old friend, "dark-eyed" Maura. Long married and the mother of six children, Ethel takes to writing passionate, seductive letters to Maura. She finally arranges a reunion in New York where she lures Maura to some pay toilets in Penn Station and makes her desires known in a passionate release of physical fondling and kissing. Maura is awakened to her own repressed love for Ethel and when asked if she would spend at least a week with her, "sleep with her," Maura decides, lucidly, carelessly, "Why not?" One "knife" in the story is the knife of long-repressed sexual desire and a desire to be free (another instance of this common proclivity) of society's expectations and conventions. "Why not?" as Maura announces it, is at once a cry of liberation and a leveling of self-restraint in the face of larger instincts. The actual descriptions of physical contact between the two women seem tame if not quaint by today's no-holds-barred erotic accounts. But in the context of the story, the passion seems anything but silly and allows the reader insights into just how far in the history of the short story the freedom to deal with issues of homosexuality has extended. In this sense Williams needs as much recognition as E. M. Forster and others whose homosexual stories were by and large only published posthumously. Whether his homosexual stories were intended by Williams as a kind of apology for those of homosexual persuasion among his painter and poet friends, or a working out of his own feelings for others of the same sex, as is suggested by Reed Whittemore about Williams and Robert McAlmon, is perhaps beside the point.

The homosexual stories in *Knife* hold forth the possibility—most especially to readers of more conventional (Williams would say puritanical) persuasion and those contemporary with the era in which these stories were written—that male-male friendship or love may be a kind of shield against female barbs and other kinds of knives of the times. Moreover, lesbian or homosexual love, if that is the person's inclination, is presented—more shockingly for Williams's time, and somewhat more ironically in the 1980s given the hysteria over AIDS—as something to be accepted without inhibitions if that is the nature of those involved. All three gender combinations—male-male, female-female, and female-male are accepted throughout Williams's early stories as ways of attempting to get through life, as observed by an author who sees human sexuality and behavior for what it is, diverse as it may be, and vulnerable as it may be, both in fidelity and infidelity, and set against the social and psychological, mental and emotional slicings of the "knife of the times."

The nineteen stories in *Life Along the Passaic River* continue some of the same themes and techniques Williams develops in *Knife.* A half dozen of these stories are among Williams's best, and at least two of them, **"The Girl with a Pimply Face,"** and **"Jean Beicke,"** are among Williams's own favorites. In *Passaic* subject and tone turn darker, tending more than in *Knife* to the cynical, the grotesque, and the tragic. Part of the darkness of these stories is attributable to the familiar "knife" of the times:

the worries, fears, and miseries of humanity, now focused more on children than on adults of middle age. Although the crises and conflicts in *Passaic* do involve adults peripherally, children's presences are closer to the center of things. Place (setting, locale, ambiance—Williams regarded "place" broadly) also assumes greater importance, reflecting Williams's belief that "In a work of art place is everything." In these stories, the Passaic River itself gives a nodality to Williams's portrayal of character and action.

Williams appears again, quite autobiographically, as the physician-writer, the narrator, the overarching persona who, in watching the Passaic and describing the urban liabilities of lives whose rare presences captivate him, is so moved to empathy that he passes beyond voyeur to participant through the telling and retelling of their lives. Few of these stories involve country interludes, retreats, farms, or the summer cottages on the shore known to the more affluent middle-class protagonists who appeared as the "employers" in *Knife.* Here there is only a provisional escape from the city squalor in which the working-class, proletarian families portrayed in *Passaic* live. Part of the cynicism and part of the hostility expressed here by Williams and his personae is due to the inequalities in class, education, income, intelligence and sensibilities between those who see and those who are seen, those who are told about and those who tell. Here, too, hard times are recorded on more than one level. Williams's own middle-class respectability and security adds to the poignancy of the disparities between class and economic status of the individuals living along the Passaic.

One thing is felt by the author and shared by the reader vividly in story after story: Williams feels the "hard history" of the people, the society, the country. And he takes his job as physician and as chronicler seriously. It is that feeling, again, that turns ordinary presences into rare ones. Williams empathizes with these individuals, with their predicament, with their humanity in a caring, far from condescending way, even though his own status in life could easily distance him from them, and cause him to be disparaging rather than empathetic.

In *Passaic* more than in any other collection of his stories, memorable characters come to the forefront as living people, people with names and desires that at once typify and transcend their kind. For example, the title story, **"Life Along the Passaic River,"** is a wonderfully tough but impassioned overview of the place and the people. Both the river and the local inhabitants of the valley virtually compel Williams and his narrator(s) to pay attention to them, to speak up for them, to say in various ventriloquisms that they matter very much in spite of the larger world's indifference, in spite, to some degree, of their own indifference. The stories could be, and usually are, capable of their own individual meanings, but read together, they gain a special rhythm and structure. As a whole, the volume personalizes the human "swarm," bringing moment and distinction to the larger, generational and historical process that Williams tried to define throughout his career, from "The Wanderer" to *Paterson,* from *In the American Grain* to *Pictures from Brueghel.* He credited

James Laughlin with saying that the form of *Passaic,* with its attention to the river as a metaphor for history, might also be well suited to a long poem—a poem that turned out to be *Paterson.* Similar presuppositions about history as process, the flowing of events and persons along time's river also infuse the organic and nature metaphors of *In the American Grain.*

In *Life Along the Passaic River* the point of view shifts and blends (now limited, then omniscient); specific scene merges with limited editorializing; vignette dissolves into vignette; showing and telling mix and separate as styles of story; the story proper is reinforced by smaller, internalized stories; the river is knowable first as place and then as idea; the historical past alternates with the present; the language, the vocabulary, the diction, the intonations not only reflect but help define the nature of these lives and their riverscape, or, conversely, the riverscape and its lives. The resultant effect is that of a large canvas done in hasty but impassioned brush strokes. The stories are all essentially Williams—person, physician, narrator, character all combined—teller and technique shaping and being shaped by subject.

As Williams the physician well knew, life is defined ultimately in terms of death and in these stories about life along the Passaic, death is always ready to intrude. This irony of death threatening life is made part of the rhythmic structure of the story in one anecdote after another. The "Polacks" in the city try to cope, like the narrator, with the predicament they are born into, generation after generation. Some, like the young anonymous male hitchhiker in one of the vignettes, possess the saving ambition of wanderlust—the gumption to leave the hometown, like Boone, and travel to "the coast." The hitchhiker at least has the story of his traveling to tell when he gets in the narrator's car. He has been to one geographical limit, found no work there or anywhere else during his journey "back again through the whole country," and now his glorious westering comes down to a ride to "Westover" just "up here a way."

The small canoe, in the summer-hot, dye-waste, polluted water of the river, which the narrator watches and describes intermittently in the story, is not really going any place very far either. The boy who made the canoe and now floats in it has fashioned hope more than anything else. Others of the youths described are resourceful, if not successful, in their schemes. The intentions of the girls are presented with an air of tragic indulgence and sympathy for their attempts to get their oversized feet into undersized shoes. The narrator's conversation with some listener other than the reader clarifies the attitude: "If your shoes fit you and they're made of good leather, if you know what good leather is, . . . you're getting somewhere. What did you say? The girls' feet look like flat tires in most of the things they don't know enough not to buy and to wear."

And in another vignette, Williams makes clear that the teenage girl lying on the autopsy slab in the hospital never went very far at all. Neither did her aborted twins. Not just children and youths but young girls especially have Williams's feeling about their hard, rare presences. The pimply-faced girl; Jean Beicke; the young Olson girl in

"The Use of Force"; this girl long gone on the slab—all of them face dead-end lives with precious few like the narrator/physician caring to help even if it is only for the sake of helping more than for wondrous "results."

The narrator does not know for sure what the dead girl's story is. She is dead, he sees, a suicide whose death was gruesome, as evidenced by the burn down her throat caused by some concoction she drank. Indignation at the probable motive and the waste of it all, and yet the possible, painful blessing of it, is heard in the narrator's Greek chorus-like judgment: "Good legs. A fine pair of breasts. Well-shaped arms. She's dead all right, and if you get what I mean, that's not such a bad thing either. But good God, what for?" Trying to deduce the details of her story is not worth it, finally, for the narrator/observer. A woman, a mother, a worker—a waste. But Williams at least makes that point. The reader is convinced that the details would be ghastly whatever they are.

Death in the form of murder along the Passaic cuts short these lives too, as the two bodies fished up out of the river testify—one of them without a head, arms, or feet. And the narrator of this vignette with his "ain'ts" and "gonnas" and "wannas" puts the case plain and hard about those who kill and are killed, "punks," and "suckers" and "gorillas" and "mugs" who as kids grow up to be either cops or criminals. All are still there—". . . they ain't moved away none; that's what I'm saying. They're still here. Still as dumb as ever."

In addition to presenting the narrator's flinging of words and throwing of voice, his impersonations of these peoples' voices and views, Williams paints heart-rending and soul-tearing verbal descriptions of the river. Two bridges, one upstream by the new Third Street Bridge between Passaic and Wallington, and the other downstream at the Country Bridge, frame the story's opening and closing. Above the Country Bridge the "Polacks" walk looking for, of all things, gold coins out of some rumored, softer past. And Williams watches them in their looking—for coins, at a diver, at each other; watches one turn up an 1864 copper coin; watches one sit amidst the roots of an upturned tree; watches young, muscular men; watches them want to see "The Babe knock it, just once, out of the lot"—laughs and says, "good luck to you." . . .

In Williams's most popular story, **"The Use of Force,"** the reader is taken again into the house of another such Passaic River family, where a strange, intimate presence is played out, a battle of wills, of love and hate, cool reason and mindless rage. A relatively simple challenge faces the physician in the story: to examine the girl's throat for infection and signs of possible diphtheria. But out of fear or defiance, the girl, Mathilda Olson, refuses to open her mouth, violently scratches at the doctor's glasses, bites a tongue depressor into splinters, and generally behaves—while in her father's lap—as if the doctor were the embodiment of the disease itself, rather than the means to a cure.

Irony compounds irony and Mathilda's mother and father make matters worse with each word they say to the child.

And Williams uses the implications of the semantics in the "argument" at hand to great effectiveness. "He won't *hurt* you," says the mother. "Hurt" is the wrong word to use and irritates the doctor—and the doctor (also the first-person narrator) makes this clear to the reader although he restrains himself in his "professional" dialogue with the parents and girl. "You *bad* girl . . . , The *nice* man . . . , You'll have to go the *hospital*," the mother continues, and Williams, again through the first-person point of view, calls attention to the words and the wrong psychology behind them. Finally he blurts out a remonstrance to the mother with her "bad girl"/"nice man [doctor]" designations: "For heaven's sake, I broke in. Don't call me a nice man to her."

Since the doctor/narrator (and behind him, Williams) is so keenly tuned to these loaded words in context, it is significant to note that he describes his own persistence toward the end of the struggle with Mathilda as "a final unreasoning *assault*," by which he "overpowers the child's neck and jaw" (my italics).

Williams utilizes his familiar undertones of violent eroticism in **"The Use of Force"** as well. The doctor's admiration for the girl's beauty (that is, he speaks of her as "an unusually attractive little thing"), which is met by devouring him with her eyes, combined with his hostility to her whimpering mother, become a kind of "rape of the girl's will." The doctor's confessed feeling of "adult shame" notwithstanding, the end justifies the means—the use of force (also exerted by the father) is necessary because Mathilda's tonsils are seriously infected. She cares nothing of such matters, however, and the story ends in her tear-blinded, furious attempt to brutalize the doctor—force returned for force—her own kind of violent attempted "rape of his will." Neither Williams nor his narrator is naive about the sexual implications of the episode. And even if the narrator says, "I had to smile to myself. After all, I had already fallen in love with the savage brat . . ." in an essentially nonliteral way, the adequacy and inadequacy of words in relation to action become a theme of the story.

"Love," "bad," "nice," "savage"—all of the words to which Williams and the narrator call attention, are useless in the face of the infection threatening the girl's very life. The doctor knows the infection is the most powerful force in the equation of forces at work in the small, squalid room. Even the word "diphtheria" with all of its forceful connotations is just a word. The force lies behind the word in the disease and in the will and anger and beauty of the girl's presence, her human essence. But words, inadequate as they are, do have a certain limited, albeit primitive, magical, incantatory persuasive force that will enable the doctor to see, to know the truth of the ailment once he can convince the girl to relinquish her stubbornness. He sees his need to open her mouth, to examine her, as stupidly but admirably thwarted by the girl's resoluteness. Does she hate him? Does he love her? The word "love," as used—perhaps intended figuratively but revealing a more subconscious literalness—and the psychology of the emotion(s) expressed, make for intriguing speculation. Life along the Passaic, like the river itself and the aborigine in Williams's psyche, has its violent, savage aspect. . . .

Although not all of the stories in ***Passaic,*** beautiful and significant as they all are, can be discussed here, two other stories do bear mentioning. **"Danse Pseudomacabre"** and **"The Accident"** (two of Williams's earliest stories, first published in 1920 and 1921, respectively) raise the general/specific, specific/general rhythm of Williams's narration to further heights of the abstract and the philosophical. For Williams was desperately trying not just to report and describe, but to piece together some meaning to the misery he witnessed, some self-reflexive, word-way of coping with it, of solacing the people, the situation and himself—of reconciling life being born unto death.

In **"Danse"** a man meditates, in a Kafkaesque way, about life and death, health and illness, time and historical process, self and others—all the metaphysical queries about being and awareness. That process, the living of life, the "doctoring" becomes "la danse" as Williams suggests. The premise from which the man's ruminations radiate is a paradox: "That which is possible is inevitable," he thinks, the "normality of every distortion to which the flesh is susceptible, every disease, every amputation." It is the paradox of death in life, of morbidity in health, of the reversals of every kind that physicians see in their training and in their daily practice as it accumulates over the years.

Much of his anxiety is personal as well as professional. He is awakened with an overwhelming sense of death. His wife, sleeping next to him, might die, he thinks. How could he bear such separation, his "boon companion annihilated"? He hears a taxi leave; hears the "finality" of the clock strike three. Other thoughts come—of death, of a will in need of endorsement, of sickroom talk, a wife's fear of her husband dying, of an unconscious baby with meningitis, presumably, infected at the baptismal font of all places, from "holy" water, a baby, who, if it lives will be an idiot. The moon and street lamps imagistically provide a funereal backdrop to his meditations. The moon's movements, the lighting, are part of the dance and the repetitious visitations of a physician, and the writings and rememberings that grow out of those visits: "And do I repeat the trouble of writing that which I have already written, and so drag another human being from oblivion to serve my music." Such an imagistic "dance" is confirmation in plotless but still "story" form of the significance, the meaning that writing stories such as this one brought to Williams, "Satyr-like," in counting out the tempos and rhythms heard against his music and giving form to his music, the dance of the river, the place where he happened to find himself, the compulsion to write out an accompaniment to the words, the sounds, "the tragic foot," the dance of life—to death.

In **"The Accident"** the vignettes that dramatize the event point out that "Death is difficult for the senses to alight on." For twelve days the speaker struggles to keep a girl alive, but death comes, finally, vividly, grotesquely: "She lies gasping her last: eyes rolled up till only the whites show, lids half open, mouth agape, skin a cold bluish white, pasty, hard to the touch—as the body temperature drops the tissues congeal."

Which is the accident, Williams seems to say, life or death? The girl's final moments are juxtaposed with another lesser accident, experienced by the narrator/physician, a minor cataclysm on a serendipitous "out-of-doors" trip in spring (a beginning, an "accident") to see four goats "down a red dirt path." The physician now becomes a man who wants to stop to show his son the goats. As in e. e. cummings's "Just Spring," the spring, the boy, the goats, the sexual urges felt by the man toward the woman in the car seat, "hips beside him," or in Williams's "Spring and All," out of all the lustful longing for life and its utter mystery of "death, a sign of life," the child must instinctively touch one of the goats. He does so. Then, walking back along the path, the child stumbles, falls full face into the dirt.

The child's falling is an accident of another kind than the girl's gasping and dying, which opens the account. Death is an accident and spring is an accident. The goats where they are, doing what they are doing as "goats," are an accident. The child's fall is an accident. The story is a kind of accident. Experience is an accident, life, the rarest presence of all, and the rarest absence, in death—all such "accidents" are the stuff of storytelling.

In **Knife** and **Passaic** Williams first tries his hand at doing all of it—the "danse," the "accident(s)," the poetry, the words of it—in short story form. And readers who happen across them, like the six wonderful, sun-drenched women who stop their work and stare, concerned, and finally laugh and wave at the child recovering from his fall, can be thankful Williams cared to tell each and every one of these hard histories, these beautiful stories.

---

## FURTHER READING

Baker, William. "Williams' 'The Use of Force'." *Explicator* 37, No. 1 (Fall 1978): 7-8.
   Suggests that "the power of the story is its sense of urgency and its brevity."

Bell, Barbara Currier. "Williams' 'The Use of Force' and First Principles in Medical Ethics." *Literature and Medicine,* Vol. 3, edited by William Claire, pp. 143-51. Albany: State University of New York Press, 1984.
   Demonstrates the value of "The Use of Force" to the field of medical ethics.

Breslin, James E. "The Fiction of a Doctor." In his *William Carlos Williams: An American Artist,* pp. 125-67. New York:

Oxford University Press, 1970.
   Surveys Williams's fiction of the 1930s, including his short stories.

Deutsch, Babette. "Gusty Tales from over Passaic Way." *New York Herald Tribune Book Review* 27, No. 16 (December 3, 1950): 5.
   Asserts that *Make Light of It* "helps us to realize the distinguishing features of [Williams's] contribution to American writing."

Gott, Peter H. A review of *The Doctor Stories,* by William Carlos Williams. *Saturday Review* 10, No. 2 (November/December 1984): 76-7.
   Mixed review, claiming that "as sociological studies, the stories have merit."

Graham, Theodora R. "A New Williams Short Story: 'Long Island Sound' (1961)." *William Carlos Williams Review* VII, No. 2 (Fall 1981): 1-3.
   Provides brief background information about the story, featuring the entire text.

Halsband, Robert. "'I Lived Among These People'." *The Saturday Review of Literature* 33 (December 9, 1950): 14-15.
   Assesses *Make Light of It,* suggesting that "whatever his ultimate reputation will be, [Williams] is one of the hardiest and healthiest shrubs on the landscape of American writing."

Pearson, Norman Holmes. "Williams Collected." *The Yale Review* LI, No. 2 (December 1962): 329-32.
   Positive assessment of *The Farmers' Daughters,* emphasizing the "local color" of Williams's stories.

Sorrentino, Gilbert. "Polish Mothers and 'The Knife of the Times'," in *Man and Poet,* edited by Carroll F. Terrell, pp. 391-95. Orono, Maine: The National Poetry Foundation, 1983.
   Investigates the linguistic patterns of "The Knife of the Times."

————. "A Dose of Strong Medicine." *The New York Times Book Review* 89 (October 21, 1984): 9.
   Favorable review of *The Doctor Stories,* remarking that "Williams was not so much telling stories as he was making forms."

Wagner, Linda W. "Williams' 'The Use of Force': An Expansion." *Studies in Short Fiction* IV, No. 4 (Summer 1967): 351-53.
   Studies "The Use of Force" in the context of Williams's other writings.

# Appendix:

## Select Bibliography of General Sources on Short Fiction

### BOOKS OF CRITICISM

Allen, Walter. *The Short Story in English*. New York: Oxford University Press, 1981, 413 p.

Aycock, Wendell M., ed. *The Teller and the Tale: Aspects of the Short Story* (Proceedings of the Comparative Literature Symposium, Texas Tech University, Volume XIII). Lubbock: Texas Tech Press, 1982, 156 p.

Averill, Deborah. *The Irish Short Story from George Moore to Frank O'Connor*. Washington, D.C.: University Press of America, 1982, 329 p.

Bates, H. E. *The Modern Short Story: A Critical Survey*. Boston: Writer, 1941, 231 p.

Bayley, John. *The Short Story: Henry James to Elizabeth Bowen*. Great Britain: The Harvester Press Limited, 1988, 197 p.

Bennett, E. K. *A History of the German Novelle: From Goethe to Thomas Mann*. Cambridge: At the University Press, 1934, 296 p.

Bone, Robert. *Down Home: A History of Afro-American Short Fiction from Its Beginning to the End of the Harlem Renaissance*. Rev. ed. New York: Columbia University Press, 1988, 350 p.

Bruck, Peter. *The Black American Short Story in the Twentieth Century: A Collection of Critical Essays*. Amsterdam: B. R. Grüner Publishing Co., 1977, 209 p.

Burnett, Whit, and Burnett, Hallie. *The Modern Short Story in the Making*. New York: Hawthorn Books, 1964, 405 p.

Canby, Henry Seidel. *The Short Story in English*. New York: Henry Holt and Co., 1909, 386 p.

Current-García, Eugene. *The American Short Story before 1850: A Critical History*. Twayne's Critical History of the Short Story, edited by William Peden. Boston: Twayne Publishers, 1985, 168 p.

Flora, Joseph M., ed. *The English Short Story, 1880-1945: A Critical History*. Twayne's Critical History of the Short Story, edited by William Peden. Boston: Twayne Publishers, 1985, 215 p.

Foster, David William. *Studies in the Contemporary Spanish-American Short Story*. Columbia, Mo.: University of Missouri Press, 1979, 126 p.

George, Albert J. *Short Fiction in France, 1800-1850*. Syracuse, N.Y.: Syracuse University Press, 1964, 245 p.

Gerlach, John. *Toward an End: Closure and Structure in the American Short Story*. University, Ala.: The University of Alabama Press, 1985, 193 p.

Hankin, Cherry, ed. *Critical Essays on the New Zealand Short Story*. Auckland: Heinemann Publishers, 1982, 186 p.

Hanson, Clare, ed. *Re-Reading the Short Story*. London: MacMillan Press, 1989, 137 p.

Harris, Wendell V. *British Short Fiction in the Nineteenth Century*. Detroit: Wayne State University Press, 1979, 209 p.

Huntington, John. *Rationalizing Genius: Ideological Strategies in the Classic American Science Fiction Short Story*. New Brunswick: Rutgers University Press, 1989, 216 p.

Kilroy, James F., ed. *The Irish Short Story: A Critical History*. Twayne's Critical History of the Short Story, edited by William Peden. Boston: Twayne Publishers, 1984, 251 p.

Lee, A. Robert. *The Nineteenth-Century American Short Story*. Totowa, N. J.: Vision / Barnes & Noble, 1986, 196 p.

Leibowitz, Judith. *Narrative Purpose in the Novella*. The Hague: Mouton, 1974, 137 p.

Lohafer, Susan. *Coming to Terms with the Short Story*. Baton Rouge: Louisiana State University Press, 1983, 171 p.

Lohafer, Susan, and Clarey, Jo Ellyn. *Short Story Theory at a Crossroads*. Baton Rouge: Louisiana State University Press, 1989, 352 p.

Mann, Susan Garland. *The Short Story Cycle: A Genre Companion and Reference Guide*. New York: Greenwood Press, 1989, 228 p.

Matthews, Brander. *The Philosophy of the Short Story*. New York, N.Y.: Longmans, Green and Co., 1901, 83 p.

May, Charles E., ed. *Short Story Theories*. Athens, Oh.: Ohio University Press, 1976, 251 p.

McClave, Heather, ed. *Women Writers of the Short Story: A Collection of Critical Essays*. Englewood Cliffs, N. J.: Prentice-Hall, 1980, 171 p.

Moser, Charles, ed. *The Russian Short Story: A Critical History*. Twayne's Critical History of the Short Story, edited by William Peden. Boston: Twayne Publishers, 1986, 232 p.

New, W. H. *Dreams of Speech and Violence: The Art of the Short Story in Canada and New Zealand*. Toronto: The University of Toronto Press, 1987, 302 p.

Newman, Frances. *The Short Story's Mutations: From Petronius to Paul Morand*. New York: B. W. Huebsch, 1925, 332 p.

O'Connor, Frank. *The Lonely Voice: A Study of the Short Story*. Cleveland: World Publishing Co., 1963, 220 p.

O'Faolain, Sean. *The Short Story*. New York: Devin-Adair Co., 1951, 370 p.

Orel, Harold. *The Victorian Short Story: Development and Triumph of a Literary Genre*. Cambridge: Cambridge University Press, 1986, 213 p.

O'Toole, L. Michael. *Structure, Style and Interpretation in the Russian Short Story*. New Haven: Yale University Press, 1982, 272 p.

Pattee, Fred Lewis. *The Development of the American Short Story: An Historical Survey*. New York: Harper and Brothers Publishers, 1923, 388 p.

Peden, Margaret Sayers, ed. *The Latin American Short Story: A Critical History*. Twayne's Critical History of the Short Story, edited by William Peden. Boston: Twayne Publishers, 1983, 160 p.

Peden, William. *The American Short Story: Continuity and Change, 1940-1975*. Rev. ed. Boston: Houghton Mifflin Co., 1975, 215 p.

Reid, Ian. *The Short Story*. The Critical Idiom, edited by John D. Jump. London: Methuen and Co., 1977, 76 p.

Rhode, Robert D. *Setting in the American Short Story of Local Color, 1865-1900*. The Hague: Mouton, 1975, 189 p.

Rohrberger, Mary. *Hawthorne and the Modern Short Story: A Study in Genre*. The Hague: Mouton and Co., 1966, 148 p.

Shaw, Valerie. *The Short Story: A Critical Introduction*. London: Longman, 1983, 294 p.

Stephens, Michael. *The Dramaturgy of Style: Voice in Short Fiction*. Carbondale, Ill.: Southern Illinois University Press, 1986, 281 p.

Stevick, Philip, ed. *The American Short Story, 1900-1945: A Critical History*. Twayne's Critical History of the Short Story, edited by William Peden. Boston: Twayne Publishers, 1984, 209 p.

Summers, Hollis, ed. *Discussion of the Short Story*. Boston: D. C. Heath and Co., 1963, 118 p.

Vannatta, Dennis, ed. *The English Short Story, 1945-1980: A Critical History*. Twayne's Critical History of the Short Story, edited by William Peden. Boston: Twayne Publishers, 1985, 206 p.

Voss, Arthur. *The American Short Story: A Critical Survey*. Norman, Okla.: University of Oklahoma Press, 1973, 399 p.

Walker, Warren S. *Twentieth-Century Short Story Explication: New Series, Vol. 1: 1989-1990*. Hamden, Conn.: Shoe String, 1993, 366 p.

Ward, Alfred C. *Aspects of the Modern Short Story: English and American*. London: University of London Press, 1924, 307 p.

Weaver, Gordon, ed. *The American Short Story, 1945-1980: A Critical History*. Twayne's Critical History of the Short Story, edited by William Peden. Boston: Twayne Publishers, 1983, 150 p.

West, Ray B., Jr. *The Short Story in America, 1900-1950*. Chicago: Henry Regnery Co., 1952, 147 p.

Williams, Blanche Colton. *Our Short Story Writers*. New York: Moffat, Yard and Co., 1920, 357 p.

Wright, Austin McGiffert. *The American Short Story in the Twenties*. Chicago: University of Chicago Press, 1961, 425 p.

## CRITICAL ANTHOLOGIES

Atkinson, W. Patterson, ed. *The Short-Story*. Boston: Allyn and Bacon, 1923, 317 p.

Baldwin, Charles Sears, ed. *American Short Stories*. New York, N.Y.: Longmans, Green and Co., 1904, 333 p.

Charters, Ann, ed. *The Story and Its Writer: An Introduction to Short Fiction*. New York: St. Martin's Press, 1983, 1239 p.

Current-García, Eugene, and Patrick, Walton R., eds. *American Short Stories: 1820 to the Present*. Key Editions, edited by John C. Gerber. Chicago: Scott, Foresman and Co., 1952, 633 p.

Fagin, N. Bryllion, ed. *America through the Short Story*. Boston: Little, Brown, and Co., 1936, 508 p.

Frakes, James R., and Traschen, Isadore, eds. *Short Fiction: A Critical Collection*. Prentice-Hall English Literature Series, edited by Maynard Mack. Englewood Cliffs, N.J.: Prentice-Hall, 1959, 459 p.

Gifford, Douglas, ed. *Scottish Short Stories, 1800-1900*. The Scottish Library, edited by Alexander Scott. London: Calder and Boyars, 1971, 350 p.

Gordon, Caroline, and Tate, Allen, eds. *The House of Fiction: An Anthology of the Short Story withCommentary*. Rev. ed. New York: Charles Scribner's Sons, 1960, 469 p.

Greet, T. Y., et. al. *The Worlds of Fiction: Stories in Context*. Boston, Mass.: Houghton Mifflin Co., 1964, 429 p.

Gullason, Thomas A., and Caspar, Leonard, eds. *The World of Short Fiction: An International Collection.* New York: Harper and Row, 1962, 548 p.

Havighurst, Walter, ed. *Masters of the Modern Short Story.* New York: Harcourt, Brace and Co., 1945, 538 p.

Litz, A. Walton, ed. *Major American Short Stories.* New York: Oxford University Press, 1975, 823 p.

Matthews, Brander, ed. *The Short-Story: Specimens Illustrating Its Development.* New York: American Book Co., 1907, 399 p.

Menton, Seymour, ed. *The Spanish American Short Story: A Critical Anthology.* Berkeley and Los Angeles: University of California Press, 1980, 496 p.

Mzamane, Mbulelo Vizikhungo, ed. *Hungry Flames, and Other Black South African Short Stories.* Longman African Classics. Essex: Longman, 1986, 162 p.

Schorer, Mark, ed. *The Short Story: A Critical Anthology.* Rev. ed. Prentice-Hall English Literature Series, edited by Maynard Mack. Englewood Cliffs, N. J.: Prentice-Hall, 1967, 459 p.

Simpson, Claude M., ed. *The Local Colorists: American Short Stories, 1857-1900.* New York: Harper and Brothers Publishers, 1960, 340 p.

Stanton, Robert, ed. *The Short Story and the Reader.* New York: Henry Holt and Co., 1960, 557 p.

West, Ray B., Jr., ed. *American Short Stories.* New York: Thomas Y. Crowell Co., 1959, 267 p.

# Short Story Criticism Indexes

Literary Criticism Series
Cumulative Author Index

*SSC* Cumulative Nationality Index
*SSC* Cumulative Title Index

# How to Use This Index

The main references

Calvino, Italo
1923–1985 ....... CLC 5, 8, 11, 22, 33, 39,
73; SSC 3

list all author entries in the following Gale Literary Criticism series:

*BLC* = *Black Literature Criticism*
*CLC* = *Contemporary Literary Criticism*
*CLR* = *Children's Literature Review*
*CMLC* = *Classical and Medieval Literature Criticism*
*DA* = *DISCovering Authors*
*DAB* = *DISCovering Authors: British*
*DAC* = *DISCovering Authors: Canadian*
*DAM* = *DISCovering Authors: Modules*
  *DRAM*: *Dramatists Module*; *MST*: *Most-Studied Authors Module*;
  *MULT*: *Multicultural Authors Module*; *NOV*: *Novelists Module*;
  *POET*: *Poets Module*; *POP*: *Popular Fiction and Genre Authors Module*
*DC* = *Drama Criticism*
*HLC* = *Hispanic Literature Criticism*
*LC* = *Literature Criticism from 1400 to 1800*
*NCLC* = *Nineteenth-Century Literature Criticism*
*PC* = *Poetry Criticism*
*SSC* = *Short Story Criticism*
*TCLC* = *Twentieth-Century Literary Criticism*
*WLC* = *World Literature Criticism, 1500 to the Present*

The cross-references

See also CANR 23; CA 85-88;
obituary CA116

list all author entries in the following Gale biographical and literary sources:

*AAYA* = *Authors & Artists for Young Adults*
*AITN* = *Authors in the News*
*BEST* = *Bestsellers*
*BW* = *Black Writers*
*CA* = *Contemporary Authors*
*CAAS* = *Contemporary Authors Autobiography Series*
*CABS* = *Contemporary Authors Bibliographical Series*
*CANR* = *Contemporary Authors New Revision Series*
*CAP* = *Contemporary Authors Permanent Series*
*CDALB* = *Concise Dictionary of American Literary Biography*
*CDBLB* = *Concise Dictionary of British Literary Biography*
*DLB* = *Dictionary of Literary Biography*
*DLBD* = *Dictionary of Literary Biography Documentary Series*
*DLBY* = *Dictionary of Literary Biography Yearbook*
*HW* = *Hispanic Writers*
*JRDA* = *Junior DISCovering Authors*
*MAICYA* = *Major Authors and Illustrators for Children and Young Adults*
*MTCW* = *Major 20th-Century Writers*
*NNAL* = *Native North American Literature*
*SAAS* = *Something about the Author Autobiography Series*
*SATA* = *Something about the Author*
*YABC* = *Yesterday's Authors of Books for Children*

# Literary Criticism Series
# Cumulative Author Index

**Abasiyanik, Sait Faik** 1906-1954
See Sait Faik
See also CA 123

**Abbey, Edward** 1927-1989 ......... **CLC 36, 59**
See also CA 45-48; 128; CANR 2, 41

**Abbott, Lee K(ittredge)** 1947- ......... **CLC 48**
See also CA 124; CANR 51; DLB 130

**Abe, Kobo** 1924-1993 ...... **CLC 8, 22, 53, 81; DAM NOV**
See also CA 65-68; 140; CANR 24, 60; DLB 182; MTCW

**Abelard, Peter** c. 1079-c. 1142 ....... **CMLC 11**
See also DLB 115

**Abell, Kjeld** 1901-1961 ...................... **CLC 15**
See also CA 111

**Abish, Walter** 1931- ........................... **CLC 22**
See also CA 101; CANR 37; DLB 130

**Abrahams, Peter (Henry)** 1919- ......... **CLC 4**
See also BW 1; CA 57-60; CANR 26; DLB 117; MTCW

**Abrams, M(eyer) H(oward)**
1912- .......................................... **CLC 24**
See also CA 57-60; CANR 13, 33; DLB 67

**Abse, Dannie**
1923- ..... **CLC 7, 29; DAB; DAM POET**
See also CA 53-56; CAAS 1; CANR 4, 46; DLB 27

**Achebe, (Albert) Chinua(lumogu)**
1930- ........ **CLC 1, 3, 5, 7, 11, 26, 51, 75; BLC; DA; DAB; DAC; DAM MST, MULT, NOV; WLC**
See also AAYA 15; BW 2; CA 1-4R; CANR 6, 26, 47; CLR 20; DLB 117; MAICYA; MTCW; SATA 40; SATA-Brief 38

**Acker, Kathy** 1948- ........................... **CLC 45**
See also CA 117; 122; CANR 55

**Ackroyd, Peter** 1949- .................. **CLC 34, 52**
See also CA 123; 127; CANR 51; DLB 155; INT 127

**Acorn, Milton** 1923- .............. **CLC 15; DAC**
See also CA 103; DLB 53; INT 103

**Adamov, Arthur**
1908-1970 ....... **CLC 4, 25; DAM DRAM**
See also CA 17-18; 25-28R; CAP 2; MTCW

**Adams, Alice (Boyd)**
1926- .................. **CLC 6, 13, 46; SSC 24**
See also CA 81-84; CANR 26, 53; DLBY 86; INT CANR-26; MTCW

**Adams, Andy** 1859-1935 ................ **TCLC 56**
See also YABC 1

**Adams, Douglas (Noel)** 1952- .... **CLC 27, 60; DAM POP**
See also AAYA 4; BEST 89:3; CA 106; CANR 34; DLBY 83; JRDA

**Adams, Francis** 1862-1893 ............. **NCLC 33**

**Adams, Henry (Brooks)**
1838-1918 ....... **TCLC 4, 52; DA; DAB; DAC; DAM MST**
See also CA 104; 133; DLB 12, 47

**Adams, Richard (George)**
1920- ............... **CLC 4, 5, 18; DAM NOV**
See also AAYA 16; AITN 1, 2; CA 49-52; CANR 3, 35; CLR 20; JRDA; MAICYA; MTCW; SATA 7, 69

**Adamson, Joy(-Friederike Victoria)**
1910-1980 .................................. **CLC 17**
See also CA 69-72; 93-96; CANR 22; MTCW; SATA 11; SATA-Obit 22

**Adcock, Fleur** 1934- ........................... **CLC 41**
See also CA 25-28R; CAAS 23; CANR 11, 34; DLB 40

**Addams, Charles (Samuel)**
1912-1988 .................................. **CLC 30**
See also CA 61-64; 126; CANR 12

**Addams, Jane** 1860-1935 .............. **TCLC 76**

**Addison, Joseph** 1672-1719 ................ **LC 18**
See also CDBLB 1660-1789; DLB 101

**Adler, Alfred (F.)** 1870-1937 ......... **TCLC 61**
See also CA 119; 159

**Adler, C(arole) S(chwerdtfeger)**
1932- .......................................... **CLC 35**
See also AAYA 4; CA 89-92; CANR 19, 40; JRDA; MAICYA; SAAS 15; SATA 26, 63

**Adler, Renata** 1938- ...................... **CLC 8, 31**
See also CA 49-52; CANR 5, 22, 52; MTCW

**Ady, Endre** 1877-1919 ................... **TCLC 11**
See also CA 107

**A.E.** 1867-1935 .......................... **TCLC 3, 10**
See also Russell, George William

**Aeschylus** 525B.C.-456B.C. **CMLC 11; DA; DAB; DAC; DAM DRAM, MST; WLCS**
See also DLB 176

**Africa, Ben**
See Bosman, Herman Charles

**Afton, Effie**
See Harper, Frances Ellen Watkins

**Agapida, Fray Antonio**
See Irving, Washington

**Agee, James (Rufus)**
1909-1955 ....... **TCLC 1, 19; DAM NOV**
See also AITN 1; CA 108; 148; CDALB 1941-1968; DLB 2, 26, 152

**Aghill, Gordon**
See Silverberg, Robert

**Agnon, S(hmuel) Y(osef Halevi)**
1888-1970 ............. **CLC 4, 8, 14; SSC 29**
See also CA 17-18; 25-28R; CANR 60; CAP 2; MTCW

**Agrippa von Nettesheim, Henry Cornelius**
1486-1535 ..................................... **LC 27**

**Aherne, Owen**
See Cassill, R(onald) V(erlin)

**Ai** 1947- ................................... **CLC 4, 14, 69**
See also CA 85-88; CAAS 13; DLB 120

**Aickman, Robert (Fordyce)**
1914-1981 ................................... **CLC 57**
See also CA 5-8R; CANR 3

**Aiken, Conrad (Potter)**
1889-1973 ..... **CLC 1, 3, 5, 10, 52; DAM NOV, POET; SSC 9**
See also CA 5-8R; 45-48; CANR 4, 60; CDALB 1929-1941; DLB 9, 45, 102; MTCW; SATA 3, 30

**Aiken, Joan (Delano)** 1924- ............. **CLC 35**
See also AAYA 1; CA 9-12R; CANR 4, 23, 34; CLR 1, 19; DLB 161; JRDA; MAICYA; MTCW; SAAS 1; SATA 2, 30, 73

**Ainsworth, William Harrison**
1805-1882 ................................. **NCLC 13**
See also DLB 21; SATA 24

**Aitmatov, Chingiz (Torekulovich)**
1928- .......................................... **CLC 71**
See also CA 103; CANR 38; MTCW; SATA 56

**Akers, Floyd**
See Baum, L(yman) Frank

**Akhmadulina, Bella Akhatovna**
1937- .................... **CLC 53; DAM POET**
See also CA 65-68

**Akhmatova, Anna**
1888-1966 ......... **CLC 11, 25, 64; DAM POET; PC 2**
See also CA 19-20; 25-28R; CANR 35; CAP 1; MTCW

**Ambler, Eric** 1909- ........................ **CLC 4, 6, 9**
See also CA 9-12R; CANR 7, 38; DLB 77;
MTCW

**Amichai, Yehuda** 1924- .......... **CLC 9, 22, 57**
See also CA 85-88; CANR 46, 60; MTCW

**Amichai, Yehudah**
See Amichai, Yehuda

**Amiel, Henri Frederic** 1821-1881 ... **NCLC 4**

**Amis, Kingsley (William)**
1922-1995 .... **CLC 1, 2, 3, 5, 8, 13, 40,
44; DA; DAB; DAC; DAM MST, NOV**
See also AITN 2; CA 9-12R; 150; CANR 8,
28, 54; CDBLB 1945-1960; DLB 15, 27,
100, 139; DLBY 96; INT CANR-8; MTCW

**Amis, Martin (Louis)**
1949- .................... **CLC 4, 9, 38, 62, 101**
See also BEST 90:3; CA 65-68; CANR 8, 27,
54; DLB 14; INT CANR-27

**Ammons, A(rchie) R(andolph)**
1926- ..... **CLC 2, 3, 5, 8, 9, 25, 57; DAM
POET; PC 16**
See also AITN 1; CA 9-12R; CANR 6, 36, 51;
DLB 5, 165; MTCW

**Amo, Tauraatua i**
See Adams, Henry (Brooks)

**Anand, Mulk Raj** 1905-... **CLC 23, 93; DAM
NOV**
See also CA 65-68; CANR 32; MTCW

**Anatol**
See Schnitzler, Arthur

**Anaximander**
c. 610B.C.-c. 546B.C. ............. **CMLC 22**

**Anaya, Rudolfo A(lfonso)**
1937- ...... **CLC 23; DAM MULT, NOV;
HLC**
See also AAYA 20; CA 45-48; CAAS 4;
CANR 1, 32, 51; DLB 82; HW 1; MTCW

**Andersen, Hans Christian**
1805-1875 .... **NCLC 7; DA; DAB; DAC;
DAM MST, POP; SSC 6; WLC**
See also CLR 6; MAICYA; YABC 1

**Anderson, C. Farley**
See Mencken, H(enry) L(ouis); Nathan, George
Jean

**Anderson, Jessica (Margaret) Queale**
1916- .......................................... **CLC 37**
See also CA 9-12R; CANR 4, 62

**Anderson, Jon (Victor)**
1940- ..................... **CLC 9; DAM POET**
See also CA 25-28R; CANR 20

**Anderson, Lindsay (Gordon)**
1923-1994 .................................. **CLC 20**
See also CA 125; 128; 146

**Anderson, Maxwell**
1888-1959 .......... **TCLC 2; DAM DRAM**
See also CA 105; 152; DLB 7

**Anderson, Poul (William)** 1926-....... **CLC 15**
See also AAYA 5; CA 1-4R; CAAS 2; CANR
2, 15, 34; DLB 8; INT CANR-15; MTCW;
SATA 90; SATA-Brief 39

**Anderson, Robert (Woodruff)**
1917- .................... **CLC 23; DAM DRAM**
See also AITN 1; CA 21-24R; CANR 32; DLB
7

**Anderson, Sherwood**
1876-1941 ...**TCLC 1, 10, 24; DA; DAB;
DAC; DAM MST, NOV; SSC 1; WLC**
See also CA 104; 121; CANR 61; CDALB
1917-1929; DLB 4, 9, 86; DLBD 1; MTCW

**Andier, Pierre**
See Desnos, Robert

**Andouard**
See Giraudoux, (Hippolyte) Jean

**Andrade, Carlos Drummond de** ........ **CLC 18**
See also Drummond de Andrade, Carlos

**Andrade, Mario de** 1893-1945 ....... **TCLC 43**

**Andreae, Johann V(alentin)**
1586-1654 ...................................... **LC 32**
See also DLB 164

**Andreas-Salome, Lou**
1861-1937 ................................. **TCLC 56**
See also DLB 66

**Andress, Lesley**
See Sanders, Lawrence

**Andrewes, Lancelot** 1555-1626 ............. **LC 5**
See also DLB 151, 172

**Andrews, Cicily Fairfield**
See West, Rebecca

**Andrews, Elton V.**
See Pohl, Frederik

**Andreyev, Leonid (Nikolaevich)**
1871-1919 ....................................**TCLC 3**
See also CA 104

**Andric, Ivo** 1892-1975 ........................ **CLC 8**
See also CA 81-84; 57-60; CANR 43, 60; DLB
147; MTCW

**Androvar**
See Prado (Calvo), Pedro

**Angelique, Pierre**
See Bataille, Georges

**Angell, Roger** 1920- .......................... **CLC 26**
See also CA 57-60; CANR 13, 44; DLB 171

**Angelou, Maya** 1928-..... **CLC 12, 35, 64, 77;
BLC; DA; DAB; DAC; DAM MST,
MULT, POET, POP; WLCS**
See also AAYA 7, 20; BW 2; CA 65-68; CANR
19, 42; DLB 38; MTCW; SATA 49

**Annensky, Innokenty (Fyodorovich)**
1856-1909 ............................... **TCLC 14**
See also CA 110; 155

**Annunzio, Gabriele d'**
See D'Annunzio, Gabriele

**Anodos**
See Coleridge, Mary E(lizabeth)

**Anon, Charles Robert**
See Pessoa, Fernando (Antonio Nogueira)

**Anouilh, Jean (Marie Lucien Pierre)**
1910-1987 **CLC 1, 3, 8, 13, 40, 50; DAM
DRAM**
See also CA 17-20R; 123; CANR 32; MTCW

**Anthony, Florence**
See Ai

**Anthony, John**
See Ciardi, John (Anthony)

**Anthony, Peter**
See Shaffer, Anthony (Joshua); Shaffer, Peter
(Levin)

**Anthony, Piers** 1934- .... **CLC 35; DAM POP**
See also AAYA 11; CA 21-24R; CANR 28, 56;
DLB 8; MTCW; SAAS 22; SATA 84

**Antoine, Marc**
See Proust, (Valentin-Louis-George-Eugene-)
Marcel

**Antoninus, Brother**
See Everson, William (Oliver)

**Antonioni, Michelangelo** 1912- ........ **CLC 20**
See also CA 73-76; CANR 45

**Antschel, Paul** 1920-1970
See Celan, Paul
See also CA 85-88; CANR 33, 61; MTCW

**Anwar, Chairil** 1922-1949 ............. **TCLC 22**
See also CA 121

**Apollinaire, Guillaume**
1880-1918 **TCLC 3, 8, 51; DAM POET;
PC 7**
See also Kostrowitzki, Wilhelm Apollinaris de
See also CA 152

**Appelfeld, Aharon** 1932- ............ **CLC 23, 47**
See also CA 112; 133

**Apple, Max (Isaac)**
1941-........................................ **CLC 9, 33**
See also CA 81-84; CANR 19, 54; DLB 130

**Appleman, Philip (Dean)** 1926- ........ **CLC 51**
See also CA 13-16R; CAAS 18; CANR 6, 29,
56

**Appleton, Lawrence**
See Lovecraft, H(oward) P(hillips)

**Apteryx**
See Eliot, T(homas) S(tearns)

**Apuleius, (Lucius Madaurensis)**
125(?)-175(?) ............................ **CMLC 1**

**Aquin, Hubert** 1929-1977 ................ **CLC 15**
See also CA 105; DLB 53

**Aragon, Louis**
1897-1982 CLC 3, 22; DAM NOV, POET
See also CA 69-72; 108; CANR 28; DLB 72;
MTCW

**Arany, Janos** 1817-1882 ................ NCLC 34

**Arbuthnot, John** 1667-1735 .................. LC 1
See also DLB 101

**Archer, Herbert Winslow**
See Mencken, H(enry) L(ouis)

**Archer, Jeffrey (Howard)** 1940- ...... CLC 28;
DAM POP
See also AAYA 16; BEST 89:3; CA 77-80;
CANR 22, 52; INT CANR-22

**Archer, Jules** 1915- ........................... CLC 12
See also CA 9-12R; CANR 6; SAAS 5; SATA
4, 85

**Archer, Lee**
See Ellison, Harlan (Jay)

**Arden, John** 1930- ........ CLC 6, 13, 15; DAM
DRAM
See also CA 13-16R; CAAS 4; CANR 31; DLB
13; MTCW

**Arenas, Reinaldo**
1943-1990 ...... CLC 41; DAM MULT;
HLC
See also CA 124; 128; 133; DLB 145; HW

**Arendt, Hannah** 1906-1975 ......... CLC 66, 98
See also CA 17-20R; 61-64; CANR 26, 60;
MTCW

**Aretino, Pietro** 1492-1556 ................... LC 12

**Arghezi, Tudor** ................................... CLC 80
See also Theodorescu, Ion N.

**Arguedas, Jose Maria**
1911-1969 ............................. CLC 10, 18
See also CA 89-92; DLB 113; HW

**Argueta, Manlio** 1936- ...................... CLC 31
See also CA 131; DLB 145; HW

**Ariosto, Ludovico** 1474-1533 ................ LC 6

**Aristides**
See Epstein, Joseph

**Aristophanes**
450B.C.-385B.C. ... CMLC 4; DA; DAB;
DAC; DAM DRAM, MST; DC 2; WLCS
See also DLB 176

**Arlt, Roberto (Godofredo Christophersen)**
1900-1942 ....... TCLC 29; DAM MULT;
HLC
See also CA 123; 131; HW

**Armah, Ayi Kwei** 1939- ..... CLC 5, 33; BLC;
DAM MULT, POET
See also BW 1; CA 61-64; CANR 21; DLB
117; MTCW

**Armatrading, Joan** 1950- ................. CLC 17
See also CA 114

**Arnette, Robert**
See Silverberg, Robert

**Arnim, Achim von (Ludwig Joachim von
Arnim)** 1781-1831 ..... NCLC 5; SSC 29
See also DLB 90

**Arnim, Bettina von** 1785-1859 ...... NCLC 38
See also DLB 90

**Arnold, Matthew**
1822-1888 ........ NCLC 6, 29; DA; DAB;
DAC; DAM MST, POET; PC 5; WLC
See also CDBLB 1832-1890; DLB 32, 57

**Arnold, Thomas** 1795-1842 ........... NCLC 18
See also DLB 55

**Arnow, Harriette (Louisa) Simpson**
1908-1986 ........................... CLC 2, 7, 18
See also CA 9-12R; 118; CANR 14; DLB 6;
MTCW; SATA 42; SATA-Obit 47

**Arp, Hans**
See Arp, Jean

**Arp, Jean** 1887-1966 ........................... CLC 5
See also CA 81-84; 25-28R; CANR 42

**Arrabal**
See Arrabal, Fernando

**Arrabal, Fernando** 1932- .... CLC 2, 9, 18, 58
See also CA 9-12R; CANR 15

**Arrick, Fran** ......................................... CLC 30
See also Gaberman, Judie Angell

**Artaud, Antonin (Marie Joseph)**
1896-1948 .... TCLC 3, 36; DAM DRAM
See also CA 104; 149

**Arthur, Ruth M(abel)** 1905-1979 ..... CLC 12
See also CA 9-12R; 85-88; CANR 4; SATA 7,
26

**Artsybashev, Mikhail (Petrovich)**
1878-1927 ............................... TCLC 31

**Arundel, Honor (Morfydd)**
1919-1973 ............................... CLC 17
See also CA 21-22; 41-44R; CAP 2; CLR 35;
SATA 4; SATA-Obit 24

**Arzner, Dorothy** 1897-1979 ............. CLC 98

**Asch, Sholem** 1880-1957 ................... TCLC 3
See also CA 105

**Ash, Shalom**
See Asch, Sholem

**Ashbery, John (Lawrence)**
1927- ... CLC 2, 3, 4, 6, 9, 13, 15, 25, 41,
77; DAM POET
See also CA 5-8R; CANR 9, 37; DLB 5, 165;
DLBY 81; INT CANR-9; MTCW

**Ashdown, Clifford**
See Freeman, R(ichard) Austin

**Ashe, Gordon**
See Creasey, John

**Ashton-Warner, Sylvia (Constance)**
1908-1984 .................................. CLC 19
See also CA 69-72; 112; CANR 29;
MTCW

**Asimov, Isaac**
1920-1992 .... CLC 1, 3, 9, 19, 26, 76, 92;
DAM POP
See also AAYA 13; BEST 90:2; CA 1-4R;
137; CANR 2, 19, 36, 60; CLR 12; DLB
8; DLBY 92; INT CANR-19; JRDA;
MAICYA; MTCW; SATA 1, 26, 74

**Assis, Joaquim Maria Machado de**
See Machado de Assis, Joaquim Maria

**Astley, Thea (Beatrice May)**
1925- ........................................... CLC 41
See also CA 65-68; CANR 11, 43

**Aston, James**
See White, T(erence) H(anbury)

**Asturias, Miguel Angel**
1899-1974 .. CLC 3, 8, 13; DAM MULT,
NOV; HLC
See also CA 25-28; 49-52; CANR 32; CAP
2; DLB 113; HW; MTCW

**Atares, Carlos Saura**
See Saura (Atares), Carlos

**Atheling, William**
See Pound, Ezra (Weston Loomis)

**Atheling, William, Jr.**
See Blish, James (Benjamin)

**Atherton, Gertrude (Franklin Horn)**
1857-1948 .................................. TCLC 2
See also CA 104; 155; DLB 9, 78

**Atherton, Lucius**
See Masters, Edgar Lee

**Atkins, Jack**
See Harris, Mark

**Atkinson, Kate** ..................................... CLC 99

**Attaway, William (Alexander)**
1911-1986 ......... CLC 92; BLC; DAM
MULT
See also BW 2; CA 143; DLB 76

**Atticus**
See Fleming, Ian (Lancaster)

**Atwood, Margaret (Eleanor)**
1939- . CLC 2, 3, 4, 8, 13, 15, 25,
44, 84; DA; DAB; DAC; DAM
MST, NOV, POET; PC 8; SSC 2;
WLC
See also AAYA 12; BEST 89:2; CA 49-
52; CANR 3, 24, 33, 59; DLB 53; INT
CANR-24; MTCW; SATA 50

**Aubigny, Pierre d'**
See Mencken, H(enry) L(ouis)

**Aubin, Penelope**
1685-1731(?) .................................. LC 9
See also DLB 39

Auchincloss, Louis (Stanton)
1917- .. CLC 4, 6, 9, 18, 45; DAM NOV;
SSC 22
See also CA 1-4R; CANR 6, 29, 55; DLB 2;
DLBY 80; INT CANR-29; MTCW

Auden, W(ystan) H(ugh)
1907-1973 ... CLC 1, 2, 3, 4, 6, 9, 11, 14,
43; DA; DAB; DAC; DAM DRAM,
MST, POET; PC 1; WLC
See also AAYA 18; CA 9-12R; 45-48; CANR
5, 61; CDBLB 1914-1945; DLB 10, 20;
MTCW

Audiberti, Jacques
1900-1965 ........... CLC 38; DAM DRAM
See also CA 25-28R

Audubon, John James 1785-1851 . NCLC 47

Auel, Jean M(arie)
1936- ..................... CLC 31; DAM POP
See also AAYA 7; BEST 90:4; CA 103; CANR
21; INT CANR-21; SATA 91

Auerbach, Erich 1892-1957 .......... TCLC 43
See also CA 118; 155

Augier, Emile 1820-1889 ............... NCLC 31

August, John
See De Voto, Bernard (Augustine)

Augustine, St. 354-430 .......... CMLC 6; DAB

Aurelius
See Bourne, Randolph S(illiman)

Aurobindo, Sri 1872-1950 ............. TCLC 63

Austen, Jane
1775-1817 ..... NCLC 1, 13, 19, 33, 51;
DA; DAB; DAC; DAM MST, NOV;
WLC
See also AAYA 19; CDBLB 1789-1832; DLB
116

Auster, Paul 1947- ............................ CLC 47
See also CA 69-72; CANR 23, 52

Austin, Frank
See Faust, Frederick (Schiller)

Austin, Mary (Hunter)
1868-1934 ............................... TCLC 25
See also CA 109; DLB 9, 78

Autran Dourado, Waldomiro
See Dourado, (Waldomiro Freitas) Autran

Averroes 1126-1198 .......................... CMLC 7
See also DLB 115

Avicenna 980-1037 ......................... CMLC 16
See also DLB 115

Avison, Margaret
1918- ......... CLC 2, 4, 97; DAC; DAM
POET
See also CA 17-20R; DLB 53; MTCW

Axton, David
See Koontz, Dean R(ay)

Ayckbourn, Alan
1939-. CLC 5, 8, 18, 33, 74; DAB; DAM
DRAM
See also CA 21-24R; CANR 31, 59; DLB 13;
MTCW

Aydy, Catherine
See Tennant, Emma (Christina)

Ayme, Marcel (Andre)
1902-1967 ..................................... CLC 11
See also CA 89-92; CLR 25; DLB 72; SATA
91

Ayrton, Michael 1921-1975 ................. CLC 7
See also CA 5-8R; 61-64; CANR 9, 21

Azorin ..................................................... CLC 11
See also Martinez Ruiz, Jose

Azuela, Mariano
1873-1952 ....... TCLC 3; DAM MULT;
HLC
See also CA 104; 131; HW; MTCW

Baastad, Babbis Friis
See Friis-Baastad, Babbis Ellinor

Bab
See Gilbert, W(illiam) S(chwenck)

Babbis, Eleanor
See Friis-Baastad, Babbis Ellinor

Babel, Isaac
See Babel, Isaak (Emmanuilovich)

Babel, Isaak (Emmanuilovich)
1894-1941(?) ......... TCLC 2, 13; SSC 16
See also CA 104; 155

Babits, Mihaly 1883-1941 ............. TCLC 14
See also CA 114

Babur 1483-1530 .................................. LC 18

Bacchelli, Riccardo 1891-1985 ......... CLC 19
See also CA 29-32R; 117

Bach, Richard (David)
1936-.............. CLC 14; DAM NOV, POP
See also AITN 1; BEST 89:2; CA 9-12R;
CANR 18; MTCW; SATA 13

Bachman, Richard
See King, Stephen (Edwin)

Bachmann, Ingeborg 1926-1973 ...... CLC 69
See also CA 93-96; 45-48; DLB 85

Bacon, Francis 1561-1626 ............. LC 18, 32
See also CDBLB Before 1660; DLB 151

Bacon, Roger 1214(?)-1292 .......... CMLC 14
See also DLB 115

Bacovia, George ............................... TCLC 24
See also Vasiliu, Gheorghe

Badanes, Jerome 1937- ..................... CLC 59

Bagehot, Walter 1826-1877 ........... NCLC 10
See also DLB 55

Bagnold, Enid 1889-1981 ...... CLC 25; DAM
DRAM
See also CA 5-8R; 103; CANR 5, 40; DLB 13,
160; MAICYA; SATA 1, 25

Bagritsky, Eduard 1895-1934 ........ TCLC 60

Bagrjana, Elisaveta
See Belcheva, Elisaveta

Bagryana, Elisaveta .......................... CLC 10
See also Belcheva, Elisaveta
See also DLB 147

Bailey, Paul 1937- ............................. CLC 45
See also CA 21-24R; CANR 16, 62; DLB
14

Baillie, Joanna 1762-1851 ............... NCLC 2
See also DLB 93

Bainbridge, Beryl (Margaret)
1933-...... CLC 4, 5, 8, 10, 14, 18, 22, 62;
DAM NOV
See also CA 21-24R; CANR 24, 55; DLB 14;
MTCW

Baker, Elliott 1922- ........................... CLC 8
See also CA 45-48; CANR 2

Baker, Jean H. ............................. TCLC 3, 10
See also Russell, George William

Baker, Nicholson
1957-....................... CLC 61; DAM POP
See also CA 135

Baker, Ray Stannard
1870-1946 ................................. TCLC 47
See also CA 118

Baker, Russell (Wayne) 1925-........... CLC 31
See also BEST 89:4; CA 57-60; CANR 11, 41,
59; MTCW

Bakhtin, M.
See Bakhtin, Mikhail Mikhailovich

Bakhtin, M. M.
See Bakhtin, Mikhail Mikhailovich

Bakhtin, Mikhail
See Bakhtin, Mikhail Mikhailovich

Bakhtin, Mikhail Mikhailovich
1895-1975 ................................... CLC 83
See also CA 128; 113

Bakshi, Ralph 1938(?)- ..................... CLC 26
See also CA 112; 138

Bakunin, Mikhail (Alexandrovich)
1814-1876 .......................... NCLC 25, 58

Baldwin, James (Arthur)
1924-1987 .... CLC 1, 2, 3, 4, 5, 8, 13,
15, 17, 42, 50, 67, 90; BLC; DA;
DAB; DAC; DAM MST, MULT,
NOV, POP; DC 1; SSC 10; WLC
See also AAYA 4; BW 1; CA 1-4R; 124;
CABS 1; CANR 3, 24; CDALB 1941-
1968; DLB 2, 7, 33; DLBY 87; MTCW;
SATA 9; SATA-Obit 54

**Bass, Kingsley B., Jr.**
See Bullins, Ed

**Bass, Rick** 1958- ............................... **CLC 79**
See also CA 126; CANR 53

**Bassani, Giorgio** 1916- ...................... **CLC 9**
See also CA 65-68; CANR 33; DLB 128, 177;
MTCW

**Bastos, Augusto (Antonio) Roa**
See Roa Bastos, Augusto (Antonio)

**Bataille, Georges** 1897-1962 ............. **CLC 29**
See also CA 101; 89-92

**Bates, H(erbert) E(rnest)**
1905-1974 ... **CLC 46; DAB; DAM POP;**
**SSC 10**
See also CA 93-96; 45-48; CANR 34; DLB
162; MTCW

**Bauchart**
See Camus, Albert

**Baudelaire, Charles**
1821-1867 .. **NCLC 6, 29, 55; DA; DAB;**
**DAC; DAM MST, POET; PC 1; SSC 18;**
**WLC**

**Baudrillard, Jean** 1929- ................... **CLC 60**

**Baum, L(yman) Frank** 1856-1919 .... **TCLC 7**
See also CA 108; 133; CLR 15; DLB 22;
JRDA; MAICYA; MTCW; SATA 18

**Baum, Louis F.**
See Baum, L(yman) Frank

**Baumbach, Jonathan**
1933- ....................................... **CLC 6, 23**
See also CA 13-16R; CAAS 5; CANR 12;
DLBY 80; INT CANR-12; MTCW

**Bausch, Richard (Carl)**
1945- ........................................ **CLC 51**
See also CA 101; CAAS 14; CANR 43, 61;
DLB 130

**Baxter, Charles**
1947- ................. **CLC 45, 78; DAM POP**
See also CA 57-60; CANR 40; DLB 130

**Baxter, George Owen**
See Faust, Frederick (Schiller)

**Baxter, James K(eir)** 1926-1972 ....... **CLC 14**
See also CA 77-80

**Baxter, John**
See Hunt, E(verette) Howard, (Jr.)

**Bayer, Sylvia**
See Glassco, John

**Baynton, Barbara** 1857-1929 ........ **TCLC 57**

**Beagle, Peter S(oyer)** 1939- ........ **CLC 7, 104**
See also CA 9-12R; CANR 4, 51; DLBY 80;
INT CANR-4; SATA 60

**Bean, Normal**
See Burroughs, Edgar Rice

**Beard, Charles A(ustin)**
1874-1948 ................................. **TCLC 15**
See also CA 115; DLB 17; SATA 18

**Beardsley, Aubrey** 1872-1898 ......... **NCLC 6**

**Beattie, Ann** 1947-...... **CLC 8, 13, 18, 40, 63;**
**DAM NOV, POP; SSC 11**
See also BEST 90:2; CA 81-84; CANR 53;
DLBY 82; MTCW

**Beattie, James** 1735-1803 .............. **NCLC 25**
See also DLB 109

**Beauchamp, Kathleen Mansfield** 1888-1923
See Mansfield, Katherine
See also CA 104; 134; DA; DAC; DAM
MST

**Beaumarchais, Pierre-Augustin Caron de**
1732-1799 ................................... **DC 4**
See also DAM DRAM

**Beaumont, Francis**
1584(?)-1616 ........................ **LC 33; DC 6**
See also CDBLB Before 1660; DLB 58, 121

**Beauvoir, Simone (Lucie Ernestine Marie**
**Bertrand) de**
1908-1986 ... **CLC 1, 2, 4, 8, 14, 31, 44,**
**50, 71; DA; DAB; DAC; DAM MST,**
**NOV; WLC**
See also CA 9-12R; 118; CANR 28, 61; DLB
72; DLBY 86; MTCW

**Becker, Carl (Lotus)** 1873-1945 .... **TCLC 63**
See also CA 157; DLB 17

**Becker, Jurek** 1937-1997 .............. **CLC 7, 19**
See also CA 85-88; 157; CANR 60; DLB 75

**Becker, Walter** 1950- ...................... **CLC 26**

**Beckett, Samuel (Barclay)**
1906-1989 ... **CLC 1, 2, 3, 4, 6, 9, 10, 11,**
**14, 18, 29, 57, 59, 83; DA; DAB; DAC;**
**DAM DRAM, MST, NOV; SSC 16;**
**WLC**
See also CA 5-8R; 130; CANR 33, 61;
CDBLB 1945-1960; DLB 13, 15; DLBY
90; MTCW

**Beckford, William** 1760-1844 ....... **NCLC 16**
See also DLB 39

**Beckman, Gunnel** 1910- ................... **CLC 26**
See also CA 33-36R; CANR 15; CLR 25;
MAICYA; SAAS 9; SATA 6

**Becque, Henri** 1837-1899 ................ **NCLC 3**

**Beddoes, Thomas Lovell** 1803-1849 **NCLC 3**
See also DLB 96

**Bede** c. 673-735 ............................. **CMLC 20**
See also DLB 146

**Bedford, Donald F.**
See Fearing, Kenneth (Flexner)

**Beecher, Catharine Esther**
1800-1878 ................................. **NCLC 30**
See also DLB 1

**Beecher, John** 1904-1980 .................... **CLC 6**
See also AITN 1; CA 5-8R; 105; CANR 8

**Beer, Johann** 1655-1700 ........................ **LC 5**
See also DLB 168

**Beer, Patricia** 1924- ........................ **CLC 58**
See also CA 61-64; CANR 13, 46; DLB 40

**Beerbohm, Max**
See Beerbohm, (Henry) Max(imilian)

**Beerbohm, (Henry) Max(imilian)**
1872-1956 ........................... **TCLC 1, 24**
See also CA 104; 154; DLB 34, 100

**Beer-Hofmann, Richard**
1866-1945 ................................. **TCLC 60**
See also CA 160; DLB 81

**Begiebing, Robert J(ohn)** 1946- ....... **CLC 70**
See also CA 122; CANR 40

**Behan, Brendan** 1923-1964 **CLC 1, 8, 11, 15,**
**79; DAM DRAM**
See also CA 73-76; CANR 33; CDBLB 1945-
1960; DLB 13; MTCW

**Behn, Aphra** 1640(?)-1689 ..... **LC 1, 30; DA;**
**DAB; DAC; DAM DRAM, MST, NOV,**
**POET; DC 4; PC 13; WLC**
See also DLB 39, 80, 131

**Behrman, S(amuel) N(athaniel)**
1893-1973 ................................. **CLC 40**
See also CA 13-16; 45-48; CAP 1; DLB 7, 44

**Belasco, David** 1853-1931 ................ **TCLC 3**
See also CA 104; DLB 7

**Belcheva, Elisaveta** 1893-................. **CLC 10**
See also Bagryana, Elisaveta

**Beldone, Phil "Cheech"**
See Ellison, Harlan (Jay)

**Beleno**
See Azuela, Mariano

**Belinski, Vissarion Grigoryevich**
1811-1848 ................................. **NCLC 5**

**Belitt, Ben** 1911- ............................. **CLC 22**
See also CA 13-16R; CAAS 4; CANR 7; DLB
5

**Bell, Gertrude** 1868-1926 .............. **TCLC 67**
See also DLB 174

**Bell, James Madison** 1826-1902 ... **TCLC 43;**
**BLC; DAM MULT**
See also BW 1; CA 122; 124; DLB 50

**Bell, Madison Smartt** 1957- ...... **CLC 41, 102**
See also CA 111; CANR 28, 54

**Bell, Marvin (Hartley)** 1937- ....... **CLC 8, 31;**
**DAM POET**
See also CA 21-24R; CAAS 14; CANR 59;
DLB 5; MTCW

**Bell, W. L. D.**
See Mencken, H(enry) L(ouis)

**Bernhardt, Sarah (Henriette Rosine)**
  1844-1923 ................................ **TCLC 75**
  See also CA 157

**Berriault, Gina** 1926- ........................ **CLC 54**
  See also CA 116; 129; DLB 130

**Berrigan, Daniel** 1921- ........................ **CLC 4**
  See also CA 33-36R; CAAS 1; CANR 11, 43;
  DLB 5

**Berrigan, Edmund Joseph Michael, Jr.**
  1934-1983
  See Berrigan, Ted
  See also CA 61-64; 110; CANR 14

**Berrigan, Ted** ...................................... **CLC 37**
  See also Berrigan, Edmund Joseph Michael,
  Jr.
  See also DLB 5, 169

**Berry, Charles Edward Anderson** 1931-
  See Berry, Chuck
  See also CA 115

**Berry, Chuck** ...................................... **CLC 17**
  See also Berry, Charles Edward Anderson

**Berry, Jonas**
  See Ashbery, John (Lawrence)

**Berry, Wendell (Erdman)**
  1934- ......... **CLC 4, 6, 8, 27, 46; DAM
  POET**
  See also AITN 1; CA 73-76; CANR 50; DLB
  5, 6

**Berryman, John**
  1914-1972 ... **CLC 1, 2, 3, 4, 6, 8, 10, 13,
  25, 62; DAM POET**
  See also CA 13-16; 33-36R; CABS 2; CANR
  35; CAP 1; CDALB 1941-1968; DLB 48;
  MTCW

**Bertolucci, Bernardo** 1940- .............. **CLC 16**
  See also CA 106

**Berton, Pierre (Francis De Marigny)**
  1920- .......................................... **CLC 104**
  See also CA 1-4R; CANR 2, 56; DLB 68

**Bertrand, Aloysius** 1807-1841 ....... **NCLC 31**

**Bertran de Born** c. 1140-1215 ......... **CMLC 5**

**Besant, Annie (Wood)** 1847-1933 ..... **TCLC 9**
  See also CA 105

**Bessie, Alvah** 1904-1985 .................. **CLC 23**
  See also CA 5-8R; 116; CANR 2; DLB 26

**Bethlen, T. D.**
  See Silverberg, Robert

**Beti, Mongo** ....... **CLC 27; BLC; DAM MULT**
  See also Biyidi, Alexandre

**Betjeman, John**
  1906-1984 ... **CLC 2, 6, 10, 34, 43; DAB;
  DAM MST, POET**
  See also CA 9-12R; 112; CANR 33, 56;
  CDBLB 1945-1960; DLB 20; DLBY 84;
  MTCW

**Bettelheim, Bruno** 1903-1990 .......... **CLC 79**
  See also CA 81-84; 131; CANR 23, 61;
  MTCW

**Betti, Ugo** 1892-1953 ........................ **TCLC 5**
  See also CA 104; 155

**Betts, Doris (Waugh)** 1932- ....... **CLC 3, 6, 28**
  See also CA 13-16R; CANR 9; DLBY 82; INT
  CANR-9

**Bevan, Alistair**
  See Roberts, Keith (John Kingston)

**Bialik, Chaim Nachman**
  1873-1934 ................................ **TCLC 25**

**Bickerstaff, Isaac**
  See Swift, Jonathan

**Bidart, Frank** 1939- .......................... **CLC 33**
  See also CA 140

**Bienek, Horst** 1930- ....................... **CLC 7, 11**
  See also CA 73-76; DLB 75

**Bierce, Ambrose (Gwinett)**
  1842-1914(?) ... **TCLC 1, 7, 44; DA;
  DAC; DAM MST; SSC 9; WLC**
  See also CA 104; 139; CDALB 1865-1917;
  DLB 11, 12, 23, 71, 74

**Biggers, Earl Derr** 1884-1933 ....... **TCLC 65**
  See also CA 108; 153

**Billings, Josh**
  See Shaw, Henry Wheeler

**Billington, (Lady) Rachel (Mary)**
  1942- ........................................... **CLC 43**
  See also AITN 2; CA 33-36R; CANR 44

**Binyon, T(imothy) J(ohn)** 1936- ....... **CLC 34**
  See also CA 111; CANR 28

**Bioy Casares, Adolfo**
  1914- ..... **CLC 4, 8, 13, 88; DAM MULT;
  HLC; SSC 17**
  See also CA 29-32R; CANR 19, 43; DLB 113;
  HW; MTCW

**Bird, Cordwainer**
  See Ellison, Harlan (Jay)

**Bird, Robert Montgomery**
  1806-1854 ................................. **NCLC 1**

**Birney, (Alfred) Earle**
  1904- ....... **CLC 1, 4, 6, 11; DAC; DAM
  MST, POET**
  See also CA 1-4R; CANR 5, 20; DLB 88;
  MTCW

**Bishop, Elizabeth**
  1911-1979 ..... **CLC 1, 4, 9, 13, 15,
  32; DA; DAC; DAM MST, POET;
  PC 3**
  See also CA 5-8R; 89-92; CABS 2; CANR
  26, 61; CDALB 1968-1988; DLB 5,
  169; MTCW; SATA-Obit 24

**Bishop, John** 1935- ......................... **CLC 10**
  See also CA 105

**Bissett, Bill** 1939- ................ **CLC 18; PC 14**
  See also CA 69-72; CAAS 19; CANR 15; DLB
  53; MTCW

**Bitov, Andrei (Georgievich)** 1937- ... **CLC 57**
  See also CA 142

**Biyidi, Alexandre** 1932-
  See Beti, Mongo
  See also BW 1; CA 114; 124; MTCW

**Bjarme, Brynjolf**
  See Ibsen, Henrik (Johan)

**Bjornson, Bjornstjerne (Martinius)**
  1832-1910 ........................... **TCLC 7, 37**
  See also CA 104

**Black, Robert**
  See Holdstock, Robert P.

**Blackburn, Paul** 1926-1971 ......... **CLC 9, 43**
  See also CA 81-84; 33-36R; CANR 34; DLB
  16; DLBY 81

**Black Elk**
  1863-1950 ......... **TCLC 33; DAM MULT**
  See also CA 144; NNAL

**Black Hobart**
  See Sanders, (James) Ed(ward)

**Blacklin, Malcolm**
  See Chambers, Aidan

**Blackmore, R(ichard) D(oddridge)**
  1825-1900 ............................... **TCLC 27**
  See also CA 120; DLB 18

**Blackmur, R(ichard) P(almer)**
  1904-1965 ............................... **CLC 2, 24**
  See also CA 11-12; 25-28R; CAP 1; DLB 63

**Black Tarantula**
  See Acker, Kathy

**Blackwood, Algernon (Henry)**
  1869-1951 ................................. **TCLC 5**
  See also CA 105; 150; DLB 153, 156, 178

**Blackwood, Caroline** 1931-1996 ... **CLC 6, 9,
  100**
  See also CA 85-88; 151; CANR 32, 61; DLB
  14; MTCW

**Blade, Alexander**
  See Hamilton, Edmond; Silverberg, Robert

**Blaga, Lucian** 1895-1961 ................. **CLC 75**

**Blair, Eric (Arthur)** 1903-1950
  See Orwell, George
  See also CA 104; 132; DA; DAB; DAC; DAM
  MST, NOV; MTCW; SATA 29

**Blais, Marie-Claire**
  1939- **CLC 2, 4, 6, 13, 22; DAC; DAM MST**
  See also CA 21-24R; CAAS 4; CANR 38; DLB
  53; MTCW

**Blaise, Clark** 1940- ........................... **CLC 29**
  See also AITN 2; CA 53-56; CAAS 3; CANR
  5; DLB 53

**Blake, Fairley**
See De Voto, Bernard (Augustine)

**Blake, Nicholas**
See Day Lewis, C(ecil)
See also DLB 77

**Blake, William**
      1757-1827   **NCLC 13, 37, 57; DA; DAB;**
      **DAC; DAM MST, POET; PC 12; WLC**
See also CDBLB 1789-1832; DLB 93, 163;
MAICYA; SATA 30

**Blake, William J(ames)** 1894-1969 ..... **PC 12**
See also CA 5-8R; 25-28R

**Blasco Ibanez, Vicente**
      1867-1928 ............ **TCLC 12; DAM NOV**
See also CA 110; 131; HW; MTCW

**Blatty, William Peter** 1928- .... **CLC 2; DAM**
      **POP**
See also CA 5-8R; CANR 9

**Bleeck, Oliver**
See Thomas, Ross (Elmore)

**Blessing, Lee** 1949- ........... **CLC 54**

**Blish, James (Benjamin)**
      1921-1975 ................................... **CLC 14**
See also CA 1-4R; 57-60; CANR 3; DLB 8;
MTCW; SATA 66

**Bliss, Reginald**
See Wells, H(erbert) G(eorge)

**Blixen, Karen (Christentze Dinesen)**
      1885-1962
See Dinesen, Isak
See also CA 25-28; CANR 22, 50; CAP 2;
MTCW; SATA 44

**Bloch, Robert (Albert)** 1917-1994.... **CLC 33**
See also CA 5-8R; 146; CAAS 20; CANR 5;
DLB 44; INT CANR-5; SATA 12; SATA-
Obit 82

**Blok, Alexander (Alexandrovich)**
      1880-1921 .................................. **TCLC 5**
See also CA 104

**Blom, Jan**
See Breytenbach, Breyten

**Bloom, Harold** 1930- ................ **CLC 24, 103**
See also CA 13-16R; CANR 39; DLB 67

**Bloomfield, Aurelius**
See Bourne, Randolph S(illiman)

**Blount, Roy (Alton), Jr.** 1941- .......... **CLC 38**
See also CA 53-56; CANR 10, 28, 61; INT
CANR-28; MTCW

**Bloy, Leon** 1846-1917 .................... **TCLC 22**
See also CA 121; DLB 123

**Blume, Judy (Sussman)** 1938- ...**CLC 12, 30;**
      **DAM NOV, POP**
See also AAYA 3; CA 29-32R; CANR 13, 37;
CLR 2, 15; DLB 52; JRDA; MAICYA;
MTCW; SATA 2, 31, 79

**Blunden, Edmund (Charles)**
      1896-1974 ............................... **CLC 2, 56**
See also CA 17-18; 45-48; CANR 54; CAP 2;
DLB 20, 100, 155; MTCW

**Bly, Robert (Elwood)**
      1926- ....... **CLC 1, 2, 5, 10, 15, 38; DAM**
      **POET**
See also CA 5-8R; CANR 41; DLB 5; MTCW

**Boas, Franz** 1858-1942 ................... **TCLC 56**
See also CA 115

**Bobette**
See Simenon, Georges (Jacques Christian)

**Boccaccio, Giovanni**
      1313-1375 ................ **CMLC 13; SSC 10**

**Bochco, Steven** 1943- ........................ **CLC 35**
See also AAYA 11; CA 124; 138

**Bodenheim, Maxwell** 1892-1954 ... **TCLC 44**
See also CA 110; DLB 9, 45

**Bodker, Cecil** 1927- ........................... **CLC 21**
See also CA 73-76; CANR 13, 44; CLR 23;
MAICYA; SATA 14

**Boell, Heinrich (Theodor)**
      1917-1985 ...   **CLC 2, 3, 6, 9, 11, 15, 27,**
      **32, 72; DA; DAB; DAC; DAM MST,**
      **NOV; SSC 23; WLC**
See also CA 21-24R; 116; CANR 24; DLB 69;
DLBY 85; MTCW

**Boerne, Alfred**
See Doeblin, Alfred

**Boethius** 480(?)-524(?) ................... **CMLC 15**
See also DLB 115

**Bogan, Louise**
      1897-1970 ........**CLC 4, 39, 46, 93; DAM**
      **POET; PC 12**
See also CA 73-76; 25-28R; CANR 33; DLB
45, 169; MTCW

**Bogarde, Dirk** .................................... **CLC 19**
See also Van Den Bogarde, Derek Jules
Gaspard Ulric Niven
See also DLB 14

**Bogosian, Eric** 1953- ........................... **CLC 45**
See also CA 138

**Bograd, Larry** 1953- ........................... **CLC 35**
See also CA 93-96; CANR 57; SAAS 21; SATA
33, 89

**Boiardo, Matteo Maria** 1441-1494 ....... **LC 6**

**Boileau-Despreaux, Nicolas**
      1636-1711 ........................................ **LC 3**

**Bojer, Johan** 1872-1959 .................. **TCLC 64**

**Boland, Eavan (Aisling)** 1944- ..**CLC 40, 67;**
      **DAM POET**
See also CA 143; CANR 61; DLB 40

**Bolt, Lee**
See Faust, Frederick (Schiller)

**Bolt, Robert (Oxton)** 1924-1995 ...... **CLC 14;**
      **DAM DRAM**
See also CA 17-20R; 147; CANR 35; DLB 13;
MTCW

**Bombet, Louis-Alexandre-Cesar**
See Stendhal

**Bomkauf**
See Kaufman, Bob (Garnell)

**Bonaventura** .................................... **NCLC 35**
See also DLB 90

**Bond, Edward**
      1934-..... **CLC 4, 6, 13, 23; DAM DRAM**
See also CA 25-28R; CANR 38; DLB 13;
MTCW

**Bonham, Frank** 1914-1989 ............... **CLC 12**
See also AAYA 1; CA 9-12R; CANR 4, 36;
JRDA; MAICYA; SAAS 3; SATA 1, 49;
SATA-Obit 62

**Bonnefoy, Yves**
      1923-.......... **CLC 9, 15, 58; DAM MST,**
      **POET**
See also CA 85-88; CANR 33; MTCW

**Bontemps, Arna(ud Wendell)**
      1902-1973 ......... **CLC 1, 18; BLC; DAM**
      **MULT, NOV, POET**
See also BW 1; CA 1-4R; 41-44R; CANR 4,
35; CLR 6; DLB 48, 51; JRDA; MAICYA;
MTCW; SATA 2, 44; SATA-Obit 24

**Booth, Martin** 1944- ........................... **CLC 13**
See also CA 93-96; CAAS 2

**Booth, Philip** 1925- ............................ **CLC 23**
See also CA 5-8R; CANR 5; DLBY 82

**Booth, Wayne C(layson)** 1921-......... **CLC 24**
See also CA 1-4R; CAAS 5; CANR 3, 43; DLB
67

**Borchert, Wolfgang** 1921-1947 .......**TCLC 5**
See also CA 104; DLB 69, 124

**Borel, Petrus** 1809-1859 ................ **NCLC 41**

**Borges, Jorge Luis**
      1899-1986 ...   **CLC 1, 2, 3, 4, 6, 8, 9, 10,**
      **13, 19, 44, 48, 83; DA; DAB; DAC;**
      **DAM MST, MULT; HLC; SSC 4; WLC**
See also AAYA 19; CA 21-24R; CANR 19, 33;
DLB 113; DLBY 86; HW; MTCW

**Borowski, Tadeusz** 1922-1951 ......... **TCLC 9**
See also CA 106; 154

**Borrow, George (Henry)**
      1803-1881 .................................. **NCLC 9**
See also DLB 21, 55, 166

**Bosman, Herman Charles**
      1905-1951 ............................... **TCLC 49**
See also Malan, Herman
See also CA 160

**Bosschere, Jean de**
      1878(?)-1953 ............................ **TCLC 19**
See also CA 115

**Boswell, James**
1740-1795 ........ **LC 4; DA; DAB; DAC; DAM MST; WLC**
See also CDBLB 1660-1789; DLB 104, 142

**Bottoms, David** 1949- ........................ **CLC 53**
See also CA 105; CANR 22; DLB 120; DLBY 83

**Boucicault, Dion** 1820-1890 .......... **NCLC 41**

**Boucolon, Maryse** 1937(?)-
See Conde, Maryse
See also CA 110; CANR 30, 53

**Bourget, Paul (Charles Joseph)**
1852-1935 ............................... **TCLC 12**
See also CA 107; DLB 123

**Bourjaily, Vance (Nye)** 1922- ........ **CLC 8, 62**
See also CA 1-4R; CAAS 1; CANR 2; DLB 2, 143

**Bourne, Randolph S(illiman)**
1886-1918 ................................ **TCLC 16**
See also CA 117; 155; DLB 63

**Bova, Ben(jamin William)** 1932- ...... **CLC 45**
See also AAYA 16; CA 5-8R; CAAS 18; CANR 11, 56; CLR 3; DLBY 81; INT CANR-11; MAICYA; MTCW; SATA 6, 68

**Bowen, Elizabeth (Dorothea Cole)**
1899-1973 ........ **CLC 1, 3, 6, 11, 15, 22; DAM NOV; SSC 3, 28**
See also CA 17-18; 41-44R; CANR 35; CAP 2; CDBLB 1945-1960; DLB 15, 162; MTCW

**Bowering, George** 1935- .............. **CLC 15, 47**
See also CA 21-24R; CAAS 16; CANR 10; DLB 53

**Bowering, Marilyn R(uthe)** 1949-.... **CLC 32**
See also CA 101; CANR 49

**Bowers, Edgar** 1924- .......................... **CLC 9**
See also CA 5-8R; CANR 24; DLB 5

**Bowie, David** ...................................... **CLC 17**
See also Jones, David Robert

**Bowles, Jane (Sydney)**
1917-1973 ............................... **CLC 3, 68**
See also CA 19-20; 41-44R; CAP 2

**Bowles, Paul (Frederick)**
1910- ................ **CLC 1, 2, 19, 53; SSC 3**
See also CA 1-4R; CAAS 1; CANR 1, 19, 50; DLB 5, 6; MTCW

**Box, Edgar**
See Vidal, Gore

**Boyd, Nancy**
See Millay, Edna St. Vincent

**Boyd, William** 1952- .............. **CLC 28, 53, 70**
See also CA 114; 120; CANR 51

**Boyle, Kay**
1902-1992 ......... **CLC 1, 5, 19, 58; SSC 5**
See also CA 13-16R; 140; CAAS 1; CANR 29, 61; DLB 4, 9, 48, 86; DLBY 93; MTCW

**Boyle, Mark**
See Kienzle, William X(avier)

**Boyle, Patrick** 1905-1982 ................. **CLC 19**
See also CA 127

**Boyle, T. C.** 1948-
See Boyle, T(homas) Coraghessan

**Boyle, T(homas) Coraghessan**
1948-.. **CLC 36, 55, 90; DAM POP; SSC 16**
See also BEST 90:4; CA 120; CANR 44; DLBY 86

**Boz**
See Dickens, Charles (John Huffam)

**Brackenridge, Hugh Henry**
1748-1816 ................................. **NCLC 7**
See also DLB 11, 37

**Bradbury, Edward P.**
See Moorcock, Michael (John)

**Bradbury, Malcolm (Stanley)**
1932-................ **CLC 32, 61; DAM NOV**
See also CA 1-4R; CANR 1, 33; DLB 14; MTCW

**Bradbury, Ray (Douglas)**
1920-........ **CLC 1, 3, 10, 15, 42, 98; DA; DAB; DAC; DAM MST, NOV, POP; SSC 29; WLC**
See also AAYA 15; AITN 1, 2; CA 1-4R; CANR 2, 30; CDALB 1968-1988; DLB 2, 8; MTCW; SATA 11, 64

**Bradford, Gamaliel** 1863-1932 ...... **TCLC 36**
See also CA 160; DLB 17

**Bradley, David (Henry, Jr.)**
1950-.......... **CLC 23; BLC; DAM MULT**
See also BW 1; CA 104; CANR 26; DLB 33

**Bradley, John Ed(mund, Jr.)**
1958-.......................................... **CLC 55**
See also CA 139

**Bradley, Marion Zimmer** 1930- ...... **CLC 30; DAM POP**
See also AAYA 9; CA 57-60; CAAS 10; CANR 7, 31, 51; DLB 8; MTCW; SATA 90

**Bradstreet, Anne**
1612(?)-1672 ........ **LC 4, 30; DA; DAC; DAM MST, POET; PC 10**
See also CDALB 1640-1865; DLB 24

**Brady, Joan** 1939- .............................. **CLC 86**
See also CA 141

**Bragg, Melvyn** 1939- ........................ **CLC 10**
See also BEST 89:3; CA 57-60; CANR 10, 48; DLB 14

**Braine, John (Gerard)**
1922-1986 ........................... **CLC 1, 3, 41**
See also CA 1-4R; 120; CANR 1, 33; CDBLB 1945-1960; DLB 15; DLBY 86; MTCW

**Bramah, Ernest** 1868-1942 ........... **TCLC 72**
See also CA 156; DLB 70

**Brammer, William** 1930(?)-1978 ...... **CLC 31**
See also CA 77-80

**Brancati, Vitaliano** 1907-1954....... **TCLC 12**
See also CA 109

**Brancato, Robin F(idler)** 1936- ........ **CLC 35**
See also AAYA 9; CA 69-72; CANR 11, 45; CLR 32; JRDA; SAAS 9; SATA 23

**Brand, Max**
See Faust, Frederick (Schiller)

**Brand, Millen** 1906-1980 .................... **CLC 7**
See also CA 21-24R; 97-100

**Branden, Barbara** .............................. **CLC 44**
See also CA 148

**Brandes, Georg (Morris Cohen)**
1842-1927 ................................. **TCLC 10**
See also CA 105

**Brandys, Kazimierz** 1916- ............... **CLC 62**

**Branley, Franklyn M(ansfield)**
1915-.......................................... **CLC 21**
See also CA 33-36R; CANR 14, 39; CLR 13; MAICYA; SAAS 16; SATA 4, 68

**Brathwaite, Edward Kamau**
1930-..................... **CLC 11; DAM POET**
See also BW 2; CA 25-28R; CANR 11, 26, 47; DLB 125

**Brautigan, Richard (Gary)**
1935-1984 ...... **CLC 1, 3, 5, 9, 12, 34, 42; DAM NOV**
See also CA 53-56; 113; CANR 34; DLB 2, 5; DLBY 80, 84; MTCW; SATA 56

**Brave Bird, Mary** 1953-
See Crow Dog, Mary (Ellen)
See also NNAL

**Braverman, Kate** 1950- .................... **CLC 67**
See also CA 89-92

**Brecht, (Eugen) Bertolt (Friedrich)**
1898-1956 ........ **TCLC 1, 6, 13, 35; DA; DAB; DAC; DAM DRAM, MST; DC 3; WLC**
See also CA 104; 133; CANR 62; DLB 56, 124; MTCW

**Brecht, Eugen Berthold Friedrich**
See Brecht, (Eugen) Bertolt (Friedrich)

**Bremer, Fredrika** 1801-1865 .......... **NCLC 11**

**Brennan, Christopher John**
1870-1932 ................................ **TCLC 17**
See also CA 117

**Brennan, Maeve** 1917-...................... **CLC 5**
See also CA 81-84

**Brentano, Clemens (Maria)**
1778-1842 ................................... **NCLC 1**
See also DLB 90

**Brent of Bin Bin**
See Franklin, (Stella Maraia Sarah) Miles

**Brown, Sterling Allen**
 1901-1989 ... **CLC 1, 23, 59; BLC; DAM
 MULT, POET**
 See also BW 1; CA 85-88; 127; CANR 26;
 DLB 48, 51, 63; MTCW

**Brown, Will**
 See Ainsworth, William Harrison

**Brown, William Wells**
 1813-1884 ........... **NCLC 2; BLC; DAM
 MULT; DC 1**
 See also DLB 3, 50

**Browne, (Clyde) Jackson** 1948(?)- ... **CLC 21**
 See also CA 120

**Browning, Elizabeth Barrett**
 1806-1861 .. **NCLC 1, 16, 61; DA; DAB;
 DAC; DAM MST, POET; PC 6; WLC**
 See also CDBLB 1832-1890; DLB 32

**Browning, Robert**
 1812-1889 .. **NCLC 19; DA; DAB; DAC;
 DAM MST, POET; PC 2; WLCS**
 See also CDBLB 1832-1890; DLB 32, 163;
 YABC 1

**Browning, Tod** 1882-1962 ................. **CLC 16**
 See also CA 141; 117

**Brownson, Orestes (Augustus)** 1803-1876
 **NCLC 50**

**Bruccoli, Matthew J(oseph)** 1931- ... **CLC 34**
 See also CA 9-12R; CANR 7; DLB 103

**Bruce, Lenny** ...................................... **CLC 21**
 See also Schneider, Leonard Alfred

**Bruin, John**
 See Brutus, Dennis

**Brulard, Henri**
 See Stendhal

**Brulls, Christian**
 See Simenon, Georges (Jacques Christian)

**Brunner, John (Kilian Houston)**
 1934-1995 ........... **CLC 8, 10; DAM POP**
 See also CA 1-4R; 149; CAAS 8; CANR 2,
 37; MTCW

**Bruno, Giordano** 1548-1600 ................ **LC 27**

**Brutus, Dennis** 1924- ...**CLC 43; BLC; DAM
 MULT, POET**
 See also BW 2; CA 49-52; CAAS 14; CANR
 2, 27, 42; DLB 117

**Bryan, C(ourtlandt) D(ixon) B(arnes)**
 1936- ................................................. **CLC 29**
 See also CA 73-76; CANR 13; INT CANR-
 13

**Bryan, Michael**
 See Moore, Brian

**Bryant, William Cullen**
 1794-1878**NCLC 6, 46; DA; DAB; DAC;
 DAM MST, POET; PC 20**
 See also CDALB 1640-1865; DLB 3, 43, 59

**Bryusov, Valery Yakovlevich**
 1873-1924 ................................. **TCLC 10**
 See also CA 107; 155

**Buchan, John** 1875-1940 .... **TCLC 41; DAB;
 DAM POP**
 See also CA 108; 145; DLB 34, 70, 156; YABC
 2

**Buchanan, George** 1506-1582 ............... **LC 4**

**Buchheim, Lothar-Guenther** 1918- ... **CLC 6**
 See also CA 85-88

**Buchner, (Karl) Georg**
 1813-1837 ................................ **NCLC 26**

**Buchwald, Art(hur)** 1925- ................ **CLC 33**
 See also AITN 1; CA 5-8R; CANR 21; MTCW;
 SATA 10

**Buck, Pearl S(ydenstricker)**
 1892-1973 ......**CLC 7, 11, 18; DA; DAB;
 DAC; DAM MST, NOV**
 See also AITN 1; CA 1-4R; 41-44R; CANR 1,
 34; DLB 9, 102; MTCW; SATA 1, 25

**Buckler, Ernest**
 1908-1984 ... **CLC 13; DAC; DAM MST**
 See also CA 11-12; 114; CAP 1; DLB 68; SATA
 47

**Buckley, Vincent (Thomas)**
 1925-1988 ................................. **CLC 57**
 See also CA 101

**Buckley, William F(rank), Jr.**
 1925- .............. **CLC 7, 18, 37; DAM POP**
 See also AITN 1; CA 1-4R; CANR 1, 24, 53;
 DLB 137; DLBY 80; INT CANR-24; MTCW

**Buechner, (Carl) Frederick**
 1926- ............. **CLC 2, 4, 6, 9; DAM NOV**
 See also CA 13-16R; CANR 11, 39; DLBY 80;
 INT CANR-11; MTCW

**Buell, John (Edward)** 1927- ............. **CLC 10**
 See also CA 1-4R; DLB 53

**Buero Vallejo, Antonio** 1916- ..... **CLC 15, 46**
 See also CA 106; CANR 24, 49; HW; MTCW

**Bufalino, Gesualdo** 1920(?)- ............ **CLC 74**

**Bugayev, Boris Nikolayevich** 1880-1934
 See Bely, Andrey
 See also CA 104

**Bukowski, Charles**
 1920-1994 ..... **CLC 2, 5, 9, 41, 82; DAM
 NOV, POET; PC 18**
 See also CA 17-20R; 144; CANR 40, 62; DLB
 5, 130, 169; MTCW

**Bulgakov, Mikhail (Afanas'evich)**
 1891-1940 ... **TCLC 2, 16; DAM DRAM,
 NOV; SSC 18**
 See also CA 105; 152

**Bulgya, Alexander Alexandrovich**
 1901-1956 ................................ **TCLC 53**
 See also Fadeyev, Alexander
 See also CA 117

**Bullins, Ed**
 1935-...**CLC 1, 5, 7; BLC; DAM DRAM,
 MULT; DC 6**
 See also BW 2; CA 49-52; CAAS 16; CANR
 24, 46; DLB 7, 38; MTCW

**Bulwer-Lytton, Edward (George Earle Lytton)**
 1803-1873 ............................. **NCLC 1, 45**
 See also DLB 21

**Bunin, Ivan Alexeyevich**
 1870-1953 ...................... **TCLC 6; SSC 5**
 See also CA 104

**Bunting, Basil**
 1900-1985 ......... **CLC 10, 39, 47; DAM
 POET**
 See also CA 53-56; 115; CANR 7; DLB 20

**Bunuel, Luis**
 1900-1983 .... **CLC 16, 80; DAM MULT;
 HLC**
 See also CA 101; 110; CANR 32; HW

**Bunyan, John**
 1628-1688 ........ **LC 4; DA; DAB; DAC;
 DAM MST; WLC**
 See also CDBLB 1660-1789; DLB 39

**Burckhardt, Jacob (Christoph)**
 1818-1897 ................................ **NCLC 49**

**Burford, Eleanor**
 See Hibbert, Eleanor Alice Burford

**Burgess, Anthony ... CLC 1, 2, 4, 5, 8, 10, 13,
 15, 22, 40, 62 , 81, 94; DAB**
 See also Wilson, John (Anthony) Burgess
 See also AITN 1; CDBLB 1960 to Present;
 DLB 14**

**Burke, Edmund**
 1729(?)-1797 ........ **LC 7, 36; DA; DAB;
 DAC; DAM MST; WLC**
 See also DLB 104

**Burke, Kenneth (Duva)**
 1897-1993 ................................... **CLC 2, 24**
 See also CA 5-8R; 143; CANR 39; DLB 45,
 63; MTCW

**Burke, Leda**
 See Garnett, David

**Burke, Ralph**
 See Silverberg, Robert

**Burke, Thomas** 1886-1945 ............. **TCLC 63**
 See also CA 113; 155

**Burney, Fanny** 1752-1840 ........ **NCLC 12, 54**
 See also DLB 39

**Burns, Robert** 1759-1796 ..................... **PC 6**
 See also CDBLB 1789-1832; DA; DAB; DAC;
 DAM MST, POET; DLB 109; WLC

**Burns, Tex**
 See L'Amour, Louis (Dearborn)

**Burnshaw, Stanley**
 1906-................................ **CLC 3, 13, 44**
 See also CA 9-12R; DLB 48

Charles I 1600-1649 .............................. LC 13

Charyn, Jerome 1937- .............. CLC 5, 8, 18
See also CA 5-8R; CAAS 1; CANR 7, 61;
DLBY 83; MTCW

Chase, Mary (Coyle) 1907-1981 ............ DC 1
See also CA 77-80; 105; SATA 17; SATA-Obit
29

Chase, Mary Ellen 1887-1973 ............ CLC 2
See also CA 13-16; 41-44R; CAP 1; SATA 10

Chase, Nicholas
See Hyde, Anthony

Chateaubriand, Francois Rene de 1768-
1848 ............................................ NCLC 3
See also DLB 119

Chatterje, Sarat Chandra 1876-1936(?)
See Chatterji, Saratchandra
See also CA 109

Chatterji, Bankim Chandra 1838-
1894 .......................................... NCLC 19

Chatterji, Saratchandra ................. TCLC 13
See also Chatterje, Sarat Chandra

Chatterton, Thomas 1752-
1770 .......................... LC 3; DAM POET
See also DLB 109

Chatwin, (Charles) Bruce 1940-
1989 ............. CLC 28, 57, 59; DAM POP
See also AAYA 4; BEST 90:1; CA 85-88; 127

Chaucer, Daniel
See Ford, Ford Madox

Chaucer, Geoffrey 1340(?)-
1400LC 17; DA; DAB; DAC; DAM MST,
POET; PC 19; WLCS
See also CDBLB Before 1660; DLB 146

Chaviaras, Strates 1935-
See Haviaras, Stratis
See also CA 105

Chayefsky, Paddy ............................... CLC 23
See also Chayefsky, Sidney
See also DLB 7, 44; DLBY 81

Chayefsky, Sidney 1923-1981
See Chayefsky, Paddy
See also CA 9-12R; 104; CANR 18; DAM
DRAM

Chedid, Andree 1920- ........................ CLC 47
See also CA 145

Cheever, John 1912-
1982CLC 3, 7, 8, 11, 15, 25, 64; DA; DAB;
DAC; DAM MST, NOV, POP; SSC 1;
WLC
See also CA 5-8R; 106; CABS 1; CANR 5,
27; CDALB 1941-1968; DLB 2, 102; DLBY
80, 82; INT CANR-5; MTCW

Cheever, Susan 1943- .................. CLC 18, 48
See also CA 103; CANR 27, 51; DLBY 82;
INT CANR-27

Chekhonte, Antosha
See Chekhov, Anton (Pavlovich)

Chekhov, Anton (Pavlovich)
1860-1904 ....... TCLC 3, 10, 31, 55; DA;
DAB; DAC; DAM DRAM, MST; SSC 2,
28; WLC
See also CA 104; 124; SATA 90

Chernyshevsky, Nikolay Gavrilovich
1828-1889 ................................ NCLC 1

Cherry, Carolyn Janice 1942-
See Cherryh, C. J.
See also CA 65-68; CANR 10

Cherryh, C. J. ...................................... CLC 35
See also Cherry, Carolyn Janice
See also DLBY 80; SATA 93

Chesnutt, Charles W(addell)
1858-1932 ....... TCLC 5, 39; BLC; DAM
MULT; SSC 7
See also BW 1; CA 106; 125; DLB 12, 50, 78;
MTCW

Chester, Alfred
1929(?)-1971 ............................... CLC 49
See also CA 33-36R; DLB 130

Chesterton, G(ilbert) K(eith)
1874-1936 ...TCLC 1, 6, 64; DAM NOV,
POET; SSC 1
See also CA 104; 132; CDBLB 1914-1945;
DLB 10, 19, 34, 70, 98, 149, 178; MTCW;
SATA 27

Chiang Pin-chin 1904-1986
See Ding Ling
See also CA 118

Ch'ien Chung-shu 1910- .................. CLC 22
See also CA 130; MTCW

Child, L. Maria
See Child, Lydia Maria

Child, Lydia Maria 1802-1880 ........ NCLC 6
See also DLB 1, 74; SATA 67

Child, Mrs.
See Child, Lydia Maria

Child, Philip 1898-1978 .............. CLC 19, 68
See also CA 13-14; CAP 1; SATA 47

Childers, (Robert) Erskine
1870-1922 ................................ TCLC 65
See also CA 113; 153; DLB 70

Childress, Alice
1920-1994 CLC 12, 15, 86, 96; BLC;
DAM DRAM, MULT, NOV; DC 4
See also AAYA 8; BW 2; CA 45-48; 146;
CANR 3, 27, 50; CLR 14; DLB 7, 38;
JRDA; MAICYA; MTCW; SATA 7, 48,
81

Chin, Frank (Chew, Jr.) 1940- .............. DC 7
See also CA 33-36R; DAM MULT

Chislett, (Margaret) Anne 1943- ...... CLC 34
See also CA 151

Chitty, Thomas Willes 1926- ........... CLC 11
See also Hinde, Thomas
See also CA 5-8R

Chivers, Thomas Holley
1809-1858 ................................ NCLC 49
See also DLB 3

Chomette, Rene Lucien 1898-1981
See Clair, Rene
See also CA 103

Chopin, Kate TCLC 5, 14; DA; DAB; SSC 8;
WLCS
See also Chopin, Katherine
See also CDALB 1865-1917; DLB 12, 78

Chopin, Katherine 1851-1904
See Chopin, Kate
See also CA 104; 122; DAC; DAM MST, NOV

Chretien de Troyes
c. 12th cent. - ........................... CMLC 10

Christie
See Ichikawa, Kon

Christie, Agatha (Mary Clarissa)
1890-1976 CLC 1, 6, 8, 12, 39, 48; DAB;
DAC; DAM NOV
See also AAYA 9; AITN 1, 2; CA 17-20R; 61-
64; CANR 10, 37; CDBLB 1914-1945;
DLB 13, 77; MTCW; SATA 36

Christie, (Ann) Philippa
See Pearce, Philippa
See also CA 5-8R; CANR 4

Christine de Pizan 1365(?)-1431(?) ....... LC 9

Chubb, Elmer
See Masters, Edgar Lee

Chulkov, Mikhail Dmitrievich
1743-1792 ........................................ LC 2
See also DLB 150

Churchill, Caryl
1938-........................... CLC 31, 55; DC 5
See also CA 102; CANR 22, 46; DLB 13;
MTCW

Churchill, Charles 1731-1764................ LC 3
See also DLB 109

Chute, Carolyn 1947- ....................... CLC 39
See also CA 123

Ciardi, John (Anthony)
1916-1986 CLC 10, 40, 44; DAM POET
See also CA 5-8R; 118; CAAS 2; CANR 5,
33; CLR 19; DLB 5; DLBY 86; INT CANR-
5; MAICYA; MTCW; SATA 1, 65; SATA-
Obit 46

Cicero, Marcus Tullius
106B.C.-43B.C. ........................ CMLC 3

Cimino, Michael 1943- ..................... CLC 16
See also CA 105

Cioran, E(mil) M. 1911-1995 ........... CLC 64
See also CA 25-28R; 149

**Coleridge, Mary E(lizabeth)**
1861-1907 ................................ **TCLC 73**
See also CA 116; DLB 19, 98

**Coleridge, Samuel Taylor**
1772-1834 ........ **NCLC 9, 54; DA; DAB; DAC; DAM MST, POET; PC 11; WLC**
See also CDBLB 1789-1832; DLB 93, 107

**Coleridge, Sara** 1802-1852 ............. **NCLC 31**

**Coles, Don** 1928- .............................. **CLC 46**
See also CA 115; CANR 38

**Colette, (Sidonie-Gabrielle)**
1873-1954 .. **TCLC 1, 5, 16; DAM NOV; SSC 10**
See also CA 104; 131; DLB 65; MTCW

**Collett, (Jacobine) Camilla (Wergeland)**
1813-1895 ................................ **NCLC 22**

**Collier, Christopher** 1930- ............... **CLC 30**
See also AAYA 13; CA 33-36R; CANR 13, 33; JRDA; MAICYA; SATA 16, 70

**Collier, James L(incoln)**
1928- ...................... **CLC 30; DAM POP**
See also AAYA 13; CA 9-12R; CANR 4, 33, 60; CLR 3; JRDA; MAICYA; SAAS 21; SATA 8, 70

**Collier, Jeremy** 1650-1726 ..................... **LC 6**

**Collier, John** 1901-1980 ..................... **SSC 19**
See also CA 65-68; 97-100; CANR 10; DLB 77

**Collingwood, R(obin) G(eorge)**
1889(?)-1943 ............................ **TCLC 67**
See also CA 117; 155

**Collins, Hunt**
See Hunter, Evan

**Collins, Linda** 1931- .......................... **CLC 44**
See also CA 125

**Collins, (William) Wilkie**
1824-1889 ............................ **NCLC 1, 18**
See also CDBLB 1832-1890; DLB 18, 70, 159

**Collins, William**
1721-1759 .......... **LC 4, 40; DAM POET**
See also DLB 109

**Collodi, Carlo** 1826-1890 .............. **NCLC 54**
See also Lorenzini, Carlo
See also CLR 5

**Colman, George**
See Glassco, John

**Colt, Winchester Remington**
See Hubbard, L(afayette) Ron(ald)

**Colter, Cyrus** 1910- ........................... **CLC 58**
See also BW 1; CA 65-68; CANR 10; DLB 33

**Colton, James**
See Hansen, Joseph

**Colum, Padraic** 1881-1972 ................ **CLC 28**
See also CA 73-76; 33-36R; CANR 35; CLR 36; MAICYA; MTCW; SATA 15

**Colvin, James**
See Moorcock, Michael (John)

**Colwin, Laurie (E.)**
1944-1992 ................... **CLC 5, 13, 23, 84**
See also CA 89-92; 139; CANR 20, 46; DLBY 80; MTCW

**Comfort, Alex(ander)**
1920- .......................... **CLC 7; DAM POP**
See also CA 1-4R; CANR 1, 45

**Comfort, Montgomery**
See Campbell, (John) Ramsey

**Compton-Burnett, I(vy)**
1884(?)-1969 ........ **CLC 1, 3, 10, 15, 34; DAM NOV**
See also CA 1-4R; 25-28R; CANR 4; DLB 36; MTCW

**Comstock, Anthony** 1844-1915 ...... **TCLC 13**
See also CA 110

**Comte, Auguste** 1798-1857 ............ **NCLC 54**

**Conan Doyle, Arthur**
See Doyle, Arthur Conan

**Conde, Maryse**
1937- .............. **CLC 52, 92; DAM MULT**
See also Boucolon, Maryse
See also BW 2

**Condillac, Etienne Bonnot de**
1714-1780 ...................................... **LC 26**

**Condon, Richard (Thomas)** 1915-
1996 ... **CLC 4, 6, 8, 10, 45, 100; DAM NOV**
See also BEST 90:3; CA 1-4R; 151; CAAS 1; CANR 2, 23; INT CANR-23; MTCW

**Confucius**
551B.C.-479B.C. . **CMLC 19; DA; DAB; DAC; DAM MST; WLCS**

**Congreve, William**
1670-1729 ... **LC 5, 21; DA; DAB; DAC; DAM DRAM, MST, POET; DC 2; WLC**
See also CDBLB 1660-1789; DLB 39, 84

**Connell, Evan S(helby), Jr.**
1924- ............... **CLC 4, 6, 45; DAM NOV**
See also AAYA 7; CA 1-4R; CAAS 2; CANR 2, 39; DLB 2; DLBY 81; MTCW

**Connelly, Marc(us Cook)**
1890-1980 ...................................... **CLC 7**
See also CA 85-88; 102; CANR 30; DLB 7; DLBY 80; SATA-Obit 25

**Connor, Ralph** ................................ **TCLC 31**
See also Gordon, Charles William
See also DLB 92

**Conrad, Joseph** 1857-1924 **TCLC 1, 6, 13, 25, 43, 57; DA; DAB; DAC; DAM MST, NOV; SSC 9; WLC**
See also CA 104; 131; CANR 60; CDBLB 1890-1914; DLB 10, 34, 98, 156; MTCW; SATA 27

**Conrad, Robert Arnold**
See Hart, Moss

**Conroy, Donald Pat(rick)**
1945- ....... **CLC 30, 74; DAM NOV, POP**
See also AAYA 8; AITN 1; CA 85-88; CANR 24, 53; DLB 6; MTCW

**Constant (de Rebecque), (Henri) Benjamin**
1767-1830 ................................ **NCLC 6**
See also DLB 119

**Conybeare, Charles Augustus**
See Eliot, T(homas) S(tearns)

**Cook, Michael** 1933- ......................... **CLC 58**
See also CA 93-96; DLB 53

**Cook, Robin** 1940- ........ **CLC 14; DAM POP**
See also BEST 90:2; CA 108; 111; CANR 41; INT 111

**Cook, Roy**
See Silverberg, Robert

**Cooke, Elizabeth** 1948- ..................... **CLC 55**
See also CA 129

**Cooke, John Esten** 1830-1886 .......... **NCLC 5**
See also DLB 3

**Cooke, John Estes**
See Baum, L(yman) Frank

**Cooke, M. E.**
See Creasey, John

**Cooke, Margaret**
See Creasey, John

**Cook-Lynn, Elizabeth**
1930- ................... **CLC 93; DAM MULT**
See also CA 133; DLB 175; NNAL

**Cooney, Ray** ....................................... **CLC 62**

**Cooper, Douglas** 1960- ....................... **CLC 86**

**Cooper, Henry St. John**
See Creasey, John

**Cooper, J(oan) California** ...... **CLC 56; DAM MULT**
See also AAYA 12; BW 1; CA 125; CANR 55

**Cooper, James Fenimore**
1789-1851 ...................... **NCLC 1, 27, 54**
See also AAYA 22; CDALB 1640-1865; DLB 3; SATA 19

**Coover, Robert (Lowell)**
1932- ...... **CLC 3, 7, 15, 32, 46, 87; DAM NOV; SSC 15**
See also CA 45-48; CANR 3, 37, 58; DLB 2; DLBY 81; MTCW

**Copeland, Stewart (Armstrong)**
1952- ........................................... **CLC 26**

**Coppard, A(lfred) E(dgar)**
1878-1957 ..................... **TCLC 5; SSC 21**
See also CA 114; DLB 162; YABC 1

**Crews, Harry (Eugene)**
1935- ................................ **CLC 6, 23, 49**
See also AITN 1; CA 25-28R; CANR 20, 57;
DLB 6, 143; MTCW

**Crichton, (John) Michael**
1942- ...... **CLC 2, 6, 54, 90; DAM NOV,**
**POP**
See also AAYA 10; AITN 2; CA 25-28R;
CANR 13, 40, 54; DLBY 81; INT CANR-
13; JRDA; MTCW; SATA 9, 88

**Crispin, Edmund** ................................ **CLC 22**
See also Montgomery, (Robert) Bruce
See also DLB 87

**Cristofer, Michael**
1945(?)- .............. **CLC 28; DAM DRAM**
See also CA 110; 152; DLB 7

**Croce, Benedetto** 1866-1952 .......... **TCLC 37**
See also CA 120; 155

**Crockett, David** 1786-1836 .............. **NCLC 8**
See also DLB 3, 11

**Crockett, Davy**
See Crockett, David

**Crofts, Freeman Wills**
1879-1957 ................................... **TCLC 55**
See also CA 115; DLB 77

**Croker, John Wilson**
1780-1857 ................................ **NCLC 10**
See also DLB 110

**Crommelynck, Fernand**
1885-1970 ................................... **CLC 75**
See also CA 89-92

**Cronin, A(rchibald) J(oseph)**
1896-1981 .................................... **CLC 32**
See also CA 1-4R; 102; CANR 5; SATA 47;
SATA-Obit 25

**Cross, Amanda**
See Heilbrun, Carolyn G(old)

**Crothers, Rachel**
1878(?)-1958 ............................. **TCLC 19**
See also CA 113; DLB 7

**Croves, Hal**
See Traven, B.

**Crow Dog, Mary (Ellen)** (?)- ............. **CLC 93**
See also Brave Bird, Mary
See also CA 154

**Crowfield, Christopher**
See Stowe, Harriet (Elizabeth) Beecher

**Crowley, Aleister** ................................ **TCLC 7**
See also Crowley, Edward Alexander

**Crowley, Edward Alexander** 1875-1947
See Crowley, Aleister
See also CA 104

**Crowley, John** 1942- ......................... **CLC 57**
See also CA 61-64; CANR 43; DLBY 82;
SATA 65

**Crud**
See Crumb, R(obert)

**Crumarums**
See Crumb, R(obert)

**Crumb, R(obert)** 1943- ..................... **CLC 17**
See also CA 106

**Crumbum**
See Crumb, R(obert)

**Crumski**
See Crumb, R(obert)

**Crum the Bum**
See Crumb, R(obert)

**Crunk**
See Crumb, R(obert)

**Crustt**
See Crumb, R(obert)

**Cryer, Gretchen (Kiger)** 1935- ......... **CLC 21**
See also CA 114; 123

**Csath, Geza** 1887-1919 ................... **TCLC 13**
See also CA 111

**Cudlip, David** 1933- .......................... **CLC 34**

**Cullen, Countee**
1903-1946 **TCLC 4, 37; BLC; DA; DAC;**
**DAM MST, MULT, POET; PC 20;**
**WLCS**
See also BW 1; CA 108; 124; CDALB
1917-1929; DLB 4, 48, 51; MTCW;
SATA 18

**Cum, R.**
See Crumb, R(obert)

**Cummings, Bruce F(rederick)** 1889-1919
See Barbellion, W. N. P.
See also CA 123

**Cummings, E(dward) E(stlin)**
1894-1962 .. **CLC 1, 3, 8, 12, 15, 68; DA;**
**DAB; DAC; DAM MST, POET; PC 5;**
**WLC 2**
See also CA 73-76; CANR 31; CDALB 1929-
1941; DLB 4, 48; MTCW

**Cunha, Euclides (Rodrigues Pimenta) da**
1866-1909 ................................ **TCLC 24**
See also CA 123

**Cunningham, E. V.**
See Fast, Howard (Melvin)

**Cunningham, J(ames) V(incent)**
1911-1985 ............................... **CLC 3, 31**
See also CA 1-4R; 115; CANR 1; DLB 5

**Cunningham, Julia (Woolfolk)**
1916- ......................................... **CLC 12**
See also CA 9-12R; CANR 4, 19, 36;
JRDA; MAICYA; SAAS 2; SATA 1,
26

**Cunningham, Michael** 1952- ........... **CLC 34**
See also CA 136

**Cunninghame Graham, R(obert) B(ontine)**
1852-1936 .............................. **TCLC 19**
See also Graham, R(obert) B(ontine)
Cunninghame
See also CA 119; DLB 98

**Currie, Ellen** 19(?)- ........................... **CLC 44**

**Curtin, Philip**
See Lowndes, Marie Adelaide (Belloc)

**Curtis, Price**
See Ellison, Harlan (Jay)

**Cutrate, Joe**
See Spiegelman, Art

**Cynewulf** c. 770-c. 840 ................. **CMLC 23**

**Czaczkes, Shmuel Yosef**
See Agnon, S(hmuel) Y(osef Halevi)

**Dabrowska, Maria (Szumska)**
1889-1965 ................................... **CLC 15**
See also CA 106

**Dabydeen, David**
1955- ............................................. **CLC 34**
See also BW 1; CA 125; CANR 56

**Dacey, Philip**
1939- ............................................. **CLC 51**
See also CA 37-40R; CAAS 17; CANR 14, 32;
DLB 105

**Dagerman, Stig (Halvard)**
1923-1954 ................................ **TCLC 17**
See also CA 117; 155

**Dahl, Roald**
1916-1990 ........ **CLC 1, 6, 18, 79; DAB;**
**DAC; DAM MST, NOV, POP**
See also AAYA 15; CA 1-4R; 133; CANR 6,
32, 37, 62; CLR 1, 7, 41; DLB 139; JRDA;
MAICYA; MTCW; SATA 1, 26, 73; SATA-
Obit 65

**Dahlberg, Edward**
1900-1977 ............................. **CLC 1, 7, 14**
See also CA 9-12R; 69-72; CANR 31, 62; DLB
48; MTCW

**Daitch, Susan** 1954- ........................ **CLC 103**

**Dale, Colin** ........................................ **TCLC 18**
See also Lawrence, T(homas) E(dward)

**Dale, George E.**
See Asimov, Isaac

**Daly, Elizabeth**
1878-1967 ................................... **CLC 52**
See also CA 23-24; 25-28R; CANR 60; CAP
2

**Daly, Maureen**
1921- ............................................. **CLC 17**
See also AAYA 5; CANR 37; JRDA; MAICYA;
SAAS 1; SATA 2

**Damas, Leon-Gontran**
1912-1978 ................................... **CLC 84**
See also BW 1; CA 125; 73-76

**Deighton, Leonard Cyril** 1929-
See Deighton, Len
See also CA 9-12R; CANR 19, 33; DAM NOV,
POP; MTCW

**Dekker, Thomas**
1572(?)-1632 .......... **LC 22; DAM DRAM**
See also CDBLB Before 1660; DLB 62, 172

**Delafield, E. M.** 1890-1943 ........... **TCLC 61**
See also Dashwood, Edmee Elizabeth Monica
de la Pasture
See also DLB 34

**de la Mare, Walter (John)**
1873-1956 ...... **TCLC 4, 53; DAB; DAC;
DAM MST, POET; SSC 14; WLC**
See also CDBLB 1914-1945; CLR 23; DLB
162; SATA 16

**Delaney, Franey**
See O'Hara, John (Henry)

**Delaney, Shelagh**
1939- ................... **CLC 29; DAM DRAM**
See also CA 17-20R; CANR 30; CDBLB 1960
to Present; DLB 13; MTCW

**Delany, Mary (Granville Pendarves)**
1700-1788 ...................................... **LC 12**

**Delany, Samuel R(ay, Jr.)**
1942- ......... **CLC 8, 14, 38; BLC; DAM
MULT**
See also BW 2; CA 81-84; CANR 27, 43; DLB
8, 33; MTCW

**De La Ramee, (Marie) Louise** 1839-1908
See Ouida
See also SATA 20

**de la Roche, Mazo** 1879-1961 .......... **CLC 14**
See also CA 85-88; CANR 30; DLB 68; SATA
64

**De La Salle, Innocent**
See Hartmann, Sadakichi

**Delbanco, Nicholas (Franklin)**
1942- ...................................... **CLC 6, 13**
See also CA 17-20R; CAAS 2; CANR 29, 55;
DLB 6

**del Castillo, Michel** 1933- ................. **CLC 38**
See also CA 109

**Deledda, Grazia (Cosima)**
1875(?)-1936 ............................. **TCLC 23**
See also CA 123

**Delibes, Miguel** ............................... **CLC 8, 18**
See also Delibes Setien, Miguel

**Delibes Setien, Miguel** 1920-
See Delibes, Miguel
See also CA 45-48; CANR 1, 32; HW;
MTCW

**DeLillo, Don**
1936- ....... **CLC 8, 10, 13, 27, 39, 54, 76;
DAM NOV, POP**
See also BEST 89:1; CA 81-84; CANR 21;
DLB 6, 173; MTCW

**de Lisser, H. G.**
See De Lisser, H(erbert) G(eorge)
See also DLB 117

**De Lisser, H(erbert) G(eorge)**
1878-1944 ................................. **TCLC 12**
See also de Lisser, H. G.
See also BW 2; CA 109; 152

**Deloria, Vine (Victor), Jr.** 1933- ...... **CLC 21;
DAM MULT**
See also CA 53-56; CANR 5, 20, 48; DLB 175;
MTCW; NNAL; SATA 21

**Del Vecchio, John M(ichael)**
1947- ........................................... **CLC 29**
See also CA 110; DLBD 9

**de Man, Paul (Adolph Michel)**
1919-1983 ................................. **CLC 55**
See also CA 128; 111; CANR 61; DLB 67;
MTCW

**De Marinis, Rick** 1934- ..................... **CLC 54**
See also CA 57-60; CAAS 24; CANR 9, 25,
50

**Dembry, R. Emmet**
See Murfree, Mary Noailles

**Demby, William**
1922- .......... **CLC 53; BLC; DAM MULT**
See also BW 1; CA 81-84; DLB 33

**de Menton, Francisco**
See Chin, Frank (Chew, Jr.)

**Demijohn, Thom**
See Disch, Thomas M(ichael)

**de Montherlant, Henry (Milon)**
See Montherlant, Henry (Milon) de

**Demosthenes** 384B.C.-322B.C. ..... **CMLC 13**
See also DLB 176

**de Natale, Francine**
See Malzberg, Barry N(athaniel)

**Denby, Edwin (Orr)** 1903-1983 ........ **CLC 48**
See also CA 138; 110

**Denis, Julio**
See Cortazar, Julio

**Denmark, Harrison**
See Zelazny, Roger (Joseph)

**Dennis, John** 1658-1734 ...................... **LC 11**
See also DLB 101

**Dennis, Nigel (Forbes)** 1912-1989 ..... **CLC 8**
See also CA 25-28R; 129; DLB 13, 15;
MTCW

**Dent, Lester** 1904(?)-1959 ............. **TCLC 72**
See also CA 112

**De Palma, Brian (Russell)** 1940- ...... **CLC 20**
See also CA 109

**De Quincey, Thomas** 1785-1859 ...... **NCLC 4**
See also CDBLB 1789-1832; DLB 110; 144

**Deren, Eleanora** 1908(?)-1961
See Deren, Maya
See also CA 111

**Deren, Maya** 1917-1961 ........... **CLC 16, 102**
See also Deren, Eleanora

**Derleth, August (William)**
1909-1971 .................................. **CLC 31**
See also CA 1-4R; 29-32R; CANR 4; DLB 9;
SATA 5

**Der Nister** 1884-1950 ..................... **TCLC 56**

**de Routisie, Albert**
See Aragon, Louis

**Derrida, Jacques** 1930- .............. **CLC 24, 87**
See also CA 124; 127

**Derry Down Derry**
See Lear, Edward

**Dersonnes, Jacques**
See Simenon, Georges (Jacques Christian)

**Desai, Anita**
1937-........ **CLC 19, 37, 97; DAB; DAM
NOV**
See also CA 81-84; CANR 33, 53; MTCW;
SATA 63

**de Saint-Luc, Jean**
See Glassco, John

**de Saint Roman, Arnaud**
See Aragon, Louis

**Descartes, Rene** 1596-1650 ........... **LC 20, 35**

**De Sica, Vittorio** 1901(?)-1974 ......... **CLC 20**
See also CA 117

**Desnos, Robert** 1900-1945 .............. **TCLC 22**
See also CA 121; 151

**Destouches, Louis-Ferdinand**
1894-1961 .............................. **CLC 9, 15**
See also Celine, Louis-Ferdinand
See also CA 85-88; CANR 28; MTCW

**de Tolignac, Gaston**
See Griffith, D(avid Lewelyn) W(ark)

**Deutsch, Babette** 1895-1982 ............. **CLC 18**
See also CA 1-4R; 108; CANR 4; DLB 45;
SATA 1; SATA-Obit 33

**Devenant, William** 1606-1649 ............. **LC 13**

**Devkota, Laxmiprasad**
1909-1959 ............................... **TCLC 23**
See also CA 123

**De Voto, Bernard (Augustine)**
1897-1955 ............................... **TCLC 29**
See also CA 113; 160; DLB 9

**De Vries, Peter**
1910-1993 ......**CLC 1, 2, 3, 7, 10, 28, 46;
DAM NOV**
See also CA 17-20R; 142; CANR 41; DLB 6;
DLBY 82; MTCW

**Dexter, John**
See Bradley, Marion Zimmer

**Dexter, Martin**
See Faust, Frederick (Schiller)

**Dexter, Pete**
1943- ................. **CLC 34, 55; DAM POP**
See also BEST 89:2; CA 127; 131; INT 131; MTCW

**Diamano, Silmang**
See Senghor, Leopold Sedar

**Diamond, Neil** 1941- .......................... **CLC 30**
See also CA 108

**Diaz del Castillo, Bernal**
1496-1584 ...................................... **LC 31**

**di Bassetto, Corno**
See Shaw, George Bernard

**Dick, Philip K(indred)**
1928-1982 . **CLC 10, 30, 72; DAM NOV,
POP**
See also CA 49-52; 106; CANR 2, 16; DLB 8; MTCW

**Dickens, Charles (John Huffam)**
1812-1870 ..... **NCLC 3, 8, 18, 26, 37, 50;
DA; DAB; DAC; DAM MST, NOV; SSC
17; WLC**
See also CDBLB 1832-1890; DLB 21, 55, 70,
159, 166; JRDA; MAICYA; SATA 15

**Dickey, James (Lafayette)**
1923-1997 ...... **CLC 1, 2, 4, 7, 10, 15, 47;
DAM NOV, POET, POP**
See also AITN 1, 2; CA 9-12R; 156; CABS 2;
CANR 10, 48, 61; CDALB 1968-1988;
DLB 5; DLBD 7; DLBY 82, 93, 96; INT
CANR-10; MTCW

**Dickey, William** 1928-1994 .......... **CLC 3, 28**
See also CA 9-12R; 145; CANR 24; DLB 5

**Dickinson, Charles** 1951- ................. **CLC 49**
See also CA 128

**Dickinson, Emily (Elizabeth)**
1830-1886 .. **NCLC 21; DA; DAB; DAC;
DAM MST, POET; PC 1; WLC**
See also AAYA 22; CDALB 1865-1917; DLB
1; SATA 29

**Dickinson, Peter (Malcolm)**
1927- ...................................... **CLC 12, 35**
See also AAYA 9; CA 41-44R; CANR 31, 58;
CLR 29; DLB 87, 161; JRDA; MAICYA;
SATA 5, 62, 95

**Dickson, Carr**
See Carr, John Dickson

**Dickson, Carter**
See Carr, John Dickson

**Diderot, Denis** 1713-1784 .................... **LC 26**

**Didion, Joan**
1934- .... **CLC 1, 3, 8, 14, 32; DAM NOV**
See also AITN 1; CA 5-8R; CANR 14, 52;
CDALB 1968-1988; DLB 2, 173; DLBY 81,
86; MTCW

**Dietrich, Robert**
See Hunt, E(verette) Howard, (Jr.)

**Dillard, Annie**
1945- ................. **CLC 9, 60; DAM NOV**
See also AAYA 6; CA 49-52; CANR 3, 43, 62;
DLBY 80; MTCW; SATA 10

**Dillard, R(ichard) H(enry) W(ilde)**
1937- ............................................. **CLC 5**
See also CA 21-24R; CAAS 7; CANR 10; DLB
5

**Dillon, Eilis** 1920-1994 ...................... **CLC 17**
See also CA 9-12R; 147; CAAS 3; CANR 4,
38; CLR 26; MAICYA; SATA 2, 74; SATA-
Obit 83

**Dimont, Penelope**
See Mortimer, Penelope (Ruth)

**Dinesen, Isak** ............... **CLC 10, 29, 95; SSC 7**
See also Blixen, Karen (Christentze Dinesen)

**Ding Ling** ........................................... **CLC 68**
See also Chiang Pin-chin

**Disch, Thomas M(ichael)** 1940- .... **CLC 7, 36**
See also AAYA 17; CA 21-24R; CAAS 4;
CANR 17, 36, 54; CLR 18; DLB 8;
MAICYA; MTCW; SAAS 15; SATA 92

**Disch, Tom**
See Disch, Thomas M(ichael)

**d'Isly, Georges**
See Simenon, Georges (Jacques Christian)

**Disraeli, Benjamin** 1804-1881 ... **NCLC 2, 39**
See also DLB 21, 55

**Ditcum, Steve**
See Crumb, R(obert)

**Dixon, Paige**
See Corcoran, Barbara

**Dixon, Stephen** 1936- .......... **CLC 52; SSC 16**
See also CA 89-92; CANR 17, 40, 54; DLB
130

**Doak, Annie**
See Dillard, Annie

**Dobell, Sydney Thompson**
1824-1874 ................................ **NCLC 43**
See also DLB 32

**Doblin, Alfred** ................................ **TCLC 13**
See also Doeblin, Alfred

**Dobrolyubov, Nikolai Alexandrovich**
1836-1861 .................................. **NCLC 5**

**Dobyns, Stephen** 1941- ..................... **CLC 37**
See also CA 45-48; CANR 2, 18

**Doctorow, E(dgar) L(aurence)**
1931- ........ **CLC 6, 11, 15, 18, 37, 44, 65;
DAM NOV, POP**
See also AAYA 22; AITN 2; BEST 89:3; CA
45-48; CANR 2, 33, 51; CDALB 1968-
1988; DLB 2, 28, 173; DLBY 80; MTCW

**Dodgson, Charles Lutwidge** 1832-1898
See Carroll, Lewis
See also CLR 2; DA; DAB; DAC; DAM MST,
NOV, POET; MAICYA; YABC 2

**Dodson, Owen (Vincent)**
1914-1983 . **CLC 79; BLC; DAM MULT**
See also BW 1; CA 65-68; 110; CANR 24;
DLB 76

**Doeblin, Alfred** 1878-1957 ............. **TCLC 13**
See also Doblin, Alfred
See also CA 110; 141; DLB 66

**Doerr, Harriet** 1910- .......................... **CLC 34**
See also CA 117; 122; CANR 47; INT 122

**Domecq, H(onorio) Bustos**
See Bioy Casares, Adolfo; Borges, Jorge Luis

**Domini, Rey**
See Lorde, Audre (Geraldine)

**Dominique**
See Proust, (Valentin-Louis-George-Eugene-)
Marcel

**Don, A**
See Stephen, Leslie

**Donaldson, Stephen R.**
1947- ........................ **CLC 46; DAM POP**
See also CA 89-92; CANR 13, 55; INT CANR-
13

**Donleavy, J(ames) P(atrick)**
1926- ...................... **CLC 1, 4, 6, 10, 45**
See also AITN 2; CA 9-12R; CANR 24, 49,
62; DLB 6, 173; INT CANR-24; MTCW

**Donne, John**
1572-1631 . **LC 10, 24; DA; DAB; DAC;
DAM MST, POET; PC 1**
See also CDBLB Before 1660; DLB 121, 151

**Donnell, David** 1939(?)- .................... **CLC 34**

**Donoghue, P. S.**
See Hunt, E(verette) Howard, (Jr.)

**Donoso (Yanez), Jose**
1924-1996 .... **CLC 4, 8, 11, 32, 99; DAM
MULT; HLC**
See also CA 81-84; 155; CANR 32; DLB 113;
HW; MTCW

**Donovan, John** 1928-1992 ................. **CLC 35**
See also AAYA 20; CA 97-100; 137; CLR 3;
MAICYA; SATA 72; SATA-Brief 29

**Don Roberto**
See Cunninghame Graham, R(obert) B(ontine)

**Doolittle, Hilda**
1886-1961 **CLC 3, 8, 14, 31, 34, 73; DA;
DAC; DAM MST, POET; PC 5; WLC**
See also H. D.
See also CA 97-100; CANR 35; DLB 4, 45;
MTCW

**Dorfman, Ariel** 1942- ....... **CLC 48, 77; DAM
MULT; HLC**
See also CA 124; 130; HW; INT 130

**Dorn, Edward (Merton)** 1929- ... **CLC 10, 18**
See also CA 93-96; CANR 42; DLB 5; INT
93-96

**Dorsan, Luc**
See Simenon, Georges (Jacques Christian)

**Dorsange, Jean**
See Simenon, Georges (Jacques Christian)

**Dos Passos, John (Roderigo)**
1896-1970 ... **CLC 1, 4, 8, 11, 15, 25, 34,
82; DA; DAB; DAC; DAM MST, NOV;
WLC**
See also CA 1-4R; 29-32R; CANR 3; CDALB
1929-1941; DLB 4, 9; DLBD 1, 15; DLBY
96; MTCW

**Dossage, Jean**
See Simenon, Georges (Jacques Christian)

**Dostoevsky, Fedor Mikhailovich**
1821-1881 ... **NCLC 2, 7, 21, 33, 43; DA;
DAB; DAC; DAM MST, NOV; SSC 2;
WLC**

**Doughty, Charles M(ontagu)**
1843-1926 .............................. **TCLC 27**
See also CA 115; DLB 19, 57, 174

**Douglas, Ellen** ..................................... **CLC 73**
See also Haxton, Josephine Ayres; Williamson,
Ellen Douglas

**Douglas, Gavin** 1475(?)-1522 .............. **LC 20**

**Douglas, Keith (Castellain)**
1920-1944 ................................. **TCLC 40**
See also CA 160; DLB 27

**Douglas, Leonard**
See Bradbury, Ray (Douglas)

**Douglas, Michael**
See Crichton, (John) Michael

**Douglas, Norman** 1868-1952 ........ **TCLC 68**

**Douglass, Frederick**
1817(?)-1895 ..... **NCLC 7, 55; BLC; DA;
DAC; DAM MST, MULT; WLC**
See also CDALB 1640-1865; DLB 1, 43, 50,
79; SATA 29

**Dourado, (Waldomiro Freitas) Autran**
1926- ...................................... **CLC 23, 60**
See also CA 25-28R; CANR 34

**Dourado, Waldomiro Autran**
See Dourado, (Waldomiro Freitas) Autran

**Dove, Rita (Frances)**
1952- ......... **CLC 50, 81; DAM MULT,
POET; PC 6**
See also BW 2; CA 109; CAAS 19; CANR 27,
42; DLB 120

**Dowell, Coleman** 1925-1985 ............ **CLC 60**
See also CA 25-28R; 117; CANR 10; DLB 130

**Dowson, Ernest (Christopher)**
1867-1900 .................................... **TCLC 4**
See also CA 105; 150; DLB 19, 135

**Doyle, A. Conan**
See Doyle, Arthur Conan

**Doyle, Arthur Conan**
1859-1930 **TCLC 7; DA; DAB; DAC;
DAM MST, NOV; SSC 12; WLC**
See also AAYA 14; CA 104; 122; CDBLB
1890-1914; DLB 18, 70, 156, 178; MTCW;
SATA 24

**Doyle, Conan**
See Doyle, Arthur Conan

**Doyle, John**
See Graves, Robert (von Ranke)

**Doyle, Roddy** 1958(?)- ....................... **CLC 81**
See also AAYA 14; CA 143

**Doyle, Sir A. Conan**
See Doyle, Arthur Conan

**Doyle, Sir Arthur Conan**
See Doyle, Arthur Conan

**Dr. A**
See Asimov, Isaac; Silverstein, Alvin

**Drabble, Margaret**
1939-.... **CLC 2, 3, 5, 8, 10, 22, 53; DAB;
DAC; DAM MST, NOV, POP**
See also CA 13-16R; CANR 18, 35; CDBLB
1960 to Present; DLB 14, 155; MTCW;
SATA 48

**Drapier, M. B.**
See Swift, Jonathan

**Drayham, James**
See Mencken, H(enry) L(ouis)

**Drayton, Michael** 1563-1631 ................ **LC 8**

**Dreadstone, Carl**
See Campbell, (John) Ramsey

**Dreiser, Theodore (Herman Albert)**
1871-1945 ....... **TCLC 10, 18, 35; DA;
DAC; DAM MST, NOV; WLC**
See also CA 106; 132; CDALB 1865-
1917; DLB 9, 12, 102, 137; DLBD 1;
MTCW

**Drexler, Rosalyn** 1926- ................... **CLC 2, 6**
See also CA 81-84

**Dreyer, Carl Theodor** 1889-1968 ..... **CLC 16**
See also CA 116

**Drieu la Rochelle, Pierre(-Eugene)**
1893-1945 ................................. **TCLC 21**
See also CA 117; DLB 72

**Drinkwater, John**
1882-1937 ................................. **TCLC 57**
See also CA 109; 149; DLB 10, 19, 149

**Drop Shot**
See Cable, George Washington

**Droste-Hulshoff, Annette Freiin von**
1797-1848 ................................... **NCLC 3**
See also DLB 133

**Drummond, Walter**
See Silverberg, Robert

**Drummond, William Henry**
1854-1907 .............................. **TCLC 25**
See also CA 160; DLB 92

**Drummond de Andrade, Carlos**
1902-1987 ................................. **CLC 18**
See also Andrade, Carlos Drummond de
See also CA 132; 123

**Drury, Allen (Stuart)** 1918- ............. **CLC 37**
See also CA 57-60; CANR 18, 52; INT CANR-
18

**Dryden, John**
1631-1700 ... **LC 3, 21; DA; DAB; DAC;
DAM DRAM, MST, POET; DC 3; WLC**
See also CDBLB 1660-1789; DLB 80, 101,
131

**Duberman, Martin** 1930- ................... **CLC 8**
See also CA 1-4R; CANR 2

**Dubie, Norman (Evans)** 1945- ......... **CLC 36**
See also CA 69-72; CANR 12; DLB 120

**Du Bois, W(illiam) E(dward) B(urghardt)**
1868-1963 ... **CLC 1, 2, 13, 64, 96; BLC;
DA; DAC; DAM MST, MULT, NOV;
WLC**
See also BW 1; CA 85-88; CANR 34; CDALB
1865-1917; DLB 47, 50, 91; MTCW; SATA
42

**Dubus, Andre**
1936- ................. **CLC 13, 36, 97; SSC 15**
See also CA 21-24R; CANR 17; DLB 130; INT
CANR-17

**Duca Minimo**
See D'Annunzio, Gabriele

**Ducharme, Rejean** 1941- ................... **CLC 74**
See also DLB 60

**Duclos, Charles Pinot** 1704-1772 ......... **LC 1**

**Dudek, Louis** 1918- ...................... **CLC 11, 19**
See also CA 45-48; CAAS 14; CANR 1; DLB 88

**Duerrenmatt, Friedrich**
1921-1990 ..**CLC 1, 4, 8, 11, 15, 43, 102;
DAM DRAM**
See also CA 17-20R; CANR 33; DLB 69, 124;
MTCW

**Duffy, Bruce** (?)- ............................... **CLC 50**

**Duffy, Maureen** 1933- ....................... **CLC 37**
See also CA 25-28R; CANR 33; DLB 14;
MTCW

**Dugan, Alan** 1923- ......................... **CLC 2, 6**
See also CA 81-84; DLB 5

**du Gard, Roger Martin**
See Martin du Gard, Roger

**Duhamel, Georges** 1884-1966 ............. **CLC 8**
See also CA 81-84; 25-28R; CANR 35; DLB
65; MTCW

Fagen, Donald  1948-............................. CLC 26

Fainzilberg, Ilya Arnoldovich  1897-1937
  See Ilf, Ilya
  See also CA 120

Fair, Ronald L.  1932- ........................ CLC 18
  See also BW 1; CA 69-72; CANR 25; DLB
  33

Fairbairn, Roger
  See Carr, John Dickson

Fairbairns, Zoe (Ann)  1948-............. CLC 32
  See also CA 103; CANR 21

Falco, Gian
  See Papini, Giovanni

Falconer, James
  See Kirkup, James

Falconer, Kenneth
  See Kornbluth, C(yril) M.

Falkland, Samuel
  See Heijermans, Herman

Fallaci, Oriana  1930-........................... CLC 11
  See also CA 77-80; CANR 15, 58; MTCW

Faludy, George  1913- ........................ CLC 42
  See also CA 21-24R

Faludy, Gyoergy
  See Faludy, George

Fanon, Frantz  1925-1961 ...... CLC 74; BLC;
  DAM MULT
  See also BW 1; CA 116; 89-92

Fanshawe, Ann  1625-1680 .................. LC 11

Fante, John (Thomas)
  1911-1983 ................................... CLC 60
  See also CA 69-72; 109; CANR 23; DLB 130;
  DLBY 83

Farah, Nuruddin
  1945- ......... CLC 53; BLC; DAM MULT
  See also BW 2; CA 106; DLB 125

Fargue, Leon-Paul  1876(?)-1947 .... TCLC 11
  See also CA 109

Farigoule, Louis
  See Romains, Jules

Farina, Richard  1936(?)-1966 ........... CLC 9
  See also CA 81-84; 25-28R

Farley, Walter (Lorimer)
  1915-1989 ................................... CLC 17
  See also CA 17-20R; CANR 8, 29; DLB 22;
  JRDA; MAICYA; SATA 2, 43

Farmer, Philip Jose  1918- ............. CLC 1, 19
  See also CA 1-4R; CANR 4, 35; DLB 8;
  MTCW; SATA 93

Farquhar, George
  1677-1707 ............. LC 21; DAM DRAM
  See also DLB 84

Farrell, J(ames) G(ordon)
  1935-1979 ..................................... CLC 6
  See also CA 73-76; 89-92; CANR 36; DLB
  14; MTCW

Farrell, James T(homas)
  1904-1979 ... CLC 1, 4, 8, 11, 66; SSC
  28
  See also CA 5-8R; 89-92; CANR 9, 61; DLB
  4, 9, 86; DLBD 2; MTCW

Farren, Richard J.
  See Betjeman, John

Farren, Richard M.
  See Betjeman, John

Fassbinder, Rainer Werner
  1946-1982 ................................... CLC 20
  See also CA 93-96; 106; CANR 31

Fast, Howard (Melvin)
  1914-....................... CLC 23; DAM NOV
  See also AAYA 16; CA 1-4R; CAAS 18;
  CANR 1, 33, 54; DLB 9; INT CANR-33;
  SATA 7

Faulcon, Robert
  See Holdstock, Robert P.

Faulkner, William (Cuthbert)
  1897-1962 CLC 1, 3, 6, 8, 9, 11, 14, 18,
  28, 52, 68; DA; DAB; DAC; DAM
  MST, NOV; SSC 1; WLC
  See also AAYA 7; CA 81-84; CANR 33;
  CDALB 1929-1941; DLB 9, 11, 44, 102;
  DLBD 2; DLBY 86; MTCW

Fauset, Jessie Redmon
  1884(?)-1961 ... CLC 19, 54; BLC; DAM
  MULT
  See also BW 1; CA 109; DLB 51

Faust, Frederick (Schiller)
  1892-1944(?) ........ TCLC 49; DAM POP
  See also CA 108; 152

Faust, Irvin  1924-................................. CLC 8
  See also CA 33-36R; CANR 28; DLB 2, 28;
  DLBY 80

Fawkes, Guy
  See Benchley, Robert (Charles)

Fearing, Kenneth (Flexner)
  1902-1961 ................................... CLC 51
  See also CA 93-96; CANR 59; DLB 9

Fecamps, Elise
  See Creasey, John

Federman, Raymond  1928-........... CLC 6, 47
  See also CA 17-20R; CAAS 8; CANR 10, 43;
  DLBY 80

Federspiel, J(uerg) F.  1931- .............. CLC 42
  See also CA 146

Feiffer, Jules (Ralph)
  1929-........... CLC 2, 8, 64; DAM DRAM
  See also AAYA 3; CA 17-20R; CANR 30, 59;
  DLB 7, 44; INT CANR-30; MTCW; SATA
  8, 61

Feige, Hermann Albert Otto Maximilian
  See Traven, B.

Feinberg, David B.  1956-1994 .......... CLC 59
  See also CA 135; 147

Feinstein, Elaine  1930- ...................... CLC 36
  See also CA 69-72; CAAS 1; CANR 31; DLB
  14, 40; MTCW

Feldman, Irving (Mordecai)  1928- .... CLC 7
  See also CA 1-4R; CANR 1; DLB 169

Felix-Tchicaya, Gerald
  See Tchicaya, Gerald Felix

Fellini, Federico  1920-1993 ........ CLC 16, 85
  See also CA 65-68; 143; CANR 33

Felsen, Henry Gregor  1916- ............. CLC 17
  See also CA 1-4R; CANR 1; SAAS 2; SATA
  1

Fenton, James Martin  1949-............. CLC 32
  See also CA 102; DLB 40

Ferber, Edna  1887-1968 ............. CLC 18, 93
  See also AITN 1; CA 5-8R; 25-28R; DLB 9,
  28, 86; MTCW; SATA 7

Ferguson, Helen
  See Kavan, Anna

Ferguson, Samuel  1810-1886 ......... NCLC 33
  See also DLB 32

Fergusson, Robert  1750-1774 .............. LC 29
  See also DLB 109

Ferling, Lawrence
  See Ferlinghetti, Lawrence (Monsanto)

Ferlinghetti, Lawrence (Monsanto)
  1919(?)- .......... CLC 2, 6, 10, 27; DAM
  POET; PC 1
  See also CA 5-8R; CANR 3, 41; CDALB 1941-
  1968; DLB 5, 16; MTCW

Fernandez, Vicente Garcia Huidobro
  See Huidobro Fernandez, Vicente Garcia

Ferrer, Gabriel (Francisco Victor) Miro
  See Miro (Ferrer), Gabriel (Francisco Victor)

Ferrier, Susan (Edmonstone)
  1782-1854 ................................... NCLC 8
  See also DLB 116

Ferrigno, Robert  1948(?)- ................. CLC 65
  See also CA 140

Ferron, Jacques
  1921-1985 ........................ CLC 94; DAC
  See also CA 117; 129; DLB 60

Feuchtwanger, Lion  1884-1958 ........ TCLC 3
  See also CA 104; DLB 66

Feuillet, Octave  1821-1890 ........... NCLC 45

Feydeau, Georges (Leon Jules Marie)
  1862-1921 ........ TCLC 22; DAM DRAM
  See also CA 113; 152

Ford, Richard ...................................... CLC 99

Ford, Richard
1944- .............................................. CLC 46
See also CA 69-72; CANR 11, 47

Ford, Webster
See Masters, Edgar Lee

Foreman, Richard
1937- .............................................. CLC 50
See also CA 65-68; CANR 32

Forester, C(ecil) S(cott)
1899-1966 .......................................... CLC 35
See also CA 73-76; 25-28R; SATA 13

Forez
See Mauriac, Francois (Charles)

Forman, James Douglas  1932- ......... CLC 21
See also AAYA 17; CA 9-12R; CANR 4, 19,
42; JRDA; MAICYA; SATA 8, 70

Fornes, Maria Irene
1930- ........................................... CLC 39, 61
See also CA 25-28R; CANR 28; DLB 7; HW;
INT CANR-28; MTCW

Forrest, Leon  1937- ............................. CLC 4
See also BW 2; CA 89-92; CAAS 7; CANR
25, 52; DLB 33

Forster, E(dward) M(organ)
1879-1970 ...CLC 1, 2, 3, 4, 9, 10, 13,
15, 22, 45, 77; DA; DAB; DAC;
DAM MST, NOV; SSC 27; WLC
See also AAYA 2; CA 13-14; 25-28R;
CANR 45; CAP 1; CDBLB 1914-1945;
DLB 34, 98, 162, 178; DLBD 10;
MTCW; SATA 57

Forster, John  1812-1876 ................. NCLC 11
See also DLB 144, 184

Forsyth, Frederick
1938- .... CLC 2, 5, 36; DAM NOV, POP
See also BEST 89:4; CA 85-88; CANR 38, 62;
DLB 87; MTCW

Forten, Charlotte L. ............... TCLC 16; BLC
See also Grimke, Charlotte L(ottie) Forten
See also DLB 50

Foscolo, Ugo  1778-1827 ................... NCLC 8

Fosse, Bob ......................................... CLC 20
See also Fosse, Robert Louis

Fosse, Robert Louis  1927-1987
See Fosse, Bob
See also CA 110; 123

Foster, Stephen Collins
1826-1864 ................................. NCLC 26

Foucault, Michel
1926-1984 ...................... CLC 31, 34, 69
See also CA 105; 113; CANR 34; MTCW

Fouque, Friedrich (Heinrich Karl) de la Motte
1777-1843 ................................. NCLC 2
See also DLB 90

Fourier, Charles  1772-1837 .......... NCLC 51

Fournier, Henri Alban  1886-1914
See Alain-Fournier
See also CA 104

Fournier, Pierre  1916- ...................... CLC 11
See also Gascar, Pierre
See also CA 89-92; CANR 16, 40

Fowles, John
1926-.... CLC 1, 2, 3, 4, 6, 9, 10, 15, 33,
87; DAB; DAC; DAM MST
See also CA 5-8R; CANR 25; CDBLB 1960
to Present; DLB 14, 139; MTCW; SATA
22

Fox, Paula  1923- ............................... CLC 2, 8
See also AAYA 3; CA 73-76; CANR 20, 36,
62; CLR 1, 44; DLB 52; JRDA; MAICYA;
MTCW; SATA 17, 60

Fox, William Price (Jr.)
1926- ........................................... CLC 22
See also CA 17-20R; CAAS 19; CANR 11;
DLB 2; DLBY 81

Foxe, John  1516(?)-1587 ..................... LC 14

Frame, Janet
1924-.... CLC 2, 3, 6, 22, 66, 96; SSC 29
See also Clutha, Janet Paterson Frame

France, Anatole ................................. TCLC 9
See also Thibault, Jacques Anatole Francois
See also DLB 123

Francis, Claude  19(?)- ...................... CLC 50

Francis, Dick
1920-..... CLC 2, 22, 42, 102; DAM POP
See also AAYA 5, 21; BEST 89:3; CA 5-8R;
CANR 9, 42; CDBLB 1960 to Present; DLB
87; INT CANR-9; MTCW

Francis, Robert (Churchill)
1901-1987 ................................. CLC 15
See also CA 1-4R; 123; CANR 1

Frank, Anne(lies Marie)
1929-1945 .. TCLC 17; DA; DAB; DAC;
DAM MST; WLC
See also AAYA 12; CA 113; 133; MTCW;
SATA 87; SATA-Brief 42

Frank, Elizabeth  1945- ...................... CLC 39
See also CA 121; 126; INT 126

Frankl, Viktor E(mil)  1905- .............. CLC 93
See also CA 65-68

Franklin, Benjamin
See Hasek, Jaroslav (Matej Frantisek)

Franklin, Benjamin
1706-1790 ........ LC 25; DA; DAB; DAC;
DAM MST; WLCS
See also CDALB 1640-1865; DLB 24, 43,
73

Franklin, (Stella Maraia Sarah) Miles
1879-1954 ................................. TCLC 7
See also CA 104

Fraser, (Lady) Antonia (Pakenham)
1932- .............................................. CLC 32
See also CA 85-88; CANR 44; MTCW; SATA-
Brief 32

Fraser, George MacDonald
1925- .............................................. CLC 7
See also CA 45-48; CANR 2, 48

Fraser, Sylvia  1935- .......................... CLC 64
See also CA 45-48; CANR 1, 16, 60

Frayn, Michael
1933-.... CLC 3, 7, 31, 47; DAM DRAM,
NOV
See also CA 5-8R; CANR 30; DLB 13, 14;
MTCW

Fraze, Candida (Merrill)  1945- ........ CLC 50
See also CA 126

Frazer, J(ames) G(eorge)
1854-1941 ................................. TCLC 32
See also CA 118

Frazer, Robert Caine
See Creasey, John

Frazer, Sir James George
See Frazer, J(ames) G(eorge)

Frazier, Ian  1951- ............................. CLC 46
See also CA 130; CANR 54

Frederic, Harold  1856-1898 .......... NCLC 10
See also DLB 12, 23; DLBD 13

Frederick, John
See Faust, Frederick (Schiller)

Frederick the Great  1712-1786 .......... LC 14

Fredro, Aleksander  1793-1876 ........ NCLC 8

Freeling, Nicolas  1927- ..................... CLC 38
See also CA 49-52; CAAS 12; CANR 1, 17,
50; DLB 87

Freeman, Douglas Southall
1886-1953 ................................. TCLC 11
See also CA 109; DLB 17

Freeman, Judith  1946- ...................... CLC 55
See also CA 148

Freeman, Mary Eleanor Wilkins
1852-1930 ...................... TCLC 9; SSC 1
See also CA 106; DLB 12, 78

Freeman, R(ichard) Austin
1862-1943 ................................. TCLC 21
See also CA 113; DLB 70

French, Albert  1943- .......................... CLC 86

French, Marilyn
1929-...... CLC 10, 18, 60; DAM DRAM,
NOV, POP
See also CA 69-72; CANR 3, 31; INT CANR-
31; MTCW

French, Paul
See Asimov, Isaac

**Garcia Lorca, Federico**
1898-1936 ..... **TCLC 1, 7, 49; DA; DAB;
DAC; DAM DRAM, MST, MULT,
POET; DC 2; HLC; PC 3; WLC**
See also CA 104; 131; DLB 108; HW; MTCW

**Garcia Marquez, Gabriel (Jose)**
1928- ... **CLC 2, 3, 8, 10, 15, 27, 47, 55,
68; DA; DAB; DAC; DAM MST, MULT,
NOV, POP; HLC; SSC 8; WLC**
See also AAYA 3; BEST 89:1, 90:4; CA 33-
36R; CANR 10, 28, 50; DLB 113; HW;
MTCW

**Gard, Janice**
See Latham, Jean Lee

**Gard, Roger Martin du**
See Martin du Gard, Roger

**Gardam, Jane** 1928- ......................... **CLC 43**
See also CA 49-52; CANR 2, 18, 33, 54; CLR
12; DLB 14, 161; MAICYA; MTCW; SAAS
9; SATA 39, 76; SATA-Brief 28

**Gardner, Herb(ert)** 1934- ................. **CLC 44**
See also CA 149

**Gardner, John (Champlin), Jr.**
1933-1982 .. **CLC 2, 3, 5, 7, 8, 10, 18, 28,
34; DAM NOV, POP; SSC 7**
See also AITN 1; CA 65-68; 107; CANR 33;
DLB 2; DLBY 82; MTCW; SATA 40;
SATA-Obit 31

**Gardner, John (Edmund)** 1926- ...... **CLC 30;
DAM POP**
See also CA 103; CANR 15; MTCW

**Gardner, Miriam**
See Bradley, Marion Zimmer

**Gardner, Noel**
See Kuttner, Henry

**Gardons, S. S.**
See Snodgrass, W(illiam) D(e Witt)

**Garfield, Leon** 1921-1996 ................. **CLC 12**
See also AAYA 8; CA 17-20R; 152; CANR 38,
41; CLR 21; DLB 161; JRDA; MAICYA;
SATA 1, 32, 76; SATA-Obit 90

**Garland, (Hannibal) Hamlin**
1860-1940 .................... **TCLC 3; SSC 18**
See also CA 104; DLB 12, 71, 78

**Garneau, (Hector de) Saint-Denys**
1912-1943 ............................... **TCLC 13**
See also CA 111; DLB 88

**Garner, Alan**
1934- ........... **CLC 17; DAB; DAM POP**
See also AAYA 18; CA 73-76; CANR 15; CLR
20; DLB 161; MAICYA; MTCW; SATA 18,
69

**Garner, Hugh** 1913-1979 ................. **CLC 13**
See also CA 69-72; CANR 31; DLB 68

**Garnett, David** 1892-1981 ................. **CLC 3**
See also CA 5-8R; 103; CANR 17; DLB
34

**Garos, Stephanie**
See Katz, Steve

**Garrett, George (Palmer)**
1929- ................................. **CLC 3, 11, 51**
See also CA 1-4R; CAAS 5; CANR 1, 42; DLB
2, 5, 130, 152; DLBY 83

**Garrick, David** 1717-1779 ....... **LC 15; DAM
DRAM**
See also DLB 84

**Garrigue, Jean** 1914-1972 ............... **CLC 2, 8**
See also CA 5-8R; 37-40R; CANR 20

**Garrison, Frederick**
See Sinclair, Upton (Beall)

**Garth, Will**
See Hamilton, Edmond; Kuttner, Henry

**Garvey, Marcus (Moziah, Jr.)**
1887-1940 ......... **TCLC 41; BLC; DAM
MULT**
See also BW 1; CA 120; 124

**Gary, Romain** ..................................... **CLC 25**
See also Kacew, Romain
See also DLB 83

**Gascar, Pierre** ..................................... **CLC 11**
See also Fournier, Pierre

**Gascoyne, David (Emery)**
1916- ............................................ **CLC 45**
See also CA 65-68; CANR 10, 28, 54; DLB
20; MTCW

**Gaskell, Elizabeth Cleghorn**
1810-1865 .. **NCLC 5; DAB; DAM MST;
SSC 25**
See also CDBLB 1832-1890; DLB 21, 144,
159

**Gass, William H(oward)**
1924-..... **CLC 1, 2, 8, 11, 15, 39; SSC 12**
See also CA 17-20R; CANR 30; DLB 2;
MTCW

**Gasset, Jose Ortega y**
See Ortega y Gasset, Jose

**Gates, Henry Louis, Jr.**
1950-................... **CLC 65; DAM MULT**
See also BW 2; CA 109; CANR 25, 53; DLB
67

**Gautier, Theophile**
1811-1872 ... **NCLC 1, 59; DAM POET;
PC 18; SSC 20**
See also DLB 119

**Gawsworth, John**
See Bates, H(erbert) E(rnest)

**Gay, Oliver**
See Gogarty, Oliver St. John

**Gaye, Marvin (Penze)** 1939-1984 ..... **CLC 26**
See also CA 112

**Gebler, Carlo (Ernest)** 1954- ........... **CLC 39**
See also CA 119; 133

**Gee, Maggie (Mary)** 1948- ............... **CLC 57**
See also CA 130

**Gee, Maurice (Gough)** 1931- ........... **CLC 29**
See also CA 97-100; SATA 46

**Gelbart, Larry (Simon)** 1923- .... **CLC 21, 61**
See also CA 73-76; CANR 45

**Gelber, Jack** 1932- ............... **CLC 1, 6, 14, 79**
See also CA 1-4R; CANR 2; DLB 7

**Gellhorn, Martha (Ellis)**
1908-..................................... **CLC 14, 60**
See also CA 77-80; CANR 44; DLBY 82

**Genet, Jean**
1910-1986 ....**CLC 1, 2, 5, 10, 14, 44, 46;
DAM DRAM**
See also CA 13-16R; CANR 18; DLB 72;
DLBY 86; MTCW

**Gent, Peter** 1942- ............................... **CLC 29**
See also AITN 1; CA 89-92; DLBY 82

**Gentlewoman in New England, A**
See Bradstreet, Anne

**Gentlewoman in Those Parts, A**
See Bradstreet, Anne

**George, Jean Craighead**
1919-..................................... **CLC 35**
See also AAYA 8; CA 5-8R; CANR 25; CLR
1; DLB 52; JRDA; MAICYA; SATA 2, 68

**George, Stefan (Anton)**
1868-1933 ............................. **TCLC 2, 14**
See also CA 104

**Georges, Georges Martin**
See Simenon, Georges (Jacques Christian)

**Gerhardi, William Alexander**
See Gerhardie, William Alexander

**Gerhardie, William Alexander**
1895-1977 ..................................... **CLC 5**
See also CA 25-28R; 73-76; CANR 18; DLB
36

**Gerstler, Amy** 1956-........................... **CLC 70**
See also CA 146

**Gertler, T.** ............................................ **CLC 34**
See also CA 116; 121; INT 121

**Ghalib** ................................................. **NCLC 39**
See also Ghalib, Hsadullah Khan

**Ghalib, Hsadullah Khan** 1797-1869
See Ghalib
See also DAM POET

**Ghelderode, Michel de**
1898-1962 ....... **CLC 6, 11; DAM DRAM**
See also CA 85-88; CANR 40

**Ghiselin, Brewster** 1903-................... **CLC 23**
See also CA 13-16R; CAAS 10; CANR 13

**Ghose, Zulfikar** 1935-........................ **CLC 42**
See also CA 65-68

**Ghosh, Amitav** 1956- ..................... **CLC 44**
See also CA 147

**Giacosa, Giuseppe** 1847-1906 .......... **TCLC 7**
See also CA 104

**Gibb, Lee**
See Waterhouse, Keith (Spencer)

**Gibbon, Lewis Grassic** ...................... **TCLC 4**
See also Mitchell, James Leslie

**Gibbons, Kaye**
1960-................. **CLC 50, 88; DAM POP**
See also CA 151

**Gibran, Kahlil**
1883-1931 ....... **TCLC 1, 9; DAM POET,
POP; PC 9**
See also CA 104; 150

**Gibran, Khalil**
See Gibran, Kahlil

**Gibson, William**
1914-... **CLC 23; DA; DAB; DAC; DAM
DRAM, MST**
See also CA 9-12R; CANR 9, 42; DLB 7; SATA
66

**Gibson, William (Ford)**
1948-................. **CLC 39, 63; DAM POP**
See also AAYA 12; CA 126; 133; CANR
52

**Gide, Andre (Paul Guillaume)**
1869-1951 ... **TCLC 5, 12, 36; DA; DAB;
DAC; DAM MST, NOV; SSC 13; WLC**
See also CA 104; 124; DLB 65; MTCW

**Gifford, Barry (Colby)** 1946- .......... **CLC 34**
See also CA 65-68; CANR 9, 30, 40

**Gilbert, Frank**
See De Voto, Bernard (Augustine)

**Gilbert, W(illiam) S(chwenck)**
1836-1911 ........ **TCLC 3; DAM DRAM,
POET**
See also CA 104; SATA 36

**Gilbreth, Frank B., Jr.**
1911-........................................... **CLC 17**
See also CA 9-12R; SATA 2

**Gilchrist, Ellen**
1935-... **CLC 34, 48; DAM POP; SSC 14**
See also CA 113; 116; CANR 41, 61; DLB 130;
MTCW

**Giles, Molly** 1942- ............................. **CLC 39**
See also CA 126

**Gill, Patrick**
See Creasey, John

**Gilliam, Terry (Vance)** 1940-........... **CLC 21**
See also Monty Python
See also AAYA 19; CA 108; 113; CANR 35;
INT 113

**Gillian, Jerry**
See Gilliam, Terry (Vance)

**Gilliatt, Penelope (Ann Douglass)**
1932-1993 .................... **CLC 2, 10, 13, 53**
See also AITN 2; CA 13-16R; 141; CANR 49;
DLB 14

**Gilman, Charlotte (Anna) Perkins (Stetson)**
1860-1935 ............. **TCLC 9, 37; SSC 13**
See also CA 106; 150

**Gilmour, David**
1949- ........................................... **CLC 35**
See also CA 138, 147

**Gilpin, William** 1724-1804 ............. **NCLC 30**

**Gilray, J. D.**
See Mencken, H(enry) L(ouis)

**Gilroy, Frank D(aniel)**
1925- ............................................. **CLC 2**
See also CA 81-84; CANR 32; DLB 7

**Gilstrap, John** 1957(?)-...................... **CLC 99**
See also CA 160

**Ginsberg, Allen**
1926-1997 .... **CLC 1, 2, 3, 4, 6, 13, 36,
69; DA; DAB; DAC; DAM MST, POET;
PC 4; WLC 3**
See also AITN 1; CA 1-4R; 157; CANR 2, 41;
CDALB 1941-1968; DLB 5, 16, 169;
MTCW

**Ginzburg, Natalia**
1916-1991 .................... **CLC 5, 11, 54, 70**
See also CA 85-88; 135; CANR 33; DLB 177;
MTCW

**Giono, Jean**
1895-1970 ................................ **CLC 4, 11**
See also CA 45-48; 29-32R; CANR 2, 35; DLB
72; MTCW

**Giovanni, Nikki**
1943- ....... **CLC 2, 4, 19, 64; BLC; DA;
DAB; DAC; DAM MST, MULT, POET;
PC 19; WLCS**
See also AAYA 22; AITN 1; BW 2; CA 29-
32R; CAAS 6; CANR 18, 41, 60; CLR 6;
DLB 5, 41; INT CANR-18; MAICYA;
MTCW; SATA 24

**Giovene, Andrea**
1904- ............................................. **CLC 7**
See also CA 85-88

**Gippius, Zinaida (Nikolayevna)** 1869-1945
See Hippius, Zinaida
See also CA 106

**Giraudoux, (Hippolyte) Jean**
1882-1944 ...... **TCLC 2, 7; DAM DRAM**
See also CA 104; DLB 65

**Gironella, Jose Maria** 1917- ............. **CLC 11**
See also CA 101

**Gissing, George (Robert)**
1857-1903 ...................... **TCLC 3, 24, 47**
See also CA 105; DLB 18, 135, 184

**Giurlani, Aldo**
See Palazzeschi, Aldo

**Gladkov, Fyodor (Vasilyevich)**
1883-1958 ................................. **TCLC 27**

**Glanville, Brian (Lester)** 1931- .......... **CLC 6**
See also CA 5-8R; CAAS 9; CANR 3; DLB
15, 139; SATA 42

**Glasgow, Ellen (Anderson Gholson)**
1873(?)-1945 ........................... **TCLC 2, 7**
See also CA 104; DLB 9, 12

**Glaspell, Susan** 1882(?)-1948 ........ **TCLC 55**
See also CA 110; 154; DLB 7, 9, 78; YABC
2

**Glassco, John** 1909-1981 ..................... **CLC 9**
See also CA 13-16R; 102; CANR 15; DLB 68

**Glasscock, Amnesia**
See Steinbeck, John (Ernst)

**Glasser, Ronald J.** 1940(?)- .............. **CLC 37**

**Glassman, Joyce**
See Johnson, Joyce

**Glendinning, Victoria** 1937- ............. **CLC 50**
See also CA 120; 127; CANR 59; DLB 155

**Glissant, Edouard**
1928-.............. **CLC 10, 68; DAM MULT**
See also CA 153

**Gloag, Julian** 1930-........................... **CLC 40**
See also AITN 1; CA 65-68; CANR 10

**Glowacki, Aleksander**
See Prus, Boleslaw

**Gluck, Louise (Elisabeth)**
1943-... **CLC 7, 22, 44, 81; DAM POET;
PC 16**
See also CA 33-36R; CANR 40; DLB 5

**Glyn, Elinor** 1864-1943 ................. **TCLC 72**
See also DLB 153

**Gobineau, Joseph Arthur (Comte) de**
1816-1882 ................................. **NCLC 17**
See also DLB 123

**Godard, Jean-Luc** 1930- .................. **CLC 20**
See also CA 93-96

**Godden, (Margaret) Rumer**
1907-........................................... **CLC 53**
See also AAYA 6; CA 5-8R; CANR 4, 27, 36,
55; CLR 20; DLB 161; MAICYA; SAAS 12;
SATA 3, 36

**Godoy Alcayaga, Lucila** 1889-1957
See Mistral, Gabriela
See also BW 2; CA 104; 131; DAM MULT;
HW; MTCW

**Godwin, Gail (Kathleen)**
1937-... **CLC 5, 8, 22, 31, 69; DAM POP**
See also CA 29-32R; CANR 15, 43; DLB 6;
INT CANR-15; MTCW

**Godwin, William** 1756-1836 .......... **NCLC 14**
See also CDBLB 1789-1832; DLB 39, 104,
142, 158, 163

**Goebbels, Josef**
See Goebbels, (Paul) Joseph

**Goebbels, (Paul) Joseph**
1897-1945 .................................. TCLC **68**
See also CA 115; 148

**Goebbels, Joseph Paul**
See Goebbels, (Paul) Joseph

**Goethe, Johann Wolfgang von**
1749-1832 .. NCLC **4, 22, 34; DA; DAB;
DAC; DAM DRAM, MST, POET; PC 5;
WLC 3**
See also DLB 94

**Gogarty, Oliver St. John**
1878-1957 .............................. TCLC **15**
See also CA 109; 150; DLB 15, 19

**Gogol, Nikolai (Vasilyevich)**
1809-1852 .. NCLC **5, 15, 31; DA; DAB;
DAC; DAM DRAM, MST; DC 1; SSC 4,
29; WLC**

**Goines, Donald**
1937(?)-1974 .......... CLC **80; BLC; DAM
MULT, POP**
See also AITN 1; BW 1; CA 124; 114; DLB
33

**Gold, Herbert**
1924- ............................. CLC **4, 7, 14, 42**
See also CA 9-12R; CANR 17, 45; DLB 2;
DLBY 81

**Goldbarth, Albert** 1948- .............. CLC **5, 38**
See also CA 53-56; CANR 6, 40; DLB 120

**Goldberg, Anatol**
1910-1982 .................................. CLC **34**
See also CA 131; 117

**Goldemberg, Isaac** 1945- ................. CLC **52**
See also CA 69-72; CAAS 12; CANR 11, 32;
HW

**Golding, William (Gerald)**
1911-1993 ... CLC **1, 2, 3, 8, 10, 17, 27,
58, 81; DA; DAB; DAC; DAM MST,
NOV; WLC**
See also AAYA 5; CA 5-8R; 141; CANR 13,
33, 54; CDBLB 1945-1960; DLB 15, 100;
MTCW

**Goldman, Emma** 1869-1940 ......... TCLC **13**
See also CA 110; 150

**Goldman, Francisco** 1955- ............... CLC **76**

**Goldman, William (W.)**
1931- ...................................... CLC **1, 48**
See also CA 9-12R; CANR 29; DLB 44

**Goldmann, Lucien**
1913-1970 .................................. CLC **24**
See also CA 25-28; CAP 2

**Goldoni, Carlo**
1707-1793 .............. LC **4; DAM DRAM**

**Goldsberry, Steven** 1949- .................. CLC **34**
See also CA 131

**Goldsmith, Oliver**
1728-1774 ....... LC **2; DA; DAB; DAC;
DAM DRAM, MST, NOV, POET; WLC**
See also CDBLB 1660-1789; DLB 39, 89,
104, 109, 142; SATA 26

**Goldsmith, Peter**
See Priestley, J(ohn) B(oynton)

**Gombrowicz, Witold**
1904-1969 .......... CLC **4, 7, 11, 49; DAM
DRAM**
See also CA 19-20; 25-28R; CAP 2

**Gomez de la Serna, Ramon**
1888-1963 .................................. CLC **9**
See also CA 153; 116; HW

**Goncharov, Ivan Alexandrovich**
1812-1891 ............................. NCLC **1, 63**

**Goncourt, Edmond (Louis Antoine Huot) de**
1822-1896 .................................. NCLC **7**
See also DLB 123

**Goncourt, Jules (Alfred Huot) de**
1830-1870 .................................. NCLC **7**
See also DLB 123

**Gontier, Fernande** 19(?)- .................. CLC **50**

**Gonzalez Martinez, Enrique**
1871-1952 .............................. TCLC **72**
See also HW

**Goodman, Paul** 1911-1972 ...... CLC **1, 2, 4, 7**
See also CA 19-20; 37-40R; CANR 34; CAP
2; DLB 130; MTCW

**Gordimer, Nadine**
1923-..... CLC **3, 5, 7, 10, 18, 33, 51, 70;
DA; DAB; DAC; DAM MST, NOV; SSC
17; WLCS**
See also CA 5-8R; CANR 3, 28, 56; INT
CANR-28; MTCW

**Gordon, Adam Lindsay**
1833-1870 .............................. NCLC **21**

**Gordon, Caroline**
1895-1981 .... CLC **6, 13, 29, 83; SSC 15**
See also CA 11-12; 103; CANR 36; CAP 1;
DLB 4, 9, 102; DLBY 81; MTCW

**Gordon, Charles William** 1860-1937
See Connor, Ralph
See also CA 109

**Gordon, Mary (Catherine)**
1949-.................................... CLC **13, 22**
See also CA 102; CANR 44; DLB 6; DLBY
81; INT 102; MTCW

**Gordon, N. J.**
See Bosman, Herman Charles

**Gordon, Sol** 1923- ............................. CLC **26**
See also CA 53-56; CANR 4; SATA 11

**Gordone, Charles**
1925-1995 ......... CLC **1, 4; DAM DRAM**
See also BW 1; CA 93-96; 150; CANR 55;
DLB 7; INT 93-96; MTCW

**Gore, Catherine** 1800-1861 ............ NCLC **65**
See also DLB 116

**Gorenko, Anna Andreevna**
See Akhmatova, Anna

**Gorky, Maxim ........** TCLC **8; DAB; SSC 28;
WLC**
See also Peshkov, Alexei Maximovich

**Goryan, Sirak**
See Saroyan, William

**Gosse, Edmund (William)**
1849-1928 .............................. TCLC **28**
See also CA 117; DLB 57, 144, 184

**Gotlieb, Phyllis Fay (Bloom)**
1926- ...................................... CLC **18**
See also CA 13-16R; CANR 7; DLB 88

**Gottesman, S. D.**
See Kornbluth, C(yril) M.; Pohl, Frederik

**Gottfried von Strassburg**
fl. c. 1210- .............................. CMLC **10**
See also DLB 138

**Gould, Lois ...................................** CLC **4, 10**
See also CA 77-80; CANR 29; MTCW

**Gourmont, Remy (-Marie-Charles) de**
1858-1915 .............................. TCLC **17**
See also CA 109; 150

**Govier, Katherine** 1948- .................... CLC **51**
See also CA 101; CANR 18, 40

**Goyen, (Charles) William**
1915-1983 .................... CLC **5, 8, 14, 40**
See also AITN 2; CA 5-8R; 110; CANR 6; DLB
2; DLBY 83; INT CANR-6

**Goytisolo, Juan**
1931-........ CLC **5, 10, 23; DAM MULT;
HLC**
See also CA 85-88; CANR 32, 61; HW;
MTCW

**Gozzano, Guido** 1883-1916 ................. PC **10**
See also CA 154; DLB 114

**Gozzi, (Conte) Carlo**
1720-1806 .............................. NCLC **23**

**Grabbe, Christian Dietrich**
1801-1836 .................................. NCLC **2**
See also DLB 133

**Grace, Patricia** 1937-........................ CLC **56**

**Gracian y Morales, Baltasar**
1601-1658 ...................................... LC **15**

**Gracq, Julien ............................... CLC **11, 48**
See also Poirier, Louis
See also DLB 83

**Grade, Chaim** 1910-1982 ................. CLC **10**
See also CA 93-96; 107

**Graduate of Oxford, A**
See Ruskin, John

Griffin, Peter 1942- ........................... CLC 39
See also CA 136

Griffith, D(avid Lewelyn) W(ark)
1875(?)-1948 ........................... TCLC 68
See also CA 119; 150

Griffith, Lawrence
See Griffith, D(avid Lewelyn) W(ark)

Griffiths, Trevor 1935- ............... CLC 13, 52
See also CA 97-100; CANR 45; DLB 13

Grigson, Geoffrey (Edward Harvey)
1905-1985 ........................... CLC 7, 39
See also CA 25-28R; 118; CANR 20, 33; DLB
27; MTCW

Grillparzer, Franz 1791-1872 ......... NCLC 1
See also DLB 133

Grimble, Reverend Charles James
See Eliot, T(homas) S(tearns)

Grimke, Charlotte L(ottie) Forten
1837(?)-1914
See Forten, Charlotte L.
See also BW 1; CA 117; 124; DAM MULT,
POET

Grimm, Jacob Ludwig Karl
1785-1863 ........................... NCLC 3
See also DLB 90; MAICYA; SATA 22

Grimm, Wilhelm Karl 1786-1859 ... NCLC 3
See also DLB 90; MAICYA; SATA 22

Grimmelshausen, Johann Jakob Christoffel
von 1621-1676 ........................... LC 6
See also DLB 168

Grindel, Eugene 1895-1952
See Eluard, Paul
See also CA 104

Grisham, John
1955- ........................... CLC 84; DAM POP
See also AAYA 14; CA 138; CANR 47

Grossman, David 1954- ............... CLC 67
See also CA 138

Grossman, Vasily (Semenovich)
1905-1964 ........................... CLC 41
See also CA 124; 130; MTCW

Grove, Frederick Philip ............... TCLC 4
See also Greve, Felix Paul (Berthold Friedrich)
See also DLB 92

Grubb
See Crumb, R(obert)

Grumbach, Doris (Isaac)
1918- ........................... CLC 13, 22, 64
See also CA 5-8R; CAAS 2; CANR 9, 42; INT
CANR-9

Grundtvig, Nicolai Frederik Severin
1783-1872 ........................... NCLC 1

Grunge
See Crumb, R(obert)

Grunwald, Lisa 1959- ............... CLC 44
See also CA 120

Guare, John
1938-... CLC 8, 14, 29, 67; DAM DRAM
See also CA 73-76; CANR 21; DLB 7;
MTCW

Gudjonsson, Halldor Kiljan 1902-
See Laxness, Halldor
See also CA 103

Guenter, Erich
See Eich, Guenter

Guest, Barbara 1920- ............... CLC 34
See also CA 25-28R; CANR 11, 44; DLB 5

Guest, Judith (Ann)
1936-......... CLC 8, 30; DAM NOV, POP
See also AAYA 7; CA 77-80; CANR 15; INT
CANR-15; MTCW

Guevara, Che ........................... CLC 87; HLC
See also Guevara (Serna), Ernesto

Guevara (Serna), Ernesto 1928-1967
See Guevara, Che
See also CA 127; 111; CANR 56; DAM MULT;
HW

Guild, Nicholas M. 1944- ............... CLC 33
See also CA 93-96

Guillemin, Jacques
See Sartre, Jean-Paul

Guillen, Jorge
1893-1984 CLC 11; DAM MULT, POET
See also CA 89-92; 112; DLB 108; HW

Guillen, Nicolas (Cristobal)
1902-1989 ....... CLC 48, 79; BLC; DAM
MST, MULT, POET; HLC
See also BW 2; CA 116; 125; 129; HW

Guillevic, (Eugene) 1907- ............... CLC 33
See also CA 93-96

Guillois
See Desnos, Robert

Guillois, Valentin
See Desnos, Robert

Guiney, Louise Imogen
1861-1920 ........................... TCLC 41
See also CA 160; DLB 54

Guiraldes, Ricardo (Guillermo)
1886-1927 ........................... TCLC 39
See also CA 131; HW; MTCW

Gumilev, Nikolai Stephanovich
1886-1921 ........................... TCLC 60

Gunesekera, Romesh
1954-........................... CLC 91
See also CA 159

Gunn, Bill ........................... CLC 5
See also Gunn, William Harrison
See also DLB 38

Gunn, Thom(son William)
1929-......... CLC 3, 6, 18, 32, 81; DAM
POET
See also CA 17-20R; CANR 9, 33; CDBLB
1960 to Present; DLB 27; INT CANR-33;
MTCW

Gunn, William Harrison 1934(?)-1989
See Gunn, Bill
See also AITN 1; BW 1; CA 13-16R; 128;
CANR 12, 25

Gunnars, Kristjana 1948- ............... CLC 69
See also CA 113; DLB 60

Gurdjieff, G(eorgei) I(vanovich)
1877(?)-1949 ........................... TCLC 71
See also CA 157

Gurganus, Allan
1947-........................... CLC 70; DAM POP
See also BEST 90:1; CA 135

Gurney, A(lbert) R(amsdell), Jr.
1930-....... CLC 32, 50, 54; DAM DRAM
See also CA 77-80; CANR 32

Gurney, Ivor (Bertie)
1890-1937 ........................... TCLC 33

Gurney, Peter
See Gurney, A(lbert) R(amsdell), Jr.

Guro, Elena 1877-1913 ............... TCLC 56

Gustafson, James M(oody)
1925-........................... CLC 100
See also CA 25-28R; CANR 37

Gustafson, Ralph (Barker) 1909-..... CLC 36
See also CA 21-24R; CANR 8, 45; DLB 88

Gut, Gom
See Simenon, Georges (Jacques Christian)

Guterson, David 1956-........................... CLC 91
See also CA 132

Guthrie, A(lfred) B(ertram), Jr.
1901-1991 ........................... CLC 23
See also CA 57-60; 134; CANR 24; DLB 6;
SATA 62; SATA-Obit 67

Guthrie, Isobel
See Grieve, C(hristopher) M(urray)

Guthrie, Woodrow Wilson 1912-1967
See Guthrie, Woody
See also CA 113; 93-96

Guthrie, Woody ........................... CLC 35
See also Guthrie, Woodrow Wilson

Guy, Rosa (Cuthbert) 1928-............. CLC 26
See also AAYA 4; BW 2; CA 17-20R; CANR
14, 34; CLR 13; DLB 33; JRDA; MAICYA;
SATA 14, 62

Gwendolyn
See Bennett, (Enoch) Arnold

H. D. ............... CLC 3, 8, 14, 31, 34, 73; PC 5
See also Doolittle, Hilda

Harjo, Joy 1951- ....... **CLC 83; DAM MULT**
See also CA 114; CANR 35; DLB 120, 175;
NNAL

Harlan, Louis R(udolph) 1922- ........ **CLC 34**
See also CA 21-24R; CANR 25, 55

Harling, Robert 1951(?)- ................... **CLC 53**
See also CA 147

Harmon, William (Ruth) 1938- ....... **CLC 38**
See also CA 33-36R; CANR 14, 32, 35; SATA
65

Harper, F. E. W.
See Harper, Frances Ellen Watkins

Harper, Frances E. W.
See Harper, Frances Ellen Watkins

Harper, Frances E. Watkins
See Harper, Frances Ellen Watkins

Harper, Frances Ellen
See Harper, Frances Ellen Watkins

Harper, Frances Ellen Watkins
1825-1911 .......... **TCLC 14; BLC; DAM
MULT, POET**
See also BW 1; CA 111; 125; DLB 50

Harper, Michael S(teven)
1938- ....................................... **CLC 7, 22**
See also BW 1; CA 33-36R; CANR 24; DLB
41

Harper, Mrs. F. E. W.
See Harper, Frances Ellen Watkins

Harris, Christie (Lucy) Irwin
1907- ............................................. **CLC 12**
See also CA 5-8R; CANR 6; CLR 47; DLB
88; JRDA; MAICYA; SAAS 10; SATA 6,
74

Harris, Frank 1856-1931 ................ **TCLC 24**
See also CA 109; 150; DLB 156

Harris, George Washington
1814-1869 ................................ **NCLC 23**
See also DLB 3, 11

Harris, Joel Chandler 1848-1908... **TCLC 2;
SSC 19**
See also CA 104; 137; DLB 11, 23, 42, 78, 91;
MAICYA; YABC 1

Harris, John (Wyndham Parkes Lucas)
Beynon 1903-1969
See Wyndham, John
See also CA 102; 89-92

Harris, MacDonald ............................ **CLC 9**
See also Heiney, Donald (William)

Harris, Mark 1922- ........................... **CLC 19**
See also CA 5-8R; CAAS 3; CANR 2, 55; DLB
2; DLBY 80

Harris, (Theodore) Wilson
1921- ......................................... **CLC 25**
See also BW 2; CA 65-68; CAAS 16; CANR
11, 27; DLB 117; MTCW

Harrison, Elizabeth Cavanna 1909-
See Cavanna, Betty
See also CA 9-12R; CANR 6, 27

Harrison, Harry (Max) 1925-........... **CLC 42**
See also CA 1-4R; CANR 5, 21; DLB 8; SATA
4

Harrison, James (Thomas)
1937-............. **CLC 6, 14, 33, 66; SSC 19**
See also CA 13-16R; CANR 8, 51; DLBY 82;
INT CANR-8

Harrison, Jim
See Harrison, James (Thomas)

Harrison, Kathryn 1961- .................. **CLC 70**
See also CA 144

Harrison, Tony 1937-.......................... **CLC 43**
See also CA 65-68; CANR 44; DLB 40;
MTCW

Harriss, Will(ard Irvin) 1922- .......... **CLC 34**
See also CA 111

Harson, Sley
See Ellison, Harlan (Jay)

Hart, Ellis
See Ellison, Harlan (Jay)

Hart, Josephine
1942(?)- ................... **CLC 70; DAM POP**
See also CA 138

Hart, Moss
1904-1961 ...........**CLC 66; DAM DRAM**
See also CA 109; 89-92; DLB 7

Harte, (Francis) Bret(t)
1836(?)-1902 ..... **TCLC 1, 25; DA; DAC;
DAM MST; SSC 8; WLC**
See also CA 104; 140; CDALB 1865-1917;
DLB 12, 64, 74, 79; SATA 26

Hartley, L(eslie) P(oles)
1895-1972 ............................ **CLC 2, 22**
See also CA 45-48; 37-40R; CANR 33; DLB
15, 139; MTCW

Hartman, Geoffrey H. 1929-............. **CLC 27**
See also CA 117; 125; DLB 67

Hartmann, Sadakichi 1867-1944... **TCLC 73**
See also CA 157; DLB 54

Hartmann von Aue
c. 1160-c. 1205........................ **CMLC 15**
See also DLB 138

Hartmann von Aue 1170-1210...... **CMLC 15**

Haruf, Kent 1943- .............................. **CLC 34**
See also CA 149

Harwood, Ronald 1934- ........ **CLC 32; DAM
DRAM, MST**
See also CA 1-4R; CANR 4, 55; DLB 13

Hasek, Jaroslav (Matej Frantisek)
1883-1923 ................................**TCLC 4**
See also CA 104; 129; MTCW

Hass, Robert 1941-....**CLC 18, 39, 99; PC 16**
See also CA 111; CANR 30, 50; DLB 105;
SATA 94

Hastings, Hudson
See Kuttner, Henry

Hastings, Selina ................................. **CLC 44**

Hathorne, John 1641-1717.................. **LC 38**

Hatteras, Amelia
See Mencken, H(enry) L(ouis)

Hatteras, Owen ............................... **TCLC 18**
See also Mencken, H(enry) L(ouis); Nathan,
George Jean

Hauptmann, Gerhart (Johann Robert)
1862-1946 .......... **TCLC 4; DAM DRAM**
See also CA 104; 153; DLB 66, 118

Havel, Vaclav 1936- ... **CLC 25, 58, 65; DAM
DRAM; DC 6**
See also CA 104; CANR 36; MTCW

Haviaras, Stratis ............................... **CLC 33**
See also Chaviaras, Strates

Hawes, Stephen 1475(?)-1523(?) ......... **LC 17**

Hawkes, John (Clendennin Burne, Jr.)
1925-. **CLC 1, 2, 3, 4, 7, 9, 14, 15, 27, 49**
See also CA 1-4R; CANR 2, 47; DLB 2, 7;
DLBY 80; MTCW

Hawking, S. W.
See Hawking, Stephen W(illiam)

Hawking, Stephen W(illiam)
1942-..................................... **CLC 63, 105**
See also AAYA 13; BEST 89:1; CA 126; 129;
CANR 48

Hawthorne, Julian 1846-1934 ....... **TCLC 25**

Hawthorne, Nathaniel
1804-1864 .. **NCLC 39; DA; DAB; DAC;
DAM MST, NOV; SSC 29; WLC**
See also AAYA 18; CDALB 1640-1865; DLB
1, 74; YABC 2

Haxton, Josephine Ayres 1921-
See Douglas, Ellen
See also CA 115; CANR 41

Hayaseca y Eizaguirre, Jorge
See Echegaray (y Eizaguirre), Jose (Maria
Waldo)

Hayashi Fumiko 1904-1951 .......... **TCLC 27**
See also DLB 180

Haycraft, Anna
See Ellis, Alice Thomas
See also CA 122

Hayden, Robert E(arl)
1913-1980 . **CLC 5, 9, 14, 37; BLC; DA;
DAC; DAM MST, MULT, POET; PC 6**
See also BW 1; CA 69-72; 97-100; CABS 2;
CANR 24; CDALB 1941-1968; DLB 5, 76;
MTCW; SATA 19; SATA-Obit 26

Horney, Karen (Clementine Theodore Danielsen) 1885-1952 ............. **TCLC 71**
See also CA 114

Hornung, E(rnest) W(illiam) 1866-1921 ..................... **TCLC 59**
See also CA 108; 160; DLB 70

Horovitz, Israel (Arthur) 1939- ....... **CLC 56; DAM DRAM**
See also CA 33-36R; CANR 46, 59; DLB 7

Horvath, Odon von
See Horvath, Oedoen von
See also DLB 85, 124

Horvath, Oedoen von 1901-1938 ............................... **TCLC 45**
See also Horvath, Odon von
See also CA 118

Horwitz, Julius 1920-1986 ................ **CLC 14**
See also CA 9-12R; 119; CANR 12

Hospital, Janette Turner 1942- ........ **CLC 42**
See also CA 108; CANR 48

Hostos, E. M. de
See Hostos (y Bonilla), Eugenio Maria de

Hostos, Eugenio M. de
See Hostos (y Bonilla), Eugenio Maria de

Hostos, Eugenio Maria
See Hostos (y Bonilla), Eugenio Maria de

Hostos (y Bonilla), Eugenio Maria de 1839-1903 ................................. **TCLC 24**
See also CA 123; 131; HW

Houdini
See Lovecraft, H(oward) P(hillips)

Hougan, Carolyn 1943- ..................... **CLC 34**
See also CA 139

Household, Geoffrey (Edward West) 1900-1988 .............................................. **CLC 11**
See also CA 77-80; 126; CANR 58; DLB 87; SATA 14; SATA-Obit 59

Housman, A(lfred) E(dward) 1859-1936 ........ **TCLC 1, 10; DA; DAB; DAC; DAM MST, POET; PC 2; WLCS**
See also CA 104; 125; DLB 19; MTCW

Housman, Laurence 1865-1959 ........ **TCLC 7**
See also CA 106; 155; DLB 10; SATA 25

Howard, Elizabeth Jane 1923- ..... **CLC 7, 29**
See also CA 5-8R; CANR 8, 62

Howard, Maureen 1930- ......... **CLC 5, 14, 46**
See also CA 53-56; CANR 31; DLBY 83; INT CANR-31; MTCW

Howard, Richard 1929- ........... **CLC 7, 10, 47**
See also AITN 1; CA 85-88; CANR 25; DLB 5; INT CANR-25

Howard, Robert E(rvin) 1906-1936 ................................... **TCLC 8**
See also CA 105; 157

Howard, Warren F.
See Pohl, Frederik

Howe, Fanny 1940- ........................... **CLC 47**
See also CA 117; CAAS 27; SATA-Brief 52

Howe, Irving 1920-1993 ................... **CLC 85**
See also CA 9-12R; 141; CANR 21, 50; DLB 67; MTCW

Howe, Julia Ward 1819-1910 ........ **TCLC 21**
See also CA 117; DLB 1

Howe, Susan 1937- ........................... **CLC 72**
See also CA 160; DLB 120

Howe, Tina 1937- ............................. **CLC 48**
See also CA 109

Howell, James 1594(?)-1666 ............... **LC 13**
See also DLB 151

Howells, W. D.
See Howells, William Dean

Howells, William D.
See Howells, William Dean

Howells, William Dean 1837-1920 ...................... **TCLC 7, 17, 41**
See also CA 104; 134; CDALB 1865-1917; DLB 12, 64, 74, 79

Howes, Barbara 1914-1996 .............. **CLC 15**
See also CA 9-12R; 151; CAAS 3; CANR 53; SATA 5

Hrabal, Bohumil 1914-1997 ....... **CLC 13, 67**
See also CA 106; 156; CAAS 12; CANR 57

Hsun, Lu
See Lu Hsun

Hubbard, L(afayette) Ron(ald) 1911-1986 ............... **CLC 43; DAM POP**
See also CA 77-80; 118; CANR 52

Huch, Ricarda (Octavia) 1864-1947 ............................... **TCLC 13**
See also CA 111; DLB 66

Huddle, David 1942- ......................... **CLC 49**
See also CA 57-60; CAAS 20; DLB 130

Hudson, Jeffrey
See Crichton, (John) Michael

Hudson, W(illiam) H(enry) 1841-1922 ............................... **TCLC 29**
See also CA 115; DLB 98, 153, 174; SATA 35

Hueffer, Ford Madox
See Ford, Ford Madox

Hughart, Barry 1934- ....................... **CLC 39**
See also CA 137

Hughes, Colin
See Creasey, John

Hughes, David (John) 1930- ............. **CLC 48**
See also CA 116; 129; DLB 14

Hughes, Edward James
See Hughes, Ted
See also DAM MST, POET

Hughes, (James) Langston 1902-1967 ........ **CLC 1, 5, 10, 15, 35, 44; BLC; DA; DAB; DAC; DAM DRAM, MST, MULT, POET; DC 3; PC 1; SSC 6; WLC**
See also AAYA 12; BW 1; CA 1-4R; 25-28R; CANR 1, 34; CDALB 1929-1941; CLR 17; DLB 4, 7, 48, 51, 86; JRDA; MAICYA; MTCW; SATA 4, 33

Hughes, Richard (Arthur Warren) 1900-1976 .......... **CLC 1, 11; DAM NOV**
See also CA 5-8R; 65-68; CANR 4; DLB 15, 161; MTCW; SATA 8; SATA-Obit 25

Hughes, Ted 1930-... **CLC 2, 4, 9, 14, 37; DAB; DAC; PC 7**
See also Hughes, Edward James
See also CA 1-4R; CANR 1, 33; CLR 3; DLB 40, 161; MAICYA; MTCW; SATA 49; SATA-Brief 27

Hugo, Richard F(ranklin) 1923-1982 .. **CLC 6, 18, 32; DAM POET**
See also CA 49-52; 108; CANR 3; DLB 5

Hugo, Victor (Marie) 1802-1885 .. **NCLC 3, 10, 21; DA; DAB; DAC; DAM DRAM, MST, NOV, POET; PC 17; WLC**
See also DLB 119; SATA 47

Huidobro, Vicente
See Huidobro Fernandez, Vicente Garcia

Huidobro Fernandez, Vicente Garcia 1893-1948 ............................... **TCLC 31**
See also CA 131; HW

Hulme, Keri 1947- ........................... **CLC 39**
See also CA 125; INT 125

Hulme, T(homas) E(rnest) 1883-1917 ............................... **TCLC 21**
See also CA 117; DLB 19

Hume, David 1711-1776 ....................... **LC 7**
See also DLB 104

Humphrey, William 1924-1997 ....... **CLC 45**
See also CA 77-80; 160; DLB 6

Humphreys, Emyr Owen 1919- ........ **CLC 47**
See also CA 5-8R; CANR 3, 24; DLB 15

Humphreys, Josephine 1945- ...... **CLC 34, 57**
See also CA 121; 127; INT 127

Huneker, James Gibbons 1857-1921 ............................... **TCLC 65**
See also DLB 71

Hungerford, Pixie
See Brinsmead, H(esba) F(ay)

Hunt, E(verette) Howard, (Jr.) 1918- ............................................ **CLC 3**
See also AITN 1; CA 45-48; CANR 2, 47

Jibran, Khalil
See Gibran, Kahlil

Jiles, Paulette 1943- .................... **CLC 13, 58**
See also CA 101

Jimenez (Mantecon), Juan Ramon
1881-1958 .......... **TCLC 4; DAM MULT,
POET; HLC; PC 7**
See also CA 104; 131; DLB 134; HW; MTCW

Jimenez, Ramon
See Jimenez (Mantecon), Juan Ramon

Jimenez Mantecon, Juan
See Jimenez (Mantecon), Juan Ramon

Joel, Billy ............................................ **CLC 26**
See also Joel, William Martin

Joel, William Martin 1949-
See Joel, Billy
See also CA 108

John of the Cross, St. 1542-1591 ......... **LC 18**

Johnson, B(ryan) S(tanley William)
1933-1973 .................................. **CLC 6, 9**
See also CA 9-12R; 53-56; CANR 9; DLB 14,
40

Johnson, Benj. F. of Boo
See Riley, James Whitcomb

Johnson, Benjamin F. of Boo
See Riley, James Whitcomb

Johnson, Charles (Richard)
1948- .......... **CLC 7, 51, 65; BLC; DAM
MULT**
See also BW 2; CA 116; CAAS 18; CANR 42;
DLB 33

Johnson, Denis 1949- .......................... **CLC 52**
See also CA 117; 121; DLB 120

Johnson, Diane 1934- .............. **CLC 5, 13, 48**
See also CA 41-44R; CANR 17, 40, 62; DLBY
80; INT CANR-17; MTCW

Johnson, Eyvind (Olof Verner)
1900-1976 .................................. **CLC 14**
See also CA 73-76; 69-72; CANR 34

Johnson, J. R.
See James, C(yril) L(ionel) R(obert)

Johnson, James Weldon
1871-1938 ....... **TCLC 3, 19; BLC; DAM
MULT, POET**
See also BW 1; CA 104; 125; CDALB 1917-
1929; CLR 32; DLB 51; MTCW; SATA
31

Johnson, Joyce 1935- .......................... **CLC 58**
See also CA 125; 129

Johnson, Lionel (Pigot)
1867-1902 ................................ **TCLC 19**
See also CA 117; DLB 19

Johnson, Mel
See Malzberg, Barry N(athaniel)

Johnson, Pamela Hansford
1912-1981 ............................ **CLC 1, 7, 27**
See also CA 1-4R; 104; CANR 2, 28; DLB 15;
MTCW

Johnson, Robert 1911(?)-1938 ....... **TCLC 69**

Johnson, Samuel
1709-1784 ....... **LC 15; DA; DAB; DAC;
DAM MST; WLC**
See also CDBLB 1660-1789; DLB 39, 95, 104,
142

Johnson, Uwe 1934-1984 ... **CLC 5, 10, 15, 40**
See also CA 1-4R; 112; CANR 1, 39; DLB 75;
MTCW

Johnston, George (Benson) 1913- .... **CLC 51**
See also CA 1-4R; CANR 5, 20; DLB 88

Johnston, Jennifer 1930- ..................... **CLC 7**
See also CA 85-88; DLB 14

Jolley, (Monica) Elizabeth 1923- .... **CLC 46;
SSC 19**
See also CA 127; CAAS 13; CANR 59

Jones, Arthur Llewellyn 1863-1947
See Machen, Arthur
See also CA 104

Jones, D(ouglas) G(ordon) 1929- ..... **CLC 10**
See also CA 29-32R; CANR 13; DLB 53

Jones, David (Michael)
1895-1974 ................ **CLC 2, 4, 7, 13, 42**
See also CA 9-12R; 53-56; CANR 28; CDBLB
1945-1960; DLB 20, 100; MTCW

Jones, David Robert 1947-
See Bowie, David
See also CA 103

Jones, Diana Wynne 1934- ................. **CLC 26**
See also AAYA 12; CA 49-52; CANR 4, 26,
56; CLR 23; DLB 161; JRDA; MAICYA;
SAAS 7; SATA 9, 70

Jones, Edward P. 1950- ..................... **CLC 76**
See also BW 2; CA 142

Jones, Gayl
1949- ....... **CLC 6, 9; BLC; DAM MULT**
See also BW 2; CA 77-80; CANR 27; DLB
33; MTCW

Jones, James 1921-1977 ...... **CLC 1, 3, 10, 39**
See also AITN 1, 2; CA 1-4R; 69-72; CANR
6; DLB 2, 143; MTCW

Jones, John J.
See Lovecraft, H(oward) P(hillips)

Jones, LeRoi ................. **CLC 1, 2, 3, 5, 10, 14**
See also Baraka, Amiri

Jones, Louis B. ..................................... **CLC 65**
See also CA 141

Jones, Madison (Percy, Jr.)
1925- ........................................... **CLC 4**
See also CA 13-16R; CAAS 11; CANR 7, 54;
DLB 152

Jones, Mervyn
1922-....................................... **CLC 10, 52**
See also CA 45-48; CAAS 5; CANR 1;
MTCW

Jones, Mick 1956(?)- ........................... **CLC 30**

Jones, Nettie (Pearl)
1941-............................................. **CLC 34**
See also BW 2; CA 137; CAAS 20

Jones, Preston 1936-1979 ................. **CLC 10**
See also CA 73-76; 89-92; DLB 7

Jones, Robert F(rancis)
1934-............................................... **CLC 7**
See also CA 49-52; CANR 2, 61

Jones, Rod 1953- ............................... **CLC 50**
See also CA 128

Jones, Terence Graham Parry
1942-............................................. **CLC 21**
See also Jones, Terry; Monty Python
See also CA 112; 116; CANR 35; INT 116

Jones, Terry
See Jones, Terence Graham Parry
See also SATA 67; SATA-Brief 51

Jones, Thom 1945(?)- ........................ **CLC 81**
See also CA 157

Jong, Erica
1942-.... **CLC 4, 6, 8, 18, 83; DAM NOV,
POP**
See also AITN 1; BEST 90:2; CA 73-76;
CANR 26, 52; DLB 2, 5, 28, 152; INT
CANR-26; MTCW

Jonson, Ben(jamin)
1572(?)-1637 ....... **LC 6, 33; DA; DAB;
DAC; DAM DRAM, MST, POET; DC 4;
PC 17; WLC**
See also CDBLB Before 1660; DLB 62,
121

Jordan, June
1936-........ **CLC 5, 11, 23; DAM MULT,
POET**
See also AAYA 2; BW 2; CA 33-36R; CANR
25; CLR 10; DLB 38; MAICYA; MTCW;
SATA 4

Jordan, Pat(rick M.) 1941- .............. **CLC 37**
See also CA 33-36R

Jorgensen, Ivar
See Ellison, Harlan (Jay)

Jorgenson, Ivar
See Silverberg, Robert

Josephus, Flavius c. 37-100 .......... **CMLC 13**

Josipovici, Gabriel 1940- .............. **CLC 6, 43**
See also CA 37-40R; CAAS 8; CANR 47; DLB
14

Joubert, Joseph 1754-1824 .............. **NCLC 9**

Jouve, Pierre Jean 1887-1976........... **CLC 47**
See also CA 65-68

**Joyce, James (Augustine Aloysius)**
1882-1941 ... **TCLC 3, 8, 16, 35, 52; DA; DAB; DAC; DAM MST, NOV, POET; SSC 26; WLC**
See also CA 104; 126; CDBLB 1914-1945; DLB 10, 19, 36, 162; MTCW

**Jozsef, Attila**
1905-1937 ............................. **TCLC 22**
See also CA 116

**Juana Ines de la Cruz** 1651(?)-1695 ..... **LC 5**

**Judd, Cyril**
See Kornbluth, C(yril) M.; Pohl, Frederik

**Julian of Norwich**
1342(?)-1416(?) ............................... **LC 6**
See also DLB 146

**Juniper, Alex**
See Hospital, Janette Turner

**Junius**
See Luxemburg, Rosa

**Just, Ward (Swift)**
1935- .................................... **CLC 4, 27**
See also CA 25-28R; CANR 32; INT CANR-32

**Justice, Donald (Rodney)**
1925- ........ **CLC 6, 19, 102; DAM POET**
See also CA 5-8R; CANR 26, 54; DLBY 83; INT CANR-26

**Juvenal** c. 55-c. 127 ........................ **CMLC 8**

**Juvenis**
See Bourne, Randolph S(illiman)

**Kacew, Romain** 1914-1980
See Gary, Romain
See also CA 108; 102

**Kadare, Ismail** 1936- ...................... **CLC 52**

**Kadohata, Cynthia** ............................. **CLC 59**
See also CA 140

**Kafka, Franz**
1883-1924 ..... **TCLC 2, 6, 13, 29, 47, 53; DA; DAB; DAC; DAM MST, NOV; SSC 29; WLC**
See also CA 105; 126; DLB 81; MTCW

**Kahanovitsch, Pinkhes**
See Der Nister

**Kahn, Roger** 1927- ............................. **CLC 30**
See also CA 25-28R; CANR 44; DLB 171; SATA 37

**Kain, Saul**
See Sassoon, Siegfried (Lorraine)

**Kaiser, Georg**
1878-1945 ................................... **TCLC 9**
See also CA 106; DLB 124

**Kaletski, Alexander**
1946- ...................................... **CLC 39**
See also CA 118; 143

**Kalidasa** fl. c. 400- ........................ **CMLC 9**

**Kallman, Chester (Simon)**
1921-1975 ................................... **CLC 2**
See also CA 45-48; 53-56; CANR 3

**Kaminsky, Melvin** 1926-
See Brooks, Mel
See also CA 65-68; CANR 16

**Kaminsky, Stuart M(elvin)**
1934- ........................................ **CLC 59**
See also CA 73-76; CANR 29, 53

**Kane, Francis**
See Robbins, Harold

**Kane, Paul**
See Simon, Paul (Frederick)

**Kane, Wilson**
See Bloch, Robert (Albert)

**Kanin, Garson** 1912- ........................ **CLC 22**
See also AITN 1; CA 5-8R; CANR 7; DLB 7

**Kaniuk, Yoram** 1930- ........................ **CLC 19**
See also CA 134

**Kant, Immanuel** 1724-1804 .......... **NCLC 27**
See also DLB 94

**Kantor, MacKinlay** 1904-1977 .......... **CLC 7**
See also CA 61-64; 73-76; CANR 60; DLB 9, 102

**Kaplan, David Michael** 1946- ........... **CLC 50**

**Kaplan, James** 1951- ........................ **CLC 59**
See also CA 135

**Karageorge, Michael**
See Anderson, Poul (William)

**Karamzin, Nikolai Mikhailovich**
1766-1826 ................................... **NCLC 3**
See also DLB 150

**Karapanou, Margarita** 1946- ........... **CLC 13**
See also CA 101

**Karinthy, Frigyes** 1887-1938 ........ **TCLC 47**

**Karl, Frederick R(obert)**
1927- ........................................ **CLC 34**
See also CA 5-8R; CANR 3, 44

**Kastel, Warren**
See Silverberg, Robert

**Kataev, Evgeny Petrovich** 1903-1942
See Petrov, Evgeny
See also CA 120

**Kataphusin**
See Ruskin, John

**Katz, Steve** 1935- ............................. **CLC 47**
See also CA 25-28R; CAAS 14; CANR 12; DLBY 83

**Kauffman, Janet** 1945- ..................... **CLC 42**
See also CA 117; CANR 43; DLBY 86

**Kaufman, Bob (Garnell)**
1925-1986 ................................... **CLC 49**
See also BW 1; CA 41-44R; 118; CANR 22; DLB 16, 41

**Kaufman, George S.** 1889-1961 ...... **CLC 38; DAM DRAM**
See also CA 108; 93-96; DLB 7; INT 108

**Kaufman, Sue** .................................. **CLC 3, 8**
See also Barondess, Sue K(aufman)

**Kavafis, Konstantinos Petrou** 1863-1933
See Cavafy, C(onstantine) P(eter)
See also CA 104

**Kavan, Anna** 1901-1968 .......... **CLC 5, 13, 82**
See also CA 5-8R; CANR 6, 57; MTCW

**Kavanagh, Dan**
See Barnes, Julian (Patrick)

**Kavanagh, Patrick (Joseph)**
1904-1967 ................................... **CLC 22**
See also CA 123; 25-28R; DLB 15, 20; MTCW

**Kawabata, Yasunari**
1899-1972 .......... **CLC 2, 5, 9, 18; DAM MULT; SSC 17**
See also CA 93-96; 33-36R; DLB 180

**Kaye, M(ary) M(argaret)** 1909- ....... **CLC 28**
See also CA 89-92; CANR 24, 60; MTCW; SATA 62

**Kaye, Mollie**
See Kaye, M(ary) M(argaret)

**Kaye-Smith, Sheila** 1887-1956 ...... **TCLC 20**
See also CA 118; DLB 36

**Kaymor, Patrice Maguilene**
See Senghor, Leopold Sedar

**Kazan, Elia** 1909- ..................... **CLC 6, 16, 63**
See also CA 21-24R; CANR 32

**Kazantzakis, Nikos**
1883(?)-1957 ..................... **TCLC 2, 5, 33**
See also CA 105; 132; MTCW

**Kazin, Alfred** 1915- ..................... **CLC 34, 38**
See also CA 1-4R; CAAS 7; CANR 1, 45; DLB 67

**Keane, Mary Nesta (Skrine)** 1904-1996
See Keane, Molly
See also CA 108; 114; 151

**Keane, Molly** ....................................... **CLC 31**
See also Keane, Mary Nesta (Skrine)
See also INT 114

**Keates, Jonathan** 19(?)- .................... **CLC 34**

**Keaton, Buster** 1895-1966 ................. **CLC 20**

**Keats, John**
1795-1821 .... **NCLC 8; DA; DAB; DAC; DAM MST, POET; PC 1; WLC**
See also CDBLB 1789-1832; DLB 96, 110

**Keene, Donald** 1922- ........................ **CLC 34**
See also CA 1-4R; CANR 5

**La Fayette, Marie (Madelaine Pioche de la Vergne Comtes** 1634-1693 ............ **LC 2**

**Lafayette, Rene**
See Hubbard, L(afayette) Ron(ald)

**Laforgue, Jules**
1860-1887 .. **NCLC 5, 53; PC 14; SSC 20**

**Lagerkvist, Paer (Fabian)**
1891-1974 ........ **CLC 7, 10, 13, 54; DAM DRAM, NOV**
See also Lagerkvist, Par
See also CA 85-88; 49-52; MTCW

**Lagerkvist, Par** ..................................... **SSC 12**
See also Lagerkvist, Paer (Fabian)

**Lagerloef, Selma (Ottiliana Lovisa)**
1858-1940 ............................ **TCLC 4, 36**
See also Lagerlof, Selma (Ottiliana Lovisa)
See also CA 108; SATA 15

**Lagerlof, Selma (Ottiliana Lovisa)**
See Lagerloef, Selma (Ottiliana Lovisa)
See also CLR 7; SATA 15

**La Guma, (Justin) Alex(ander)**
1925-1985 ............. **CLC 19; DAM NOV**
See also BW 1; CA 49-52; 118; CANR 25; DLB 117; MTCW

**Laidlaw, A. K.**
See Grieve, C(hristopher) M(urray)

**Lainez, Manuel Mujica**
See Mujica Lainez, Manuel
See also HW

**Laing, R(onald) D(avid)**
1927-1989 ................................... **CLC 95**
See also CA 107; 129; CANR 34; MTCW

**Lamartine, Alphonse (Marie Louis Prat) de**
1790-1869 .. **NCLC 11; DAM POET; PC 16**

**Lamb, Charles** 1775-1834 ..... **NCLC 10; DA; DAB; DAC; DAM MST; WLC**
See also CDBLB 1789-1832; DLB 93, 107, 163; SATA 17

**Lamb, Lady Caroline** 1785-1828 .. **NCLC 38**
See also DLB 116

**Lamming, George (William)**
1927- ........ **CLC 2, 4, 66; BLC; DAM MULT**
See also BW 2; CA 85-88; CANR 26; DLB 125; MTCW

**L'Amour, Louis (Dearborn)**
1908-1988 ...... **CLC 25, 55; DAM NOV, POP**
See also AAYA 16; AITN 2; BEST 89:2; CA 1-4R; 125; CANR 3, 25, 40; DLBY 80; MTCW

**Lampedusa, Giuseppe (Tomasi) di**
1896-1957 ............................... **TCLC 13**
See also Tomasi di Lampedusa, Giuseppe
See also DLB 177

**Lampman, Archibald** 1861-1899 .. **NCLC 25**
See also DLB 92

**Lancaster, Bruce** 1896-1963 ............ **CLC 36**
See also CA 9-10; CAP 1; SATA 9

**Lanchester, John** ................................ **CLC 99**

**Landau, Mark Alexandrovich**
See Aldanov, Mark (Alexandrovich)

**Landau-Aldanov, Mark Alexandrovich**
See Aldanov, Mark (Alexandrovich)

**Landis, Jerry**
See Simon, Paul (Frederick)

**Landis, John** 1950- ........................... **CLC 26**
See also CA 112; 122

**Landolfi, Tommaso** 1908-1979 ... **CLC 11, 49**
See also CA 127; 117; DLB 177

**Landon, Letitia Elizabeth**
1802-1838 .............................. **NCLC 15**
See also DLB 96

**Landor, Walter Savage**
1775-1864 .............................. **NCLC 14**
See also DLB 93, 107

**Landwirth, Heinz** 1927-
See Lind, Jakov
See also CA 9-12R; CANR 7

**Lane, Patrick**
1939- .................... **CLC 25; DAM POET**
See also CA 97-100; CANR 54; DLB 53; INT 97-100

**Lang, Andrew** 1844-1912 .............. **TCLC 16**
See also CA 114; 137; DLB 98, 141, 184; MAICYA; SATA 16

**Lang, Fritz** 1890-1976 .............. **CLC 20, 103**
See also CA 77-80; 69-72; CANR 30

**Lange, John**
See Crichton, (John) Michael

**Langer, Elinor** 1939- ......................... **CLC 34**
See also CA 121

**Langland, William**
1330(?)-1400(?) **LC 19; DA; DAB; DAC; DAM MST, POET**
See also DLB 146

**Langstaff, Launcelot**
See Irving, Washington

**Lanier, Sidney** 1842-1881 ..... **NCLC 6; DAM POET**
See also DLB 64; DLBD 13; MAICYA; SATA 18

**Lanyer, Aemilia** 1569-1645 ........... **LC 10, 30**
See also DLB 121

**Lao Tzu** ........................................... **CMLC 7**

**Lapine, James (Elliot)** 1949- ............ **CLC 39**
See also CA 123; 130; CANR 54; INT 130

**Larbaud, Valery (Nicolas)**
1881-1957 ................................ **TCLC 9**
See also CA 106; 152

**Lardner, Ring**
See Lardner, Ring(gold) W(ilmer)

**Lardner, Ring W., Jr.**
See Lardner, Ring(gold) W(ilmer)

**Lardner, Ring(gold) W(ilmer)**
1885-1933 ........................... **TCLC 2, 14**
See also CA 104; 131; CDALB 1917-1929; DLB 11, 25, 86; DLBD 16; MTCW

**Laredo, Betty**
See Codrescu, Andrei

**Larkin, Maia**
See Wojciechowska, Maia (Teresa)

**Larkin, Philip (Arthur)**
1922-1985 **CLC 3, 5, 8, 9, 13, 18, 33, 39, 64; DAB; DAM MST, POET**
See also CA 5-8R; 117; CANR 24, 62; CDBLB 1960 to Present; DLB 27; MTCW

**Larra (y Sanchez de Castro), Mariano Jose de**
1809-1837 ................................ **NCLC 17**

**Larsen, Eric** 1941- ........................... **CLC 55**
See also CA 132

**Larsen, Nella**
1891-1964 ......... **CLC 37; BLC; DAM MULT**
See also BW 1; CA 125; DLB 51

**Larson, Charles R(aymond)** 1938- .. **CLC 31**
See also CA 53-56; CANR 4

**Larson, Jonathan** 1961(?)-1996 ........ **CLC 99**

**Las Casas, Bartolome de** 1474-1566 ... **LC 31**

**Lasch, Christopher** 1932-1994 ....... **CLC 102**
See also CA 73-76; 144; CANR 25; MTCW

**Lasker-Schueler, Else** 1869-1945 .. **TCLC 57**
See also DLB 66, 124

**Latham, Jean Lee** 1902- .................... **CLC 12**
See also AITN 1; CA 5-8R; CANR 7; MAICYA; SATA 2, 68

**Latham, Mavis**
See Clark, Mavis Thorpe

**Lathen, Emma** ..................................... **CLC 2**
See also Hennissart, Martha; Latsis, Mary J(ane)

**Lathrop, Francis**
See Leiber, Fritz (Reuter, Jr.)

**Latsis, Mary J(ane)**
See Lathen, Emma
See also CA 85-88

**Lattimore, Richmond (Alexander)**
1906-1984 ................................... **CLC 3**
See also CA 1-4R; 112; CANR 1

Laughlin, James 1914- ..................... **CLC 49**
    See also CA 21-24R; CAAS 22; CANR 9, 47;
    DLB 48; DLBY 96

Laurence, (Jean) Margaret (Wemyss)
    1926-1987 ... **CLC 3, 6, 13, 50, 62; DAC;**
    **DAM MST; SSC 7**
    See also CA 5-8R; 121; CANR 33; DLB 53;
    MTCW; SATA-Obit 50

Laurent, Antoine 1952- ..................... **CLC 50**

Lauscher, Hermann
    See Hesse, Hermann

Lautreamont, Comte de
    1846-1870 .................. **NCLC 12; SSC 14**

Laverty, Donald
    See Blish, James (Benjamin)

Lavin, Mary
    1912-1996 ............. **CLC 4, 18, 99; SSC 4**
    See also CA 9-12R; 151; CANR 33; DLB 15;
    MTCW

Lavond, Paul Dennis
    See Kornbluth, C(yril) M.; Pohl, Frederik

Lawler, Raymond Evenor
    1922-............................................ **CLC 58**
    See also CA 103

Lawrence, D(avid) H(erbert Richards)
    1885-1930 .... **TCLC 2, 9, 16, 33, 48,**
    **61; DA; DAB; DAC; DAM MST,**
    **NOV, POET; SSC 4, 19; WLC**
    See also CA 104; 121; CDBLB 1914-
    1945; DLB 10, 19, 36, 98, 162;
    MTCW

Lawrence, T(homas) E(dward)
    1888-1935 ................................ **TCLC 18**
    See also Dale, Colin
    See also CA 115

Lawrence of Arabia
    See Lawrence, T(homas) E(dward)

Lawson, Henry (Archibald Hertzberg)
    1867-1922 .................. **TCLC 27; SSC 18**
    See also CA 120

Lawton, Dennis
    See Faust, Frederick (Schiller)

Laxness, Halldor ............................... **CLC 25**
    See also Gudjonsson, Halldor Kiljan

Layamon fl. c. 1200- ..................... **CMLC 10**
    See also DLB 146

Laye, Camara
    1928-1980 ........ **CLC 4, 38; BLC; DAM**
    **MULT**
    See also BW 1; CA 85-88; 97-100; CANR 25;
    MTCW

Layton, Irving (Peter)
    1912-....... **CLC 2, 15; DAC; DAM MST,**
    **POET**
    See also CA 1-4R; CANR 2, 33, 43; DLB 88;
    MTCW

Lazarus, Emma 1849-1887 ............. **NCLC 8**

Lazarus, Felix
    See Cable, George Washington

Lazarus, Henry
    See Slavitt, David R(ytman)

Lea, Joan
    See Neufeld, John (Arthur)

Leacock, Stephen (Butler)
    1869-1944 ... **TCLC 2; DAC; DAM MST**
    See also CA 104; 141; DLB 92

Lear, Edward 1812-1888 ................. **NCLC 3**
    See also CLR 1; DLB 32, 163, 166; MAICYA;
    SATA 18

Lear, Norman (Milton) 1922- .......... **CLC 12**
    See also CA 73-76

Leavis, F(rank) R(aymond)
    1895-1978 ................................ **CLC 24**
    See also CA 21-24R; 77-80; CANR 44;
    MTCW

Leavitt, David 1961- ..... **CLC 34; DAM POP**
    See also CA 116; 122; CANR 50, 62; DLB 130;
    INT 122

Leblanc, Maurice (Marie Emile)
    1864-1941 ................................ **TCLC 49**
    See also CA 110

Lebowitz, Fran(ces Ann)
    1951(?)- ................................. **CLC 11, 36**
    See also CA 81-84; CANR 14, 60; INT CANR-
    14; MTCW

Lebrecht, Peter
    See Tieck, (Johann) Ludwig

le Carre, John .................. **CLC 3, 5, 9, 15, 28**
    See also Cornwell, David (John Moore)
    See also BEST 89:4; CDBLB 1960 to Present;
    DLB 87

Le Clezio, J(ean) M(arie) G(ustave)
    1940- ........................................... **CLC 31**
    See also CA 116; 128; DLB 83

Leconte de Lisle, Charles-Marie-Rene
    1818-1894 ................................ **NCLC 29**

Le Coq, Monsieur
    See Simenon, Georges (Jacques Christian)

Leduc, Violette 1907-1972 ................. **CLC 22**
    See also CA 13-14; 33-36R; CAP 1

Ledwidge, Francis 1887(?)-1917 ... **TCLC 23**
    See also CA 123; DLB 20

Lee, Andrea 1953-........**CLC 36; BLC; DAM**
    **MULT**
    See also BW 1; CA 125

Lee, Andrew
    See Auchincloss, Louis (Stanton)

Lee, Chang-rae 1965- ........................ **CLC 91**
    See also CA 148

Lee, Don L. .................................... **CLC 2**
    See also Madhubuti, Haki R.

Lee, George W(ashington)
    1894-1976 ........ **CLC 52; BLC; DAM**
    **MULT**
    See also BW 1; CA 125; DLB 51

Lee, (Nelle) Harper
    1926-....... **CLC 12, 60; DA; DAB; DAC;**
    **DAM MST, NOV; WLC**
    See also AAYA 13; CA 13-16R; CANR 51;
    CDALB 1941-1968; DLB 6; MTCW; SATA
    11

Lee, Helen Elaine 1959(?)- ............... **CLC 86**
    See also CA 148

Lee, Julian
    See Latham, Jean Lee

Lee, Larry
    See Lee, Lawrence

Lee, Laurie
    1914-1997 .... **CLC 90; DAB; DAM POP**
    See also CA 77-80; 158; CANR 33; DLB 27;
    MTCW

Lee, Lawrence 1941-1990 ................ **CLC 34**
    See also CA 131; CANR 43

Lee, Manfred B(ennington)
    1905-1971 ................................ **CLC 11**
    See also Queen, Ellery
    See also CA 1-4R; 29-32R; CANR 2; DLB 137

Lee, Shelton Jackson 1957(?)- ....... **CLC 105;**
    **DAM MULT**
    See also Lee, Spike
    See also BW 2; CA 125; CANR 42

Lee, Spike
    See Lee, Shelton Jackson
    See also AAYA 4

Lee, Stan 1922-................................. **CLC 17**
    See also AAYA 5; CA 108; 111; INT 111

Lee, Tanith 1947- .............................. **CLC 46**
    See also AAYA 15; CA 37-40R; CANR 53;
    SATA 8, 88

Lee, Vernon ........................................ **TCLC 5**
    See also Paget, Violet
    See also DLB 57, 153, 156, 174, 178

Lee, William
    See Burroughs, William S(eward)

Lee, Willy
    See Burroughs, William S(eward)

Lee-Hamilton, Eugene (Jacob)
    1845-1907 ................................ **TCLC 22**
    See also CA 117

Leet, Judith 1935- ............................ **CLC 11**

Le Fanu, Joseph Sheridan
    1814-1873 **NCLC 9, 58; DAM POP; SSC**
    **14**
    See also DLB 21, 70, 159, 178

**Leffland, Ella** 1931- .......................... **CLC 19**
See also CA 29-32R; CANR 35; DLBY 84;
INT CANR-35; SATA 65

**Leger, Alexis**
See Leger, (Marie-Rene Auguste) Alexis Saint-
Leger

**Leger, (Marie-Rene Auguste) Alexis Saint-
Leger** 1887-1975 ......... **CLC 11; DAM
POET**
See also Perse, St.-John
See also CA 13-16R; 61-64; CANR 43;
MTCW

**Leger, Saintleger**
See Leger, (Marie-Rene Auguste) Alexis Saint-
Leger

**Le Guin, Ursula K(roeber)**
1929- ....... **CLC 8, 13, 22, 45, 71; DAB;
DAC; DAM MST, POP; SSC 12**
See also AAYA 9; AITN 1; CA 21-24R;
CANR 9, 32, 52; CDALB 1968-1988;
CLR 3, 28; DLB 8, 52; INT CANR-
32; JRDA; MAICYA; MTCW; SATA 4,
52

**Lehmann, Rosamond (Nina)**
1901-1990 ........................... **CLC 5**
See also CA 77-80; 131; CANR 8; DLB 15

**Leiber, Fritz (Reuter, Jr.)**
1910-1992 ........................... **CLC 25**
See also CA 45-48; 139; CANR 2, 40; DLB 8;
MTCW; SATA 45; SATA-Obit 73

**Leibniz, Gottfried Wilhelm von**
1646-1716 ........................... **LC 35**
See also DLB 168

**Leimbach, Martha** 1963-
See Leimbach, Marti
See also CA 130

**Leimbach, Marti** ............................... **CLC 65**
See also Leimbach, Martha

**Leino, Eino** ........................................ **TCLC 24**
See also Loennbohm, Armas Eino Leopold

**Leiris, Michel (Julien)**
1901-1990 ........................... **CLC 61**
See also CA 119; 128; 132

**Leithauser, Brad**
1953- ........................... **CLC 27**
See also CA 107; CANR 27; DLB 120

**Lelchuk, Alan** 1938- ........................... **CLC 5**
See also CA 45-48; CAAS 20; CANR 1

**Lem, Stanislaw**
1921- ................................. **CLC 8, 15, 40**
See also CA 105; CAAS 1; CANR 32;
MTCW

**Lemann, Nancy** 1956- ........................ **CLC 39**
See also CA 118; 136

**Lemonnier, (Antoine Louis) Camille**
1844-1913 ............................... **TCLC 22**
See also CA 121

**Lenau, Nikolaus** 1802-1850 ............ **NCLC 16**

**L'Engle, Madeleine (Camp Franklin)**
1918- ....................... **CLC 12; DAM POP**
See also AAYA 1; AITN 2; CA 1-4R; CANR
3, 21, 39; CLR 1, 14; DLB 52; JRDA;
MAICYA; MTCW; SAAS 15; SATA 1, 27,
75

**Lengyel, Jozsef**
1896-1975 ...................................... **CLC 7**
See also CA 85-88; 57-60

**Lenin** 1870-1924
See Lenin, V. I.
See also CA 121

**Lenin, V. I.** ........................................ **TCLC 67**
See also Lenin

**Lennon, John (Ono)**
1940-1980 ............................. **CLC 12, 35**
See also CA 102

**Lennox, Charlotte Ramsay**
1729(?)-1804 ............................. **NCLC 23**
See also DLB 39

**Lentricchia, Frank (Jr.)**
1940- ....................................... **CLC 34**
See also CA 25-28R; CANR 19

**Lenz, Siegfried**
1926- ............................................. **CLC 27**
See also CA 89-92; DLB 75

**Leonard, Elmore (John, Jr.)**
1925- ............ **CLC 28, 34, 71; DAM POP**
See also AAYA 22; AITN 1; BEST
89:1, 90:4; CA 81-84; CANR 12, 28,
53; DLB 173; INT CANR-28;
MTCW

**Leonard, Hugh** ................................... **CLC 19**
See also Byrne, John Keyes
See also DLB 13

**Leonov, Leonid (Maximovich)**
1899-1994 ............. **CLC 92; DAM NOV**
See also CA 129; MTCW

**Leopardi, (Conte) Giacomo**
1798-1837 ............................... **NCLC 22**

**Le Reveler**
See Artaud, Antonin (Marie Joseph)

**Lerman, Eleanor**
1952- ............................................... **CLC 9**
See also CA 85-88

**Lerman, Rhoda**
1936- ............................................. **CLC 56**
See also CA 49-52

**Lermontov, Mikhail Yuryevich**
1814-1841 ................... **NCLC 47; PC 18**

**Leroux, Gaston**
1868-1927 ............................... **TCLC 25**
See also CA 108; 136; SATA 65

**Lesage, Alain-Rene** 1668-1747 ............ **LC 28**

**Leskov, Nikolai (Semyonovich)**
1831-1895 ............................... **NCLC 25**

**Lessing, Doris (May)**
1919-.. **CLC 1, 2, 3, 6, 10, 15, 22, 40, 94;
DA; DAB; DAC; DAM MST, NOV; SSC
6; WLCS**
See also CA 9-12R; CAAS 14; CANR 33, 54;
CDBLB 1960 to Present; DLB 15, 139;
DLBY 85; MTCW

**Lessing, Gotthold Ephraim**
1729-1781 ...................................... **LC 8**
See also DLB 97

**Lester, Richard** 1932- ...................... **CLC 20**

**Lever, Charles (James)**
1806-1872 ............................... **NCLC 23**
See also DLB 21

**Leverson, Ada** 1865(?)-1936(?) ...... **TCLC 18**
See also Elaine
See also CA 117; DLB 153

**Levertov, Denise**
1923-........ **CLC 1, 2, 3, 5, 8, 15, 28, 66;
DAM POET; PC 11**
See also CA 1-4R; CAAS 19; CANR 3, 29,
50; DLB 5, 165; INT CANR-29; MTCW

**Levi, Jonathan** ................................... **CLC 76**

**Levi, Peter (Chad Tigar)** 1931- ........ **CLC 41**
See also CA 5-8R; CANR 34; DLB 40

**Levi, Primo**
1919-1987 ............... **CLC 37, 50; SSC 12**
See also CA 13-16R; 122; CANR 12, 33, 61;
DLB 177; MTCW

**Levin, Ira** 1929- ........... **CLC 3, 6; DAM POP**
See also CA 21-24R; CANR 17, 44; MTCW;
SATA 66

**Levin, Meyer**
1905-1981 ................. **CLC 7; DAM POP**
See also AITN 1; CA 9-12R; 104; CANR 15;
DLB 9, 28; DLBY 81; SATA 21; SATA-Obit
27

**Levine, Norman** 1924- ...................... **CLC 54**
See also CA 73-76; CAAS 23; CANR 14; DLB
88

**Levine, Philip**
1928-........ **CLC 2, 4, 5, 9, 14, 33; DAM
POET**
See also CA 9-12R; CANR 9, 37, 52; DLB 5

**Levinson, Deirdre** 1931- .................... **CLC 49**
See also CA 73-76

**Levi-Strauss, Claude** 1908- .............. **CLC 38**
See also CA 1-4R; CANR 6, 32, 57; MTCW

**Levitin, Sonia (Wolff)** 1934- ............ **CLC 17**
See also AAYA 13; CA 29-32R; CANR 14,
32; JRDA; MAICYA; SAAS 2; SATA 4,
68

**Levon, O. U.**
See Kesey, Ken (Elton)

**Locke, John** 1632-1704 ..................... **LC 7, 35**
See also DLB 101

**Locke-Elliott, Sumner**
See Elliott, Sumner Locke

**Lockhart, John Gibson**
1794-1854 ................................. **NCLC 6**
See also DLB 110, 116, 144

**Lodge, David (John)** 1935- ... **CLC 36; DAM POP**
See also BEST 90:1; CA 17-20R; CANR 19, 53; DLB 14; INT CANR-19; MTCW

**Loennbohm, Armas Eino Leopold** 1878-1926
See Leino, Eino
See also CA 123

**Loewinsohn, Ron(ald William)**
1937- ............................................. **CLC 52**
See also CA 25-28R

**Logan, Jake**
See Smith, Martin Cruz

**Logan, John (Burton)** 1923-1987 ....... **CLC 5**
See also CA 77-80; 124; CANR 45; DLB 5

**Lo Kuan-chung** 1330(?)-1400(?) ......... **LC 12**

**Lombard, Nap**
See Johnson, Pamela Hansford

**London, Jack** . **TCLC 9, 15, 39; SSC 4; WLC**
See also London, John Griffith
See also AAYA 13; AITN 2; CDALB 1865-1917; DLB 8, 12, 78; SATA 18

**London, John Griffith** 1876-1916
See London, Jack
See also CA 110; 119; DA; DAB; DAC; DAM MST, NOV; JRDA; MAICYA; MTCW

**Long, Emmett**
See Leonard, Elmore (John, Jr.)

**Longbaugh, Harry**
See Goldman, William (W.)

**Longfellow, Henry Wadsworth**
1807-1882 ........ **NCLC 2, 45; DA; DAB; DAC; DAM MST, POET; WLCS**
See also CDALB 1640-1865; DLB 1, 59; SATA 19

**Longley, Michael** 1939- ..................... **CLC 29**
See also CA 102; DLB 40

**Longus** fl. c. 2nd cent. - ..................... **CMLC 7**

**Longway, A. Hugh**
See Lang, Andrew

**Lonnrot, Elias** 1802-1884 .............. **NCLC 53**

**Lopate, Phillip** 1943- ......................... **CLC 29**
See also CA 97-100; DLBY 80; INT 97-100

**Lopez Portillo (y Pacheco), Jose**
1920- ........................................... **CLC 46**
See also CA 129; HW

**Lopez y Fuentes, Gregorio**
1897(?)-1966 ............................... **CLC 32**
See also CA 131; HW

**Lorca, Federico Garcia**
See Garcia Lorca, Federico

**Lord, Bette Bao** 1938- ..................... **CLC 23**
See also BEST 90:3; CA 107; CANR 41; INT 107; SATA 58

**Lord Auch**
See Bataille, Georges

**Lord Byron**
See Byron, George Gordon (Noel)

**Lorde, Audre (Geraldine)**
1934-1992 ....... **CLC 18, 71; BLC; DAM MULT, POET; PC 12**
See also BW 1; CA 25-28R; 142; CANR 16, 26, 46; DLB 41; MTCW

**Lord Houghton**
See Milnes, Richard Monckton

**Lord Jeffrey**
See Jeffrey, Francis

**Lorenzini, Carlo** 1826-1890
See Collodi, Carlo
See also MAICYA; SATA 29

**Lorenzo, Heberto Padilla**
See Padilla (Lorenzo), Heberto

**Loris**
See Hofmannsthal, Hugo von

**Loti, Pierre** ......................................... **TCLC 11**
See also Viaud, (Louis Marie) Julien
See also DLB 123

**Louie, David Wong** 1954- .................. **CLC 70**
See also CA 139

**Louis, Father M.**
See Merton, Thomas

**Lovecraft, H(oward) P(hillips)**
1890-1937 ...... **TCLC 4, 22; DAM POP; SSC 3**
See also AAYA 14; CA 104; 133; MTCW

**Lovelace, Earl**
1935- ............................................. **CLC 51**
See also BW 2; CA 77-80; CANR 41; DLB 125; MTCW

**Lovelace, Richard**
1618-1657 ....................................... **LC 24**
See also DLB 131

**Lowell, Amy**
1874-1925 ... **TCLC 1, 8; DAM POET; PC 13**
See also CA 104; 151; DLB 54, 140

**Lowell, James Russell**
1819-1891 ................................... **NCLC 2**
See also CDALB 1640-1865; DLB 1, 11, 64, 79

**Lowell, Robert (Traill Spence, Jr.)**
1917-1977 ... **CLC 1, 2, 3, 4, 5, 8, 9, 11, 15, 37; DA; DAB; DAC; DAM MST, NOV; PC 3; WLC**
See also CA 9-12R; 73-76; CABS 2; CANR 26, 60; DLB 5, 169; MTCW

**Lowndes, Marie Adelaide (Belloc)**
1868-1947 ................................. **TCLC 12**
See also CA 107; DLB 70

**Lowry, (Clarence) Malcolm**
1909-1957 ............................. **TCLC 6, 40**
See also CA 105; 131; CANR 62; CDBLB 1945-1960; DLB 15; MTCW

**Lowry, Mina Gertrude** 1882-1966
See Loy, Mina
See also CA 113

**Loxsmith, John**
See Brunner, John (Kilian Houston)

**Loy, Mina** ........ **CLC 28; DAM POET; PC 16**
See also Lowry, Mina Gertrude
See also DLB 4, 54

**Loyson-Bridet**
See Schwob, (Mayer Andre) Marcel

**Lucas, Craig** 1951- ........................... **CLC 64**
See also CA 137

**Lucas, E(dward) V(errall)**
1868-1938 ................................. **TCLC 73**
See also DLB 98, 149, 153; SATA 20

**Lucas, George** 1944- ......................... **CLC 16**
See also AAYA 1; CA 77-80; CANR 30; SATA 56

**Lucas, Hans**
See Godard, Jean-Luc

**Lucas, Victoria**
See Plath, Sylvia

**Ludlam, Charles** 1943-1987 ........ **CLC 46, 50**
See also CA 85-88; 122

**Ludlum, Robert** 1927- ..... **CLC 22, 43; DAM NOV, POP**
See also AAYA 10; BEST 89:1, 90:3; CA 33-36R; CANR 25, 41; DLBY 82; MTCW

**Ludwig, Ken** ....................................... **CLC 60**

**Ludwig, Otto** 1813-1865 .................. **NCLC 4**
See also DLB 129

**Lugones, Leopoldo** 1874-1938 ....... **TCLC 15**
See also CA 116; 131; HW

**Lu Hsun** 1881-1936 ............ **TCLC 3; SSC 20**
See also Shu-Jen, Chou

**Lukacs, George** .................................. **CLC 24**
See also Lukacs, Gyorgy (Szegeny von)

**Lukacs, Gyorgy (Szegeny von)** 1885-1971
See Lukacs, George
See also CA 101; 29-32R; CANR 62

**Luke, Peter (Ambrose Cyprian)**
1919-1995 .................................... **CLC 38**
See also CA 81-84; 147; DLB 13

**Lunar, Dennis**
See Mungo, Raymond

**Lurie, Alison** 1926- ............. **CLC 4, 5, 18, 39**
See also CA 1-4R; CANR 2, 17, 50; DLB 2;
MTCW; SATA 46

**Lustig, Arnost** 1926- ......................... **CLC 56**
See also AAYA 3; CA 69-72; CANR 47; SATA
56

**Luther, Martin** 1483-1546 ............... **LC 9, 37**
See also DLB 179

**Luxemburg, Rosa** 1870(?)-1919 .... **TCLC 63**
See also CA 118

**Luzi, Mario** 1914- .............................. **CLC 13**
See also CA 61-64; CANR 9; DLB 128

**Lyly, John** 1554(?)-1606 ......................... **DC 7**
See also DAM DRAM; DLB 62, 167

**L'Ymagier**
See Gourmont, Remy (-Marie-Charles) de

**Lynch, B. Suarez**
See Bioy Casares, Adolfo; Borges, Jorge Luis

**Lynch, David (K.)** 1946- .................... **CLC 66**
See also CA 124; 129

**Lynch, James**
See Andreyev, Leonid (Nikolaevich)

**Lynch Davis, B.**
See Bioy Casares, Adolfo; Borges, Jorge Luis

**Lyndsay, Sir David** 1490-1555 ............. **LC 20**

**Lynn, Kenneth S(chuyler)**
1923- ............................................. **CLC 50**
See also CA 1-4R; CANR 3, 27

**Lynx**
See West, Rebecca

**Lyons, Marcus**
See Blish, James (Benjamin)

**Lyre, Pinchbeck**
See Sassoon, Siegfried (Lorraine)

**Lytle, Andrew (Nelson)**
1902-1995 .................................... **CLC 22**
See also CA 9-12R; 150; DLB 6; DLBY 95

**Lyttelton, George** 1709-1773 ............. **LC 10**

**Maas, Peter** 1929- ............................. **CLC 29**
See also CA 93-96; INT 93-96

**Macaulay, Rose**
1881-1958 ............................ **TCLC 7, 44**
See also CA 104; DLB 36

**Macaulay, Thomas Babington**
1800-1859 ................................ **NCLC 42**
See also CDBLB 1832-1890; DLB 32, 55

**MacBeth, George (Mann)**
1932-1992 ............................. **CLC 2, 5, 9**
See also CA 25-28R; 136; CANR 61; DLB 40;
MTCW; SATA 4; SATA-Obit 70

**MacCaig, Norman (Alexander)**
1910- ........ **CLC 36; DAB; DAM POET**
See also CA 9-12R; CANR 3, 34; DLB 27

**MacCarthy, (Sir Charles Otto) Desmond**
1877-1952 ................................ **TCLC 36**

**MacDiarmid, Hugh** .... **CLC 2, 4, 11, 19, 63;
PC 9**
See also Grieve, C(hristopher) M(urray)
See also CDBLB 1945-1960; DLB 20

**MacDonald, Anson**
See Heinlein, Robert A(nson)

**Macdonald, Cynthia** 1928- ......... **CLC 13, 19**
See also CA 49-52; CANR 4, 44; DLB
105

**MacDonald, George** 1824-1905 ....... **TCLC 9**
See also CA 106; 137; DLB 18, 163, 178;
MAICYA; SATA 33

**Macdonald, John**
See Millar, Kenneth

**MacDonald, John D(ann)**
1916-1986 ... **CLC 3, 27, 44; DAM NOV,
POP**
See also CA 1-4R; 121; CANR 1, 19, 60; DLB
8; DLBY 86; MTCW

**Macdonald, John Ross**
See Millar, Kenneth

**Macdonald, Ross** ........ **CLC 1, 2, 3, 14, 34, 41**
See also Millar, Kenneth
See also DLBD 6

**MacDougal, John**
See Blish, James (Benjamin)

**MacEwen, Gwendolyn (Margaret)**
1941-1987 ............................. **CLC 13, 55**
See also CA 9-12R; 124; CANR 7, 22; DLB
53; SATA 50; SATA-Obit 55

**Macha, Karel Hynek** 1810-1846 ... **NCLC 46**

**Machado (y Ruiz), Antonio**
1875-1939 .................................. **TCLC 3**
See also CA 104; DLB 108

**Machado de Assis, Joaquim Maria**
1839-1908 ........ **TCLC 10; BLC; SSC 24**
See also CA 107; 153

**Machen, Arthur** ................... **TCLC 4; SSC 20**
See also Jones, Arthur Llewellyn
See also DLB 36, 156, 178

**Machiavelli, Niccolo**
1469-1527 ... **LC 8, 36; DA; DAB; DAC;
DAM MST; WLCS**

**MacInnes, Colin** 1914-1976 ......... **CLC 4, 23**
See also CA 69-72; 65-68; CANR 21; DLB
14; MTCW

**MacInnes, Helen (Clark)**
1907-1985 ............... **CLC 27, 39; DAM POP**
See also CA 1-4R; 117; CANR 1, 28, 58; DLB
87; MTCW; SATA 22; SATA-Obit 44

**Mackay, Mary** 1855-1924
See Corelli, Marie
See also CA 118

**Mackenzie, Compton (Edward Montague)**
1883-1972 .................................... **CLC 18**
See also CA 21-22; 37-40R; CAP 2; DLB 34,
100

**Mackenzie, Henry** 1745-1831 ........ **NCLC 41**
See also DLB 39

**Mackintosh, Elizabeth** 1896(?)-1952
See Tey, Josephine
See also CA 110

**MacLaren, James**
See Grieve, C(hristopher) M(urray)

**Mac Laverty, Bernard** 1942- ............ **CLC 31**
See also CA 116; 118; CANR 43; INT 118

**MacLean, Alistair (Stuart)**
1922(?)-1987 ....**CLC 3, 13, 50, 63; DAM
POP**
See also CA 57-60; 121; CANR 28, 61;
MTCW; SATA 23; SATA-Obit 50

**Maclean, Norman (Fitzroy)**
1902-1990 .. **CLC 78; DAM POP; SSC
13**
See also CA 102; 132; CANR 49

**MacLeish, Archibald**
1892-1982 ......... **CLC 3, 8, 14, 68; DAM
POET**
See also CA 9-12R; 106; CANR 33; DLB 4, 7,
45; DLBY 82; MTCW

**MacLennan, (John) Hugh**
1907-1990 ... **CLC 2, 14, 92; DAC; DAM
MST**
See also CA 5-8R; 142; CANR 33; DLB 68;
MTCW

**MacLeod, Alistair**
1936- ............. **CLC 56; DAC; DAM MST**
See also CA 123; DLB 60

**Macleod, Fiona**
See Sharp, William

**MacNeice, (Frederick) Louis**
1907-1963 ....... **CLC 1, 4, 10, 53; DAB;
DAM POET**
See also CA 85-88; CANR 61; DLB 10, 20;
MTCW

**MacNeill, Dand**
See Fraser, George MacDonald

**Macpherson, James**
1736-1796 ...................................... **LC 29**
See also DLB 109

**Macpherson, (Jean) Jay**
1931- ............................................. **CLC 14**
See also CA 5-8R; DLB 53

MacShane, Frank 1927- ................... **CLC 39**
See also CA 9-12R; CANR 3, 33; DLB
111

Macumber, Mari
See Sandoz, Mari(e Susette)

Madach, Imre 1823-1864 .............. **NCLC 19**

Madden, (Jerry) David
1933- ....................................... **CLC 5, 15**
See also CA 1-4R; CAAS 3; CANR 4, 45; DLB
6; MTCW

Maddern, Al(an)
See Ellison, Harlan (Jay)

Madhubuti, Haki R.
1942- .... **CLC 6, 73; BLC; DAM MULT,
POET; PC 5**
See also Lee, Don L.
See also BW 2; CA 73-76; CANR 24, 51; DLB
5, 41; DLBD 8

Maepenn, Hugh
See Kuttner, Henry

Maepenn, K. H.
See Kuttner, Henry

Maeterlinck, Maurice
1862-1949 .......... **TCLC 3; DAM DRAM**
See also CA 104; 136; SATA 66

Maginn, William 1794-1842 ........... **NCLC 8**
See also DLB 110, 159

Mahapatra, Jayanta 1928- ... **CLC 33; DAM
MULT**
See also CA 73-76; CAAS 9; CANR 15, 33

Mahfouz, Naguib (Abdel Aziz Al-Sabilgi)
1911(?)-
See Mahfuz, Najib
See also BEST 89:2; CA 128; CANR 55; DAM
NOV; MTCW

Mahfuz, Najib ............................. **CLC 52, 55**
See also Mahfouz, Naguib (Abdel Aziz Al-
Sabilgi)
See also DLBY 88

Mahon, Derek 1941- ........................ **CLC 27**
See also CA 113; 128; DLB 40

Mailer, Norman
1923- ... **CLC 1, 2, 3, 4, 5, 8, 11, 14, 28,
39, 74; DA; DAB; DAC; DAM MST,
NOV, POP**
See also AITN 2; CA 9-12R; CABS 1;
CANR 28; CDALB 1968-1988; DLB
2, 16, 28; DLBD 3; DLBY 80, 83;
MTCW

Maillet, Antonine
1929- ................................ **CLC 54; DAC**
See also CA 115; 120; CANR 46; DLB 60;
INT 120

Mais, Roger
1905-1955 .................................. **TCLC 8**
See also BW 1; CA 105; 124; DLB 125;
MTCW

Maistre, Joseph de 1753-1821 ....... **NCLC 37**

Maitland, Frederic 1850-1906 ....... **TCLC 65**

Maitland, Sara (Louise)
1950-.......................................... **CLC 49**
See also CA 69-72; CANR 13, 59

Major, Clarence
1936-.......... **CLC 3, 19, 48; BLC; DAM
MULT**
See also BW 2; CA 21-24R; CAAS 6; CANR
13, 25, 53; DLB 33

Major, Kevin (Gerald)
1949-................................ **CLC 26; DAC**
See also AAYA 16; CA 97-100; CANR 21, 38;
CLR 11; DLB 60; INT CANR-21; JRDA;
MAICYA; SATA 32, 82

Maki, James
See Ozu, Yasujiro

Malabaila, Damiano
See Levi, Primo

Malamud, Bernard
1914-1986 .... **CLC 1, 2, 3, 5, 8, 9, 11,
18, 27, 44, 78, 85; DA; DAB; DAC;
DAM MST, NOV, POP; SSC 15;
WLC**
See also AAYA 16; CA 5-8R; 118; CABS
1; CANR 28, 62; CDALB 1941-1968;
DLB 2, 28, 152; DLBY 80, 86; MTCW

Malan, Herman
See Bosman, Herman Charles; Bosman,
Herman Charles

Malaparte, Curzio 1898-1957 ....... **TCLC 52**

Malcolm, Dan
See Silverberg, Robert

Malcolm X ................... **CLC 82; BLC; WLCS**
See also Little, Malcolm

Malherbe, Francois de 1555-1628......... **LC 5**

Mallarme, Stephane
1842-1898 ... **NCLC 4, 41; DAM POET;
PC 4**

Mallet-Joris, Francoise
1930-.......................................... **CLC 11**
See also CA 65-68; CANR 17; DLB
83

Malley, Ern
See McAuley, James Phillip

Mallowan, Agatha Christie
See Christie, Agatha (Mary Clarissa)

Maloff, Saul 1922-................................ **CLC 5**
See also CA 33-36R

Malone, Louis
See MacNeice, (Frederick) Louis

Malone, Michael (Christopher)
1942-.......................................... **CLC 43**
See also CA 77-80; CANR 14, 32, 57

Malory, (Sir) Thomas
1410(?)-1471(?) ........ **LC 11; DA; DAB;
DAC; DAM MST; WLCS**
See also CDBLB Before 1660; DLB 146; SATA
59; SATA-Brief 33

Malouf, (George Joseph) David
1934-....................................... **CLC 28, 86**
See also CA 124; CANR 50

Malraux, (Georges-)Andre
1901-1976 ........ **CLC 1, 4, 9, 13, 15, 57;
DAM NOV**
See also CA 21-22; 69-72; CANR 34, 58; CAP
2; DLB 72; MTCW

Malzberg, Barry N(athaniel)
1939-.............................................. **CLC 7**
See also CA 61-64; CAAS 4; CANR 16; DLB
8

Mamet, David (Alan)
1947-.......... **CLC 9, 15, 34, 46, 91; DAM
DRAM; DC 4**
See also AAYA 3; CA 81-84; CABS 3; CANR
15, 41; DLB 7; MTCW

Mamoulian, Rouben (Zachary)
1897-1987 .................................. **CLC 16**
See also CA 25-28R; 124

Mandelstam, Osip (Emilievich)
1891(?)-1938(?) ......... **TCLC 2, 6; PC 14**
See also CA 104; 150

Mander, (Mary) Jane 1877-1949 ... **TCLC 31**

Mandeville, John
fl. 1350- .................................... **CMLC 19**
See also DLB 146

Mandiargues, Andre Pieyre de .......... **CLC 41**
See also Pieyre de Mandiargues, Andre
See also DLB 83

Mandrake, Ethel Belle
See Thurman, Wallace (Henry)

Mangan, James Clarence
1803-1849 ................................ **NCLC 27**

Maniere, J.-E.
See Giraudoux, (Hippolyte) Jean

Manley, (Mary) Delariviere
1672(?)-1724 .................................... **LC 1**
See also DLB 39, 80

Mann, Abel
See Creasey, John

Mann, Emily 1952- ............................. **DC 7**
See also CA 130; CANR 55

Mann, (Luiz) Heinrich
1871-1950 .................................. **TCLC 9**
See also CA 106; DLB 66

Mann, (Paul) Thomas
1875-1955 **TCLC 2, 8, 14, 21, 35, 44, 60;
DA; DAB; DAC; DAM MST, NOV;
SSC 5; WLC**
See also CA 104; 128; DLB 66; MTCW

**Martinson, Harry (Edmund)**
1904-1978 ................................. **CLC 14**
See also CA 77-80; CANR 34

**Marut, Ret**
See Traven, B.

**Marut, Robert**
See Traven, B.

**Marvell, Andrew**
1621-1678 ........ **LC 4; DA; DAB; DAC;
DAM MST, POET; PC 10; WLC**
See also CDBLB 1660-1789; DLB 131

**Marx, Karl (Heinrich)**
1818-1883 ................................. **NCLC 17**
See also DLB 129

**Masaoka Shiki** ................................. **TCLC 18**
See also Masaoka Tsunenori

**Masaoka Tsunenori** 1867-1902
See Masaoka Shiki
See also CA 117

**Masefield, John (Edward)**
1878-1967 ...... **CLC 11, 47; DAM POET**
See also CA 19-20; 25-28R; CANR 33; CAP
2; CDBLB 1890-1914; DLB 10, 19, 153,
160; MTCW; SATA 19

**Maso, Carole** 19(?)- ........................... **CLC 44**

**Mason, Bobbie Ann** 1940-... **CLC 28, 43, 82;
SSC 4**
See also AAYA 5; CA 53-56; CANR 11, 31,
58; DLB 173; DLBY 87; INT CANR-31;
MTCW

**Mason, Ernst**
See Pohl, Frederik

**Mason, Lee W.**
See Malzberg, Barry N(athaniel)

**Mason, Nick** 1945- ........................... **CLC 35**

**Mason, Tally**
See Derleth, August (William)

**Mass, William**
See Gibson, William

**Masters, Edgar Lee**
1868-1950 ........ **TCLC 2, 25; DA; DAC;
DAM MST, POET; PC 1; WLCS**
See also CA 104; 133; CDALB 1865-1917;
DLB 54; MTCW

**Masters, Hilary** 1928- ........................ **CLC 48**
See also CA 25-28R; CANR 13, 47

**Mastrosimone, William** 19(?)- .......... **CLC 36**

**Mathe, Albert**
See Camus, Albert

**Mather, Cotton** 1663-1728 ................. **LC 38**
See also CDALB 1640-1865; DLB 24, 30, 140

**Mather, Increase** 1639-1723 .............. **LC 38**
See also DLB 24

**Matheson, Richard Burton** 1926- .... **CLC 37**
See also CA 97-100; DLB 8, 44; INT 97-100

**Mathews, Harry** 1930- ................. **CLC 6, 52**
See also CA 21-24R; CAAS 6; CANR 18, 40

**Mathews, John Joseph** 1894-1979 .. **CLC 84;
DAM MULT**
See also CA 19-20; 142; CANR 45; CAP 2;
DLB 175; NNAL

**Mathias, Roland (Glyn)** 1915- .......... **CLC 45**
See also CA 97-100; CANR 19, 41; DLB 27

**Matsuo Basho** 1644-1694 ..................... **PC 3**
See also DAM POET

**Mattheson, Rodney**
See Creasey, John

**Matthews, Greg** 1949- ....................... **CLC 45**
See also CA 135

**Matthews, William** 1942- ................. **CLC 40**
See also CA 29-32R; CAAS 18; CANR 12, 57;
DLB 5

**Matthias, John (Edward)** 1941- ......... **CLC 9**
See also CA 33-36R; CANR 56

**Matthiessen, Peter**
1927-...**CLC 5, 7, 11, 32, 64; DAM NOV**
See also AAYA 6; BEST 90:4; CA 9-12R;
CANR 21, 50; DLB 6, 173; MTCW; SATA
27

**Maturin, Charles Robert**
1780(?)-1824 ............................... **NCLC 6**
See also DLB 178

**Matute (Ausejo), Ana Maria**
1925- ........................................... **CLC 11**
See also CA 89-92; MTCW

**Maugham, W. S.**
See Maugham, W(illiam) Somerset

**Maugham, W(illiam) Somerset**
1874-1965 .... **CLC 1, 11, 15, 67, 93; DA;
DAB; DAC; DAM DRAM, MST, NOV;
SSC 8; WLC**
See also CA 5-8R; 25-28R; CANR 40; CDBLB
1914-1945; DLB 10, 36, 77, 100, 162;
MTCW; SATA 54

**Maugham, William Somerset**
See Maugham, W(illiam) Somerset

**Maupassant, (Henri Rene Albert) Guy de**
1850-1893 ........ **NCLC 1, 42; DA; DAB;
DAC; DAM MST; SSC 1; WLC**
See also DLB 123

**Maupin, Armistead**
1944- ........................ **CLC 95; DAM POP**
See also CA 125; 130; CANR 58; INT
130

**Maurhut, Richard**
See Traven, B.

**Mauriac, Claude** 1914-1996 .............. **CLC 9**
See also CA 89-92; 152; DLB 83

**Mauriac, Francois (Charles)**
1885-1970 ............. **CLC 4, 9, 56; SSC 24**
See also CA 25-28; CAP 2; DLB 65; MTCW

**Mavor, Osborne Henry** 1888-1951
See Bridie, James
See also CA 104

**Maxwell, William (Keepers, Jr.)**
1908- ........................................... **CLC 19**
See also CA 93-96; CANR 54; DLBY 80; INT
93-96

**May, Elaine** 1932- ............................ **CLC 16**
See also CA 124; 142; DLB 44

**Mayakovski, Vladimir (Vladimirovich)**
1893-1930 ............................. **TCLC 4, 18**
See also CA 104; 158

**Mayhew, Henry** 1812-1887 ............ **NCLC 31**
See also DLB 18, 55

**Mayle, Peter** 1939(?)- ........................ **CLC 89**
See also CA 139

**Maynard, Joyce** 1953- ....................... **CLC 23**
See also CA 111; 129

**Mayne, William (James Carter)**
1928- ........................................... **CLC 12**
See also AAYA 20; CA 9-12R; CANR 37; CLR
25; JRDA; MAICYA; SAAS 11; SATA 6,
68

**Mayo, Jim**
See L'Amour, Louis (Dearborn)

**Maysles, Albert** 1926- ....................... **CLC 16**
See also CA 29-32R

**Maysles, David** 1932- ........................ **CLC 16**

**Mazer, Norma Fox** 1931-................... **CLC 26**
See also AAYA 5; CA 69-72; CANR 12, 32;
CLR 23; JRDA; MAICYA; SAAS 1; SATA
24, 67

**Mazzini, Guiseppe** 1805-1872 ........ **NCLC 34**

**McAuley, James Phillip**
1917-1976 ................................. **CLC 45**
See also CA 97-100

**McBain, Ed**
See Hunter, Evan

**McBrien, William Augustine**
1930-........................................... **CLC 44**
See also CA 107

**McCaffrey, Anne (Inez)**
1926-.............. **CLC 17; DAM NOV, POP**
See also AAYA 6; AITN 2; BEST 89:2; CA
25-28R; CANR 15, 35, 55; DLB 8;
JRDA; MAICYA; MTCW; SAAS 11;
SATA 8, 70

**McCall, Nathan** 1955(?)- ................... **CLC 86**
See also CA 146

**McCann, Arthur**
See Campbell, John W(ood, Jr.)

**Mehta, Ved (Parkash)** 1934- ............. **CLC 37**
See also CA 1-4R; CANR 2, 23; MTCW

**Melanter**
See Blackmore, R(ichard) D(oddridge)

**Melikow, Loris**
See Hofmannsthal, Hugo von

**Melmoth, Sebastian**
See Wilde, Oscar (Fingal O'Flahertie Wills)

**Meltzer, Milton** 1915- ........................ **CLC 26**
See also AAYA 8; CA 13-16R; CANR 38; CLR 13; DLB 61; JRDA; MAICYA; SAAS 1; SATA 1, 50, 80

**Melville, Herman**
1819-1891 ..... **NCLC 3, 12, 29, 45, 49; DA; DAB; DAC; DAM MST, NOV; SSC 1, 17; WLC**
See also CDALB 1640-1865; DLB 3, 74; SATA 59

**Menander**
c. 342B.C.-c. 292B.C. .... **CMLC 9; DAM DRAM; DC 3**
See also DLB 176

**Mencken, H(enry) L(ouis)**
1880-1956 ................................ **TCLC 13**
See also CA 105; 125; CDALB 1917-1929; DLB 11, 29, 63, 137; MTCW

**Mendelsohn, Jane** 1965(?)- ............... **CLC 99**
See also CA 154

**Mercer, David** 1928-1980 ........ **CLC 5; DAM DRAM**
See also CA 9-12R; 102; CANR 23; DLB 13; MTCW

**Merchant, Paul**
See Ellison, Harlan (Jay)

**Meredith, George**
1828-1909 ... **TCLC 17, 43; DAM POET**
See also CA 117; 153; CDBLB 1832-1890; DLB 18, 35, 57, 159

**Meredith, William (Morris)**
1919- ... **CLC 4, 13, 22, 55; DAM POET**
See also CA 9-12R; CAAS 14; CANR 6, 40; DLB 5

**Merezhkovsky, Dmitry Sergeyevich**
1865-1941 ................................ **TCLC 29**

**Merimee, Prosper** 1803-1870 .... **NCLC 6, 65; SSC 7**
See also DLB 119

**Merkin, Daphne** 1954- ...................... **CLC 44**
See also CA 123

**Merlin, Arthur**
See Blish, James (Benjamin)

**Merrill, James (Ingram)**
1926-1995 **CLC 2, 3, 6, 8, 13, 18, 34, 91; DAM POET**
See also CA 13-16R; 147; CANR 10, 49; DLB 5, 165; DLBY 85; INT CANR-10; MTCW

**Merriman, Alex**
See Silverberg, Robert

**Merritt, E. B.**
See Waddington, Miriam

**Merton, Thomas**
1915-1968 ...**CLC 1, 3, 11, 34, 83; PC 10**
See also CA 5-8R; 25-28R; CANR 22, 53; DLB 48; DLBY 81; MTCW

**Merwin, W(illiam) S(tanley)**
1927-.... **CLC 1, 2, 3, 5, 8, 13, 18, 45, 88; DAM POET**
See also CA 13-16R; CANR 15, 51; DLB 5, 169; INT CANR-15; MTCW

**Metcalf, John** 1938- .......................... **CLC 37**
See also CA 113; DLB 60

**Metcalf, Suzanne**
See Baum, L(yman) Frank

**Mew, Charlotte (Mary)**
1870-1928 ................................... **TCLC 8**
See also CA 105; DLB 19, 135

**Mewshaw, Michael** 1943- .................... **CLC 9**
See also CA 53-56; CANR 7, 47; DLBY 80

**Meyer, June**
See Jordan, June

**Meyer, Lynn**
See Slavitt, David R(ytman)

**Meyer-Meyrink, Gustav** 1868-1932
See Meyrink, Gustav
See also CA 117

**Meyers, Jeffrey** 1939- ........................ **CLC 39**
See also CA 73-76; CANR 54; DLB 111

**Meynell, Alice (Christina Gertrude Thompson)**
1847-1922 ................................... **TCLC 6**
See also CA 104; DLB 19, 98

**Meyrink, Gustav** .............................. **TCLC 21**
See also Meyer-Meyrink, Gustav
See also DLB 81

**Michaels, Leonard**
1933- .......................... **CLC 6, 25; SSC 16**
See also CA 61-64; CANR 21, 62; DLB 130; MTCW

**Michaux, Henri** 1899-1984 .......... **CLC 8, 19**
See also CA 85-88; 114

**Micheaux, Oscar** 1884-1951 ......... **TCLC 76**
See also DLB 50

**Michelangelo** 1475-1564 ...................... **LC 12**

**Michelet, Jules** 1798-1874 .............. **NCLC 31**

**Michener, James A(lbert)**
1907(?)-1997 ........ **CLC 1, 5, 11, 29, 60; DAM NOV, POP**
See also AITN 1; BEST 90:1; CA 5-8R; CANR 21, 45; DLB 6; MTCW

**Mickiewicz, Adam** 1798-1855 .......... **NCLC 3**

**Middleton, Christopher** 1926- .......... **CLC 13**
See also CA 13-16R; CANR 29, 54; DLB 40

**Middleton, Richard (Barham)**
1882-1911 ............................... **TCLC 56**
See also DLB 156

**Middleton, Stanley** 1919- .............. **CLC 7, 38**
See also CA 25-28R; CAAS 23; CANR 21, 46; DLB 14

**Middleton, Thomas**
1580-1627 .. **LC 33; DAM DRAM, MST; DC 5**
See also DLB 58

**Migueis, Jose Rodrigues** 1901- ......... **CLC 10**

**Mikszath, Kalman** 1847-1910 ........ **TCLC 31**

**Miles, Jack** ....................................... **CLC 100**

**Miles, Josephine (Louise)**
1911-1985 ... **CLC 1, 2, 14, 34, 39; DAM POET**
See also CA 1-4R; 116; CANR 2, 55; DLB 48

**Militant**
See Sandburg, Carl (August)

**Mill, John Stuart** 1806-1873 .... **NCLC 11, 58**
See also CDBLB 1832-1890; DLB 55

**Millar, Kenneth** 1915-1983 ... **CLC 14; DAM POP**
See also Macdonald, Ross
See also CA 9-12R; 110; CANR 16; DLB 2; DLBD 6; DLBY 83; MTCW

**Millay, E. Vincent**
See Millay, Edna St. Vincent

**Millay, Edna St. Vincent**
1892-1950 ........ **TCLC 4, 49; DA; DAB; DAC; DAM MST, POET; PC 6; WLCS**
See also CA 104; 130; CDALB 1917-1929; DLB 45; MTCW

**Miller, Arthur**
1915-...... **CLC 1, 2, 6, 10, 15, 26, 47, 78; DA; DAB; DAC; DAM DRAM, MST; DC 1; WLC**
See also AAYA 15; AITN 1; CA 1-4R; CABS 3; CANR 2, 30, 54; CDALB 1941-1968; DLB 7; MTCW

**Miller, Henry (Valentine)**
1891-1980 ..... **CLC 1, 2, 4, 9, 14, 43, 84; DA; DAB; DAC; DAM MST, NOV; WLC**
See also CA 9-12R; 97-100; CANR 33; CDALB 1929-1941; DLB 4, 9; DLBY 80; MTCW

**Miller, Jason** 1939(?)- ......................... **CLC 2**
See also AITN 1; CA 73-76; DLB 7

**Miller, Sue**
1943- ...................... **CLC 44; DAM POP**
See also BEST 90:3; CA 139; CANR 59; DLB 143

**Montherlant, Henry (Milon) de**
1896-1972 ....... **CLC 8, 19; DAM DRAM**
See also CA 85-88; 37-40R; DLB 72; MTCW

**Monty Python**
See Chapman, Graham; Cleese, John
(Marwood); Gilliam, Terry (Vance); Idle,
Eric; Jones, Terence Graham Parry; Palin,
Michael (Edward)
See also AAYA 7

**Moodie, Susanna (Strickland)**
1803-1885 ................................. **NCLC 14**
See also DLB 99

**Mooney, Edward** 1951-
See Mooney, Ted
See also CA 130

**Mooney, Ted** ........................................ **CLC 25**
See also Mooney, Edward

**Moorcock, Michael (John)**
1939- ................................... **CLC 5, 27, 58**
See also CA 45-48; CAAS 5; CANR 2, 17, 38;
DLB 14; MTCW; SATA 93

**Moore, Brian**
1921- ....... **CLC 1, 3, 5, 7, 8, 19, 32, 90;**
**DAB; DAC; DAM MST**
See also CA 1-4R; CANR 1, 25, 42;
MTCW

**Moore, Edward**
See Muir, Edwin

**Moore, George Augustus**
1852-1933 ..................... **TCLC 7; SSC 19**
See also CA 104; DLB 10, 18, 57, 135

**Moore, Lorrie** .......................... **CLC 39, 45, 68**
See also Moore, Marie Lorena

**Moore, Marianne (Craig)**
1887-1972 .... **CLC 1, 2, 4, 8, 10, 13, 19,**
**47; DA; DAB; DAC; DAM MST, POET;**
**PC 4; WLCS**
See also CA 1-4R; 33-36R; CANR 3, 61;
CDALB 1929-1941; DLB 45; DLBD 7;
MTCW; SATA 20

**Moore, Marie Lorena** 1957-
See Moore, Lorrie
See also CA 116; CANR 39

**Moore, Thomas** 1779-1852 .............. **NCLC 6**
See also DLB 96, 144

**Morand, Paul** 1888-1976 .... **CLC 41; SSC 22**
See also CA 69-72; DLB 65

**Morante, Elsa** 1918-1985 ............. **CLC 8, 47**
See also CA 85-88; 117; CANR 35; DLB 177;
MTCW

**Moravia, Alberto**
1907-1990 ... **CLC 2, 7, 11, 27, 46; SSC**
**26**
See also Pincherle, Alberto
See also DLB 177

**More, Hannah** 1745-1833 .............. **NCLC 27**
See also DLB 107, 109, 116, 158

**More, Henry** 1614-1687 ......... **LC 9**
See also DLB 126

**More, Sir Thomas** 1478-1535 ........ **LC 10, 32**

**Moreas, Jean** ................................... **TCLC 18**
See also Papadiamantopoulos, Johannes

**Morgan, Berry** 1919- .......... **CLC 6**
See also CA 49-52; DLB 6

**Morgan, Claire**
See Highsmith, (Mary) Patricia

**Morgan, Edwin (George)**
1920- ......................................... **CLC 31**
See also CA 5-8R; CANR 3, 43; DLB
27

**Morgan, (George) Frederick**
1922- ......................................... **CLC 23**
See also CA 17-20R; CANR 21

**Morgan, Harriet**
See Mencken, H(enry) L(ouis)

**Morgan, Jane**
See Cooper, James Fenimore

**Morgan, Janet** 1945- .......... **CLC 39**
See also CA 65-68

**Morgan, Lady** 1776(?)-1859 ......... **NCLC 29**
See also DLB 116, 158

**Morgan, Robin** 1941- .......... **CLC 2**
See also CA 69-72; CANR 29; MTCW; SATA
80

**Morgan, Scott**
See Kuttner, Henry

**Morgan, Seth** 1949(?)-1990 .............. **CLC 65**
See also CA 132

**Morgenstern, Christian**
1871-1914 ................................. **TCLC 8**
See also CA 105

**Morgenstern, S.**
See Goldman, William (W.)

**Moricz, Zsigmond** 1879-1942 ........ **TCLC 33**

**Morike, Eduard (Friedrich)**
1804-1875 ................................. **NCLC 10**
See also DLB 133

**Mori Ogai** ......................................... **TCLC 14**
See also Mori Rintaro

**Mori Rintaro** 1862-1922
See Mori Ogai
See also CA 110

**Moritz, Karl Philipp** 1756-1793 ........... **LC 2**
See also DLB 94

**Morland, Peter Henry**
See Faust, Frederick (Schiller)

**Morren, Theophil**
See Hofmannsthal, Hugo von

**Morris, Bill** 1952- ............................. **CLC 76**

**Morris, Julian**
See West, Morris L(anglo)

**Morris, Steveland Judkins** 1950(?)-
See Wonder, Stevie
See also CA 111

**Morris, William** 1834-1896 ............. **NCLC 4**
See also CDBLB 1832-1890; DLB 18, 35, 57,
156, 178, 184

**Morris, Wright** 1910- ..... **CLC 1, 3, 7, 18, 37**
See also CA 9-12R; CANR 21; DLB 2; DLBY
81; MTCW

**Morrison, Arthur** 1863-1945 ......... **TCLC 72**
See also CA 120; 157; DLB 70, 135

**Morrison, Chloe Anthony Wofford**
See Morrison, Toni

**Morrison, James Douglas** 1943-1971
See Morrison, Jim
See also CA 73-76; CANR 40

**Morrison, Jim** ..................................... **CLC 17**
See also Morrison, James Douglas

**Morrison, Toni**
1931-.... **CLC 4, 10, 22, 55, 81, 87; BLC;**
**DA; DAB; DAC; DAM MST, MULT,**
**NOV, POP**
See also AAYA 1, 22; BW 2; CA 29-32R;
CANR 27, 42; CDALB 1968-1988; DLB 6,
33, 143; DLBY 81; MTCW; SATA 57

**Morrison, Van** 1945- .......... **CLC 21**
See also CA 116

**Morrissy, Mary** 1958- .......... **CLC 99**

**Mortimer, John (Clifford)**
1923-... **CLC 28, 43; DAM DRAM, POP**
See also CA 13-16R; CANR 21; CDBLB
1960 to Present; DLB 13; INT CANR-21;
MTCW

**Mortimer, Penelope (Ruth)** 1918- ...... **CLC 5**
See also CA 57-60; CANR 45

**Morton, Anthony**
See Creasey, John

**Mosca, Gaetano** 1858-1941 ........... **TCLC 75**

**Mosher, Howard Frank** 1943- ......... **CLC 62**
See also CA 139

**Mosley, Nicholas** 1923- ............... **CLC 43, 70**
See also CA 69-72; CANR 41, 60; DLB 14

**Mosley, Walter**
1952-........... **CLC 97; DAM MULT, POP**
See also AAYA 17; BW 2; CA 142; CANR 57

**Moss, Howard** 1922-1987 **CLC 7, 14, 45, 50;**
**DAM POET**
See also CA 1-4R; 123; CANR 1, 44; DLB 5

**Mossgiel, Rab**
See Burns, Robert

**O'Hara, Frank**
1926-1966 ......... **CLC 2, 5, 13, 78; DAM POET**
See also CA 9-12R; 25-28R; CANR 33; DLB 5, 16; MTCW

**O'Hara, John (Henry)**
1905-1970 ....... **CLC 1, 2, 3, 6, 11, 42; DAM NOV; SSC 15**
See also CA 5-8R; 25-28R; CANR 31, 60; CDALB 1929-1941; DLB 9, 86; DLBD 2; MTCW

**O Hehir, Diana** 1922- ......................... **CLC 41**
See also CA 93-96

**Okigbo, Christopher (Ifenayichukwu)**
1932-1967 ....... **CLC 25, 84; BLC; DAM MULT, POET; PC 7**
See also BW 1; CA 77-80; DLB 125; MTCW

**Okri, Ben** 1959- ................................. **CLC 87**
See also BW 2; CA 130; 138; DLB 157; INT 138

**Olds, Sharon** 1942- .... **CLC 32, 39, 85; DAM POET**
See also CA 101; CANR 18, 41; DLB 120

**Oldstyle, Jonathan**
See Irving, Washington

**Olesha, Yuri (Karlovich)**
1899-1960 ..................................... **CLC 8**
See also CA 85-88

**Oliphant, Laurence**
1829(?)-1888 ............................. **NCLC 47**
See also DLB 18, 166

**Oliphant, Margaret (Oliphant Wilson)**
1828-1897 ........... **NCLC 11, 61; SSC 25**
See also DLB 18, 159

**Oliver, Mary** 1935-................**CLC 19, 34, 98**
See also CA 21-24R; CANR 9, 43; DLB 5

**Olivier, Laurence (Kerr)**
1907-1989 ................................. **CLC 20**
See also CA 111; 150; 129

**Olsen, Tillie** 1913- ......**CLC 4, 13; DA; DAB; DAC; DAM MST; SSC 11**
See also CA 1-4R; CANR 1, 43; DLB 28; DLBY 80; MTCW

**Olson, Charles (John)**
1910-1970 ....... **CLC 1, 2, 5, 6, 9, 11, 29; DAM POET; PC 19**
See also CA 13-16; 25-28R; CABS 2; CANR 35, 61; CAP 1; DLB 5, 16; MTCW

**Olson, Toby** 1937- ............................. **CLC 28**
See also CA 65-68; CANR 9, 31

**Olyesha, Yuri**
See Olesha, Yuri (Karlovich)

**Ondaatje, (Philip) Michael**
1943- .. **CLC 14, 29, 51, 76; DAB; DAC; DAM MST**
See also CA 77-80; CANR 42; DLB 60

**Oneal, Elizabeth** 1934-
See Oneal, Zibby
See also CA 106; CANR 28; MAICYA; SATA 30, 82

**Oneal, Zibby** ........................................ **CLC 30**
See also Oneal, Elizabeth
See also AAYA 5; CLR 13; JRDA

**O'Neill, Eugene (Gladstone)**
1888-1953 ... **TCLC 1, 6, 27, 49; DA; DAB; DAC; DAM DRAM, MST; WLC**
See also AITN 1; CA 110; 132; CDALB 1929-1941; DLB 7; MTCW

**Onetti, Juan Carlos** 1909-1994....**CLC 7, 10; DAM MULT, NOV; SSC 23**
See also CA 85-88; 145; CANR 32; DLB 113; HW; MTCW

**O Nuallain, Brian** 1911-1966
See O'Brien, Flann
See also CA 21-22; 25-28R; CAP 2

**Opie, Amelia** 1769-1853 ................. **NCLC 65**
See also DLB 116, 159

**Oppen, George** 1908-1984 ...... **CLC 7, 13, 34**
See also CA 13-16R; 113; CANR 8; DLB 5, 165

**Oppenheim, E(dward) Phillips**
1866-1946 ..................................... **TCLC 45**
See also CA 111; DLB 70

**Origen** c. 185-c. 254 ...................... **CMLC 19**

**Orlovitz, Gil** 1918-1973 .................... **CLC 22**
See also CA 77-80; 45-48; DLB 2, 5

**Orris**
See Ingelow, Jean

**Ortega y Gasset, Jose** 1883-1955 ... **TCLC 9; DAM MULT; HLC**
See also CA 106; 130; HW; MTCW

**Ortese, Anna Maria** 1914- ............... **CLC 89**
See also DLB 177

**Ortiz, Simon J(oseph)**
1941-.... **CLC 45; DAM MULT, POET; PC 17**
See also CA 134; DLB 120, 175; NNAL

**Orton, Joe** ..................... **CLC 4, 13, 43; DC 3**
See also Orton, John Kingsley
See also CDBLB 1960 to Present; DLB 13

**Orton, John Kingsley** 1933-1967
See Orton, Joe
See also CA 85-88; CANR 35; DAM DRAM; MTCW

**Orwell, George** **TCLC 2, 6, 15, 31, 51; DAB; WLC**
See also Blair, Eric (Arthur)
See also CDBLB 1945-1960; DLB 15, 98

**Osborne, David**
See Silverberg, Robert

**Osborne, George**
See Silverberg, Robert

**Osborne, John (James)**
1929-1994 ........ **CLC 1, 2, 5, 11, 45; DA; DAB; DAC; DAM DRAM, MST; WLC**
See also CA 13-16R; 147; CANR 21, 56; CDBLB 1945-1960; DLB 13; MTCW

**Osborne, Lawrence** 1958- ................. **CLC 50**

**Oshima, Nagisa** 1932-....................... **CLC 20**
See also CA 116; 121

**Oskison, John Milton**
1874-1947 ......... **TCLC 35; DAM MULT**
See also CA 144; DLB 175; NNAL

**Ossoli, Sarah Margaret (Fuller marchesa d')**
1810-1850
See Fuller, Margaret
See also SATA 25

**Ostrovsky, Alexander** 1823-1886 . **NCLC 30, 57**

**Otero, Blas de** 1916-1979 ................. **CLC 11**
See also CA 89-92; DLB 134

**Otto, Whitney** 1955- ......................... **CLC 70**
See also CA 140

**Ouida** ................................................. **TCLC 43**
See also De La Ramee, (Marie) Louise
See also DLB 18, 156

**Ousmane, Sembene** 1923- ...... **CLC 66; BLC**
See also BW 1; CA 117; 125; MTCW

**Ovid**
43B.C.-18(?) ... **CMLC 7; DAM POET; PC 2**

**Owen, Hugh**
See Faust, Frederick (Schiller)

**Owen, Wilfred (Edward Salter)**
1893-1918 ... **TCLC 5, 27; DA; DAB; DAC; DAM MST, POET; PC 19; WLC**
See also CA 104; 141; CDBLB 1914-1945; DLB 20

**Owens, Rochelle** 1936- ....................... **CLC 8**
See also CA 17-20R; CAAS 2; CANR 39

**Oz, Amos**
1939-...... **CLC 5, 8, 11, 27, 33, 54; DAM NOV**
See also CA 53-56; CANR 27, 47; MTCW

**Ozick, Cynthia**
1928-........ **CLC 3, 7, 28, 62; DAM NOV, POP; SSC 15**
See also BEST 90:1; CA 17-20R; CANR 23, 58; DLB 28, 152; DLBY 82; INT CANR-23; MTCW

**Ozu, Yasujiro** 1903-1963 ................... **CLC 16**
See also CA 112

**Pacheco, C.**
See Pessoa, Fernando (Antonio Nogueira)

**Paulin, Tom** ............................................ CLC 37
   See also Paulin, Thomas Neilson
   See also DLB 40

**Paustovsky, Konstantin (Georgievich)**
   1892-1968 ....................................... CLC 40
   See also CA 93-96; 25-28R

**Pavese, Cesare**
   1908-1950 ........ **TCLC 3; PC 13; SSC 19**
   See also CA 104; DLB 128, 177

**Pavic, Milorad** 1929- .......................... CLC 60
   See also CA 136; DLB 181

**Payne, Alan**
   See Jakes, John (William)

**Paz, Gil**
   See Lugones, Leopoldo

**Paz, Octavio**
   1914- ... CLC 3, 4, 6, 10, 19, 51, 65; DA;
   DAB; DAC; DAM MST, MULT, POET;
   HLC; PC 1; WLC
   See also CA 73-76; CANR 32; DLBY 90; HW;
   MTCW

**p'Bitek, Okot**
   1931-1982 ......... **CLC 96; BLC; DAM**
   **MULT**
   See also BW 2; CA 124; 107; DLB 125;
   MTCW

**Peacock, Molly** 1947- ......................... CLC 60
   See also CA 103; CAAS 21; CANR 52; DLB
   120

**Peacock, Thomas Love**
   1785-1866 ................................. NCLC 22
   See also DLB 96, 116

**Peake, Mervyn** 1911-1968 ............ CLC 7, 54
   See also CA 5-8R; 25-28R; CANR 3; DLB 15,
   160; MTCW; SATA 23

**Pearce, Philippa** ................................. CLC 21
   See also Christie, (Ann) Philippa
   See also CLR 9; DLB 161; MAICYA; SATA 1,
   67

**Pearl, Eric**
   See Elman, Richard

**Pearson, T(homas) R(eid)** 1956- ....... CLC 39
   See also CA 120; 130; INT 130

**Peck, Dale** 1967- ................................ CLC 81
   See also CA 146

**Peck, John** 1941- ................................ CLC 3
   See also CA 49-52; CANR 3

**Peck, Richard (Wayne)** 1934- .......... CLC 21
   See also AAYA 1; CA 85-88; CANR 19, 38;
   CLR 15; INT CANR-19; JRDA; MAICYA;
   SAAS 2; SATA 18, 55

**Peck, Robert Newton**
   1928- ... CLC 17; DA; DAC; DAM MST
   See also AAYA 3; CA 81-84; CANR 31; CLR
   45; JRDA; MAICYA; SAAS 1; SATA 21,
   62

**Peckinpah, (David) Sam(uel)**
   1925-1984 ..................................... CLC 20
   See also CA 109; 114

**Pedersen, Knut** 1859-1952
   See Hamsun, Knut
   See also CA 104; 119; MTCW

**Peeslake, Gaffer**
   See Durrell, Lawrence (George)

**Peguy, Charles Pierre** 1873-1914 .. TCLC 10
   See also CA 107

**Pena, Ramon del Valle y**
   See Valle-Inclan, Ramon (Maria) del

**Pendennis, Arthur Esquir**
   See Thackeray, William Makepeace

**Penn, William** 1644-1718 ..................... LC 25
   See also DLB 24

**PEPECE**
   See Prado (Calvo), Pedro

**Pepys, Samuel**
   1633-1703 ........ LC 11; DA; DAB; DAC;
   DAM MST; WLC
   See also CDBLB 1660-1789; DLB 101

**Percy, Walker**
   1916-1990 ... CLC 2, 3, 6, 8, 14, 18, 47,
   65; DAM NOV, POP
   See also CA 1-4R; 131; CANR 1, 23; DLB 2;
   DLBY 80, 90; MTCW

**Perec, Georges** 1936-1982 ................. CLC 56
   See also CA 141; DLB 83

**Pereda (y Sanchez de Porrua), Jose Maria de**
   1833-1906 ................................. TCLC 16
   See also CA 117

**Pereda y Porrua, Jose Maria de**
   See Pereda (y Sanchez de Porrua), Jose Maria
   de

**Peregoy, George Weems**
   See Mencken, H(enry) L(ouis)

**Perelman, S(idney) J(oseph)**
   1904-1979 ... CLC 3, 5, 9, 15, 23, 44, 49;
   DAM DRAM
   See also AITN 1, 2; CA 73-76; 89-92; CANR
   18; DLB 11, 44; MTCW

**Peret, Benjamin** 1899-1959 ........... TCLC 20
   See also CA 117

**Peretz, Isaac Loeb**
   1851(?)-1915 ............. TCLC 16; SSC 26
   See also CA 109

**Peretz, Yitzhok Leibush**
   See Peretz, Isaac Loeb

**Perez Galdos, Benito**
   1843-1920 ................................. TCLC 27
   See also CA 125; 153; HW

**Perrault, Charles** 1628-1703 ................. LC 2
   See also MAICYA; SATA 25

**Perry, Brighton**
   See Sherwood, Robert E(mmet)

**Perse, St.-John** ........................... CLC 4, 11, 46
   See also Leger, (Marie-Rene Auguste) Alexis
   Saint-Leger

**Perutz, Leo** 1882-1957 ................... TCLC 60
   See also DLB 81

**Peseenz, Tulio F.**
   See Lopez y Fuentes, Gregorio

**Pesetsky, Bette** 1932- .......................... CLC 28
   See also CA 133; DLB 130

**Peshkov, Alexei Maximovich** 1868-1936
   See Gorky, Maxim
   See also CA 105; 141; DA; DAC; DAM
   DRAM, MST, NOV

**Pessoa, Fernando (Antonio Nogueira)**
   1888-1935 ......... TCLC 27; HLC; PC 20
   See also CA 125

**Peterkin, Julia Mood** 1880-1961 ...... CLC 31
   See also CA 102; DLB 9

**Peters, Joan K(aren)** 1945- .............. CLC 39
   See also CA 158

**Peters, Robert L(ouis)** 1924- .............. CLC 7
   See also CA 13-16R; CAAS 8; DLB 105

**Petofi, Sandor** 1823-1849 .............. NCLC 21

**Petrakis, Harry Mark** 1923- .............. CLC 3
   See also CA 9-12R; CANR 4, 30

**Petrarch**
   1304-1374 ... CMLC 20; DAM POET;
   PC 8

**Petrov, Evgeny** ................................. TCLC 21
   See also Kataev, Evgeny Petrovich

**Petry, Ann (Lane)**
   1908-1997 ........................... CLC 1, 7, 18
   See also BW 1; CA 5-8R; 157; CAAS 6;
   CANR 4, 46; CLR 12; DLB 76; JRDA;
   MAICYA; MTCW; SATA 5; SATA-Obit
   94

**Petursson, Halligrimur** 1614-1674 ....... LC 8

**Phaedrus** 18(?)B.C.-55(?) ............. CMLC 24

**Philips, Katherine** 1632-1664 ............. LC 30
   See also DLB 131

**Philipson, Morris H.** 1926- ............... CLC 53
   See also CA 1-4R; CANR 4

**Phillips, Caryl**
   1958- ................... CLC 96; DAM MULT
   See also BW 2; CA 141; DLB 157

**Phillips, David Graham**
   1867-1911 ................................. TCLC 44
   See also CA 108; DLB 9, 12

**Phillips, Jack**
   See Sandburg, Carl (August)

**Polidori, John William**
1795-1821 ............................... NCLC 51
See also DLB 116

**Pollitt, Katha** 1949- ........................... CLC 28
See also CA 120; 122; MTCW

**Pollock, (Mary) Sharon**
1936- ....... CLC 50; DAC; DAM DRAM,
MST
See also CA 141; DLB 60

**Polo, Marco** 1254-1324 ................. CMLC 15

**Polonsky, Abraham (Lincoln)**
1910- .......................................... CLC 92
See also CA 104; DLB 26; INT 104

**Polybius** c. 200B.C.-c. 118B.C. ..... CMLC 17
See also DLB 176

**Pomerance, Bernard** 1940- ... CLC 13; DAM
DRAM
See also CA 101; CANR 49

**Ponge, Francis (Jean Gaston Alfred)**
1899-1988 ........ CLC 6, 18; DAM POET
See also CA 85-88; 126; CANR 40

**Pontoppidan, Henrik** 1857-1943 ... TCLC 29

**Poole, Josephine** ................................. CLC 17
See also Helyar, Jane Penelope Josephine
See also SAAS 2; SATA 5

**Popa, Vasko** 1922-1991 ..................... CLC 19
See also CA 112; 148; DLB 181

**Pope, Alexander**
1688-1744 ........ LC 3; DA; DAB; DAC;
DAM MST, POET; WLC
See also CDBLB 1660-1789; DLB 95, 101

**Porter, Connie (Rose)** 1959(?)- ......... CLC 70
See also BW 2; CA 142; SATA 81

**Porter, Gene(va Grace) Stratton**
1863(?)-1924 ............................ TCLC 21
See also CA 112

**Porter, Katherine Anne**
1890-1980 .... CLC 1, 3, 7, 10, 13, 15, 27,
101; DA; DAB; DAC; DAM MST, NOV;
SSC 4
See also AITN 2; CA 1-4R; 101; CANR 1; DLB
4, 9, 102; DLBD 12; DLBY 80; MTCW;
SATA 39; SATA-Obit 23

**Porter, Peter (Neville Frederick)**
1929- ................................. CLC 5, 13, 33
See also CA 85-88; DLB 40

**Porter, William Sydney** 1862-1910
See Henry, O.
See also CA 104; 131; CDALB 1865-1917;
DA; DAB; DAC; DAM MST; DLB 12, 78,
79; MTCW; YABC 2

**Portillo (y Pacheco), Jose Lopez**
See Lopez Portillo (y Pacheco), Jose

**Post, Melville Davisson** 1869-1930 TCLC 39
See also CA 110

**Potok, Chaim**
1929- ......... CLC 2, 7, 14, 26; DAM NOV
See also AAYA 15; AITN 1, 2; CA 17-20R;
CANR 19, 35; DLB 28, 152; INT CANR-
19; MTCW; SATA 33

**Potter, (Helen) Beatrix** 1866-1943
See Webb, (Martha) Beatrice (Potter)
See also MAICYA

**Potter, Dennis (Christopher George)**
1935-1994 ............................. CLC 58, 86
See also CA 107; 145; CANR 33, 61;
MTCW

**Pound, Ezra (Weston Loomis)**
1885-1972 ... CLC 1, 2, 3, 4, 5, 7, 10, 13,
18, 34, 48, 50; DA; DAB; DAC; DAM
MST, POET; PC 4; WLC
See also CA 5-8R; 37-40R; CANR 40; CDALB
1917-1929; DLB 4, 45, 63; DLBD 15;
MTCW

**Povod, Reinaldo** 1959-1994 .............. CLC 44
See also CA 136; 146

**Powell, Adam Clayton, Jr.**
1908-1972 ......... CLC 89; BLC; DAM
MULT
See also BW 1; CA 102; 33-36R

**Powell, Anthony (Dymoke)**
1905- ..................... CLC 1, 3, 7, 9, 10, 31
See also CA 1-4R; CANR 1, 32, 62; CDBLB
1945-1960; DLB 15; MTCW

**Powell, Dawn** 1897-1965 .................. CLC 66
See also CA 5-8R

**Powell, Padgett** 1952- ....................... CLC 34
See also CA 126

**Power, Susan** 1961- ........................... CLC 91

**Powers, J(ames) F(arl)**
1917- ................... CLC 1, 4, 8, 57; SSC 4
See also CA 1-4R; CANR 2, 61; DLB 130;
MTCW

**Powers, John J(ames)** 1945-
See Powers, John R.
See also CA 69-72

**Powers, John R.** ................................. CLC 66
See also Powers, John J(ames)

**Powers, Richard (S.)** 1957- .............. CLC 93
See also CA 148

**Pownall, David** 1938- ......................... CLC 10
See also CA 89-92; CAAS 18; CANR 49; DLB
14

**Powys, John Cowper**
1872-1963 ..................... CLC 7, 9, 15, 46
See also CA 85-88; DLB 15; MTCW

**Powys, T(heodore) F(rancis)**
1875-1953 ................................... TCLC 9
See also CA 106; DLB 36, 162

**Prado (Calvo), Pedro** 1886-1952 ... TCLC 75
See also CA 131; HW

**Prager, Emily** 1952- ........................... CLC 56

**Pratt, E(dwin) J(ohn)**
1883(?)-1964 ......... CLC 19; DAC; DAM
POET
See also CA 141; 93-96; DLB 92

**Premchand** ...................................... TCLC 21
See also Srivastava, Dhanpat Rai

**Preussler, Otfried**
1923- .......................................... CLC 17
See also CA 77-80; SATA 24

**Prevert, Jacques (Henri Marie)**
1900-1977 ..................................... CLC 15
See also CA 77-80; 69-72; CANR 29, 61;
MTCW; SATA-Obit 30

**Prevost, Abbe (Antoine Francois)**
1697-1763 ......................................... LC 1

**Price, (Edward) Reynolds**
1933- ....... CLC 3, 6, 13, 43, 50, 63; DAM
NOV; SSC 22
See also CA 1-4R; CANR 1, 37, 57; DLB 2;
INT CANR-37

**Price, Richard**
1949- ...................................... CLC 6, 12
See also CA 49-52; CANR 3; DLBY 81

**Prichard, Katharine Susannah**
1883-1969 ................................... CLC 46
See also CA 11-12; CANR 33; CAP 1; MTCW;
SATA 66

**Priestley, J(ohn) B(oynton)**
1894-1984 ............ CLC 2, 5, 9, 34; DAM
DRAM, NOV
See also CA 9-12R; 113; CANR 33; CDBLB
1914-1945; DLB 10, 34, 77, 100, 139;
DLBY 84; MTCW

**Prince** 1958(?)- ................................. CLC 35

**Prince, F(rank) T(empleton)**
1912- ........................................... CLC 22
See also CA 101; CANR 43; DLB 20

**Prince Kropotkin**
See Kropotkin, Peter (Aleksieevich)

**Prior, Matthew** 1664-1721 .................... LC 4
See also DLB 95

**Prishvin, Mikhail** 1873-1954 ......... TCLC 75

**Pritchard, William H(arrison)**
1932- .......................................... CLC 34
See also CA 65-68; CANR 23; DLB 111

**Pritchett, V(ictor) S(awdon)**
1900-1997 ........ CLC 5, 13, 15, 41; DAM
NOV; SSC 14
See also CA 61-64; 157; CANR 31; DLB 15,
139; MTCW

**Private 19022**
See Manning, Frederic

**Probst, Mark** 1925- ........................... CLC 59
See also CA 130

**Rizal, Jose** 1861-1896 ..................... **NCLC 27**

**Roa Bastos, Augusto (Antonio)**
    1917- .........**CLC 45; DAM MULT; HLC**
  See also CA 131; DLB 113; HW

**Robbe-Grillet, Alain**
    1922- ........... **CLC 1, 2, 4, 6, 8, 10, 14, 43**
  See also CA 9-12R; CANR 33; DLB 83;
  MTCW

**Robbins, Harold**
    1916- ........................ **CLC 5; DAM NOV**
  See also CA 73-76; CANR 26, 54; MTCW

**Robbins, Thomas Eugene** 1936-
  See Robbins, Tom
  See also CA 81-84; CANR 29, 59; DAM NOV,
  POP; MTCW

**Robbins, Tom** ........................... **CLC 9, 32, 64**
  See also Robbins, Thomas Eugene
  See also BEST 90:3; DLBY 80

**Robbins, Trina** 1938- ........................ **CLC 21**
  See also CA 128

**Roberts, Charles G(eorge) D(ouglas)**
    1860-1943 ............................... **TCLC 8**
  See also CA 105; CLR 33; DLB 92; SATA 88;
  SATA-Brief 29

**Roberts, Elizabeth Madox**
    1886-1941 ............................... **TCLC 68**
  See also CA 111; DLB 9, 54, 102; SATA 33;
  SATA-Brief 27

**Roberts, Kate** 1891-1985 .................. **CLC 15**
  See also CA 107; 116

**Roberts, Keith (John Kingston)**
    1935- ................................................. **CLC 14**
  See also CA 25-28R; CANR 46

**Roberts, Kenneth (Lewis)**
    1885-1957 ............................... **TCLC 23**
  See also CA 109; DLB 9

**Roberts, Michele (B.)** 1949- ............. **CLC 48**
  See also CA 115; CANR 58

**Robertson, Ellis**
  See Ellison, Harlan (Jay); Silverberg, Robert

**Robertson, Thomas William**
    1829-1871 ........ **NCLC 35; DAM DRAM**

**Robeson, Kenneth**
  See Dent, Lester

**Robinson, Edwin Arlington**
    1869-1935 .... **TCLC 5; DA; DAC; DAM**
  **MST, POET; PC 1**
  See also CA 104; 133; CDALB 1865-1917;
  DLB 54; MTCW

**Robinson, Henry Crabb**
    1775-1867 ............................... **NCLC 15**
  See also DLB 107

**Robinson, Jill** 1936- ........................ **CLC 10**
  See also CA 102; INT 102

**Robinson, Kim Stanley** 1952- .......... **CLC 34**
  See also CA 126

**Robinson, Lloyd**
  See Silverberg, Robert

**Robinson, Marilynne** 1944- ............. **CLC 25**
  See also CA 116

**Robinson, Smokey** .............................. **CLC 21**
  See also Robinson, William, Jr.

**Robinson, William, Jr.** 1940-
  See Robinson, Smokey
  See also CA 116

**Robison, Mary** 1949- .................. **CLC 42, 98**
  See also CA 113; 116; DLB 130; INT 116

**Rod, Edouard** 1857-1910 ............... **TCLC 52**

**Roddenberry, Eugene Wesley** 1921-1991
  See Roddenberry, Gene
  See also CA 110; 135; CANR 37; SATA 45;
  SATA-Obit 69

**Roddenberry, Gene** ............................ **CLC 17**
  See also Roddenberry, Eugene Wesley
  See also AAYA 5; SATA-Obit 69

**Rodgers, Mary** 1931- ........................ **CLC 12**
  See also CA 49-52; CANR 8, 55; CLR 20;
  INT CANR-8; JRDA; MAICYA; SATA
  8

**Rodgers, W(illiam) R(obert)**
    1909-1969 ................................ **CLC 7**
  See also CA 85-88; DLB 20

**Rodman, Eric**
  See Silverberg, Robert

**Rodman, Howard** 1920(?)-1985 ....... **CLC 65**
  See also CA 118

**Rodman, Maia**
  See Wojciechowska, Maia (Teresa)

**Rodriguez, Claudio** 1934- ................ **CLC 10**
  See also DLB 134

**Roelvaag, O(le) E(dvart)**
    1876-1931 ................................ **TCLC 17**
  See also CA 117; DLB 9

**Roethke, Theodore (Huebner)**
    1908-1963 .. **CLC 1, 3, 8, 11, 19, 46, 101;**
  **DAM POET; PC 15**
  See also CA 81-84; CABS 2; CDALB 1941-
  1968; DLB 5; MTCW

**Rogers, Thomas Hunton** 1927- ......... **CLC 57**
  See also CA 89-92; INT 89-92

**Rogers, Will(iam Penn Adair)**
    1879-1935 ..... **TCLC 8, 71; DAM MULT**
  See also CA 105; 144; DLB 11; NNAL

**Rogin, Gilbert** 1929- ........................ **CLC 18**
  See also CA 65-68; CANR 15

**Rohan, Koda** .................................. **TCLC 22**
  See also Koda Shigeyuki

**Rohlfs, Anna Katharine Green**
  See Green, Anna Katharine

**Rohmer, Eric** ....................................... **CLC 16**
  See also Scherer, Jean-Marie Maurice

**Rohmer, Sax** ..................................... **TCLC 28**
  See also Ward, Arthur Henry Sarsfield
  See also DLB 70

**Roiphe, Anne (Richardson)**
    1935-............................................... **CLC 3, 9**
  See also CA 89-92; CANR 45; DLBY 80; INT
  89-92

**Rojas, Fernando de** 1465-1541 ........... **LC 23**

**Rolfe, Frederick (William Serafino Austin
    Lewis Mary)** 1860-1913 ........ **TCLC 12**
  See also CA 107; DLB 34, 156

**Rolland, Romain** 1866-1944 .......... **TCLC 23**
  See also CA 118; DLB 65

**Rolle, Richard** c. 1300-c. 1349 ...... **CMLC 21**
  See also DLB 146

**Rolvaag, O(le) E(dvart)**
  See Roelvaag, O(le) E(dvart)

**Romain Arnaud, Saint**
  See Aragon, Louis

**Romains, Jules** 1885-1972 .................. **CLC 7**
  See also CA 85-88; CANR 34; DLB 65;
  MTCW

**Romero, Jose Ruben** 1890-1952 .... **TCLC 14**
  See also CA 114; 131; HW

**Ronsard, Pierre de** 1524-1585 .. **LC 6; PC 11**

**Rooke, Leon** 1934- .. **CLC 25, 34; DAM POP**
  See also CA 25-28R; CANR 23, 53

**Roosevelt, Theodore** 1858-1919 .... **TCLC 69**
  See also CA 115; DLB 47

**Roper, William** 1498-1578 ................... **LC 10**

**Roquelaure, A. N.**
  See Rice, Anne

**Rosa, Joao Guimaraes** 1908-1967 .... **CLC 23**
  See also CA 89-92; DLB 113

**Rose, Wendy**
    1948-........ **CLC 85; DAM MULT; PC 13**
  See also CA 53-56; CANR 5, 51; DLB 175;
  NNAL; SATA 12

**Rosen, R. D.**
  See Rosen, Richard (Dean)

**Rosen, Richard (Dean)** 1949- ........... **CLC 39**
  See also CA 77-80; CANR 62; INT CANR-
  30

**Rosenberg, Isaac** 1890-1918 ......... **TCLC 12**
  See also CA 107; DLB 20

**Rosenblatt, Joe** ................................... **CLC 15**
  See also Rosenblatt, Joseph

**S. S.**
See Sassoon, Siegfried (Lorraine)

**Saba, Umberto** 1883-1957 ............. **TCLC 33**
See also CA 144; DLB 114

**Sabatini, Rafael** 1875-1950 ........... **TCLC 47**

**Sabato, Ernesto (R.)**
1911- ........**CLC 10, 23; DAM MULT;
HLC**
See also CA 97-100; CANR 32; DLB 145; HW;
MTCW

**Sacastru, Martin**
See Bioy Casares, Adolfo

**Sacher-Masoch, Leopold von**
1836(?)-1895 ............................ **NCLC 31**

**Sachs, Marilyn (Stickle)**
1927- .................................... **CLC 35**
See also AAYA 2; CA 17-20R; CANR 13, 47;
CLR 2; JRDA; MAICYA; SAAS 2; SATA
3, 68

**Sachs, Nelly** 1891-1970 ............... **CLC 14, 98**
See also CA 17-18; 25-28R; CAP 2

**Sackler, Howard (Oliver)**
1929-1982 ................................. **CLC 14**
See also CA 61-64; 108; CANR 30; DLB
7

**Sacks, Oliver (Wolf)** 1933- ................ **CLC 67**
See also CA 53-56; CANR 28, 50; INT CANR-
28; MTCW

**Sadakichi**
See Hartmann, Sadakichi

**Sade, Donatien Alphonse Francois, Comte de**
1740-1814 ................................ **NCLC 47**

**Sadoff, Ira** 1945- ................................. **CLC 9**
See also CA 53-56; CANR 5, 21; DLB 120

**Saetone**
See Camus, Albert

**Safire, William** 1929- ......................... **CLC 10**
See also CA 17-20R; CANR 31, 54

**Sagan, Carl (Edward)**
1934-1996 ................................ **CLC 30**
See also AAYA 2; CA 25-28R; 155; CANR
11, 36; MTCW; SATA 58; SATA-Obit
94

**Sagan, Francoise** ............. **CLC 3, 6, 9, 17, 36**
See also Quoirez, Francoise
See also DLB 83

**Sahgal, Nayantara (Pandit)**
1927- .......................................... **CLC 41**
See also CA 9-12R; CANR 11

**Saint, H(arry) F.** 1941- ...................... **CLC 50**
See also CA 127

**St. Aubin de Teran, Lisa** 1953-
See Teran, Lisa St. Aubin de
See also CA 118; 126; INT 126

**Saint Birgitta of Sweden**
c. 1303-1373 ............................. **CMLC 24**

**Sainte-Beuve, Charles Augustin**
1804-1869 .................................. **NCLC 5**

**Saint-Exupery, Antoine (Jean Baptiste
Marie Roger) de**
1900-1944 ........       **TCLC 2, 56; DAM
NOV; WLC**
See also CA 108; 132; CLR 10; DLB 72;
MAICYA; MTCW; SATA 20

**St. John, David**
See Hunt, E(verette) Howard, (Jr.)

**Saint-John Perse**
See Leger, (Marie-Rene Auguste) Alexis Saint-
Leger

**Saintsbury, George (Edward Bateman)**
1845-1933 ................................. **TCLC 31**
See also CA 160; DLB 57, 149

**Sait Faik** ........................................ **TCLC 23**
See also Abasiyanik, Sait Faik

**Saki** ....................................... **TCLC 3; SSC 12**
See also Munro, H(ector) H(ugh)

**Sala, George Augustus** .................... **NCLC 46**

**Salama, Hannu** 1936- ...................... **CLC 18**

**Salamanca, J(ack) R(ichard)**
1922- ............................................ **CLC 4, 15**
See also CA 25-28R

**Sale, J. Kirkpatrick**
See Sale, Kirkpatrick

**Sale, Kirkpatrick**
1937- ............................................ **CLC 68**
See also CA 13-16R; CANR 10

**Salinas, Luis Omar**
1937- ......... **CLC 90; DAM MULT;
HLC**
See also CA 131; DLB 82; HW

**Salinas (y Serrano), Pedro**
1891(?)-1951 ............................. **TCLC 17**
See also CA 117; DLB 134

**Salinger, J(erome) D(avid)**
1919- ......... **CLC 1, 3, 8, 12, 55, 56; DA;
DAB; DAC; DAM MST, NOV, POP;
SSC 2, 28; WLC**
See also AAYA 2; CA 5-8R; CANR 39;
CDALB 1941-1968; CLR 18; DLB 2,
102, 173; MAICYA; MTCW; SATA
67

**Salisbury, John**
See Caute, David

**Salter, James**
1925- ............................................ **CLC 7, 52, 59**
See also CA 73-76; DLB 130

**Saltus, Edgar (Everton)**
1855-1921 ................................. **TCLC 8**
See also CA 105

**Saltykov, Mikhail Evgrafovich**
1826-1889 ............................... **NCLC 16**

**Samarakis, Antonis** 1919- .................. **CLC 5**
See also CA 25-28R; CAAS 16; CANR 36

**Sanchez, Florencio** 1875-1910 ....... **TCLC 37**
See also CA 153; HW

**Sanchez, Luis Rafael** 1936- .............. **CLC 23**
See also CA 128; DLB 145; HW

**Sanchez, Sonia** 1934- ..... **CLC 5; BLC; DAM
MULT; PC 9**
See also BW 2; CA 33-36R; CANR 24, 49;
CLR 18; DLB 41; DLBD 8; MAICYA;
MTCW; SATA 22

**Sand, George**
1804-1876 .. **NCLC 2, 42, 57; DA; DAB;
DAC; DAM MST, NOV; WLC**
See also DLB 119

**Sandburg, Carl (August)**
1878-1967 ...... **CLC 1, 4, 10, 15, 35; DA;
DAB; DAC; DAM MST, POET; PC 2;
WLC**
See also CA 5-8R; 25-28R; CANR 35; CDALB
1865-1917; DLB 17, 54; MAICYA; MTCW;
SATA 8

**Sandburg, Charles**
See Sandburg, Carl (August)

**Sandburg, Charles A.**
See Sandburg, Carl (August)

**Sanders, (James) Ed(ward)** 1939- .... **CLC 53**
See also CA 13-16R; CAAS 21; CANR 13, 44;
DLB 16

**Sanders, Lawrence**
1920- ....................... **CLC 41; DAM POP**
See also BEST 89:4; CA 81-84; CANR 33, 62;
MTCW

**Sanders, Noah**
See Blount, Roy (Alton), Jr.

**Sanders, Winston P.**
See Anderson, Poul (William)

**Sandoz, Mari(e Susette)** 1896-1966 . **CLC 28**
See also CA 1-4R; 25-28R; CANR 17; DLB
9; MTCW; SATA 5

**Saner, Reg(inald Anthony)** 1931- ....... **CLC 9**
See also CA 65-68

**Sannazaro, Jacopo** 1456(?)-1530 .......... **LC 8**

**Sansom, William**
1912-1976 .. **CLC 2, 6; DAM NOV; SSC
21**
See also CA 5-8R; 65-68; CANR 42; DLB 139;
MTCW

**Santayana, George** 1863-1952 ....... **TCLC 40**
See also CA 115; DLB 54, 71; DLBD 13

**Santiago, Danny** ............................... **CLC 33**
See also James, Daniel (Lewis)
See also DLB 122

Schulz, Charles M(onroe)
1922-　...................................... **CLC 12**
See also CA 9-12R; CANR 6; INT CANR-6;
SATA 10

Schumacher, E(rnst) F(riedrich)
1911-1977　.................................. **CLC 80**
See also CA 81-84; 73-76; CANR 34

Schuyler, James Marcus
1923-1991　....... **CLC 5, 23; DAM POET**
See also CA 101; 134; DLB 5, 169; INT
101

Schwartz, Delmore (David)
1913-1966　.... **CLC 2, 4, 10, 45, 87; PC 8**
See also CA 17-18; 25-28R; CANR 35; CAP
2; DLB 28, 48; MTCW

Schwartz, Ernst
See Ozu, Yasujiro

Schwartz, John Burnham 1965-　....... **CLC 59**
See also CA 132

Schwartz, Lynne Sharon 1939-　........ **CLC 31**
See also CA 103; CANR 44

Schwartz, Muriel A.
See Eliot, T(homas) S(tearns)

Schwarz-Bart, Andre 1928-　............ **CLC 2, 4**
See also CA 89-92

Schwarz-Bart, Simone 1938-　.............. **CLC 7**
See also BW 2; CA 97-100

Schwob, (Mayer Andre) Marcel
1867-1905　............................... **TCLC 20**
See also CA 117; DLB 123

Sciascia, Leonardo
1921-1989　........................... **CLC 8, 9, 41**
See also CA 85-88; 130; CANR 35; DLB 177;
MTCW

Scoppettone, Sandra 1936-　.............. **CLC 26**
See also AAYA 11; CA 5-8R; CANR 41; SATA
9, 92

Scorsese, Martin 1942-　............... **CLC 20, 89**
See also CA 110; 114; CANR 46

Scotland, Jay
See Jakes, John (William)

Scott, Duncan Campbell
1862-1947　........................ **TCLC 6; DAC**
See also CA 104; 153; DLB 92

Scott, Evelyn 1893-1963　.................... **CLC 43**
See also CA 104; 112; DLB 9, 48

Scott, F(rancis) R(eginald)
1899-1985　.................................... **CLC 22**
See also CA 101; 114; DLB 88; INT
101

Scott, Frank
See Scott, F(rancis) R(eginald)

Scott, Joanna 1960-　........................... **CLC 50**
See also CA 126; CANR 53

Scott, Paul (Mark) 1920-1978....... **CLC 9, 60**
See also CA 81-84; 77-80; CANR 33; DLB
14; MTCW

Scott, Walter
1771-1832 ..**NCLC 15; DA; DAB; DAC;
DAM MST, NOV, POET; PC 13; WLC**
See also AAYA 22; CDBLB 1789-1832; DLB
93, 107, 116, 144, 159; YABC 2

Scribe, (Augustin) Eugene
1791-1861 ...　**NCLC 16; DAM DRAM;
DC 5**

Scrum, R.
See Crumb, R(obert)

Scudery, Madeleine de 1607-1701......... **LC 2**

Scum
See Crumb, R(obert)

Scumbag, Little Bobby
See Crumb, R(obert)

Seabrook, John
See Hubbard, L(afayette) Ron(ald)

Sealy, I. Allan 1951-............................ **CLC 55**

Search, Alexander
See Pessoa, Fernando (Antonio Nogueira)

Sebastian, Lee
See Silverberg, Robert

Sebastian Owl
See Thompson, Hunter S(tockton)

Sebestyen, Ouida 1924-..................... **CLC 30**
See also AAYA 8; CA 107; CANR 40; CLR
17; JRDA; MAICYA; SAAS 10; SATA 39

Secundus, H. Scriblerus
See Fielding, Henry

Sedges, John
See Buck, Pearl S(ydenstricker)

Sedgwick, Catharine Maria
1789-1867　................................. **NCLC 19**
See also DLB 1, 74

Seelye, John 1931-.............................. **CLC 7**

Seferiades, Giorgos Stylianou 1900-1971
See Seferis, George
See also CA 5-8R; 33-36R; CANR 5, 36;
MTCW

Seferis, George ................................ **CLC 5, 11**
See also Seferiades, Giorgos Stylianou

Segal, Erich (Wolf)
1937-................... **CLC 3, 10; DAM POP**
See also BEST 89:1; CA 25-28R; CANR 20,
36; DLBY 86; INT CANR-20; MTCW

Seger, Bob 1945-................................ **CLC 35**

Seghers, Anna ....................................... **CLC 7**
See also Radvanyi, Netty
See also DLB 69

Seidel, Frederick (Lewis) 1936-........ **CLC 18**
See also CA 13-16R; CANR 8; DLBY 84

Seifert, Jaroslav 1901-1986 ..**CLC 34, 44, 93**
See also CA 127; MTCW

Sei Shonagon c. 966-1017(?) .......... **CMLC 6**

Selby, Hubert, Jr.
1928-....................**CLC 1, 2, 4, 8; SSC 20**
See also CA 13-16R; CANR 33; DLB 2

Selzer, Richard 1928-......................... **CLC 74**
See also CA 65-68; CANR 14

Sembene, Ousmane
See Ousmane, Sembene

Senancour, Etienne Pivert de
1770-1846　................................. **NCLC 16**
See also DLB 119

Sender, Ramon (Jose)
1902-1982 ...**CLC 8; DAM MULT; HLC**
See also CA 5-8R; 105; CANR 8; HW; MTCW

Seneca, Lucius Annaeus
4B.C.-65 ....　　**CMLC 6; DAM DRAM;
DC 5**

Senghor, Leopold Sedar
1906-.........**CLC 54; BLC; DAM MULT,
POET**
See also BW 2; CA 116; 125; CANR 47;
MTCW

Serling, (Edward) Rod(man)
1924-1975　.................................... **CLC 30**
See also AAYA 14; AITN 1; CA 65-68; 57-60;
DLB 26

Serna, Ramon Gomez de la
See Gomez de la Serna, Ramon

Serpieres
See Guillevic, (Eugene)

Service, Robert
See Service, Robert W(illiam)
See also DAB; DLB 92

Service, Robert W(illiam)
1874(?)-1958........ **TCLC 15; DA; DAC;
DAM MST, POET; WLC**
See also Service, Robert
See also CA 115; 140; SATA 20

Seth, Vikram
1952-.............. **CLC 43, 90; DAM MULT**
See also CA 121; 127; CANR 50; DLB 120;
INT 127

Seton, Cynthia Propper
1926-1982　.................................... **CLC 27**
See also CA 5-8R; 108; CANR 7

Seton, Ernest (Evan) Thompson
1860-1946　................................. **TCLC 31**
See also CA 109; DLB 92; DLBD 13; JRDA;
SATA 18

Seton-Thompson, Ernest
See Seton, Ernest (Evan) Thompson

Settle, Mary Lee
1918- ..................................... CLC 19, 61
See also CA 89-92; CAAS 1; CANR 44; DLB 6; INT 89-92

Seuphor, Michel
See Arp, Jean

Sevigne, Marie (de Rabutin-Chantal) Marquise de 1626-1696 ................................ LC 11

Sewall, Samuel
1652-1730 ...................................... LC 38
See also DLB 24

Sexton, Anne (Harvey)
1928-1974 ..... CLC 2, 4, 6, 8, 10, 15, 53;
DA; DAB; DAC; DAM MST, POET; PC 2; WLC
See also CA 1-4R; 53-56; CABS 2; CANR 3, 36; CDALB 1941-1968; DLB 5, 169; MTCW; SATA 10

Shaara, Michael (Joseph, Jr.)
1929-1988 ............... CLC 15; DAM POP
See also AITN 1; CA 102; 125; CANR 52; DLBY 83

Shackleton, C. C.
See Aldiss, Brian W(ilson)

Shacochis, Bob .................................... CLC 39
See also Shacochis, Robert G.

Shacochis, Robert G. 1951-
See Shacochis, Bob
See also CA 119; 124; INT 124

Shaffer, Anthony (Joshua) 1926- .... CLC 19;
DAM DRAM
See also CA 110; 116; DLB 13

Shaffer, Peter (Levin)
1926- ........ CLC 5, 14, 18, 37, 60; DAB;
DAM DRAM, MST; DC 7
See also CA 25-28R; CANR 25, 47; CDBLB 1960 to Present; DLB 13; MTCW

Shakey, Bernard
See Young, Neil

Shalamov, Varlam (Tikhonovich)
1907(?)-1982 ................................ CLC 18
See also CA 129; 105

Shamlu, Ahmad 1925- ...................... CLC 10

Shammas, Anton 1951- ..................... CLC 55

Shange, Ntozake
1948- ...... CLC 8, 25, 38, 74; BLC; DAM
DRAM, MULT; DC 3
See also AAYA 9; BW 2; CA 85-88; CABS 3; CANR 27, 48; DLB 38; MTCW

Shanley, John Patrick
1950- ............................................. CLC 75
See also CA 128; 133

Shapcott, Thomas W(illiam)
1935- ............................................. CLC 38
See also CA 69-72; CANR 49

Shapiro, Jane ..................................... CLC 76

Shapiro, Karl (Jay) 1913- ... CLC 4, 8, 15, 53
See also CA 1-4R; CAAS 6; CANR 1, 36; DLB 48; MTCW

Sharp, William 1855-1905 ............. TCLC 39
See also CA 160; DLB 156

Sharpe, Thomas Ridley 1928-
See Sharpe, Tom
See also CA 114; 122; INT 122

Sharpe, Tom ....................................... CLC 36
See also Sharpe, Thomas Ridley
See also DLB 14

Shaw, Bernard ................................... TCLC 45
See also Shaw, George Bernard
See also BW 1

Shaw, G. Bernard
See Shaw, George Bernard

Shaw, George Bernard
1856-1950 ..... TCLC 3, 9, 21; DA; DAB;
DAC; DAM DRAM, MST; WLC
See also Shaw, Bernard
See also CA 104; 128; CDBLB 1914-1945; DLB 10, 57; MTCW

Shaw, Henry Wheeler
1818-1885 ................................ NCLC 15
See also DLB 11

Shaw, Irwin
1913-1984 ............ CLC 7, 23, 34; DAM
DRAM, POP
See also AITN 1; CA 13-16R; 112; CANR 21; CDALB 1941-1968; DLB 6, 102; DLBY 84; MTCW

Shaw, Robert 1927-1978 .................... CLC 5
See also AITN 1; CA 1-4R; 81-84; CANR 4; DLB 13, 14

Shaw, T. E.
See Lawrence, T(homas) E(dward)

Shawn, Wallace 1943- ...................... CLC 41
See also CA 112

Shea, Lisa 1953- ................................ CLC 86
See also CA 147

Sheed, Wilfrid (John Joseph)
1930- ...............................CLC 2, 4, 10, 53
See also CA 65-68; CANR 30; DLB 6; MTCW

Sheldon, Alice Hastings Bradley 1915(?)-1987
See Tiptree, James, Jr.
See also CA 108; 122; CANR 34; INT 108; MTCW

Sheldon, John
See Bloch, Robert (Albert)

Shelley, Mary Wollstonecraft (Godwin)
1797-1851 ....... NCLC 14, 59; DA; DAB;
DAC; DAM MST, NOV; WLC
See also AAYA 20; CDBLB 1789-1832; DLB 110, 116, 159, 178; SATA 29

Shelley, Percy Bysshe
1792-1822 .. NCLC 18; DA; DAB; DAC;
DAM MST, POET; PC 14; WLC
See also CDBLB 1789-1832; DLB 96, 110, 158

Shepard, Jim 1956- ........................... CLC 36
See also CA 137; CANR 59; SATA 90

Shepard, Lucius 1947- ...................... CLC 34
See also CA 128; 141

Shepard, Sam
1943- ...... CLC 4, 6, 17, 34, 41, 44; DAM
DRAM; DC 5
See also AAYA 1; CA 69-72; CABS 3; CANR 22; DLB 7; MTCW

Shepherd, Michael
See Ludlum, Robert

Sherburne, Zoa (Morin) 1912- ......... CLC 30
See also AAYA 13; CA 1-4R; CANR 3, 37; MAICYA; SAAS 18; SATA 3

Sheridan, Frances 1724-1766 ............... LC 7
See also DLB 39, 84

Sheridan, Richard Brinsley
1751-1816 .... NCLC 5; DA; DAB; DAC;
DAM DRAM, MST; DC 1; WLC
See also CDBLB 1660-1789; DLB 89

Sherman, Jonathan Marc .................. CLC 55

Sherman, Martin 1941(?)- ................. CLC 19
See also CA 116; 123

Sherwin, Judith Johnson 1936- .... CLC 7, 15
See also CA 25-28R; CANR 34

Sherwood, Frances 1940- .................. CLC 81
See also CA 146

Sherwood, Robert E(mmet)
1896-1955 .......... TCLC 3; DAM DRAM
See also CA 104; 153; DLB 7, 26

Shestov, Lev 1866-1938 .................. TCLC 56

Shevchenko, Taras 1814-1861 ....... NCLC 54

Shiel, M(atthew) P(hipps)
1865-1947 ................................. TCLC 8
See also Holmes, Gordon
See also CA 106; 160; DLB 153

Shields, Carol 1935- ............... CLC 91; DAC
See also CA 81-84; CANR 51

Shields, David 1956- ........................ CLC 97
See also CA 124; CANR 48

Shiga, Naoya 1883-1971 ..... CLC 33; SSC 23
See also CA 101; 33-36R; DLB 180

Shilts, Randy 1951-1994 ................... CLC 85
See also AAYA 19; CA 115; 127; 144; CANR 45; INT 127

Shimazaki, Haruki 1872-1943
See Shimazaki Toson
See also CA 105; 134

**Shimazaki Toson** 1872-1943 ............ **TCLC 5**
See also Shimazaki, Haruki
See also DLB 180

**Sholokhov, Mikhail (Aleksandrovich)**
1905-1984 ............................... **CLC 7, 15**
See also CA 101; 112; MTCW; SATA-Obit 36

**Shone, Patric**
See Hanley, James

**Shreve, Susan Richards** 1939- .......... **CLC 23**
See also CA 49-52; CAAS 5; CANR 5, 38; MAICYA; SATA 46, 95; SATA-Brief 41

**Shue, Larry**
1946-1985 ........... **CLC 52; DAM DRAM**
See also CA 145; 117

**Shu-Jen, Chou** 1881-1936
See Lu Hsun
See also CA 104

**Shulman, Alix Kates** 1932- .......... **CLC 2, 10**
See also CA 29-32R; CANR 43; SATA 7

**Shuster, Joe** 1914- .............................. **CLC 21**

**Shute, Nevil** ........................................ **CLC 30**
See also Norway, Nevil Shute

**Shuttle, Penelope (Diane)** 1947- ......... **CLC 7**
See also CA 93-96; CANR 39; DLB 14, 40

**Sidney, Mary** 1561-1621 ................ **LC 19, 39**

**Sidney, Sir Philip**
1554-1586 ........ **LC 19, 39; DA; DAB; DAC; DAM MST, POET**
See also CDBLB Before 1660; DLB 167

**Siegel, Jerome** 1914-1996 ................ **CLC 21**
See also CA 116; 151

**Siegel, Jerry**
See Siegel, Jerome

**Sienkiewicz, Henryk (Adam Alexander Pius)**
1846-1916 ....................... **TCLC 3**
See also CA 104; 134

**Sierra, Gregorio Martinez**
See Martinez Sierra, Gregorio

**Sierra, Maria (de la O'LeJarraga) Martinez**
See Martinez Sierra, Maria (de la O'LeJarraga)

**Sigal, Clancy** 1926- .............................. **CLC 7**
See also CA 1-4R

**Sigourney, Lydia Howard (Huntley)**
1791-1865 ............................... **NCLC 21**
See also DLB 1, 42, 73

**Siguenza y Gongora, Carlos de**
1645-1700 ............................... **LC 8**

**Sigurjonsson, Johann**
1880-1919 ............................... **TCLC 27**

**Sikelianos, Angelos** 1884-1951 ...... **TCLC 39**

**Silkin, Jon** 1930- ......................... **CLC 2, 6, 43**
See also CA 5-8R; CAAS 5; DLB 27

**Silko, Leslie (Marmon)**
1948- ........ **CLC 23, 74; DA; DAC; DAM MST, MULT, POP; WLCS**
See also AAYA 14; CA 115; 122; CANR 45; DLB 143, 175; NNAL

**Sillanpaa, Frans Eemil**
1888-1964 ................................. **CLC 19**
See also CA 129; 93-96; MTCW

**Sillitoe, Alan**
1928- ..................... **CLC 1, 3, 6, 10, 19, 57**
See also AITN 1; CA 9-12R; CAAS 2; CANR 8, 26, 55; CDBLB 1960 to Present; DLB 14, 139; MTCW; SATA 61

**Silone, Ignazio** 1900-1978 .................. **CLC 4**
See also CA 25-28; 81-84; CANR 34; CAP 2; MTCW

**Silver, Joan Micklin** 1935- ................ **CLC 20**
See also CA 114; 121; INT 121

**Silver, Nicholas**
See Faust, Frederick (Schiller)

**Silverberg, Robert**
1935-.......................... **CLC 7; DAM POP**
See also CA 1-4R; CAAS 3; CANR 1, 20, 36; DLB 8; INT CANR-20; MAICYA; MTCW; SATA 13, 91

**Silverstein, Alvin** 1933- ..................... **CLC 17**
See also CA 49-52; CANR 2; CLR 25; JRDA; MAICYA; SATA 8, 69

**Silverstein, Virginia B(arbara Opshelor)**
1937-........................................... **CLC 17**
See also CA 49-52; CANR 2; CLR 25; JRDA; MAICYA; SATA 8, 69

**Sim, Georges**
See Simenon, Georges (Jacques Christian)

**Simak, Clifford D(onald)**
1904-1988 ............................... **CLC 1, 55**
See also CA 1-4R; 125; CANR 1, 35; DLB 8; MTCW; SATA-Obit 56

**Simenon, Georges (Jacques Christian)**
1903-1989 ........ **CLC 1, 2, 3, 8, 18, 47; DAM POP**
See also CA 85-88; 129; CANR 35; DLB 72; DLBY 89; MTCW

**Simic, Charles**
1938-........ **CLC 6, 9, 22, 49, 68; DAM POET**
See also CA 29-32R; CAAS 4; CANR 12, 33, 52, 61; DLB 105

**Simmel, Georg** 1858-1918 ............. **TCLC 64**
See also CA 157

**Simmons, Charles (Paul)** 1924- ........ **CLC 57**
See also CA 89-92; INT 89-92

**Simmons, Dan**
1948-....................... **CLC 44; DAM POP**
See also AAYA 16; CA 138; CANR 53

**Simmons, James (Stewart Alexander)**
1933-........................................... **CLC 43**
See also CA 105; CAAS 21; DLB 40

**Simms, William Gilmore**
1806-1870 ............................... **NCLC 3**
See also DLB 3, 30, 59, 73

**Simon, Carly** 1945- ........................... **CLC 26**
See also CA 105

**Simon, Claude**
1913- ........ **CLC 4, 9, 15, 39; DAM NOV**
See also CA 89-92; CANR 33; DLB 83; MTCW

**Simon, (Marvin) Neil**
1927-........... **CLC 6, 11, 31, 39, 70; DAM DRAM**
See also AITN 1; CA 21-24R; CANR 26, 54; DLB 7; MTCW

**Simon, Paul (Frederick)**
1941(?)- ................................. **CLC 17**
See also CA 116; 153

**Simonon, Paul** 1956(?)- .................... **CLC 30**

**Simpson, Harriette**
See Arnow, Harriette (Louisa) Simpson

**Simpson, Louis (Aston Marantz)**
1923- ............ **CLC 4, 7, 9, 32; DAM POET**
See also CA 1-4R; CAAS 4; CANR 1, 61; DLB 5; MTCW

**Simpson, Mona (Elizabeth)**
1957-........................................... **CLC 44**
See also CA 122; 135

**Simpson, N(orman) F(rederick)**
1919-........................................... **CLC 29**
See also CA 13-16R; DLB 13

**Sinclair, Andrew (Annandale)**
1935-........................................ **CLC 2, 14**
See also CA 9-12R; CAAS 5; CANR 14, 38; DLB 14; MTCW

**Sinclair, Emil**
See Hesse, Hermann

**Sinclair, Iain** 1943- ........................... **CLC 76**
See also CA 132

**Sinclair, Iain MacGregor**
See Sinclair, Iain

**Sinclair, Irene**
See Griffith, D(avid Lewelyn) W(ark)

**Sinclair, Mary Amelia St. Clair** 1865(?)-1946
See Sinclair, May
See also CA 104

**Sinclair, May** ................................. **TCLC 3, 11**
See also Sinclair, Mary Amelia St. Clair
See also DLB 36, 135

**Sinclair, Roy**
See Griffith, D(avid Lewelyn) W(ark)

**Snow, Frances Compton**
    See Adams, Henry (Brooks)

**Snyder, Gary (Sherman)**
    1930- ... **CLC 1, 2, 5, 9, 32; DAM POET**
    See also CA 17-20R; CANR 30, 60; DLB 5,
    16, 165

**Snyder, Zilpha Keatley** 1927- .......... **CLC 17**
    See also AAYA 15; CA 9-12R; CANR 38; CLR
    31; JRDA; MAICYA; SAAS 2; SATA 1, 28,
    75

**Soares, Bernardo**
    See Pessoa, Fernando (Antonio Nogueira)

**Sobh, A.**
    See Shamlu, Ahmad

**Sobol, Joshua** ...................................... **CLC 60**

**Soderberg, Hjalmar** 1869-1941 ..... **TCLC 39**

**Sodergran, Edith (Irene)**
    See Soedergran, Edith (Irene)

**Soedergran, Edith (Irene)**
    1892-1923 ................................ **TCLC 31**

**Softly, Edgar**
    See Lovecraft, H(oward) P(hillips)

**Softly, Edward**
    See Lovecraft, H(oward) P(hillips)

**Sokolov, Raymond** 1941- ..................... **CLC 7**
    See also CA 85-88

**Solo, Jay**
    See Ellison, Harlan (Jay)

**Sologub, Fyodor** ................................ **TCLC 9**
    See also Teternikov, Fyodor Kuzmich

**Solomons, Ikey Esquir**
    See Thackeray, William Makepeace

**Solomos, Dionysios** 1798-1857 ....... **NCLC 15**

**Solwoska, Mara**
    See French, Marilyn

**Solzhenitsyn, Aleksandr I(sayevich)**
    1918- ... **CLC 1, 2, 4, 7, 9, 10, 18, 26, 34,
    78; DA; DAB; DAC; DAM MST, NOV;
    WLC**
    See also AITN 1; CA 69-72; CANR 40; MTCW

**Somers, Jane**
    See Lessing, Doris (May)

**Somerville, Edith** 1858-1949 ......... **TCLC 51**
    See also DLB 135

**Somerville & Ross**
    See Martin, Violet Florence; Somerville, Edith

**Sommer, Scott** 1951- .......................... **CLC 25**
    See also CA 106

**Sondheim, Stephen (Joshua)**
    1930- ........... **CLC 30, 39; DAM DRAM**
    See also AAYA 11; CA 103; CANR 47

**Sontag, Susan**
    1933-.... **CLC 1, 2, 10, 13, 31, 105; DAM
    POP**
    See also CA 17-20R; CANR 25, 51; DLB 2,
    67; MTCW

**Sophocles**
    496(?)B.C.-406(?)B.C. ..... **CMLC 2; DA;
    DAB; DAC; DAM DRAM, MST; DC 1;
    WLCS**
    See also DLB 176

**Sordello** 1189-1269 ........................ **CMLC 15**

**Sorel, Julia**
    See Drexler, Rosalyn

**Sorrentino, Gilbert**
    1929-................... **CLC 3, 7, 14, 22, 40**
    See also CA 77-80; CANR 14, 33; DLB 5, 173;
    DLBY 80; INT CANR-14

**Soto, Gary**
    1952-.... **CLC 32, 80; DAM MULT; HLC**
    See also AAYA 10; CA 119; 125; CANR 50;
    CLR 38; DLB 82; HW; INT 125; JRDA;
    SATA 80

**Soupault, Philippe** 1897-1990 .......... **CLC 68**
    See also CA 116; 147; 131

**Souster, (Holmes) Raymond**
    1921-...... **CLC 5, 14; DAC; DAM POET**
    See also CA 13-16R; CAAS 14; CANR 13, 29,
    53; DLB 88; SATA 63

**Southern, Terry** 1924(?)-1995 ............. **CLC 7**
    See also CA 1-4R; 150; CANR 1, 55; DLB 2

**Southey, Robert** 1774-1843 ............. **NCLC 8**
    See also DLB 93, 107, 142; SATA 54

**Southworth, Emma Dorothy Eliza Nevitte**
    1819-1899 ................................ **NCLC 26**

**Souza, Ernest**
    See Scott, Evelyn

**Soyinka, Wole** 1934- .... **CLC 3, 5, 14, 36, 44;
    BLC; DA; DAB; DAC; DAM DRAM,
    MST, MULT; DC 2; WLC**
    See also BW 2; CA 13-16R; CANR 27, 39;
    DLB 125; MTCW

**Spackman, W(illiam) M(ode)**
    1905-1990 .................................. **CLC 46**
    See also CA 81-84; 132

**Spacks, Barry (Bernard)** 1931- ........ **CLC 14**
    See also CA 154; CANR 33; DLB 105

**Spanidou, Irini** 1946-........................ **CLC 44**

**Spark, Muriel (Sarah)**
    1918-.. **CLC 2, 3, 5, 8, 13, 18, 40, 94;
    DAB; DAC; DAM MST, NOV; SSC
    10**
    See also CA 5-8R; CANR 12, 36; CDBLB
    1945-1960; DLB 15, 139; INT CANR-12;
    MTCW

**Spaulding, Douglas**
    See Bradbury, Ray (Douglas)

**Spaulding, Leonard**
    See Bradbury, Ray (Douglas)

**Spence, J. A. D.**
    See Eliot, T(homas) S(tearns)

**Spencer, Elizabeth** 1921- ................... **CLC 22**
    See also CA 13-16R; CANR 32; DLB 6;
    MTCW; SATA 14

**Spencer, Leonard G.**
    See Silverberg, Robert

**Spencer, Scott** 1945-.......................... **CLC 30**
    See also CA 113; CANR 51; DLBY 86

**Spender, Stephen (Harold)**
    1909-1995 ....... **CLC 1, 2, 5, 10, 41, 91;
    DAM POET**
    See also CA 9-12R; 149; CANR 31, 54;
    CDBLB 1945-1960; DLB 20; MTCW

**Spengler, Oswald (Arnold Gottfried)**
    1880-1936 ................................ **TCLC 25**
    See also CA 118

**Spenser, Edmund**
    1552(?)-1599 ........ **LC 5, 39; DA; DAB;
    DAC; DAM MST, POET; PC 8; WLC**
    See also CDBLB Before 1660; DLB 167

**Spicer, Jack**
    1925-1965 .......... **CLC 8, 18, 72; DAM
    POET**
    See also CA 85-88; DLB 5, 16

**Spiegelman, Art** 1948- ...................... **CLC 76**
    See also AAYA 10; CA 125; CANR 41, 55

**Spielberg, Peter** 1929- ........................ **CLC 6**
    See also CA 5-8R; CANR 4, 48; DLBY 81

**Spielberg, Steven** 1947- ..................... **CLC 20**
    See also AAYA 8; CA 77-80; CANR 32; SATA
    32

**Spillane, Frank Morrison** 1918-
    See Spillane, Mickey
    See also CA 25-28R; CANR 28; MTCW; SATA
    66

**Spillane, Mickey** ............................ **CLC 3, 13**
    See also Spillane, Frank Morrison

**Spinoza, Benedictus de** 1632-1677 ........ **LC 9**

**Spinrad, Norman (Richard)** 1940-... **CLC 46**
    See also CA 37-40R; CAAS 19; CANR 20;
    DLB 8; INT CANR-20

**Spitteler, Carl (Friedrich Georg)**
    1845-1924 ................................ **TCLC 12**
    See also CA 109; DLB 129

**Spivack, Kathleen (Romola Drucker)**
    1938-................................................ **CLC 6**
    See also CA 49-52

**Spoto, Donald** 1941- .......................... **CLC 39**
    See also CA 65-68; CANR 11, 57

**Springsteen, Bruce (F.)** 1949- .......... **CLC 17**
    See also CA 111

**Summers, Hollis (Spurgeon, Jr.)**
1916-................................. CLC 10
See also CA 5-8R; CANR 3; DLB 6

**Summers, (Alphonsus Joseph-Mary Augustus)**
**Montague** 1880-1948 ............. TCLC 16
See also CA 118

**Sumner, Gordon Matthew** 1951-...... CLC 26

**Surtees, Robert Smith**
1803-1864 ................................. NCLC 14
See also DLB 21

**Susann, Jacqueline** 1921-1974............ CLC 3
See also AITN 1; CA 65-68; 53-56;
MTCW

**Su Shih** 1036-1101 .......................... CMLC 15

**Suskind, Patrick**
See Sueskind, Patrick
See also CA 145

**Sutcliff, Rosemary**
1920-1992 ........ CLC 26; DAB; DAC;
**DAM MST, POP**
See also AAYA 10; CA 5-8R; 139; CANR 37;
CLR 1, 37; JRDA; MAICYA; SATA 6, 44,
78; SATA-Obit 73

**Sutro, Alfred** 1863-1933 ................... TCLC 6
See also CA 105; DLB 10

**Sutton, Henry**
See Slavitt, David R(ytman)

**Svevo, Italo**
1861-1928 ............. TCLC 2, 35; SSC 25
See also Schmitz, Aron Hector

**Swados, Elizabeth (A.)**
1951-........................................ CLC 12
See also CA 97-100; CANR 49; INT 97-
100

**Swados, Harvey** 1920-1972 ................ CLC 5
See also CA 5-8R; 37-40R; CANR 6; DLB
2

**Swan, Gladys** 1934- ......................... CLC 69
See also CA 101; CANR 17, 39

**Swarthout, Glendon (Fred)**
1918-1992 ................................. CLC 35
See also CA 1-4R; 139; CANR 1, 47; SATA
26

**Sweet, Sarah C.**
See Jewett, (Theodora) Sarah Orne

**Swenson, May**
1919-1989 ..... CLC 4, 14, 61; DA; DAB;
**DAC; DAM MST, POET; PC 14**
See also CA 5-8R; 130; CANR 36, 61; DLB 5;
MTCW; SATA 15

**Swift, Augustus**
See Lovecraft, H(oward) P(hillips)

**Swift, Graham (Colin)**
1949-........................................ CLC 41, 88
See also CA 117; 122; CANR 46

**Swift, Jonathan**
1667-1745 . LC 1; DA; DAB; DAC;
**DAM MST, NOV, POET; PC 9;**
**WLC**
See also CDBLB 1660-1789; DLB 39, 95, 101;
SATA 19

**Swinburne, Algernon Charles**
1837-1909 ....... TCLC 8, 36; DA; DAB;
**DAC; DAM MST, POET; WLC**
See also CA 105; 140; CDBLB 1832-1890;
DLB 35, 57

**Swinfen, Ann** ...................................... CLC 34

**Swinnerton, Frank Arthur**
1884-1982 ................................. CLC 31
See also CA 108; DLB 34

**Swithen, John**
See King, Stephen (Edwin)

**Sylvia**
See Ashton-Warner, Sylvia (Constance)

**Symmes, Robert Edward**
See Duncan, Robert (Edward)

**Symonds, John Addington**
1840-1893 ................................. NCLC 34
See also DLB 57, 144

**Symons, Arthur** 1865-1945 ............. TCLC 11
See also CA 107; DLB 19, 57, 149

**Symons, Julian (Gustave)**
1912-1994 ..........................CLC 2, 14, 32
See also CA 49-52; 147; CAAS 3; CANR
3, 33, 59; DLB 87, 155; DLBY 92;
MTCW

**Synge, (Edmund) J(ohn) M(illington)**
1871-1909 .. TCLC 6, 37; DAM DRAM;
**DC 2**
See also CA 104; 141; CDBLB 1890-1914;
DLB 10, 19

**Syruc, J.**
See Milosz, Czeslaw

**Szirtes, George** 1948-........................ CLC 46
See also CA 109; CANR 27, 61

**Szymborska, Wislawa** 1923-............. CLC 99
See also CA 154; DLBY 96

**T. O., Nik**
See Annensky, Innokenty (Fyodorovich)

**Tabori, George** 1914-........................ CLC 19
See also CA 49-52; CANR 4

**Tagore, Rabindranath**
1861-1941 ... TCLC 3, 53; DAM DRAM,
**POET; PC 8**
See also CA 104; 120; MTCW

**Taine, Hippolyte Adolphe**
1828-1893 ................................. NCLC 15

**Talese, Gay** 1932- ............................. CLC 37
See also AITN 1; CA 1-4R; CANR 9, 58; INT
CANR-9; MTCW

**Tallent, Elizabeth (Ann)** 1954- ......... CLC 45
See also CA 117; DLB 130

**Tally, Ted** 1952- ................................. CLC 42
See also CA 120; 124; INT 124

**Tamayo y Baus, Manuel**
1829-1898 ................................. NCLC 1

**Tammsaare, A(nton) H(ansen)**
1878-1940 ................................. TCLC 27

**Tam'si, Tchicaya U**
See Tchicaya, Gerald Felix

**Tan, Amy (Ruth)**
1952-....... CLC 59; DAM MULT, NOV,
**POP**
See also AAYA 9; BEST 89:3; CA 136; CANR
54; DLB 173; SATA 75

**Tandem, Felix**
See Spitteler, Carl (Friedrich Georg)

**Tanizaki, Jun'ichiro**
1886-1965 ........... CLC 8, 14, 28; SSC 21
See also CA 93-96; 25-28R; DLB 180

**Tanner, William**
See Amis, Kingsley (William)

**Tao Lao**
See Storni, Alfonsina

**Tarassoff, Lev**
See Troyat, Henri

**Tarbell, Ida M(inerva)**
1857-1944 ................................. TCLC 40
See also CA 122; DLB 47

**Tarkington, (Newton) Booth**
1869-1946 ................................. TCLC 9
See also CA 110; 143; DLB 9, 102; SATA 17

**Tarkovsky, Andrei (Arsenyevich)**
1932-1986 ................................. CLC 75
See also CA 127

**Tartt, Donna** 1964(?)- ...................... CLC 76
See also CA 142

**Tasso, Torquato** 1544-1595 ................... LC 5

**Tate, (John Orley) Allen**
1899-1979 ....... CLC 2, 4, 6, 9, 11, 14, 24
See also CA 5-8R; 85-88; CANR 32; DLB 4,
45, 63; MTCW

**Tate, Ellalice**
See Hibbert, Eleanor Alice Burford

**Tate, James (Vincent)**
1943-..................................CLC 2, 6, 25
See also CA 21-24R; CANR 29, 57; DLB 5,
169

**Tavel, Ronald** 1940- ........................... CLC 6
See also CA 21-24R; CANR 33

**Taylor, C(ecil) P(hilip)**
1929-1981 ................................. CLC 27
See also CA 25-28R; 105; CANR 47

Taylor, Edward
1642(?)-1729 .... **LC 11; DA; DAB; DAC; DAM MST, POET**
See also DLB 24

Taylor, Eleanor Ross 1920- ................ **CLC 5**
See also CA 81-84

Taylor, Elizabeth
1912-1975 ........................... **CLC 2, 4, 29**
See also CA 13-16R; CANR 9; DLB 139;
MTCW; SATA 13

Taylor, Frederick Winslow
1856-1915 ............................... **TCLC 76**

Taylor, Henry (Splawn) 1942- ......... **CLC 44**
See also CA 33-36R; CAAS 7; CANR 31; DLB
5

Taylor, Kamala (Purnaiya) 1924-
See Markandaya, Kamala
See also CA 77-80

Taylor, Mildred D. ............................. **CLC 21**
See also AAYA 10; BW 1; CA 85-88; CANR
25; CLR 9; DLB 52; JRDA; MAICYA;
SAAS 5; SATA 15, 70

Taylor, Peter (Hillsman)
1917-1994 ....    **CLC 1, 4, 18, 37, 44, 50,
71; SSC 10**
See also CA 13-16R; 147; CANR 9, 50; DLBY
81, 94; INT CANR-9; MTCW

Taylor, Robert Lewis 1912- ............. **CLC 14**
See also CA 1-4R; CANR 3; SATA 10

Tchekhov, Anton
See Chekhov, Anton (Pavlovich)

Tchicaya, Gerald Felix
1931-1988 ................................ **CLC 101**
See also CA 129; 125

Tchicaya U Tam'si
See Tchicaya, Gerald Felix

Teasdale, Sara 1884-1933 ................. **TCLC 4**
See also CA 104; DLB 45; SATA 32

Tegner, Esaias 1782-1846 ................ **NCLC 2**

Teilhard de Chardin, (Marie Joseph) Pierre
1881-1955 ................................... **TCLC 9**
See also CA 105

Temple, Ann
See Mortimer, Penelope (Ruth)

Tennant, Emma (Christina)
1937- ................................... **CLC 13, 52**
See also CA 65-68; CAAS 9; CANR 10, 38,
59; DLB 14

Tenneshaw, S. M.
See Silverberg, Robert

Tennyson, Alfred
1809-1892 .. **NCLC 30, 65; DA; DAB;
DAC; DAM MST, POET; PC 6;
WLC**
See also CDBLB 1832-1890; DLB 32

Teran, Lisa St. Aubin de .................... **CLC 36**
See also St. Aubin de Teran, Lisa

Terence
195(?)B.C.-159B.C. ...... **CMLC 14; DC 7**

Teresa de Jesus, St. 1515-1582 ........... **LC 18**

Terkel, Louis 1912-
See Terkel, Studs
See also CA 57-60; CANR 18, 45;
MTCW

Terkel, Studs ..................................... **CLC 38**
See also Terkel, Louis
See also AITN 1

Terry, C. V.
See Slaughter, Frank G(ill)

Terry, Megan 1932- ........................... **CLC 19**
See also CA 77-80; CABS 3; CANR 43; DLB
7

Tertz, Abram
See Sinyavsky, Andrei (Donatevich)

Tesich, Steve
1943(?)-1996 ......................... **CLC 40, 69**
See also CA 105; 152; DLBY 83

Teternikov, Fyodor Kuzmich 1863-1927
See Sologub, Fyodor
See also CA 104

Tevis, Walter 1928-1984 ................... **CLC 42**
See also CA 113

Tey, Josephine ................................. **TCLC 14**
See also Mackintosh, Elizabeth
See also DLB 77

Thackeray, William Makepeace
1811-1863 **NCLC 5, 14, 22, 43; DA;
DAB; DAC; DAM MST, NOV;
WLC**
See also CDBLB 1832-1890; DLB 21, 55, 159,
163; SATA 23

Thakura, Ravindranatha
See Tagore, Rabindranath

Tharoor, Shashi 1956- ...................... **CLC 70**
See also CA 141

Thelwell, Michael Miles
1939- ..................................... **CLC 22**
See also BW 2; CA 101

Theobald, Lewis, Jr.
See Lovecraft, H(oward) P(hillips)

Theodorescu, Ion N. 1880-1967
See Arghezi, Tudor
See also CA 116

Theriault, Yves
1915-1983 ... **CLC 79; DAC; DAM MST**
See also CA 102; DLB 88

Theroux, Alexander (Louis)
1939- ..................................... **CLC 2, 25**
See also CA 85-88; CANR 20

Theroux, Paul (Edward)
1941- ...... **CLC 5, 8, 11, 15, 28, 46; DAM
POP**
See also BEST 89:4; CA 33-36R; CANR 20,
45; DLB 2; MTCW; SATA 44

Thesen, Sharon 1946- ....................... **CLC 56**

Thevenin, Denis
See Duhamel, Georges

Thibault, Jacques Anatole Francois 1844-1924
See France, Anatole
See also CA 106; 127; DAM NOV; MTCW

Thiele, Colin (Milton) 1920- ............. **CLC 17**
See also CA 29-32R; CANR 12, 28, 53; CLR
27; MAICYA; SAAS 2; SATA 14, 72

Thomas, Audrey (Callahan)
1935- ................... **CLC 7, 13, 37; SSC 20**
See also AITN 2; CA 21-24R; CAAS 19;
CANR 36, 58; DLB 60; MTCW

Thomas, D(onald) M(ichael)
1935- .......................... **CLC 13, 22, 31**
See also CA 61-64; CAAS 11; CANR 17, 45;
CDBLB 1960 to Present; DLB 40; INT
CANR-17; MTCW

Thomas, Dylan (Marlais)
1914-1953 ..... **TCLC 1, 8, 45; DA; DAB;
DAC; DAM DRAM, MST, POET; PC 2;
SSC 3; WLC**
See also CA 104; 120; CDBLB 1945-1960;
DLB 13, 20, 139; MTCW; SATA 60

Thomas, (Philip) Edward
1878-1917 ........ **TCLC 10; DAM POET**
See also CA 106; 153; DLB 19

Thomas, Joyce Carol 1938- ............. **CLC 35**
See also AAYA 12; BW 2; CA 113; 116;
CANR 48; CLR 19; DLB 33; INT 116;
JRDA; MAICYA; MTCW; SAAS 7; SATA
40, 78

Thomas, Lewis 1913-1993 ................ **CLC 35**
See also CA 85-88; 143; CANR 38, 60; MTCW

Thomas, Paul
See Mann, (Paul) Thomas

Thomas, Piri 1928- ........................... **CLC 17**
See also CA 73-76; HW

Thomas, R(onald) S(tuart)
1913- .......... **CLC 6, 13, 48; DAB; DAM
POET**
See also CA 89-92; CAAS 4; CANR 30;
CDBLB 1960 to Present; DLB 27;
MTCW

Thomas, Ross (Elmore) 1926-1995 .. **CLC 39**
See also CA 33-36R; 150; CANR 22

Thompson, Francis Clegg
See Mencken, H(enry) L(ouis)

Thompson, Francis Joseph
1859-1907 ................................. **TCLC 4**
See also CA 104; CDBLB 1890-1914; DLB
19

Treitel, Jonathan 1959- .................... CLC 70

Tremain, Rose 1943- .......................... CLC 42
See also CA 97-100; CANR 44; DLB 14

Tremblay, Michel
1942- ... CLC 29, 102; DAC; DAM MST
See also CA 116; 128; DLB 60; MTCW

Trevanian ............................................ CLC 29
See also Whitaker, Rod(ney)

Trevor, Glen
See Hilton, James

Trevor, William
1928- ........ CLC 7, 9, 14, 25, 71; SSC 21
See also Cox, William Trevor
See also DLB 14, 139

Trifonov, Yuri (Valentinovich)
1925-1981 .................................. CLC 45
See also CA 126; 103; MTCW

Trilling, Lionel 1905-1975 ...... CLC 9, 11, 24
See also CA 9-12R; 61-64; CANR 10; DLB
28, 63; INT CANR-10; MTCW

Trimball, W. H.
See Mencken, H(enry) L(ouis)

Tristan
See Gomez de la Serna, Ramon

Tristram
See Housman, A(lfred) E(dward)

Trogdon, William (Lewis) 1939-
See Heat-Moon, William Least
See also CA 115; 119; CANR 47; INT 119

Trollope, Anthony
1815-1882 ........ NCLC 6, 33; DA; DAB;
DAC; DAM MST, NOV; SSC 28; WLC
See also CDBLB 1832-1890; DLB 21, 57, 159;
SATA 22

Trollope, Frances 1779-1863 ......... NCLC 30
See also DLB 21, 166

Trotsky, Leon 1879-1940 ................ TCLC 22
See also CA 118

Trotter (Cockburn), Catharine
1679-1749 ........................................ LC 8
See also DLB 84

Trout, Kilgore
See Farmer, Philip Jose

Trow, George W. S. 1943- ................ CLC 52
See also CA 126

Troyat, Henri 1911- .......................... CLC 23
See also CA 45-48; CANR 2, 33; MTCW

Trudeau, G(arretson) B(eekman) 1948-
See Trudeau, Garry B.
See also CA 81-84; CANR 31; SATA 35

Trudeau, Garry B. ............................ CLC 12
See also Trudeau, G(arretson) B(eekman)
See also AAYA 10; AITN 2

Truffaut, Francois
1932-1984 .......................... CLC 20, 101
See also CA 81-84; 113; CANR 34

Trumbo, Dalton 1905-1976 .............. CLC 19
See also CA 21-24R; 69-72; CANR 10; DLB
26

Trumbull, John 1750-1831 ............. NCLC 30
See also DLB 31

Trundlett, Helen B.
See Eliot, T(homas) S(tearns)

Tryon, Thomas
1926-1991 .......... CLC 3, 11; DAM POP
See also AITN 1; CA 29-32R; 135; CANR 32;
MTCW

Tryon, Tom
See Tryon, Thomas

Ts'ao Hsueh-ch'in 1715(?)-1763 ............ LC 1

Tsushima, Shuji 1909-1948
See Dazai, Osamu
See also CA 107

Tsvetaeva (Efron), Marina (Ivanovna)
1892-1941 ................ TCLC 7, 35; PC 14
See also CA 104; 128; MTCW

Tuck, Lily 1938- ................................ CLC 70
See also CA 139

Tu Fu 712-770 ...................................... PC 9
See also DAM MULT

Tunis, John R(oberts) 1889-1975 ..... CLC 12
See also CA 61-64; CANR 62; DLB 22, 171;
JRDA; MAICYA; SATA 37; SATA-Brief 30

Tuohy, Frank ...................................... CLC 37
See also Tuohy, John Francis
See also DLB 14, 139

Tuohy, John Francis 1925-
See Tuohy, Frank
See also CA 5-8R; CANR 3, 47

Turco, Lewis (Putnam) 1934- ..... CLC 11, 63
See also CA 13-16R; CAAS 22; CANR 24, 51;
DLBY 84

Turgenev, Ivan 1818-1883 ..... NCLC 21; DA;
DAB; DAC; DAM MST, NOV; DC 7; SSC
7; WLC

Turgot, Anne-Robert-Jacques
1727-1781 ...................................... LC 26

Turner, Frederick 1943- .................... CLC 48
See also CA 73-76; CAAS 10; CANR 12, 30,
56; DLB 40

Tutu, Desmond M(pilo)
1931- .......... CLC 80; BLC; DAM MULT
See also BW 1; CA 125

Tutuola, Amos 1920-1997 ...... CLC 5, 14, 29;
BLC; DAM MULT
See also BW 2; CA 9-12R; 159; CANR 27;
DLB 125; MTCW

Twain, Mark ..... TCLC 6, 12, 19, 36, 48, 59;
SSC 6, 26; WLC
See also Clemens, Samuel Langhorne
See also AAYA 20; DLB 11, 12, 23, 64, 74

Tyler, Anne
1941- .......CLC 7, 11, 18, 28, 44, 59, 103;
DAM NOV, POP
See also AAYA 18; BEST 89:1; CA 9-12R;
CANR 11, 33, 53; DLB 6, 143; DLBY 82;
MTCW; SATA 7, 90

Tyler, Royall 1757-1826 .................. NCLC 3
See also DLB 37

Tynan, Katharine 1861-1931 ............ TCLC 3
See also CA 104; DLB 153

Tyutchev, Fyodor 1803-1873 ......... NCLC 34

Tzara, Tristan 1896-1963 ...... CLC 47; DAM
POET
See also Rosenfeld, Samuel; Rosenstock, Sami;
Rosenstock, Samuel
See also CA 153

Uhry, Alfred 1936- ... CLC 55; DAM DRAM,
POP
See also CA 127; 133; INT 133

Ulf, Haerved
See Strindberg, (Johan) August

Ulf, Harved
See Strindberg, (Johan) August

Ulibarri, Sabine R(eyes)
1919- .................... CLC 83; DAM MULT
See also CA 131; DLB 82; HW

Unamuno (y Jugo), Miguel de
1864-1936 ...... TCLC 2, 9; DAM MULT,
NOV; HLC; SSC 11
See also CA 104; 131; DLB 108; HW; MTCW

Undercliffe, Errol
See Campbell, (John) Ramsey

Underwood, Miles
See Glassco, John

Undset, Sigrid
1882-1949 .... TCLC 3; DA; DAB; DAC;
DAM MST, NOV; WLC
See also CA 104; 129; MTCW

Ungaretti, Giuseppe
1888-1970 ........................ CLC 7, 11, 15
See also CA 19-20; 25-28R; CAP 2; DLB 114

Unger, Douglas 1952- ........................ CLC 34
See also CA 130

Unsworth, Barry (Forster) 1930- ..... CLC 76
See also CA 25-28R; CANR 30, 54

Updike, John (Hoyer)
1932-... CLC 1, 2, 3, 5, 7, 9, 13, 15, 23,
34, 43, 70; DA; DAB; DAC; DAM MST,
NOV, POET, POP; SSC 13, 27; WLC
See also CA 1-4R; CABS 1; CANR 4, 33, 51;
CDALB 1968-1988; DLB 2, 5, 143; DLBD
3; DLBY 80, 82; MTCW

**Very, Jones** 1813-1880 .................... **NCLC 9**
See also DLB 1

**Vesaas, Tarjei** 1897-1970 ................. **CLC 48**
See also CA 29-32R

**Vialis, Gaston**
See Simenon, Georges (Jacques Christian)

**Vian, Boris** 1920-1959 ...................... **TCLC 9**
See also CA 106; DLB 72

**Viaud, (Louis Marie) Julien** 1850-1923
See Loti, Pierre
See also CA 107

**Vicar, Henry**
See Felsen, Henry Gregor

**Vicker, Angus**
See Felsen, Henry Gregor

**Vidal, Gore**
1925- ....... **CLC 2, 4, 6, 8, 10, 22, 33, 72;**
**DAM NOV, POP**
See also AITN 1; BEST 90:2; CA 5-8R;
CANR 13, 45; DLB 6, 152; INT CANR-
13; MTCW

**Viereck, Peter (Robert Edwin)**
1916- ........................................ **CLC 4**
See also CA 1-4R; CANR 1, 47; DLB 5

**Vigny, Alfred (Victor) de**
1797-1863 ........... **NCLC 7; DAM POET**
See also DLB 119

**Vilakazi, Benedict Wallet**
1906-1947 ............................... **TCLC 37**

**Villiers de l'Isle Adam, Jean Marie Mathias**
**Philippe Auguste Comte**
1838-1889 .................... **NCLC 3; SSC 14**
See also DLB 123

**Villon, Francois** 1431-1463(?) .............. **PC 13**

**Vinci, Leonardo da** 1452-1519 ........... **LC 12**

**Vine, Barbara** ..................................... **CLC 50**
See also Rendell, Ruth (Barbara)
See also BEST 90:4

**Vinge, Joan D(ennison)**
1948- ............................ **CLC 30; SSC 24**
See also CA 93-96; SATA 36

**Violis, G.**
See Simenon, Georges (Jacques Christian)

**Visconti, Luchino** 1906-1976 ........... **CLC 16**
See also CA 81-84; 65-68; CANR 39

**Vittorini, Elio** 1908-1966 .......... **CLC 6, 9, 14**
See also CA 133; 25-28R

**Vizenor, Gerald Robert** 1934- ....... **CLC 103;**
**DAM MULT**
See also CA 13-16R; CAAS 22; CANR 5, 21,
44; DLB 175; NNAL

**Vizinczey, Stephen** 1933- .................. **CLC 40**
See also CA 128; INT 128

**Vliet, R(ussell) G(ordon)**
1929-1984 ................................... **CLC 22**
See also CA 37-40R; 112; CANR 18

**Vogau, Boris Andreyevich** 1894-1937(?)
See Pilnyak, Boris
See also CA 123

**Vogel, Paula A(nne)** 1951- ................ **CLC 76**
See also CA 108

**Voight, Ellen Bryant** 1943- .............. **CLC 54**
See also CA 69-72; CANR 11, 29, 55; DLB
120

**Voigt, Cynthia** 1942- ......................... **CLC 30**
See also AAYA 3; CA 106; CANR 18, 37, 40;
CLR 13; INT CANR-18; JRDA; MAICYA;
SATA 48, 79; SATA-Brief 33

**Voinovich, Vladimir (Nikolaevich)**
1932- ..................................... **CLC 10, 49**
See also CA 81-84; CAAS 12; CANR 33;
MTCW

**Vollmann, William T.**
1959- .............. **CLC 89; DAM NOV, POP**
See also CA 134

**Voloshinov, V. N.**
See Bakhtin, Mikhail Mikhailovich

**Voltaire**
1694-1778 ........ **LC 14; DA; DAB; DAC;**
**DAM DRAM, MST; SSC 12; WLC**

**von Daeniken, Erich** 1935- ................ **CLC 30**
See also AITN 1; CA 37-40R; CANR 17,
44

**von Daniken, Erich**
See von Daeniken, Erich

**von Heidenstam, (Carl Gustaf) Verner**
See Heidenstam, (Carl Gustaf) Verner von

**von Heyse, Paul (Johann Ludwig)**
See Heyse, Paul (Johann Ludwig von)

**von Hofmannsthal, Hugo**
See Hofmannsthal, Hugo von

**von Horvath, Odon**
See Horvath, Oedoen von

**von Horvath, Oedoen**
See Horvath, Oedoen von

**von Liliencron, (Friedrich Adolf Axel) Detlev**
See Liliencron, (Friedrich Adolf Axel) Detlev
von

**Vonnegut, Kurt, Jr.**
1922-.... **CLC 1, 2, 3, 4, 5, 8, 12, 22, 40,**
**60; DA; DAB; DAC; DAM MST, NOV,**
**POP; SSC 8; WLC**
See also AAYA 6; AITN 1; BEST 90:4; CA
1-4R; CANR 1, 25, 49; CDALB 1968-
1988; DLB 2, 8, 152; DLBD 3; DLBY 80;
MTCW

**Von Rachen, Kurt**
See Hubbard, L(afayette) Ron(ald)

**von Rezzori (d'Arezzo), Gregor**
See Rezzori (d'Arezzo), Gregor von

**von Sternberg, Josef**
See Sternberg, Josef von

**Vorster, Gordon** 1924- ...................... **CLC 34**
See also CA 133

**Vosce, Trudie**
See Ozick, Cynthia

**Voznesensky, Andrei (Andreievich)**
1933- .......... **CLC 1, 15, 57; DAM POET**
See also CA 89-92; CANR 37; MTCW

**Waddington, Miriam** 1917- ............. **CLC 28**
See also CA 21-24R; CANR 12, 30; DLB
68

**Wagman, Fredrica** 1937- .................... **CLC 7**
See also CA 97-100; INT 97-100

**Wagner, Linda W.**
See Wagner-Martin, Linda (C.)

**Wagner, Linda Welshimer**
See Wagner-Martin, Linda (C.)

**Wagner, Richard**
1813-1883 ................................... **NCLC 9**
See also DLB 129

**Wagner-Martin, Linda (C.)**
1936- ........................................ **CLC 50**
See also CA 159

**Wagoner, David (Russell)**
1926- ................................. **CLC 3, 5, 15**
See also CA 1-4R; CAAS 3; CANR 2; DLB 5;
SATA 14

**Wah, Fred(erick James)**
1939- ........................................ **CLC 44**
See also CA 107; 141; DLB 60

**Wahloo, Per**
1926-1975 ................................... **CLC 7**
See also CA 61-64

**Wahloo, Peter**
See Wahloo, Per

**Wain, John (Barrington)**
1925-1994 ................... **CLC 2, 11, 15, 46**
See also CA 5-8R; 145; CAAS 4; CANR 23,
54; CDBLB 1960 to Present; DLB 15, 27,
139, 155; MTCW

**Wajda, Andrzej** 1926- ...................... **CLC 16**
See also CA 102

**Wakefield, Dan** 1932- ......................... **CLC 7**
See also CA 21-24R; CAAS 7

**Wakoski, Diane**
1937- .......... **CLC 2, 4, 7, 9, 11, 40; DAM**
**POET; PC 15**
See also CA 13-16R; CAAS 1; CANR 9, 60;
DLB 5; INT CANR-9

**Wakoski-Sherbell, Diane**
See Wakoski, Diane

**Walcott, Derek (Alton)**
1930- ..... CLC 2, 4, 9, 14, 25, 42, 67, 76;
BLC; DAB; DAC; DAM MST, MULT,
POET; DC 7
See also BW 2; CA 89-92; CANR 26, 47; DLB
117; DLBY 81; MTCW

**Waldman, Anne** 1945- ......................... CLC 7
See also CA 37-40R; CAAS 17; CANR 34;
DLB 16

**Waldo, E. Hunter**
See Sturgeon, Theodore (Hamilton)

**Waldo, Edward Hamilton**
See Sturgeon, Theodore (Hamilton)

**Walker, Alice (Malsenior)**
1944-.... CLC 5, 6, 9, 19, 27, 46, 58, 103;
BLC; DA; DAB; DAC; DAM MST,
MULT, NOV, POET, POP; SSC 5;
WLCS
See also AAYA 3; BEST 89:4; BW 2; CA 37-
40R; CANR 9, 27, 49; CDALB 1968-1988;
DLB 6, 33, 143; INT CANR-27; MTCW;
SATA 31

**Walker, David Harry**
1911-1992 .................................. CLC 14
See also CA 1-4R; 137; CANR 1; SATA 8;
SATA-Obit 71

**Walker, Edward Joseph** 1934-
See Walker, Ted
See also CA 21-24R; CANR 12, 28, 53

**Walker, George F.**
1947-..... CLC 44, 61; DAB; DAC; DAM
MST
See also CA 103; CANR 21, 43, 59; DLB
60

**Walker, Joseph A.** 1935-........ CLC 19; DAM
DRAM, MST
See also BW 1; CA 89-92; CANR 26; DLB
38

**Walker, Margaret (Abigail)**
1915-.... CLC 1, 6; BLC; DAM MULT;
PC 20
See also BW 2; CA 73-76; CANR 26, 54; DLB
76, 152; MTCW

**Walker, Ted** ......................................... CLC 13
See also Walker, Edward Joseph
See also DLB 40

**Wallace, David Foster** 1962-............. CLC 50
See also CA 132; CANR 59

**Wallace, Dexter**
See Masters, Edgar Lee

**Wallace, (Richard Horatio) Edgar**
1875-1932 .................................. TCLC 57
See also CA 115; DLB 70

**Wallace, Irving**
1916-1990 ...... CLC 7, 13; DAM NOV,
POP
See also AITN 1; CA 1-4R; 132; CAAS
1; CANR 1, 27; INT CANR-27;
MTCW

**Wallant, Edward Lewis**
1926-1962 .............................. CLC 5, 10
See also CA 1-4R; CANR 22; DLB 2, 28, 143;
MTCW

**Walley, Byron**
See Card, Orson Scott

**Walpole, Horace** 1717-1797 .................. LC 2
See also DLB 39, 104

**Walpole, Hugh (Seymour)**
1884-1941 .................................. TCLC 5
See also CA 104; DLB 34

**Walser, Martin** 1927- ......................... CLC 27
See also CA 57-60; CANR 8, 46; DLB 75, 124

**Walser, Robert**
1878-1956 ................... TCLC 18; SSC 20
See also CA 118; DLB 66

**Walsh, Jill Paton** ............................... CLC 35
See also Paton Walsh, Gillian
See also AAYA 11; CLR 2; DLB 161; SAAS 3

**Walter, Villiam Christian**
See Andersen, Hans Christian

**Wambaugh, Joseph (Aloysius, Jr.)**
1937- ........ CLC 3, 18; DAM NOV, POP
See also AITN 1; BEST 89:3; CA 33-36R;
CANR 42; DLB 6; DLBY 83; MTCW

**Wang Wei** 699(?)-761(?) ...................... PC 18

**Ward, Arthur Henry Sarsfield** 1883-1959
See Rohmer, Sax
See also CA 108

**Ward, Douglas Turner** 1930-............ CLC 19
See also BW 1; CA 81-84; CANR 27; DLB 7,
38

**Ward, Mary Augusta**
See Ward, Mrs. Humphry

**Ward, Mrs. Humphry** 1851-1920 .. TCLC 55
See also DLB 18

**Ward, Peter**
See Faust, Frederick (Schiller)

**Warhol, Andy** 1928(?)-1987 .............. CLC 20
See also AAYA 12; BEST 89:4; CA 89-92; 121;
CANR 34

**Warner, Francis (Robert le Plastrier)**
1937- ............................................... CLC 14
See also CA 53-56; CANR 11

**Warner, Marina** 1946- ....................... CLC 59
See also CA 65-68; CANR 21, 55

**Warner, Rex (Ernest)** 1905-1986 ...... CLC 45
See also CA 89-92; 119; DLB 15

**Warner, Susan (Bogert)**
1819-1885 ................................ NCLC 31
See also DLB 3, 42

**Warner, Sylvia (Constance) Ashton**
See Ashton-Warner, Sylvia (Constance)

**Warner, Sylvia Townsend**
1893-1978 ................ CLC 7, 19; SSC 23
See also CA 61-64; 77-80; CANR 16, 60; DLB
34, 139; MTCW

**Warren, Mercy Otis** 1728-1814 ..... NCLC 13
See also DLB 31

**Warren, Robert Penn**
1905-1989 ... CLC 1, 4, 6, 8, 10, 13, 18,
39, 53, 59; DA; DAB; DAC; DAM MST,
NOV, POET; SSC 4; WLC
See also AITN 1; CA 13-16R; 129; CANR 10,
47; CDALB 1968-1988; DLB 2, 48, 152;
DLBY 80, 89; INT CANR-10; MTCW;
SATA 46; SATA-Obit 63

**Warshofsky, Isaac**
See Singer, Isaac Bashevis

**Warton, Thomas**
1728-1790 ............... LC 15; DAM POET
See also DLB 104, 109

**Waruk, Kona**
See Harris, (Theodore) Wilson

**Warung, Price** 1855-1911 ............... TCLC 45

**Warwick, Jarvis**
See Garner, Hugh

**Washington, Alex**
See Harris, Mark

**Washington, Booker T(aliaferro)**
1856-1915 ......... TCLC 10; BLC; DAM
MULT
See also BW 1; CA 114; 125; SATA 28

**Washington, George** 1732-1799 ......... LC 25
See also DLB 31

**Wassermann, (Karl) Jakob**
1873-1934 .................................. TCLC 6
See also CA 104; DLB 66

**Wasserstein, Wendy**
1950-..... CLC 32, 59, 90; DAM DRAM;
DC 4
See also CA 121; 129; CABS 3; CANR 53;
INT 129; SATA 94

**Waterhouse, Keith (Spencer)**
1929-............................................... CLC 47
See also CA 5-8R; CANR 38; DLB 13, 15;
MTCW

**Waters, Frank (Joseph)** 1902-1995 .. CLC 88
See also CA 5-8R; 149; CAAS 13; CANR 3,
18; DLBY 86

**Waters, Roger** 1944- ......................... CLC 35

**Watkins, Frances Ellen**
See Harper, Frances Ellen Watkins

**Watkins, Gerrold**
See Malzberg, Barry N(athaniel)

**Watkins, Gloria** 1955(?)-
See hooks, bell
See also BW 2; CA 143

Watkins, Paul 1964- .......................... CLC 55
See also CA 132; CANR 62

Watkins, Vernon Phillips
1906-1967 ...................................... CLC 43
See also CA 9-10; 25-28R; CAP 1; DLB
20

Watson, Irving S.
See Mencken, H(enry) L(ouis)

Watson, John H.
See Farmer, Philip Jose

Watson, Richard F.
See Silverberg, Robert

Waugh, Auberon (Alexander)
1939- .............................................. CLC 7
See also CA 45-48; CANR 6, 22; DLB 14

Waugh, Evelyn (Arthur St. John)
1903-1966 .... CLC 1, 3, 8, 13, 19, 27, 44;
**DA; DAB; DAC; DAM MST, NOV,
POP; WLC**
See also CA 85-88; 25-28R; CANR 22;
CDBLB 1914-1945; DLB 15, 162;
MTCW

Waugh, Harriet 1944- ......................... CLC 6
See also CA 85-88; CANR 22

Ways, C. R.
See Blount, Roy (Alton), Jr.

Waystaff, Simon
See Swift, Jonathan

Webb, (Martha) Beatrice (Potter)
1858-1943 ................................. TCLC 22
See also Potter, (Helen) Beatrix
See also CA 117

Webb, Charles (Richard) 1939- ......... CLC 7
See also CA 25-28R

Webb, James H(enry), Jr. 1946- ....... CLC 22
See also CA 81-84

Webb, Mary (Gladys Meredith)
1881-1927 ................................. TCLC 24
See also CA 123; DLB 34

Webb, Mrs. Sidney
See Webb, (Martha) Beatrice (Potter)

Webb, Phyllis 1927- .......................... CLC 18
See also CA 104; CANR 23; DLB 53

Webb, Sidney (James)
1859-1947 ................................. TCLC 22
See also CA 117

Webber, Andrew Lloyd ...................... CLC 21
See also Lloyd Webber, Andrew

Weber, Lenora Mattingly
1895-1971 ................................... CLC 12
See also CA 19-20; 29-32R; CAP 1; SATA 2;
SATA-Obit 26

Weber, Max 1864-1920 .................. TCLC 69
See also CA 109

Webster, John
1579(?)-1634(?) ....... LC 33; DA; DAB;
**DAC; DAM DRAM, MST; DC 2; WLC**
See also CDBLB Before 1660; DLB 58

Webster, Noah 1758-1843 .............. NCLC 30

Wedekind, (Benjamin) Frank(lin)
1864-1918 ......... TCLC 7; **DAM DRAM**
See also CA 104; 153; DLB 118

Weidman, Jerome 1913- ...................... CLC 7
See also AITN 2; CA 1-4R; CANR 1; DLB 28

Weil, Simone (Adolphine)
1909-1943 ................................. TCLC 23
See also CA 117; 159

Weinstein, Nathan
See West, Nathanael

Weinstein, Nathan von Wallenstein
See West, Nathanael

Weir, Peter (Lindsay) 1944- .............. CLC 20
See also CA 113; 123

Weiss, Peter (Ulrich)
1916-1982 .......... CLC 3, 15, 51; **DAM
DRAM**
See also CA 45-48; 106; CANR 3; DLB 69,
124

Weiss, Theodore (Russell)
1916- ................................... CLC 3, 8, 14
See also CA 9-12R; CAAS 2; CANR 46; DLB
5

Welch, (Maurice) Denton
1915-1948 ................................. TCLC 22
See also CA 121; 148

Welch, James
1940- ....... CLC 6, 14, 52; **DAM MULT,
POP**
See also CA 85-88; CANR 42; DLB 175;
NNAL

Weldon, Fay
1933- ...... CLC 6, 9, 11, 19, 36, 59; **DAM
POP**
See also CA 21-24R; CANR 16, 46; CDBLB
1960 to Present; DLB 14; INT CANR-16;
MTCW

Wellek, Rene
1903-1995 ................................. CLC 28
See also CA 5-8R; 150; CAAS 7; CANR 8;
DLB 63; INT CANR-8

Weller, Michael 1942- .................. CLC 10, 53
See also CA 85-88

Weller, Paul 1958- ........................... CLC 26

Wellershoff, Dieter 1925- ................. CLC 46
See also CA 89-92; CANR 16, 37

Welles, (George) Orson
1915-1985 .......................... CLC 20, 80
See also CA 93-96; 117

Wellman, Mac 1945- ......................... CLC 65

Wellman, Manly Wade 1903-1986 ... CLC 49
See also CA 1-4R; 118; CANR 6, 16, 44; SATA
6; SATA-Obit 47

Wells, Carolyn 1869(?)-1942 ......... TCLC 35
See also CA 113; DLB 11

Wells, H(erbert) G(eorge)
1866-1946 ... TCLC 6, 12, 19; DA; DAB;
**DAC; DAM MST, NOV; SSC 6; WLC**
See also AAYA 18; CA 110; 121; CDBLB
1914-1945; DLB 34, 70, 156, 178; MTCW;
SATA 20

Wells, Rosemary 1943- ...................... CLC 12
See also AAYA 13; CA 85-88; CANR 48; CLR
16; MAICYA; SAAS 1; SATA 18, 69

Welty, Eudora
1909-...... CLC 1, 2, 5, 14, 22, 33, 105;
**DA; DAB; DAC; DAM MST, NOV; SSC
1, 27; WLC**
See also CA 9-12R; CABS 1; CANR 32;
CDALB 1941-1968; DLB 2, 102, 143;
DLBD 12; DLBY 87; MTCW

Wen I-to 1899-1946 ........................ TCLC 28

Wentworth, Robert
See Hamilton, Edmond

Werfel, Franz (V.) 1890-1945 ........... TCLC 8
See also CA 104; DLB 81, 124

Wergeland, Henrik Arnold
1808-1845 ................................. NCLC 5

Wersba, Barbara 1932- ...................... CLC 30
See also AAYA 2; CA 29-32R; CANR 16, 38;
CLR 3; DLB 52; JRDA; MAICYA; SAAS
2; SATA 1, 58

Wertmueller, Lina 1928- ................... CLC 16
See also CA 97-100; CANR 39

Wescott, Glenway 1901-1987 ........... CLC 13
See also CA 13-16R; 121; CANR 23; DLB 4,
9, 102

Wesker, Arnold
1932- .......... CLC 3, 5, 42; **DAB; DAM
DRAM**
See also CA 1-4R; CAAS 7; CANR 1, 33;
CDBLB 1960 to Present; DLB 13; MTCW

Wesley, Richard (Errol) 1945- ........... CLC 7
See also BW 1; CA 57-60; CANR 27; DLB
38

Wessel, Johan Herman 1742-1785 ....... LC 7

West, Anthony (Panther)
1914-1987 ................................. CLC 50
See also CA 45-48; 124; CANR 3, 19; DLB
15

West, C. P.
See Wodehouse, P(elham) G(renville)

West, (Mary) Jessamyn
1902-1984 ............................... CLC 7, 17
See also CA 9-12R; 112; CANR 27; DLB 6;
DLBY 84; MTCW; SATA-Obit 37

**West, Morris L(anglo)** 1916- ........ **CLC 6, 33**
See also CA 5-8R; CANR 24, 49; MTCW

**West, Nathanael**
1903-1940 ........ **TCLC 1, 14, 44; SSC 16**
See also CA 104; 125; CDALB 1929-1941;
DLB 4, 9, 28; MTCW

**West, Owen**
See Koontz, Dean R(ay)

**West, Paul** 1930- ...................... **CLC 7, 14, 96**
See also CA 13-16R; CAAS 7; CANR 22, 53;
DLB 14; INT CANR-22

**West, Rebecca** 1892-1983 .... **CLC 7, 9, 31, 50**
See also CA 5-8R; 109; CANR 19; DLB 36;
DLBY 83; MTCW

**Westall, Robert (Atkinson)**
1929-1993 .................................. **CLC 17**
See also AAYA 12; CA 69-72; 141; CANR 18;
CLR 13; JRDA; MAICYA; SAAS 2; SATA
23, 69; SATA-Obit 75

**Westlake, Donald E(dwin)**
1933- .................... **CLC 7, 33; DAM POP**
See also CA 17-20R; CAAS 13; CANR 16, 44;
INT CANR-16

**Westmacott, Mary**
See Christie, Agatha (Mary Clarissa)

**Weston, Allen**
See Norton, Andre

**Wetcheek, J. L.**
See Feuchtwanger, Lion

**Wetering, Janwillem van de**
See van de Wetering, Janwillem

**Wetherell, Elizabeth**
See Warner, Susan (Bogert)

**Whale, James** 1889-1957 ............... **TCLC 63**

**Whalen, Philip** 1923- .................... **CLC 6, 29**
See also CA 9-12R; CANR 5, 39; DLB 16

**Wharton, Edith (Newbold Jones)**
1862-1937 ........ **TCLC 3, 9, 27, 53; DA;
DAB; DAC; DAM MST, NOV; SSC 6;
WLC**
See also CA 104; 132; CDALB 1865-1917;
DLB 4, 9, 12, 78; DLBD 13; MTCW

**Wharton, James**
See Mencken, H(enry) L(ouis)

**Wharton, William (a pseudonym)**... **CLC 18,
37**
See also CA 93-96; DLBY 80; INT 93-96

**Wheatley (Peters), Phillis**
1754(?)-1784 ...... **LC 3; BLC; DA; DAC;
DAM MST, MULT, POET; PC 3; WLC**
See also CDALB 1640-1865; DLB 31, 50

**Wheelock, John Hall**
1886-1978 .................................. **CLC 14**
See also CA 13-16R; 77-80; CANR 14; DLB
45

**White, E(lwyn) B(rooks)**
1899-1985 ...**CLC 10, 34, 39; DAM POP**
See also AITN 2; CA 13-16R; 116; CANR 16,
37; CLR 1, 21; DLB 11, 22; MAICYA;
MTCW; SATA 2, 29; SATA-Obit 44

**White, Edmund (Valentine III)**
1940- ...................... **CLC 27; DAM POP**
See also AAYA 7; CA 45-48; CANR 3, 19, 36,
62; MTCW

**White, Patrick (Victor Martindale)**
1912-1990 ...**CLC 3, 4, 5, 7, 9, 18, 65, 69**
See also CA 81-84; 132; CANR 43;
MTCW

**White, Phyllis Dorothy James** 1920-
See James, P. D.
See also CA 21-24R; CANR 17, 43; DAM
POP; MTCW

**White, T(erence) H(anbury)**
1906-1964 .................................. **CLC 30**
See also AAYA 22; CA 73-76; CANR 37; DLB
160; JRDA; MAICYA; SATA 12

**White, Terence de Vere**
1912-1994 .................................. **CLC 49**
See also CA 49-52; 145; CANR 3

**White, Walter F(rancis)**
1893-1955 .................................. **TCLC 15**
See also White, Walter
See also BW 1; CA 115; 124; DLB 51

**White, William Hale** 1831-1913
See Rutherford, Mark
See also CA 121

**Whitehead, E(dward) A(nthony)**
1933- .............................................. **CLC 5**
See also CA 65-68; CANR 58

**Whitemore, Hugh (John)** 1936- ........ **CLC 37**
See also CA 132; INT 132

**Whitman, Sarah Helen (Power)**
1803-1878 .................................. **NCLC 19**
See also DLB 1

**Whitman, Walt(er)**
1819-1892 ........ **NCLC 4, 31; DA; DAB;
DAC; DAM MST, POET; PC 3; WLC**
See also CDALB 1640-1865; DLB 3, 64; SATA
20

**Whitney, Phyllis A(yame)**
1903- ...................... **CLC 42; DAM POP**
See also AITN 2; BEST 90:3; CA 1-4R;
CANR 3, 25, 38, 60; JRDA; MAICYA;
SATA 1, 30

**Whittemore, (Edward) Reed (Jr.)**
1919- .............................................. **CLC 4**
See also CA 9-12R; CAAS 8; CANR 4; DLB
5

**Whittier, John Greenleaf**
1807-1892 .................................. **NCLC 8, 59**
See also DLB 1

**Whittlebot, Hernia**
See Coward, Noel (Peirce)

**Wicker, Thomas Grey** 1926-
See Wicker, Tom
See also CA 65-68; CANR 21, 46

**Wicker, Tom** .......................................... **CLC 7**
See also Wicker, Thomas Grey

**Wideman, John Edgar**
1941-...... **CLC 5, 34, 36, 67; BLC; DAM
MULT**
See also BW 2; CA 85-88; CANR 14, 42; DLB
33, 143

**Wiebe, Rudy (Henry)**
1934-........ **CLC 6, 11, 14; DAC; DAM
MST**
See also CA 37-40R; CANR 42; DLB 60

**Wieland, Christoph Martin**
1733-1813 ............................ **NCLC 17**
See also DLB 97

**Wiene, Robert** 1881-1938 .............. **TCLC 56**

**Wieners, John** 1934- ........................... **CLC 7**
See also CA 13-16R; DLB 16

**Wiesel, Elie(zer)**
1928-........ **CLC 3, 5, 11, 37; DA; DAB;
DAC; DAM MST, NOV; WLCS**
See also AAYA 7; AITN 1; CA 5-8R; CAAS
4; CANR 8, 40; DLB 83; DLBY 87; INT
CANR-8; MTCW; SATA 56

**Wiggins, Marianne** 1947- .................. **CLC 57**
See also BEST 89:3; CA 130; CANR 60

**Wight, James Alfred** 1916-
See Herriot, James
See also CA 77-80; SATA 55; SATA-Brief
44

**Wilbur, Richard (Purdy)**
1921-...... **CLC 3, 6, 9, 14, 53; DA; DAB;
DAC; DAM MST, POET**
See also CA 1-4R; CABS 2; CANR 2, 29;
DLB 5, 169; INT CANR-29; MTCW;
SATA 9

**Wild, Peter** 1940- .............................. **CLC 14**
See also CA 37-40R; DLB 5

**Wilde, Oscar (Fingal O'Flahertie Wills)**
1854(?)-1900 ..... **TCLC 1, 8, 23, 41; DA;
DAB; DAC; DAM DRAM, MST, NOV;
SSC 11; WLC**
See also CA 104; 119; CDBLB 1890-1914;
DLB 10, 19, 34, 57, 141, 156; SATA 24

**Wilder, Billy** ...................................... **CLC 20**
See also Wilder, Samuel
See also DLB 26

**Wilder, Samuel** 1906-
See Wilder, Billy
See also CA 89-92

**Wilder, Thornton (Niven)**
1897-1975 ....**CLC 1, 5, 6, 10, 15, 35, 82;
DA; DAB; DAC; DAM DRAM, MST,
NOV; DC 1; WLC**
See also AITN 2; CA 13-16R; 61-64; CANR
40; DLB 4, 7, 9; MTCW

Xenophon c. 430B.C.-c. 354B.C. .. **CMLC 17**
See also DLB 176

Yakumo Koizumi
See Hearn, (Patricio) Lafcadio (Tessima Carlos)

Yanez, Jose Donoso
See Donoso (Yanez), Jose

Yanovsky, Basile S.
See Yanovsky, V(assily) S(emenovich)

Yanovsky, V(assily) S(emenovich)
1906-1989 ................................ **CLC 2, 18**
See also CA 97-100; 129

Yates, Richard 1926-1992 ......... **CLC 7, 8, 23**
See also CA 5-8R; 139; CANR 10, 43; DLB 2; DLBY 81, 92; INT CANR-10

Yeats, W. B.
See Yeats, William Butler

Yeats, William Butler
1865-1939 ....... **TCLC 1, 11, 18, 31; DA; DAB; DAC; DAM DRAM, MST, POET; PC 20; WLC**
See also CA 104; 127; CANR 45; CDBLB 1890-1914; DLB 10, 19, 98, 156; MTCW

Yehoshua, A(braham) B.
1936- ..................................... **CLC 13, 31**
See also CA 33-36R; CANR 43

Yep, Laurence Michael 1948- ........... **CLC 35**
See also AAYA 5; CA 49-52; CANR 1, 46; CLR 3, 17; DLB 52; JRDA; MAICYA; SATA 7, 69

Yerby, Frank G(arvin)
1916-1991 ..... **CLC 1, 7, 22; BLC; DAM MULT**
See also BW 1; CA 9-12R; 136; CANR 16, 52; DLB 76; INT CANR-16; MTCW

Yesenin, Sergei Alexandrovich
See Esenin, Sergei (Alexandrovich)

Yevtushenko, Yevgeny (Alexandrovich)
1933- ........ **CLC 1, 3, 13, 26, 51; DAM POET**
See also CA 81-84; CANR 33, 54; MTCW

Yezierska, Anzia 1885(?)-1970 ......... **CLC 46**
See also CA 126; 89-92; DLB 28; MTCW

Yglesias, Helen 1915- .................... **CLC 7, 22**
See also CA 37-40R; CAAS 20; CANR 15; INT CANR-15; MTCW

Yokomitsu Riichi 1898-1947 ......... **TCLC 47**

Yonge, Charlotte (Mary)
1823-1901 ................................ **TCLC 48**
See also CA 109; DLB 18, 163; SATA 17

York, Jeremy
See Creasey, John

York, Simon
See Heinlein, Robert A(nson)

Yorke, Henry Vincent 1905-1974 ..... **CLC 13**
See also Green, Henry
See also CA 85-88; 49-52

Yosano Akiko 1878-1942 .... **TCLC 59; PC 11**

Yoshimoto, Banana ........................... **CLC 84**
See also Yoshimoto, Mahoko

Yoshimoto, Mahoko 1964-
See Yoshimoto, Banana
See also CA 144

Young, Al(bert James)
1939- .......... **CLC 19; BLC; DAM MULT**
See also BW 2; CA 29-32R; CANR 26; DLB 33

Young, Andrew (John) 1885-1971 ...... **CLC 5**
See also CA 5-8R; CANR 7, 29

Young, Collier
See Bloch, Robert (Albert)

Young, Edward 1683-1765 ............... **LC 3, 40**
See also DLB 95

Young, Marguerite (Vivian)
1909-1995 ................................. **CLC 82**
See also CA 13-16; 150; CAP 1

Young, Neil 1945- ............................. **CLC 17**
See also CA 110

Young Bear, Ray A. 1950- ..... **CLC 94; DAM MULT**
See also CA 146; DLB 175; NNAL

Yourcenar, Marguerite
1903-1987 ..... **CLC 19, 38, 50, 87; DAM NOV**
See also CA 69-72; CANR 23, 60; DLB 72; DLBY 88; MTCW

Yurick, Sol 1925- ................................. **CLC 6**
See also CA 13-16R; CANR 25

Zabolotskii, Nikolai Alekseevich
1903-1958 ............................... **TCLC 52**
See also CA 116

Zamiatin, Yevgenii
See Zamyatin, Evgeny Ivanovich

Zamora, Bernice (B. Ortiz)
1938- .......... **CLC 89; DAM MULT; HLC**
See also CA 151; DLB 82; HW

Zamyatin, Evgeny Ivanovich
1884-1937 ............................. **TCLC 8, 37**
See also CA 105

Zangwill, Israel 1864-1926 ........... **TCLC 16**
See also CA 109; DLB 10, 135

Zappa, Francis Vincent, Jr. 1940-1993
See Zappa, Frank
See also CA 108; 143; CANR 57

Zappa, Frank ..................................... **CLC 17**
See also Zappa, Francis Vincent, Jr.

Zaturenska, Marya 1902-1982 ..... **CLC 6, 11**
See also CA 13-16R; 105; CANR 22

Zeami 1363-1443 ................................... **DC 7**

Zelazny, Roger (Joseph)
1937-1995 ............................... **CLC 21**
See also AAYA 7; CA 21-24R; 148; CANR 26, 60; DLB 8; MTCW; SATA 57; SATA-Brief 39

Zhdanov, Andrei A(lexandrovich)
1896-1948 ................................ **TCLC 18**
See also CA 117

Zhukovsky, Vasily 1783-1852 ....... **NCLC 35**

Ziegenhagen, Eric ............................ **CLC 55**

Zimmer, Jill Schary
See Robinson, Jill

Zimmerman, Robert
See Dylan, Bob

Zindel, Paul
1936- ........ **CLC 6, 26; DA; DAB; DAC; DAM DRAM, MST, NOV; DC 5**
See also AAYA 2; CA 73-76; CANR 31; CLR 3, 45; DLB 7, 52; JRDA; MAICYA; MTCW; SATA 16, 58

Zinov'Ev, A. A.
See Zinoviev, Alexander (Aleksandrovich)

Zinoviev, Alexander (Aleksandrovich)
1922-............................................. **CLC 19**
See also CA 116; 133; CAAS 10

Zoilus
See Lovecraft, H(oward) P(hillips)

Zola, Emile (Edouard Charles Antoine)
1840-1902 **TCLC 1, 6, 21, 41; DA; DAB; DAC; DAM MST, NOV; WLC**
See also CA 104; 138; DLB 123

Zoline, Pamela 1941- ........................ **CLC 62**

Zorrilla y Moral, Jose 1817-1893 ... **NCLC 6**

Zoshchenko, Mikhail (Mikhailovich)
1895-1958 ................... **TCLC 15; SSC 15**
See also CA 115; 160

Zuckmayer, Carl 1896-1977 ............. **CLC 18**
See also CA 69-72; DLB 56, 124

Zuk, Georges
See Skelton, Robin

Zukofsky, Louis
1904-1978 ....... **CLC 1, 2, 4, 7, 11, 18; DAM POET; PC 11**
See also CA 9-12R; 77-80; CANR 39; DLB 5, 165; MTCW

Zweig, Paul 1935-1984 ............... **CLC 34, 42**
See also CA 85-88; 113

Zweig, Stefan 1881-1942 ............... **TCLC 17**
See also CA 112; DLB 81, 118

Zwingli, Huldreich 1484-1531 ............. **LC 37**
See also DLB 179

# *Short Story Criticism*
# Cumulative Nationality Index

de la Mare, Walter (John)  **14**
Dickens, Charles (John Huffam)  **17**
Doyle, Arthur Conan  **12**
du Maurier, Daphne  **18**
Forster, E(dward) M(organ)  **27**
Galsworthy, John  **22**
Gaskell, Elizabeth Cleghorn  **25**
Greene, Graham (Henry)  **29**
Hardy, Thomas  **2**
James, Montague (Rhodes)  **16**
Jolley, (Monica) Elizabeth  **19**
Kipling, (Joseph) Rudyard  **5**
Lawrence, D(avid) H(erbert Richards)  **4, 19**
Lessing, Doris (May)  **6**
Lowry, (Clarence) Malcolm  **31**
Maugham, W(illiam) Somerset  **8**
Pritchett, V(ictor) S(awdon)  **14**
Rhys, Jean  **21**
Saki  **12**
Sansom, William  **21**
Trollope, Anthony  **28**
Warner, Sylvia Townsend  **23**
Wells, H(erbert) G(eorge)  **6**
Wilson, Angus (Frank Johnstone)  **21**
Wodehouse, P(elham) G(renville)  **2**
Woolf, (Adeline) Virginia  **7**

**FRENCH**
Balzac, Honore de  **5**
Barbey d'Aurevilly, Jules Amedee  **17**
Baudelaire, Charles  **18**
Beckett, Samuel (Barclay)  **16**
Camus, Albert  **9**
Colette, (Sidonie-Gabrielle)  **10**
Flaubert, Gustave  **11**
Gautier, Theophile  **20**
Gide, Andre (Paul Guillaume)  **13**
Jarry, Alfred  **20**
Laforgue, Jules  **20**
Lautreamont, Comte de  **14**
Maupassant, (Henri Rene Albert) Guy de  **1**
Mauriac, Francois (Charles)  **24**
Merimee, Prosper  **7**
Morand, Paul  **22**
Nerval, Gerard de  **18**
Nin, Anais  **10**
Stendhal  **27**
Villiers de l'Isle Adam, Jean Marie Mathias Philippe Auguste, Comte de  **14**
Voltaire  **12**

**GERMAN**
Arnim, Achim von (Ludwig Joachim von Arnim)  **29**
Boell, Heinrich (Theodor)  **23**
Hesse, Hermann  **9**
Hoffmann, E(rnst) T(heodor) A(madeus)  **13**

Kleist, Heinrich von  **22**
Mann, (Paul) Thomas  **5**
Storm, (Hans) Theodor (Woldsen)  **27**
Tieck, (Johann) Ludwig  **31**

**INDIAN**
Narayan, R(asipuram) K(rishnaswami)  **25**

**IRISH**
Beckett, Samuel (Barclay)  **16**
Bowen, Elizabeth (Dorothea Cole)  **3, 28**
Joyce, James (Augustine Aloysius)  **3, 26**
Lavin, Mary  **4**
Le Fanu, Joseph Sheridan  **14**
McGahern, John  **17**
Moore, George Augustus  **19**
O'Brien, Edna  **10**
O'Connor, Frank  **5**
O'Faolain, Sean  **13**
O'Flaherty, Liam  **6**
Trevor, William  **21**
Wilde, Oscar (Fingal O'Flahertie Wills)  **11**

**ISRAELI**
Agnon, S(hmuel) Y(osef Halevi)  **30**

**ITALIAN**
Boccaccio, Giovanni  **10**
Calvino, Italo  **3**
Levi, Primo  **12**
Moravia, Alberto  **26**
Pavese, Cesare  **19**
Pirandello, Luigi  **22**
Svevo, Italo  **25**
Verga, Giovanni (Carmelo)  **21**

**JAPANESE**
Kawabata, Yasunari  **17**
Mishima, Yukio  **4**
Oe, Kenzaburo  **20**
Shiga, Naoya  **23**
Tanizaki, Jun'ichiro  **21**

**MEXICAN**
Fuentes, Carlos  **24**
Rulfo, Juan  **25**

**NEW ZEALANDER**
Frame, Janet  **29**
Mansfield, Katherine  **9, 23**

**POLISH**
Agnon, S(hmuel) Y(osef Halevi)  **30**
Conrad, Joseph  **9**
Peretz, Isaac Loeb  **26**
Schulz, Bruno  **13**
Singer, Isaac Bashevis  **3**

**RUSSIAN**
Babel, Isaak (Emmanuilovich)  **16**
Bulgakov, Mikhail (Afanas'evich)  **18**
Bunin, Ivan Alexeyevich  **5**
Chekhov, Anton (Pavlovich)  **2, 28**
Dostoevsky, Fedor Mikhailovich  **2**
Gogol, Nikolai (Vasilyevich)  **4, 29**
Gorky, Maxim  **28**
Nabokov, Vladimir (Vladimirovich)  **11**
Pasternak, Boris (Leonidovich)  **31**
Pushkin, Alexander (Sergeyevich)  **27**
Tolstoy, Leo (Nikolaevich)  **9, 30**
Turgenev, Ivan  **7**
Zoshchenko, Mikhail (Mikhailovich)  **15**

**SCOTTISH**
Oliphant, Margaret (Oliphant Wilson)  **25**
Spark, Muriel (Sarah)  **10**
Stevenson, Robert Louis (Balfour)  **11**

**SOUTH AFRICAN**
Gordimer, Nadine  **17**

**SPANISH**
Cervantes (Saavedra), Miguel de  **12**
Pardo Bazán, Emilia  **30**
Unamuno (y Jugo), Miguel de  **11**

**SWEDISH**
Lagerkvist, Par  **12**

**SWISS**
Hesse, Hermann  **9**
Keller, Gottfried  **26**
Walser, Robert  **20**

**URUGUAYAN**
Onetti, Juan Carlos  **23**

**WELSH**
Machen, Arthur  **20**
Thomas, Dylan (Marlais)  **3**

# *Short Story Criticism*
# Cumulative Title Index

Title Index

Title Index

Title Index

Title Index